D1471142

LET'S GO PUBLICATIONS

TRAVEL GUIDES

Australia
Austria & Switzerland
Brazil
Britain
California
Central America
Chile
China
Costa Rica
Costa Rica, Nicaragua & Panama
Eastern Europe
Ecuador
Egypt
Europe
France
Germany
Greece
Guatemala & Belize
Hawaii
India & Nepal
Ireland
Israel
Italy
Japan
Mexico
New Zealand
Peru
Puerto Rico
Southeast Asia
Spain & Portugal with Morocco
Thailand
USA
Vietnam
Western Europe
Yucatán Peninsula

ROADTRIP GUIDE

Roadtripping USA

ADVENTURE GUIDES

Alaska
Pacific Northwest
Southwest USA

CITY GUIDES

Amsterdam
Barcelona
Berlin, Prague & Budapest
Boston
Buenos Aires
Florence
London
London, Oxford, Cambridge & Edinburgh
New York City
Paris
Rome
San Francisco
Washington, DC

POCKET CITY GUIDES

Amsterdam
Berlin
Boston
Chicago
London
New York City
Paris
San Francisco
Venice
Washington, DC

LET'S GO

CENTRAL AMERICA

RESEARCHERS

Eli Berger   Asa Bush

Charles Fisher-Post   Maryam Janani

Dan Normandin   Alison Tarwater

Ethan Waxman

HOW TO USE THIS BOOK

COVERAGE LAYOUT. *Let's Go Central America* covers all seven countries in Central America. Beginning in Belize and ending in Panama, the coverage in each individual country chapter is organized geographically, to facilitate linking transportation from place to place. For connections between destinations, information is generally listed under both the arrival and departure cities. Parentheticals usually provide the trip duration followed by frequency, then the price. For more general information on travel, consult Essentials (p. 5).

COVERING THE BASICS. The first chapter, **Discover Central America** (p. 1), contains highlights of the country. The **Essentials** (p. 5) section contains practical information on planning a budget, making reservations, and other useful tips for traveling throughout these countries, including price diversity charts (see below for more information). Take some time to peruse the **Life and Times** (Belize p. 46, Guatemala p. 117, Honduras p. 216, El Salvador p. 310, Nicaragua p. 373, Costa Rica p. 439, and Panama p. 555) sections and brush up on your Latin American history. The **Appendix** (p. 630) features climate information, a list of national holidays for each country, measurement conversions, and a glossary. For study abroad, volunteer, and work opportunities throughout the region, **Beyond Tourism** (p. 34) has all the resources you need.

RANKINGS, TIP BOXES, AND FEATURES. Our researchers list establishments in order of value from best to worst, with absolute favorites denoted by the *Let's Go* thumbpick (◼). Since the lowest price does not always equal the best value, we've incorporated a system of price ranges (❶-❺) for food and accommodations—the ranges are different for each country, and you will find price diversity charts for all three in the **Life and Times** sections (Belize p. 46, Guatemala p. 117, Honduras p. 216, El Salvador p. 310, Nicaragua p. 373, Costa Rica p. 439, and Panama p. 555). Tip boxes come in a variety of flavors: warnings (◼), helpful hints and resources (◼), inside scoops (◼), and a variety of other things you should know. When you want a break from transportation info and listings, check out our features for unique opportunities, surprising insights, and fascinating stories.

PHONE CODES AND TELEPHONE NUMBERS. 505 is the area code for all of Nicaragua, 506 for Costa Rica, and 507 for Panama, but when calling within the country, it is not necessary to use these numbers. Phone numbers are all preceded by the ☎ icon.

A NOTE TO OUR READERS. The information for this book was gathered by Let's Go researchers from May through August of 2009. Each listing is based on one researcher's opinion, formed during his or her visit at a particular time. Those traveling at other times may have different experiences since prices, dates, hours, and conditions are always subject to change. You are urged to check the facts presented in this book beforehand to avoid inconvenience and surprises.

CONTENTS

RESEARCHERS

Elias Berger
Western, Central, and Southern Guatemala

Armed with a semester of Spanish, a love for geography, and a friendly disposition, Eli took on Guatemala's biggest cities and most isolated villages with equal good cheer. Tirelessly searching for the best deals and the tastiest mojitos, this first-time Let's Go Researcher won us over with his sharp wit and determination to overcome food poisoning and unreliable bus schedules alike. From the bars and clubs of Panajachel to the most ancient Mayan ruins to the smoggy streets of Guatemala City, Eli wrote with candor and honesty—charming his editors and adding characteristic pizzazz to his coverage throughout the book.

Asa E. Bush
Nicaragua

A first-time researcher, Asa coped with 15-hour ferry rides in the rain, hostile taxi drivers, and two-story climbs with the calm and determination of an old hand. This Idaho native conquered volcano craters and jungle hikes with the same focus that he devoted to finding the best deals and the safest routes for our readers. His hilarious blogs and penchant for adventure kept us on the edge of our seats, while his ability to get out of a sticky situation continually impressed even the toughest of Let's Go veterans.

Maryam Janani
Costa Rica

This neurobio major from San Antonio spent much of her time in Costa Rica trying to avoid overly forward men, and the rest of it keeping her distance from, as she puts it, Costa Rica's "animal-infested rainforest." Characteristically one who avoids animals not in cages, Maryam put her best foot forward in this country known for its wildlife, traveling all over the country from Golfito to Tortuguero to Nicoya. Her attention to detail made for meticulous coverage, but she still managed to have some fun—going ziplining and bungee jumping in her free time, making those of us in the office green with envy.

Daniel Normandin
Belize and Northern Guatemala

Apparently, there is nothing that Dan can't do. Overcoming early obstacles, this Let's Go veteran never complained, never missed a deadline, and never stopped impressing us with his incredible work ethic and passion for travel. Whether wading through waist-deep water on jungle treks, befriending local hostel owners, or traversing the hallowed grounds of a Mayan temple, Dan traveled—and researched—with the boundless enthusiasm that pervades his entertaining and informative coverage of Belize and Guatemala.

RESEARCHERS

Charles Fisher-Post
Honduras

After conquering the Australian outback for *Let's Go Australia*, Charles was ready for a new challenge and some place with a few more beaches. During his time in Honduras, Charles got that and a whole lot more. A stolen laptop, a military coup, and an emergency national curfew didn't stop this intrepid Let's Go veteran from conducting quality research and writing some of our website's most fascinating blogs. Whether following in the footsteps of Robinson Crusoe on the Bay Islands, driving across the swamps of La Moskitia in the back of a pickup truck, or exploring the ancient ruins of Copán, Charles proved once again that he is as tough as he is fearless.

Alison Tarwater
Eastern Guatemala

Street gangs, active volcanoes, and giant spiders were no match for Alison as she trekked through Honduras, El Salvador, and Guatemala. Braving city bus routes, remote mountain hikes, and even a suburban mega-mall or two, this three-time Let's Go veteran embodied the spirit of independent travel throughout her journey. Intrepid and fearless, Alison is also a keen observer of people. Keeping her finger on the pulse of Central American culture, she injected her coverage with the insight and experience of a local. Fueled by ever elusive fresh garden salads, Alison consistently completed comprehensive and detailed work along the way.

Ethan Waxman
Panama

Given that his favorite book is *The Three Musketeers*, we knew from the outset that Ethan would be a great fit for the wild jungles of Panama. He forged his way through the overgrown and unexplored Darién, island-hopped via boats filled with leaky gasoline tanks in the San Blas archipelago, and got chased by wild dogs in Panama City. With an eye for adventure, and an enthusiasm for getting to know locals, we knew we could trust Ethan to give us honest coverage.

STAFF WRITERS

Charlotte Alter	Megan Amram	Allison Averill
Dan Barbero	Lauren Brown	Billy Eck
Charles Fisher-Post	Anna Kendrick	Megan Michelson
Colleen O'Brien	Meg Popkin	C. Harker Rhodes
Maria Vassileva	Sara Joe Wolansky	

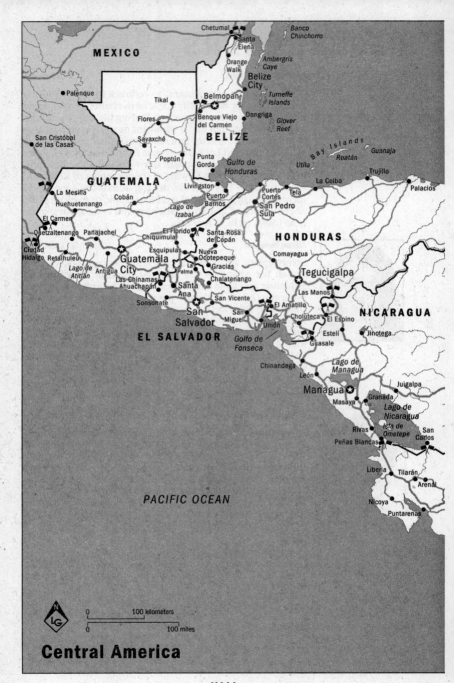

Central America

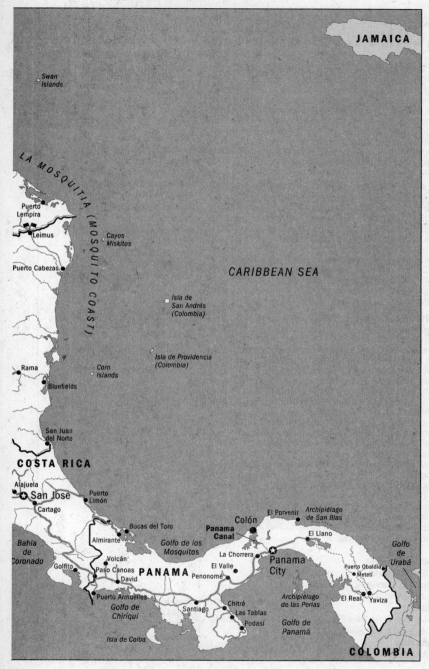

JAMAICA

Swan
Islands

LA MOSQUITIA (MOSQUITO COAST)

Puerto
Lempira

Leimus

Cayos
Miskitos

Puerto Cabezas

CARIBBEAN SEA

Isla de
San Andrés
(Colombia)

Isla de Providencia
(Colombia)

Rama

Corn
Islands

Bluefields

San Juan
del Norte

COSTA RICA

Alajuela

San José

Puerto
Limón

Cartago

El Porvenir   Archipiélago
de San Blas

Colón

Panama
Canal

El Llano

Bahía
de
Coronado

Golfito

Bocas del Toro

Almirante

Volcán

Paso Canoas

David

Golfo de los
Mosquitos

La Chorrera

Panama
City

El Valle

Puerto Obaldía

Metetí

PANAMA

Penonomé

Golfo
de
Urabá

Puerto Armuelles

Golfo de
Chiriquí

Santiago

Chitré

Archipiélago
de las Perlas

El Real   Yaviza

Las Tablas

Pedasí

Golfo de
Panamá

Isla de Coiba

COLOMBIA

ACKNOWLEDGMENTS

JOSEPH THANKS: Ashley, for letting me get her coffee and be her stay-at-home dad. But really for being a great boss and friend—never simma down. Asa, for being the man. The other RM's for keeping the office fun and the poetry erotic. The eds for their hard work/summer UnFun. The whole LG office for being quaint, Bohemian, and tasty. My friends for letting me stay in on the weekends and stay here for the summer. Florence, NJ for still being home, and Mom, Dad, Jim, Mike, and Russ for keeping it that way.

CLAIRE THANKS: Let's Go's 9-5 work day for helping me maintain a normal sleep schedule for the first time since middle school, Maryam and Ethan for all their hard work, my fellow Research Managers for all the bonding and fun times in the pod, Kavita for the swine flu piglet that sat on my desk all summer, Molly for being my aloe buddy and putting up with my many whackings of the snooze button in the morning, my family (and little brother) for their guidance with my various cooking experiments, and my friends for an adventure-packed and fun-filled summer.

EDITORS THANKS: The Ed Team would first and foremost like to thank our lord (Jay-C) and savior (Starbucks, Terry's Chocolate Orange). We also owe gratitude to Barack Obama (peace be upon Him), the Oxford comma, the water cooler, bagel/payday Fridays, the HSA "Summer-Fun" team for being so inclusive, Rotio (wherefore art thou Rotio?), the real Robinson Crusoe, the Cambridge weather and defective umbrellas, BoltBus, Henry Louis Gates, Jr. (sorry 'bout the phone call), the office blog, gratuitous nudity, the 20-20-20 rule and bananas (no more eye twitches), the Portuguese flag, trips to the beach (ha!), sunbathing recently-married Mormon final club alums, non-existent free food in the square, dog-star puns, and last but not least, America. The local time in Tehran is 1:21am.

But seriously, to the MEs and RMs, our researchers (and all their wisdom on table-cloths and hipsters), LGHQ, HSA, our significant others (future, Canadian, and otherwise), and families (thanks Mom).

Managing Editor
Ashley R. Laporte
Research Managers
Claire Shepro, Joseph Molimock
Editors
Courtney A. Fiske, Sara Plana, Russell Ford Rennie, Charlie E. Riggs, Olga I. Zhulina
Typesetter
C. Alexander Tremblay

LET'S GO

Publishing Director
Laura M. Gordon
Editorial Director
Dwight Livingstone Curtis
Publicity and Marketing Director
Vanessa J. Dube
Production and Design Director
Rebecca Lieberman
Cartography Director
Anthony Rotio
Website Director
Lukáš Tóth
Managing Editors
Ashley Laporte, Iya Megre, Mary Potter, Nathaniel Rakich
Technology Project Manager
C. Alexander Tremblay
Director of IT
David Fulton-Howard
Financial Associates
Catherine Humphreville, Jun Li

President
Daniel Lee
General Manager
Jim McKellar

DISCOVER CENTRAL AMERICA

Spider monkeys, camouflaged vine snakes, and lizards that walk on water. Vibrant wildlife, thundering waterfalls, and tropical rainstorms. From green mountains and white-sand beaches to expansive coffee fields and active volcanoes, Central America is waiting. Grab your hiking shoes and go explore 2000-year-old ruins in Guatemala, or learn to read hieroglyphics in Honduras. Tan on the Caribbean coast, hike in Nicaragua's lush jungles, explore ancient temples in Nicaragua, or zipline through the canopy in Costa Rica. Although Central America makes only a modest dent in the map, these seven countries are rich in culture and adventure.

Our Researchers have gathered the best advice on how to get around, how to stay safe, what to eat, where to sleep, and how to plan your trip. Whether you're interested in visiting all of Central America in a month or just hitting up Honduras, El Salvador, and Nicaragua in two weeks, we've got you covered.

WHEN TO GO

The most important factor to consider when planning a trip to Central America is the **rainy season,** or *invierno* (winter). Central America's rainy season generally occurs between May and November. Predictably, the rest of the year is called the **dry season,** or *verano* (summer). The seasons are particularly distinct on the Pacific Coast, while on the Caribbean Coast, some rain should be expected regardless of the season. The temperature in Central America is determined by altitude rather than season; the highlands experience moderate highs and pleasantly cool nights, while the costal and jungle lowlands swelter. For a country-specific temperature chart, see the **Appendix,** p. 631.

The dry season is the tourist "high season," meaning crazy crowds and elevated prices. Budget travelers should consider a rainy season trip. Even then, the sun generally shines all day, excluding furious but fleeting afternoon rainstorms. Dry season travel is for those in search or a tan or access to areas where roads and trains can be washed out for weeks during the rainy season. The region's best parties are using during **Semena Santa,** the week-long Easter holiday. For more destination-specific info, see the specific country introductions.

WHAT TO DO

🔲 PUT ME IN THE WATER

If you're looking for a place to explore the deep blue, Central America is the place for you. With the Carribbean Sea to the east and the Pacific Ocean to the west, the region is literally surrounded by some of the best snorkeling and diving sites in the world. We know that jumping into the Belize's Blue Hole takes more than just big *cajones*, so we've singled out the best budget options from a sea of tourst traps.

DIVE RIGHT IN	SNORKEL SHMORKEL
THE BLUE HOLE (P. 74). This 400 ft. deep wonder is Belize's most famous attraction.	**AMBERGRIS CAYE (P. 70).** Spy on rays and sharks off the coast of this famous island.
CAYE CAULKER (P. 63). Ambergris' sidekick, Caulker is must-see.	**TOBACCO CAYE (P. 100)** Swim off the shores of this tiny Caye in Southern Belize.
PLAYA HERMOSA (P. 507). Swim with eels, octopi, and seahorses in Costa Rica's Nicoya Peninsula.	**CORN ISLANDS (P. 427).** This Nicaraguan island is a snorkeler's paradise.
TURNEFFE ATOLL (P. 74). Boasting beautiful coral reef formations, this is one of the most exhilarating places to dive in Belize.	**HOPKINS (P. 103).** Explore the deep blue with local Garífuna in this little town in southern Belize.

YOU DIG?

Over 2000 years ago, the inhabitants of Northern Guatemala begin hauling huge slabs of limestone out of the ground in order to build temples and palaces more than 70m high. The structures embody the mystery and grandeur of the great Maya cities, whose earliest remnants may date back more than 4000 years. The awesome temples, hieroglyphics, carvings, and statues that immortalize the ancients can be visited today at more than 30 sites in Guatemala, Belize, Honduras, and El Salvador. Below are just a few of the incredible sites we cover in this guide.

HISTORICAL SITES
ACTUN TUNICHIL (P. 92). An unforgettable trip to the underworld. Come see human skeletons in cathedral-like spaces 1km inside this enormous jungle cave in Belize.
TIKAL (P. 207). Camp beside soaring temples and catch a stunning sunset before the crowds come to attack this Guatemalan jewel.
COPÁN (P. 249). Explore ancient monuments and heiroglypics in Copán, Honduras.
ANTIGUA (P. 136). This well-preserved Colonial city with its cobblestone streets and grand architecture deserves its fame.
GRANADA (P. 395). Nicragua's Colonial city, Granada (like Antigua) offers a glimpse into Colonial Central America.
SANTA ANA (P. 350). When exploring this city in El Salvador, be sure to stop by the Santa Ana Cathedral--it will take your breath away.

RIDE THE WAVES

In August of 2009, 35 different countries participated in the ICA Surfing Championships at Playa Hermosa in Costa Rica. The pros know what's up: Central America's coasts are picture-perfect places to ride the waves. Whether you're looking to find the best hidden spots where only the seasoned dare tear it up, or simply trying to stand up on a board for the first time, Central America is the place to be. And when it comes to finding the best beaches, surfing lessons, and rentals, we've got your back.

SURF AND SPLASH

ISLA GRANDE (P. 584). The eastern part of this Panamanian island offers prime waves for surfing.

JACÓ (P. 521). After a long day on your board, enjoy a drink with fellow surfers at this partygoing paradise.

BOCAS DEL TORO (P. 619). There are many places to surf at this mecca in Panama; we recommend north of Carenero Key.

LA LIBERTAD (P. 329). The tourquoise waters off the shore of this beach in El Salvador attract pros and beginners alike.

MAL PAIS (P. 513). Despite its name ("bad place"), Mal Pais is actually a really good place to surf.

PROTECTED AREAS

Blessed with one of the most breathtaking and extensive park systems in the world, Central America is a nature-lover's paradise. The diversity of the region caters to every whim—whether you're looking to stroll along well-maintained trails or machete you way through thousands of kilometers of jungle, Central America will not disappoint.

ALWAYS USE PROTECTION

REFUGIO NACIONAL CAÑO NEGRO (P. 488). This lush reserve is home to 160 different speices of mammals, and over 315 species of birds.

VOLCÁN SAN SALVADOR (P. 326). Hike around the volcanic crater or just sit and take in the facinating views.

TURNEFFE ATOLL (P. 74). Boasting beautiful coral reef formations, this is one of the most exhilarating places to dive in Belize.

BEACH BUMMING

Okay, so maybe ripping tasty waves isn't for you. Perhaps the idea of trekking through jungles makes you nauseous. Maybe you're the type that gets claustrophobic in a snorkel mask. Don't worry, we're not judging, and we've thought of you too. Here is our list of the best beaches in Central America. From the shores of the Caribbean Sea in Belize to the quiet coasts of the Pacific in Costa Rica, we've found the best places to lay out with a mixed drink in hand. All you have to do is bring the sunscreen.

LIFE'S A BEACH

HOPKINS (P. 103). Catch some rays by the sea, take in the incredible views, and visit the local Garifuna village while visitng this Belizean town.

LAGO DE COATEPEQUE (P. 356). Just a short daytrip from El Salvador's Santa Ana, this lake provides quiet shores and beautiful scenery.

ISLA EL TIGRE (P. 226). This island off the coast of El Salvador plays host to Playa Grande, an incredible beach with a glistening cave, Cueva de la Sirena.

PLAYA EL TORO (P. 611). Just 3km from Pedasí, this beach is a cheap and accessible for those looking to cool off on Panama's Azuero Peninsula.

DISCOVER

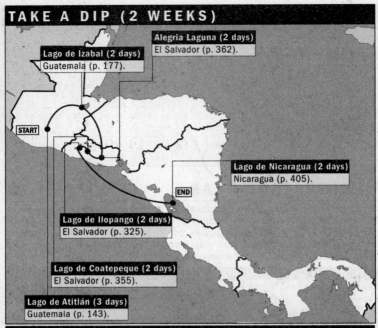

TAKE A DIP (2 WEEKS)

Alegria Laguna (2 days)
El Salvador (p. 362).

Lago de Izabal (2 days)
Guatemala (p. 177).

START

Lago de Nicaragua (2 days)
Nicaragua (p. 405).

END

Lago de Ilopango (2 days)
El Salvador (p. 325).

Lago de Coatepeque (2 days)
El Salvador (p. 355).

Lago de Atitlán (3 days)
Guatemala (p. 143).

THE BIGGEST AND MOST BADASS

Snorkeling in the Blue Hole
Belize (p. 74).

Belize Barrier Reef
Belize (p. 104).

Volcán Pacaya
Guatemala (p. 138).

Volcán Maderas
Isla de Ometepe,
Nicaragua (p. 408).

San Ramón Waterfalls
Isla de Ometepe,
Nicaragua (p. 408).

ESSENTIALS

PLANNING YOUR TRIP

ENTRANCE REQUIREMENTS
Passport (p. 5). Required for all visitors.
Visa (p. 6). See specific country chapters for visa-specific entrance info.
Inoculations (p. 14). Travelers coming from nations with endemic yellow fever need proof of vaccination.
Work Permit (p. 6). Required for all foreigners planning to work in Central America.

DOCUMENTS AND FORMALITIES

See individual country chapters for for specific info on **Consular Services** and **Tourist Offices**.

PASSPORTS

REQUIREMENTS

Citizens of Australia, Canada, Ireland, New Zealand, the UK, and the US need valid passports to enter Central America and to re-enter their home countries. Central American nations generally do not allow entrance if the holder's passport expires in under 3 months; returning home with an expired passport is illegal and may result in a fine. Your passport will prove your most convenient method of identification and, if the photo was taken long ago, a source of humorous conversation.

NEW PASSPORTS

Citizens of Australia, Canada, Ireland, New Zealand, the UK, and the US can apply for a passport at any passport office or at selected post offices and courts of law. Citizens of these countries may also download passport applications from the official website of their country's government or passport office. Any new passport or renewal applications must be filed well in advance of the departure date, though most passport offices offer rush services for a steep fee. Note, however, that "rushed" passports still take up to two weeks to arrive.

PASSPORT MAINTENANCE

Make photocopies of the page of your passport with your photo as well as your visas, traveler's check serial numbers, and any other important documents. Carry one set of these copies in a safe place, apart from the originals, and leave another set at home. Consulates also recommend that you carry an expired passport or an official copy of your birth certificate separate from other documents.

If you lose your passport, immediately notify the local police and your home country's nearest embassy or consulate. To expedite its replacement, you must show photo ID and proof of citizenship; it also helps to know all information previously recorded in the passport. In some cases, a replacement may take weeks to process, and it may be valid only for a limited time. Any visas stamped in your old passport will be lost forever. In an emergency, ask for immediate temporary traveling papers that will permit you to re-enter your home country.

VISAS AND WORK PERMITS

See specific country chapters for **visa** specific entrance information. Entering Central America to study or work requires a special visa. For more information on these visas, see **Beyond Tourism, p. 34.**

IDENTIFICATION

Always carry at least two forms of identification on your person, including a photo ID. A passport and a driver's license will usually suffice. Never carry all of your IDs together; split them up in case of theft or loss and keep photocopies in your luggage and at home.

STUDENT, TEACHER, AND YOUTH IDENTIFICATION

The **International Student Identity Card (ISIC),** the most widely accepted form of student ID, provides discounts on some sights, accommodations, food, and transportation, access to a 24hr. emergency help line, and insurance benefits for US cardholders. In Central America, most ISIC discounts will be found in the major cities, and usually apply at hotels or restaurants, with the odd boat cruise in there. Applicants must be full-time secondary or post-secondary school students, and at least 12 years old. Because of the proliferation of fake ISICs, some services (particularly airlines) require additional proof of student identity. For travelers who are under 26 years old and are not students, the **International Youth Travel Card (IYTC)** also offers similar benefits to the ISIC.

Each of these identity cards costs US$22. ISICs and IYTCs are valid for one year from the date of issue. To learn more about ISICs and IYTCs, visit www.myisic.com. Many student travel agencies (p. 18) issue these cards; for a list of issuing agencies and more information, see the **International Student Travel Confederation (ISTC)** website at www.istc.org.

The **International Student Exchange Card (ISE Card)** is a similar identification card available to students, faculty, and children aged 12 to 26. The card provides discounts, medical benefits, access to a 24hr. emergency help line, and the ability to purchase discounted airfares. An ISE Card costs US$25; visit www.isecard.com for more info. The ISE is only accepted in Costa Rica and Nicaragua.

CUSTOMS

Upon entering Central America, you must declare certain items from abroad and pay a duty on the value of those articles if they exceed the allowance established by the country's customs service. These include alcohol, cigarettes, perfume and cash. Contact the nearest consulate to determine the allowance amounts. Jot down a list of any valuables brought from home and register them with customs before traveling abroad. Goods and gifts purchased at duty-free shops abroad are not exempt from duty or sales tax; "duty-free" means that you won't pay tax in the country of purchase. Upon returning home, you must likewise declare all articles acquired abroad and pay a duty on the value of articles in excess of your home country's allowance. It's a good idea to keep receipts for all goods acquired abroad.

MONEY

CURRENCY AND EXCHANGE

Check the currency converter on websites like www.xe.com or www.bloomberg.com for the latest exchange rates. As a general rule, it's cheaper to convert money in Central America than at home. While your arrival airport will probably have a currency exchange, it's wise to bring enough foreign currency to last for at least 24-72hr.

When changing money abroad, try to go only to banks or *casas de cambio* that have at most a 5% margin between their buy and sell prices. Since you lose money with every transaction, it makes sense to convert large sums at one time (unless the currency is depreciating rapidly).

If you use traveler's checks or bills, carry some in small denominations (the equivalent of US$50 or less) for times when you are forced to exchange money at poor rates. Bring a range of denominations since charges may be applied per check cashed. Store your money in a variety of forms. Ideally, at any given time you will be carrying some cash, some traveler's checks, and an ATM and/or credit card. All travelers should also consider carrying some US dollars (about US$50 worth), which are often preferred by local tellers. For this reason, most prices listed by *Let's Go* will be in US dollars.

TRAVELER'S CHECKS

Traveler's checks are one of the safest and most convenient means of carrying funds. American Express and Visa are the best-recognized brands. Many banks and agencies sell them for a small commission. Check issuers provide refunds if the checks are lost or stolen, and many provide additional services, such as toll-free refund hotlines abroad, emergency message services, and assistance with lost or stolen credit cards or passports. In Central America, traveler's checks are accepted in most capitals and in larger cities. Note that they are only accepted in US dollars, and that American Express is heavily preferred to Visa. Nicaragua is a notoriously bad place for traveler's checks.

American Express: Checks available with commission at AmEx offices and select banks (www.americanexpress.com). AmEx cardholders can also purchase checks by phone (☎+1-800-528-4800). Cheques for Two can be signed by either of 2 people traveling together. For purchase locations or more information, contact AmEx's service centers: in Australia ☎2 9271 8666, in Canada and the US 800-528-4800, in New Zealand 9 583 8300, in the UK 44 1273 571 600.

Visa: Checks available at banks worldwide. For the location of the nearest office, call the Visa Travelers Cheque Global Refund and Assistance Center: in the UK ☎800 895 078, in the US 800-227-6811; elsewhere, call the UK collect at +44 2079 378 091. Checks available in American, British, Canadian, European, and Japanese currencies, among others. Visa also offers TravelMoney, a prepaid debit card that can be reloaded online or by phone. For more information on Visa travel services, see http://usa.visa.com/personal/using_visa/travel_with_visa.html.

CREDIT, DEBIT, AND ATM CARDS

Where they are accepted, credit cards often offer superior exchange rates—up to 5% better than the retail rate used by banks and other currency-exchange establishments. Credit cards may also offer services such as insurance or emergency help and are sometimes required to reserve hotel rooms or rental cars. **MasterCard** and **Visa** are the most frequently accepted in Central America; **American Express** cards work at some ATMs, AmEx offices, and at major airports. Credit cards are widely accepted in the capitals and larger cities of Central America, especially at major hotels and restaurants. In particular, Nicaragua is surprisingly credit card-friendly in rural areas. Outside the cities, count on using cash.

The use of **ATM cards** is increasingly common in Central America. ATM machines are ubiquitous in larger cities and generally available in towns with banks. Still, err on the side of caution; even if there is an ATM, it might not work or accept your card. The safest bet is to withdraw cash in larger cities. Depending on the system that your bank at home uses, you can most likely access your personal bank account from abroad. ATMs get the same wholesale exchange rate as credit cards, but there is often a limit on the amount of money you can withdraw per day (usually around US$500). There is also typically a surcharge of US$1-5 per withdrawal, so it pays to be efficient.

Debit cards are as convenient as credit cards but withdraw money directly from the holder's checking account. A debit card can be used wherever its associated credit card company (usually MasterCard or Visa) is accepted.

The two major international money networks are **MasterCard/Maestro/Cirrus** (for ATM locations ☎+1-800-424-7787; www.mastercard.com) and **Visa/PLUS** (for ATM locations visit http://visa.via.infonow.net/locator/global/). In Central America, **Visa** is heavily preferred, and MasterCard might not be accepted at local ATMs. Most ATMs charge a transaction fee that is paid to the bank that owns the ATM. It is a good idea to contact your bank or credit card company before going abroad; frequent charges in a foreign country can sometimes prompt a fraud alert, which will freeze your account.

GETTING MONEY FROM HOME

If you run out of money while traveling, the easiest and cheapest solution is to have someone back home make a deposit to your bank account. Otherwise, consider one of the following options.

WIRING MONEY

It is possible to arrange a **bank money transfer,** which means asking a bank back home to wire money to a bank in Central America. This is the cheapest way to transfer cash, but it's also the slowest, usually taking several days or more. Note that some banks may only release your funds in local currency, potentially sticking you with a poor exchange rate; inquire about this in advance. Money transfer services like **Western Union** are faster and more convenient than bank transfers—but also much pricier. Western Union has many locations worldwide. To find one, visit www.westernunion.com, or in Australia call ☎1800 173 833, in Canada and the US 800-325-6000, in the UK 0800 735 1815. There is no number to call from Central America. To find agent locations, check the website instead. To wire money using a credit card, in Canada and the US call ☎800-CALL-CASH (800-2255-2274), in the UK 0800 833 833. Money transfer services, like remittances and access to emergency funds, are also available to **American Express** cardholders at selected travel offices in Central America; check www.amextravelresources.com before leaving.

US STATE DEPARTMENT (US CITIZENS ONLY)

In serious emergencies only, the US State Department will forward money within hours to the nearest consular office, which will then disburse it according to instructions for a US$30 fee. If you wish to use this service, you must contact the **Overseas Citizens Services** division of the **US State Department** (☎+1-202-501-4444, from US 888-407-4747).

COSTS

The cost of your trip will vary considerably, depending on where you visit, how you travel, and where you stay. For more on expenses, see the individual country chapters. The most significant expenses will probably be your round-trip (return) airfare to Central America (see **Getting to Central America: By Plane**, p. 18).

TIPPING AND BARGAINING

THE ART OF THE DEAL. Bargaining in Central America is a given: no price is set in stone, and vendors and drivers will automatically quote you a price that is several times too high. It's up to you to get them down to a reasonable rate. With the following tips and some finesse, you might be able to impress even the most hardened hawkers:

1. **Bargaining needn't be a fierce struggle laced with barbs.** Quite the opposite—good-natured wrangling with a cheerful face may prove your best weapon.

2. **Use your poker face.** The less your face betrays your interest in the item the better. If you touch an item to inspect it, the vendor will be sure to "encourage" you to name a price or make a purchase. Coming back again and again to admire a trinket is a good way of ensuring that you pay a ridiculously high price. Never get too enthusiastic about the object in question; point out flaws in workmanship and design. Be cool.

3. **Know when to bargain.** In most cases, it's quite clear when it's appropriate to bargain. Most private transportation fares and things for sale in outdoor markets are all fair game. Don't bargain on prepared or pre-packaged foods on the street or in restaurants. In some stores, signs will indicate whether "fixed prices" prevail. When in doubt, ask tactfully, "Is that your lowest price?" or whether discounts are given.

4. **Never underestimate the power of peer pressure.** Bargaining with more than one person at a time always leads to higher prices. Alternatively, try having a friend discourage you from your purchase—if you seem to be reluctant, the merchant will want to drop the price to interest you again.

5. **Know when to turn away.** Feel free to refuse any vendor or driver who bargains rudely and don't hesitate to move on to another vendor if one will not be reasonable about his final price. However, to start bargaining without an intention to buy is a major faux pas. Agreeing on a price and declining it is also poor form. Turn away slowly with a smile and "thank you" upon hearing a ridiculous price—it may plummet.

6. **Start low.** Never feel guilty offering a ludicrously low price. Your starting price should be no more than one-third to one-half the asking price.

Tipping and especially bargaining in Central America are quite different than what you may be accustomed to; there are many unspoken rules to which tourists must adhere. In tourist and upscale restaurants, a 10% tip is common. In smaller restaurants frequented by locals, tipping is rare. Tour guides generally appreciate something extra, though taxi drivers do not expect to be tipped. At outdoor markets, handicraft markets, and some handicraft shops, bargaining is expected and essential. Prices at supermarkets and most indoor stores, on the other hand, are non-negotiable. Bargaining for hotel rooms is often a good idea, particularly in the low season (or if the hotel obviously has vacancies).

TAXES

Each country in Central America has either a **sales tax** or a **value-added tax (VAT)** that is assessed as a percentage of an item's price. The rate ranges from 5% in Panama to 15% in Nicaragua. Certain goods and services, like food, are exempt or taxed at a reduced rate. Some businesses list prices without tax, so make sure you know how much you'll be paying before you purchase.

PACKING

Pack lightly: lay out only what you think you absolutely need, then take half the clothes and twice the money. If you plan to do a lot of hiking, also consult **The Great Outdoors,** p. 27.

Converters and adapters: All of the countries in Central America run on 110V/60Hz electricity, the same kind as in the United States. Appliances use North American two- and three-prong plugs. Travelers from outside the US will need both an adapter (to change the plug) and a converter (to change the voltage).

Important documents: Don't forget your passport, traveler's checks, ATM and/or credit cards, adequate ID, and photocopies of all of the aforementioned in case these documents are lost or stolen. Also check that you have any of the following that might apply to you: a hosteling membership card, driver's license, travel insurance forms (p. 14), ISIC (p. 6), and/or railpass or bus pass.

SAFETY AND HEALTH

GENERAL ADVICE

In any type of crisis, the most important thing to do is **stay calm.** Your country's embassy abroad (see p. 43 for Belize and p. 112 for Guatemala) is usually your best resource in an emergency; registering with that embassy upon arrival in the country is a good idea. The government offices listed in the **Travel Advisories** box (p. 12) can provide information on the services they offer their citizens in case of emergencies abroad.

LOCAL LAWS AND POLICE

Central American legal systems are notoriously ineffective and police are sometimes corrupt. Tourist police are present in larger cities for peacekeeping and informational purposes. To learn which towns have tourist police, contact the **tourism bureau** in each country, listed in the respective country chapters.

Most Central American countries run aggressive campaigns against sexual tourism; sexual activity with a minor is typically punishable by imprisonment.

Homosexuality is legal in all Central American countries except Belize.In Belize, homosexuality is punishable by imprisonment. There are no reports of tourists being prosecuted, but discretion is probably the wisest course of action. See **Specific Concerns** (p. 11) for more information.

DRUGS AND ALCOHOL

Because of Central America's serious narcotics problem, penalties are severe for drug possession. Your home embassy will be of minimal assistance should you get into trouble. If you carry **prescription drugs** while you travel, have a copy of the prescriptions themselves and a note from your doctor. Avoid public drunkenness; in certain areas it is against the law, and can also jeopardize your safety and earn the disdain of locals.

SPECIFIC CONCERNS

NATURAL DISASTERS

FLOODS. The rainy season in Central America runs from May to November. Many countries see over 200cm (80 in.) of rainfall annually. The extensive flooding that results can destroy bridges and roads, making travel dangerous and occasionally impossible. Areas along the Caribbean coast and near rivers are most prone to flooding. **Mudslides** due to the rain are a very real danger in Central America and in recent years have caused the destruction of entire villages. Mountainous areas are the most prone to mudslides, especially during the rainy season. Exercise caution when traveling during the rainy season; check the weather and know your route before heading out.

SEISMIC ACTIVITY. Most of Central America lies along the boundary of several tectonic plates, making it the sight of frequent and often unpredictable earthquakes. Tremors are more common, but large-scale earthquakes are still a danger. If an earthquake occurs, be sure to stay away from anything that could fall on you. If indoors, stand in a doorway or crouch under a desk. If you're driving, pull over to the side of the road until the quake passes. Most Central American countries are sites of active **volcanoes.** They erupt infrequently and generally with several weeks' warning.

CRIME

Unfortunately, crime rates are extremely high in Central America, and pose very real risks for travelers. Petty theft and pickpocketing occur frequently (see **Personal Safety: Possessions and Valuables,** p. 12). Carjackings and armed robbery have risen to alarmingly high levels in recent years, especially those involving tourists. Foreigners are assumed to have money, making them instant (and often easy) targets for thieves. If you are held up, do not attempt to resist, since robbers will not hesitate to shoot or stab. Many tourist murders in recent years have stemmed from resistance to robbers.

DEMONSTRATIONS AND POLITICAL GATHERINGS

Political demonstrations are a frequent sight in Central America, often due to labor problems or electoral results. While demonstrations are usually nonviolent, groups will often block roads or airports. These areas are better avoided during times of political unrest. Very rarely, tourists are taken hostage for short periods of time as a ploy to bait the government. Such incidents are usually not physically dangerous to tourists, as they are safely returned as soon as the conflict is over.

TERRORISM

While crime is a major problem, terrorism is limited in Central America. Drug and street gangs exist, especially in capital cities, but their activity is generally local, and financial in nature. See below for more information.

> **TRAVEL ADVISORIES.** The following government offices provide travel information and advisories by telephone, by fax, or via the web:
> **Australian Department of Foreign Affairs and Trade:** ☎+61 2 6261 1111; www.dfat.gov.au.
> **Canadian Department of Foreign Affairs and International Trade (DFAIT):** ☎+1-800-267-8376; www.dfait-maeci.gc.ca. Call or visit the webside for the free booklet *Bon Voyage...But.*
> **New Zealand Ministry of Foreign Affairs:** ☎+64 4 439 8000; www.mfat. govt.nz.
> **United Kingdom Foreign and Commonwealth Office:** ☎+44 20 7008 1500; www.fco.gov.uk.
> **US Department of State:** ☎+1-888-407-4747, 202-501-4444 from abroad; http://travel.state.gov.

PERSONAL SAFETY

EXPLORING AND TRAVELING

To avoid unwanted attention, try to blend in as much as possible. Respecting local customs (in many cases, dressing more conservatively than you would at home) may ward off would-be hecklers. Familiarize yourself with your surroundings before setting out and carry yourself with confidence. Check maps in shops and restaurants rather than on the street. If you are traveling alone, be sure someone at home knows your itinerary. Never tell anyone you meet that you're by yourself. When walking at night, stick to busy, well-lit streets and avoid dark alleyways. There is no sure-fire way to avoid all the threatening situations that you might encounter while traveling, but a good **self-defense course** will give you concrete ways to react to unwanted advances. **Impact, Prepare,** and **Model Mugging** (www.modelmugging.org) can refer you to local self-defense courses in Australia, Canada, Switzerland, and the US.

POSSESSIONS AND VALUABLES

Never leave your belongings unattended; crime can occur in even the most safe-looking hostel or hotel. Bring your own padlock for hostel lockers. Be particularly careful on **buses** and **trains;** horror stories abound about determined thieves who wait for travelers to fall asleep. Carry your bag or purse in front of you where you can see it. When traveling with others, sleep in alternate shifts. When alone, be careful in selecting a train compartment: never stay in an empty one and always use a lock to secure your pack to the luggage rack. Use extra caution if traveling at night or on overnight trains. Try to sleep on top bunks with your luggage stored above you (if not in bed with you) and keep important documents and other valuables on you at all times.

Bring as little with you as possible. Buy a few combination **padlocks** to secure your belongings. Next, **carry as little cash as possible.** Keep your traveler's checks and ATM/credit cards in a **money belt** along with your passport and ID cards. Lastly, **keep a small cash reserve separate from your primary stash.** This should be about US$50 (US dollars are best) sewn into or stored in the depths of your pack, along with your traveler's check numbers and photocopies of your important documents.

In large cities, **con artists** often work in groups and may involve children in their schemes. Beware of certain classics: sob stories that require money, rolls of bills "found" on the street, mustard spilled (or saliva spit) onto your shoulder to distract you while they snatch your bag. **Never let your passport or your bags out of your sight.** Hostel workers will sometimes stand at bus and train arrival points to recruit tired and disoriented travelers to their hostel; never believe strangers who tell you that theirs is the only hostel open. Beware of **pickpockets** in city crowds, especially on public transportation. Also, be alert in public telephone booths. If you must say your calling-card number, do so very quietly; if you punch it in, make sure no one can look over your shoulder.

If you will be traveling with electronic devices, such as a laptop computer, check whether your homeowner's insurance covers loss, theft, or damage when you travel. If not, you might consider purchasing a separate, low-cost insurance policy. **Safeware** (☎ +1-800-800-1492; www.safeware.com) specializes in covering computers and charges US$90 for 90-day comprehensive international travel coverage up to US$4000.

PRE-DEPARTURE HEALTH

In your passport, write the names of any people you wish to be contacted in case of a medical emergency and list any allergies or medical conditions. Matching a prescription to a foreign equivalent is not always easy, safe, or possible, so, if you take **prescription drugs,** carry up-to-date prescriptions or a statement from your doctor stating the medications' trade names, manufacturers, chemical names, and dosages. While traveling, be sure to keep all medication with you in your carry-on luggage.

INOCULATION RECOMMENDATIONS.
There are several inoculations recommended for travel in Central America. Yellow fever inoculations are required throughout Central American for visitors who have previously visited nations where it is endemic. Panama is the only nation in which yellow fever is a health risk.
Hepatitis A, or immunoglobulin (IG). Requires a series of shots, so consult your doctor a few weeks in advance.
Hepatitis B, particularly if you expect to be exposed to blood (e.g. health-care workers), have sexual contact, stay longer than 6 months, or undergo medical treatment. The Hepatitis B vaccine is now recommended for all infants and for children 12 years old or younger who did not receive the series as infants.
Rabies, for travel in rural areas or anticipated contact with animals.
Typhoid, for travel in rural areas.
Yellow fever, if traveling to rural areas in Panama.

The names in Spanish for common drugs are: *aspirina* (aspirin), *paraceta-mol* or *acetaminofén* (acetaminophen), *penicilina* (penicillin), *ibuprofeno* (ibuprofen), and *antihistamínico* (antihistamine/allergy medicine). Brand names like Tylenol®, Advil®, and Pepto Bismol® are also well known.

IMMUNIZATIONS AND PRECAUTIONS

Travelers over two years old should make sure that the following vaccines are up to date: **MMR** (for measles, mumps, and rubella); **DTaP or Td** (for diphtheria, tetanus, and pertussis); **IPV** (for polio); **Hib** (for *Haemophilus influenzae* B); and **HepB** (for Hepatitis B). See **Inoculation Recommendations,** p. 13, for details on vaccination.

For recommendations on immunizations and prophylaxis, consult the **Centers for Disease Control and Prevention** (CDC; below) in the US or the equivalent in your home country and check with a doctor for guidance. For country-specific information about malaria and other vaccinations, see the **Health** section for each country chapter.

INSURANCE

Travel insurance covers four basic areas: medical and health problems, property loss, trip cancellation and interruption, and emergency evacuation. Though regular insurance policies may well extend to travel-related accidents, you may consider purchasing separate travel insurance if the cost of potential trip cancellation, interruption, or emergency medical evacuation is greater than you can afford. Prices for travel insurance generally run about US$50 per week for full coverage, while trip cancellation and interruption coverage may be purchased separately at a rate of US$3-5 per day, depending on length of stay.

Medical insurance can cover costs incurred abroad; check with your provider. **Homeowners' insurance** (or your family's coverage) often covers theft during travel and loss of travel documents (passport, plane ticket, railpass, etc.) up to US$500. **American Express** (☎+1-800-528-4800; www.americanexpress.com) grants most cardholders automatic collision and theft car-rental insurance on rentals.

USEFUL ORGANIZATIONS AND PUBLICATIONS

The American **Centers for Disease Control and Prevention** (**CDC;** ☎+1-800-CDC-INFO/232-4636; www.cdc.gov/travel) maintains an international travelers' hotline and an informative website. Consult the appropriate government agency in your home country for consular information on health, entry requirements, and other issues for various countries. See **Travel Advisories,** p. 12. For quick information on health and other travel warnings, call the **Overseas Citizens Services** (☎+1-202-647-5225) or contact a passport agency, embassy, or consulate abroad. For information on medical evacuation services and travel insurance firms, see the US government's website at http://travel.state.gov/travel/abroad_health.html or the **British Foreign and Commonwealth Office** (www.fco.gov.uk). For general health information, contact the **American Red Cross** (☎+1-202-303-5000; www.redcross.org).

STAYING HEALTHY

ONCE IN CENTRAL AMERICA

ENVIRONMENTAL HAZARDS

Heat exhaustion and dehydration: Avoid heat exhaustion and **heatstroke** by drinking plenty of fluids, eating salty foods (e.g. crackers), abstaining from dehydrating beverages (e.g. alcohol, coffee, and tea), and wearing sunscreen. If showing symptoms, cool off with wet towels and see a doctor.

Hypothermia: A rapid drop in body temperature, shivering, exhaustion, and hallucinations are the clearest sign of overexposure to cold. Do not let hypothermia victims fall asleep. To avoid it, keep dry, wear layers, and use common sense.

Sunburn: Always wear sunscreen (SPF 30 or higher) when spending significant amounts of time outdoors. If you get sunburned, apply some aloe and wear more sunblock the next time out.

E S S E N T I A L S

INSECT-BORNE DISEASES

Many diseases are transmitted by insects—mainly mosquitoes, fleas, ticks, and lice. Be aware of insects in wet or forested areas, especially while hiking and camping. Wear long pants and long sleeves, tuck your pants into your socks, and use a mosquito net. Use insect repellents such as DEET and soak or spray your gear with permethrin (licensed in the US only for use on clothing).
Mosquitoes—responsible for malaria, dengue fever, and yellow fever—can be particularly abundant in wet, swampy, or wooded areas.

Dengue fever: An "urban viral infection" transmitted by *Aedes* mosquitoes that bite during the day. The incubation period is usually 4-7 days. Early symptoms include a high fever, severe headaches, swollen lymph nodes, and muscle aches. Patients also suffer from nausea, vomiting, and rash. To reduce the risk of contracting Dengue fever, use mosquito repellent and wear clothing that covers the arms and legs. See a doctor immediately upon noticing symptoms, drink plenty of liquids, and take a fever-reducing medication such as acetaminophen (Tylenol®).

Malaria: Transmitted by *Anopheles* mosquitoes that bite at night. The incubation period varies anywhere between 10 days and 4 weeks. Early symptoms include fever, chills, aches, and fatigue, followed by high fever and sweating, sometimes with vomiting and diarrhea. See a doctor if you experience flu-like symptoms after traveling in a risk area. To reduce the risk of contracting malaria, use mosquito repellent, particularly in the evenings and when visiting forested areas. See a doctor at least 4-6 weeks before a trip to a high-risk area to get up-to-date malaria prescriptions and recommendations. A doctor may prescribe oral prophylactics, like mefloquine or doxycycline. Know that mefloquine can have serious side effects, including paranoia, psychosis, and nightmares. Halofantrine (often marketed as Halfan) is commonly prescribed overseas, but be aware that it has serious heart-related side effects.

Other insect-borne diseases: Lymphatic filariasis is a roundworm transmitted by mosquitoes. Infection causes lymphedema and enlargement of extremities. **Leishmaniasis,** a parasite transmitted by sand flies, usually occurs in rural Central America. Symptoms include fever, weakness, swelling of the spleen, and skin sores weeks to months after the bite. **Chagas' disease (American trypanomiasis)** is a relatively common parasite transmitted by the cone nose or "kissing" bug, which infests mud, adobe, and thatch. Its immediate symptoms include fever, fatigue, headache, and nausea. If untreated in the long term, Chagas' can lead to fatal, debilitating conditions of the heart and intestines. There are no vaccines for these ailments, and tropical specialists offer the only (limited) treatment available.

FOOD- AND WATER-BORNE DISEASES

Prevention is the best cure: be sure that your food is properly cooked and that the water you drink is clean. Watch out for food from markets or street vendors that may have been cooked in unhygienic conditions. Other culprits are raw shellfish, unpasteurized milk, and sauces containing raw eggs. Buy bottled water or purify your own water by bringing it to a rolling boil or treating it with **iodine tablets.**

Dysentery: Results from an intestinal infection caused by bacteria in contaminated food or water. Common symptoms include bloody diarrhea, fever, and abdominal pain and tenderness. The most common type of dysentery generally only lasts a week, but it is highly contagious. Seek medical help immediately. Dysentery can be treated with the drugs norfloxacin or ciprofloxacin (commonly known as Cipro). If you are traveling in high-risk (especially rural) regions, consider obtaining a prescription before you leave.

Giardiasis: Transmitted through parasites and acquired by drinking untreated water from streams or lakes. Symptoms include diarrhea, cramps, bloating, fatigue, weight loss, and nausea. If untreated, it can lead to severe dehydration. Giardiasis occurs worldwide.

Hepatitis A: A viral infection of the liver acquired through contaminated water or shellfish from contaminated water. Symptoms include fatigue, fever, loss of appetite, nausea, dark urine, jaundice, vomiting, aches and pains, and light stools. The risk is highest in rural areas and the countryside, but Hepatitis A is also present in urban areas. Ask your doctor about the Hepatitis A vaccine or an injection of immunoglobulin.

Traveler's diarrhea: Results from drinking fecally contaminated water or eating uncooked and contaminated foods. Symptoms include nausea, bloating, and urgency. Try non-sugary foods with protein and carbohydrates to keep your strength up. Over-the-counter anti-diarrheals (e.g., Imodium®) may counteract the problem. The most dangerous side effect is dehydration; drink uncaffeinated soft drinks and eat salted crackers. If you develop a fever or your symptoms don't go away after 4-5 days, consult a doctor.

Typhoid fever: Caused by the salmonella bacteria, which are common in villages and rural areas in Central America. Mostly transmitted through contaminated food and water, typhoid may also be acquired by direct contact with another person. Early symptoms include high fever, headaches, fatigue, appetite loss, constipation, and a rash on the abdomen or chest. Antibiotics can treat typhoid, but a vaccination (70-90% effective) is recommended.

OTHER INFECTIOUS DISEASES

The following diseases exist all over the world. Travelers should know how to recognize them and what to do if they suspect they have been infected.

AIDS and HIV: For detailed information on Acquired Immune Deficiency Syndrome (AIDS) in Central America, call the CDC's 24hr. National AIDS Hotline at ☎+1-800-232-4636. Belize, Nicaragua, and Panama require HIV test results for those applying for extended residency, and only rarely grant residency to people with positive tests. Provisions exist in Panama to deport those with HIV/AIDS, but they do not screen visitors.

Hepatitis B: A viral liver infection transmitted via blood or other bodily fluids. Symptoms, which may not surface until years after infection, include jaundice, appetite loss, fever, and joint pain. Hepatitis B is transmitted through unprotected sex and unclean needles. A 3-shot vaccination sequence is recommended for sexually active travelers and anyone planning to seek medical treatment abroad. The vaccine series must begin 6 months before traveling.

Rabies: Transmitted through the saliva of infected animals (often dogs and bats); fatal if untreated. By the time symptoms (thirst and muscle spasms) appear, the disease is in its terminal stage. Wash the wound, seek immediate medical care, and try to have the animal located. There is a vaccine, but it is only semi-effective.

Sexually transmitted infections (STIs): Gonorrhea, chlamydia, genital warts, syphilis, herpes, HPV, and other STIs are easier to catch than HIV and can be just as serious. Though condoms may protect you from some STIs, oral or even tactile contact can lead to transmission. If you think you may have contracted an STI, see a doctor immediately.

Swine influenza: "Swine flu", also known by its subtype H1N1, is a highly infectious strain of flu that originated in Mexico in 2009. Cases have been reported in Central

America, but have been rarely fatal. Symptoms include fever, fatigue, chills, muscle pain, and congestion. Wash your hands and go to the hospital if you have symptoms. There is currently no vaccine.

OTHER HEALTH CONCERNS

MEDICAL CARE ON THE ROAD

In general, medical facilities in Central America are fairly basic. Only in the capital cities are you likely to find facilities equipped for advanced surgery or trauma treatment. In some countries (Belize, Nicaragua) you'll have trouble finding adequate care. Most hospitals and doctors expect to be paid upfront in cash. Public hospitals are often crowded, and can't provide appropriate care in many cases. Private hospitals are better (though don't offer comprehensive services), but are much more expensive. Ambulance services, available in cities, are often just transportation to the hospital. It is important to let the driver know which kind of hospital you need. While some countries (Guatemala, Panama) have many English-speaking personnel, don't count on receiving adequate care unless you can communicate your needs in Spanish. Check with your embassy or consulate to see if they have a list of local doctors.

If you are concerned about obtaining medical assistance while traveling, you may wish to employ special support services. The **International Association for Medical Assistance to Travelers (IAMAT;** US ☎+1-716-754-4883, Canada +1-416-652-0137; www.iamat.org) has free membership, lists English-speaking doctors worldwide, and offers details on immunization requirements and sanitation. For those whose insurance doesn't apply abroad, it is possible to purchase additional coverage (See **Insurance,** p. 14).

Those with medical conditions (such as diabetes, allergies to antibiotics, epilepsy, or heart conditions) may want to obtain a **MedicAlert** membership (US$40 per year), which includes, among other things, a stainless-steel ID tag and a 24hr. collect-call number. Contact the MedicAlert Foundation International (from the US ☎888-633-4298, outside the US +1-209-668-3333; www.medicalert.org).

WOMEN'S HEALTH

Women traveling in unsanitary conditions are vulnerable to **urinary tract (including bladder and kidney) infections.** Over-the-counter medicines can sometimes alleviate symptoms, but if they persist, see a doctor. Since tampons, pads, and reliable contraceptive devices are sometimes hard to find when traveling, bring supplies with you.

SANITATION

It's best to avoid food from street vendors in Central America, especially if you can't see it being prepared. Stick to bottled water, as local tap water is often unpotable. Be on the lookout for ice in your drinks made from tap water. Likewise, fresh vegetables and fruit that have been washed in tap water are often unsafe. In general, keep away from raw, unpeeled, and uncooked food.

Toilets are often subpar in Central American countries, especially outside of the cities. Make sure to bring toilet paper with you everywhere, and remember that the plumbing systems are not, as a rule, equipped to handle paper waste.

GETTING TO CENTRAL AMERICA

BY PLANE

When it comes to airfare, a little effort can save you a bundle. Last-minute specials, airfare wars, and charter flights are often the these best. The key is to hunt around, be flexible, and ask about discounts. Students, seniors, and those under 26 should never pay full price for a ticket.

AIRFARES

Airfares to Central America peak between December and April. Holidays, especially Christmas and *Semana Santa* (the week before Easter), are also expensive. The cheapest times to travel are late spring and November. Midweek (M-Th morning) round-trip flights run cheaper than weekend flights, but they are generally more crowded and less likely to permit frequent-flier upgrades. Not fixing a return date ("open return") or arriving in and departing from different cities ("open-jaw") can be pricier than round-trip flights. Patching one-way flights together is the most expensive way to travel. Flights between Central American capitals will tend to be cheaper.

If Central America is only one stop on a more extensive globe-hop, consider a **round-the-world (RTW)** ticket. Tickets usually include at least five stops and are valid for about a year; prices range US$3000-8000. Try the airline consortiums **Oneworld** (www.oneworld.com), **Skyteam** (www.skyteam.com), and **Star Alliance** (www.staralliance.com).

Fares for round-trip flights to capital cities from the US or Canada's east coast cost around $US250-300 in the low season. Flights from the US or Canada's west coast are around US$200-300; from the UK, UK£400-600; from Australia AUS$3000-3500; from New Zealand NZ$4000-4500.

FLIGHT PLANNING ON THE INTERNET. The internet may be the budget traveler's dream when it comes to finding and booking bargain fares, but the array of options can be overwhelming. Many airline sites offer special last-minute deals on the web. Check the websites of **Taca** (www.taca.com) and **Copa** (www.copaair.com) for sweet fares.

STA (www.statravel.com) and **StudentUniverse** (www.studentuniverse. com) provide quotes on student tickets, while **Orbitz** (www.orbitz.com), **Expedia** (www.expedia.com), and **Travelocity** (www.travelocity.com) offer full travel services. **Priceline** (www.priceline.com) lets you specify a price and obligates you to buy any ticket that meets or beats it; **Hotwire** (www.hotwire. com) offers bargain fares but won't reveal the airline or flight times until you buy. Other sites that compile deals include www.bestfares.com, www.flights. com, www.lowestfare.com, www.onetravel.com, and www.travelzoo.com.

Cheapflights (www.cheapflights.co.uk) is a useful search engine for finding—you guessed it—cheap flights. **Booking Buddy** (www.bookingbuddy.com), **Kayak** (www.kayak.com), and **SideStep** (www.sidestep.com) are online tools that let you enter your trip information and search multiple sites at once. *Let's Go* does not endorse any of these websites. As always, be cautious and research companies before you hand over your credit card number.

BUDGET AND STUDENT TRAVEL AGENCIES

Travelers holding **ISICs** and **IYTCs** (p. 6) qualify for big discounts from student travel agencies. Most flights from budget agencies are on major airlines, but note that in high season some may sell seats on less reliable chartered aircraft.

> **STA Travel,** 2871 Broadway, New York City, NY 10025, USA (24hr. reservations and info ☎+1-800-781-4040; www.statravel.com). A student and youth travel organization with offices worldwide, including US offices in Los Angeles, New York City, Seattle, Washington, DC and a number of other college towns. Ticket booking, travel insurance, railpasses, and more. Walk-in offices are located throughout Australia (☎+61 134 782), New Zealand (☎+0800 474 400), and the UK (☎+44 8712 230 0040).

BY BUS

Getting to Central America is possible by bus via Mexico. Buses leave from the border town of **Chetumal** and go to **Belize City** and cost about US$10 or $BZ20. There is a US$20(BZ$40) fee for foreigners crossing the border into Belize. From the border, buses continue on to **Flores, Guatemala** (US$25).

BORDER CROSSINGS

Coming overland from North America means traveling through Mexico via bus (see above) or car. If driving, remember that Mexican insurance should be obtained before heading into Mexico. Preparation and planning is essential. Traveling to Panama from Colombia overland is impossible—to do so you must cross the **Darién gap,** an often dangerous jungle with no roads or trails. For country-specific border crossings, see the **Transportation** section for each country chapter.

GETTING AROUND CENTRAL AMERICA

BY PLANE

AIRCRAFT SAFETY. The airlines of developing-world nations do not always meet safety standards. The **Official Airline Guide** (www.oag.com) and many travel agencies can tell you the type and age of aircraft on a particular route. This can be especially useful in Central America, where less reliable equipment is often used for internal flights. The **International Airline Passengers Association** (www.iapa.com) provides region-specific safety information to its members. The **Federal Aviation Administration** (www.faa.gov/passengers/international_travel) reviews the airline authorities for countries whose airlines enter the US. **US State Department** travel advisories (www.travel.state.gov) sometimes involve foreign carriers, especially when terrorist bombings or hijackings may be a threat, though it hasn't been a problem in Central America.

Copa Airlines and Taca (see **Getting to Central America: By Plane, p. 18**) offer flights between all capitals in Central America (usually US$100-200). Once again, Belize is the exception. Check the airlines' websites for last-minute deals and special offers.

BY BUS

INTERNATIONAL BUSES

The cheapest way to get from country to country in Central America is by **international coach bus.** There are two main lines that serve Central America. These buses feature amenities like air conditioning and reclining seats that you won't find on local buses, but they come at a higher price.

King Quality (☎+502 2369 7070; www.king-qualityca.com). Coach trips from Tapachula, Mexico through all of Central America (except for Belize and Panama). Mexico to Costa Rica, one-way US$98; round-trip $181.

Tica Bus (www.ticabus.com). Services destinations all the way from Tapachula, Mexico to Panama City. Tickets allow you to hop on and off at the stops along the way. Mexico to Panama City, one-way US$105; round-trip $210.

LOCAL BUSES

Buses are the only way to get from place to place within countries in Central America. In intercity travel, the beastly **Toyota Coaster** is the vehicle of choice; people far in excess of the theoretical capacity (21) routinely cram into these white beauties. In more rural areas you'll most often ride the famous **camionetas,** or **"chicken buses"**—garishly painted American schoolbuses—to get from place to place. Worn shocks help passengers feel every bump in the rough and often unpaved roads. Drivers have few qualms about putting it into high gear down hills. Snag a window seat (unless you're tall) to enjoy the view. Keep in mind that those who travel by bus in Central America occasionally fall prey to hijackers and roadside bandits. Traveling by bus at night can be particularly dangerous. Buses may break down, run behind schedule, or fill with hot, cramped passengers. But all in all, buses are generally cheap and reliable, and usually the only option.

BY CAR

Driving in Central America frees you from cramped, overheated buses never will, but also promises bad roads and bad conditions. Getting around Central America by car is a challenge—make sure to do your homework beforehand. Visit the **Association for Safe International Road Travel** (www.asirt.org) for more information.

DRIVING PERMITS AND CAR INSURANCE

INTERNATIONAL DRIVING PERMIT (IDP)

If you plan to drive a car while in Central America, you must be over 18 and have an **International Driving Permit (IDP),** though all the countries in Central America allow travelers to drive for a limited number of months with a valid license from your home country. It may be a good idea to get an IDP anyway, in case you're in a situation (e.g., an accident or stranded in a small town) where the police do not know English.

Your IDP, valid for one year, must be issued in your own country before you depart. An application for an IDP usually requires one or two photos, a current local license, an additional form of photo identification. You will also be charged a fee. To apply, contact your home country's automobile association. Be vigilant when purchasing an IDP online or anywhere other than your home automobile association. Many vendors sell permits of questionable legitimacy for higher prices.

CAR INSURANCE

Most credit cards cover standard car insurance. If you rent, lease, or borrow a car, you will need a **green card,** or **International Insurance Certificate,** to certify that you have liability insurance and that it applies abroad. Green cards can be obtained at car-rental agencies, car dealers (for those leasing cars), some travel agents, and some border crossings. Rental agencies may require you to purchase theft insurance in countries in which they believe there is a high risk of auto theft.

RENTING

While renting a car in Central America allows you to travel comfortably and at your own pace, it comes with its own set of hassles. In general, the cheaper the car, the less reliable and more difficult it is to handle, which can pose problems on the often dangerous roads.

With reliable public transportation in most cities, it is often unnecessary to rent a car. Parking and city driving are often exhausting, and rental cars are often a target for theft in cities.

While regular cars might suffice during the dry season (November to April), four-wheel-drive (4WD) vehicles are often essential in the rainy season, especially in rural areas. Less expensive 4WDs, however, tend to be more top heavy and can topple over when navigating particularly bumpy roads.

RENTAL AGENCIES

You can generally make reservations before you leave by calling major international offices in your home country. It's a good idea to cross-check this information with local agencies as well. *Let's Go* includes local desk numbers in town listings.

To rent a car from most establishments in Central America, you need to be at least 21 years old. Some agencies require renters to be 25, and most charge those aged 21-24 an additional insurance fee (around US$10 per day). Small local operations occasionally rent to people under 21, but be sure to ask about the insurance coverage and deductible. Always check the fine print.

Budget: ☎+1-800-472-3325; www.budgetcentroamerica.com. Rental cars available in Belize, (US$70 per day), Costa Rica (US$25), El Salvador (US$30), Guatemala (US$25-45), Honduras (US$25-40), Nicaragua (US$20), and Panama (US$20). Insurance is another US$10/day. 24hr. roadside assistance in Belize, El Salvador, and Nicaragua.

National: ☎+1-877-222-9058; www.nationalcar.com. Rental cars available in Costa Rica (US$20 per day), El Salvador (US$20-25), Guatemala (US$20), Honduras (US$20), Nicaragua (US$40), and Panama (US$20). US$25 surcharge for those under 25.

Thrifty: ☎+1-918-669-2168; www.thrifty.com. Rental cars available in Costa Rica (US$30-40 per day), El Salvador (US$25-30), Guatemala (US$20), Honduras (US$40), Nicaragua (US$20), and Panama (US$15-20). Surcharges apply to drivers under 25.

ESSENTIALS

COSTS AND INSURANCE

Rental-car prices start at around US$20 per day for national companies. Local agencies start around US$25. Expect to pay more for larger cars and for four-wheel-drive. Cars with **automatic transmission** can cost up to US$20 more per day than cars with manual transmission (stick shift), and, in some places, automatic transmission is nearly impossible to find.

Remember that if you are driving a conventional rental vehicle on an unpaved road in a rental car, you are almost never covered by insurance. Be aware that cars rented on an **American Express** or **Visa/MasterCard Gold** or **Platinum** credit card in Central America might not carry the automatic insurance that they would in some other countries; check with your credit card company before renting. Insurance plans from rental companies almost always come with an **deductible** (or excess) of around US$750-1000 for conventional vehicles; excess can reach US$1500 for younger drivers and for four-wheel-drive vehicles. This means that the insurance purchased from the rental company only applies to damages over the deductible; damages below that amount must be covered by your existing insurance plan. Some rental companies in Central America require you to buy a **collision damage waiver (CDW)**, which will waive the deductible in the case of a collision. **Loss damage waivers (LDWs)** do the same in the case of theft or vandalism. It is important to note that CDWs only cover collisions with other cars.

National chains often allow one-way rentals (picking up in one city and dropping off in another). There is usually a minimum hire period and sometimes an extra drop-off charge of several hundred dollars.

ON THE ROAD

In Central America, defensive driving is imperative. The rules of the road (those that exist) are rarely enforced and rarely obeyed. Speed limits are often not posted, and thus somewhat discretionary. Passing on blind corners is not uncommon. In addition, roads outside of cities are unpaved, unlit, poorly maintained, and seasonally damaged by flooding and other natural disasters.

Children under 40 lb. should ride only in specially designed car seats, available for a small fee from most car-rental agencies. For long drives in desolate areas, invest in a cell phone and a roadside assistance program (p. 23). Sleeping in your car is the most dangerous way to get your rest, and it's also illegal in many countries.

Gasoline (petrol) prices vary, ranging from around US$2.50 per gallon in Honduras to about US$5 per gallon in Belize. Unleaded gas is available in most places, but not everywhere. If you must use leaded gasoline, always use the high grade/premium kind. Park your vehicle in garages or well-traveled areas, and keep valuables out of sight.

DANGERS

The biggest driving hazard in Central America is the road itself. Urban roads and highways are generally well-maintained, but outside of these areas the roads are unpaved. Be careful driving during the rainy season (May-Oct.), when roads are often in poor condition and **landslides** are common. In many areas the added safety of a four-wheel-drive vehicle may be well worth the extra rental cost. When approaching a one-lane bridge, labeled *"puente angosto"* or *"solo carril,"* the first driver to flash headlights has the right of way.

Carjacking and **armed vehicular robbery** are becoming problems in many parts of Central America. Robbers target tourists, often at night, on highways, small roads, and crowded urban streets. It is advisable to avoid driving at night altogether. Foreign brands and sports cars—anything that signals to strangers that you are foreign or have money—should be avoided.

CAR ASSISTANCE

There are few resources to help out in case of a breakdown or accident in Central America. Some rental agencies offer 24hr. roadside assistance—ask about this when you're shopping around. Your best bet is to make sure your vehicle is ready for the road. Parts, gas, and service stations are hard to come by, so be prepared for every possible contingency. Mechanically inclined drivers might want to bring tools for any problems that arise.

If you are involved in an accident, you should wait until the police arrive to move your vehicle so that an officer can prepare a report. Unless this is done immediately and reported to insurers, it is difficult or impossible to file claims and receive coverage.

BY THUMB

 LET'S NOT GO. *Let's Go* urges you to consider the risks before you choose to hitch. We do not recommend hitching as a safe means of transportation, though it is common in many parts of Central America.

KEEPING IN TOUCH

BY EMAIL AND INTERNET

Internet access is widely available in Central America. In the capitals and larger cities, internet cafes are ubiquitous, fairly cheap, and connections are faster. In smaller cities and towns, internet access is slower and spottier but still available. In general, large hotels offer internet to their guests. Some larger restaurants, as well as American chains like McDonalds and Starbucks, often have it as well. Travelers with laptops may be able to take advantage of an increasing number of "hotspots" where they can get online for free or for a small fee. Central America is short on free Wi-Fi hotspots; the best bets are large hotels and restaurants and some hostels. **Internet cafes** and the occasional free internet terminal at a public library are listed in the **Practical Information** sections of major cities. If you do have to pay, prices vary by region, but internet generally costs US$1-3 per hr., except in Belize, where it runs around US$5 per hr.

Take advantage of free **web-based email accounts** (e.g., www.gmail.com).

 WARY WI-FI. Wireless hot spots make internet access possible in public and remote places. Unfortunately, they also pose **security risks.** Hot spots are public, open networks that use unencrypted, unsecured connections. They are susceptible to hacks and "packet sniffing"—the theft of passwords and other private information. To prevent problems, disable "ad hoc" mode, turn off file sharing and network discovery, encrypt your email, turn on your firewall, beware of phony networks, and watch for over-the-shoulder creeps.

BY TELEPHONE

CALLING HOME FROM CENTRAL AMERICA

Prepaid phone cards are a common and relatively inexpensive means of calling abroad. Each one comes with a Personal Identification Number (PIN) and a toll-free access number. Call the access number and then follow the directions for dialing your PIN. To purchase prepaid phone cards, check online for the best rates; www.callingcards.com is a good place to start. Online providers generally send your access number and PIN via email, with no actual "card" involved. You can also call home with prepaid phone cards purchased in Central America (see **Calling Within Central America,** p. 24).

Another option is to purchase a **calling card,** linked to a major national telecommunications service in your home country. Calls are billed collect or to your account. Cards generally come with instructions for dialing both domestically and internationally.

Placing a **collect call** through an international operator can be expensive but may be necessary in case of an emergency. You can frequently call collect without even possessing a company's calling card just by calling its access number and following the instructions.

PLACING INTERNATIONAL CALLS. To call Central America from home or to call home from Central America, dial:

1. The **international dialing prefix.** To call from **Australia,** dial ☎0011; **Canada** or the **US,** ☎011; **Ireland, New Zealand,** or the **UK,** ☎00; **Belize, Costa Rica, Honduras,** and **Nicaragua,** ☎00; **El Salvador,** ☎00 or ☎144 + 00; **Guatemala,** ☎00 or 130 + 00; **Panama,** ☎0.

2. The **country code** of the country you want to call. To call **Australia,** dial ☎61; **Canada** or the **US,** ☎1; **Ireland,** ☎353; **New Zealand,** ☎64; the **UK,** ☎44; **Belize,** ☎501; **Costa Rica,** ☎506; **El Salvador,** ☎503; **Guatemala,** ☎502; **Honduras,** ☎504; **Nicaragua,** ☎505; **Panama,** ☎507.

3. The **city/area code.** *Let's Go* lists the city/area codes for cities and towns in Central America opposite the city or town name, next to a ☎, as well as in every phone number. If there's no number, then there's no area code.

4. The **local number.**

CALLING WITHIN A SINGLE COUNTRY IN CENTRAL AMERICA

The simplest way to call within one country is to use a **card-based telephone,** as coin-based phones are increasingly unavailable. Prepaid phone cards, available at newspaper kiosks and convenience stores, usually save time and money in the long run. Phone rates typically tend to be highest in the morning, lower in the evening, and lowest on Sundays and late at night.

CELL PHONES

Cell phone service is reliable and widely available in Central America. The best option is to buy a cell phone when you arrive—they're often just US$20-30—and buy minutes in prepaid increments. The rates on the prepaid cards are comparable to the rates of payphones. If you need to make lots of local calls, or need people to be able to contact you, this is the best option. Cellular rates for international calls can be prohibitively expensive. Still, phone cards are a better option for calling abroad. It is possible to bring your own cell phone, as long as it is not SIM-locked and operates on the same band as the country you are in. Be aware that expensive cell phones are ostentatious in Latin America and are begging to be stolen.

The international standard for cell phones is **Global System for Mobile Communication (GSM)**. To make and receive calls in Central America, you will need a GSM-compatible phone and a **SIM (Subscriber Identity Module) card,** a country-specific, thumbnail-size chip that gives you a local phone number and plugs you into the local network. Many SIM cards are prepaid, and incoming calls are frequently free. You can buy additional cards or vouchers (usually available at convenience stores) to "top up" your phone. For more information on GSM phones, see below and check out www.telestial.com. Companies like **Cellular Abroad** (www.cellularabroad.com) rent cell phones that work in a variety of destinations around the world.

GSM PHONES. Just having a GSM phone doesn't mean you're necessarily good to go when you travel abroad. The majority of GSM phones sold in the US operate on a different frequency (1900) than international phones (900/1800) and will not work abroad. Tri-band phones work on all three frequencies (900/1800/1900) and will operate through most of the world. Additionally, some GSM phones are SIM-locked and will only accept SIM cards from a single carrier. You'll need a SIM-unlocked phone to use a SIM card from a local carrier when you travel. Central America is a patchwork of GSM frequencies. Costa Rica operates at 1800 MHz (like most European phones), while the other countries use the 850/1900 MHz bands. In Panama, you'll need to buy a phone, since the carriers there only operate at 850.

BY MAIL

SENDING MAIL FROM CENTRAL AMERICA

Airmail is the best way to send mail home from Central America, though quality and timeliness of service varies within the region. Belize and Costa Rica are quite efficient, while Guatemala's tends to be more temperamental. Surface mail is by far the cheapest, though slowest, way to send mail. Mail takes one to two months to cross the Atlantic and one to three to cross the Pacific.

SENDING MAIL TO CENTRAL AMERICA

To ensure timely delivery, mark envelopes "airmail," *"par avion,"* or *"por avión."* In addition to the standard postage system whose rates are listed below, **Federal Express** (☎ +1-800-463-3339; www.fedex.com) handles express mail services from most countries to Central America. Sending a postcard within Central America costs about US$0.20, while sending letters within Central America should not exceed US$0.50. Postal service can be slow and only moderately reliable. Mail theft is not uncommon, so avoid sending expensive items or money through the mail. In general, mail sent to and from cities has a better chance of arriving.

There are several ways to arrange pick-up of letters sent to you by friends and relatives while you are abroad. Mail can be sent via **Poste Restante** ("General Delivery" in Belize, "*Lista de Correos*" in most of Central America, "*Entrega General*" in Panama) to almost any city or town with a post office. While the service is available in all seven countries, few continue to see it as a valuable and necessary system—service suffers accordingly. Address letters like so:

Liz Purcell	Patrick Connor Hines
Lista de Correos	General Delivery
Correo Central	City, Belize
City, Country (except Belize)	

The mail will go to a special desk in the central post office, unless you specify a post office by street address or postal code. It's best to use the largest post office, since mail may be sent there regardless. It is usually safer and quicker, though more expensive, to send mail express or registered. Bring your passport for pickup. You may be charged a small fee. If the clerks insist that there is nothing for you, ask them to check under your first name as well. *Let's Go* lists post offices in the **Practical Information** section for each city and most towns.

ACCOMMODATIONS

HOTELS AND HOSPEDAJES

Hotels are the most common kind of accommodation in Central America. Hotels go by many different names. *Hospedajes* or *casas de huéspedes* are usually the cheapest. *Hoteles, pensiones, and posadas* are slightly more expensive. Standards vary greatly, but generally speaking a basic room includes nothing more than a bed, a light bulb, and perhaps a fan; other amenities are a bonus. The very cheapest places may not provide towel, soap, or toilet paper. Spending a little more gets you a room with a private bath, and if you're lucky, hot water. For a modest amount more you might find a place with some character and charm.

Hotel singles in Central America cost about US$15 per night; doubles are around US$30. Prices are generally higher in the high season and around certain Central American holidays. *Let's Go* quotes room prices with and without private bath. Note that "with bath" means a sink, toilet, and basic shower in the room, not an actual tub. Communal baths are typically the same sort of thing, just off the hall. **Hot shower** is a relative term in Central America, as "hot" can often be tepid at best. In rural areas and sometimes in cities, the water heating device can be electric coils in the shower head. Such devices work best at low water pressure.

In sea level areas, try to get a room with a fan or a window with a nice coastal breeze. In more upscale hotels, air conditioning will probably be available. Look for screens and mosquito netting in more tropical areas. At higher elevations, hot showers and extra blankets are a must.

HOSTELS

Many hostels are laid out dorm-style, often with large single-sex rooms and bunk beds. Private rooms that sleep from two to four are becoming more common. Hostels sometimes provide kitchens and utensils for your use, break-fast and other meals, storage areas, laundry facilities, internet, transportation to airports, and bike or moped rentals. Some hostels impose a maximum stay, close during certain daytime "lockout" hours, have a curfew, don't accept res-ervations, or, less frequently, require that you do chores. In Central America, a dorm bed in a hostel will average around US$8-10 and a private room around US$15-20. Rooms and beds in Belize cost about twice as much.

A HOSTELER'S BILL OF RIGHTS. There are certain standard fea-tures that we do not include in our hostel listings. Unless we state otherwise, you can expect that every hostel has no lockout, no curfew, free hot showers, some system of secure luggage storage, and no key deposit.

LONG-TERM ACCOMMODATIONS

Travelers planning to stay in Central America for extended periods of time may find it most cost-effective to rent an **apartment.** A basic one-bedroom (or studio) apartment in a capital city (except Belize) will be less than US$200 per month. For US$300-400, you can often find more comfortable two-bedroom digs with a kitchen, full bath, and other amenities. There are plenty of luxury condos for rent, especially beachfront properties, but unless you have a few thousand to blow per month, it's not worth it. Besides the rent itself, prospective tenants are typically required to front a security deposit (frequently one month's rent) and the last month's rent.

The biggest hurdles to overcome when renting an apartment in Central America are learning the local laws related to property rental, hammering out the contract, and the language barrier. Consult your consulate, talk to locals about your rights and responsibilites as a tenant, and ask around to see if you are getting a good price.

CAMPING

Camping in Central America is a pleasant way to save money and sleep a little closer to nature. That said, there are few proper campgrounds, public or pri-vate. Many hotels and hostels will let you sleep on their property for a nominal fee, a fraction of what a room costs. Some travelers report that many residents will let you sleep on their land, as long as you ask beforehand. Some also charge a small fee. Some national park services (e.g., Costa Rica's) will allow you to sleep in certain parks for free.

Lugging your camping gear to Central America is unnecessary. Tents, ham-mocks, and mosquito nets are widely available at cheap rates. In addition to having to carry any equipment you bring with you, customs officials may disin-fect it at the airport, adding travel time to your trip.

THE GREAT OUTDOORS

The **Great Outdoor Recreation Page** (www.gorp.com) provides excellent general information for travelers planning on camping or enjoying the outdoors.

LEAVE NO TRACE. *Let's Go* encourages travelers to embrace the "leave no trace" ethic, minimizing their impact on natural environments and protecting them for future generations. Trekkers and wilderness enthusiasts should set up camp on durable surfaces, use cookstoves instead of campfires, bury human waste away from water supplies, bag trash and carry it out with them, and respect wildlife. For more detailed information, contact the **Leave No Trace Center for Outdoor Ethics,** P.O. Box 997, Boulder, CO 80306, USA (☎+1-800-332-4100 or 303-442-8222; www.lnt.org).

NATIONAL PARKS

Ecotourism is becoming a major economic force in Central America thanks to the abundance of natural beauty and biodiversity in the area, best maintained in nature reserves in each country. National park systems across Central America vary in quality, upkeep, and regulations. Some national parks have regulations they follow stringently, with a good ranger force and plenty of financial support. Costa Rica has far and away the best system of protected land. The country's effort is repaid by the droves of visitors that come visit and pay for the parks' maintenance. Other countries have less financial support and lack upkeep of paths and hiking trails, as well as maintenance of roads and entrances.

Not all parks and reserves are open to the public. Admission is generally US$5-10, though some charge more for tourists. Costa Rica is the only country whose conservation department, **Sistema Nacional de Areas de Conservacion (SINAC),** has a dedicated website (www.sinac.go.cr), which provides comprehensive information about services, prices, and hours. For information about national parks in other Central American nations, the best bet is to go to the tourist office or visit their websites—see **Tourist Offices** in each country chapter.

WILDLIFE

The jungles and streets of Central America are home to a variety of poisonous and harmful critters that will ruin your day.

THINGS WITH STINGS. Venomous snakes inhabit the jungles of the region. The most dangerous is the fer-de-lance (*terciopelo* in Spanish or "Tommy Goff" in Belize), a nocturnal snake that lives in and around settled areas. Snakebites are uncommon and usually accidental, but to minimize the risk, always wear shoes and avoid stepping off the path. Bites can be fatal if left untreated. **Tarantulas** also prowl the jungles of Central America. Bites are usually not fatal, but should be treated immediately. More common are **scorpions** (*alacranes*), some of which can grow up to 8 inches in length. To avoid these guys, shake out your shoes before putting them on and watch where you walk.

BUGGIN' OUT. Mosquitoes and other bugs can be a huge, highly infectious bother. Yellow fever, malaria, and dengue fever are all transmitted through mosquito bites. Mosquitoes can bite through thin fabric, so cover up as much as possible with thicker material. **100% DEET** is useful, but mosquitoes are so ravenous that nothing short of a mosquito hood and netting really stops every jab. Another villain is the "kissing bug," which causes **Chagas disease** in humans. Sleeping inside and using a mosquito net are the best measures against the bug. See **Staying Healthy** (p. 14) for more information.

NOT YOUR BEST FRIEND. Stay away from dogs, especially the stray variety. **Rabies** is frighteningly prevalent in Central America. If bitten, get treatment immediately. By the time you're foaming at the mouth, it's too late.

CAMPING AND HIKING EQUIPMENT

WHAT TO BUY

Note that good camping equipment is both sturdy and light.

Sleeping bags: Bags are made of **down** (durable, warm, and light, but expensive, and miserable when wet) or of **synthetic** material (heavy, durable, and warm when wet).

Tents: The best tents are freestanding (with their own frames and suspension systems), set up quickly, and only require staking in high winds. Consider getting a **tarp** and a **ground cloth.**

Backpacks: Internal-frame packs mold well to your back, keep a lower center of gravity, and flex adequately to allow you to hike difficult trails, while **external-frame** packs are more comfortable for long hikes over even terrain, as they carry weight higher and distribute weight more evenly. Make sure your pack has a strong, padded hip belt to transfer weight to your legs. Any serious backpacking requires a pack of at least 4000 cu. in. (16,000cc), plus 500 cu. in. for sleeping bags in internal-frame packs.

Boots: Be sure to wear hiking boots with good **ankle support.** They should fit snugly and comfortably over 1-2 pairs of **wool socks** and a pair of thin **liner socks.**

Other necessities: Synthetic layers, like those made of polypropylene or polyester, will keep you warm even when wet. A **space blanket** will help you to retain body heat and doubles as a **ground cloth. Water bottles** are vital; look for metal ones that are shatter- and leak-resistant. Carry **water-purification tablets** for when you can't boil water. Although most campgrounds provide campfire sites, you may want to bring a small **metal grate** or **grill.** For those places that forbid fires, you'll need a **camp stove** and a propane-filled fuel bottle to operate it. Also bring a **first-aid kit, pocketknife, insect repellent,** and a tool for lighting things on fire.

SPECIFIC CONCERNS

SUSTAINABLE TRAVEL

As the number of travelers on the road rises, the detrimental effect they can have on natural environments is an increasing concern. With this in mind, *Let's Go* promotes the philosophy of sustainable travel. Through a sensitivity to issues of ecology and sustainability, today's travelers can be a powerful force in preserving and restoring the places they visit.

Ecotourism, a rising trend in sustainable travel, focuses on the conservation of natural habitats—mainly, on how to use them to build up the economy without exploitation or overdevelopment. Travelers can make a difference by doing advance research, by supporting organizations and establishments that pay attention to their carbon footprint, and by patronizing establishments that strive to be environmentally friendly.

Deforestation and **biodiversity loss** are the greatest ecological problems facing Central America. It is estimated that Central America has lost 20% of its forest cover in the past 20 years, most of it turning to pasture for cattle to graze in to supply the North American beef market. Deforestation causes soil erosion, loss of wildlife and their habitats, and greater carbon dioxide emissions. As a consumer, there are plenty of ways to combat this, from using recycled paper to eating fewer hamburgers. On the road, you can help by visiting the national parks and reserves. The admission fee and any donations you make will go toward the upkeep of the parks, and your visit will educate you about the specific environmental concerns of the country.

The **illegal wildlife trade** is also a problem in Central America. Be conscious of what animal products you might be buying, as it may be processed from an endangered species. Seaturtle eggs, though illegal, are sold in many places in Central America, and tortoise shells are often peddled as souvenirs. It's also illegal to traffic in these items. If you're caught at customs, you might be thrown in jail.

For opportunities to volunteer and work toward sustainable travel and consevation in Central America, see **Beyond Tourism, p. 34.**

ECOTOURISM RESOURCES. For more information on environmentally responsible tourism, contact one of the organizations below:
Conservation International, 2011 Crystal Dr., Ste. 500, Arlington, VA 22202, USA (☎+1-800-429-5660 or 703-341-2400; www.conservation.org).
Green Globe 21, Green Globe vof, Verbenalaan 1, 2111 ZL Aerdenhout, the Netherlands (☎+31 23 544 0306; www.greenglobe.com).
International Ecotourism Society, 1301 Clifton St. NW, Ste. 200, Washington, DC 20009, USA (☎+1-202-506-5033; www.ecotourism.org).
United Nations Environment Program (**UNEP;** www.unep.org).

RESPONSIBLE TRAVEL

Your tourist dollars can make a big impact on the destinations you visit. The choices you make during your trip can have powerful effects on local communities—for better or for worse. Be aware of the social and cultural implications of their choices. Simple decisions such as buying local products, paying fair prices for products or services, and attempting to speak the local language can have a strong, positive effect on the community.

Community-based tourism aims to channel tourist dollars into the local economy by emphasizing tours and cultural programs that are run by members of the host community. This type of tourism also benefits the tourists themselves, as it often takes them beyond the traditional tours of the region.

Because the Central American economy is so dependent on tourism, it is especially important to be concious of your actions as a tourist. Commodification of tradition, loss of authenticity, and income inequality are all issues that have been exacerbated by tourism here in the last decades. Strive to practice **minimum-impact travel.** Leave the land and the cultural landscape the way you found it. Be conscious of all of your transactions and what they mean for both parties.

WOMEN TRAVELERS

Women exploring on their own inevitably face some additional safety concerns. Solo female travelers should consider staying in hostels that offer single rooms that lock from the inside. It's a good idea to stick to centrally located accommodations and to avoid late-night treks or bus rides. Always carry extra cash for a phone call, bus, or taxi. **Hitchhiking** is never safe. Look as if you know where you're going and approach older women or couples for directions if you're lost or feeling uncomfortable in your surroundings.

Generally, the less you look like a tourist, the better off you'll be. Central American women seldom travel without the company of men; foreign women who travel alone often draw attention. Awareness of Central American social standards and dress codes may help to minimize unwanted attention. More traditional areas of the country generally require conservative dress; wear a long skirt and sleeved blouses in churches or very religious towns. If you are traveling with a male friend, it may help to pose as a couple; this will make it easier to share rooms and will also chill the blood of potential Romeos. Wearing a conspicuous **wedding band** sometimes helps to prevent unwanted advances.

Your best answer to verbal harassment is no answer at all; feigning deafness, sitting motionless, and staring straight ahead at nothing in particular will usually do the trick. The extremely persistent can sometimes be dissuaded by a firm, loud, and very public "Go away!"—in Spanish, *"¡Vete!"* or *"¡Déjame en paz!"* Don't hesitate to seek out a police officer, store clerk, or passerby if you're being harassed. Some countries have a **policía turística** specifically geared toward travelers. Memorize the emergency numbers in places you visit and and carry a whistle on your keychain. A **self-defense course** will prepare you for a potential attack and raise your level of awareness of your surroundings (see **Personal Safety,** p. 12). Also, it might be a good idea to talk with your doctor about the health concerns that women face when traveling (p. 30).

GLBT TRAVELERS

Attitudes toward gay, lesbian, bisexual, and transgender (GLBT) travelers can vary drastically from region to region in Central America. In **Belize,** homosexual activity is illegal, while the cities of San Jose, Manuel Antonio, and Quepos in **Costa Rica** are surprisingly tolerant. While Costa Rica has the most travel-friendly infrastructure for GLBT travelers, other Central American countries are becoming increasingly open and tolerant. Gay bars are also beginning to open in major cities and particularly touristy areas. This is a very recent development, however—be careful about open association and realize that *machismo* and very strict gender role expectations are the norm. Keeping a low profile about your sexuality is probably your best bet. **Homosociality** (camaraderie between members of the same sex, particularly men) is much more common than you may be accustomed to. Handholding between two men, for example, is quite common.

International Lesbian and Gay Association (ILGA), 17 Rue de la Charité, 1210 Brussels, Belgium (☎+32 2 502 2471; www.ilga.org). Provides political information, such as homosexuality laws of individual countries.

TRAVELERS WITH DISABILITIES

Traveling in Central America with disabilities can be very difficult, especially on a budget. Sidewalks are narrow and in disrepair; streets are busy and disorganized. Transportation is generally not wheelchair accessible, so planning with a tour group, though expensive, may be the best (or only) option.

Travelers with disabilities should inform airlines and hotels of their disabilities when making reservations, as some time may be needed to prepare special accommodations. Call ahead to restaurants, museums, and other facilities to find out if they are wheelchair accessible. Guide-dog owners should inquire as to the quarantine policies of each country.

For those who wish to rent cars, some major car-rental agencies (e.g., Hertz) offer hand-controlled vehicles. The listings below are some organizations that can help plan your trip.

Mobility International USA (MIUSA), 132 E. Broadway, Ste. 343, Eugene, OR 97401, USA (☎+1-541-343-1284; www.miusa.org). Provides a variety of books and other publications containing information for travelers with disabilities.

MINORITY TRAVELERS

More likely than not, if you are a tourist in Central America, you are the minority, especially if you are white. No matter what you may try to do to disguise it, Central Americans can spot a "*gringo*" from a mile away.

Tourists with darker skin should be aware that they are an uncommon sight in Central America, and will attract curious stares and attention, but probably not any outright racism. *Chinita*, *negra*, and *india* are terms that will be thrown out, often inaccurately, at minority travelers. Understand that in Central America these are considered descriptive terms. These terms, along with other misperceptions, stem from unfamiliarity with people of different backgrounds. Reports of racism and discrimination from minority travelers are far from the norm.

Tourists are at an especially high risk in some of the region's more dangerous areas. Anti-Western, and especially Anti-American sentiment may still be strong in some of the more war-torn countries where the US funded and trained military forces during the Cold War. Travelers need to always be aware of the fact that they not only stick out, but are a prime target for Central America's less scrupulous residents.

DIETARY CONCERNS

Central American cuisine does not always cater to the traveler with specific eating concerns. **Vegetarian cuisine** is not hard to find in the more touristed, cosmopolitan cities, but in more remote areas, beans and rice may become the only option. Many eateries in Central America do not consider pork or chicken to be "meat." Make sure to ask for *vegetariano* food, not just a meal *sin carne*. If you are concerned about the specific ingredients of dishes listed on the menu, be sure to ask very specific questions.

Travelers who keep **kosher** should contact synagogues in larger cities for information on kosher restaurants, which are a rare sight in Central America. Your own synagogue or college Hillel should have access to lists of Jewish institutions across the nation. If you are strict in your observance, you may have to prepare your own food on the road. Travelers looking for **halal** restaurants may find www.zabihah.com a useful resource.

LET'S GO ONLINE. Plan your next trip on our newly redesigned website, **www.letsgo.com**. It features the latest travel info on your favorite destinations as well as tons of interactive features: make your own itinerary, read blogs from our trusty Researchers, browse our photo library, watch exclusive videos, check out our newsletter, find travel deals, and buy new guides. We're always updating and adding new features, so check back often!

BEYOND TOURISM

A PHILOSOPHY FOR TRAVELERS

> **HIGHLIGHTS OF BEYOND TOURISM IN CENTRAL AMERICA**
>
> **REHABILITATE** macaws and parrots in Atenas, Costa Rica (p. 446).
>
> **SPEAK** K'iche' Mayan like a local in one of Quetzaltenango's excellent full-immersion language schools (p. 39).
>
> **VOLUNTEER** at a rural clinic in Guatemala or Honduras (p. 35).

As a tourist, you are always a foreigner. Sure, hostel-hopping and sightseeing can be great fun, but connecting with a foreign country through studying, volunteering, or working can extend your travels beyond tourist traps. We don't like to brag, but this is what's different about a *Let's Go* traveler. Instead of feeling like a stranger in a strange land, you can understand Central America like a local. Instead of being that tourist asking for directions, you can be the one who gives them (and correctly!). All the while, you get the satisfaction of leaving Central America in better shape than you found it. It's not wishful thinking—it's Beyond Tourism.

As a **volunteer** Central America, you can roll up your sleeves, cinch down your Captain Planet belt, and get your hands dirty doing anything from learning the language of the ancient Mayans to cleaning up after endangered jaguars. This chapter is chock-full of ideas to get involved, whether you're looking to pitch in for a day or run away from home for a whole new life in activism.

Ahh, to **study** abroad! It's a student's dream, and when you find yourself deciphering 2000 year old Mayan hieroglyphics, it actually makes you feel sorry for those poor tourists who don't get to do any homework while they're here. Not surprisingly, archaelogy, zoology, Latin American studies, and urban development programs are common in the region.

Working abroad is one of the best ways to immerse yourself in a new culture, meet locals, and learn to appreciate a non-US currency. Yes, we know you're on vacation, but we're not talking about normal desk jobs. However, Let's Go strongly encourages those considering employment in developing countries to only pursue positions that do not involve competing for jobs with locals. Teaching English or helping to develop small businesses allow travelers to utilize their unique skills and aid development in Belize or Guatemala rather than hinder it.

 SHARE YOUR EXPERIENCE. Have you had a particularly enjoyable volunteer, study, or work experience that you'd like to share with other travelers? Post it to our website, www.letsgo.com!

VOLUNTEERING

Feel like saving the world this week? Volunteering can be a powerful and fulfilling experience, especially when combined with the thrill of traveling in a new place. Central America abounds with chances to make a difference—whether in a school, a zoo, or a protected nature reserve. Social causes and ecological initiatives make up the bulk of volunteer opportunities in the region, so travelers interested in education, healthcare, and environmental issues are sure to find the perfect cause.

Most people who volunteer in Central America do so on a short-term basis at organizations that make use of drop-in or once-a-week volunteers. The best way to find opportunities that match your interests and schedule may be to go through intermediary organizations designed to connect volunteers with local NGO's and community service organizations. **Global Vision International** (☎+44(0) 1727 250 250; www.gvi.gov.uk) offers wode-range of volunteer opportunities in Central America, from working with children in Guatemala to embarking on a wildlife expedition in Costa Rica. **The International Volunteer Programs Association** (☎646 505 8209; www.volunteerinternational.org) provides an up-to-date database of hundreds of volunteer and internship opportunities around the world. **The Institute for Field Research Expeditions** (☎214-666-3169; www.ifrevolunteers. org) offers a variety of volunteer opportunities in Central America for a fee. As always, read up before heading out.

Those looking for longer, more intensive volunteer opportunities usually choose to go through a parent organization that takes care of logistical details and often provides a group environment and support system—for a fee. There are two main types of organizations—religious and secular—although there are rarely restrictions on participation for either. Websites like **www.volunteerabroad.com, www.servenet.org,** and **www.idealist.org** allow you to search for volunteer openings both in your country and abroad.

I HAVE TO PAY TO VOLUNTEER? Many volunteers are surprised to learn that some organizations require large fees or "donations," but don't go calling them scams just yet. While such fees may seem ridiculous at first, they often keep the organization afloat, covering airfare, room, board, and administrative expenses for the volunteers. (Other organizations must rely on private donations and government subsidies.) If you're concerned about how a program spends its fees, request an annual report or finance account. A reputable organization won't refuse to inform you of how volunteer money is spent. Pay-to-volunteer programs might be a good idea for young travelers who are looking for more support and structure (such as pre-arranged transportation and housing) or anyone who would rather not deal with the uncertainty of creating a volunteer experience from scratch.

ENVIRONMENTAL AND WILDLIFE CONSERVATION

It isn't always easy being GREEN, but volunteers in Central America help to make it a whole lot easier. In a region known for its natural beauty and biodiversity, environmental and wildlife conservation are essential to preserving the unique, indigenous flora and fauna. These organizations are committed to doing just that and are always in need of volunteers.

Center for Ecological Living and Learning (CELL), An organization in partnership with Lesley University, CELL offers a 12-week sustainability project that takes place in 3 countries: Nicaragua, Honduras, and Costa Rica. Help develop renewable energy in Nicaragua, teach a Honduran community how to achieve environmental sustainability, and learn about the conservation of natural resources in a Costa Rican rainforest. College credit granted through Lesley University. US$12500 (airfare not included).

Go Eco (☎972 3647 4208; www.goeco.org). Save sea turtles in Costa Rica or iguanas in Honduras. Offers wildlife conservation volunteer opportunities in Central America and around the world.

Involvement Volunteers, P. O. Box 218 Port Melbourne, VIC 3207 Australia (☎+61 (3) 9646 9392; www.volunteering.org.au). Volunteer for 4 to 12 weeks (US$350 per month includes food and accommodation) on various conservation projects. Park maintenance, trail building, reforestation, helping in a tree nursery, and teaching about environmental conservation in addition to optional US$5 per hour Spanish lessons.

Rainforest and Reef, P.O. Box 141543, Grand Rapids, Michigan 49514-1543, USA (☎ +1 877-255-3721; rainforestandreef.org). An organization dedicated to marine and rainforest ecology. Offers field courses in Belize, Costa Rica, Guatemala, Honduras, Nicaragua, and Panama. Semester abroad experiences are offered at several field course sites. For details on dates and fees email info@rainforestandreef.org.

Trekforce Expeditions, 530 Fulham Road London SW6 5NR, UK (☎+44 (0) 207 384 3343; www.trekforce.org.uk). Combines adventure, conservation, and community service in treks through Belize and Guatemala ranging from one month (US$3300) to five months (US$6700). Longer itineraries include Spanish language training.

SOCIAL ACTIVISM, EDUCATION, AND RURAL DEVELOPMENT

What better way to make an impact on a country than to work directly with its people? Youth outreach initiatives, work in orphanages and domestic violence shelters, and non-profit organizations working to reduce poverty await do-gooders of all backgrounds in Central America.

Amigos de las Américas, 5618 Star Lane, Houston, Texas 77057 (☎713-782-5290; www.amigoslink.org/Amigos). Programs in Honduras, Panama, and Nicaragua for high school and college-aged students. Teach young people about leadership and environmental health. Programs fill up fast, so apply early.

Travel to Teach (www.travel-to-teach.org). An organization developed in Thailand in 2002, Travel to Teach has several programs in Central America. Education programs include teaching English and sports in San Jose, Costa Rica, and teaching computer in Santa Tecla, El Salvador. Alternatively, volunteers can work at an El Salvadoran orphanage or Costa Rican daycare. Volunteer programs US$750-5113 (includes orientation, accommodation, Spanish and cooking classes, and, for Costa Rican programs, meals.)

MEDICAL OUTREACH

Health-related concerns plague many areas of Central America, especially in impoverished rural areas and within indigenous communities. Volunteers in rural clinics and hospitals often provide the only medical care to which many people have access.

Global Crossroad, (☎+1-866-387-7816; www.globalcrossroad.com). Volunteer programs around the world, including medical projects in Guatemala, Costa Rica, and Honduras. Participants assist at a clinic and hospital and engage in health-related community education. Healthcare background and Spanish skills necessary. Application fee of US$350, prices vary depending on length of stay but room and board are included with fee.

STUDYING

VISA INFORMATION. Country-specific visa information is available in the introduction chapters of Costa Rica (p. 433), Nicaragua (p. 370), and Panama (p. 551).

It's completely natural to want to play hookey on the first day of school when it's raining and first period Trigonometry is meeting in the old cafeteria, but when your campus is Antigua, Guatemala and your meal plan revolves around warm, hand-rolled burritos and a refreshing midday mojito, what could be better than the student life?

A growing number of students report that studying abroad is the highlight of their learning careers. If you've never studied abroad, you don't know what you're missing—and, if you have studied abroad, you do know what you're missing.

Study-abroad programs range from basic language and culture courses to university-level classes, often for college credit (sweet, right?). In order to choose a program that best fits your needs, research as much as you can before making your decision—determine costs and duration as well as what kinds of students participate in the program and what sorts of accommodations are provided. Don't forget to read up on the city or town where the program takes place too—rural Central American villages aren't exaclty known for the wild frat parties and all-night keggers that some students might be used to at home.

In programs that have large groups of students who speak English, there is a trade-off. You may feel more comfortable in the community, but you will not have the same opportunity to practice a foreign language or to befriend other international students. For accommodations, dorm life provides a better opportunity to mingle with fellow students, but there is less of a chance to experience the local scene. If you live with a family, you could potentially build lifelong friendships with natives and experience day-to-day life in more depth, but you might also get stuck sharing a room with their pet iguana. Conditions can vary greatly from family to family.

UNIVERSITIES

Most university-level study-abroad programs are conducted in Spanish, although many programs offer classes in English as well as lower-level language courses. Savvy linguists may find it cheaper to enroll directly in a university abroad, although getting college credit may be more difficult. You can search **www.studyabroad.com** for various semester-abroad programs that meet your criteria, including your desired location and focus of study. If you're a college student, your friendly neighborhood study-abroad office is often the best place to start. For university programs in Central America, check individual curriculuma and course offerings before paying application fees or a deposit.

AMERICAN PROGRAMS

AFS International Programs,, 71 West 23rd St., 17th fl., New York, NY 10010-4102, USA (☎+1 800-237-4636 or 212-807-8668; www.afs.org). Runs study abroad and community service programs for high school and college students as well as educators in countries around the world, including Guatemala, Honduras, Panama, and Costa Rica. Volunteers live with host families and programs last from several months to one year. Cost varies based on the program type and duration.

Center for Global Education at Augsburg College, 2211 Riverside Avenue, Minneapolis, MN 55454 USA (☎+1 800-299-8889 or 612-330-1159; www.augsburg.edu/global). Offers a semester long program for college students called Sustainable Development and Social Change in Central America. Participants spend five weeks in Guatemala, four in El Salvador, and six in Nicaragua for the equivalent of 4 courses or 16 credits. Basic Spanish knowledge required. Costs US$16,375 and includes tuition, room and board, medical/emergency insurance, travel within Central America, and in-country costs.

CENTRAL AMERICAN PROGRAMS

No matter what your interests are, you're likely to find an exciting study abroad opportunity in Central America. There are two universities within Belizean borders, both of which are eager to include visiting students for study abroad semesters or summers. Guatemala has one public university and nine private universities—some secular and some religiously affiliated. Most are located in Guatemala City, but several also operate smaller campuses in other parts of the country. Universidad Centroamericana José Simeón Canas has a foreign

BEYOND TOURISM

exchange program and represents one of the many universities in the El Sal- vadorian capital, San Salvador. The capital cities of both Honduras and Nica- ragua—Tegucigalpa and Managua, respectively—are home to several universi- ties, some of which offer study abroad and exchange programs. Costa Rica has a wide variety of study abroad opportunities, whether you'd prefer to live in a bustling metropolis, on a deserted beach, or in a tropical rainforest. Some pro- grams specialize in Spanish and academics, while others focus more heavily on field research. The Universidad Tecnológica de Panamá is just one of many schools in Panama that offer study abroad opportunities.

LANGUAGE SCHOOLS

Old lady making snarky comments to you in the plaza? Imprudent cashier at the mercado? Cute moped girl that is totally into you? To communicate is to be human, and without the local language in your toolbelt, you're up a creek without a *pala*. Fear not! Language school is here to help—and particular regions of Central America are chock full of them.

While language school courses rarely count for college credit, they do offer a unique way to get acquainted with Guatemalan culture and language. Schools can be independently run or university affiliated, local or international, youth- oriented or full of old people—the opportunities are endless. Many language schools are part of a package deal including meals and accommodation, often a homestay with a local family, about 5 hours of instruction five or six days per week, and group activities or community service opportunities. From the bustling streets of Guatemala City to the quietest highland village, it seems that Spanish (and an occasional Mayan dialect!) is being taught in every setting imaginable. Local language schools can be found under Beyond Tourism in the Practical Information sections of most cities and towns throughout the book. US embassy websites also offers an extensive list of Spanish language schools; the site for Guatemela, for instance, is http://guatemala.usembassy. gov. Below are a couple places to begin your search; sites may take a com- mission or have booking fees:

A2Z Languages, 3219 East Camelback Road 806, Phoenix, AZ 85018, USA (☎+1 800-496-4596; www.a2zlanguages.com). Helps students find suitable language immer- sion programs in several countries, including Costa Rica and Guatemala.

AmeriSpan Study Abroad, 1334 Walnut St, 6th Floor, Philadelphia, PA 19107, USA (☎215-751-1100; www.amerispan.com). Offers language immersion programs in Costa Rica, Honduras, Nicaragua, Guatemala, and Panama.

Language Immersion Institute, State University of New York at New Paltz, 1 Hawk Dr., New Paltz, NY 12561, USA (☎+1-845-257-3500; www.newpaltz.edu/lii). Short, inten- sive summer language courses and some overseas courses in Spanish. Program fees are around US$1000 for a 2-week course, not including accommodations.

Languages Abroad, (☎+1 800-219-9924; www.languagesabroad.com). Offers 1- to 12-week standard and intensive language programs for all levels in Costa Rica, Guate- mala, Honduras, and Panama.

WORKING

Some travelers want **long-term** jobs that enable them to get to know another part of the world while immersing themselves in another culture and develop- ing international connections. Most of these jobs are confined to the tourist industry or involve teaching English. Others seek **short-term** employment to finance their travel. However, Let's Go does not reccommend competing for employment in developing countries where jobs for locals may already be scarce. Instead, English speakers and those with a particular area of expertise (education, healthcare, small business development) can use their unique skills to positively impact Belize or Guatemala through teaching or some other under-served field. **Transitions Abroad** (www.transitionsabroad.com) offers updated online listings for work over any time period.

Note: working abroad often requires a special work visa.

MORE VISA INFORMATION. Due to high unemployment rates in many Central American countries, natives are wary of allowing foreign workers to come in and contribute to those discouraging statistics. Still, finding work as a foreigner is not impossible. Work permit requirements vary widely in different countries. In Guatemala, the company intending to hire you must receive permission from immigration authorities. In order to obtain a job in Nicaragua, you have to seek extended residency; to do so, you must be able to present your birth certificate and police record, among other official documents. Websites offer conflicting information about working in Central American countries, and so your best option is to contact a country's embassy in Washington, D.C. for employment details.

LONG-TERM WORK

If you're planning on spending a substantial amount of time (more than 3 months) working in Central America, search for a job well in advance. International placement agencies are often the easiest way to find employment abroad, especially for those interested in teaching. Although they are often only available to college students, **internships** are a good way to ease into working abroad. Many students say the interning experience is well worth it, despite low pay (if you're lucky enough to get paid at all). Be wary of advertisements for companies offering to get you a job abroad for a fee—often times, these same listings are available online or in newspapers.

TEACHING ENGLISH

Suffice t to say that teaching jobs abroad pay more in personal satisfaction and emotional fulfillment than in actual cash. Nevertheless, even volunteer teachers often receive some sort of a daily stipend to help with living expenses. Salaries may be low for English teachers, but, considering the low cost of living in Central America, your Quetzals could go a long way. Most legitimate schools will only hire long-term teachers with a bachelor's degree or equivalent, although college undergraduates can sometimes get special summer positions teaching or tutoring. Many schools require teachers to have a **Teaching English as a Foreign Language (TEFL)** certificate. You may still be able to find a teaching job without one, but certified teachers often find higher-paying jobs.

The Spanish-impaired don't have to give up their dream of teaching, either. Private schools usually hire native English speakers for English-immersion classrooms where no Spanish is spoken. (Teachers in public schools will more likely work in both English and Spanish.) Placement agencies or university fellowship programs are the best resources for finding teaching jobs. The alternatives are to contact schools directly or try your luck once you arrive. In the latter case, the best time to look is several weeks before the start of the school year.

SHORT-TERM WORK

Some travelers find short-term work in tourist centers like Antigua, Lago de Atitlan, and Quetzaltenango. Bartending or working for English-language tour companies are common. Some knowledge of Spanish can also be helpful in finding temporary work. Another popular option is to work several hours a day at a hostel in exchange for free or discounted room and/or board. Most often, these short-term jobs are found by word of mouth or by expressing interest to the owner of a hostel or restaurant.

FURTHER READING ON BEYOND TOURISM

Alternatives to the Peace Corps: A Guide of Global Volunteer Opportunities, edited by Paul Backhurst. Food First, 2005.

The Back Door Guide to Short-Term Job Adventures: Internships, Summer Jobs, Seasonal Work, Volunteer Vacations, and Transitions Abroad, by Michael Landes. Ten Speed Press, 2005.

Green Volunteers: The World Guide to Voluntary Work in Nature Conservation, by Fabio Ausenda. Universe, 2009.

How to Get a Job in Europe, by Cheryl Matherly and Robert Sanborn. Planning Communications, 2003.

How to Live Your Dream of Volunteering Overseas, by Joseph Collins, Stefano DeZerega, and Zahara Heckscher. Penguin Books, 2001.

International Job Finder: Where the Jobs Are Worldwide, by Daniel Lauber and Kraig Rice. Planning Communications, 2002.

Live and Work Abroad: A Guide for Modern Nomads, by Huw Francis and Michelyne Callan. Vacation Work Publications, 2001.

Volunteer Vacations: Short-Term Adventures That Will Benefit You and Others, by Doug Cutchins, Anne Geissinger, and Bill McMillon. Chicago Review Press, 2009.

Work Abroad: The Complete Guide to Finding a Job Overseas, edited by Clayton A. Hubbs. Transitions Abroad, 2002.

Work Your Way Around the World, by Susan Griffith. Vacation Work Publications, 2008.

BEYOND TOURISM

BELIZE

The least inhabited country in Central America, tiny, English-speaking Belize is graced with nearly untouched natural beauty and stable politics, leading to one of the most developed tourist infrastructures in the region. With a diverse population of 300,000 and a predominantly Caribbean atmosphere, Belize is also the only country in Central America where reggae is more common than salsa. Though a bit pricier than its neighbors, Belize is extremely accessible; transportation is relatively easy, and few other places in the world offer such mind-boggling biological and geographic diversity in such a small space (23,000 sq. km). In fact, ecotourism has turned into the nation's leading money-maker; luckily, commercial development still remains modest, particularly in the south and the interior. While Belize has its share of Mayan ruins, they are less outstanding than their Guatemalan counterparts; the nation's most popular destinations are the dozens of coastal cayes and national parks, nearly twenty of which have been set aside for conservation.

In one day, an enthusiastic traveler could snorkel the second-largest barrier reef in the Northern and Western hemispheres, scale Mayan temples, and slide down waterfalls in a pine forest, stopping along the way at a jaguar or baboon reserve. After savoring inexpensive lobster and sipping smooth Belikin beers on one of the country's many idyllic beaches, many find they never want to move again. Thousands of travelers come each year to explore the country's wonders and affirm the tourist bureau's slogan, "You better Belize it."

ESSENTIALS

PLANNING YOUR TRIP

BEFORE YOU GO

Passport (p. 5). Required of all visitors.

Visa (p. 6). Not required for citizens of the US, UK, Australia, Canada, Costa Rica, Ireland, New Zealand, Mexico, and the European Union. Valid for 30 days. Extensions of up to 90 days granted by the Immigration Department.

Onward or Return Ticket. Required of all visitors.

Proof of Funds. If requesting to remain in country for more than 30 days, visitors must show proof of sufficient funds for the duration of the extension of their stay. Belize requires a minimum of US$50 per person per day.

Work Permit. Required for all foreigners planning to work in Belize. Must reside in Belize for at least 6 months prior to application. For more information, contact the **Immigration and Nationality Department** (☎011 501 822 2423).

Recommended Vaccinations. Hepatitis A, Hepatitis B, Typhoid, and Rabies.

Required Vaccinations. None required.

Inoculations (p. 13). Travelers who have been to nations with endemic yellow fever must present proof of vaccination.

Other Health Concerns: Malaria pills are recommended for those traveling to Belize. If your regular medical insurance policy (p. 14) does not cover travel abroad, you may wish to purchase additional coverage.

Departure Tax. US$35 if leaving by air, US$19 if by land.

EMBASSIES AND CONSULATES

BELIZEAN CONSULAR SERVICES ABROAD

An updated list of Belizean embassies and consulates is available on the web at http://bz.embassyinformation.com/list.php.

Australia: 5/1 Oliver Road Roseville, NSW, Roseville (☎+61 298 807 160).

Canada: 1800 McGill College, Suite 2480, H3A 3J6, Montreal, Quebec (☎514-288-1687; fax 514-288-4998). **Consulates:** 2321 Trafalgar Street, V6K 3T1, British Colombia, Vancouver (☎604-730-1224); McMillan Binch, Suite 3800, South Tower, Royal Bank Plaza, Ontario, Toronto (☎416-865-7000; fax 416-864-7048); Suite 100, 1122-8th Avenue S.W. Calgary, Alberta (☎403-215-6072; fax 403-242-9907).

Ireland: Christchurch Square, Dublin (☎+35 314 544 333).

UK: Third Floor, 45 Crawford Place, W1H 4LP, London (☎+44 207 723 3603).

US: 2535 Massachusetts Ave. NW, Washington, D.C. 20008 (☎202-332-9636; fax 202-332-6888; www.embassyofbelize.org). **Consulates:** Korean Trade Center Park Mile Plaza 4801 Wilshire Blvd Suite #250, Los Angeles, CA 90010 (☎323-469-7343; fax 213-469-7346); 4173 S Le Jeune Rd., Coconut Grove, FL 33146 (☎305-666-1121); 4318 Ridgecrest Dr., Las Vegas, NV 89121 (☎702-451-8444); 7101 Breen, Houston, TX 77086 (☎281-999-4484; fax 281-999-0855); c/0 Eztech Manufacturing, Inc. 1200 Howard Drive West Chicago, IL 60185 (☎630-293-0010; fax 630-293-0463).

CONSULAR SERVICES IN BELIZE

Australia: (☎+52 555 531 5225)

Canada: 80 Princess Margaret Drive, PO Box 610, Belize City (☎+501 231 060).

Ireland and the UK: P.O. Box 94, Belmopan (☎+501 822 2146; fax 501 822 2764).

US: 29 Gabourel Lane, P.O. Box 286, Belize City (☎+501 227 7161; fax 501 230 802).

UK: Embassy Squarew, P.O. Box 91, Belmopan (☎+44 207 723 3603).

TOURIST OFFICES

Belize Tourism Board, P.O. Box 325, 64 Regent St., Belize City (☎+011 501 227 2420; fax 011 501 227 2423; www.travelbelize.org).

MONEY

The currency chart below was accurate as of August 2009. Check websites like www.xe.com or www.bloomberg.com for the latest exchange rates.

BELIZEAN DOLLAR ($)		
	AUS$1 = BZ$1.55	BZ$1 = AUS$0.64
	CDN$1 = BZ$1.77	BZ$1 = CDN$0.56
	EUR€1 = BZ$2.74	BZ$1 = EUR€0.36
	NZ$1 = BZ$1.23	BZ$1 = NZ$0.81
	UK£1 = BZ$3.17	BZ$1 = UK£0.32
	US$1 = BZ$2.00	BZ$1 = US$0.50

The **Belizean dollar** (BZ$) is locked in to the US dollar at a rate of two to one. American paper currency is accepted nearly everywhere, but US coins are not. As a result of this constant and straightforward exchange rate, US dollars

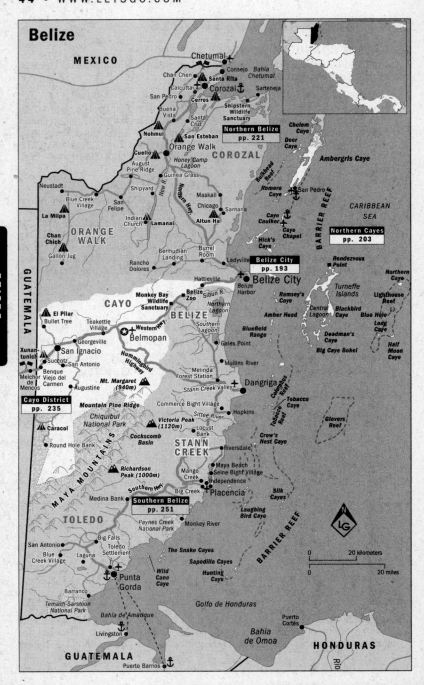

Belize

MEXICO

Chetumal
Consejo
Chan Chen
Bahía Chetumal
Calcutta
Santa Rita
San Pedro
Corozal
Sarteneja
Cerros
Shipstern Wildlife Sanctuary
Buena Vista
Santa Cruz

Northern Belize
pp. 221

Nohmul
San Esteban
Orange Walk
COROZAL

Cuello
Honey Camp Lagoon
August Pine Ridge
Guinea Grass

Neustadt
Shipyard
New R.
Maskall
Chicago
Santana

Blue Creek Village
San Felipe
Indian Church
Lamanal
Altun Ha

La Milpa
ORANGE WALK
Bermudian Landing
Burrel Boom

Chan Chich
Gallon Jug
Rancho Dolores
Ladyville

Hattieville
Belize City
pp. 193
Belize City
Belize Harbor

CAYO
Monkey Bay Wildlife Sanctuary
Belize Zoo
Sibun R.
Northern Lagoon

El Pilar
Bullet Tree
Teakettle Village
Western Hwy.
BELIZE

Georgeville
Belmopan
Southern Lagoon

Xunantunich
San Ignacio
Succotz
San Antonio
Hummingbird Highway
Gales Point

Melchor de Mencos
Benque Viejo del Carmen
Augustine
Mt. Margaret (940m)
Melinda Forest Station
Mullins River

Cayo District
pp. 235
Mountain Pine Ridge
Stann Creek Valley
Dangriga

Chiquibul National Park
Commerce Bight Village
Sittee River
Hopkins

Caracol
Cockscomb Basin
Victoria Peak (1120m)
Locust Bank

Round Hole Bank
STANN CREEK
Riversdale

Richardson Peak (1000m)
Maya Beach
Seine Bight Village
Independence

Mango Creek
Placencia

Medina Bank
Big Creek
Silk Cayes

Southern Hwy.
Southern Belize
pp. 251

TOLEDO
Paynes Creek National Park
Monkey River
Laughing Bird Caye

San Antonio
Big Falls
Toledo Settlement
The Snake Cayes
Sapodilla Cayes
Hunting Caye

Blue Creek Village
Laguna
Punta Gorda
Wild Cane Caye

Barranco
Temash-Sarstoon National Park
Bahía de Amatique

Livingston
Golfo de Honduras

GUATEMALA
Puerto Barrios
Bahía de Omoa
HONDURAS

GUATEMALA
Bullhead Reef
Romero Caye
San Pedro
Ambergris Caye

Chelem Caye
Deer Caye

Caye Caulker

Caye Chapel

Northern Cayes
pp. 203

Hick's Caye
Rendezvous Point
Northern Caye

Ramsey's Caye
Turneffe Islands
Lighthouse Reef

Amber Head
Central Lagoon
Blackbird Caye
Blue Hole
Long Caye

Bluefield Range
Deadman's Caye
Half Moon Caye

Big Caye Bokel

Columbus Reef
Tobacco Caye
Glovers Reef

Tobacco Reef

Crow's Nest Caye

BARRIER REEF

Puerto Cortés

CARIBBEAN SEA

BELIZE

0   20 kilometers
0   20 miles

are almost universally accepted; be careful, however, to specify which "dollars" you are referring to when bargaining or you could end up paying twice as much. Internationally accessible **ATMs** are located only in major cities and tourist hotspots. Use ATMs as a backup measure while traveling, rather than as a primary source of funds. **MasterCard** and **Visa** are the most frequently accepted credit cards; **American Express** cards work at some ATMs and at AmEx offices and major airports. **Traveler's checks** are accepted at most hotels, but are not welcomed at many restaurants and stores.

COSTS

Belize is significantly more expensive than its Central American neighbors. A day without frills—a cheap hotel, transportation, and basic food—will set you back US$30-40. A stay in a nicer hotel, with a private bathroom, hot water showers, and a kitchenette raises costs to US$80-150 per day. The sky's the limit for spending in heavily touristed and resort areas. Prices rise in high season (Dec.-May) and holidays (Christmas, New Years, and *Semana Santa*), but are negotiable in low season.

PRICE DIVERSITY

Our Researchers list establishments in order of value from best to worst, honoring our favorites with the Let's Go thumbs-up (🖪). Because the best *value* is not always the cheapest *price*, we have incorporated a system of price ranges based on a rough expectation of what you will spend. For **accommodations,** we base our range on the cheapest price for which a single traveler can stay for one night. For **restaurants,** we estimate the average amount one traveler will spend in one sitting. The table below tells you what you'll *typically* find in Panama at the corresponding price range, but keep in mind that no system can allow for the quirks of individual establishments.

ACCOMMODATIONS	RANGE	WHAT YOU'RE *LIKELY* TO FIND
❶	Under US$10	Campgrounds and some cheaper dorm rooms. Expect bunk beds, a shared bath, and rustic conditions.
❷	US$10-15	Most hostels and lower-end hotels. Most likely a shared bathroom.
❸	US$16-22	A small room with a private bath. Should have decent amenities. If you're lucky, maybe even a TV.
❹	US$ 23-30	Should have bigger rooms than a ❸, with cable TV, A/C, and a private bath with hot water.
❺	Over US$30	Large hotels or resorts. If it's a ❺ and it doesn't have the perks you want, you've paid too much.

FOOD	RANGE	WHAT YOU'RE *LIKELY* TO FIND
❶	Under US$3	Market food and street stalls. Typically a take-out meal.
❷	US$3-5	Burgers, small salads, burritos, or fajitas. You may have the option to actually sit down at these places.
❸	US$6-8	Mid-priced entrees and pasta dishes. Since you'll have the luxury of a waiter, tip will set you back a little extra.
❹	US$9-15	Edging toward the fancier side of things, with heartier or more elaborate entrees. Most seafood dishes fall within this range.
❺	Over US$15	Your meal might cost more than your room, but there's a reason—it's something fabulous, famous, or both. Fancier dress wear might be expected.

BELIZE

SAFETY AND HEALTH

Violent crime is on the rise in Belize, especially in urban areas. Tourists at resorts or on the road are particularly vulnerable targets for sexual assault, theft, purse snatching, pick pocketing, and car jacking. The incidence of such crimes significantly increases during spring and winter breaks. Victims who resist when attacked run the risk of serious physical injuries.

BORDER CROSSINGS

GUATEMALA. See p. 116.

MEXICO. Buses cross at **Chetumal**, Mexico from **Belize City** and **Corozal**, Belize.

HONDURAS. Weekly boats run between **Placencia**, Belize and **Puerto Cortés**, Honduras and between **Dangriga**, Belize and Puerto Cortés.

LIFE AND TIMES

HISTORY

MAYAN TIMES. The roots of Belize are with the Maya, whose ruins still lie beneath the forests of the country. The oldest dated settlement is the city of Cahal Pech, built in 1200 BC, but the Maya people are estimated to have arrived centuries before. Other cities built in the very beginning include Altun Ha, Lubaantun, Lamanai, and Caracol, of which the latter two remain preserved to this day. In the centuries that followed, stone *sakbé* roads sprang up, crisscrossing the entire Maya civilization, of which Belize was one corner. The cities of Belize were built by the Mopan Maya, the tribe with the longest history in Belize, while the Yucatec would later migrate from the west and the Kekchi from the south. Several centers for the distant trade carried out amongst these tribes and cities were located in Belize; Moho Caye, Santa Rita, and Ambergris Caye. The Mayan culture began to decline at the end of the first millennium AD; in Belize, dramatic wars between the kings, or *ajaw*, of the city of Caracol and the kings of Tikal in Guatemala resulted in much bloodshed and an eventual victory for Water Lord, the ruler of Caracol. The cities were soon after abandoned in the mysterious decline of the entire Maya people.

ENTER THE EXPLORERS. In 1502, Columbus sailed along the coast of Belize, but it would be decades until Europeans entered in force. That venture, the 1540 invasion by a small force of conquistadors from the Yucatán, brought diseases that killed off 90% of the 250,000 Mayans living in the Belize. The Spanish, however, were never able to hold on to the trackless mountains and forests of the country, and soon left, leaving a scattered, depopulated Belize behind.

About a century later, the increase in European settlement and trade in the Caribbean brought more traffic, mostly of the pirating variety. British marauders in particular favored the region's coasts, and became known as the Baymen. Near the wealthy hubs of Havana, Mexico, and Panama, the seas presented an ungoverned wilderness. In 1638, the Scottish pirate captain Peter Wallace laid the crude foundations of what would become Belize City. The pirates also discovered other, more industrious work: the logging of the valuable forests of the countryside. Of course, much of this work was done by the forced labor of Africans and Creoles who also found their way to the colony.

By the 18th century, however, the British authorities had reined in the region, putting it under Britain's law and watchful eye. The Spanish came to envy the wealthy little colony, and mounted several assaults, both military and diplomatic. Belize City was burned down in 1779, but a few years later, the Baymen bested the Spaniards in the Battle of St. George's Caye, pushing them out for good. September 10th, the day of the battle is now remembered as a holiday.

BRITISH HONDURAS. In 1840, after the tumult of the Napoleonic Wars and the growth of Britain's overseas empire, the unruly coast was officially named British Honduras, and more properly drawn into the imperial orbit. In 1862, it was elevated to the status of a crown colony, a multicultural, English-speaking enclave in the middle of the Caribbean. The tensions between Europeans, Africans, and Creoles deepened with the first British-Maya encounters in the middle of the 19th century, as logging operations and plantation clearings began to cut deeper into the forests. Initial strife was soon overshadowed by the massive Maya revolt against the Mexican elite in the Yucatán, known as the Caste War. Tens of thousands of refugees, many Yucatec Maya, fled to Belize over the course of the conflict. One futile uprising against the British, the Battle of Orange Walk, failed, consigning the Maya to marginalization for a century. Belize slowly modernized during the century, with roads finally linking its cities in the 1920s.

A PLACE IN THE SUN. The 1930s brought economic hardship that sparked mass resistance to British rule. The next economic blow, the devaluation of the British Honduras dollar in 1949, prompted the formation of the People's Committee, which became the powerful People's United Party (PUP). A few years later, Britain granted constitutional reforms, and in 1964 the PUP leader, George Price, became the colony's prime minister. Price held on to power in various forms for decades, becoming the head of government of a formally independent Belize in 1981, though British troops remained to guard against a Guatemala that claimed the whole region for itself. The opposition party, the United Democratic Party (UDP), took power for the second half of the 1980s, and has traded power with the PUP in recent decades as the country struggled to find peace with Guatemala, fight corruption, and foster growth. In 2005, Dean Barrow of the UDP became the country's first black prime minister.

TODAY

Current events in Belize are dominated by a few constants: scandals and corruption in the nation's small-scale politics, disputes with Guatemala and occasionally Mexico, and general economic ups and downs. Issues of local politics have had the highest profile in the last few years, with one hot-button issue: a proposed sweeping amendment to the Belizean constitution. Known as Amendment 7, it would make the international Caribbean Court of Justice the country's final court of appeal, allow dual citizens to sit in the National Assembly, and allow non-legislators to be appointed Attorney General. The United Democratic Party has taken criticism for these amendments, but with allegations of corruption still swirling around the People's United Party, no one is safe from attack. Ex-Prime Minister Said Musa of the People's United Party remains extremely controversial for his government's huge public spending and diversion of foreign aid into hospitals with undisclosed ownership. In February 2009, a lower court ruled that Musa could be tried in the Supreme Court of Belize. Similar scandals at the local level are epidemic, with recent news focusing on misdoings in the Treasury.

Robberies and violent crimes have become more pervasive in recent years in the capital and cities like San Pedro, Caye Caulker, and Placencia. One unusual case of property damage involved not a street ruffian but the Mexican billionaire Ricardo Salinas Pliego, whose careening yacht severely damaged Belize's tropical reefs—he was made to pay a huge fine and run Belize-promoting advertisements on his personal television networks.

In the still-poor country of Belize, the fate of the immigration industry is closely linked the country's future. Recently, Tropic Air, one of the main airlines serving Belize, opened a new $4.6 million dollar terminal in San Pedro to facilitate tourism and travel—but few tourists are coming as the global economic crisis resonates in the travel industry. In 2009, a drop in remittances from Belizeans working abroad, the fall in tourism, and an inflation rate above 12% combined to put the country in dire straits. Since 2007, the rise in global grain prices has put enormous pressure on the small country, and even before the last few years, the nation had received over $4 billion in international debt relief, which the government promised to continue spending on poverty alleviation. All the while, government salaries have drawn more and more from the public purse. As the government tries to cut costs, it has run into the powerful National Trade Union Congress of Belize, which accused it in July 2009 of amending the country's labor laws to squeeze the nation's workers.

Belize's foreign relations, on the other hand, have been mostly quiet, though the dispute with Guatemala has persisted in recent years. The failure of the Organization of American States to arbitrate the dispute led to both parties agreeing in December 2008 to go before the International Court of Justice in the Hague. The International Court of Justice is estimated to take six years to resolve the dispute, at least. Relations with Mexico have improved of late: a new bridge connecting the two countries was finished in the summer of 2009, and Mexico is on the verge of abolishing the visa requirement for Belizean citizens.

ECONOMY AND GOVERNMENT

Belize still bows to Queen Elizabeth, but is independent in every other regard. Its highest official is the **Prime Minister,** currently **Dean Barrow** of the United Democratic Party. His party swept into power in 2008 after years of rule by the People's United Party, the party that led the decades-long movement for independence and that was the main force in negotiations with Britain for autonomy. Only the third Prime Minister since that independence was achieved in 1981, Barrow is the first black Belizean to serve in the office. The **National Assembly of Belize** contains two familiar chambers: the lower, the House of Representatives, and the upper, the Senate. Party politics are particularly polarized in Belize, and American travelers will even recognize the dueling parties' colors: red and blue. Justice is administered through a British-style common law courts system, which, like most of Belize's institutions, comes off as a hothouse replica of the institutions of other English-speaking countries.

Real economic activity in Belize derives from tourism, agriculture, and a few small industries, like apparel production; yet the country remains the second poorest in Central America. Logging was once the lifeblood of the forested country, but valuable timber was exhausted decades ago, leaving the scarred forests to heal. Banana and citrus plantations blanket the arable land. But tourism, which has taken off in the last decades, employs over a quarter of Belizeans and has transformed Belize into a country heavily reliant on the traveler, as visitors will find out. The country's beautiful land and shorelines and diversity of flora and fauna have contributed to this transformation; the recent discovery of oil in the mountains has some worried about the continued survival of Belize's wilderness.

PEOPLE

DEMOGRAPHICS

Belize's diverse heritage draws upon the many nations that have come to the country by land or sea. Belize's largest ethnic group is the Spanish-speaking **mestizos.** The *mestizos* constitute 40% of the population and are of mixed Mayan and European heritage. Europeans, mostly of Spanish origins, are another 10% of the population. Large numbers of *mestizo* and Yucatec Maya were driven into Belize by the Caste War of the 1800s. Immigrants of similar backgrounds followed from Guatemala, Honduras, Nicaragua, and El Salvador in the last few decades. Maya natives still make up about 10% of the population, principally Kekchi-, Yucatec-, or Mopan-Mayan-speakers. The **Kriol** make up a third of Belize's population and are traditionally the largest group and one of the most culturally influential. The term Kriol encompasses those of mixed African and British descent. The **Garífuna** are another distinct group of mixed African and Carib Indian descent. They are located mostly in the south of the country, and have retained their indigenous language and lifestyle.

Adding to this mélange are the rural communities of **German Mennonite farmers** who emigrated from Mexico. These farmers are permitted a measure of autonomy, as they are free from the obligation of military service. They are, however, excluded from voting. Members of the South Asian, Arab, and Chinese communities also occupy key positions in the urban and commercial life of Belize. Very small American and British expatriate communities also exist.

LANGUAGE

The official language of Belize is **English,** although less than a tenth of the country speaks it in the home. **Kriol,** the day-to-day language of a good 40% of Belizeans, is a mishmash of English, West African languages, and Central American vernaculars like Miskito and Caliche slang. Another 40% of Belizeans (primarily *mestizos*) speak **Spanish** as their main language. The remainder of Belize speaks the various Mayan dialects (Kekchi, Yucatec, and Mopan), the Plautdietsch German of the Mennonites, and the Garifuna language, itself a mixture of Arawak, Carib, French, and English.

With such a profusion of languages, it has been estimated that over half of the population is either bilingual or trilingual. Anglophone travelers should take heart: approximately 80% of Belizeans have at least some knowledge of English and over half the population speaks it proficiently. English is spoken primarily in the cities, however, and it becomes less prevalent as one travels further into the countryside.

RELIGION

Belize is home to many faiths, but little religious polarization. *Mestizos*, Maya, and Central American transplants tend to identify themselves as **Roman Catholics** and exist in the fold of the Diocese of Belize City-Belmopan. Various strains of Protestantism account for another third of the population. Belize, like many of its neighbors, has been affected by the recent wave of evangelism from North

American missionaries of the Assemblies of God, the Seventh-Day Adventists, the Jehovah's Witnesses, and the Church of Latter-day Saints. The numerous immigrants in the urban centers maintain the religious traditions of their home-lands; communities of Hindus, Muslims, and Greek Orthodox, among others, thrive in the cities. Further out, among the Maya and Garífuna, old folk beliefs are mixed with elements of official Christianity.

LAND

The beautiful enclave that is Belize sits along 386km of marshy **Caribbean coast,** shielded by a string of **Caye Islands.** Behind this pleasant front rise the **Maya Mountains** in the south, which give way to the southern coastal plain and north-ern forested lowlands, which are crisscrossed by rivers and lagoons.

GEOGRAPHY AND GEOLOGY

Belize sits atop the limestone shelf of the Yucatán Peninsula. In the south-west, it shares a steep, mountainous border with Guatemala. The Maya Mountains dominate this region. These rugged karst hills and ridges give way to the fertile fields and gentle, rolling frontier of the north. Important rivers of Belize include the **Sibun,** the **New River,** and the Belize, or the **"Old River."** What may be Belize's greatest geographical feature is sunken off-shore, in the form of the **Belize Barrier Reef,** the second-largest coral reef in the world. Around it rise hundreds of tiny islands called the **Cayes,** among which the most notable are **Ambergris** (p. 70) and **Caulker** (p. 63).

WILDLIFE

This tropical country features an unsurprisingly lush, not to mention profit-able, array of flora and fauna. Logging was once the backbone of the Belizean economy, but much of the forest cover is no longer old-growth. All the same, over 700 tree species, including logwood, coconut, apple, papaya, cashew, pineapple, guava, and mahogany (the country's national tree), shade the soil of Belize. An estimated 4000 species of native flowering plants, including 250 varieties of orchids, adorn the landscape, and as the wilderness is catalogued and categorized, many plants are finding medicinal use.

Belize's national animal is the "mountain cow," or tapir. Hundreds of migratory birds winter in Belize, including wood storks, white ibis, and keel-billed toucans.

WEATHER

Belize, as a **tropical country,** has only the **wet** and the **dry season,** though tem-peratures vary with elevation, proximity to the coast, and coastal trade winds. Average temperatures range from 24°C in January to 27°C in July and are higher further inland. Change in season entails less change in tempera-ture than it does in humidity and rainfall, especially in the north and central regions of the country, which see practically no rain between January and May. This dry season is markedly shorter in the south.

BELIZE CITY

Blighted by crime, poverty, and drugs for years, Belize City (pop. 70,000) is nobody's idea of an ideal tourist stop. In fact, it's nobody's idea of Belize; travelers and Belizeans alike will agree that the nation's sole metropolis has little to do with the majestic beauty, natural wonders, and relaxed lifestyle that characterize the rest of the country. Most tourists pass through the city without a look back, taking advantage of its status as the country's main transit hub, but avoiding the crowded and claustrophobic streets themselves. The view from a taxi window isn't exactly a coastal getaway: canals filled with trash and sewage, seaside ghettos with dilapidated shacks, beggars sprawled on the hot, dusty streets, and aggressive hustlers looking to sell drugs or women.

Once upon a time, the Belize City was a much quieter colonial capital. Settled in the 1700s, the city was reportedly founded on a pile of mahogany chips and rum bottles discarded by British lumberjacks. Soon it developed into the center of colonial rule in British Honduras, with a white ruling class mingling with a growing population of Creoles. In 1961, Hurricane Hattie virtually destroyed the city, killing hundreds. Belize's capital was forced to move to Belmopan. Since then, Belize City has stagnated, the toll of drugs and crime growing by the year.

Caribbean paradise this isn't, but cautious travelers willing to brave an uncertain environment can escape the crowds in this decidedly untouristed area of the country. The city is the best place to see Belize's remarkable multiculturalism in action, with Creoles, Mestizos, Garinagu, East and South Asians, and the occasional Mennonite selling their wares. Their languages, foods, and music come together and create a unique city. Despite its problems, Belize City remains the country's commercial center. With its many teeming shops and tourist agencies, this city is also the best place to find quick supplies and prepare for further inland or aquatic adventures.

◧ INTERCITY TRANSPORTATION

Since Belize City is the country's main transit hub, getting to or (more commonly) away from the city is a cinch. The city is the only international point of entry and departure from the air. Domestic service, though often rustic (prepare to relive your preteen years on American school buses), is quick and usually painless.

Flights: The **Philip Goldson International Airport** (☎225 2045; www.pgiabelize.com), located 11 miles northwest of the city. Since no public transportation services the airport, you'll need to take a taxi from the airport exit (BZ$40-50).

Continental Airways (☎227 8309; www.continental.com), Belize offices at 80 Regent St. Flights to: **Houston** (3 daily); **Newark** (Sa).

US Airways (☎225 3589; www.usairways.com), offices in Belize Global Travel Services at 41 Albert St.. Flights to: **Charlotte** (daily).

American Airlines (☎225 4145; www.aa.com), offices in Sancas Plaza at Belcan Junction. Flights to: **Miami** (2 daily); **Dallas** (daily).

Delta Airlines (☎225 3423; www.delta.com), offices in the Goldson airport. Flights to: **Atlanta** (1 per day M-Tu and F-Su).

Grupo Taca (☎221 2163; www.taca.com), offices in Belize Global Travel Services at 41 Albert St.. Flights to **San Salvador, El Salvador** (daily); **Houston** (daily).

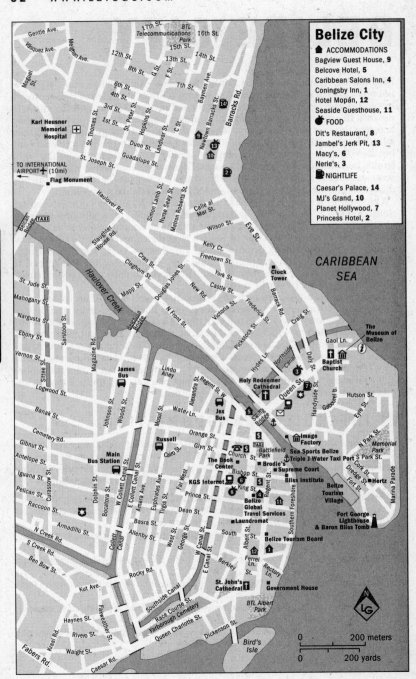

BELIZE CITY

Belize City

ACCOMMODATIONS
Bagview Guest House, 9
Belcove Hotel, 5
Caribbean Salons Inn, 4
Coningsby Inn, 1
Hotel Mopán, 12
Seaside Guesthouse, 11

FOOD
Dit's Restaurant, 8
Jambel's Jerk Pit, 13
Macy's, 6
Nerie's, 3

NIGHTLIFE
Caesar's Palace, 14
MJ's Grand, 10
Planet Hollywood, 7
Princess Hotel, 2

CARIBBEAN SEA

Maya Island Air (☎225 2219; www.mayaislandair.com), offices in the Goldson Airport. Flights to: **Flores, Guatemala** (2 daily).

Tropic Air (☎225 2302; www.tropicair.com), offices in the Goldson airport. Flights to: **Flores, Guatemala** (2 daily).

Domestic Flights: **Maya Island Air** and **Tropic Air,** both Belizean homegrown companies, offer flights to various cities within Belize. These flights are always more expensive than the bus or boat options, but travel time is considerably shortened. Both airlines leave both from the **Goldson Airport** and the **Municipal Airstrip,** located 2 mi. north of the city. Since flights leaving Goldson will stop at the airstrip en route anyway, it's a better bet to fly from the airstrip, where flights are less expensive.

Maya Island Air (airstrip office ☎223-1140; www.mayaislandair.com) flies from the airstirp to **San Pedro** (25min., every hr. 7:30am-5:30pm, one-way BZ$70, round-trip BZ$140);

Caye Caulker (25min., every 2 hr. 7:30am-3:30pm, BZ$70/BZ$140); **Dangriga** (30min., every hr. 8-10am and every 2hr. noon-4pm, BZ$86/BZ$166); **Placencia** (50min., every hr. 8-10am and every 2hr. noon-4pm, BZ$159/BZ$318); **Punta Gorda** (1hr. 20min., every 2hr. 8am-4pm, BZ$204/408).

Tropic Air (airstrip office ☎223-5671; www.tropicair.com) flies from the airstrip to **San Pedro** (25min.; every hr. 7:30am-5:30pm; one-way BZ$70, round-trip BZ$134); **Caye Caulker** (20min., every 2hr. 7:30am-4:30pm, BZ$70/134); **Dangriga** (15min., every 2hr. 8:30 am-4:30pm, BZ$83/159); **Placencia** (35min., every 2hr. 8:30am-4:30pm, BZ$159/310); **Punta Gorda** (1hr., every 2hr. 8:30am-4:30pm, BZ$204/401).

Intercity Buses: Belize City's main bus station is located next to the Collet Canal; just walk up King Street or Orange Street from downtown (be careful; the surrounding neighborhood is gritty). A dizzying array of bus companies now serve Belize after the meltdown of the former bus monopoly, Novelo's (whose name is still emblazoned on the colorful bus station). Since their prices, destinations, and durations are the same, don't worry about distinguishing between them. Just look for the cardboard destination sign in the front window and hop on.

Eastbound buses travel to **Belmopan** (1½hr., BZ$4); **San Ignacio** (2½hr., BZ$5); **Benque Viejo del Carmen** (3hr., BZ$7) every 30min. 5am-9:30pm.

Southbound buses travel to **Belmopan** (1½hr., BZ$4); **Dangriga** (2½hr., BZ$5); **Independence,** near Placencia (4½hr., BZ$7); **Punta Gorda** (6½hr., BZ$12) every 30min. 5:15am-6:15pm.

Northbound buses travel to **Orange Walk** (2hr., BZ$5); **Corozal** (3hr., BZ$6); **Chetumal, Mexico**(3½hr., BZ$7) every 30min. 9am-6pm.

Express Buses: These buses resemble charter or Greyhound buses rather than school buses, will cost a bit more, but won't stop as often at points in between. Buses to **Flores** (near Tikal) in Guatemala and other points in neighboring countries, including destinations in the **Yucatan,** leave from the front of the Caye Caulker Water Taxi Terminal. Just across the Swing Bridge on North Front St. BZ$50-110. Inquire and buy tickets at the **Mundo Maya Deli** desk inside the terminal (☎223 2923; mundomayatravels@yahoo.com).

Local Buses: Smaller and more specialized lines have their own bases in the city. Since these services are extremely informal, unpredictable and subject to change, ask locals for the details of departure. **Jex & Sons** buses to **Crooked Tree** (3 per day, 1hr., BZ$3.50) leave from the corner of Regent Street West and W Canal Street. **Russell buses** to **Bermudian Landing** (2 per day, 1hr., BZ$5) leave from the intersection of Cairo Street and Euphrates Avenue; to **Sarteneja** (3 per day, 2½hr., BZ$7) leave from the back of the Supreme Court building on the Southern Foreshore.

Boats: Belize City also offers the country's best and easiest access to the popular cayes off the coast.

Caye Caulker Water Taxi (☎203 1969, www.cayecaulkerwatertaxi.com) has its dock at 10 North Front Street, directly to the right after crossing the Swing Bridge. Boats leave for **Caye Caulker** (50min., one-way BZ$15, round-trip BZ$25) and **San Pedro** on Ambergris Caye (1½hr., one-way BZ$20, round-trip BZ$35) at 7:30, 8, 9, 10:30am, noon, 1:30, 3, 4:30, and 5:30pm. MC/V.

San Pedro-Belize Express (☎226 2194; www.sanpedrowatertaxi.com) has its dock just north, right next to the Fish Co-Op building, a 5min. walk along North Front St. from the Swing Bridge.

Boats leave for **Caye Caulker** (50min., one-way BZ$13, round-trip BZ$25) and **San Pedro** (1½hr., one-way BZ$25, round-trip BZ$45) at 8, 9, 10:30am, noon, 1:30, 3, 4, and 5:30pm (express to San Pedro). MC/V.

Triple J Express (☎207 7777 or 223 5752; www.triplejbelize.com), on the Southern Foreshore in front of the courthouse. Boats leave for **Caye Caulker** (one-way BZ$15, round-trip BZ$25) and **San Pedro** (one-way BZ$20, round trip BZ$35) at 7:30, 10am, 1, and 5:15pm. Cash only.

Car Rental: Driving yourself around Belize is the best (though certainly not the cheapest) way to avoid confusing and unreliable bus schedules and far-flung locales. You must be 25 to rent a car in Belize.

Crystal Auto Rental (☎223 1600; www.crystal-belize.com), offices at Mile 5 Northern Highway. BZ$107-270 per day; BZ$640-1700 per week. MC/V.

Budget Car Rental (☎223 2435; www.budget-belize.com), offices at Mile 2½ Northern Highway and at the Goldson airport. BZ$140-210 per day; BZ$840-1260 per week. MC/V.

Euphrates Auto Rental (☎227 5752; www.ears.bz), offices at 143 Euphrates Ave. in the city. BZ$130-150 per day. MC/V.

Avis (☎225 2629; www.avis.com.bz), offices at the Goldson airport and at 1 Poinsetta St. in Ladyville, a village near the airport. BZ$150-210 per day.

Hertz (☎223 0886, www.hertzbelize.com), offices at the Goldson airport and at 11A Cork St. in the city. BZ$140-220 per day.

 BUSES GOT BACK. If you're carrying heavy luggage and trying to flag down a bus by the road, it might be a better—and more efficient—option to board the bus from the back. Don't worry about the door alarm; you're not in middle school anymore, and local riders jump on and off from this end all the time. Ask someone on the bus hoist your bags up for you.

⊞ ▞ ORIENTATION

Haulover Creek, emptying into the Caribbean Sea, neatly divides Belize City in two. To the south is the rough **Southside district** (between Collet and Southside Canals). Also to the south of the creek are the more affluent residential neighborhoods of **Fort George, Newtown Barracks,** and **Kings Park.** The **Swing Bridge,** spanning Haulover Creek, connect the two halves. **Albert Street,** the city's main road lined with banks, shops, and restaurants, extends south of the bridge. Two blocks south of the bridge on Albert St. is **Battlefield Park,** the city's center. Next to the Swing Bridge on the north side is the **water taxi terminal.** To the right along the seafront is **Tourist Village,** a shopping section closed off from the street and set aside for cruise-ship passengers. The main **bus station,** surrounded by fruit sellers and other vendors, is located on **Collet Canal** to the west of the Southside district. Twenty minutes north of the creek, a small cluster of restaurants, hotels, and clubs sits next to the **Newtown Barracks Green,** just north of the Princess Hotel & Casino (p. 59).

Travelers should take extra precautions when traveling through the Southside district at any time of day to reach the bus station. Taxis are available on Albert St. around Battlefield Park to get you there safely for a small fee. The same goes for traveling into the city from the bus station, where many taxis are also parked. Always take a taxi at night when going anywhere in the city; ask your hotel to call one if necessary. Khaki-shirted **tourist police** patrol the downtown area (☎227 6082).

◧ LOCAL TRANSPORTATION

Since the city does not have a public transportation system (given its size, it doesn't really need one), taxis are the best resource for traveling safely within the city. You'll most likely be offered a taxi before you find one, but the best places to get a ride are the main bus station and along Albert St. by Battlefield Park. Licensed taxis are marked by green license plates; make sure the cab is reputable before getting in. Most rides within the city cost around US$1.50-3.50. Unless you're in a large group, **always take a taxi at night.**

◧ ▱ PRACTICAL INFORMATION

TOURIST AND FINANCIAL SERVICES

Tourist Offices: Several throughout Belize City lead tours and distribute information.

Belize Tourism Board, 64 Regent St. (☎227 2420; www.travelbelize.org.), toward the south end of the city. Map and brochure selection especially helpful for those seeking to explore the country's interior as well as coastal hotspots. Open M-F 8am-5pm.

Belize Global Travel Services, 41 Albert St. (☎227 7185; www.belizeglobal.bz). Guided tours to Mayan ruins at Altun Ha (5hr., US$65), Xunantunich (6½hr., US$90), the Baboon (4hr., US$55), and Crooked Tree (4hr., US$55) Sanctuaries. The nautically inclined can sign up for dive tours (7hr., US$110) and snorkeling trips (6½hr., US$100) in the Barrier Reef. Open M-F 8am-noon and 1-5pm, Sa 8am-noon. AmEx/MC/V.

Discovery Expeditions (☎223 0748; www.discoverybelize.com), at the Philip Goldson International Airport. A substantial array of tours exploring remote areas of Belize and the Cayes. Office in San Pedro on Ambergris Caye.

Hugh Parkey Belize Dive Connection (☎223 4526; www.belizediving.com), in the Radisson Fort George Hotel. Specializes in diving (US$80-225) and snorkeling (US$60-130) expeditions. A sister company, **Hugh Parkey's Jaguar Adventure Travel and Tours,** promises inland adventures.

S & L Travel and Tours, 91 North Front St. (☎227 7593 or 227 5145; www.sltravelbelize.com). This 30-year-old agency offers ½, full, and even multi-day tours in Belize's interior.

Sea Sports Belize, 83 North Front St. (☎223 5505; www.seasportsbelize.com). Diving US$120-220, snorkeling US$90-150, fishing US$400-700, and diving classes US$150-330.

Embassies and Consulates: See **Belmopan,** p. 86.

Banks: American travelers may not even need to exchange money; most businesses in Belize accept both US and Belize dollars. Most ATMs will dispense Belize dollars, but be sure to check at each bank or machine before withdrawing. All of the following banks have **24hr. ATMs:**

Belize Bank, 60 Market Sq. (☎227 7132). Open M-Th 8am-3pm, F 8am-4:30pm.

First Caribbean International Bank, 21 Albert St. (☎227 7211). Open M-Th 8am-2:30pm, F 8am-2:30pm.

Scotiabank, 4A Albert St. (☎227 7027). Open M-Th 8am-2:30pm, F 8:30am-4pm, Sa 9am-noon.

Atlantic Bank, 6 Albert St. (☎227 1225). Open M-Th 8am-3:30m, F 9am-3pm, Sa 9am-noon.

LOCAL SERVICES

Bookstore: The Book Center, 4 Church St. (☎227 7457). A tiny but well-stocked bookstore with magazines, newspapers, and paperbacks. Open M-Th and Sa 8am-5:30pm; F 8am-9pm. Cash only.

Laundry: G's Laundromat, 22 Dean St. (☎207 4461). Open 7:30am-5:30pm. US$6 per load.

EMERGENCY AND COMMUNICATIONS

Police: Raccoon St., at the intersection of Queen St. and New Rd. in the west side of the city. For **emergencies** call ☎911 or ☎90. **Tourist police** ☎227 6082.

BELIZE CITY

THE LOCAL STORY

PRINCE CHARLES

"I shall make you an ambassador of Belize!" Prince Charles ntones knighting me. We're standng on Albert Street, Belize City's crowded main drag, where vendors, taxi drivers, and the homeless rub shoulders. Jacks-of-all-trades line Albert St. and Prince Charles is one of the more renowned. No, not the floppy-eared successor to he British throne, but a disheveled, middle-aged Belizean who offers personal tours of the city when he's not washing down cars and working the docks.

We head through the Fort George district, making a roundabout loop ending at the Bliss omb and lighthouse. Prince Charles, his voice a mixture of stentorian authority and eccentric urns of phrases ("put a tack in hat" instead of "remember that"), uns through his topics with the slight professionalism of the best tour guides. He talks about Belize's history, about its many people, about the Garinagu and heir drum rhythms, about the Mennonites and their problems with inbreeding, about crippled Baron Bliss and the ancient Mayan princess-goddess who gave a form of her name to Belikin beer.

We come to the lighthouse. He completes the knighting ceremony, making me an official representative of Belizean culture, and commands me to spread the word.

-Dan Normandin

Pharmacy: Central Drugstore (☎227 2138), Albert St., right next to Swing Bridge. Open daily 8am-9:30pm. AmEx/MC/V. **Brodie's** (see **Food**, p. 57) also has a pharmacy.

Hospitals: The public **Karl Heusner Memorial Hospital** (☎223 1548; www.khmh.bz.), Princess Margaret Dr. Belize's main referral hospital offers 24hr. emergency service. **Belize Medical Associates,** 5791 St Thomas St. (☎223 0302; www.belizemedical.com), a private hospital, also with 24hr. service.

Telephones: Several pay phones are located around the downtown area, but travelers seeking longer and cheaper conversations can head to **BTL,** 1 Church St. (☎227 7085). Booths for international calls. Open M-F 8am-6pm.

Internet Access: Many hostels have internet service, but several internet cafes also dot the city.

Angelus Press, 10 Queen St. (☎223 5777). US$3.50 per hr. Open M-F 7:30am-5:30pm, Sa 8am-noon. MC/V.

KGS Internet, 60 King St. (☎207 7130). US$2.50 per hr. In a gritty area, but well crowded and safe inside. Open M-F 8am-7pm, Sa 8am-6pm, Su 9:30am-2:30pm. Cash only.

Post Office: (☎223 2201), Paslow building at the intersection of North Front and Queen St. Open M-F 8am-noon and 1-4:30pm. Belize does not use a postal code.

▟ ACCOMMODATIONS

There's no shortage of hotels in Belize City, from backpacker meccas to luxury options for cruise-ship passengers. The city's status as a transportation hub translates into plenty of sleeping space. As always here, safety is of primary concern. Accommodations in downtown Belize City are generally more dangerous than those on the outskirts. Hotels in the northern **Fort George** and **Newtown Barracks** districts of the city are the quietest, while those closer to the center will likely offer more security.

▧ **Seaside Guest House,** 3 Prince St. (☎227 8339; www.seasideguesthouse.org).This old backpacker favorite is one of the best (and cheapest) options in the city. 19th-century coastal house lined with mahogany, quiet rooms provide a much-needed respite from the nervous bustle of the city. Common room, kitchen and dining room, and hammock-lined porches facing the sea. Breakfast US$2-5. Free WiFi. Dorms US$20; singles US$25, with bath US$35; doubles US$45, with bath US$55. MC/V. ❷

Caribbean Palms Inn, 26 Regent St. (☎227 0472). This converted house close to downtown has comfortable and clean rooms that vary in size. Enjoy the beautiful outdoor terrace facing away from the street. Dorm rooms US$18-23; single with bath US$20-30; double with bath US$30-50; rooms with A/C US$35-70. MC/V. ❶

Bayview Guest House, 58 Baymen Ave. (☎223 4179; www.belize-guesthouse-hotel.com). In the quiet, residential neighborhood that is Northern Barracks district, this guesthouse offers fantastically decorated rooms with quirky names to match. You can sleep in the Lavender Room, the Sunrise Room, the Blue Iris, or even the Pink Lady. All rooms with cable TVs and private baths. Free WiFi. Rooms with double bed and fan US$25; rooms with 1 double bed and A/C US$35-45; rooms with 2 double beds and A/C US$45. AmEx/MC/V. ❷

Belcove Hotel, 9 Regent St. (☎227 3054; www.belcove.com). Be warned, this hotel is located north of the Swing Bridge, in a somewhat dangerous neighborhood. Still, Belcove's convenient location on Haulover Creek is as scenic as budget accommodations get. A verandah provides a relaxing space from which to survey the center of town. The staff can arrange diving and fishing tours. Singles US$28, with bath US$35, with A/C, TV, and bath US$50; doubles US$35/40/52; triples US$59. Beware hidden fees: there's a US$5-6 tax per person. MC/V. ❷

Freddie's Guest House, 86 Eve St. (☎223 3851). 3 quiet, sizable, cozy rooms. Shared bath. US$25 each. Cash only. ❷

Hotel Mopan, 55 Regent St. (☎227 7351; www.hotelmopan.com), toward the western side of downtown, near the Government House and St. John's Cathedral. A sprawling mansion with elegant, clean rooms. Outdoor patios provide shade and views of the neighborhood. Some rooms with balconies and A/C. Rooms US$45-75. US$10 tax per person. MC/V. ❺

Coningsby Inn, 76 Regent St. (☎227 1566; www.coningsby-inn.com). Next to the Hotel Mopan, this colonial-era house offers serious old-school grandeur. 10 spotless rooms, each with a small patio space. All rooms have A/C, cable TVs, and baths. Doubles US$50; triples US$60. MC/V. ❹

◪ FOOD

Belizean food is as varied as its population, and Belize City is the best place to sample the whole shebang. Downtown, near Albert St., is a carnival of cuisines. Taco stands brush shoulders with Creole restaurants and fruit hawkers, old Mayan recipes are preserved in tiny food stalls, and sizable immigrant populations offer Chinese and Indian food. Seek out the cowfoot soup (trust us, it's better than it sounds). Try the food stands that pop up on Albert St. near the Swing Bridge at night. It's the best opportunity to enjoy Belizean hot dogs and spicy chicken burgers, tacos, and beans-rice-chicken mixtures on the cheap (US$1-2). For groceries, head to the ever-reliable **Brodie's** at 2 Albert St. (☎227 7070. Open M-F 8am-10pm, Sa-Su 8am-6pm; AmEx/MC/V).

Dit's Restaurant, 50 King St. (☎227 3350). Entering its 51st year, Dit's is the oldest restaurant in the city and is still owned by the founding family. Along with its wide selection of local pastries—johnny cakes, jam rolls, coconut tarts, meat, rice, and bread puddings (USZ$1-2.50)—you can get a good start on Belizean favorites like bean-and-rice stews (US$1.50). Desserts US$2-6; entrees US$2-5. Open M-Sa 7am-8pm, Su 8am-4pm. Cash only. ❷

Nerie's (☎223 4028), corner of Queen and Daly Streets in the Fort George district. A spacious, 2-floor local favorite serving an elaborate selection of Belizean dishes. For breakfast, try those beans, ham, and eggs, or try the ever-popular fry jacks (biscuits). For dinner, lap up some cowfoot soup and finish it off with one of Nerie's excellent puddings (rice, meat, or cassava). Entrees US$3-9. Drinks US$1-3. Open M-Sa 7am-9pm. Cash only. ❷

Macy's, 18 Bishop St. (☎207 3419). Macy's is the definition of Belizean cooking. Bravely order deer and boar (US$4.50-7). Their fish fillets—served, of course, with rice and beans (US$3)—are local favorites. There are only 5 tables, so hurry up for that cherished slab of game. Open M-Sa 8am-9pm. Cash only. ❷

Jambel's Jerk Pit, 164 Newtown Barracks Rd. (☎223 1966). Jambel's has gone through several chapters in its history: starting on Ambergris Caye, opening a branch on King St. in Belize City, and recently moving north to a safer neighborhood by the Princess Hotel. What hasn't changed is the popular Jamaican-style cuisine and welcoming staff. Try the jerk. Those willing to splurge can try the jerked lobster (US$15). Entrees US$8-15. Open M-Sa 11-3pm and 6-10pm. Cash only. ❸

◎ SIGHTS

Most travelers see Belize City only as a travel hub. For those interested in the country's culture and history, several sites are worth a quick look.

MUSEUM OF BELIZE. Built as Queen's Prison in 1857, rid of criminals in 1993, and refurbished as a museum in 2002, this stately brick building now houses exhibits on Belize's wildlife, landscape, culture, and history. The 3D model of the Great Western Barrier Reef will interest prospective divers. The Mayan exhibits include a replica of the gorgeous jade head uncovered in a tomb at Altun Ha in 1968. Prison aficionados will appreciate the preserved 19th-century cell, graffiti and all. (*Gabourel Lane in the Fort George District.* ☎223 4524. Open M-F 8am-4pm. US$5.)

SWING BRIDGE. Chances are, you'll be crossing this unique structure at some point during your stay. Currently the only manually operated "swinging" bridge in the world, this overpass has become a symbol for Belize City. M-Sa at 6am and 6pm, six to eight operators use cranks to rotate the bridge open, letting boats pass. An illustration of this procedure holds a proud place on the back of some Belizean banknotes.

GOVERNMENT HOUSE. This seaside two-story colonial mansion was built in 1814 and housed British governors until the end of colonial rule in 1981. Historical exhibits are juxtaposed with showcases of modern Belizean art. Stroll the finely tended grounds by the sea. (*Open M-F 8:30am-4:30pm, exhibit hours 9am-4pm. BZ$10.*)

ST. JOHN'S CATHEDRAL. This Anglican church, the oldest in Central America, stands directly across from the Government House. Built from 1812 to 1820, this church was constructed using bricks that functioned as ballast during a sea journey from Britain. Tombstones dating from the earliest years of settlement line the front of the church. (*Services M, W, and Sa 6:30am; Tu 9am; Th 7pm; F 6:30pm; Su 9:30am. Spanish mass Sa 6pm.*)

SUPREME COURT BUILDING AND BATTLEFIELD PARK. This graceful building, designed in 1926 by a New Orleans-based firm, replaced an older structure that burned to the ground in 1918. Apparently a burning flagpole fell on the head of the British governor, who died of his injuries a few days later. Battlefield Park occupies the area in front of the building. Several demonstrations for Belizean independence were held here throughout the 20th century. It's now common ground for street vendors, the homeless, hustling taxi drivers, tour guides, and unwitting tourists.

FORT GEORGE LIGHTHOUSE AND BARON BLISS TOMB. Henry Edward Ernest Victor Bliss (1869-1926) was a wealthy and polio-afflicted English petroleum speculator who spent his last years traversing the Caribbean in his luxury yacht, the *Sea King II*. He chose Belize Harbour as his final yachting place and fell in love with Belize's climate and people, though because of his condition he never managed to step onto Belizean soil. Upon his death Mr. Henry Bliss willed some US$2 million to the country. Today, the Bliss Center for the Performing Arts and the Bliss School of Nursing mark the influence of the baron's generosity. Baron Bliss Day is celebrated nationwide on March 9. This slender lighthouse was built and is still maintained using Bliss's funds; appropriately, the generous baron lies beneath it, having finally reached the mainland.

IMAGE FACTORY. This exhibit space for Belizean contemporary art has been doing its best to enrich the city's cultural scene since 1995. Exhibits usually last for a month; check the website for up-to-date information. The building is located right on the harbor and includes a deck with a sea view. On your way out, stop by the museum's shop, which has a respected collection of local crafts, artwork, and a relatively wide selection of books. *(91 North Front St. ☎223 4093; www.imagefactory-bz. Open M-F 9am-5pm. Free.)*

NIGHTLIFE AND ENTERTAINMENT

There's no shortage of nightlife opportunities in the city, but travelers are warned to take extreme care when traveling around at night. Always take a taxi, even for short distances. Travel in groups, preferably of three or more. If you do go out, we suggest the area north of the Swing Bridge. And if you don't want to take the risk, don't worry; countless nocturnal adventures await you in the rest of Belize, most of them far safer than what's offered in this city. Plus, Belize City offers numerous other forums for entertainment. Some of them are listed below.

Bliss Center for the Performing Arts (☎227 2110; www.nichbelize.org), on the Southern Foreshore. Another offspring of the ever-generous Baron Bliss trust, this relatively new theater hosts a range of drama, music, and dance performances. It also houses the headquarters of the Institute of Creative Arts, which encourages local creative expression and holds shows and exhibits. The broad gray building, located right on the coast, is sure to capture your attention as you approach the city by boat. Check postings by the entrance for show dates and times. Cash only.

Princess Hotel & Casino (☎223 2670; www.princessbelize.com). While the rooms at this luxury hotel are well beyond the average backpacker's budget (US$110 per night, anyone?), the complex's entertainment center attempts to provide diversified nightlife. For starter's, there's the **Calypso Club,** a restaurant offering high-end Belizean seafood (US$15-30) and drinks (US$2.50-7.50). True nighthawks can chill at the **Vogue Bar & Lounge,** with its 40-person capacity, 4 TVs, DJs Th-Sa 9am-2pm, and an occasional live Mariachi band (drinks US$2-6; open M-W noon-midnight and Th-Sa noon-2am). The Princess also houses the city's only **movie theater,** with 2 screens usually showing standard blockbuster films (screenings 6-9pm, 3pm on weekends, "adult showings" on weekend nights; US$5). At this pace, why not throw in some bowling? The hotel's 8-lane alley and arcade are open daily 11am-11pm. Last, but certainly not least, is the **casino,** with over 400 machines alongside blackjack, Caribbean poker, and more. (open daily noon-4am, 18+).

Caesar's Palace, 190 Newtown Barracks Rd. (☎223 7624). Another name poached from an American nightlife institution, another unique establishment. Latin music and dancing reign in this small and packed club on the city's northern shore. Expect some familiar pop hits too. Things get going around 11pm. Drinks US$2-3. Open Th-Sa 10pm-2am. Cash only.

MJ's Grand, 160 Newtown Barracks Rd. A local favorite blaring punta rock and reggae blare while pouring Belikin beer (US$1.50). Relax at the pool tables and on the outside verandah. Open M-F 7pm-1am and Sa-Su 5pm-2am. Cash only.

Planet Hollywood, at the corner of Queen and Handyside streets. No relation to the American brainchild of Arnold Schwarzenegger and Sylvester Stallone. Instead, this bustling, 2nd-floor dance hall hosts a largely Latin crowd and a handful of tourists. Groove to local punta rock, reggae, and salsa. The fun starts around 11:30pm. Open Th-Sa 10:30pm-2am. Drinks US$1-3. Cash only.

▟ DAYTRIPS FROM BELIZE CITY

ALTUN HA

Getting to Altun Ha without a car is very difficult, as it's located along rarely traveled routes. It is difficult to travel back and forth in one day with the bus schedules being fairly unreliable. An overnight stay might be a better option. If driving from Belize City, head north along the Northern Highway. Turn right on the Old Northern Highway and head toward Maskall. Turn left at the sign for Altun Ha and continue for the 3km. Buses to Maskall from Belize City (Sa and M, 1pm, US$1.50) can drop you off at the junction with the road leading to site, but infrequent service makes this an inconvenient option. The easiest, though more expensive, option is to find a taxi driver in Belize City willing to drive you to Altun Ha, wait, then drive you back. This usually costs US$75-100. In a group of 3 or 4, the rate per person can drop to US$25. The bus station is the best place to find willing drivers. From Belize City, Belize Global Adventure Tours, Discovery Expeditions, and S & L Travel and Tours run guided tours to the site and back (4½hr., US65-75). Open daily 7am-4pm. US$5.

These beautifully preserved and recently refurbished ruins stood at the ceremonial plaza of a city of 8,000 to 10,000 people from about AD 300 to 1000. Once a trading point between inland and coastal settlements, now Altun Ha is almost entirely overgrown by jungle. The 13 structures are organized around two plazas (marked A and B) and date from the sixth and seventh centuries. Turn right from the entrance to reach plaza A; turn left for Plaza B. The highlight of Plaza A is the elegant **Temple of the Green Tomb** (A-1), where the tomb of a seventh-century king was uncovered alongside a variety of ceremonial artifacts. The most famous temple is found in plaza B and is called the **Temple of the Masonry Altars,** or the **Sun God Temple** (B-4). You might recognize the temple from Belikin beer bottle labels. Inside the box-like structure, excavators found another tomb containing the body of an elderly, highly-respected priest. Among the jade objects buried with him was a beautifully carved head of the Mayan sun god Kinich Ahau. A replica of this piece can be viewed at the **Museum of Belize** in Belize City (p. 58). The top of B-4 gives the best view of the site as a whole. Behind B-6, half a mile down a pleasant rain forest, is a small pond that served as the city's reservoir.

 MAKE NEW FRIENDS. Getting to Altun Ha by taxi can suck up a few days' worth of money—find a buddy to tag along with you to lower the price of transportation. A taxi to Altun Ha usually costs around US$75-100, so you'll be looking at saving at least US$37.

COMMUNITY BABOON SANCTUARY

If driving from Belize City, head up the Northern Highway and turn left at the turnoff for Burrell Boom. Turn right into Burrell Boom village and continue straight for 9 mi. to Bermudian Landing. Russell buses leave from Belize City for Bermudian Landing at the intersection of Euphrates Ave. and Cairo St., next to the school lot; buses run M-Sa at around noon and 4pm (US$1.50). They head through Bermudian Landing to Belize City 3 times M-Sa between 6am and 7am. From Belize City, Belize Global

Adventure Tours, Discovery Expeditions, and S & L Travel and Tours run guided tours to the sanctuary and back (4hr., US$55-65).

Thirty miles west of Belize City, this unique sanctuary is the product of an entirely grassroots effort to combine wildlife preservation with local economic development. The effort began in 1985 when 12 landowners in several villages promised to conserve their land for local baboons. In return, they hoped, this new tourist attraction would supplement the cost of using their land, while encouraging local economic growth. Today, over 200 landowners in seven villages have made the pledge, creating a sanctuary of over 20 sq. mi. Rather than making the area an untouchable wilderness, the program lets villagers share space—in an environmentally friendly way, of course—with these neighborhood primates. The black howler population has expanded dramatically, with over 2000 living in the protected areas. The sanctuary also protects a wide range of wildlife and flora within its grounds and has established various educational programs aimed at local citizens. For more information on the sanctuary, visit www.howlermonkeys.org.

The monkeys at the center of this effort are known for their incredibly loud guttural growls. You'll hear them well before you see them. If you do see a baboon (and it's never guaranteed), you'll probably be surprised by the discrepancy between the baboon's mighty cry and tiny body.

The village of Bermudian Landing is the best point of access for visitors. The small **CBS visitor's center** (☎220 2181) has small exhibits on the monkeys and other wildlife. Included with the admission fee (US$5) is a 45-60min. guided walk through the jungle. The center also offers river tours (US$25 per hr.), horseback riding (US$23 per hr.), and crocodile night tours on the river (US$50 per hr.). The daring can try the night walks (US$12 per hr.) through the jungle.

The **Nature Resort** (☎610 1378), right behind the visitor's center, offers bare but clean cabanas with electricity, a fan, and a cold-water private bath (US$30-60). The family-run **Howler Monkey Lodge** (☎220 2158; www.howlermonkeylodge.org), 400 yards down the road after turning right from the visitor's center, has slightly more luxurious digs. The Lodge offers cabanas on the river (some with air-conditioning and a river view), and occasionally complimentary dinner and breakfast. In addition to local tours, the lodge also arranges longer expeditions to surrounding sites like Lamanai, Crooked Tree, and Altun Ha. *(Rooms with jungle view and fan: singles US$35; doubles US$4; triples US$65. Rooms with river view and A/C: BZ$87/114/147.)*

LAMANAI

For many, getting to Lamanai is half the adventure. Belize Global Adventure Tours, Discovery Expeditions, and S & L Travels and Tours run tours from Belize City (8hr., US$105-110). Most travelers visit the site via the New River. From Orange Walk, Jungle River Tours is the go-to company, with experienced tours of both the ruins and the wildlife. Many hotels in Orange Walk also arrange tours. The standard rate for a guided tour is US$40, not including the US$5 admission fee. Trips last 6-7hr.; lunch is usually included. Tillet's buses occasionally run from the market in Orange Walk to Indian Church, the closest village to the ruins (2hr.; M, W, and F 3pm; US$2). Open daily 8am-5pm.

One of the true highlights of Belize, a jewel nestled deep inside the northern jungles beside the New River Lagoon, Lamanai ("submerged crocodile," a reference to a Mayan creation myth) has enticed countless visitors by the boatload since its excavation in the early 1970s. Lamanai is famous for its ruins which date as far back as 1500 BC and nestled near 17th-century Spanish relics. Lamanai's location on the New River established the city as a major trading point between Belizes inland and the coast. Between 200 BC and AD

700, Lamanai became known as a major economic and religious center, with a population of about 35,000. When the Spanish arrived in the early 16th century, the Mayan population in the city was still quite active. The Spanish brought several fatal European diseases which devastated the community despite its successful efforts to destroy the Spanish mission in the 1600s. By the late 18th century Lamanai was a mere vestige of its former self.

A walk through Lamanai can take up to 2hr. give that the site is large and spread out. The first major ruin as you enter from the river is the **Jaguar Temple** (Structure N10-9), which dates from the AD sixth century. Two jaguar faces glare from the temple's base. The holes in these patterns were once used as small incense chambers. Across the plaza lie several royal bedrooms, with stone beds that are nearly 1000 years old. On your right, another temple, fronted by a stone tablet, is intricately carved with glyphs and a royal portrait. This is **Stela 9,** a replica dating from AD 625 that was used to commemorate the royal accession of Lord Smoking Shell. Moving to the west, walk through the ball court to the tallest structure, **N10-43,** which rises well above tree level and affords gorgeous views of the surrounding jungle and river. A six minute walk through the jungle brings you to the **Mask Temple,** whose lower-right-hand corner bears the huge facial relief of a proud ruler. Excavators found this relief under a staircase constructed by another ruler who had sought to erase the memory of his predecessor. If you have any energy left at the end of your visit, head 400 yards south from the docks to the remains of two Colonial churches. These structures were built by Mayan slave labor and later were destroyed in Mayan rebellion. There are gift stores and a small museum near the entrance by the docks.

NORTHERN CAYES

Few travelers overlook Belize's exquisite Cayes (pronounced KEYS), strung along the second-largest barrier reef in the world. As Belize's number-one tourist destination, the Cayes feature some of the best diving in the world. Although there are several hundred cayes off Belize's aquamarine coast, visitors primarily concern themselves with Ambergris Caye, with its top-end resorts and dive shops. The more rugged Caye Caulker, is also popular and is a budget traveler's haven. While the Cayes are nice, it is the reef and its 400 species of fish that sets the Belizean Cayes apart.

CAYE CAULKER

Caye Caulker (population 800) is Ambergris Caye's scruffy younger cousin, lounging in a hammock, and most likely smoking a joint. The streets here are unpaved, the waterfront is relatively uncluttered, and the pace of life is set by the ubiquitous street sign and the island's unofficial motto: "Go slow."

Maya populated Caye Caulker thousands of years ago. Modern settlement began with *mestizo* refugees, fleeing the Yucatán Peninsula during the Caste War. A fishing community soon developed and continues to this day. In the 1970s, backpackers and hippies making their way from Tulum, Mexico, to Antigua, Guatemala made the island an established budget stop. Since then, possibilities for adventure on or below the seas have grown to almost rival those of Ambergris Caye's. So hit the water, groove to the reggae beat, lounge in a hammock by the sea, and go slow.

▣ TRANSPORTATION

Located directly along the Belize City-San Pedro boat route, Caye Caulker is easy to travel to and away from. Flying out from the island's airstrip is also possible, but it's an extremely costly option considering the relatively cheap water taxi prices.

Flights: The **Caye Caulker Airstrip** is located well south of the village, about a 10-15min. walk from town along the coast or on Back Street. **Maya Island Air** (☎226 0012; www.mayaislandair.com) flies from the airstrip to **Belize City,** stopping at the Philip Goldson International Airport (10min.; one-way US$62, round-trip US$125) and at the **Municipal Airstrip** (15min., US$62/256) at 7:10, 9:10, 11:10am, 1:10, and 3:10pm. Flights to **San Pedro** (10min., US$35/70) leave at 7:45, 9:45am, 1:45, and 3:45pm. **Tropic Air** (☎226 0040; www.tropicair.com) flies from the airstrip to **Belize City,** stopping at the Goldson International Airport (10min.; one-way US$63, round-trip US$120) and the Municipal Airstrip (15min., US$35/65), at 7:10, 9:10, 11:10am, 1:10, 3:10, and 5:10pm. Flights to **San Pedro** (10min., US$35/65) leave at 7:50, 8:50, 9:50, 10:50, 11:50am, 12:50, 1:50, 2:50, 3:50, and 4:50pm.

Boats: Caye Caulker Water Taxis (☎223 5752; www.cayecaulkerwatertaxi.com) arrive at and leave from the **arrival pier** in the middle of the village. Boats leave for **Belize City** (50min.; one-way US$7.50, round-trip US$12.50) at 6:30, 7:30, 8:30, 10, 11am, noon, 1:30, 3, 4, and 5pm. Boats leave for **San Pedro** (30min., US$7.50/12.50) at 7, 8:20, 8:45, 9:50, 11:20am, 12:50, 2:20, 3:50, 5:20, and 6:15pm. You can buy tickets at the pier, the Tropical Paradise Restaurant, or Femi's Restaurant and Lounge. **San**

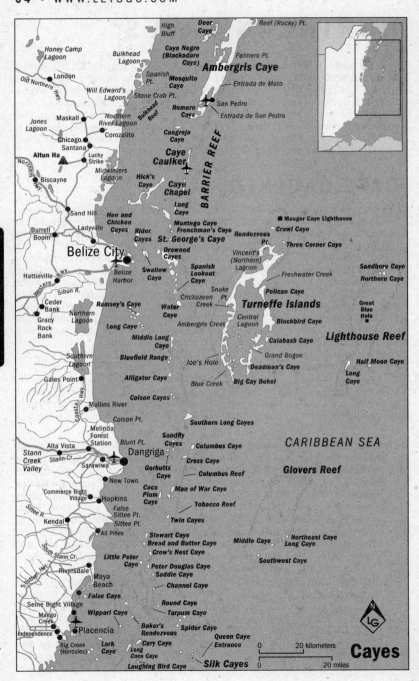

Honey Camp Lagoon
London
Old Northern Hwy.
Bulkhead Lagoon
Will Edward's Lagoon
Spanish Pt.
Mosquito Caye
Stone Crab Pt.
High Bluff
Deer Caye
Reef (Rocky) Pt.
Cayo Negro (Blackadore Caye)
Palmero Pt.
Ambergris Caye
Entrada de Mato
San Pedro
Romero Caye
Entrada de San Pedro
Jones Lagoon
Maskall
Chicago
Santana
Altun Ha
Corozalito
Lucky Strike
Midwinters Lagoon
Biscayne
Northern River Lagoon
Cangrejo Caye
Caye Caulker
Hick's Caye
Caye Chapel
BARRIER REEF
Sand Hill
Ladyville
Hen and Chicken Cayes
Rider Cayes
Long Caye
Montego Caye
Frenchman's Caye
St. George's Caye
Rendezvous Pt.
Mauger Caye Lighthouse
Crawl Caye
Three Corner Caye
Burrell Boom
Belize City
Belize Harbor
Swallow Caye
Drowned Cayes
Spanish Lookout Caye
Vincent's (Northern) Lagoon
Freshwater Creek
Sandbore Caye
Northern Caye
Hattieville
Western Hwy.
Sibun R.
Ceder Bank
Gracy Rock Bank
Ramsey's Caye
Northern Lagoon
Long Caye
Water Caye
Crickozeen Creek
Snake Creek
Turneffe Islands
Pelican Caye
Central Lagoon
Blackbird Caye
Calabash Caye
Great Blue Hole
Lighthouse Reef
Ambergris Creek
Middle Long Caye
Bluefield Range
Joe's Hole
Grand Bogoe
Deadman's Caye
Half Moon Caye
Long Caye
Southern Lagoon
Gales Point
Alligator Caye
Blue Creek
Big Cay Bokel
Colson Cayes
Mullins River
Colson Pt.
Coastal Hwy.
Melinda Forest Station
Alta Vista
Blunt Pt.
Dangriga
Stann Creek Valley
Stann Cr.
Sarawiwa
Southern Long Cayes
Sandfly Cayes
Columbus Caye
CARIBBEAN SEA
Cross Caye
Gorbutts Caye
Columbus Reef
Glovers Reef
Commerce Bight Village
New Town
Hopkins
False Sittee Pt.
Sittee Pt.
Coco Plum Caye
Man of War Caye
Tobacco Reef
Sittee R.
Kendal
All Pines
Twin Cayes
Stewart Caye
Bread and Butter Caye
Crow's Nest Caye
Middle Caye
Northeast Caye
Long Caye
Southwest Caye
South Stann Cr.
Riversdale
Little Peter Caye
Peter Douglas Caye
Saddle Caye
Maya Beach
Channel Caye
Southern Hwy.
Seine Bight Village
False Caye
Round Caye
Mango Creek
Wippari Caye
Tarpum Caye
Independence
Placencia
Baker's Rendezvous
Spider Caye
Queen Caye Entrance
Big Creek (Hercules)
Lark Caye
Cary Caye
Long Coco Caye
Silk Cayes
Laughing Bird Caye

0   20 kilometers
0   20 miles

Cayes

Pedro-Belize Express boats (☎226 2194; www.sanpedrowatertaxi.com) arrive at and depart from the pier just north of the Caye Caulker Water Taxi arrival pier. Boats leave for **Belize City** (50min.; one-way US$3.50, round-trip US$6) at 7:30, 8:30, 10am, noon, 1:30, 3, 4, and 5pm. Boats leave for **San Pedro** (30min.; one-way US$6, round-trip US$10) at 8:40, 9:40, 11:10am, 12:40, 2:10, 3:40, and 4:40pm. Buy tickets at the **Xtreme Adventures office** on Front St. one minute north of the arrival pier. **Triple J Water Taxis** (☎207 7777; www.triplejbelize.com) arrive at and depart from the pier in front of the Rainbow Bar and Grill. Boats leave for **Belize City** (50min.; one-way US$5, round-trip US$12.50) at 7:30, 8:30, 11am, 1:30, 3, and 4pm. Boats leave for **San Pedro** (30min., US$7.50/12.50) at 8:45, 11:15am, 12:45, 2:15, 3:45, and 5:15pm.

Taxis: Golf cart taxis usually congregate around the **arrival pier,** but in most cases they're not necessary for getting around the small village.

TAKE A HIKE. For a small island, Caye Caulker is mysteriously teeming with taxi drivers who descend, vulture-like, on new arrivals from the water taxis. Unless you're a wimp, don't take them up on their offer—most destinations on the Caye are within 10 minutes' walking distance of one another.

NORTHERN CAYES

✴ 🛐 ORIENTATION AND PRACTICAL INFORMATION

Three main north-south drags constitute Caye Caulker's village. **Front Street** is closest to the eastern coast and the arrival piers. **Middle Street,** which begins farther south, and **Back Street** are the other main roads. Front St. is lined with hotels, restaurants, and tour companies. The more residential and less developed Middle St. and Back St. feature a few restaurants and services. More restaurants, beach bars, and hotels stretch along the eastern shore. At the very north of town, the **Split,** a water channel created by a hurricane, separates the village from the northern section of the island. Fifteen minutes south of town are the **Caye Caulker Forest Reserve** and the **airstrip.** Expensive resorts perch on the coasts to the north and south of town.

Tours and Agencies: See **Outdoor Activities,** p. 73.

Bank: Atlantic Bank, Middle St. (☎226 0207). Open M-F 8am-2pm, Sa 8:30am-noon.

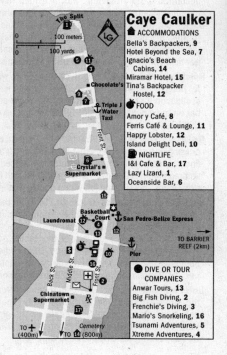

Caye Caulker

🏠 **ACCOMMODATIONS**
Bella's Backpackers, **9**
Hotel Beyond the Sea, **7**
Ignacio's Beach Cabins, **14**
Miramar Hotel, **15**
Tina's Backpacker Hostel, **12**

🍴 **FOOD**
Amor y Café, **8**
Ferris Café & Lounge, **11**
Happy Lobster, **12**
Island Delight Deli, **10**

🎵 **NIGHTLIFE**
I&I Cafe & Bar, **17**
Lazy Lizard, **1**
Oceanside Bar, **6**

⬤ **DIVE OR TOUR COMPANIES**
Anwar Tours, **13**
Big Fish Diving, **2**
Frenchie's Diving, **3**
Mario's Snorkeling, **16**
Tsunami Adventures, **5**
Xtreme Adventures, **4**

Laundromat: Coin Laundromat (☎226 0137), on the street leading in from the dock . Wash US$2; dry US$2. Open daily 7am-9pm. **Ruby's Coin Laundromat,** down the street and under the same owner (☎226 0137). Wash US$2; dry US$2.50. Open daily 8am-9pm.

Police Station, Front St. (☎206 0179). A large, yellow building, with a large, drug warning plastered on its front.

24hr. Pharmacy: R&M's Pharmacy (☎226 0190) next to the post office. Open M-Sa 8am-noon and 1:30-7pm, Su 9am-noon and 5-7pm. MC/V.

Internet Access: Cayeboard Connection, Front St. US$5 per hr. Printing and copying services. Selection of used books. Open daily 8am-7pm. **Cyber Cafe,** Front St. (☎226 0402). US$7 per hr. Open daily 7am-10pm.

Post Office: Just off Front St. at the southern end of the village. Open M-Th 8:45am-noon and 1-4pm.

⌐ ACCOMMODATIONS

The budget traveler arriving at Caye Caulker from Ambergris Caye has reached the Promised Land. From luxury hotels, our weary pilgrim arrives at a backpacker's paradise of cheap hostels. Here, affordable views of the beach aren't just possible—they're the norm.

▨ **Tina's Backpacker Hostel** (☎226 0351; www.tinashostelbelize.com), on the beachfront. From the arrival pier, walk right on the beach for 1min. After 11 years, Tina's is still the most convenient and satisfying budget option on the island. An elaborately decorated 2-story building, with a garden full of palm trees, hammocks, and chairs, affording expansive ocean views. Deck with hammocks right on the shore. The rooms are clean, but you'll be spending most of your time chilling with other guests in the garden (parties are plentiful during the winter months). A new annex provides dorms with A/C, large common rooms, a kitchen, couch, and cable TV. Free Wi-Fi. Computer rental US$2 per hr. Dorms in main building US$11, in annexUS$15; doubles US$27. MC/V. ❷

Hotel Beyond the Sea, Front St. (☎624 9258; www.hotelbeyondthesea.com). Formerly the Taj Hotel, a new American owner has transformed the space into yet another Caye Caulker destination for backpackers. Rooms are bright and clean, but the highlight is the open-air bar on the ground-floor, which offers internet access (US$1.25 per hr.) and Skype. Dorms US$10, extended stay US$9; singles US$20/18; doubles US$27/25. Cash only. ❷

Bella's Backpackers (☎226 0360), off Front St. at the northern end of the village. From the arrival pier, turn right onto Front St. and turn left at the sign for Bella's after 5min. You won't find much privacy in these rustic, airy halls stuffed with beds, but the digs are cheap. Central common room with cable TV and a kitchen with fridge. Free Wi-Fi and internet. Free canoe use. Dorms US$10; high loft with a double mattress US$13. Cash only. ❷

Ignacio's Beach Cabins (☎226 0175). From the arrival pier, turn left and walk along the coast for 15-20min. Cheap, blue-painted cabins on a beachfront space. The area itself isn't exactly picturesque—the water is murky, a destroyed palm tree blights any clean views of the water, and many of the cabins themselves are aging and rustic—but the effect of solitude is complete. Each cabin comes with 2 beds, a porch with a chair and hammock, a private bath, and a fan. Kayak rental US$8 per hr.; US$13 per 2hr.; US$15 per 3hr. Beachfront cabins US$20; back cabins US$15. MC/V. ❸

Hotel Miramar (☎206 0357), on the beachfront. Verandahs with beachfront views are the strongest attraction of this centrally located hotel which lacks amenities. Barebones but clean rooms. Small cafe on the ground floor sells coffee and pastries. All rooms with fans. Singles with shared bath US$13, with private bath US$27; doubles US$27/25. Triples US$30. Cash only. ❷

❐ FOOD

Caye Caulker is the place to be for Caribbean and Belizean seafood specials. Waterfront views, great food, and friendly service more than compensate for the high prices. For groceries, try **Crystal's Supermarket** (Front St.; ☎226 0033; open daily 7am-11pm.) and **Chinatown Supermarket** (Middle St.; ☎226 4585; open daily 8am-10pm).

Femi's Cafe and Lounge, Front St. (☎226 8963), 5min. north of the arrival pier. With prime waterfront real estate, Femi's is the ideal spot to relax after a day at sea. Seafood dishes US$6-15. The famous "Nacho Blast" US$6. Coffee US$2-5; smoothies US$3-6. For a stronger beverage, try a rum or colada (US$4.50-7.50) during the long happy hour (3-9pm). Open daily 8am-10pm. AmEx/MC/V. ❸

Happy Lobster Restaurant and Bar, Front St. (☎226 0064), 1min. north of the arrival pier. Cheerfully serves a wide range of Mexican and Belizean breakfasts like *huevos rancheros,* eggs, bacon, beans, and fruit plates (US$4-8). Seafood US$7.50-15. Open 8am-10pm. MC/V. ❸

Island Delight Deli, Front St., just south of the arrival pier. A tiny eatery with a mighty menu. Mexican salutes US$1. Belizean rice and beans US$3.50. Fried dishes US$4.50-10. Burgers US$2-7.50. The deli is take-out only, so grab your food and chill on the beach. Open daily 9am-7pm. Cash only. ❶

Amor Y Cafe, Front St. (☎601 4458). A small cafe that's been the locals' go-to breakfast stop for years. Homemade bread, cakes, and brownies along with more filling fare like scrambled eggs with bacon and tomatoes and grilled sandwiches. A wide variety of smothies, milkshakes, and fresh natural juices. You can take it to go or, if there's room, sit outside on the porch and watch the village wake up. Entrees US$4-8; drinks US$2-5. Open daily M and W-Su 6am-11am. Cash only. ❷

▤ ♫ NIGHTLIFE AND ENTERTAINMENT

Caulker is as relaxed at night as it is during the day, preferring relaxed drinking to sweaty crowds. These are just a few options for the groove-happy.

I&I Reggae Bar (☎625 0344), just off the southern end of Front St. 3-story I&I features a dance floor on the ground level, swings hanging from the ceiling on the 2nd fl., and hammocks for lounging and drinking on the 3rd. Beer US$2; mixed drinks US$4.50-8.50. Open daily 6pm-midnight. Cash only.

Oceanside Nightclub, Front St. Locals congregate here for frenetic punta and reggae dancing after 10:30pm on the weekend. Don't miss the dance contests; check the front door for flyers announcing dates and times. Drinks US$2.50-7.50. Open daily 7am-midnight. Cash only.

Lazy Lizard Bar & Grill (☎226 0280), on the Split. Proclaiming itself "a sunny place for shady people," the Lizard is perfectly placed next to the public swimming area. Local rum US$2.50; Belikin beer US$2. Happy hour 5-7pm. Open daily 11am-10pm. Cash only.

▣ OUTDOOR ACTIVITIES

It may not have Ambergris's range of companies, but Caye Caulker still manages to offer access to Belize sea adventures. Most likely, the crowds won't be as stifling. Though trips visit many of the same sites accessed from Ambergris, Caulker also offers treasures of its own.

DIVING AND SNORKELING DESTINATIONS FROM CAYE CAULKER

CAYE CAULKER MARINE RESERVE (CCMR). Established in 1998, the CCMR covers the local section of the barrier reef as well as a turtle grass lagoon closer to shore. Angelfish, parrotfish, colorful sponges, Christmas tree worms, shrimps, crabs, and lobsters all call the reserve their home. The reserve boasts its own **Shark Ray Alley** (not to be confused with Hol Chan's) and a brilliant array of coral formations at **Coral Gardens**. *(Diving and snorkeling ½-day trips leave at 9am and 2pm. Diving US$80-90; snorkeling US$23-30.)*

SWALLOW CAYE WILDLIFE SANCTUARY. One of the best spots in the world to catch a glimpse of **manatees** (sea cows), the sanctuary stretches over 9,000 acres southwest of Caye Caulker. Swimming with the manatees is forbidden. The sanctuary was created after excessive disturbance damaged the population. Still, several tour companies allow snorkelers to watch and share space with these delicate sea creatures.

GOFF'S CAYE AND SERGEANT'S CAYE. It's hard to believe, but tiny **Goff's Caye** was once home to a colonial fishing settlement and cemetery. Today, snorkelers take advantage of its location in a particularly healthy section of the barrier reef. The area northwest of the caye is a foraging area for sea turtles. **Sergeant's Caye** is just a tiny scrap of sand, but the plentiful coral sites around it make the caye a popular snorkeling site. These cayes are most often visited in snorkeling trips, but Frenchie's Diving (see below) also offers diving trips around the area (US$95-100).

DIVING COMPANIES

Frenchie's Diving (☎226-0234; www.frenchiesdivingbelize.com), on a dock by the Split. Diving in the local reef, Hol Chan, Spanish Bay, St. George's Caye, Turneffe Atoll, and Blue Hole. The kicker is an overnight diving and camping trip to Half Moon Caye in the Lighthouse Reef (US$500). AmEx/MC/V.

Big Fish Dive Center, Front St. (☎226-0450; www.bigfishdivebelize.com). 5min. south of the arrival pier. Run by a Caye Caulker native, Big Fish offers diving tours to 7 locations, including the local reef, Hol Can, and Blue Hole. MC/V.

Xtreme Adventures, Front St. (☎206-0065 or 206-0225; xadventures@hotmail.com). 1min. north of the arrival pier. Dive trips to the local reef, Hol Chan, and Blue Hole. You can also buy tickets for the San Pedro-Belize Express Water Taxi here. AmEx/MC/V.

Mario's Snorkeling and Inland Tours, Front St. (☎226-0056). 5min. south of the arrival pier. Diving trips to Blue Hole. MC/V.

Tsunami Adventures, Front St. (☎226-0462; www.tsunamiadventures.com). 5min north of the arrival pier. Diving at Hol Chan, Blue Hole, and Turneffe North and South. MC/V.

SNORKELING COMPANIES

Raggamuffin Tours, Front St. (☎226 0348; www.raggamuffintours.com). Snorkeling trips to the local reef (US$23), Hol Chan (US$45) and Turneffe (US$75). Their most famous tour is a 3-day sailing trip down to Placencia, stopping for fishing, snorkeling, and camping on small, deserted cayes along the way (US$225-300). MC/V.

Tsunami Adventures, Front St. (☎226 0462; www.tsunamiadventures.com), 5min. north of the arrival pier. Snorkeling trips to the Caye Caulker Marine Reserve, Hol Chan, Blue Hole, and Turneffe. Night snorkeling US$33. MC/V.

Mario's Snorkeling and Inland Tours, Front St. (☎226 0056), 5min. south of the arrival pier. Snorkeling tours to the Caye Caulker Marine Reserve, Hol Chan, and Caye Chapel. MC/V.

Blackhawk Tours, Front St. (☎607 0323), 2min. north of the arrival pier, across the street from the merchandise booths. Snorkeling trips to the Caye Caulker Marine Reserve (US$23) and Hol Chan (US$37). MC/V.

Star Tours (☎226 0374; www.startoursbelize.com), offices in front of the Tropics Hotel on Front St. Local reef, manatee, and Hol Chan snorkeling trips. AmEx/MC/V.

MANATEE WATCHING

Chocolate's Manatee Tours, Front St. (☎226 0151). 5min. north of the arrival pier. One of the most renowned manatee tour services, founded by a pioneer of the manatee cause. Full-day tours to Swallow Caye and Sergeant's Caye (US$60-65). Also rents kayaks (single US$5 per hr.; double US$7.50 per hr.). Chocolate's gift store open M-Sa 9am-9:30pm. MC/V.

French Angel Expeditions. Occasionally runs trips to Goff's Caye with a barbeque on the tiny beach there (US$60). MC/V.

WINDSURFING AND KITEBOARDING

Kitexplorer, Front St. (☎226 0303; www.kitexplorer.com), near the Split . 9hr. windsurfing and kiteboarding adventures, including instruction, lunch, and gear. MC/V.

FISHING

Shallow flats near the caye make for some of the best fishing in Belize. Many tour companies offering diving and snorkeling trips can also arrange fishing expeditions for a negotiated price.

Anglers Abroad (☎226 0303; www.anglersabroad.com), at the Sea Dreams Hotel. This fly fishing shop also offers fly fishing instruction and ½-day, full-day, and overnight trips. MC/V.

Tsunami Adventures, Front St. (☎226 0462; www.tsunamiadventures.com), 5min. north of the arrival pier. ½-day local fishing trips US$175; 4hr. fly fishing trips US$200, 6hr. US$300. MC/V.

INLAND TRIPS

Xtreme Adventures (☎206 0065 or 206 0225; xadventures@hotmail.com). Inland trips to Altun Ha and Lamanai.

Mario's Snorkeling and Inland Tours (☎226 0056). Offers inland trips to Lamanai and to the Belize Zoo with cave tubing. MC/V.

Tsunami Adventures, Front St. (☎226 0462; www.tsunamiadventures.com), 5min. north of the arrival pier. Inland trips to Altun Ha, Lamanai, cave tubing, zip lining, and the Xunantunich Mayan ruins with a tour of San Ignacio. MC/V.

AMBERGRIS CAYE

Ambergris has avoided Mexican rule thanks only to a narrow canal dug by the Maya 500 years ago, separating the peninsula from the mainland. Once a hideout for European pirates, the island developed into a coconut plantation and fishing center before the tourist boom hit in the 1960s. Now chock full of resorts, Ambergris is hardly the best option for backpackers looking for chill island vibes (thankfully, the neighboring Caye Caulker has picked up that slack). Still, the range of sea adventures offered here is unbeatable, and at times the island's strained attempt to resemble a tropical paradise works.

San Pedro (population 11,300), is the center of civilization on Ambergris Caye. Belize's main tourist destination is full of peddling, diving, snorkeling, and fishing expeditions crowding the beach and the docks. Watch out for golf carts flying along narrow cobblestone streets past countless flashy gift shops, restaurants, and hotels; get ready to encounter aging resort denizens in polo shirts and golf caps mingling with Rastafarians. You've landed on Belize's largest Caye.

⌐ TRANSPORTATION

You can't throw a diving tank without hitting a service renting out golf carts and bikes, though they're only good for exploring the areas lying well beyond San Pedro. Ambergris's popularity ensures that a steady stream of boats floats constantly to and from San Pedro's piers.

Flights: The **San Pedro Airstrip** is located directly south of town, beginning just south of Esmerelda St. **Maya Island Air** (☎225 2219; www.mayaislandair.com) and **Tropic Air** (☎225 2302; www.tropicair.com) fly from the airstrip to **Belize City** (25min.; one-way US$63, round-trip US$125); **Caye Caulker** (10min., US$350/70); and **Corozal** (20min., US$50/100).

Boats: Thunderbolt skiffs leave from the western shore of San Pedro at the end of Black Coral St. at 7am and 3pm for **Corozal** (1½hr.; one-way US$23, round-trip US$33), with a stop in **Sarteneja** if requested (1hr., one-way US$23). The **Triple J Water Taxi** (☎207 7777; www.triplejbelize.com) leaves for **Caye Caulker** (40min.; one-way US$5, round-trip US$10) and **Belize City** (1½hr.; one-way US$7.50, round-trip US$14) at 7, 8, 10:30am, 1, 2:30, and 3:30pm. The **Caye Caulker Water Taxi** (☎223 5752; www. cayecaulkerwatertaxi.com), dock in front of the Blue Tang Hotel, leaves for **Caye Caulker** (45min.; one-way US$7.50, round-trip US$13) and **Belize City** (1½hr.; US$10/15) at 6, 7, 8, 9:30, 10:30, 11:30am, 1, 2:30, 3:30, and 4:30pm. The **San Pedro-Belize Express** (☎226-2194; www.sanpedrowatertaxi.com) leaves for **Caye Caulker** (30-40min.; one-way US$4, round-trip US$6) and **Belize City** (1½hr.; US$6/11) at 7 (express to Belize City), 8, 9:30, 11:30am, 1, 2:30, 3:30, and 4:30pm.

Taxis: Cabs wait midway up Barrier Reef Drive, by the public seating area on the shore.

Golf Cart: Polo's Golf Cart Rentals (☎226 3542), at the northern end of Barrier Reef Dr. Rentals US$13 per hr., US$25 per 2hr., US$30 per 3hr., US$62 per day. Open daily 9am-6pm. **Castle Car Rentals** (☎226 2421; www.castlecarsbelize.com), on the corner of Barrier Reef Dr. and Tarpon St. Rentals US$40 per 3hr., US$55 per 8hr., US$65 per day, and US$270 per week. **Ultimate Golf Cart Rentals** (☎226 3326), on the corner of Pescador Dr. and Tarpon St. **4-seater rentals:** US$15 per hr., US$25 per 2hr., US$50 per 8hr., US$70 per day, and US$300 per week. **6-seater rentals:** US$24 per hr., US$40 per 2hr., US$70 per 8hr., US$100 per day, and US$500 per week.

Biking: Joe's Bike Rental (☎226 4371), on the corner of Pescador Dr. and Caribena St. Rental US$2.50 per hr., US$10 per day, US$40 per week. Open daily 8am-6pm. **Los Quapos Bicycle Rental,** Pelican St (☎621 2505). Bike rental US$2 per hr., US$3 per 2hr., US$4 per 3hr., US$10 per day, and US$40 per week. **Calvio's Bike Rental** (☎661 7143), southern end of Pescador Dr. Rentals BZ$5 per hr., US$10 per 5hr., US$6 per day.

✦ 🛈 ORIENTATION AND PRACTICAL INFORMATION

SAN PEDRO

San Pedro is nestled near the southern end of the Caye. Behind it, a lagoon stretches into the **Hol Chan Marine Reserve.** The more remote areas north and south of town are dotted with expensive resorts, but scenic biking opportunities are plentiful there. Within San Pedro itself, three drives stretch from north to south: **Barrier Reef Drive, Pescador Drive,** and **Angel Coral Drive.** Small streets intersect the drives. Below **Tarpon Street,** at the southern end of the town center, the **airstrip** stretches south; paralleling it, **Coconut Drive** leads into unpaved, more residential sections of town. The **eastern coast** is lined with restaurants, bars, hotels, and docks laden with tour companies and ferry terminals. The quieter **western shore,** meanwhile, is mostly full of fishing boats.

Tourist Office: The San Pedro offices of the **Belize Tourism Board** (☎226 4531; www. travelbelize.org or www.belizetourism.org) are located at the southern end of Barrier Reef Dr. Open M-Th 8am-noon and 1-5pm, F 8am-noon and 1-4pm. A small **Tourist Information** booth loaded with pamphlets and other information is midway up Barrier Reef Dr. next to the opening on the beach.

Tours and Agencies: See **Outdoors Activities,** p. 73.

Banks: Atlantic Bank (☎226 2195), at the intersection of Barrier Reef Dr. and Buccaneer St. Open M-F 8am-3pm, Sa 8am-noon. **First Caribbean International Bank,** at the intersection of Barrier Reef Dr. and Buccaneer St. Open M-Th 8am-2:30pm, F 8am-4:30pm. **Belize Bank** (☎226 2450), at the north end of Barrier Reef Dr. Open M-Th 8am-3pm, F 8am-4:30pm, Sa 9am-noon.

Bookstore: Pages, Tarpon St., toward the south end of town. Decent selection of new and used books. Open M-Sa 8am-5pm.

Laundromat: Candace's Laundromat (☎226 2052), toward the northern end of Barrier Reef Dr. US$10 per load with service, US$7.50 without. Open daily 9am-7pm. Cash only.

Police Station: Midway up Barrier Reef Dr., by the opening to the sea.

Pharmacy: Ambergris Hope's Pharmacy (☎226 2983), at the northern end of Pescador Dr. Open M-Th 8am-9:30pm, F 8am-5pm, Sa 6-9pm, Su 9am-1pm and 5-9pm.

Internet Access: The **"D" Surf Shop,** on the beach at the northern end of Barrier Reef Dr. Internet US$7.50 per hr.; international calls US$0.50 per min. Open daily 8am-9pm. **Pelican Internet,** on Barrier Reef Dr. between Pelican St. and Caribena St. Internet US$0.50 per 5min.; use for over 20min. and get free unlimited calls to the US and Canada. MC/V. **Caribbean Connection** (☎226 4664; www.sanpedrointernet. com), on the corner of Barrier Reef Dr. and Black Coral St. A deluxe internet cafe, featuring outdoor seating, actual coffee, and with jewelry for sale to boot. Internet US$5 per hr. International phone service also available.

Post Office: near the corner of Barrier Reef Dr. and Buccaneer St. Open M-Th 8am-noon and 1-4pm, F 8am-noon and 1-3:30pm.

🏠 ACCOMMODATIONS

Hotels seem to breed like rabbits on Ambergris, but a satisfying range of backpacker options has yet to develop. Still, a stable subset of hostels and cheap hotels survive the suffocating presence of the more affluent establishments nearby.

Pedro's Inn, Sea Grape Dr. (☎226 3825; www.backpackersbelize.com). Despite its distance from the docks, this is the cheapest and best backpacker option in San Pedro. Spread over 3 white clapboard houses in a quiet, mostly untouristed area of town. High-ceiling rooms and spotless beds. Pool, free kayaks, and golf cart rentals. Well-stocked, popular bar and pizza joint, decorated with Jagermeister bottles, complete with pool table and card room. Singles US$10; doubles US$12.50. Rooms with private baths, cable TVs, and A/C US$50. MC/V. ❷

Ruby's Hotel, Barrier Reef Dr. (☎226 2063; www.ambergriscaye.com/rubys). Ruby's convenient location and ample verandah space by the beach has made it a budget haven for years. Rooms with stark white walls, wooden floors, and fans are a bit dark (especially on the street side). Arranges snorkeling, diving, and inland tours. Singles with shared bath US$20; singles and doubles with private bath US$30. MC/V. ❸

Lily's Hotel (☎206 2059; www.ambergriscaye.com/lilys). This family-run hotel features large rooms by the ocean with shaded balconies. All rooms with A/C and private baths; some with cable TVs. Restaurant downstairs. Singles US$55-65; doubles US$65-75. Seaside singles US$45-55; doubles US$55-65. AmEx/MC/V. ❺

San Pedrano Hotel (☎226 2054), on corner of Barrier Reef Dr. and Caribena St. Family-run for over 30 years. Clean, comfortable, wood-floor rooms, each with a private bath. Ocean views are rare, but some glimpses can be caught from the verandah upstairs. Singles and doubles with fan US$32.50, with A/C BZ$43.50; triples BZ$37/49. MC./V. ❺

🍴 FOOD

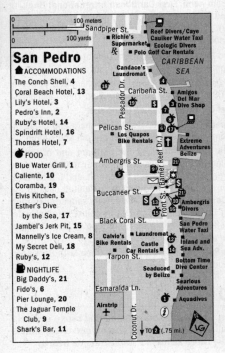

San Pedro

🏠 ACCOMMODATIONS
The Conch Shell, **4**
Coral Beach Hotel, **13**
Lily's Hotel, **3**
Pedro's Inn, **2**
Ruby's Hotel, **14**
Spindrift Hotel, **16**
Thomas Hotel, **7**

🍴 FOOD
Blue Water Grill, **1**
Caliente, **10**
Coramba, **19**
Elvis Kitchen, **5**
Esther's Dive
  by the Sea, **17**
Jambel's Jerk Pit, **15**
Mannelly's Ice Cream, **8**
My Secret Deli, **18**
Ruby's, **12**

🎵 NIGHTLIFE
Big Daddy's, **21**
Fido's, **6**
Pier Lounge, **20**
The Jaguar Temple
  Club, **9**
Shark's Bar, **11**

Jam-packed with restaurants, Ambergris doesn't skimp on the grub; finding food that's affordable is another story. The many cafes and snack shops will offer sustenance to the budget traveler; there are also a few restaurants in town that are easy on the wallet. For groceries, try **Richie's Supermarket,** at the northern end of Pescador Dr. (open M-Sa 7am-10pm, Su 7am-9pm) or **San Pedro Supermarket Ltd.,** next to Richie's (☎226-3446; open M-Sa 7am-11pm and Su 7am-10pm).

🔳 **Estel's Diner by the Sea** (☎226 2019), on the beach at the end of Pelican St. Floors lined with beach sand, walls decorated with Belizean and American memorabilia, ceiling covered in flags, and a corner piano outfitted with country albums make Estel's worth a visit. Large, delicious, and reasonably priced breakfasts and lunches. Extensive breakfast menu (US$7-8.50), loaded with the traditional Belizean egg-meat mixtures and gems like Estel's Special (Mayan eggs with fried tortillas; US$7.50). The lunch menu (US$6-15) is heavy on Mexican dishes with burritos (US$5.50-7) and Mexican platters (US$10.50). Open M and W-Su 6am-5pm. Cash only. ❸

Ruby's Cafe, Barrier Reef Dr. (☎226 2063), next to Ruby's Hotel toward the south end of town. A local favorite satisfying desires for pastries and Mexican food. Pick up cinnamon rolls, rum cake, and banana bread (US$2.50-5) in the morning and return for burritos and tostadas in the afternoon or evening (US$3-6). Open M-Tu and F-Sa 6am-7:30pm, W 6am-2pm, Su 6am-noon. Cash only. ❷

Jambel's Jerk Pit, Barrier Reef Dr. (☎226 3515), beneath the Coral Beach Hotel. An old-time San Pedro favorite that wears its Jamaican affiliation proudly on its sleeve. Come here for "jerked" (a Jamaican process of grilling and spicing) seafood and meat dishes (US$10-17.50). Stay for the reggae beats, sometimes live. W buffet nights. Open daily 10am-10pm. Another location in Belize City. MC/V. ❹

Mannelly's Ice Cream, Barrier Reef Dr. (☎226 2285). There's no shortage of ice cream shops in San Pedro, but Mannelly's rises above the rest with its range of Belizean home-made options like bubble gum, coconut, rum n' raisin, and piña colada flavors. Single cone US$1.50-2.50; double scoop US$3-5. Cash only. ❶

🎭🎵 NIGHTLIFE AND ENTERTAINMENT

SAN PEDRO

San Pedro is full of night venues. Most of them are open-air bars, strung along the beachfront. San Pedro's compact layout makes bar and club-hopping easy: just walk along the beach beginning at around 9pm and follow the music. As with everything else in San Pedro, the scene is busier during the popular winter season.

Fido's Restaurant and Bar (☎226 2056; www.fidosbelize.com). At 10pm each night, this massive, beachside seafood restaurant turns into one of San Pedro's main nightspots. Come drink and dance to live music under a thatched roof. Extensive list of special shots—Buttery Nipple and Mayan Dragon among them (2 for US$5). The party often spills over onto the beach, where Fido's owns its own pier. Drinks US$2-7.50. Live music (reggae, punta, R&B, classic rock, and funk) begins around 8pm. Open daily 11am-2am. Cash only.

Jaguar's Temple Club (☎226 4077; www.jaguarstemple.com). One of the most recognizable buildings in town, proudly lording over Barrier Reef Dr., next to the beachfront park. This jungle and Mayan-inspired "temple" can fit hundreds within its exotic walls. Light shows and live DJs playing remixes of old R&B hits along with the newest Caribbean sounds. You can be pretty sure that this nightclub won't attract the older resort crowd. Open Th-Sa 10pm-midnight. MC/V.

Pier Lounge (☎226 2002), in the Spindrift Hotel. For the full San Pedro entertainment experience, a visit to the Pier Lounge on W evenings at 6pm to see the "World Famous Chicken Drop" is a must. The Drop is a 20-year-old tradition wherein tourists drop a well-fed chicken onto a board of squares and bet on which square the bird will inevitably take a crap. For those who want a night free of bird poop, the Lounge features a daily happy hour daily 4-6pm (2 for 1 rum shots; US$4) and live music F-Sa at 8pm. Open daily 11am-10pm. Cash only.

🏄 OUTDOOR ACTIVITIES

Ambergris Caye's location next to the Mesoamerican Barrier Reef System, the second-largest barrier reef in the world, has made the island a draw for divers, snorkelers, and other watersports enthusiasts who flock here by the thousands every year.

DIVING AND SNORKELING DESTINATIONS

BLUE HOLE NATURAL MONUMENT. Probably Belize's most famous and photographed site, this 1000-ft-diameter circle has become a diving mecca ever since Jacques Cousteau explored and publicized it in the early 1970s. The Hole, lying at the center of Lighthouse Reef, started its life as a limestone cave during the last glacial period. Rising waters put an end to its above-ground existence, flooding it and collapsing its roof. Now extending over 400ft. below water, the Hole is filled with huge stalactites. Divers winding their way through these odd shapes can also see an abundant display of wildlife, including hammerhead sharks and Caribbean reef sharks. Word on the diving street is that the Blue Hole, for all its popularity and iconic status, is not as captivating as dives on Turneffe and even some other sites in the Lighthouse Reefs. If you're only planning on one dive in the Cayes, make sure you consult veterans before hitting the poster-friendly monument. *(The Blue Hole is an all day trip from San Pedro, with 1 or 2 additional stops elsewhere in the Lighthouse Reef. Trips usually leave at 5-7am and return at dusk. Diving trips cost US$225-250, including the US$40 marine park fee entrance. Snorkelers can also head out to see the monument, but be prepared to share the ride home with divers who have had a better experience than you fpr US$125-150.)*

LIGHTHOUSE REEF. Besides the Blue Hole, the reef boasts many other attractions. Divers can visit the **Painted Wall,** which features a teeming sponge community. The **Aquarium** boasts a huge collection of small reef fish. The (above-ground) bird sanctuary at **Half Moon Caye** is well worth the visit (park fee US$10), as is the abundant coral spurs and grooves at **Pete's Palace.** These sites are usually visited as part of a trip to Blue Hole.

TURNEFFE ATOLL. Perhaps the best site for divers, this huge atoll—the largest and closest—is 30 mi. long, 10 mi. wide, and packed with over 200 cayes. Exotic marine life is especially attracted to the area due to the preponderance of mangroves. You'll usually see signs for specific destinations within the atoll, i.e. "Turneffe Elbow" or "Turneffe South." **The Elbow,** one of the most exciting dives in Belize, lies at the atoll's southernmost tip. Its location at the convergence point of several ocean currents makes it a boisterous breeding and feeding ground for underwater life (you'll have to glance rather than stare, though; predictably, drift diving is the only option here). Visitors flock to **Myrtle's Turtle** to catch a glimpse of its famous eponymous resident. Head to **Three Anchorsto** to see the remnants of an old shipwreck. **Rendezvous Point,** at the atoll's northern end, features 3,000-ft. wall dives, with turtles and groupers for company. *(The Turneffe is an all-day, 3-dive trip, with a common cost of US$160-180.)*

HOL CHAN MARINE RESERVE. Located around the southern end of Ambergris, just four miles southwest of San Pedro, Hol Chan is a hugely popular and convenient stop for divers and snorkelers alike. The **Hol Chan Cut,** at the center of the reserve, is a 75 ft wide, 30 ft deep break in the reef that hosts a enormous population of striking corals and small fish life. Other "zones" in the reserve include a collection of **mangrove cayes** and **Shark Ray Alley,** whose residents—predominately nurse sharks and southern sting rays—are acclimated to boats and human visitors; they'll most likely come to visit even before you hit the water. For more information, visit the **Hol Chan Visitor's Center** in San Pedro on the corner of Angel Coral Dr. and Caribena St. *(☎ 226 2247; www.holchanbelize.org. Open M-F 8am-5pm, Sa 1-5pm. Diving and snorkeling trips to Hol Chan are usually a ½ day from Ambergris, leaving at 9am and 2pm and lasting 3-4 hours. 1 dive US$45; 2 dives US$75; 3 dives US$105.)*

Snorkeling trips are US$40-50. From Caye Caulker, trips last 9am-5pm, including a few hours for lunch and exploring in San Pedro. Diving trips US$190-200; snorkeling US$40-50. Be prepared to factor equipment into your total price. Diving gear US$15-17; snorkeling gear US$6-10.)

MEXICO ROCKS AND TRES COCOS. Often visited in tandem, these nearby snorkeling sites lie directly off the northern shore of Ambergris. Mexico Rocks is located between the caye and the reef. It is very shallow (only 6-12ft. deep), but water visibility can reach 50ft. at times. Large, rare corals house small but plentiful creatures like conch, hermit crabs, and stingrays. Tres Cocos sits nearby on the reef, sporting elaborate 50ft. coral heads and schools of snapper and spotted eagle rays. *(Trips to Mexico Rocks and Tres Cocos are ½ day, leaving at 9am and 2pm and lasting 3-4 hours. US$35-45.)*

COMPANIES OFFERING DIVING AND SNORKELING TRIPS

Bottom Time Dive Center (☎226 3788), on the dock behind Ruby's. Diving and snorkeling around the local reef, Hol Chan, Turneffe's, and Blue Hole. MC/V.

Amigos del Mar Dive Shop (☎226 2706; www.amigosdive.com), on the dock at the end of Caribena St. Diving only; trips to the local reef, Turneffe, and Blue Hole. MC/V.

Karibbean Water Sports (☎226 3205, www.karibbeanwatersports.com), on the dock at the end of Bucaneer St. Pontoon boats head on snorkeling trips to Hol Chan (US$40), Mexico Rocks (US$40), and Tres Cocos (US$35). You can explore on jet ski (single ridger US$150, double rider US$175). MC/V.

Extreme Adventures Belize (☎226 3513; www.belizeextremeadventure.com), on the Fido's dock. Snorkeling only; trips to Hol Chan, Shark Ray Alley, Mexico Rocks, and other local destinations. MC/V.

Reef Adventures (☎226 2538; www.reefadventures.net), on the dock behind the Blue Tang Inn. Diving at Blue Hole and Turneffe, snorkeling at Hol Chan and Mexico Rocks. Manatee-watching tours from US$45. MC/V.

Ecologic Divers (☎226 4118; www.ecologicdivers.com), on the dock by the end of Caribena St. Diving trips in the local reef, Turneffe, Blue Hole; snorkeling at Hol Chan, Mexico Rocks, and Tres Cocos. MC/V.

DIVING INSTRUCTION

You can't dive without certification, but the classes offered on the Cayes are often cheaper than those offered elsewhere. For safety's sake, beware of slipshod classes and make sure that your instructors are PADI-certified. "Resort" or "beginner" classes (for those who want the bare-bones minimum instruction) run around US$125-135. If you've been certified but need a once-over, refresher courses are also US$125-135. To go the whole nine yards, take the open-water or certification courses (US$350-375). Companies offering diving instruction are listed below.

Aquadives (☎226 3415; www.aquadives.com), on a dock south of town, behind the Blue Water Grill. MC/V.

Ambergris Divers (☎226 2634; www.ambergrisdivers.com), on the dock by the end of Black Coral St. MC/V.

Chuck and Robbie's Scuba Diving and Instruction (☎610 4424; www.ambergriscayediving.com), on a dock towards the north end of town. Exit to the beach at the northern end of Barrier Reef Dr. MC/V.

FISHING

The reef is a fishing paradise. The tarpon and coral palaces are home to barracuda, jacks, snappers, and groupers. The Big Kahuna of reef fishing in Belize is the famous **Grand Slam.** Some opt to go beyond the reef, where the pickings are slimmer but still include a healthy array of marlin and sailfish. Half-day fishing trips in the reef run for about BZ$350-400; full-day trips are BZ$550-600. Half-day deep-sea fishing expeditions cost between US$300 and US$400, while full-day trips beyond the reef are US$550-600.

Freedom Tours (☎226 3308; www.fishingunlimited.bz), dock on the western shore of the island near the end of Pelican St. Run by the expert "Hilly Boo," this company specializes in reef and deep sea fishing. Also offers snorkeling and inland trips. MC/V.

Bottom Time Dive Center (☎226 3788), on the dock behind Ruby's. Reef and deep sea fishing. MC/V.

Amigos del Mar Dive Shop (☎226 2706; www.amigosdive.com), on the dock at the end of Caribena St. Reef and deep sea fishing. MC/V.

Reef Adventures (☎226 2538; www.reefadventures.net), on the dock behind the Blue Tang Inn. Reef fishing only. MC/V.

WIND SPORTS

Though diving and snorkeling rule the roost on the cayes, thrill-seekers have created a niche for faster-paced adventure on the water. Though winds here are not as strong as the most hardcore aficionados might hope—the reef creates a huge protected area, freeing the sea of passing boats and other nuisances that plague these sports. The best winds blow through between February and June at 12-20 knots. **Windsurfing** is still the most popular water adventure sport here. **Kiteboarding** is also a favorite here. In this sport, the boarder is rocketed across the water by a high sail. For those who want to experience the sea from a higher elevation, check out Ambergris's abundant **parasailing** opportunities.

Seasports Belize (☎226 4488; www.sailsportsbelize.com), on the beach a ten-minute walk south of town. The Ambergris mecca for windsurfing and kiteboarding. Windsurfing board rentals US$22-27 per hr.; US$50 per day. 1hr. windsurfing lessons US$50. Kiteboarding rental US$82 per day; US$142 per 3 days; US$330 per week. Kite control lessons (2½hr.) US$165; board skill lessons (2½hr.) US$165; supervised rentals for beginners (2hr.) US$166. MC/V.

Extreme Adventures Belize (☎226 3513; www.belizeextremeadventure.com), on the Fido's dock. Parasailing US$70 for 1; US$1300 for 2. MC/V.

SAILING AND CRUISES

Several companies rent out sailboats and provide instruction. If you don't want to man the boat yourself, small cruises—especially those that set off to watch the setting sun—are popular.

Bottom Time Dive Center (☎226 3788), on the dock behind Ruby's. Sunset cruises US$55; manatee watching expeditions US$105; tours around the Bacalar Chico Marine Reserve with snorkeling stops US$105. MC/V.

Karibbean Water Sports (☎226 3205, www.karibbeanwatersports.com), on the dock at the end of Bucaneer St. The center for jet-ski excitement. Watersport enthusiasts leisurely embark on tours around the island (US$150 for single, US$140 for two), or cut loose on raucous 1hr. thrill rides (US$175). Pontoon boat cruises US$40-50. "Booze cruise" around the various seaside pubs on the island US$45. MC/V.

Reef Adventures (☎226 2538; www.reefadventures.net), on the dock behind the Blue Tang Inn. Sunset cruises US$45. MC/V.

Seasports Belize (☎226 4488; www.sailsportsbelize.com), on the beach a 10min. walk south of town. Sailboat rentals US$22-100, depending on the make of the boat. Beginner sail course US$275; Catamaran course US$65; monohull course US$65. MC/V.

SEArious Adventures (☎226 4202), on the dock behind Ruby's. Catamaran sailing US$60. MC/V.

Seaduced by Belize (☎226 2254; www.seaducedbybelize.com), on the beach behind Ruby's. Also has an office in the Vilma Linda Plaza off Tarpon St. Catamaran day sailing to Caye Caulker with snorkeling stops US$75; sunset cruise US$50. Manatee watch and snorkeling US$105. MC/V.

INLAND TRIPS

Many companies run one-day or overnight trips to the best sites in inland Belize. You'll either boat or fly to Belize City and continue on river or road to the site. If you are spending any time on the mainland, it's a better idea to take the far cheaper tours run from nearby towns, where guides are often more knowledgeable. Common trips from the Cayes include tours of the Mayan ruins at **Altun Ha** (US$75-85) and **Lamanai** (US$125-150); these trips are often combined with cave tubing, raising the price to US$50. Trips to the **Belize Zoo** are also usually combined with cave tubing (US$150-160). If you want to skip the ruins and wildlife and cut to the adventurous chase, combined **cave tubing** and **zip lining** tours (US$205-230) are available.

Bottom Time Dive Center (☎226-3788), on the dock behind Ruby's. Trips to Altu Ha, Lamanai, Belize Zoo with cave tubing, and Tikal, Guatemala (US$402-420). MC/V.

Extreme Adventures Belize (☎226 3513; www.belizeextremeadventure.com), on the Fido's dock (p. 73). Cave tubing ½-day US$250; full-day with zip line and Mayan ruin trip US$450. MC/V.

Reef Adventures (☎226 2538; www.reefadventures.net). Altun Ha, Lamanai, and Belize Zoo with cave tubing. MC/V.

Ecologic Divers (☎226 4118; www.ecologicdivers.com), on the dock by the end of Caribena St. Altun Ha with cave tubing. Lamanai, cave tubing and zip line. MC/V.

NORTHERN BELIZE

Northern Belize is a low-lying area of pine savannas, swamps, jungles, and coastal lagoons. The region has feels a lot more like its neighbor Mexico than other parts of the country do, and Spanish is prevalent in many areas. Given the long stretches of cane fields, smokestacks jutting up from refineries, and the abundance of cheap rum, it's easy to see that sugar is the basis of the northern economy. After reaching most of the region's landlocked Mayan ruins and nature reserves, the Northern Highway turns inland. It doesn't return to the coast until it reaches Corozal eight miles from the Mexican border. Highlights of the region include the impressive Mayan site of Lamanai, accessible from mellow Orange Walk. Look for the rare Jaribu stork at Crooked Tree Wildlife Sanctuary, and marvel the many different species at the Shipstern Nature Reserve.

CROOKED TREE WILDLIFE SANCTUARY

Birds are the star attraction in the tiny, lagoon-bound village of Crooked Tree (population 900), 33 miles northwest of Belize City. With 286 species spread over 16,400 acres, the sanctuary is one of the largest of its kind in Central America. Bird watchers with binoculars flood this relaxed farming community, eager to catch a glimpse of the famous Jaribu storks (with a 12-foot wingspan), ospreys, whistling ducks, and the many other of migrating ilk who flock to the lagoon between December and May. Those who aren't as passionate about double-crested cormorants will enjoy the calm peace and quiet dirt paths of the village. Subsistence farmers tend their small plots while horses, cows, and bulls have the run of the village roads. The tranquility belies a rich history. Mayas lived in the lagoon thousands of years ago; small, scattered ruins here mark their previous existence. One of the first inland European settlements was established here around 1750 by British loggers, who named the island for a gnarled cashew tree that grew by the shore. Today, the cashew business is booming in Crooked Tree. Check out the **Cashew Festival** in mid-May that offers cashew products, animal rides, shows, and late-night music and dancing devoted to the almighty nut.

▐▀ TRANSPORTATION

The 3 mi. dirt road to Crooked Tree begins at the Northern Highway 32 miles from Belize City. Despite its isolated lagoon position, the village is actually not too difficult to access with some advance planning.

Buses: Jex & Sons buses leave Belize City at the intersection of Regent St. West and West Canal St. at around 10:30am and 5pm, M-Sa (1hr., US$1.50). The buses leave from the bus yard in Crooked Tree next to the visitor's center for Belize City M-Sa at 5am and 7am.

Northbound buses leave Belize City for Orange Walk. Ask the driver to let you off at the Crooked Tree turnoff (45min., US$1). Arrange a day in advance with your accommodation to be picked up at the turnoff. Some travelers have found hitchhiking to Crooked Tree a convenient option. Let's Go never recommends hitchhiking as a safe means of transportation, and none of the information presented here is intended to do so. **Belize Global Adventure Tours, Discovery Expeditions,** and **S & L Travel and Tours** run guided tours from Belize City to the village and back (4hr., US$55-60).

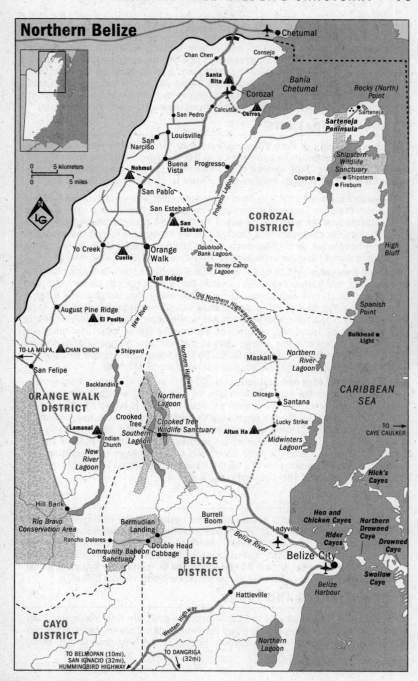

Northern Belize

NORTHERN BELIZE

Chetumal

Chan Chen
Consejo

Santa
Rita
Calcutta
Corozal
Cerros

*Bahía
Chetumal*

*Rocky (North)
Point*

Sarteneja

**Sarteneja
Peninsula**

San Pedro
Louisville

San
Narciso

*Shipstern
Wildlife
Sanctuary*

Nohmul
Buena
Vista
Progresso

Cowpen
Shipstern
Fireburn

San Pablo

San Esteban

*Doubloon
Bank Lagoon*

**COROZAL
DISTRICT**

San
Esteban

*Honey Camp
Lagoon*

Yo Creek
Cuello
Orange
Walk

*High
Bluff*

Toll Bridge

Old Northern Highway (unpaved)

*Spanish
Point*

August Pine Ridge
El Pozito

New River

TO LA MILPA,
CHAN CHICH
Shipyard

Maskall

*Northern
River
Lagoon*

*Bulkhead
Light*

San Felipe

Backlanding

Northern Highway

Chicago
Santana

**CARIBBEAN
SEA**

TO
CAYE CAULKER

**ORANGE WALK
DISTRICT**

*Northern
Lagoon*

Crooked
Tree
*Southern
Lagoon*

*Crooked Tree
Wildlife Sanctuary*

Lucky Strike

Altun Ha

*Midwinters
Lagoon*

Lamanai
Indian
Church

*New
River
Lagoon*

*Hick's
Cayes*

Hill Bank

*Río Bravo
Conservation Area*

Rancho Dolores

Bermudian
Landing

Burrell
Boom

Belize River
Ladyville

*Hen and
Chicken Cayes*

*Rider
Cayes*

*Northern
Drowned
Caye*

*Drowned
Caye*

Belize City

*Community Baboon
Sanctuary*
Double Head
Cabbage

**BELIZE
DISTRICT**

*Belize
Harbour*

*Swallow
Caye*

Hattieville

**CAYO
DISTRICT**

Western Highway

*Northern
Lagoon*

TO BELMOPAN (10mi),
SAN IGNACIO (32mi),
HUMMINGBIRD HIGHWAY

TO DANGRIGA
(32mi)

0   5 kilometers
0   5 miles

⊞ ☷ ORIENTATION AND PRACTICAL INFORMATION

The sanctuary's **visitor's center** (open daily 8am-4:30pm) is directly to the right as you enter the village. Pay the entrance fee of US$5 here, sign your name in the guestbook, and pick up a map of the sanctuary. A 5min. walk up the road from the center and through the bus yard will bring you to the village's **main road,** along which lies the village **police station,** cemetery, school, and a varied group of churches. Walking trails leave mostly from the eastern side of the village.

☷ ACCOMMODATIONS

The recent passing of Sam Tillett, a legendary bird-watcher who operated a lodge and tours around the sanctuary, has left a considerable lacuna in the village's tourist scene. Still, several excellent lodges provide comfortable accommodations and even tours for those who want to stay for more than a day.

> **Rhaburn's Rooms** (☎225 7035). From the visitor's center, walk up to the main road and turn left. Cross the field next to the church on your right (you'll see a sign) and walk through the path that leads into the woods. The Rhaburns' house is through the first gate on your left. The cheapest find in Crooked Tree. The Rhaburns, a friendly Creole couple, offer 4 humble but comfortable rooms on the 2nd floor of their home. All rooms with fans and shared hot-water baths. Singles US$10; doubles US$15. Cash only. ❶
>
> **Crooked Tree Lodge** (☎626 3820; crookedtreelodgebelize.com). Turn right along the main road, fork left just before the cemetery. Turn right at the sign for the lodge, and continue for 10 min. In a remote corner of the village, this fantastic new lodge is worth a stay just to soak up its breathtaking views. Friendly owners Mick and Angie Webb keep 5 spotless *cabañas*, each with lovely decor, double beds, and private bath. Spacious dining hall, outdoor bar, deck on the lagoon shore, and manmade pools. The Webbs can also arrange tours of the sanctuary. Singles US$50; doubles US$70; family suite (fitting 7) US$100. The truly frugal can camp on the spacious front lawn for US$10 and have access to showers inside. MC/V. ❷
>
> **Bird's Eye View Lodge and Restaurant** (☎203 2040 or 225 7027; www.birdseyeview-belize.com). From the visitor's center, take the path leading left along the shore and continue for 10 min. This grand hotel set along a lagoon is hardly a budget option, but it does offer the village's best range of tours around Crooked Tree and inland Belize. Stately, well-lit roms with fans and private bathrooms. 2nd floor patio with the best views of the lagoon in town. The restaurant below is pricey (US$10-18) but with an extensive menu. The lodge offers tours of the sanctuary (see **Activities and Tours,** p. 80) and explorations of sites throughout Belize. Singles US$50-60; doubles US$60-80; triples US$90-100. AmEx/MC/V. ❺

☷ FOOD

Don't expect any fine dining in Crooked Tree (unless you're willing to shell out at the **Bird's Eye View Lodge;** p. 80. The village includes a few small restaurants, but hours are very unpredictable. The few stands near the main road are your best bet if you want to venture out of your lodge for food. For easily accesible, down-home Belizean offerings, try **A & B's Fast Food Stand ❷**, next to the bus yard, 3 min. from the visitor's center. (Rice-bean-chicken stew US$3; drinks US$1-2).

☷ ☷ ACTIVITIES AND TOURS

Bird-watching is the name of the game here, so grab the visitor's center map, generously apply bug repellent, strap on your walking shoes, bring your binoculars, and head out into the lagoon. Spring is the best time to see birds, but satisfying sightings happen here year-round. A highlight is the large **viewing boardwalk** three miles north of town, accessible via the **Trogan Trail.** (Walk to the main street from the visitor's center, turn right, then head left at the sign for the trail.) Several trails, leaving directly from the visitor's center, wind along the shore and provide ample views of waterfowl.

Novices may want a guided tour of the sanctuary. The **Bird's Eye View Lodge and Restaurant** (p. 80) offers guided nature walks (US$7.50-10 per hr.), boat tours (US$35-75), and horseback riding (US$7.50 per hr.) around the area. From Belize City, **Belize Global Adventure Tours, Discovery Expeditions,** and **S & L Travel and Tours** run guided tours to the sanctuary and back (4hr., US$55-60).

SARTENEJA AND THE SHIPSTERN NATURE RESERVE

A tiny fishing village perched on Belize's northeastern corner, Sarteneja serves as an entry point to the Shipstern Nature Reserve three and a half miles inland. Sarteneja is an ideal spot to observe the gentle rhythms of coastal life. Watch villagers paint or repair their wooden boats, while fishermen ply their trade in the waters nearby.

⬛ TRANSPORTATION. The most convenient way to reach the village is by **Thunderbolt boat** (☎422 0026).Thunderbolts leave **Corozal** and **San Pedro** at 7am and 3pm. They only stop in Sarteneja by request, so be sure to tell the boat crew your plans before departure. If you're leaving from Sarteneja by water, call Thunderbolt (☎422-0026) well in advance of departure time so they can pick you up. Trips to Corozal are US$12.50; to San Pedro US$23.

There's also a select **bus** service that travels to and from Sarteneja, Orange Walk, and Belize City. To get a ride from the village, wake up early. Two to three buses leave Monday-Saturday from Sarteneja for Orange Walk and Belize City between 5am-7am. They'll circle the village to wake potential passengers up, but the most convenient point to grab one is by the road leading into and out of town.

◼🈂 ORIENTATION AND PRACTICAL INFORMATION. Like Corozal, Sarteneja is arranged in a fairly straightforward grid pattern by the coast. Unlike Corozal, the streets aren't numbered. You probably won't get lost in this tiny village, though, so feel free to stroll the tranquil streets without worry. The **dirt entry and exit road** can be reached by walking one block into town from the coast and turning right. After 10-15min., you'll reach the "Welcome to Sartneja" sign and the turnoff to Backpacker's Paradise.

🛏 ACCOMMODATIONS. There are a few inns and guesthouses in the village, but the true backpacker will want to head a little out of town to find his ideal home at **Backpacker's Paradise ❶.** Walk down the entry road to the "Welcome to Sarteneja" sign (15min.) and turn left. The Paradise is a one minute walk further down. Not just any place to stay, Backpacker's Paradise stretches over 27 acres of Sarteneja's environs. The grounds are filled with jungles, orchards, and farmland. You can take several trails through the wilderness or, if you like, go by horse. The large screen windows in the *cabañas* will make you feel like you're in the midst of the jungle. When you wake up, pluck some fresh mangos from the trees overhead. The friendly young French couple who run the place operate a small restaurant serving crepes (US$2-7) and other French and Caribbean specialties. (☎403 2051; www.blueandgreen.org. *Cabañas* with shared bathroom US$10, with private bathroom BZ$35. Camping BZ$6. Restaurant open 8am-8pm. Cash only.)

☐ FOOD. Sarteneja has a few modest eateries, but nothing of particular note. If you find yourself yearning for a bite in the village, stroll around and select from the number of small fast food shacks selling cheap Belizean and Mexican snacks. If you're willing to take a short walk (or if you're staying there anyway), check out **Backpacker's Paradise** (p. 81). Chances are you'll meet a few colorful locals and some fellow travelers.

☑ DAYTRIPS FROM SARTENEJA: THE SHIPSTERN NATURE RESERVE. Covering 27,000 acres in the driest area in Belize, Shipstern includes a remarkable variety of climates, terrains, and wildlife. The Reserve is one of Belize's top destinations for birdwatchers, who gaze admirably at the more than 300 species who call Shipstern home, including the endangered American Woodstork. Other creatures, including the full gamut of Belize's large cat population (Ocelots, Margays, Pumas, Jaguars, and Jaguaroundis), countless bats and butterflies (over 270 species), and 70 reptile and amphibian species, reside in the protected zone. Baird's Tapir, another rare species, lives in and around the Xo-Pol pond region, one of the main attractions for visitors.

The Shipstern forest, devastated by Hurricane Janet in 1955, has been re-growing ever since and now holds dozens of tree species and ten different vegetation types. The headquarters by the road includes a small visitor's **museum** with exhibits describing the Reserve's history, flora, and fauna, as well as a **butterfly garden** displaying local species. To fully explore the region beyond the botanical trail (with almost 100 tree species labeled), look into renting the reserve's vehicles. A 45min. drive will bring you to an overlook nestled in the trees, providing views of a remote pond with accompanying wildlife (deer, crocodiles, and a range of waterfowl like the Reddish Egret and Roseate Spoonbill). You can also take guided boat tours of the lagoon areas. The wetlands attract many mosquitoes and other pests, so dress accordingly (long sleeves and pants, closed-toe shoes) and bring plenty of bug spray.

The Reserve's remote location makes arrival difficult for those without cars. To reach it you can take a very early morning **bus** (a few 5-7am) from Sarteneja and ask to be dropped off at the entrance to the Reserve (you'll have to wait a bit for the 8am opening). Ask the visitor's center for a ride back to the village (though it's never guaranteed). Otherwise, ask your lodgings for rides in and out of the area. Many Sarteneja guesthouses are partners with the Reserve. (*Headquarters along the Orange Walk-Sarteneja road 3½ mi. from the village; www.shipstern.org. US$5. Open daily open 8am-5pm.*)

COROZAL   ☎04

A sleepy seaside town that has miraculously avoided the tourist plague, Corozal (population 9100) lies just nine miles south of the Mexican border. The place is perfect for relaxing: ocean breezes seem to have lulled the town into a languid state far removed from the market bustle of Orange Walk and the tourist frenzy of San Pedro. Most use Corozal as a transit point on the way to and from Mexico or the northern Cayes. Still, a stay of more than a few hours here can provide cool and uncrowded relaxation under the shaded *palapas* in the waterfront parks.

▣ TRANSPORTATION

Flights: Corozal's **airstrip** is located about 1 mi. south of the city. To avoid a walk, take a taxi (BZ$8-10) to and from the city. **Maya Island Air** (☎225 2219; www.mayaislandair.com) and **Tropic Air** (☎225 2302; www.tropicair.com) both fly to **San Pedro** (20-25min.; every 2hr. 7:30am-3:30pm; one-way US$45, round-trip US$45).

Buses: The bus station is on the corner of 7th Ave. and 1st St. South. **Southbound** buses leave for **Orange Walk** (1¼hr., US$1.50) and **Belize City** (2¾hr., US$2.50) every 30min. 3:45am-7:30pm. Additional buses head only to **Orange Walk** (1¼hr., US$1.50) every 30min. from noon-4pm. **Northbound** buses leave Santa Elena on the border with Mexico (15min., US$0.25) every 30min. between 8:30am and 10pm.

Taxis: Taxi stands are located on the corner of Park St. and 1st St. South and in Central Park at the corner of 5th Ave. and 1st St. South.

Water Taxis: Thunderbolt water taxis (☎422 0026) leave from the dock at the end of 2nd St South for **Sarteneja** (30min.; one-way US$12.50, round-trip US$25) and **San Pedro** (2hr.; US$23/43) daily at 7am and 3pm.

◼◼ ORIENTATION AND PRACTICAL INFORMATION

Corozal spreads out along the bay of the same name in a grid pattern (a vestige of the rebuilding done after Hurrican Janet devastated the town in 1955), so navigation is easier than in most Belizean towns. However, many street signs are missing, especially in areas farther from the center. **Avenues run parallel to the coast (north-south) and streets run east-west.** Directions are complicated by the duplication of streets—1st St. North, for example, has a southern counterpart. Buses drop passengers off at **7th Avenue** and **1st Street South.** Walking down **2nd Street South,** you'll pass the **Central Park,** with its sky-blue **clock tower.** The **pier** for Thunderbolt skiffs leaving for San Pedro lies at the coastal end of 2nd St. South.

Tours and Agencies: Vitalino Reyes (☎602 8975; www.cavetubing.bz) is a travel agent, offering cave tubing and other adventures around the country from his home base in Corozal. He'll also take you to the Belize Zoo. The **George and Esther Moralez Travel Service** (☎422 2485; www.gettransfers.com), based out of the Corozal Airstrip, 1 mi. to the south of town, arranges tours to Altun Ha, the Belize Zoo, Lamanai, Placencia, and more. Travel service to the Mexican border and to all points in Belize.

Banks:Scotiabank, 4th Ave. Open M-Th 8am-2pm, F 8am-3:30pm, Sa 9-11:30am. **Atlantic Bank,** corner of 3rd St. North and 4th Ave. Open M-Th 8am-3pm and F 8am-4pm. **Belize Bank,** 5th Ave. by Central Park. Open M-Th 8am-3pm, F 8am-4:30pm.

Police Station: (☎422 2022), corner of 5th Ave. and 1st St. North.

Pharmacy: Annie's Pharmacy, 7th Ave. near the bus station. Open M-F 8am-10pm, Su 8am-7pm.

Hospital: The **Corozal Hospital,** (☎422 2076), 1 mi. northwest of town on the way to Chetumal.

Internet: BluePC, corner of 1st St. South and 4th Ave. (☎422 2828). Above the Shun Li Fashion Shop. US$1.50 per hr. Open M-Sa 9am-8pm. **Stellar Links,** 4th Ave. and 3rd St. N. (☎402 2043). Internet US$2 per hr. International calls US$2.50 per 15min. Skype access. Open M-F 8am-7pm, Sa 8am-5pm.

Post Office: 5th Ave. by Central Park. Open M-Th 8:30am-noon and 1-4pm, F 8:30am-noon and 1-4:30pm.

◤ ACCOMMODATIONS

Like Orange Walk, Corozal's location has given rise to a number of lodgings, from bare bones to luxury seacoast. Luckily, you can find quiet rooms on the coast with plenty of amenities for a small charge.

Sea Breeze Hotel, 23 1st Ave. (☎422 3051, www.theseabreezehotel.com). From the park, walk down to 1st Ave. by the sea and head left for 10min. There may be a Welsh flag flying above (the owner's proud declaration of nationality), but the decor inside, with its fishing maps and aquatic blue walls, pledges allegiance only to the sea. Bar on 2nd floor (drinks US$1-4.50) and a verandah overlooking the bay. All rooms with double beds, cable TVs, and private baths. Free Wi-Fi. Budget rooms with fan US$17.50; economy rooms with fan US$20; premium rooms with A/C US$25-30. 9% tax for each guest. MC/V. ❺

Maya World Guest House, 16 2nd St. (☎666 3577), north between 6th and 7th Avenues (☎666 3577). From the bus station, walk right on 7th Ave. and turn left on 2nd St. North. This 2-story house near the bus station holds several spacious, breezy rooms with large windows. Hammocks strung up on the porch for lounging. Kitchen and cooking areas downstairs. All rooms with fans. Singles US$22.50; doubles US$25.50. Cash only. ❹

Corozal Guest House, 22 6th Ave (☎402 0634). From the bus station, turn right on 6th Ave. Convenient (if not spectacular coastal) location and a double bed, fan, and private bath in each spare, clean room. This cheap offering will appeal to those just passing through town. Rooms US$17.50. Cash only. ❸

🍴 FOOD

The streets may be lazy, but the kitchens are busy preparing a teeming multitude of local and foreign fare. Nearly every block has a few eateries to satisfy the cravings of hungry travelers. For groceries, try **Gabrielle Hoare market,** with outdoor fruit stands and a two-story building with small restaurants on the upper level (right behind the bus station between 6th Ave. and 7th Ave. and 1st St. North and 1st St. South). Likewise, **Central Supermarket** (Park St.; ☎422-0096; open daily 7am-9pm). **Amelio Reyes & Sons Supermarket,** 4th Ave., 2 blocks away from Central Park. Open M-Sa 8am-7pm, Su 8am-noon.

Romantic Bar and Restaurant (☎422 0013), in the basement of the Mirador Hotel. A highlight of the countless Chinese restaurants that populate Corozal, this ground-floor component of the 4-story Mirador Hotel serves Chinese standards in a large, sparse room hung with Chinese lanterns and cooled by strategically placed fans. Order take out and eat by the shore. Meals US$3.50-7; salads US$5-8. Open daily 11am-10pm. Cash only. ❷

RD's Diner (☎422 3796), near the corner of 4th Ave. and 4th St. North. A spiffy, sit-down restaurant offering Belizean standards (rice, bean, and meat combos US$3.50-4.50) as well as international food and swankier nightly specials (US$7.50-10). Open daily 8am-8pm. AmEx/MC/V. ❸

Marcello's Pizza, corner of 4th Ave. and 3rd St. North. If you're feeling homesick for American cooking, Marcello's—promising "a taste of America"—is the ideal cure. Pizza US$3.50-5; BBQ chicken and ribs US$3-4.50; ice cream US$1-2. Open daily 11am-10pm. Cash only. ❷

👁 SIGHTS

A stroll along the waterfront parks may be the best thing to do in Corozal

SANTA RITA. The "ancient Corozal" once occupied roughly the same area as the modern Corozal. Today, Santa Rita is a small ruin site mainly consisting of one pyramid. The structure itself is by no means the most remarkable find in Belize, but from the top you can catch a view of the turquoise waters lapping Corozal's shores. Enjoy the breeze and imagine the old glory of this town that once took advantage of the trade routes on the Rio Hondo and New River to carve out its place in the Mayan world. *(To reach the ruins, head north on Santa Rita Rd. (stretching north of the bus station) and turn left after about 15-20min. at the Super Santa Rita store. After 10min., you'll see a forested area on the right that houses the Santa Rita ruins. Free.)*

CAYO DISTRICT

The Western Highway bisects Belize horizontally, cutting across the Cayo District and offering an avenue to rugged jungle adventure for those tired of the sandy beaches. Far from the sea and the grassy savannas of northern Belize, and nestled within the lush greenery of the Maya Mountains, this area is Belize's only highland region. Along the Western Highway, Monkey Bay Wildlife Sanctuary and Guanacaste National Park tease travelers with hints of the tropical forests to come. From Mennonite farmland to the Maya village of San José Sucotz, this may be Belize's most culturally diverse district. Cayo is a mecca for outdoor adventure tourists. San Ignacio makes a good base from which to explore the ruins, caves, and rivers of the region. Highlights include the Mountain Pine Ridge Reserve, with caves, waterfalls, and refreshingly cool temperatures, and Caracol, the largest Mayan site in Belize.

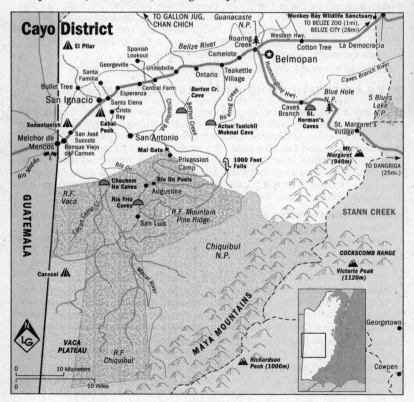

BELMOPAN

Charmless Belmopan (pop. 17,500) is strategically placed at the junction of the Western and Hummingbird highways, making the city a convenient transit point for those heading south to Dangriga or west to Belize City. Otherwise, Belmopan holds little of interest for travelers. Founded in 1971 to provide Belize with a new capital after Hurricane Hattie wiped out Belize City ten years before, the city is mostly suburbia spreading out from a small center. Most of this center consists of unappealing government buildings placed around grassy plazas, many of them overgrown. The most interesting area by far is conveniently around the bus station, where shops, restaurants, and outdoor markets share space in the intriguing chaos. If you have to wait for a bus, you might as well pay a quick visit.

▐ TRANSPORTATION

Since it's at the junction of the Western Highway (leading to San Ignacio) and the Hummingbird Highway (leading to Dangriga), Belmopan is a major hub for bus traffic.

Buses: The **bus station** is in Market Sq., at the corner of Constitution Dr. and Bliss Parade. Buses to: **Belize City** (1½hr., every 30 min. 4am-7:30 pm, US$1.50); **San Ignacio** (1hr., every 30min. 7:30am-midnight, US$1.50); **Benque Viejo del Carmen** (1½hr., every 30min. 7:30am-midnight, US$2); **Dangriga** (1¼hr., every 30min. 6:30am-7:30pm, US$1.50), **Independence** (2½hr., every 30min. 6:30am-5pm, US$2.50); **Punta Gorda** (4hr., every 30min. 6:30am-5pm, US$4).

Taxis: Cabs and drivers wait outside (and sometimes inside) the bus station.

✦ ▐ ORIENTATION AND PRACTICAL INFORMATION

Belmopan is just southeast of the junction between the **Western** and **Hummingbird Highways;** two turnoffs connect the city with the Hummingbird. The heart of town—the government center and the market area—is surrounded by **North Road, South Road,** and **East Ring Road.** The western side is formed by **Constitution Drive.** The **bus station** is at the corner of Constitution Drive and **Bliss Parade,** which curves to meet **South Ring Road.** Around the bus station is a bustling shopping center known as **Market Square.** To the east, several **pedestrian walkways** cut through the grassy plazas, the largest of which is **Independence Plaza.**

Embassies and Consulates: US Embassy, Floral Park Rd. (☎822 4011; www.usembassy. state.gov/belize). From North Ring Rd., turn left on Floriana Ave. Open M-F 8am-noon and 1-5pm. **Mexican Embassy,** Embassy Sq. (☎822 0406; www.sre.gob.mx/belice), at the corner of Constitution Dr. and North Ring Rd. Open M-F 9am-12:30pm. **British High Commission,** Embassy Sq. (☎822 2146; www.britishhighcommission.gov.uk), next to the Mexican Embassy. Open M-Th 8am-noon and 1-4pm, F 8am-2pm.

Bank: First Caribbean International Bank, Courthouse Pl., off Melhado Parade. Open M-Th 8am-2:30pm, F 8am-4:30pm. **Belize Bank** (☎822 2303), corner of Constitution Dr. and Melhado Parade. Open M-Th 8am-3pm, F 8am-4:30pm. **Scotiabank,** across from Belize Bank. Open M-Th 8am-2pm, F 8am-3:30pm, Sa 9am-11:30am.

Police Station: Off Bliss Parade, 5min. from the bus station.

Pharmacy: No less than 5 pharmacies dot the market area around the bus station. **Cardinal Pharmacy,** Constitution Dr. (☎822 3065). Open M-F 8:30am-7pm, Sa 9am-2pm. **Friendly Pharmacy** (☎822 2807), in Market Sq., across the street from the bus station. Open M-F 7:30am-6pm, Sa 8am-5pm.

Hospital: Belmopan Hospital (☎822 2264), enter at the corner of Constitution Dr. and North Ring Rd. 24hr. emergency service.

Internet Access: Angelus Press, Constitution Dr. (☎822 3866). US$1.50 per hr. Open M-F 7:30am-5:30pm, Sa 8am-noon. **Pross Computers,** Constitution Dr. (☎601 3529). Internet US$2.25 per hr. **PC.Com** (☎822 2449), in Market Square. Internet US$2 per hr. Open M-F 8am-7pm, Sa 8am-noon.

Post Office: Off Bliss Parade, 5min. from the bus station. Open M-Th 8am-noon and 1-5pm, F 8am-4:30pm.

⚑ ACCOMMODATIONS

If you're forced to spend a night in Belmopan, be aware that true budget options are sorely lacking.

El-Rey Inn, 23 Moho St. (☎822 3438; www.belmopan hotels). From Constitution Dr., turn onto North Ring Rd., walk north for 15min., turn right on Nanche St., and turn right on Moho St. The cheapest rooms in Belmopan are bare, with white walls and linoleum floors. Despite its inconvenient location, the inn is clean and quiet. Rooms with fan US$22.20; family rooms US$37.50. MC/V. ❹

Hibiscus Hotel (☎822 1418; www.belmopanhotels.com), off Melhado Parade. Turn right on Melhado Pde. from Constitution Dr. Owned by the same family who runs El-Rey, the Hibiscus offers much more appealing digs: rooms are colorful, decorated, and spotless. They're also more expensive. Singles with fan US$32.50; doubles with A/C and TV BZ$47.50; triples US$55. MC/V. ❺

Belmopan Hotel, Bliss Parade (☎822 2340). The rooms here are a bit grungy for the price, with splotched carpets and bare walls. However, Belmopan's location next to the bus station and pool in the middle of the courtyard more than compensate. Free Wi-Fi. Doubles with A/C and cable TV BZ$60; triples BZ$65. MC/V. ❺

◘ FOOD

The area around the bus station, **Market Square,** is packed with small fast food restaurants. North of the station stretches a large **outdoor market** full of stands selling fruit, clothes, handicrafts, and bootlegged DVDs.

Caladium Restaurant, Market Sq. (☎822 2754), across from the bus station. A Belmopan favorite, this convenient restaurant serves Belizean specialties (rice and bean plates, US$4-6), grilled food (steak and pork, US$9-11), and Caribbean seafood (shrimp creole and fish fillet, US$7.50-15) in an immaculate and well-decorated setting cooled by fans. Burgers US$2-5.50. Salads US$-6. MC/V. ❷

Seri's Restaurant, Market Sq. (☎809 3970), across from the bus station. This 2nd-floor Chinese restaurant boasts better decor than most in Belize, with a large Chinese gate protecting the entrance to the restrooms. Curry dishes BZ$7.50-10; fried rice US$2.50-7.50; chow mein BZ$3-7.50. Open daily 9am-9pm. Cash only. ❸

◙ SIGHTS

GUANACASTE NATIONAL PARK

Catch any westbound bus (heading toward Benque Viejo del Carmen), and ask to be let off at the park, right along the Western Highway, at the turnoff to Belmopan (15min., BZ$1). Open daily 8am-4:30pm. BZ$5.

The smallest of Belize's many national parks (250,000 sq. yd.) provides a welcome and ready escape from the dullness of Belmopan. Named for the huge guanacaste tree that grows on its grounds, the park offers hiking trails with marked plants and trees. Though it's difficult to spend more than a few hours here, the park may be best used as a place to lounge and relax; the grounds are shady and there's a small pool for swimming open to visitors. On the weekends, local families from nearby towns and villages often have picnics on the park ground.

SAN IGNACIO

Sprawling over the hilly terrain of the western Cayo district, San Ignacio (population 19,000) is a picturesque Belizean town. Upper verandahs open out on views of busy, winding streets and verdant hills dotted with houses. Ideally located near a plethora of outdoor activities, San Ignacio has become Belize's second most popular tourist destination. The wilds of Cayo are unforgettable destinations, but spend some time in town too—good restaurants are plentiful, the locals friendly, and the banks of the Macal River wonderful resting grounds.

▣ TRANSPORTATION

Intercity Buses: Arrive at and depart from an unmarked stand in the square in the town center, next to the Savannah Taxi Drivers' Co-Op building. Buses to: **Belmopan** (1hr., every 30min. 6:30am-8pm, US$1.50); **Belize City** (2hr., every 30min. 6:30am-8pm, US$2.50); **Benque Viejo del Carmen** (30min., every 30min. 7am-6:30pm, US$1). **Amigos Bus Service** (☎626 6795 or 804 4676), at the foot of the Hawkesworth Bridge on the Santa Elena side, still arranges pickups with the San Juan and Linea dorada bus lines. Express buses to: **Chetumal, Mexico** (4hr., daily 9am, US$25); **Flores, GUA** (3hr., daily 8am, US$17.50). You must register your name with the company at least a day in advance to have a seat on this bus.

Local buses: Depart from the sandy lot next to the grassy expanse by the river, just north of the main bus stop on Savannah St. Buses to: **Bullet Tree Falls** (15min.; daily 10:30am, 1, and 4:30pm; US$.50); **Spanish Lookout** (30min.; daily 10:30am, 1, and 4:30pm; US$1.50); **San Antonio** (50min., daily 11:30am, US$1.50). Be sure to check times with the bus drivers before boarding since these schedules are subject to change.

Taxis: Next to the bus stop. **The Savannah Taxi Drivers' Co-Op** (☎824 2155) is the main service provider. The **Bullet Tree Falls Taxi Association** runs **collectivos** to **Bullet Tree Falls** (15min., every 20min. 8am-9:30pm, US$1), leaving from the corner of Wyatt St. and Burns Ave., next to the Hot Summer Chinese restaurant.

✦ ❷ ORIENTATION AND PRACTICAL INFORMATION

San Ignacio is actually one of the "twin towns" split by the Macal River; its sibling is the more residential **Santa Elena,** which lies on the river's eastern side. The web of roads in San Ignacio is confusing and difficult to navigate. Two bridges span the river: the small wooden **New Bridge,** which provides an entrance into town, and the large, suspended **Hawkesworth Bridge** (look for it on bank notes). From the New Bridge, **Savannah Street** leads past the outdoor market and the football field into the **town square** (sometimes known as **Savannah Plaza**), where buses pick up and drop off passengers, while taxis hunt for customers. The plaza is a tangled five-way intersection with no stop signs. **Burn's Avenue,** San Ignacio's main commercial strip (and tour company stomping ground), heads north, while **Waight's Avenue** curves west. South of the plaza, Burns Avenue leads uphill to the new, eye-grabbing **Town Hall** and the small columned park in front of it. From here, **Buena Vista Road** heads southwest.

Tours and Agencies: San Ignacio is packed to the brim with companies offering adventure tours around the Cayo district, it's never too hard to find a tour. Trips operate on a per-person basis rather than on a fixed schedule. Most tours need a minimum of 2 people, although the larger ones—**ATM, Caracol,** and **Tikal**—often require a minimum of 4. This can be frustrating for independent travelers, but if you spend a few days in San Ignacio and keep your schedule flexible, your desired tour is likely to attract members. Prices for the tours do not vary much between companies. All of the companies listed below offer tours to Caracol, cave tubing at Nohoch Che'en, Barton Creek Cave, and Mountain Pine Ridge. Pacz, Mayawalk, Eva's, K'Atun Ahaw, and Hun Chi'ik offer trips to Altun Tunichil Muknal. For details on the destinations themselves, see **Daytrips,** p. 93. In addition, nearly all companies offer full-day tours to Tikal in Guatemala; there's usually a change in vehicle and driver at the border. These tours leave at 7am and return at 5 or 6pm, running US$130-135.

Pacz Tours, Burns Ave. (☎822 0536; www.pacztours.com). Pacz is a San Ignacio stalwart, distinguishing itself from the crowded tour company crowd with its excellent personnel and wide variety of trips on offer. Their 8 guides are incredibly knowledgeable yet personal, offering some of the best, most comprehensive tours of ATM, Caracol, and the other usual destinations. MC/V.

Mayawalk Tours, Burns Ave (☎824 3070; www.mayawalktours.com). One of the original guide companies to set up shop in San Ignacio, Mayawalk is a sort of mothership: many of the guides have gone on to start their own companies in town. The parent company is still going strong, offering a huge variety of tours with professional and irreverent guides.

Eva's Daily Tours, Burns Ave. (☎625 4880 or 620 5616), in Eva's Restaurant. Max and Sergio, the affable owners of this company, also run all the tours, keeping it personal and professional. All the usual destinations are offered here.

K'Atun Ahaw, Burns Ave. (☎824 2080; www.belizeculturetours.com), in the Casa Blanca hotel. Friendly service headed by Elias Cambranes, one of the few Belizeans licensed to guide in Tikal, Guatemala. Also offers a full-day tour to nearby Mayan sites at Cahal Pech, El Pilar, and Xunantunich. MC/V.

Bank: Scotiabank, Burns Ave. (☎824 4190), by the Town Hall. Open M-Th 8am-2pm, F 8am-3:30pm, Sa 9-11:30am. **Atlantic Bank,** across the street from Scotiabank. Open M-F 8am-3pm, Sa 8:30am-noon. **Belize Bank** (☎824 2031), corner of Waight Ave. and Hudson St., next to the town square. Open M-Th 8am-3pm, F 8am-4:30pm, Sa 9am-noon.

Laundromat: On Wyatt St. (☎824 2820). US$3 per load. Open M-Sa 8am-noon and 1-8pm, Su 9am-noon. **Martha's Guesthouse** also offers a public laundromat service. US$3.50 per load. Open 6am-9pm.

Police Station: In the Town Hall building next to the Hawkesworth Bridge.

Pharmacy: On West St. (☎824 0317). Open M-Sa 8am-noon, 1-5pm, 7-9pm; Su 9am-noon. MC/V.

Hospital: La Loma Luz Hospital, Western Highway (☎804 2985), in Santa Elena. 24hr. service.

Internet Access: Tradewinds Internet Cafe, corner of Waight Ave. and West St. Internet in an air-conditioned setting. Grab a free cup of coffee while you surf. US$2.50 per hr. Open M-Sa 7am-11pm, Su 10am-10pm. **D+J Internet Cafe,** Burns Ave. (☎661 5712). Open 9am-8pm. **Data Link Cafe,** in the town square. US$2 per hr. Open M-Sa 8am-9pm.

Post Office: Hudson St. (☎824 2049), near the town square. Open M-Th 8am-noon and 1-5pm, F 8-noon and 1-4pm.

ACCOMMODATIONS

San Ignacio is full of lodgings of all conceivable prices, from cheap guesthouses above family homes near the town center to expansive lodges perched on the tops of nearby hills. Backpackers won't have to venture far; the guesthouses and cheap hotels are intimate, affordable, and never more than 5min. from the bus stop.

Mana Kai Camp and Cabins, Branch Mouth Rd. (☎824 2317; www.manakaibelize.com), just north of the outdoor market. Rooms are clean and comfortable. Some, perched high on stilts, offer decent views. Well-kept grounds. Book well in advance. Camping US$5 per person; cabins with shared baths US$12.50, with private baths US$17.50-22.50. Cash only. ❶

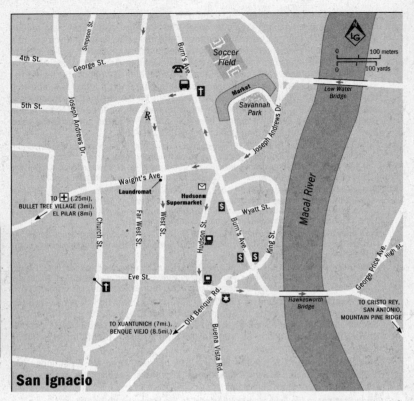

San Ignacio

Cosmos Camping Branch Mouth Rd. (☎824 2116 or 669 0153), a 10min. walk from town. A beautiful, quiet spot for camping. Well-maintained grounds with lots of shade. You can pitch your tent behind the owners' home or head across the street and sleep by the river. Camping US$5 per person. Showers provided. ❶

Hi-Et Guest House, 12 West St. (☎824 2828). Spread out over 2 buildings, this expansive house affords views of town from the small, breezy verandahs attached. You have to walk through the living and dining rooms to reach the rooms upstairs, but the friendly family is used to it. Tiny rooms, each with fan. Beds remade every day. Rooms with shared bath US$10-12.50, with private bath US$20. Cash only. ❷

Tropicool Hotel, 30 Burns Ave. (☎824 3052), behind the Pacz Tours building. Conveniently located next to several tour companies on Burns Ave. Rooms, situated around a back yard, are mostly sheltered from street noise. Budget travelers snatch up the cheap, spare rooms quickly, but Tropicool also rents spacious rooms (resembling cabins) with private baths and TVs. Rooms with shared bath US$11.50, with private bath US$37.50. MC/V. ❷

Central Hotel, Burns Ave. (☎628 2361). The building shows its age, with rustic rooms and old wooden walls. The shared bathrooms could be cleaner, but these are some of the cheapest rooms in town, with a great location on one of San Ignacio's main streets. A massage room and a verandah with hammocks are pleasant surprises. Singles US$10; doubles US$12; triples US$15. Cash only. ❷

◈ FOOD

Several fruit stands cluster around Savannah Plaza, but the large **outdoor market** itself is located five minutes behind the bus stop along Savannah St.; you'll pass it on your way in. On Saturdays, farmers from near and far gather at 6am to sell produce and finger foods; it's your best chance to buy both Mennonite and Garifuna cuisine at the same place. For groceries, try **Hudson Supermarket,** on Hudson St (☎092 4623; open daily 7am-9pm), **Tai San Shop,** right across from the Hudson (☎824 3550; open daily 8am-9pm), or **Celina's Superstore,** on Burns Ave. (open M-Sa 8am-noon and 1-7pm).

Hannah's, 5 Burns Ave. (☎824 3014). The motto here is "Ko-Ox Hannah" ("Let's Go Eat"), and the diners heed the call. The prices relatively cheap and the food comes from local farms. You can go for the Belizean breakfasts, heavy with scrambled eggs (BZ$12-14), or stop in later for the smattering of lamb and steak (US$10-15). Sizable Indian and Asian food menu featuring a variety of curry meals (US$10-12.50). Lunch and dinner US$7-10. Open 6am-10pm; last orders at 9pm. MC/V. ❸

Pop's Restaurant, West St. (☎824 3366). One of the top breakfast spots in town, serving up delicious omelettes (US$6) along with small breakfast appetizers (US$2.50-4.50) in a diner-style setting. Breakfast meals US$5-6. Open M-Sa 6:30am-2pm. MC/V. ❷

Mickey's Fast Food, Burns Ave. This section of Burns Ave. is lined with snack stands, but Mickey's always seems to attract the largest crowds. Cheap, tasty, and quickly prepared Mexican standards: *tostades, garnaches,* and *salbutes* US$.25-.50. Burritos US$1.25. You can get a full breakfast plate (US$3.25), or just go for a breakfast burrito or quesadilla (US$1.75). Open daily 7am-3pm. Cash only. ❶

Eva's Restaurant, 22 Burns Ave. (☎804 2267). A restaurant, bar, tour company, and internet cafe rolled into one. Posters of popular Cayo trips line the walls of the dining space. The menu offers breakfast (US$4.50-7.50), lunch, and dinner (US$5-8), ranging from Mexican dishes to Belizean specials. Open daily 7am-10pm. MC/V. ❸

◉ SIGHTS

 THANKS, BUT NO THANKS. Don't be fooled into taking guided tours to nearby sites like Cahal Pech or Xunantunich. Both sites are easily accessible—Cahal Pech by walking from San Ignacio, Xunantunich by taking the bus to San Jose Succotz—so all you should be paying is the admission fee (US$5 each).

CAHAL PECH. A vist to a Mayan ruin doesn't get any easier: a 30min. walk up a steep hill or a quick taxi (US$2.50) gets you to this site named "Place of the Ticks" (a reminder of more cattle-pervasive and tick-plentiful times). Cahal Pech is the oldest site in area, with signs of settlement dating back to 1500 BC; the ruins here, though, all date from AD 400-850, when the area declined along with the rest of the Mayan civilization. The shaded grounds contain **seven plazas,** but the real attraction here are the **royal residences** at the rear of the site, some of the most extensive in the area. You can climb down narrow staircases and through small passages to visit the dark rooms that once were home to the town's elite. Caretakers sometimes give tours, and expect a tip. *(From the police station, take Buena Vista St. out of town. You will pass the San Ignacio Resort Hotel on your left, after the road curves to the right the sign for Cahal Pech will appear shortly. Follow it and take a left onto a gravel road; continue to the top. Entry to the ruins on your left. Taxi US$2.50. The ruins*

LOCAL LEGEND

HOT, SPICY, AND SHARP

Walk into your local Walmart superstore and you might just find a spicy taste of Belize. Marie Sharp's habanero pepper sauce, named after the company's founder, has become an irreplaceable staple of Belizean cuisine. Sixp. 93e year old Marie Sharp's all-natural sauces and jellies may be sold worldwide, but their owner's roots are as humble as they come. While working as a secretary, Marie began growing her own peppers and combining them with other local produce as a hobby. When friends suggested that she sell them, Marie got to work in her own kitchen and Marie Sharp's hot sauce was born—sort of. Originally naming her product Melinda, after her family's farm, the name was trademarked by an American company. Mary lost the rights to the name when she ended her relationship with the company. Undaunted, Marie renamed her company, focused on the Belizean market, and the rest is history.

Today, Marie spends most of her day in the company plant or traveling to food shows around the world. Despite her success, Marie still enjoys many traditional Belizean activities. The avid fisherwoman casts a line as often as she can. Marie's favorite fishing spot? The small private island that she and her family own off of the coast.

are also accessible by any bus bound for Benque Viejo; ask to get off by the ruins (US$.50). Open daily 6am-6pm. US$5.)

NIGHTLIFE AND ENTERTAINMENT

San Ignacio is quiet most nights, with a limited nightlife scene focusing on a small handful of bars. Weekends are livelier, with the usual Belizean stew of beats animating the center and a few entertainment venues attracting crowds farther out from town.

Faya Wata, Burns Ave. (☎824 2660). Easily the best nightspot in town. Crowds of locals gather to drink, listen to live music shows, play darts and poker, shoot pool, or just chill by the open windows overlooking Market Sq. The wide mixed drink menu, scattered along the walls and including Faya Wata itself, runs US$4-10. Beer US$2. Open daily 5pm-midnight. Cash only.

Pitpan Tavern, Market Sq. This tiny drinking hole, distinguished by the large car sculpture above it, fills up very quickly. The bar can barely fit in the space, but the atmosphere is intimate and easy-going. Drinks US$2-7.50. Happy hour M-F 4-7pm. Open M-Sa 4pm-midnight. Cash only.

The Attic, Burns Ave. This huge 2nd fl. space, with its old name "Blue Angels" emblazoned on the windows, includes many seating areas and pool tables. Can be empty on weekdays, but a crowd gathers on weekends to enjoy the company of exotic dancers. Mixed drinks US$3.50-7.50. Beer US$2. Open M-Th 10am-midnight, F-Sa 10am-2am. Cash only.

DAYTRIPS FROM SAN IGNACIO

An ideal starting point for exploring the natural wonders and thrills of the Cayo District, San Ignacio is Belize's second most popular destination after San Pedro. Tour companies loudly announce themselves at every corner, attempting to distinguish themselves from the guys next door. Unfortunately, most sites' remote locations make visiting them on your own nearly impossible, especially if you're without a car. It's an inevitable cost, but the guides themselves are usually excellent and multitalented, as adept at explaining old Mayan rituals as they are at identifying the medicinal uses of plants. Plus, exploring the wilds of Belize with a group may be the best way to gain perspective on them.

ACTUN TUNICHIL MUKNAL

Actun Tunichil Muknal must be visited as part of a guided tour. Only certain specialized guides are licensed to give tours in the site, so there's not much selection to be had. The guides at Pacz Tours and Mayawalk (see Orientation *and Practical Information, p. 88) are especially informative and respected. Trips to ATM usually cost US$75 and last all day, leaving San Ignacio at 8am. and returning around 5pm. There's a lot of climbing and swimming involved, so be prepared for a strenuous and tiring adventure.*

Remotely located in the **Tapir Mountain Reserve** at the end of a rocky 30min. drive from the Western Highway and a 45min. hike through jungle and across three rivers, the sacred Mayan site of Actun Tunichil Muknal (ATM) is one of the true highlights of any trip to Belize. The 5km long cave, rediscovered only in the late 1980s, is one of the most stunning in Central America, but it's the artifacts found within that make the visit unforgettable. From the base camp, the adventure begins with a plunge into a cold pool lying at the cave mouth. From there, groups are led through rocky, cavernous channels (most of them wet—be prepared to be soaked for hours) 500m into the cave, passing striking rock, crystal formations, and ledges of beautiful stalactites. The trip then leaves the water, ascending a ledge to the huge natural spaces that the Maya used as sacred temples. It's not hard to see why; these dark and silent caves are distinguished by stunning crystal and stalactite formations that to the Maya resembled the roots of the world tree. This was literally **Xibalba,** the underworld. Deliberately shattered pottery lies exactly where it was found, the ashes (used in ritual cooking ceremonies) still visible. Expanses of carefully planned burial grounds stretch out beneath vaulting cave ceilings. Most fascinating of all are the five human remains on display (14 in all have been discovered in the cave): buried skeletons, cracked skulls, and, at the very end of the tour, the skeleton of a young woman, the **Crystal Maiden,** ritualistically positioned as if giving birth. Be careful when stepping amidst the artifacts; they are not protected from visiting feet, and several have been damaged by careless tourists. Many believe that the site won't be open to the public for much longer, so make a visit to this haunting site a top priority.

▓ CARACOL

Caracol lies at the end of a very rocky road leaving the Western Highway just before San Ignacio and passing through remote villages before entering the wilderness of Mountain Pine Ridge. If you're driving, follow the signs to the site. The last ten miles of the road are paved, but otherwise be prepared for a bumpy and dusty ride lasting over two hours. Since Guatemalan bandits had taken to robbing tourist vans heading to the site, a security system has been established. An armed convoy accompanies visitors from a base along the road at Douglas D'Silva to the ruins themselves. The van leaves Douglas D'Silva at 9:30am sharp and leaves Caracol at 2pm, so if you're on your own keep an eye on the time; leave San Ignacio by 7:30am to arrive at the the base on time. The easiest way to reach and explore the ruins is in a tour group. Tours leave San Ignacio 7:30-8am and return at 5pm. The return trip includes stops at the Rio Frio Cave and Rio On Pools. Trips US$75. www.caracol.org. Open daily 8am-4pm. US$7.50 (included in tour prices).

The mother of all Mayan sites in Belize, Caracol (Spanish for "snail," named either after the snail shells in the soil or the winding road leading up to the site) was once a mighty city-state inhabited by 150,000 people and covering 70 sq. mi. It reached its peak in the AD seventh century after defeating mighty Tikal, but was largely deserted by AD 900. The once vibrant, teeming city lay buried in the wilds near the Belize-Guatemala border until a logger happened upon the ruins in the 1930s. Since then, excavators have discovered over 4,000 structures and even 40 mi. of wide causeways that once served as thoroughfares connecting the city center with outlying areas. The highlight of the site is **Caana** (Sky Palace), which rises 141 ft. above Plaza B; Caana is still the tallest structure in Belize. About halfway up is a row of small rooms, complete with ledges that served as beds. At the top lies a small plaza featuring several tombs. Climb the final set of steps for a great view of the jungle spreading out in all directions from the site. The **Central Acropolis** south of the temple was an elite residential center—you can still see the beds—while **Plaza A** to the west includes the **Temple of the Wooden Lintels,** featuring wooden inserts above the doorway (one of which is original). You can also walk through two **ball courts** whose small stone altars have provided archaeologists with loads of historical information about the city.

⚔ BORDER CROSSING: INTO GUATEMALA

The road from San Ignacio, Belize to Flores, Guatemala is a well-traveled one; using public transportation to make the popular trek can be complex.

First, take a **bus** bound for **Benque Viejo del Carmen** from San Ignacio (40min., every 30min., US$1.50). From there, take a taxi to the border—trust us, they're not hard to find (US$5 per taxi). **Independent money changers** gather at the border offering Guatemalan quetzals—the changers are handy, but if you're not careful you'll be given a bad exchange. Do the conversions beforehand or bring a calculator and know how much you should receive. For more information on conversions see Money, p. 7.

You'll have to cross the border on foot and pay a US$18.75 exit fee upon leaving the country; the money goes towards national park maintenance, so no need for outrage. As soon as you cross, try to pick up a minibus.

Once in Guatemala, get your **passport stamped** in the large, open-air building to the left; beware of exorbitant fees (you shouldn't pay more than Q20 here). From here, continue straight across the bridge and into **Melchor de Mencos.** From the road in front of the gas station, **minibuses** leave for **Santa Elena** (the town right below Flores) every half-hour. The ride lasts 2½hr. and costs Q25-30. From Santa Elena's bus station, small, three-wheeled *tuk-tuks* can bring you to **Flores** (Q5).

SOUTHERN BELIZE

Southern Belize is a true smorgasbord of natural and cultural treasures. Here, you'll have your pick of near-impenetrable jungles, white beaches, imposing mountains, and vibrant coastal villages. This region hosts the country's best national parks and most beautiful terrain, as well as some of its most diverse people and vibrant culture.

South of the Hummingbird Highway—Belize's most stunning drive and a fitting introduction to the region—a patchwork of protected areas leaves huge swaths of the territory home only to wildlife. The coast, though, grooves to the percussive rhythms of the region's Garífuna culture. To the far south, where mountains give way to rolling hills, the resilient Maya continue their age-old traditions amidst reminders of a storied and ancient past.

DANGRIGA

Dangriga (pop. 10,400) dances to its own rhythm, grounded in the unique history and culture of the Garífuna people. While it serves as the main transport hub for Southern Belize, the town's own vibrant energy (belied by a somewhat dilapidated appearance) makes a short stay worthwhile. This is one of the few towns in Belize that remains active after 9pm on weekdays, with locals congregating on St. Vincent Street to the muffled, frenzied beats of Garífuna drumming. And there is always the dominating presence of the sea—fishermen mingle with boat captains shepherding tourists out to nearby cayes, the outdoor market sells fresh catch, and small beaches hug the shore.

◪ TRANSPORTATION

Flights: Dangriga's **airstrip** is located to the north of town, about a 20min. walk from the center. **Maya Island Air** (☎223 1140; www.mayaislandair.com) and **Tropic Air** (☎226 2012; www.tropicair.com) both fly to **Belize City** (30min., 5 per day, US$41.50); **Placencia** (15min., 10 per day, US$46); and **Punta Gorda** (40min., 5 per day, US$75.50).

Buses: The main bus station is located at the south end of town at the corner of Havana St. and George Price Dr. Buses go to: **Belmopan** (1¼hr.; every 30min. 5-7am and 5-6:30pm, every hr. 7:30am-3:30pm; US$3); **Belize City** (3hr.; every 30min. 5-7am and 5-6:30pm, every hr. 7:30am-3:30pm; US$5); **Independence** (1½hr.; 5:30, 7:45am, and every hr. 9:15am-6:15pm; US$4); **Punta Gorda** (3½hr.; 5:30, 7:45am, and every hr. 9:15am-6:15pm; US$7.50); **Placencia** (1¾hr.; 9, 10:30, 11am, noon, 4:30, and 6pm; US$2); **Hopkins** (¾hr., 5:15am and 10:30am, US$1.50); **Sittee Point** (1¼hr., 5:15am and 10:30am, US$2).

Boats: To **Tobacco Caye** and other central cayes leave from just east of the bridge over North Stann Creek; you can usually find captains lounging in or near the Riverside Cafe (p. 98) on South Riverside Dr. Make arrangements with them personally; it's best to check a day in advance to make sure there's room on the boats (most of which can fit 15-20 people). Most boats leave for Tobacco Caye around 9-9:30am and return to Dangriga 3-4pm (US$17.50, round-trip US$35). **Nesymein Hardy Water Taxi** (☎522 0062, 604 4738, or 605 7336) heads intermittently to **Puerto Cortez, HON.** The boat leaves from North Riverside Dr. by the North Stann Creek bridge; you can buy a ticket at the offices just north of the bridge. Direct boats to **Puerto Cortez** (3hr., M and Sa 11am, US$50). Check-in time 8:30am. A boat leaves for **Puerto Cortez** on Th at 9am, though they stop to pick up passengers in **Placencia** and **Big Creek** (4½hr., US$42.50).

Taxis: Many wait at the bus station or along St. Vincent Street, the main road in town.

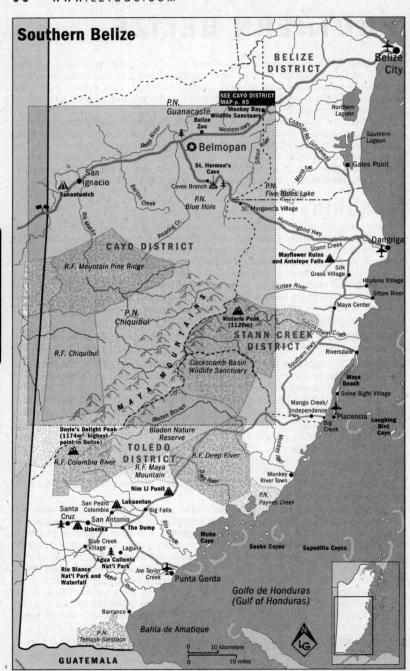

Southern Belize

SOUTHERN BELIZE

BELIZE DISTRICT

Belize City

P.N. Guanacaste

SEE CAYO DISTRICT MAP p. 85

Monkey Bay Wildlife Sanctuary

Belize Zoo

Belize River

Western Hwy.

Sibun River

Coastal Rd. (unpaved)

Northern Lagoon

Southern Lagoon

★ Belmopan

Gales Point

Manatee

San Ignacio

Xunantunich

St. Herman's Cave

Caves Branch

P.N. Blue Hole

P.N. Five Blues Lake

St. Margaret's Village

Hummingbird Hwy.

Dangriga

Barton Creek

Rio Mopán

Roaring Cr.

CAYO DISTRICT

R.F. Mountain Pine Ridge

Mayflower Ruins and Antelope Falls

Stann Creek

Silk Grass Village

Hopkins Village

Sittee River

Sittee River

P.N. Chiquibul

Victoria Peak (1120m)

Maya Center

R.F. Chiquibul

STANN CREEK DISTRICT

South Stann Creek

Southern Hwy.

Riversdale

Cockscomb Basin Wildlife Sanctuary

MAYA MOUNTAINS

Maya Beach

Seine Bight Village

Mango Creek/ Independence

Placencia

Big Creek

Laughing Bird Caye

Bladen Branch

Doyle's Delight Peak (1174m - highest point in Belize)

Bladen Nature Reserve

Monkey River

R.F. Columbia River

TOLEDO DISTRICT

R.F. Deep River

R.F. Maya Mountain

Deep River

Monkey River Town

P.N. Paynes Creek

Nim Li Punit

Santa Cruz

San Pedro Colombia

Lubaantun

Big Falls

Rio Grande

San Antonio

Uxbenka

The Dump

Blue Creek Village

Laguna

Moho

Agua Caliente Nat'l Park

Joe Taylor Creek

Moho Caye

Snake Cayes

Sapodilla Cayes

Río Blanco Nat'l Park and Waterfall

Moho River

Punta Gorda

Golfo de Honduras (Gulf of Honduras)

Barranco

Bahía de Amatique

P.N. Temash-Sarstoon

0   10 kilometers
0   10 miles

N

LG

GUATEMALA

ORIENTATION AND PRACTICAL INFORMATION

Dangriga hugs the Caribbean coast, extending almost three miles from north to south, but only about a mile inland. **George Price Drive** bounds the main part of town to the south (it becomes **Stann Creek Valley Road** as it heads west), while **Ecumenical Drive,** which leaves Stann Creek Valley Rd. about half a mile from town, provides a rough western boundary. The main road changes names a few times as it heads north. From its intersection with George Price Dr. (where you'll find the **bus station** and the **Drums of Our Fathers Monument** to **Havana Creek**, it's **Havana Street**. From Havana Creek to **North Stann Creek**, it's **St. Vincent Street** (the busiest section, lined with shops, restaurants, and services). North of North Stann, it becomes **Commerce Street.** The area to the west of this road is more residential and can be dangerous at night. By the coast where North Stann Creek empties into the sea lies **Why-Not Island,** which is actually connected to the mainland by a slight sliver of land. A small and not-too-attractive **beach** spreads out along the coast north of the creek.

Banks: Belize Bank, St. Vincent Street. Open M-Th 8am-3pm and F 8am-4:30pm. **Scotiabank,** St. Vincent Street, just south of the main bridge. Open M-Th 8am-2pm, F 8am-3:30pm, Sa 9am-11:30am. **First Caribbean International Bank,** Commerce St. Open M-Th 8am-2:30pm, F 8am-4:30pm.

Laundromat: Val's Laundry, Mahogany Rd. (☎502 3324), in Val's Backpacker Hostel (p. 98). Wash and dry US$1 per lb. Open daily 9am-7pm.

Police Station: On Commerce St., at the intersection with Court House Rd.

Pharmacy: St. Vincent Drugstore, St. Vincent Street (☎522 3124). Open M-F 8am-noon and 1:30-8pm, Sa 8am-noon and 4-8pm. MC/V.

Hospital: Southern Regional Hospital, Stann Creek Valley Rd. (☎522 2078). Follow George Price Dr. about 2 mi. north of town.

Internet Access: Val's Internet, Mahogany Rd. (☎502 3324), in Val's Backpacker Hostel (p. 98). US$2 per hr. If you have a labtop, you can hook it up with an internet cable. Open daily 9am-7pm. **Griganet Cafe,** St. Vincent Street (☎522 2096). US$2 per hr. Printing and photocopying. Open M-F 8am-8pm, Sa noon-5pm.

Post Office: Polack St. (☎522 2035), in the back of the low government office building. Open M-Th 8am-noon and 1-4:30pm, F 8am-noon and 1-4pm.

ACCOMMODATIONS

Hostels and cheap hotels abound in Dangriga, none of them too far from attractions or the shore.

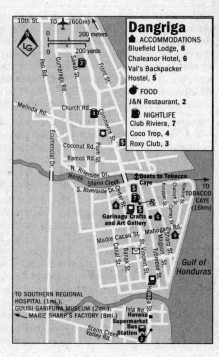

SOUTHERN BELIZE

Val's Backpacker Hostel, Mahogany Rd. (☎502 3324). Walk down Mahogany Rd. to the coast. Don't let Val's grey concrete building with an unfinished 2nd fl. turn you off. Inside you'll find one of the most backpacker-friendly atmospheres in Belize. Two large, no-frills dorm rooms are lined with comfortable bunks. Communal area houses a book exchange, internet cafe, laundry room (see **Orientation and Practical Information,** p. 97), and a deli (delicious homemade ice cream, US$0.50 per scoop). A verandah catches all the right breezes from the ocean, which is just a playground away from the building. There's little privacy, but that's the point; expect to meet other travelers on the porch. There is 1 fully stocked private double with bath and cable TV (US$30). Breakfast US$2.50. Reception 8am-7pm. Dorm beds US$11. Cash only. ❷

Bluefield Lodge, 6 Bluefield Rd. (☎522 2742). This well-established budget option was actually the childhood home of Louise, its owner. A clean, white columned verandah introduces blue walls and large, tastefully decorated rooms inside. Knowledgeable staff will answer all your tourist questions. Singles US$13.50, with bath US$22; doubles US$19/27.50. MC/V. ❷

Chaleanor Hotel, 35 Magoon St. (☎522 2587). Chaleanor makes a striking first impression: a wide, 3-story building with columned verandahs and paintings of Belize's wildlife. Regular rooms are spacious and bright, each with bath, fan, and cable TV. Budget rooms are cramped and rustic but clean and with a spotless shared bathroom. Budget singles US$11, regular singles US$31.50, with A/C US$46; doubles US$18/50/65; triples US$23.50/62.50/77. MC/V. ❷

▣ FOOD

While you're in Dangriga try some traditional Garífuna cuisine. *Hudut,* a plantain mash cooked in coconut milk, is the most common dish. The large, outdoor **Dangriga Central Market** is just north of North Stann Creek, by the coast; you can get all the fruits (and occasionally all the fish) you want there. Also try **Havana Supermarket,** on Havana St., across from the bus station (open M-Sa 8am-9pm and Su 8am-noon), **First Choice Supermarket,** on St. Vincent St. (open M-Sa 8am-9pm, Su 8am-noon), or **The Price Is Right Supermarket,** ironically right across the street from First Choice (open M-Sa 8am-8:30pm).

Riverside Cafe, South Riverside Dr. (☎502 3449). This small diner by the creek and the docks is populated by fishers, boat captains, and tourists about to head off to the Cayes. You can grab a hearty traditional Belizean breakfast in the mornings (US$3.50) and fish and meat dishes at lunch (US$4.50-6). Dinner is predictably dominated by seafood: lobster conch and a bevy of fish and shrimp plates (US$6-12.50) keep the small cafe busy all evening. Open M-Sa 8am-9pm. Cash only. ❸

Roots Kitchen, Ecumenical Dr. Walk 20min. up George Price Dr., turn right on Ecumenical Dr., and continue straight for 5min. This tiny restaurant on the outskirts of town is little more than a rustic shack, but the delicious specialties cooked inside have made it one of the most popular dinner spots in town. Breakfasts (US$2.50-3.50) are standard Belizean, but the highlight is the Garífuna cooking. It isn't prepared every day, though; come weekend nights for the best chances of sampling the coconut milk-drenched local cuisine. Entrees US$3.50-6. Open daily 6am-9pm. Cash only. ❷

J&N Restaurant, Havana St. (☎600 9570). An unpretentious eatery right across from the bus station, J&N is one of the best places to try some standard Belizean cooking, including Gariguna cuisine. *Hudut* with BBQ, chicken, and fish dishes US$6-10. If you're arriving or heading out of town early, stop in for some large breakfasts featuring fry jacks and tortillas (US$3.50-5.50). Open M-Sa 6:30am-9pm. ❸

SIGHTS

Two attractions on the outskirts of town allow for intimate looks at some of the basic ingredients of Belizean culture, while small stops in town bring you closer to the musical heart of Garífuna culture.

GULISI GARÍFUNA MUSEUM. The small museum is inconveniently located two miles from town, but is the best place to learn about the remarkable history and fascinating, unique culture of the Garífuna people. Colorful exhibits detail the story: the initial shipwreck, mixing with the native tribes, resistance to colonization, and arrival on the shores of Belize from Honduras. Music is the main focus. You can catch video footage of Dangriga's own **Pen Cayetano**, the founder of punta rock, inventor of the turtle shell as musical instrument, and noted painter. **Andy Palacios**, a more current punta legend, gets his fair share of attention as well. *(Stann Creek Valley Rd. A short bus ride (10min., US$0.50) is the quickest way to get to the museum. ☎ 669 0639; www.ngcbelize.org. Open M-F 10am-5pm, Sa 8am-noon. US$5.)*

MARIE SHARP'S FACTORY. In the early 1980s, a surplus of *habanero* peppers at her family farm prompted Mary Sharp to experiment and try out some new sauces. Nearly 30 years later, bottles of her hot sauce—from the elusive mild variety to the "Beware!" strain—adorn almost every restaurant table in Belize. This factory isn't the true home of the sauce (Marie moved here in the late 1990s), but it's close enough; you can take a tour of the creation process, sometimes with Marie herself as a guide. And, of course, a shop has the full gamut of MS sauces. Just beware. *(1 mi. down Melinda Rd. off the Southern Highway, 8 mi. from Dangriga. Ask to be let off at the turnoff for Marie Sharp's. ☎ 520 2087; www.mariesharps-bz.com. Open M-F 7am-4pm.)*

GARINAGU CARFTS AND ART GALLERY. This small shop and gallery has Garífuna wood carvings and drums for sale (US$20-100). Pick up some turtle shells, a common punta instrument, or postcards (US$1) featuring the beautiful artwork of Pen Cayetano, originator of punta rock and noted painter of Garífuna scenes. *(Tubroose St. ☎ 522 2596. Open M-F 8:30am-6pm. Cash only.)*

AUSTIN RODRIGUEZ. Mr. Rodriguez is a local drum-making legend, whose workshop is one of the more noticeable structures in town: a huge seaside *palapa* (thatched-roofed open house) on Why-Not Island by the mouth of North Stann Creek. You can buy his handcrafted cedar and mahogany drums

ON THE MENU

BELIZEAN BREWS

Anyone vacationing in a tropical climate knows the value of sitting back and enjoying a nice, cold beer. When in Belize, do as the Belizians do and gulp down a delicious Belikin, the leading domestically produced beer.

First marketed in the late 1960s, the Belikin Beer brand proudly sports the tagline, "The Only Beer Worth Drinking." Belikin is created in the Belikin Brewery by 94 full time employees who produce 52,000 barrels of beer a year. Even though their production is not large scale, their product is perfect for quenching one's thirst on a sweltering Belizian day. The name "Belikin" comesfrom the Maya language and means "Road to the East." Their label, shamelessly marketed to tourists on T-shirts and glassware at the airport gift shop, features a drawing of a Pre-Columbian, Mayan temple-pyramid at Altun Ha.

Their most popular product is a light lager beer; a premium lager and a stout beer are also brewed and sold under the Belikin name. The light lager has a golden color; it tastes soft and sweet, and is somewhat dry. So, what are you waiting for? Kick back, relax, and enjoy a Belkin.

for US$50-125; he's also been known to offer drum-making lessons to groups. (☎502 2380 or 665 3975. *Open M-Sa 9am-7pm.*)

🎵 📷 ENTERTAINMENT AND NIGHTLIFE

Be on the lookout for Garífuna drumming gatherings; they often take place in otherwise nondescript spots in the city's residential area (to the west of the main road) at night. It's best to roam these areas with a group.

Club Riviera, St. Vincent Street. Danriga's most happening night spot, no doubt because of the double promise of lubricated condoms and karaoke advertised on its front wall. On weekdays, Riviera is a popular karaoke bar; weeknights feature raucous dance parties and live performances by punta rockers and other local musicians. Drinks US$2-7. Open Tu, W, Th, and Su from 9pm-late; F and Sa from 10pm-late. Cash only.

Roxy Club, Commerce St., in Harlem Sq. The name conjures up ritz and glamor, but Dangriga's Roxy is as down-home and unassuming as they come. A small downstairs room fills up quickly with locals thirsting for cheap drinks (US$2-5). It's well north of town, so you might want to take a friend, as the area gets a little sketchy after dark. Game night Th. Open M-Sa 7-11pm. Cash only.

Coco Trop, Commerce St., right across from a church and convent. Coco Trop, serving stew dishes and Mexican snacks by day. But on Sa nights, this squat, blue eatery transforms into a club hosting dance parties with Latin, reggae, punta, and other Caribbean beats. Food US$1.50-5.50. Drinks US$1.50-5. Open M-F 7am-9pm, Sa 7am-2am. Cash only.

❄ FESTIVALS

A small group of Garinagu landed in Dangriga from Honduras in a dug-out canoe on November 19, 1832. Now, the city erupts for the **Garífuna Resettlement Day** celebrations. It's easily the best time of year to see proud, joyous celebrations of traditional Garífuna culture. November 18 and 19 are filled with drum performances and dancing, while the streets fill with food vendors. The landing is reenacted on the morning of the 19th. Be sure to book accommodations at least a week ahead if you plan on traveling here in mid-November.

🔺 DAYTRIPS FROM DANGRIGA

TOBACCO CAYE

Boats leave from South Riverside Drive by the Riverside Cafe in Dangriga. Captains linger around the cafe during the day; check with them a day in advance to arrange a trip. Boats usually leave around 9-9:30am and can bring you back to Dangriga around 2-3pm. US$17.50, round-trip US$35.

Barely four and a half acres of sand and palm trees, surrounded by clear water and coral reefs, Tobacco Caye, 12 mi. from Dangriga, is Belize's most popular island south of Caye Caulker. Just over 20 inhabitants call the island home, but a steady influx of tourists who come to fish, snorkel, swim, and lounge in hammocks keep the pace at a lazy bustle. The caye is crammed with hotels, so finding a quiet spot can be difficult. Luckily, the accommodations themselves strive for an isolated atmosphere; your daytrip may turn into an extended stay (though it's best to call ahead to arrange a lodging). All of them include three meals in their price, so you don't have to fish to survive (though some have been known to make the valiant effort). Most can also rent out snorkeling and fishing gear. On the northern edge of the island, **Tobacco Caye Paradise ❶** (☎520 5101) rents small but beautifully located *cabaña* (US$38.50) with porches extending over the shore. Rest on the porch hammocks. Plain, offshore rooms are also available (US$26, with bath US$33). The **Gaviota Lodge ❺** (☎509 5032), in the middle of the island, has a few small rooms near its gift shop for US$35-40. **Lana's on the Reef ❹** (☎520 5036) rents small, plain rooms (some without a sea view) for US$30. **Reef's End ❺** (☎522 2419; www.reefsendlodge.com), a very noticeable bar and restaurant (and the caye's most expensive accommodation) perched on its own pier at the caye's southern end, is the only nightspot in town; the expansive ocean views are reason enough to make a stop there. Call ahead if you plan to take a meal. It's also the place to ask about diving near the site; scuba trips can be arranged to the nearby **Shark Hole.**

COCKSCOMB BASIN WILDLIFE SANCTUARY
At the end of a 6 mi. access road that leaves the Southern Highway at the village of Maya Centre, about 20 mi. south of Dangriga. Taxis (US$15, round-trip US$30) are available in Maya Centre and will bring you to the visitors' center; you can find one at Nu'uk Cheil Cottages in the village, 500 yd. down the access road, or at Tutzil Nah Cottages by the highway. Open daily 7:30am-4:30pm. US$5.

This massive reserve, Belize's largest and most popular, covers over 124,000 acres in the western part of the Stann Creek District. Although Cockscomb is known as a home to jaguars, spotting one in the park's vast territory is unlikely. However, it does happen, and excited notices by tourists in the sighting book at the visitors' center testify to the finds a patient wildlife observer can come across. The sanctuary dates back to the early 1980s, when the Belize Audubon Society, concerned about jaguar hunting in the country, asked Alan Rabinowitz of the New York Zoological Society to locate the best place for a big cat sanctuary. Using gentle traps to capture jaguars and attach radio collars to them, researchers found that the present-day sanctuary housed the most populous community of jaguars and four other species of big cats. The area was created as a forest reserve in 1984; in 1986, it was declared a wildlife sanctuary. The flood of excited tourists and dedicated wildlife enthusiasts began and continues to flow through the sanctuary. The reserve continues to grow; in 1999, Victoria Peak was added to its protected territory. Today, all five of Belize's big cats call the Sanctuary home, including an estimated 60 jaguars. Ornithologists also flock to the park drawn by the 290 bird species, including scarlet macaws, toucans, and curassows. Smaller animals, including the celebrated tapir (or "mountain cow"), are often seen.

RISE AND SHINE. If you want your name next to an amazing, groundbreaking wildlife sighting in the Cockscomb visitors' log, be prepared to get there early—most of the park's wildlife (especially the birds) are most active right after dawn. Your best bet is to spend a night within the park, either on a campsite or in their dorms.

Exhibits on the park, its history, geology, and wildlife, along with information on local Mayan culture, are on display in the small **museum** by the visitors' center. An extensive, 12 mi. network of trails restricts public access to a small but beautiful section of the sanctuary around the visitors' center. The easiest loop is formed by the **River Path** (500m), the **Rubber Tree Path** (500m), and the **Curassow Path** (0.4km). The River Path leaves the access road just before the visitors' center. From the Curassow, **Ben's Bluff Trail** (3.2km) crosses a creek and goes up a steep incline to a viewpoint looking out on the Maya Mountains, including mighty Victoria Peak and Outlier Mountain. On the way back, stop by the creek to enjoy a cool swimming pool at the foot of a small **cascade.** The **Warl Loop** heads for 2½km to **South Stann Creek,** where you can tube down the river to an established exit point and walk back on the Curassow path

CAPTAIN DOGGY

"Ever drive outboard?" Captain Doggy lets go of the outboard motor and offers the handle before I've had a chance to respond.

In what seems like a split second, the front of the boat aimed directly at Dangriga's television tower, we're cutting through the choppy waves at the trembling hand of a very inexperienced pilot. We're in the middle of a back-and-forth journey between the Gari (use glyph) funa town and the cayes lying off its coast, popular rest stops those looking for that ever-elusive, affordable Caribbean getaway.

Doggy is just one of several boat captains who shepherd visitors around these waters. Unlike the water taxis that service the northern cayes, these boats are small and conducive to conversation. Especially when it's just you and the captain.

He motions for me to cut the engine. "I need a swimming break," he says, and with that we're in the warm Caribbean waters, miles away from either caye or mainland. It's beautiful out, and like in most places here, we're free from time constraints. There may be people waiting for a boat somewhere, but we could care less. This is traveling in Belize.

-Dan Normandin

(rent tubes for US$2.50). Leaving the access road about 15min. before the visitors' center, the **Tiger Fern Trail** (2km) ends at the beautiful, 75ft. **Tiger Fern Waterfall,** which features another **swimming pool** at its base. Leaving the access road 25min. before the visitors' center, the 3½km **Antelope** or **Gibnut Loop** forms the sanctuary's largest regular trail, crossing several creeks and providing plenty of opportunities to spot wildlife (especially birds in the early morning hours). Much longer trails lead to the **Outlier Mountain** (6-7hr., 14km roundtrip), which is 1920 ft. high. Guides are not necessary, but you must travel in groups of two or more. The star attraction is **Victoria Peak**—at 3675ft., it is Belize's second highest mountain. A hike of three to four days is required to reach the summit, guides are required (US$40-45 per day), and the trek is only allowed between March and May. Those are some stringent limitations, but the mountain promises some of the most amazing views in Belize.

The best way to experience the full expanse of the sanctuary's available territory (and to spot wildlife during the crucial early morning hours) is to spend the night. You can choose between **"rustic cabins"** and newly built **dorm beds** near the visitors' center; each option is US$20 per person. **Camping** (US$10) is also available; the main campsite is not far off from the visitors' center. Other camps along the Tiger Fern trail and a very distant one near Victoria Peak are also available. It may be more convenient for transportation purposes to sleep near the highway; luckily, Maya Centre has some cheap options. **Nu'uk Cheil Cottages** ❶ (☎520 3033 or 615 2091), 500 yd. down the access road (it's the last building before the park), is run by a former director of the Sanctuary and his friendly family. They rent clean bunk rooms for US$10, singles and doubles with shared bath for US$22.50, and triples with private bath for US$30. You can camp on their grounds for US$3.50. They also run a restaurant on site serving standard Belizean food and Mayan cuisine (entrees US$5-7.50; open 7am-8pm), and a gift shop. Right by the highway, the lodgings at **Tutzil Nah Cottages** ❸ (☎520 3044; www.mayacentre. com) are a bit dingier, housed in squat concrete buildings. (Rooms US$18, with bath US$22.50.) The owner offers kayak trips (US$25 for 2, US$22.50 for 3 or more), day tours (US$22.50/20), and night tours (US$20/17.50) in the Sanctuary. Both offer taxi service to the sanctuary.

HOPKINS

Miles away from Dangriga's noise and dust, Hopkins is just as proud of its vibrant Garífuna culture. The long village of Hopkins (pop. 1100) is a great off-the-beaten-path destination for those exploring southern Belize. Just two streets wide, Hopkins provides seaside tranquility for visitors looking to relax and enjoy some time by the shore. If you're looking to dive into the area's natural beauty and get right into the percussive heart of the Garínagu, Hopkins is just as fun as Dangriga. Here you'll find great snorkeling and diving opportunities, exhilarating watersports, and plenty of drumming. Hopkins isn't entirely undiscovered—there's a growing foreign population and plenty of hotels and craft shops catering to tourists.

TRANSPORTATION

Buses: Buses from **Sittee Point** pass through Hopkins on their way to **Dangria** (45min., 6:45am and 2pm, US$1.50) and will pick up passengers along the length of the village as far north as Lebeha Drumming Center.

Bike Rental: With long stretches of road by the beach, the Hopkins area is an ideal place for biking with or without a destination in mind. **Dolly's Bike Rentals,** half a mile south of the intersection just past the basketball court. US$2.50 per hr., US$10 per day. **Yugadah Cafe** (p. 104) rents bikes for US$1.50 per hr., US$5 per ½-day, and US$10 per full-day.

Kayak Rental: Tipple Tree Beya. US$7.50 per hr., US$15 per ½-day.

ORIENTATION AND PRACTICAL INFORMATION

Hopkins is connected to the Southern Highway by a rugged, mostly unpaved, four-mile **access road.** The heart of town is at the intersection of this road with the village's **main street,** which continues south to the nearby settlement of **Sittee Point**; another street closer to the shore runs for about a mile.

Tourist Office: The **green shack** at the main intersection. Open M-Sa 9am-3pm.

Police Station: At the main intersection just past the mural.

Internet Access: Hopkins Internet, at **Windschief** (p. 105). US$4 per hr. Open M-Sa 1-9pm, Su 6-9pm.

ACCOMMODATIONS AND CAMPING

Tiny Hopkins is full of hotels catering to the ever-increasing tourist flood. Managers and owners of the hotels are some of the best people to ask for information about activities around the area. They may be able to provide a boat, kayak, or bike.

Lebeha Cabana and Drumming Center (☎666 6658; www.lebeha.com), half a mile north of the intersection. One of the coolest spots in town, Lebeha rents lodgings in a few plain but comfortable *cabañas.* Best of all, you get to be near frequent nightly drumming concerts. Doubles US$15 with bath US$25; beach doubles with bath US$49. MC/V. ❷

Tania's Guest House (☎523 7058), 1 mi. south of the intersection. The two ramshackle yellow buildings here don't have any sea views and stand next to a sanitation service center. Rooms are a little dingy but well-kept, with carpeted floors. Each room comes with bath, cable TV, and fan. Singles US$13; doubles and triples US$22.50. MC/V. ❷

Kismet Beach Apartments (☎523 7280), 1 mi. north of the intersection. A funky, earthy vibe prevails in these cheap apartments on the shore. It's technically an inn, but you have to sign a lease. Rustic rooms adorned with aquatic paintings and fishing gear. Organizes fishing and snorkeling tours for BZ$300 per boat. Homemade meals eaten in the upstairs kitchen; prices negotiable. Free bike use. Singles US$12.50; doubles US$25. Cash only. ❷

⬛ FOOD

For information on Garífuna cooking see the Food section for Dangriga (p. 98). You'll most likely have to call ahead to get some real Garífuna meals. Hopkins also specializes in seafood and Belizean standards.

King Cassava Cultural Restaurant and Bar (☎503 7305), at the main intersection. Specializes in local food and seafood dishes. *Gial* (fried chicken) BZ$10. Garífuna shrimp sauteed in red onion sauce, pepper, and garlic US$12. Appetizers US$4-5. Breakfast US$5-8. Lunch US$6-10. Dinner US$8.50-12. Open Tu-Su 8:30am-9pm. MC/V. ❸

Thongs Cafe (☎602 0110), half a mile south of the intersection. Run by a German-Russian couple, Thongs is an anomalous bit of European polish in untidy Hopkins. Decorated with carved wooden masks, the cafe boasts a small book selection. Breakfast (omelets, rice and beans, cereal) US$6.50-7.50. Lunch and dinner (pastas, fajitas, eggplant) US$6-10. Delicious muffins and cinnamon rolls US$1.50. Open W-Sa 8am-1pm and 5:30-9pm, Su 8am-1pm. MC/V. ❸

Yugadah Cafe (☎503 7089), 1 mi. south of the intersection. A standard blend of seafood, Belizean basics, Mexican snacks, and friendly service. Garífuna food by order only. Breakfast US$5-6. Lunch US$3.50-6. Dinner US$9-12.50. Also rents bikes (see **Transportation,** p. 103). Open M-Tu and Th-Su 6am-2pm and 5-10pm. Cash only. ❸

The Octopus Garden (☎503 7346), 1 mi. north of the intersection. This small, laid-back, open-air restaurant serves specials like teriyaki shrimp and curry lobster with the usual burger, burrito, and rice-beans options. Appetizers US$2-3.50. Entrees US$6-7.50. Open M-Sa 10am-9pm. Cash only. ❸

🎵 ENTERTAINMENT

Lebeha Drumming Center (☎666 6658; www.lebeha.com), 1 mi. north of the intersection, is the best place in either Dangriga or Hopkins to see real and incredible Garífuna drumming in action. Informal jam sessions are held in the evenings on weeknights (usually around 7-7:30pm); you can watch these without an official fee, though donations are requested. Call or visit ahead to make sure there'll be drumming that night. Things get a bit more serious Friday and Saturday nights, when a mixture of locals and tourists come to see more polished concerts. Lebeha's drumming lessons, offered to individuals or groups, might be the best reason for an extended stay in Hopkins.

🏃 OUTDOOR ACTIVITIES

If simple relaxation was not the reason you came to Hopkins, there is diving, snorkeling, fishing, water sports, and even some drumming close at hand.

King Cassava Restaurant and Bar (☎503 7305 or 669 5499; see **Food,** p. 104) organizes tours to Mayflower Bocawina National Park (1-5:30pm, US$30 per person, 3 person minimum) and to the Cockscomb Basin Wildlife Sanctuary (8am-1pm, US$30 per person, 3 person minimum). Snorkeling tours around the nearby cayes and reef run to US$150 for up to 3 people, US$25 for each additional stop. Open Tu-Su 8:30am-9pm. MC/V.

AN's Snorkeling Gear Rentals/Noel's Fishing and Snorkeling Trips (☎523 7219 or 669 2407), 20min. south of the main intersection. Snorkeling equipment for US$5 per day. Organizes trips to the barrier reef (9am-3pm, 2 people US$75 per person, 4 people US$50 per person), including lunch on an island beach. MC/V.

Windschief Windsurfing School and Rental (☎523 7249; www.windschief.com). The multi-purpose Windschief offers 1hr. introductory windsurfing lessons for US$30. Rent equipment for US$10 for the 1st hr., US$5 each additional hr.

PLACENCIA

Crowded around the southern tip of a long peninsula which stretches into the Caribbean just south of Dangriga, Placencia village (pop. 600) enjoys its own beauty. White beaches leading to warm, clear water, and palm trees swaying in the ocean breeze—these views have transformed Placencia into a tourist village. At times the place can resemble Florida, especially toward the northern end where middle-aged North Americans and Europeans jog beside large, stately beach homes. But beneath the flashy veneer, Placencia's roots as a fishing village still exist. There are ample opportunities to mingle with the locals who catch and trap the sea-food eaten in all the swanky restaurants. If relaxing in the village becomes a bore, offshore diving and snorkeling spots are readily available.

▌ TRANSPORTATION

Flights: Placencia's **airstrip** is located about 1 mi. north of the village along the main road. **Tropic Air** (☎226 2012; www.tropicair.com) and **Maya Island Air** (☎223 1140; www.mayaislandair.com) fly to the **Belize City Municipal Airstrip** (35min.; 7:25, 10:05am, noon, 2, 4:25 pm; US$79.50) and **Punta Gorda** (20min., every 2hr. 9:10am-3:10pm and 5:40pm, US$46.50).

Buses: Stop at station at the southern end of the street by the piers. To **Dangriga** (1½hr.; 5:45, 6:15, 7am, 12:45, 2:15pm; US$2.50). Independence buses go to **Belize City** (every hr. 6-8am, every 2hr. 10am-4pm, 5, and 5:45pm) and **Punta Gorda** (9am, every hr. 10:45am-2:45pm, 4:45, 5:45, 7:45, and 8pm).

Boats: The **Hokey Pokey Water Taxi** (☎523 2376 or 601 0271) takes passengers between **Independence and Mango Creek** on the mainland and the western edge of Placencia village (20min., 8 per day, US$5). In Independence you can pick up buses traversing the Southern Highway, heading south to **Punta Gorda** or north to **Belize City**. The bus stops in front of Sherl's Restaurant, which is just off the main road, a 10min. walk from the docks. To reach the docks from the bus stop, walk to the Main Road from Sherl's, turn right, and continue straight for 10min.

Car Rental: Placencia Office Supply (☎523 3205), on the street. US$92.50 per day.

Kayak Rentals: Paradise Tours (☎642 1655 or 564 9400; www.belize123.com), on the street. US$5 per hr., US$30 per day.

✦ ⚡ ORIENTATION AND PRACTICAL INFORMATION

Placencia Village lies at the southern tip of the **Placencia Peninsula**. Bordered by a wide **lagoon** to the west and the **Caribbean Sea** to the right, the village is only about half a mile wide at its broadest point. There are two thoroughfares: the **street** which runs the length of the peninsula and down through the west end of town, and a pedestrian **sidewalk** about 100 yd. east of it. Just east of the side-walk is the long, clean **public beach**. A series of piers extend into the sea at the village's southern tip; **Placencia Caye** lies 200 yd. off the southern coastline.

Tourist Office: Placencia Tourist Center (☎523 3294; www.placencia.com), on the street. Plenty of brochures and a helpful staff. Open M-F 9am-11:30am and 1-5pm.

Tours: For mroe details on destinations and prices, see **Outdoor Activities,** p. 108.

Nite Wind Guide Services (☎523 3487), by the piers at the southern end of the village. Trips to Monkey River, snorkeling trips to Laughing Bird Caye and Silk Caye, ½-day snorkels, whale shark snorkel (US$105), manatee watching (US$35), fishing (US$330), and fly fishing (US$385). Inland trips to Cockscomb Basin Wildlife Sanctuary, Mayflower Bocawina National Park (US$80), and select southern Mayan ruins in the south. MC/V.

Splash Dive Shop (☎523 3058 or 620 6649; www.splashbelize.com), next to Nite Wind. Snorkeling trips to Laughing Bird Caye and to the reef, diving trips (US$100-175), Monkey River tours, trips to Cockscomb Basin, and tours of Mayan ruins. Scuba instruction classes US$150-350. MC/V.

Joy Tours (☎523 3325; www.belizewithjoy.com), on the street north of the football field. Diving and offshore snorkeling trips, fishing trips (fly, trolling, bottom, and casting), inland tours to Monkey River, Cockscomb Basin, and Mayan ruins. MC/V.

D-Tourz (☎523 3397 or 600 2318), on the sidewalk by the open beach expanse. Diving and snorkeling trips. Trips to Cockscomb, Xunantunich, and Blue Hole. MC/V..

Banks: Belize Bank, at the southern end of the street by the piers. Open M-Th 8am-3pm, F 8am-4:30pm. **Scotiabank,** on the street just north of the Hokey Pokey docks. Open M-Th 8am-2pm, F 8am-3:30pm, Sa 9am-11:30am. **Atlantic Bank,** on the street at the north end of the village. Open M-Th 8am-3pm, F 8am-4pm.

Laundromat: The Boson's Chair (☎523 4063 or 622 3199), on the sidewalk near the southern piers. US$6 per load. Open M-Sa 6am-6pm, Su 6am-noon.

Police Station: On the street just north of the Hokey Pokey dock.

Pharmacy: Wallen's Pharmacy, on the street above Wallen's Market. Open M-Sa 8am-noon and 1:30-5:30pm.

Internet Access: Sea House Internet and Tours, on the sidewalk. Internet US$5 per hr. Open M-Sa 9am-noon and 2:30-7:30pm. **Placencia Office Supply** (☎523 3205), on the street. Internet US$4 per hr. Printing, copying, and faxing services. Open M-F 8:30am-7pm, Sa 8:30am-5pm.

Post Office: On the street at the north edge of the village. Open M-Th 8am-noon and 1-4:30pm, F 8am-noon and 1-4pm.

ACCOMMODATIONS AND CAMPING

There are plenty of cheap rooms for rent all over town, but most have bare, unattractive rooms that lack ocean views or breezes. With a long public beach a few minutes away, though, it hardly matters. After all, no one spends too much time indoors in Placencia. The prices in the following listings reflect summer rates; during the winter (November-April) they can go up by as much as BZ$20.

Deb & Dave's Last Resort (☎523 3207), on the street. Despite the name, you'll want to try this place first out of all the budget options in town. Communal atmosphere. Small, well-lit rooms in a house behind the owners' place. A shady, sandy yard provides a free pool for guests and relaxing space away from the tourist bustle. Deb and Dave also run tours through their Toadal Agency (www.toadaladventure.com). Singles US$19; doubles US$24.50. MC/V. ❸

Omar's Guest House (☎600 8421), on the sidewalk. It's hard to miss this well-advertised budget guesthouse. Rooms on the 2nd floor above Omar's private residence are spare and the shared bathroom at the hallway's end is cramped, but the verandah with chairs and hammock serves as a good resting spot. Dorms US$10; singles US$12.50-15; doubles US$20. Cash only. ❷

Traveller's Inn (☎523 3190). This unassuming budget inn's 2 green buildings hold a variety of cramped rooms. Don't expect breathtaking postcard views, unless sandy lots are your thing, but cheap prices make this a backpacker favorite. Singles US$12.50, with bath US$15; doubles US$15/20. Cash only. ❷

Eloise's Rooms (☎523 2399), between the sidewalk and the street. Accessible from either the street or the sidewalk, Eloise's sits in a quiet, mostly untrafficked sandy lot in the middle of the village. Both stories are fronted by shaded verandahs with hammocks. Well-kept, comfortable rooms with baths. You can check in at Eliose's house behind the inn, closer to the street side. Singles US$15; doubles US$20. Cash only. ❷

⬚ FOOD

Seafood rules in Placencia, and you can often enjoy it with a cheap, breezy ocean view. The influx of expats has created culinary diversity in the small village, so there are plenty of options other than the ubiquitous fish, shrimp, and ceviche dishes. For groceries, try **Everyday Supermarket,** on the street north of the Hokey Pokey dock (☎523 3230; open daily 7:30am-9pm).

▨ **Tuttifruti Gelateria,** on the street. Some of the best ice cream in Belize is served at this Italian dessert shop. If you stay in town long enough you may find yourself addicted to the smooth, perfectly prepared creams which come in cappuccino, lime, and colada flavors. Cones US$1.75. Cups US$2.25-3.50. Milkshakes US$3. Open M-Tu and Th-Su 9:30am-9pm. Cash only. ❶

De' Tatch Seafood Restaurant (☎503 3385), on the beach off the sidewalk. It's worth eating at De' Tatch just for its beautiful beachside setting (grab a seat under the small *palapas* for full effect). Huge menu with stuffed fry jacks for breakfast, cheap seafood platters (US$6-7.50) for lunch, and beer batter shrimp for dinner. Breakfast US$3.25-5.50. Afternoon delights US$4.50-9. Dinner US$9-16. Internet available. MC/V. ❸

Pickled Parrot (☎604 0278 or 624 2651), between the street and sidewalk (accessible from either). Under a brightly colored tent. Some of the biggest crowds in town gather here all day. Pizzas US$17-21. Subs US$6-9.50. Burgers US$6-7.50. Fajitas US$7-9.50. Huge variety of mixed drinks after dark US$6-7.50. Brave souls can down the Parrot Piss, a large blend of juice and coconut rum (US$7.50). Lunch special (US$5) noon-2pm. Happy hour 5-6pm (US$2.50 appetizers). Open M-Sa noon-10pm, Su 5-9pm. MC/V. ❸

🎵 🖼 ENTERTAINMENT AND NIGHTLIFE

A range of beachside bars keeps things loud and lively at night, especially during the winter high season when tourists and locals really get to mingling. The clientele is a mostly middle-aged crowd, so expect more bars than DJs or dance parties. This is a compact village, so the stumble home shouldn't be too long or confusing.

Tipsy Tuna Sports Bar, on the beach next to the Barefoot Beach Bar. Keeps things ocean chill with sandy floors, pool tables, and high stools. Catch some soccer or basketball on the bar's TV. Drinks US$2.50-9. Open M-W 7pm-midnight, Th-Sa 7am-2am, and Su 7pm-midnight. MC/V.

J-Byrds' Bar (☎523 2412), on the waterfront by the docks at the village's southern end. Painted marine wildlife swims on windows and a giant jaguar wades through the sea above the bar. Karaoke and dancing nights F and Sa . A pool table, free darts, and a flatscreen TV keep things interesting during the weekdays. Drinks US$2.50-7.50. Open M-Th and Su 10am-midnight, F-Sa 10am-2am. MC/V.

Barefoot Beach Bar (☎523 3515), on the beach. The name explains it all: this open-air bar is as close to the shore as they come. A collection of American license plates on the walls almost rivals the collection of American tourists chatting with the bartenders. Drinks US$2.50-8. Open Tu-Th 10am-8pm, F 11am-9pm. Cash only.

❊ FESTIVALS

Along with Caye Caulker, Placencia is the place to be to celebrate the opening of lobster season. During **Lobsterfest,** during the last weekend of June, the beach pulses to live reggae and punta, vendors hawk their wares along the shore, and fishing and lobster-catching competitions take place. Book ahead for this weekend—hotels fill up quickly.

⚡ OUTDOOR ACTIVITIES

Placencia is meant for relaxing, but a variety of tour companies offer day-trips and getaways to some of Belize's most exciting attractions, off-shore and inland. Unfortunately, prices for these trips range from dismaying to shocking. Skip the guided tours of Cockscomb Basin Wildlife Sanctuary (BZ$150-170) and nearby Mayan ruins (BZ$180-230), all of which can be visited privately. If you are going to trek from the village, head for the offshore sites, most of them inaccessible from the northern cayes and appealing to hardcore divers and snorkelers.

NEARBY CAYES. The nearest sizable island is **Laughing Bird Caye,** 12 mi. off the coast, which is at the center of its own national park but lies between the shore and the reef The **Silk Cayes Marine Reserve,** on the reef an hour boat ride from the village, features abundant tropical fish and coral species, making it a popular spot for both divers and snorkelers. Just south of the Silk Cayes, **Ranguana** and **Pompian Cayes** are similar underwater attractions; they can be visited as part of a trip to the Silk Cayes or independently. *(4hr. snorkeling trips BZ$90-100 per person, 6hr. BZ$120-130 per person; 6-7 hr. fishing trips BZ$140-160 per person).*

FISHING. If you've got interest and money to spare, the seas near Placencia are much less crowded than the areas near the northern cayes. *(½-day fishing trips to the reef BZ$450-500, full-day BZ$600-650.)*

MONKEY RIVER. The Creole fishing village of Monkey River lies about 15 mi. southwest of Placencia on the coast; after (or before) a lunch stop here, trips continue 4 mi. upriver in search of howler monkeys, crocs, and birds. The trip there may include some manatee watching among nearby mangrove estuaries. *(6-7hr., BZ$110-140 per person).*

PUNTA GORDA

Belize's southernmost town (pop. 5100) lies well off the beaten track; for many it's simply a convenient crossing point to Guatemala after a stay in Placencia. But PG, as it's known here, is more than a transit hub. Though it was founded by Garinagu from Honduras in the early nineteenth century, the community has since opened up to a variety of cultures. Today, Garífuna, Creoles, Maya, East Indians, Chinese, and American expats mingle on the humid coastal streets. The town itself will probably get old after a few days, but the surrounding Toledo District is among the most beautiful in Belize, and PG serves as an ideal base for exploring.

▐ TRANSPORTATION

Flights: Punta Gorda's **airstrip** is located about a ½-mile north of town along Prince, Queen, and King St. **Tropic Air** (☎226 2012; www.tropicair.com) and **Maya Island Air** (☎223 1140; www.mayaislandair.com) fly to **Placencia** (20min., BZ$84), **Dangriga** (40min., BZ$137), **Belize City Municipal Airstrip** (1hr., BZ$185), and the

Philip Goldson International Airport in Belize City (1hr. 10min.; 7, 9:40, 11:35am, 1:35, and 4pm; BZ$218).

Buses: Punta Gorda is the home base of the **James Bus Line,** King St. (☎702 2049), which services most of southern Belize. Buses stop right in front of the offices; you can buy tickets inside or on the bus. Buses to: **Belize City** (6¼hr., BZ$23); **Belmopan** (5¼hr., BZ$20); **Dangriga** (3½hr., BZ$14); **Independence** (2hr., BZ$9) at 4, 5, 6, 8, 10am, noon, 2, 3, and 4pm. **Local buses** to Mayan villages in the Toledo district leave from Jose Maria Nunez St. between Prince, Queen, and King St. Buses for **San Antonio** (1hr., BZ$3), **Jalacte** (2hr., BZ$5), and all other villages along the route leave M-Sa between 6-7am, 11am-noon, and 4-5pm; check with the drivers for the exact time. Buses for **Silver Creek** (1hr., BZ$3) and **Indian Creek** (1½hr., BZ$5) leave between 11am-noon and 4-5pm.

Boats: Punta Gorda is a popular transportation hub for coastal towns in Guatemala. The **customs office,** Front St., answers questions about tickets and other procedures.

Marisol Boat Charters (☎702 0113). Leaves Punta Gorda daily at 4pm and arrives in Puerto Barrios at 5pm (BZ$44). Buy tickets at the **Dreamlight Computer Center** (p. 110).

Memo's Boat Service (☎625 0464 or 722 2622). Leaves Punta Gorda daily at 12:30pm and arrives in Livingston at 1:30pm (BZ$40) and in Puerto Barrios at 2pm (BZ$50).

Pichilingo (☎722 2870). Leaves Punta Gorda daily at 2pm and arrives in Puerto Barrios at 3pm (BZ$50).

Requena's Charter Services, Front. St. (☎722 2070 or 662 0042). Leaves Punta Gorda daily at 9am and arrives in Puerto Barrios at 10:30am (BZ$40).

Rigoberto James. Leaves Punta Gorda Tu and F at 10am and arrives in Livingston at 11am (BZ$40).

Kayak Rentals: Tide Tours, 41 Front St. (☎722 2129; www.tidetours.com). BZ$5 per hr., BZ$15 per ½-day, BZ$25 per day. Open M-F 8am-noon and 2-5pm, Sa 8am-noon.

✷ 🛈 ORIENTATION AND PRACTICAL INFORMATION

Punta Gorda is spread out on the shore next to the **Gulf of Honduras;** like many other coastal towns in Belize, it is longer than it is wide. Organized in a grid system, the town extends inland for about five blocks before meeting the local airstrip. **Front Street** hugs the shore while **Main, Jose Maria Nunez, West,** and **Far West Streets** march successively inland. From South to North, they are intersected by

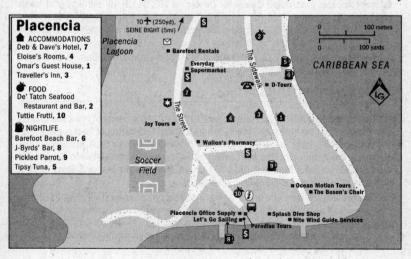

Placencia

🏠 ACCOMMODATIONS
Deb & Dave's Hotel, **7**
Eloise's Rooms, **4**
Omar's Guest House, **1**
Traveller's Inn, **3**

🍴 FOOD
De' Tatch Seafood
Restaurant and Bar, **2**
Tuttie Frutti, **10**

🍸 NIGHTLIFE
Barefoot Beach Bar, **6**
J-Byrds' Bar, **8**
Pickled Parrot, **9**
Tipsy Tuna, **5**

TO ✈ (250yd),
SEINE BIGHT (5mi)

Placencia
Lagoon

Barefoot Rentals

Everyday
Supermarket

D-Tourz

CARIBBEAN SEA

Joy Tours

Wallen's Pharmacy

Soccer
Field

Ocean Motion Tours
The Boson's Chair

Placencia Office Supply
Let's Go Sailing
Paradise Tours
Splash Dive Shop
Nite Wind Guide Services

0   100 meters
0   100 yards

Clements, Prince, Queen, King, and **North Streets.** The **town park,** distinguished by its large, sky-blue **clock tower,** serves as the locus of market activity along Main St. between Prince and Queen St.

Tourist Office: BTIA Tourist Info, Front St. (☎722 2531), in the white hexagonal building. Has information on sights in the Toledo district; the **Toledo Ecotourism Association Program** has a stand here. Open Tu-F 8am-noon and 1-5pm, Sa 8am-noon.

Tours: Tide Tours, 41 Front St. (☎722 2129; www.tidetours.com). Offers a wide array of tours in southern Belize. Kayaking trips down Joe Taylor's Creek (3hrs., BZ$40 per person). Half-day trips to Rio Blanco park and Blue Creek Cave (BZ$140-170). Full-day trips to Barranco and the Sastoon-Temash National Park, Laguna and the Agua-Caliente Wildlife Sanctuary, and Nim Li Punit and Lubaantun (BZ$170). Proceeds go to development programs in the region. Open M-F 8am-noon and 2-5pm, Sa 8am-noon. **Toledo Travel Center** (☎614 2080 or 668 8811; www.suncreeklodge.com), on the corner of Front and Queen St. Leads trips in the Toledo District. Destinations include the Mayan ruins at Lubaantun and Uxbenka and the villages of Blue Creek and Laguna. Also leads multi-day hiking trips into the Maya Mountains, including a trek up Doyle's Delight, the highest point in Belize.

Banks: Belize Bank, on the corner of Main and Queen St. Open M-Th 8am-3pm, F 8am-4:30pm. **Scotiabank,** down Main St. just south of the park. Open M-Th 8am-2pm, F 8am-3:30pm, Sa 9-11:30am.

Luggage Storage: Toledo Travel Center (☎614 2080; www.suncreeklodge.com), on the corner of Front and Queen St. BZ$2 per day.

Laundromat: P.G. Laundry, Main St. BZ$1.75 per lb. Open M-Sa 8am-5pm.

Police Station: On the corner of Front and King St.

24hr. Pharmacy: Rosalma's Pharmacy, Main St. (☎722 2444). Open M-Sa 9am-noon and 2-5pm.

Hospital or Medical Services: Punta Gorda Hospital, Main St. (☎722 2026), 20min. west of town.

Internet Access: Dreamlight Computer Center (☎702 0113), on the corner of North and Main St. Internet BZ$6 per hr. Wi-Fi. Open M-Sa 8am-9pm, Su 9am-5pm. **Tide Tours,** 41 Front St. (☎722 2129; www.tidetours.com). Internet BZ$4 per hr. Wi-Fi. Open M-F 8am-noon and 2-5pm, Sa 8am-noon. .

Post Office: Front St. (☎722 2087). Open M-Th 8am-noon and 1-5pm, F 8am-noon and 1-4:30pm.

ACCOMMODATIONS

Nature's Way Guest House, 82 Front St. (☎702 2119), at the corner of Front and Church St. Peaceful and secluded, this family-run joint is the first choice of backpackers. Sizable rooms with huge windows. Common room with TV. Small book exchange. Chet Schmidt, the owner, provides information about the area and the Toledo Ecotourism Association program. Breakfast BZ$5-8. Internet access BZ$9 per hr. Singles BZ$26; doubles BZ$36; triples BZ$46. Cash only. ❷

St. Charles Inn, 23 King St. (☎722 2149; www.toucantrail.com/st.-charles-inn.html). Make yourself at home in this long-standing mid-range favorite. Rooms run the gamut from homey and well-decorated to rustic and cramped. All rooms come with cable TV. Shaded 2nd-floor veranda with hammock space. Singles BZ$40; doubles BZ$50; with A/C BZ$65. Cash only. ❷

FOOD

Front St. and the town park are filled with vendors from Toledo villages selling produce on Monday, Wednesday, Friday, and Saturday mornings. This market is the cheapest and best way to sample local food and grab some fresh fruit. For groceries, head to Main St., where you'll find **Mel's Enterprise** (open M and W 8am-12:30pm and 2-8:30pm, Tu and Th 8am-12:30pm and 2-6pm, and F-Sa 8am-12:30pm and 2-9pm), **SuPaul's Supermarket** (open M-Sa 8am-6:30pm), and **Li Quan Supermarket** (☎722 0097; open 7am-9pm).

Earth Runnins Cafe and Bukut Bar, 13 Main Middle St. Rasta rhythm rules at Earth Runnins, easily the most distinctive restaurant in Punta Gorda. More of an experience than a mere eatery. Don't be surprised if the staff starts up a live reggae jam between taking orders and preparing meals. The menu is an amalgam of seafood, pasta, and Belizean dishes, all of them personally prepared by a dynamic chef (he's usually on vocals). Waits can be long, but they're worth it—just don't come if you're looking for a relaxing night out. Entrees BZ$12-25. Drinks BZ$4-10. Open daily M and W-Sa 9am-2pm and 5-11pm. ❸

Marian's Bayview Restaurant, Front St. (☎722 0129), across from Nature's Way Guest House. The ocean views from the high open-air deck are spectacular; the menu, with its blend of Belizean, East Indian, and vegetarian food, isn't bad either. All ingredients are organic and prepared in homemade soybean or coconut oil. Entrees from BZ$10. Open M-W and F-Sa 11am-2pm and 6-10pm, Th 11am-2pm, Su noon-2pm and 7-9pm. AmEx/MC/V. ❷

Grace's Restaurant (☎702 2414), on the corner of Main and King St. Seafood and Belizean food prepared grilled, fried, and stewed. Entrees BZ$7-12. Seafood BZ$9-34. Open daily 8am-10pm. MC/V. ❷

NIGHTLIFE

Front St. is the heart of nightlife in PG. Offerings range from dingy holes-in-the-wall overlooking the street, to breezy open-air spots with views of the sea.

Reef Bar and Restaurant, Front St. The Reef is a place to relax. The bar's hammocks are the best place to do it. Whether you're reclining or not, you can enjoy the breeze and views from this prime upper-floor, open-air location. Reggae and punta provide an undulating soundtrack. Drinks BZ$4-15. Open daily 11am-midnight. Cash only.

SOUTHERN BELIZE

GUATEMALA

Guatemala contains both Central America's most diverse landscape and the most clear class division in the region. Crisp mountain peaks, towering volcanic ridges, thick rainforest, and mellow Caribbean ports all coexist within Guatemala's borders. While possessing the strongest modern Maya presence in Central America (around 46% of the population), Guatemala is also highly urbanized, with over 40% of the population living in cities. Nevertheless, a two hour bus ride from the frenzy of Guatemala City transports you to the rolling western highlands where Maya women in colorful traditional garb weave *huipiles* on the volcanic shores of Lake Atitlán. In many highland villages, travelers will find that Spanish can take them only so far—each of Guatemala's 23 Maya populations has its own language. Take it from the swarms of returning travelers: Guatemala is *the* place for culturally adventurous travel in Latin America.

ESSENTIALS

PLANNING YOUR TRIP

ENTRANCE REQUIREMENTS
Passport (p. 5). Required for all visitors.
Visa (p. 6). Not required for citizens of the US, UK, Australia, Canada, Ireland, and New Zealand for stays of up to 90 days. Extension of the 90-day period can be granted upon application by the **Guatemalan Immigration Office** (☎502 2411 2411)
Recommended Vaccinations (p. 13). Hepatitis A, Hepatitis B, Typhoid, and Rabies.
Required Vaccinations. None required.
Inoculations (p. 13). Travelers who have been to nations with endemic yellow fever must present proof of vaccination.
Other Health Concerns: Malaria pills are recommended for those traveling to areas at high risk for malaria. If your regular medical insurance policy (p. 14) does not cover travel abroad, you may wish to purchase additional coverage.
Work Permit. Required for all foreigners planning to work in Guatemala.
Departure Tax. US$30.

EMBASSIES AND CONSULATES

GUATEMALAN CONSULAR SERVICES ABROAD

Australia: 41 Blarney Av., Killarney Heights NSW 2087, (☎02 9451 3018).

Canada: 130 Albert St., Ottawa, Ontario K1P 5G4 (☎613-233-7188).

UK: 13 Fawcett St., London, SW10 (☎44 20 7351 3042).

US: 2220 R Street NW, Washington, DC 20008 (☎202-745-4953). **Consulates:** 1605 W. Olympic Bl., Suite 422, Los Angeles, CA 900105 (☎213-365-9251); 300 Sevilla Av., Suite 210, Coral Gables, FL 33134 (☎305-443-4828); 200 N. Michigan Av., Suite 610, Chicago, IL 60601 (☎312-332-1587); 57 Park Av., New York, NY 10016 (☎212-686-3837); 3600 S. Gessner Rd., Suite 200, Houston, TX 77063 (☎713-953-9531).

CONSULAR SERVICES IN GUATEMALA

Canada: 13 C. 8-44 Zone 10, Edificio Edyma Plaza (☎50 223 634 348; fax 50 223 651 216; www.guatemala.gc.ca).

UK: Edificio Torre Internacional, Nivel 11, 16 C. 0-55, Zona 10, Guatemala City (☎44 502 2380 7300).

US: Av. de la Reforma 7-01, Zona 10, Guatemala City (50 223 264 000; fax 50 223 348 477; http://usembassy.state.gov).

TOURIST OFFICES

Guatemala Tourist Institute (INGUAT): 17A. Av. 1-17, Zona 4, Apartado Postal 1020-A, Guatemala (☎50 224 212 810). 24hr. line for security information and advice. Service avaliable in English.

MONEY

CURRENCY AND EXCHANGE

The currency chart below was accurate as of August 2009. Check the currency converter on websites like www.xe.com or www.bloomberg.com for the latest exchange rates.

QUEZTAL (Q)		
AUS$1 = Q6.49		1Q = AUS$0.15
CDN$1 = Q7.44		1Q = CDN$0.13
EUR€1 = Q11.5		1Q = EUR€0.09
NZ$1 = Q5.19		1Q = NZ$0.19
UK£1 = Q13.1		1Q = UK£0.08
US$1 = Q8.11		1Q = US$0.12

The Guatemalan currency is the **queztal** (Q). The US dollar is the only foreign currency freely exchangeable in Guatemala. Exchanging dollars for quetzals is straightforward enough at most banks, although making purchases with wads of Q100 can be difficult at small *tiendas*. Although **ATMs** are located in most locales, it is easy to find yourself in a town with no ATM and no place to change money. **Visa** and **Mastercard** are the most frequently accepted credit cards; **American Express** cards work at some ATMs and at AmEx offices and major airports. Some banks give cash advances on Visa cards and, less frequently, on MasterCard. **Traveler's checks** are not widely accepted in Guatemala.

COSTS

Guatemala makes budget travel look easy. A bare bones day will set you back US$15-20 without any substantial sacrifices. Add in hot water, a private bathroom, admission fees, and a few drinks, and you can expect to spend around US$60 per day.

PRICE DIVERSITY

Our Researchers list establishments in order of value from best to worst, honoring our favorites with the Let's Go thumbs-up (🔳). Because the best *value* is not always the cheapest *price*, we have incorporated a system of price ranges based on a rough expectation of what you will spend. For **accommodations**, we base our range on the cheapest price for which a single traveler can stay for one night. For **restaurants**, we estimate the average amount one traveler will spend in one sitting. The table below tells you what you'll *typically* find in Panama at the corresponding price range, but keep in mind that no system can allow for the quirks of individual establishments.

ACCOMMODATIONS	RANGE	WHAT YOU'RE *LIKELY* TO FIND
❶	Under Q41 Under US$5	Campgrounds and dorm rooms. Expect bunk beds and a communal bath. You may have to provide or rent towels and sheets. Found in most Guatemalan cities, with the possible exception of the capital.
❷	Q41-82 US$5-10	Upper-end hostels or lower-end hotels, sometimes with private bath. Most budget accommodations in Guatemala fall into this price range, and they're usually a good value.
❸	Q90-123 US$11-15	In Guatemala City, this will get you a comfortable dorm-style room. Anywhere else, you'll be in a hotel with small room and private bath. Decent amenities, like phone and TV. Breakfast is most likely included.
❹	Q131-148 US$16-18	Bigger rooms than a ❸, with more amenities or in a more convenient location. Breakfast probably included.
❺	Over Q18 Over US$18	Large hotels, upscale chains or intimate bed and breakfasts. If it's a ❺ and it doesn't have the perks you want, you've paid too much. You'll only find this price range in places like Guatemala City, Antigua, Reu, and Xela.

FOOD	RANGE	WHAT YOU'RE *LIKELY* TO FIND
❶	Under Q16 Under US$2	Probably street food or a low-end *comedor*-style restaurant. With food in this price range, you'll probably be eating on-the-go, and wish you would have remembered to pack Tums®.
❷	Q16-32 US$2-4	Sandwiches, pizza, appetizers at a bar, or low-priced entrees at a nicer *comedor*. Most Guatemalan eateries are a ❷. Either takeout or a sit-down meal, but only slightly more fashionable décor than a ❶.
❸	Q41-57 US$ 5-7	Some lower-end international restaurants. Fast-food restaurants in larger Guatemalan cities.
❹	Q65-82 US$8-10	A somewhat fancy restaurant. Entrees tend to be heartier or more elaborate, but you're really paying for decor and ambience. Few restaurants in this range have a dress code, but some may look down on T-shirts and sandals.
❺	Over Q82 Over US$10	Your meal might cost more than your room, but there's a reason—it's something fabulous, famous, or both. Offers foreign-sounding food and a decent wine list.

SAFETY AND HEALTH

Guatemala has one of the **highest violent crime rates** in Latin America—in 2008, an average of 40 murders per week were reported in Guatemala City alone. Tourists are directly targeted. Armed attacks are increasingly common in and around

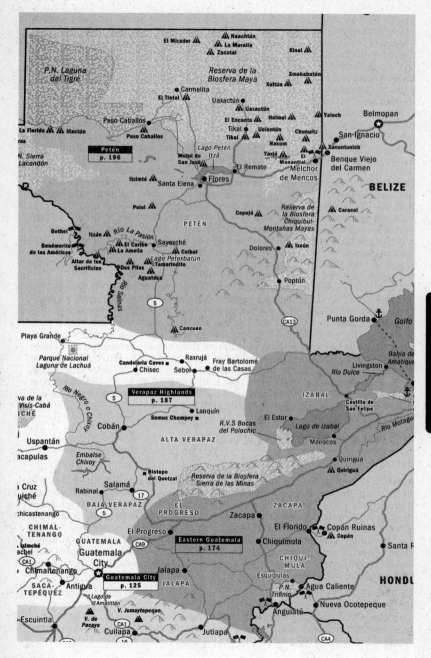

places such as Antigua, Tikal, Peten, and Lake Atitlan. Local officials, already overwhelmed and underpaid, are unable to manage the mounting problem.

Assault, theft, armed robbery, carjacking, rape, kidnapping, and murder are the most common violent crimes against tourists. **Gangs**, well-armed and eager to employ force, are increasingly prevalent in Guatemala City and rural areas. **Violent robberies** are also commonplace, and **pick-pocketing** and **petty theft** are rampant. Guatemala City is a hotspot of criminal activity, especially in the central market area. Travelers are urged to refrain from staying in or near this region. **Attacks on vehicles**, often when stopped at traffic lights, are frequent. In a common scenario, tourists are blockaded by an armed gang as their car leaves the airport; the assailants summarily proceed to slash the car's tires and steal any passports, cash, and luggage they can find. **Public and "chicken" buses**, in addition to being poorly maintained, are routinely attacked by armed robbers; private intra-city coach services are a much safer, and highly advisable, alternative. **Express kidnappings** at ATM machines, shopping centers, and around the airport area are on the rise as well. For short trips, your safest bet is to take official **taxis**. Do not hail cabs on the street or traveling in bootleg vehicles.

Do not approach or take photographs of Guatemalan children without express permission from their guardians, particularly in more remote regions such as the Quiche, Peten, San Marcos, and Chiqmula provinces. Due to widespread fear of child kidnapping and organ harvesting, tourists who have failed to take this precaution have been met with violent reactions, including attempted and actual lynchings by local mobs.

Guatemala's **Tourist Institute (INGUAT)** staffs regional offices in tourist hotspots nationwide and offers security escorts for tourist groups through its **Assistance Office (ASISTUR)**. With the purchase of an ASISTUR card policy (1 day, 15 days, 30 days, or 1 year; US$1 per day), visitors can access 24hr. telephone assistance for medical and legal issues, as well as obtain security escorts, roadside assistance, helicopter evacuation from remote areas, and assistance in the event of a robbery. Cards can be purchased at the INGUAT kiosks at the Guatemala City, Flores and Tikal airports. ASISTUR can be reached from within Guatemala by dialing ☎1500. Call toll-free at ☎888-464-8281 from within the US. INGUAT also provides a 24hr. security hotline (☎502 24 212 810 or ☎502 55 789 836; fax 502 24 212 891).

BORDER CROSSINGS

BELIZE. See p. 46.

MEXICO. There are three land crossings between Guatemala and Mexico. In the Guatemalan highlands, **La Mesilla**, 90km west of Huehuetenango, has buses to San Cristóbal de las Casas, Mexico. There is bus service from **Huehue, Guatemala City,** and other towns to **La Mesilla. El Carmen,** Guatemala is west of Quetzaltenango and Retalhuleu, near Tapachula, Mexico. On the Pacific Coast, **Ciudad Tecun Umán,** Guatemala is 75km west of Retalhuleu. Buses head to this border crossing from Quetzaltenango, Retalhuleu, and Tapachula, Mexico. There are several land and river crossings from **Flores,** Guatemala toward **Palenque,** Mexico.

EL SALVADOR. There are three land crossings between El Salvador and Guatemala. **Valle Nuevo/Las Chinamas** (Highway 8) serves from Area 1 in Zone 4 of Guatemala City (p. 173). **San Cristóbal** (Interamericana Highway, or Highway 1) has buses from Guatemala City and **Santa Ana,** El Salvador. Buses also run to **Angiatú,** Guatemala (Highway 10) from Esquipulas and **Metapán,** El Salvador.

HONDURAS. There are three land crossings between Honduras and Guatemala. **El Florido** is along a dirt road between **Chiquimula,** Guatemala and **Copán Ruinas,** Honduras. Buses run on the Guatemalan side (p. 174), and pickups run on the Honduran side. **Agua Caliente** is 10km east of Esquipulas, Guatemala near Nueva Ocotepeque, Honduras (p. 243). **Corinto,** near Puerto Barrios, Guatemala, has connections to **Omoa,** Honduras (p. 263).

LIFE AND TIMES

HISTORY

MAYA HAVE YOUR ATTENTION? (DAWN OF TIME-AD 1523). The first settlers of Guatemala were the ancestors of the great **Mayan civilization** that dominated the land until the Spanish arrived in the 16th century. The classic Mayan period lasted from AD 250-900, during which time the early villages became a mosaic of individual city-states, all constantly at war with one another. Each city-state built monumental stone temples, such as those at **Tikal** (p. 207) and **Uaxactun** (p. 205), to demonstrate power and to record victories through exquisite hieroglyphics. By the tenth century AD, the great Mayan cities had collapsed; remnants of the civilization continued to flourish until the Spanish conquest, but the days of giant stone temples were gone for good.

FROM CONQUEST TO UN-CONQUEST (AD 1523-1821). In 1523, Spanish conquistador **Pedro de Alvarado** headed to Guatemala with 120 cavalrymen, 300 foot-soldiers, four cannons, and several hundred native auxiliaries, leading a cruel and bloodthirsty campaign to conquer the highlands. By 1527, the Spanish controlled enough of the region for Alvarado to be declared Governor of Guatemala. Still, it took another 170 years before the invaders destroyed the last Mayan stronghold in Guatemala—the island city of Tayasal in the Petén region. On the whole, the Spanish found Guatemala disappointing as it lacked the rich gold and silver deposits they yearned for. Nevertheless, the Spanish held on to the entire region between California and Costa Rica until the Mexican War of Independence.

INDEPENDENTE (1821-71). On September 15, 1821, Guatemala announced its official independence from Spain, and the country's incorporation into the new Mexican Empire. Two years later, Guatemala gave up on Mexico and joined the short-lived United Provinces of Central America, which collapsed during the civil war in 1838. Guatemala's independence from the Mexican Empire was engineered in part by **Rafael Carrera.** This savvy swineherd who turned politico became Guatemala's first conservative president in 1844. Backed by large landowners and the Catholic Church, Carrera declared himself president for life in 1854. Under his rule, Guatemala recognized the boundaries of British-controlled Belize in exchange for the promise of a road connecting the two countries. The road was never built, and Guatemala and Belize continue to argue about the logistics of their border. Unlike most Central American strongmen, Carrera managed to pull off his presidency-for-life, staying in control until he died peacefully in 1865.

ILLIBERAL LIBERALS (1871-1944). Starting as a revolt in western Guatemala, the Liberal Revolution of 1871 brought **Justo Rufino Barrios** to power, where he quickly became known as "the Reformer" for his rapid program of social and economic change. After establishing freedom of religion and press, Barrios oversaw the ratification of Guatemala's first constitution, maintaining dictatorial power. He also pushed for economic modernization by promoting the coffee industry and by promoting the construction of roads, railroads, and telephone lines. In 1898, **Manuel Estrada Cabrera** continued Barrios's policies of economic modernization and dictatorial rule. He made major land deals with the American-owned United Fruit Company and later even hired them to run the postal service. Bizarrely, he also attempted to promote the worship of Minerva, the Roman goddess of wisdom, through the construction of several Greco-Roman temples within the country. **Jorge Ubico,** the last of Guatemala's dictatorial liberals, also bolstered the country's infrastructure and economic ties with the United States. Ubico earned the nickname "Little Napoleon of the Tropics" for his peculiar fondness for the French emperor. Ubico even dressed his troops in an 18th-century French style of uniform, lending credence to **Tomás Borge Martínez's** description of him as "crazier than a half-dozen opium-smoking frogs." Ubico was finally ousted by a general strike in 1944, known as the **October Revolution.**

TEN YEARS OF SPRING (1945-54). The democratic election of **Juan José Arévalo** in 1944 ushered in the **Ten Years of Spring,** a new era of spiritual socialism. Drawing much of his support from organized labor, Arévalo enacted a new labor code, established a social security system, and worked towards agrarian reform. Arévalo's successor, **Jacobo Arbenz,** pursued the same radical program and even legalized the communist Guatemalan Labor Party in 1952. Most importantly, Arbenz finally carried out agrarian reform by expropriating and redistributing uncultivated lands that had been owned by the United Fruit Company and other wealthy elites. Unfortunately for Guatemala, United Fruit had powerful allies in Washington, and the United States government quickly retaliated. In 1954, a CIA-trained army invaded, deposing Arbenz's government and establishing a military junta under **Carlos Castilla Armas.**

OPPRESSION AND CIVIL WAR (1954-96). Military rule after the 1954 coup reversed the social reforms of the last decade and violently crushed any political opposition. These oppressive tactics aroused increasingly violent resistance, and many Guatemalans joined guerrilla groups demanding land reform and democracy. The 1960s saw a series of rigged elections and puppet presidents controlled by the US military. Meanwhile, right-wing paramilitary groups like the **White Hand** and the **Secret Anti-Communist Army (ESA)** attacked students, professionals, and the lower classes suspected of leftist activity. The period from the late 1970s to the early 1980s became known as *La Violencia*, as conflict spread throughout Guatemala. General **Efraín Ríos Montt** led the military's scorched-earth campaign from 1982-1983. Soon the violence turned genocidal when the general began targeting the indigenous Maya of Guatemala, destroying hundreds of Mayan villages, and torturing and killing over 10,000 indigenous inhabitants. After Ríos Montt was deposed, the conflict receded enough to allow peace negotiations brokered by the United Nations. Finally, in 1996, **Alvaro Arzú Irigoyen** won the presidency and signed peace accords with the guerillas in the same year.

TODAY

Guatemala has experienced rapid economic growth over the past few decades, consolidated by the country's ratification of the **Dominican Republic–Central America Free Trade Agreement (DR-CAFTA)** in 2006, which took effect in 2009 and formally opened the entire region to trade with the United States. This new, open movement of goods between north and south may reach levels achieved by the vast exodus of Guatemalans themselves: between 500,000 and 1 million Guatemalans have emigrated to the United States since the 1970s, mostly due to a mixture of civil war troubles and lackluster economic opportunities. While unemployment is low, about one-third of Guatemalans live below the poverty line, and the country remains among the 10 poorest of all Latin America. However, growth over the past decades, especially in the export sector, has been robust. General well-being has tentatively improved, with infant and general mortalities as well as inflation all decreasing.

Tourism, one of the nation's largest economic sectors, has grown with the country's stability. The traditional ebb and flow of travelers is now augmented by business tourism and large events such as the International Olympic Committee's 119th assembly held in Guatemala City. American visitors comprise the largest share of this tourism. The communities that survived the brutalities of the civil war have proved resilient in the face of commercialization.

Guatemala's salient illegal drug issue feeds into the larger problem of rampant crime. While rarely affecting foreigners, crime was the focus of the 2007 presidential elections for good reason: kidnappings are unsettlingly common and the murder rate reached 45 per 100,000 in 2007, a level higher even than the one experienced during the civil war that ended in 1996. Apart from crime, natural disasters, such as the 2005 landslides, the result of the frequent hurricanes that strike Guatemala from June to November, have also plagued the country.

Guatemala's foreign relations are much less rocky than they were in the 1950s, when the acting president challenged the Mexican head of state to a duel to settle a dispute over fishing boundaries. Boundary disputes, rooted in the conflicts over Spanish and British colonial frontiers, remain a feature of Belize-Guatemala. Yet by 1991, Guatemala recognized Belize and established formal, diplomatic ties. Eight years later, however, the Guatemalan Foreign Ministry changed course. In 1999, Guatemala proposed that Belize cede half of its territory, but was met with a peaceful refusal. Guatemala has smoother relations with its other neighbors. In a foreign relations oddity characteristic of several Central American nations, Guatemala recognizes the Republic of China as legitimate rather than the People's Republic. Guatemala is the seat of **PARLACEN**, the Central American Parliament, one of the institutions of the **Central American Integration System** and the last in a long line of attempts to integrate the countries of the region in economic and political matters.

ECONOMY AND GOVERNMENT

Guatemala's economy, the largest in Central America, principally depends on subsistence agriculture with a primary focus on corn and squash. Guatemala's agriculture also consists of large-scale commercial farming on the Pacific slopes, where coffee, bananas, and sugar have been produced for mass export since the turn of the 20th century, replacing cocoa and dyes. The U.S. remains the principal export destination for Guatemalan goods, with neighboring countries such as Nicaragua coming in at a distant second. The Guatemalan economy witnessed slow growth of its industrial sector in the post-war era, but Latin America's **Lost Decade** (the misery-fraught 1980s) hit Guatemala as hard as any—GDP plummeted and inflation boomed. Since the 1990s and the decline of civil war violence, Guatemala has enjoyed marked economic growth, though poverty remains deeply entrenched in Guatemalan society and socioeconomic mobility is rare. Inflation has fallen from its previous heights, but corn prices have risen due to the global rise in food prices, a trend that threatens the well-being of a large segment of the population.

Guatemala has had a civilian government since 1985, though the early years of its democracy were marked by *autogolpe* (self-coup), intimidation, and corruption. Since the peace accords ended the 36-year civil war, power transitions have been stable and clean, and the legislative and judicial bodies have functioned coherently. The constitution provides for **22 departamentos**, each headed by a governor. Popular vote determines the election of presidents who serve four year terms, while a mix of department-based constituency elections choose the main legislative body, the **Congress of Deputies.** The current president, **Álvaro Colom,** of the social-democratic **National Unity of Hope (UNE),** the largest party in the Congress, was elected in 2007. Other parties on the ever-changing Guatemalan political scene include the right-wing **Grand National Alliance (GANA)** and **Patriotic Party (PP)** and the **Guatemalan Republican Front (FRG)** of the 1930s-era Guatemalan dictator **Efraín Montt.**

PEOPLE

DEMOGRAPHICS

The composition of Guatemala's population is similar to those of many countries of Central America. A broad **Mestizo** population of mixed Spanish and indigenous descent forms a middle band, in Guatemala only about a fifth of the population. The vast majority of Guatemala, about 60% of the population, is of indigenous origin; in this case, some nation of the **Maya.** The largest of these are the **K'iche, Kaqchikel, Mam, and Q'eqchi** tribes. The K'iche are concentrated in the province of El Quiche, the Mam in western Guatemala, the Kaqchikel in the regions around Lake Atitlan and the Midwestern highlands, and the Q'eqchi in the Petén and more broadly across Guatemala. A small community of **Creole Guatemalans** of entirely Spanish descent makes up 5% of the population, mostly concentrated in the cities. The **Garífuna** people, a mixed ethnic group of Arawak, Carib, and African descent, have lived on the east coast of Guatemala for centuries.

LANGUAGE

The primary and official language of Guatemala is **Spanish,** spoken in the Central American style, which, much like Argentine and Uruguayan Spanish, makes use of the "vos" second person singular. However, this informality is safer to avoid for the traveler, who should stick with polite forms of address. Guatemala is also a country with an extraordinarily resilient Mayan culture; Spanish is spoken by 93% of the population, but a significant portion of that usage is as a second language. A full 23 languages, including most Maya tongues as well as Xinca and Garífuna, are recognized in the slightly lower category of National Languages that are entitled to some bilingual education and other cultural rights. The Peace Accords of 1996, which ended the epic civil war, included provision of voting materials and government proceedings in indigenous languages as an important part of the attempt to form a political order more inclusive of the Maya population.

RELIGION

In Guatemala, as in most of Latin America, the principal, and once official, religion is **Roman Catholicism,** and is evident in the omnipresent churches, missions, and cathedrals of the colonial era. About 60% of *guatemaltecos* are affiliated with Rome, under the two Archdioceses of Guatemala City and Los Altos Quetzaltenango-Totonicapán. Coexisting with the Church as it has for centuries is traditional **Mayan religion,** practiced by about 1% of the population, in part in the form of syncretism and in part as a surviving worship of the old Mayan gods, veneration of sacred places, and traditional practice of divination. Unlike its neighbors, however, Guatemala also has a very strong **Protestant** presence due to forceful evangelism, mostly from the United States, over the 20th century and the massive upheavals of the civil war. Mass conversion to various evangelical churches has resulted in about 40% of the population belonging to some sect, including, prominently, the Pentecostals. The Church of Latter-day Saints has a significant presence among the population as well. Tiny communities of Jews, Muslims, Buddhists, and the non-religious also exist in the country.

CULTURE

THE ARTS

On the topic of the arts, a traveler's thoughts tend to flit to the **Maya,** whether of the crafts and artisan's works that decorate the country, or the ancient reliefs, murals, and architecture of the Mayan past. Slightly more recent in pedigree, the **colonial period** left its imprint in the churches and religious infrastructure of Guatemala. Modern artistic endeavors have a small but important role in Guatemala's history. One of the best-known painters of Guatemala is **Carlos Mérida,** a mural painter who was born in 1891 and is often compared to Diego Rivera; another classical artist of Guatemala was **Alfred Jensen,** a painter and printmaker of Danish and German descent. In recent years, modern art in Guatemala has been carried forward by avant-garde performance artists, including **Regina José Galindo,** who work on an international scene.

LITERATURE

The most ancient Guatemalan literature is the mostly vanished corpus of **Mayan writing,** referenced in their artifacts and exemplified by the **Popul Vuh,** one of the main religious texts, and the traditional play, the **Rabinal Achi.** It was not until centuries after the Spanish conquest that another major literary tradition came about. These first stirrings included the poet and historian Francisco Antonio de Fuentes y Guzmán, who chronicled the recent conquest, and, later, the poet Rafael Landívar.

Early Guatemalan authors and intellectuals quickly became partisans of independence and **romantic nationalism;** many Guatemalan figures from the period of independence, the broad era comprising the end of the 18th century and the beginning of the 19th, traveled around Latin America and were significant figures in creating the new independent identity of the continent. **Antonio José de Irisarri Antonio** was a Guatemalan journalist and statesman who was deeply involved in the nascent republics of Guatemala, Chile, and El Salvador. **María Josefa García Granados** was an influential Spanish-Guatemalan socialite of this era who became renowned as a satirist, commentator, and woman of letters. More well-known was her friend, **José Batres Montúfar,** a poet and critic.

Later, Guatemalan literature began to leave behind the poetry and nation-building that had characterized it in decades past. The **novelistic tradition** began with **José Milla y Vidaurre,** a newspaper editor, international literary figure, conservative politician, and father of the Guatemalan novel, whose work mainly was in the field of historical fiction and the realistic portraiture of life in the colonial age. **Modernism,** and a heavy dose of Francophilia, began to reach Guatemala at the *fin de siècle*, with authors like **Domingo Estrada** and Máximo Soto Hall fostering a small but energetic hub of modern literature in Guatemala.

A new element of daring was injected into Guatemalan literature by the political strife of the 20th century, and the emergence of the **"dictator novel,"** a genre criticizing the authoritarianism of Latin America. **Miguel Ángel Asturias** received the 1967 Nobel Prize for his efforts in this genre, as well as the Soviet Union's Lenin Prize. In recent years, Guatemalan literature has diversified further, with a re-examination of the Mayan contribution to Guatemalan literature; a recent winner of the prize set up in Asturias's honor was **Humberto Ak'abal,** a K'iche Maya poet who declined the prize in protest. Guatemalan literature remains largely political, and focuses on the often turbulent question of Guatemalan national identity.

MUSIC

Guatemalan folk is the country's most widely exported musical genre; several distinct traditions make up this tradition. In one corner is **traditional Maya music,** reliant on wind instruments, drums, and, for the very authentic, the conch-shell trumpet. Coming from the African-derived culture of the Garífuna is the tradition of **Garífuna music,** which brought African rhythms and styles similar to those of the marimba, Guatemala's national instrument and the cornerstone of mainstream Guatemalan popular music. Classical music in Guatemala bears strong Spanish and Church influences, but became indigenous with **José Eulalio Samayoa,** who composed the first symphonies of the New World in the early years of the 19th century. The various strains of music in Guatemala have been unified in the 20th and 21st centuries by Guatemalan composers and conductors like Dieter Lehnhoff, who has brought together Mayan, African, and Western traditions to international acclaim.

FILM AND TELEVISION

The cinematic arts have had a checkered history in Guatemala. In 1905, the first film in Guatemala was produced, a documentary of a festival in Guatemala City. Detective films were soon to follow, and in the 1930s the government began to make use of film extensively. The first all-Guatemalan film with sound, **"El sombrerón,"** was produced in 1950 under director Eduardo Fleischman. The 1970s were an age of renewed work under directors like Rafael Lanuza. For much of the post war era, however, great parts of the country were too dangerous for film or documentary work, and many films with Guatemalan subjects were filmed in neighboring countries, including Mexico. Recently, however, both film and an indigenous television industry have taken off.

FOOD AND DRINK

Corn is divine in Guatemala—literally. According to the sacred Quiché Maya text, the *Popol Vuh*, the gods unsuccessfully first tried to use mud, then wood, and finally corn in their attempts to create man. As man's original essence, it is hardly surprising that Guatemalan cuisine centers around **corn.** From **tortillas** and **tamales,** to the roasted cobs sold on street corners and the popular milky drink **atol,** visitors will find more than their typical earful of corn. Black beans, or **frijoles,** are another sure bet: while they may come refried (*volteado*) or whole (*parado*), they'll definitely be somewhere in most dishes.

Beyond the staples of corn, rice, eggs, and beans, Guatemalan cuisine features a wealth of traditional dishes and **stews** (*caldos*). In *restaurantes típicos,* thick, chili-based sauces spice up otherwise ordinary servings of vegetables, chicken, and turkey. Around Antigua, the rich sauce **pepián,** consisting of onions, tomatoes, and peppers, is particularly popular. Along the Caribbean coast, seafood reigns supreme. Savor a bowl of **tapado,** a rich, coconut-based soup in which an unlikely mix of shrimp, fish, tomatoes, and bananas are all mixed together. In the highlands, you'll find the distinct taste of indigenous Ki'iche cuisine with **Kak'Ik,** a spicy turkey stew crafted by simmering cilantro, garlic, tomatoes and dried peppers in a wholly delicious culinary affair.

If you're searching for the basics, nearly every town has a market with stalls of fresh fruits and vegetables—look out for **guanábana** (soursop), a tropical fruit with a thorny exterior and pulpy, creamy, seed-studded flesh. Coffee is the **bebida preferida,** but with Guatemalan coffee in high demand by international coffee companies, locals are often peddling cheaper, weaker brews. Guatemala's temperate climate produces some of the world's best beans, along with exceptional crops of sugar, bananas, and cocoa. Fruit juice blends known as **licuados** are lifesavers on hot days. We suggest cooling off like a local by sipping on a homegrown beer like **Gallo, Mozo, or Dorado.**

CUSTOMS AND ETIQUETTE

Although etiquette is fairly universal throughout Central America, Guatemala has a few of its own customs. As in much of Latin America, **punctuality sometimes falls by the wayside**—no one seems to be in a rush, and lateness is both tolerated and expected. Between friends, it is customary to give a kiss on one cheek as a greeting, and handshakes are the norm among men. Gifts should always be accepted with emphatic gratitude, and visitors to a Guatemalan home should consider bringing a small offering like chocolate, flowers, or souvenirs from their home country.

Most Guatemalans have two surnames: their paternal name, followed by the maternal. When addressing Guatemalans, use only the first surname. To greet a stranger or authority figure, make sure to use the formal **usted** form, while the *tú* form should suffice for friends and informal acquaintances. A soft speaking voice is considered polite in Guatemala. Be aware of the volume and tone of the people around you, and notice how your voice sounds and travels—particularly when conversing in English. Approach conversations about politics and the recent violence in Guatemala with care, as you may hit upon a particularly painful or controversial subject. Feel free, however, to demonstrate your interest in Guatemalan history, culture, or geography with a well-posed question about Guatemala's 1967 Nobel Prize in Literature (to Miguel Asturias) or the *Liga Internacional de Fútbol.*

As a visitor to a highly touristed, developing country, **be sensitive about whom you photograph.** It is considered polite to ask permission of indigenous people and locals before you take their picture out of respect for their privacy. Don't be surprised, however, if you are asked for a few *quetzales* to seal the deal. **Machismo,** a chauvinistic attitude toward women, still colors gender relations in many communities across the country. While it is perfectly acceptable for women to dine alone, it is not advisable for them to go unaccompanied to bars or clubs or to walk alone at night. Women are encouraged to dress conservatively in order to stave off catcalls and unwanted advances, and all female travelers should be aware of the alarmingly high number of violent crimes targeted at Guatemalan women over the past decade. Public displays of affection are generally acceptable, but while Guatemala has no laws prohibiting homosexuality, same-sex relationships remain taboo. As always, rules of etiquette and codes of conduct tend to be more relaxed in cosmopolitan, urban areas.

LAND

Guatemala lies between Mexico, Belize, El Salvador, and Honduras, with coasts on both the Gulf of Honduras in the east and the Pacific Ocean to the west. Divided into several areas by mountains and highlands, the landscape nevertheless retains broad similarities. Guatemala is a tropical, mostly mountainous country and a hothouse of biodiversity, ripe with forests and wetlands.

GEOGRAPHY AND GEOLOGY

Several large mountain chains split Guatemala. In the south, a string of 27 **volcanoes** reaches from Mexico to El Salvador, shielding a narrow, fertile plain huddled against the Pacific Ocean. The rectangular portion of Guatemala jutting into Mexico, the Petén region, features a thickly forested, isolated, **limestone plateau.** Part of its isolation is due to the mountains and highlands that wall it off to the south. These highlands represent the most densely populated areas of the country, including the capital of Guatemala City and other major cities, though some cities are also located in the **fertile Pacific plain.** The far east of Guatemala has high sierras and deeper valleys winding toward the tiny **Caribbean coast.**

WILDLIFE

Guatemala is internationally heralded as a wildlife hotspot. Over a third of Guatemala is under forest cover, with over half of that biosphere unlogged old-growth forest, much of it oak, pine, and otherwise coniferous. Additionally, a full 29% of the national territory is classified as protected from development, the highest ratio in Central America. In the northern lowlands of Petén, rainforest breaks into natural savanna grasslands, while in the southern lowlands of the Pacific plain most land has been cleared for agriculture.

The great forests of Guatemala host an immense variety of animal life, though some of the great mammals, including tapir, deer, ocelot, peccaries, and jaguars, are becoming rarer. The most flamboyant fauna include the birds of Guatemala. Chief among them is the vibrant emerald-and-red quetzal, the national bird, which reigns from its seat in the protected valleys of Copán.

WEATHER

The diversity of terrains in Guatemala is matched by a wide range of climates. Below 3,000ft., temperatures linger at the low end of tropical, between 21° and 27° C. The heaviest rains fall on the sierra slopes, at the Caribbean coastline, and on parts of the Pacific plain, especially during the wet season (March through December). The dry season grips the country between November and April. Severe tropical storms menace in September and October, as did Hurricane Stan in 2005.

GUATEMALA CITY

Guatemala City, or Guate (GUAH-te), is the largest urban area in Central America. Smog-belching buses and countless sidewalk vendors, together with the sheer number of people, noise, and the endless expanse of concrete, make the city center uncomfortably claustrophobic. Add to this a general concern for safety and it's easy to understand why many visitors flee Guatemala's capital for the surrounding highlands. Still, poking around Guate for a day or two does have its rewards. Fine architecture dating back to the 1700s and several worthwhile museums make for an engaging stay. After camping in the countryside and hiking through jungles, the city's modern conveniences and hot showers can be welcoming. While travelers may find comfort in Guate, many residents do not. Poverty is laid bare here, standing in harsh contrast to the antiseptic shopping malls and guarded, fortress-like mansions in the wealthiest neighborhoods. This disparity is particularly evident in Guatemala's large refugee population, mainly Maya who fled civil violence in their home villages.

Guatemala City was named the country's capital in 1775 after an earthquake in Antigua left the government scrambling for a safer center, though powerful tremors shook the new capital in 1917, 1918, and 1976. Despite the whims of Mother Nature, the city and its three million inhabitants persevere, expanding ceaselessly into the surrounding valleys.

▐ INTERCITY TRANSPORTATION

FLIGHTS:

International Flights: La Aurora International Airport (☎2334 7680), 7km south of Zona 1 in Zona 13. Services the following airlines: **American** (☎2337 1177; www. aa.com); **Continental** (☎2331 2051; www.continental.com); **Delta** (☎2337 0642; www.delta.com); **Grupo Taca** (☎2470 8222; www.taca.com); **Iberia** (☎2332 0911; www.iberia.com); **KLM** (☎2367 6179; www.klm.com); **Mexicana** (☎2366 4543; www. mexicana.com); and **United** (☎2336 9923; www.united.com).

Domestic Flights: The most common domestic flight is from Guatemala City to **Flores,** near Tikal. Two airlines serve this route: **Grupo Taca** (see above) and **TAG** (☎2360 3038; www.tag.com.gt). Taca offers more frequent flights and larger aircraft. Round-trip Q700-950. Specials are often available. During peak season, Taca offers spotty (and pricey) domestic service via its regional affiliate, **Inter.** Destinations include **Huehuetenango, Puerto Barrios, Quetzaltenango,** and **Río Dulce. Rasca** can arrange charter flights, but these also tend to be expensive.

INTERNATIONAL BUSES

Domestic and international buses also leave from various locations across Guatemala City. Only one or two companies are listed here, but there are several others that offer bus service to Central America's largest cities.

San Salvador:

Melva Internacional and J.F. Pezarossi: 3a Av. 1-38, Zona 9 (☎2331 0874). 4hr., every hr. 5:15am-4:15pm, Q90.

Pullmantur: 1a Av. 13-22, Zona 10 (☎2337 2861). 4hr.; 7am, 1, and 3pm; Q254.

Belize City: Línea Dorada, 10a Av. and 16a C., Zona 1 (☎2415 8900). 2 days, Q330; stop-over in Flores.

GUATEMALA CITY

Guatemala City

🏠 ACCOMODATIONS
Hotel Ajau, 19
Hotel Colonial, 20
Hotel Fénix, 18
Hotel Mi Casa, 8
Hotel Posada Belén, 22
Hotel Real InterContinental, 5
Hotel Spring, 23
Hotel Xamanek, 6
Otelito, 10

🍎 FOOD
Cafe León, 25
Long Wah, 27
Mexico Lindo, 3
Restaurante Altuna, 24
Sophos, 9
Tacontento, 4
Tamarindos, 11
Tasca El Rocío, 7

⚫ MUSEUMS AND SIGHTS
Casa MIMA, 21
Catedral Metropolitano, 26
Iglesia Yurrita, 15
Museo Ixchel, 12
Museo Nacional de
Arqueología y Etnología, 2
Museo de Los Niños, 1
Museo del Ferrocarril, 17
Palacio Nacional, 28
Popol Vuh Museum, 13
Torre del Reformador, 14

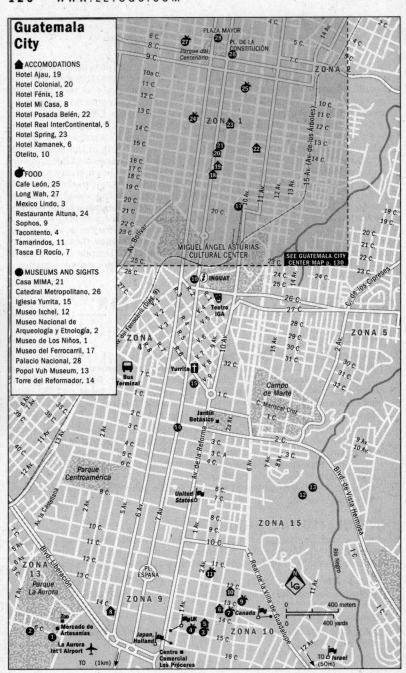

SEE GUATEMALA CITY
CENTER MAP p. 130

Copán: Hedman Alas, 2a Av. 8-73, Zona 10 (☎2362 5072 or 2362 5075). 5hr., 5 and 9am, Q271.

Tegucigalpa:

Hedman Alas, 2a Av. 8-73, Zona 10 (☎2362 5072 or 2362 5075). 12hr., 5 and 9am, Q403.

King Quality y Confort Lines, 18a Av. 1-96, Zona 15 (☎2369 0404). 2 days; 6:30am, 8am, 2, 3:30pm; Q488; involves a stop-over in San Salvador.

Managua:

Cruceros del Golfo, 18a Av. 1-96, Zona 15 (☎2369 0456). 16hr., 4am, Q424.

Tica Bus, Blvd. Los Próceres 26-55, Zona 10 (☎2366 4234). 2 days; Q347; stop-over in San Salvador.

San José:

King Quality y Confort Lines, 18a Av. 1-96, Zona 15 (☎2369 0404). 2 days; 6:30, 8am, 2, and 6:30pm; Q568; involves stop-overs in San Salvador and Managua.

Tica Bus, Blvd. Los Próceres 26-55, Zona 10 (☎2366 4234). 3 days, one bus leaves at 1pm, Q521; involves stop-overs in San Salvador and Managua.

Panama City: Tica Bus, Blvd. Los Próceres 26-55, Zona 10 (☎2366 4234). 4 days, Q781; stop-overs in San Salvador and Managua.

Tapachula:

Linea Dorada, 10a Av. and 16a C., Zona 1 (☎2415 8900). 7hr., Q280.

Trans Galgos Inter, 7a Av. 19-44, Zona 1 (☎2253 9131). 7hr., 7:30am and noon, Q194.

DOMESTIC BUSES

The **bus terminal** is located in the southwest corner of **Zona 4,** framed by Av. 4, Av. de Ferrocarril, and C. 8. Many 2nd-class services depart from here; ask around to find an exact departure point. Departures are scattered throughout the blocks surrounding the main terminal. Domestic buses that do not depart from the Zona 4 terminal depart from various locations around a few of the Zonas. See **Orientation** (p. 128) for information on how to decipher addresses in Guatemala City. Be advised that none of these bus "stations" have ticket offices. Brace yourself for chaos: you pay for the trip on the road. Make sure to have your payment ready before you step on—you don't want to fumble with your wallet on a crowded bus.

Antigua: Multiple carriers. 23a Av. and 3a C., Zona 3. 1hr., every 15min. 7am-8pm, Q5.

Biotopo del Quetzal: Escobar y Monja Blanca, 8a Av. 15-16, Zona 1 (☎2238 1409). 3½hr., every 30min. 4am-5pm, Q50.

Chichicastenango: Veloz Quichelense, 41 C., between 6a and 7a Av., Zona 8. 3hr., every hr. 5am-6pm, Q12.

Cobán: Escobar y Monja Blanca, 8a Av. 15-16, Zona 1 (☎2238 1409). 4½hr., every hr. 4am-5pm, Q50.

Esquipulas: Rutas Orientales, 19a C. 8-18, Zona 1 (☎2253-7282). 4½hr., every 30min. 4:30am-6pm, Q40.

Flores:

Fuentes del Norte, 17a C. 8-46, Zona 1 (☎2238 3894). 9-10hr., every hr., Q100.

Línea Dorada, 10a Av. and 16a C., Zona 1 (☎2415 8900; 8hr., 10am and 9pm, Q145).

Huehuetenango:

Transportes Velásquez, Calzada Roosevelt 9-56, Zona 7 (☎2440 3316). 5hr., every 30min. 8am-3pm, Q60.

Los Halcones, Calzada Roosevelt 37-47, Zona 11 (☎2432 5364). 5hr.; 7am, 2, 5pm; Q60.

Puerto de Iztapa: Multiple Carriers. 4a C. between 7a and 8a Av., Zona 12. 1½hr., every 15min. 5am-4:45pm, Q15.

La Mesilla: Transportes Velásquez, Calzada Roosevelt 9-56, Zona 7 (☎2440 3316). 7hr., 6am-3pm, Q70.

Monterrico: Transportes Cubanita, 4a C. and 8a Av., Zona 12. 3hr.; 10:30am, 12:30, 2:20pm; Q40.

Panajachel: Transportes Rebulli, 41 C. between 6a and 7a Av., Zona 8 (☎2230 2748). 3hr., every hr. 5:30am-3:50pm, Q25. Alternatively, take any bus to the western highlands and change at Los Encuentros junction.

Puerto Barrios: Transportes Litegua, 15a C. 10-40, Zona 1 (☎2220 8840). 5hr., every hr. 4:30am-6pm, Q55.

Quetzaltenango:

Transportes Alamo, 12 Av. A 0-65, Zona 7 (☎2472 2355). 4hr.; 8, 10:15am, 12:30, 3, 4:15, 5:30pm; Q55.

Transportes Galgos, 7a Av. 19-44, Zona 1 (☎2220 0238). 4hr., 5:30am and 2:30pm, Q45.

Rabinal: Transporte Dulce María, 17 C. 11-32, Zona 1 (☎2253 4618). 3½hr., every 30min. 5am-5pm, Q27.

Retalhuleu: Transportes Fortaleza del Sur, 19a C. 8-70, Zona 1 (☎2230 3390). 3hr., every 30min. 6am-6pm, Q45.

Río Dulce: Transportes Litegua, 15a C. 10-40, Zona 1 (☎2220 8840). 5hr.; 6, 9, 11:30am, 1, 4:15pm; Q55.

Salamá: Transporte Dulce María, 17 C. 11-32, Zona 1 (☎2253 4618). 3hr., every hr. 5am-5pm, Q23.

Tecpán: Transportes Poaquileña, 1a Av. between 3a and 4a C., Zona 7. 2hr., every 15min. 5:30am-7pm, Q7.

◾◾ ORIENTATION

Upon Arrival Both international and domestic flights arrive at **La Aurora International Airport**, in Zona 13. The posh hotels of **Zona 10** are close, but the budget spots in **Zona 1** require a bit more of a trek. Bus #83 departs from outside the terminal and runs to Zona 1; watch your luggage carefully. Though more expensive, a taxi (Q50) is an easier and safer way of getting to your hotel.

If arriving by bus, prepare for some confusion. Many second-class services arrive in the **Zona 4** market area, referred to as the main bus terminal. Taxis are plentiful here; if you want to take a bus to Zona 1, walk to the corner of 2 C. and 4 Av. Other second-class buses arrive at scattered locations throughout the city. Most of these are in Zona 1, within walking distance or a short taxi ride from downtown hotels. Terminal addresses are listed under Transportation (p. 129). Avoid arriving by bus at night; if you do, take a taxi from the terminal.

LAYOUT. Although Guate is overwhelmingly large, sights and services are concentrated in Zonas 1, 2, 4, 9, 10, and 13. The major thoroughfare is **6 Av.**, beginning at the Plaza Mayor in the north and continuing south through Zonas 4 and 9. **Zona 1**, the city's oldest section and the true city center, houses budget hotels and restaurants. **Zona 4** lies immediately south of Zona 1. An industrial area, Zona 4 houses the INGUAT office, the second-class bus terminal, and the market area. **Zonas 9** and **10** house the boutiques, embassies, fancy restaurants, and five-star hotels. The two zones are divided by the north-south Av. de la Reforma: Zona 9 is to the west, and Zona 10 is to the east. Avenidas run parallel to Av. de la Reforma and the street numbers increase eastward. Calles run east-west and increase southward. The southern portion of Zona 10 is the **Zona Viva** (Lively Zone), home to the bulk of the city's most happening clubs. **Zona 13** is south of Zona 9. Its two notable features are the international airport and the **Parque La Aurora**, which contains museums, a market, and a zoo. Some possible causes for confusion: 1a Av. of Zona 1 is different from the 1a Av. of Zona 5. Also, some streets are nameless for a block, and some calles in Zona 1 have secondary names. Note that many streets—especially in Zona 1—do not have street signs, so it's best to ask for directions.

SAFETY. Personal safety is a definite concern in Guatemala City. Exploring the city on your own during the day is generally not a problem; be aware of your surroundings and carry yourself as if you always know where you are going, even if completely lost. Don't be afraid to step into an establishment if you are in need of help. Wandering alone at night is strongly discouraged by locals. The streets of Zona 1 are not safe after dark. If you must, travel by taxi and never alone. Nighttime bar and restaurant hopping in Zona 10 is reasonably safe, provided you stick with the crowds and have a companion. Pickpockets are ubiquitous, especially in bus terminal areas. Always keep your money and valuables close to your body and distribute bills among multiple pockets so that you don't lose everything if you are robbed. Thigh or waist money belts are recommended. Female travelers should expect cat calls and whistles all over the city. The best response is to remain quiet and move on.

⊏ LOCAL TRANSPORTATION

Buses: Guate's city bus system is extensive and relatively efficient, but it takes a while to get the hang of it. The nicer and slightly more expensive buses, **preferenciales,** are large and red. Second-class buses are called **corrientes,** although they are not recommended for tourists due to safety concerns. Buses run from 7am until about 8pm, though you'll find the occasional bus running later. Buses have their destination clearly marked on the front; the best places to catch them in Zona 1 are 4 Av. or 10 Av. The latter is the place to go for buses headed towards the airport. Some major bus routes include:

82: Goes from the center of **Zona 1** into **Zona 4,** continuing down **Av. de la Reforma** through **Zona 9** and **Zona 10.**

83: Goes from **10a Av.** in **Zona 1** down to **La Aurora Airport** in **Zona 13,** passing through the sights of **Zona 13** and eventually returning to **9a Av.** in **Zona 1.**

101: Starts on **Av. de los Proceres** in **Zona 10,** continuing past the **INGUAT office** on its way through **Zona 4.**

Taxis: Taxis are relatively cheap in Guatemala City and necessary for travelers looking to go out after dark. A taxi ride is usually Q30-50, though prices vary depending on time of day and length of trip. If the cab is not metered, agree ahead of time on a price, as bargaining is sometimes necessary (and sometimes impossible). If there are no taxis around, you can call one of two taxi companies, named for the color of their vehicles: **Taxis Amarillos** (☎2470 1515) and **Taxis Verdes** (☎2475 9595).

Car Rental: There are about 12 car rental companies in Guatemala. Most have stations at La Aurora Airport; some have additional offices scattered throughout the city. Travelers will find both local and more expensive international options. **Avis,** 6a C. 7-64, Zona 9 (☎2339 3249; www.avis.com.gt), and at the La Aurora Airport, Zona 13 (☎2385 8781).

⁊ PRACTICAL INFORMATION

TOURIST AND FINANCIAL SERVICES

Tourist Office

INGUAT 7a Av. 1-17, Zona 4 (☎2421 2800). The INGUAT headquarters are located in this building, right in the center of Guatemala City. Staff is helpful and bilingual. City maps are free. Open M-F 8am-4pm.

Tours:

Guatemalan Adventure 13a C. 3-40, Zona 10, Edificio Atlantis (☎2410 8260 or 2410 8261; www. guatemalanadventure.com), Offers tours around Guatemala City, as well as arranging excursions

GUATEMALA CITY

Guatemala City Center

🏠 ACCOMODATIONS
Hotel Ajau, 3
Hotel Colonial, 4
Hotel Fénix, 2
Hotel Posada Belén, 6
Hotel Spring, 7

🍎 FOOD
Cafe León, 9
Long Wah, 11
Restaurante Altuna, 8

⚫ MUSEUMS AND SIGHTS
Casa MIMA, 5
Catedral Metropolitano, 10
Museo del Ferrocarril, 1
Palacio Nacional, 12

to Antigua, Chichicastenango, Lake Atitlan, or longer tours/hikes to Tikal, Copán, Aguateca, and more. English spoken. Open Mon-Fri 9am-5pm.

GuateMaya (☎5852 7780 or 4581 6507; www.guatemayatour.com), Offers trip-packages to various countries throughout Central America, as well as transportation from the airport to hotels in Guatemala City. Open M-Sa 9am-5pm.

Embassies:

United States Embassy Av. de la Reforma 7-01, Zona 10 (☎2326 4000), Open M-Th 7:30am-5pm, Fri 7:30am-12:30am.

Canada Embassy 13 C. 8-44, Zona 10 (☎2333 6102), Edyma Plaza Niv. 8. Open M-F 8am-4:30pm.

UK Embassy Av. de la Reforma 16-00, Zona 10 (☎2367 5425), Torre Internacional, 11th fl. Open M-F 9am-noon and 2pm-4pm. Citizens of Australia or New Zealand can resolve any concerns within the UK embassy.

Currency Exchange and Banks: There are hundreds of banks in Guatemala City, and while all cards are served at various locations throughout the city, Visa card holders will have the least amount of trouble with banking needs. ATMs are also very common occurrences, though you should only use an ATM that is located in a safe zona or within a bank. Almost all of the main banks in the city (G&T Continental, Banrural, Banco Industrial, etc.) have Western Unions located within them. All require photo ID (most in the form of a passport) to exchange currency. The listings below are the central offices of the following banks, which have branches all over the city.

Banco Industrial 7a Av. 5-10, Zona 4 (☎2420 1737) Edificio Centro Financiero Torre I.

Banco Agromercantil 7 Av. 7-30, Zona 9 (☎2338 6565).

G&T Continental 6 Av. 9-08, Zona 9 (☎2338 6801) Plaza G&T Continental.

Citibank Metrocentro, Blvd. de los Heroes (☎2202 5610).

American Express: 7a Av. 6-26, Zona 9, Edificio Plaza el Roble (☎2361 0909).

Western Union: There are Western Unions located within many of the banks surrounding the plaza in Zona 1, as well as in banks throughout the other zonas.

LOCAL SERVICES

Bookstores: VRISA Bookshop 15a Av. 3-64, Zona 1 (☎7761 3237). Wide range of genres in both Spanish and English. Open M-Sa 9am-7pm.

Markets: Grocery stores include **Paiz** and **Super del Ahorro,** both on 7a Av. between 17 and 18 C. in Zona 1. There is also a large **Central Market** behind the main cathedral in an underground garage. Open M-Sa 6am-6pm, Su 8am-noon. Another **crafts market** is located in Zona 13 (see **Sights,** p. 133).

Laundromats: Many of the hotels in Zonas 9 and 10 offer laundry service. **Lavanderia Passarelli,** 4a C. A 0-20, Zona 1 (☎5896 0736), has ironing and dry-cleaning services.

EMERGENCY AND COMMUNICATIONS

Emergency: Fire ☎122. Ambulance ☎123 or 128.

Police: 6a Av. 13-71 (☎120).

Pharmacy: Farmacia Batres, 6a C. and 6a Av., Zona 10 (☎2332 7425). Open 24hr.

Medical Services: Hospital General San Juan de Dios, 1a Av. 10-50, Zona 1 (☎2253 0423). **Hospital Roosevelt,** Calzada Roosevelt, Zona 11 (☎2471 1441).

Telephones: TELGUA, 7a Av. in between 12a and 13a C., Zona 1 (☎2238 1098). Open M-F 8am-6pm, Sa 8am-1pm.

Internet Access: Cafe Internet Carambola, Carretera al Atlánt. (☎2258 3684). Internet Q20 per hr. Open daily 8:30am-8:30pm. **Cafe Internet Gamanet** 5a Av. 3-78, Zona 1 (☎2232 1569). Internet Q15 per hr. Open M-Sa 9am-8pm.

Post Office: 7a Av. and 12a C., Zona 1. Open M-F 8:30am-5:30pm, Su 9am-1pm. **Postal Code:** 01000.

⛏ ACCOMMODATIONS

Almost all of Guate's budget hotels are located in Zona 1, the city's aging downtown area. Because robberies do occur here, prioritize safety when choosing a hotel: windows should be barred, balconies secure, locks functional, and the management should be conscientious. You may want to consider spending more than you would otherwise for accommodations here. Given nighttime safety concerns, a reservation or an early arrival is a good idea. Female travelers or those traveling alone may feel more comfortable paying slightly more for the safer surroundings in Zona 9 or 10.

ZONA 1

🏨 **Hotel Posada Belén,** 13a C. A 10-30 (☎2253 4530; posadabelen.com). Loaded with charm and history, this hotel is as much of an experience as it is a place to stay.

All rooms have private baths and hot water. Shuttle available for pick-up or drop-off at the airport. Breakfast C50. Laundry service available. Free Wi-Fi. Singles Q300; doubles Q400. AmEx/D/MC/V. ⑤

Hotel Colonial, 7a Av. 14-19 (☎2232 6722; www.hotelcolonial.net). Gorgeous mahogany furniture fills this accommodation's spacious rooms, most with private baths, hot water, and cable TV. Singles Q100, with bath Q140. V. ③

Hotel Spring, 8a Av. 12-65 (☎2232 2858, www.hotelspring.com). In a well-kept colonial home with an open air courtyard. Roomy and well-lit accommodations. Reserve in advance. Singles Q96, with bath Q136; doubles Q136/175. MC/V. ③

Hotel Ajau, 8a Av. 15-62 (☎2232 0488). Slightly claustrophobic, windowless rooms, some with private baths. Singles Q64, with bath Q100; doubles Q75/115. Cash only. ②

Hotel Fénix, 7a Av. 15-81 (☎2226 7343). One of the cheapest options in the city. Well-furnished rooms, some with private baths. A cafe is located downstairs. Singles Q43; doubles Q50. Cash only. ②

OTHER ZONAS

Hotel Xamanek, 13a C. 3-57, Zona 10 (☎2360 8345; www.mayaworld.net). Backpacker-friendly hotel with dorm-style and private rooms. Ideal location in the heart of Zona Viva. Breakfast included. Free internet access and Wi-Fi. Dorms Q115; private rooms Q250. Cash only. ③

Hotel Real Intercontinental, 14a C. 2-51, Zona 10 (☎2413 4444; www.intercontinental.com). Luxurious 4-star establishment in the heart of the Zona Viva. Japanese restaurant, **Tanoshii,** on the ground floor serves melt-in-your-mouth sushi. Free pool access. Continental breakfast included. Rooms from Q1130. AmEx/D/MC/V. ⑤

Otelito, 12a C. 4-51, Zona 10 (☎2339 1811; www.otelito.com). Has the intimacy of a bed-and-breakfast with the amenities (and prices) of a luxury hotel chain. Impeccably executed decor. Ground-floor bar and lounge is a prime nightlife location. Rooms from Q700. AmEx/D/MC/V. ⑤

Hotel Mi Casa, 5a Av. "A" 13-51, Zona 9 (☎2339 2246; www.hotelmicasa.com). Breakfast included. Free Wi-Fi. Free parking for guests. Airport shuttle service available. Singles with shared baths Q280, with private baths Q440; doubles Q400/520. Discounts for groups. V. ⑤

◖ FOOD

In Zona 1, sidewalk vendors offer the cheapest grub, though travelers have been known to experience stomach illness from these quick fixes. Local *comedores* are inexpensive, offering daily *típico* menus for Q10-20. There's also a fair amount of American fast food joints. The ever-developing Zonas 9 and 10 are featuring an increasing number of international options. Here, pad thai is just as common as *comida típica*.

ZONA 1

▨ **Restaurante Altuna,** 5a Av. 12-31 (www.restaurantealtuna.com). In a beautifully restored colonial home, old-fashioned, upscale Altuna has a long-standing reputation as the nicest restaurant in downtown Guate. Serves excellent Spanish food. Paella Q47. Desserts Q15-25. Open Tu-Sa noon-10pm, Su noon-4pm. Reservations recommended. AmEx/MC/V. ④

Cafe León, 8a Av. 9-15. Join intellectuals and coffee enthusiasts at this smoke-filled cafe for an exquisite *café con leche*. Decent sandwich menu (Q30-40). Cash only. ②

Long Wah, 6a C. 3-75 (☎2232 6611). Reasonably priced, authentic Chinese food in the heart of Zona 1. Entrees Q30-60. Take-out available. Open daily 9am-9pm. Cash only. ❷

ZONA 10

▓ **Tamarindos,** 11a C. 2-19A (☎2360 5630; www.tamarindos.com.gt). Extensive menu with irresistable dishes such as Pear and Ricotta Ravioli (Q85). Steak prepared any way you like it Q135. Impressive mixed drinks menu. Georgia Peach Q50. Restaurant open M-Sa noon-2:30pm and 7:30-10:30pm. Bar open until 1am most nights. AmEx/D/MC/V. ❺

▓ **Mexico Lindo,** 14a C. 2-56 (☎2337 3822 or 4132; www.mexlindo.com). This sports bar serves upscale Mexican cuisine in heaping portions. A well-stocked bar and savvy bar tender can mix you anything you want. The *tostidas Chiapanecas,* stacked with salsa, guacamole, goat cheese, shredded chicken, and a dollop of sour cream, are unreal. Open M-Sa 7am-1am, Su 7:30am-11pm. AmEx/D/MC/V. ❹

Sophos, 12a C. and 4a Av. (☎2419 7070), on the 2nd level of the Plaza Fontabella. Attached to a beautiful Spanish bookstore, this sophisticated restaurant has an extensive selection of coffees and a mouth-watering panini menu. Try the Ben Franklin (roast beef, carmelized onions, roasted red peppers and *camembert;* Q50). Pad Thai Q90. Ravioli Q60. Open M-Sa 9am-9pm, Su 10am-8pm. ❸

Tasca El Rocío, 4a Av. 12-59 (☎2366 1064 or 2336 6938), inside the Plaza Fontabella. Upscale Spanish cuisine in a refined atmosphere. Tapas from Q45. Paella from Q85. Mixed drinks Q35-Q45. Open M-Sa noon-10pm, Su noon-7pm. AmEx/D/MC/V. ❸

Tacontento, 14a C. 1-42 (☎2367 6044). Lower prices do not translate to lower quality. Tacos made on the spot in hefty portions. Burritos Q33. Wash it all down with a beer or a frozen mixed drink. Open daily noon-1am. AmEx/D/MC/V. ❷

◎ SIGHTS

ZONA 1

PLAZA MAYOR Surrounded by some of the finest architecture in the city, the Plaza Mayor has been stripped to its basic elements: a slab of concrete and a large fountain. Formerly known as "the center of all Guatemala," the space is now mostly filled with pigeons, shoeshines, and men playing card games. The exception to this rule comes on Sunday, when the plaza is flooded with indígenas selling textiles, families out for a stroll, and political protesters. *(Bounded on the west and east by 6a and 7a Av., and on the north and south by 6a and 8a C.)*

CATEDRAL METROPOLITANO The stately Catedral Metropolitana, reconstructed after the 1917 earthquake, rises dramatically against the Plaza. Inside the neoclassical structure are the usual saints and religious images—it is on the outer pillars where the magic lies. Etched into the twelve front columns are the names of all those who disappeared during the recent civil war, making the trip to the Catedral a pilgrimage for many families. It is perhaps the quietest spot in the city. Head through the building to a courtyard on the south side of the cathedral where you will see the entrance to the cathedral's museum; the museum houses some impressive religious relics and provides an interesting history of Guatemalan Christianity. *(Located on the east side of the Plaza Mayor. The Cathedral is open M-Sat 7:30am-1pm and 2pm-6pm, Su 7am-6:30pm. Free. The Cathedral's museum is open M-F 9am-1pm and 2pm-5pm, Sa 9am-1pm. Admission is Q10 for students with ID and Q30 for non-citizens.)*

PALACIO NACIONAL This grand palacio was built between 1928 and 1943 under the orders of President Jorge Ubico. Currently, the public is allowed to see only a few of the imposing palace's 350 rooms, but even the corridors are magnificent. La Sala de Recepción awes visitors with its massive Bohemian crystal chandelier, replete with graceful brass and gold quetzals. The Presidential Balcony offers commanding views of the plaza and the surrounding highlands. The second floor houses a fairly complete collection of modern Guatemalan art, including rotating exhibitions of the most renowned Guatemalan artists. In 1980, a car bomb shattered the stained glass windows of the central corridor which had depicted the 10 virtues of a good nation, and some have yet to be reconstructed. *(Located on the north side of the Plaza Mayor. Open daily 9am-11:45pm and 2-4:45pm. Free; tip expected for guided tours.)*

CASA MIMA A renovated 19th-century home, the Casa MIMA is a quirky look into the former glory of Guatemala. The house includes a fully furnished chapel and 1920s era kitchen. Relax with a cup of coffee (Q5) in the back courtyard of this truly picturesque and tranquil residence. *(8a Av. 14-12. ☎2253 4020, www.portalmuseo-sguatemala.net/m.casa.mima. Open M-Sat 10am-5pm. Admission is Q20, students Q15.)*

MUSEO DEL FERROCARRIL There was a time when Guatemala was connected by an expansive railroad system, stretching up and down the Pacific coast, across the country to the Atlantic, and even up into Petén. This museum, which also houses three trains that visitors can board and exlore, provides an extensive and interactive history of thse old railroads.*(9a Av. 18-03, ☎2238 0519. Located several blocks south east of the Plaza Mayor. Open M-F 9am-4:30pm, Sat-Sun 10am-4:30pm. Wheelchair accessible. Admission is Q2 for adults, Q1 for children.)*

ZONA 2

MAPA EN RELIEVE. Located in a park in the more quiet and suburban Zona 2, the Mapa en Relieve will satisfy any traveler trying to get their geographic bearings in Guatemala. Climb to the top of one of the two viewing towers to get a birds-eye view of this gigantic map of Guatemala, which features true-to-life topography (mountains, volcanoes, lakes, rivers, oceans, etc.), as well as countless little signs to indicate the locations of cities, towns, Mayan ruins, and more. *(Located in Zona 2. From the Plaza Mayor in Zona 1, ask a taxi driver to take you to and from the Mapa en Relieve for approximately Q40. Other than the viewing towers, this sight is wheelchair accessible. Open daily from 9am-5pm. Q25.)*

ZONA 4

IGLESIA YURRITA. Decked out in vermilion, this outlandish neo-Gothic curiosity was built in 1929. The color scheme inside the church, including an unusual window painted like the daytime sky, is nearly as blinding as the exterior. *(Ruta 6 and Via 8. Wheelchair accessible. Open Tues-Sun 7am-12pm and 4pm-6pm.)*

TORRE DEL REFORMADOR Check out this smaller (and considerably less polished) take on the Eiffel Tower, named in honor of forward-looking President Justo Rufino Barrios, who held office between 1871 and 1885. *(Located at the intersection of 7a Av. and 2a C.)*

ZONA 10

MUSEO IXCHEL DEL TRAJE INDÍGENA. A must see for any travelers interested in buying Guatemalan textiles. A detailed step-by-step of the traditional jaspee dye process and its use in indigenous garb informs those interested in purchasing items. The museum is on the campus of the Universidad Francisco Marroquín in a valley with well-landscaped picnic areas. The tranquil atmosphere here makes it a nice escape from the congested city center and an especially fine place to bring lunch. *(Take 6a C. Final east off Av. de la Reforma; the museum is located at the bottom of a large hill. ☎ 2331 3622. Open M-F 9am-5pm, Sa 9am-1pm. Wheelchair accessible. Q35, students Q15. MC/V.)*

JARDÍN BOTÁNICO. Head over to the Jardín Botánico, where there are over 700 species of plants labeled in Spanish and Latin. Perfect for a quiet picnic, and great escape from the crowded and polluted urban scenery. *(1a C. off Av.enida de la Reforma. ☎ 2333 0904. Open M-F 8am-3pm. Q5.)*

POPOL VUH MUSEUM. Named after the sacred Maya text, the museum has a first rate collection of pre-Columbian Maya pottery, as well as exhibits on colonial art and indigenous folklore. Visitors will leave this museum with a stronger understanding of a text that is extremely important to much of Guatemala's indigenous Mayan population. *(Next to the Museo Ixchel del Traje Indígena at the university; follow directions above. ☎ 2361 2301. Open M-F 9am-5pm, Sa 9am-1pm. Wheelchair accessible. Q35, Q15 for students with university ID.)*

ZONA 13

The sights of Zona 13 are clustered within the vast Parque La Aurora, near the airport. Several government-run museums and an INGUAT-sponsored artisans' market reside here. The area can be reached by bus #83.

MUSEO NACIONAL DE ARQUEOLOGÍA Y ETNOLOGÍA. This museum traces eons of Mayan history with hundreds of artifacts and an excellent scale model of Tikal. The exhibits are strikingly similar to those of the Popol Vuh Museum. *(Located in the park at the corner of 7 Av., 5 and 6 C., Edificio #5. ☎ 2472 0489. Open Tues-Fri 9am-4pm, Sa-Su 9am-noon and 1:30-4pm. Q60.)*

MERCADO DE ARTESANÍAS. La Aurora also holds an INGUAT-sponsored craft market. The traditional textiles, ceramics, and jewelry may make good gifts, but bargaining is off-limits. *(Open daily from 9am-6pm.)*

🔊 🎵 NIGHTLIFE AND ENTERTAINMENT

Although the city's frenetic pace tends to die down after dark, there are several options for evening entertainment. The capital is a good place to catch an American flick. Two convenient Zona 1 theaters are the **Capitol,** 6 Av., 12 C., and **Palace,** across the street. **La Cúpula,** 7 Av 13-01, Zona 9, is a theater conveniently close to Zona 9 and 10 hotels. Theater and opera performances (all in Spanish) are staged at **Teatro IGA,** Ruta 1 4-05, Zona 4, and in the **Teatro Nacional** on Friday and Saturday nights. For a listing of cultural events, check *La Prensa Libre* or any other local newspaper.

Though it is generally unsafe to be out after dark in the capital, there are a few places worth checking out. Clubbers and bar-hoppers should be sure to take cabs to and from their nighttime destinations. The best places to get your dance on are in **Zona 4** and the **Zona Viva (Zona 10).**The pace picks up around 10pm and winds down around 2am. The hottest club is currently **Kahlua,** 1 Av. 15-06, Zona 10, which comes complete with two dance floors, a lounge room, and a pop music. (No cover.) **SUAE,** on Vía 5 (Cuatro Grados Norte) and the **Rec Lounge** 9 Av. 0-81, are two hot-pots in Zona 4 that are worth checking out for trendy atmospheres, electronic music, and lots of dancing. If you're looking for a bar with incredible live music and room to dance, visit local haunt **Bodeguita del Centro,** 12 C. 3-55, Zona 1 (Closed Sunday and Monday).

GUATEMALA CITY

WESTERN HIGHLANDS

For many travelers, the Western Highlands are the reason to come to Guatemala. A vast expanse of rolling farmland rises up to dense jungle volcanoes and twisting roadways lead to stunning miradores. Meanwhile, the majority of Central America's indigenous population is packed into the region's untouched tiny hillside villages. Dialects of Mam, Ixil, and Cakchiquel echo in the vibrant markets; men stand outside churches swinging coffee-can censers filled with smoldering resin while chanting the cycles of the Mayan calendar.

The graceful colonial splendor of Antigua serves as a gateway to the altiplano. The unsurpassed beauty of Lago de Atitlán is ringed by traditional Mayan villages, while the colorful Mayan market of Chichicastenango is one of the country's most famous sights. Quetzaltenango, Guatemala's second-largest city, is home to increasingly popular language schools and provides easy access to hot springs. Two beautiful mountain towns offer a more serene highlands atmosphere: traditional Todos Santos, in the Cuchumatanes, and Nebaj, situated in northern Quiché.

ANTIGUA

After landing in Guatemala City, most people catch the first bus to the colonial city of Antigua, preferring to skip the country's capital in favor of a more historical and beautiful locale. From the cobblestone streets seemingly frozen in the 18th century to stunning courtyards concealed behind Mudéjar-influenced buildings, it is no wonder that Antigua remains one of the most popular destinations in Guatemala. If the colonial architecture fails to impress, Antigua's surroundings, featuring mountain ranges and three commanding volcanoes, certainly will.

Antigua was once the capital of Guatemala, but after a series of earthquakes destroyed the city, Guatemala City's solid ground seemed like a better fit. Today, Antigua is a city brimming with international influences thanks to the many tourists that flock here each year. These influences are particularly apparent in the diverse culinary scene, featuring everything from Japanese to French cuisine.

▐ TRANSPORTATION

Though its off the beaten path of the Interamericana, Antigua remains easy to reach by means of chicken bus routes and inexpensive shuttle services. Once in Antigua, the city is quite easy to navigate on foot; taxis and tuk tuks are only necessary for excursions to neighboring towns and villages. Many people rent cars, bikes, and motorcycles in order to explore the area around Antigua on their own.

Public Transportation:Buses: Station located behind Antigua's main market. While most people use private shuttles to travel from Antigua to cities throughout Guatemala (bookable through hotels, hostels, or travel agents), several chicken bus routes that originate in Antigua. **Chimaltenango** (40min., every 20min.); **Guatemala City** (1hr., every 30min.); **Panajachel** (3hr., daily, 7am); **San Antonio Aguas Calientes** (20min., every 30min.).

Taxis: Official cabs, labeled **"Antigua Guatemala,"** congregate around the Parque Central, but lack phone numbers or specific company names.

WESTERN HIGHLANDS

Western Highlands

ALTA VERAPAZ
TO COBÁN (15km)

Biotopo del Quetzal
La Cumbre Junction
Salamá
EL PROGRESO
JALAPA
SANTA ROSA

Guatemala City
Cuilapa

5

CA1

18

Chuarrancho

GUATEMALA
San Juan Sacatepéquez

Villa Nueva
Amatitlán
Lago de Amatitlán
San Vicente
Villa Canales

Mixco
Antigua
Ciudad Vieja
San Antonio Aguas Calientes

Volcán Pacaya
Palín Pacaya

CA9

Escuintla

CA2

Embalse Chixoy

BAJA VERAPAZ
Rabinal
Cubulco

Joyabaj
Zacualpa

San Martín Jilotepeque

5

Chimaltenango

Sta. María de Jesús

SACATEPÉQUEZ

Volcán de Agua

CA2

Uspantán

7W

Sacapulas
San Bartolomé Jocotenango

EL QUICHÉ

Chichicastenango

2

Los Encuentros Junction
El Cuchillo Junction

CA1

Tecpán
Iximché

Volcán Acatenango
Volcán de Fuego

Sta. Lucía Cotzumalguapa

CHIMAL-TENANGO

Nebaj

3

TO TODOS SANTOS CUCHUMATÁN (40km)

San Pedro Jocopilas
Sta. Cruz del Quiché

Sta. Lucía la Reforma

Utatlán

15

Santa Catarina
Panajachel
Sololá
Santa Cruz

San Antonio

San Lucas Tolimán
Volcán Tolimán

11

Cocales Junction

SOLOLÁ

Lago de Atitlán
Volcán Atitlán

Santiago de Atitlán

Pueblo Nuevo Tiquisate

Huehuetenango

Zaculeu

CA1

7W

Momostenango

San Francisco El Alto
TOTONICAPÁN
Totonicapán
Cuatro Caminos Junction
San Cristóbal Totonicapán
Olintepeque

Quetzaltenango (Xela)

Zunil
Volcán Sta. María

9S

Santa Clara La Laguna
San Marcos La Laguna
San Pedro
Volcán San Pedro

Mazatenango

SUCHITEPÉQUEZ

Volcán Siete Orejas
QUETZALTENANGO
Volcán Chicabal

Abaj Takalik

Colomba

CA2

Retalhuleu

9S

RETALHULEU

Champerico

Volcán Tajumulco

San Marcos
SAN MARCOS
San Pablo

12

Coatepeque

Malacatán

Coatepeque

PAMPAS EL GUAMUCHAL

Ixchiguán
Tajumulco
Volcán Tacaná
Tacaná

Unión Juárez

MEXICO

Cacahoatán
El Carmen
Tuxtla Chico

Frontera Hidalgo
Ciudad Hidalgo

19

Río Suchiate

Ciudad Tecún Umán

La Libertad

PACIFIC OCEAN

0   10 kilometers
0   10 miles

Tuk Tuks: For less than Q10, Tuk Tuks—glorified motorcycles—will take you anywhere in Antigua. Some will even take you to neighboring towns and villages for a slightly steeper fee.

Car Rental: Tabarini, 6a Av. Sur 22 (☎7832 8107 or 7832 8108). Rates start at Q309 per day. AmEx/D/MC/V.

Bike and Motorcycle Rental: Mayan Bike Tours (☎7832 3383, 24hr. cell phone 4562 3103; www.guatemalaventures.com), on the corner of 1a Av. Sur and 6a C. Oriente. Open daily 9am-5pm. Prices vary based on length and nature of rental. AmEx/D/MC/V.

🔲 🔢 ORIENTATION AND PRACTICAL INFORMATION

There are very few places in Guatemala that are as easy to navigate as this small city. With a few exceptions, Antigua's streets follow a grid where calles run east-west (*oriente-poniente*) and avenidas run north-south (*norte-sur*). The **parque central,** in the center of the city, is framed by 4/5 C. and 4/5 Av.. Providing a potential point of confusion, some street segments have reverted to their colonial names. Still, most businesses and residents refer to the numbered *calles* and *avenidas*. Many streets are also unmarked, so you may have to ask for directions.

Antigua's bus terminal is located behind the *mercado*, three blocks west of the *parque central*. Most visitors to Antigua arrive at the bus terminal; to get to the **parque central,** simply cross the tree-lined street, **Alameda Santa Lucía** (or C. Santa Lucía, depending on who you ask), and continue straight. It's hard to miss **Volcan de Agua,** the theatrical volcano looming to the south of the city. Be wary of following the INGUAT-authorized guides to your destination: they occasionally sometimes lead travelers astray. Instead, trust your instincts and take comfort in the fact that, given the relatively straightforward layout of the city, you will almost always be able to find your way around.

Tourist Office: INGUAT, 4a C. Oriente 10 (☎7832 5681; www.visitguatemala.com), inside the Casa Antigua El Jaulón courtyard. Head out of the *parque central* on 4A C. Oriente and the Casa Antigua El Jaulón is on your left; the INGUAT office is located in the back left corner of the courtyard. Helpful, English-speaking staff will answer any questions you might have. Open M-F 8am-5pm, Sa-Su 9am-5pm.

Tours: Adrenalina Tours, 5a Av. Norte 31 (☎7832 1108 or 5308 3523; www.adrenalinatours.com), just past the Arch on the right side of the street. Adrenalina Tours offers everything from jetting to Tikal (Q2,236) to excursions into Antigua and the surrounding area (Q406, 3 person minimum). If you want to hike the Pacaya Volcano, Adrenalina leads 2 tours per day, but be sure to book in advance, especially if you are banking on doing the morning tour. Flexible staff is willing to personalize any package. Offices in Antigua, Coban, Huehuetenango, Panajachel, and Quetzaltenango. AmEx/D/MC/V.

Currency Exchange and Bank: Banco Agromercantil, 4 C. Poniente (☎7832 0048). Open daily 9am-7pm.

Beyond Tourism:

Christian Spanish Academy, 6a Av. Norte 15 (☎7832 3922 or 7832 3924; www.learncsa.com). Take Spanish lessons for anywhere from 4 to 8 hours a day at this premier Spanish school in the heart of Antigua. Students stay with host families located within walking distance of the school. Open M-F. AmEx/MC/V.

Probigua, 6a Av. Norte 41B (☎7832 0860 or 7832 2998; www.probigua.org). One-on-one lessons with a local professor. Group classes avaliable for the more economically-minded. The dollars that you spend here will do more than just improve your Spanish: Probigua donates all of its profits go to the up-keep of libraries in rural villages of Guatemala.

Niños de Guatemala, 6a Av. Norte 45 (☎4379 1557; www.ninosdeguatemala.org). From the center of town, head North on 6a Av. Norte; just past La Merced on the right. Established in 2006, this non-profit organization works to endow educational projects in places where there is little to no

Antigua

ACCOMMODATIONS
Posada Asjemenou, 2

NIGHTLIFE
La Casbah, **1**
Mono Loco, **4**
Reilly's, **3**

opportunity for elementary education. Volunteers proficient in Spanish are always needed at Niños de Guatemala's newly opened school in Ciudad Vieja, a 20-min. bus ride from Antigua. Volunteers can also work in the Volunteer Center in Antigua, which focuses on fundraising and self-sustainability. Information session and tour of the school site departing from the main office W 2-4pm.

English-Language Bookstore: Rainbow Reading Room, 7a Av. Sur 8 (☎7832 1919; www.rainbowcafeantigua.com), on the northwest corner of the intersection between 7A Av. Sur and 6A C. Poniente. Tons of secondhand books that you can buy or rent for just Q2 per day. AmEx/D/MC/V.

Laundromat: Lavanderia Lily, 1a C. Poniente 12 (☎7832 2295). Walk down 2 blocks from La Merced, and the laundromat is on your right. Q12 per kg. Open daily 7am-7pm. Cash only.

Emergency: ☎1500 or 2421 2810.

Police:(☎7832 2266), on the corner of C. Santa Lucía and 4 C. Poniente. **Tourist Police:** (☎7832 7290), in the back of the *mercado* off of C. Santa Lucía.

24hr. Pharmacy: Ivori, at the intersection of 6A Av. Norte and 2A C. Pte. 19 (☎7832 1559).

Hospital: Santa Lucía Hospital, Calzada Santa Lucía Sur 7 (☎7832 0251).

Internet Access: Micronet, 3a C. Poniente 9 (☎7832 5081), between 5a Av. Norte and 6A Av. Norte. If you simply cannot decide whether to check your email or drink a beer, you can do both for the price of one at Micronet. Buying a beer snags you 15min. of free internet. 15 min. sans alcohol costs Q2, 1hr. Q6. Open M-Sa 8am-7:30pm, Su 10am-7:30pm. Cash only. **Cabaguil,** 5a C. Poniente 6 (☎7832 8316 or 5433 6671), in the Cabaguil Spanish School just down the road from the *parque central*. Internet Q4 per hr. Photocopies Q1 per page. Open daily 8am-8pm. Cash only.

Post Office: (☎7832 0485), at the intersection of 4a C. Poniente and Calzada Santa Luisa Esquina. Open M-F 8:30am-5:30pm, Sa 9am-1pm. **Postal Code:** 03001.

ACCOMMODATIONS

Antigua offers some of the nicest hotels and hostels in Guatemala. Even some of Antigua's cheapest hostels boast beautiful central courtyards and spotless communal bathrooms that would impress even the most highbrow traveler. The following establishments are all conveniently located in this small city.

- **El Hostal** (☎7832 0442). This charming and tranquil hostel is the perfect place to stay. El Hostal manages to remain quiet and peaceful even with 2 bars across the street. Quaint courtyard with a fountain and hammock, and offers laundry service ($1.25 per kg), hot showers, free Wi-Fi, and reasonably priced shuttle service to several locations around Antigua. Delicious breakfast daily 7:30-10:30am. Reception 8am-8pm. Bunkbed Q73; single bed Q89; private single Q122; double Q211; triple Q301. AmEx/D/MC/V. ❸

Las Camelias Inn (☎7832 5483 or 7832 5176; www.cameliasinn.com) 3a C. Oriente #19, between 1a and 2a Av. Norte. Just down the street from the Convent of the Capuchinas, this charming inn will immediately enchant you. Each room has a private bath and cable TV. Second-floor rooms open onto a terrace with spectacular views of the surrounding volcanoes. Laundry included. Wi-Fi. Singles Q326; doubles with one bed Q407, with two beds Q489. AmEx/MC/V. ❺

Posada Asjemenou, C. del Arco 31 (☎7832 2670), located just north of the Arch on the right-hand side. The standard of cleanliness and unbeatable location of this hotel make its slightly pricey rooms worth it. Complimentary breakfast, private baths, safes, Wi-Fi, and a beautiful courtyard. Singles Q211; doubles Q285; triples Q326. AmEx/D/MC/V. ❻

Posada Juma Ocag (☎7832 3109), located directly across the street from the large *mercado*, between 3a and 4a C. Poniente. Hotel-like accommodations for hostel-prices. Clean and comfortable Posada Juma Ocag is a peaceful place to crash. Reserve rooms in advance. Singles Q122, doubles Q146. AmEx/MC/V. ❹

FOOD

Antigua's cosmopolitan flair is especially apparent in its vibrant food scene. It is just as easy to dine on budget-friendly rice and beans as it is to devour a delicious steak-frites for Q244 or more. More touristy areas like the *parque central* and the Arch offer some international fare; you'll need to duck down into less populated side streets to dine on authentic Guatemalan food. Snag some fresh produce from a local vendor. For groceries, visit **La Bodegona** on the corner of 5a C. Poniente and Av. Santa Lucía

- **Rainbow Cafe** (☎7832 1919; www.rainbowcafeantigua.com), on the northwest corner of the intersection between 7a Av. Sur and 6a C. Poniente. Enter through a quaint secondhand bookstore to find yourself in a beautiful courtyard replete with live music and unparalleled ambience. If you can, snag one of the cushioned booths in the far corner and savor Rainbow Cafe's international cuisine while sipping on a delicious mixed drink. The chicken fajitas are incredible (Q49) and their mojito is one of the best in Antigua. AmEx/D/MC/V. ❹

Nokiate, 1a Av. Sur 7 (☎7821 2896; www.nokiate.com). This super-chic restaurant and bar in the southeast corner of Antigua serves up delicious Japanese cuisine alongside killer mixed drinks. Don't miss the *pollo teriyaki* (Q73). Tu and Th are martini nights; Q150 gets you a night of all-you-can-drink martinis. Open Tu-Th 6:30-10:30pm, F-Su 12:30-11pm. AmEx/D/MC/V. ❺

Y Tu Piña Tambien (☎5242 3574) Located at the corner of 6a C. Oriente and 1a Ave. Sur. One of the nicest cafes in town, Y Tu Piña Tambien is a perfect place to grab an omelette and some fresh juices (Q20). Espresso Q8. Free Wi-Fi. Breakfast served all day. Open M-F 7am-8pm, Sa-Su 8am-7pm. AmEx/D/MC/V. ❸

La Cuevita de Los Urquizú, 2a C. Oriente 9d (☎5656 6157 or 7832 2495). The slogan on La Cuevita's business card—"If you come to Antigua and don't eat here, it's like you never came!"—may be boastful, but it rings true. The highlight of this hole-in-the-wall is the 2 tables loaded with freshly made dishes, ranging from sumptuous guacamole to incredible sausages. Fill up a plate with whatever you're in the mood for; it's just Q65. AmEx/D/MC/V. ❹

Las Antorchas (☎7832 0806; www.lasantorchas.com), on 3a Av. Sur in between 5a C.and 6a C. Oriente. This classy restaurant offers everything from international cuisine to your standard rice and beans. Try the *churrasco típico antigüeño* (traditional Antiguan steak; Q97) accompanied by one of their delicious fresh juices (Q18). Boasts a wide selection of wines, beer, and tropical mixed drinks. AmEx/D/MC/V. ❺

⊙ SIGHTS

▓CONVENTO DE LAS CAPUCHINAS. This convent, founded by Spanish nuns in the 18th century, is one of Antigua's archictectural highlights. Though the convent has sustained significant damage from Antigua's many earthquakes, tasteful renovations have made it difficult to discern the old from the new. A beautiful museum on the second floor contextualizes the history of Christianity in Guatemala . The ruins and the underground catacombs are spectacular. *(On the corner of 2 Av. Norte and 2 C. Oriente. Open daily 9am-5pm. Q35, students Q16. Cash only.)*

CATEDRAL SAN JOSE. The Church of San Jose, located directly on the east side of the *parque central*, is certainly a sight to see, but it is the ruins of the Catedral San Jose, right behind the Church, that are truly remarkable. Inside, INGUAT guides await to debrief you on the rich history of the cathedral, which spans more than five centuries. Dominated by an angular archway juxtaposed with softer, rounded versions of the same. The cathedral's structural elements showcase the unique blend of Mayan and Spanish influences that mark much of Guatemala's architecture. Down into the catacombs, visitors learn that the region's history of discrimination is as old as the cathedral itself: the tombs of indigenous Maya are separated from those of the Spanish conquistadores. *(Entrance on 5a C. Oriente across from the Museo de Arte Colonial. Open daily 9am-5pm. Q4. Cash only)*

PALACIO DEL NOBLE AYUNTAMIENTO. On the north side of the *parque central*, the Ayuntamiento is home to two must-see museums: the **Museo del Libro Antiguo** and the **Museo de Santiago.** The Museo del Libro Antiguo—the Musuem of the Ancient Book—contains a wealth of information about the history of literature in Guatemala. This former Spanish colony was the fourth of its kind in the New World to boast its own printing press. In honor of this, the musuem houses an exact replica, in addition to the first book printed on this press and the announcement of the 1773 earthquake that leveled the city. Next door, in the Museo de Santiago, check out weapons and furniture from colonial Antigua. *(North side of the parque central. Open Tu-F 9am-4pm, Sa-Su 9am-noon and 2-4pm. Museo de Santiago is wheelchair-accessible; Museo del Libro Antiguo is not. Q32, Museo Santiago Q16. Cash only.)*

WESTERN HIGHLANDS

SAN FRANCISCO CHURCH. Built in 1579, the San Francisco Church is the burial place of the patron saint of Antigua, **Hermano Pedro,** a 17th-century Spanish missionary elevated to sacred status by Pope John Paul II. The church's stunning interior is definitely worth a peek. Its ruins, some of the most extensive and beautiful in town, are readily accessible to the general public. *(At the south end of 1a Av. Sur. Open daily 8am-6pm. Wheelchair-accessible. Dress appropriately: no shorts or bare shoulders. Ruins Q4.)*

CERRO DE LA CRUZ. You may be tempted to make fun of the fanny-pack wearing, Canon-toting tourists who scurry to Cerro de la Cruz, but they know what's up. A trip here provides a stunning panorama of Antigua and its surrounding volcanoes. Two tourist police permanently stationed on the road up the hill provide security; it is still advisable, however, to bring a friend along and to avoid nighttime excursions. *(Head north on 1a Av. Norte and follow signs. Tourist police lead group tours at 10am and 3pm.)*

MUSEO DE ARTE COLONIAL. Located in the former University of San Carlos Borromeo, this beautiful museum houses a hodgepodge of colonial art, religious artifacts, and paintings . Venture beyond the Moorish-inspired arches and check out the map of 17th century Antigua. Visitors with a knack for Where's Waldo will find a solid 10min. of fun in comparing the parts of the city that have changed to those that remain the same. *(Off of parque central on 5A C. Oriente, across from Catedral San Jose. Open Tu-F 9am-4pm, Sa-Su 9am-noon and 2-4pm. Q24.)*

IGLESIA LA MERCED. It's hard to miss this luxurious mustard yellow church just north of the Arch in the northwest corner of town. The recently repainted Baroque facade, replete with recessed statues and soaked in religious metaphor, is truly a masterpiece. Be sure to step inside to marvel at the cavernous interior. *(Located on the corner of 6A Av. Norte and 1A C. Poniente. Open daily from 8am-6pm. Wheelchair-accessible.)*

PARQUE CENTRAL. Many aspects of life in Antigua have changed since colonial times (the absence of Spanish imperial rule for starters), but one remains the same: everything revolves around the *parque central*. The park is perfect for a 15min. breather and the fountain at its center is stunning. Love-sick travelers be forewarned: the proliferation of couples locked in loving embraces may make the single more keenly aware of their solitude. *(Smack in the middle of town. Wheelchair accessible.)*

CASA POPENOE. This colonial mansion, formerly the residence of a wealthy Spaniard and his family, was renovated and restored to its former architectural glory in the early 20th century. Today, visitors can wander the house as it would have been in the 18th century, complete with a colonial-style kitchen, elegant artwork, and flowery paths through shady courtyards. *(On the corner of 5A C. Oriente and 1A Av. Sur. Open M-Sa 2-4pm. Q12.)*

🎭 🎵 NIGHTLIFE AND ENTERTAINMENT

Though most bars in Guatemala close their doors at 1am, the nightlife scene in Antigua is known for pushing the envelope. Here you'll find everything from dive bars to trendy discotheques.

- **Café No Sé,** 1 Av. Norte 11C (☎2552 2165), across from El Hostal. The perfect place to end a long day in Antigua. Friendly bartenders make this evening hangout one that every traveler should experience. Order a draft beer (Q18) or a tequila shot (Q16-89). Cash only.

- **Bistrot Cinq,** 4A C. Oriente 7 (☎7832 5510; www.bistrotcinq.com). For sophisticated mixed drinks and unparalleled ambience, travelers should head to miss Bistrot Cinq, especially during happy hour (6pm-8pm). Guava Sling Q48. Open M-Th 6-10pm, F-Su, 2-11pm. AmEx/D/MC/V.

Reilly's, 5A Av. Norte 31. Right in the thick of things, Reilly's is easily the city's most popular bar. Touted as Antigua's Irish tavern, this rowdy joint lives up to its motto, "come as strangers, leave as friends." Vodka tonic Q20. Su trivia night. Open until 1am daily. AmEx/D/MC/V.

Riki's Bar, 4A Av. Norte, in the back of the La Escudilla restaurant (☎7832 1327; www. la-escudilla.com/en/rikis.htm). Peopled by foreigners and locals alike, Riki's Bar is the perfect place to start or end your night in Antigua. Happy hour 8:30pm-10pm. Open daily until 1am. AmEx/D/MC/V.

LAGO DE ATITLÁN

Lago de Atitlan has long been shrouded in a veil of mystery and enchantment, and it is hard to grasp the beauty of this place unless you see it for yourself. According to Quiché legend, Lago de Atitlán was one of the four lakes that marked the corners of the world. The towns surrounding the lake are inhabited mostly by indigenous Maya of Cakchiquel and Tz'utujil descent with deep ties to the region, and by foreigners who came for a visit, only to find themselves unwilling to leave. What has resulted is a mosaic of cultural and natural beauty that makes this a place unlike any other. The tourist mecca of Panajachel is the first stop for almost every visitor, and this is reflected in the diversity of the population. Several of the towns that ring Atitlán—bustling Santiago Atitlan, isulated Tzununa, and captivating San Antonio Palopó—are among the few in all of Guatemala in which the men wear traditional dress. San Pedro La Laguna has become a backpacker's paradise, while San Marcos, Santa Cruz, and Jaibalito are home to beautiful lakeside hotels and houses. Whether you are jetting across the lake's blue waters on a *lancha*, haggling with Mayan vendors over the price of a colorful hand-woven *tejido*, or enjoying the unparalleled view of the lake from the summit of the Volcan San Pedro, you are bound to eventually understand the magnetism of this magical lake.

UMBRELLA EH EH. If you are traveling around Lake Atitlán during rainy season, never be deceived by brilliant morning sunshine. The weather is frequently unpredictable; you don't want to be caught unprotected in a Guatemalan downpour.

PANAJACHEL

Panajachel, located on the shore of the Lago de Atitlán, surrounded by volcanoes, teeters between staying true to its Mayan roots, and falling into a toruist trap. This town's unique past explains a lot. In the 1960s and 70s, Pana was a hippie hangout; today, the old-time peace-lovers sell goods and grub alongside traditional Mayans on the city's main thoroughfare, C. Santander. Given its status as Lake Atitlán's transportation hub, Panajachel has morphed a popular tourist destination. Though the town is more developed than other stops in the region, Pana's unique culture holds its own.

TRANSPORTATION

Panajachel is easy to access by chicken bus from any of Guatemala's major cities. Because of its small size, it's easy to get around as well. While some opt to make use of the **tuk tuks,** most people walk or bike. Panajachel is also a hub for boat travel on the lake, offering rides to almost every lakeside destination including Santiago Atitlán, San Marcos, Santa Cruz, and Tzunaná.

Buses: Chicken buses pick up and drop off passengers at the intersection of C. Principal and C. Santander. To: **Chichicastenango, Chimaltenango, Guatemala City,** and **Sololá** (15min., Q4). Aside from the trip to Sololá, prices and trip times vary by driver.

Boats: Panajachel has 2 docks, each servicing a different part of the lake. From the dock at the end of C. del Embarcadero, boats depart for cities on the northern part of the lake including **Santa Cruz** (10min., Q16), **San Marcos** (40min., Q24-32), and **Tzununá** (30min., Q24). From the 2nd dock at the end of C. Rancho Grande, boats leave for **Santiago Atitlán** (1 hr., Q32).

Bike Rental: Emanuel, C. 14 de Febrero (☎7762 2790). Mountain bikes Q57 per day.

Tuk Tuk: For Q4, they'll take you anywhere in Panajachel.

ORIENTATION AND PRACTICAL INFORMATION

Panajachel is a small city that is very easy to navigate. **C. Santander** and **C. Principal** are the city's main thoroughfares and connect the old village in the north to the lake at the south end. C. Santander is well marked with signs directing travelers toward the town's amenities.

Tourist office: INGUAT, C. Santander 1-87, Zona 2, Centro Comercial San Rafael, L-No 11 (☎7762-1106; www.visitguatemala.com).

Tours: Atitrans, C. Santander, Anexo Hotel Regis (☎7762 0152 or 7762 0146; www.atitrans.com). Tours of the lake, 2 per day, Q285 per person. Offers 24hr. shuttle service to Antigua (Q98), Guatemala City (Q179), and Flores (Q489). Reservations required.

Bank: Banco Agromercantil, C. Principal (☎7762 1145), in the Edificio Mayan Palace. M-Sa 8:30am-6pm, Su 9am-1pm.

Beyond Tourism:

Jabel Tinamit, C. Santander (☎7762 6056 or 7762 6058; www.jabeltinamit.com). This Spanish school is owned and operated by local Maya. Cash only.

Jardín de America, C. del Chalí (☎7762 2637; www.jardindeamerica.com). Excellent Spanish language instruction with low teacher-to-student ratio. Cash only.

Habitat para la Humanidad (☎7762 0408), on the alley marked by signs for the Casa Linda and Hospedaje Montufar. Information on volunteer opportunities in the Atitlán region. Open M-F 8am-1pm and 2-4pm, Sa 8am-noon.

Laundromat: Lavanderia Santander, C. Santander (☎5756 8577). Open 7am-8pm. Cash only.

Emergency: ☎1500 or 2421 2810.

Police: ☎110. **Tourist Police (Asistur):** ☎2421 2810.

24hr. Pharmacy: Farmacia Batres, C. Principal 0-32, Zona 2 (☎7762 1485).

Medical Services: Pana Medic, C. Principal 0-72, Zona 2.

Internet Access: Mayanet, C. Santander, just north of C. 14 de Febrero. Q8 per hr. Open 8am-10:30pm. Cash only. **Tecnocompu,** C. Principal, just north of intersection with C. Santander. Scanner and international calls. Internet Q5 per hr. Open daily 9am-9:30pm. Cash only.

Post Office: Correo de Panajachel, A-3 C. Santander, Zona 2, Panajachel, Sololá (☎7762 2603). M-F 8:30am-5:30pm, Sa 9am-1pm. **Postal Code:** 07010

ACCOMMODATIONS

Living up to its status as the "Gateway to the Lake," Panajachel has an impressive array of accomodations. Most establishments are conveniently located on or around the central street, C. Santander, though some are tucked away on quieter streets.

Hospedaje Garcia (☎7762 2187), follow the signs from C. Santander; once on C. de Chalí it's hard to miss. If the central location of Hospedaje Garcia isn't enough to seal the deal, its friendly staff, comfortable rooms, and great prices will do the trick. Rooms are spacious, secure, and well-kept, and the communal bathroom facilities are immaculate. Singles Q40; doubles Q81. Cash only. ❷

Hotel Dos Mundos (☎7762 2078, 7762 2140, or 7762 2865; www.hoteldosmundos.com). This resort-style hotel right on C. Santander is a pleasant, if relatively pricey, alternative to Panajachel's budget-friendly accommodations. Well-kept garden, pool, and ample outdoor seating. Singles Q325; doubles Q488. Reservations recommended. AmEx/D/MC/V. ❺

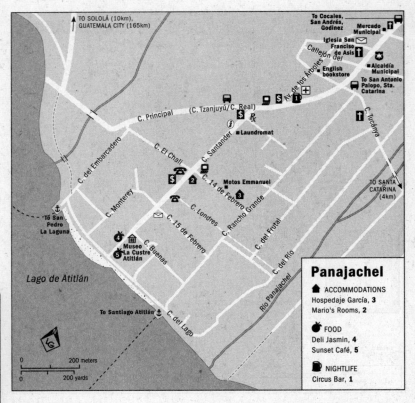

Panajachel

ACCOMMODATIONS
Hospedaje García, **3**
Mario's Rooms, **2**

FOOD
Deli Jasmin, **4**
Sunset Café, **5**

NIGHTLIFE
Circus Bar, **1**

Mario's Rooms (☎7762 1313). Smack in the middle of town on C. Santander, Mario's Rooms offers a great budget alternative to some of the more expensive hotels in town, while furnishing many of the same amenities. Rooms are clean, spacious, and equipped with safes, private baths, and cable TV. Breakfast included. Free Wi-Fi. Checkout 1pm. Singles Q122, doubles Q162. Cash only. ❸

FOOD

Featuring everything from Malaysian dishes to Uruguayan delicacies, Panajachel's international culinary influence is truly impressive. For groceries, visit **Chalos** at the intersection of C. Santander and C. Principal.

Deli Jasmin (☎7762 2585), at the south end of C. Santander, just up the road from the lake. Deli Jasmin is perfect any time of the day. Try their incredible banana pancakes (Q29) or pita pizzas (Q27). A Panajachel fixture since 1985, Deli Jasmine is not to be missed. Open M and W-Su 7am-6pm. Cash only. ❸

Las Chinitas (☎7762 2612). From the traditional Chinese decor to the delicious food, it's difficult to pull yourself away from this fun and welcoming restaurant. Try the lunch special (dumplings, Malaysian fried rice, and fresh mango; Q57). Open daily 8am-10pm. Cash only. ❹

Crossroads Cafe, 0-27 C. del Campanario (☎5292 8439; www.crossroadscafepana. com). There is no better way to start your day than with a perfectly crafted cup of coffee at the Crossroads Café. This café offers an unparalleled everybody-knows-your-name atmosphere. The cinnamon buns are out of this world. Open Tu-Sa 9am-1pm and 3-7pm. Cash only. ❷

👁 SIGHTS

MUSEO LA CUSTRE ATITLÁN. This small museum provides a comprehensive history of the peoples and cities of Lake Atitlán. Museo La Custre also houses an interesting collection of Mayan artifacts found in and around the lake. *(At the south end of C. Santander. ☎7762 2326. Open M-F and Su 8am-6pm, Sa 8am-7pm. Parking availbale in the lot of the Hotel Posada de Don Rodrigo. Museum entry Q35, students Q20, under 12 free.)*

SAN FRANCISCO DE ASIS. Dominating a small plaza in the old village, this beautiful Catholic church definitely warrants a visit. *(At the intersection of Av. de los Árboles and C. del Campanario. No bathing suits.)*

📻 NIGHTLIFE

Though the beginning of the week can be a bit slow, Panajachel's nightlife picks up as the weekend approaches.

▣ **PanaRock Café,** C. Santander 1-86 (☎7762 2194; www.panarockcafe.com). This place calls out to travelers once the sun sets. Live music, cheap happy hour, and great ambience make a night at the PanaRock Café too good to pass up. Open until 1am.

Circus Bar (☎7762 0374 or 7762 2056; www.circus-bar.com), across the street from Chapiteau on C. de los Árboles. Known for its pizza (margarita; Q57), Circus Bar has been a fixture on the Panajachel nightlife scene for more than 20 years. Open noon-midnight. AmEx/D/MC/V over Q97.

Chapiteau (☎7762 0374 or 7762 2056), at the intersection of C. de los Árboles and C. Principal. Chapiteau has been a hallmark in Panajachel since 1988. Locals and tourists alike come to dance and play pool. Open W-Sa 7pm-1am. AmEx/D/MC/V.

📌 DAYTRIPS FROM PANAJACHEL

SANTA CATARINA AND SAN ANTONIO

Minibuses depart from C. el Amante in Panajachel every 20min. Q30. Minibuses returning to Panajachel leave from Santa Catarina and San Antonio's main streets.

Visitors to Panajachel should be sure to check out Santa Catarina Palopó and San Antonio Palopó, two small towns built into the hillside southwest of Panajachel on the shores of Lake Atitlán. Both towns are known for their *tejidos* (knitting). The church in Santa Catarina, located right on the main road, is a good place to start exploring. Follow one of the many alleyways down to the stunning shore of the lake. At the edge of town is the local cemetery. Here, colorful tombstones watch over quiet Lake Atitlán.

San Antonio sits 2km down the lake's shore. This town is slightly larger than its neighbor and feels slightly more traditional. Alongside the terraced farmland that descends down the mountains enclosing this charming city, travelers can hardly avoid breathtaking lake views in the town's marketplace. Head to the area around the main church (definitely worth a peek) where old women sell homespun ceramics, knittings, and often crafts. The Mayan influences in both towns are vibrant examples of the wider Mayan influence in the Lake Atitlán region.

If you want to extend your stay in Santa Catarina, **Hospedaje Santa Catarina** ❶, on the main road through town, is a solid budget choice. In San Antonio Palopó, the **Hotel Terrazas del Lago** ❶ has reasonably priced rooms with great views of the lake.

SANTIAGO DE ATITLÁN

Though Santiago de Atitlan is accessible by road, most people arrive by lancha from Pana-jachel (20 min.; Q25). Once at the docks, the town is relatively easy to navigate. Santiago's main road originates at the dock, from which all of the city's sights are visible, and there is no shortage of locals willing to direct you. If a guide offers to show you around the city, which is unnecessary given how easy it is to get around, be prepared to pay a significant amount of money for his services. While taking pictures of people without their permission is never recommended, be particularly conscious of taking pictures of Santiago's inhabitants because some will charge. (Museo Cojolya open M-F 9am-4pm, Sa 9am-1pm; you can meet the weavers at 11am and 1pm.)

Santiago de Atitlán, Lake Atitlán's largest, and arguably most traditional, city is defined by its strong Tz'unujil Mayan culture. Nestled in a horseshoe-shaped bay in the southwest corner of Lake Atitlán, Santiago's sits between the San Pedro Volcano and the Tolimán Volcanoes. Accessible by road or by *lancha* (boat), most visitors arrive at the docks and make the 10min. walk up into the center of town. In the center of town stands a massive Catholic church, which, despite having undergone extensive renovations, still affords tourists glimpses of its original 16th-century construction. A powerful representation of Central American Catholicism, the church's walls are populated by countless life-like statues of the country's indigenous people. Santiago's residents worship the folk saint, Maximón. A shrine devoted to Maximón is constructed each year and placed in a different spot in the city, where townspeople and tourists can come to pay homage. A trip to Maximón's dwelling typically costs Q2. In addition, expect to pay a small fee to the local who shows you where to find it. After paying their dues to this effigy, visitors should be sure to check out **Museo Cojolya,** located right on the main road. The musuem is devoted to the weaving culture of the Tz'unujil Maya and features exhibits that illustrate traditional dress and the intricate process of dying and weaving. (Offers explanations in both English and Spanish. Admission is free.)

On Fridays, just a few blocks from the church, Santiago de Atitlan plays host to a large market. Street vendors fill several streets and sell everything from vegetables to underwear and soap. At the docks, tourists can rent canoes to explore the bay. Those in need of more directed activity can find guides to take them to a scenic vantage point of the city and the surrounding volcanoes.

For a place to sleep, the centrally located **Hotel Chi-Nim-Ya** ❶ (singles US$7, doubles US$10) and the **Hotel Tzan'juyú** ❶ (rooms from US$13) are convenient choices. To soothe your grumbling stomach, the main street in town has plenty of restaurants that serve *comida típica* of Santiago and the surrounding region.

SOLOLÁ. Though the city itself is nothing special, Sololá does have two draws: market days on Tuesday and Friday, and the parade of the *cofradías* on Sunday. On market days, Sololá is filled with artisans and vendors hailing from neighboring towns and villages. Though it can get a bit hectic (especially during the larger Friday market), meandering through the wealth of local fares is well-worth the experience. On Sunday, for the parade of the *cofradías*, elders of the community, wear colorful traditional dress on their way to late-morning mass. (*Chicken buses shuttle between Panajachel and Sololá every 10min. Be warned: the speed at which chicken bus drivers take the cliff-side curves will nauseate even the hardiest traveler.*)

SAN PEDRO

A dynamic city on the shores of Lake Atitlán, San Pedro never has trouble attracting visitors. Though plagued by drug problems, the town is an ideal base for those in search of outdoor adventures. From kayaking, snorkeling, and horse-back-riding, to climbing the Volcán San Pedro, which looms above the city, San Pedro will not disappoint. Having become somewhat of a backpacker's paradise in recent years, San Pedro is an exciting and ever-changing place to visit.

▐ TRANSPORTATION

San Pedro La Laguna is easily accessible by **lancha, chicken bus,** or **minibus.** Most travelers make use of the convenient *lancha* service that connects San Pedro to the other towns on Lake Atitlán.

Buses: Chicken buses depart from the central plaza, across from the church, for **Quetzaltenango** (2½hr., every 30min., last bus 11am) and **Guatemala City** (3¼hr., every 30min., last bus 2pm).

Bike Rental: Excursion Big Foot (☎7721 8203), up from the Panajachel dock. Offers a variety of outdoor activities. Bike rental Q66 (US$8) per day.

Boats: Public *lanchas* depart from San Pedro every 20-30min. *Lanchas* to **Panajachel** (30min., Q25), **Santiago** (15 min., Q15), and **Santa Cruz** (20 min., Q20). Private *lancha* service is also available, though it is significantly more expensive and only marginally more convenient than the public service.

✈ ▐ ORIENTATION AND PRACTICAL INFORMATION

Visitors to San Pedro typically arrive at either the **Panajachel** or **Santiago dock,** which serve the north and south sides of the lake respectively. *Tuk-tuks* shuttle travelers between the docks (Q5). Most of the bars, restaurants, cafes, hotels, and hostels are located on or close to the shore of the lake, while the town itself is set further back. San Pedro is surprisingly hilly; if you want to explore beyond the tourist lakeside establishments but want to save your legs, have a *tuk-tuk* take you to the center of town (*"al centro"*). Winding roads and a lack of street names make San Pedro difficult to navigate, so don't be afraid to ask for directions.

Tours and Agencies: Asoantur (☎5423 7423 or 4379 4545), off the Panajachel dock. Volcano hikes Q200 (includes taxi ride to basecamp). Kayak rental Q20 per hr. **Rancho Moises** (☎5967 3235), on the trail between the 2 docks. Offers eco-tours of San Pedro and its surroundings on horseback (Q40 per hr.) **Atitlán Adventures** (☎4130 5205), on the trail between the 2 docks. Water activities like snorkeling and canoeing on Lake Atitlán are reasonably priced.

Bank: Banrural, 2 blocks down from the main square.

Laundry: Shampoo Laundry (☎5094 4230), to the right of the Panajachel dock. Q5 per lb.

Police: (☎5534 0256), just off the main square to the right of the church.

Internet access: D'Noz (☎5578 0201), just off the Panajachel dock. Also home to a restaurant, bar, and small library. Cash only.

Post Office: (☎2476 0202), next to the church. Open M-F 8:30am-12:30pm and 1:30-5:30pm, Sa 9am-1pm. **Postal Code:** 07018.

ACCOMMODATIONS

Hotel San Antonio (☎4423 1156). From Panajachel dock, head left through town; the hotel is on the right just before the road turns into a dirt path. Spacious well-kept rooms. Stunning lake views from the 3rd floor terrace. Laundry service available. Free Wi-Fi. Singles Q50; doubles Q80. Cash only. ❷

Hotel Gran Sueño (☎7721 8110), on the right as you head left from the Panajachel dock. A tranquil place to stay. Rooms have private baths and excellent views of the lake. Singles Q75; doubles Q120. Cash only. ❷

Hospedaje Casa Maria (☎4145 0307), on the dirt path between the 2 docks. Guests will enjoy escaping the bustle of San Pedro in this somewhat hidden *hospedaje*. Rooms are clean and spacious with private baths. Singles Q40. Cash only. ❶

Hotel Maria Elena (☎5864 4628), on the left side as you head left from the Panajachel dock. A new hotel with beautiful rooms. Singles Q100; doubles Q150. Cash only. ❸

FOOD

Covering everything from chop suey to homemade apple pie, the tourist industry has shaped Pana's restaurant business. While there are some solid local options concentrated in the center of town, travelers would be remiss not to take advantage of the great international restaurants that have sprung up here.

Zoola (☎5847 4857), on the path between the 2 docks. Guests dine Middle-Eastern style, seated on floor pillows and carpets. Delicious ethnic food and local fare. Small hotel on the premises with 8 rooms available. Open 9am-9pm. Cash only. ❷

Café La Puerta (☎5098 1272 or 5284 2406), on the path between the 2 docks. A wonderful cafe that offers guests the option of sitting lakeside or in a quaint garden. Sandwiches and heartier entrees for reasonable prices. Nachos and guacamole Q25. Open daily from 8am-5pm. Cash only. ❷

Fata Morgana, just up from the Panajachel dock, on the left. Fresh baked goods and delicious coffee. Entrees include sandwiches and pizza (Q30-Q40). Amazing smoothies (*Besa Fresa*, Q20). Open M-Tu and Th-Su 8am-2pm. Cash only. ❷

Nick's Place (☎7721 8065), on the Panajachel dock. Heaping portions; appetizers (Q20) are the size of entrees. Mixed drinks and beers (Q10-Q20) are some of the cheapest in town. Open daily 7am-11pm. Cash only. ❷

SIGHTS AND OUTDOOR ACTIVITIES

VOLCÁN SAN PEDRO. Many come to San Pedro in hopes of conquering the Volcan San Pedro, which dominates the landscape of this lakeside town. Though in recent times the hike has become safer for tourists to tackle without a guide, solo hikers should be cautious as robberies are still a concern. *(Several tour companies lead hikes up Volcan San Pedro (see Asoantur, p. 149). The hike to the summit takes 4hr. It's best to get an early start.)*

THERMAL POOLS. Visitors should not miss the thermal pools naturally heated by the Volcán San Pedro. To complete the experience, most thermal pool establishments serve food and drinks to their guests. *(Just off the path between the Panajachel and Santiago docks. Most charge Q20 per hr.)*

CHICHICASTENANGO

Chichicastenango's famous Thursday and Sunday markets draw people from across Guatemala to what is considered by many to be the country's greatest attraction. The tourist invasion has had both positive and negative effects: both cheap knock-offs of traditional textiles and the most well-crafted products that the Guatemalan countryside has to offer are for sale in the packed stalls. Despite of the tour groups that flood in from Antigua and Panajachel, "Chichi," with its nearly 50,000 inhabitants, remains very much an *indígena* town.

Like the town's bustling markets, Chichi's history is tumultuous. It was built by the Spanish in the 16th century as a home for refugees from Utatlán, the Quiché capital brutally leveled by the Spaniards. During the 19th century, the Guatemalan government used forced-labor laws written during the colonial era to pull Quiché workers from the mountains to work on coffee plantations. Tensions rose again in the late 1970s and early 80s, when guerilla activity disturbed the area. Despite these periods of persecution, the region's unique meld of indigenous and Catholic religious tradition continues to thrive.

▐ TRANSPORTATION

Located in the heart of the Western highlands, Chichicastenango is relatively easy to reach. A short jaunt to **Los Encuentros** (20 min. via microbus) allows travelers to connect to **chicken buses** heading to most major destinations in Guatemala.

Buses: Buses depart from the intersection of 5a Av. and 5a C. to **Guatemala City** (3hr., every 20min. 5am-4pm, Q20) and **Santa Cruz del Quiche** (30min., every 20min. 5am-4pm, Q5). **Microbuses,** stationed on 7a Av. between 8a C. and 9a C., shuttle passengers to **Los Encuentros,** where they can catch chicken buses heading to **Quetzaltenango, Chimaltenango,** and other popular destinations. Several local travel agencies (such as **Chichi Turkaj,** p. 151) offer shuttle services to several Guatemalan cities.

Tuk-tuks: In Chichi, as in most small Guatemala cities, *tuk-tuks* are the most commonly used alternative to walking.

▐◆ ▐ ORIENTATION AND PRACTICAL INFORMATION

Chichicastenango is centered around the **parque central**. The *parque* is bordered by 4 and 5 Av. to the west and east, and 7 and 8 C. to the north and south. Reading street signs gets a bit tricky during market days, when they are hardly discernible behind a slew of market stands. Tourist services are concentrated in the area surrounding the *parque central* and the **Centro Comercial,** located on the north side of the *parque central*.

Tours and Agencies: Chichi Turkaj, 5 Av. 5-24 (☎7756 1579), just off the main squre. Offers general information and shuttle service to many Guatemalan cities.

Bank: Banco Industrial, 6a C. between 5a and 6a Av. Open M-F and Su 9am-5pm, Sa 8am-noon. **Currency exchange** and **ATM.**

Beyond Tourism: Ut'z Bat'z, 5a Av. 5-24 (☎5008 5193; www.enmisalsa.com/english), just north of the central plaza. This Mayan handicraft collective works with the *En Mi Salsa* project to make environmentally friendly sustainable products and employ impoverished citizens. Open W 1-5pm, Th 9am-5pm, Sa 10am-5pm, and Su 9am-5pm.

Police: 4 blocks past the arch, next to the school.

Pharmacy: Farmacia Girón, 5a Av. 5-70 (☎7756 1226). Open daily 7:30am-12:30pm and 2-7:30pm.

Medical Services: El Buen Samaritano, 6a C. 6-30 (☎7756 1163).

FROM THE ROAD

MY NIGHT AS A DRAG REINA

Exhausted from a day of exploring my eighth lakeside town of the week, San Pedro La Laguna, I returned to my hostel intending to take it easy until bedtime. Yeah, it was a Saturday night, but that doesn't mean anything when you're staying in the sleepy town of Santa Cruz, right? Wrong. When I arrived at the hostel, I was told that they hosted a party on Saturday nights. One detail caught me off guard: everyone was expected to cross-dress. I'm not one to get embarrassed or be a party-pooper, so I knew that I was going to be a full-fledged participant, but I didn't expect every attendee would heed to the gender-bending theme. Then again, the hostel did have a costume room dedicated to these Saturday night parties. That night, I walked down to the party, dressed in a purple lace dress, wondering what I was getting myself in to. I entered the room, and found myself surrounded by cross-dressed partiers. Apparently you don't even have to be staying at the Iguana to attend the party. You just have to tell them in advance that you're going to be there. The night included dancing, cat-walking on tables, brief moments of stopping to enjoy the stunning view of Lake Atitlán, and then more dancing.

-Elias Berger

Internet Access: Internet Café, 5a Av. 8-39 (☎7756 1215), just south of the central plaza. Internet Q8 per hr. Open daily 7am-9pm. Cash only.

Post Office: El Correo (☎2232 6101 or 2476 0202), on the corner of 4a Av. and 7a C. Open M-Sa 8:30am-5:30pm. **Postal Code:** 14006.

ACCOMMODATIONS

Most of Chichicastenango's hotels and hostels are located only a block or two from the center of town.

Hotel Chalet House, 3a C. 7-44 (☎7756 1360; www.chalethotelguatemala.com). Three-floor hotel with a homey atmosphere. Spacious rooms have private baths. Breakfast included. Free Wi-Fi. Singles Q200. ❺

Posada El Arco, 4a C. 4-36 (☎7756 1255). Well-furnished rooms with private baths and large beds centered around a stunning courtyard. English-speaking owners are welcoming and a wonderful resource for information on Chichi and environs. Rooms Q225. MC/V. ❺

Hotel Chugüilá, 5a Av. 5-24 (☎7756 1134). Spacious rooms with private baths look out over a central courtyard. Singles Q80. AmEx/D/MC/V. ❷

Hotel Posada El Teléfono, 8a C. 1-64 (☎7756 1197), behind the El Calvario. A great budget option in a quiet part of town. No-frills, institutional-looking rooms, some with views of the colorful above-ground tombs in the city's large cemetery. Immaculate communal bathrooms. Singles Q30. Cash only. ❶

Hospedaje Girón, 6a C. 4-52 (☎7756 1156). Reasonably priced rooms with private baths and cable TV. Breakfast included. Internet Q6 per hr. Singles Q85; doubles Q145. Cash only. ❸

FOOD

While the many of the restaurants clustered around the *parque* are pricey, cheap and tasty options abound in the **market,** which plays host to a colorful labyrinth of food vendors.

Casa San Juan (☎7756 2086 or 5134 8852), in the main square, opposite Santo Tomás Church, on the 2nd floor. Upscale, by Chichi's standards. *Comida típica* Q60. Sandwiches with homemade bread Q20. Occasional live music. Open Tu-W and F-Sa 9am-9pm; Th and Su 7am-10pm. V. ❸

La Villa de Los Cofrades (☎7756 1643 or 7756 1678), on the 1st floor of the Centro Comercial, on the north side of the central plaza. *Comida típica* options are a safe bet. Club sandwich Q40. Open W and Sa 9am-8pm, Th and Su 7am-4pm. AmEx/D/MC/V. ❸

Restaurant Kieq Ik Wal'm Ja (☎ 7756 1013), off the central plaza. Outdoor balcony seating offers birds-eye views of the central plaza, which are especially impressive on market days. Specializes in steak dishes (Q50). Chile *rellenos* Q35. Impressive breakfast selection (banana pancakes Q27). Open M and W-Su 7am-8pm. AmEx/D/MC/V. ❸

Restaurante La Parrilla (☎ 7756 1321 or 7756 1497). Grilled entrees Q30-50. Hearty breakfast special (eggs, sausage, beans, cheese and tortilla) Q22. Open daily 7am-9pm. AmEx/D/MC/V. ❷

Tu Café, several doors down from the Santo Tomás Church on the main plaza. Great for a quick meal or a snack. Nachos and guacamole Q18. Sandwiches Q15-30. *Plato típico* Q45. Open daily 7:30am-9pm. Cash only. ❷

📷 SIGHTS

📷 MARKET DAY. Although a few stands remain open all week, the scheduled Thursday and Sunday markets are well worth a special visit. On these days, the otherwise calm, peaceful streets of Chichi undergo a drastic transformation: every inch of space is blanketed with vendors hawking their crafts and handiwork. The main **vegetable market** is inside the **Centro Comercial** on the north side of the plaza. If you're shopping for *artesanía*, remember that bargaining is expected (aim for 30% off the asking price). While prices in Chichi certainly aren't the lowest in the country, you can still find some good deals. Asking prices for wooden masks (Q20-100), hammocks (Q80-300), and big blankets (Q80-150) vary greatly depending on quality. Shop around before making a purchase. Tourist buses arrive at around 10am and leave at around 2pm; the best bargains are found before and after the crowds of tourists clog the streets and drive up the prices.*(The market usually lasts from about 8am to 5pm.)*

IGLESIA SANTO TOMÁS. Looming over the central market, this church provides a fascinating glimpse into the Catholicism of the Quiché Maya. The church is built on an ancient Quiché Maya holy site and is therefore sacred to local indigenous communities. *Indígenas* make an elaborate ritual of ascending the steps and repeatedly kneeling. An incense fire is kept burning at the base of the church's steps and, on market days, brightly dressed *indígena* women cover the stairs with hibiscus, lilies, roses, and gladiolas; churchgoers purchase the blooms to give as offerings. Inside the altars are surrounded by candles and petals dedicated to both Catholic saints and Quiché ancestors. Check out the former monastery, located to the right of the church. *(On the corner of 5a Av. and 8a C., on the parque central. Use the side entrance, to the right; the front entrance is reserved for senior church officials and cofradías. Dress modestly. No photography allowed. Free, but small donations appreciated.)*

PASCUAL ABAJ. This Mayan shrine, dating back to the Columbian era, consists of a ceremonial rock surrounded on three sides by a low stone wall. There's usually a small fire burning in front, as well as a profusion of flowers, liquor, and candles. The best time to go is Sunday mornings, when gatherings are larger and more frequent. Visitors should try to visit during a ceremony. *(Walk downhill 1 block from the Santo Tomás church on 5 Av. Turn right on 9 C. and follow it as it curves downhill and to the left. When the road crosses a small stream and then veers to the right, follow the large sign and proceed straight up the dirt path. Pass through a courtyard and a small museum of ceremonial masks and enter a forested area. The trail zigzags up the hillside until flattening out in a small meadow dotted with pines. The shrine is about 30km farther on the right.)*

MUSEO ROSSBACH. In addition to providing a detailed history of the region, this museum houses a collection of pre- and post-Classical Maya bowls, figurines, arrowheads, and necklaces. *(On the south side of the parque central. Open Tu-W and F-Sa 8am-12:30pm and 2-4:30pm, Th 8am-4pm, Su 8am-2pm. Q5.)*

EL CALVARIO. This chapel, which looks like a smaller version of the Iglesia Santo Tomás, is worth peeking inside. Incense-burning rituals are frequently held on the front steps. Perhaps more impressive than the chapel itself is the view of Chichi's colorful **cemetery,** to the left of El Calvario (8a C.). *(On the corner of 4a Av. and 8a C., on the southwest corner of the parque central. Dress modestly. No photography allowed.)*

SANTA CRUZ DEL QUICHÉ

Located about 18km north of Chichicastenango and 40km northeast of Quetzaltenango, Santa Cruz del Quiché (pop. 22,100) is the capital of the district and an important transportation hub for those heading to more remote parts of the highlands. The town is neither particularly attractive nor exciting, though some might take comfort in the big-city comforts that Santa Cruz provides, like western clothing stores and traffic lights set this city apart from the surrounding towns. The nearby Quiché Maya ruins are perfect for a brief escape from the city.

TRANSPORTATION

Santa Cruz del Quiché is easily reached by **chicken bus, microbus,** or **shuttle.** Chicken buses connect Santa Cruz with Guatemala City, and microbuses connect Santa Cruz to Chichicastenango, Nebaj, and other nearby cities.

Buses: Chicken buses arrive at and depart from the **bus station** at 1a Av. and 10a C. To reach the central plaza from there, head north for 4 blocks on 1 Av. and make a left on 6a C. Microbuses also leave from the bus terminal, but some (especially those headed to Nebaj) will drive through the central plaza to pick up more passengers. The times and prices listed below are for **chicken buses.** Microbuses take ¾ of the time and cost an additional Q5-10.

Guatemala City: (3hr., every 30min., Q20). Makes stops at **Chichicastenango, Los Encuentros,** and **Chimaltenango.**

Chichicastenango: (30 min., every 30min., Q3). Same bus as the Guatemala City bus.

Los Encuentros: (1hr., every 30min., Q6). Also the same bus as Guatemala City. At **Los Encuentros,** there are connections to **Quetzaltenango** or **Panajachel.**

Quetzaltenango: (3hr., every hr. from 5-7am, Q20).

Nebaj: (3hr.; 5am, noon, 6pm; Q15). Passes through Sacapulas, where transfers can be made for **Huehuetenango** and **Cobán.**

ORIENTATION AND PRACTICAL INFORMATION

Santa Cruz del Quiché is laid out on a grid, making it easy to navigate. The **central plaza** is bounded by **1a and 2a Av.** and **3a and 6a C.** The **bus terminal** is located a few blocks southeast of the plaza, though many microbuses will drop passengers right in front of the whitewashed **Catholic church** that stands on the east side of the main square.

Bank: Banrural, 2a Av. 3-22 (☎7755 1540), in Zona 1. Open M-F 8am-5pm, Sat-Sun 8am-12pm.

Police: 0 Av., 4 C. (☎7755 1106), in Zona 1.

24hr. Pharmacy: Farmacia Batres, 2a Av. 6-13, in Zona 1, right on the southwest corner of the main square.

Hospital: Hospital Nacional Santa Elena (☎7755 1782), just west of the city.

Internet Access: Hotel Acuario (☎7755 1878), on the 2nd floor. Q5 per hour. Cash only.

Chichicastenango

🏠 **ACCOMMODATIONS**
Hospedaje Salvador, **7**
Hotel Chugüila, **2**
Hotel Girón, **3**
Hotel Posada Belén, **9**
Posada El Arco, **1**

🍎 **FOOD**
Cafe Restaurante La Villa
    de los Cofrades, **6**
Casa San Juan, **4**
El Baquete de los Mayas, **8**
Restaurante La Parilla, **5**

TO 🐢 (300m),
SANTA CRUZ
DEL QUICHÉ (18km)

Arco
Gucumatz

Turkaj Tours

El Buen
Samaritano

Public
Gardens

El Calvario
Chapel

Maya
Chicchi Vans

Parque
Central

Museo
Regional

Santo Tomás

Cemetery

0   200 meters
0   200 yards

TO SHRINE OF
PASCUAL ABAJ (300m)

Post Office: 3a C., (☎ 7755 1085), between 0 and 1a Av. Open M-F 8:30am-5:30pm, Sa-Su 9am-1pm. **Postal Code:** 14001.

🏠 ACCOMMODATIONS

Not many people stay in Santa Cruz del Quiché, as it is more of a jumping off point than a destination in itself. If you are looking for a place to stay, don't stray too far from the center of this somewhat sprawling town. Budget accommodations tend to be rougher around the edges than in other Guatemalan destinations, so you might consider springing for some comfort and convenience.

Hotel Acuario 5a C. 2-44 (☎ 7755 1878). Just a ½-block west of the main square on 5a C., there's a staircase that leads up to the main entrance. Clean, secure, and spacious rooms with private bath and cable television. Internet Q5 per hr. Rooms Q100. V. ❸

Hotel Monte Bello (☎ 7755 3948 or 7755 3949), on 4a Av. between 9a and 10a C. Clean and comfortable rooms. All rooms have private bath, TV, and Wi-Fi. Singles Q125; doubles Q200. Cash only. ❺

Hotel Las Vegas (☎ 7755 1464), 3a Av. between 4a and 5a C. No-frills rooms for a good price. Singles Q60; doubles Q100. Cash only. ❷

🔲 FOOD

Santa Cruz del Quiché has plenty decent *comedores*. Santa Cruz is also home to many *panaderías* (bakeries), where you can get everything from a simple roll to an elaborate pastry—either way you can't go wrong. Try the *panadería* on the corner of 2a Av. and 5a C., right on the main square. Santa Cruz's **market** on Thursdays and Saturdays has delicious fresh produce.

🔳 **El Portal de la Cruz,** just west of the *parque central* on 4a C. The place to sample *comida típica*. Open daily 8am-7pm. Cash only. ➋

   Pizza Argentina, 6a C. 3-31 (☎7755 0553), just west of the main square. Good slices for a good prices. Pizzas Q30-50. Delivery available. Open 9am-9pm. Cash only. ➋

🔳 DAYTRIP FROM SANTA CRUZ DEL QUICHÉ

UTATLÁN

Just outside of Santa Cruz del Quiché lies Utatlán, capital of the Quiché Kingdom during AD 1250-1523. Under the rule of Q'uk'ab, the Quiché domain extended from the Pacific nearly all the way to the Atlantic. The capital also encompassed nine different nations, including Tzutuhil and Cakchiquel, two major indigenous groups. The official archaeological site of **K'umarkaaj** ("Houses of Old Reeds") covers an area of eight sq. km. The only discernible structures are located around a single *parque*. Once you enter the site, there is a **Visitors Center** that houses a **museum,** where you can check out a model of what Utatlán looked like in its heyday. To reach the ruins themselves, follow the path right from the Visitors Center. Standing in what was once the **central plaza,** you can make out the few of the structures that remain. One of the most interesting features of these ruins is the tunnel that runs under the plaza. This tunnel can be found by following the steep trail to the right of the plaza ruins. Follow the sign that reads "La dirección de la Cueva." Religious healing ceremonies have taken place in this tunnel for the last 500 years. If you're lucky, you may stumble across one. You need a flashlight to see into the cave; bring your own. *(To get to the ruins of Utatlán, follow C. 10 out of town (begin at the bus terminal), which eventually passes by La Colonia. At the sign for the SCEP, take a right up the hill to the park entrance. The walk from there is 3km (about 30min.). A tuk-tuk will take you from the main square in Santa Cruz (10 min.; Q50). Museum open daily 8am-4pm; gates close a little later. Q30.)*

NEBAJ

Though a mere 40km north of Santa Cruz del Quiché, winding dirt roads and imposing mountain passes make Nebaj (pop. 19,600) feel very isolated. Situated in a fertile, stream-fed valley high in the Cuchumatanes, Nebaj marks the southwest point of the Ixil Triangle. With Chajul to the north and Cotzal to the east, this is the homeland of the Ixil Maya. Nebaj is a beautiful, traditional town; the local clothing is striking. Women dress in deep-red *cortes* and adorn themselves with elegant, forest-green shoulder drapes with sewn golden birds and matching head wraps. Fires and landmines wrecked the land during Guatemala's civil war in the late 70s and early 80s. Today, the town's natural beauty makes it difficult to imagine its scarred past.

▐ TRANSPORTATION

The only way to get to Nebaj is via bus or microbus from Santa Cruz del Quiche (which goes through Sacapulas) or from Cobán.

Buses: The **bus station** is on 7a C., across from the market. The bus service is somewhat erratic, so it is best to check the schedules at the station. Buses run out of Nebaj to **Santa Cruz del Quiché** (2.5hr., every hr., Q20). These buses pass through **Sacapulas,** where passengers can connect to buses to **Huehuetenango,** and the intersection that heads to **Uspantán,** where passengers can connect to a bus to **Cobán.** Buses also head to **Cotzal** (30min., every hr.; Q5) and **Chajul** (30min., every hr., Q5).

✈ ℤ ORIENTATION AND PRACTICAL INFORMATION

Arriving in the **parque central** of Nebaj, you'll see the large, whitewashed Catholic church towering over the south side of the plaza. For the most part, Nebaj's streets are organized on a grid (*calles* run east-west with *avenidas* going north-south), with the exception of **Calzada 15 de Septiembre,** which heads northeast (in the direction of Chajul and Cotzal) from the northeast corner of the *parque central.* Both the market and the bus terminal are located two blocks down from the southeast corner of the plaza.

Tourist Office: 3a C. between 5a and 6a Av. (☎4516 2059; www.nebaj.org), in the same building as El Descanso Café. Bilingual staff. Open M-Sa 8am-5pm, Su 8am-noon.

Tours and Agencies: Pablo's Tours, 3a C. between 5a and 6a Av. (☎4090 4924). Offers guided hikes to Acul (6hr., Q150) and other nearby towns. Also offers shuttle service to Santa Cruz del Quiche, Huehuetenango, Quetzaltenango, and other cities. Oddly enough, they also offer a **laundry service** for Q10 per lb. **Guías Ixiles,** 3a C. between 5a and 6a Av. (☎7756 0207 or 5847 4747), in the same building as El Descanso Café. Guided hikes to various locations around Nebaj, including Acul (5 hr.), Cocop (3-4 hr.) and the waterfalls (2 hr.). Cash only.

Bank: Banrural, on the 1st fl. of the Palacio Municipal, on the north side of the plaza. ATM. Open M-F 8am-4:30pm.

Beyond Tourism: Nebaj Spanish School, 3a C. between 5a and 6a Av. (☎7756 0207 or 5847 4747), in the same building as the El Descanso Cafe. Offers the unique opportunity to learn Spanish and Ixil. Offers a homestay program.

Police: (☎7756 0055), on the 1st fl. of the Palacio Municipal, on the north side of the main plaza.

Pharmacy: Farmacia Emanuel (☎5743 0798), on the northeast corner of the main square. Open daily 8am-9pm.

Hospital or Medical Services: Clínica Médica Familiar, 7a Av. between 5a and 6a C. (☎5784 8448). Open M-F 4:30am-8:30pm, Sa 9am-1pm.

Internet Access: El Descanso, 3a C. between 5a and 6a Av. (☎7756 0207 or 5847 4747). Internet Q10 per hr. Printing Q1 per page. Cash only.

Post Office: 4a C. 4-37 (☎7756 0239). Open M-F 8:30am-12:30pm and 1:30-5:30pm, Sa 9am-1pm. **Postal Code:** 14013.

▐ ACCOMMODATIONS

Here, in Nebaj, a little luxury won't set you back a significant amount. As more and more travelers discover the amazing hiking and outdoor activities that this town has to offer, the number of hotels and hostels is increasing dramatically.

☒ **Hotel del Centro Naab'a,** 3a C. 3-18 (☎4145 6243 or 5722 6736), 2 blocks north of the main square. Friendly, quiet, and comfortable. All rooms have private bath and television. Singles Q65; doubles Q130. Cash only. ❷

Hotel Villa Nebaj, Calzada 15 de Septiembre 2-37 (☎7756 0005 or 7715 1651). Comfortable rooms at reasonable prices. Singles Q80, with private bath Q195; doubles Q150/275. ❸

Hotel Casa Shalom, Calzada 15 de Septiembre (☎7755 8028), across from G&T Bank. Clean and comfortable. All rooms with private baths and double beds. Singles Q75; doubles Q140. Cash only. ❷

▣ FOOD

Nebaj's food scene is continually expanding. Whether you're in the mood for pizza, tacos, or *comida típica*, you won't go hungry around here. Head to the **market,** two blocks east of the plaza on 2a Av. and 7a C., for food on-the-go.

☒ **El Descanso,** 3a C. between 5a and 6a Av. (☎7756 0207 or 5847 4747). Founded by a Peace Corps volunteer in 2001, El Descanso is not to be missed. In addition to its menu of international breakfasts (French toast Q18), local dishes (traditional Ixil *boxboles* on Th) and great desserts, El Descanso has a bar, a Spanish school, an internet cafe, and a tourist office. Open daily from 6:30am-9:30pm. ❷

Café Restaurante Maya Ixil (☎7755 8168), on the north side of the main square. Grab a filling and well-prepared meal. Extensive breakfast selection. *Comida típica* offerings include *churrascos* (Guatemalan steak Q32). Open daily 7am-9:30pm. Cash only. ❷

Chévere (☎5765 0067). An abbreviated menu with *chévere* (Q7), hamburgers (Q12), and a few other grilled items. Open daily 8am-7pm. Cash only. ❶

◉ ▣ SIGHTS AND OUTDOOR ACTIVITIES

Beyond taking in the scenery, there isn't much to do in Nebaj proper. Before heading off on the many hikes and daytrips for which Nebaj serves as an ideal starting point, make sure to head over to the bustling fruit and vegetable **market** (especially on Sundays). The colorful market sells everything from coffee beans to mangos and chili peppers.

ACUL. A challenging hike leads to the village of Acul and the cheese farm **Hacienda San Antonio.** From the police station on the *parque*, head north past Comedor Irene and down the hill. After 15min., continue over a small concrete bridge to a rougher, wider road. About 30-45min. after the bridge, turn right, leaving the smaller path. About an hour into the hike, the path flattens out and runs past a long, thin field. At the end of the field, take the well-worn path to the right (the left path will get you there, too; it's just longer). After 10-15min., you'll go around a bend and the village of Acul will come into sight. Follow the road through Acul with the fields on the left and the village on the right. About 10min. up the same road on the left is the Hacienda San Antonio.

Set in a picturesque pasture with a forested hillside rising behind it, the *finca* seems more like something out of the Swiss Alps. The farmers inside will show you a room filled with circular blocks of fine Swiss cheese they produce (Q30 per lb). The surrounding valley is perfect for a picnic. Small *tiendas* in the village sell drinks and snacks. Allow 3-5hr. for the whole trip and set out early in the morning when the air is cool and the skies are clear.

LA PISTA DE ATZUMAL. A hike to the old military airfield in the tiny town of Atzumal provides a peak into the area's violent history. Atzumal was built partly by foreign volunteers in the 80s. During the war, displaced Ixil families lived here after their homes were razed. The new homes contrast with the traditional lifestyle of their inhabitants. At the top of town is the old military airfield, a barren and silent strip of ground surrounded by a minefield. The minefield has been cleared, leaving the landscape awkwardly uneven. Watch out for barbed wire.

From the church in town, follow the road to Chajul until you reach the Quetzal gas station, where you should follow the left fork. When the paved road ends, take a quick left, and then immediately turn right onto the dirt road heading down the hill. After following this for about 30-45min., you'll come to the only junction (at the tall Feliz Viaje sign); take the right fork down the slope. After passing a couple of houses and *tiendas*, make a left onto the path just past a blue-painted *papelería*. At the end of the path, turn right, then left. You should now see La Pista in front of you.

LAS CASCADAS DE PLATA. Las Cascadas de Plata is a less rigorous hike than the others listed above. The largest *cascada* (1-1½hr. from Nebaj) is a jagged rock face carved out of a tree-lined hillside. The water here divides into many small cascades, making for a stunning display. The walk to the falls is a leisurely stroll through the pastures and valleys surrounding Nebaj. From the church in town, follow the road west to Chajul until you reach the first bridge. Take the road that veers left just before the bridge and stay on it for the rest of the walk. About ten minutes from the bridge, the valley narrows and the hillsides grow steeper. Less than one hour from the town, there's a small waterfall on the left and some small waterfalls on the right. Continuing on, the road soon curves sharply to the left and drops steeply downhill to the largest fall. Allow at least 2½hr. for the entire trip.

COCOP. A half-day of hiking will bring you to the remote, newly rebuilt village of Cocop. Like Atzumal and Acul, the village saw more than its fair share of activity during the war. Particularly harrowing were the massacres, when 98 villagers were brutally slaughtered. The few who were out in the fields working returned to find the village smoldering without a single survivor. After that, many left the village to avoid the 'poisonous' spirits lurking in the hills. Only recently have inhabitants begun to return.

To get to Cocop, start at the BanCafé on the market street in Nebaj and head east. At the end of the street, take a right, then a left down the hill. Cross over the small stream and continue on the well-worn path to a collection of wooden houses in the village of Xemamatzé. Take a left and follow the rutted road uphill for 2hr.

There is one shop in Cocop; the owners there will put you up in a room at the school for the night (Q15 per person). Otherwise, take the path towards Río Azul down the valley. Río Azul is on the road to Coatzal; from there you can walk the couple of hours back to Nebaj.

▶ DAYTRIPS FROM NEBAJ

CHAJUL AND SAN JUAN COTZAL

Chajul's market days are on Tu and F; Cotzal's are on W and Sa. On these days, buses leave the Nebaj station around 6am. Regular microbuses now connect Nebaj to Cotzal and Chajul. In Nebaj, head to the corner of Calzada 15 de Septiembre and 3a C., where all microbuses to Chajul and Cotzal pass by. The destination of the microbus is usually painted on the bus; the driver's helper is usually screaming the destination as well. Buses to Chajul and Cotzal leave approximately every hr.; the same is true in the opposite direction. Once in Cotzal and Chajul, have the driver drop you off in the main square; here wait for a microbus back to Nebaj. Buses from Nebaj to Cotzal and Nebaj to Chajul (Q5); from Cotzal to Chajul (Q3).

Chajul and San Juan Cotzal, the towns that with Nebaj form the **Ixil Triangle,** are set in the stunning hills of the Cuchumatanes. Though out of the way, the strong sense of tradition and natural beauty in both of these towns make them worth a visit. New paved roads connect all three towns of the Ixil Triangle, making getting from one to another very easy.

CHAJUL

The most remote of the three towns, Chajul is composed mostly of smoke-filled, adobe homes. Women weave their fantastic *trajes* in front of these huts. In the plaza, the colonial church, **Iglesia de San Gaspar,** is relatively bare inside. Still, there are two notable elements: the trough of fire in the aisle, devoted to the assassinated Father José María Gran, and the gold-plated altar of Christ of the Golgotha, for whom a pilgrimage is made on the second Friday of Lent. Two angels stand guard on either side of the altar wearing the traditional Nebaj male dress. Many of the other religious figurines inside the church are also colorfully dressed in traditional Ixil garb. The artfully carved wood at the main entrance displays fine Mayan designs.

Market days are a sight to be seen, with people from all three villages meeting to buy and sell local wares in Chajul's plaza. Occasionally men will wear their white pants and blue sash *trajes:* women always wear their colorful blue *huipiles* and *pom-pom* head wraps.

If you are staying the night in Chajul, head to the **Posada Vetz K'aol** ❷ (☎7765 6114), a 5-10 minute walk south of the plaza (follow signs). Located in a converted clinic, this old building has comfortable rooms and a friendly staff (singles Q80). Alternatively, some travelers opt to stay with families who rent out beds in their houses.

SAN JUAN COTZAL

Along the road that branches away from to Chajul sits San Juan Cotzal. Larger, more developed, and closer to Nebaj, Cotzal remains a tranquil, traditional town set in a rolling green valley. The town's central plaza is picturesque, with flower-covered pergolas and fountains decorating the area in front of the whitewashed Catholic church on the east side of the plaza. Cotzal celebrates its patron saint with a festival the week of June 24. The festival features religious ceremonies and costumed dances in the afternoon.

For those who are spending the night in Cotzal, the **Hotel El Maguey** ❶ (☎5789 1009), across from the police station and up from the left side of the church, rents clean, basic rooms (singles Q45). Communal bathrooms are clean and have hot water; the *comedor* downstairs serves great *comida típica*. As in Chajul, some families offer the option of renting out a bed in their home.

QUETZALTENANGO

Quetzaltenango is more commonly known as Xela (SHAY-lah), meaning "under the 10" in reference to the ten mountain gods believed to inhabit the peaks surrounding the city. Xela is the largest and most important city in Guatemala's Western Highlands, lying at the intersection of major roads from the capital, the Pacific coast, and Mexico. Aside from the often bitter-cold evenings, it's a pleasant place, with polite locals, interesting architecture, and an increasingly cosmopolitan nightlife. There isn't a whole lot to see in town beyond the well-maintained *parque central*, but daytrips into the surrounding countryside promise hot springs, rugged volcanic peaks, and colorful markets.

TRANSPORTATION

Quetzaltenango is easily accessible from cities throughout Guatemala. In addition to being connected to various parts of the country via **chicken bus** and **microbus,** there are also many tourist agencies that provide **shuttles** to various destinations. The **Minerva Bus Terminal,** the main terminal located in the northwest corner of the city, sends chicken buses and microbuses to: **Chichicastenango** (2½hr., every hr., Q12); **Guatemala City** (4½hr., every 30min., Q25; stops in **Chimaltenango** (Q20), where buses connect to Antigua); **Huehuetenango** (2½hr., every 30min., Q15); **La Mesilla** (4hr., every hr., Q20); **Momostenango** (1½hr., every hr., Q8; stops in **San Francisco El Alto** (Q6) and **Cuatro Caminos** (Q5)); **Panajachel** (2½hr., every 2 hr., Q15); and **Retalhuleu** (1½hr., every 30min., Q10). Microbuses shuttle people from **Zona 1** (6a C. and 14 Av. A) to the Minerva Bus Terminal regularly for Q1.25. There are other intracity microbus routes, but most travelers stay within Zona 1 and the bus terminal.

ORIENTATION AND PRACTICAL INFORMATION

Quetzaltenango follows the mighty Guatemalan Grid. The **Parque Centroamérica,** the *parque central,* at the center of town in **Zona 1,** is bordered by 11

Quetzaltenango Center

ACCOMMODATIONS   FOOD   NIGHTLIFE

Hostal Altense, **5**   Cardinali, **2**   Salon Tecún, **3**
Hotel Don Diego, **4**   Royal Paris, **1**

Av. on the east, 12 Av. on the west, 4 C. to the north, and 7 C. to the south. Walk a few blocks east or west of the *parque* and you'll find "diagonals" thrown into the mix. Most hotels, restaurants and services can be found in Zona 1 near the *parque*. The **Minerva Bus Terminal**, the second-class bus station, is in **Zona 3**, northwest of the city center. If you arrive here, walk straight through the bustling **market** and then across an empty lot to the street on the other side. Any of the city buses heading to the left will take you to the *parque central* (Q1.25; buses marked *parque*.)

Tourist Office: INGUAT, 11-35 C. de las Animas (☎7761 4931; www.visitguateamala. com), on the south side of the *parque central*. Open M-F 9am-4pm, Sa 9am-1pm. Many brochures and business cards for hotels and Spanish schools in Xela.

Tours and Agencies: Adrenalina Tours, 13 Av. 4-25 (☎7761 4509; www.adrenalina-tours.com), inside the Pasaje Enriquez. Shuttle services to many Guatemalan cities (Antigua Q210, Coban Q330, Panajachel Q125, Chichicastenango Q140). Twice daily round-trip shuttles to and from the Fuentes Georginas Q50. V.

Bank:Banrural, 12a Av. 5-2A, on the east side of the *parque central*. Open M-F 9am-7pm and Sa 9am-1pm.

Beyond Tourism: Miguel Angel Asturias Spanish School, 8a C. 16-23 (☎7765 3707; www. spanishschool.com). 1-on-1 instruction. Volunteer opportunities. **Sakribal Spanish School,** 6a C. 7-42 (☎7763 0717; www.sakribal.com), 3 blocks east of the *parque central*. Spanish instruction, homestays, and cultural activities such as field trips to local attractions.

Laundromat: Rapi-Servicio Laundromat, 7a C. 13-25a, less than 2 blocks from the *parque central*. Laundry Q22 per 4 kg. Cash only.

Police: 14a Av. (☎7765 4990 or 7761 0042), in the Hospital Antiguo.

24hr. Pharmacy: Farmacia Batres, 10a Av. and 6a C. (☎7761 4531). Open daily 8:30am-7:30pm. AmEx/D/MC/V.

Hospital: Hospital Privado Sagrada Familia, 13 Av. 5-38 (☎7763 2344).

Internet Access: The Buddha, 7a C. (☎4087 9751), between 12 and 13 Av., off the south end of the *parque central*. Q5 per hour. Cash only.

Post Office:El Correo, 4a C. 15-07 Zona 1 (☎7761 2671). Open M-F 8:30am-5:30pm, Sa 9am-1pm. **Postal Code:** 09001.

ACCOMMODATIONS

Hotels of all price ranges have cropped up around the city center, catering to the increasing number of students and travelers passing through Xela. Most are quite reasonable and are located within a few blocks of the *parque central*. Weekends tend to be busiest, when crowds of new Spanish language students wait for homestay assignments. Xela can be cool and damp at night; ask for hot water and extra blankets. All hotels listed are in Zona 1.

Black Cat Hostal, 13 Av. 3-33 (☎7765 8951; www.blckcathostels.net). Young travelers won't be disappointed by a stay at this very popular hostel. Dorms are social, comfortable, and cleaned daily. Laundry Q30. Breakfast included. Free Wi-Fi. Dorms Q60; private rooms Q120. ❷

Hostal Don Diego, 6a C. 15-12 (☎5308 5106 or 1489). Clean and comfortable rooms. Dorms feel a bit cramped when full. Breakfast included. Free Wi-Fi. Dorms Q40. Cash only. ❶

Villa de Don Andrés, 13 Av. 6-16 (☎7761 2014 or 5557 8313). Spacious rooms with private bath and cable TV. Rooms surround a beautiful courtyard. Singles Q80. AmEx/D/MC/V. ❷

Hotel Modelo, 14 Av. A 2-31 (☎7761 2529 or 7763 1376). An upscale option. Rooms are tastefully furnished with private bathrooms, cable TV, and closets. Picturesque courtyard and adjoining restaurant. Breakfast included. Singles Q318; doubles Q380. AmEx/D/MC/V. ❺

⚑ FOOD

Xela's affordable *típico* is supplemented by fast-food joints and a thriving cafe and bar scene that caters to the entire community. Most upscale places have both international and local offerings. All listed restaurants are in Zona 1.

▨ **Royal Paris,** 14 Av. A 3-06 (☎7761 1942). The menu of this elegant yet laid-back French restaurant quickly reveals its sophistication; try the *camembert* (Q43) or the house special trout *a la Florentine* (Q95). For a quick bite, the sandwiches (*croque monsieur* Q35) will satisfy. Quetzalteco special Q69. Live jazz on Sa night. Open M 6-11pm, Tu-Sa noon-11pm, Su noon-10pm. AmEx/D/MC/V. ❸

Pasaje El Mediterraneo, Pasaje Enriquez (☎5515 6724). Tapas dishes (Q35-60) make for good appetizers. Entrees Q80-120. Mixed drinks Q40. Open Tu-Su 4pm-midnight. AmEx/D/MC/V. ❹

Cardinali, 14 Av. 3-25 (☎7761 0924 or 7761 0922; www.restaurantecardinali.com). Walls covered in wine bottles and Italian flags attest to this restaurant's attempt create an authentic Italian experience. Diverse pizza toppings include mozzarella, walnuts, and asparagus. Small pizzas Q25-40, larges Q50-75. V. Open daily from noon-10pm. ❷

◎ SIGHTS

PARQUE CENTROAMÉRICA. No matter how many central plazas you have seen on your trip to Guatemala, Xela's Parque Centroamérica does not fail to impress. With stunning Neo-classical architecture on all sides and beautiful landscaping and fountains throughout, this is the perfect place to relax and take in the surroundings. A three-sided sign on the west side of the *parque* gives a comprehensive description of this historical plaza. On the east side of the *parque* presides the **Municipalidad,** a stately structure built in 1897. There's a courtyard inside the main entrance. The first Sunday of each month explodes with the commotion of traditional clothing, outdoor concerts, and impromptu street performances.

MUSEO DE HISTORIA NATURAL. Located in the Casa de la Cultura, the collection includes a few Maya artifacts, ceramics, and a collection of soda bottles from throughout the ages. Don't miss the traditional **funeral urn.** Legend has it that a small donation to the urn can bring good luck. The strange collection of deceased animals (some with strange deformities) is entertaining, to say the least. Though the exhibits don't have the most polished displays, this charming museum is certainly worth checking out. *(On the southern side of the Parque Centroamérica. Open M-F 8am-noon and 2-6pm. Q6.)*

TEATRO MUNICIPAL. This beautiful Neoclassical structure hosts sporadic performances of traditional music and dance; call ahead or consult the tourist office for a show schedule. On a clear day, come enjoy the stunning views of the Volcán Santa Maria in the distance. *(1a C. in between 14 Av. and 14 Av. "A".)*

⚐ ⚑ NIGHTLIFE AND ENTERTAINMENT

Unlike its neighbors in the Western Highlands, Xela will not fail to impress those seeking something to do after the sun sets. Many cafes are open late and play live music most nights. Travelers looking for a rowdier evening can choose from a wide selection of places where they can dance salsa all night.

▨ **Salon Tecun,** inside Pasaje Enriquez, between 12 and 13 Av., just off the *parque central.* The perfect place to start an evening out in Xela. Bar food is cheap and tasty (*hamburguesa simple,* Q23). Beer Q35 per L. Cuba Libre Q14. Open daily from 8am-1pm. AmEx/D/MC/V.

⌨ **La Parranda,** 14 Av. 4-41 (☎5535 6163), down 7a C. to the west of the *parque central.* Devoted clientele flocks here for free salsa lessons (W 9pm). Reasonably priced drinks. Cover Sa-Su Q15-20. Open Tu-Sa 7pm-1am.

Ojalá, 15 Av. A 3-33 (☎7763 0206). Hookah and bean-bags make Ojalá a great place to start or end the night. Open Tu-Sa 5pm-1am, Su noon-10pm.

⚑ DAYTRIPS FROM QUETZALTENANGO

VOLCÁN SANTA MARÍA

The hike starts from Llanos del Pinal, which is served by buses from Xela's Minerva termi-nal every hr. 5am-6pm. However, most tour agencies will pick you up from your hostel and guide you for the whole experience. Most tours leave very early (4am-5am). The hike up is 5hr., the descent about 3hr. Take note that most tour agencies have a minimum amount of people that they will lead, and the price adjusts accordingly. Ask around at your hostel if you need some fellow hikers.

Visible from downtown Quetzaltenango on a clear day, the inactive Volcán Santa María (3772m) forms a perfect cone 10km southwest of the city. The climb to the top is rigorous and sweaty, but well worth it for the view of the whole valley. As the unmarked trail is confusing at times, and is the site of occasional robberies, *Let's Go* does not recommend hiking here alone. Adren-alina Tours and Altiplano's Tours lead trips regularly (both Q100). It is possible to do it as a long daytrip from Xela, but watching the sun rise is well worth hauling along some camping gear. The weather tends to be cold and wet; arm yourself with lots of water, warm clothes, and rain gear.

HUEHUETENANGO

With fewer than 30,000 inhabitants, Huehue (WAY-way) is an inviting small city with welcome comforts like ice cream and real milk. Though there's not much to do here, it's a nice stopover on the way to or from the Mexican border. Huehue began as a suburb of Zaculeu, the capital of the Mam, an indigenous Mayan people. Since the Spanish conquest, Huehuetenango has witnessed a couple of minor silver rushes and a region-wide coffee boom. The mineral has since petered out, but coffee still holds its own here.

⚑ TRANSPORTATION

Huehuetenango is an important transportation hub for the Western highlands. As such, it is easily accessible from cities as far as Antigua and Cobán. Most traveling to and from the city do so by **chicken bus** or **microbus.** Shuttles can be arranged by agencies such as Adrenalina Tours.

Buses: The **bus terminal** is 2km outside of town. From here, buses depart to **Guatemala City** (5hr., every hr., Q25). Use this bus to transfer to **Antigua** (4hr., transfer at Chi-maltenango), **Chichicastenango** (3hr., transfer at Los Encuentros) or **Panajachel** (3hr., transfer at Los Encuentros). Buses also leave for **Quetzaltenango** (2hr., every hr., Q20) and **Todos Santos Cuchumatán** (2hr., every hr., Q25), although microbuses departing every 2hr. from El Calvario make the trip for the same price.

Taxis: in the *parque central* or at the intersection of 3a C. and 7a Av.

⚡🔁 ORIENTATION AND PRACTICAL INFORMATION

Huehue adheres to Guatemala's grid system. The **parque central** is in **Zona 1**, bounded by **2 C.** on the north, **3 C.** on the south, **4 Av.** on the east, and and **5 Av.** on the west. Most services, hotels, and restaurants are located within a few blocks of the *parque central*. Buses pull into the well laid-out station about 2km outside of town.

Tours and Agencies: Adrenalina Tours, 4 C. 6-54 (☎7768 1538; www.adrenalinatours. com), in Zone 1. Offers tours to Todos Santos Cuchumatanes and multi-day packages to places like Rio Chixoy and Laguna Braba. Horseback riding packages in the countryside around Huehuetenango. Shuttle service from Huehuetenango to Nebaj Q164 (US$20), Coban Q247 (US$30), Quetzaltenango Q164 (US$20), Antigua Q330 (US$40), Guatemala City Q410 (US$50), and other cities.

Bank: G&T Continental Bank, 2a C. 4-66, on the northwest corner of the *parque central*. Open M-F 8am-8pm, Sa 8am-1pm. **ATM** outside.

Beyond Tourism: Xinabajul Spanish School, 4a Av. 14-14 (☎7764 6631 or 5326 6525), in Zone 5. 1-on-1 teaching with homestay and volunteer opportunities.

Police (☎7764 1465).

Pharmacy: Farmacia Batres, 6a Av. 3-21 (☎7768 1354 or 7768 1499), in Zone 1. Open 24hr.

Hospital: Hospital de Especialidades, 5a Av. (☎7764 1414), in between 6a C. and 7a C.

Internet Access: Génesis Internet, 6a C. (☎7762 7820), across from Doña Estercita. Internet Q5 per hr. Open M-Sa 9am-7pm.

Post Office: 2a C. 3-51 (☎7764 1123). Open M-F 8:30am-5:30pm, Sa 9am-1pm.

🛏 ACCOMMODATIONS

Huehuetenango has accommodations in all shapes and sizes, whether you're looking for a nice hotel or just a bed to crash on. Most places to stay in Huehue are centered around the **parque central** in Zona 1, though there are also budget accommodations located close to the bus terminal, 2km outside of the town center. Accommodations in Zona 1, though slightly more expensive, tend to be nicer and safer than those near the terminal.

Hotel Zaculeu (☎7764 1086 or 1575), ½ block from the *parque central*. Spacious and beautifully furnished rooms with private bath and cable TV. Free Wi-Fi. Singles Q120; doubles Q225; triples Q300. V. ❸

Hotel La Sexta (☎7764 6612 or 7559), several blocks south of the *parque central*. Comfortable, if slightly underfurnished, rooms for reasonable prices. Rooms are clean and include private baths and cable TV. Singles Q60; doubles Q120. Cash only. ❷

Hotel Vasquez (☎7764 1338), 2 blocks west of the *parque central*. Singles Q100; doubles Q175. Cash only. ❸

🍴 FOOD

Excellent local options abound in Huehue. Make sure to grab yourself a cup of joe when in town: the Huehue blend is one of Guatemala's finest. Market days on Thursday and Sunday are ideal for stocking up on fresh fruits and vegetables.

La Cabaña de Cafe, 2a C. 6-50 (☎7764 8903). Charming cafe modeled after a log cabin. Impressive selection of coffee and espresso drinks (Q6-15) alongside great

ON THE MENU

FURTHER SOUTH OF THE BORDER

Cuisine from "south of the border" (Mexico) has become popular not only with the country's neighbor to the north, but around the world. From China to Finland, South Africa to New Zealand, words like "taco," "enchilada," and "tamale" evoke images of delectable, spicy Mexican fare. Try to order the same dishes in Guatemala and you'll get a quick reminder that you're south of a very different border.

Guatemalans and other Central Americans use many of the same culinary terms as Mexicans, but Guatemalans use different ingredients and methods of preparation. Guatemalan cooks typically cook with corn rather than flour tortillas and place less importance on "spicy;" they also favor rice, plantains, and potatoes more often than their Mexican counterparts.

Think you know what a taco is? Guess again: in Guatemala they are corn tortillas rolled with meat and vegetable filling, deep-fried, and served with steamed cabbage and Guatemalan cheese. Quesadillas are far from the Mexican variety; instead they're spongy, cheesy cupcakes served as a treat to deserving children. Eating a Guatemalan enchilada, you might be surprised to stumble across ingredients like hard-boiled egg, tomato sauce, and even pickled beets!

sandwiches (Q20-30) and hard-to-pass-up crepes (Q10-15). Open M-Sa 8am-9pm. AmEx/MC/V. ❷

Doña Estercita, 2a C. 6-40 (☎7764 2212). This *cafeteria y pasteleria* is sure to satisfy your sweet tooth. Desserts range from apple pie (Q10) to cakes of all shapes and sizes. Quesadillas Q10. Open daily from 7am-9pm. Cash only. ❶

Mi Tierra, 4a C. 6-46 (☎7764 1473). A great place to take a break from the busy streets of Huehue. Try the Mexican-style fajitas (Q20) or the fries with your choice of toppings (Q15-25). Open M-Sa 7am-9pm, Su 2-9pm. Cash only. ❷

🔅 SIGHTS

EL MIRADOR. If you have the time, be sure to head to El Mirador, a lookout point that provides stunning views of Huehue and the surrounding Cuchumatan Mountains. Though getting here takes a bit of time, El Mirador provides a great way to escape the bustle of the city. *(To get to El Mirador, head to El Calvario on 7a C. in the NE corner of the city, where all of the buses to the Cuchumatanes leave. Find a microbus heading to El Mirador (45min.; Q15) and hop on.)*

🔲 NIGHTLIFE

Kaktus Disco, 6a C. 6-38. Come to this Huehue staple to dance to latin, salsa, and electronic music. Open F-Sa 9pm-1am.

La Biblioteca, 6a C., next to the Kaktus Disco. This recently opened pub-sports bar is a great place to catch an afternoon game. Open Tu-Sa 2-11pm.

PACIFIC SLOPE

Guatemala's Pacific Slope is a sweltering plain that contrasts sharply with the mountain vistas of the highland region. Here, on fertile land divided into vast *fincas* (plantations), bountiful crops like sugarcane, bananas, and rubber make a vital contribution to the nation's economy. The Pacific Slope does not, however, usually make the tourist's hit list. The dusty inland trade towns tend to be busy but unappealing for visitors, and the black-sand coast is too often marred by trash and debris. There are exceptions: along the busy coastal highway between the Mexican border and Guatemala City, **Retalhuleu** is a pleasant town with the ruins of Abaj Takalik and a few beaches nearby. Farther east, as the coast makes its way toward the border, laid-back **Monterrico** captivates visitors with hammock-lined stretches of fine beach and a verdant nature reserve.

RETALHULEU

Reu (RAY-oo), as Retalhuleu (pop. 36,400) is concisely nicknamed, is a pleasant city on the Pacific slope. Buildings surrounding the *parque central* testify to Reu's colonial pretensions, from its stately neoclassical city hall to its snow-white church flanked by royal palms. Laid-back Reu is a logical stopover on the way to or from the Mexican border. Visit the Maya ruins of Abaj Tabalik, slide down fake ruins at the Xocomil water park, or take a trip to nearby Pacific beaches.

◼ TRANSPORTATION

Because Reu is just 5km southwest of El Zarco junction, where the coastal highway (CA2) meets the road to Quetzaltenango, there are plenty of buses heading toward the Mexican border and the Guatemalan highlands. Retalhuleu's main bus terminal, **La Galera**, is marked by food stands between 7 Av. and 8 on 10 C. To: **El Carmen** (2½hr., every hr., Q20); **Escuintla** (2½hr., every hr., Q20), transfer available to Antigua; **Guatemala City** (3½hr., every hr., Q25) via Escuintla; **Quetzaltenango** (1½hr., every hr., Q13) connections available to most destinations in the Western Highlands; **Tecún Umán** (1½hr., every 30 min., Q15). A second **bus terminal** a few blocks west of the *parque* serves **Champerico** and the coast. Grab a bus along 8 Av. and ask to be dropped off at the terminal (Q1) or take a taxi (Q10 from the main bus terminal). Walking from the park, follow 5 Av. until it runs into 2 C., turn left onto 6a Av., then right, and walk until you see parked buses.

◼◼ ORIENTATION AND PRACTICAL INFORMATION

Reu is organized on a grid with the *parque central* in the center. To reach the *parque central* from the main bus terminal, turn left on 7 Av., walk four blocks to 6 C., then turn right and go straight one block. The *parque* is bordered by 5 and 6 Av. and 5 and 6 C. Most services are near the *parque* or on 7 Av. between the bus stop and the center of town. Because the city is somewhat sprawling, you might want to hop in a *tuk-tuk*, which will take you wherever you need to go for Q5.

Tours and Agencies: REUXtreme and **REUXtours,** 4a C. 4-13 Zona 1 (☎7771 0443 or 5202 8180; www.reuxtreme.com or www.reuxtours.com), in the same facility as the Hostal Casa Santa Maria. Offers day tours of Abaj Takalik and Parque Xocomil, natural

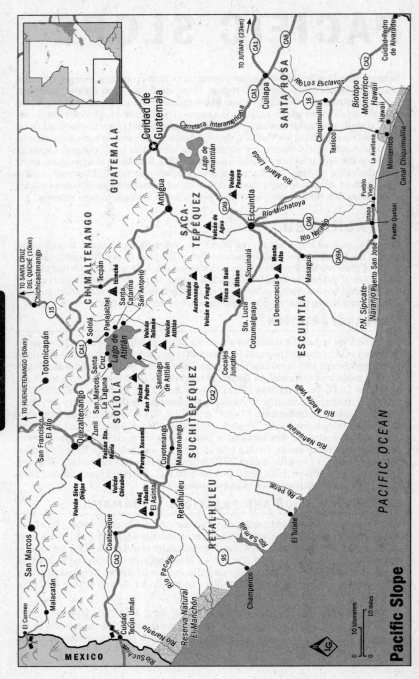

Pacific Slope

tours of the nearby mangrove reserves, kayaking and mountain biking, and shuttles to several Guatemalan cities, including Antigua, Chichi, Panajachel, and Xela.

Bank: Banco Agromercantil, 5a Av. on the *parque central.* Currency exchange inside. Open M-F 8:30am-7pm, Sa 9am-1pm. **ATM** outside.

Police: (☎7771 0120), on the *parque central.*

Pharmacy: Farmacia Las Palmas II, on the *parque central.* Open daily 8:30am-7:30pm.

Internet Access: Asys Computación (☎7771 5272), on the *parque central.* Q10 per hour. Open daily 8am-7pm. Cash only.

Post Office: El Correo, on the *parque central.* Open M-F 8:30am-5:30pm, Sa 9am-1pm.

ACCOMMODATIONS

Reu's tropical climate and proximity to the beach make it a prime vacation destination; its hotel offerings reflect this. Very few budget options exist, as the majority of hotels are nicer establishments geared towards families and older guests on vacation. Still, there are deals to be found, and some of the nicest places in town are quite reasonably priced.

Hostal Casa Santa Maria, 4a C.4-23 (☎7771 6136 or 5202 8180). Spacious and comfortable rooms, each with private bath, A/C, cable TV, and hot water. Free Wi-Fi. Parking available. Singles Q150; doubles Q225. V. ❺

Posada Don Jose, 5a C. 3-67 (☎7771 0180 or 7771 0841). Large rooms with private bath, hot water, A/C, and cable TV. Gym access and breakfast included. Free Wi-Fi. Singles Q332; doubles Q390. AmEx/D/MC/V. ❻

Hotel Modelo, 5a C. 4-53 (☎7771 0256). Well-priced alternative to the more upscale resort-style hotels nearby. Rooms are spacious with ceiling fans and private baths (though hot water is intermittent). Singles Q65; doubles Q90. Cash only. ❷

Hospedaje San Francisco, 6a C. 8-30. A budget option that might leave you wishing you hadn't opted for a budget option. Rooms are barebones, but they get the job done. Singles Q20, with fan Q30, with private bath Q50; doubles Q40/50/70. Cash only. ❶

FOOD

📷Cafe Posada Don Jose, 5a C. 5-67 (☎7771 0180), in the Posada Don Jose. Excellent pasta dishes (Q60) and fresh seafood options (Q80-Q110) are only some of the diverse offerings at this lovely restaurant. Outdoor seating overlooks the beautiful hotel pool. Breakfast until 10:30am. Open 7:30am-10:30pm. AmEx/D/MC/V. ❹

Cafetería La Luna, 5 Av. and 5a C., on the *parque central.* Convenient spot to grab some *comida típica.* Always busy, in spite of the slew of *comedors* surrounding the *parque.* Lunch special Q20. Open daily 7:30am-10pm. Cash only. ❷

Restaurante El Patio, 5a C. If you're not immediately sold by the fact that the *almuerzo del día* is only Q12, then perhaps you'll be roped in by the hamburgers and sandwiches (Q10). The food won't disappoint, either. Open daily 7am-9:30pm. Cash only. ❶

SIGHTS

MUSEO DE ARQUEOLOGÍA Y ETNOLOGÍA. This musuem has a sizable collection of Mayan artifacts from the pre- to post-classical periods, and a rotating gallery with photographs of Reu's early history. *(On the parque central in the municipal building. Open Tu-Sa 8:30am-5:30pm, Su 9am-12:30pm.)*

PACIFIC SLOPE

NIGHTLIFE

Bar La Carreta, 5a C. 4-60 (☎7771 2559 or 0475), in the Hotel Astor. Sophisticated ambience with well-priced mixed drinks (Q30-40) and beer (Q20). A somewhat older crowd. Open Tu-Sa 5-10pm. AmEx/D/MC/V.

DAYTRIPS FROM RETALHULEU

ABAJ TAKALIK. Though only partially open and excavated, Abaj Takalik is one of the more interesting Mayan sites outside of Petén. The settlement, probably occupied between 800 BC and AD 900, once covered 9 sq. km. Today, you can see several temple platforms and a series of carved sculptures and stelae. *(From Reu, take a bus to El Asintal (45min., Q3) to the end of the line, which stops at the parque central. From there, it's a 4km walk continuing up the road, which will take you through a coffee plantation and to the ruins. Between 6am and 5pm there are pickups for hire near the parque that will take you to the site. Admission Q25, including guide. Tour companies offer round-trip shuttle service to and from the ruins, but at higher prices than the taxis at the parque.)*

THE COASTAL HIGHWAY. East of Retalhuleu, the highway passes Cuyote-nango, where a side road runs 45km south to the nondescript beach of **El Tulate.** Further east on the highway are the towns of **Mazatenango** and **Cocales.** Buses from here run north to Santiago Atitlán and Panajachel. After another 23km, the coastal highway reaches **Santa Lucía Cotzumalguapa,** famous for its archaeological sites. Next up on the highway is run-down **Siquinalá.** A branch road serviced by a bus heads to the coast by way of La Democracia. The site of **Monte Alto** is east of La Democracia, but the town plaza houses its highlight: massive stone heads that may be as many as 4000 years old. Continuing all the way down to the coast from Siguinalá and La Democracia, you will arrive at **Sipacate,** located in the **Parque Natural Naranjo.** Sipacate is a more low-key, up-and-coming beach town with mangrove reserves and beautiful stretches of beach. Before winding its way to Guatemala City, the coastal highway from Retalhuleu runs though **Escuintla,** a transportation hub. From here, one road goes to **Taxisco,** a town en route to Monterrico and Guatemala's southernmost border with El Salvador. Another road runs to the large, scruffy beach "resort" of **Puerto San José** and the tiny beach town of **Iztapa.** Yet another road heads north to Antigua and Guatemala City.

MONTERRICO

If you have time to visit just one spot along the Pacific coast, this is the place to go. Separated from the mainland by the Chiquimulilla Canal and encircled by a mangrove swamp, Monterrico (pop. 1000) lives by the motto *"pura vida"* (literally, "pure life"). Its narrow stretch of black-sand beach and powerful surf are some of Guatemala's finest, drawing both fishermen and itinerant students. A sand shelf protects Monterrico from the rain, ensuring sunny, cloudless days. The shelf also allows visitors to watch the frequent lightning storms a few kilometers offshore. So, grab a hammock and let the crashing waves of the Pacific lull you to sleep in relaxing Monterrico.

TRANSPORTATION

Getting to Monterrico by bus can be a bit tricky as it involves multiple transfers.

Buses: Buses from Guatemala City leave from the south-coast terminal at 8a Av. and 4a C. in Zona 12 (2½hr., 5 daily, Q20). Alternatively, you can take a bus bound for Iztapa or

Puerto San Jose, and then transfer to a microbus heading to Monterrico. Buses depart from **Taxisco** (1 hr., every hr., Q10). These bus stop in **La Avellana,** where travelers can transfer to a ferry heading to Monterrico.

Ferries: Ferries connect Monterrico with **La Avellana** (40min., 8 per day, Q5). A ferry leaves Monterrico for La Avellana 30min. before each bus to Taxisco.

Microbuses: Most people opt to get to Monterrico on a microbus from Antigua. Travelers should book 1-2 days in advance, as these shuttles tend to fill up quickly. **Don Quijote Travel** (☎7832 7513), in Antigua, makes 2 trips to and from Monterrico each day. Departs from Antigua at 8am and 1pm; departs from Monterrico at 11am and 4pm; round-trip Q100.

⬛ 🔢 ORIENTATION AND PRACTICAL INFORMATION

Monterrico has **one main road,** which begins at the *lancha* dock and ends at the beach. All of the town's hotels and restaurants are either on this street, along the beach, or set back one block from the beach. The higher-end hotels and restaurants tend to be located off of the main road. A street sign located where the main road hits the beach will point you in the direction of many hotels and restaurants. Though Monterrico is a fairly safe town, female travelers should exercise caution at night, particularly on the weekends. Check the town's website (www.monterrico-guatemala.com) for up-to-date information on lodging and tourist attractions.

Bank: There are no banks in Monterrico. **Super Monterrico,** just up from the beach on the main road, has an **ATM.** Open daily 8am-6pm.

Tourist Police: C. Principal (☎5551 4075).

Beyond Tourism: Proyecto Linguistico (www.monterrico-guatemala.com/spanish-school), on the main road, across the street from the internet cafe. One-on-one Spanish instruction. US$90 for 20 hr. AmEx/D/MC/V.

Post Office: C. Principal. Open M-F 8:30am-5:30pm, Sa 9am-1pm.

🔰 ACCOMMODATIONS

Hotels prices tend to rise dramatically on weekends, during the high season (July and August), and during Guatemalan holidays, especially *Semana Santa*. Make sure to get a room with mosquito netting, or bring your own. Most of the nicer accommodations in Monterrico are off of the beaten path, so don't be afraid to explore a bit before settling down.

🏨 Hotel Brisas del Mar (☎5517 1142), 100m east of the main road. An unbeatable bargain for the amenities offered. Spotless rooms with private baths and fans are complemented by a beautiful pool and incredibly friendly staff. 2nd-floor restaurant and lounge area has hammocks and spectacular views of the ocean. Singles Q60. V. ❷

Hotel El Mangle (☎5514 6517 or 5490 1336). From the beach at the end of the main road, head to the left a few 100 meters. Beautiful hotel organized around a central courtyard. Rooms come with mosquito nets and fans. Pool and on-site restaurant. Singles Q200; doubles Q300. Discounts for groups. V. ❺

Hotel Cafe del Sol (☎5810 0821), on the beach, 100m west of C. Principal. Breathtaking ocean views and comfortable rooms with private baths and fans. Singles Q200; doubles Q300. V. ❺

Hotel El Delfin (☎5702 6701), on the beach, off of C. Principal. Popular with Guatemalans and backpackers. Simple accommodations with mosquito nets. Well-kept swimming pool and abundant hammocks. Decent *comedor* on-site. Singles M-F Q35, Sa-Su Q50. Cash only. ❶

🔲 FOOD

If there's any place in Guatemala to order yourself a plate of fresh seafood, it's Monterrico. Though seafood dishes tend to be more expensive than the more common menu items, they are an incredible deal considering the freshness and the portion size offered at most places. *Comedor*-style restaurants line the main street; more upscale restaurants with international offerings grace the ocean-front. For groceries, visit **Super Monterrico**, located just up the main street from the beach (open daily 8am-6pm).

Taberna El Pelicano (☎5409 6775 or 4001 5885), 350m east of the C. Principal on the road that runs parallel to the beach. For a great meal at a reasonable price, dine under the huge thatched roof of Taberna El Pelicano in the company of the restaurant's impressive pet pelican. Fresh seafood dishes (fish filets Q75, jumbo shrimp entree Q110) are the main draw, but there are also delicious daily specials (Q65-Q75). Top off your meal with their homemade ice cream (Q20) or a frozen mixed drink (strawberry daiquiri Q28). Open W-Sa noon-2pm and 5:30-10pm, Su noon-3pm and 6-10pm. V. ❶

Cafe del Sol (☎5810 0821; www.cafe-del-sol.com), in Hotel Cafe del Sol, 100m west of the main road. Stunning beachfront views and tasty entrees. Splurge on seafood (Q80-120) or feast on a hamburger with their special sauce (Q45, includes fries). Wash it down with a drink from their extensive mixed drink menu (Amaretto Sour, Q28). Open daily 7am-10pm. V. ❸

Johnny's Place (☎5812 0409; www.johnnysplacehotel.com), across from El Pelicano. Johnny's Place, which doubles as a hotel, is a social and laid-back place to grab a tasty bite to eat. Hefty breakfast special Q35. Extensive panini selection (tuna panini Q35). Well-priced seafood entrees Q40-Q70. Mixed drink specials Q20-30. Open daily 7am-9:30pm. V. ❸

🔳 🎵 NIGHTLIFE AND ENTERTAINMENT

El Animal Desconocido, on the beach. Beers and mixed drinks are well-priced (Q15). Try their signature drink, El Animal Desconocido, a sublime mixture of Malibu, milk, and cacao. Happy hour 8-10pm. Open daily 5pm-1am. Cash only.

El Punto Disco (☎4211 5201), next to Hotel El Marlin, 300m east of C. Principal. If a long day of lounging on the beach leaves you feeling energized, head to El Punto Disco to dance the night away. The DJ blasts Latin and electronic music. Reasonably-priced drink menu (beer Q15, mixed drinks Q15-Q25). Open Sa-Su 7pm-1am, later in summer. Cash only.

🔺 🏞 OUTDOOR ACTIVITIES AND BEACHES

Biotopo Monterrico-Hawaii. Established to protect three species of nesting sea turtles, Biotopo Monterrico-Hawaii encompasses 2800 hectares, including Monterrico and several smaller towns. In addition to housing thousands of birds, the Biotopo preserves one of Guatemala's last remaining mangrove swamps. Pole-pushed sunrise boat tours offer a chance to catch the animals in their natural habitat. Plus, you'll get to see a spectacular view of Volcán Tecuamburro. *(Iguanatours, off the main street and down the road across from the soccer field, arranges tours. 2hr. tour Q40.)*

Reserva Natural de Monterrico (CECON). This natural reserve offers an up close and personal view of iguanas, baby turtles, and caimans. The volunteers at the Reserva organize turtle races to the sea every Saturday morning during the hatching season (September and November). The lucky winner gets a free dinner for two at the local restaurant of their choice. *(Next to the Hotel Baule Beach. Open 8am-noon and 2-5pm. Q8, Guatemalans Q3.)*

BORDER WITH EL SALVADOR

Chiquimulilla and **Taxisco** are the best places to catch a ride to the border (45min., every hr. 5am-5pm, Q10). If you're entering Guatemala at this border crossing, **buses** head toward Guatemala City via Chiquimulilla and Taxisco. Pullman buses run (4hr., every 30min. 9am-4pm, Q30) as do 2nd-class buses (4½hr., every hr. 6am-3:30pm, Q15). Taxisco is the transfer point for Monterrico. On the El Salvador side, frequent buses run to Sonsonate. The **immigration office** is open daily 6am-10pm.

The bustling crossroad of **Ciudad Pedro de Alvarado** sits at Guatemala's southernmost border crossing with El Salvador, dominated by long-distance truckers on the Interamerican Highway and government officers. La Hachadura on the Salvadoran side provides easy access to Sonsonate, though it's not the most convenient way to reach San Salvador. Americans and Canadians must buy a US$10 tourist visa in El Salvador. At the border, street exchangers will change US dollars and quetzals. Keep a close eye on their calculations, as they are prone to dropping a zero here and there. (Open daily 6am-9pm.)

> **WHEN CROSSING.** Beware of shady men carrying thick wads of cash. Independent money changers on the border are convenient but tend to be unscrupulous—know your conversion rates and make sure you're getting a good deal. To avoid the haggling process, change your money beforehand at a bank with a fixed rate.

PACIFIC SLOPE

EASTERN GUATEMALA

Guatemala's short Caribbean coastline, squeezed between Belize and Honduras, is a world away from the jungles and highlands of the rest of the country. Populated mainly by people of African descent, the towns along the coast boast delicious seafood, numerous boating and hiking opportunities, and a distinct local culture. The region's two main attractions are laid-back Livingston, a well-known and tourist-friendly town, and the Río Dulce, which begins at the northeastern end of Lago Izabal and flows into Livingston.

There are two ways to get to the Caribbean coast. The first is to take the Atlantic Hwy. to its end in Puerto Barrios, where boats leave for Livingston. The highway passes numerous historically significant sites: the ruins of Quiriguá, home to some of the best preserved Maya stelae; a branch road to Esquipulas, one of the most important pilgrimage sites in all Central America; and Chiquimula, a gateway to the Mayan ruins of Copán in Honduras. The second option is to head to Fronteras, at the beginning of the Río Dulce on the Lago de Izabal, and boat down the river.

CHIQUIMULA

A transport hub for the Salvadoran and Honduran borders, Chiquimula is hot and bustling with a big market, lots of buses. This is also a great location for heading off to Honduras's Copán ruins.

TRANSPORTATION. Buses enter Chiquimula on 2a C., turning right on 11a Av. and into the terminal on 10a Av. between 1 C. and 2 C. The bus station is hectic, and departing buses are often not in a specific spot but along the road shouting out destinations. Few buses are marked; tell your destination to anyone in the station and they will point you to the next departing bus. Pay on board. Buses go to: **Esquipulas** (1hr., every 10min. 5am-7pm, Q15); **Guatemala City** (3½hr., every 30min. 2am-4:30pm, Q40); **Puerto Barrios** (4hr., every hr. 4:30am-3:30pm, Q40); **El Florido/Frontera Honduras** (2½hr., every 30min 6:30am-4pm, Q25); **Zacapa** (30min., every 30min. 4:30am-5:30pm, Q10); **Flores**(8hr.; daily 6, 10am, 3pm; Q80) via **Río Dulce** (Q35, 3hr.).

ORIENTATION AND PRACTICAL INFORMATION. Hilltop Chiquimula is laid out in a grid. *Avenidas* run across the hill, while *calles* follow the slope down. As you head downhill, *avenida* numbers increase; *calle* numbers increase from left to right. The bus station is at 10 Av., 1/2 C. The *parque central* is at 7 Av., 3 C.

Currency exchange can be found at **Bancafé**, 2 C. 9-99 (☎7942 2335; open M-F 8am-4pm, Sa 8am-noon) where a **24 hr. ATM** also accepts international credit cards. Other services include: **police** (☎7942 0256), 8a Av. across from the station; **Farmacia Universal**, 8a Av. 3-61 (☎7943 8275; open 24hr.; delivery service available); **Hospital Centro Clínico de Especialidades**, 9 Ave., 4 C. (☎7942 4202; open 24hr.); **internet access** at **Enet Cafe**, 3 C. and 9/10 Av. (☎7942 4367; Q5 per hr.; open 9am-9pm); **post office**, 10 Av. and 2 C., across from the bus station (☎7942 0109; open M-F 8:30am-5pm, Sa 9am-1pm).

ACCOMMODATIONS. Chiquimula has a fair number of budget options near the market; quieter rooms can be found on 2a C. before its intersection

Eastern Guatemala

EASTERN GUATEMALA

HONDURAS

TO TEGUCIGALPA (100km)

TO HONDURAS

30 kilometers
30 miles

Golfo de Honduras

Omoa
Puerto Cortés
Tegucigalpita
Cuyamelito
San Pedro Sula
Quimistán
Petoa
San Marcos
Azacualpa
Macuelizo
La Entrada
Protección
Nueva Arcadia
Dulce Nombre de Copán
Sta. Rosa de Copán
Cucuyagua
Corquín
Nueva Ocotepeque
El Poy
La Palma
Dulce Nombre de María
Guarita

Puerto Barrios
Finca Inca
El Cinchado
Punta de Manabique
Biotopo Punta de Manabique
Bahía de Amatique

BELIZE

TO POPTÚN (70km)

Modesto Méndez
Biotopo Chocón Machaca
Livingston
Fronteras (Río Dulce)
Río Dulce
Entre Ríos
San Francisco
Montañas del Mico
Bananera
Morales

Lago de Izabal
Castillo de San Felipe
El Estor
Mariscos
Finca Tatín
Finca Paraíso
La Ruidosa

Chahal
Cahabón
Panzós
La Tinta
R.V.S. Bocas del Polochic
Montaña Rubelpec

SIERRA DE SANTA CRUZ
SIERRA DEL ESPÍRITU SANTO
SIERRA DEL MERENDÓN
SIERRA DE LAS MINAS
SIERRA DEL GALLINERO

Montañas del Gallinero
Quiriguá
Quiriguá
Amates
Los Amates
La Unión
Copán Ruinas
Copán
El Florido
Florida

IZABAL
ZACAPA
CHIQUIMULA
OCOTEPEQUE

Zacapa
El Rancho
El Rancho Junction
Río Hondo
Chiquimula
Agua Caliente
Quetzaltepeque
Concepción
Las Minas
Esquipulas
Agua Blanca
Anguiatú

Lago de Güija
EL SALVADOR

Las Chinamas
Las Chinamas

Las Mojadas

Playa Grande (Ixcán)
Parque Nacional Laguna de Lachuá
Xuctzul
Chisec
Raxrujá
Frey Bartolomé de las Casas
Sebol
Candelaria Caves
Lanquín Caves
Lanquín
Semuc Champey
Montañas Piedras Blancas
Biotopo del Quetzal
Purulhá
Reserva de la Biósfera Sierra de las Minas

ALTA VERAPAZ
BAJA VERAPAZ
SIERRA DE CHAMÁ
QUICHÉ
SIERRA DE CHUACÚS
EL PROGRESO
CHIMALTENANGO
GUATEMALA
SANTA ROSA
JALAPA
JUTIAPA

Cobán
San Pedro Carchá
San Cristóbal Verapaz
Cubulco
Rabinal
San Miguel Chicaj
Salamá
San Jerónimo
Uspantán
Sacapulas
Nebaj
Santa Cruz del Quiché
Chichicastenango
Totonicapán
Sololá
Panajachel
Utatlán
Lago de Atitlán

San Luis Jilotepeque
Montaña de Pinula
Jalapa
Volcán Jumay
Sanarate
Guastatoya
Los Mixcos
Mataquescuintla
Sta. María Ixhuatán
Cuilapa
Barberena
Pueblo Nuevo Viñas
Jutiapa
Yupiltepeque

Ciudad de Guatemala
Mixco
Villa Nueva
Antigua
Amatitlán
Lago de Amatitlán
Los Dolores
S. Vicente Pacaya
Volcán de Pacaya
Volcán Agua
Esquintla

with 11a Av. **Hotel y Restaurante Grandorado** ❷, 2a C. 1-30, a few blocks from 11a Av., offers small, amenity-filled rooms. All rooms have fans, cable TV, and glistening private baths with color-coordinated decor. (☎7942 7644. Restaurant open 7am-9pm. Singles with fan Q60, with A/C Q85; doubles Q100/150. Cash only.) **Hotel Posada Perla de Oriente** ❸, 2a C. betwee 11/12 Av., with a massive walled-in complex, offers a large and relaxing setting to wait for your next bus. The hotel contains a pool for guest use, rooms with cable TV, private baths, restaurant on-site, balconies, and use of social space including billiards area. (☎7942 0014. Free parking. Rooms with fan Q80 per person, with A/C Q125 per person. AmEx/D/MC/V.) **Hotel La Palmera** ❷, 2a C. and 11a Av., on the corner, has second and third floor rooms with breezy balconies overlooking the street and perfect for people-watching. The complex is super secure, with a small side entrance watched day and night. All rooms have private cold water baths and cable TV. (☎7942 4647. Singles with fan Q70, with A/C Q95; doubles Q120/Q150; triples Q150 with fan. Cash only.)

◘ FOOD. Chiquimula is filled with the standard selection of *comedores*, cafeterias, and low-key restaurants; for more refined dining, you'll have to go to a hotel or look elsewhere. For groceries, visit **Supermercado Paiz,** 3 C. and 7a Av., on the corner. (☎7942 6232. Open M-Sa 7am-8:30pm, Su 7am-7pm. Cash only.) **◪Anda Pícate** ❶, 8a Av. 2-60, provides cheap, tasty Mexican specialties in a chilled patio-area just blocks from the center and the bus station. (☎7942 7886. Platters of tacos Q10-20. Fajitas Q30. Burritos Q20. Nachos Q20-30. Open daily 10am-10pm. Cash only.) **Joe's Pizza** ❷, 11a Av., is a consistent winner for filling up any empty stomach, with its pizza-diner interior, quick delivery, and delicious menu including sandwiches, burgers, calzones (Q15-25), and huge pizzas (Q25-85). The service is friendly and fast, and the restaurant is a cool break from the heat of Chiquimula's busy streets. (☎7942 7530 and 7723 6118. Free delivery. Open daily 9am-11pm. Cash only.) **El Tesoro** ❷, 7a Av. and 4/5 C., draws in a consistent crowd of locals with its great prices and large portions of Guate-Chinese food and standard *típico*. (☎7942 3521. Chinese food Q20-37. *Típico* dishes Q20-45. Open daily 11am-9pm. Cash only.)

QUIRIGUÁ

Part of Guatemala's Ruta Maya, Quiriguá boasts a grand collection of *stelae*, altars, and human and animal-shaped zoomorphs. The site, in a hot field between the lowlands of Guatemala's Caribbean coast and the cooler hills of the Honduran-Salvadoran border, has been traced back to AD 300. Quiriguá developed into a major power after defeating Copán around AD 737. As the rest of the Mayan Empire slowly died out, Quiriguá lost its prominence and was completely abandoned by AD 900. The impressive carved sculptures that decorated the city during its successful years in the late-Mayan period now sit under tents in a visitor's center.

◧ TRANSPORTATION. There is no direct bus service to Quirigua or the ruins. The following buses service **Los Amayos,** on the highway: **Chiquimula** (2hr., every 30min. 6am-6pm, Q20); **Chiquimula** (2hr., every 30min. 6am-6pm, Q20); **Puerto Barrios** (2hr., every 30min. 5am-9pm, Q20). From Los Amayos, it is 1½km to Quirigua and another 2½km to the ruins. A regular bus service runs from the drop-off to the **ruins** (10min., every 30min. 7:30am-5:30pm, Q4), passing by the village of Quiriguá. For pickup, head to the village from Los Amayos; service is irregular (5min., Q1). You can walk to the Ruins from Los Amayos; it's about 4km down the road to Quiriguá. There is fairly frequent traffic and the road is safe to walk, though mosquitos and heat are a guarantee.

ACCOMMODATIONS AND FOOD. There are several restaurants and hotels along the highway to and from Los Amatos, but only one option in town. **Hotel and Restaurante Royal ❶**, C. Principal, has a fairly large variety of rooms available, from basic singles (Q30) and doubles (Q60) with fairly-clean shared bathrooms, to tidy, en-suite singles (Q50) and doubles (Q90). The **restaurant** in front serves standard Guatemalan fare at reasonable prices. (☎7947 3639. Q15-Q35; vegetarian meals available. Open daily 7am-8pm. Cash only.)

SIGHTS. The ruins' location in a hot field can be sweltering. Still, the ruins themselves are well organized. The main entrance has a bilingual guide to the site's history (Q10). There is also a free museum with photos and historical information. Past the museum and kiosk, the ruins are organized under thatched-roof huts connected by paved walking paths. The 22 *stelae* and zoomorphs (designated with letters of the alphabet) stand like sentinels in the site's central plaza. The plaza is an open field, making sunscreen and mosquito repellent a necessity. **Stela E**, a towering 12m, is the tallest in Central America and is on the Guatemalan 10-centavo coin. **Stela D** contains some of the most fantastically designed and best-preserved artwork in the region. Look for the **ball court** at the southwest end of the plaza (near the mango tree) and the **Acropolis**, the residence of the elite, to the south of the plaza. *(Entrance to the ruins Q25. Open daily 7:30am-5pm.)*

LAGO DE IZABAL AND FRONTERAS (RÍO DULCE)

The largest lake in Guatemala, Lago de Izabal is slowly becoming a major tourist attraction. The waterfront backpacker crowd in Rio Dulce is lured by calm, safe waters and beautiful scenery. The expansive lake to the west borders the marshes of Bocas del Polochic. Visitors have easy access to Castillo de San Felipe, the Spanish fortress turned beach destination. The swimming holes and waterfalls of Finca El Paraiso and El Boquerón are sandwiched between Rio Dulce and El Estor.

The land gateway to Río Dulce and Lago de Izabal, Fronteras—commonly referred to as Río Dulce—lies on the north side of a 1km bridge spanning the river. The peaceful waters of the river and lake are just fast enough to keep the mosquito population manageable, and the river's low-key atmosphere is a perfect contrast to Atitlán's gringo-party vibe. Most hotels are in isolated inlets along the river, and transportation by boat is more common than by bus. Yet, despite the influx of tourists and sailboats, Fronteras remains a humble town; upscale marinas are only blocks from worn-down playgrounds and small local fish-markets. The combination is both gritty and relaxing, making it a great option for an idyllic but budget-friendly hideaway.

TRANSPORTATION

Buses: Stop on the north side of the bridge in front of the Litegua/Fuente del Norte offices. Each company services different destinations in their large, semi-luxury buses.

Purchase tickets in the **Litegua** (☎ 7930 5251; open daily 3am-7pm) and **Fuente del Norte** (open daily 7:30am-5:30pm) offices.

Litegua Buses to **Antigua** (7hr., daily 8am and noon, Q100) and **Guatemala City** (5hr.; daily 3, 6, 8am, noon, 3:15pm; Q60).

Fuente Del Norte Buses to **Flores** (4hr., every hr. 7am-6:30pm, Q70), **Guatemala City** (5hr., 7:15am and every hr. 10:30am-4:30pm, Q60), **Jutiapa** (5hr., daily 9am and 9:30am, Q60), and **San Salvador** (7hr., daily 10am, Q125).

Local Buses departing two blocks north of the Puente service **El Castillo de San Felipe** (15min., every 30min. 6am-4pm, Q3) and **El Estor** (1hr., every hr. 7am-3pm, Q18-20).

Boats: Lanchas from **Trasportes Maritimo** (☎ 5561 9657), on the water underneath the north side of the bridge, can be hired for private trips. Daily departures for **Livingston** (1-3hr., 2 daily 9am and 1:30pm, Q130) leave from the dock as well. Buy tickets at the *colectivo*'s ticket office on the dock. *Lanchas* to hotels in the area are mostly free; you can call or radio them at **Sundog Cafe** or **Restaurante Rio Bravo,** where the main dock is.

◀▦ 🛈 ORIENTATION AND PRACTICAL INFORMATION

The town of Fronteras lies on the north side of the bridge that crosses the Rio Dulce. The highway stemming from the bridge doubles as the **C. Principal.** About 300m north of the bridge is the turnoff to the Castillo de San Felipe and El Estor; there are no other main streets. Most hotels and restaurants are on the water, either under the bridge or in secluded inlets accessible only by boat. *Lanchas* leave from Restaurante Río Bravo on the right just 50m past the bridge to most destinations.

Tourist Office: Tijax Express (☎ 7930 5196), on the north side of the bridge. Info about hotels and transportation in the area. Open Tu-Sa 9am-5pm. If Tijax is closed, **Restaurante Río Bravo** and **Sundog Café** are your best bets for info.

Bank: Banrural (☎ 7930 5161), 300m from the north side of the bridge on C. Principal. **Currency exchange. 24hr. ATM** accepts international cards. Open M-F 9am-5pm, Sa 9am-1pm.

Police: Km 277 (☎ 7930 5406), on the south side of the bridge. Open 24hr.

Medical Services: Centro de Salud, C. Principal (☎ 7930 5209), on the north side of the bridge. Open 24hr. for emergencies.

Internet Access: Bruno's Internet Cafe (☎ 7930 5721), under the bridge on the north side. Internet Q10 per hr. Open daily 7am-8pm.

Post Office: C. Principal, 500m north of the bridge. Open M-F 9am-5pm.

🅿 ACCOMMODATIONS

Though there are a couple lodging options in Fronteras, the best options by far are along the water. Waterfront hotels cater to practically every budget. If you haven't already booked when you get in town, your best bet is to contact Restaurante Rio Bravo and Sundog Cafe. Both of these establishments can call a *lancha* for you. They also give basic information on the types of accommodations available.

Hacienda Tijax (☎ 7930 5505; www.tijax.com), on the water. *Lanchas* leave from the Río Bravo dock. Practically an institution in Río Dulce, Tijax does it all, with a restaurant, marina, and hotel on its lakeside property, and an information booth at the bus stop at the entrance to town. The hotel offers reasonably priced bungalows connected by wooden walkways to the pool area, and patio-style restaurant. Rooms have hot-water baths, mosquito nets, fans, and Wi-Fi. Single Q150, with private bath Q320, with bath and A/C Q560; double Q240/380/600; triple Q325/540/760. AmEx/D/MC/V. ❺

Casa Périco (☎7930 5666), accessible via *lancha* from Restaurante Río Bravo/Sundog Cafe. Though you'll need a fair supply of mosquito repellent for your stay, it is well worth the peace and budget-friendly rates at this Swiss-run backpacker favorite. Set back in the marshes along the Río, Casa Périco offers a secluded, swampy paradise. Thatched-roof dorms supplied with ample mosquito nets, a waterfront dining area, and free kayaks for guest use. Hot-water bathrooms and free safe for guests. Dorms Q40-45; private rooms with shared bath Q50-60 per person; 2-person bungalow with private hot water bath Q200. Restaurant open daily 7:30am-9pm. Cash or traveler's checks only. ❶

Hotel Backpackers (☎7930 5169), on the south side of the bridge; *lanchas* leave from the main dock in Rio Dulce. Though it's in a vintage, waterfront mansion on the south side of the Río, Hotel Backpackers manages to turn its old furnishings into authentic charm with one of the most relaxing atmospheres around. Run by the center for troubled youth, **Casa Guatemala,** Hotel Backpackers offers a communal kitchen, dorm rooms, private rooms, and space for hammocks. The outdoor bar and restaurant have reasonably priced food and is one of the best social spaces in town, especially if you like a little Latin music. Restaurant open daily 7am-9:30pm. Laundry Q20 per load. Bunks Q24-40; simple rooms Q80; private rooms with bath Q160-325. Cash only. ❶

◖ FOOD

There are many restaurants in Río Dulce, though they're all about the same. Most restaurants serve the standard *típico* dishes with a few fresh seafood options thrown in for good measure; some of the hotel restaurants have slightly more extensive menus, but you'll have to shop around a bit if you're looking for anything out of the ordinary. For groceries, there is a **Despensa Familiar** on C. Principal, two blocks north of the bridge. (Open M-Sa 7am-8pm, Su 7am-7pm. Cash only.)

Sundog Cafe (☎5760 1844 or 4645 3192), in front of Restaurante Río Bravo just past the Tijax office. The best option in town for something outside the standard grilled dishes, Sundog serves up delicious sandwiches on homemade bread (Q24-38), smoothies and *licuados* (Q10-15), and daily specialties including fresh salads and curries. Open-air patio style dining, replete with lounging couches, a book exchange, and drink specials on W, Sa, and Su nights. Open M, Th-F, Su 10am-8pm; W and Sa 10am-midnight. Cash only. ❷

Pizzeria Rio Bravo (☎7930 5167), in front of the *lancha* dock. Right on the water, Rio Bravo gets the most traffic for its *lancha*-calling service, but it also serves up huge pizzas and standard Guatemalan fare in its restaurant internet cafe. Entrees Q30-55. Pizza Q12-115. Open daily 7am-10pm. AmEx/D/MC/V. ❷

Cafeteria Bendicion de Dios (☎7930 5421), next to the *colectivo* dock under the bridge. With its cavernous wood-plank interior and on-the-water porch area, this cafeteria feels more like an old ship than the standard cafeteria-*comedor*; the food is tasty and a bargain relative to other options in town. Great breakfast (Q10-23), seafood dishes (Q45-75), meat entrees (Q35), and sandwiches (Q15-35), served by friendly family members. Open daily 7am-7pm. Cash only. ❷

🖪 DAYTRIPS FROM FRONTERAS AND RÍO DULCE

🖪 BOCAS DEL POLOCHIN AND EL ESTOR

To get to Bocas del Polochin, take a minibus or bus from Río Dulce headed to El Estor (1½hr., daily 5:30am-3pm, Q18-20). Buses depart from the intersection of C. Principal and the road to El Castillo and El Estor; make sure to bring water. From El Estor, there are community lanchas serving Bocas del Polochic and Selempim (1hr.; M, W, Sa at noon; Q30). Return boats from Selempim (6am on M, W, Sa). Multi-day tours organized through Defensa de la Naturaleza usually provide transportation but must be arranged in advance.

Accessible only by boat and home to 250-plus animal species including the elusive manatee, Bocas del Polochin wildlife refuge is the crowning jewel of Lago de Izabal's undertouristed beauty. Often overlooked because of its remote location, the reserve offers hiking, boat trips, and visits to the nearby village of Selempim. The wetlands have the country's largest manatee populations and are also home to monkeys, birds, ocelots, and jaguars. The site is equipped with walking trails and guides giving visitors a chance to see wildlife up-close. The Selempim Research Station functions as a tourist and research center for the reserve, has its own restaurant, dorm rooms and cabins with shared bathrooms, solar-powered electricity, and a peaceful outdoor hammock lounge. Defensa de la Naturaleza, which runs the refuge, offers multi-day and custom packages and manages reservations for the Station. Visit their office in El Estor. (2a C. ☎7949 7237. Open M-F 9am-5pm.) It is also possible to see the wetlands on a 4hr. boat trip from El Estor; there are *lanchas* at the dock that can be hired for rental (Q250-400 per trip), though you'll have to bargain.

EL CASTILLO DE SAN FELIPE

San Felipe and the castle are a 45min. walk from Fronteras. Heading away from the bridge, take the 1st left at Pollito Tienda; bear left at the fork. Boats coming from Livingston will drop you off in San Felipe if you ask, and Río Dulce boat tours often include a stop here. Direct lancha from Río Dulce Q37. Minibuses from Fronteras leave from the intersection of C. Principal and the road to El Estor (15min., every 30min. 6:30am-5pm, Q3). Open daily 8am-5pm. Grounds open daily 7am-6pm. Q30.

Resting on its original foundations, the Castillo de San Felipe is a reconstructed Spanish fortress turned tourist hotspot. Originally built in 1651 to stave off plundering pirates from looting warehouses on Lake Izabal, the *castillo* is now a stopping point on most Rio Dulce cruises. This is also a popular destination for tourists searching for the lake's elusive beaches. There is a special swimming area on the beach, equipped with underwater nets to keep pesky fish away. The truly fish-o-phobic can stay in the pristine pool area at the castle itself, replete with lounge chairs and a snack bar. There is an on-site picnic area as well.

FINCA EL PARAISO

The Finca is occasionally included on Río Dulce boat tours. It's also reachable on any bus traveling between Fronteras and El Estor. From Fronteras, you can get to Finca El Paraíso and Boquerón by hopping on a bus to El Estor (Q15). Otherwise, from El Estor grab a bus to Fronteras and tell the driver where you want to get off (Q4). From either city, it's no problem to see both the canyon and the waterfalls in a day. The last bus back to Fronteras passes the Finca at 4:30pm. Buses from Fronteras leave from the turnoff to El Castillo de San Felipe, 200m north of the bridge. Transportation and tours can also be arranged through Hacienda Tijax in Fronteras. ☎ 7949 7122. Entry Q10. Cash only.

Along the north side of the lake between San Felipe and El Estor, the beautiful Finca el Paraíso is a working ranch just a 10min. walk from a sauna and a fascinating hot waterfall that cascades into clear, cold pools perfect for swimming. Caves are nearby (bring a flashlight). Horse and rowboat rentals are available. (Horses Q50 per hr., boats Q25 per 30min.) The ranch has its own restaurant along with areas for camping (Q25, hammock rentals Q25) and more luxurious cabins with private baths (doubles Q240). A bit farther down the road to El Estor is El Boquerón. A 500m hike down a dirt path from the bus drop-off leads to an outhouse and a small collection of unmanned canoes. One of the guys around will paddle you (Q20) into the dramatic limestone canyon until a series of impassable river rapids and a rocky beach appear. You can also rent a canoe and paddle yourself (Q15). Across from the rapids is a series of stalactites hanging over the water and a large cave used for Mayan rituals. To get back, jump into the lime green waters and float down the lazy river.

PUERTO BARRIOS

United Fruit Company exports once made Puerto Barrios (pop. 51,500) the nation's most crucial port. Commerce has since shifted to Pacific ports and the city's significance has faded. Today, the city's dusty, palm tree-lined streets function as a market and passageway for travelers and residents of Livingston, Belize, and Honduras. Walking the streets at night is not recommended.

▐ TRANSPORTATION

Buses: Bus traffic is centered around the railroad tracks and the market. **Litegua Buses** (☎7948 1172) leave from the west side of the railroad tracks at their intersection with 6a Av. To: **Guatemala City** (5-6hr.; every 30min. 1am-noon, every hr. noon-4pm; Q80), via **Quirigua** (2½hr., Q50) and **Rio Hondo** (3½hr., Q65) where you connect to buses headed to **Esquipulas** or **El Salvador**. Other buses leave from destination-specific stops, with service to **Chiquimula,** departing from the east side of the railroad tracks (4hr., every hr. 5am-5pm, Q45) and **Frontera Honduras,** departing from the north side of the market on 6a Av. (1hr., every 10min. 5am-5pm, Q15).

Boats: The dock is at the western end of 12 C. **Ferries** to **Livingston** (1½hr., 2 daily 10am and 7pm, Q20). **Lanchas** also make the trip to **Livingston** (30min., every hr. or when full 6:30am-5pm, Q30), and **Punta Gorda, BZE** (50min., Q100).

▐ ▐ ORIENTATION AND PRACTICAL INFORMATION

The center of Puerto Barrios is the **market,** between **8a/9a C.** and **6a/7a Av.**. *Avenidas* increase in number from the western waterfront towards the eastern inland side of town. **1a C.** sits at the far north side of town; *calles* increase in number going south. The **railroad tracks** where most buses stop run diagonally through the intersection of **6a Av.** and **9a C.** before hitting the **Container Port,** where mercantile ships enter the city. The passenger port is several blocks south, at the **Muelle Municipal,** located at the western end of **12a C.**.

Bank: Banco Internacional, 6a Av. and 8a C. (☎7948 2531). Open M-F 9am-6pm, Sa 9am-1pm. **Currency exchange** and has Western Union services. **24hr. ATM** accepts international cards.

Police: 5a C. and 6a Av. (☎7947 0484). Open 24hr.

24hr. Pharmacy: Farmacia 24 Horas, 13 C. and 5a Av. (☎7948 5518), on the corner.

Medical Services: Hosptial Nacional de la Amistad Japón (☎7948 3071 or 3073), at the turnoff to Santo Tomas de Castillo. Open 24hr.

Internet Access: Telgua, 10 C. and 8a Av. (☎7948 2198). Open M-F 8am-6pm. Internet, phones, and fax services. Internet Q10 per hr.

Post Office: 6a C. and 6a Av. (☎7948 7992). Open M-F 8:30am-5:30pm.

ACCOMMODATIONS

There are many lodging options in Puerto Barrios. Since the city is not the safest at night, be sure to get a room you don't mind spending time in after the sun sets.

Hotel Miami, 3a Av. and 11/12 C. (☎7948 0537). Close to the dock, this hotel offers cheap and simple rooms with fans and basic private baths. Rooms are clean and secure. Singles Q45, with A/C Q100; doubles Q90, with A/C Q170. Cash only. ❷

Hotel Europa, 3a Av. and 11/12 C. (☎7948 1292), next to Hotel Miami. With a relaxing courtyard and friendly service, Europa offers a pleasant atmosphere and basic, clean rooms with fans and private baths. Q50 per person; Cash only. ❷

Hotel Lee, 5 Av. and 9/10 C. (☎7948 0830 or 0685). Though it's a walk from the port, Hotel Lee is quiet and offers rooms with fans, private baths, and cable TV within a few blocks of the center. Singles Q65; doubles Q115. Cash only. ❷

FOOD

Puerto Barrios has a suprising variety of food options, from the standard *tapado* and seafood dishes, to more exotic Portuguese and Chinese options. For groceries, visit **Despensa Familiar,** 8 C. and 7a Av. (☎7948 0462. Open M-Sa 7am-8pm, Su 7am-7pm.)

Pizza Luigi, 5a Av. and 13a C. (☎7948 0284). A local standard, Luigi's pies are some of the best in town. Pizzas Q45-125. Free delivery. Open Tu-Su 10am-1pm and 4-9pm. Cash only. ❸

Restaurante Safari, 1 C. and 5a Av. (☎7948 0563). On the prettier side of the water and out of sight of the port, this breezy spot is the most popular place around for seafood dishes (Q60-130). The open air-dining room is busy on weekends, but relaxing and quiet the rest of the week. Open daily 11am-11pm. AmEx/D/MC/V. ❹

BORDER CROSSING: HONDURAS

BORDER WITH HONDURAS
Minibuses run from Puerto Barrios, across from the Despensa Familiar on 8 C. and 6 Av., to the Honduran border (1 hr., about every 20min., Q15).

The minibus from Puerto Barrios drops you off across the border in no-man's land. From there, Honduran **pickup trucks** (L5) shuttle you 3km to their immigration office in **Corinto,** where money changers swarm outside. From Corinto, buses leave for Omoa and Puerto Cortés, Honduras on the Caribbean coast (every hour at about 20 past the hour). The trip from Puerto Barrios to Omoa takes about 4hr. in decent weather; rains sometimes close the road on the Honduran side. The jungle trail and boat crossings to Honduras are no longer used.

LIVINGSTON   007

Life is sweet in Livingston (pop. 11,300), where the Río Dulce meets the waves of the Atlantic and the Belizean Cayes are just minutes away. With a large Garífuna population, the descendants of African slaves and Carib Indians, the town has a unique language and culture, providing a taste of the laid-back Belizean lifestyle that waits just across the border. The Garífuna have a wandering history, having constantly been shuttled from island to island by Spanish and English invaders. Sizably cut down by disease, the Garífuna finally settled down in southern Belize at the beginning of the 19th century. Today's 6000 Guatemalan Garífuna seem to have departed from their highland compatriots; basketball is the chosen sport and reggae and rap the popular genres of music. Traditional *punta*-drumming music continues to play a significant role in Garífuna culture, though.

Once the largest port in Central America, Livingston now spends its days partying and transporting tourists to an array of breathtaking nearby sites, including the cascades of the Seven Altars and the effervescent *aguas calientes* (hot springs). The greatest tourist attraction is the beautiful Río Dulce boat ride, which starts in Livingston and heads to Lago de Izabal. In town, steady infusions of coconut bread, fresh fish, and reggae jams redefine *tranquilo*. Be aware that some crime (mainly drug-related) has found a way to disturb the peace.

▐ TRANSPORTATION

Livingston is accessible only by boat. There are two ferries per day arriving from and leaving for Puerto Barrios. Many quicker *lanchas* traveling around the gulf and the Rio Dulce. The town itself is small and walkable; because of its island location, most traffic is on foot or bike.

Ferries: Depart from the main dock, go to **Puerto Barrios** (1½hr., daily 5am and 2pm, Q20).

Lanchas: Depart from the main dock, offer quicker service to: **Puerto Barrios** (30min., every hr. 6:30am-5pm, Q30); **Rio Dulce** (1-2hr., 2 per day 9am and 1:30pm, Q85-125); **Punta Gorda, BLZ** (1hr., leaves when full, Q120); **Omoa and Puerto Cortés, HND** (3hr., minimum groups of 6, Q300 each). For international trips, remember to get your passport stamped at immigration.

✚ ❓ ORIENTATION AND PRACTICAL INFORMATION

It's almost impossible to get lost in Livingston. The town's main street, **C. Principal,** leads directly up a hill from the **main dock** and hooks to the right at the public school painted with big, blue Pepsi signs. Most of the action occurs along C. Principal. **C. del Cementario** (a left turn off C. Principal) is similarly active. **C. Marcos Sánchez-Díaz** runs parallel to the **Río Dulce.** C. Marcos Sánchez-Díaz has a number of good budget hotels and restaurants. **C. del Capitánia** runs parallel to the beach on the gulf side.

Tours: Exotic Travel Agency (☎7947 0151), in Bahía Azul restaurant, halfway up C. Principal. Free maps and advice on border crossings, tours, and transportation. Little English spoken. Open daily 7am-midnight.

Bank: Bancafe (☎7947 0491), just above Bahia Azul on C. Principal. Changes travelers checks and gives cash advances on MC/V. **Currency exchange. 24hr. ATM** serves international credit cards. Open M-F 9am-5pm, Sa 9am-1pm.

Beyond Tourism: Livingston Spanish School (☎4151 0397; www.livingstonspanish-school.com), in Hotel Salvador Gaviota, 15 min. from the center in a taxi. Offers in residence 1-on-1 Spanish language tutoring. All-inclusive US$205 per week. For more **Beyond Tourism** opportunities, see p. 34.

Police: (☎7948 0120).

24hr. Pharmacy: Farmacia Sucey, on C. del Cementario, 400m past C. Principal. Open daily 8am-9pm.

Medical Services: Centro de Salud de Livingston (☎ 7947 0143), on C. Principal right after Restaurante Tiburón. Open 24hr.

Internet Access: Telgua (☎ 7947 0196), 20m right off C. Principal just before the Alcadia Municipal. Offers telephone service and 20min. free internet.

Post Office: (☎ 7947 0070), next to Telgua off C. Principal. Open M-F 8am-1pm and 3-5:30pm.

ACCOMMODATIONS

Budget rooms are around every corner, but the rush of visitors during the high season leaves only the nicest rooms available. Be sure to book in advance. The heat in Livingston can be sweltering, so it's worth it to check out rooms first and make sure you aren't buying yourself a night in a ventilation-free inferno.

Hotel Rios Tropicales (☎ 7947 0158), on C. Principal, 2 blocks north of the dock. In the center of town, Rios Tropicales provides affordable lodging with a little beach-flavor. The wooden building with a small courtyard, hammocks, lounging areas, and its own small cafe has great Wi-Fi and computers for guest use. Reasonably priced

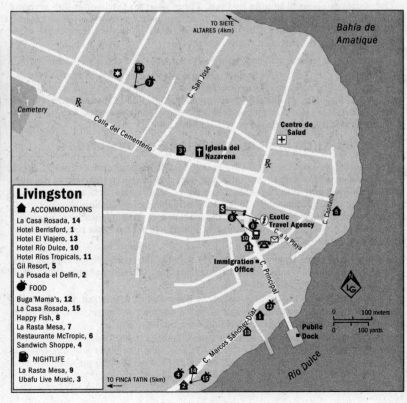

TO SIETE
ALTARES (4km)

*Bahía de
Amatique*

C. San José

Cemetery

Calle del Cementerio

℞

Centro de
Salud

Iglesia del
Nazarena

℞

C. Capilañia

Livingston

ACCOMMODATIONS

La Casa Rosada, **14**
Hotel Berrisford, **1**
Hotel El Viajero, **13**
Hotel Río Dulce, **10**
Hotel Ríos Tropicales, **11**
Gil Resort, **5**
La Posada el Delfin, **2**

FOOD

Buga Mama's, **12**
La Casa Rosada, **15**
Happy Fish, **8**
La Rasta Mesa, **7**
Restaurante McTropic, **6**
Sandwich Shoppe, **4**

NIGHTLIFE

La Rasta Mesa, **9**
Ubafu Live Music, **3**

Exotic
Travel Agency

C. a la Playa

Immigration
Office

C. Principal

C. Marcos Sánchez Díaz

Public
Dock

Río Dulce

TO FINCA TATIN (5km)

0   100 meters
0   100 yards

rooms with comfy beds, and fans. Cafe open 7am-6pm. Singles Q50, with bath Q150; doubles Q50/200. Cash only. ❷

Hotel Berrisford (☎7947 0471), on C. Diaz right before Buga Mama's. Though quiet is a hard to find here—between the ferries arriving at the dock and partiers arriving for the basement-level live concerts—Berrisford cranks up the amenities as well, with A/C, cable TV, and private baths for just Q100 per person. The rooms are by no means new, but the water views and blasting A/C attempt to make the midday heat more bearable. Cash only. ❸

Gil Resort (☎7947 0039; www.gilresorthotel.com), in front of the beach on C. del Capitania. An upscale option that won't kill your budget, Gil Resort offers rooms with A/C, private hot water baths, and modern furnishings. Its beachside complex has a private dock, jacuzzi, Wi-Fi, kayaks, and its own section of the beach. Some rooms have ocean views; request in advance. On-site restaurant. Singles Q325; doubles Q410; triples Q490. AmEx/D/MC/V. ❺

La Casa Rosada, C. Diaz (☎7947 0303; www.hotelcasarosada.com), 400m. west of the main dock. Exotic furniture, peaceful gardens, hammocks on a gazebo over the water, a patio, and ocean views make this worth the extra quetzals. Bungalows are artfully simple, with mosquito netting, fans, and hand-painted furnishings. Clean, shared hot baths. English spoken. Excellent food and tours. Laundry Q2.50 per piece. Wi-Fi. 2-person bungalows Q150. MC/V. ❺

◖ FOOD

Livingston's Garífuna population has blessed it with some of the best food in Guatemala. *Tapado,* seafood and plantains drenched in a spicy coconut broth is a delicious local favorite. Far superior to inland beans and rice, Caribbean rice and beans are stir-fried in coconut milk. Curries are common, and spice is popular, making for some flavorful hot and sweet delicacies. Because it's an island, expect Livingston's food to be a little more expensive.

La Casa Rosada, C. Diaz (☎7947 0303; www.hotelcasarosada.powerhost.be), 400m west of the main dock. Though it serves tasty and affordable breakfast and lunch (Q30-35), the real star here is the dinner. Orders must be put in by 6pm. The menu changes everyday to incorporate the freshest available seafood, meat, and vegetable entrees. All dinners (Q65-100) include fresh salad, coconut bread, and a dessert. Popular options include vegetarian pasta, *tapado,* lobster, and shrimp. Breakfast open from 6:30am to closing. Dinner open 7-9pm. Cash only. ❹

Buga Mama's, C. Diaz (☎7947 0891), 50m west of the dock. Run by non-profits dedicated to promoting job-training for young Maya, Buga Mama's offers one of the best locations and most varied menus around. Homemade pastas (Q45-55), breakfasts (Q15-25), seafood (Q70-100), curries (Q40-50), and pizzas (Q30-115) enjoyed on a waterfront patio overlooking the gulf. As a training restaurant, the service can be slower than normal, but the prices are some of the best around. Open daily 9am-9pm. AmEx/D/MC/V. ❷

Happy Fish (☎7947 0661), on C. Principal, 3 blocks from the dock. With large portions of the local seafood specialties (Q60-110), Happy Fish is the place to come for your fix of *tapado,* shrimp, fish, and lobster, all served up with rice and beans or french fries and salad. Popular with the weekend loungers, it also has a drinks menu and the ever popular *coco loco* (Q30). Open daily 7am-9pm. AmEx/D/MC/V. ❹

NIGHTLIFE

A mellow village by day, Livingston apparently conserves its energy for nighttime partying. Most establishments are open until 3am but people stay out until dawn. Things are wild during the **Garífuna festival** from November 20 to 27. The cemetery has a happening party November 1 and 2 **(All Saints Day)** and **(All Souls Day)**.

Ubafu Live Music, 50m down the C. del Cemeterio leg of the C. Principal. The Garífuna music scene and dance party begins and ends with Ubafu Live Music. The live music here never disappoints. *Coco loco* Q30. Open daily until 3am.

La Rasta Mesa, Barrio Nevago (☎4200 4371). With live reggae and Garífuna music every night, Rasta Mesa is your best bet for non-sketchy and creative nightlife in town. Music every night from 8pm until the last customer leaves. Cash only.

DAYTRIPS FROM LIVINGSTON

UP THE RÍO DULCE

Visits may be arranged in either Livingston or Fronteras/Río Dulce. Head to the docks to arrange a trip with any of the boaters, or book at almost any of the hotels in Livingston or Río Dulce for about the same price. (Q125 or round-trip Q200.) Trips last 2hr. and leave from Livingston at 9:30am and 1pm; they leave from Río Dulce at 9am and 1:30pm. Lanchas will deliver you to the dock of your hotel in Río Dulce; just tell the driver where you are staying.

The most enjoyable way to travel from Izabal to Livingston bypasses the dirty, crowded streets of Puerto Barrios and heads down the scenic cliffs, marshes, and islands of the Río Dulce on a 2hr. *lancha* ride. Boats travel in both directions down the river, stopping at the sulfuric *aguas calientes*, where the hot egg-smelling water mixes with cool river water. These trips also pass by the **Isla de los Pajaros,** a tiny island swarming with *garzas* (storks). The *lanchas* float passes by the bridge over the Río Dulce, considered the longest bridge in Central America, and gives riders a glimpse of the **Castillo de San Felipe.** You'll also see the opening to the calm, blue **Lago de Izabal**at the western end of the Río Dulce. The most impressive parts of the trip are the sheer cliffs and intense greenery around the river as it spills into the **Golfo de Honduras.** The stretch near Fronteras is peaceful, with lily pads and magnificent sailboats around each turn.

The trips go rain or shine; it is a good idea to have a rain jacket and sunscreen available, as the weather can change rapidly and the sun shines brightly in this part of Guatemala, regardless of the season. The boats usually make a bathroom and refreshment stop, and then another at the hot springs. If you want to visit Finca Tatin or the Biotopo, you should ask the driver in advance and be prepared to wait for the next scheduled boat, which may be overnight.

VERAPAZ HIGHLANDS

No great geographic divide separates the Verapaces from the Western Highlands, though travelers will immediately sense the difference between Baja Verapaz's unique combination of near-desert and tropical forests and the densely-forested green hills of Alta Verapaz. Cobán, the capital of Alta Verapaz and the region's transportation hub, is a convenient base from which to explore the surrounding highlands, including Chisec, which is itself a wonderful jumping off point for numerous outdoor wonders.

The cloud-covered Alta Verapaz exists in sharp contrast with the high-pines of the highlands. It consists of limestone pockmarked with sinkholes, humid tropical forest, and mammoth caves. When oil was discovered here, the region's first road—the Transversal del Norte—was built, and K'ekchi' from the war-torn highlands settled the area. Today, it remains a sparsely populated agricultural frontier criss-crossed by a baffling web of routes built by the oil and cardamon industry. If you're looking for an off-the-beaten-path adventure, a trip through the region is worth the hassle. Its magnificent natural sites, the Candelaria Caves and Parque Nacional Laguna de Lachuá, remain little touristed. Its reconstructed towns ring with K'ekchi' and are scented with caldo de chunto, and although the region may not boast the vibrant colors of the highlands, the Maya here remain undisturbed in their traditional lifestyle. The festive towns of Salamá and Rabinal are in Baja Verapaz, near the highway from Guatemala City to Cobán.

SALAMÁ

Despite being the capital of the Baja Verapaz region, Salamá is an intimate city whose isolated location wards off the tourist crowds. An added perk: Salamá makes a great hub for exploring the small villages of Cubulco or Rabinal.

▌ TRANSPORTATION

Buses: All chicken buses departing from Salamá pass through the *parque central*. The bus to **Guatemala City** (3¼hr., every hr., Q25) passes through the La Cumbre junction, where connections are possible.

Microbuses: Microbuses also leave from the *parque central* and head to **Coban** (2hr., every hr., Q20), **Cubulco** (1hr., Q10), **La Cumbre** (via San Jeronimo; 45min., Q8), and **Rabinal** (30min., Q5).

Taxis: Try **Veliz y Amigos** taxi service (☎5616 5537; available 24hr.).

▊▊ ORIENTATION AND PRACTICAL INFORMATION

For a regional capital, Salamá is a small city. If you are standing in the *parque central*, it is quite possible that you will be able to see the establishment that you're looking for. Banks, pharmacies, fast food restaurants, and the main cathedral are clustered around the **main plaza**, while most hotels and restaurants are only a block or two from the center of town.

Bank: Banrural (☎7954 0984 or 1110), on the west side of the *parque central*.**ATM.** Open M-F 8:30am-5pm, Sa 9am-1pm.

Police: 7a Av. 6-36, Zona 1 (☎7940 2240 or 0050).

Pharmacy: Farmacia Batres, 7a Av. 6-99, Zona 1 (☎7954 5175). Open 24hr.

Hospital or Medical Services: Hospital Nacional y Centro de Salud, 1a C. 1-01, Zona 4 (☎7940 0125).

Internet Access: Cafe Internet, 8a Av. 6-70, Zona 1, 1 block from the *parque central.* Q8 per hr. Open daily 8am-8pm.

ACCOMMODATIONS

Salamá does not play host to a large number of backpackers. As a result, the city lacks the standard budget options that the student traveler might normally find.

Hotel Real Legendario, 8a Av. 3-57, Zona 1 (☎2833 0827 or 2709 8011), 2 blocks south of the *parque central.* A great value. All rooms have private baths, cable TVs, and hot showers. Free internet. Singles Q90; doubles Q160. Cash only. ❸

Hotel San Ignacio, 4a C. "A" 7-09, Zona 1 (☎2833 0827 or 2709 8011). Well-kept rooms with private baths. On-site restaurant. Parking available. Singles Q83; doubles Q150. Cash only. ❸

Hotel Posada de Don Maco, 3a C. 8-26, Zona 1 (☎2833 0827 or 2709 8011). Slightly more expensive than nearby options, despite the fact that it provides nearly identical amenities. All rooms have private baths, TVs, and hot water. Parking available. Singles Q100. V. ❸

FOOD

With a few exceptions, cuisine in Salamá is straightforward, with *comedores* on every street corner.

Deli Donas, 5a C. 6-61, Zona 1 (☎7940 1121). Cafe-style restaurant offering delicious *comida típica* (enchiladas Q11) and a variety of sandwiches (Q16). Open daily from 7:30am-9pm. Cash only. ❶

La Cascada, 10a Av., 2 blocks southwest of the *parque.* Serves decent international entrees at reasonable prices (Q50-80). Open M-Sa for lunch and dinner. Cash only. ❸

COBÁN

Though touristed enough to be home to plenty of cosmopolitan pleasures, Cobán (pop. 51,100) gives the distinct impression that nature is never too far away. The lush green heart of the Alta Verapaz appears within arm's reach as the city's edges quickly fade into country terrain. Even though rain is common, the sun does show most days, and tourists use Cobán as an attractive base for exploring the natural wonders nearby, including the Biotopo del Quetzal, Rey Marcos, Semuc Champey, and the Grutas de Lanquín. When you need a break from the outdoors, Cobán is happy to oblige: sip a cup of the famous local coffee in a cafe and rest your head at one of several charming hotels.

TRANSPORTATION

Buses: Unless otherwise noted, buses leave from the main terminal at 1/3 Av., 2/3 C. in Zona 4. Coming into town, some buses stop conveniently to the west of the *parque,* on 1 C. near the Telgua offices. Buses heading south also depart from this location. Make sure to get to the terminal at least 30min. early, especially for destinations toward Alta Verapaz and the Petén. Ask ahead for the latest info—services change frequently. Buses depart to:

Biotopo del Quetzal: 1hr., every 30min., Q6. Depart on any Guatemala City bound bus.

Chisec: 45min., every30 min., Q10.

Fray Bartolomé de las Casas: 7 hr., every hr., Q40.

Guatemala City: 5hr., every hr., Q30.

Lanquín: 3hr.; 5:30, 11:30am, 1:30, and 5:30pm; Q25.

Raxrujá: 1½hr., every hr., Q15.

Salamá: 1½hr., every hr., Q20. Take a bus to La Cumbre junction and transfer to a minibus.

Sayaxche: 3hr., every 2hr., Q25. Make sure to ask if it's a direct bus; some buses transfer at Raxrujá.

Taxis: Around the *parque central* and the bus terminal. *Parque central* to bus terminal Q5.

ORIENTATION AND PRACTICAL INFORMATION

The two main streets in Cobán, **1 Av.** and **1 C.**, adhere to the standard grid. They divide the city into **quadrants:** northwest Zona 1, southwest Zona 2, southeast Zona 3, and northeast Zona 4. The city's **cathedral** towers at 1 Av., 1 C. The neighboring **parque central** is directly west in Zona 2. The cathedral and *parque* rest atop a hill that encompasses Cobán. Numbered *avenidas* and *calles* continue through different zonas. Addresses on 1 Av. and 1 C. may be in any of the zonas they run through, depending which side of the street they lie on.

Tourist Office: There is no INGUAT office in Cobán, but both **Adrenalina Tours** and the staff at the **Hostal D'Acuña** will be able to provide any tourist services.

Tours: Adrenalina Tours (☎5356 8821), in the southwest corner of the *parque central*. Open M-F 8am-6pm. Offers tours to all surrounding attractions, including an excellent package for Semuc Champey (Q330 or US$40).

Bank: G&T Continental Bank, 1a C. 4-25, Zona 1 (☎7951 3939). Open M-F from 9am-7pm, Sa 9am-1pm.

Pharmacy: Farmacia Botica Central, 1a C. 3-23, Zona 1 (☎7951 2075 or 3721). Open daily 8am-9pm.

Hospital: Poliolínica Galeno, 3a Av. 1-47, Zona 3 (☎7951 3175). This well-equipped private clinic has emergency service, though not always 24hr. Walk-in hours M-Sa 10am-noon and 4-8pm.

Internet Access: Internet y Más L&M, 1a C., west of the *parque central* (☎7941 7371). Open daily 8:30am-9:30pm. Also offers tourist information.

Post Office: 3a C. 2-02, Zona 3. Open M-F 8:30am-5:30pm, Sat 9am-1pm. **Postal Code:** AV002.

ACCOMMODATIONS

Cobán has plenty of accommodation options, offering everything from hostel bunkbeds to king-sized beds in gorgeous boutique hotels. Most hotels and hostels are located wihthin one or two blocks of the *parque central.*

FROM THE ROAD

CHICKEN BUSES

Of my past few months on the road, I would estimate about 1/6 of my time to be spent in buses. Despite crowded, small space, bus rides can be one of the best parts of traveling.

While at the museums, or on hikes, or at the beach, I usually see people outside of their daily routines. I may occasionally see a local fisherman out on his boat while on water taxi, but the only people I see in their daily roles are service workers.

On a bus, I am doing the same thing as locals. It's a leveling ground that makes it easy to meet people.

At bus stops, cracking jokes with the other lone person waiting for that bus has led to some of the best conversations I've had on the road. A book, map, or article can bridge even more gaps; I've entertained 5 year olds with my meager Spanish music knowledge; I've discussed Latin American literature with old men.

Spending time on a bus isn't always fun. The smells can be ridiculous, the dust flying through the open window can leave you coated in dirt, and fitting 20 people into a 10-person vehicle has never ended comfortably. Still, it's a shared sense of discomfort, a sense that allows for training camp-style bonding, because damn it, you might be suffering, but at least for these few hours, you're all suffering together.

-Alison Tarwater

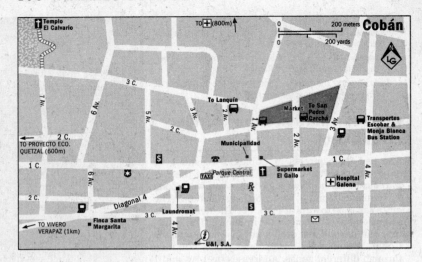

Casa D'Acuña, 4a C. 3-11, Zona 2 (☎7951 0482 or 0484), 2 blocks south of the *parque central*. With a colorful, inviting atmosphere, this is the best budget option and the center of tourist activity in Cobán. Bunkbeds are arranged in homey rooms for 2 or 4 people. Laundry Q35. Small courtyard garden and on-site restaurant. Hot water and dressers with padlocks. Dorms Q50 per person; private rooms Q150. AmEx/D/MC/V. ❷

Hotel La Posada, 1a C. 4-12, Zona 2 (☎7952 1495 or 7951 0588), on the west side of the *parque central*. This huge, beautiful hotel has impeccably furnished rooms, all spacious and with private baths. Sit in a chair outside your room and enjoy the views of the large, leafy courtyards within the walls of the hotel. Singles Q315; doubles Q395. AmEx/D/MC/V. ❺

Hotel Central, 1a C. 1-79, Zona 4 (☎7952 1442; www.hotelcentralcoban.com), 1 block east of the *parque central*. This bright and airy hotel has spacious rooms surrounding an attractive central courtyard. All rooms have private baths, TVs, and hot water. Free Wi-Fi. Singles Q98; doubles Q170. AmEx/D/MC/V. ❸

Casa Luna, 5a Av. 2-28, Zona 1 (☎7951 3528), northwest of the *parque central*. This is a great option for backpackers in Cobán. Staff couldn't be friendlier. Shuttle service available to many cities around Guatemala (Antigua Q164, Chichi Q290, Semuc Q65, Panajachel Q290). Dorms Q50; private rooms Q75 per person. V. ❷

🔲 FOOD

For groceries, visit the **Dispensa Familiar** one block east of the *parque central* on 1a C. (Open daily from 7am to 8pm.) Food prices are slightly higher than most Guatemalan cities because of the town's remote location.

⬛ Casa D'Acuña, 4a C. 3-11, Zona 2 (☎7951 0482 or 0484). This 1st-class restaurant offers European-style candlelit dining, good service, delicious home-cooked food, and plenty of *música tranquila*. Grab a table by the fire or on the terrace and enjoy a crepe with chicken and light parsley cream sauce (Q60), delicious ravioli (Q60), or a brownie (Q10). Open daily from 7am-10:30pm. AmEx/D/MC/V. ❹

Xkape Kob'an Diagonal, 4 5-13, Zona 2. This great option is a cultural center in a rebuilt colonial home. Legends and a Q'eqchi' dictionary are included on the menu. A wide array of Q'eqchi' books are scattered on the wooden tables. *Kaq-ik* (traditional duck soup) Q40. *Horchata* (milky cinnamon drink) Q6. Wide cappuccino selection starts at Q7. Open daily from 6am-7pm. ❸

La Posada Restaurante, 1a C.4-12, Zona 2 (☎7952 1495), within the walls of the Hotel La Posada. High-class Spanish-decor restaurant with both international and *típico* dishes. Chili rellenos with beef Q56. Delicous breakfast specials Q45. Try to get a table on the veranda overlooking the beautiful walled gardens of the hotel. Open daily from 7am-9:30pm. AmEx/D/MC/V. ❸

👁 SIGHTS

TEMPLO EL CALVARIO. For a bird's eye view of Cobán, head out to Templo El Calvario. The hillside church dates back to 1559, but it's the expansive view from the church, reached by climbing 135 steps, that really makes the visit worthwhile. *(Follow 7a Av. north until you reach the stairs. Travel in a group, if possible.)*

VÍVERO VERAPAZ. Located within walking distance of the *parque central*, this orchid farm showcases thousands of different species, including the *monja blanca* (white nun), the national flower of Guatemala. *(Follow Diagonal 4 that begins at the end of the parque, to the left of Hotel la Posada. At the bottom of the hill turn left and continue for 15min. Open M-Sa 9am-noon and 2-5pm. Q5.)*

FINCA SANTA MARGARITA. Cobán's passion for coffee spills outside the town's cafes and into the surrounding *fincas*, many of which were once owned by wealthy Germans. For insight into the coffee culture, check out **Finca Santa Margarita,** 3 C. 4-12, Zona 2. Guided tours of the plantation explain the *finca's* history and give a detailed look at modern coffee production; some provide coffee samples for visitors to savor and compare. Spanish and English-speaking guides are available. *(3a C. 4-12, Zona . ☎7951 3067. Open M-F 8am-12:30pm and 1:30-5pm, Sa 8am-noon. Q20.)*

🎵 NIGHTLIFE

Milenio, 3a Av., half a block north of 1a C. in Zona 4. The front bar has a more upscale feel, but the atmosphere stays relaxed, with *fútbol* on the widescreen TV and a dance floor in back. There are 2 main lounges. Salsa is the music of choice. Pool tables. Open daily until 1am. Cash only.

🔖 DAYTRIPS FROM COBÁN

BIOTOPO DEL QUETZAL

Buses on the route between Cobán and Guatemala City pass the biotopo. Buses also leave the biotopo to Guatemala City (3hr., every 30min. 3-7am, every hr. 7am-5pm) and Cobán (1hr., every hr. 7am-8pm, Q6). Open daily 7am-5:30pm; last entrance 4pm.

About 30km southeast of Cobán is the Biotopo Mario Dary Rivera, commonly known as the Biotopo del Quetzal (Quetzal Reserve), an expanse of rugged cloud forest home to Guatemala's national bird, the elusive quetzal. Two trails twist their way through the park: **Sendero los Helechos** (1hr., 2km) is the shorter trail, while **Sendero los Musgos** (2hr., 3½km) takes you deep into the dense forest. The longer route provides better vistas while the shorter leads to a waterfall, but both give excellent tours of the forest and an equally good chance of spotting the elusive quetzal. The road at the entrance to the reserve is actually one of the best places to catch a glimpse of the beautiful birds; they're seen most often in April and September in the early morning. Take time to look into the large leaves of the *aguacatillo;* its small green fruit is a favorite treat for elusive quetzals. But even if the bird eludes you (and odds are, it will), the beautiful forest canopy and a swim in the waterfalls are still worth a visit. You can stay the night at **Hospedaje Los Ranchitos** ❶, just down the road toward Cobán from the entrance to the reserve. It offers rustic accommodations and is a good place to look for the elusive quetzal. The *hospedaje* has its own patch of forest, complete with a private trail and a basic *comedor*. (Breakfast Q15-20. Lunch or dinner Q18-25. Singles Q30, with bath Q50; doubles Q60/80; triples Q90/100. Camping is also available inside the reserve for Q10 per person.)

GRUTAS DEL REY MARCOS AND BALNEARIO CECILINDA

To reach the Grutas from Cobán, take a bus to Chamelco from 5 Av., 5 C. in Zona 3 (20min., Q2), where you can find morning buses or pickups to Chamil. Ask to be dropped off at the road to Rey Marcos/Balneario Cecilinda, then walk about 500m to the entrance; follow the sign. Coming back, pickups to Chamelco are less frequent in the afternoon but still pass by. The last bus to Cobán departs in the late afternoon.

For adventure seekers who enjoy crawling and climbing through unlit caves, the Grutas del Rey Marcos are not to be missed. Listen to the roar of a sacred, underground Maya river, and splash around under gorgeous natural waterfalls. Discovered in May 1998 and open to the public since January 1999, the caves are believed to be the site of religious ceremonies that took place in pre-Columbian times; the Maya still hold the site sacred and ceremonies continue even today. The inner sanctuary of the cave is rumored to be the source of a large, mystic energy field, and Iván, the owner and occasional tour guide, warns that everyone who enters will leave carrying a blessing or a curse. Mysticism aside, a tour of Rey Marcos is an exhilarating experience and makes for a worthwhile daytrip from Cobán. After getting muddy exploring, cool off in the Balneario Cecilinda, the natural swimming area set into the mountainside below the caves. (Open daily 8am-5pm. Admission including guided tour, rubber boots, helmet, and flashlight. Q25.) For those adventurers who just can't get enough of Grutas, a pleasant farm and hostel has opened 500m from the entrance. **Don Jeronimo's** ❺, run by an American, is an all-inclusive resort. (For Q200 per day or Q360 for a couple, you get 3 full vegetarian meals and a pleasant *cabaña* next to a gurgling river.)

LANQUÍN

About 40km northeast of Cobán rests the village of Lanquín. Nearby are two natural wonders, the beautiful pools of Semuc Champey and the cave network known as the Grutas de Lanquín. Guided tours from Cobán are convenient and often a good deal for one or two travelers; the guides are excellent and will point out the sights' hidden marvels. Hostal D'Acuña in Cobán offers a "Semuc Special," which includes transportation, breakfast, lunch, and guides (Q280 per person, 4 person minimum). The Hostal can also organize transportation to Semuc Champey (Q205 per person, 4 person minimum; discounts for larger groups).

⌨ TRANSPORTATION

Many travelers make daytrips to Lanquín, catching the 6am bus from Cobán and returning on the 2:30pm bus. Buses from **Cobán** (2½hr., 6 per day 6am-3pm, Q10) and return buses from **Lanquín** (2½hr.; 6 per day 3:30am-2:30pm; Q10, minibus Q15) make several trips per day. Pickups also happen in the mornings, heading from Lanquín to Pujal and then on to Cobán. Go early and be prepared to wait.

ACCOMMODATIONS

While many travelers opt to visit Semuc Champey and Grutas de Lanquín in one day, there are options for those who want to spend the night in Lanquín. Below are some of the accommodation options that provide easy access to both the caves and Semuc Champey.

Casa Marbella (☎7983 0009), on the shore of the Lanquín River, 10min. east of town. This legendary hostel's laid-back style, beautiful setting, and terrific vegetarian food captures backpackers for weeks at a time. Arrive early as dorms fill up quickly. Free pickup is available at the bus stop. Dinner Q45. Dorms Q40; private bungalows Q80 per person, with bath Q100 per person. ❶

Hotel El Recreo (☎7983 0056), about 100m downhill from the town entrance. Spacious rooms, most with private baths. Decent budget bungalows with clean communal bath in forested grounds. Bungalows Q25 per person. Singles and doubles Q100 per person. Prices vary seasonally. MC/V. ❶

Hospedaje La Divina Providencia (☎7983 0041), uphill and to the right of the town entrance. All rooms have hot water. On-site *comedor* and pharmacy. Rooms Q25 per person. ❶

FOOD

Eating in Lanquín is straightforward—if you're not eating a home-cooked meal at the hostel or hotel that you are staying at, you'll be enjoying *comida típica* (local food) in a *comedor*.

DAYTRIPS FROM LANQUÍN

SEMUC CHAMPEY

If you are not on a tour and need to get to Semuc Champey on your own, make sure to leave early so that you can catch the 9am minibus that links Lanquín to Semuc Champey. There are also plenty of tour buses passing through that may be able to give you a ride for a small fee. The ride should not cost more than Q10. Open 8am-5pm daily. Q20 collected in the parking lot.

Semuc Champey is best reached by pickup, but you can do the 3hr. (8km) uphill hike by following the gravel road heading away from the river. Bring water. Pickups (Q10) pass by Café Semuc, most frequently on market days (M and Th), but the best bet is to take a round-trip pickup from El Retiro (daily 9am, Q30).

The 300m natural limestone bridge of Semuc Champey creates quite a show, with the mighty Cahabón River thundering into the depths below. The top of the bridge, in contrast to the chaos below, is pure tranquility. A descending series of clean pools, perfect for swimming, flow above the river. Framed by steep forested hillsides, the waters turn marvelous shades of blue and green as the sun moves across the sky. Alongside the pools is a covered rancho for camping and picnicking; the rancho also has bathrooms. To reach the departure point for the Cahabón River, start with the parking lot at your back and follow the trail that crosses over to the right side of the pools and continues past the picnic tables. Follow the slippery rocks carefully and don't get too close to the waterfalls. The trail which branches to the right before the changing rooms, continues steeply uphill for 30-45min. to a spot overlooking the entire series of pools.

If you don't want to bother with transportation and want to spend several days at the pools, the new **Posada Las Marias** ❷ (☎7861 2209) is the place to hang. Popular with travelers, the full service Las Marias is only 1km away from the Semuc Champey parking lot. The hostel has both dorm rooms and loft space. It can be a bit buggy, so bring a mosquito net or a strong bottle of DEET. Although it is isolated, Las Marias offers tasty *típico* grub so travel back and forth to Lanquín is not necessary. Minibus drivers from Cobán are more than happy to drop you off for a few extra quetzals.

CHISEC

Long a traveler-forbidden frontier territory, new roads have made Chisec (pop. 13,500) and its natural beauty accessible to all. Dominated by the K'ekchi' Maya, the area remained virtually unpopulated until 40 years ago when refugees entered en masse to escape the civil war. Unfortunately, the war found them. The town itself was burned and bulldozed twice during the 80's and is still recovering. Little Spanish is spoken; at times, creative hand motions are necessary. The main attractions are the turquoise rivers and limestone cave systems that dot the region, though they are well off the beaten track.

▎▛ TRANSPORTATION

Buses: Microbuses connect Chisec to the various other cities in the Alta Verapaz region. All microbuses leave from a parking lot on the south side of the *parque central.* To: **Cobán** (1½hr., every 30min., Q20); **Flores** (4hr., every 15min., Q50); and **Raxrujá** (40min., every 15 min., Q10), where connections to Sayaxche and Flores are possible.

▟▞ ORIENTATION AND PRACTICAL INFORMATION

The main road, or **C. Principal,** runs directly through town and passes by the *parque central.*

Bank: Banco Agromercantil, on the north side of the *parque central.* Has **currency exchange** and **ATM.** Open M-F 9am-5pm, Sa 9am-1pm.

Police: (☎7983 2121), just south of the *parque central.* Open 24hr.

Pharmacy: Farmacia Arteaga, C. Principal (☎5325 7500), north of the *parque central.* Open daily 7am-8pm.

Internet Access: Restaurante Don Miguel, C. Principal (☎5156 7470 or 5439 8712), north of the *parque central.* Internet and Wi-Fi Q6 per hr. Open daily 7am-10pm.

Post Office: In Barrio El Centro. Open M-F 8am-12:30pm and 1:30-5:30pm. **Postal Code:** 16013.

▐ ACCOMMODATIONS

All accommodations either border the *parque central* or line C. Principal.

Hotel La Estancia, C. Principal (☎7983 2010 or 5514 7444), north of the *parque central.* All rooms have private baths, A/C, and cable TVs. Outdoor hammocks and a beautiful pool with a theme-park-style waterslide. Restaurant in the lobby, as well as a small *tienda* selling everything from toothpaste to booze. Singles Q122; doubles Q150. V. ❶

Hotel Nopales (☎5514 0624), on the east side of the *parque central.* The best budget option in Chisec. Clean and simple rooms all have private baths and fans. Singles Q45; doubles Q86. Cash only. ❷

Hotel Elizabeth, on C. Principal, north of the *parque central,* across from Hotel La Estancia. No-frills, slightly shabby rooms. Singles Q44. Cash only. ❷

🔲 FOOD

Chisec's dining options are limited, but that doesn't mean there aren't a few places worth visiting. You'll find more exotic *comida típica* options than in larger villages (there might be deer on the menu), as well as a few international options limited mainly to burgers and pasta.

Restaurante Bonapek (☎5736 7699), on the north side of the *parque central.* Don't be intimidated by the stuffed animal decor: the creatures may prove helpful if you don't understand one of the entrees, as the waiter will point to the animal in the dish they are describing. Breakfast (eggs, beans, *plátanos,* cheese, and tortillas) Q30. *Lomito a la plancha* Q40. Open daily 7am-9pm. Cash only. ❸

Restaurante Hotel La Estancia (☎5514 7444 or 7983 2010), in the lobby of the Hotel La Estancia. Giant flatscreen TV plays a constant stream of soccer. *Comida típica* Q30. Hamburgers Q25. Beer Q15. Open daily from 7am-9pm. V. ❷

Restaurante Don Miguel, C. Principal (☎5156 7470 or 5439 8712), north of the *parque central.* Half internet cafe, half restaurant. *Pollo frito* Q20. Free Wi-Fi. Open daily 7am-10pm. Cash only. ❷

🔲 DAYTRIPS FROM CHISEC

CANDELARIA CAVES
From Chisec, take any bus to Raxrujá and ask to be dropped at Candelaria Camposanto. Bring a flashlight. Tours are 2 hr. Dry tour Q30. Tubing tour Q40.

The beautiful and remote Candelaria Caves, located halfway between Chisec and Raxrujá, are part of an underground system more than 30km long. Now part of a national park, these caves are widely considered the most awe-inspiring in Central America. French spelunker Daniel Dreux discovered the caves in 1974, following a six-year search that began when he read about a sacred underground river in the *Popol Vuh,* the Quiché Maya holy book. Of particular note is the Ventana de Seguridad cave: a cathedral-sized vault with a large opening in the roof. Partially collapsed from a 1976 earthquake, the roof lets in a filtered column of light from the jungle above. Deeper in the cave are a series of unmarred stalactite, crystalline formations. Part of the caves are not open to tourists as they are still thought to be a sight sacred to the K'ekchi'.

VERAPAZ HIGHLANDS

PETÉN

Guatemala's northernmost region once boasted one of the world's most advanced civilizations, but ever since the Maya mysteriously abandoned their power center at Tikal, humans have more or less avoided this foreboding area. The thick forest and thin soil here kept the Spanish settlers away, and today the Petén region contains a third of Guatemala's land mass but less than 3% of its population. Even so, nature's dominance is being threatened by new residents, slash-and-burn agriculture, and ranching. Conservation efforts have helped slow the destruction. With roads rolling over cleared grasslands dotted with banana trees, jaguars prowling, and stone pyramids hidden behind hanging jungle vines, Petén feels like something out of a movie.

The region's great attraction is Tikal, arguably the most beautiful of all Mayan sites. Flores and its sister city, Santa Elena, have the most visitor services in Petén and serve as pleasant bases from which to travel. El Remate, between Flores and Tikal, is a quiet lakeside village. Sayaxché provides river access to smaller Mayan sites, while the famous traveler's hangout of Finca Ixobel lies along the coastal highway to Guatemala City. North of Tikal are some isolated Mayan ruins, including Uaxactún and spectacular El Mirador.

SAYAXCHÉ

Sleepy Sayaxché (pop. 7800) sits on the Río de La Pasión about 50km southwest of Flores. Although there's little to do here, the town makes a great launching point for trips to El Ceibal, Aguateca, and other ruins in the southwest Petén. Sayaxché also makes for a good stop over before heading south toward Tikal or Cobán and the Verapaz Highlands. During the rainy season, however, the river often floods its banks, making travel through the area exciting but dangerous.

▐ TRANSPORTATION

All buses and microbuses leave Sayaxché from the waterfront and pass through the *parque central*. To: **Cobán** (4¼hr.; 6, 11am, and 3pm; Q45); **Flores** (1½hr., every 20min., Q15); and **Raxrujá** (2hr., every 30min., Q25).

✈ 🛈 ORIENTATION AND PRACTICAL INFORMATION

Most travelers arrive to Sayaxché on microbuses which stop in the *parque central*, just three blocks from the river. Most hotels and restaurants line the streets that run along or parallel to the river.

Tourist Office: There is no tourist office in Sayaxche, but Cecilia at **Restaurante Yaxkín** (☎4144 7334) is a wealth of information on happenings in Sayaxché and environs.

Bank:Banrural: on a corner of the *parque central*. Open M-F 8:30am-5pm, Sa 9am-1pm. Has **ATM** and **currency exchange.**

Police: (☎7928 6144), 1 block from the waterfront, across from Restaurante Yaxkín.

Pharmacy: Farmacia Arteaga (☎7928 6104), 2 blocks from the *parque central* and 2 blocks up from the waterfront. Open daily 7am-9pm.

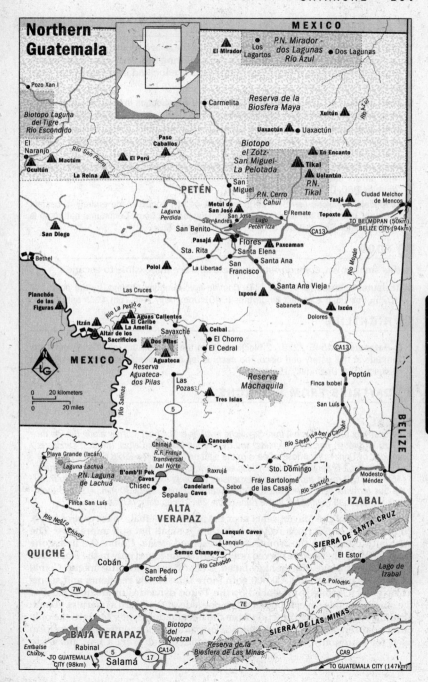

Northern Guatemala

MEXICO

Pozo Xan I

P.N. Mirador-
dos Lagunas
Río Azul

El Mirador
Los
Lagartos
Dos Lagunas

Carmelita

Reserva de la
Biosfera Maya

Xultún

Biotopo Laguna
del Tigre
Río Escondido

Uaxactún   Uaxactún

El
Naranjo
Río San Pedro

Mactún
El Perú
Paso
Caballos

Biotopo
el Zotz-
San Miguel-
La Pelotada
En Encanto

Tikal

Ocultún
La Reina

PETÉN
San
Miguel
Uolantún

P.N.
Tikal

San Diego
Laguna
Perdida
Metul de
San José
San Andrés
San José

P.N. Cerro
Cahuí
El Remate

Yaxjá
Ciudad Melchor
de Mencos

San Benito
Lago
Petén Itzá
Pasajá
Flores
Topoxte

TO BELMOPAN (50km)
BELIZE CITY (94km)

Bethel

Pancam

Sta. Rita
Santa Elena
Paxcaman

CA13

Poloi
La Libertad
San
Francisco
Santa Ana
Río Mopán

Planchón
de las
Figuras
Las Cruces
Santa Ana Vieja

Ixponé
Sabaneta

Itzán
Río La Pasión
Aguas Callentes
El Caribe
La Amelia
Sayaxché

Ixcún

Dolores

CA13

Altar de los
Sacrificios
Dos Pilas
Ceibal
El Chorro
El Cedral

MEXICO
Aguateca
Reserva
Aguateca-
dos Pilas
Las
Pozas

Reserva
Machaquila
Finca Ixobel
Poptún

0   20 kilometers
0   20 miles
5
Tres Islas
San Luís

Cancuén
Río Santa Isabel o Cancón

Chinajá
R.F. Franja
Transversal
Del Norte
Sto. Domingo
Modesto
Méndez

Playa Grande (Ixcán)
B'omb'll Pek
Caves
Raxrujá
Fray Bartolomé
de las Casas
Río Sarstún

Laguna Lachuá
P.N. Laguna
de Lachuá
Chisec
Sepalau
Candelaria
Caves
Sebol

IZABAL

Finca San Luís
ALTA
VERAPAZ
SIERRA DE SANTA CRUZ

BELIZE

Río Negro
Chixoy
El Estor
Lago de
Izabal

QUICHÉ
Lanquín Caves
Lanquín

Cobán
Semuc Champey
Río Cahabón
R. Polochic

San Pedro
Carchá

7W

7E

BAJA VERAPAZ
Biotopo
del
Quetzal
SIERRA DE LAS MINAS

Embalse
Chixoy
Rabinal
5   17
CA14
Reserva de la
Biosfera de Las Minas
CA9

TO GUATEMALA
CITY (98km)
Salamá
TO GUATEMALA CITY (147km)

PETÉN

ACCOMMODATIONS

There are no luxury hotels in Sayaxché, but there are plenty of accommodations that are perfect to use as a base for exploring the area around Sayaxché and Lake Petexbatun. Most accommodations are located in between the river and the *parque central*.

- **Hotel del Río** (☎7928 6138 or 5150 1231). The nicest option in town. Spacious rooms have private baths and hot water. Rooms with fans Q150, with A/C Q225. Cash only. ❹
- **Hotel Guayacán** (☎7928 6111), 1 block from the waterfront. Clean, secure rooms in a convenient location. All rooms have private baths and fans. Singles Q100; doubles Q150. Cash only. ❸
- **Hotel la Pasión** (☎5170 7913), across the street from the Hotel Guayacán. Rooms with private baths, fans, and cable TVs. The staff couldn't be friendlier. Singles Q60; doubles Q80. Cash only. ❷
- **Hospedaje Sayaxché** (☎4576 1905 or 5914 4454). Rooms made entirely of cement are dark, drab, and furnished with cruelly uncomfortable beds. Communal bathroom is clean enough. Singles Q30; doubles Q60. Cash only. ❶

FOOD

In this small town, *comedor*-style restaurants are impossible to escape.

- **Restaurante Yaxkín** (☎4144 7334). *Comida típica* options abound. Try the *pollo frito* (Q25). Box lunch is perfect for daytrips (Q40). Open daily 7am-7pm. Cash only. ❷

NIGHTLIFE

- **El Botanero** (☎4545 2229), 2 blocks up from the river, on the left. It's all about the attitude at this eatery and disco. The decor is log cabin meets discotheque. *Pollo a la plancha* Q34. Open daily 10am-8pm.

DAYTRIPS FROM SAYAXCHÉ

CEIBAL

The best way to reach Ceibal from Sayaxché involves a 1hr. boat journey along the Río de la Pasión through pastures, hamlets, and the Parque Nacional Ceibal. The best service is provided by Don Pedro, whose office is to the right on the water (☎7928 6109. Q250-300 round trip for 1-5 people.) A slightly less expensive option is to hire a direct pickup truck (45min., Q150 round trip). The least expensive option is to take a collective pickup from the bus terminal across the river to Aldea Paraíso (10min., every 30 min., Q3) and then walk the dirt road veering left to the ruins (8km, 2hr.). Open daily 7:30am-5pm.

The grandest of the Mayan ruins near Sayaxché is Ceibal, 15km east of town. With only 3% of the ruins restored, the site is small but still impressive. The main attractions are the wonderfully preserved *stelae*. Unlike the limestone *stelae* of Tikal, these were carved out of hard stone found only in the small area surrounding the site; the monkey-faced "*stelae* 2" is particularly unique. Ceibal reached its peak around AD 900 with more than 10,000 residents and seems to have been strongly influenced by the Toltec dynasties of Mexico. Most of the site surrounds several plazas off to one side of the guard's quarters. A path heading in the opposite direction from the information center leads to the only other restored structure, the *pirámide circular*, a Toltec-influenced platform used for astronomy. Free camping is permitted, but bring a tent, mosquito netting, water, and enough food to share with the guards (no joke). For tours of the ruins, hire a guide at the entrance.

LAKE PETEXBATÚN

A 30-45min. speed boat ride will take you from Sayaxche to the northern tip of Lake Petexbatún.

From Sayaxché, a short ride down the southern branch of the Río de la Pasión leads to the secluded Lake Petexbatún (Peh-tesh-bah-TOON), surrounded by forest and teeming with wildlife. The area was once an important trading center for the Maya, and the ruins of Aguateca overlook the southern edges of the lake. Occupied until about AD 790, the site has plazas, unexcavated temples, well-preserved *stelae*, and the only known Mayan bridge. The ruins are undergoing restorations scheduled for completion in 2004. The guards will show you around and let you camp if you bring food and equipment. Rain gear, mosquito netting, and plenty of bug repellent are advisable. Nearby is the **Petexbatún Lodge ❺**, a well-maintained hotel on the shores of the lake. (☎7926 0501. Dorms Q80; singles Q285.) A second Maya site, **Dos Pilas**, is a 13km (3½hr.) hike west of the lake. Find guides at the Posada el Caribe (☎7928 6114). Built in a unique east-west linear pattern, these ruins include *stelae* and hieroglyphic stairways.

AGUATECA

Aguateca is a 1½hr. boat ride from Sayaxché. The walk to the path to Dos Pilas takes 45min.; the walk to Aguateca is another 3hr. from there. Servicio de Lanchas Don Pedro arranges trips to Aguateca and Dos Pilas. During the dry season (Jan.-May), a four-wheel-drive pickup sometimes runs to Dos Pilas, departing from Sayaxché at 7am.

One of the shortest-lived Maya sites in the Petén region, Aguateca has recently become one of the area's most heavily excavated and studied sites. Occupied between early AD 700 and AD 790, the city was thought to be closely aligned with nearby Dos Pilas. There have even been similar *stelae* found at both sites chronicling the defeat of El Ceibal. Set high on a limestone platform and protected on three sides by a large rock wall and gorge, Aguateca's geology is both unique and fascinating. A slippery two-hour walk around the edge of the site delves into the gorge and ventures deep into the surrounding jungle which monkeys, snakes, mosquitoes, and sloths call home. The city came to its surprising end during the construction of the palace dedicated to the fifth governor, when an enemy attack forced locals to flee. The massive pile of rocks waiting to be erected still sits in the center of the main plaza.

FLORES

Far more than a mere jumping off point for Tikal, Flores (pop. 2000) is an island world unto itself. Just a short causeway across from noisy Santa Elena, narrow cobblestone streets wind their way past bright pastel facades and up steep inclines. Beautiful Lago de Petén Itza is never far from sight, encircled by lush jungle hills. Still, don't expect a peaceful oasis free of tourist bustle; Flores wears its charm on its sleeve. Every street seems to hold at least five hotels, signs in English are unavoidable, and travel agencies flaunt their tour and shuttle deals from every corner. But all that fades into irrelevance when you're enjoying dinner by the waterfront at dusk, watching the brilliant sunset ripple on the water.

PETÉN

▐ TRANSPORTATION

Flores is Guatemala's northernmost destination for most travelers; there are plenty of options for journeying south into the rest of Guatemala or heading into nearby Mexico and Belize. If you're really wheelin' it, you can even catch direct but long bus rides into bordering El Salvador and Honduras.

Flights: Mundo Maya International Airport, on the Santa Elena side, southeast of the causeway. *Tuk-tuks* from Flores Q20-25. There is a Q20 airport tax for all flights. **Transportes Aeoreos Guatemaltecos (TAG)** (☎2380 9494; www.tag.com.gt) flies to **Guatemala City** (1hr., daily 4:30pm, Q915-1000). **Grupo TACA** (☎2470 8222; www.taca.com) flies to **Guatemala City** (1hr.; 8:05am, 4:10, 7:20pm; Q915-1000), **Cancun, MEX** (3hr., 11:25am, Q1900-2080), and **Belize City** (2hr., 12:30 and 1pm, Q3080-3400). **Tropic Air** (☎1-800-422-3435; www.tropicair.com) flies to **Belize City** (1hr., 9:45am and 4:15pm, Q950). **Continental Airlines** (www.continental.com) flies to **Houston, Texas** W and Sa.

Tourist Buses: Seats on these buses must be reserved at least a day in advance; you can usually book them at your accommodation and, in some cases, arrange to be picked up there. **Aventuras Turisticas minibuses** go to: **Antigua** (10hr., 10pm, Q245; 1st class 10hr., 9:30pm, Q285); **Coban** (5hr., 9am, Q150); **Guatemala City** (8hr., 10 and 11pm, Q175; 1st class 8hr., 9 and 11pm, Q250); **Lanquin** (7hr., 9am, Q150); **Panajachel** (12hr., 10pm, Q300); **Rio Dulce** (5hr., every 30min. 5:30-8:30am, Q125; 1st-class 5hr., 10am, Q210); **San Pedro Sula, HON** (12hr., 5:30am, Q300); **San Salvador, El Salvador** (12hr., 5:30am, Q300); **Semuc Champey** (7hr., 9am, Q150); **Tegucigalpa, HON** (14hr., 5:30am, Q330). San Juan buses go to **Belize City, Belize** (6hr., 5 and 7:30am, Q160), **Chetumal, MEX** via Belize City (8hr., 5am, Q225), and **Palenque, MEX** (8hr., 5am, Q265).

Public buses: Main bus station in Santa Elena, 1 mi. south of the bridge on 6a Av. *Tuk-tuk* ride from Flores Q5. Minibuses and buses also leave from inside the Santa Elena market along 5a C., but most of these rides start at the main station and are just trying to pick up more passengers among the crowds. **1st-class ADN** buses go to **Guatemala City** (8hr., 9 and 11pm, Q165). **AMCAS buses** go to: **Bethel** (3¼hr.; 11:30am, noon, 3:30pm; Q45); **La Tecnica** (3½hr., 8 and 9am, Q50); **San Andres** (25min., every 15min. 5am-6:30pm, Q9); **San Jose** (25min., every 15min. 5am-6:30pm, Q9). **ATIM minibuses** got to **El Remate** (45min., every 30min. 8am-6:30pm, Q25-30). **Fuente del Norte buses** go to **Guatemala City** (9hr., every 1½hr. 3:30am-10:30pm, Q110; 1st class 8hr.; 10am, 2, 9, 10pm; Q160), **Melchor de Mencos** (1½hr., Q30), and **San Salvador, El Salvador** (10hr., 6am, Q210). **1st-class Linea Dorada** buses go to **Guatemala City** (8hr., 9am and 8:45pm, Q150; luxury buses 8hr., 9:30pm, Q190). **Microbuses del Norte** go to **Sayaxche** (1hr. 20min., every 15min. 5:30am-6pm, Q20). **Rapidos del Sur buses** go to **Guatemala City** (7hr., 10 and 11pm, Q120). **Transportes Maria Elena** go to **Chiqimula** (7hr.; 6, 10am, 2pm; Q95), **Esquipulas** (8hr.; 6, 10am, 2pm; Q110), and **Rio Dulce** (4hr.; 6, 10am, 2pm; Q70). **Transportes Rosario** chicken buses go to **Guatemala City** (9hr., 7 and 8:30pm, Q95).

▐▐ ▐ ORIENTATION AND PRACTICAL INFORMATION

Flores is connected to the mainland by a 1600 ft. causeway. **Playa Sur** (or **C. Sur**) heads left from the bridge; **Av. Santa Ana, Av. Barrios,** and **C. 30 de Junio** head north up the hill. At the hill's top is the **parque central**, with a basketball court, stone benches arranged in a circle, and a large cathedral (visible from Santa Elena). **C. Union** circles around the northern edge of the island, becoming **C. 15 de Septiembre** on the eastern side.

Tourist Office: There's a tourist information booth on Pl. Sur right by the causeway. Open M-Su 7am-11am and 2-6pm. **INGUAT,** Av. Santa Ana (☎7867 5334). Open M-F 8am-4pm.

Tours: Flores is littered with companies offering tour packages to various destinations in the Petén, many of them indistinguishable from or tied to the travel agencies in town. Most hostels and hotels will be able to arrange tours as well. Some companies have offices; with others it is best to simply contact in advance through phone or online (see **Sights Around Flores and Santa Elena**, p. 202, for details on trip destinations).

Martsam Tour and Travel, C. 30 de Junio (☎7867 5093; www.martsam.com). One of the best tour providers, offering a huge range of trips to the top destinations in Petén. Full-day trips to Tikal, Uaxactun, Yaxha, Nakum, Ceibal, and Aguateca; 3-day tours of El Zotz and Tikal; 5-day trips to El Mirador; 2- and 3-day trips to the Laguna del Tigre National Park. MC/V.

Quetzal Travel (☎4188 7883; www.mayanprincesstouroperator.com). Tours to Tikal, Uaxactun, Yaxha, El Mirador, El Zotz, and Ceibal.

Turismo Aventura (☎7926 0398 or 5510 2965; www.toursguatemala.com). Full-day and overnight tours of Tikal, full-day tours of Uaxactun, regular and sunset tours of Yaxha, 5-day trip to El Mirador, 3-day tours of El Zotz and Tikal.

Cafe Arqueologico Yaxha, C. 15 de Septiembre (☎5830 2060). Restaurant also offers tours to **La Blanca** and **Yaxha** (8am-5pm; 2 people Q620 per person, 3 people Q440 per person, 4 people Q350 per person, 5 people Q290 per person, plus Q80 park fee); **Topoxte** and **Yaxha** (8am-4pm; 2 people Q700 per person, 5 people Q500 per person, 4 people Q375 per person, 3 people Q315 per person); **Yaxha** and **Nakum** (2 days, 2 people Q1540 per person, 3 people Q1455 per person, 4 people Q1250 per person, plus Q80 park fee); **El Zotz** and **Tikal** (3 days, 1 person Q2200, 2 people Q1370 per person, 4 people Q1120 per person, + Q415 for English-speaking guide); **El Mirador** (5 days, 1 person Q3450, 2 people Q2450 per person, 4 people Q1800 per person, plus Q415 for English-speaking guide). MC/V.

Bank: Banrural, Av. Flores. Open M-Sa 8am-3pm. The only **ATM** in Flores is next to the Hotel Petén on C. 30 de Junio.

Laundromat: Mayan Princess Travel Agency, C. 30 de Junio. Wash and dry Q30. Open M-Sa 9am-6pm. **Lavafacil,** C. Jon el Crucero. Wash and dry Q35. Also has an internet cafe (Q8 per hr.). Open daily 9am-7pm.

Canoe Rental: La Villa del Chef, C. Union (see **Food,** p. 202). Rents canoes for Q40 per hr.

Police Station: In *parque central.*

Internet Access: Tikal Net, C. Centroamerica. Q10 per hr. Open daily 8am-9pm. **Peten Net,** C. Centroamerica, next to Tikal Net. Q10 per hr. Open daily 9m-10pm. **Maya Net,** corner of Av. La Reforma and C. Jon El Crucero. Q12 per hr. Book exchange and chocolate-dipped fruit. Open daily 9am-9pm.

Post Office: At the corner of C. Central and Av. Barrios. Open M-Sa 8am-5pm.

🏠 📷 ACCOMMODATIONS AND CAMPING

Countless hotels running the full price gamut crowd the narrow streets, most of them with their own restaurants. Many allow guests to book tourist shuttles, which can pick you up at the hotel's door.

▣ **Los Amigos Hostel,** C. Central (☎5584 8795; www.amigoshostel.com). Easily the best budget option in Flores, Los Amigos is always full of backpackers who flock to its groovy, jungle-like interior. It's a perfect example of controlled chaos—dogs and cats run through haphazardly placed plants, crowds of backpackers lounge in hammocks, and nonstop music provides eclectic background noise. There's also a restaurant that serves delicious vegetarian breakfasts (Q18-30), *tortas* (Q22-35), burritos (Q25-35; try the massive "Ay Caramba!"), pastas (Q30-35), and brownies (Q12). Internet Q10 per hr. Free Wi-Fi. You can also book bus and plane tickets here. Hammocks Q20; outdoor dorms with tin roofing Q25; indoor dorms Q30-40; singles with shared bath Q70; doubles with shared bath Q70, with private bath Q140; triples Q90/150; quads Q120/140. MC/V. ❶

Hospedaje Dona Gona 1 and 2, C. Union (☎ 7867 5513 or 7926 3538). Two buildings on C. Union form one of the most popular backpacker destinations in Flores. The 2nd building sports an interior waterfall and viewing hammocks under thatched roofs. Dorms Q25; singles Q60, with bath Q80; doubles Q80/100. MC/V. ❶

Inka Ti Jesh Maach Hostal, Pl. Sur (☎ 7867 5599 or 5818 3273). Basic rooms in a convenient location. Doubles as a travel agency. Free internet. Singles Q35; doubles Q70; triples Q105. Cash only. ❶

Hotel Mirador del Lago, C. 15 de Septiembre (☎ 7926 3276). Cheap lakeside lodging in appropriately blue rooms. The small, quiet garden area by the shore is perfect for unwinding. All rooms with private baths. Singles Q45; doubles Q60. MC/V. ❷

🚩 FOOD

Flores's restaurants, like its hotels (sometimes they're the same thing), are numerous. Their menus feature an eclectic range of offerings, mixing local specialties (including Mayan dishes) with international fare. Many restaurants hug the waterfront, providing spectacular views and cool breezes.

Cool Beans, C.15 de Septiembre. "El Cafe Chilero" definitely lives up to its name, attempting eccentricities in every corner: a book exchange, board games, movies for sale, hammocks, and quirky decorations. If you don't want to stay for a meal, snatch up some homemade bread, muffins, and rolls (Q15-25). Breakfast served all day (Q25-32). Sandwiches Q18-35. Lunch and dinner options Q28-60. Drinks Q5-18. Open M-Sa 6am-9pm. V. ❷

Cafe Arqueologico Yaxha, C. 15 de Septiembre (☎ 5830 2060). The Cafe Yaxha proudly represents the Petén in more ways than one. With a small library of books, a handmade packet of information on the area, and a wide range of tours on offer, the cafe is an ideal base from which to plan explorations. The walls, lined with photographs of the region's archaeological treasures, are worth a close look. Check out the pictures from Tikal's earliest stages of excavation, when the ruins were still buried under moss and vegetation. Oh, and then there's the delicious food; a huge menu offering breakfast (Q20-30), beef, chicken, and pasta. Mayan specialties Q30-60. Entrees Q20-90. AmEx/MC/V. ❷

La Villa del Chef, C. Union. German expats offer fish dishes with fresh catches from the lake (Q110-120), lasagna and pasta (Q39-44), pizza (Q61-79), Guatemalan specialties (Q30-74), and Arabic food, including falafel and shish kebabs (Q34-64). La Villa is also the only place in town where you can puff on a hookah pipe (Q65). Come at sunset; the views from the waterfront seating are spectacular. Rents canoes for Q40 per hr. (maximum 2 people). Open daily 8am-10pm. AmEx/MC/V. ❷

Capitan Tortuga, C. 30 de Junio (☎ 7867 5089). A spacious restaurant and pizzeria with lakeside seating. Get after the burritos and tacos (Q30-45) or opt for the grill food (Q55-110), seafood (Q95-105), or pizzas (small Q39-44, grande Q79-87). Try Capitan Tortuga pizza, with mushrooms, eggplant, chicken, ham, and cheese. Open daily 11am-10pm. ❷

⬤ SIGHTS AROUND FLORES

So, you've seen Tikal. Maybe you've even made the grueling jungle trek to El Mirador. You think you've "done" the Petén and are ready to book it. Well don't. You'll be missing out on the region's smaller, more painlessly accessible treasures: beautiful outlooks, thrilling parks, and quiet beaches all lie within navigable distance of Flores.

BOAT TRIPS. *Lancheros* (small boats) lurk along the island's coasts, offering service to all nearby points on the lake. The best place to find them is along Playa Sur right next to the causeway, but if you're heading to a northern point it will probably be cheaper to find a boat along the northern shore. These

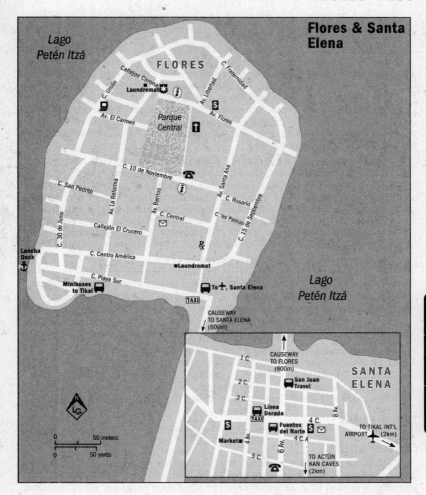

Flores & Santa Elena

prices are general; hone your haggling chops by negotiating for a smaller fare. You can catch a ride to **Arcas** (one-way Q50, round-trip Q200), the **Petencito Zoo** (Q50/200), the lookout at **El Mirador** (one-way Q100), the **Playita beach** (one-way Q100), and the nearby lakeside towns of **San Jose** (Q250/350) and **San Andres** (Q200/300). You can also try to snag a relaxing **lake tour** (2hr., Q100-150).

PARQUE NATURAL IXPANPAJUL. Like a natural amusement park, this small nature preserve just south of Flores and Santa Elena provides a variety of thrilling ways to explore the rainforest. A network of high, hanging bridges is an ideal way to view the greenery. Or, to really give that fear of heights a workout, try the Tarzan Canopy Tour, where you can speed through the treetops on a zipline. Other opportunities here include horseback, bike tours, and night walks through the jungle. (*Take a Rio Dulce-bound bus or a minibus from the Santa*

Elena bus station and ask to be let off at Ixpanpajul (Q10-15). ☎ 2336 0576 or 5619 0513; www. ixpanpajul.com. Q200. Open M-Sa 9am-5pm.)

EL MIRADOR. Not to be confused with the large Mayan site on Guatemala's northern edge, the closer and humbler El Mirador is easily accessed—no five-day jungle treks here. High up on the sliver of land cutting into the lake north of Flores, a lookout provides a bird's-eye view of the island. Ask a *lanchero* (boatman) to take you to the village of San Miguel; from there, a trail climbs for 1 mi. up the lookout spot. Several small Mayan ruins dot the area, many of them under excavation—expect to meet a few archaeologists along the way. Relax on the walk back by stopping at the small beach near the trail, literally called "El Playita." *(One-way Q100.)*

THE ASOCIACION DE RESCATE Y CONSERVACION DE VIDA SILVESTRE (ARCAS). The Wildlife Rescue and Conservation Association was founded to aid animals abused in the illegal smuggling trade and to protect them before reintroduction into the wild. The NGO is based near the village of San Benito, on the shore northeast of Flores. The center offers a mile-long trail for visitors with opportunities for viewing some of the actual wildlife. *(A boat leaves for the center 7:30-8:30am by the arch in the middle of the causeway between Flores and Santa Elena. Free. A one-way lanchero Q50. ☎ 2478 4096 or 2480 7270; www.arcasguatemala.com. Q10.)*

🎵 🎬 ENTERTAINMENT AND NIGHTLIFE

Flores is mostly quiet at night, with the few drinking establishments closing around 10pm. Most of the restaurants (see **Food**, p. 202) also have a bar with happy hours in the early evening, so if you want to have a few drinks and meander through the quaint streets you'll be able to do it. **C. Sur** on the island's southern edge is the best place to seek out rowdier restaurants and a few bars.

Cafe Bar El Tropico, C. Sur (☎5769 1281). There's a flatscreen TV above the bar and a small aquarium to entertain you if the view of Santa Elena across the lake gets boring. Beers Q15-20. Mixed drinks Q25-30. Try the *michelador* (Q25), a Guatemalan specialty aiming for a spicier Bloody Mary: salt, pepper, lime, hot sauce, and Gallo beer make for a delicious mix—if you can handle it. Open M-Sa 11am-10pm. Cash only.

⛰ HIKING

MAYAN RUINS

If Tikal didn't satiate your curiosity and you feel the old familiar tug of adventure, northern Guatemala hides many other Mayan ruins. Most are visited through a guided tour, and some require strenuous multi-day hikes through the most isolated of wildernesses. The romantic prospect of hidden ruins and beautiful views attracts the bold and willing, but don't expect comfort.

EL MIRADOR

El Mirador is only accessible via multi-day hiking and camping trips that last 5-6 days in total. Trips leave from Flores and begin walking from the northern village of La Carmelita, the last outpost of civilization before the jungle. You can book your trip at one of the tour companies in Flores (see Orientation and Practical Information, p. 200); a minimum of 4 people is usually required (though you can book solo trips at Cafe Yaxha for Q3450). With a group of 4, the cost per person runs between Q1750 and Q2080. All mules, equipment, and food are provided.

El Mirador is for the die-hards, those who either obsess over Mayan ruins or relish any chance for serious jungle adventure. "Getting there is half the fun" has never been so true—the long hiking and camping treks (5-6 days) are major tests of endurance (with 27-30hr. of rough walking). At the end of the journey lies one of the true hidden treasures of the Mayan civilization—a relic of the distant origins of the great civilization. El Mirador was one of the earliest cities in all of North America. Settled as early as 800 BC, it flourished during the late Pre-classic period, between 300 BC and AD 150. With over 80,000 inhabitants, El Mirador quickly became the first superpower of the Mayan world, lassoing all surrounding cities, including Tikal, into obedience. The excavated portion of the city covers 2 sq. km and includes the largest concentration of buildings ever found yet among Mayan ruins. The main structure here is **El Tigre,** a temple 55m high (180 ft.) and with a surface area six times that of **Templo IV,** the largest structure at Tikal. Enjoy a sunset from the top, with vistas of the unbroken jungle stretching as far as the eye can see. The **Danta Complex** consists of ascending platforms holding up three pyramids at the top. The structure is carefully laid out in an elegant geometric structure: the base is 7m high, the next platform 7m higher, the next platform is 21m higher, and the pyramids themselves are 21m high. All in all, it stands 70m tall, with each side of the base measuring 300m. Longer (6-day) trips circle around to visit the nearby ruins at **Nakbe,** another impressive site; by 800 BC a small city had been established there.

UAXACTUN

Uaxactun is located 23km down a road leading off from Tikal. A bus from Santa Elena's bus station heads to Uaxactun village (3hr., daily 1-3pm, Q50); ask at the bus station for the exact time, as it changes often. You'll have to wait a day to catch the return bus; it heads back to Santa Elena between 5 and 6am. If you want to visit straight from Tikal, you can catch this bus on its way through. San Juan Travel (☎5461 6010) runs a shuttle to Uaxactun at 6am (returning at noon), but they must be contacted in advance and require a minimum of 2 people (round-trip Q500). Otherwise, you can try to catch a ride from Tikal or (the easiest and most popular method) come on a tour (see Tours in Orientation and Practical Information, p. 200). Full-day tours Q415-580.

Uaxactun's original name was **Siaan K'aan,** "Born in Heaven"; the existing name was coined by the site's first excavator. Uaxactun is now contained within the grounds of the **Parque Nacional Tikal.** Its chronology roughly aligns with that of Tikal: primitive settlement in the Pre-classical Era, establishment of a flourishing, advanced civilization from about AD 500-800, and collapse by AD 1000. The city's subservient status frustrated any chance of growth comparative to that of Tikal, though, and travelers looking for the hidden grandeur like that of El Mirador will be disappointed. There is a village situated around the airstrip. Of most interest here is the **E group,** which provides evidence of the advanced state of Mayan science. Structures **E-1, E-2,** and **E-3** form an astronomical observatory. Structure **E-VII-B,** a truncated pyramid, with staircases on all four sides and decorated with stucco masks of sacred animals, is believed to have been a main point of observation, perfectly placed to record solstices and equinoxes. Groups **A** and **B,** about a 20min. walk away, have some comparatively unremarkable temple ruins. **Aldana's Lodge** ❶ near the ruins has campsites (Q20) and rooms with shared baths (Q35).

YAXHA

Yaxha lies 14km north of the main Flores/Santa Elena-Belize road. There are 3 options for reaching it without a car. You can take a guided tour from Flores (full-day tours US$70-90; see Orientation and Practical Information, p. 200), take a taxi from Flores (Q500), or take a bus in the direction of Melchor de Mencos and the Belizean border and ask to be let off at the turnoff to Yaxha. Site Q80.

Just 30 km southeast of Tikal, the hilltop Mayan ruins at Yaxha give evidence of yet another powerful city in the region. With over 500 structures discovered—and excavation still ongoing (you're likely to see archaeologists at work)—Yaxha is the third-largest discovered city in Guatemala. Because of its inconvenient location, it usually lacks the teeming crowds of its neighbor to the northwest. So, a trip to these ruins, surrounded by rich flora and fauna ("Yaxha means "green water"), is likely to be a quiet one. Yaxha was even deemed remote enough to provide the setting for *Survivor: Guatemala* in 2005. Known mainly as a ceremonial center, Yaxha contained some 20,000 people during its eighth-century peak. Evidence points to a highly advanced culture: two astronomical observatories, three ball courts, and a well-established *sacbe* system connecting the city to the lake. Tikal's close presence was probably the greatest factor in establishing Yaxha's importance. Similarities between the two sites indicate that the larger city's protection and trade secured Yaxha, especially against the hostile Naranjo to the northeast. The *stelae* discovered at Yaxha seem to show that Naranjo finally defeated its rival. During the collapse of the Maya, it's believed that the city's elite fled to the nearby island of Topoxte. You can reach Topoxte via boat, which you can rent at El Sombrero.

Plaza F, distinguished by a pyramid affording great views of the other temples, is the first stop from the entrance. Just north is the **Grupo Mayer complex,** whose layout—twin temples separated by a plaza—is reminscent of Tikal's Gran Plaza. The temple-heavy **Acropolis Norte** features an unusual 22m structure with rounded edges. Southeast lies Yaxha's greatest pride, **Templo 216,** the tallest building here. Views of the lakes and lagoons make the tough climb worth it; go at sunset if you can, but check the park's closing times. Yaxha lies in the **Parque Nacional Yaxha-Nakum-Naranjo,** which covers over 91,000 acres and protects a huge range of wildlife, including over 22 species of fish that live in the region's lakes. For those who want to spend the night near the ruins, Campamento Ecologico El Sombrero (☎7861 1688 or 1691; www.ecosombrero.com) lies just off the road on the southern shore of the lake. Beautiful bungalows by the shore provide peace and views; there's also a restaurant on site. Singles Q140, with bath Q240; doubles Q240/312. Horseback riding tours available. Rent canoes and boats for trips around the lake, including the island ruins of Topoxte.

EL ZOTZ

Though a 25km road connects El Zotz with Uaxactun, the site is most easily visited as part of a guided tour. Hiking and camping trips usually last 3 days and include a visit to Tikal. (This grueling hike to see unrestored ruins will really separate the men from the boys among the Maya-obsessed.) Tours are Q2200 for 1 person, Q1370 for 2, and Q1120 for 3 (see Orientation and Practical Information, p. 200).

Thirty kilometers west of Tikal, El Zotz is an almost completely buried site just outside the Parque Nacional Tikal. The area was settled during the Classical era (AD 200-900) and was probably vassal to Tikal for most of its existence—wooden lintel carvings of Tikal's rulers were discovered here. On display are the careful tunnels of grave robbers who have looted the site for centuries. The tallest structure is the 148 ft. high **Devil's Pyramid,** which includes a large cave formation housing thousands of bats. Bats are the main residents here now—"Zotz" means "bat" in several Mayan languages—and those who camp nearby at night will most likely meet a few. The area around El Zotz is its own biotope and functions as a conservation protecting the bats and a variety of other wildlife, including jaguars, monkeys, and many bird species.

PETÉN

LAGUNA DE TIGRE NATIONAL PARK AND EL PERU RUINS

Trips to El Peru last 3 days and cost BZ$100-150 (US$200-300) per person. For tour companies, see Orientation and Practical Information, p. 200.

Guatemala's largest national park covers 335,080 hectares of lowland forest and wetlands. This is Central America's largest protected wetland. Unfortunately, the region is under attack from illegal immigrants, drug traffickers, ranchers, and oil drillers. Tourism in the area is strictly limited to the Waka'-Peru archaeological site and a few biological stations located in the park's southeastern corner. Trips to the ruins at El Peru start in Paso Cabelleros, a Kekchi Mayan village on the southeastern outskirts of the park. Tours continue on boat down the Rio San Pedro river. An hour-long hike leads to the small ruins, organized around four plazas. The highest structure is **El Mirador de los Monos** (the Monkeys' Lookout), a hilltop temple that provides expansive views of the jungle and Laguna El Peru. Hikes farther into the surrounding area offer sightings of local wildlife. The most fascinating are the threatened species of Scarlet Macaw (*Guacamaya*), who are unique to this area of Guatemala.

TIKAL

The greatest reminder of the ancient Mayan world spreads over 10km in northern Guatemala—and that's just the excavated part, a mere fraction of the glorious city-empire that once dominated the region. The ruins proudly display their own kind of glory, an awesome majesty that transcends the defeated look characteristic of many other Mayan sites. High temples still reach above the jungle, in some cases visible from dozens of kilometers away. Meanwhile, in the surrounding 220km of wilderness that makes up the Parque Nacional Tikal, a bevy of exotic flora and fauna offer another brand of excitement. Go early and you'll catch howler monkeys swinging through the trees and countless bird species nesting among the ruins.

█ TRANSPORTATION. Almost every travel agency in Flores offers their own deal for heading to the site, and several bus companies operating from the Santa Elena station run buses there. But the easiest way to reach Tikal is with **San Juan Travel** (☎5461 6010), which runs **minibuses** leaving Flores (they can pick you up at your hotel) every hr. 5-10am and 2pm. Return trips head from Tikal back to Flores at 12:30pm and then every hr. 2-6pm. You can book by phone, at San Juan's offices along C. Sur in Flores, or in Santa Elena just south of the causeway. Round-trip cost is Q60. **Guided tours** of Tikal run between Q450 and Q600. If you're with a group, you can try to snag a guide at the park's entrance (about Q300).

█ ORIENTATION. The ruins lie 13 mi. inside the **Tikal National Park**. You'll pass the large arched **gate** about 30min. before reaching the site itself. Directly before reaching the **tourist information booth** and **ticket stand,** you'll pass the **Museo Litico** and the **Visitors' Center** on the left and a few *comedores* (eateries and restaurants) on the right. The **Museo Tikal** lies just ahead. The path to the ruins heads off to the left; you can buy your ticket (Q150) and a map (Q40) right at the trail's start. Any ticket bought after 3pm is valid for the next day. A 5min. walk toward the ruins will bring you to the **ticket control booth;** from there, it's about another 10-15min. to the **Gran Plaza.** The park is open daily from 6am to 6pm.

ACCOMMODATIONS AND FOOD. Watching the sunrise from a temple at Tikal is a legendary and elusive—given the mists that often descend at dawn—experience that can only be had by spending the night by the ruins. A few camping options exist for the budget traveler. The park's own **campsite** lies just south off the entrance road by the tourist information center. You can pitch your own tent for Q10 or rent one for Q60. **Jaguar Inn ❷**, to the right of the tourist information center, offers comfy and expensive bungalows with hammocks. You can also rent tents and put them in the backyard. (☎7926 0002; www.jaguartikal.com. Tent sites Q30; rented tent Q60; hammocks Q50; single bungalows; doubles Q470; triples Q590; quads Q710. MC/V.)

A small selection of restaurants provides relaxation and nourishment for the eager or exhausted explorer. A few small open-air eateries line the right side of the road as you approach Flores, serving cheap meals for Q20-60. They open as early as 6am, so you can enjoy a breakfast even if you're on the first morning shuttle.

MUSEUMS. The two on-site museums present a more detailed look at life in Tikal; they're perfect for either whetting your appetite or satiating the curiosity you've worked up while strolling the main ruins. A ticket to one museum buys access to both. **Museo Litico** is to the left of the entrance road right before the ticket booth. *Stelae* depicting important historical and cultural information are housed here, along with pottery fragments and carvings. (Open daily 8am-4pm. Q10.) **Museo Tikal** is straight ahead as you enter the visiting center from the access road. Smaller than its definitive name suggests, this museum nevertheless attempts to convey the cultural weight of the site, displaying more small carved objects: *stelae*, pottery, tools, jewelry, and even bones. The spectacular **tomb** of Lord Chocolate uncovered in **Templo I** is reconstructed here in all its splendor, including over 150 carved jade objects. (Open M-F 9am-5pm and Sa-Su 9am-4pm. Q10.)

THE RUINS OF TIKAL

HISTORY

Tikal was already a small village by about 900 BC, though the oldest excavated buildings only date from 500-400 BC. By 200 BC a variety of ceremonial structures had been built, including the first buildings at what is now the **Acropolis del Norte**. Over the centuries, Tikal developed, its art becoming more ornate and its political influence more widely felt, but with the domineering presence of the great city of El Mirador to the north, it never managed to attain superstate status. The collapse of El Mirador in the AD third century and the defeat of neighboring Uaxactun as a potential rival in AD 378 finally established the city as the region's main strongman. It was even able to apparently avoid an attempted takeover by Teotihuacan (today near Mexico City), assimilating the northern city's cultural styles but maintaining its own autonomy. During this time the city's population is believed to have been over 100,000.

In 562 AD, though, the city's growth was suddenly halted. *Stelae* reveal that Lord Water of Caracol (now in southern Belize), reacting against Tikal's attemped takeover of his kingdom, crushed the greater city, sacrificed its king Double Bird, destroyed temples, and forced it into subservience. Thus began what is known as Tikal's "hiatus" period—130 years during which no new building or development seems to have been attempted.

PETÉN

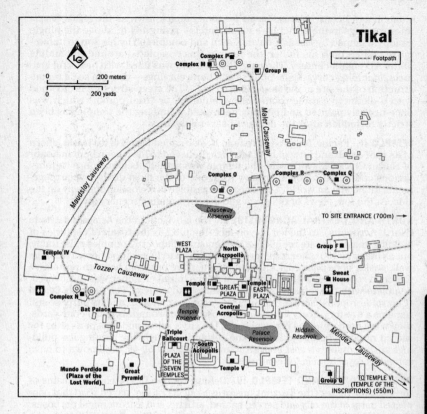

In the late seventh century, Hasaw Cha'an K'awil, sometimes known as Ah Cacau or "Lord Chocolate," came to power and defeated Caracol's ally Calakmul in AD 711. Tikal's central, autonomous role was restored, and the city began a building spree that saw the construction of most of the existing structures, including the five main temples. Lord Chocolate was buried in **Templo I**, while his wife was entombed across the Gran Plaza in **Templo II**. During the AD ninth and tenth centuries Tikal fell victim to the general and still mysterious collapse of the Mayan civilization. By AD 1000 the city was abandoned. Local peoples knew of the site for centuries, but its existence wasn't publicized until 1848, when a *chiclero* (street vendor) reported his find. Serious archaeological work commenced only in the 1950s, led by researchers from the University of Pennsylvania. Tikal was declared a UNESCO World Heritage Site in 1979.

THE MAIN SITE

THE GREAT PLAZA. A path leads about 1 mi. from the ticket booth to the first main sight, the Great Plaza. The cultural and ceremonial heart of city is surrounded by temples to its east and west and acropolises to its north and south. It's dominated by Tikal's most famous structure, emblazoned on

Guatemalan license plates: **Templo I**—sometimes known as the **Jaguar Temple** after carvings in the structure's wood lintels—rising 144 ft. above the jungle canopy. Planned by Hasan Cha'an K'awil and completed by his son to immortalize and entomb his father, the temple was completed around the middle of the AD eighth century. The magnificent tomb was filled with beautiful artifacts, including carved jade objects and bone carvings—you can see a reconstruction of the site in the **Museo Tikal** (p. 208). The steep structure is crowned with a distinctive three-room hollow building, or "roof comb," which was once brightly painted and lavishly decorated. Climbing the temple has been strictly forbidden after the deaths of several visitors.

TEMPLO II. Facing Templo I is Templo II, also called **Temple of the Masks,** shorn of its roof comb and now only 124 ft. high. Believed to have been built in honor of Hasan Cha'an K'awil's wife, the temple was actually begun before its more famous counterpart. Together, they form one of the most distinctive arrangements in the Mayan world. This one is accessible via a wooden stairway on the side. At the top, views of the plaza and the surrounding scenery await.

NORTH AND CENTRAL ACROPOLISES. The labyrinth of the **Acropolis del Norte** (North Acropolis), to the left as you face Templo I, is the result of centuries of building and deliberate rebuilding; the remains of about 12 temples exist today, but as many as 100 other structures are believed to have stood here. Two huge wall masks, once painted scarlet and green, stare out from beneath protective thatched roofs. Below the acropolis, a ruler's burial chamber was discovered, complete with the remains of nine servants and pottery. The **Acropolis Central** (Central Acropolis) across the plaza is even more complex, and its purpose still remains a mystery. Forty five rooms are organized around six small courtyards; they were used either as residences for the city's rulers and elite or as sites for sacred rituals. There is at least some certainty, though: the rectangular buildings at the complex's east end, structures **5D-45** and **5D-46,** are known to have served as royal homes for centuries.

CALZADA TOZZER AND TEMPLO IV. Behind Templo II stretch the remains of the Calzada Tozzer (the Tozzer Causeway), once a raised, paved road that connected parts of the city and served sacred, artistic, and astronomical purposes. To the right of the causeway behind the temple is the **Plaza Oueste** (West Plaza), with a late Classical temple; to the left is **Templo III,** still largely unexcavated and buried beneath mounds of earth. It was built around AD 810, very late in the city's history and unusually close to the Mayan collapse. On the left as you walk along the causeway, **Complejo N** (Complex N) features the distinctive twin-temple design, the Great Plaza in smaller form. A range of *stellae* honoring Hasan Cha'an K'awil lie around the site; he is believed to have built the complex to celebrate the completion of a *katun* (20-year cycle in the calendar). The causeway leads up to **Templo IV,** at 212 ft. the tallest of Tikal's buildings. Built in AD 741 by Hasaw's son, perhaps as his own burial tomb, the lower half of the temple is still covered in earth, the excavated top rising out of the ground. The views here are probably the most impressive, and the temple is popular among those looking to catch a good surise or sunset.El Mundo Perdido and Plaza de los Siete Templos. A path leads southwest from Templo IV into the most evocatively named of Tikal's areas, **El Mundo Perdido** (The Lost World). The purpose of most of the 38 buildings here remains a mystery, though the large **pyramid** dominating the site and rising 105 ft. was believed to have served an astronomical function. The existing structure was built over four existing pyramids, the earliest of which, dating back to 500 BC, is the earliest discovered structure in Tikal. Just west is the **Plaza de los Siete Templos** (Plaza of the Seven

Temples). The purpose of these temples, which date back to the Preclassical era, is also unclear. Aligned in a row, they offer a good example of the various states of repair and disrepair that can befall Mayan ruins; the central temple is almost fully restored, while the outlying ones are still mostly heaps of rubble. Excavation is noticeably ongoing here. A **triple ball court** lies to the north. The mostly unexcavated **Acropolis del Sur** (South Acropolis) lies to the west of the plaza, featuring structures built over a thousand years—some date from the Preclassical era, some from the late Classical.

TEMPLO V. The path continues on, circling around the back end of Templo V, whose restoration was completed only in 2004. Evidence suggests that the structure is the earliest of the six main temples here, built in a 50-year period between AD 600 and 700. The rounded edges are unusual for a Mayan temple. The temple is 190 ft. high, and you'll feel every foot as you stand at the rope-free top after a nearly vertical climb up a wooden staircase. The views are amazing, with the roof combs of Templos I and II jutting above the treetops. Just don't look down.

TEMPLO VI. Templo VI is the last discovered and most distant of Tikal's main structures, located about a 10min. walk (1km) down the Calzada Mendez from the Great Plaza (you can pick up the path while walking back from Templo V). It was completed in AD 766 by Hasaw's son Yik'in Chan K'awil, who also finished Templo I and built Templo IV. In fact, Yik'in is believed to be buried in either Templo IV or Templo VI. Also known as the **Temple of the Inscriptions,** it is famous for the long glyph text carved on the back of its roof comb. Almost 200 glyphs record the city's history, from a legendary founding date in 1139 BC to the overthrow of Caracol and the takeover of Calakmul in AD 711. The text is very faded, though, so you might want to practice your Mayan glyph-reading skills elsewhere.

OTHER STRUCTURES. From Templo VI, the path circles around and heads back to the ticket control booth, making for a pleasant nature walk and wildlife spotting. Smaller complexes and reservoirs (so effective that they were used by archaeologists excavating the site in the 19th and 20th centuries) lie to the north of the main site. In all, thousands of structures lie buried amidst the jungles, entombed remnants of a city far larger than the already expansive ruins suggest.

PETÉN

HONDURAS

A land of jagged mountains and dense jungle, Honduras has the most rugged geography in the region. Ironically, the indomitable terrain that once kept the country isolated is now a huge draw for tourists. Pristine cloudforests full of wildlife, long stretches of Caribbean beach, pine-covered ridges, and tropical rainforest all beckon adventurers. For the more subdued visitor, western Honduras hosts the magnificent Maya ruins at Copán, attracting professors of archaeology and laymen alike. Non-Maya indigenous groups survive alongside colonial architecture elsewhere in the country, displaying Honduras' wide cultural array. Years of military oppression in the 80s rendered Honduras one of Central America's poorest countries—and, for better or worse, one of the cheapest to visit. Though Honduras isn't known for tourism, the gringo trail is well defined. Copán, Tela, and the Bay Islands have well-established tourist industries, but it's the back country's scattered frontier towns, and engaging locals that truly make Honduras worth visiting.

ESSENTIALS

PLANNING YOUR TRIP

PASSPORTS, VISAS, AND CUSTOMS.

Passport. Required of all visitors. Must be valid for a full 3 months after arrival.

Visa (p. 6). Not required of citizens from the US, UK, EU, Canada, Australia, NZ and many other countries. Valid for 30 days. Others may purchase a single-entry visa for L30, renewable upon application.

Onward Ticket. Required of all visitors.

Work Permit (p. 6). Required for all foreigners planning to work in Honduras.

Required Vaccinations. Travelers who have visited nations with endemic yellow fever need proof of vaccination.

Driving Permit. Valid driver's license from your home country or an International Driving Permit is required.

Departure Tax. US$35.

EMBASSIES AND CONSULATES

For a list of embassies and consulates in Honduras, see the **Practical Information** section for Tegucigalpa.

Canada: Embassy, 151 Slater Street, Suite 805-A, Ottawa, Ontario, KIP 5-H3 (☎+1 613-233-8900).

UK: Embassy, 115 Gloucester Place, London W1U 6JT (☎+44 020 7486 4880).

US: Embassy, 3007 Tilden Street, NW, Suite 4M, Washington DC 20008 (☎+1 202-966-7702).

Honduras

50 miles
50 kilometers
0

Western Highlands p. 136

Caribbean Coast p. 255

Bay Islands p. 280

La Mosquitia

Olancho p. 299

Southern Honduras p. 224

Tegucigalpa p. 223

BELIZE

GUATEMALA

EL SALVADOR

NICARAGUA

CARIBBEAN SEA

PACIFIC OCEAN

LA MOSQUITIA

GRACIAS A DIOS

COLÓN

OLANCHO

EL PARAÍSO

FRANCISCO MORAZÁN

COMAYAGUA

YORO

ATLÁNTIDA

CORTÉS

SANTA BÁRBARA

COPÁN

OCOTEPEQUE

LEMPIRA

INTIBUCÁ

LA PAZ

VALLE

CHOLUTECA

BAY ISLANDS

MONTAÑAS DE COLÓN

MONTAÑAS DE PATUCA

CORD. ENTRE RÍOS

Gulfo de Honduras

Golfo de Fonseca

HONDURAS

VISA INFORMATION

Citizens of the US, UK, Canada, the EU, Australia, and Ireland do not need a visa to stay in Honduras for the first 30 days. Unfortunately, there are scant resources to tell you which countries need what, so your best bet is to contact an embassy and ask. **Visa extensions** are available for up to six months, and must be renewed every month for L30.

All foreigners wishing to study or work in Honduras must first apply for a **resident visa.** To apply for a resident visa, submit a valid passport, four passport size pictures, notarized medical certificate, bank letter, income tax references, work contract (if needed), copies of a birth or naturalization certificate, letter of good conduct, and a marriage certificate (if applicable) to the Honduran Consulate in your home country (p. 212). Once all documents are processed at the consulate, your passport will be stamped with the appropriate visa.

TOURIST OFFICES

The **Instituto Hondureño de Turismo** (☎+504 222 2124; www.letsgohonduras. com) is the tourism board for Honduras. The website is only somewhat useful; it's probably better to call or to head into the main office in Tegucigalpa, at Col. San Carlos, Edificio Europa.

MONEY

LEMPIRAS (L)		
AUS$1 = L15.1		L1 = AUS$0.07
CDN$1 = L17.3		L1 = CDN$0.06
EUR€1 = L26.8		L1 = EUR€0.04
NZ$1 = L12.1		L1 = NZ$0.08
UK£1 = L30.6		L1 = UK£0.03
US$1 = L19.1		L1 = US$0.05

The currency chart above is based on August 2009 exchange rates. The Honduran currency is the **lempira.** Bills are divided into 100 *centavos* and come in denominations of one, two, five, 10, 20, 50, and 100. The 10-*centavo* coin is sometimes called a *daime;* you'll occasionally hear a 20-centavo coin called a *búfalo* and a 50-*centavo* piece called a *tostón.* Large banks, exchange shops, hotels, and international airports will change **traveler's checks,** but prepare for long forms and high charges. **Western Union** can be found in many towns, and banks occasionally have money-wiring systems. Most banks give cash advances on credit cards. Banks don't change currencies of other Central American countries, but officials at border crossings will.

PRICE DIVERSITY

Our Researchers list establishments in order of value from best to worst, honoring our favorites with the Let's Go thumbs-up (🖤). Because the best *value* is not always the cheapest *price,* we have incorporated a system of price ranges based on a rough expectation of what you will spend. For **accommodations,** we base our range on the cheapest price for which a single traveler can stay for one night. For **restaurants,** we estimate the average amount one traveler will spend in one sitting. The table below tells you what you'll *typically* find in

Panama at the corresponding price range, but keep in mind that no system can allow for the quirks of individual establishments.

ACCOMMODATIONS	RANGE	WHAT YOU'RE *LIKELY* TO FIND
❶	Under L100 (Under US$5)	Campgrounds and dorm rooms, both in hostels and actual universities. Expect bunk beds and a communal bath. You may have to provide or rent towels.
❷	L100-300 (US$ 5-15)	Hostels in heavily-touristed areas or shabby hotels. Sometimes private bathrooms, but most likely communal facilities. May have a TV.
❸	L301-500 (US$ 16-25)	A comfortable room with a private bath. Should have decent amenities such as A/C and TV. Breakfast may be included.
❹	L501-1000 (US$ 26-50)	Bigger rooms than a ❸, with more amenities, and often in a more convenient location. Breakfast may be included.
❺	Over L1000 (Over US$50)	Large hotels or upscale chains. If it's a ❺ and it doesn't have the perks you want, you've paid too much.

FOOD	RANGE	WHAT YOU'RE *LIKELY* TO FIND
❶	Under L40 (Under US$2)	Probably food stalls, university cafeterias, and rural Honduran eateries. It's yummy and cheap, but you'll be reaching for the Honduran version of Tums post pig out.
❷	L41-80 (US$2-4)	National restaurant chains and some international fast food. Expect typical Honduran platters and sandwiches, food at a bar, and low-priced entrees. The average Honduran eatery is a ❷.
❸	L81-150 (US$4-8)	Mid-priced entrees, seafood, and exotic pasta dishes. More upscale Honduran eateries. Check the menu to see if tax is included in prices.
❹	L151-300 (US$8-15)	The cheapest entrees at an upscale restaurant. Entrees tend to be heartier or more elaborate, but you'll mostly be throwing down for ambiance. Few restaurants in this range have a dress code, but you'll feel out of place in a T-shirts and sandals.
❺	Over L300 (Over US$15)	Your meal might cost more than your room, but there's a reason—it's something fabulous, famous, or both. Extensive drink options. Only found in big cities or the most heavily-touristed areas.

COSTS

Honduras is definitely made for budget travelers. Comfortable lodging can be found in many places for a few bucks, and food and beer are just a hair above free.

TRANSPORTATION

Taca Regional (www.tacaregional.com) offers relatively low domestic fares. The easiest way to get around Honduras is by bus. Each destination in the extensive bus system is served by a different company from a large city. Be especially cautious riding buses at night, as hold-ups and robberies do occur. For information on driving, see **Essentials,** p. 5.

BORDER CROSSINGS

Travelers can cross into Honduras by land or sea. Remember to carry enough money to pay any entrance or exit fees.

HONDURAS

GUATEMALA. There are three land crossings: **El Florido** (p. 254) and **Agua Caliente** (p. 245), 16km west of Nueva Ocotepeque and 10km east of Esquipulas. The one at **Omoa** crosses to Corinto, Guatemala.

BELIZE. Weekly boats link Puerto Cortés and coastal Belize.

EL SALVADOR. There are three land crossings. **El Poy** is south of Nueva Ocotepeque (p. 243), **El Amatillo** is near Choluteca, and **Sabanetas** is 165km southeast of Gracias. Ferries connect El Salvador and Honduras in the Gulf of Fonseca.

NICARAGUA. There are three land crossings. **Guasaule** is 50km southeast of Choluteca, **San Marcos/El Espino** is 70km east of Choluteca, and **Las Manos** is 150km east of Tegucigalpa.

SAFETY

Small Honduran towns are relatively safe, but urban centers are extremely dangerous. Street crime and gang violence are very serious problems in some areas such as San Pedro Sula, rural Olancho, and parts of Tegucigalpa. In Tegus, armed gang members are a more common sight than police officers. The Caribbean coast has also suffered from escalated crime. Don't walk the streets at night or carry anything valuable. For more info, see **Essentials**, p. 10.

HEALTH

Prophylaxis for **malaria** is recommended for travelers going to altitudes below 1000m. Prophylaxis is also recommended if traveling in the Mosquitia region, and on Roatán and other Bay Islands. Malaria also poses a risk in the outskirts of Tegucigalpa and San Pedro Sula. For more information, see **Essentials**, p. 13. Nearly every Honduran town has a **pharmacy** open from 8am to 6pm.

LIFE AND TIMES

HISTORY

LONG LONG AGO (DAWN OF TIME-AD 1502). Since before the first millennium BC, a thriving **Mayan civilization** sprawled across Honduras. The country's most impressive ruins are found at **Copán.** Founded around AD 200, this city flourished until the mysterious collapse of the Mayans in the 10th century. The **Lenca** also thrived in the region in the pre-colonial era and were known for their fierce resistance against the Spanish conquerors.

NOT SO INDEPENDENT (1502-1838). Shortly after Columbus arrived in Honduras in 1502, the conquistador **Pedro de Alvarado** led the Spanish takeover. Spanish colonists founded towns in modern-day Trujillo, Comayagua, and Tegucigalpa, driving ever deeper into the jungle in their all-consuming quest for gold and silver. Despite attacks by Caribbean pirates and a British push for control of the coast, the area remained in Spanish hands until all of Central America gained independence in 1821. Honduras briefly joined the new United Provinces of Central America, sending liberal leader **Francisco Morazán** to head the federation in 1830. Rising conservative opposition led Honduras to break from the United Provinces and declare absolute independence on November 5, 1838.

HONDURAS

A NATION DIVIDED (1838-99). Once free, Honduras struggled to establish national unity in the face of constant British, US, and Central American interventions. The federal capital bounced between liberal **Tegucigalpa** and conservative **Comayagua**. Eventually, the liberals won out, and Tegucigalpa became the permanent capital in 1880. Liberal presidents like **Marco Aurelio Soto** and **Luis Bográn** in the latter half of the century managed to calm things down, expanding the education system and improving infrastructure.

BANANA REPUBLIC (1899-1954). In the 20th century, **bananas** took over. The American-owned United Fruit Company bought huge tracts of Honduran land, set up its own railroads and security forces, and created a powerful political machine. In addition to bankrolling pliable politicians, the banana companies won backing from the US military, which intervened in Honduras seven times between 1903 and 1925. In 1954, the famous **Banana Strike** began among dock workers for United Fruit, and spread throughout the country. For 69 days, thousands of people protested the business practices of the foreign-owned banana industry. The strike was mostly successful and prompted the legal recognition of labor unions in Honduras.

TOUGH TIMES (1954-98). A military coup put **Colonel Oswaldo López Arellano** in control of the government in 1963. His rule saw social and political tensions mount with neighboring El Salvador, culminating in the four-day **Soccer War** of 1969 when a particularly intense soccer match led to riots. Though brief, the war left 2000 Honduran civilians dead and 300,000 Salvadoran refugees homeless. The military remained in control until 1981, when a civilian government came to power through election. Honduras wasn't quite done with army troubles yet: US President Ronald Reagan saw Honduras as an ideal launching pad for an attack against the Sandinista government in Nicaragua, and the intervention led to a massive and long-term US military and CIA presence in the region. CIA-trained death squads also went to work on Honduran soil, murdering leftist political opponents. Under the pressure from **President Rafael Leonardo Callejas Romero**, elected in 1989, the Nicaraguan Contras finally left Honduran soil. Though Callejas's term was marked by economic adjustment policies and a falling poverty rate, he was also charged with overseeing another kind of "economic adjustment" — embezzling US$11 million into a secret presidential bank account. Honduras saw a more natural disaster in 1998 when **Hurricane Mitch** swept over the country, killing some 5000 people and leaving behind nearly US$3 billion worth of damage.

TODAY

Honduras continues to suffer from natural and political disasters that hit at the end of the last century. Even after more than a decade of rebuilding, the damage to industry and infrastructure done by Hurricane Mitch has left Honduras one of the least developed countries in the region. Poverty and economic inequality still plague the country, with about half the population below the poverty line and nearly a third unemployed. In turn, Honduras's economic problems have led to social ones; the country has high rates of infant mortality, malnutrition, and violence. Criminal youth gangs known as *maras* control the poorer districts in many towns and cities, perpetrating high-profile murders and profiting from drug trafficking. Estimates say the larger gangs may have tens of thousands of members.

In 2005, the mustachioed, Stetson-wearing **Manuel Zelaya** narrowly won the presidency, taking home a slim victory margin of less than 65,000 votes after 10 days of recounting. Zelaya ran on a hard-line, anti-crime platform, promising to double the number of police officers, give convicted murderers and rapists life sentences, and establish a re-education campaign to integrate former *mara* members back into society. He also swore to stimulate the economy and tackle the corruption in government, a major problem in recent Honduran administrations. Zelaya's initiatives have met with mixed success at best. Faced with dropping approval ratings, he blamed the media and in 2007 declared that all TV and radio stations would be required to carry government propaganda at least two hours a day. In a controversial move, he also recommended in 2008 that the United States legalize recreational drug use, to help him fight drug-related violence in Honduras. New presidential elections in November of 2009 pitted the Liberal Party's **Elvin Ernesto Santos** against the National Party's **Porfirio Pepe Lobo**.

ECONOMY AND GOVERNMENT

After Nicaragua, Honduras remains the second poorest country of Central America. Its economic growth depends largely on the United States, for two reasons: first, because the US is its largest trading partner, and second, because more than a quarter of Honduras's GDP comes from checks sent home by Honduran workers in the US (The US government granted Temporary Protection Status to tens of thousands of Hondurans in the aftermath of Hurricane Mitch, allowing them to work legally in the US; the "temporary" status has since been renewed repeatedly, up to the present day.) Honduras has seen greater foreign investment and growth since signing on to the US-Central America Free Trade Agreement (CAFTA) in 2006. Nevertheless, the country still relies on a limited set of agricultural exports (like those good ol' bananas), and so remains vulnerable to dropping food prices or natural disasters.

The Honduran political scene, meanwhile, is dominated by the National Party and the Liberal Party, who have passed the presidency back and forth since 1982. There is also a handful of minor parties, each of which generally picks up a few seats in the country's unicameral legislature. Though the military remains a potent force, it no longer seems tempted, at least in recent years, to interfere by coup or coercion. The failing economy and tremendous crime rates remain Honduras's major political issues to date.

PEOPLE

THEM DEMOGRAPHICS. Honduran people are primarily *mestizo*, a mixture of Central American Indian (Mayan and other) and European. The *mestizo* demographic makes up 90% of the Honduran population. Pure Central American Indians make up 7% of Honduras's people, while the rest is made up of black (2%) and white (1%) Hondurans.

PEOPLE WHO NEED PEOPLE. Honduras currently has a population of over six million people. That's somewhere between the populations of Los Angeles and the number of workers at Disney World. Over 700,000 of those Hondurans dwell in Tegucigalpa, the country's capital, while 600,000 reside in San Pedro Sula, Honduras' largest industrial city. The population is growing at an annual rate of about 3%, though urban areas are expanding much more quickly.

SPANISH MAIN: The official language of Honduras is Spanish. Go figure. However, English is also widely spoken as a secondary language. Americans never fear – it looks like you don't have to learn anyone else's language after all! American Indian Dialects are also spoken in more rural areas.

DIOS MÍO: The vast majority (97%) of Hondurans are Roman Catholic. The rest belong to a variety of Protestant minority groups. In the 1950s, the Roman Catholic Church launched a comprehensive campaign to increase the number of evangelic churches in Honduras. However, in the 60s and 70s, evangelism turned into activism against government and military oppression. After violent activist uprisings in 1975, the Catholic Church changed its stance on evangelism and fanaticism. Protestant churches have greatly increased since the 1980s, especially in the lower classes. The most popular denominations are Methodist, Church of God, Seventh Day Adventist, and Assembly of God. The growing Protestant population (thought only estimated at 100,000 in 1990) is somewhat seen as a threat by the Roman Catholic Church in Honduras.

LAND

GEOGRAPHY

With over 500 miles of coastline, Honduras is a beach lover's paradise. Don't be fooled, though: those who prefer adventure to sunbathing will not be disappointed by this geographically diverse country. **Roatam**, the largest of several offshore islands, boasts pristine sands and easy access to the Belize Barrier Reef, the second largest coral reef in the world. Just inland from the coastal plains of both coasts, mountains dominate the inner terrain of the country. Dense cloud forests lay nestled among mountaintops while tropical rainforests and mangrove swamps abound at lower elevations.

WILDLIFE

Honduras plays host to a colorful array of creatures, both on land and underwater. Venturing into the country's forests, you're bound to spot, or at least hear, several different species of monkeys and parrots. The forests are also home to elusive cougars, jaguars, and ocelots. For those willing to head for the water, manatees, one of many endangered species residing in Honduras, can be found in shallow waters along the coast and in estuaries among the mangroves, along with a variety of other marine life.

WEATHER

The coastal lowlands of Honduras enjoy a tropical climate with high temperatures year-round. While the Caribbean lowlands receive consistent and plentiful rainfall throughout the year, the Pacific lowlands and the highland interior of the country experience a dry season from November to April. The highlands, including the capital city of Tegucigalpa, experience a more temperate climate with temperatures declining as the elevation increases.

ARTS

LITERATURE

The literature of Honduras came into its own in the 20th century. The poet **Clementina Suárez** became an object of national intrigue and pride in the early decades of the century for her brilliant verses and Bohemian lifestyle. Suárez defied the traditional gender roles of the time period, spending time in the company of men, especially artists, and wearing shorts. A highly public figure, Suárez was known as the "new woman." Many people considered her lifestyle scandalous, while others respected her for her great intellect. Other modern Honduran writers and poets have taken as their themes the political and social problems of their country. Among these is the man who conducted the final interview of Suárez before her death in 1991, the poet **Roberto Sosa**. Sosa was born into a poor Honduran family in the 1930s and lived through the oppressive sixteen-year rule of president Tiburcio Carías Andino. Many of Sosa's works reflect on poverty, inequality, and political oppression. Sosa gained international attention though his collection of poems *Los Pobres*, literally, *The Poor*.

VISUAL ARTS

Like Honduran literature, some of the greatest Honduran artwork depicts scenes of poverty. **Anibal Cruz**, born in 1944, expressed the desperation of poverty through the lens of surrealist painting. Other Honduran artists, such as **Carlos Garay**, have chosen to depict the natural beauty of the country's landscapes and the colorful culture of the Honduran people. While the fine arts are not as historically established in Honduras as in European countries, the **Escuela Nacional de Bellas Artes** in Tegucigalpa is working to help Honduran artists develop their talent and achieve international recognition. Most visitors to Honduras will experience art more locally, through murals found on city walls and handicrafts produced by the native population.

MUSIC

The sounds of Honduras are as diverse as the cultures that produce them. Traditional Mayan rhythms play alongside modern reggaeton beats. Perhaps the most striking of the musical traditions of Honduras is **Garífuna** music. The Garífuna are an Afro-Caribbean people who emigrated to Honduras and the neighboring Central American countries after the British colonized their native home, St. Vincent, in 1797. In its most basic form, their music combines singing and percussion, but it's not uncommon to hear guitars and other instruments incorporated into modern Garífuna music. The music is strongly influenced by traditional African rhythms, but maintains its own distinct sound.

CUSTOMS AND ETIQUETTE

TIP OF THE DAY. In many Honduran restaurants, gratuity is automatically added to your bill, so don't worry about trying to calculate anything on your cell phone. Note that it is also customary to tip housekeepers with a few dollars at the end of a hotel stay.

KEEP IN TOUCH. If you hate PDA (Public Displays of Affection), you're in for an experience. Hondurans tend to stand fairly close to each other while chatting, and they often touch each other's hands, shoulders, and arms during conversation. Personal space on public transportation is virtually nonexistent.

CATCH YOU LATER. Throwing things to another person is generally taboo. The act, reminiscent of feeding an animal or a dog, is considered demeaning.

FORMAL WHERE? Honduras is a little more prim and proper than some of its Central American cousins. Men are expected to remove their hats before entering churches or homes.

FOOD AND DRINK

SO CORNY. Like many Central American countries, corn is a vital staple of the diet. Manifestations include corn tortillas for breakfast, tamales (corn husks stuffed with cornmeal and a myriad of different fillings) and corn tortillas for lunch, *tamales de elote* (corncakes served with cheese, chilies, or raisins) and corn tortillas for dinner.

I'LL DRINK TO THAT. Salva Vida, Port Royal, Barena and Imperial are all popular Honduran beers. If you're looking for something a little stronger, go for Guaro, a sugarcane liquour, or Giffity, a spicy Garífuna potable.

THE SWEET LIFE: There are plenty of ways to indulge your sweet tooth in Honduras. *Pasel de tres leches* is a cake made of three types of "milk": evaporated milk, sweetened condensed milk, and cream. *Arroz con leche*, Honduran rice pudding, pairs rice soaked in warm milk and sugar with spices like cinnamon.

BEYOND TOURISM

VOLUNTEERING

COMMUNITY OUTREACH

Global Volunteer Network Ltd., PO Box 30-968, Lower Hutt, New Zealand (☎+1 800-963-1198 from US or Canada, 0800 032 5035 from UK; www.volunteer. org). Founded in 2000, the Global Volunteer Network helps communities in need by supporting local organizations. Offers several volunteer opportunities in the poverty-stricken nation of Honduras, including programs in medicine, childcare, teaching, building, and conservation. Volunteers in certain programs will have homestays; others will be stationed accordingly. US$350 application fee; total program cost ranges from US$716 (2 weeks) to US$1924 (12 weeks).

Students Helping Honduras (SHH), 1213 Dandridge St., Fredericksburg, VA 22401, USA (☎540-322-3471; www.studentshelpinghonduras.org). An organization that brings students to Honduras to empower orphans that live in impoverished conditions. Week-long service trips are offered in the summer, fall, and winter. Past groups of SHH volunteers have begun sustainability

ON THE MENU

TOP TEN THINGS TO DRINK IN HONDURAS

1. Fresco: Light and refreshing, these juicy treats are made from fruit, water, and sugar.

2. Guaro: A delicious liquor distilled from cane sugar. It sweetens any cocktail.

3. Beer: The popular brands like Salva Vida or Port Royal are unrivaled in the hot, Honduran sun.

4. Chicha: Originally the drink of the Incas and made from fermented corn, chicha is still common and can be served alcoholic or plain.

5. Bottled water: Not kidding here, folks. Don't be adventurous; the results will not be pretty.

6. Licuado: The Honduran milkshake, this godly creation is a simple mixture of milk and fruit, but will make your day.

7. Garifuna Gaffity: As funky as its name, this spicy drink is a combination of extremely hot herbs and spices and Garifuna liquor.

8. Coffee: These magic beans have trouble making it out of the country, so make sure to try it while you're down here.

9. Horchata: Made from rice and seeds, this delicious milky drink tastes like rice pudding, or arroz con leche.

10. Tea: Hondurans make their tea from scratch, so unlike the Lipton's bag lurking in the bottom of your backpack, it's always fresh and flavorful.

projects in Honduras, and built homes and schools. Service trips US$750-900 (airfare not included).

United Planet, 11 Arlington Street, Boston MA, 02116, USA (☎617-267-7763; www. unitedplanet.org). Offers long-term (6-12 months) volunteer opportunities in Honduras, with projects focusing on disabled youth, education, healthcare, and other social issues. Fees range from US$5265 (6 months) to US$7965 (1 year).

STUDYING

AMERICAN PROGRAMS

Rainforest and Reef, P.O. Box 141543, Grand Rapids, Michigan 49514-1543, USA (☎877-255-3721; rainforestandreef.org). An organization dedicated to marine and rainforest ecology. Offers a 12-day and 11-night field course program in Honduras. In addition to classroom work, students itineraries is chock-full of adventures, from visiting Mayan ruins, to chilling with toucans in a national park. Contact Rainforest and Reef for date and fee information for the Honduras program; some meals are included, but airfare is not. Also offers field courses in Belize, Costa Rica, Guatemala, Nicaragua, and Panama, as well as full semester abroad opportunities in many of its field sites. For more details, email info@rainforestandreef.org.

HONDURAN LANGUAGE SCHOOLS

Central American Spanish Schools (CASS), P.O. Box 1142, La Ceiba, Atlantida, Honduras (La Ceiba ☎504 440 1061; www.ca-spanish.com). Offers programs in both La Ceiba and Roatán, Honduras. Upon arrival, students take a placement exam to determine their Spanish language skill level. When the textbooks are closed, CASS arranges several excursions (US$5-125) and activities, including cooking and dance classes. Diving course offered with intensive language program in Roatán. One-week La Ceiba course US$170-250; 1-week Roatan course US$480-1125.

Ixbalanque Spanish School, Copán Ruinas, Honduras, Central America (☎504 651 4432; www.ixbalanque.com). With a campus in the center of Copán Ruinas, Ixbalanque allows students to learn Spanish in the midst of Mayan history. Most students will live with local families. Both activities and volunteer opportunities available. US$210 per week (with homestay).

 THERE'S MORE? For more information on volunteer and study abroad opportunities in other areas of Central America, see **Beyond Tourism, p. 34**. To learn more about opportunities all over the world, visit our website at ▨ **www.letsgo.com**.

TEGUCIGALPA

Tegucigalpa (pop. 897,000) and its sister city of Comayagüela (not to be confused with Comayagua) were incorporated into a "central district" constituting the official national capital in 1938. Over the past four hundred years, the city has maintained a more provincial air than that of a capital city. At 3000 ft. above sea level, Tegus (as the city is familiarly called) sprawls out across river-cut valleys and emerald mountains, scattering the rough terrain with a hodgepodge of clay roofs. While Tegus looks picturesque from afar, a closer look reveals contaminated rivers, homelessness, blaring horns, and intense gang violence. Tegus boasts gourmet restaurants, colorful fruit stands, and flashy malls.

On July 28, 2009, President Manuel Zelaya was ousted by the military in the Honduran capital and placed on a plane to Costa Rica. This event—deemed a coup d'état by the international community—was the culmination of months of unease over the President's scheduled referendum to change the Constitution of Honduras, presumably to facilitate his re-election to a second term. The first in Central America since the fall of the Berlin Wall, the coup was entirely non-violent and resulted in the succession of Roberto Micheletti, the Speaker of Parliament, to the presidency. Although the Honduran government claims that Zelaya's arrest was constitutional, as of August 2009, no foreign government had recognized the Micheletti regime. Let's Go's Researchers did not generate new coverage of Teguicigalpa for 2009.

Daytripping in a Coup

A CLOSER LOOK

I noticed the machine guns on soldiers' backs as my bus passed the Choluteca bridge. I handed my passport to the soldiers who boarded the bus to check the IDs of its passengers. And I greeted the soldiers at the lancha dock in Coyolito as I got off the boat from El Tigre.

But this is Central America, and guns are nothing new. If anything, being here has desensitized me to a constant military presence. In countries that struggle with corruption, gangs, and drug trade, guns are the norm, not the exception.

So I went about my day, and nothing seemed odd. The buses were full, the mango vendors were in full force, and no one appeared perturbed. I finished my work, stopped at the grocery store, and came home to relax before dinner.

When I turned on CNN, I could only laugh. Mixed in with the Iranian protests and Michael Jackson remembrances was another story: one about a military coup in Honduras that had ousted President Manuel Zelaya.

CNN explained that leftist Zelaya had been under siege for a referendum on his re-election. Zelaya threatened to fire a leading general if he did not provide him with military protection during the poll; instead, he woke up to a free ride to Costa Rica. Hugo Chavez and the Cuban foreign minister were urging Obama to condemn the coup; the EU was also throwing in its two cents.

As I attempted to decipher exactly what all of this meant for my planned trip across the border to El Salvador, I was at a loss. The local news was had shifted its coverage to soccer games. CNN kept telling me to check its website, but I had no internet. And with a national curfew of 9pm, the streets were more silent than ever. There were no newspapers to be found, all of the stores were closed, and even Pizza Hut—my last hope for dinner—was shutting down early.

So there I was, in the middle of an international crisis, and I couldn't say much more about it. My lunch and dinner had shrunk to a bottle of water, a bag of Cheetos, and some Trident gum. My TV now rotated between Honduran news and CNN, in lieu of my standard CSI. I wrote my copy, packed my things, and made sure to stay inside.

-Alison Tarwater

SOUTHERN HONDURAS

A thin part of Honduras runs south to the Golfo de Fonseca, giving the country all-important access to the Pacific Ocean. Travelers here are usually going somewhere else: both El Salvador and Nicaragua are an easy trip down the Carretera Panamericana. From Choluteca, tourists head to Isla El Tigre, the only completely Honduran island in the gulf, with relaxing black-sand beaches.

CHOLUTECA ☎504

Though primarily a stopover on the Panamerican Highway between both Nicaraguan and Salvadoran borders, residents of Honduras' fourth largest city argue for its architectural and environmental merits; the city has some of Honduras' best colonial architecture, and the region around it is known for its anti-deforestation efforts. Though it's not a tourist attraction in itself, Choluteca is easy on the eyes, as is the landscape around it.

▐ TRANSPORTATION

Due to Choluteca's size and weather, getting around on foot can be a hassle. **Taxis** abound around town, and it is not unusual for them to pick up separate passengers at the same time; rides within the city limits cost L15-25. After dark, taxis are a must; the largest concentration is near the old market and the bus station. There are two **bus** stations in Choluteca within two blocks of each other.

Main Terminal, 3a Av. northeast, off Blvd. Carranza. To: **Amatillo** (2hr., every 15min. 3:30am-5:30pm, L41); **Guasaule** (1hr., every 30min. 5:30am-5pm, L20); **San Marcos de Colón** (1½hr., every 30min. 6am-5pm, L25); and **Tegucigalpa** (4hr., every 30min. from 5am-6pm, L65).

Mi Esperanza Terminal, 1½ blocks north on 3a Av. northeast, has private buses to: **Guasaule** (45min., 9am, L12); **Tegucigalpa** (3hr., every hr. 6am-5pm, L100); **San Marcos de Colón** (1hr., every 2hr. 7am-5pm, L25).

Tica Bus: On the highway toward El Amatillo, in front of the Puma Gas Station (☎504 962 9102). Buses pass by on the *carretera* to **Managua** (US$20), **Panama** (US$65), **San José** (US$40), **San Salvador** (US$15), **Guatemala City** (US$30), and **Tapachula, Mexico** (USD$45).

✠ ▐ ORIENTATION AND PRACTICAL INFORMATION

Choluteca is big and confusing; most locals can't tell you what street they are standing on, preferring to navigate by landmarks. The town is technically organized along the standard Honduran grid, except the *parque central* (also called **Parque Valle**) is on 6 C., 6 Av. Nte. instead of in the middle of town. The main commercial strip is **4 Calle,** two blocks south of the *parque*. Buses come into Choluteca via the bridge on the northwest edge of town, turning left onto **Blvd. Enrique Weddle,** which goes west to east along the northern edge of town, heading toward San Marcos de Colón and the Espino border with Nicaragua.

Currency Exchange and Bank: Banco de America Central, C. Vicente Williams (☎504 782 0085), 1 block from Ciber Cafe. Open M-F 8am-4pm, Sa 8am-noon. Credomatic **24hr. ATM** accepts AmEx/MC/V.

Emergency: ☎198.

Police: (☎782 0951). Northwest side of the *parque central*.

24hr. Pharmacy: Farmacia San Luis, C. Vicente Williams (☎782 7274). Open M-Sa 7am-8pm. Cash only.

Hospital or Medical Services: Hospital del Sur, 5a C. Ote. (☎782 0231 or 782 0211).

Telephone: Corner of 4a Av. and 2a C. (☎882 2990). Open M-F 8am-4pm.

Internet Access: Ciber Cafe, C. Vicente Williams (☎9999 1600), 2 blocks from Av. Valle. Internet L20 per hr. International calls available as well; prices vary. Open daily 8am-9pm.

Post Office: 4a Av. (☎882 2513), next to Hondutel. Open M-F 8am-4pm and Sa 8am-noon.

ACCOMMODATIONS

Choluteca has plenty of accommodations options. Rooms in the center cost a bit more, as do those with air-conditioning.

Hotel Rivera, Blvd. Enrique Wedle, Carreterra Panamericana (☎782 0828 or 780 0050). The nicest budget option in Choluteca, Rivera has the advantage of a quiet but convenient location, pleasing decor, and quality A/C. Well-kept rooms are arranged around a small, plant-filled courtyard and have cable TV and private baths. Free parking. Reception 24hr. On-site restaurant open daily 6am-2pm and 6-10pm. Singles and doubles L500; triples L650. AmEx/D/MC/V. ❸

Hotel Bonsai Centro Av. Valle (☎782 2648), 1 block from the *parque central.* Bonsai's location is convenient, but be prepared to pay for it. The lovely courtyard with an open grass area and covered porch lined with tables is undeniably attractive; rooms, however, are more functional with an occasional painting to spruce things up. Each room has a clean and aged private bath, cable TV, and fan or A/C. Singles with fan L300, with A/C L375; doubles with A/C L425; extra person L50. V. ❸

Hotel Pacifico, 4 C. (☎782 3249), 1 block east and 3 blocks north of the bus station. With 2 sets of rooms on either side of the same street, Hotel Pacifico is one of the larger options around. Rooms are a bit dated and the private bathrooms could be cleaner, but all have cable TV and A/C. Free parking. Singles L300; doubles L400; triples L450. Cash only. ❸

Hotel Jerusalem (☎782 7760), 1 block east and half a block south of the bus station. Though it's a bit oddly located, the prices are some of the most reasonable around and the rooms some of the nicest. All rooms have A/C, sparkling new private baths, and cable TV. Free parking. Singles L250; doubles L300; triples L350. Cash only. ❸

FOOD

Choluteca's many dining options are spread out across the city. Fast-food establishments are found on Blvd. Enrique Wedle/Carreterra Panamericana; small *comedores* and fried chicken shops are mostly found in the city center. Supermarket **Maxi Bodega** (☎782 1251), on Blvd. Enrique Wedle, behind Pizza Hut, has a huge supply of groceries and virtually every other household item. (Open daily 7am-8pm. MC/V.)

Restaurante Aquariun (☎782 7002), on the *parque central,* at the corner of Av. Valle. This pleasant spot is the perfect mix of old-world architecture and down-home charm. Summery orange and yellow tablecloths and friendly service complement the delicious *ceviche* (L80-120), seafood (L110-250), and meat (L180-240) dishes. Open daily 11am-10pm. AmEx/D/MC/V. ❹

Restaurante Canton, Av. Valle (☎782 6700), across from Hotel Bonsai. This small but well-cooled and decorated Cantonese spot delivers good rice (L45-140), chicken (L120-170), beef (L120-140), and shrimp (L150-165) dishes at dark wooden tables. Open daily 9am-10pm. Cash only. ❸

Restaurante Asado El Gordo, 4 C. (☎780 3196), behind Wendy's. Dine with the animals in this meat-lover's paradise, complete with a dining room full of dead ones;

the welcome mat is an animal hide, and the walls are decorated with the heads of various hunters' trophies. The menu is not vegetarian friendly. Entrees L84-200. Open daily 11am-9pm. AmEx/D/MC/V. ❸

ISLA EL TIGRE

In the sunny waters of the Gulf of Fonseca, Isla El Tigre offers world-class views and beautiful weather with a small-town feel. Only 10min. from Coyolito, Isla El Tigre has several beaches of its own as well as access to the peaceful waters of nearby Isla La Exposición. For the more adventurous, the island offers the peak of La Cima (783m), from which you can see the vast expanses of El Salvador, Honduras, and Nicaragua.

▛ TRANSPORTATION

Isla El Tigre is beautiful, but a bit of a trek to get to. *Lanchas* travel from the docks at **Coyolito** to **Amapala** (10min., leave whenever full; last boat from Coyolito at 4pm, from Amapala to Coyolito at 3pm; L20) and **Playa El Burro** (10min., every 10min. from 6am-4pm, L15). To get to Coyolito, take any bus on the InterAmerican Highway to **San Lorenzo**; from **Choluteca**, any bus to **El Amatillo** or **Tegucigalpa** (1hr., every 15 min. 4:30am-8pm, L15). An old school bus runs from **San Lorenzo** to **Coyolito** (45min.; every 40min. M-Sa 6am-4:30pm, Su every hour 6am-4pm; L20). The last bus from Coyolito back to San Lorenzo leaves at 4:20pm; make sure to be at the Coyolito docks by 4pm in order to make the bus.

Once on Isla El Tigre, there are **mototaxis** and **taxis** that can transport you around the island; rates are per person. Expect to pay L10 from Amapala to Playa El Burro and L15-20 to Playa Negra or Playa Grande. Taxis line up by the dock in Amapala and the beach in Playa El Burro.

✈ 🛈 ORIENTATION AND PRACTICAL INFORMATION

All services are located in **Amapala**, the island's main town. From the ferry drop-off, walk about 300m on the dirt road to get to **Parque Bonilla** and the church. Turn left directly after you walk past the *parque* to access the road that goes around the island; **Hotel Mirador** (5min.) and **Playa El Burro** (40min.) are both down this road. There is **no bank or pharmacy** on Isla El Tigre; the nearest services in this regard are in San Lorenzo.

Tourist Office: (☎795 8643), on the dock. Maps and information on accommodations and transportation on the island. Open M-F 8am-noon and 2-5pm, Sa 8am-noon.

Police: (☎795 8502), to the left of the main square coming from the docks.

Hospital or Medical Services: Red Cross (☎795 8563), 50m from the docks on the way to the square. Open M-F 8am-5pm.

Post Office: (☎795 8524), on the 2nd floor of the Alcadia. Open M-F 8am-noon and 2-4pm.

Telephones: Hondutel (☎795 8500), across from the Casa de Cultura on the west side of the park. Open M-F 8am-noon and 2-5pm, Sa 8am-noon.

▟ ACCOMMODATIONS

Hotel Mirador de Amapala (☎795 8407 or 3377 9278; www.miradordeamapala.com), 4 blocks east of the main square in Amapala; follow the road downhill when it forks to the left. The only lodging option within walking distance of the docks, Hotel Mirador is also the nicest option on the island, and its abundant services are worth the splurge. Beautiful rooms have private hot-water baths, A/C, fans, and cable TV. There is a swimming pool and lounge area for guest use. Room prices include breakfast, dinner, transportation from the beach, and free pick-up from the docks in Amapala for those with reservations. Singles L700; doubles L900-1200; triples L1300-1600. AmEx/D/MC/V. ❹

Hotel Veleros, Playa El Burro (☎795 8040). Cheapest lodging on the island, practically on the beach. Simple rooms with beds, fans, and private cold-water baths. Veleros's restaurant is the most popular on the beach (entrees L60-160; open daily 10am-9pm; cash only). Doubles L350; triples L450. Cash only. ❸

FOOD

Most hotels on the island have their own restaurants. Still, there are a couple spots in Amapala where you can get a meal if you're just in town for the day. Most of the beaches also have *comedores* or **food stands** (food L20-L50, open M-Sa 6am-4pm, cash only).

Faro Victoria (☎795 8543), on C. La Marina, 200m to the right of the docks in Amapala. With a patio dining area overlooking the Gulf, Faro is a pleasant, relaxing, and reasonably priced dining option. Seafood specialties and occasional live entertainment at the bar. Meals L65-140. Open daily 10am-10pm. Cash only. ❸

Golosinas Sarahy (☎795 8408), 150m east of the *parque municipal* in Amapala. The smell of fresh food wafts in from the kitchen in this small family-run spot. Basic menu with meat, pork, and chicken plates (L85) to complement hamburgers and sandwiches (L60-80). Open 10am-9pm daily. Cash only. ❷

SIGHTS AND OUTDOOR ACTIVITIES

PLAYAS. There are swimmable beaches on almost every side of the island, but the three most popular are **Playa El Burro, Playa Grande,** and **Playa Negra.** Playa El Burro is best for dining and lodging; its sand is marred by trash and the water is filled with *lanchas.* Playa Grande is the best for tanning and swimming; it also has its own cave, the **Cueva de la Sirena,** which is only accessible during low tide. Playa Negra is named after its black volcanic sand. For a less busy option, you can hire a *lancha* at Playa El Burro (L20-40) to **Isla La Exposición,** a small island in between El Tigre and Coyolito that has a peaceful, secluded beach in a small cove. Make sure to arrange for transport back ahead of time; La Exposición is deserted except for a few swanky villas. *(All of El Tigre's beaches are most easily accessed by taxi; L10-20 per person. Playa El Burro can also be reached by lancha from Coyolito; 10min., every 10min. 6am-4pm, L15 per person)*

LA CIMA. The defining physical element of El Tigre, La Cima's conical form and towering heights make it an appealing venture. The panoramic views of Nicaragua, Honduras, and El Salvador from the top are a great reason to visit. The hike is about 2-3 hours; guides are recommended (L150-200 total). To get to the base of the hike, follow the road out of Amapala toward Playa El Burro; you can hire guides at the entrance to the trail. Make sure to bring plenty of water along; Isla El Tigre is very hot and sunny.

WESTERN HIGHLANDS

The highland's star attraction is undoubtedly the magnificent Maya site of Copán, but there's so much more: forest-covered mountain ranges call to the outdoor enthusiast while time-warped colonial towns charm romantics. Along the busy highway between Tegus and San Pedro Sula, the first noteworthy stop is colonial Comayagua, the country's first capital. Not far north lies the relaxing Lago de Yojoa, the country's largest lake, and the fabulous waterfall, Catarata de Pulhapanzak. The rest of the region's attractions are farther west, most easily accessible from San Pedro Sula or across the border in Guatemala and El Salvador. After exploring the majesty of Parque Nacional Celaque, travelers recoup in the nearby colonial towns of Gracias and Santa Rosa de Copán.

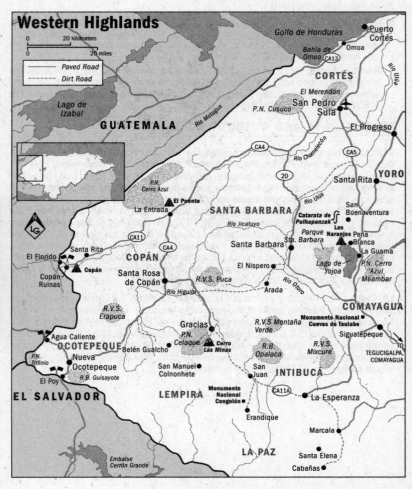

COMAYAGUA

Comayagua, founded in 1537 by Spanish captain Alonso de Caceres, was the nation's capital for over 300 years. A popular rumor claims that in 1880, the unpopular wife of President Marco Aurelio Soto took her revenge on Comayagua's social elite by convincing her husband to move the capital to Tegucigalpa. Even stripped of its capital title, the colonial nucleus has remained intact as the main focus of a neat, manageable city. Its location midway between San Pedro Sula and Tegucigalpa, on the nation's most heavily trafficked highway, has brought commercialization; the influx of money has spurred restoration and reconstruction efforts—colonial-style porticos frame stone plazas that front 16th-century churches that are today as freshly painted as the day they were built.

⌐ TRANSPORTATION

Buses: Buses run regularly from both Tegus and San Pedro Sula. The **Catracho** bus station (☎772 0260; office open M-F 7:30-12pm and 1:30-5pm, Sa 7:30am-12pm) is 4½ blocks south of the *parque central* and sends buses to **Tegucigalpa** (every 30min. 5:20am-5:20pm, L38). **Transporte Rivera** bus company (☎772 1208) has a station 6 blocks south of the *parque* that sends buses to **San Pedro Sula** (3½hr., express 1½hr.; every hr. 5am-4pm, express every 2hr. 9am-3pm; L62, express L100) via **La Guama/Lago de Yojoa** (2hr., L50).

Taxis: (☎8980 2702), alongside the *parque central*. To anywhere in the city L20.

▎▊ ORIENTATION AND PRACTICAL INFORMATION

The **San Pedro Sula-Tegus** highway runs along the western edge of the town. *Avenidas* run east-west and *calles* run north-south with the **parque central** at the center of the grid pattern. Standing in the center of the *parque*, the **cathedral** lies directly to the east and the **municipal building** lies to the north.

Tourist Information: Municipal Tourism Office (☎772 2028; www.comayagua.hn), next to the municipal building in the northeast corner of the *parque*. Bilingual tourist information and hotel and restaurant information. Open Tu-Su 8am-5pm. **Casa Cultura Comayaguense,** in the southeast corner of the *parque*. Also provides tourist tips and sells maps (L20) of the town. Open Tu-F 9am-5pm, Sa 9am-9pm, Su 9am-12pm.

Tours: Latin American Travel and Tours (☎771 7125), 4½ blocks south of the southwest corner of the *parque*, upstairs and across from the Catracho bus station. Package tours to Roatan and the Copán Ruins. Four days and 3 nights at Pura Vida resort in Rotan, including round-trip airfare from Teguc L7145 per person. Four days, 3 nights at Plaza Copán, including transportation to and from Comayagua L4280 per person. Day tours to the Lago Yojoa, including the Cuevas Taulabe and Pulhapanzak waterfall L665 per person. Open M-F 8am-5pm, Sa 8am-12pm. AmEx/MC/V.

Banks: Line the edge of the *parque*. **Banco Ficensa** (☎772 0016), on the west side. Cash advances on MC. Open M-F 9am-3pm, Sa 8:30-11:30am. **Banco Occidente** (☎772 1501), on the north side of the *parque*. **Western Union** available. Open M-F 8am-4pm, Sa 8am-11:30am. **Banco Atlantida** (☎772 2492), 2 blocks south of the *parque*'s southwest corner on Av. 1, has an **ATM**. Open M-F 8:30am-3:30pm, Sa 8:30-11:30am.

Laundry: Idal Colonial (☎772 0082), 3 blocks north and 1 block west of the *parque central*, around the corner from the movie theater in a white, unmarked building. L8 per lb., minimum L20. Open M-Sa 7am-6pm, Su 7am-noon.

Police: (☎772 0080, emergency 3040), 2 blocks east of the *parque*, in a yellow building unmarked except for a small *"operacional"* sign. Open 24hr.

Pharmacy: Farmacia Genesis (☎771 7544), 1 block east of the *parque*. Open M-F 8am-5:30pm, Sa 8am-noon. Pharmacies in Camayagua operate on a rotation—every day there are at least 2 in town open from 8am-9:30pm.

Medical Services: Hospital Santa Teresa (☎772 0208), 3 blocks west and 8 blocks south of the *parque*. Open 24hr. for emergency care.

Telephones and Internet: La Red (☎772 4162), on the east side of the *parque*. Internet L25 per hr. Open daily 9am-7pm. **Medi@Net** (☎772 1897), 1 block north of the *parque's* northwest corner. Internet L20 per hr. Calls to US and Canada L1.50 per min. Open M-F 8am-9pm, Sa-Su 8am-8pm. **Hondutel** (☎772 0260), 1 block east of the *parque,* next to the Post Office. Calls to US L2 per min. Open M-F 8am-4pm.

Post Office: (☎772 0089), 1 block east of the *parque*. Open M-F 8am-4pm, Sa 8-11am. **Post Code:** 12101.

▶ ACCOMMODATIONS

Comayagua has a wide selection of accommodations; a large number can be found southwest of the *parque.*

Hotel America Inc. (☎772 0360), 3 blocks south of the southwest corner of the *parque*. Clean rooms with cable TV, fans, telephones, and private hot-water baths. Pool available. Free Wi-Fi. Singles L292, with A/C L361; doubles L402/466. AmEx/MC/V. ❷

Hotel Emperador (☎772 0354), 4 blocks south and 3 blocks west of the *parque's* southwest corner. Rooms with A/C, hot-water baths, telephones, cable TV, and free filtered water. Ask for a room with a balcony—they're brighter. Singles L325; doubles L384. Cash only. ❸

Hotel Norimax Colonial (☎722 1703), 4 blocks south and 1 block east of the *parque*. Rooms close to the center of town with cable TVs, fans, and private hot-water baths. Singles L250; doubles L400, with A/C L500. Cash only. ❷

Hotel Norimax (☎772 1210), 4 blocks south and 2 blocks west of the *parque,* near Hotel Emperador. Rooms comparable to those at the Colonial. Singles L250, with A/C L300; doubles L300/350. Cash only. ❷

Hospedaje La Esperanza (☎772 4762), 1 block west and 1 block north of the northwest corner of the *parque*. Friendly and family-run. Rents small rooms with fans, and has limited shared cooking facilities. Gate locks 10:30pm. Singles L85; doubles L100. Cash only. ❶

Hospedaje Primavera (☎715 8253), 2 blocks south of the *parque*. Tiny, clean square compartments with beds in a great location. The front desk is also a *pulperia*. Curfew 10pm. L100 per person. Cash only. ❶

◖◗ FOOD AND NIGHTLIFE

Pricier cafes and restaurants line the plazas by the cathedrals, while the streets surrounding the bus stations are full of cheap *comedors.* For groceries **Supermercado Carol,** one block south of the southwest corner of the *parque,* has a wide selection and is one of several locally owned supermarkets. (☎772 0071. Open M-Sa 8am-noon and 2-6pm, Su 8am-noon. AmEx/MC/V.)

Gota de Limon (☎771 8446), 1 block east of the northeast corner of the *parque*. An extensive array of platters of different meats priced by size (8 oz. platter L130, 12 oz. L160, 16 oz. L190) served at polished wooden tables by a small courtyard. The bar upstairs becomes a *discoteca* on weekends. Bar menu L60-150. Porkchop with a beer combo L90. Fries with meat L75. Beer L25. Th live music. Restaurant open M 10am-7pm, Tu-Su 10am-midnight. Bar open Tu-W and Su 6pm-midnight, Th 6pm-2am, F-Sa 6pm-3am. AmEx/MC/V. ❷

La Fonda (☎772 4585), 1 block south and 1 block west of the southwest corner of the *parque*. Large menu including a whole slew of Mexican-style options. *Taquitos Mexica-*

nas with chicken, pork, and beef mix L60. Chimichanga L30. Pork, beef, or chicken faji-tas L100. *Baleadas* L20-25. Skewers of chicken, pork, or beef L120, mix L130. *Tajaditas* with meat L45. Garlic shrimp L160. Beer L25. Open M-Sa 9:30am-9pm. MC/V. ❷

El Patio de Alicia (☎ 772 0676), 2 blocks south and 1 block west of the southwest corner of the *parque*. Breakfast and lunch served in a quiet, shaded courtyard. Soup of the day L50. Kids menu L40. Pork-chop or steak platters L60. Fried chicken L53. Beer L25. Open M-Sa 8am-5pm. Cash only. ❷

Comida Rapida Vencia (☎ 772 1734), 1 block south of the southwest corner of the *parque*. Where the famished and time-pressed can get fed heartily in a hurry from the buffet of *comida típica*. Breakfast/lunch L70. Open M-Sa 7am-4pm. Cash only. ❷

Villa Real (☎ 772 01011), 1 block east and 1 block south of the *parque central*. Originally constructed in the 16th century, the building has served as the living quarters of two Honduran presidents, including José Trinidad Cabañas (the dude on the 10 lempira bill). More recently, it has been converted into Comayagua's most popular *discoteca*. A stone fountain and shady coconut trees create an elegant atmosphere in delightful contrast to the bass-heavy pup music moving those on the dance floor. Open Th-Sa 9pm-late.

◼ SIGHTS

◼**MUSEO REGIONAL DE ARQUEOLOGÍA.** Housed in the 400-year-old former presidential palace, the museum's prized exhibits include leg bones of a megatherium (a prehistoric gigantic bear), the printing press used to make the first Honduran book, and rooms full of Lenca artifacts. The library once served as Honduras's first court of justice. (*1 block north of the cathedral, across from the Plaza San Francisco. ☎ 772 0386. Open daily 8:30am-4pm. L78. Tour guides to Comayagua in Spanish and English L20.*)

CASA CULTURA COMAYAGUENSE. Apart from offering information about the town, the Casa has a few rooms displaying signs in Spanish and English on Comayaguan history, and a diorama of what the colonial city used to look like. (*On the southeast corner of the parque. Open Tu-F 9am-5pm, Sa 9am-9pm, Su 9am-noon. Free; donations suggested.*)

COMAYAGUA'S CATHEDRAL. The city's Cathedral is an astounding display of 17th-century colonial architecture. Originally built by the Moors for the Alhambra Palace in Granada, Spain, the clock in the church's towers is a recreation of the nearly 500-year-old clock given to the town by Spain's Philip II; it is the oldest working clock in the Western Hemisphere. The Roman numeral four is written as "IIII," a reflection of Moorish influence. Check out the magnificent golden altar and small side chapel. (*Alongside the parque central. Open daily 8am-5pm.*)

OTHER CHURCHES. Built in 1536, **Iglesia San Merced** is the oldest church in Honduras. Inside, the statues are made of *balsa* wood; these statues were sent over from Spain, and were constructed with this type of wood so that they would float to shore in the event of a shipwreck. (*Three blocks south and 1 block east of the cathedral. Open daily 5-7pm.*) **Iglesia de la Caridad,** built in the 16th century, integrates Spanish and indigenous cultural influences. (*Three blocks north and 3 blocks west of the parque. Open daily 2-4pm.*) **San Sebastián Church** is famed for the altar and the tomb of ex-president General José Trinidad Cabañas, both of which reside here. (*Eleven blocks south and 3 blocks east of the parque. Open daily 8-10am. Service daily 6pm.*)

PEÑA BLANCA

Nestled at the base of dramatic green peaks rising on all sides, the little town of Peña Blanca sits just north of the serene waters of Lago de Yojoa. The lake supports large populations of tilapia and large mouth bass as well as legions of fisherman plying their trade on boats throughout the lake. Originally populated by the Lenca, ancient ruins here are a dramatic reminder that the lake has sustained communities for centuries. Peña Blanca, named after the white rock cliffs outside of town, offers accommodations for exploring the area. But to best appreciate the tranquility of the lake, choose among the waterside resorts, off the highway between the town and La Guama.

☐ TRANSPORTATION

Buses running between **San Pedro Sula** (1½hr., L45) and **Tegucigalpa** (4hr., L90) via **Comayagua** (2hr., L50) stop at the town of **La Guama** (in front of the *pulpería* of the same name), which lies along the main highway on the east edge of the lake. Buses also run regularly between La Guama and **Peña Blanca** (20min., every 20min. 7am-5:20pm, L12), the main town on the northern side of the lake. Catch buses in Peña Blanca from the stop just north of the La Guama's one intersection. Buses marked "Mochito" head to **San Pedro Sula** (1½hr., L45) or **Catarata Pulhapanzak** (20min., every 30min. 6am-5:30pm, L10). Buses marked "Etimol" travel once daily to **Santa Barbara** from the intersection of the two main streets in Peña Blanca (1½hr., 5:30am, L45); alternatively, flag it down from anywhere along the road to La Guama.

☐☐ ORIENTATION AND PRACTICAL INFORMATION

Ten kilometers from La Guama and the main highway between San Pedro Sula and Tegucigalpa, Peña Blanca is a small, one intersection village. Just across a short concrete bridge, the road continues north-south through town, while in the center the only other paved road peels off to the west before heading northwest towards Catarata de Pulhapanzak.

Banks: No banks cash traveler's checks and the nearest ATM is in Santa Cruz, a small town 6km northeast off the road between Peña Blanca and La Guama. You can wire money at **Banco Occidente** (☎650 0158), south of the main intersection; also has a Western Union. Open M-F 8am-4pm, Sa 8am-noon.

Police: (☎608 2030), across the street from Hotel Maranata. Open 24hr.

Medical Services: Centro Medico Santa Cecilia (☎394 5796), half a block up from Peña Blanca's intersection on the side road. Pharmacy and 24hr. medical assistance. Pharmacy open daily 8am-5pm.

Pharmacy: Farmacia Monte Sinai (☎898 8132), on the northern end of town. Open M-Sa 8am-5pm. **Hotel Maranata** (☎898 8106), on the same road, has a small pharmacy. Open daily 5am-10pm.

Internet Access: Explor@dores Cyber Cafe (☎608 1695), down a dirt driveway, half a block south of the bus stop. Computers equipped with Skype headsets. Internet L15 per hr. Open M-F 8am-8pm, Sa-Su 9am-8pm. **Antojitos y Mas** (☎650 0215), south of the intersection past Banco Occidente, has internet on the 2nd floor above the restaurant. Internet L10 per hr. Open daily 8am-8pm.

☐ ACCOMMODATIONS

A stay at one of the lakeside resorts can be well worth the price, but more economical options are available in Peña Blanca. All resorts have restaurants and boats for fishing and recreation. Local guide **Jorge Medrano** (☎9901 6582) will open his house to those looking to go on tours of nearby parks; he lives a few doors down from the entrance to Agua Azul toward Peña Blanca, in the house with the "Centro de Acopia" sign out front. (Rooms L200 per night. Meals around L40. Fish L25 per lb.).

Hotel Las Glorias (☎566 0461; www.hotellasglorias.com), 8km from La Guama, down the long pathway beside Las Brisas. A secluded, waterfront setting, large fields for sports, Wi-Fi, and a pool. All rooms have balconies, hammocks, A/C, private hot-water baths, and cable TV. Reception 7am-9pm. Restaurant meals L80-250. Singles L870; doubles L928; triples L1044. AmEx/MC/V. ❹

Hotel Auga Azul (☎991 7244), 3km up the road from La Guama. Cabins perched on a small wooden peninsula jutting out into the lake; also has an outdoor pool. Rooms have A/C, private hot-water baths, and cable TV. Restaurant meals L70-150. Triples L490; cabins for up to 6 L825. AmEx/MC/V. ❸

Las Brisas del Lago (☎608 7229), 4km north of Agua Azul, on an overlook above the lake. The most expansive views of all the resorts as well as the most impressive poolside patio. All rooms have balconies, cable TVs, A/C, and hot-water private baths. Restaurant meals L75-230. Recreation facilities open Sa-Su. Reception 7am-10pm. Singles L599; doubles L750; triples L835. AmEx/MC/V. ❹

Cortijo del Lago (☎608 5527), 1½km from La Guama, down a long driveway in the woods. The smallest of the resorts. Hot-water baths and rooms with fans; also allows camping. Restaurant meals L35-110. Reception 7am-7pm. Camping L100 per person; dorms L180; triples L500. Cash only. ❷

Hotel Maranata (☎898 8106), in Peña Blanca, just north of the bus stop. *Sencillos* with shared baths and rooms with private baths, fans, and cable TV. Curfew 10pm. Singles L200, with bath L300; doubles and triples L400, with bath L500. Cash only. ❷

Hotel Las Chicanas (☎9725 5706), just north of town, to the left off the road just past the Dippsa Station; veer to the left and continue 2 more blocks until you see it on the left. Modern, well-appointed rooms above a family home with hot-water private baths, cable TV, and Wi-Fi. Singles L300; quads L400. Cash only. ❷

🍴 FOOD

Cheap *comedors* and mini markets line the main road around the intersection in Peña Blanca, while each resort has its own restaurant. **Mini Supermercado Mas Por Menos,** just south of the main intersection, has the largest selection of goods. (☎9613 6082. Open daily 7am-5pm. Cash only.)

Coffee & Pizza (☎3225 0547), south of the intersection across from Banco Occidente. Serves its namesake fare and more in a small, open-air shop. Slice of pizza L25. Regular and large pies: cheese L120/140, pepperoni L140/185, veggie L140/185, chicken L180/210, Hawaiian L195/225. Coffee L8, with milk L10, iced L16. Hamburger with fries L45. Chicken fajitas L55. Natural juices L15. Open daily 9am-7pm. Cash only. ❷

Hao King (☎650 0238), just north of town past Hotel Maranata, across from the Dippsa station. The only Chinese restaurant in the area. Wanton soup L85. Fried rice L100-135. Chop suey L100-135. Chicken and beef dishes L110-135. Special for 4 including fried wanton, fried rice, and chicken and vegetable dishes L340. Beer L20. Open daily 10am-9pm. Cash only. ❸

Antojitos y Mas (☎650 0215), south of the main intersection near the bridge marking the beginning of Peña Blanca's center on the highway from La Guama. Typical Honduran cuisine served in a bright, tiled dining room. Fried chicken with *tajadas* L40. *Carne asada* L60. Hamburger with fries L50. Internet L10. Wi-Fi available. Open daily 8am-8pm. Cash only. ❷

Cafeteria la Roca (☎9753 4063), 1 block towards La Guama from the bus stop. Typical Honduran fare. Hamburgers L40. *Comida corriente* L40-60. Open daily 7am-9pm. Cash only. ❷

⚠ OUTDOOR ACTIVITIES

See **Accommodations,** p. 232, for contact information for the various resorts offering activities.

Fishing: As the dozens of vendors lining the road just before La Guama demonstrate, fishing is the lake's main attraction for Hondurans (though the famed black bass have all but died out due to chemicals from the local mine). Bring your own equipment to the lake, as only **Agua Azul** rents fishing poles (L50 per hr.). **Cortijo del Lago** provides fishing lines, hooks, and worms from their compost heap free to guests, and can arrange guides especially for large mouth bass fishing (L600 per day, L300 for 2-3hr.).

Boat Rentals: Each resort has rentals for touring the lake. **Las Glorias** rents paddle boats and canoes (L100 per hr.), as well as motorboats for up to 6 (L600 per hr.), and offers large groups rides on its catamaran (L100 per person, minimum 10). **Agua Azul** rents water bicycles, canoes, kayaks, motorboats, and a big motor boat for large groups (maximum 20 people) for L100 per person per hr. **Las Brisas** rents kayaks (L50 per person per hr.), as well as small (maximum 4 people) and large (maximum 12 people) motorboats (L600 per 1000hr.). **Cortjio** rents canoes and rowboats at the cheapest rates (L100 per boat for up to 3hr.). **Jorge Medrano** also has a few canoes for rent (L100 per hr.). He points tourists in the direction of La Isla El Benado, a short 30min. paddle from the shore near his house. Agua Azul is a small island full of birds and butterflies, with a small mountain that takes about 30min. to climb. The mountain offers expansive views of the lake (personal tour L100 per person per hr.).

Horseback Riding: Las Glorias (L100 per hr.), **Las Brisas** (L50 per hr.), and **El Cortijo** (L25 per hr.) can organize horseback rides for their guests.

▶ DAYTRIPS AROUND LAGO DE YOJOA

CUEVAS DE TAULABE
Take any bus headed to San Pedro Sula from Comayagua (L40) or to Teguc from La Guama (L15), and ask to get off at the Cuevas de Taulabe. You can also get off at the regular stop of Taulabe City and then walk back up the highway 20min. to the Km104 marker. The cuevas will be on your right. Alternatively, Jorge Medrano (see Accommodations, p. 232) offers daytrips to the caves, including round-trip transportation, with a standard rate of L1800 for up to 12 people—smaller groups should negotiate. Cuevas ☎898 8705. Open daily 8am-7pm. L40 plus tip for your guide.

The caverns at Taulabe were discovered by accident in 1969 and have only recently opened to tourists. A paved and lit path leads 300m in from the mouth of the cave, revealing millions of years worth of nature's underground artwork. Stalactites along the path, with a little creative interpretation from your tour guide, may look like a sombrero, a frog, a pig, or a map of Honduras. The caves were formed when Honduras was still submerged under the ocean, before the volcanic formation of Central America. Small bats hang from the walls inside the caves; the seeds from their guano have sprouted along the floor of the cave. At the end of the path comes a rare opportunity for adventurers; if you bring your own flashlight and lots of water, you can explore beyond the touristed area. Though a guide must accompany you, you are free to travel for as long and as far back as you like. The truly ambitious spelunker can set his or her sights on finding an exit to the caves, which has yet to be discovered.

WESTERN HIGHLANDS

CATARATA DE PULHAPANZAK

Take a Tima company bus labeled "Mochito" toward San Pedro Sula from the bus stop in Peña Blanca and get off in San Buena Ventura. (20min., every 30min. 6am-5:30pm, L10.) A yellow sign points the way to Centro Turístico Pulhapanzak. Follow the main concrete road for about 1km and bear left at the cul-de-sac at the top of the hill. After about 15min., a sign on your right will direct you inside the gated entrance to the Centro Turístico. Return buses to San Pedro Sula and Peña Blanca leave from the drop-off about every hr. until 5pm and 6pm, respectively. Alternatively, Jorge Medrano (see Accommodations, p. 232) offers daytrips to the waterfall, including round-trip transportation, with a standard rate of L1800 for up to 12 people—smaller groups should negotiate. Waterfalls ☎ 995 1010. Open daily 6am-6pm. L80; camping free, but bring your own gear.

An easy trip from San Pedro Sula or Lago de Yojoa, this 43m waterfall along the Río Lindo has carved out a spectacular natural water park beneath its cooling mist. The water at the top of the falls is a refreshing place for a dip, and a cement stairway about 100m downstream will take you to the base of the falls. Once at the falls, you'll notice the numerous swimming holes abound, many deep enough to jump into from the overhanging rocks; use caution. Beneath the blinding spray and torrential pour of the main shoot hides the narrow entrance to a **small cave** where the non-claustrophobic can find some very unique calcite formations. For a mere L100 tip, guides will ensure your safety while revealing all of these secret nooks. If a guide doesn't appear on your way down to the falls, the men working the entrance to the park will find one for you. The area around the falls is a public park that allows camping and has a small **restaurant** (with public **bathrooms**) just upstream from the falls. (Meals L60.) Next to the restaurant is the **Plaza Ceremonial**, an unexcavated archaeological site believed to have been a center of Lenca religious ceremonies.

LOS NARANJOS ECO-ARCHAEOLOGICAL PARK

Take the small yellow school bus marked "El Jaral" from the bus stop in Peña Blanca (10min., every hr. 6:30-11:30am and 1-6pm, L8) or look for the large green "Los Naranjos" sign 3km down the road that begins in Las Peñas. Jorge Medrano (see Accommodations, p. 232) offers guided trips through the park including round-trip transportation, with a standard rate of L1800 for up to 12 people—smaller groups should negotiate. Camping is technically not permitted within the park; the nearest lodging is in Peña Blanca. A cafeteria operates within the park serving meals for L60. Park ☎ 394 8102. Open daily 8am-4pm. L80. Spanish audio guide L60 at the gift shop.

On the west side of the lake, Los Naranjos Eco-Archaeological Park reveals the area's Lenca influence as well as stunning flora and fauna. The yellow-tailed montezuma oropendola, the largest oriole in the Americas, is just one of the myriad species in this incredibly diverse bird population. There are four side excursions off the main pathway. **El Jaral,** named after the earliest period of Lenca inhabitance, is the principal trail and leads past an enormous, old tree into the forest. The first trail to the left, **Sobre Polines,** leads down a poorly-maintained boardwalk to a picnic area looking out on the lake. Sobre Polines connects to **Gualiqueme,** which tours a wide variety of tropical plants and ends at a rickety suspension bridge with a breathtaking view of the canal. The bridge is in serious disrepair. Across the bridge, **Isla Las Ventanas** leads to a smaller archaeological site and panoramic lake vista at the base of Santa Bárbara National Park. Pathways from all the trails lead to the **Los Naranjos ruins.** Three mounds represent some of the earliest architecture in Mesoamerica, dating from around 800 BC. The site is not fully excavated, but with a little imagination the ancient Lenca village comes to life, showing visitors a basalt column, cutaway steps, and a stone statue on display at the park's entrance.

PARQUE NACIONAL CERRO AZUL MEAMBAR

Las Pavas trail (11km) is the most scenic route to the Los Pinos visitor center. The trail begins behind Restaurante La Naturaleza, located right before La Guama on the road from Tegus. After 2km, you will come to a sign that directs you through the village of Santa Elena. Follow a 2nd sign that directs you along a 4.5km winding path to the visitor center. The visitor center has maps and drinking water, as well as guides for hire. (☎ 951 3754. Open daily 7am-6pm.) Alternatively, Jorge Medrano (see Accommodations, p. 232) offers guided daytrips through the park including round-trip transport, with a standard rate of L1800 for up to 12 people—smaller groups should negotiate. To reserve basic rooms with hot water and fans at the Los Pinos hotel at the visitor center, call ☎ 9865 9082 and speak to Alba; alternativel,y ask at the La Naturaleza restaurant. Meals served at Los Pinos must be arranged in advance (L60-80). There are 2 designated camping areas, one next to the visitor center, and the other at the top of the mountain (L100 per person, bring your own equipment). For more info, contact the national parks administrators office in San Pedro Sula (☎ 504 1138; panacamtours@paghonduras.org).

The park features dense rain forest, and cloud forest at higher elevations. Three well-marked trails radiate from Los Pinos visitor center, revealing cascading waterfalls and stunning vistas within the cloud forest. **El Sinai,** the longest trail, is a steep 8km climb through secondary forest to a 10m waterfall with a swimming hole and a lookout point over the lake (keep an eye out as it's easy to miss). **El Venado** is a shorter 1.2km hike leading through the forest to the park's most famous waterfall. This trail also goes to a refuge for white-collared swifts and the park's mascot, the *pisote*. The waterfall can also be reached from the short and well-maintained **Los Vencejos** trail.

SANTA BÁRBARA

A mountain town with its center on the top of a hill, to the west of Lago de Yojoa, Santa Barbara (pop. 15,000) is bigger than it looks. Dwarfed by some of the largest peaks in Honduras to its north and west, the city is regarded internationally for the crafts produced by local artisans, especially woven baskets. Nearby fresh spring-water spas, where many locals relax, epitomize the pace of life in town. Recently, local churches purchased the only *discotecas* in Santa Barbara, bringing the town relief from late night delinquency problems that plague most Honduran cities, although don't be surprised by particularly loud, late-evening church services—they have great sound systems.

◤ TRANSPORTATION

Buses: Most buses stop across the *parque central* from the church. Just down the hill from the northeast corner of the *parque,* east 1 block, and northeast 1½ blocks, terminal **Cotisba** (☎643 2308) runs buses to **San Pedro Sula** (2hr., every 30min. 4am-5pm, L40.) 1½ blocks south from the southwest corner of the *parque,* above Restaurante Cebollas, **Terminal Junqueños** (☎643 2113) runs 3 buses per day to **Siguatepeque** (1½hr., L45), **La Esperanza** (2½hr., L60), and **Tegucigalpa** (3½hr., L126).

Public Transportation: Directly across the park from the church, city buses marked **Urbano** run to the *balnearios,* Nispero, and some of the *junco* villages on their routes through the surrounding settlements of Santa Bárbara—ask drivers if they're headed to the spa or town you're looking for.

Taxis: (☎9839 5451), along the main road on the east side of town. To anywhere in town L20. To the spas outside of town L40-60. To and from the *castillo* above town L80-100.

⚡ 🏨 ORIENTATION AND PRACTICAL INFORMATION

The **parque central** marks the center of Santa Bárbara. On the west side of the *parque* is the large **church**. The main street, **Avenida Independencia,** runs north-south along the east side of the *parque*. Here, Av. Independencia connects with the main highway heading towards Tegucigalpa via Siguatepeque, and San Pedro Sula.

Tourist Information: Tourism Office (☎643 2910), 1 block south of the southeast corner of the *parque*, down the main road, and then a few meters downhill to the east in the yellow and green painted building through the unmarked door just before the SKOTELC sign. Provides maps and pamphlets about the area, and can help with organizing a trip to nearby natural sites. No English spoken. Open M-F 8:30am-noon and 2-5pm.

Banks: Banco Atlántida (☎643 2300), 1 block south from the southwest corner of the *parque*. Cashes traveler's checks, gives advances, and has an **ATM.** Open M-F 8:30am-4pm, Sa 8:30-11:30am. **Banco Occidente** (☎643 2450), 1 block north of the northeast corner of the *parque*. Has a Western Union. Open M-F 8:30am-4:30pm, Sa 8:30am-noon.

Pharmacy:Farmacia Nueva (☎643 2009), across from the northwest corner of the *parque*. Open M-F 8am-8pm, Sa 8am-noon. Pharmacies operate on a system of rotations, whereby at least 2 throughout town are open everyday from 8am-8pm—check on pharmacy doors for a schedule noting extended hours.

Police: (☎643 2120), just south of the hospital, across the bridge along the highway. Open 24hr.

Hospital: (☎646 2721), south of the *parque* and a 10min. walk down Av. Independencia, just past where the road meets the highway. Open 24hr. for emergencies.

Telephones: For international calls, **Hondutel** (☎643 2422), 1 block north of the northwest corner of the *parque*. Open M-F 8am-5pm.

Internet: Blessing Ciber Cafe, half a block south of the southeast corner of the *parque*. Internet L13 per hr., Open daily 9am-6pm. **Cibernet** (☎643 3823), 1 block south of the *parque*, across from Hotel San Juan. Skype headsets and the fastest internet in town. Internet L15 per hr. Open daily 9am-9pm.

Post Office: (☎643 2121), 1 block north of the northwest corner of the *parque*, just west of the Hondutel store. Open M-F 8am-4pm, Sa 8am-noon.

🏨 ACCOMMODATIONS

Most accommodations in Santa Barbara are situated about one block from the *parque central* to the north, west, and south.

Hotel Gran Colonial (☎643 2625), 1½ blocks to the west of the northwest corner of the *parque central*. Tidy, comfortable rooms with private hot-water baths, fans, and cable TV. Singles and doubles L250, with A/C L390, with fridges, flatscreen TVs, and bathtubs L550. AmEx/MC/V. ❷

Boarding House Moderno (☎643 2203), 1 block north and 1 block west from the northwest corner of the *parque*. A wide variety of rooms. Those with A/C are the nicest. All rooms have private hot-water private baths, cable TV, and fans. Singles L250, with A/C L500; doubles L250/600. MC/V. ❷

Hotel Anthony Deluxe (☎643 0483; www.hotelanthonydeluxe.hn), 2km outside of town to the south along the main highway (taxi from center L20). Comfortable and well-equipped. Situated in a secure private compound, with a restaurant, outdoor swimming pool, and lounge area. All rooms have A/C, hot water private baths, flatscreen TVs with cable, telephones, and Wi-Fi. Restaurant open 7am-8pm; buffet meals L70-90. Reception 7am-10pm. Singles L696; doubles L928; triples L1044. AmEx/MC/V. ❸

FOOD

The cheapest *comedores* are downhill from the *parque central* to the east, south, and west. For groceries, **Bodega Elmer,** two blocks north of the northeast corner of the *parque*, is well stocked. (☎643 0343. Open M-Sa 9am-5pm. Cash only.) For fresh produce, check out the **market** one block downhill west of the *parque*. (Open daily 8am-5pm.)

Casablanca (☎643 2839), 2 blocks north and 1 block west from the *parque*'s northwest corner. Vegetarian friendly options served in a handsome, plaster dining room full of antique decorations. Lunch is a buffet, while dinner is a plate that changes daily. Breakfast *típico* L75. Lunch buffet L85. Dinner plate L85. Open M-Sa 7am-8pm. Cash only. ❸

Restaurante Cebollas (☎643 2329), 1½ blocks south of the *parque*'s southwest corner. Specializes in Honduran style meat dishes—if you have a carnivorous craving, Cebollas can satisfy your tastes. Beef tacos L50. Enchiladas L30. Hamburger with fries L45. Porkchop or steak lunch platter L55. Dinner *típica* (beans, tortillas, cheese, plantains, with eggs, beef, chicken, or pork) L55. Open M-Sa 8am-8:30pm, Su 8am-3pm. Cash only. ❷

Delivery Pizza (☎643 2903), 3½ blocks south, downhill from the southwest corner of the *parque*. Pizzas come in 4 sizes. Pepperoni L70-165. Ham and cheese L70-160. Vegetarian L80-180. Garlic bread L40. Delivery L10. Open M-Sa 9am-9pm. Cash only. ❷

SIGHTS AND OUTDOOR ACTIVITIES

JUNCO CRAFTS. Local villagers come into the city to sell baskets, purses, dolls, mats, and their famous woven hats, made in Santa Barbara's signature junco style. It is easy to visit the to nearby areas where the crafts are produced. Some recommended villages are **Santa Rita Oriente, La Zona**, and **Ilama**. Different towns specialize in different *artesanía* products; the tourist office can help you find transportation to each *pueblo*. Stores in Santa Bárabra specialize in different crafts. **Tersenia Tencoa,** one block north of the northwest corner of the *parque*, specializes in high quality wood and woven baskets. *(☎643 2188. Open daily 7:30am-5pm. Cash only.)* **Artesanías Yahamala,** two blocks north of Tersenia Tencoa, has a wide selection of different locally made items. *(☎643 2387. Open daily 7:30am-noon and 2-5pm. Cash only.)* **Estrella de Zamora,** to the right of the *parque*, 1½ blocks up the main street, has been making hats for 30 years. *(☎643 2689. Hats L80-L300. Open daily 8am-6pm. Cash only.)*

EL CASTILLO. High above the city, the 180-year-old weekend castle of President Luis Bogran has spectacular views of the city and valley below—be sure to bring your camera. *(The castle is just a cab ride away from town; tell your cab driver to wait. Round-trip L80-100. Open daily. Free.)*

BALNEARIOS. Five natural spas and thermal springs can be found in the area surrounding Santa Bárbara. **Balneario Torre,** 4½ blocks west of the southwest corner of the *parque central*, is the only one of the five located within the city. *(☎643 2440. L50. Open daily 10am-5pm.)* **Balneario Santa Rosita,** 3km north of town, is across from the Hotel Guacamaya. *(☎9868 7316. Open daily 8am-5pm. L50.)* **Balneario Tencoa** is 7km down the highway towards Tegucigalpa. *(☎643 2661. L30-50. Open F-Su 9am-5pm.)* **Balneario Bella Vista** is just a little further up the highway past Tencoa, and owned by the same owners as the Hotel Gran Colonial. *(☎643 1414. L45. Open F-Su 7am-6pm.)* **Balneario Santa Lucia** is 13km past the hospital on the side of the highway, is the only spa with natural thermal waters. It's also free to enter if you purchase a meal at the on-site restaurant. *(Open daily 9am-9pm.)*

⚡ DAYTRIP FROM SANTA BÁRBARA

PARQUE NACIONAL SANTA BÁRBARA. There are few areas in all Honduras with more rugged and unscathed wilderness than these 30,000 hectares. The park is home to **Maroncho Mountain** (2740m), the second highest peak in Honduras and the largest limestone formation in Central America. **Aguila Arpía,** the largest eagle in the Americas, also calls the park home. Lack of access keeps the park pristine, but presents a challenge for any hiker. *(Mario Orellana, who has his office 13km up the road past El Castillo, is the best source of information about the park. Mario can also provide info on the caves in the surrounding area. He also serves as a guide for the park free of charge (though he accepts tips). This is highly recommended: the park is enormous and it is difficult to follow scarcely marked trails. All cab drivers know where he lives, and the tour office can put you in touch with him. Alternatively, Jorge Medrano (see p. 232) offers guided days trips through the park from Lago Yojoa; includes round-trip transportation, with a standard rate of L1800 for up to 12 people—smaller groups should negotiate. An urbano bus leaves from east of the parque in Santa Bárbara at 5am and goes up to the entrance to the national park for L25.)*

LA ESPERANZA

With one of the highest altitudes of all major settlements in Honduras, La Esperanza has a noticeably cooler climate than cities elsewhere in the country. Though the small town is composed mostly of dirt roads, there is a diversity of accommodations options and shops to satisfy most needs. Up the paved street that runs along the east edge of the *parque central*, steps carved out of the stone lead up to La Gruta, you'll find a shrine to the Virgin Mary and with expansive views of the town and forest beyond.

⬛ TRANSPORTATION

Buses: La Esperanza has 2 bus stations. The main terminal is 7 blocks south and 1 block east of the southeast corner of the *parque central*. To **San Pedro Sula** (3½hr., every 2hr. 4:30am-2:30pm, L90) and **Tegucigalpa** (3¼hr., every hr. 4:45am-2pm, L90). The Tegus bus also stops in **Siguatepeque** (1½hr., L50). For buses to **San Juan** (1½hr., every hr. 6am-noon and 4pm, L35) and other small villages in the area, the main stop is 1 block east of the *parque central*, across from the Banco Atlantida.

Taxis: At the main bus station and 1 block east of the *parque central*.

⬛ ⬛ ORIENTATION AND PRACTICAL INFORMATION

The **parque central** sits to the northwest of the expanded settlement. The **main street** runs along the east side of the *parque*, continuing straight uphill to the white-framed **shrine** to the Virgin Mary and the **mirador** overlooking the town.

Banks: Banco de Occidente (☎783 0229), across from the southeast corner of the *parque*. Cashes traveler's checks and has a Western Union office. Open M-F 8:30am-4pm, Sa 8:30am-noon. **Banco Atlantida** (☎783 0043), 1 block east of the *parque*, has a **24hr. ATM** for MC/V. Open M-F 8:30am-3:30pm, Sa 8:30-11:30am.

Police: (☎783 7272), in the turreted building on the east side of the *parque*.

Medical Services: Hospital (☎783 0184), 2km south on the main street running along the west side of the *parque*. Open 24hr. There are many medical clinics around the *parque*. **Clínica Médica San Carlos** (☎783 0290), 1 block south of the southwest corner of the *parque*. Open 24hr.

Pharmacy: Farmacia Tres Marias (☎ 783 0986), 1 block east and 1 block south of the southeast corner of the *parque*. Open M-Sa 8am-6pm, Su 8am-2pm.

Telephones and Internet: Hondutel (☎ 783 1860), across from the northwest corner of the *parque*. Calls to US L2 per min. Open daily 8am-6pm. **Explored Net** (☎ 783 1048), 1 block north of the *parque*. Internet L12 per hr. Calls to US L1 per min. Open daily 8am-midnight.

Post Office: (☎ 783 0072), across from the northwest corner of the *parque*, next to the Hondutel. Open M-F 8am-noon and 2-5pm, Sa 8-10am.

ACCOMMODATIONS

Most accommodations lie within a few blocks south and east of the *parque central*.

Hotel Mejin Batres (☎ 783 7086), 1 block north of the northwest corner of the *parque central*. Colorful, neatly decorated rooms with private hot-water baths and cable TV. Rooms with double bed L250; 2 beds L400. Cash only. ❷

Hotel Urquia (☎ 783 0435), 1 block south and 2 blocks east of the southeast corner of the *parque*. *Sencillas* with a bed, table, chair, and shared bathroom L70 per personk, 2 person maximum. Rooms in the older part of the hotel with private hot-water baths and cable TVs L130 per person. Newer rooms with more modern versions of the same amenities L200 per person. Cash only. ❶

Hotel Mina (☎ 783 1071), 4 blocks south and 1 block east of the southeast corner of the *parque*. Boasts elegant, spotless rooms with hot-water baths and cable TV in a secure compound. On-site restaurant. Restaurant 7am-8pm; meals L65-85. Rooms for up to 2 people L350-550; rooms with 2 double beds L600. AmEx/MC/V. ❸

FOOD

Comedors abound a few blocks south and east of the *parque*. For groceries, visit **Supermercado La Canasta,** one block north of the northeast corner of the *parque*. (☎ 783 0565. Open M-Sa 8am-8pm, Su 8am-12:30pm. AmEx/MC/V.) For fresh produce check out the local **market,** one block east of the *parque*, across from the Banco Atlantida and next to the bus stop. (Open daily 8am-5pm).

Opalaca's Restaurant (☎ 783 0503), southeast of the *parque*. The nicest interior decor, largest array of options, and the best choice for a memorable, relaxing meal in town. Onion steak L117. Grilled meat fillet platters L120-140. BBQ platter with beef, chicken, pork, and fries L135. Garlic shrimp L162. Mixed meat skewers L125. Chicken sandwich L85. Open daily 10am-9:30pm. AmEx/MC/V. ❸

Restaurante Pollito Indio (☎ 783 0570), 6 blocks south and 1 block east of the *parque*. Large, modern dining room and an extensive menu. Chicken fajitas L110. *Sopa marinera* L90. Two-person BBQ platter with chicken, steak, and sausage or pork with fries and salad L200. Bloody Mary L60. Beer L25. Open daily 6:30am-9:30pm. AmEx/MC/V. ❸

Restaurante Cantonese (☎ 783 0931), 2 blocks south of the southwest corner of the *parque*. Brings the cuisine of southern China to the culinary scene in La Esperanza. Vegetable curry L65. Chicken with broccoli L80, with mushrooms L95. Beef with tomato L80. Mixed fried rice or chap suey L55. Beer L25. Open daily 9am-9pm. Cash only. ❷

SIGHTS AND FESTIVALS

The crisp weather here makes La Esperanza an ideal place to cool off while soaking up small-town Honduran life. The dramatic **shrine** to the Virgin Mary, poised conspicuously at the end of the main street running uphill along the east edge of the *parque*, is the main city landmark. Staircases hewn into the stone on both sides of the shrine lead to the top of the hill, presenting a view of the entire town. Cool spring baths wait at the end of the path that leads to the left of the shrine. (Open during daylight hours. Free.)

On the third Sunday in June, elegant floral altars decorate every street corner in honor of **Cuerpo de Cristo.**

SANTA ROSA DE COPÁN

Santa Rosa is 1km uphill from the main highway that separates San Pedro Sula and the border crossings for El Salvador and Guatemala. Travelers arriving at the bus station located along the ugly, commercialized stretch of road may be surprised by the pretty, cobblestone streets of colonial Santa Rosa de Copán. For centuries, the city and the surrounding area have been known to produce Honduras's finest tobacco, a practice that continues to this day at the Flor de Copán cigar factory in town and in the nearby villages. The town also makes for a decent base from which to plan excursions to Parque Nacional Celaque, as well as the forested areas of the Honduran highlands. A yearly festival on August 30 honors Santa Rosa, the city's patron saint.

▐ TRANSPORTATION

Buses: Santa Rosa's **terminal,** on the northwest outskirts of the city, about 1km downhill from the city center, can be a frenzied place, with bus companies in constant competition. Buses to **San Pedro Sula** (3½hr., every 30min., 4am-5:15pm, L65. Express 2½hr.; 8, 9:30am, 2pm; L85.) To get to **Tegucigalpa,** take any bus to San Pedro and transfer there, or look for the less frequent **Sultana** buses (7½hr.; 6, 8, 9, 10, 11am; L200). If you are headed to **Copán Ruins,** catch a bus to **La Entrada** (45min., every 30min. 4am-5:15pm, L35); and connect to the ruins from there (2hr., every hr. 6am-5pm, L55). Buses also run to: **Nueva Ocotepeque** (1½hr., every hr. 6am-5:30pm, L65); **Gracias** (1½hr., roughly every hr. 6:30am-6:30pm, L40); **Agua Caliente** (2hr., every hr. 9:30am-3:30pm and 5pm, L80); and **San Salvador** (daily 7:30am, L270).

Taxis: Line up along the southern edge of the *parque central.*

◀▶ ORIENTATION AND PRACTICAL INFORMATION

Once you get to the **parque central,** the city is easy to navigate; most activity can be found within a short distance of the *parque.* The main drag, **Calle Centenario,** runs east-west along the *parque*'s south side. The yellow **Cathedral of Santa Rosa** is on the east side of the *parque.* The paved road uphill from the main highway running to the north of town enters the city alongside Hotel Casa Real, three blocks west and a block north of the northwest corner of the *parque.*

Tourist Information: The **Office of Tourism** (☎662 2234; www.visitsantarosadecopan. org), in a kiosk in the middle of the *parque.* has 4 computers, free maps of the city, English-speaking representatives, and an upper patio with food and drinks. Open M-F 8am-6pm, Sa 9am-noon and 1:30-5pm.

Tours: Lenca Land Trails (☎9997 5340), 2½ blocks west of the southwest corner of the *parque.* This company is run by English-speaking Max Elvir. Max arranges a variety of tours in and around Santa Rosa de Copán. Ask about the Tobacco Tour and the Quetzal Hill and Parque National Celaque tours.

Banks: Banco de Occidente (☎662 0022), in the southeast corner of the *parque,* has a Western Union. 2nd branch next to the bus terminal. Open M-F 8:30am-noon and 2-4:30pm, Sa 8:30-11:30am. **Banco Atlántida** (☎662 0138), 1½ blocks west of the northwest corner of the *parque,* with a branch across from the bus terminal. Open M-F

8:30am-3:30pm, Sa 8:30-11:30am. A **24hr. UNIBANC ATM,** half a block south of the southeast corner of the *parque*, across from Flamingo's, accepts AmEx/Cirrus/Plus/Visa.

Laundry: Lavandería Wash and Dry (☎662 1653), 2½ blocks east of the northeast corner of the *parque*. L100 per load. Open daily 6am-9pm.

Police: (☎662 0840, emergency ☎199), in the yellow building across from the northwest corner of the *parque.*

Medical Services: Hospital de Occidente (☎662 0112). Take C. Centenario 8 blocks west of the *parque*, turn left just before the soccer field, and head up the hill 1 block. Open 24hr. for emergencies.

Pharmacy: Farmacia Central (☎662 0465). One of many pharmacies across from the southeast corner of the *parque.* Open M-Sa 8am-6pm.

Telephones: Hondutel (☎662 3550), on the west side of the *parque.* Permits collect calls but no foreign phone cards. Calls to US L2 per min. Open daily 7am-10pm.

Internet Access: Zona Digital (☎9999 6095), 2 blocks east of the northeast corner of the *parque.* Internet L18 per hr. Open daily 8am-10pm. **Bonsay Ciber Cafe** (☎662 5717), 2 blocks west of the southwest corner of the *parque.* Internet L15 per hr. Calls to US L2 per min. Open daily 7am-10pm.

Post Office: (☎662 0162), next to the Hondutel office on the west side of the *parque.* Open M-F 8am-noon and 2-5pm, Sa 8am-noon. **Postal Code:** 040101.

ACCOMMODATIONS

For such a large town, Santa Rosa de Copan does not have quite as many lodging options as you might expect. Hotels cluster a few blocks west of the *parque central*, and spread among the blocks to the south and east of the *parque.*

Hotel Maya Central (☎662 0073), 3 blocks west of the northwest corner of the *parque.* May be the best deal in town, offering clean, spacious rooms with private baths. Singles L150, with cable TV and hot water L200; doubles L200/250. Cash only. ❷

Hotel VIP Copán (☎662 0265), 2 blocks east of the northeast corner of the *parque.* Exquisite lobby, dark wooden ceilings, Mayan-themed decorations, a pool, and handsome baths. Singles L445, with A/C L695; doubles L645/845. Restaurant open 7am-1pm and 5-10pm. AmEx/MC/V. ❸

Hotel San Jorge (☎662 2521; www.hotelsanjorge.4t.com), 1 block west and 2 blocks south of the southwest corner of the *parque.* Offers what might be the largest rooms in Santa Rosa, as well as free Wi-Fi and computer access for guests, an English-speaking staff, laundry service (L10 per article). Provides rides to the airport, Copán Ruinas, or elsewhere (L4000 for up to 10 people). Rooms have cable TV, fans, and private hot-water baths. Singles L400; doubles L600; triples L800. AmEx/MC/V. ❸

FOOD

Santa Rosa has a large selection of good, high-end restaurants, especially in the blocks surrounding the *parque*. Cheaper meals can be found at the *comedors* a few blocks outside the *parque*. For groceries, head to **Manzanitas Supermarket,** one block down C. Centenario to the west of the *parque*. (☎662 0029. Open daily 8am-6:30pm. AmEx/MC/V.) Fresh produce can be purchased at the indoor **market,** three blocks south and five blocks east of the southeast corner of the *parque central*. (Open daily 8am-4pm.)

Pizza Pizza (☎662 1104; www.pizzapizza.vze.com), 4 blocks east of the southeast corner of the *parque.* Bakes brick-oven pizza with numerous topping choices. While you wait for your pizza, check out the English-language book exchange. Open M-Tu and

Th-Su, 11:30am-9pm. Personal pizza L40-65. Vegetarian L41. Pizza prima with mushrooms and ham, L47. Spaghetti boloñese L57. Garlic bread L25. Cash only. ❷

Restaurante Las Haciendas (☎662 3518), 1 block south and 2 blocks east of the *parque*. With black and white photos of Santa Rosa de Copán lining the courtyard walls, Restaurante Hacienda serves wood-grilled international specialties. Maps of the city L30. Meat dishes L90-150.*Típico* L85. Cordon Bleu L120. Beer L28. Open M-Sa 10am-10pm. AmEx/MC/V. ❸

Ten Napel Cafe (☎662 3238), 1½ blocks west of the northwest corner of the *parque*. Serves coffee, smoothies, and homemade treats and desserts in a colorfully decorated hall, or out back on a patio next to a verdant garden. Free Wi-Fi for customers. Paninis L55. Cappuccino L22. Tiramisu L45. Open M-Sa 9-12pm, 2-7pm. Cash only. ❷

El Rodeo (☎662 0697), 2 blocks south of the *parque*'s southeast corner. A Western-style restaurant known for its steak and a decor which includes mounted cow heads and a stuffed snake. Open M-Th 10am-11pm, F-Sa 10am-1am. Live music Th-Sa after 9pm. Rodeo Chicken L125. Steak L135. Prairie Oysters (Bull Testicles) L150. Surf & Turf skewer L185. Tequila Sunrise L55. Beer L30. AmEx/MC/V. ❸

👁 SIGHTS

▓FLOR DE COPÁN. The cigar factory hand-rolls Honduran *puros*, said to rival their Cuban counterparts. Watch the grueling and meticulous process. *(3 blocks toward the city, to the right of the bus terminal. ☎662 0185. L40 for Spanish guided tours. Open M-F 10am and 2pm.)*

CATEDRAL DE SANTA ROSA. This cathedral features wooden altars displaying devotional items particular to different saints. *(On the parque's east side. Open M-Sa 8am-7pm, Su 5:45am-9pm; mass M-Sa 5-6pm, Su 10am, 7pm.)*

EL CERRITO. Climb the steps to the top of the hill to see the sculpture of an AD 753 Mayan king dressed with an extravagant headdress. Demonstrating more modern iconography, the "18" graffitied on the statue's chest is the mark of the local gang. *(At the western end of C. Centenario, past the soccer fields.)*

🏔 OUTDOOR ACTIVITIES

Balneario Ecoturístico Las Tres Jotas (JJJ). A swimming spot filled with mountain spring water. The pools and cafeteria are on the site of an old fish and tobacco farm. A 15min. ride on the bus headed to Gracias (L20). Be sure to remind the driver when you get close. Admission and swimming L20-60. Lunch L55-75. Open daily 7am-6:30pm.

La Montañita. A similarly pleasant spot for picnicking, La Montañita also features a swimming hole. 5min. ride on the bus to Gracias L13.

NUEVA OCOTEPEQUE AND THE BORDER

Nueva Ocotepeque is situated in the extreme southwest corner of Honduras, at the confluence of the highways to border crossings at El Poy to El Salvador and Agua Caliente to Guatemala. The settlement serves as little more than a glorified bus depot for those just passing through. If the town's layout design seems modern in its strict regularity, that's because it is—the old city was wiped out years ago by a flashflood.

TRANSPORTATION

Buses: The **San José** bus company, 2 blocks north of the park on 1 C. Shuttles people to the Salvadoran border at **El Poy** (15min., every 30min. 7am-7pm, L15), the Guatemalan Border at **Agua Caliente** (30min., every 30min. 5am-6pm, L20), and **San Pedro Sula** (5hr., every 2hr. 6am-1pm, L125) via **Santa Rosa de Copán** (L60). **Torito/Copanecos**, a ½ block towards the park on the same side of 1 C. Runs to **San Pedro Sula** (L125) with stops at **Santa Rosa de Copán** (L60) and **La Entrada** (4½hr., every hr. 4am-6pm, L100); express to **Tegus** (8hr., every hr. 4am-10am, L210); and shuttles to **Agua Caliente** (30min., every 30min. 5am-7pm, L20). Across from the southwest corner of the *parque* beneath the large chief logo, **Congolón** leaves daily for **San Pedro Sula** stopping at the major cities along the way (5hr., 9 per day, L125); **Guatemala City** (7½hr., 9:45am, L160); and **San Salvador** (1½hr., 10:30am, L125). More frequent buses to cities in Guatemala and El Salvador can be found just after crossing the border.

Taxis: The local **Punto de Taxis** is across the street from the San José bus terminal.

ORIENTATION AND PRACTICAL INFORMATION

Just south of the highway junction towards Agua Caliente (22km), the main road to El Poy (10km) becomes Nuevo Ocotepeque's **Calle Principal.** Three blocks south of the edge of town is the **parque central,** with C. Principal running along its western edge. Another main street a block east and parallel to C. Principal runs south and turns into the main path bisecting the *parque.*

Banks: Banco Atlántida (☎653 3254), 1 block north from the northwest corner of the *parque* toward the San José terminal. Gives cash advances on Visa. Open M-F 8:30am-3:30pm, Sa 8:30-11:30am. Across the street, **Banco de Occidente** (☎653 3469) wires money and exchanges traveler's checks for US dollars or *lempiras,* but not *colones* or quetzals. Open M-F 8am-4pm, Sa 8-11am.

Police: (☎653 3199), 1 block south and 5 blocks west of the southwest corner of the *parque.*

Pharmacy: Farmacia Nueva (☎653 8756), along C. Principal 1 block north of the *parque*'s northwest corner. Open M-F 8am-5pm, Sa 8am-noon.

Medical Service: Periferica (☎653 2221), a 10min. ride north of town towards Agua Caliente. Turn left down the dirt road at the sign indicating medical care. Provides 24hr. medical service.

Telephones: Hondutel (☎653 3001), ½ block down the street that bisects the *parque.* Calls to US L2 per min. Open daily 7am-9pm.

Internet Access: Cyber.com (☎653 3592), 1 block west of the northwest corner of the *parque central.* Internet L20 per hr. Open daily 8am-7pm.

Post Office: (☎653 0221), across from the east side of the *parque central.* Open M-F 8am-noon and 2-5pm, Sa 8am-noon.

ACCOMMODATIONS

Accommodations options in Nueva Ocotepeque line the main street through town. Be aware that hotels tend to fill up in the late afternoons as travelers realize they've gone as far as they want to for the day.

Hotel International (☎653 2357), opposite the northwest corner of the *parque.* The choicest rooms in town with private baths, hot water, fans, and complementary breakfast. Most rooms also have balconies. Reception 24hr. Singles L365, with A/C L464; doubles L524/623. MC/V. ●

Hotel Congolón (☎653 3092), adjacent to the Congolón terminal. Convenient, inexpensive rooms. Reception 5am-noon. Singles L100, with private bath and cable TV L150; doubles L120/250. Cash only. ❶

Hotel Ocotepeque (☎653 3310), next to Torito/Copanecos terminal on 1 C., 2 blocks north of the *parque*. Rooms with private hot-water baths and cable TV in 3 classes of comfort increasing in size and modernity of amenities. Reception 24hr. Singles L150/200/250; doubles L250/300/350. Cash only. ❷

Hotel Turista (☎653 3639), 2 blocks north of the *parque* and 1 block east of C. Principal. *Sencillas* as well as rooms with private bathrooms. *Sencillas* with shared bathroom L130 per person, rooms with fan, cable TV, and private bath L180 per person, rooms with private hot-water bathrooms L230 per person. Cash only. ❷

🍴 FOOD

Comedors cluster within a block and along C. Principal. For groceries, visit **Supermercado San Jose,** three blocks north of the *parque* and one block east of C. Principal. (☎653 3218. Open daily 8am-7pm. AmEx/MC/V.)

Restaurante Sandoval (☎653 3098), 1 block north of the *parque* and 1 block east of C. Principal. Clean, well-lit, modern restaurant. A varied menu offers chicken soup (L60), tacos (L22), onion steak platters (L90), and spaghetti bolognese (L65), as well as a hamburger combo including fries, drink, and dessert (L85). Breakfast L40-70. Dinner L85-160. Beer L25. Open daily 6am-9pm. MC/V. ❸

El Reno (☎653 2098), on C. Principal, 2 blocks north of the *parque*. A typical Honduran eatery that also features a bar upstairs with karaoke 4 nights per week. Enchiladas L25. *Baleada especial* L16. *Cena típica* L45. Beer L25. Restaurant open daily 8am-10pm. Bar open daily 8pm-2am. Cash only. ❷

Restaurante San Marino (☎9609 8800), a *comedor* along C. Principal 1 block south of the *parque*. Specializes in simple dishes featuring beef or chicken (L70-130). Filet mignon L110. Seafood L82-90. Breakfast L20-41. Open daily 8am-10pm. Cash only. ❷

🏞 DAYTRIPS FROM NUEVA OCOTEPEQUE

EL POY: BORDER WITH EL SALVADOR

To get to the border, take a bus (15min., every 30min. 7am-7pm, L15) from the San José terminal in Nueva Ocotepeque, 2 blocks north of the park on 1 C., marked El Poy. Border open 24hr. While there is no fee to leave Honduras, there is a fee for both exiting Guatemala (Q10) and entering Honduras (L60). To the left of the immigration booths, a tourist office provides bus info and free country maps. In El Salvador, Route 119 buses leave from a parking lot down the street from the gate, running regularly to La Palma (30min., every 30min. 4am-4pm) and continuing on to San Salvador (3hr.). King Quality buses also go to San Salvador (2hr., 10:30am and 5pm).

The border at El Poy is about 10km south of Nueva Ocotepeque. Banco Occidente, just before the border crossing, has Western Union service but does not exchange currency or accept traveler's checks or credit cards. (☎653 3400. Open M-F 8:30am-noon and 1-4:30pm, Sa 8:30-11:30am.) Money changers usually offer good exchange rates for lempiras, quetzals, or US dollars.

AGUA CALIENTE: BORDER WITH GUATEMALA

The San José terminal 2 blocks north of the park on 1 C. and the Torito/Copanecos is ½ block toward the park on the same side of 1 C. Both terminals run buses from Nueva Ocotepeque (30min., every 30min. 5am-6pm, L20). Border open 24hr. Enter Guatemala free of charge for 90 days. Shuttle runs up the hill whenever it is full from the bus drop point to the border (3:30am-8pm, L15). In Guatemala, minibuses run to Esquipulas (Q20), where you can connect to destinations throughout the country.

The crossing into Guatemala is 22km from Nueva Ocotepeque. Money changers trade US dollars, quetzals, lempiras, and pesos. The border police are around the corner from the immigration booths. (☎652 3839. Open 24hr.)

COPÁN RUINAS

In a picturesque valley of Honduras's western mountains, the busy modern town is perched on a small hill 1km to the west of its more famous ruins. Around the central park, narrow streets are trafficked by locals, backpackers, archaeologists, and expats well into the night. Only a few blocks away in all directions, quiet streets attest to fact that even with modern changes, technological trappings, and mass tourism, the tranquil peace of Copán remains. The effects of recent political instability have been felt in Copán, where the community depends on the flow of tourism that has recently slowed to a trickle as foreigners decide to take their vacations elsewhere; it is possible that many businesses in town will shut down in the near future.

▐ TRANSPORTATION

Buses: Hedman Alas provides luxury bus service (with A/C, bathroom, and videos) to **San Pedro Sula** (daily 5:15, 10:30am, 2:30pm; L290), with connections to **Tegus** or **La Ceiba** (each L480), departing from their terminal 4 blocks south of the southeast corner of the *parque,* across from Casa Marias on the highway to La Entrada. All other long-distance buses depart from the lot 2 blocks east and 1 block north of the *parque's* northeast corner. **Casasola** (☎651 4078; office open daily 7am-8pm), across from Casa de Todo 2 blocks east of the *parque,* provides direct shuttle service to **San Pedro Sula** (daily 5, 6, 7am, 2pm; L110) which stops at **La Entrada** (L45). **Etumi** also runs direct buses to **San Pedro Sula** (3hr.; 8am, 1pm; L110) as well as to **La Entrada** (1hr., every 40min. 6:30am-5pm, L45).

Shuttles: Plus Travel (☎651 4088, 24hr. cell ☎9589 6414; open daily 8am-11:45am and 2-7pm), 1½ blocks north of the *parque's* northeast corner. Shuttles into Guatemala leave at 6am and 2pm to **Puerto Barrios** (L385), **Rio Dulce** (L385), **Coban** (L385), and **Tikal** (6am only; L580); all buses make a change at Rio Hondo. **Copán Tours** leaves daily at noon to **Antigua** (L230), **Guatemala City** (L230), **Río Dulce** (L230), and **Panajachel** (L480). **Basecamp Tours** also runs shuttles to Guatemala leaving at 5:30am and noon: **Antigua/Guatemala City/Rio Hondo** (L230), **Rio Dulce/Puerto Barrios/ Coban** (L425), and **Tikal** (L620)..

Minivans: Run regularly by **Etumi** bus service. Leave from the bridge 1 block west of the *parque's* northwest corner to the Guatemalan Border at **El Florido,** 10km away (30min.; leave when full 6am-5:30pm; L20).

Taxis: A few small, red, 3-wheeled vehicles transport passengers around town as well as to Macaw Mountain, Enchanted Wings, and the ruins, congregating along the north of the *parque* (L20-L80 per person).

▐ ▐ ORIENTATION AND PRACTICAL INFORMATION

Most buses stop at the bottom of the short, steep hill on the eastern edge of Copán Ruinas two blocks east and one block north of the *parque's* corner, along the path leading from town to the ruins. To get to the **parque central,** head straight uphill and take your second left; you'll be at the *parque's* northeast corner, marked by Banco de Occidente. The **church** sits on the east side of the *parque*, and the town hall and museum of archaeology along the west side. The entrance to the ruins is 1km from Copán Ruinas on the road east of the northeast corner of the *parque;* the road north from the northeast corner of the *parque* heads to the hot springs (23km); to the west of town the main highway continues to the El Florido border with Guatemala (10km).

Tourist Information: Tourism Office (☎651 3829; www.copanhonduras.org), 1 block south of the *parque* under the "free tourist info" sign. Has city maps (L20) and can help with hotel and restaurant reservations. Open M-F 8am-5pm, Sa 8am-noon.

Tour Agencies:

Yaragua Tours (☎651 4147; www.yaragua.com), next to the Yaragua Hotel. Office across from the southeast corner of the *parque*, next to the restaurant. Internet (L20 per hr.), tour packages to a number of local attractions, and free maps. Hot Springs tour L580. Horse tour (3hr.) L385. Open daily 8am-7pm. Call beforehand to arrange tours. Traveler's checks accepted. AmEx/MC/V.

Basecamp Tours (☎651 4695; www.basecamphonduras.com) at the Via Via Cafe. Run by former world-traveling backpackers who share their wealth of travel info. Tours include horseback riding (3hr., L290, "no experience necessary"), Finca El Cisne coffee farm (daytrip, L1140, overnight L1490), bushwhacking (2-8hr., leave at 7:30am daily, L155-675), and the Aguas Termales (3-4hr., shuttles at 8am and 2pm, L195-290 per person plus entrance fee). Also rents motorcycle tours with hot springs admission included but not gas costs (3hr. L775, 5hr. L970) and plans Moskitia rainforest trips (all inclusive starting from L8220 per person).

Copán Tours (☎9999 6127; 24hr. cell ☎9960 7174), half a block east of the northeast corner of the *parque*. Offers similar tour deals to Yaragua and shuttles into Guatemala. Open daily 9am-7pm.

Banks: Banco Atlántida (☎651 4505), on the *parque*'s south side. Gives Visa advances. **24hr. ATM.** Open M-F 8:30am-4pm, Sa 8:30-11:30am. **Banco Credomatic** (☎651 4686), next door to Atlántida, has a **24hr. ATM** that accepts AmEx/Cirrus/MC/Plus/V. Open daily 9am-5pm. **Banco de Occidente** (☎651 4085), on the *parque*'s northeast corner, has a **Western Union.** Open M-F 8:30am-4:30pm, Sa 8:30am-noon. All banks cash traveler's checks.

Police: FUSEP (☎651 4060), 4½ blocks west of the southwest corner of the *parque*. A 2nd outpost is on the road to the ruins. Both open 24hr.

Pharmacy: Farmacia Ángel (☎651 3676), ½ block south of the *parque*'s southeast corner. Open M-Sa 8:30am-8pm, Su 1pm-7pm. AmEx/MC/V.

Medical Services: Dr. Luis Castro (☎651 4504), west from the northwest corner of the *parque*, across the street from the cemetery toward the Guatemalan border. English-spoken. Open M-Sa 8am-5pm. **Medical Clinic,** 1 block south and ½ block to the west of the *parque*'s southwest corner. Open M-F 8am-3pm.

Telephones: Hondutel (☎651 4687), ½ block west of the *parque*'s southwest corner on the right. Calls to US L2 per min. Open daily 7am-9pm.

Internet Access: Maya Connections (☎651 4669), 1 block south of the *parque*'s southwest corner. Souvenir shop with internet. L20 per hr. charged in 15min. blocks. Open daily 7am-9pm. Also offers **laundry service**. L20 per lb. for a same day wash, dry, and fold, min. L100. Open daily 7am-9pm. **Internet Angel** (☎651 3533), 1 block north uphill from the *parque*'s corner. Internet L20 per hr. Open daily 8am-10pm.

Post Office: (☎651 4447), ½ block west of the southwest corner of the *parque*. Open M-F 8am-noon and 2-5pm, Sa 8am-noon. **Postal Code:** 41209.

ACCOMMODATIONS

The priciest accommodations cluster immediately around the *parque central*, or sit one kilometer or more out of town, while budget accommodations occupy the middle range edges of town.

■ **En la Manzana Verde** (☎9791 0896), 1½ blocks north of the *parque*'s northeast corner on the left. May be one of Central America's best hostels. Dorm-style rooms with a sense of humor have individually named beds, fans, and hot water showers. Full kitchen, TV lounge, sink for washing clothes, and luggage storage. Run by the owners of Via Via. Dorms L95. Cash only. ❶

■ **Via Via Copán** (☎651 4652; www.viaviacafe.com), 1½ blocks west of the *parque*'s southwest corner. An environment worth the price tag. Run by 4 world travelers, Via Via Copán has become a Mecca for all who pass though Copán. Spotless rooms all have hot baths, fans, and free iced lemonade or coffee and unlimited purified water. Eclectic cafe. Reception 24hr. Check-out 10am. Reservations recommended. Singles L230; doubles L300. Discounts for longer stays. MC/V. ❸

Hostel Iguana Azul (☎651 4620). From the *parque*'s southwest corner go 1 block south, west 5 blocks, then south again 1 block toward the blue building. Clean dorm-style hostel with friendly management, communal showers, hot water, and comfy beds. Dorms L100; singles L200; doubles L250. Cash only. ❷

⬛ 🍴 FOOD AND NIGHTLIFE

The most upscale restaurants are grouped to the south and west area surrounding the *parque central*, while cheap *comedors* are downhill a few blocks east of the *parque*. For groceries, visit **Mini Super Daniela**, across from the southwest corner of the *parque*. (☎651 4738. Open daily 7am-9pm. Cash only.)

■ **Via Via Café** (☎651 4652; www.viaviacafe.com), in the hotel of the same name (see **Accommodations**). A traveler's heaven. With a delectable health food menu including 24 daily vegetarian entrees and freshly baked bread (loaves for L50), every meal will bowl you away with savory flavor. At night, candle-lit tables set the scene while international music keeps the atmosphere hopping. Granola L15. Pancakes with fruit salad L60. Via Via sandwich L65. Breakfast *típico* L70. Beer L30. Tequila sunrise L55. Restaurant open daily 7am-10pm. Bar open 7pm-midnight. MC/V. ❸

■ **Vamos a Ver** (☎651 4627; www.vamosaver.com), ½ block south of the southwest corner of the *parque* on the right. A friendly Dutch couple serves fresh baked bread (L35) in a fun multilingual environment. Patrons entertain each other on a guitar borrowed from the owners. Vegetarian dishes available. Granola and fruit L80. Veggie or meat lasagna L120. *Baleadas* L30. Dutch sandwich L80. Happy hour 6-7pm: 2-for-1 mixed drinks. Open daily 7am-10pm. AmEx/MC/V. ❸

Jim's Pizza Copan (☎651 4381), ½ block south of the southwest corner of the *parque*. An American sailor cooks up 1 ft. handmade pizzas using fresh local cheese and vegetables. Pizza *"con todo"* L200. Veggie L150. Occasional movies at 7pm, most often on weekends. Open daily 11am-9pm. Cash only. ❹

Carnitas Nia Lola (☎651 4196), 2 blocks south of the southwest corner of the *parque*, at the end of the street on the right. Fun bungalow atmosphere with a book exchange, open hearth cooking, and waitresses who bring your drinks balanced on their heads. Free nachos with meal. The house specialty is the grilled meat skewers (*pinchos*, L280-315). Beer L32. 2-for-1 daiquiris 4-6pm. Happy hour 6:30-8pm: 2-for-1 mixed drinks. Open 7am-10pm. AmEx/MC/V. ❹

Yaragua Restaurant (☎651 4147), across from the southeast corner of the *parque central*. Feels like a Mediterranean bodega inside. The menu is full of different meal choices. French toast L58. Philly cheese steak L120. *Típico Maya* L110. Moon jaguar steak L170. Fajitas mixtos L130. Beer L25. Open daily 6am-10pm. AmEx/MC/V. ❹

Twisted Tanya (☎651 4182), 1 block south and 1 block to the west of the *parque*. Tanya is known among the locals for having the best drinks in town. Enjoy the fine dining on the 2nd fl. seating and 2-for-1 mixed drinks during Happy hour (4-6pm). Daily backpackers menu of soup, pasta, and carrot cake (4-6pm, L120). Tequila L65. Open M-Sa 10am-10pm. AmEx/MC/V. ●

SIGHTS

CASA K'INICH MUSEUM. The museum hosts interactive displays that teach visitors of all ages how to read the symbols in Mayan hieroglyphics, how *stela* are dressed, and the rules of the ancient ball games. *(5 blocks to the north uphill from the northwest corner of the parque. www.casakinich.com. Open daily 8am-noon and 1-5pm. L20.)*

THE COPÁN MUSEUM OF ARCHAEOLOGY. This museum contains detailed information on countless aspects of Mayan civilizations and stunning displays of well-preserved ceramics, stone carvings, and human fossils. *(On the parque's east side, across from the church. ☎651 4437. Open daily 9am-5pm. L57.)*

EL PABELLON MAYA. This art cooperative deals in handmade crafts from all over Honduras as well as parts of Guatemala. Pieces include paintings, weavings, and woodwork. *(1 block south of the parque central, across from the tourist office. ☎651 4066. Open daily 9am-7pm. AmEx/MC/V.)*

ENCHANTED WINGS BUTTERFLY HOUSE. More than 15 butterfly species flutter around the 3200 sq. ft. terraced enclosure in this Butterfly House, above 200 species of native orchids. *(From the northwest corner of the parque, located west down the road to Guatemala past the cemetery at the highway intersection. ☎651 4133; www.hondurasecotours.com. Open daily 8am-5pm. L100. Bilingual tour guides L50. Best time to see orchids is Apr.-May.)*

THE RUINS OF COPÁN

Dubbed the "Athens of the New World" by archaeologist Sylvanus Morley, the Classic Maya settlement of Copán contains over 4500 ruins and more *stelae* and altars than any other Mayan site in Central America. Visitors see firsthand the extensive hieroglyphics of Mesoamerica's most developed ancient written language along with the longest inscribed text in the New World. Although Copán has given archaeologists one of the most complete pictures of the civilization's culture, a sense of mystery and wonderment still lives inside these walls.

HISTORY

Called Xukpi by the Maya, Copán's impressive history is inscribed on the surface of **Altar Q,** dedicated to the founder of the Copán dynasty: **Yax K'uk' Mo'.** The inscription explains that in AD 426, Yax K'uk' Mo' rose to power in a city far from Copán. On September 8th of that year, he left his kingdom, setting out for Copán. When he arrived in Copán, he displaced the ruler and erected a new palace of his own. Part of Yax K'uk Mo's success was that his arrival coincided with the end of a Baktun, a symbolically important 400-year-long period on the Mayan calendar.

Yax K'uk' Mo' solidified his god-like image by transforming Copán into a majestic city. Building on the people's religious beliefs, he commissioned four new structures (the ball court and structures 7, 11, and 26) reflecting the four corners of the cosmos and commemorating the 400-year-long period that ended with his arrival. By inscribing the name of his son into the floor of one of the structures, Yax K'uk' Mo' gave supernatural legitimacy to his dynasty and created an intense belief in numerology that eventually led to Copán's desertion.

WESTERN HIGHLANDS

In AD 763 a new king, Yax Pasah, rose to the throne without any blood relation to Yax K'uk' Mo. With the end of another 400-year period on the horizon and the original bloodline no longer on the throne, Yax Pasah foresaw the end of the Copán dynasty. The city had been ruled by 16 kings, four sets of four over a 400 year period: a perfectly calculated end to a great civilization. He dedicated his rule to finishing the projects started by his predecessors. When all of the structures were completed, Yax Pasah ordered the construction of Altar Q, which depicts the end of the dynasty. When Yax Pasah died in AD 820, the people accepted the dynasty's end and burned his funerary temple. Before the city was abandoned, one last stela was erected depicting Yax Pasah passing the dynasty's emblem to "a king who never rules, on an altar that is never completed."

In 1834, Spaniard Juan Galindo drew the first map of the ruins, sparking the interest of Americans John L. Stephens and Frederick Catherwood, whose 1841 book *Incidents of Travel in Central America, Chiapas, and the Yucatán* introduced Copán to the world. In 1891, the first archaeological study was made and today this UNESCO site is the most studied Maya site in the world.

⚑ 🛈 ORIENTATION AND PRACTICAL INFORMATION

The main entrance to the ruins is a 15min. walk from town via a stone pathway that runs along the road to La Entrada. The **visitor center** just left of the main entrance houses the ticket booth, and a small exhibition on the site's history. Just before the center is a desk to arrange for guides in English, French, Italian, or Spanish; get together with other travelers for cheaper rates. The fabulous **Museum of Maya Sculpture** is near the entrance, to the right of the visitor center. The main site is open daily 8am-5pm (last entry 3:30pm). A number of attractions have entrance fees. Las Sepulturas archaeological site is 1km farther along the road to La Entrada on the right. (Ruins and Las Sepulturas L290, Museum of Maya Sculpture L116, both tunnels L230, 2hr. guided tour with a certified, multilingual guide L775 per group.)

More detailed information about the ruins is available in a booklet entitled *History Carved in Stone*, available in the gift shop or in souvenir shops in town (L100-150). For the full experience, hire one of the many uniformed guides at the booth outside the visitor center (L375). Antonio Ríos (or "Tony Rivers"), the very first guide at Copán, and Juan Marroquín are highly recommended English-speaking guides. One restaurant, **Cafetería Rosalila,** to the right as you enter, serves sandwiches (L50), bottled water (L10), and ice cream (L25).

🏛 RUINS

THE WEST COURT AND THE RESIDENTIAL ZONE. Temple 11, constructed by Yax-Pac in AD 773, portrays the Maya theory of Central America as a crocodile floating on the head of *pauahtuns* (old men). **Stela P** (AD 623) is a portrait of the 11th ruler Butz' Chan. **Altar Q** (AD 775) displays each of the 16 rulers with the 'creation story' of Copán written on top. The rulers sit chronologically, beginning with on the western side Yax K'uk' Mo' whose glyph reads simply "lord." Beneath Altar Q is the partially unexcavated **Rosalila Structure,** which shows what the structures looked like upon discovery. While originally thought to be a burial ground, **El Cementerio** is now considered to have been a residential area for Copán's elites. **Structure 41** demonstrates the importance of water and maize in Maya culture. **Structure 29** is thought to be the sleeping house for ancestors' souls with thirteen stepped niches that symbolize cave entrances to the underworld.

THE EAST COURT (PLAZA OF THE JAGUARS). The discovery of **Temple 18** (AD 801), the tomb of Yax-Pac, in the "Temple of the Rain" revealed that rulers weren't buried communally with their families, but instead in a sacred location. Two **jaguar sculptures,** symbols of courage and greatness, overlook the plaza, where the dance of the jaguar was practiced to honor the king. **Temple 22,** built by 18 Rabbit, has some of Copán's most intricate carvings and elaborate symbolism. Used as the king's seat for ceremonies, the plateau represents the mouth of a cave or earth monster. Atop **Structure 22A** sat the throne of Smoke Monkey and the Council House, or Popol Nah. The nine figures that once stood here pointed towards the divisions they controlled, all wearing loincloths to show their rank, but each with different headdresses from their regions. White flowers indicate that the soul of the community resides in this place.

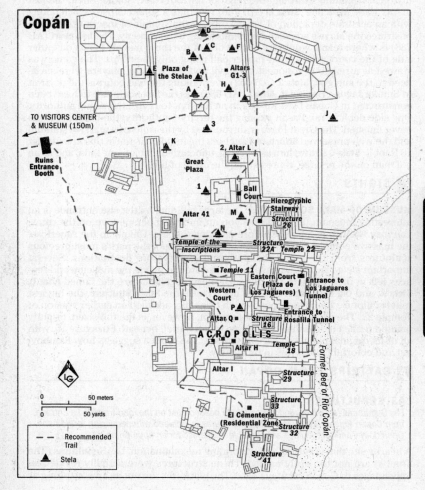

TUNNELS. Many travelers find the **Rosalila Tunnel** and **Los Jaguares Tunnel** overpriced (L225) and overrated. Without an expert's eye it's hard to appreciate the architecture, but they are an interesting experience just the same. Excavations within Structure 16 found the beautifully preserved stucco Rosalila Structure (AD 571), which honors the sun god. This building was so sacred the Maya did not destroy and rebuild it as they did with most other structures. For this reason, Rosalila is one of the most well-preserved underground temples on earth. The Los Jaguares tunnel displays evidence of an advanced draining system and the only private bath in all of Maya civilization.

THE GREAT PLAZA. The **Hieroglyphic Stairway** is the longest known piece of hieroglyphic writing in the Americas. The intricate carvings and inscriptions on the 63 steps depict the genealogy of Copán's rulers and the city's history from its mythical beginnings through the reign of its 15th ruler, Smoke Shell, the last of Yax K'uk' Mo's line. **Stela M** (AD 756) recounts a solar eclipse, which, along with an accurate depiction of Venus' orbit in the Temple of Inscriptions, demonstrates the Maya's advanced understanding of astronomy. The **ball court** (AD 738) is where teams would try hitting one of the three macaw heads on either side of the court with a solid rubber ball using only their hips. The game was viewed as a religious conquest over evil and the winning players were sacrificed to the sun god. **Stela 2** (AD 652) overlooking the ball court is the portrait of Smoke Jaguar. Behind it, **Altar L** (AD 882) has the last sculpture to have been constructed in Copán by U Kit Tok in an attempt to revive the ruling authority. One side depicts Yax Pasah passing the torch of authority; the other side was never finished. The Great Plaza is surrounded by the ruins of a massive stadium and the well-preserved **Structure 4** anchors the middle. *Stelae* in this area depict 18 Rabbit. **Stela C** shows him as a young, unbearded man on one side, and as an old man on the reverse, representing the cycle of life.

⊙ SIGHTS

MUSEUM OF MAYA SCULPTURE. The large building by the site entrance is an interesting museum that will give you an informed perspective on the ruins; you may want to come here before entering the site. Unique in the Americas, the massive complex was built to house and protect the park's most precious sculptures from the area's moisture and temperature fluctuations. Several important *stelae* and altars have been relocated to inside the museum and replicas left in their place in the ruins. Of these, highlights are the famed **Altar Q, Stela A,** and **Old Man Head.** Be sure not to miss the **Hijole Structure,** the highest relief sculpture found at Copán, which originally adorned an earlier version of Temple 22. The centerpiece of the museum, however, is the full-sized, brightly painted replica of Rosalila, the temple found buried beneath Structure 16, with all of its original paint and carvings intact. The replica suggests how flamboyant and colorful Copán was in its heyday.

⊡ DAYTRIPS FROM COPÁN

LAS SEPULTURAS

Las Sepulturas is 1km beyond the main site headed east on the road towards La Entrada from Copán Ruinas. Admission to Las Sepulturas is included with admission to the ruins. Open daily 7am-4pm. Guides are available in Spanish for an appropriate tip.

A nearby site that is getting an invigorating reexamination, Las Sepulturas (The Tombs) are not too aptly named. These structures were actually residential appendages to Copán for Maya elite. The platforms are not as awe-inspiring as the ruins at Copán, but they've sparked a small frenzy among archaeologists intrigued with the social stratification of the Copán dynasty. When approaching the site on foot, take the small trail off to the right rather than continuing on the dirt road. The trail winds through pleasant green foliage before opening up to the first series of residential dwellings. As you continue, buildings get taller, culminating with the residences of the rich and powerful and the impressive scribe's palace. The palace features scribes on either side holding ink pots and styluses and a central figure above the doorway portraying the owner.

LOS SAPOS

To walk to the Hacienda from Copán Ruinas, head south from the parque's southeast corner on the street in front of the church. Stay to the right as the dirt road begins, passing the car wash. Continue to the bridge, cross the river, and turn left. Up the hill, Hacienda San Lucas on the right has great trail maps included with a L50 entrance. The trail to Los Sapos, marked by white painted rocks, is off to the left just past the farmhouse (10min.). To reserve rooms at the farmhouse or schedule a guide for your trip, check in with the Hacienda's office in town, next to the tourism office (☎651 4106; open daily 9am-5pm). Lunch L200. Taxi to San Lucas (L80). Entrance fee is included in the package trips run by the information center.

One small piece of the Copán story, Los Sapos (The Toads) sits on the town's outlying hills, about a 30min. walk from Copán Ruinas. A group of rock outcroppings carved around AD 300 features two amphibious-looking beings, which has led some archaeologists to believe the site was a birthing site for Maya women. Toads are the Maya symbol of fertility and one of the stones resembles a pregnant woman. Others have postulated that the pregnant woman is not a woman at all, but an abnormally well-endowed man holding a perforator for self-sacrifice.

The stones sit on the grounds of the **Hacienda San Lucas** ❺, a beautifully restored *hacienda* with views overlooking the entire valley. The property also includes a network of birdwatching trails and a small waterfall. Meals and lodging with hot private baths are available. Horseback rides around the *hacienda* (US$25) are a fun way to spend the afternoon. (☎651 4495. Breakfast included. Singles L2440; doubles L2800; triples L3385. AmEx/MC/V.)

POOLS AND CAVES

The hot springs are open daily 8am-8pm for L100. Half of the springs is occupied by the Luna Jaguar spa, which charges a separate L195 entrance fee (☎651 4746; www.lunajaguar.com; open daily 9am-9pm, last entry 4:30pm). Both Vamos a Ver and Yaragua Tours organize trips (L567 per person). Basecamp Tours at Via Via also arranges transport to the springs (2 person min.; L195-290). Cave trips are led by Yaragua Tours (L675 per person). Ruby Waterfall (3-4hr., L386) and river tubing (2-3hr., L290) excursions are run by Yaragua Tours.

A respite from civilizations past and present, the hot springs 23km north of town are a welcome sight for the weary. Lounge in the two large stone pools or stroll down to where the springs meet the river to find your favorite water temperature. Take a short hike above the pools and watch the spring water bubbling up from its volcanic roots, but be cautious—the water here is extremely hot. There are several caves near town, but you must hire a guide to access them. A good option is to explore the extensive cave system and underground river of **Cueva de Boqueron.** While a November 2001 machete attack made Ruby Waterfall a less frequented destination, Yaragua Tours now organizes trips led by two armed guides to this watering hole, which has smooth rock banks and deep water. Yaragua also offers one of the most popular activities for people with extra time: tubing down the river, which allows visitors to enjoy a tour of the countryside in the slow, relaxing flow.

EL FLORIDO: BORDER WITH GUATEMALA

Border open daily 6am-7pm (☎651 4442). Pickups run back and forth 6am-5:30pm (L20). Transportes Vilma (open 6am-6pm), on the Guatemalan side, runs buses to Chiquimula (1½hr.; M-Sa every hr., Su every 30min. 5:30am-4:30pm; Q16); Guatemala City (4½hr.; M-Sa 4:15am, Su noon; Q45); and Petén (daily 6am, Q50).

A commonly attempted scam is for border officials to charge travelers for a US$20 passport extension instead of the required US$3 pass. Those entering Honduras just to see Copán should request a longer stamp than the 72hr. permit to avoid having to pay the US$20 fee on the way back. A 24hr. Guatemalan police office is just beyond the border on the left. Banrural does not accept traveler's checks or credit cards but does wire money. (Open M-F 8am-5pm, Sa 8am-1pm.) Money changers offer good rates on lempira, quetzal, or US dollar exchanges.

CARIBBEAN COAST

Honduras's long, hot Caribbean coastline is lined with beaches, national parks, wildlife reserves, old Spanish forts, and tiny Garífuna villages. La Ceiba, the region's urban center, is the country's main party town. Other cities include backpacker favorite Tela, Caribbean hub Puerto Cortés, and Trujillo, the gateway to La Mosquitia. The region has a gregarious Caribbean atmosphere where English and Creole are as common as Spanish.

The 17th century saw this region marred by the African slave trade. As slaves escaped or were emancipated, they intermarried with South American indigenous people. Their descendants built fishing communities along the northern shores as well as a distinctive culture and language. Today, the Garífuna (as they came to be called) are one of the fastest-growing ethnic groups in Central America. Their thatched-roof villages, dugout canoes, and colorful *punta* music are among the most captivating highlights of the Caribbean coast.

SAN PEDRO SULA ☎504

San Pedro Sula, Honduras's industrial heart, is built upon big business. Gaudy advertisements for international brands are visible in all directions and on practically every surface. San Pedro Sula is a vast, sprawling city, with so many nondescript streets, densely packed malls, and empty lots that from any given street corner it is difficult to appreciate the enormity of what surrounds you. Perhaps the only good way to grasp the full effect is from the vantage point of the Merendon Mountains, looming to the west of the city. To the traveler, San Pedro is nothing more than a concrete jungle and transport hub, rife with the problems that plague most big cities—noise, pollution, and crime. Come to visit and to shop or attend a big sporting event; otherwise, its best to do what San Pedro best facilitates: moving on elsewhere.

▬ TRANSPORTATION

Flights: Villeda Morales International Airport is located 15 km east of the city in the town of Lima. A cab ride to the city costs about L250. **American Airlines** (☎668 3243) flies to **Miami; Continental Airlines** (☎668 3208) to **Houston; Delta Airlines** (☎668 0233) to **Atlanta; Aeromexico** (☎668 4022) to **Mexico City; Copa Airlines** (☎233 2672) to **Panama City; Isiena** (☎237 3410) and **Sosa** (☎668 3223) to **Roatan.**

Buses: All intercity buses leave from the **Terminal Gran Metropolitana** (☎504 516 1616), south of the city center on the Blvd. del Sur. The terminal is open 24hr. Schedules change frequently and many destinations are accessed by multiple companies. For help with figuring out what company to take and where to find your bus, stop in the **Oficina de Transporte Gran Central,** down the hallway under the sign for Anden 57, although English may not be spoken.

Casa Sol: (☎516 2031). To **Copán Ruinas** (3 hr., 4 per day, L110).

Catista-Tupsa: (☎509 0442). To: **Progreso** (40min., L30); **Tela** (1½hr., L80); **La Ceiba** (3hr., every 30min. 5:30am-5:30pm, L94).

COTRAIPBAL: (☎990 81509). To **Trujillo** (5½hr., every 1½hr. 6am-4pm, L164).

El Rey de Oro: (☎516 2179). To **Tela/La Ceiba** (every 2hr. 8:30-5:30pm, L70/90) and **Tegucigalpa** (4hr., every 2hr. 6:30-5:30pm, L120).

El Paisano: (☎516 2015). To **Tegucigalpa** (4hr., 4 per day, L90).

Transportes Liberteños: (☎609 2599). 6 per day to: **La Guama** (L35); **Comayagua** (L70); **La Cuesta** (L80); **Libertad** (L100).

Saenz: (☎816 2222). 6 per day to **Tegucigalpa** (L365) and **Choluteca** (L590).

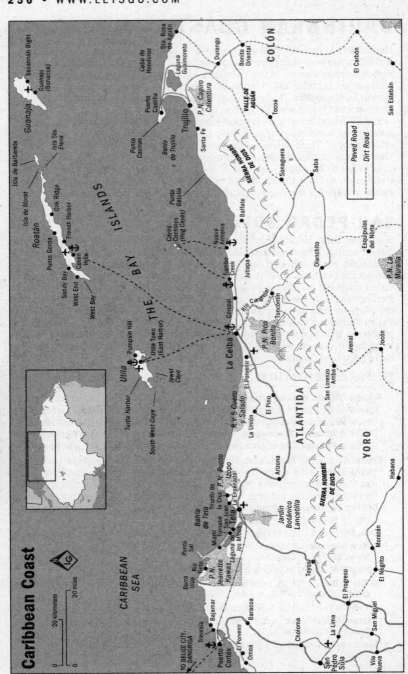

CARIBBEAN COAST

Juda: (☎443 4078). 6 per day to: **Tela** (L75); **La Ceiba** (L90); **Saba** (L130); **Olanchito** (L155).

Tica: (☎516 2022; www.ticabus.com). Daily 5am to: **Managua** (L608); **San Jose** (L988); **Panama City** (L1653).

Hedman Alas: (☎516 2273). To: **Tegucigalpa** (6 per day, L342); **La Ceiba** (4 per day, L380); **Tela** (2 per day, L304); **Copán Ruinas** (2 per day, L320); **Guatemala** (2 per day, L1122).

Impala: (☎553 3111). Small buses leave from the north side of the terminal for **Puerto Cortes** (every 15min. 6am-6pm, L35) and towns to the north of San Pedro Sula.

Toritos (☎553 4930) and **Copanecos** (☎553 1954): Small buses leave from the south side of the terminal by Andenes 54/56 for **Santa Rosa de Copán** and towns to the west of San Pedro Sula (every 15min. 6am-6:40pm, L70).

Alejandro Express: Small buses leave from the south side of the terminal by Anden 59 for **El Progreso**, El **Negrito, Morazan,** and towns to the east of San Pedro (every 15min. 6am-6pm, L20).

Taxis: Taxi Central (☎557 4020). Taxis congregate along C. 1 and the Av. de Circunvalación. They'll honk to flag you down. Taxis within the city should not cost more than L50.

Car Rental: Omega Rental, C. 3/4, Ave. 3 Northwest (☎552 7625). Rents cars and SUVs. 25+. Open M-F 8am-5pm, Sa 8am-1pm, or by appointment.

📑 🔢 ORIENTATION AND PRACTICAL INFORMATION

The streets of San Pedro Sula are organized along a grid pattern divided into four quadrants, with *avenidas* running north to south and *calles* running east to west. **Calle 1** runs past the **parque central** and divides the north and south halves of the city center. **Avenida 1** runs alongside old, unused railroad tracks and divides the east and west halves. Tourists should stay in the northwest and southwest quadrants of town—everything a traveler could need is found in these areas. **The eastern part of the city is significantly more dangerous.** Running in a loop around the city center is the **Avenida de Circunvalación,** a highway replete with gas stations, chain restaurants, and shopping malls. The main **bus terminal** and **estadio olímpico** are both outside of the center—a cab ride from the center of town to either should cost no more than L80. The areas just south of the *parque* tend to be much more heavily trafficked, while the north is noticeably quieter and more secure. After dark, however, all bets are off.

Tourist Office: C. 2 Av. 4 Southwest (☎550 3920), 3rd floor of the Gran Via building #305. Open M-F 8am-5pm.

Tours: Astro Tours, (☎557 2550). Specializes in organizing private tours. Runs many to the ruins at Copán. English spoken by some employees. Open M-F 8am-5:30pm, Sa 8am-12pm.

Financial Services: Banks line the western length of Av. de Circunvalación and C. 1 between Av. 3 and 7. All offer money exchange and cash traveler's checks. **HSBC,** on the corner of Av. 7, has a **24hr. ATM.** Most banks open M-F 9am-4pm, Sa 9am-12pm. Many gas stations along Circ. also have ATMs inside their minimarts. **Western Union,** C. 1/2 Av. 8 NO (☎552 1288). Open M-F 8:30am-6pm, Sa 8:30am-5pm, Su 8:30am-3pm.

Laundromat: Lavanderia Jil, C. 4, Av. 7/8 Northwest. Laundry services for loads up to 10 lbs. Wash L40. Dry L40. Open M-Sa 7am-6pm.

Emergency: ☎199, fire ☎198.

Tourist Police: C. 1, Av. 12 Northwest (☎550 3452). Open 24hr. English may not be spoken.

Pharmacy: Competing pharmacies are located all around the *parque central* and along the western part of the Av. Circunvalación. **Farmacia Kielsa** offers two 24 hr. options along Av. Circunvalación, across from C. 6/7 Northwest, and C. 8/9 Southwest.

Hospital: Hospital Leonardo Martinez, C. 7/8, Av. 10 Southwest (☎550 3411). Open 24hr.

Internet Access: Diosita.net (☎550 1307), on the 1st floor of the Gran Via building, below the tourist office. Internet L25 per hr. Open daily 7:30am-7pm. **Terranet,** C. 2/3,

Ave. 4 Northwest (☎557 9560), across from Astro Tours. Internet L15 per hr. Open M-F 7am-6pm, Sa 10am-6pm.

Post Office: C. 9, Ave. 3 Southwest (☎552 3185). Open M-F 8am-5pm, Sa 8am-12pm. **Postal Code:** 21101.

🏠 ACCOMMODATIONS

While hostels are rare in San Pedro, there is a abundance of cheap to moderately priced hotels, especially in the blocks just south of the city center around the *parque*. Unfortunately, this also happens to be among the most dangerous parts of the city, especially at night. Be sure to examine your room before paying for the night.

Hostal Tamarindo, C. 9A, Av. 10/11 Northwest (☎557 0123; www.tamarindohostel. com). Possibly San Pedro Sula's only option for a traditional hostel. Away from the bustle of the city center, but only blocks from Guamilito (the city's best crafts market). The communal lounge and kitchen downstairs are conducive to socializing. Adequate dorms and private rooms with bath and cable TV. Reserve beds ahead of time if possible. The neighborhood can be unsafe, particularly at night. Free Wi-Fi. Dorms L220; private rooms L650. AmEx/MC/V. ●

Hostal E y N (☎504 0374; www.hostaleyn.com), along C. 5, between Av. 15 and 16 Northwest. Despite its name, Hostal E y N is more of a modern B&B than a hostel, but is a good option for those seeking comfortable lodging in one of the city's safer areas. Much more economical for those traveling in groups. Rooms with A/C, cable TV, hot water, and private bathrooms. Continental breakfast included. Free Wi-Fi. Singles L855; doubles L951; triple L1047. AmEx/MC/V. ❹

Hotel Maya Copan (☎552 1516), on C. 5, Ave. 8 NO. A colorful and cozy lobby leads to clean, modern rooms. The hotel is among the pricier options in San Pedro Sula. Rooms come with A/C, cable TV, and private bathrooms with hot water. Breakfast included and served in the small, adjoining restaurant. Free Wi-Fi. Singles L875; doubles L1100; triples L1250. AmEx/MC/V. ❹

⬛ FOOD

In the city center, surrounding streets, and along the **Avenida Circunvalacion,** international brand name restaurants and fast food joints of all types and origins hawk their mediocre, generic cuisine. For a less corporate and more intimate eating experience, explore the neighborhoods between these areas (though remember not to walk anywhere unfamiliar at night, especially if alone). As a general rule of thumb: the smaller, less visible, and more obscure the name and advertisement of an eatery, the more authentic the experience. To load up on groceries, head to the new and enormous **Supermercados Junior's,** C. 7, Av. 14 Southwest (☎550 9222; open daily 8am-8:30pm).

Cafe Skandia (☎552 9999), on C. 1 in the city center at the back of the lobby of the massive Grand Sula Hotel. Models its logo after what appears to be a Viking ship, but its counter-seating, metal tables, and menu selections call to mind a 50s American diner. Grab a late-night coffee (with milk L32) and a slice of apple pie (L35), or cool off with a real fruit smoothie (pineapple, papaya, watermelon; L30). Club sandwich L95. Spaghetti L95. Open 24hr. ❸

Casa de Campo, C. 8, Av. 15 Southwest (☎504 2272). Serves "typical Honduran" grilled fare—that is, succulent meats served on carved wooden tables. Try the *parrillada tres delicias,* chicken, pork and beef (L150, for 6 people L800). Various seafood dishes including different styles of shrimp L170-200. Open M-Th 10am-3pm and 6pm-11pm, F-Su 10am-11pm. ❷

Euphoria (☎516 8100), in the Jardines del Valle neighborhood outside of the Av. de Circunvalacion (a cab ride before dark from the center should cost L50). Patrons come here to escape the city for a while within the walls of this gardened compound. Air-conditioned dining rooms are situated around a central fish pond, gardens provide a peaceful atmosphere. Menu options range from pork-chops served with plantains, rice, and beans (L150) to pizzas (personal L188-98; 12 piece L320-40), grilled skewers of chicken (L179), shrimp (L205), and a mix of meats and seafood (L185). Entrees L150-260. Open M-Sa 11am-2pm and 5pm-10pm, Su 9am-5pm. AmEx/MC/V. ❷

Deriva, C. 9A, Av. 11 Northwest (☎552 0535), across from Hostal Tamarindo. First and foremost a *vinoteca* (wine bodega) with vintages personally selected by the owner from Chile, Argentina, and France. With a quiet, sophisticated ambience Deriva offers a unique dining experience. Specializing in seafood, the *Jalea Peruana* features shrimp, squid, and fish prepared Peruvian style with yuca (L350). Appetizers L180-275. *Vinoteca* open M-Sa 10am-8pm; restaurant open M-Sa 12pm-2:30pm and 6pm-10pm. AmEx/MC/V. ❹

🜚 🗗 SIGHTS AND SHOPPING

🜚MUSEO DE ANTROPOOGÍA E HISTORIA. Two large exhibition halls take visitors through the history of the area, from the Pre-Columbian era through colonial history and the turn of the century. Informative signs in Spanish and English are supplemented by impressive arrays of artifacts from ancient times up until the 20th century. To fully appreciate the entire collection visitors must set aside at least two hours. Also on site is a separately run theater. *(C. 3/4, Av. 3 Northwest. ☎ 557 1496. Open M and W-Sa 9am-4pm, Su 9am-3pm. Library open daily 8am-5pm. Adjacent outdoor cafeteria closes at 6pm. L38, Children L5.)*

MUSEO DE LA NATURALEZA. Twenty-two rooms enlighten visitors about the diverse ecology of Honduras. Come here to learn about the contamination and pollution that are affecting some of the country's most precious wildlife reserves. *(Entrance on Av. 12 Northwest around the side of the museum and next to the tourist police station. ☎ 550 1832. Open M-F 8am-12pm, 1pm-4pm. L20.)*

ASOCIACION NACIONAL DE ARTESANOS DE HONDURAS. Besides being a good source of traditional food, the **Mercado Guamilito** houses the best Honduran artisans' market. Wander through the maze of handmade carvings and ceramics. Across the street on C. 6, **Casa del Sol** offers similar crafts at slightly higher prices. Be prepared to bargain. *(C. 6, Av. 8/9. Casa del Sol ☎ 557 1371. Guamilito open M-Sa 6am-4:30pm. Casa del Sol open M-Sa 7am-6pm, Su 8:30-3pm. 15% discount for cash payments; 10% discount for credit cards. AmEx/MC/V.)*

CENTRO CULTURAL SAMPEDRANO. Next to the *comida típica* food plaza, the center has both permanent and rotating gallery spaces which display traditional handicrafts and contemporary paintings. There are a plethora of merchants eager to sell you works. *(C. 3, Av. 3/4. ☎ 553 3911. Open M-Sa 8am-5pm, Su 8am-4pm.)*

🜚 🎵 NIGHTLIFE AND ENTERTAINMENT

Much of San Pedro's nightlife centers on bars and *discotecas* located on or near the western half of the Av. de Circunvalación. At the clubs, men arrive dressed to impress—don't wear sandals, shorts, or T-shirts. Women should be aware that *machismo* is the norm around here; they should expect blatant come-ons. All should be aware that San Pedro is a dangerous city, especially at night, and that it is advisable to take taxis everywhere.

Klein Bohemia, C. 7, Av. 8 Southwest. Situated on the 2nd floor above a corner store, it doesn't look like much from the outside, but the vibe inside is comfortable and relaxed. Swiss-owned and popular with foreigners. Occasionally hosts cultural events like movie showings or live music performances. Open W-Sa 7pm-midnight.

Caribbean Bar, C. 10, Av. 16 Southwest. Features an array of mixed drinks, with music varying from pop to alternative. Open M-Sa 7pm-2am or later.

Grand Sula Bar, to the right in the main lobby of the Hotel on C. 1, Av. 4 Northwest. A popular hangout for expats.

Kawama Bay Disco, on the Av. Circunvalacion near Ave. 10 Northwest. One of the most established *discotecas* in San Pedro Sula. Full service bar. Expect to pay a cover.

Geminis Theater, C. 1, Av. 12 Northwest (☎ 550 9060). Newly released movies showing daily on 4 screens. L50, Tu L25. Th couples pay L80.

FESTIVALS

San Pedro Sula's only major festival is the **Juniana,** celebrated throughout the month of June. The biggest crowds and largest festival events occur on the weekends. Parades feature Garífuna dancers, drum corps, and young beauty queens. Marching through the streets, these characters entertain crowds in the city center. Along the Av. de Circunvaluation, large empty lots are turned into fairgrounds, with food vendors and mechanical rides. The last night of the Juniana is **carnaval;** acquire your own cardboard mask to join the throngs in costumed celebration.

PUERTO CORTES

Puerto Cortes (pop. 47,100), Honduras' largest port, is situated on a deep natural harbor 64km north of San Pedro Sula. The city is mostly frequented by travelers on their way to Belize, Omoa, and the Guatemalan border to the west. Puerto Cortes is also used as a stop-over for those headed to the Garífuna villages to the north. The many shops and banks in the city make it a good place to stock up on the way to more beautiful environs, but there are enough of beaches and people-watching spots to make a more extended stay worthwhile.

TRANSPORTATION

Buses generally drop new arrivals to town on Av. 4, C. 3. The center of town, around the *parque*, is one block south (towards the tall loading cranes) and one block east. Most buses also depart from this area.

Buses: Impala (☎553 3111), on Av. 4 by the corner with C. 3, runs buses to **San Pedro Sula** (1 hr., every 15 min. 5am-7pm, L35.). Direct buses to **Omoa** leave from the parking lot across the street (30min., every 30 min. 6am-7pm, L15.). Many buses going to Omoa also continue on to the Guatemalan border, eventually dropping travelers at the border crossing by **Corinto** (3 hr., every hr. 6am-4pm, L45). Buses to the nearby Garífuna villages of **Travesia** (15 min., every hr. 6am-4pm, L8) and **Bajamar** (30min. every hr. 6am-4pm, L10) leave from Av. 4, C. 4 in the empty lot. Travelers bound for **Tela** should take a bus to **San Pedro Sula** and catch a connection there.

Boats: Two regularly scheduled boats operated by **Nesyumein Neydy** (☎501 522 0062) run between Puerto Cortes and Dangriga. The boats leave from by the fish market, to the east of the bridge. It is a good idea to arrive at least an hour before departure; come the day before to make sure the boat is running.

Taxis: A queue forms around the *parque* and near the Hotel Formosa on Av. 3. A ride from the center to the *laguna* where the boats leave for Belize should cost about L30.

ORIENTATION AND PRACTICAL INFORMATION

Puerto Cortes occupies a peninsula surrounded by the Caribbean to the north and west, the **Bahia de Cortes** to the south, and the inland **Laguna de Alvarado** to the southeast. The docks, recognizable by the loading cranes, line the south side of downtown. *Avenidas* run east-west, parallel to the docks, starting with Av. 1 and increasing numerically as you head north into the city. *Calles* run perpendicular to the *avenidas*. The large **parque central** sits between Av. 2/3, C. 4/5. Beaches to the north, **Marejada** and **Vacacional,** are reached by long walks down dirt roads (taxis L30; arrange a pickup beforehand); many chose to head to the calmer waters of the **municipal beach,** to the south on the other side of the bay.

Tours and Agencies: Bahia, C. 2/3 Av. 3 (☎665 5803). Provides travel advice and rents vehicles. Open M-F 8am-5pm, Sa 8am-12pm.

Banks: Banco de Occidente, C. 4, Ave. 3, off the northwest corner of the *parque,* Cashes traveler's checks and **exchanges currency.** The small supermarket on Ave. 4, C. 2 has a Unibank **ATM** which draws money from most account types. Open daily 8am-7:30pm.

Pharmacy: Different pharmacies, many of them around the central *parque,* take turns staying open until 10pm. Check pharmacy doors for the schedule.

Hospital: Hospital Cemeco, C. 8, Av. 5 (☎665 0460). English speaking doctor on-call 24hr. Open 24 hr.

Internet Access: Rudon's Cyber Net, C. 3, Av. 1/2 (☎665 5822). Also offers call service to the United States. Open M-Sa 8am-5pm. internet L20 per hr. Calls to US L1 per min. **Cortes Net,** C. 2, Av. 2/3 (☎665 2585), has even cheaper rates. Internet L15 per hr.; calls to US L1 per min. Open daily 8:30am-7pm.

Post Office: C. 1, near Av. 1 (☎665 0455). Open M-F 8:30am-4pm.

ACCOMMODATIONS

For a fairly large town, Puerto Cortes lacks a variety of lodging options. Many who spend a night in Puerto Cortes stay away from the center at more distant, more expensive accommodations. Along Ave. 1 and near the docks, certain hotels offer hourly rates, encouraging travellers to look for rooms closer to the center of town if they choose to stay in Puerto Cortes.

Hotel Formosa, C. 2, Ave. 3 (☎665 0823). Small, battered, adequate rooms with private bathrooms, fans, and cable TV. Try to get a room upstairs if noise from the street might bother you. For those returning at night, the entrance changes to a door down a long alley to the right of the normal entrance. A/C L100. Singles L250; double L350. ❷

Hotel Spring Palace (☎665 1471), on Ave. 2, between C. 4 and 5, across from the *parque.* Nice, clean, modern rooms with A/C, cable TV, and private bathrooms for those willing to pay more. A much better deal for groups. Singles L522; doubles L580; triples L638. ❹

FOOD

Most chain restaurants are in the center of town. While walking away from the *parque,* especially towards C. 2, there are a number of more authentic, local options. For groceries, visit **Supermercado Rigo,** C. 4, Ave. 2. (☎665 0117. Open M-Sa 7am-7pm, Su 8am-12:30pm.)

Reposteria and Pasteleria, C. 2, Ave. 3 (☎665 2383). Serves buffet-style breakfast and lunch, with plenty of sweets to satisfy snacking urges. Meals L75-95. Desserts L7-25. AmEx/MC/V. ❷

Golosinas Alex (☎665 4447), on Ave. 3 between C. 3 and 4, down a green, tunnel-like hallway. Escape into a small air-conditioned dining room where typical Honduran cuisine is sold at good prices. Meals L20-60. Open M-Sa 7am-9pm, Su 7-12pm. ❶

DAYTRIPS FROM PUERTO CORTES

TRAVESIA

To get to Travesia, take a bus marked Etumesca or Urbano from the empty lot on 4 Ave. C. 5/6 in Puerto Cortes (15min, every hr. 7am-5pm, L8.). A taxi will take about 10min. and cost L80-100.

While only a few kilometers from the busy, industrial Puerto Cortes, the small Garífuna community of Travesia has an entirely different feel from the nearby city. Wood- and grass-covered huts are interspersed with typical Honduran cement houses, most situated along the one main road that runs through town and parallels the beach. Miles of empty beaches stretch in either direction from the *parque central*. The *parque* is on the beach side of town and is marked by colorful gazebos. Every year the **Feria de Travesia** is held in the middle two weekends of June, featuring Garífuna *bailes de punta*, horseback riding, fishing, traditional food, and dancing in the *parque central*. Nightly dancing takes place at Glorieta la 3a Edad, on the far side of the *parque*.

Hotel Fronteras del Caribe ●, located about 1½km outside of town towards Puerto Cortes, is the only place to stay in town. Cozy second-story rooms have fans, cable TV, and private bathrooms (L350 per room up to 3 people). The downstairs restaurant serves breakfast, lunch, and dinner. Look for the sign and long driveway on the beach side of the road. To catch a bus back to town head towards Puerto Cortes (about 100m0, to the fork in the road, where more buses pass by. (☎665 5001. Reception 24hr. Restaurant open 8am-6:30pm. Breakfast L80. Beer L28.)

OMOA

What was intended to be a short stay in Omoa (pop. 2500) can easily extend to a week or more. The massive Fortaleza de San Fernando de Omoa, an 18th-century Spanish fort, is the best-known attraction, but the town is quickly becoming a popular tourist stopover for the epic coastline views. Though lacking in traditional flavor and already rife with expat settlers, Omoa's palm-shaded beaches and clean waters are great places to kick back and go for a swim. If the beach isn't good enough, two spectacular waterfalls are a short walk from the beach.

▐ TRANSPORTATION

Buses headed to the Guatemalan border tend to stop 1km outside of town (at the turnoff on the main road towards the beach). Other buses continue all the way to the dock. Buses run to **Puerto Cortes** (5:45am-5pm, L10), 18km away. Buses also run to **Corinto** and the **Guatemalan border** (51km in the opposite direction). (2½hr., 6am-4pm, L45.) To get to **San Pedro Sula**, you'll need to return to Puerto Cortes.

▐▐ ORIENTATION AND PRACTICAL INFORMATION

It takes a special kind of traveler to get lost in this one-road town. The **street** connects the highway from Puerto Cortes to the beach, snaking by the **Fortaleza de San Fernando** along the way. At the beach, a road lined with restaurants and hotels folllows the curve of the bay. The **town center** sits at the intersection of the highway and the road to the beach.

Bank: Banco Occidente (☎658 9283), to the south at the highway intersection. The 1 bank in town and doesn't have an ATM, but will exchange currency, although the rate is better nearer the border. Open M-F 8:30am-4pm, Sa 8:30am-11:30am.

Pharmacy: Farmacia VI Ana (☎658 9198), across the highway from the bank. Open M-Sa 8am-5pm, Su 8am-12pm.

Internet Access: Internet and Video Club (☎933 0271), along the main road between the Fortaleza and the highway intersection. Internet L20 per hr. Open daily 9am-10pm.

▐ ACCOMMODATIONS

Hotels along the beach tend to be pricier, while *hospedajes* along the main road offer more economical options—that is, if and when they are open.

Roll's Place (☎658 9082), along the main road about 150m from the dock. Operated by a veteran backpacker and situated on lush, shady grounds. Guests get a cheap and comfortable, if somewhat shabby place to stay, with free access to a kitchen, bikes, and a sea kayak. This is also the place to go if you have any questions about the town or about catching buses. Reception 7am-9pm. Laundry 5 lb. for L35, L7 per additional lb. Camping L50; hammocks L60; dorms L80; doubles L250. ❷

Suenos de Mar (☎658 9047; www.suenosdemar.com), to the right facing the dock, to the left when the road forks, and then down to the end of the road. Canadian-owned bed and breakfast with comfortable, well appointed rooms and a pleasant, well furnished lobby. Rooms come with private bathrooms, hot water, cable TV, and A/C. Free Wi-Fi. Singles and doubles L660. Additional person L283 up to 5. AmEx/MC/V. ❹

Flamingo's Hotel (☎658 9199), to the left from the dock along the beach. The most luxurious accommodation in town. Rooms with A/C, cable TV, private bathrooms, hot water, and private terraces. Singles L870; doubles L1044; triples L1770. ❹

▐ FOOD

Cheap *comedors* line the stretch of road extending from the beach towards the highway. Many similar restaurants line the shore, frequently offering American staples, but at prices much higher than eateries more towards the center of town.

Suenos de Mar (☎658 9047; www.suenosdemar.com), at the B&B of the same name. North American fare for breakfast and lunch. French toast and juice L80. Pancakes and juice L60. Bacon, eggs, hashbrowns L100. Tuna salad sandwich L75. Ham and cheese L80. Open daily 8am-5pm. ❷

Champa Johnson (☎658 9328), to the right along the beachside road from the dock. Serves fish (L100-350), as well as hamburgers (L60) in a small, open-air patio. Ham and cheese sandwich L45. Beer L25. Open daily 9am-10pm. ❷

Flamingo's Restaurant (☎658 9199), to the left on the beachside road from the docks. One of Omoa's most established and most upmarket restaurants. Second-floor dining room has a great view of the bay. Flamingo's specialty rice comes with lobster, shrimp, and fish (L275). Chicken L180. Open M-F and Su 10am-9pm, Sa 9am-10pm. ❹

◉ ▲ SIGHTS AND OUTDOOR ACTIVITIES

▓**FORTALEZA DE SAN FERNANDO DE OMOA.** The best-preserved Spanish fort in Honduras, this national monument was built between 1759 and 1775 to protect gold and silver shipments from buccaneers and the British navy. The Brits seized the fort for five months in 1779; some 40 years later, famed pirate Luis Aury controlled it for a brief but glorious period. During the first half of the 20th century, once the foreign threat dissipated, the damp, dark cellars of the Fortaleza were used to hold political prisoners of the Honduran government. In the nearby **museum,** exhibits display swords and rifles from the fort's former pirate aggressors. (☎658 9167. Open M-F 8am-4pm, Sa-Su 9am-5pm. L76. Guide books in English L9.)

WATERFALLS. Both of the nearby waterfalls are located up the dirt road south of the intersection on the highway, and past the Baneo de Occidente and the cemetary. Climbing up to the waterfall is an exhilarating, if dangerous, experience; successful attempts reward climbers with two refreshing swimming holes. The closer of the two falls is a 45 min. hike (4km) from the beach; the second one is about 15min. longer (5½km). Both hikes involve walking up the river a bit, so wear shoes that can get wet. When you reach the river (stick to the right at the first two forks in the bank), walk alongside until the trail end; trek upstream to the right for the farther waterfall and to the left for the closer one. Ask any local for the location of the *chorros* if you get lost or aren't sure of the way.

TELA

An ideal beach town, Tela's compact layout is easy to navigate; its center remains authentically Honduran, and its municipal beach is atypically appealing, set behind a thin grove of palms. East, west, and south of the city are ecological attractions well worth experiencing—Punta Izopo Reserve, Punta Sal, and the Lancetilla Botanical Gardens, a vestige of the United Fruit Company's former dominant hold on the region. Be sure not to miss out on a visit to nearby Garífuna villages, resplendent in a culture distinct from that of greater Honduras. Don't put off your visit—a large luxury resort and golf course under construction near the villages to the west are sure to change the peaceful small communities in the area, not to mention Tela itself.

☞ TRANSPORTATION

Many long distance buses between San Pedro Sula and La Ceiba don't actually enter Tela, but drop riders 1km from town at the Dippsa gas station across from the road into Tela, where taxis await (L20 to the town center).

Buses: Long distance buses leave from Empresa de Transportes LTDA (☎448 2235) on C. Principal, 3 blocks east of the *parque central*. To: **La Ceiba** (2hr., every 25min. 4:10am-6pm, L38) and **El Progreso** (1¾hr., every 25min. 4:30am-6pm, L30), from which they continue to **San Pedro Sula. Terminal Trasul/Tela Express** sends direct buses to **San Pedro Sula** from the corner of 2 Av., 6 C. (1½hr., 8 per day, L75). Local buses leave from the lot on Blvd. Playero to **Triunfo** via **La Enseñada** (1hr., every hr. 6am-6pm, L15) and **Tornabé** via **San Juan** (1hr., every 40min. 6am-6pm, L17). **Hedman Alas** (☎448 0570) buses leave from Hotel Villas Telemar at 6:30am and 12:45pm to: **Antigua** (L1122); **Copan Ruins** (L456); **Guatemala City** (L989); **San Pedro Sula** (L304); **Tegucigalpa** (L456). Other direct buses to **Tegucigalpa** (L241) leave from the terminal on the main highway running between El Progreso and La Ceiba about 150m east of the Dippsa gas station on the north side of the highway. **Transporte Cristina** (☎448 1300) leaves every 3hr. 4:55am-5:30pm; **Kamaldy** (☎448 3056) leaves at 8:55, 10:30am, and 3:30pm.

Taxis: Congregate along the *parque central* and outside of town at the Dippsa station.

Bike Rental: Garífuna Tours, via the Mango hotel. L190 per day, L95 per half-day. See **Practical Information**, p. 265.

✈ 🛈 ORIENTATION AND PRACTICAL INFORMATION

With the sea to the north, the city is divided in two by the Rio Tela; east of the river is **Tela Vieja** and west of the river is **Tela Nueva.** *Calles* run east and west parallel to the beach; *avenidas* run north and south parallel to the river. The street closest to the beach is called **Boulevard Playero,** while two blocks south is **Calle Principal,** which runs along the southern edge of the **parque central.** From the river eastward, the *avenidas* are:: Costa Rica, Nicaragua, Uruguay, Guatemala, Panama, Honduras, Mexico, Cuba, and Colombia. However, since road signs are non-existent, it's easiest to refer to them in terms of their distance from the river. **Avenida Panama** and **Avenida Honduras,** the fifth and sixth *avenidas* east of the river, border the *parque*.

Tourist Office: (☎448 1473), in the Municipal Building on the southeast corner of the *parque*. Info is limited, however, and only Spanish is spoken. Open M-F 8am-4pm. More helpful are the tour companies, where English is spoken. For information about nearby national parks, head to the **PROLANSATE** office (☎448 1686) on the 9th Av. east of the river, 2 blocks south of the C. Principal. It sells maps (L10) and pamphlets (L25) that give details about the preserves. Open M-F 7am-noon and 2-5pm.

Tours: Several companies offer similar tours (L500-675) to nearby nature preserves.

Garífuna Tours (☎448 2904; www.garifunatours.com), on the C. Principal, 1 block west of the *parque*. A great source for info and packages to nearby attractions as well as maps of Tela. 4 day, 3 night package to Roatan, Pura Vida Hotel from L5000 per person. Horseback riding US$29 per hr. Open 7:30am-6:30pm.

Honduras Caribbean Tours (☎448 2623; www.honduras-caribbean.com). Packaged tours to regional attractions identical to those offered by Garífuna Tours, although arrangements are much more negotiable, especially if you want to take several tours. Cayos Cuchinos day trip L1135 per person. Open M-Sa 7:30am-6:30pm, Su 7:30am-1pm.

Banks: Banks with **24hr. ATMs** line the C. Principal. **Banco Occidente,** on the northeast corner of the *parque*, also has a **Western Union.** Open M-F 8:30am-4pm, Sa 8:30am-12pm.

Beyond Tourism: Spanish Language School for students of all abilities runs through Garífuna Tours, with lodging at Mango Hotel. Courses are scheduled for the week. 20hr. basic courses in Spanish US$119, in English US$139; intermediate US$129; advanced US$149. 15hr. courses US$109/124/109/129. 10hr. courses US$89/109/95/109. Lodging: 6 nights US$74-169. For more **Beyond Tourism** opportunities, see p. 34.

Public Toilets: On Blvd. Playero, at the corner with the 8th Av. east of the river and across from the local bus departure lot, L3.

Police: (☎448 2909). Follow the C. Principal east until the 9th Av. from the river, then climb the stairs to the top of the hill. **Tourist Police** (☎448 3535) on Blvd. Playero, at the corner of the 4th Av. east of the river. Free Tela and Honduras maps. Open 24hr.

Pharmacy: Farmacia San Ramon (☎448 1007), on the C. Principal, 1 block east from the *parque*. Open M-F 8am-6pm, Sa 8am-2pm.

Hospital: Centro Médico Tela (☎448 0297), 2 blocks south of the C. Principal on the 7th Av. from the river. Some English-speaking doctors. Open 24hr.

Telephones: Hondutel (☎448 2002), on the 4th Av. east of the river, 2 blocks south of the C. Principal. Fax available. Open daily 7am-8pm.

Internet Access: Fusion Net, on the 2nd Av. from the river, 1 block south of the C. Principal on the far side of the parking lot. L12 per hr. Open daily 8am-7pm.

Post Office: White building on the 4th Av. from the river, 2 blocks south of the C. Principal, next to the Hondutel. Open M-F 8am-4pm, Sa 8-11am. **Postal Code:** 31301.

♠ ACCOMMODATIONS

Tela has many beautiful beachside hotels. Cozy, budget-friendly cabins fill the surrounding villages.

Hotel Marazul (☎448 2313), on Blvd. Playero on the corner of the 4th Av. east of the river. 1 block from the beach. Run by a friendly staff. Rooms with fans and private baths. For the location, the price is right. Reception 5am-10pm. Rooms L100 per person. Cash only. ❷

Hotel Sinai (☎448 1486), on the 6th Av. east of the river, 6 blocks from the beach past the post office. Cozy and tranquil. Singles L150, with bath L250, with bath and A/C L300; doubles L250/300/350. Cash only. ❷

Mango Hotel (☎448 0338), on the corner of the 8th *calle* from the beach and the 6th Av. east of the river. Clean and comfortable rooms near the center of town. Rooms with TVs. Ask about Garífuna tours. Singles L290, with A/C L360; doubles L320/460. AmEx/MC/V. ❸

♠ FOOD

For the cheapest food, head south away from the beach to *comedors* frequented by locals. *Baleadas* will cost around L25. For groceries, visit **Dispensa Familiar** on the C. Principal across from the *parque central*. (Open M-Sa 7am-7pm, Su 7am-6pm. AmEx/MC/V.)

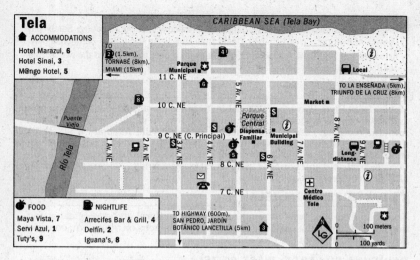

Maya Vista (☎448 1497; www.mayavista.com). Walk east on the C. Principal 3 blocks past the *parque central* until you see the steep flight of stairs ascending the hill. The view alone is reason enough to try this restaurant, even if you can only afford a beer. Food is served elegantly, and in large portions. Baked chicken L115. Vegetarian pasta L105. Lobster L285-425. Cake of the day L35. Beer L25. Tax not included. Open daily 7am-10pm. AmEx/MC/V. ❹

Servi Azul (☎448 0250), 1 block south of the C. Principal on the 5th Av. from the river. Heaping plates of buffet-style breakfast (L50) and lunch (L70), with juice included—and free refills. Choose from typical Honduran cuisine—fish, pork, chicken, beef, rice, beans, and different vegetable salads. Soda L10. Open M-Sa 7am-3pm. Lunch begins service at 9am. Cash only. ❷

Arrecifes Bar and Grill, right on the beach at the end of the 4th Av. east of the river, is the best choice for quality cuisine at affordable prices among the beachside establishments. A good place to go for a meal or a drink, whether a coffee in the morning or a beer at night. Garlic steak L160. Conch soup L120. Hamburger L45. Porkchop platter L100. Beer L20. Coffee L20. Open Tu-Su 8am-3pm. Cash only. ❸

Tuty's (☎448 0013), on the C. Principal just west of the *parque central*. Huge breakfasts (L56; served until 11am), delicious mango *licuados* (L20), and baked treats (L10-15) make this a local favorite. *Tajadas con pollo* (L40) are a tasty, inexpensive lunch. Grilled chicken L45. Open daily 7am-8pm. Cash only. ❷

🅚 NIGHTLIFE

Nightlife in Tela is generally unsafe. The place listed below are worth checking out, but use caution.

🅜 Delfín (☎448 2196), at the Hotel Villas Telemar in Tela Nueva. Walk west on Blvd. Playero across the river for about 1½km (taxi L20). Boogie barefoot to modern Latin pop in a huge gazebo right on the beach. No cover, but drinks cost an arm and a leg. Open F-Sa 9am-3pm. Cash only.

Iguana's Sports Bar, on the 2nd Av. east from the river, 1 block south of the C. Principal. Plays modern hits on a massive dance floor. Balcony and floor seating. Safety pat-downs at the door. Cover L75-100. Drinks from L50. Open Th-Su 8pm-3am. Cash only.

Arrecifes Bar and Grill. A good place to relax with a beer and listen to the waves. Beer L20. Open Tu-Su 8am-3am. Cash only.

BEACHES

Meters from Blvd. Playero, Tela's public beaches are at times devoid of people and often strewn with trash. To the west of Tela Vieja, the beach sits farther from the road and can be a little cleaner. At Hotel Villa Telemar (☎448 2196), the beach is patrolled and well maintained—access is free to patrons of any store or restaurant within the compound. For a fee, visitors also get use of the pool, jacuzzi, and golf course. *(1.5km west of Tela Vieja. ☎ 448 2196. Pool and jacuzzi M-F L100, Sa-Su L150. Golf course L250 per hr.)*

DAYTRIPS FROM TELA

Tela is an excellent base for exploring nearby cultural and ecological attractions. To eliminate the hassle of getting to these places on your own, consider signing up with one of the tour offices in town.

GARÍFUNA VILLAGES: WEST OF TELA

Buses (M-Sa every 40min., Su every hr. 7:40am-5pm; L17) leave for Tornabe from the local bus departure lot at the corner of Blvd. Playero and Av. Cuba, the 8th Av. to the east paralleling the Rio Tela. From there, Miami is a further 7km.

Past the village of San Juan and about 8km from Tela is the seaside village of **Tornabe.** An easy bikeride, the town is also accessible daily by bus. **Victor Hotel ❷**, to the right along the main road through town about 200m from the inlet of the lagoon where the bus stops, has several small rooms right by the beach. (☎9856 4245. Rooms L200).

Another 8km to the west, ▨**Miami** is a small fishing community of thatched houses on a narrow sand peninsula between an inland lagoon and the ocean. Most days, a truck leaves twice per day from the far end of the main road through Tornabe at 6:30am and 1:30pm (L20s), but otherwise the village is difficult to access—part of its appeal. If you want to walk to it, consider following the beach; the roads to Miami move inland, cross through many intersections of converging, unmarked roads, and are overwhelmed by the construction of a major resort in the area (a good reason to get to Miami as soon as you can, before the crowds start to descend). **Raimunda Vallerio ❷** rents small, thatched huts for L100 and cooks breakfast (L40), lunch (L100), and dinner (L40) for guests.

GARÍFUNA VILLAGES: EAST OF TELA

Walk along the beach from Tela to La Ensenada for about 2hr. If alone, it's safer to take a taxi from Tela L100. Buses run to Triunfo via La Ensenada (every hr. 7am-5pm, L15) from the local bus departure lot in Tela.

The smaller of the two villages to the east, **La Ensenada** is easy to reach and has calm waters and a cozy family feel. Locals flock here on weekends and there are restaurants and a couple of small hotels. To get to **Hotel Mirtha ❷**, take a right at the entrance to the village. Guests stay in wooden huts with cold outdoor baths. (☎984 6551. Huts L150; doubles with private baths L250; triples with garage L300). **Hotel Budari ❸**, down the left fork from the city entrance on the left, offers nice doubles with fans and hot baths. Prices are often negotiable. (☎381 0234; perlaandrea2001@yahoo.com. Doubles L450, with A/C L650). The food huts by the beach are mainly open on weekends and serve delicious fresh grilled fish and conch soup for around L120. Dozens of these huts line the fluffy-white beaches, inviting visitors to stay a little longer.

Farther from Tela, **Triunfo de la Cruz** (pop. 10,000) is the second largest Garífuna village in the country. It was here that Cristobal de Olid first landed under orders from Hernan Cortés with the intention of conquering Honduras. Several hotels and rooms are available in town for around L200 a night, and restaurants are easy to find. Though some huts are being replaced by concrete boxes, thatched roofs still populate the beach. The **Playas Miramar Restaurant ❸**, in the west end of town right next to the cemetery, serves delicious and authentic Garífuna seafood in grass-hut seating on the beach. (☎981 3533. Entrees start at L80. Open daily 8am-11pm).

PARQUE NACIONAL JEANETTE KAWAS

By far the easiest way to visit the park is with a guided tour. Honduras Caribbean Tours and Garífuna Tours lead expeditions to Punta Sal (8am-3pm, about L655 including lunch at Garífuna village). Birdwatching tours leave for Laguna de Los Micos and also include a lunch of local cuisine at Miami (same hours and rates). If you are traveling alone and plan on camping in the park, arrange pickup/transfer with one of the tour companies, or hire a boat in Miami (around L200). PROLANSATE can also help you plan your trip.

To the west of Tela, Parque Nacional Jeanette Kawas (formerly called Parque Nacional Punta Sal) supports rare species and diverse ecosystems, from jungles to coral reefs. **Laguna de los Micos** boasts mangrove waterways, an abundance of birds, and, farther west, the white sand beaches of the **Punta Sal Peninsula**. On the west side of the peninsula **Puerto Escondido,** a sheltered cove, provides great snorkeling in a pristine coral reef that is home to many manatees. In the 18th century the famed pirate Captain Morgan used this port, and supposedly his treasure still remains buried somewhere on the sandy shores. For home-cooked meals (L100) on the east side by the beach, head to the tiny, two-family Garífuna village of **Cocalito**. From Cocalito, you can take a steep 0.6km trail to the left to the top of a cliff for panoramic views from the Punta Sal **lighthouse**. A trail to the right of the village leads up to another lookout point and then down a steep wooden stairway to a beach popular with monkeys and Montezuma's Oriole (1-1½hr.). The park's namesake, naturalist Jeanette Kawas, was a strong defender of the preserve.

LA CEIBA

Honduras's third largest city, La Ceiba is known especially for its nightlife—particularly appropriate because a stay in northern Honduras's transportation hub probably shouldn't last longer than a night anyway. Surprising for a city of its size, La Ceiba is for the most part a one street town—or, more precisely, a town of two or three streets running parallel past the central park toward the narrow, nondescript stretch of beach, where most everything the city offers can be found. As a gateway city to the Bay Islands and numerous nearby natural parks such as Pico Bonito and Cuero y Salado Reserve, La Ceiba attracts a multitude of different types of people. If it's not the weekend, though, they're most likely moving on toward bigger and better things.

⬛ TRANSPORTATION

Flights: Aeropuerto Goloson is 6km west of town on the road to Tela. Snag any Tela-bound bus and ask to be let off at the airport (L10). Alternatively, take a taxi from where they line up west of the *parque* (L100). **Islena** and **SOSA** have offices to the east opposite the *parque*. Call ahead to make a reservation.

Islena/Taca (☎441 2390) to: **Grand Caymen** (2hr., Th and Su 6pm, round-trip L9,935); **Roatan** (15 min.; daily 6am, noon, 2:30, 4, 5:30pm; round-trip L1,900); **San Pedro Sula** (25min.; daily 7:40, 10am, 1, 4pm; round-trip L2,580); **Tegucigalpa** (40 min.; M-Sa 7:30am and 2pm, Su 2pm; round-trip L3,120). Taca flies daily to: **San Jose, Belize City, Panama City, Guatemala City, Managua,** and most other major Central American cities. Airport office open daily 6am-7pm; *parque* office open M-F 7am-5pm, Sa 7am-11am.

SOSA (☎443 1399; www.aerolineassosa.com) to: **Bros Laguna** (55min., M and F, L2268); **Guanaja** (26min., daily M-Sa, L1392); **Puerto Lempira** (75min., M-Sa 6am, L2470); **Roatan** (15min.; daily 6:15, 11:15am, 3:30pm; L1056); **San Pedro Sula** (25min.; M-Sa 7:30am and 1:30pm, Su 9:45am; L1392); **Utila** (10min.; M, W, F; L1056). Airport office open M-Sa 5am-5:30pm, Su 6:30am-4:30pm; park office open M-F 7am-5pm, Sa 7am-noon.

Buses: The **station** is about 3km from Av. San Isidro west on Blvd. 15 de Septiembre; accessible by taxi (L20). Buses to: **El Porvenir** (30min., every hr. 6:30am-5pm, L15); **La Union** (1¼hr., every hr. 6:30am-3pm, L17); **Olanchito** (2hr., every 30min. 6:30am-4:30pm, L60); **San Pedro Sula** (4hr., every 1½hr. 6am-5:30pm, L90); **Tegucigalpa** (6½hr., 7 per day 3:30am-3pm, L180); **Tela** (2hr., every 30min. 4:20am-6pm, L40); **Trujillo** (4hr., every hr. 5:30am-4:30pm, L90).

Ferries: Nuevo Muelle de Cabotaje serves as the departure point for boats to the Bay Islands. The harbor is 5km east of La Ceiba and takes 15min. by taxi (L50-100). The **Galaxy II** (☎445 1795) heads daily to **Roatan** (1½hr., daily 9:30am and 1:30pm, L524), landing near **Coxen Hole.** The **Utila Princess** (☎425 3390) heads daily to **Utila** (1hr., daily 9:30am and 1:30pm, L425). With a little luck and lots of patience, you can catch a cheaper, longer ride on a cargo boat or motorized *cayuco*—ask around at the dock.

Taxis: A queue forms on the southwest side of *parque*. Fares around town L20. To the harbor or airport L100. Remember to negotiate (or try).

Car Rental: Union (☎440 0439; www.unionrentacar.com) on Av. San Isidro next to Hotel Iberia. Open M-F 8am-12pm and 1:30-5:30pm, Sa 8am-12pm.

✈ 🔒 ORIENTATION AND PRACTICAL INFORMATION

La Ceiba uses the same old grid system; *avenidas*, (labeled by name as opposed to number) run north-south and *calles* run east-west. Extending from the east side of the *parque* toward the water is **Avenida San Isidro**, the main drag. One block to the east is **Avenida Atlantida**; another block east is **Avenida 14 de Julio**. **Calle 1** runs along the shore. The **cathedral** is opposite the southeast corner of the *parque*. Most nightclubs are along C. 1 east of the Estuary. The **bus station** is 1½km west down **Boulevard 15 de Septiembre** from where it crosses Av. San Isidro, two blocks south of the *parque*. The area between Av. San Isidro and Av. 14 de Julio from C. 1 to 11 is the safest part of town.

Tourist Office: (☎440 3045), 1 block east of the *parque's* northeast corner. Open M-F 8:30am-4pm.

Tours: Garifuna Tours (☎440 3252; www.garifunatours.com), on the corner of C. 1 and Av. San Isidro. Tours to Pico Bonito L655 per person; rafting on Rio Cangrejal L750 per person; trips to Cayos Cochinos L750 per person. Most tours 8am-3pm. Open M-Sa 7:30am-12:30pm and 2-6:30pm. **Jungle River** (☎440 1268; www.jungleriverlodge. com) operates out of the Banana Republic Guesthouse on Av. La Republica. See **Outdoor Activities**, p. 273 for more details.

Budget Travel: Agencia de Viajes Lafitte, Av. San Isidro (☎443 0115), next to Hotel Iberia, 4 blocks south of C. 1. English-speaking travel agents.

Banks: All along both sides of Av. San Isidrio toward the beach. **Banco Credomatic,** Av. San Isidro, by C. 5 and across the street from Hotel Iberia. Cash advances on AmEx/MC/V. Open M-F 8am-12pm and 1:30-7pm, Sa 8am-2pm.

Police: Preventiva (☎441 0995), off Blvd. 15 de Septiembre, next to the bus station. **Tourist Police** (☎441 6288), in the same building. Both open 24hr.

Pharmacy: Farmacia Central (☎443 0075), on Av. San Isidro across from the *parque*. Open M-F 8am-11:30am and 1:30pm-5:30pm, Sa 8am-12pm.

Hospital: Centro Medico Ceiba, C. 8 (☎442 2195), 4 blocks east of the *parque*. 24hr. emergency service.

Internet Access: Video Planet, on Av. Atlantida, 4 blocks south of C. 1. Internet L28 per hr. International calls to US L1 per min. Open M-Sa 8:30am-6pm. **Internet San Isidro,** on Av. San Isidro, next to the Hotel Iberia, offers the same services at the same prices. The **Pizza Hut** across from the *parque* on Av. San Isidro has free Wi-Fi for customers. Open daily 7am-10pm.

Post Office: Av. Morazan, C. 13, in the southwest part of town. EMS Express Mail in the same building. Open M-F 8am-3pm, Sa 8am-noon. **Postal Code:** 31301.

ACCOMMODATIONS

Hotel Amsterdam 2001 (☎443 2311). just off C. 1, 7 blocks east of Av. San Isidro, on Av. Miguel Paz Barahoa. Located close to the beach and to the best nightlife spots, Hotel Amsterdam is the best deal in town. 24hr. reception at the adjacent Dutch Cafe

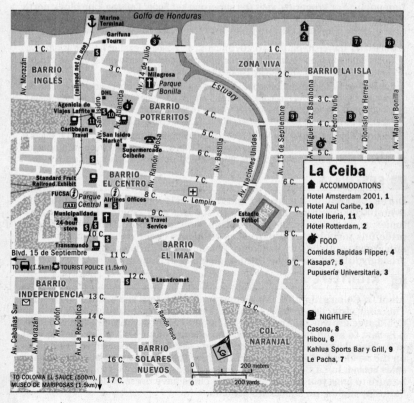

La Ceiba

🏠 **ACCOMMODATIONS**
Hotel Amsterdam 2001, **1**
Hotel Azul Caribe, **10**
Hotel Iberia, **11**
Hotel Rotterdam, **2**

🍎 **FOOD**
Comidas Rapidas Flipper, **4**
Kasapa?, **5**
Pupuseria Universitaria, **3**

🍸 **NIGHTLIFE**
Casona, **8**
Hibou, **6**
Kahlua Sports Bar y Grill, **9**
Le Pacha, **7**

(on the corner of C. 1). Dorms L100; singles and doubles with bath L200; triples L300. Cash only. ❷

Hotel Rotterdam (☎440 0321), next to the Hotel Amsterdam 2001, about 25m from the water. All rooms have private baths and overlook a garden courtyard. Singles and doubles L250; triples L350. Cash only. ❷

Hotel Azul Caribe (☎443 1857), on C. 5 between Av. San Isidro and Av. Atlantida. Large rooms all have private bathrooms. Reception 24hr. Singles and doubles L225; triples and quads with A/C and cable L350. Cash only. ❷

Hotel Iberia (☎443 0401), on Ave. San Isidro, 4 blocks south of C. 1. Hotel Iberia has a few more amenities and a little more comfort than most La Ceiba lodgings. Large rooms have private bath, cable, A/C and free Wi-Fi. Singles L580; doubles L696; triples L696. AmEx/MC/V. ❹

🗇 FOOD

You'll find a bunch of fast food joints in the city center and along Av. San Isidro. Head a few blocks south and east of the *parque* to find cheaper *comedors* and buffets serving *comida típica*. The **San Isidro Market** C. 6, a block east of Av. San Isidro, is one of the biggest markets in Honduras. Here, crowds and produce stalls fill an indoor space and spill out onto the street. (Open M-Sa 7am-7pm, Su 7am-noon.) For groceries, visit the supermarket **Super Ceibeno,** one block north of the *parque* on Av. La Republica, which runs along the *parque's* western edge. (Open M-Sa 7am-7pm, Su 7am-noon.)

Pupuseria Universitaria (☎440 1070), on C. 1, 2 blocks east of Av. San Isidro. Two-room eatery with bamboo paneling and polished wooden ornaments. *Pupusas* L15-80. Tacos L31. Beer L30. Open daily 10am-11pm. Cash only. ❷

Kabasa? on Av. Miguel Paz Barahona, 4 blocks south from C. 1. Specializes in seafood. Eat outdoors under a wooden canopy, or indoors where ocean-themed murals decorate the air-conditioned dining room. T-bone steak platter L65. Fried fish from L89. Panamanian-style octopus L189. Conch soup L159. Beer from L20. Open daily 11am-10pm. AmEx/MC/V. ❸

Comidas Rapidas Flipper (☎440 1796), on Av. Atlantida, 2 blocks south of C. 1. Offers a slightly different menu each day. *Plato económico* L45; stand at a buffet and point at what you want on your plate. All sorts of *comida típica* L60-L80. Open M-Sa 7am-8pm. Cash only. ❷

❄ FESTIVALS

During **Carnaval,** in the second and third weeks of May, La Ceiba fills with over 100,000 visitors. They come to see the wild tangle of parades, costumes, and tributes to the local patron saint, San Isidro. The great *ceibaño* pride fills neighborhood parties as residents cheer on contestants in the numerous youth beauty pageants. When it's not Carnaval time, there's surprisingly little to see in the third largest city in Honduras.

💡 NIGHTLIFE

All of La Ceiba's nightlife is concentrated in the **Zona Viva** section of the city. This zone stretches from C. 1 along the beach before heading south through C. 5. Large crowds on Thursday, Friday, and Saturday nights keep you safe. It is best to avoid the area around the estuary along C. 1, a few blocks east of Av. San Isidro. Most clubs hire private security to keep an eye on things on the weekend. Still, use common sense: **stay alert, take taxis, and leave valuables behind.** In La Ceiba, minors (under 18) aren't allowed in nightspots, so be sure to **bring your ID** with you. Some clubs have dress codes on Thursday-Saturday nights: no shorts, no sandals.

La Casona, 2 blocks east of Av. Miguel Paz Barahona and 3 blocks south of C. 1. Casona is a major club in Ceiba. The local's favorite spot. Cover Th-Sa L150 for men. Open W-Su 9pm-late.

Hibou, to the east on C. 1, past Le Pacha. Another beachside club option. Beer L30. Cover Th-Sa L150 for men.

Kahlua Sports Bar y Grill, on C. 4, just east of the estuary. An alternative option for those looking for something other than discos. *Fútbol* is usually projected on the large screen on the outdoor deck. The Canadian owner sometimes plays big sports games popular in the United States. The upstairs seating area becomes a lounge Th-Sa. Beers from L25; bucket of 6 L125. *Baleada familiar* for 3 or 4 L365. Cover M-Th L60 for men, includes drink. Open Tu-Su 6pm-3am. MC/V.

🔦 OUTDOOR ACTIVITIES

La Ceiba's proximity to nearby national parks and reserves has inspired several local tour companies to offer relatively similar outdoor excursions. Shop around and to find the best activities offered at the best price. All tours include lunch and transportation to and from the location; overnight tours include accommodations.

GARÍFUNA TOURS. This company leads tours to a number of nearby outdoor attractions. At **Pico Bonito National Park** (8:30am-2:30pm, L655 per person), a hike up through the lush jungle leads to expansive views of the Caribbean coast, encounters with butterflies and many different types of birds. The grand finale is the Zacate Waterfall. This company also offers tours of **Cuero y Salado Wildlife Refuge** (7am-3pm, L945 per person), where after taking the old railway from La Union, you can explore the mangrove lagoons where monkeys, alligators, manatees, and tropical birds coexist. **Cayos Cuchinos** (7am-3pm, L750 per person), has snorkeling among 13, sparsely inhabited coral cayes. The tour includes a lunch of Garífuna-style fish. At **Rio Cangrejal** (8:30am-2pm, L750 per person) you can raft through class IV and V rapids through the Pico Bonito tropical forest before hiking the Bejuco trail to a waterfall. (☎ 440 3252; www.garifunatours.com. MC/V.)

JUNGLE RIVER TOURS. Shuttles leave from the Banana Republic Guesthouse on Av. La Republic at 8am and 1pm. Tours head to the company lodge on the banks of the Rio Cangrejal where they have a canopy zipline. From here the company offers rafting and hiking tours. (☎ 440 1268; www.jungleriverlodge.com. MC/V.)

🔦 DAYTRIP FROM LA CEIBA

CUERO Y SALADO RESERVE

Take the direct bus to La Union (every hr. 6:30am-3pm, L17). The park entrance is 9km from La Union. The visitor center has trail maps and a cafeteria (to your right, at the end of the tracks in Saldo Burra). Guides for up to 7 people L150. Boat use L300-450 for up to 7 people, plus mandatory guide. The FUCSA office is to the left of the visitor center. Only 30 people may enter the refuge per day, so call ahead to reserve a spot. For more info, check www.cueroysalado.org. Entrance fee L200, children L100, students L100.

The Cuero y Saladao Wildlife Refuge, 33km west of La Ceiba, is one of the most biologically diverse regions of Honduras. Spilling out into the Caribbean Sea, the 13,225 hectares of freshwater wetlands, saltwater marshes, and coastline protect 350 different species of animals, including jaguars, ocelots, sloths, and boa constrictors. Two hundred species of birds—more than a quarter of all those in Honduras—can also be found here. Topping it off, 10% of all the manatees in the world live in the Refuge.

There are four designated trails through the park; three are aquatic and one is terrestrial. Of the aquatic trails, **El Espejo** is the most easily accessible. It follows the **Estero de Garcia** river that runs south to Rios Termita, Bujaja, and Monos. **El Olingo** breaks off from El Espejo and heads up the Rio Salado to the Rio Limon, and into Rio Cocodrillo (famous for its crocodile sightings) and Marinero. From the coast, **Boca Cerrada,** the longest trail, follows the Rio Cuero through the entire length of the park, starting near the visitor center and going past Barra Rio Cuero to **Lago Boca Cerrada**; the majority of the park's manatees reside in Lago Boca Cerrada. **El Coco** (9km), the park's only land trail, heads east from the visitor center and runs along the coast. For those staying overnight, FUSCA rents four-person **tents** (L200 per night). There are also newly built cabins; bring your own sheets. Camping on the beach is permitted (L35 per night), but bring your own food, water, and bug repellent.

PARQUE NACIONAL PICO BONITO

Pico Bonito National Park, named for the jagged peak looming 7500 ft. overhead, is home to a diverse set of terrain and wildlife. Dirt roads to simple ecolodges and visitors centers penetrate the northern lowlands, but the rest of the park's jungled acres remain in the hands of jaguars, butterflies, white-faced monkeys, and spectacularly colorful species of tropical birds. Similarly undisturbed, sheer cliffs, deep canyons, and mist-enshrouded peaks are absolutely jaw-dropping. Trails through the park can be accessed from: the **Zacate River entrance** (just past the El Pino Community, 19km from La Ceiba on the Highway west to Tela), the **Rio Cangrejal** area (specifically at the El Bejuco trail entrance 8.8km east of La Ceiba), and at the **El Naranjo** (10km east) and **Las Mangas** (12km east) communities.

EL PINO COMMUNITY (ZACATE RIVER ENTRANCE)

TRANSPORTATION. Take any **bus** from La Ceiba headed for **Tela** (6am-6pm, L20). Tell the driver you wish to get off at the **Rio Zacate;** the park entrance is 1km after passing a pineapple plantation. El Pino is a few kilometers to the east. Alternatively, arrange your trip with a tour operator out of La Ceiba.

ACCOMMODATIONS. The town of El Pino has simpler, budget accommodations. The **Natural View Eco Lodge** has cabins and allows camping. The **Good Shepard** provides breakfast with its simple singles and doubles. **The Lodge at Pico Bonito** ➏ is Honduras's first true eco lodge, located up a 1½km driveway from the highway entrance sign. The mountain resort sits on lush, spectacular land between two rivers and offers guests access to numerous walking trails in secluded forests. Guided walks and excursions are offered, including a 5hr. trek to Unbelievable Falls (L580 per person) and a daytrip to see the endangered Emerald Humming bird in a secluded area of the park (L580). Access to the hotel is also granted to non-guests for a fee (L586, includes entrance to hotel's on-site serpentarium and butterfly farm, lunch, and a walk; L782 per person for dinner.) Cabins come with a fan, private veranda with hammock, private bath, and kitchen with organic coffee. Cabins L4255 (US$220) per night for up to 2, add L775 for third; with A/C L5125 (US$265). (☎440 0388. AmEx/MC/V.)

SIGHTS. The **El Zacate Waterfall Trail** (2½hr., 2½km) is located immediately following the Quebrada Seca Bridge. Follow the road to the left toward the mountains. The trail wanders along the clear, crisp waters of the Zacate Giver, passing multiple enticing swimming spots before reaching the 30m high waterfall. Keel-billed toucans are a common sight along the trail. Up the path on the west bank of the Coloradito River, heading out of the El Pino community, is the **Coloradito Riverwalk** (4hr., 4km). After an hour of walking by plantations, pasteurs, and cocoa fields, the path peels off to Pile Welles, a pleasant swimming hole on the Coloradito river. On the grounds of the Lodge at Pico Bonito, the **Butterfly Farm and Serpentarium** contains over 20 species of butterflies; the dozen species of reptiles here rival the colors of the winged insects. (☎440 0388. Entrance to both L100, children L60. Open Tu-Su 8am-4pm. English spoken.)

TRUJILLO

A healthy lack of billboards, national international chainstores, and traffic make Trujillo a great change of pace from other northern Honduras cities. The old cobbled streets of Trujillo give the town a colonial feel. The town is spread out along the steep hillside, skirting the curved coastline of the Bay of Trujillo. To the east are the alluring wilds of the Moskitia, and to the south is El Olancho.

▐ TRANSPORTATION

Flights: The airstrip, 1½km from the town's center, down C. Río Negro, is rarely used. **SOSA** (☎440 0692 or 441 2513; www.aerolineassosa.com) planes arrive 2 times per week to drop off passengers. Planes only pick up passengers if there are more than 3. A call must be made to **La Ceiba** (SOSA office at La Ceiba airport ☎443 1399) ahead of time.

Buses: Buses leave from the bus terminal next to the Texaco gas station. The station is a 15min. walk or L20 taxi ride east and downhill from the *parque*, on C. Río Negro, 1km along the main road out of town. To get to **La Unión**, take a bus to **Saba.** Buses to **Santa Fé** leave in front of the old cemetery on C. de Mercado (1hr.; 9, 10:45am, noon, 3pm, returns 6:30, 11am; L12). **Puerto Castilla** buses depart from the empty lot on C. Río Negro at the bottom of the hill, headed away from the park (30min., every 2hr. 7:30am-6pm, L14). **Cotraipbal** (☎434 4932) to: **Tocoa** (45min., every 30 min. 1am-2:15pm, L40); **Saba** (1¼hr., every 45min. 1am-2:15pm, L60); **La Ceiba** (3hr., every 45min. 1:15am-2:15pm, L100); **Tela** (4½hr., every hr. 1am-2:15pm, L120); **El Progreso** (5½hr., every 45min. 1am-2:15pm, L165); **San Pedro Sula** (6hr., every 45min. 1:15am-2:15pm, L165); **Tegucigalpa** (9hr., 12:30am and 2am, L280). To get to **La Moskitia** take a bus to Tocoa, and then catch a ride with one of the 4WD trucks that line up next to the bus station to **Palacios** (daily, 9am, L500).

Boats: Ocean Tours (☎3285 2118), based on Guanaja runs boats to and from the island. Ask at the municipal docks, a block north off C. Rio Negro, for information. (Donald Thompson, boat manager, ☎9949 9737; departs Th and Su noon to Guanaja, Tu and F noon from Guanaja, L720). Boats occassionally travel to the **Bay Islands, Palacios, Everta Lempira,** and other places in **La Moskitia** at irregular times and frequently take passengers.

Taxis: Queue at the southeast corner of the *parque.* Any point with in the city, including the bus station and airport L20. To FUCAGUA office L30. At night, prices jump to L30-L50. Taxis are recommended for anyone going to or from the bus station at night. Arrange for a taxi to pick you up in advance for L100.

▐▐ ▐ ORIENTATION AND PRACTICAL INFORMATION

Trujillo's main street, **Calle Conventillo,** parallels the beach, one block south of the **parque central.** One block to the south of the *parque* is the **mercado central**—most every service offered in town is located around these two areas. All streets in Trujillo are *calles* and are marked by wooden signs at major intersections. The beaches in **Barrio Cristales,** to the west of the *parque central* and downhill, are excellent and rarely crowded, but best avoided at night. **Calle Rio Negro** leaves Trujillo to the southeast of the *parque* curving downhill past the docks, crosses a small bridge, and becomes the main road out of town, passing the airport and bus station.

Tourist Information: Tourism Office (☎434 3120), east of the *parque central,* in the same building as the Fortaleza admissions office. No English spoken. Open M-F 9am-4pm. **FUCAGUA** (☎434 4294). Sells maps (L30) of nearby national parks and can help arrange a guide, from their office 2km southeast on the main road out of Trujillo, past the bus station in a small green building. Open M-F 8am-4pm.

Banks: Both banks cash traveler's checks. **Banco de Occidente,** C. Conventillo, C. Cafe Colon (☎434 4990) has a Western Union. Open M-F 8:30am-4:30pm, Sa 8:30am-noon. **Banco Atlántida** (☎434 4830), on the park's northwest corner. Cash advances and a **24hr. ATM.** Open M-F 9am-4pm, Sa 8:30-11:30am.

Laundry: Lavandería Colón (☎988 4433), west on C. Conventillo heading toward Barrio Cristales, 1½ blocks from Banco Occidente. Minimum L75 per load, L15 per lb. Open M-Sa 8am-5pm.

Police: Preventiva (☎434 4038), in the northwest corner of the *parque.* Open 24hr.

Hospital: Dr. Salvador Paredes Hospital (☎434 4093), 1 block east of the *parque* on C. Río Negro. English-speaking doctor on-call. Open 24hr.

Pharmacies: Elizabeth Farmacia (☎434 4124), on C. Rio Negro, half a block east of the hospital. Open M-F 8am-5:30pm, Sa 9am-1pm.

Telephones: Hondutel, beside the post office, 1 block behind the cathedral on C. Señorita Aguilar. International and collect calls. Calls to the US L3 per min. Calls within Honduras L2.50 per min. Open M-F 7am-5pm, Sa 7am-noon.

Internet: Cyber Net Cafe (☎9999 4731). Internet L20 per hr. Calls to US L3 per min. Open daily 8am-10pm.

Post Office: (☎434 4543). Open M-Sa 8am-midnight and 1-4pm. **Post Code:** 32101.

ACCOMMODATIONS

Trujillo only has a couple hotels, and they happen to be spread around town. It's a good idea to have a sense of which one you're headed to before arriving in town.

Villa Brinkley (☎434 4444), built like a colonial stone manor 1km from the center, up the steep hill from the southeast corner of the market, toward PN Capiro y Calentura. Boasts an unforgettable view of the entire Bay of Trujillo all the way out to Punta Caxinas. With 2 swimming pools, a sauna, and a turtle-inhabited courtyard, this is the best place in town. Rooms have hot baths and hand-carved mahogany headboards. Doubles with balconies. Breakfast L75, open to non-guests and includes unlimited fresh-squeezed orange juice, coffee, toast, and an awesome view. Rooms L350-563. Cash only. ❸

Hotel Plaza Central (☎434 3006), on C. Mercado next to the market and across from the Emperador. Small, well-kept rooms with cable TV, fans, and private baths in a cement courtyard. Negotiate deals for longer stays. Doubles L250, with A/C L350. Cash only. ❷

Hotel Emperador (☎434 4446), on C. Mercado next to the market. A well-kept and colorful hotel offering clean rooms with cold baths, fans, TVs, and low ceilings. The owner, a professor, can share useful info about the area. Singles and doubles L200. Open 24hr. Cash only. ❷

FOOD

The eateries in town are unexciting, but a plethora of bars and restaurants with seafood and Gantuna specials line the beach all along Barrio Cristales. For groceries, head to **Supermercado Popular** at the southwest corner of the *parque* on C. Cafe Colon (☎434 4458. Open M-Sa 7:30am-6pm, Su 8am-noon.).

Restaurante Playa Dorado (☎434 3121), on the beach, west of the municipal dock. Offers pancakes for breakfast (L70 with honey, coffee, and orange juice). Simple cuisine (chicken sandwich L50), and specialty entrees (filet mignon L120; garlic shrimp L165). Open daily 8am-10pm. Cash only. ❷

Perla del Caribe (☎434 4486), on the beach east of Restaurante Cocopando. Another option for a beachside meal, with a more extensive menu. Fish fillet L145-160. Hamburger with fries L60. Chicken tortilla dishes L80. Lobster L313. Fried fish L67-168. Beer L25. Open daily 9am-8pm. Cash only. ❸

Restaurante Cocopando (☎434 4748), on the beach across from the Hotel. Offers clients the opportunity to eat breakfast, lunch, and dinner while watching the waves. *Desayuno típico* with plaintain chips or bread L50. Lunch L60-130. Steak L70. Pork chops L80. Fried fish L90-250. *Sopa marinera* L220. Beer L17. Open daily 8am-9pm. Cash only. ❷

👁 SIGHTS

LA FORTALEZA DE SANTA BÁRBARA. This fort was built in 1575 to defend the town from pirate attacks, a duty it fulfilled with only modest success. The fort's faded ramparts looking out on the glistening bay, are one of the most serene spots in Honduras. *(Just east of the parque. Open daily 9am-noon and 1-5pm. Foreigners L57, citizens with student ID L10.)*

CEMENTERIO VIEJO. Here lies William Walker. After unsuccessfully trying to impose plantation slavery on Central America, Walker was executed in 1860. The gate is usually locked, but the cemetery is always open and locals tend to

Trujillo

🏨 ACCOMMODATIONS
Hotel Emperador, **10**
Hotel Plaza Central, **4**
Villa Brinkley, **11**

🍴 FOOD
Cocopando Restaurant, **1**
Perla del Caribe, **3**
Playa Dorada, **5**

🎵 NIGHTLIFE
El Black, **2**
Playa Dorada, **6**
Truxillio, **8**

just climb the walls. *(Near El Museo Riveras del Peregal. Walk down the main street with the sea to your right and turn left at Hotel Mar de Plata.)*

GARÍFUNA ART STORE. Downstairs, GaríArte sells beautiful, authentic Garífuna works of art, while upstairs is a small exhibit on Garífuna. *(In Barrio Cristales next to the Hotel Cocopando. ☎ 444 4365. Open daily 8am-noon and 2:30-6pm.)*

🎵 NIGHTLIFE

The Garífuna know how to do party. This is especially true during the last full week of June, when Trujillo has its annual festival. Each *barrio* holds a block party with huge speakers, contests, beer, and dancing. The last night culminates in a huge party with the biggest bands in Honduras coming to play. Barrio Cristales throbs until dawn, with beachfront bar patrons spilling out onto the sand—usually face-first. Beers are an unbelievably cheap (L15-L20), and bars often break out in *punta* and Garífuna dance performances.

> **El Truxillo,** up C. Conventillo, at the top of the hill, next to Hotel Mar de Plata; look for the giant beer bottle. Currently the hottest disco around, with TVs, black lights, good security, and a large dance floor. Beer L25. Cover L50. Open Th-Su 8pm-5am.

> **Arenas Discotec** (☎ 434 2776), on the beach east of Cocopando and Perla del Caribe. A relaxed place to have a beer during the day near the water. Big crowds on weekend nights. Pool tables. Meals L50. Beer L25. Open M-W and Su 10am-midnight, Th-Sa 10am-2am. Cash only.

> **El Black** (a.k.a. "Disco Black and White"), in front of the Hotel Cocopando. Partiers usually shuffle up to the 2nd floor terrace for some cool air when the dance floor gets hot. Beer L17. Almost never has a cover. Open F-Su 9pm-4am.

🏔 OUTDOOR ACTIVITIES

For info on the nearby parks and lagoons, stop by the **FUCAGUA office** a small green building 2km southeast of town on the main road out of Trujillo, past the bus terminal. (☎ 434 4294. Open M-F 8am-4pm.)

PARQUE NACIONAL CAPIRO Y CALENTURA. Named for the towering peaks Cerro Capiro (eastern) and Cerro Calentura (western), this park covers the forested slopes behind Trujillo. The best time to go is around 4am, when animals are most likely to appear. Even if you can't pull yourself out of bed, the view from the top in the afternoon is still worth the effort. On clear days you can see Roatán. To reach the summit, walk (3-4hrs.) or take a 4WD taxi up the hill. The entrance is 1km uphill past Villa Brinkley Hotel. It's a 9km hike to the top. Although guides are not necessary, FUCAGUA can arrange for one (L150) with a day's notice.

PARQUE NACIONAL LAGUNA GUAIMORETO. A park centered around a lagoon northeast of Trujillo, Parque National Laguna Guaimoreto is an excellent place to birdwatch and spot the occasional crocodile. It is best visited very early in the morning or late afternoon via a guided boat tour. Make arrangements a day in advance through the FUCAGUA office for a guide. Alternatively, call Natarin, who takes people on his boat for a tour of the laguna. (☎ 9580 6130, Spanish only. Boat tour L1300; 12 people maximum.)

CABO DE HONDURAS This beach has excellent, uncrowded beaches. Take a bus from the lot on C. Rio Negro a block from the Municipal Dock. (30min. every 2hr. 7am-5pm, L14).

⬛ DAYTRIP FROM TRUJILLO

SANTA FE

Buses from Trujillo from in front of the old cemetery on C. de Mercado (1hr., 4 per day 9am-3pm, L18).

A 9km trek west along the beach or a 1hr. bus ride through the *campo* ends at the beautiful and friendly Garífuna community, with picture-perfect beaches, excellent food, and great hotels. Santa Fé celebrates the *Virgen del Carmen* with three weeks of festivities beginning in July. Sports tournaments and a range of dramatic and celebratory dances occur during the first weekend.

BAY ISLANDS

Though the silky white-sand beaches and world-class diving off the Bay Islands are Honduras' biggest tourist attraction, the islands feel less commercialized than many other Caribbean destinations. Dive prices and certifications are among the cheapest in the world and jungle coastline still outnumbers beachfront estates. Bay Island reef diversity is unmatched, so if you don't want to bother with scuba certification, snorkeling in the crystal clear water is almost as fun. Utila, just 32km by boat from La Ceiba, is the most budget-friendly island and is famous for sightings of the rare whale shark, the biggest fish in the sea. Roatán is the most developed of the islands with gorgeous beaches and phenomenal snorkeling. Once ravaged by Hurrican Mitch, Guanaja is now a sparsely populated island, perfect for private romantic getaways. Cayos Cochinos, with their beautiful tropical vegetation, are a miniature version of the main islands.

UTILA

Local legend has it that the real-life Robinson Crusoe spent a lot of time in Utila in the 17th century. Today, travelers have an easier time finding boats to the mainland, but still find it hard to leave behind the excellent seafood, nightly beach parties, and the best budget diving on the planet. Locals joke about how the most frequent lie heard in Utila is, "I'm leaving tomorrow."

⌐ TRANSPORTATION

Flights: Morgan's Travel (☎425 3161), at the foot of the main dock, is the best place to buy plane tickets. Open M-Sa 8am-noon and 2:30-5:30pm. **Isleña** (☎425 3364) has an office across from the fire station west of the dock. Open M-F 8:30am-4pm. **SOSA** (☎425 3166) flies to **La Ceiba** (15min.; M-Sa 6am and 3:30pm, Su 3:30pm).

Ferries: Utila Princess (☎425 3390; open 8am-4:30pm), across from Morgan's Travel, runs to **La Ceiba** (1hr., 6:30am and 2:30pm, L400). **San Ramon Express** (☎425 3979) also runs a small boat to La Ceiba from the dock at the Mariposa Cafe, 50m to the east from the Municipal Dock (daily 7am, L350). Note that the immigration officer on the Main Dock must look at your passport before he will let you leave. **Captain Vern** (vfine@hotmail.com) runs a Catamaran most days from Utila to **Roatan** (4hr., daily 7am, L1060), leaving either from Driftwood Cafe's dock to the west, or the UDC dock to the east. Reserve in advance.

Taxis: (☎425 3311).

Rentals: Rental Roney (☎425 3931) to the west from the dock just past the Methodist church. Bicycles L100 per day. Motorscooters L575 per day. Motorcycles from L675 per day. ATVs L1155 per day.

◄▮ ⚡ ORIENTATION AND PRACTICAL INFORMATION

Utila Town clings to the **East Harbour** on the south side of the island. **Main Street** runs from the decommissioned airstrip on the eastern lip of the harbor and hugs the bay until it reaches **Crepes Beach** on the western tip of the bay. Ferries land at the **Municipal Dock** which is directly in the middle of main street. **Cola de Mico Road** leads inland from the dock to **Pumpkin Hill** and the **airport**. Most services on the island take US dollars but also accept lempiras.

Tourist Information: (www.aboututila.com). Most dive shops offer free maps of the island; the one at Alton's (p. 283) is particularly good. Many dive shop representatives meet new arrivals from the incoming ferries with maps and information; these locals are also helpful for answering other questions.

Banks and Financial Services: BGA (☎425 3257), the first building up from the dock on the eastern side of the main road, exchanges travelers' Visa checks and does cash advances. Open M-F 8:30am-3:30pm, Sa 8:30-11:30am. **Banco Atlántida** (☎425 3374), to the east from the dock. Open M-F 9am-4pm, Sa 8:30-11:30am. **Bush's Supermarket** (☎425 3147), three buildings east of Banco Atlántida, exchange traveler's checks and does currency exchange. **Reef Cinema,** further to the east, gives cash advances on AmEx/MC/V (with a 6% commission).

Laundry: Alice Laundry (☎425 3785), next to Caye Caulker. L65-90 per bag, depending on size. Open daily 7am-8pm. **Tropical Hotel,** to the west from the dock, charges L80 per load. Open 8am-9pm.

Bookstore: Funky Town Library, underneath the Reef Cinema. Sells books and rents them for L20 per week (L200 deposit). Also rents DVDs for L40 per day (L500 deposit). Special deals on Tu and F. Open M-F 9am-7:30pm.

Police: (☎425 3255), upstairs from the post office, by the Municipal Dock, in the municipal office. Open M-F 9am-noon and 2-5pm. For after-hour emergencies, call **Preventiva** (☎425 3145), next to the football field, up Mamey Lane. Open 24hr.

Medical Services: Community Medical Clinic (☎425 3137), to the west of the dock, across from the Methodist church. Open M-F 8am-3pm. **Medical Store Utila** (☎425 3154), next to Banco Atlántida. Open M-Sa 8am-8pm.

Pharmacy: Utila Pharmacy (☎425 3632), to the west from the dock. Open M-Sa 8am-noon and 2pm-7pm.

Telephones and Internet: Caye Caulker, across from Reef Cinema. Internet L40 per hr. Calls to the US L3 per min. Open daily 8am-8pm. **Mermaid's Fast Food** offers free Wi-Fi to customers.

Post Office: Beneath the municipal building, on the dock, marked by a yellow headboard. Open M-F 9am-noon and 2-5pm, Sa 9-11:30am. **Postal code: 34201.**

ACCOMMODATIONS

From the dock, lodging is available down all three roads. To the east after Cooper's Inn, all accommodations tend to be reserved for divers or for those looking to stay longer. Reservations are necessary during the high season (July-Sept. and Dec.-Apr.). Most dive centers include or discount lodging as part of diving deals.

Rubi's (☎425 3240), east of the main dock next to Reef Cinema. Cozy rooms with hot baths. Large coral courtyard. Communal kitchen and free Wi-Fi. Singles L345; doubles L480, with A/C L770. Cash only. ❹

Cooper's Inn (☎425 3184), east of the dock just past Zanzibar Cafe, and after Rubi's. A friendly spot with good-sized rooms. All rooms equipped with fans, a common room, a communal kitchen, and shared cold bath. Singles L200; doubles L250; apartments from L7,700 per month. Cash only. ❷

Mango Hotel (☎425 3335), up Cola de Mico Rd., at the 2nd intersection. Beautiful resort-style rooms with wooden floors. Amenities include cable TV, hot baths, and phones. Pool and sauna on site. Shared 3- to 4- person rooms are the real steal. Reception 6am-8pm. Shared rooms L200. Doubles L975, with A/C 1075. Cash only. ❸

Backpacker's Lodge (☎425 3350), across from Gunter's Dive Shop (p. 283), west of the dock, past the fire station. Clean private rooms with a double bed and shared cold bath, just minutes from Chepe's beach. Check in at Gunter's Dive shop. Dorms L50; private rooms L190. Cash only. ❶

▸ FOOD

Heaping fruit salads and vegetarian entrees are refreshingly common among the assortment of local, European, and North American menu choices here in Utila. To cook your own food, purchase groceries at **Bush's Supermarket** (☎425 3147), a few houses east of the Banco Atlántida. (Open M-Sa 6:30am-7pm, Su 6:30am-10:30am.)

Ultra Light (☎425 3514), to the west from the dock, past the Methodist church. Get your Middle Eastern fix here with authentic Israeli food. Stuffed breakfast pitas L75-85. *Shakshurka* (tomatoes, onions, pepper, eggs, zalabia, with 2 salads) L140. Hummus L95. Falafel L95. Chicken curry L140. Open Su-F 7am-10pm. Cash only. ❸

Driftwood Cafe (☎408 5168), to the west of the dock, past Gunther's Dive Shop. Texas-style cuisine (meat, in large portions) on a shaded dock. Half-pound cheeseburger L130. BBQ Pork Ribs L195. Beer from L25. Cash only. ❹

Bundu Café, east of the dock, across from Banco Atlántida. A cozy place to lounge, with expansive open-air seating mercifully sheltered from the rains of the Monsoon season. Large book exchange. Backpacker breakfast L40. Super *baleadas* L50. Deep dish veggie pizza L158. Occasional all-you-can-eat M nights. Open M-Tu, Th, Sa-Su 9am-9:30pm. Cash only. ❷

▸ NIGHTLIFE AND ENTERTAINMENT

Utila seems to always find an excuse to party; locals celebrate the rising of the sun and moon. The annual Sun Jam (www.sunjamutila.com), typically held the first Saturday in August, draws a crowd second only to La Ceiba's carnaval (p. 272).

Coco Loco's, a thatched-roof bar on its own pier, to the west from the dock. A good place to start out the evening. Dip your feet in the ocean through the jacuzzi-like hole in the pier, laze in a hammock overlooking all the action, or dance to an eclectic mix of music. Beer L25. Happy hour 4-7pm. Open daily 4pm-midnight and later on weekends.

Tranquilo Bar, on the pier next to Coco Loco's. A relaxed scene (as the name implies). Beer L25. Open daily 3pm-midnight.

Bar in the Bush, at the 3rd intersection up Cola de Mico Rd. Popular for cheap drinks and late-night volleyball. W Techno Night draws a lot of expats; F reggaeton and hip-hop brings out more locals. Beer L25. Open W and F 9pm-3am.

▸ GUIDED TOURS

A number of agencies lead tours to attractions in the area around Utila.

Utila Tours. Behind Munchie's. Tours to water caye (L400) and the freshwater caves (L250). Open M-Sa 6:30am-9:30pm, Su 6:30am-1:30pm.

BAY ISLANDS

Bay Islands Conservation Association. A unique, historically apocryphal tour of the life of Daniel Defoe's Robinson Crusoe. Open M-F 9am-noon and 2-4pm.

Whale Shark Oceanic Research Center, to the west from the docks. Snorkling trips with whale sharks M, W, F 12:30-5:30pm. L1135 per person. Center open M-F and Su 9am-noon and 2-5pm.

Iguana Station. Walk up Mammy Ln. and turn left at the first intersection, just before Stuart's Hill. Offers tours to local bat caves (L150). Also houses a visitor's center with exhibits about Utila's iguana, known commonly as "swamper." Open M, W, F 2-5pm.

⚠ OUTDOOR ACTIVITIES

Divers come from around the world for a chance to spot the biggest fish in these seas: the bespeckled **Whale Shark,** which is frequently seen on Utila's north side during morning trips. The Whale Shark high season lasts from the end of February to the end of June. The south side has fewer big fish but compensates with greater coral diversity and unbelievable wall drops. In fact, some of the best diving can be found right outside the harbor on the east side, where eagle rays flap past in huge numbers. Divers also enjoy the open hull and pilot house of the submerged **Haliburton ship** (40m down). A little farther east, Utila's most popular dive site, **Black Hills,** is an underwater mountain that houses turtles, big schools of fish, and barracuda.

Because of steep competition among the various dive shops on the island, prices have been standardized for all open water activities. **Snorkel** equipment rental costs L95 per day for non-divers; **kayak** rentals cost L190 per day for non-divers. Both are free for those signed up for diving courses or other dives. A ride on a boat to various snorkel spots around the island costs L190. Receiving your **PADI certification** requires 3-4 days to complete the Open Water Divers course, costs L5000, and always includes at least two free fun dives after certification. If you want to try **scuba diving,** take a half-day Discover Scuba Diving class (L1500), which can count towards your certification if you decide to continue. To become a Dive Master requires a one-month internship (for more information visit www.padi.com) and costs L14,450 (US$750); on Utila, all dive shops offer the added perk of free dives for life if you train with them. Fun dives cost L1,060, although with groups of eight people or more the price drops to around L480 per dive. Shops open daily 7am-6pm and accept AmEx/MC/V.

Captain Morgan's (☎425 3349; www.divingutila.com), directly across from the Municipal Dock. Captain Morgan's is the only dive shop based on the cayes to the southwest of Utila. If you take a course with them, you stay at their lodge on the islands and have greater access to less touristed dive sites on the north side of the island. For divers, transfer to the cayes is always free, but for those wishing to stay at the lodge without diving, each ride costs L100 per person.

Utila Dive Center (UDC), halfway to the airport beach, east of the dock that is next to Seven Seas. The most heavily publicized and one of the most popular dive shops on the island. Dive masters teach in 9 languages. The shop is also has a bar.

Alton's Dive Shop (☎425 3108; www.divealtons.com), to the east near UDC. One of the most popular dive shops on the island, featuring a very young, social crew and nightly parties during high season. Fast boats make daily trips to the north side (weather permitting). Underwater camera rentals, a water polo net, and waterfront accommodation included with courses.

Gunter's Dive Shop (☎425 3350), west from the dock near Crepe's beach. The oldest shop on the island. With a maximum class size of 4, Gunter's focuses on quality and personal attention. Daily north side trips (weather permitting). Divers are hosted in the Backpacker Lodge (p. 282).

Cross Creek Dive Center (☎425 3326), across the street from UDC. Canal-side rooms with private showers.

ROATÁN

Roatan is Honduras's contribution to the Caribbean tropical paradise circuit, a destination at present still closer to "recently discovered" than "saturated" on the timeline of inevitable tourism decay. On the south side of the island are the ferry and cruise ship docks, the airport, and the small, bustling capital town, Coxen Hole. To the east past French Harbor, the terrain turns to green, rolling ridges offering expansive views across the island. Only a few exclusive resorts have opened and the villages remain largely untouched by tourism. The vast majority of the resorts, like to the west. The resort-village West Bay and the ex-pat rich West End also lie to the west; these are the only places on the island for budget travelers. Sandy Bay, on the highway between Coxen Hole and the West End, is near ecological foundations and parks, and sits on a sparsely utilized beach..

⊑ TRANSPORTATION

Flights: Manuel Galvez International Airport (☎445 1880), 1½km east of Coxen Hole, is accessible by taxi and microbus. **Isleña** (☎445 1559; www.flyislena.com; open daily 5:30am-6pm) flies to: **La Ceiba** (15min.; 6:50, 9am, 1, 3pm; L1000); **San Pedro Sula** (40min.; 6:50, 9am, 1pm; L1385); **Tegucigalpa** (55min., 6:50am and 1pm, L1560). **Taca** (☎445 1918; www.taca.com) partners with Isleña to provide international service to: **Houston** (Sa 11am); **Miami** (Su 8:45am); and **San Salvador** (Su 3:30pm). **SOSA** (☎445 1154; www.aerolineassosa.com; open daily 5:30am-5pm) flies to: **La Ceiba** (15min.; 6:30, 9am, 2:30, 4pm; L1060); **San Pedro Sula** (40min.; 7, 9am, noon; L1350); and **Tegucigalpa** (45min., 7am and noon, L1560).

Ferries: The Galaxy II Ferry (☎445 1795), leaves from their dock east of Coxen Hole daily for La Ceiba (1½hr., 7am and 2pm, L500).

Car Rentals: A&G Rent a Car (☎445 0423), **Budget** (☎445 2290), **Best Car Rental** (☎445 1494), and **Caribbean Rent a Car** (☎445 6950) all have offices inside the airport.

Local Transportation: Microbuses run daily, every 15min. 6am-6pm. **Coxen Hole** to **West End** (L20); Coxen Hole to **Sandy Bay** (L13). Another set of microbuses run daily, every 2 hr. 6am-6pm. **Oak Ridge** to **French Harbor** (L20). Oak Ridge to **Coxen Hole** (L30). Oak Ridge to the **West End** (L40). Before the 2pm ferry, some microbuses run all the way to the **ferry** (L40).

Car Rental: Roatán Rentals (☎445 1171; www.roatansalesandrentals.com), across the street from Cannibal Cafe, south of the intersection on the main drag. Most rentals L1185-1885 per day. Open M-Sa 7:30am-6pm. AmEx/MC/V. **Best Car Rental** (☎445 4322), on the corner of the main intersection. The Beach House Information Office has various vehicles for L960-1250 per day.

Bike and Motorcycle Rental: Captain Van's (☎445 4076), south of the main intersection, just before Cannibal Cafe ,on the main road toward West Bay. Bikes L175 per day, L690 per week; scooters L750/3560; motorcycles L865/3850. All come with free treasure map and 10-point safety orientation. Open daily 9am-4pm. AmEx/MC/V.

Taxis: **English Speaking Taxi Drivers** (☎445 7478). **Colectivo taxis** between Coxen Hole and the West End, or French Harbor, should cost no more than L40. Hiring a taxi will cost L200.

⚡ ORIENTATION

The **Manuel Galvez International Airport** is just to the east of Island capital **Coxen Hole;** Galaxy ferries and Carnival cruises arrive just east of the airport at **Dixon Cove,** while Royal Caribbean cruises arrive just west of Coxen Hole. The main highway passed **Sandy Bay** (6km) to the north; it then moves west to **West End** (11km) where you'll find the most tourist facilities, housing options, and dive shops. Roatán's best beach, **West Bay** (15km), is 2km south of the West End and features more expensive beachfront resorts and restaurants.

COXEN HOLE

Once a sleepy fishing village, Coxen Hole has been transformed in recents years, like much of the western half of the island, with the sudden influx of tourism dollars. These changes have manifested themselves equally in the construction of tourist villages like the West End, and in the traffic, noise, and confusion that now fill the small city. Coxen Hole does see its fair share of tourists, most of whom immediately move on to greener pastures and bluer waters.

⚡ ⟐ ORIENTATION AND PRACTICAL INFORMATION

From the cruiseship dock **Main Street** runs eastward along the coastline until it's junction with **Thicket Mouthe Road** (which marks the edge of the town center). Further on, the Main St. runs around a bend until it meets **Back Market Road.** Main St. continues east towards the airport where it meets the main Highway heading toward French Harbor and the ferry dock. Back Market Rd. runs around the north side of the town center, and swings around to form a

BAY ISLANDS

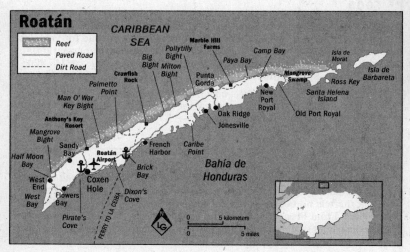

T-intersection with Thicket Mouthe Rd. Thicket Mouthe Rd. runs north to the main highway and toward the West End.

Tourist Information: Bay Islands Conservation Association (☎445 1424), on the 2nd fl. of the green Cooper Building next to the (also green) Municipal Building. Open M-F 8am-5pm.

Banks: Banco Credomatic, along Main St. eastward from H.B. Warrens, gives cash advances and has a **24hr. ATM.** Open M-F 8:30am-4:30pm, Sa 9am-noon. **Banco Atlantida,** 2 buildings to the west of H.B. Warren's, on the left. **24hr. ATM.** Open M-F 8:30am-4:30pm, Sa 8:30-11:30am.

Police: Preventiva (☎445 3449), up Thicket Rd. on the left, next to the hospital.

Hospital: Hospital Roatán (☎445 1499), on Thicket Rd., 2 blocks up from Front St. 24hr. emergency medical assistance. English spoken.

Pharmacies: Farmacia Roatán, 1 block up Thicket Rd. from Front St. Open M-F 8am-5pm, Sa 8am-noon.

Internet Access: Hondusoft Internet Cafe (☎445 1415), around back in the building next to H.B. Warren's. Internet L40 per hr. International phone calls L4 per min. Open M-Sa 8am-6pm. **Traveler's Internet Cafe** (☎445 1816), on the corner of Front St. and Thicket Rd. Internet L40 per min. International calls L4 per min. Open M-Sa 8am-9pm.

Post Office: On the Ocean side of Main St., just west of the bend. Receives but does not send packages. Open M-F 8am-5pm, Sa 8am-noon.

ACCOMMODATIONS

Hotel Sarita (☎445 1541), towards the east of town on Main St. The best option for budget travelers trying to make the best of Coxen Hole. Rooms feature private baths, TVs, and fans, while the hotel itself sits right on the edge of the harbor—some rooms offer rare panoramic views of the sea. Singles L350; doubles L400. Cash only. ❸

Hotel Coral (☎445 4714), on Main St., west of Hotel Sarita. Another budget option, with rooms on the 2nd floor of a small store. Fans, TVs, and shared bathrooms. Singles and doubles L300. Cash only. ❷

FOOD

Your best options for Food can be found along coastside **Main Street.** This road is just east from Thick Mouth road, the main access road for vehicles arriving from the West End. For groceries, an **H.B Warrens** supermarket, to the east of the intersection along Main St., is your best bet. (☎445 4208. Open M-Sa 7am-6pm. AmEx/MC/V.)

Tirza's Snacks, just across the street from H.B. Warrens on Main St. Typical Honduran food at prices that will make you, and your wallet, happy. Breakfast *típico* L50. *Baleada* L25. Beer L20. Open 8am-9pm. Cash only. ❷

DAYTRIP

EAST OF COXEN HOLE

French Harbour, the island's biggest fishing port, lies 10km east along a curvy paved road that traverses rolling green hills and great ocean views. Yachts stop here, but there is no beach. There are some inexpensive hotels. Try **Britos** or **Dixon's Plaza.** From French Harbour, the main road runs across the mountain ridge at the center of the island. Along the way, a side road branches out to **Oak Ridge,** a charming fishing village.

From Oak Ridge, boat tours hit the beautiful Jonesville mangroves and go through a mangrove tunnel. Stop and get a snack at the **Hole in the Wall** restaurant. A 1½hr. boat ride will cost around L375-L400. A good place to spend the night in Oak Ridge is the comfortable **San José Hotel ☉**. (☎435 2328. L220, with fan and bath L250.) The rustic and small **Reef House Resort ☉** may be too expensive for budget travelers, but its attached restaurant is a great place to grab a drink and watch the dolphins pass by. (All-inclusive package L1880.) **Buses** run to Oak Ridge from Coxen Hole (about 1hr., L15). Once in Oak Ridge, all transportation is by **water taxi** (L20).

Around 5km from Oak Ridge, the paved road ends at **Punta Gorda,** the oldest town on the island and the oldest Garífuna community in Honduras. The village celebrates its founding every year from April 8 to 12; Garífuna from all over come to join the celebration. **Ben's Restaurant,** along the coast south of the village, rents moderately-priced cabins. Beyond Punta Gorda a dirt road continues past new resorts to **Camp Bay,** a beach now partially closed. The road ends at **Port Royal,** site of the remains of a British fort. The fort is surrounded by the rather inaccessible **Port Royal Park and Wildlife Refuge.**

SANDY BAY

A small community (pop. 1100) 6km west of Coxen Hole and halfway to West End, Sandy Bay holds a few interesting diversions spread along the passing highway. The town boasts outstanding snorkeling in the well-protected **Sandy Bay Marine Reserve.** You can also visit the **Carambola Botanical Gardens,** across the highway from Anthony's Key Resort, where just about every kind of plant and lizard native to the tropics thrives. One of the best trails ascends to the summit of Carambola Mountain, from which you can see Roatán's reefs and Utila in the distance. (☎445 4117. Entrance L150, with tour L230. Open daily 7am-5pm.)

Make sure to check out the **Tropical Bird Park,** between Anthony's Key Resort and Coxen Hole. Tell the bus driver that you want to go there and he'll drop you off. The large collection of tropical birds includes birds that have been rehabilitated and saved from hunters. (☎444 4314. Open Tu-Sa 9am-4pm.) **Anthony's Key Resort** houses the **Roatán Museum** and the **Roatán Institute of Marine Sciences** (Anthony's Key ☎445 3003; www.anthonyskey.com). The museum has a small display on the history of the island, with exhibits in English. (L150. Open Th-Tu 8am-5pm.) The Institute features an enclosure with dolphin shows, as well as up close tours that allow you to swim with the seafaring mammals. (L135. Swim with dolphins L1615. In open ocean L2385. Open M-F 10:30am and 4:30pm; Sa and Su 11:30am and 1:30pm. Call to arrange dolphin swims.)

Sandy Bay is a 2hr. walk from Coxen Hole; buses running between Coxen Hole and the West End stop regularly at the front of Anthony's Key Resort (every 10min. 6am-7pm, L13).

THE WEST END

The West End has by far the best concentration of resources useful to travelers on the island. Lodging options alternate with restaurants and dive shops. Many of the locals here were once travelers themselves, sidetracked by the beauty that is the Bay Islands. The spectacular views down the coast line, and the offshore presence of magnificent coral reefs do make a powerful argument for lingering awhile.

BAY ISLANDS

ORIENTATION AND PRACTICAL INFORMATION

Almost all of West End surrounds one main drag which runs along the shore. To the north, this road passes **Half Moon Bay**; to south, towards **West Bay**. The road's main intersection is with the highway, a little north of the center of town where *colectivos* and buses wait to pick up passengers. The intersection faces Half Moon Bay, home to great snorkeling and a popular public beach. Most hotels, restaurants, bars and services are south, towards West Bay. While many prices are written in US dollars for tourists, items can be paid for with lempiras.

Tourist information: For up-to-date hotel, dive shop, resort, restaurant, and attraction info, visit www.roatanet.com. At the airport, the **Island Information and Hotel Reservation Center** sells island maps (L20) and can help you get organized before you arrive in West End. Open daily 8am-6pm. **Beach House Information Center** (☎445 4260), located just north of the main intersection, is open daily 8am-5pm. **Roatan Tourist Information Center** (☎9815 4163) operates a tourist information kiosk about 50m south of the main intersection. Open daily 9am-5pm; the kiosk is occasionally unmanned, especially when a cruise ship has just arrived. Keep in mind, however, that each of these tourist information centers earns commission by selling tours. That said, prices aren't any higher to arrange tours with these centers. Plus, they provide useful information.

Banks: Banco Lafise (☎455 5643), 800m up the main highway toward Coxen Hole. Open M-F 9am-4pm, Sa 9am-12pm. **Unibank ATM,** south from the main intersection just past Vallerie's. Open 24hr.

Laundry: Bamboo Hut Laundry, next to Rudi's, south of the main intersection, past Eagle Ray's. Wash and dry L15 per lb.; minimum load L75. Open M-Sa 8am-4pm. Laundry service also available at Valerie's (p. 288) for L200 per load.

Police: (☎445 1199 or 1138). **Tourist Police** have an office to the north of the main intersection, next to Woody's Grocery. Open 24hr., but has no phone number.

Pharmacy: West End Farmacia (☎445 4173), just before West End Divers, south of the intersection on the main drag, toward West Bay Beach. Open M-Sa 8:30am-7:30pm.

Medical Services: Cornerstone Emergency Medical Service (☎ 445 3003), at Anthony's Key Resort, up the highway, toward Coxen Hole. Has a hyperbaric chamber; 2 doctors who speak English. **Fantasy Island Resort** on the south side of the island by French Harbor also has a hyperbaric chamber (☎455 7506).

Telephone and Internet Access: Barefoot Charlie's (☎445 4286; fax 445 4278) across from Fosters, south of the main intersection. Satellite internet service (L2 per min.), Skype, and fax. Two weeks of internet for L200 per person. Open daily 9am-9pm. **Paradise Computers** (☎445 4028), to the south of the main intersection between Dolfin Hotel and Capt Van's rental. Internet L2 per minute. Calls to the US L10 per minute. Open daily 8am-10pm.

ACCOMMODATIONS

Mid-priced hotels are far more common than budget accommodations. The few budget options that do exist are, for the most part, south of the main intersection. Many dive shops offer discounted lodging, especially for those taking their dive courses.

Valerie's Youth Hostel (☎3263 2415; www.roatanonline.com/valleries), south of the main intersection, just past Cannibal Cafe, up a narrow boardwalk that's easy to miss. Stairs rise on all sides of the compound to rooms and patios on different levels, some with hammocks and ocean views. Communal kitchen. Longer-term apartment with A/C, balcony, private bath, cable TV, and kitchen available. Dorms L150; private rooms with shared bath L300; apartment price varies—ask for rates. Cash only. ❷

Tina's Backpackers (☎445 4144), far to the south of town, past Foster's Bar. Run by Barefeet Bar, Tina's offers a few beds in a small dorm room with a communal kitchen, fans, shared bath, living room, and cable TV. Lockers available. Dorms L135. Cash only. ❷

Chillie's (☎445 1214; www.nativesonsRoatan.com), north of the main junction, behind Native Sons Diving. Rooms accommodate up to 3 people. Guests have access to communal kitchen and courtyard. Most rooms have porches; all have private baths. Reception 8am-7pm. Quiet hours after 9pm. Doubles L385; triples L520; quads L615. Two-person cabin with kitchen L460, 3-person L580; 2-person hot water cabin L580, 3-person L675. AmEx/MC/V. ❸

◪ FOOD

A dizzying array of competing establishments line the main shore drag. Despite the competition, you'll be hard-pressed to find a meal that costs less than L100. Travelers on a budget might consider stopping by **Woody's Grocery Store** (☎445 4469) which lies to the north from the main intersection, near where the road curves away from the beach. (Open M-Th and Su 7am-6pm, F 7am-5pm. AmEx/MC/V.) Otherwise, the cheapest food you'll find are late night *baleadas* sold to the daring by street vendors for L25.

Lighthouse Restaurant (☎445 4201), south of the main intersection, across the street from Captain Van's. Enjoy glorious views of West Bay from the deck. Internet free until noon (with purchase of breakfast). Breakfast *típico* with choice of ham or bacon L80. Large fish tacos L120. Shrimp cooked in Lighthouse's famous coco sauce L265. Fruit smoothie L50. Fresh-squeezed juice L30. Beer L30. Open M-Sa 7am-10pm. AmEx/MC/V. ❹

Brick Oven Pizza (☎991 2690, delivery ☎8928 0066), to the south past West End Divers. Follow the signs up the path inland, take a right at the intersection, and follow the road around to the right and downhill again before taking another right—the most worthwhile 10min. walk you'll take on the island. Genuine brick-oven pizza prepared by Tony from Bologna. Mouth-watering 10 in. pizza L200-230. Focaccia L265. Rich homemade juices L37. Delivery 5-9pm. Open daily 5-10pm. Cash only. ❹

Cannibal Cafe (☎445 4026), south of the main intersection just after Captain Van's. This mainly Mexican restaurant serves rich feasts. Be sure to try the Big Kahuna Burrito (L150-225); if you can eat the entire thing on your own, you eat for free. The *Grande* quesadillas (L146), banana smoothies with a hint of chocolate (L55), and guacamole (L44) are all excellent. Vegetarian options available. Open M-Sa 7am-10pm. Cash only. ❹

Ali Baba's (☎445 4150), to the south of the main intersection, just before Rocket Burger, just after Nova. Middle Eastern cuisine like hummus (L115), falafel (L135), shawarma (L150), and chicken gyros (L135). *Shisha* pipe L150. Open M and W-Su 11am-10:30pm, Tu 5-10:30pm. Cash only. ❸

◪ NIGHTLIFE

The Blue Channel, to the south of the main intersection near Cannibal Cafe, shows movies in English most nights at 8pm. (☎445 4133. L50.)

The Twisted Toucan, just past Barefoot Charlie's, to the south from the main intersection. Hard to miss—patrons inevitably spill out into the streets when stools run out. Grab a Jamaican-me-crazy (L80) or a chocolate-banana daiquiri (L60). Open M-Th 11am-midnight, F-Sa 11am-2am, Su 2-10pm. Happy hour M-Sa 4-7pm, Su 24hr.; 2-for-1 mixed drinks.

BAY ISLANDS

Sundowners (www.sundownersroatan.com), to the north from the main intersection next to the Beach House. A favorite for its Su quiz night. Bar menu L70-150. Mixed drinks from L50. Happy hour daily 5-7pm; beer L30. Open daily 4-10pm.

Good Vibrations, with a deck right over the water, just past Cannibal Cafe. Plays a solid soundtrack of reggae. Beer L25. Reggae-Punch L60. Open M-Th and Su 4-10pm, F and Sa noon-2am.

Foster's (☎403 8005; www.fostersroatan.com), to the south of town and out on its own pier. A good place to kick back and ponder the stars above. Beer and philosophy are standard weeknight pastimes, while Fridays feature a more lively atmosphere, occasional DJs, and live music. Beer L30. Mixed drinks from L95. Tu 2-for-1 beers. Th L100 beer buckets. Open M-Th and Su 11am-midnight, F-Sa 11am-2am.

▣ OUTDOOR ACTIVITIES

The West End Village is right next to spectacular coral reefs. You need only don snorkel gear and swim out a hundred feet into Half Moon Bay to witness stunning underwater environments. Dive shops and equipment rentals jostle for your services all the way down the shore drive. Tourist Information Centers sell watersports packages, many of which actually run out of Half Moon Bay; in the West End, these tours cost less and include transport to and from the beach 2km south.

DIVING

Half Moon Bay Wall, just a short swim out from the main intersection, remains one of the best in Roatán with spectacular wall drops and colorful marine life. **Mary's Place,** the island's premier dive site, covers an impressive span of reef along the south shore. **Peter's Place,** at the end of Marine Park, has tons of big fish, deep canyons, and vertical walls. **Pablo's Place,** boasts the island's highest and healthiest coral diversity. **West End Wall,** another wall densely packed with marine life, features terrific drift-diving. Nearby, **Overheat** and **Ulysess reefs** are great shallow dives. **Las Palmas** is an exhilarating dive while the famous **Hole in the Wall,** a sand-chute that swimmers can wriggle through, is suited for advanced divers. **Bear's Den,** with enclosed canyons, is also an unique experience for highly skilled divers. A popular tune-up for rusty divers, **Blue Channel** is a shallow dive (35ft.) through a natural channel packed with bright fish and the occasional octopus. The most popular wreck dive is massive **El Águila,** near Sandy Bay. Experienced divers find thrills at the deep and dark **Texas.** Recently sunk for recreational purposes, the **Odyssey** is drawing large crowds as the third largest wreck this side of the Caribbean.

Roatan's West End features a number of large dive shops, as well as several smaller, more personal establishments. Many resorts have their own equipment and guides for visitors. Similar to Utila, prices tend to be consistent between dive shops for individual dives, or dive courses. The shops differ in the deals they offer on multiple-dive packages; some include discounted lodging. **Open-water certification** costs L5390 ($280) plus PADI books, and **Discover Scuba courses** cost L1920 ($100). **Advanced certification** costs L5390 ($280) plus books. A single fun dive will cost L675 ($35). Experienced Roatan dive veteran William Welbourn maintains a website that divers should check out (www.bayislandsdiver.com).

Pura Vida Dive Center (☎445 4110; www.puravidaresort.com), to the south next to West End Divers. Pura Vida has earned PADI 5-star Gold Palm Resort distinction for its equipment, fast boats, and experienced instructors. Expert instructors lead dives to destinations for divers at all skill levels. Dives for guests L480. Underwater camera rental L385. Dive Master L17,312 ($900). Daily boats 9, 11:30am, 2:30pm. Open daily 8am-5pm. AmEx/MC/V.

Coconut Tree Divers (☎445 4081, in the US 813 964 7214, UK ☎0151 324 0701; www.coconuttreedivers.com), right at the main intersection. The only dive shop in the West End with an instructor development center that offers technical advanced dive training. Coconut Tree also has 4 daily dives on their 2 covered boats. Dive shop also an equipment retailer. Two-tank dives L1830 ($95). Dive Master including all materials L13,465 ($700), without materials L9620 ($500). Open M, W, F-Su 8am-5pm; Tu and Th 8am-8pm. AmEx/MC/V.

West End Divers (☎445 4289; www.westendivers.com), to the south, next to Pura Vida Dive Resort. One of the most frequented dive shops in the West End, with an experienced and friendly staff, and all female dive instructors. Dives conducted with covered boats. Special 2-tank trips include lunch L1830 ($95). Dive Master L13,465 ($700). Boats daily at 9am, 11:30, 2:30pm. Open daily 8am-5pm. AmEx/MC/V.

SNORKELING

You don't have to blow a lot of cash to enjoy the remarkable reefs, considering two of the best dive spots are even easier to enjoy when snorkeling. All dive shops have snorkeling equipment (free for divers), L95-135 for non-divers (plus deposit). Half Moon Bay, at the north end of town, is nearly impossible to avoid—roll out of bed anytime you want and wade into its refreshing waters with your gear for a look around the coral megalopolis. Some of the best snorkeling on the island is in nearby West Bay.

On the Top of the Water Sports (☎445 0020). In West Bay, above the Cannibal Cafe, south of the main intersection. Rents snorkeling gear through the restaurant. L190 ($10) plus deposit. Open 9am-5pm. Cash only.

Roatan Tourist Info Center (☎9815 4163). In West Bay. Rents snorkel equipment. L95 ($5), plus L950 ($50) deposit; 6% commission from credit card transaction. Also hires snorkel boat trips for L940 ($49) per hr. (minimum of 2 people). Kiosk, south of main intersection, open daily 9am-5pm. AmEx/MC/V.

Beach House Info Center (☎445 4260; www.gumbalimbapark.com). In West Bay. Rents snorkel equipment for L95 ($5), plus deposit. Runs snorkel boat outings at nearby Gumbalimba Park for L675 ($35) per person, including transportation. Open 8am-5pm. AmEx/MC/V.

KAYAKING

Roatan Tourist Info Center. Rents 2-person kayaks. (L480 per 2 hr.) Clear 2-person kayak L675 per 2hr.

Beach House Info Center. Rents single kayaks. (L290 per 2 hr.) Doubles L480 per 2 hr.

HORSEBACK RIDING

Cayefites Ranch. Offers 1-1½hr. horseback rides along the beach, through the jungle, to destinations with incredible views. L1060 ($55) per person; sunset ride L1250 ($65). Organize ride through Roatan Tourist Info Center.

Shirkie Bodden Ranch (☎9555 4880; www.barriodorcasranch.com). Offers 2hr. rides at reasonable prices. Daytime, sunset, and full moon tours for L770 ($40) per person.

SAILING/BOAT CHARTERS

Stray Cat Sailing Adventures (☎3385 7457). Offers 3 hr. sunset cruises for L1250 ($65) per person as well as more personalized excursions. Organize in the West End through the Beach House Info Center.

Roatan Tourist Information Center (☎9815 4163). 3hr. sunset tris L1250 ($65) per person. 5hr. trips L1710 ($89) per person, includes 1-2hr. of snorkeling, refreshments, lunch, and open bar. 8hr. cruises L2480 ($129) per person. Overnight cruises to Cayos Cuchinos, Utila, or Guanaja L5480 ($285). Trips leave from West Bay; transportation from West End included. AmEx/MC/V.

Action Sailing (☎916 7654) runs 5hr. sailing trips daily. Trips include snorkel rental and free beer. Leaves from Suenos de Mar, at the south end of the shore road, near Barefeet Bar. L865 ($45) per person plus tax. Organize trips with Action Sailing through the Beach House Info Center in the West End.

WATER SPORTS

On the Top of the Water Sports (☎445 0020). above the Cannibal Cafe, south of the main intersection. Rents wake board, inner tubes, knee boards and water skis. Each L1830 ($95) per hr. or L1250 ($65) per 30min.

Roatan Tourist Information Center (☎9815 4163). Wakeboarding, waterskiing, kneeboarding, and tubing outings L1830 ($95) per 2hr. This center also offers parasailing and rents jet skis. Transportation to and from West Bay included. Open daily 9am-5pm. AmEx/MC/V.

OTHER OUTDOOR ACTIVITIES

Happy Divers (☎9898 7452). Organizes sea fishing trips for up to 6 people. L1350 ($70) per hr.

Stanley Submersibles (www.stanleysubmarines.com), at their dock on Half Moon Bay. Submarine tours in their custom-built submarine "Idabel" to a depth of 2000 ft. Tours from 1½hr (L11,540 per person) up to 8hr. (L28,855 per person). The Roatan Tourist Information Center (p. 288) can arrange tours.

Gumbalimba Park (☎9914 9196; www.gumbalimbapark.com). A park built for tourists near West Bay has ropewalks, monkeys and tropical birds, and canopy zipline tours. Park admission L385 ($20 per person). Canopy Tours L865 ($45). Park & Canopy Tour L1060 ($55). Canopy tour, Park admission, and Glass Bottom Boat Ride L1440 ($75), with scuba diving L2115 ($110). Organize at the Beach House in the West End for included transportation to and from the park. Open daily 7am-5am.

WEST BAY

West Bay is where tourists go to forget the stresses of everyday life. Opulent resorts line the length of the beach; these are at once enticing and appalling. There's no shortage of reclining chairs or reclining people. The boats for hire offer a comprehensive assortment of watersports; any ocean-related activity you wish to try is available. The beach here is long and sandy. The reefs offer spectacular snorkeling 20 yards from each end of the beach; especially nice is the southern section near the cliffs. If you want to keep your expenses down, consider bringing your own picnic supplies.

From West End, West Bay is a 45min. walk along the beach. You will need to navigate an awkwardly placed, tall, rusting metal bridge. Leave valuables at home, go in groups, and avoid walking after dark. You can also wave down a water taxi from any dock along the shore; you can also try the ones that regularly stop on the dock opposite West End Divers (5min., L50). Bring repellent to ward off sandflies.

GUANAJA

When Christopher Columbus first sighted Guanaja in 1502, he named it "island of the pines." He probably came up with this name partly because by his fourth expedition he was running out of names (there are only so many saints), but mainly because, unlike the other Bay Islands, Guanaja's forests are largely conifer. Similarly unique is the island's terrain—**Michael Rock Peak,** at 1350 ft, is the highest point on the Bay Islands. The peak offers hikers expansive vistas across the small island's mountainous terrain. One dirt road connects Mangrove Bight (at the island's northeast corner) with Savannah Bight, (an hour and a half drive south and across the water from Barocca Town); this means that most travel around the island is done by boat. Resorts are spread along the coastline, far from each other. Here in Guanaia, peaceful seclusion is almost inevitable.

Reservations are a must for most Guanaja accommodations. Resorts are full-service, but tiny. The cheapest rooms can be found at hotels in Bonacca Town. Savannah Bight, on a coral caye about 1km offshore, also has cheap rooms. One option is to simply inquire if anyone in these towns lets rooms.

All resorts offer pickup services from the airport or various small ports in Guanaja. On the sparsely settled northern side of Guanaja, **Island House,** run by Bo Bush has two guesthouses that can fit up to 12 people. The guesthouses have balconies and Spanish-tile floors. (☎9963 8551. L11,540 per week includes transfers and all meals. L13,465 per week includes 2 daily dives. Daily rates available upon request.) **The West Peak Inn,** on the western beach of the island, 3 mi. from its closest neighbor, runs on solar power and preaches sustainability—cool showers in the morning and sun-warmed showers in the afternoon. Rates include all meals and taxes. Unlimited access to kayaks, snorkel gear, hiking trails, and transportation. Cabins have private porches and private baths. (L11,930 per week per person, L1830 per night per person; singles extra L290 per day.)

Dive sights are plentiful around Guanaja. Explore reefs, volcanic caverns, and shipwrecks. Recently discovered **Mestizo Reef** features 16th-century Spanish artifacts under 65 feet of water.

Islena (☎453 4208; www.flyislena.com) and **Sosa Airlines** (☎443 1399; www.aerolineassosa.com) fly to Guanaja from **La Ceiba** (L1392). Additionally, a boat run by **Ocean Tour** leaves from the municipal dock of **Trujillo** (☎3285 2118; 2 per week, L720). From **Roatan** and **Utila,** Captain Vern will charter trips to Guanaja. (☎3346 2600; L1060 per person. Reservations required.)

CAYOS COCHINOS

Those looking for an isolated alternative to the Bay Islands need look no further than Cayos Cochinos. Only 18km offshore from La Ceiba, a cluster of 16 mostly uninhabited islands wait for travelers looking for some quiet. All but two of the islands are actually composed of coral; 66 species directly off-shore make up this National Marine Monument. The Smithsonian Institute has been conducting marine research here since 1994. (For more information about research projects, email fundcayos@caribe.hn.)

BAY ISLANDS

⊡ TRANSPORTATION. Getting to the islands without an organized tour requires a bit of patience and an extra day for travel. You must arrive in one of the villages opposite the cayes a day early; head over to the Cochinos the next morning as early-morning departures are necessary to avoid the wind that kicks up later. **Sambo Creek** is easier to reach from La Ceiba (1hr., every 35min. 5am-6:10pm, L15), but is not the best base for reaching the cayes, since the direction of the waves can make transportation difficult. **Nueva Armenia,** the village across from the cayes, takes longer to reach from La Ceiba (2hr., 5 per day, L35), but has regular daily transportation to the cayes. From **Roatan,** it is possible to arrange trips by boat to the Cayos Cochinos. Captain Vern (☎3346 2600; vfine@hotmail.com) offers trips on his catamaran leaving from the West End, Roatan, or from Utila (L1060 per person. Reserve departure times). Captain Hank (☎3355 8705; sailsunyata@yahoo.com) offers three-day, two-night getaways to the Cayos Cochinos on his 55 foot sailing sloop "Sunyata." (L5770/US$300 per person includes all services, beach BBQ, snorkel rental. Alcohol and dives not included. Boat leaves from Dixon Cove, by the Galaxy ferry dock.)

🖼 ISLANDS. Cayo Menor, the smaller of the two largest islands, hosts the headquarters of the **Cayos Cochinos Foundation**: the Turtle and Coral Marine Research Center. They can arrange island tour guides for visitors. (☎443 4075; www.cayoscochinos.com. Ask about extra beds in one of their dorm bungalows, or camping nearby. Open daily 8am-5pm.)

Cayo Mayor, the larger of the two largest islands, is occupied on the western side by the only resort in Cayos Cochinos, the all-inclusive **Plantation Beach Resort** (☎442 0974). Diving packages include seaside accommodation with private hot-water baths and fans, three dives per day, unlimited shore dives, kayaking, snorkeling, and fishing and hiking tours of the islands. For those not staying at the resort, 12 complementary moorings are available for sea vessels; dive gear can be rented here too. For L290 (US$15), visitors can use all of the resort facilities. For guests, there is a transportation service from the La Ceiba docks east of the city. The eastern side of the Cayo Mayor is home to **East End**, the small fishing village where recreational trails to the lighthouse begin. Francisco Velásquez coordinates most tourist activities and has recently completed cabins with shared cold baths for L80-100 per night (☎382 1159. Spanish only. Advance reservations preferred). Ask around in the village for beds that usually run for L100 per night. Women in the community cook solely traditional food (L70). In the middle of the village their is a small *pulpería* with drinks, snacks, and beer. Francisco and others offer tours of **Cayo Grande** on foot or in a motorboat around the cayes (L300). Travelers can also try their luck fishing in a *cayuco* off the eastern coast (L150).

Beware of the sometimes treacherous weather. If the severe winds pick up around the islands, it's no longer safe for small crafts to make the trip. You could wind up stuck on an island for up to several days, so plan accordingly. Also, be ware of scams; some canoe operators have been known to overcharge visitors for the ride back to the mainland once alternatives are no longer possible. Get recommendations on reputable operators before leaving, and hold your ground for as long as possible, but be prepared to pay more (L190-290) to get back.

BAY ISLANDS

LA MOSKITIA

The magnificent tropical forests, coastal marshlands, and flat savannah of the Moskitia create an terrain unlike any other. Getting to the northeast coast of Honduras is half the adventure; the few towns are frontier settlements, and travel requires patience and good Spanish skills. A growing tourist industry has made trips possible, but they're not cheap. The Biosfera Río Plátano, known as "the little Amazon," is the largest tract of virgin tropical rainforest north of the equator. Travelers to the Biosfera will find themselves in virtually unexplored territory. Most visitors come on guided tours that reach otherwise inaccessible regions. Though expensive, the extra service is well worth the added cost.

One of the main reasons why the area continues to be so pleasantly unpopulated is the difficulty and expense of getting there—a few settlements have sparsely utilized airstrips, while four-wheel-drive vehicles offer the only overland access. There are no bus routes. Within the Moskitia, motorboats taking advantage of natural highways are the primary mode of transport, and most settlements sit on a river or lake. Some towns have electricity, but only from private generators which are active only during certain periods of the day. Village clinics and stores have limited supplies and irregular hours.

Travelers to the Moskita should plan ahead: Puerto Lempira is the only settlement with a bank. Do not bring bills larger than L100, as few stores can offer change for large notes. Hiring boats to travel between settlements is expensive (e.g., Palacios to Las Marias L3500) and there are no *colectivos*, so be sure to bring enough cash for the distances you plan on covering. Also, be sure to bring a cell phone—technology has only recently arrived to the Moskitia, but every *pulpería* in the area will likely sell phone credit.

CREEPY CRAWLERS. Mosquitoes and other insects are everywhere, especially at night, and can carry dangerous diseases like **malaria** and **dengue fever** (p. 15). Never go barefoot or use open-toed shoes or you may encounter **niguas,** small insects that lay egg sacs in your cuticles. **"Kissing bugs"** carry the incurable **Chagas disease** and commonly bite around the lips of sleeping hikers, so be sure to tuck your mosquito netting into your mattress. **Chiggers,** similar to ticks, are common in Las Marias; tuck the bottoms of your pants into your socks and use a rubber band for added protection. Also make sure to shake clothing and shoes before getting dressed as **scorpions** are common. Because of the humidity and frequent rains in the Biosfera, bug bites or small cuts can lead to **impetigo** or **tropical ulcers** if untreated. If you see any strange marks or discoloration on your skin, seek medical attention immediately.

Even experienced travelers should take certain precautions. Don't let these helpful tips scare you away; just keep them in mind as you plan and execute your trip. Most of the Biosfera, including Las Marías, is dry: **no alcohol** is sold and bringing your own is a no-no. Where there are *cantinas*, they tend to attract unsavory criminal-types. Travelers should never walk along trails without a guide and women should never travel alone.

Some travel companies operating out of La Ceiba offer package tours of the Moskitia. **La Moskitia Ecoaventuras** (☎414 5798; www.lamoskitiaecoaventuras.com) offers rafting on the Rio Platano (group of four for four days L7970; 10 days L25,790) as well as hiking adventures around Las Marias (5-7 days L4040 for 4 people). Check out www.larutamoskitia.com for up-to-date information on travel in the region.

PALACIOS

Palacios is the northwestern access point to the Moskitia. With a hospital, airstrip, and a couple of stores and hotels with electricity in the evenings, the settlement is a good jumping off point for joyrneys throughout the region.

E TRANSPORTATION. A fleet of **four-wheel-drive trucks** make the journey every day between Palacios and Tocoa over beaches, across streams, and down dirt roads—it's a rugged and memorable journey. The trucks actually arrive and depart from **Pueblo Nuevo,** just across the narrow lagoon from Palacios (from Pueblo Nuevo: 5am; from Tocoa: 9am; 4-5 hr. L500, L400 in back).

The main way of getting around in the Moskitia is by **boat.** A *colectivo* from Pueblo Nuevo to Palacios (L20) is significantly cheaper than a **water taxi** (L50). The two types of boat look the same so be sure to agree on a price before getting in. For longer trips, *colectivos* are rare, and a boat must be hired. Try negotiating. Boats generally can hold at least eight. Destinations from Palacios include: **Belen** (1½hr., L900); **Brus Laguna** (3hr., L2000); **Las Marias** (6hr., L3500); **Papalaya** (30min., L350); **Raista** (1¼hr., L800). Ana Argelia Marmol, owner of the Río Tinto Lodge (see **Accommodations and Food**) and the *pulpería* near the runway, can help you set up transportation.

⬛🔢 ORIENTATION AND PRACTICAL INFORMATION. Palacios is on the south side of the lagoon; Pueblo Nuevo is on the north. An air strip stretches to the west of town. Almost all services offered in town are found just to the east of the airport and then along the path that parallels the shoreline. On the south side of the airstrip, **Hospital Bayan** is open 24hr. for emergencies and has an extensive pharmacy. (Open for consultation M-F 8am-noon and 2-4pm. L50.) Across the runway, the **police station** is open M-Sa 8am-4pm and can be called by radio.

🔢🔲 ACCOMMODATIONS AND FOOD. Hotel La Moskitia ❸, located to the west of town on the water, to the north of the airstrip, offers the nicest accommodations in town as well as the longest hours of electricity. Rooms have private bathrooms, fans, and cable TV. (☎9996 5648. Electricity 6pm-11pm. Reception 24hr. Rooms L350. Cash only.) **Rio Tinto Lodge ❷** is down the main path east of the airstrip, just across from where most boats arrive from Pueblo Nuevo. Rooms have clean cold baths, electricity from 6-10pm, and balconies that overlook the river. (☎408 4675. Singles and doubles L200; triples L200. Cash only.) **Pulperia Paty ❷** rents dark, cement rooms with hammocks and a rudimentary shared toilet with no shower in Pueblo Nuevo, 50 ft. from where the trucks leave for Tocoa early in the morning. It's a good option for those who might not otherwise wake up early enough to make the cars. (Rooms L100. Cash only.)

Palacios only has a couple of restaurants. **Cafeteria Ida ❶,** just to the east of the airport, in the small shop complex next to the beauty salon, serves typical Honduran cuisine on the shaded porch. (Meals L50. Open daily 7am-8pm. Cash only.) **Restaurante Palacios ❸,** next to the Rio Tinto Lodge to the east, offers meals on its dock overlooking the water. On Saturdays, ranchers from all over the surrounding area come in to party as the restaurant becomes a blaring *discoteca.* (Breakfast *tipico* L50. *Carne Asado* L70. Fried chicken L80. Fried fish L65-100. Beer L25. Open M-F and Su 8am-9pm, Sa 8am-2am. Cash only.)

LAS MARIAS

Las Marías, 25km up the Río Plátano from Belén, is a jungle outpost at the heart of the Biosfera. A trip to Las Marías and the interior of the Biosfera is unforgettable, but getting there takes a while and the trip can be expensive. The surrounding area offers numerous hikes with plenty of tropical wildlife as well as ancient petroglyphs of unknown date and origin.

TRANSPORTATION. Motorized boats, easiest to hire from Palacios (6hr., L3500) or Raista/Belén (5hr., L3000) are the only proper way to get to Las Marias. Boats usually hold around eight people. This fare assumes a three-day stay in Las Marías—those who want to stay longer will need to negotiate the price. Try to make arrangements the night before, as river guides will not leave after 1pm. The journey is long and you need to come prepared; bring a raincoat and sun protection, and make sure your gear is waterproof. Transportation farther up the river can only be completed in an unmotorized **pipante** from Las Marías (about L200 per day for the boat and L400 per day for two operators).

A scenic way to reach Las Marías is to hike in. The breathtaking 7-8hr. walk winds through dense jungle on the far side of the lagoon, passing through several farming communities. During the rainy season, hikers often have to wade through waist-deep water and mud. Let's Go does not recommend this hike unless you have a guide and the proper supplies.

PRACTICAL INFORMATION. The Centro de Salud, on the edge of the soccer field, provides medical service. (Open M-F 8am-noon and 2-4pm.) The closest **hospital** is in Palacios, for which the town has an emergency transport vehicle. Halfway between Hospedaje Tinglas and Hospedaje Justa, **Pulpería Yehiny** has toothpaste and snacks. (Open M-Sa 5am-6pm, Su 8am-noon.)

ACCOMMODATIONS AND FOOD. All *hospedajes* are of excellent quality, with meals of beans, rice, and super-thick tortillas (L40-60). They do not have electricity, and travelers should bring their own mosquito netting. Many have hammocks or dorms that can be slightly cheaper, but prices generally run between L80-100 per night at the five or six *hospedajes* in this small town. The lack of electricity makes reservations by phone near-impossible without the help of a packaged tour.

SIGHTS AND OUTDOOR ACTIVITIES. Though Las Marías is fascinating in and of itself, the wilderness areas that surround it are stunning beyond description. Guided adventures are planned and coordinated by the **Ecotourism Committee of Las Marías.** Guides cater each trip to the group size and experience level of travelers. Prices vary, but have been known to hover between L150 and L200. Seven trips are offered around Las Marías.

Two river tours are offered. The first is a one-day *pipante* ride to the petroglyphs of **Walpaulban Şirpi** (4km upriver), which includes a moderate hike (1-2hr.) through a jungle trail, wildlife sightings, and a chance to swim in the river. Bring lunch, mosquito repellent, rain gear, and a swimsuit. The whole trip lasts 9hr. The second is a two-day extension of the previous trip to visit the second set of petroglyphs at **Walpaulban Tara.** The trip (2 days) includes riverside camping and additional hikes upon request.

Hikers can also make a difficult two-day trek through jungle trails and across the lowlands to the northwest of Las Marías. There, one can ascend

Cerro Baltimore, the highest peak in the region (1083m). From this viewpoint, enjoy sweeping views of the Laguna de Ibans and the sea beyond. A good compromise hike for those with limited time is **Cerro de Zapote,** which goes halfway up the trail to Cerro Baltimore and has large tracts of primary forest and great early-morning birdwatching. In heavy rains, water levels may be too high to cross; wear your fording outfit either way (1 day).

The most grueling of the regularly arranged trips is a three-day guided trek to **Pico Dama** (863m). After a 1-2hr. *pipante* ride upriver, the trail leads through farmland and forests, before turning steep and muddy as it heads into the mountains. The summit rewards with spectacular views of the entire region. For a less rigorous trip nearby, a two-day hike to the peak of **Cerro Mico** begins along the same trail and then makes a loop through less frequented jungle known as **"Monkey Hill"** (2 days).

The **Village Trail** is an easy hike that begins along the river, winds up through the forest, and comes down to the village (2-3hr.). Customized trips to more remote destinations can be arranged by sitting down with a map and a local tour guide manager in the village.

OLANCHO

In what might be called the "Wild Wild East" of Honduras, imposing mountain ranges rise between far-flung cattle ranches, coffee plantations, and vast swathes of dense pine forest that give parts of Olancho a strangely un-Central-American appearance. Making up more than 20% of the country and inhabited by fiercely loyal Olancheños, the region has been nicknamed "the Independent Republic of Olancho." The friendly mountain towns belie the area's war-torn history. Travelers ought to stick to day-buses as private transportation is often unsafe.

LA UNIÓN

An isolated village set among the picturesque mountains of Olancho, La Unión (pop. 3800) is a three hour ride on winding, dirt roads from the nearest town of any size. The village is only 14km from rarely visited Parque Nacional La Muralla. Surrounding the town are rolling coffee farms and cattle ranches, separating the settlement from the pine forests. Not many people venture to La Unión, so the village's residents may overwhelm you with attention upon your arrival.

▐ TRANSPORTATION

To catch a **bus,** either wait at the stop at the southeast corner of the *parque central,* or flag it down as it drives down the main street. From La Unión there are daily buses to **Tegucigalpa** (4-5hr., 2 per day, L90) and **Juticalpa** (2½hr., 2 per day, L65); it's possible to take Juticalpa or Tegus buses to **Limones** (2hr., L45) and catch buses to a wider array of destinations. Ask the bus driver to alert you upon arrival to Limones, as it might otherwise be unclear that you have actually arrived at your destination. The bus to Trujillo passes through town at 11am, stopping in **Mame** (2hr., L70) and **Saba** (3hr., L85). To get to **La Ceiba,** catch a bus to Mame and transfer.

◢ ▐ ORIENTATION AND PRACTICAL INFORMATION

La Unión operates on the standard grid system centered around the **parque central. Calle Principal** runs north-south uphill until the *parque central,* forming the *parque's* western edge. Most businesses are found on C. Principal or on the parallel street running along the park's eastern edge, one block away; the municipal building is on the south side. C. Principal heads south to Tegus and north to Parque Nacional La Muralla.

> **Tourist Information: ICF,** 3 blocks south of the *parque's* southeast corner. Administrative office in Tegus (☎223 8491). Info on Parque Nacional La Muralla and answers to general questions about the town. Open M-F 8am-4pm.

> **24hr. ATM:** There is no bank in town, but there is an **ATM** at the *tienda* (☎754 9205; open daily 8am-8pm), 1 block south of the southwest corner of the *parque,* with a big Tigo sign. Be forewarned that the ATM occasionally lacks funds; plan ahead and bring cash to La Unión.

> **Police:** (☎754 9541), 4 blocks south of the *parque's* southwest corner on C. Principal. Open daily 5am-midnight; knock hard for after-hour emergencies.

> **Medical Services: Centro de Salud** (Dr. Octavio ☎9895 9183), 4 blocks south and half a block west of the *parque's* southwest corner. Consultations and a **pharmacy.** Open M-F 8am-3:30pm.

> **Telephones: Hondutel** (☎885 0032 or 3021), 3 blocks south of the *parque's* southeast corner.

Internet Access: Playnet is in the unmarked, yellow building 1 block east and half block south of the northeast corner of the *parque*—locals know where to direct confused looking gringos. Internet L20 per hr. Open daily 8am-8pm.

Post Office: Located 1½ blocks east of the *parque's* southeast corner. Open M-F 8am-5pm, Sa 7am-noon.

ACCOMMODATIONS

Hotel La Muralla (☎754 0795), 3 blocks south of the *parque's* southwest corner on C. Principal. Easily the most comfortable option in town. Rooms are large and have cable TV and private baths. Single L250; double L300. Cash only. ❷

Hotel Los Arcos (☎754 8629), 2 blocks south of the *parque's* southwest corner and half a block east. Simple rooms with shared baths as well as small private rooms with cable TV and private hot-water baths. Singles L80, with bath L150; doubles L200. Cash only. ❶

Hotel Karol (☎754 1638), 2 blocks south of the southeast corner of the *parque*. Tiny rooms with a common kitchen for the cheapest prices in town. Singles L70; doubles L140; larger triples with cable TV, fans, and private bathrooms L200. Cash only. ❶

FOOD

Cafeteria Muralla (☎754 9030), on C. Principal, 1 block south of the *parque's* southwest corner. Serves almost every type of Honduran dish. Chicken or beef tacos L20. *Comida corriente* L45. Banana *tajaditas* L55. Fried fish L80-100. Hamburger L25. Fried chicken with fries L60. Soda L9. Open daily 9am-9pm. Cash only. ❶

Restaurante Bola de Oro (☎754 9359), 2 blocks south and 1 block east of the *parque's* southeast corner. Serves fried chicken (L50) or *comida corriente* (L40-60). Fried rice L40. Chop suey L50. Open daily 6am-9pm. Cash only. ❷

DAYTRIPS FROM LA UNIÓN

PARQUE NACIONAL LA MURALLA

Transportation can be arranged through the ASECUM office on C. Principal, 2 blocks south of the southwest corner of the parque. Round-trip car rides L500. Alternatively, the 14km (5-6hr.) hike to the park entrance is rigorous but pleasant. Follow C. Principal north out of town; take a right at the main intersection. Schedule a pickup in advance for the return trip. Info is available at the ICF office in Tegus (☎223 8491). Guides can be hired at the ASECUM office for L300 per day for up to 20 people (office open M-Sa 8am-5pm). The visitors center has bilingual info on park plants, insects, and topography; the center also has bathrooms and a trail register. The park has 2 campgrounds (with latrines) on the trails. Bring your own food and water. Admission and camping free; donations appreciated.

High in the hills behind La Unión, Parque Nacional La Muralla is best known for its birds; toucans, peacocks, parrots, eagles, and, of course, the elusive quetzal all inhabit Muralla's cloud forest canopy. While the toucan is the official park mascot, this may be the only place in Central America where quetzals actually flock right by the visitor center, usually between February and June. Monkeys, white-tailed deer, jaguars, and pumas are among the 58 species of mammals that share the park along with 822 species of plants, 179 species of birds, 51 species of reptiles, and 294 species of insects.

There are five well-marked trails in the park. The shortest trail is **El Liquidambar**, a one-kilometer loop through the primary forest south of the visitor center. **El Pizote**, the most popular hike, makes a 3.78km (2-3hr.) loop up the south side of the mountain range and is great for quetzal sightings. A shoot off the eastern side of this trail, **Las 4 Pavas**, has a **campground** with a latrine. **El Jaguar** (3hr.) is a 4km. hike north through the heart of the park. The challenging 10km **Monte Escondido** is a 5-6hr. climb through several different levels of primary forest; there is a campsite with a latrine along the way.

JUTICALPA

With all the traffic, noise, and garish advertisements typical of any urban hub in Honduras, the largest city in the eastern part of the country sits like an anti-oasis in the midst of the majestic mountains and pine forests of Olancho. The city serves as a departure point for stocking up on supplies for wilderness adventures, and is an entry point for transitioning back to the conveniences of civilization, Juticalpa (pop. 19,600) crams enough shops and services into its compact center to satisfy the needs of any traveler. That said, don't expect businesses that cater especially to tourists.

⌐ TRANSPORTATION

Buses: There are 2 bus stations, the **Regional Transport Center** (known commonly as the main bus station) and the **Discovery** (☎785 2237; office open daily 4:30am-6pm) bus terminal, located across the street from one another at the intersection of 5 Av. and 12 C. From the Regional Transport Center, buses leave for **Catacamas** (1hr., every 30min. 6am-6pm, L24); **Gualaco** (1½hr., every 2hr., 5am-2pm, L45); **San Esteban** (3hr., daily 6am and noon, L60); **La Unión** (3hr., daily 1am and noon, L65). Discovery sends buses to **Tegucigalpa** (3hr., express 2½hr.; 15 per day 5am-6pm; L75, express 60), via **Campamento** (L35) and **Limones** (L25).

Taxis: Outside the bus terminal at Av. 5, C. 12. Anywhere within city L20.

◄ 🛈 ORIENTATION AND PRACTICAL INFORMATION

Avenidas run north-south, increasing in numbers from east to west, while *calles* run east-west, increasing in number from north to south. The main drag is **Avenida 5**, usually referred to as the **Boulevard**, which runs north-south from the Tegus-Catacamas highway, past the bus station eight blocks, until running along the eastern side of the **parque central** in front of the cathedral. **Calle 3,** the main east-west drag, runs along the *parque's* south side, passing in front of the Casa de Cultura and the Shell station, leading to the hospital.

Information: ICF, 7 Av., 13/12 C. (☎785 2252). From the main bus station, cross 5 Av. on 12 C., and walk 2 blocks; turn left onto 7 Av.; the office is 50m down on your right. Administers Parque Nacional Sierra Agulta but has limited tourist info. Open M-F 8am-4pm.

Banks: Banco Atlántida, 2 C., 5 Av. (☎785 2020), on the northeast corner of the *parque.* Changes traveler's checks, gives cash advances on Visa, and has a **24hr. ATM.** Open M-F 8am-3:30pm, Sa 8:30-11:30am. **Banco Occidente,** 2 C., 6 Av., (☎785 2255), across from the northwest corner of the *parque.* **Western Union** available. Open M-F 8am-4pm, Sa 8am-noon.

Medical Services and Pharmacies: Clínica Médica PMQ, 7 Av., 1/2 C. (☎785 2086). Open 24hr. Attached, **Pharmacy Suyapa** is open M-F 8:30am-1pm and 2:30-6pm, Sa 8:30am-1pm. **Farmacia Juticalpa,** 2 C., 6 Av., across from the northwest corner of the *parque.* Open M-F 9am-6pm, Sa 8am-1pm. Pharmacies in Juticalpa operate on on a rotation—every day there are at least 2 open in town; all pharmacies post a list of the rotation.

Police: Station at Barrio Belén, 9 Av. 4 C. (☎785 2110 or 2111), accessible from 8 Av. next to the Centro Penal. Open 24hr.

Internet Access: Internet_Sa Central (☎785 3804), on 5 Av. between C. 6/7. Internet L20 per hr. Calls to the US L1.50 per min. Open M-Sa 7am-7pm. **Ciber Espacios**

OLANCHO

(☎785 7060), on 3 C. between 4 and 5 Av. offers the same services for the same prices. Open M-Sa 8am-7pm.

Post Office: (☎785 2269), hidden in a shopping complex just off 5 Av. at 10 C., behind the Bahncafe. Open M-F 8am-4pm, Sa 8am-noon. .

ACCOMMODATIONS

Most of Juticalpa's hotels are west of the *parque*, behind the *municipalidad*.

Hotel El Paso (☎785 4642), on 5 Av. by 9 C. The most comfortable place to stay in town at a good price. Rooms have large TVs with an extensive list of channels, private bathrooms with hot water, telephones, fans, and free Wi-Fi. Singles L242, with A/C L424; doubles L424/605; triples L508/725. MC/V. ❷

Hotel Honduras (☎785 1331), on 7 Av., between 2 and 3 C. Clean rooms with good amenities only 2 blocks from the *parque central*. Rooms have TVs, private hot-water baths, telephones, and cable TV. Singles L300, with A/C L400, doubles L430/600. AmEx/MC/V. ❷

Hotel Reyes (☎785 2232), 7 Av., 3/4 C., 1 block west and half a block south of the *parque*. Big, worn rooms, each with cold bath, fan, and cable TV. Curfew 10pm. Rooms L140 per person. Cash only. ❷

FOOD

Cheap *comedors* line **5 Avenida** heading south towards the bus station. After nightfall, several cheap food stands pop up along the perimeter of the park. For groceries, visit **Supermercado Santa Gema**. (☎785 2523. Open M-Sa 7am-7pm. AmEx/MC/V.) The freshest quality produce is available at **Bodega de Frutas y Verduras La Sureana** on 5 Av., between 4/5 C. (☎785 3125. Open daily 6am-8pm.)

El Rancho (☎785 1202), Av. 4, C. 2/3, 1 block east and ½ a block south of the *parque*'s northeast corner. Mean BBQ served on a patio. Grilled porkchop and steak platter L95. Fish fillet platter L120. Double hamburger L100. Beer L25. Open M-Sa 11am-10:30pm. Cash only. ❸

Antonioni's Pizza, 7 Av., 3/4 C. (☎785 2621), near Hotel Reyes. Quick and thick-crusted pizza, complimented by friendly service; delivery available (L10). Vegetarian pizza available. Personal pizzas L100. Open daily 8am-9pm. Cash only. ❸

Dragon Dorado (☎785 3648), on 5 Av. south of 13 C. Adds authentic Chinese food options to the Juticalpa culinary scene. Fried rice L55-70. Chop suey L55-70. Wonton soup L50. Vegetable dish with mushrooms L100. Beer L25. Open daily 9am-10pm. Cash only. ❷

DAYTRIPS FROM JUTICALPA

MONUMENTO NATURAL EL BOQUERÓN

El Boquerón is easily accessible from Juticalpa—hop on one of the frequent Catacamas buses and ask to be let off at El Boquerón at the base of the mountain. L10. Ask for information at the ICF office in Juticalpa.

Halfway between Juticalpa and Catacamas, El Boquerón captures a broad cross-section of Olancho's ecological diversity in a relatively small area. Both dry and wet tropical forests, in addition to cloud forests, are nestled around the **Agua Buena Mountain** (1433m) and bisected by the **Río Olancho. Las Cuevas de Tepescuintle** line the **Laguna de Agua Buena,** which provides water for many Olancheños. An abandoned little cement house at the entrance can be used as shelter from the rain, though it is best to bring a tent. There are three marked **trails** as well as innumerable **hikes** once you reach the mountains. The most popular and accessible hike is **Sendero Río Arriba** (6km, 3½hr.), which is great for spotting birds and bluemMorph butterflies. This hike follows the river up the mountain to caves. There are crystal-clear swimming holes and 2-3 ft. waterfalls all along the trail. Bring a flashlight if you want to crawl into the caves for a fun but dirty adventure. **Sendero Tempiscapa,** the shortest and most accessible of the hikes (4km, 2hr.), is a nature trail with frequent toucan sightings amidst the medicinal plants.

CATACAMAS

The last sizeable town in eastern Olancho as the highway heads towards Dulce Nombre de Culmi, Catacamas is situated near the Monumento El Boquerón, Parque Nacional Sierra de Agalta, and the Cuevas de Talgua. The town has numerous options for accommodations and supplies but surprisingly lacks any tourism-related facilities. Catacamas is distinguished by its particularly lush and verdant *parque central.*

▐ TRANSPORTATION

The **Cotical** bus station, five blocks south of the *parque*'s southeast corner down Av. La Independencia and a half block to the east, sends **buses** to **Juticalpa** (1hr., every 45min. 5:50am-4:45pm, L24). **Discovery** buses (Juticalpa ☎785 2237) headed to **Tegucigalpa** pass through town 1hr. before heading onward to **Juticalpa** (4hr., express 3hr.; 15 per day 5am-6pm; L95/75). **Sur-Rubano** buses leave from the Mercado on Blvd. Las Acacias heading to **Cuevas de Talgua** (45min., every hr. 6am-5pm, L15).

◢▌ ORIENTATION AND PRACTICAL INFORMATION

Catacamas is organized on the standard grid system around the **parque central,** with most activity in the eastern part of town. The main drag, **Avenida La Independencia,** runs north-south along the eastern side of the *parque,* eight blocks north of the highway between Tegus and Dulce Nombre de Culmi. One block south of the *parque,* **2 Calle,** commonly referred to as the **Boulevard,** runs east-west and is the town's largest cross street. The **Boulevard Las Acacias** is a divided commercial highway that runs north-south parallel to Av. La Independencia (three blocks east of the *parque*) past the **mercado** (three blocks south of the *parque*). The **cathedral** and **municipalidad** are three blocks north of the *parque* on what is known as the **parque arriba.**

Tourist Information: The best source of tourist and park info as well as city maps (L35) is the ticket office for the Cuevas de Talgua (p. 304), 8km out of town.

Banks: BGA (☎899 4422), 1 block east and 2 blocks north of the *parque*'s northeast corner. **24hr. ATM.** Open M-F 8:30am-3:30pm, Sa 8:30-11:30am. **Banco de Occidente** (☎899 4458), on the northwest corner of the market along the Boulevard. Western Union available. Open M-F 8am-4pm, Sa 8am-1:30pm. There is another **24hr. ATM** 1 block north and 1 block east of the *parque.*

Police: Preventiva (☎899 4367), 3 blocks east and 5 blocks south of the southeast corner of the *parque.* Open 24hr.

Pharmacy: Farmacia Barahonia (☎799 2032), across from the northeast corner of the *parque.* Open daily 7am-9pm. Doctors present 9am-2:30pm and 4-9pm.

Medical Services: Medicentro (☎899 5554), 1 block south of the *parque*'s southwest corner and 2 blocks east on the Boulevard. Open 24hr. for emergencies.

Internet: Ciber as.com (☎799 2032), across from the northeast corner of the *parque.* L15 per hr. Open M-Sa 9am-9:30pm. **Mundinet** (☎799 1181), 1 block east of the *parque*'s southeast corner. Internet L15 per hr. Telephone calls to US L3 per min. Open M, Th, F 8am-8pm; Tu and Th 8am-6pm, Sa 9am-8pm.

Post Office: (☎899 4091), 1 block north of the *parque*'s northeast corner. Open M-F 8am-4pm, Sa 8-noon.

ACCOMMODATIONS

Most accommodations in Catacamas are either within several blocks of the west side of the *parque* or on the east side of the Blvd. Las Acacias.

Hotel Meyling (☎799 4523), 2 blocks south of the *parque*'s southeast corner, just west off Av. La Independencia. The most comfortable lodging options in town. Rooms with hot-water private bathrooms, cable TVs, and fans. Singles L260, with A/C L300; doubles L350/400; triples L450/500. Cash only. ❷

Hotel Rapalo (☎899 4348), 2 blocks south of the *parque*'s southwest corner and just west of Hotel Meyling. Small but bright and colorful rooms with private hot-water baths, cable TV, and fans. Singles L250, with A/C L300; doubles L350/450; triples L400/500. Cash only. ❷

Hotel Catacamas (☎799 4082), 4 blocks east of the *parque*'s southeast corner, just east of the Blvd. Las Acacias. Budget room options as well as small rooms with private baths, fans, and cable TV. Singles with shared baths L90, with private baths L180; doubles L160 260/240; triples with private baths L300. Cash only. ❶

FOOD

Food options surround the *parque central* and line **Boulevard Las Acacias.** For groceries head to **Su Hogar Supermercado,** on the corner of the Boulevard (2 C.) and Blvd. Las Acacias. (☎899 4430. Open daily 6:30am-9pm. AmEx/MC/V.) For fresh fruits and produce, visit **Frutas y Verduras La Surena** on the Boulevard, one block west of the Blvd. Las Acacias. (☎9589 7525. Open daily 6am-8pm. Cash only.)

TakiMex (☎899 4463), 3 blocks east of the northwest corner of the *parque*. Excellent Mexican delicacies. Don't miss the mountainous *chilaquiles* (L25) and plump burritos wrapped in thick tortillas. *Baleadas* L10. Burritos L10. Open daily 10am-9:30pm. Cash only. ❶

Restaurante Típico As de Oro (☎889 4663), 1 block east of the *parque*'s southeast corner and 7 blocks south, just north of the main highway. This open-air BBQ joint is decorated appropriately with bulls horns. *Anafres* (maiz tortillas, beans, cheese, cream, and beef or pork) L60. Hamburgers L60. Fish fillet platter L150. Bull testicles L140-180. Grilled chicken skewer L150. Open daily 9am-9pm. Cash only. ❷

Tilapia Centro (☎799 4544), 1 block east and 2½ blocks north of the northeast corner of the *parque*. Looks like a standard *comedor* from the street, but opens up into grassy courtyard seating in the back with an excellent array of seafood options. Garlic shrimp L170. *Sopa marinera* L150. Grilled porkchop or steak platter L120. Hamburger with fries L50. Beer L27. Open daily 9am-9pm. Cash only. ❷

DAYTRIP FROM CATACAMAS

CUEVAS DE TALGUA

Sur-Rubano buses leave from the Mercado on Blvd. Las Acacias to Cuevas de Talgua (45min., every hr. 6am-5pm, L15). Admission (L120) must be paid at the security office. Mandatory tour guides wait at the ticket office and cost an additional L20 per person. Public restrooms are across the path.

The famous Cuevas de Talgua Archaeological Park, 8km from Catacamas on the edge of Parque National Sierra de Agalta, is a series of million-year-old caves filled with massive calcite formations. The caves once served as the ceremonial burial site for an enigmatic ancient people whose chronology and customs don't fit in with any other known Mesoamerican civilization. Over 250 fossilized individuals have been discovered in the cave walls or beneath subterranean river sediment. The remains are made even more mysterious by the calcite coating that gives the skulls an eerie sheen. Farther up the trail, a small **museum** documents the park's discovery and has several well-preserved artifacts including copies of the unearthed skulls.

Two caves are currently open to visitors. **Cueva Principal,** whose entrance is just below the ticket office, has a path over the subterranean river to the entrance of the ceremonial burial site. If you're lucky, your guide will spot one of the cave's residents, the longest-legged scorpion in the world (don't worry, it's not poisonous). Thirty minutes up the trail, **Cueva Grande** beckons adventurers into its three tremendous caverns. While the river that formed it has dried up, parts of the cave are still flooded with knee-high water; bring your own flashlight. Just beyond the museum is a designated **camping area.**

OLANCHO

EL SALVADOR

The smallest country in Central America, El Salvador (pop. 6,587,541) is also the most densely populated. Memories of a long and bloody civil war in the 1980s and 90s tend to keep tourists at bay; however, now that peace has been restored, the country is safer and wide open for discovery. Mountain towns, black-sand beaches, and picturesque volcanoes eagerly await ecotourists. Perhaps more inviting than the landscape are the people. Salvadorans will spend endless hours helping you find hidden hotels, discussing the state of US-Salvadoran relations, or just shooting the breeze. These conversations are perhaps the most rewarding part of any visit, allowing you to see first-hand a nation on the road to recovery.

ESSENTIALS

PLANNING YOUR TRIP

PASSPORTS, VISAS, AND CUSTOMS.
Passport (p. 5). Required of all visitors. Must be valid for a full 6 months after arrival.
Visa (p. 6). Citizens of the US, UK, EU, Canada, Australia, New Zealand, and Ireland must either apply for a visa from the consulate before departing or purchase a US$10 tourist card upon arrival, both good for 90 days.
Onward Ticket. Required of all visitors.
Work Permit (p. 6). Required for all foreigners planning to work in El Salvador.
Required Vaccinations. Travelers who have visited nations with endemic yellow fever need proof of vaccination.
Driving Permit. Valid Americanor Canadian driver's license (along with passport) or an International Driving Permit is required.
Departure Tax. US$32.

EMBASSIES AND CONSULATES

For a list of embassies in El Salvador, see the **Practical Information** section for San Salvador (p. 319).

Australia: Consulate, Level 3, 499 St Kilda Rd., Melbourne VIC 3004 (☎+61 03 9867 4400 or 9867 1361). Open M-F 9am-5pm.

Canada: Embassy, 209 Kent St., Ottawa, Ontario, K2P 1Z8 (☎+1 613-238-2939).

NZ: Consulate, 1/644 Manukau Rd., Epsom 1003, Auckland (☎+64 9625 4770).

UK: Embassy, 8 Dorset Sq., London, NW1 6PU (☎+44 0207 224 9800).

US: Embassy, 1400 16th St. NW, Washington, DC 20036 (☎+1 202-265-9671 or 9672). **Consulate,** 2332 Wisconsin Av. NW, Washington, DC 20007 (☎+1 202-337-4032).

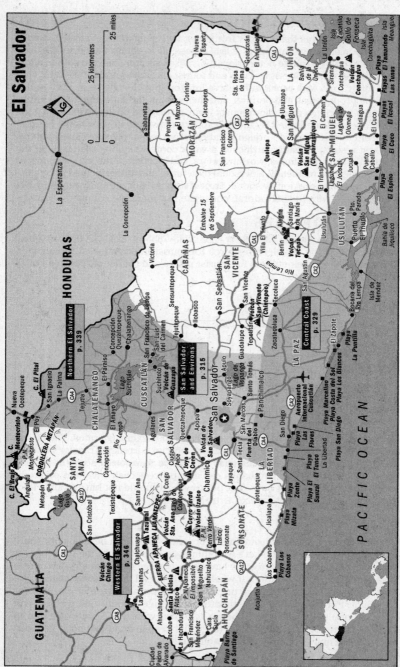

El Salvador

Northern El Salvador
p. 339

San Salvador
and Environs
p. 315

Central Coast
p. 329

Western El Salvador
p. 346

HONDURAS

GUATEMALA

PACIFIC OCEAN

EL SALVADOR

VISA INFORMATION

El Salvador requires that visitors from most nations purchase a **tourist card** for US$10 upon entering the country. It is also possible to obtain a **visa** from the nearest embassy or consulate before departing. Visas are free, but you should allow several weeks for processing. Visas and tourist cards are good for 90 days.

To apply for a **work permit** in El Salvador, you must legally be in El Salvador with the proper visas and permits, and then submit the following to the Ministry of the Interior: a residency request form, an original birth certificate, a good conduct certificate issued by the Salvadoran consulate in your home country and from the Ministry of Foreign Relations, two recent passport-sized photos, HIV test results, a health certificate, a work contract stating the terms of the contract (salary, job duties, working hours, and location of the job), a notarized letter requesting residency, a personal data form, and authenticated photocopies of everything previously stated. **Student visas** are not normally required, but double check with the Salvadoran consulate in your home country.

TOURIST OFFICES

The **Ministerio de Turismo** (**MITUR;** ☎+503 2243 7835 or 2241 3200; www.elsalvador.travel) is the traveler's resource for tourist information in El Salvador. The website lists the numbers for tourist police and tourist offices in all of El Salvador's major cities.

MONEY

US DOLLARS($)		
AUS$1 = US$0.80		US$1 = AUS$1.24
CDN$1 = US$0.92		US$1 = CDN$01.09
EUR€1 = US$1.41		US$1 = EUR€0.71
NZ$1 = US$0.64		US$1 = NZ$1.56
UK£1 = US$1.62		US$1 = UK£0.62

The currency chart above is based on August 2009 exchange rates. The **US dollar** has replaced the *colón* as El Salvador's official currency. Traveler's checks are difficult to cash. **Banco Cuscutlan** and **Banco Salvadoreño** sometimes cash traveler's checks. These two banks can also process cash advances on credit cards. Some **ATMs** accept only Visa, but travelers should not have trouble finding machines that accept AmEx/Cirrus/MC as well.

PRICE DIVERSITY

Our Researchers list establishments in order of value from best to worst, honoring our favorites with the Let's Go thumbs-up (🖼). Because the best *value* is not always the cheapest *price*, we have incorporated a system of price ranges based on a rough expectation of what you will spend. For **accommodations**, we base our range on the cheapest price for which a single traveler can stay for one night. For **restaurants**, we estimate the average amount one traveler will spend in one sitting. The table below tells you what you'll *typically* find in Panama at the corresponding price range, but keep in mind that no system can allow for the quirks of individual establishments.

ACCOMMODATIONS	RANGE	WHAT YOU'RE *LIKELY* TO FIND
❶	Under US$7	Campgrounds usually. Sometimes a simple room with a fan in a remote area. Either way, you won't be staying in a tourist hotspot.
❷	US$7-12	A dorm room or other basic lodging. Probably has a cold water bah, fan, and occasionally a TV.
❸	US$13-17	You're looking at basic amenities: private rooms with private baths, fans, and cable TV in a newer facility.
❹	US$18-23	Finally, some A/C. Expect a private bath with hot water, Cable TV, and spiffier rooms.
❺	Over US$24	Just like a ❹, but with some added perks like internet.

FOOD	RANGE	WHAT YOU'RE *LIKELY* TO FIND
❶	Under US $1	Usually street or market food. Tasty, fattening, and probably heartburn causing, but at least it won't burn a hole in your wallet.
❷	US$1-4	*Comida a la vista*, basic sandwiches, and tacos. Look for the *comedores* and bakeries.
❸	US$5-8	Full entrees in establishments that seem to care a little about ambiance.
❹	US$9-12	Fresh seafood, some pasta dishes, and other international fare. Most likely in a more urban area or other touristed spots.
❺	Over US$12	Movin' up in the world. This meal may cost more than your room, but it'll be worth it. Mostly in San Salvador or other major cities.

COSTS

A 5-10% tip is appropriate for the majority of restaurants. For more info on this, see **Tipping and Bargaining,** p. 9. Expect to pay more for lodgings and food in El Salvador than elsewhere in Central America. Reasonably priced rooms cost around US$7-15 per night, while meals cost around US$5-15.

TRANSPORTATION

Buses are the easiest way to get around El Salvador. There are many local and inter-city bus systems. Every bus route has a number assigned to it and the dispatcher at every bus station has the most recent schedules. Buses labeled *ordinario* will be slower than ones labeled *directo*. Radio-dispatched taxis are the safest way to travel if you don't have a car. **Pickups** have become a semi-formal mode of transport in some areas with regular schedules and fixed fares, but always be sure the vehicle is safe and that your destination and fare are agreed upon before leaving.

BORDER CROSSINGS

Travelers can cross into El Salvador by land or sea. Remember to carry enough money to pay any entrance or exit fees.

GUATEMALA. There are four land crossings. The northernmost is **La Hachadura/ Ciudad Pedro de Alvarado** on the Pacific Coast 66km west of Sonsonate. Farther south is **Las Chinamas/Valle Nuevo,** 25km west of Ahuachapán. Below that, **San**

Cristóbal, 30km from Santa Ana, sends buses to Guatemala City. The southern-most crossing is **Anguiatú,** 12km north of Metapán, near Esquipulas.

HONDURAS. There are three land crossings. **El Poy** (p. 245), in the northern highlands, is closest to Nueva Ocotepeque, Honduras (p. 243). **El Amatillo,** in the east, is 15km east of Santa Rosa de Lima, and near Choluteca, Honduras. Last is **Sabanetas,** near Perquín north of San Miguel; see San Miguel for bus info. There is no Salvadoran immigration at this crossing, so you won't be able to get your passport stamped. There are irregular **ferry** departures from **La Unión** (p. 366) to ports in Honduras and Nicaragua in the Gulf of Fonseca.

SAFETY

El Salvador has one of the highest homicide rates in the world. Most criminals and robbers are armed and unafraid to shoot. Travelers should refrain from traveling at night or alone. Always exercise extreme caution while conducting financial exchanges either inside the bank or at ATMs.

The tourist police, mostly found in national parks, will accompany travelers to volcanoes and mountain peaks for free. In some cases a formal request for a police guide may be necessary. Ask park headquarters for more information regarding tourist police guides.

Although demonstrations and sit-ins were common in 2002, El Salvador has recently become much more politically stable. The emergency phone number throughout the country was recently changed to ☎911; the Red Cross number for emergencies is ☎+503 222 5755 or 222 5155. For other safety tips, see **Personal Safety,** p. 12.

HEALTH

People traveling to Santa Ana, Ahuachapán, and La Unión departments should seek preventive **malaria** treatment. For more info, see **Health,** p. 13. Risk is minimal in San Salvador.

LIFE AND TIMES

HISTORY

SPANIARDS COME, SPANIARDS GO (PRE-COLUMBIAN — AD 1838). A number of Mesoamerican cultures once flourished in present-day El Salvador, including the **Nahua, Olmec,** and **Maya.** By the time the Spanish arrived in 1522, the area was mainly inhabited by the **Pipils,** descendents of the Aztecs, their neighbors to the north. The Spanish conquest was brief and brutal, and Spanish overlords dominated the country for the next 300 years.

In 1811, the Salvadoran priest **José Matías Delgado** rang the bells of his church in the first call for Central American independence. Though this uprising was quickly crushed, it inspired the successful 1821 revolts that drove the Spanish out of the New World. After an unsuccessful attempt at joining the US, El Salvador wound up as part of the United Provinces of Central America until the federation fell apart in 1838.

COFFEE BREAK (1838-1931). El Salvador's wealth originally came from indigo exports, but when chemical dyes replaced indigo in the mid-19th century, the rich landowners turned to **coffee** to earn their fortunes. The powerful planters pushed through legislation driving the indigenous population off their land and giving the elite **Fourteen Families** a stranglehold on the country's government and money. Between 1870 and 1914, nearly 60% of the government's revenue came from the coffee plantations, called *fincas*. Political instability in the late 19th century saw six new constitutions drafted between 1871 and 1886 and ongoing efforts to reunite Central America under a single government. After an 1898 coup by **General Tomás Regalado,** peace and coffee reigned until the Great Depression.

MASSACRE AND CIVIL WAR (1931-91). The collapse of coffee prices during the Great Depression opened the door to dictatorship in El Salvador. A military coup in 1931 put the fascist-loving **General Maximiliano Hernandéz Martínez** into power; less than two months later, plantation workers under the Communist leadership of **Farabundo Martí** instigated a brief revolt, which the government proceeded to crush. In a bloody massacre known as **La Matanza,** some 10,000 to 40,000 Salvadorans were slaughtered under suspicion of rebel sympathies. Martínez was ousted by a general strike in 1944, but was succeeded by a series of dictators and juntas.

A new liberalism emerged in the 1960s under **José Napoleón Duarte** and his **Christian Democratic Party (PDC),** which regularly came up against the military-backed, right-wing **National Conciliation Party (PCN)** at the polls. Salvadorans temporarily lay internal strife aside during the 1969 **Soccer War** against Honduras, as nationalist tensions led El Salvador to invade its neighbor after a particularly fiery World Cup match. Partisan warfare came back with a vengeance in 1972 when a blatantly rigged election gave the military's **Colonel Arturo Armando Molina** the presidency over the liberal Duarte, who was promptly exiled. Popular unrest throughout the 1970s, spurred by a radical Roman Catholic clergy, brought significant public protests and strikes. The ruling regime responded with brutal oppression. In one deadly episode, government troops gunned down university students when they protested lavish public spending on the 1975 Miss Universe pageant.

A 1979 coup by the reform-minded Military Youth led to Duarte's return from exile and launched El Salvador's bloody **civil war.** Right-wing forces united under **Major Roberto D'Aubuisson** to form the **Alianza Republicana Nacionalista (ARENA),** while left-wing guerrilla groups came together as the **Frente Farabundo Martí para la Liberación Nacional (FMLN).** In 1980, ARENA provoked international indignation when its operatives assassinated the liberal **Archbishop Óscar Romero** in the middle of mass. Nevertheless, between 1980 and 1990 the US sent the El Salvadoran government over US$4 billion to fight the FMLN insurgency in the name of Cold War communist containment. Finally, in 1992, the warring factions agreed to a UN-mediated peace treaty, ending twelve years of conflict that caused over 75,000 deaths and US$2 billion of damage.

TODAY

Since the end of the civil war, a shaky but gradually stabilizing peace has appeared in Salvadoran politics, with both ARENA and FMLN participating in democratically elected post-war governments. The parties have traded power in the legislative branch several times over the past years, though ARENA held the presidency continuously for two decades until the 2009 election of FMLN's **Mauricio Funes.** In accordance with the peace agreement, El Salvador's military was cut nearly in half, while the FMLN armed forces were completely disbanded. Re-integration of the country's erstwhile commandos and guerrillas became a major government priority in the 1990s, including a land redistribution scheme intended to help former fighters start a new civilian life. Though the process had some difficulty getting off the ground, over 35,000 Salvadorans

EL SALVADOR

eventually received land through the transfer program. Meanwhile, a civilian police force was created to maintain public security.

Though the democratic process has kept party strife in control, the violent paramilitary gangs of the civil war have been replaced by violent criminal gangs known as *maras*, inspired by Los Angeles street gangs. As a result, the murder rate in El Salvador is among the highest in the world and robbery and assault in broad daylight remain common throughout the country.

Elected in 1999, **President Francisco Flores Pérez** adopted an extremely pro-American foreign policy that included a free-trade agreement and the adoption of the US dollar as El Salvador's currency. In addition, Flores authorized the sending of 380 Salvadoran troops to support the US-led invasion of Iraq, a decision that proved unpopular. Flores' successor, **Antonio Saca,** finally withdrew the last of the country's forces from Iraq in 2009.

As if the devastation caused by the civil war weren't enough, El Salvador has been plagued by a series of natural disasters in recent years. **Hurricane Mitch** hit in 1998, destroying agricultural production and cl cartoony aiming over 200 lives. Things got worse in 2001, when two severe **earthquakes** hit within a month of each other, killing at least 1,200 in massive landslides and leaving more than a million homeless. That summer, El Salvador's woes continued with a drought that destroyed 80% of the nation's agriculture, wrecking the rural economy. Mother Nature smacked the country again in the fall of 2005, simultaneously sending a volcanic eruption and heavy rains from Hurricane Stan.

ECONOMY AND GOVERNMENT

The economy of El Salvador depends almost entirely on trade with the US. In 2001, El Salvador switched from its historical currency, the *colón*, to the US dollar, making accounting easier but ceding control of its monetary policy. The bulk of the country's income comes from money sent home by Salvadoran workers in the US, remittances that are worth as much as the total value of all the country's exports. As the first country to ratify the **US-Central America Free Trade Agreement (CAFTA),** El Salvador has benefited from increased exports to and investment from its North American neighbor.

The political scene in El Salvador continues to be dominated by old civil war rivals, the conservative ARENA and the liberal FMLN, with FMLN temporarily on top. The January 2009 victory of Mauricio Funes over Rodrigo Ávila in the Salvadoran presidential election marked the first time an FMLN candidate had ever won the nation's highest office. Funes, a former journalist and TV personality, is also the first FMLN party leader who did not fight in the country's civil war, a symbol of the party's progress away from its violent past. Congressional elections held at the same time gave FMLN the most seats in the legislative body, the National Assembly, but it is still well short of an absolute majority.

PEOPLE

Although El Salvador shares a border with Guatemala (the Latin American country with the highest percentage of indigenous peoples on the continent), such peoples constitute only 1% of its population. This miniscule figure is in part due to a 1932 event known as *La Matanaza*, in which the Salvadoran military slaughtered as many as 30,000 peasants, most of them indigenous, in response to a local rebellion. Since this tragic event, many autochthonous citizens have been reluctant to preserve their cultural traditions and self-identify as indigenous, preferring instead to call themselves *mestizos*. As a result, *mestizos* boast the status of El Salvador's largest ethnic group and represent 90% of the population. The remainder 10% of the population is composed of whites predominately of European descent.

Because of El Salvador's status as a former Spanish colony, Spanish is the country's official language. Alternative linguistic traditions coexist alongside the state-sanctioned tongue: Nahua, a family of indigenous dialects grounded in Aztec languages, is still spoken among Amerindians in parts of the country. Though El Salvador has no official religion, over 57% of Salvadorans are Roman Catholic and an additional 21% are Protestant. While El Salvador's Catholic heritage extends back to the Spanish conquest, Protestantism has gained a strong footing in recent times. First introduced by English and German immigrants in the late 19th century, Protestant conversions skyrocketed in the 1970s and 1980s due to the work of evangelical missionaries.

CUSTOMS AND ETIQUETTE

When greeting a Salvadoran, a handshake is customary, but it is not an opportunity for a display of superhuman strength: here, handshakes are typically less firm and longer lasting than their American counterparts. When a man and a woman meet, it is proper for the woman to extend her hand first. Once you've moved beyond introductions and onto small talk, try to avoid controversial topics such as local politics and religion; you could find yourself digging up uncomfortable tensions between Catholics and born-again evangelical Protestants. If you are a guest in someone's home, remember to bring a gift for your host, but steer clear of lilies and marigolds, as these flowers are commonly associated with funerals. There is a formality to Salvadoran culture: refrain from addressing new acquaintances by their first names until invited to and be careful not to offend the dignity or honor of any local with whom you interact.

FOOD AND DRINK

The first rule of dining in El Salvador is to embrace corn. Expect corn tortillas with every meal, breakfast included, but don't mistake the cuisine for boring because of it. With menu specialties like *sopa de pata*, a soup made from corn, plantains, cow's feet, and tripe, the less adventurous among us will find comfort in those tortillas. But do not fret—there is still an amazing and palatable variety to be had.

The influence of corn extends even to drinks. Atol is a thick, corn based, warm beverage, flavored with cinnamon, vanilla, and sometimes chocolate or fruit. Sweetened juices made from tropical fruits of the region are also quite popular, as well as Kolachampan, a sugarcane flavored soda. On a night out, beer is the beverage of choice among Salvadorans.

BEYOND TOURISM

VOLUNTEERING

COMMUNITY OUTREACH AND SOCIAL ACTIVISM

ArtCorps Artist for Social Change (☎+1 978 927-2404; www.artcorp.org). Volunteer artists lead community projects, promoting the visual arts as a means of communicating about important issues. Through mural-painting and other activities, volunteers teach participants about improving the health and environment of their communities. For more information, email artcorps@nebf.org.

Centro di Intercamio y Solidaridad (Center for Exchange and Solidarity), Av. Aguilares y Av. Bolivar #103, Colonia Libertad, San Salvador, El Salvador (☎ +(503) 2235 1330 or 1 866-887-2665; www.cis-elsalvador.org). Simultaneously teach English and help El Salvadorans fight for justice. Volunteers work with members of political parties, members of women's organizations, and wounded war veterans, helping to give them a voice. Program fee of US$100; weekly living expenses range from US$280-400.

Travel to Teach (www.travel-to-teach.org). An organization developed in Thailand in 2002, Travel to Teach has El Salvadoran projects in Santa Tecla and Meanguera Island. Opportunities include teaching English or computer to children, and working at a local orphanage. Programs range from 2 weeks (US$837) to 24 weeks (US$2423); each extra week costs an additional US$73. Fee includes accommodations, cooking classes, and Spanish classes. Email kerstin@travel-to-teach.org for information.

STUDYING

EL SALVADORAN PROGRAMS

Casa de la Solidaridad, Santa Clara University, International Programs Office, 500 El Camino Real, Santa Clara, CA, 95053-0639, USA (☎ 408-554-6940; www.scu.edu/studyabroad/casa). Offered through the Association of Jesuit Colleges and Universities (AJCU), the University of Central America (UCA) in El Salvador, and Santa Clara University, an academic program that allows you to learn about El Salvadoran poverty firsthand. Applicants must be juniors or seniors at the time of the program. Participants will live in simple conditions and should be comfortable with learning about Ignatian spirituality and community. Summer US$4600; semester US$15,800.

El Salvador Spanish Schools, (www.salvaspan.com) An organization that offers Spanish study language programs in Santa Ana, San Salvador, San Miguel, and in El Zunsal and Puerto La Libertad, all surfing hotspots. Some programs include three weekly excursions to volcanoes, Mayan ruins, and more. Both semester and summer programs are offered; homestays are available for both. Prices range range from US$3200 (summer) to US$5600 (semester). Shorter programs are also available.

La Libertad Spanish & Surf (www.studyspanishandsurf.com). Located in La Libertad, the prime surfers' haven in El Salvador, the school offers intensive Spanish courses for no more than 8 students per class. One-on-one instruction is available, and a homestay is an option for accommodation. Some US institutions allow students to receive credit for the program. Email info@studyspanishandsurf.com for further details, including fees.

SAN SALVADOR

Sprawling, intense, and colorful, San Salvador is a city of multiple, often conflicting identities. Though ravaged by earthquakes and a bloody civil war, it has refused to quit moving, and the kindness and helpfulness of its people deserve at least as much attention as the gang violence that continues to plague the city. In the bustling *centro*, locals hawk wares at *mercados* while tourists explore the sights of the old city. The city's young elite flock to the Zona Rosa, where modern, upscale restaurants, bars, and clubs belie the frantic pace of life elsewhere. In the avant-garde area around C. San Antonio Abad, local artists mingle with expats and backpackers, while the Blvd. de los Héroes offers every variety of fast food imaginable in an often uncanny display of the city's quickly growing consumer culture. Though San Salvador is in many ways a newly growing city, its history is long and rich. The sprawling shantytowns that have developed on the outskirts of the city are a constant reminder of the country's more troubled past. While the conflict between this history and the bustle of modern business can sometimes seem painfully obvious, it is also a testament to the tenacity of San Salvador's people. No matter what confronts them, they keep moving along, always willing to trade jokes or lend a helping hand.

✈ INTERCITY TRANSPORTATION

FLIGHTS

San Salvador International Airport (SAL; www.aeropuertoelsalvador.gob.sv), about 60km from San Salvador, on the coast. SAL services all international flights into and out of El Salvador. There are currently no operating domestic flights within El Salvador. The airport is accessible by bus, shuttle, taxi, and car. Taxis from the airport have a fixed fare; a ride to San Salvador or La Libertad costs US$25. Most leave from the parking lot right behind the exit from customs. Shuttles (US$4) and buses both go to El Centro from the airport, though buses can take considerably longer, perhaps because they only cost US$0.70. Shuttles and buses both leave from the parking area to the left of the customs exit. Airlines servicing SAL include: **American** (☎2239 9621); **Continental** (☎2260 2180); **Copa** (☎2366 3126 or 2209 2631); **Delta** (☎2264 2081); **Iberia** (☎1-800-772-4642); **Mexicana** (☎2243 3633); **Taca,** (☎2366 7410); **United** (☎2245 0959); **Aviateca** (☎2236 3212); **LACSA** (☎2366 7410); **Lufthansa; Amerijet** (☎2339 9720 or 9725); **Arrow Air** (☎2264 2111). Arrive at the airport at least 2hr. early for all international flights.

DOMESTIC BUSES

There are **three terminals** serving domestic bus routes in San Salvador. Each terminal serves different geographical regions, but none of the terminals have bus schedules posted; if you need help, the locals will point you to the correct bus.

Terminal del Oriente, 1 km from the city center; take bus 9, 29, or 34 from the city center. Bus 29 or 52 (from Blvd. de los Héroes), buses 7C and 34 (from Terminal de Occidente), and bus 21 (from Terminal de Sur) all go to Terminal del Oriente as well. Buses to the Terminal drop you off at roundabout, opposite the terminal; cross on the pedestrian walkway, which leads right into the terminal. This terminal serves destinations to the north and east of the city. Buses go to:

Chalatenango: Bus 125. 2hr., every 10min. 4am-6:40pm, US$0.90.

El Amatillo: Bus 306 or 346. *Directo* 4hr., every 30min. 3:45am-3:45pm, US$3, *super especial* 4hr.; 3 per day 5:20, 11:40am, 2:20pm; US$5.

El Poy: Bus 119. 3hr., every 30 min. 4am-4pm, US$1.60. To go to **La Palma,** take this bus; the stop is 15min. before El Poy (US$1.50).

Ilobasco: Bus 111. 1½ hr., every 10-15min. 5am-8pm, US$0.70.

La Unión: Bus 304. *Directo* 4hr., every 30 min. 4:30am-4pm, US$3, *especial* 3hr., 1 per day 1pm, US$5.

San Francisco Gotera: Bus 305. 3½hr.; 3 per day 6:40am, 12:30, 2:33pm; US$3.

San Miguel Bus 301. *Directo* 2½hr., every 10min. 3am-5:10pm, US$2.10, *super especial,* 2hr.; 9 per day 7, 8, 11, 11:40am, 12:20, 1, 1:40, 2:20, 3pm; US$4.

San Sebastián: Bus 110. 1½hr., every 20min. 5:30am-7pm, US$0.68.

San Vincente: Bus 116. *Directo* 1½hr., every 10min. 4:40am-9pm, US$0.83, *especial* 1hr.; 8 per day at 6, 6:20, 6:40, 7am, 4:20, 5, 5:30, 6pm; US$0.83.

Sesuntepeque: Bus 112. 2hr., every 15-30min. 4:20am-6pm, US$1.

Suchitoto: Bus 129. 1½hr., every 20min. 4:35am-8:15pm, US$0.66.

Usulután: Bus 302. 3hr., 2 per day 7am and 8am, US$1.50. Also serviced by **Terminal de Sur.**

Terminal de Occidente, on Blvd. Venezuela. Bus 34 passes by here from the city center, but you can also take bus 44 from Blvd. de los Héroes and buses 7C and 34 from Terminal de Oriente. Serves destinations to the west of San Salvador. Buses leaving from this terminal include:

Ahuachapán: Bus 202. *Directo* 2¼hr., every 10min. 4:50am-7:10pm, US$1. *Especial* 1hr., every 20min. 7am-6pm, US$2.

Joya de Ceren: Bus 108 (to **San Juan Opico**), 1¼hr., every 10min. 5:30am-8pm, US$0.52.

La Libertad: Bus 102. 1hr., every 10min. 4:30am-8pm, US$0.55. Leaves from the front of the terminal.

Metapán: Bus 201A. 2hr., every 30min. 6am-6:30pm, US$2.50.

San Cristóbal: Bus 498. 3hr.; 3 per day M-F at 4:10pm, 4:50pm, 5:20pm; M and F 7:20am; Sa 12:20pm; US$1.25. No buses Su.

Santa Ana: Bus 201. *Directo* 1¼hr., every 10min. 4am-8:10pm, US$0.80, *especial* 1hr., every 20min. 6am-7:40pm, US$1.25.

Sonsonate: Bus 205. *Directo* 1½hr., every 5-10min. 4:20am-8pm, US$0.70, *especial* 1¼hr., every 15min. 5:30am-7pm, US$1.

Terminal de Sur. Can be reached on bus route 26 or 11B from the center or bus 21 from Terminal de Oriente. Services a few destinations to the south of San Salvador. Buses leaving from this terminal go to:

Costa del Sol: Bus 495. C. Vieja (Old Road) 2½hr., every 30min. 6am-6pm, US$1.10. C. Nueva (New Road) 1½hr., 2 per day 8am and 4pm, US$1.10.

Puerto El Triunfo: Bus 185. 2hr.; 6 per day 9:05, 11:10am, 12:50, 1:35, 2:10, 5:30pm; US$1.50.

Usulután: Bus 302. *Directo* 2½hr., every 10min. 4am-4:55pm, US$1.50, *especial* 1½hr.; 10 per day at 8, 9:10, 11:15am, 12:35, 1, 1:30, 2, 2:40, 3, 4:25pm; US$2.

Zacatecoluca: Bus 133. C. Vieja (Old Road) 1½hr., every 10min. 4:30am-8:10pm, US$0.68. C. Nueva (New Road) 1hr., every 10min. 4:30am-8:10pm, US$0.68.

INTERNATIONAL BUSES

Puerto Bus Terminal, off 3A C. Pte., just after 19a Av. Nte. International bus traffic arrives and departs from this terminal. Bus routes 7C, 101D, and 29 all pass by on their way from **El Centro.** This is the safest bus terminal in San Salvador, but it is still a good idea to watch your bags closely. Buses from **Puerto Bus Terminal** go to:

Guatemala City: Second class service 5hr., every hour from 4am-3pm, US$10. First class buses serviced by King Quality (6hr., 2 per day 6am and 3:30pm, US$26) and Comfort Lines (6hr., 2 per day at 7:30am and 1:30pm, US$22).

Tegucigalpa: King Quality has 2 buses per day, 6hr., 6am and 1:30pm, US$28.

San Pedro Sula: King Quality has 2 buses per day, 6hr.; 5am and 12:30pm; US$28.

San Jose: King Quality has 1 bus per day, 18hr., 3:30am, US$48.

Hotel San Carlos, C. Concepción #121 (☎2222 4808; www.ticabus.com). **Tica Bus** services most of Central America. Buses depart from this hotel that also has a ticket booking office. It is best to book these tickets a day or two in advance. Open daily from 8am-4:30pm. Be at the hotel at least a ½hr. before the bus is scheduled to leave. MC/V.

Panamá City: Executive Service: 36hr., 1 per day 3am, US$93. Tourist Service: 68hr. (night in Managua and San Jose), 1 per day 5am, US$77.

Costa Rica: Executive Service: 30hr., 1 per day 3am, US$58. Tourist Service: 36hr. (night in Managua), 1 per day 5am, US$50.

Managua: Executive Service: 9hr., 1 per day 3am, US$44. Tourist Service: 12hr., 1 per day 5am, US$30.

Guatemala City: 6hr., 2 per day 6am and 1pm, US$15.

Tapachula: 12hr., 1 per day 6am, US$30.

Tegucigalpa: 8hr., 1 per day noon, US$15.

ORIENTATION

Though El Salvador is a tiny country, San Salvador has the second-largest population of any Central American city. The sheer number of people living here is evident in the sprawling, often confusing mass of neighborhoods that make up the city. Like other cities in Central America, San Salvador operates on a grid system; *avenidas* run north to south while *calles* go east to west. At the center is the **Catedral Metropolitana.** From here, *avenidas* to the west have odd numbers, while those to the east have even ones. *Calles* increase in odd numbers as you go north from the Catedral and increase even numbers to the south. *Avenidas* are divided by **Calle Arce** and **Calle Delgado.** *Avenidas* are labeled *norte* (north) or *sur* (south) depending on their location north or south of this main street. Likewise, *calles* are divided by **Avenida Espana** and **Avenida Cuscatlan,** those going west labeled O (from Oriente) and P (Poniente) for those moving East.

The **city center** is located in the eastern section of San Salvador, and is generally safe during the day but best visited by taxi at night. Northwest of the center is the university district, bounded by **Calle San Antonio Abad** and **Boulevard de los Héroes.** Popular with students and backpackers, this area is generally one of the city's safest, though the abundance of malls and American fast-food chains may not feel particularly authentic. To the southwest is the upscale **Zona Rosa** and **Colonia Las Palmas,** where San Salvador's young and stylish elite hang in swanky restaurants and bars. Most visitors to San Salvador will spend most, if not all of their time, in these areas, which are usually safe during the day. As a rule, it is best to always take a taxi when out in San Salvador after dusk; though crime in the city is usually not targeted at tourists, taxis are cheap and can prevent mugging and pickpocketing, especially around the city center.

 WATCH OUT! El Salvador's homicide rate is consistently high. It has also been rising in recent years to over 50 homicides per 100,000 people each year. Because most of this violence is gang related, most tourists will never encounter it during their stay. The eastern suburb of Soyapango is considered a hub of infamous gang Mara Salvatrucha, or M-13. There is no reason for tourists to go here. The biggest dangers for tourists are pickpocketing, mugging, and theft, all of which are perhaps worst in the city center and around the bus stations. When traveling in these areas, avoid carrying large bags, and if you have luggage, take a taxi, even for a short ride.

San Salvador Center

ACCOMMODATIONS
Hotel Bella, **4**
Hotel Pasadena II, **2**
Hotel Villa Florencia, **3**

FOOD
Cafeteria Bella Napoles, **1**
Cafeteria El Exclusivo, **5**
Fernanda's, **6**

LOCAL TRANSPORTATION

Buses: Run every 5-10min. from 5am to 10pm, though some routes end earlier; it is best to ask a local or driver when the last bus is if you plan on being out late; it's generally best to take a taxi after dusk anyway. Buses go all over San Salvador, including to the suburbs and the airport. There are no officially printed schedules, and timing is generally approximate. Ask locals and drivers for information. Also, most buses have a route number on the front and the names of the major destinations. Major bus stops include **El Centro** (1a C. Oriente/1a C. Poniente), **MetroSur, Blvd. de los Héroes,** and **Blvd. el Hipodromo** in the Zona Rosa. Most buses cost US$0.20, while **minibuses** run at US$0.25. It is a good idea to have exact change, or a collection of quarters. Many buses will barely stop, if they do at all; be prepared to board on the run. To return on a bus, catch it in the opposite direction; some of the loops are rather long and you don't want to make a detour through a remote suburb. Some major bus routes include:

29: From **MetroSur** into **El Centro,** continuing on to **Terminal del Oriente.**

30: From **MetroSur** into **El Centro,** passing by the Universidad Tecnológica area at 19a Av. Nte. on its way to **Parque Libertad.**

30B: Along **Blvd. De Los Héroes** (catch it in front of the Pizza Hut) down past **Galerias** into the Zona Rosa, where it stops along **Blvd. el Hipódromo** before returning back along the same route.

34: Starts at **Terminal Del Oriente**, running to **Metrocentro** then into the **Zona Rosa** and the Museum of Arte of El Salvador/Monumento a la Revolución, before passing back by **Terminal del Occidente**.

44: Starts at **Blvd. de los Héroes** by **Metrocentro** and heads by **Terminal del Occidente**. To get to this terminal, you should get off at **Av. Venezuela** and walk several blocks west.

101: Starts in **El Centro** at Plaza Barrios, passing by **MetroSur** and **Av. de la Revolución** on its way to **Santa Tecla**, where you can get taxis to El Boquerón.

138: Starts south of Plaza Barrios in **El Centro**, and goes out to the **Airport**. Ask driver to stop at the airport; minibuses (US$0.60) do not enter the terminal area.

Taxis: Taxis are cheap in San Salvador and necessary for travelers looking to go out after dark. A taxi ride is usually US$4-6, though prices can go up or down depending on time of day and length of trip. Agree ahead of time on a price, as taxis are not metered and bargaining is sometimes necessary. If there are no taxis around, you can call **Taxis Acaya** (☎2271 4937).

Car Rental: There are not many rental companies in San Salvador, due to stringent permit requirements. Roads in the city are generally well kept, but traffic can be hectic. Minimum rental age is 21, although a few companies require drivers to be at least 23 or 25. Some companies will rent to those 18-21 but require double or triple the deposit.

Alamo Rent a Car, C. Cuscatlán. #448, Col. Escalón (☎2211 2111; www.alamoelsalvador.com).

Avis, 43a Av Sur #127 (☎2500 2847; www.avis.com.sv). Open M-Sa 7:30am-6:30pm, Su 7:30am-5pm. Also at the airport (☎2339 9268). Open daily 5:45am-9pm. US$10 per day surcharge for those under 25 years old.

Thrifty Car Rental, C. Circunavalación #304, Zona Rosa (☎2263 7799; www.thrifty.com). Also in the airport (☎2339 9947).

Quick Rent a Car (☎2229 6959; www.quickrentacar.com.sv). Has an office in La Libertad but will deliver cars to the airport or your hotel. Rates from US$20 per day plus taxes.

7 PRACTICAL INFORMATION

TOURIST AND FINANCIAL SERVICES

Tourist Offices: MITUR (Ministry of Tourism), Edificio Carbonel #1, Col. Roma (☎2243 7835 or 2241 3200). Free country and city maps and brochures. Open M-F 9am-5pm.

AVA (Association of Travel Agencies Authorized in El Salvador), Av. La Revolución #3 (☎2212 0504; www.ava.org.sv). Up-to-date information on travel agencies in El Salvador. Open M-F 9am-5pm.

Tours:

Turismo El Salvador, Paseo General Escalón Condominio Balam Quize #16 (☎2534 3215, English 7930 6541; www.turismoelsalvadorsv.com). Hosts tours around El Salvador and Central America and arranges transportation and lodging in San Salvador. English spoken. Open daily 9am-5pm. MC/V.

Eco-Mayan Tours, Paseo General Escalón #3658. (☎2298 2844 or 2283 0220; www.ecomayan-tours.com). Tours of artisan workshops, colonial towns, beaches, and Ruta de las Flores, as well as the Ruta Maya. Also arranges airport transfers and hotel bookings. Open M-Sa 9am-5pm. AmEx/D/MC/V.

Avitours DMC El Salvador, Centro Comercial El Amate, Av. Masferrer #139, Col. Escalón (☎2510 7619 or 7620; www.avitours.com.sv). Specializes in tours within El Salvador and even in San Salvador. Huge variety of tours through the country's national parks, beaches, forests, and volcanoes. Open daily 10am-7pm.

Eva Tours, 3a C. Pte. #3737, Col. Escalón (☎2209 8888). Organizes private tour guides, transport, and hotel bookings throughout El Salvador, especially in the San Salvador region. Open M-F 9am-5pm.

Embassies: See **Essentials** (p. 5).

Banks: There are hundreds of banks in San Salvador, and nearly all of them have Cirrus/Plus/Visa **24hr. ATMs,** sometimes labeled "ATH." **HSBC** and **Procredit** banks also have **Western Union** services. All require photo ID for **currency exchange,** and most require passport and charge 1% commission to cash traveler's checks. Listed below are the main offices.

Banco Cuscatlán/Citibank, Av. Cuscatlán/6a C. Pte (☎2243 3333). Open M-F 9am-5pm, Sa 9am-noon.

Banco Agricola, Metrocentro, Blvd. de los Héroes (☎2514 8700). Open M-F 9am-5pm, Sa 9am-noon. **24hr. ATM.**

HSBC, Metrocentro (☎2214 2000). Open M-F 10am-6pm, Sa 10am-5pm.

Banco de America Central, Metrocentro (☎2278 4601). Open M-F 9am-6pm, Sa 9am-5pm.

Citibank, Metrocentro, Blvd. de los Héroes (☎2202 5610). Open M-F 9am-5pm, Sa 9am-noon.

American Express: Scotiabank, Av. Espana and 1a C. Pte. (☎2250 1111). Passport required to cash traveler's checks. Open M-F-9am-6pm, Sa 9am-5pm.

Beyond Tourism: For complete listings, see p. 34.

LOCAL SERVICES

English-Language Bookstores: Bookmarks, Centro Comercial Basilea, Blvd. el Hipodromo, Zona Rosa (☎2279 0833). Extensive selection of English-language books, magazines, and travel guides. Open M-Sa 10am-6pm.

Markets and Malls: You can find anything you could ever need (though you might lose your wallet if you aren't careful) at the **Mercado Central,** on C. Geraldo Barrios between 5a Av. Sur and 7a Av. Sur. Open daily dawn-late, but it is really only safe to go during daylight. For a less dangerous but still affordable shopping trip, **Metrocentro** and its next-door neighbor, **MetroSur** (both along Blvd. de los Héroes) have enough stores to satisfy any traveling needs. Open daily, hours depend on particular store. The **Mercado Ex-Cuartel,** 8a Av. Nte./C. Delgado, the town's army barracks turned market space has a selection of arts and crafts. For more upscale shopping, including decent clothing stores, take bus 30B from Blvd. de los Héroes to **Galerias,** another mega-mall near the Zona Rosa.

Laundromat: Most hostels and hotels in San Salvador will do your laundry for a small fee. If you need to do your own laundry, **Lavapronto Calle,** Los Sisimiles #2949, has washers and dryers for use. US$5 per load. Open M-F 7am-6pm, Sa 7am-5pm. Cash only.

Public Toilets: There are no public toilets in El Centro; your best bet is to find a **Pollo Campero** or other fast food place, though you may still have to buy something to use the restroom. On Blvd. de los Héroes, there are free public restrooms in the **MetroCentro;** you can find public restrooms in most of San Salvador's other malls as well.

EMERGENCY AND COMMUNICATIONS

Emergency: ☎911.

Police: ☎2261 0630. C. Berlin. **Tourist Police,** ☎2298 9982.

Pharmacy: Farmacía San Nicolás, 1a Av. Sur #119 (☎2283 3010 or 3011). ATM inside. Open M-F 7:45am-7pm, Sa 7:45am-6pm, Su 8am-2pm. AmEx/D/MC/V. Second location 1a C. Oriente #217 (☎2283 3050 or 2283 3051). Open M-F 7:45am-8pm, Sa 7:45am-6pm, Su 9am-5pm.

Medical Services: Hospital Bloom, Blvd. De Los Héroes/Av. Gustavo Guerrero (☎2225 4114). **Hospital Diagnóstico Escalón,** 3a C. Pte. (☎2264 4422).

Telephones: Most Salvadorans call the US using the internet or a cell phone; cell phone service to the US is relatively cheap and often comes as a package deal. Both internet cafes listed below have international calling. For a call center, go to **El Salvador IVR,** 13 C. Pte. #4425, Col. Escalón (☎2528 0303). Open M-Sa 8am-7pm. Cash only.

Internet Access: Internet cafes abound in San Salvador, and many hotels have either computers for use or wireless internet.

PC Station, Metrosur, Blvd. de los Héroes. Open M-Sa 7am-10pm, Su 9am-7pm. Internet US$1 per hr.

Cafe Internet, MetroCentro, Blvd. de los Héroes (☎2261 0148; www.cafeinternet.ejje.com). Open M-Sa 9am-8pm.

Post Office: Off of 29a Av. Nte., across from the Shell station, Centro Gobierno. Open M-F 7:30am-5pm, Sa 8am-Noon. **Postal Code:** 1120.

ACCOMMODATIONS

Each of San Salvador's seemingly infinite neighborhoods has numerous accommodation options. Most travelers choose to stay near Blvd. de los Héroes or the Universidad Tecnológica, though it is possible to get lodging near Terminal de Oriente. The safest and arguably most relaxed of these locations is **Boulevard de los Heroés;** a popular university area, it is relatively safe (though still not walkable at night), and close to a plethora of restaurants, bars, and clubs frequented by both expats and young Salvadorans. This area has both small hotels and hostel-style guesthouses, catering to independent travelers, Peace Corps workers, and backpackers. Away from the tree-lined streets around Blvd. de los Héroes, accommodations are less social, with family-owned hotels forming the majority of options for budget travelers. The **Universidad Tecnológica** area is safer than that of **Terminal de Oriente,** but neither area is completely free of nighttime conflict, and Terminal de Oriente is known for daytime theft.

BETWEEN LOS HÉROES AND THE UNIVERSITY

Ximena's Guesthouse, C. San Salvador 202 (☎2260 2481; www.ximenasguesthouse. com). San Salvador's most established backpacker hostel, Ximena's draws a young, bohemian crowd to its peaceful enclave a few blocks from the bustling Boulevard de los Héroes. Dorms are simple with beds, fans, and little else. Small courtyard and a patio-style dining area. Cable TV available for guest use. Internet US$2 per hr., US$2 flat fee for wireless key. Beer US$1.60. Breakfast US$2-6. Dinner US$3-7. Reception 24hr. Dorms without hot water US$7, with hot water US$9.50; private doubles US$19-35; triples US$41; quads US$47. MC/V. ❶

La Estancia, Av. Cortés 216, Located in a lilac-colored home 2 blocks south of Ximena's Guesthouse. Clean dorm rooms with fans and shared hot showers, but the real finds are the double rooms, which have A/C, cable TV, glistening private hot-water showers, and private patios. Common areas have a kitchen for public use, a TV room with cable, and a sunny front porch with a table and chairs for lounging. Internet US$2 per hr. Key deposit US$2. Reception 24hr. Dorms US$7-10; doubles US$25-30. Cash only. ❶

Hotel Tazumal House, 35 Av. Nte. #3 (☎2235 0156 or 2506; www.hoteltazumalhouse. com). Its prices are high for the area, but the comfort, amenities, and location make it a good option. Well-decorated rooms with comfortable beds, desks, phone, cable TV, private hot water bathrooms, A/C, and free breakfast and coffee. Rental cars US$25 per day. Tours (including Suchitoto, La Libertad, Chalatenango) US$100 for 1-4 people. Free internet. Singles US$32; doubles US$42; triples US$53. AmEx/D/MC/V. ❺

EL CENTRO/UNIVERSIDAD TECNOLÓGICA

Hotel Villa Florencia, 3a. C. P. #1023 (☎2221 1706 or 2271 0190; www.hotelvillaflorencia.com), 1 block off of major bus routes and 2 blocks from the Universidad Tecnológica. The stucco walls, graceful wooden pillars, and tiled courtyards filled with hanging plants and wrought-iron tables seem almost surreally tranquil. All rooms have clean private baths (though without hot water), fans, cable TV, and Wi-Fi. Free on-site parking area and cafeteria as well. Reception 24hr. Singles US$13, with A/C US$20; doubles US$19/30; triples US$21; quads US$30. MC/V. ❸

Hotel Pasadena II, 3a. C. P. #1037 (☎2221 4786 or 2782). Clean, dark rooms overlooking a courtyard. Offers a secure atmosphere with simple rooms each with a private bath, cable TV, and fan. Cafeteria on-site as well. Reception 24hr. Singles US$12; doubles US$17; triples US$20; quads US$30. US$5 extra for A/C. Cash only. ❷

Hotel Bella Luz, 3a. C. P. (☎2222 5158), across the street from Hotel Villa Florencia. Though its mismatched pastel, sponge-painted rooms win no decorating awards, Bella Luz offers clean rooms with private baths, cable TV, and fans. There are several small courtyard areas with tables and chairs as well. Reception 24hr. Singles US$12, with A/C US$17; doubles US$17/23; triples US$20. Cash only. ❷

NEAR THE TERMINAL DE ORIENTE

Hotel Princess One, Av. Peralta #1110 (☎2221 1600). The most comfortable option near Terminal de Oriente, this hotel has clean rooms with queen size beds, large hot-water private bathrooms, TVs, and A/C just 1 block from the station. The individual door locks vary in quality, so check yours before moving in, but the entire hotel is located behind locked, gated doors. The roof surrounded with barbed wire. Singles US$15; doubles US$20. Cash only. ❸

⬛ FOOD

San Salvador provides culinary options for almost everyone; *pupuserias* sell the local beans-and-cheese fried specialty, while the ubiquitous sight of McDonald's, Wendy's, and other American fast food chains blend in with Salvadoran versions like Mister Donut and the amusingly named Biggest. Those sick of burgers and beans can explore international options on Blvd. de los Héroes and in the Zona Rosa, where upscale restaurants offer the latest in foreign cuisine. Vegetarians have a surprising number of options in San Salvador, though local vegetarian cuisine is heavy on beans and not much else. Still, there are several vegetarian-friendly options around the University and Blvd. de los Héroes. The truly desperate or homesick can always find something to eat at one of the city's many mega-malls, which have food courts and restaurants serving everything from Argentinian to Chinese to Mexican and local cuisine. Food is generally reasonably priced; *pupusas* and other local specialties cost less than US$1, and most mid-range places will serve up a meal for US$3-6.

EL CENTRO/UNIVERSIDAD TECNOLOGICA

For groceries, **Super Selectos,** 1a C. Poniente/1a C. Nte. (☎2222 3011), is open daily 7am-10pm. MC/V.

▨ Cafe Bella Napoles, 4a Av. Sur/C. Delgado (☎2222 6879). The quiet, air-conditioned dining area of this cafeteria and *panadería* is a welcome respite from the grimy, exhaust-filled streets of the city center. The food is understated, but the taste is good, the service quick, and the original landscape paintings lining the walls tranquil. Entrees US$2-5. Pizza US$3-5. Cakes US$4-5. Open M-Sa 7am-8pm. Cash only. ❷

Fernanda's, C. Arce/21a Av. Sur. Next door to the Universidad Tecnológica, this sandwich and smoothie shop caters to a predominantly student crowd, as evidenced by the Ramen noodle and toast special (US$1). However, the variety of *licuados* (US$1.15) here is unparalleled, and the bright blue and yellow art-deco decor is comical. Sandwiches US$2-4. Open M-Sa 6am-8pm, Su 6am-1pm. Cash only. ❷

Cafeteria La Exclusiva, C. Arce/21a Av. Sur. Just down the block from the Universidad Tecnológica, this no-frills cafeteria serves up a hearty variety of entrees (US$2-5) and *licuados* (US$1.25) in its tile-floored, airy dining area with cafeteria-style picnic tables. Open M-F 7am-7pm, Sa 7am-3pm. Cash only. ❸

CALLE SAN ANTONIO ABAD

▨ **Sol y Luna,** Av. C/Blvd. Universitario. Across the street from El Establo. The plain stucco exterior of this rare vegetarian find belies the peaceful garden-like dining area, complete with its own trickling waterfall, painted glass light fixtures, and pretty wood tables. The food is cafeteria-style vegetarian and reasonably priced; friendly staff. Entrees US$2-5. Open M-Sa 8am-6pm. Cash only. ❸

Las Fajitas S.A., 39 Av. Nte./Blvd. Universitario (☎2211 3233 or 2223 4655). Brightly painted walls, strings of paper cut-out wall hangings, a mural-map of Mexico, and a few token *sombreros* create a festive vibe in this affordable Mexican restaurant. Fans and a tile floor keep the interior cool despite the heat outside. Tacos US$3.50. *Tortas* US$4-4.50. Entrees US$6-7.50. Beer US$1.70-2.50. Margaritas US$2-4. Open daily 10:30am-2:30pm and 5pm-10pm. MC/V. ❸

Pupusería y Cafeteria El Rincon Familiar, Av. San Jose/C. San Antonio Abad (☎2235 5342). In the midst of more upscale restaurants and busy bars, this family-run *pupusería* offers standard Salvadoran fare at prices that fit anyone's budget. The wooden-log style building and bright murals of happy eaters add to the rustic but cheery ambience, and the cheap beers (US$1) help too. *Pupusas* US$0.40-0.85. Breakfast US$1-2.50. Open daily 6:30am-9pm. Cash only. ❷

ZONA ROSA

Shaw's (☎2223 0959, www.shaws.com.sv), Centro Basilea, off Blvd. del Hippodromo. A little pricier than the average sandwich shop, this bakery and cafe's true selling point is its location; the outside patio has panoramic views of the city. The inside is blissfully air-conditioned, and there is a tree-filled courtyard for those who want something in-between. Pick from a huge variety of coffee drinks (US$1.50-4) or head to the homemade chocolates counter. Free Wi-Fi. Breakfast US$3.50-7. Sandwiches and entrees US$4-7. Open M-W 6:45am-10pm, Th-Sa 6:45am-midnight, Su 7:30am-11pm. MC/V. ❷

Shen Zhuan, Av. La Revolución #5 (☎2243 0424 or 2533 6428), down the street from the Guzman Museum. This family run Taiwanese restaurant serves up affordable vegetarian cuisine despite its location in one of the most expensive neighborhoods in the city. With a cool, quiet interior and an indoor mini-waterfall, the dining experience is as agreeable for the weary as it is for the wallet. Lunch special US$4. Rice dishes US$4-5. Noodles US$3.50-4.50. Open M-Sa 10am-9:30pm. Cash only. ❷

Tre Fratelli (☎2223 0838), Blvd. El Hipodromo #307. Those looking to splurge on something different than standard sandwiches and tacos can indulge at this upscale Italian spot in the Zona Rosa. The menu changes daily, and diners have a choice between the beautifully appointed, air-conditioned interior or the breezy *al fresco* dining on the patio. Lots of fish and vegetarian options. Pizza US$10. Pastas US$10.50-15. Entrees US$12-18. Open daily noon-11pm. AmEx/D/MC/V. ❹

⑤ SIGHTS

CATEDRAL METROPOLITANA. The center of San Salvador's grid system, the Catedral Metropolitana is still undergoing minor restorations after suffering from fire and earthquake damage. The blue and yellow dome of the Catedral is visible throughout El Centro. The tomb of famous Archbishop Romero, perhaps El

Salvador's most widely known theologian and war hero, is buried underneath the Catedral. *(Av. Cuscatlàn/2a C. Oriente. Main entrance on 2 C., on the cathedral's south side. Open M-Sa 6am-6pm, Su noon-6pm. Free.)*

IGLESIA EL ROSARIO AND PARQUE LIBERTAD. Strikingly simple in its modernity, the church of El Rosario is composed of two arcs 30m apart. This graffiti-covered church depicts religious scenes through modern sculptures made of steel rebar and other scraps. The lights in the interior blend with the sculptures to create an intense scene. Across the street, performers and locals make Parque Libertad a popular people-watching spot, though the need to watch one's wallet can detract from the amusement. *(6a Av. Sur/4a C. Oriente. Open daily during daylight hours. Free.)*

MERCADO NACIONAL DE ARTESANIAS. This market, on the site of the international fairgrounds, sells *artesanía* from all over the country. Prices tend to be quite a bit higher than in the towns where the pieces originate, but the selection is unbeatable. *(C. Manuel Enrique Araujo. Accessible by bus #30B. Open daily until 6pm.)*

MONUMENTO A LA REVOLUCIÓN/MUSEO DE ARTE DE EL SALVADOR. San Salvador's newest museum, housing a growing contemporary art collection, is just behind the monument to the revolution, celebrating the 1948 revolution and the freedom of Central America's oppressed peoples. The museum itself has a permanent collection of work by Salvadoran artists, and its temporary collections often included modern works from other Central American countries. *(Av. de la Revolución Final, up the hill from the Guzman museum. ☎ 2243 6099. Open Tu-Su 10am-6pm. US$1.50, free on Su. If you don't want to pay to see the museum, you can stop and see the Monumento without entering the museum proper.)*

BOTANICAL GARDENS. If you prefer flora over fauna, the Botanical Gardens provide a relaxing retreat where you can walk trails lined with thousands of indigenous and foreign plant species. The gardens sit at the base of a dormant volcanic crater, which was a lagoon until the 18th-century eruption. *(☎ 2243 2012. #101C bus from 3 Av. Sur and C. Rubén Darío; get off in Antiguo Cuzcatlan and follow the signs. The #44 minibus from Blvd. de los Héroes also stops here. Open Tu-Su 9am-5pm. US$0.50.)*

MUSEO NACIONAL DE ANTROPOLOGIA DAVID GUZMAN. San Salvador's most famous museum, this massive complex, complete with multiple galleries, a sculpture garden, and landscaped pathways displays artifacts from El Salvador's pre-colonial and post-colonial history. *(Av. de la Revolución, across from the Convention Center. ☎ 2243 3927; www.munaelsalvador.com. Guided tours (1½hr.) are available, but must be booked in advance. Open Tu-Su 9am-5pm. US$3 for non-Central Americans, US$1 Central Americans, free for kids under 8.)*

MUSEO DE CIENCIAS/STEPHEN HAWKING MUSEUM. Central America's only physical science museum, the Stephen Hawking Museum caters primarily to student groups with its interactive exhibits. The museum focuses primarily on El Salvador's environment. *(C. la Reforma #179. ☎ 2223 3027. Open M-Sa 10am-4pm. US$1.15.)*

NIGHTLIFE

San Salvador's nightlife is one of the most attractive points of the city. Students, hipsters, leftists, art-lovers, and broke travelers alike head to **Calle San Antonio Abad,** where live music, beer, or coffee can be found almost any day of the week. Zona Rosa is home to the city's more upscale clubbing scene, where visitors can expect to pay a cover of US$5-10 to join the crowds of well-dressed Salvadorans mingling and dancing until the wee hours of the morning. For those who can't get their fix at these hotspots, San Salvador's massive mega-malls are becoming the new nightlife favorite; though most of these clubs are relatively similar, they have the convenience of being stuffed together in one building, making transport a bit easier. All nightlife in San Salvador is best reached by taxi or car. Remember to get a taxi instead of walking home.

BLVD. DE LOS HÉROES AND CALLE SAN ANTONIO ABAD

Cafe La T, C. San Antonio Abad 2233 (☎2225 2090), next door to Bar y Restaurant GYF. Offers a more tranquil alternative, with artsy film screenings on W and Th and the occasional live music show as well. It's also impossible to miss, with a bright mural depicting El Salvador's recent struggles and natural beauty covering the entrance. Open M-W 10am-10pm, Th-Sa 10am-11pm. Cash only.

La Luna Casa Y Arte, C. Berlin 228 (☎2260 2921, www.lalunacasayarte.com). One of San Salvador's best live music venues. Extensive program of local reggae, jazz, ska, and rock bands performing almost daily in its painting-covered lounge area that also hosts theatrical acts or film screenings. Cover for most concerts US$2-3. Food US$2-7. Mixed drinks US$3. Beer US$1-2. Open M-F 10am-2am, Sa 5pm-2am. Cash only.

Bar y Restaurante GYF's, C. San Antonio Abad 229. A chilled out reggae cafe by day, GYF's transforms into a lively bar and club at night, with expats and locals lounging in the side rooms or turning the bar's main space into a dance floor. The drinks are cheap (US$1-2), and the music an eclectic mix of reggae, hip-hop, and reggaeton. Drink specials M-Tu. Open M-Sa 11am-2am. Cash only.

ZONA ROSA

Tekilas, Esq. Av. La Capilla/Blvd. El Hipodromo (☎2243 4397). For those unmoved by the artsy splendor of the university district, Tekilas provides loud, pumping, club-style beats accompanied by the occasional karaoke song and late-night revelry. Cover US$5. Open M-Sa 7pm-late. Beer US$1.70. Cash only.

Los Rinconcitos, Blvd. El Hipodromo #310 (☎2298 4799 or 4798), just past Av. Las Gardenias. Restaurant by day, popular bar scenes by night. Los Rinconcitos and its sister restaurant-bar **Puerto Escondido,** conveniently located next door, offer drink specials every night including 2-for-1 deals and discounts on bottles. Rinconcitos is a popular middle ground for those who like their music and drinks to come with a little fresh air and a little less dance party. Beer US$2. Open M-Sa 5pm-Late. MC/V.

Jala la Jarra, Av. Las Magnolias #206 (☎2245 2486), connected to the Guadalajara Grill. A disco-bar that is easily accessed from Blvd. el Hipodromo. Blasting a consistent mix of salsa, reggaeton, and hip hop music in a breezy location, with lots of tequila thrown in for good measure. The dancing doesn't really get going till about midnight, but the bar is fairly busy before then. Beer US$1.75. Open M-Sa 5pm-Late. MC/V.

⚌ DAYTRIPS FROM SAN SALVADOR

LAGO DE ILOPANGO

For the Turicentro, take bus #15 from the bus stop in front of the Palacio Nacional (55min., every 15min. until 7pm, US$0.35). From the Terminal de Oriente or Blvd. de los Héroes, an easier and faster option is to take the #29 bus to the town of Ilopango (tell the driver where you're going), where you can catch the #15 to Apulo (6am-8pm, US$0.35). Turicentro open daily 8am-5pm. Boat trips US$5 per 30min. for up to 6 people; tubing US$1 per 30min.; water-skiing US$10 per 30 min. Admission US$0.80.

Lago de Ilopango, just 16km east of the capital, is the largest and deepest crater lake in El Salvador. Steep lush hillsides drop rapidly onto the shores of the lake, and several uninhabited islands poke up through the placid surface of the deep-blue water. The easily accessible **Turicentro** ❶, at Apulo on the north shore of the lake, is the accommodation of choice for weekenders looking for a little waterfront relaxation; on weekdays you'll have the place to yourself. Picnic areas, showers, changing rooms, two clean pools, and several restaurants line the lake shore, and small bungalows on the edge of the beach can be rented for the day. (Bungalows US$4; key deposit US$2. Meals US$1-3.) Watersports and boat trips are popular. *Lanchas* are plentiful and their owners are willing to take you for a spin. For the best views of the lake, the crater, and the volcanoes to the east, take the bus a few kilometers uphill back towards San Salvador to **Restaurante Mirador 70** ❸, where you can have a drink or a relaxing meal on the terrace overlooking the lake. The restaurant is right on the highway; ask the driver to let you off. (☎ 295 4768. Meals US$8-14. Open daily noon-7pm.)

VOLCÁN SAN SALVADOR

Volcán San Salvador overlooks most of San Salvador. Access to the crater is through the tiny village of El Boquerón. To get to to El Boquerón (the crater), you need to first take a bus to Santa Tecla. Bus #101 goes from Plaza Barrios to Santa Tecla, and Bus #101D goes from Metrosur to the town as well (both US$0.20). From Santa Tecla, hire a cab to take you to the entrance of the park (US$5-7); bus #103, leaving from 4 Av. Nte. and C. Daniel Hernández (45min., every 45min. 6am-4pm, US$0.50), will drop you off outside of El Boquerón village, but the remaining 1 km to the park entrance is steep and not safe for tourists. Unless in a private car, taxis are your only option. Once at the crater, travelers have found that negotiating with a taxi to wait, having the front desk guard call a taxi, or hitchhiking down have been successful means of returning to ground level. Keep in mind that Let's Go does not recommend hitchhiking. Never try walking the road through El Boquerón with any valuables or without a local escort. Park open daily 8am-5pm. Entrance US$1 per person, US$1 per private car, US$2 per minibus or pick-up.

Volcán San Salvador, situated northwest of the capital, 11km north of Santa Tecla, stuns travelers with its breathtaking views. **El Boquerón** (Big Mouth) gapes open at the top of a 5mi. hike. Several *miradores* provide a panoramic view of the volcano's crater and a perfect 50m high cone, the result of a 1917 eruption, that rises out from inside the crater. One path winds its way down to the bottom of the crater (about 2hr.), another leaves from the right of the viewpoint and follows the rim of the crater all the way around (2-3hr.). The path around the edge of the crater is relatively safe, though it should not be attempted alone. Don't descend into the crater without a local guide; the cone traps tourists trying to run from muggers.

JOYA DE CERÉN

Take bus #108 going to the town of Opico from Terminal Occidente (40min., every 10min., US$0.50). Get off immediately after crossing the bridge over the Río Sucio, at the sign for the entrance to the site. If you feel adventurous, you can find guides at San Andrés who will take you here on horseback. Site and museum open Tu-Su 9am-5pm. Entry US$3.

Fourteen hundred years ago, the residents of Joya de Cerén were forced to flee their homes after the eruption of nearby Ilopango Volcano threatened their lives. The entire city was frozen under 3m of volcanic ash. The town was wakened from its extended slumber when bulldozers accidentally unearthed it in 1976. Full-scale excavations began in 1989, yielding the discovery of 18 structures, ranging from adobe houses, to a steam bath, to the office of the local shaman. Cerén's findings have helped to shed light on the daily sustenance, commerce, and familial relations of the ancient Maya. In 1993, Joya de Cerén was declared a **UNESCO World Heritage Site.** Its archaeological significance was augmented by the discovery of manioc planting, making Joya de Cerén the earliest example of such farming in the Americas. The small but comprehensive on-site museum contains intriguing examples of ceramics, utensils, and food-stuffs from the period. Keep in mind that the information in the museum is exclusively in Spanish; knowledgeable Spanish-speaking guides are available to take you around the three main excavation sites.

SAN ANDRES

Take bus #201 from Terminal Occidente heading to Santa Ana (US$0.50), get off at Km 33 at the sign for San Andrés, then walk about 200m down the dirt road to the ruins. From Joya de Cerén, hop on the #108 and ride to the junction with the highway to Santa Ana (10min., US$0.20) to catch a westbound #201 to San Andrés (10min., US$0.20), stopping at the Km 33 sign. Open Tu-Su 9am-4pm. US$3, includes tour. Visitor center has a cafeteria.

Occupied by Maya and Pipil, San Andrés was constructed from AD 600 to 900 and originally consisted of nearly 200 structures. The cause of the city's decline is unclear, but all that remains today are several pyramids and mound structures that have been restored to their original stone and mortar state. Enter the site on the **South Plaza**, near the **Acropolis**, a partially restored mound. North of the Acropolis, most of the structures have not been excavated and remain relatively untouched. The most interesting part of the ruins, the base of structure five, is under a thatched roof in this section.

The sprawling visitor center and museum complex, before the entrance to the ruins, are perhaps more interesting than the site itself. The museum gives an extensive overview of Maya culture in the area and San Andrés in particular. Interesting exhibits cover El Salvador's colonial past, including a display on El Obraje, the best preserved indigo factory in the world. When exiting the visitor's center to the north, El Obraje is to the right; the ruins are to the left. Guides wait at the museums' entrance and exit.

LOS PLANES DE RENDEROS

Bus #12 (US$0.50, every 10min. 6am-8pm) leaves from Av. 29 de Agosto and 12 C. Pte. on the southeastern edge of the mercado central in front of the government building and goes to Parque Balboa. La Puerta del Diablo is a 40min. walk/hike through the park from the entrance. Parque Balboa open daily 6am-8pm, US$0.90.

A rarely visited southern suburb of the city, Los Planes de Renderos is home to **Parque Balboa**, a local turi-centro with walking trails, playgrounds, and landscapes with sculptures. It is also the entrance to **La Puerta del Diablo,** a 40min. walk from the park entrance, where two massive boulders frame an impressive view of the city. During the civil war, the Puerta lived up to its name ("gate of hell") by serving as a popular execution spot. Today, the presence of tourist police make it a bit more tranquil; you'll likely encounter a mix of families, couples, and even rappellers along the way. For more information on rappelling and climbing in the area, contact **Alligatours** *(Calle La Reforma #232, 2nd fl., Zona Rosa, ☎2245 3341, Open M-F 9am-5pm.)* On your way back, **Pupusería Toñita ❶**, conveniently located at the entrance of Parque Balboa, is the place to stop for delicious traditional *pupusas*. (Small US$0.50, large US$0.80. Open daily 10am-9pm. Cash only.)

PANCHIMALCO

Bus #17 leaves from Av. 29 de Agosto and 12 C. Pte. on the southeastern edge of the mercado central in front of the government building and goes to Panchimalco (45min.). If you want to get to Panchimalco from Puerto del Diablo or Parque Balboa, go back out the entrance of the park to el triangulo, a crossroad just down Parque Balboa. From here, you can catch bus #17 (20min., US$0.50) the rest of the way to Panchimalco.

Twenty minutes past *el triangulo*, Panchimalco is a village of cobblestone streets and workshops inhabited by the Pancho Indians, some of whom still wear the traditional dress of their ancestors. The local church, **Santa Cruz,** has an octagonal dome with eight saints blessing the town from each side. Built in 1725, it is the oldest building of its kind in the country. The main attraction in Panchimalco is its festivals; though calm and quiet most of the year, the entire city turns out for these celebrations, the most famous of which is its **Palm Sunday parade** (March 28 in 2010).

THE CENTRAL COAST

El Salvador's most popular beaches hug the Central Coast south of the capital. Just 34km from San Salvador, La Libertad draws surfers from around the world. The town of Zacatecoluca is a gateway to the seemingly endless palm-fringed coastline of the Costa del Sol, the country's premier resort area. Farther east is the mangrove-lined Bahía de Jiquilisco.

LA LIBERTAD AND BEACHES

Reputed to have the best surfing in Central America, the stars have aligned to bless La Libertad (pop. 40,000) with a rare combination of wind, current, and

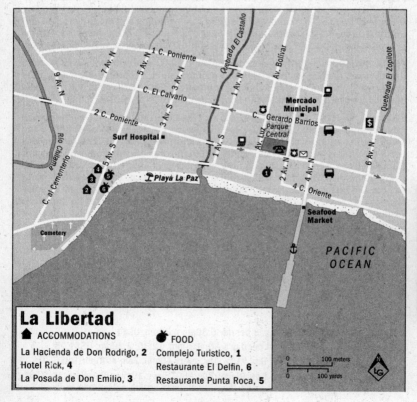

La Libertad

🏠 ACCOMMODATIONS

La Hacienda de Don Rodrigo, **2**
Hotel Rick, **4**
La Posada de Don Emilio, **3**

🍎 FOOD

Complejo Turistico, **1**
Restaurante El Delfin, **6**
Restaurante Punta Roca, **5**

shore that yields constant swells of at least 1½m. Surf culture has definitely over-taken the town; local fishermen rush to The Point after work to catch a few breaks. Serious surfers rise with the sun to ride the best waves off the famed Punta Roca. When the ocean's flat, the most interesting sight (and smell) is the bustling fish market on the pier—if it lives in the sea and can be eaten, it's for sale here. But the town is not all flip-flops and bleached hair; drugs (see **Surfing**, p. 334) and crime are all too common and tourists are frequent targets. To escape this, more and more people head west to the smaller towns of Playa El Tunco and Playa Zunzal, where the waves are still big but the streets more safe.

PLAYA EL TUNCO. A fun beach with a young crowd of Salvadoran teens in town for the weekend, Playa El Tunco is decent for swimming and surfing. It has developed into the backpacker's beach, with an abundance of hostels and beach-side lodges for surfers and loungers. *(A 20min. bus ride from La Libertad, the beach is about 800m from the town of El Tunco; signs mark the access road on both sides of the highway.)*

PLAYA ZUNZAL. West of El Tunco, this wide beach is less rocky, with consistent waves far from shore. Recommended for beginning and advanced surfers, Zunzal is also one of the best options for swimming. *(Walk west on the beach from Río Tunco until you reach Punta Zunzal.)*

PLAYA EL PALMARCITO. Less crowded, this soft curve of a beach seems to be a bit of a secret. A 400m walk down a cobblestone road from the sign reading "Puente El Palmar," the calm water is great for swimming and the sand is nice and toasty. *(Take Bus #192 to La Perla and ask to be let off at Palmarcito. Alternatively, buses from the La Libertad terminal in San Salvador also go directly to La Perla, though service is fairly irregular.)*

PLAYA ZONTE. A slightly isolated, smaller beach, Zonte draws surfers and a local crowd despite its rocky shore and dark sand. Stunning trees and cliffs make up for the drab shacks along the beach. *(Only 15min. beyond Zunzal, buses deposit you on the unmarked road which leads to the beach; stay to the right.)*

BEACHES EAST OF LA LIBERTAD. East of La Libertad are two beaches, each large enough to make finding a peaceful spot easy. **Playa las Flores,** below the section of road known as La Cerra, a few kilometers east of La Libertad, has parts that are relatively clean. About 15min. farther on Bus #80 brings you to **Playa San Diego,** a long gray beach lined with houses; public beach access paths every 100m. The beach is wide and more or less clean; at the farthest point (where the bus stops to turn around) is an estuary, a cluster of beach shacks, and *comedores.* To enjoy the sand, hop off the bus along the road to San Diego 7km after it leaves the highway (at any of the many little groups of stores or small restaurants), and take an access path to the shore.

◧ TRANSPORTATION

The main bus station is at 4a Av. Nte. and 1a C. Ote., on the northeast corner of town. Buses head to:

San Salvador: Bus #102. 1hr., every 10min. 4:30am-6pm, US$1.50. Leaves from C. Barrios and 4a Av.

Zacatecoluca: Bus #540. 2hr., 8 per day 5:30am-4:30pm, US$1.

Sonsonate: Bus #287. 3hr.; 4 per day 5:30, 8:30am, 12:30, 2:30pm; US$1.25.

La Perla and Playa El Zonte: Bus #192. 1hr., every 40min. 7am-4:40pm, US$0.70.

Zunzal, El Tunco, and Playa San Diego: Bus #80. Every 10min. 6am-6pm, US$0.25. Going west, stops in El Tunco and then Playa Zunzal; going east, stops in Playa San

Diego. Ask which destination buses service, or stand along the main highway east or west of town to catch the bus as it heads out.

◢ ⚡ ORIENTATION AND PRACTICAL INFORMATION

Buses enter La Libertad from San Salvador at the Esso gas station before turning on the *carreterra*, which becomes **2a Calle Poniente** in the port. One block north, the main street, **Calle Barrios/Calle Calvario,** runs along the north side of the **parque central.** The northwest corner of the *parque* and the intersection of **Avenida Bolivar** and **Avenida Luz** is the center for the town's grid system. Two blocks south of C. Barrios, **4a Calle** runs along the beach and meets 5 Av. on the town's west side before heading to **La Punta Roca** on the west side of the bay.

Tourist Office: MITUR (☎2233 7835), on the *carreterra* just before the entrance to La Libertad from San Salvador. Provides info on guides, hotels, and surfing in the area. Regional maps available. Open M-F 8am-4pm, Sa-Su 8am-noon.

ATM: In Centro Comercial El Faro. **24hr. Credomatic ATM** accepts all international credit cards.

Beyond Tourism: El Salvador Spanish School (☎7051 4171; www.salvaspan.com). Offers class in Playa Zunzal and in La Libertad. For more **Beyond Tourism** opportunities, see p. 313.

Police: 2a C. Pte. (☎2327 7900), across from Complejo Turistico.

Pharmacy: Farmacía Jerusalem, 1a Av./Bolivar, C. Calvario (☎2335 3508). Open M-Sa 7am-6pm.

Medical Services: Clinica San Lucas, C. El Calvario #40 (☎2335 3206). Open 24hr.

Internet Access: Ciber Fenix, 2a C. Pte. (☎2312 9000), in Edificio Eco-Maritano. US$0.75 per hr. before 6pm, US$1 per hr. after 6pm. Open daily 10am-8pm.

Post Office: 2a C. Pte. (☎2335 3002), next to the police. Open M-F 8am-5pm, Sa 8am-noon.

⌂ ACCOMMODATIONS

The majority of La Libertad's lodging options are in popular surf spot Punta Roca, which also tends to be the safest and most tourist-friendly part of town. There are lots of small *hospedajes* around the town center and on the beachfront, but the crime and gang problems in the area make staying in PUnta Roca worth the extra splurge.

La Hacienda de Don Rodrigo, 5a Av. Sur (☎2335 3166), at the end of the Punta. The nicest option in Punta Roca. Comfortable doubles with A/C, cable TV, and private baths. The real appeals are the outdoor attractions; La Hacienda's rooms have huge terraces with outdoor dining areas, hammocks, and access to the mariachi music-filled pool area. Doubles US$50. AmEx/D/MC/V. ❺

La Posada de Don Lito, 5a Av. Sur (☎2335 3166), across from Restaurante El Delfin. This 2-part hotel, rooms in front of a small pool area, has slightly pricey but comfortable accommodations with A/C, cable TV, and private baths. On-site restaurant open daily 8am-10pm, Breakfast US$1.75-4.50. Seafood US$6-12. Meat entrees US$6-11. Full bar. Doubles US$50. AmEx/D/MC/V. ❺

Hotel Rick, 5a Av. Sur and 4a C. Pte. (☎2335 3361). The cheapest option around, Hotel Rick has clean rooms with cable TV and small private baths in its slightly worn building. Singles and doubles US$20, with A/C US$25; triples US$30/35. Cash only. ❹

PUNTA ROCA

Hotel Punta Roca (☎2346 1753; www.puntaroca.com.sv), affiliated with Restaurante Punta Roca. Offers surfing lessons, tour packages, and board rental from its location in San Blas, just west of La Libertad. US$10 per day for surfboard rental and about US$10-20 per hr. for surfing lessons. ❷

EL TUNCO

El Tunco has the most varied and backpacker-friendly accommodation options around La Libertad. The small town is fairly safe and has a cluster of hotels, hostels, and lodges all within 100 yards of the beach. Most establishments have either kitchens or restaurants for guest use.

Papaya's Lodge (☎2389 6231), 100 yards from the beach just before Hostel Mangle. Run by a local surfer nicknamed Papaya, the lodge offers low prices and suprisingly clean bathrooms. Guests have kitchen access and 2 open-air thatched-roof *cabañas* lined with hammocks, along with Wi-Fi and surfboard storage. Surf lesson with board rental US$15. Dorms US$7; singles US$10; doubles US$15. Cash only. ❷

Roca Sunzal Surf Resort (☎2389 6126; www.rocasunzal.net), just before Erika's Restaurant at the main beach. The perfect splurge, Sunzal has it all: beachfront location, sparkling pool and lounge area, restaurant overlooking the water, and private porches with hammocks for each room. Ask to stay in the boat-shaped suite. Breakfast included. Doubles US$50-100; triples US$90-100; apartments US$100-140. AmEx/D/MC/V. ❺

Hostel El Mangle (☎2389 6126), next to Papaya's Lodge just before the beach. Sister hotel to the pricier Roca Sunzal Lodge, El Mangle has dorms and a couple private rooms along with kitchen access, a popular porch on the water, and free Wi-Fi in the attached cafe (open daily 6am-5pm). Dorms US$7; doubles US$26. AmEx/D/MC/V. ❷

PLAYA EL PALMARCITO

Hotel Ver Mar 1 (☎7867 8845), a 2min. walk from the beach along the road from the highway. Clean, cheap rooms ideal for the budget traveler. Ask Mario about special group rates, surf trips, or lessons. Hammocks US$3; dorms US$6; 1-6 person rooms US$20, with A/C and private bath US$30. Camping US$2 per person. ❶

Atami 5 (☎2274 6206), east on Playa Palmar. An idyllic oasis perched on a cliff. A manicured resort with great beach access, 3 pools, deck chairs, bathrooms, showers, and requisite waterslide (US$7). Rooms US$70-80. ❺

PLAYA ZONTE

Other accommodations can be found by asking locals about spare rooms; prices and quality vary.

▨ **Surf Camp Horizonte 2** (☎2323 0099). Run by friendly surfer Saburo. Extremely comfortable environment for enjoying the beach, along with the camp's own landscaped pool area and porch-style lounging spaces. Kitchen available. Board rental (US$10 per day) includes 1hr. of free instruction. Cabin-style rooms have A/C, private baths, mini-fridges, and beachfront views. Singles US$30; doubles US$35; triples US$40. MC/V. ❸

BEACHES EAST OF LA LIBERTAD

Hostal El Roble (☎7252 8498; www.elrobleelsalvador.blogspot.com). Rooms with access to gardens and the beach. Breakfast included. Airport shuttle US$10. Surfing, hiking, rappelling and zipline tours available. Food US$1-7. Dorms US$7; doubles US$18. Cash only. ❷

🖸 FOOD

There are *comedores* around the *parque central* and *pupusa* stands lining 2a C. on the way towards Playas Tunco, Zunzal, and Zonte. More upscale restaurants line the water, and the most popular spots are toward Punta Roca. For groceries, visit **SuperSelectos,** Centro Comercial El Faro, behind the Esso gas station. (☎2346 1807. Open M-Sa 7am-8pm, Su 7am-7pm. MC/V.)

Restaurante El Delfin (☎2335 3361), next to Restaurante Punta Roca on 5a Av. Sur. Overlooking the water on the east side of Punta Roca. A large menu of seafood dishes served to a mostly local crowd. Mixed drinks US$5-15. Seafood US$9-15. Meat dishes US$5-10. Open daily 7am-9pm. MC/V. ❸

Complejo Turístico, 2a C. Pte., overlooking the water next to the Muelle. Two upscale seafood restaurants and a couple ice cream shops in a massive modern, concrete complex with the best views in town. Sandwiched between the Muelle and Punta Roca, you can watch the fishermen and surfers on the beach as you enjoy your meal. Parking US$0.50. Open Tu-Sa 10am-9pm. AmEx/D/MC/V. ❷

Restaurante Punta Roca, 4a C. (☎2346 1753 or 2335 3261; www.puntaroca.com.sv), at the entrance to Punta Roca. A surfer's haven and the spot to go to catch the latest surf updates and indulge in some delicious seafood and amazing views. The owner is a Miami native who serves the best food in town. Free Wi-Fi. Mixed drinks US$6-6.50. Seafood US$8-15. Soups US$5-12. Open daily 9am-8pm. MC/V. ❷

EL TUNCO

There are a couple restaurants on the beach that double as bars on the weekend. For the best cheap food in town, check out the **pupusa stand,** across from Hostel El Mangle; it's only open on the weekends (F-Su 6am-9am and 5pm-9pm), but the *pupusas* (US$0.35-0.50) are delicious and the most affordable option around.

Restaurante y Bar La Bocana (☎2389 6238), on the beach in front of the rock formation. This restaurant and bar is packed on the weekends with visiting Salvadorans. During the week it keeps busy with tourists enjoying the spectacular views over the beach; the 2nd floor deck overlooks the water. Mixed drinks US$4-7. Seafood US$9-15. Meat dishes US$4-5.50. Drinks US$2.50-4. Open Su-Th 7:30am-8pm; F-Sa 7:30am-2am. Cash only. ❷

Restaurante Erika (☎7878 2101; www.restauranteerika.com), on the shores of Rio Tunco just before La Bocana. This popular spot serves up fresh and hearty portions of fish (US$5-10), shrimp (US$7.50-9), and lobster (US$15-18), as well as meat dishes (US$4.50-7) and mixed drinks (US$4.50-9). Beer and cigarettes also available. Open daily 7am-11:30pm. Cash only. ❷

Pizzeria Mopelia (☎2389 6265), 100 yards before turn off to beach, on the left side of the access road. The most popular pizzeria around, this cafe-restaurant attached to the hotel of the same name offers reasonably priced, tasty pizzas at backpacker prices. The quiet location away from the crowds doesn't hurt either. Pizzas US$4-12. Open daily 10am-9pm. Cash only. ❷

PLAYA ZUNZAL

Café Zunzal 4 (☎2328 0132 or 0098), Km 43.5 on the coastal highway. One of the best restaurants around with a great view of the beach and amazing seafood. Entrees US$5-15. Open Tu-Su 11am-5pm. ❷

☎ SURFING

If you're not a surfer, the rocky, polluted waters of the bay of La Libertad hold little appeal. Have no fear: cleaner, sandier beaches dot the coast on both sides of town. However, if ripping tasty waves is your thing, Punta Roca, just a few hundred meters away from La Libertad, has the best waves around. (If you're looking for stretches of sand and good swimming, head east.) Crowds of day-trippers from San Salvador hit the beaches on the weekends, but Monday to Thursday finds empty expanses of sand, quieter restaurants, and (sadly) fewer *pupusa* stands.

Standing on the pier looking back at the shore, Playa el Malecón is on the right side, while Punta Roca extends off the end of Playa la Paz to the left. The best and biggest waves in the area break off Punta Roca, with 1½-5m swells. Surfing the point is only for experts. Playa El Tunco and Playa El Zonte have medium-sized waves good for surfing and swimming, though waves can get much wilder during the rainy season. During high tide, waves pummel the whole beach, so make sure to leave your belongs high up or they may drift out to sea. The smaller, inconsistent waves that come into Playa la Paz are good for beginners, but the beach is rather rocky and polluted, making Playa El Tunco/Zunzal to the west a more attractive option. Prime surfing months are April to October. For non-surfers, the beaches are sandiest and the waves smallest in December. *(Bus #80, leaving from 4 Av. south of C. Barrios in La Libertad, runs east to Playa San Diego (every 20min. 6am-6pm, US$0.25) and west to Playas Conchalio, Majahual, El Tunco, and El Zunzal (every 10min. 6am-6pm, US$0.25). Bus #192, leaving for La Perla from 4 Av. and 1 C., passes the same eastern beaches but goes farther to Playa El Palmercito and Playa Zonte (35min., every 40min. 5am-4:40pm, US$0.30). Minibuses (US$0.30) to Playa las Flores cruise 2 Av.)*

LA COSTA DEL SOL

La Costa del Sol, a popular beach getaway of the Salvadoran elite, is a seemingly endless peninsula of whitish-gray sand. Though its relatively calm surf and flat beaches make it an appealing relaxation spot, it's quite upscale; most hotels run above US$100 per night; the majority of vacationers here stay in private villas on the water, making it a difficult trip on a backpacker's budget.

▓PLAYA LOS BLANCOS. This is the best beach on Costa del Sol. If you're looking to tan and swim, this is where you should be. The beach is accessible from pathways every 100m or so along the Carreterra. Keep in mind that most hotels here are very expensive.

PLAYA SAN MARCELINO. More popular with fishermen than swimmers, Playa San Marcelino is visited mostly for its towering sea-side restaurants offering fresh *mariscos* to the hordes of vacationing Salvadorans. *(The first beach on the road towards La Puntilla, Playa San Marcelino is on the dirt road branching right off the main highway just before ritzy Hotel Pacific Paradise.)*

TURICENTRO AND PLAYA COSTA DEL SOL. If only visiting Costa del Sol for a day, the Turicentro is the place to go. Playa Costa del Sol, between Los Blancos and La Puntilla, offers decent swimming and a fairly clean beach. The beach boasts a host of other amenities like swimming pools, football field, basketball court, and a secure place to store your belongings when you go for a swim. (☎2338 2050. Entrance US$0.90, *cabañas* US$3. Open daily 7am-4pm.)

LA PUNTILLA. The tip of the Costa del Sol, La Puntilla prides itself in its beautiful views of the estuary, Isla Tasajera, and the Pacific Ocean. Primarily a dining area, it offers ocean-side restaurants on the beach and hammock-filled picnic-style lounge areas where you can bring your own meal. La Puntilla also serves as the unofficial dock for the Costa del Sol; from here, catch boats to Isla Tasajera (US$10), Isla de los Pájaros (US$20), the Río Lempa (US$50), and any other destination you can negotiate with the boat captain. Boats leave when passengers arrive; departures from 6am-4pm.

ISLA TASAJERA. A small fishing island off of La Puntilla, Isla Tasajera is a world-away from the honking horns and hawking vendors of the Costa del Sol; its long white beaches face the estuary and the ocean. The island has a couple small *tiendas* that offer basic snacks and drinks, but the main tourist center is 10min. across the beach from the *lancha* drop-off at Hotel y Restaurante Oasis de Tasajera p. 336. *(Take a lancha from La Puntilla (US$10 per person, departs upon arrival from 6am-4pm) to La Palmera, on the north side of the island. From there, walk along the beach 10min. to Hotel y Restaurante Oasis—it's the only other non-residential building on the island.)*

▞ TRANSPORTATION

Buses run along the length of the Costa del Sol along the *carreterra*, stopping for anyone standing on the side of the road. The closest thing the coast has to a terminal is **La Puntilla,** where buses line up in a parking lot just before the restaurants. If you catch a bus along the road, be prepared to stand, especially on the weekends; the relatively infrequent service means buses are full to the aisles. Buses go from La Puntilla to:

San Salvador: #495. 2hr., every 30min. 4:30am-5pm, US$1.40.

Zacatecoluca: #193. 1½hr., 6 per day 8am-4pm, US$1.50.

San Vicente: #193-D. 2½hr., 2 per day 6:30am and 8am, US$1.70.

◪ ▞ ORIENTATION AND PRACTICAL INFORMATION

The Costa del Sol is one long strip, with the beach on the Pacific side and the boats on the estuaries of the Río Jiboa and Lempa on the other. Bus routes follow the **Carretera Costa del Sol,** which bisects the peninsula, and passes the town of **Las Isletas,** where most services are located. The main beaches, in increasing distance from Las Isletas, are **Playa Marcelino, Costa del Sol, Los Blancos,** and **Puntilla** at the tip of the peninsula.

ATM: HSBC has an ATM at the Hotel Pacific Paradise, at the entrance to Playa San Marcelino. Open 24hr. MC/V.

Tourist Police: Playa Los Blancos (☎2338 2077), behind the *comedor.* Open 24hr.

Pharmacy: Farmacia San Ernesto (☎2354 4010), 1 block from the center of Las Isletas. Open M-Sa 8am-8pm.

Medical Services: Hospital Unidad de Salud Canton Las Isletas (☎2354 4045). Walk 1 block up from the pharmacy, then 2 blocks left and half a block right. Open 24hr.

⚓ ACCOMMODATIONS

▧PLAYA LOS BLANCOS

Mini Hotel y Restaurante Mila (☎2338 2074), across from the *comedor* and the tourist police. Comfortable, clean rooms with private baths and cable TV at budget rates. On-site pool and restaurant (open daily 8am-late, entrees US$4-10), as well as a hammock lounge overlooking Playa Los Blancos. Hammock rental US$1.25. Singles and doubles with fan US$25, with A/C US$35. Cash only. ❶

Hotel y Restaurante HayDeeMar (☎2338 2046), just before Restaurante Mila on the *carreterra*. Though the worn walls and old fixtures show that HayDeeMar is a bit past its prime, the electric blue rooms with cable TV and private baths are still serviceable, and the prices, popular restaurant, and pool area make it a good option. Singles with fan US$20, with A/C US$30; doubles US$25/35; triples with A/C US$40. Restaurant open daily 7am-6pm. Breakfast US$2.50-3. Seafood US$5-10. AmEx/D/MC/V. ❹

ISLA TASAJERA

Hotel y Restaurante Oasis de Tasajera (☎2888 0526). Comfortable rooms with fans, hammocks, private baths, and constant beach access, and a picturesque courtyard. Singles US$22; doubles US$30; quads US$40. ❹

▢ FOOD

▧PLAYA LOS BLANCOS

For everything you need from food to beach supplies, visit **Supermercado Costa del Sol**, at Km 57.5 on Carretera Costa del Sol. (☎2338 2589. Open daily 9am-6pm.)

Comedor Ruth (☎2338 2147), in front of the Tourist Police at Playa Los Blancos. One of the only food options at Los Blancos that's not part of a hotel, Comedor Ruth serves up quick and hearty portions of meat (US$3) and fish (US$4) at the most reasonable prices in town. Open daily 6:30am-4pm. Cash only. ❷

PLAYA SAN MARCELINO

Restaurante KennyMar (☎2338 2578), on the beachfront. Known for its stellar seafood, KennyMar offers a variety of entrees (US$7-15) to go along with its full bar service. Patio views are relaxing and breezy. Breakfast US$2-3.50. Drinks US$1-3.50. Open daily 7am-1am. AmEx/D/MC/V. ❷

Restaurante Yessenia (☎2338 2576; www.playasanmarcelino.com). Best views around, with a 4-level terraced dining area overlooking the water and the beach from Marcelino to the end of the Costa del Sol. Strings of conch shells hang from the rafters. Heaping plates of *mariscos* US$7-17. Mixed drinks US$4-8. Meat entrees US$4-8. Open daily 6am-9pm. AmEx/D/MC/V. ❸

LA PUNTILLA

Rancho Rafael Antonio, just to the right of the entrance to La Puntilla, on the water. A bit rustic, with no bathroom and an open-air cooking area near the road, Rancho Rafael Antonio has the biggest variety of food around and the best views; you can see Isla Tasajera, the Río, and the Pacific from its 2nd floor dining area. Lounge in the hammocks downstairs on the water. Seafood US$5-12. Meat entrees US$3-8. Mixed drinks US$3-7, Beer US$1-1.50. Open daily 6am-8pm. Cash only. ❷

CENTRAL COAST

La Posada de Don Emilio (☎2411 3521), on the right side of La Puntilla when coming from Los Blancos. Though it lacks the beachfront location of Rancho Rafael, La Posada offers a shadier option. Dining area with tables next to hammocks and a sunny pool for kids to enjoy while waiting for food. Seafood US$4-12. Mixed drinks US$4-12. Open daily 6am-7:30pm. Cash only. ❷

PUERTO EL TRIUNFO AND BAHÍA DE JIQUILISCO

A small fishing town that doubles as the entrance to the mangrove-dotted Bahía de Jiquilisco, Puerto El Triunfo is worn and somewhat dilapidated, but provides access to some of El Salvador's most beautiful and remote locales. The town's highlight is its abundant seafood; the marina serves up delicious fresh lobster, shrimp and fish all day long as local fishermen bring in their catch just feet away. For those with a little more time, excursions onto the semi-deserted islands around the bay afford some of the most beautiful scenery on the eastern shores of El Salvador.

⌐ TRANSPORTATION

Puerto El Triunfo is only about four blocks long, making transportation in town quite simple. Buses enter and leave town one block east of the *parque central* on the north-bound *avenida*. Buses from Puerto El Triunfo go to:

Usulután: Bus #363 or 377. 45min., every 10min. 4am-5pm, US$0.55.

San Miguel: Bus #377. 2½hr., every 30min. 4am-3:30pm, US$1.55.

Jiquilisco: Bus #363. 15min., every 10min. 4am-5pm, US$0.25.

San Salvador: Bus #185. 2½hr.; 6 per day 4:30, 5, 5:30, 6, 6:30am, 3pm; US$2.

◢◤ 🛈 ORIENTATION AND PRACTICAL INFORMATION

Puerto el Triunfo is a small town with only two main streets. The **Avenida Principal, or 1a Avenida,** runs along the west side of the **parque central**, ending at the **Marina Turística,** where the majority of the town's restaurants and boat services are. One block east of the *parque central*, **Avenida Francisco Seguena** serves as a de facto bus station for the town. There are few services in town; nearby **Jiquilisco** has the closest bank, **Banco Agricola** 3 C. Pte. and 1a Av. Nte. (☎2210 0000. Visa cash advances. Open M-F 8am-4pm, Sa 8am-noon).

Police: 1a Av. Sur #41 (☎2663 6885 or 6154), right before the marina.

Pharmacy: Farmacia Alfalfa, 1a Av. Nte. (☎2634 8257), 1 block north of the *parque central*. Open daily 6:30am-8pm.

Hospital or Medical Services: Clínica Médica, 1a Av. Nte. (☎2634 6211), next door to the pharmacy. Open M-F 9am-5pm.

Internet Access: Ciber Center, Av. Francisco Seguena (☎7418 7796). Internet US$0.75 per hr. Open daily 8am-8pm.

⌂ ACCOMMODATIONS

Hotel y Restaurante El Jardín, 1a Av. Nte. (☎7729 2188), 1 block north of the *parque central*. The bathrooms have a few bugs, but the rooms are clean enough in Puerto's only lodging option. Only a couple blocks from the Marina, Jardín offers safe rooms with A/C, cable TV, and very basic private baths in its enclosed courtyard. On-site restaurant open daily from 8am-midnight. Singles and doubles US$17; triples US$20. Cash only. ❷

⬛ FOOD

Puerto El Triunfo's restaurants, with the exception of the restaurant at Hotel Jardín, all food options are located at the marina. Expect to eat lots of fresh seafood. The standard chicken, steak, and Mexican options are available at some places.

Restaurante El Chipotle (☎2663 6939), on the 2nd level of the marina. Views overlook the small boats at the marina's harbor. A menu of meat entrees (US$4-7) and tacos (US$1.50-3) to go along with the shrimp (US$9), lobster (US$12-14), fish (US$5.50-9), and seafood cocktails (US$4.-9.50). Open daily 9am-9pm. Cash only. ❷

El Cayukito (☎2633 7426), on the level 1 pavilion at the marina. Though it doesn't have the upstairs view, El Cayukito is still right on the water, and its bright blue picnic benches are a popular local dining spot. Dine on fresh versions of shrimp (US$9), fish (US$4.25-7.50), lobster (US$12.50) cocktails and *ceviches* (US$4-8). Finish it all off with a cold beer (US$1-2) or *licuado* (US$1.30). Open daily 9am-10:30pm. Cash only. ❷

👁 SIGHTS AND OUTDOOR ACTIVITIES

THE MARINA. The marina area jumps all day with fishermen bringing in catch, women selling fish, and families returning to the Bay Islands. Decaying steel-hulled trawlers at the end of the main pier are remainders of the collapse of the local fishing industry in the mid-1980s, after the Farabundo Martí National Liberation Front bombed nearby bridges and effectively cut off the port from San Salvador. *(At the south end of 1a Av. Sur/Av. Principal, right after the police office. Open 24hr.; most restaurants open 9am-11pm.)*

LA PENINSULA DE CORAL DE MULAS. La Península de Coral de Mulas protects the Bahia from the Pacific Ocean; with mangrove islands on one side and rough waves and deserted beaches on the other. The only regular boat service is to **Isla Coral de Mula** (US$2; departs when passengers arrive). Before leaving, buy food, drinks, and bring your own hammock, since the island is void of facilities. **Isla Menéndez,** on the peninsula's western end, has a sea turtle nursery. In town you can buy refreshments. A 30min. walk brings you to the isolated Pacific beaches. There's not much to see most of the year, except mid-August through September when the 1,500 eggs hatch. On the eastern end of the peninsula is the small community of **Coral de Mulas,** from where you can cross the peninsula to another deserted Pacific beach. It is a hot walk, but the scenery is wonderful. *(Boats run from dawn to dusk from the Marina in Puerto El Triunfo. 20min. US$2 per person. Make sure to arrange transportation back before departing, or be at the Coral de Mulas docks by 2:30pm; boast stop running fairly early.)*

ISLA EL JOBAL. Swanky Barillas Marina does trips out to Isla El Jobal, where locals run a **Cooperativa de Cocos**—a coconut farm that decided to make money by showing off how to use coconuts for unconventional purposes. They also happen to sell coconuts. *(☎2632 1802. Boat to the island US$30.)*

NORTHERN EL SALVADOR

North of the capital, pastures yield to remote mountains that hide treasures for those tourists willing to cross the poorly maintained roads. Suchitoto's fine architecture, beautiful scenery, and traditional lifestyle attract travelers drawn by El Salvador's cultural history. Local artesanía thrives in several areas, including La Palma and Ilobasco, towns known for pottery and hammocks. Nature lovers enjoy Lago Suchitlán's 14 species of fish and more than 200 types of birds, while more restless travelers heed the call of El Pital, El Salvador's highest peak.

SUCHITOTO

Suchitoto calls itself the cultural capital of El Salvador, and if such a thing is measured in number of resident artists, local pride, and distinctive architectural style, they may not be far off. Though it can swelter during the day, the city cools at dusk; it as at this time that residents emerge to wander about, eating *pupusas* in the Plaza Central, determined to create a nightlife scene, be it in a park or at a bar. For those not compelled by the town's artsy, colonial charm, the nearby Lake Suchitlán presents visitors with miles of panoramic vistas, waterfalls, caves, and hikes just minutes from the town center.

▟ TRANSPORTATION

Buses: Suchitoto does not have an official bus station; buses coming in and out of town stop at the corner of 1a C. Pte. and 4a Av. Sur. To: **Aguilares** (#163, 30 min., every 40min. 4am-8pm, US$0.50); **Ilobasco** (#482, 2hr., 2 per day 9:30am and 2pm, US$1.70); **San Salvador** (#129, 1½hr., every 15min. 4am-8pm, US$0.75). Travelers bound for **Chalatenango** should take the Aguilares bus; be prepared to stand most of the trip.

Boat: Several boats cross to **San Luis del Carmen** on the other side of Lake Suchitlán. The **docks** are at **San Luis del Carmen** and **San Francisco Lempa,** 2km from the town center. A taxi or truck ride from the center costs about US$4; the roads are unpaved and in some areas practically nonexistent. **Ferries** (US$1) run 6am-4pm. **Lanchas** (US$5) will depart on your arrival. For both ferries and *lanchas*, be sure to leave before 1pm; buses on the other side stop at 2:30pm and you should leave about an hour for the ride across. From the other side, it is a 30min. bus ride to **Chalatenango** (30min., 7 per day 6am-2:30pm, US$0.80).

✦ 🛈 ORIENTATION AND PRACTICAL INFORMATION

Suchitoto is a fairly small city with a compact center. Buses enter Suchitoto on the **Carretera de Oro,** also known as **Boulevard del Ejército Nacional.** Once in Suchitoto, they stop at the corner of 1a C. Pte. and 4a Av. Sur. One block north of this is the **Oficina de Turismo.** The **Plaza Central** is bounded by **1a Avenida Sur, 1a Calle Pte., 1a Avenida Norte,** and **1a Calle Ote.** At the east side of the Plaza Central is the **Iglesia de Santa Lucía.** The majority of restaurants and hotels are located within a few blocks of this Plaza; to get to **Lago Suchitlán** and the docks there, continue north two blocks from the Plaza Central and take a right, walking about 2km downhill to the ferry docks.

Tourist Office: C. San Martín 2 (☎2335 1739; www.suchitoto-el-salvador.com), 1 block west of the Plaza Central. Open M-F 8am-4pm. Maps and information on guides, hotels, and restaurants.

Tours and Agencies: Vista Conga Tours, (☎2335 1679 or 7118 1999), on the road into Suchitoto, just before El Tejado. Private transportation and tours from Suchitoto around El Salvador, including boating, kayaking, waterfall jumping tours.

Banks: Banco Procredit, 2a Av. Nte. and 2A C. Pte. (☎2335 1021). Open M-F 9am-5pm, Sa 9am-Noon. A **24hr. ATM** operates in the main square, just south of the Catedral, next to La Lupita del Portal.

Beyond Tourism: Pájaro Flor, 4a C. Pte. 22 (☎2327 2366; www.pajaroflor.com). Offers specialized Spanish-language classes for both individuals and groups. For more **Beyond Tourism** opportunities, see p. 313.

Police and Touris Police: 1a C. Pte. (☎2335 1147), 1 block north of plaza central.

Pharmacy: Farmacia San Rafael (☎2335 1340), in the Plaza Central. Open daily 8am-8pm.

Internet Access: X-Streme Speed Cyber Cafe, 1 C. Pte. Barrio Cantario 8 (☎2235 1722), 1 block south of the Plaza Central, High-speed internet, playstation, and international calling online. Internet US$1 per hr. Open daily 8am-8pm.

Post Office: 1a Av. Nte. (☎2335 1040), 1 block west of the Plaza Central. Open M-F 8am-noon and 2pm-5pm, Sa 8am-noon.

ACCOMMODATIONS

Hostal Vista Lago, 6a C. Pte., 2a Av. Nte. #18 (☎2335 1357 or 7880 3076). At the far north end of town, this sleeply little hostel has 4 private rooms with a shared bathroom. A panoramic view of Lake Suchitlan is visible from both the small hammock area and the memento-decorated patio. Acoustic flute versions of old Beatles songs play as the sun goes down. Rooms US$7. Beer US$1. Cash only. ❷

Hotel/Posada Blanca Luna, 1a C. Ote. (☎2335 1661), just 1 block south of the Catedral. The private cold-water baths, in-room cable TV, communal kitchen, and tranquil tree-lined patio with hammocks make up for the rooms' drab concrete interiors. Rooms US$7 per person. Cash only. ❷

Posada Alta Vista, 1a Av. 8 (☎2335 1645 or 1648), just 20 ft. north of the Plaza Central. Though its rooms are considerably pricier than most budget options in town, Posada Alta Vista has the amenities to go with it; every room has cable TV and A/C, and have private hot-water baths. Decorations are simple but pleasant, and there is beer for sale and movie rentals available at reception. Beer US$1. 24hr. movie rental US$1. Singles with shared bath US$21, with private bath US$26; doubles US$42; 4-bed rooms for 4-7 people US$70. Cash only. ❸

Hotel Obraje, 2a C. Oriente #3 (☎2335 1173), just north of the Catedral. Conveniently located just half a block from the Plaza Central, this small hotel and restaurant has reasonably priced, clean rooms with fans and private cold-water bathrooms. Rooms US$12 Restaurant on-site. Beer US$1. Entrees US$2-8. Cash only. ❷

FOOD

Stalls at the the Suchitoto **market,** open from dawn to dusk, sell fruits, vegetables, cooked foods, and other groceries. The market is indoors, across the street from the tourist office.

La Lupita del Portal, (☎2335 1429), in the central square, to the left of the front of the church. Tucked under the awning of the strip of stores on the south side of the central park, this restaurant serves up breakfast (US$2.50-4), mostly-grilled entrees (US$3-10), and *pupusas* (US$0.50-0.85) at its wooden tables with bright tablecloths. There is a faux-courtyard inside, with plant-covered trellises overlooking a bar area. Vegetarian options. Service is quick and friendly. Beer US$1.50. Open daily 7:30am-9pm. Cash only. ❷

Panadería Liliana (☎2335 1114), half a block west of the Plaza Central. This bakery is a local favorite, with lots of space, comfortable wood tables with checkered tableclothes. The delicious pastries (US$0.50-2.50) and sandwiches (US$1.50-4) sold here are served to a busy morning and afternoon crowd. Breakfast US$1-3.50. Open daily 7am-6pm. Cash only. ❷

Artex Cafe/Bar (☎2335 1410; www.centroartex.org), on the south side of the Plaza Central. Part bar, part cafe, part internet cafe, and part artisan shop. Bright red-and-yellow tables and a selection of coffee (US$0.50-2.50), breakfast (US$1.50-3.50), and alcohol (US$1-2.50). Book exchange and free Wi-Fi. There are also computers available for customers. Open M and Sa-Su 7:30am-8pm, Tu-F 9am-8pm. Cash only. ❷

2 Gardenias/Zuka Fe Bar, 3A Av. Nte. 48 (☎2335 1868 or 7035 4573), 2 blocks south of the Plaza Central. This bar, restaurant, and galleria also houses a hostel, but its main draw is the artsy dining area, where you can mingle, have a drink, and browse local art. Beer US$1-2.50; mixed drinks US$1.50-4. Entrees US$3-10. Open daily 11am-10pm. MC/V. ❷

👁 SIGHTS AND OUTDOOR ACTIVITIES

IGLESIA DE SANTA LUCÍA. On the east end of the Plaza Central. The center of Suchitoto, the church was constructed in 1853; its whitewashed exterior epitomizes the style of construction that has made Suchitoto famous in El Salvador. Just in front of the Cathedral, the Plaza Central is a popular hang-out spot home to street vendors selling delicious *pupusas* and other Salvadoran specialties. *(Open daily from dawn to dusk. Free.)*

PARQUE SAN MARTÍN. The Parque San Martín has views of Lago de Suchitlán and an open-air art gallery; the town's artists have transformed the small park using sculptures incorporating "war garbage." Tranquil during the daytime, its a local and sometimes uncomfortable hangout at night; women may find themselves getting more attention than they would like from the mostly male visitors at this time. *(On the corner of 4 Av. Nte. and 4 C. Poniente.)*

LAGO DE SUCHITLÁN. The lake used to be a good swimming spot, but overtime the dam's construction has made the water too still; swimming isn't a good idea unless you fancy a dip among ferry trash, in murky, green water. For all of the filth, it's still a strikingly beautiful and peaceful spot. *(30min. from town by foot. Take 3 Av. Nte. north until the 3-way fork. Continuing straight ahead, you will be rewarded with views of the lake before you descend to the shore. Trucks and taxis run from the bottom of the hill (US$4 per person, less for a group ride). Bearing right makes for a longer but more gradual walk to the shore. Some travelers thumb for rides back to town, since either route back is a 45min. uphill hike; Let's Go does not recommend hitchhiking.)*

GALLERIES. In a shaded villa overlooking Lago de Suchitlán, the home and museum of famed artist **Alejandro Cotto** houses a bevy of works representing the artist's life and the culture of El Salvador and Suchitoto. It has odd hours, but it's a must-see for those interested in the culture and history of the region. *(Open daily 2-5pm. US$4)* Another of the area's well-known artists, **Víctor Manuel Sanabria,** nicknamed "Shanay," has a studio and gallery on 3 Av. Nte. between 2 and 4 C. Oriente. *(Knock any time during the day and he'll be happy to show you around.)*

LOS TERCIOS. The tourist office organizes horse rides to Los Tercios, a 25m high waterfall with strange cubic-rock formations To get to the waterfall on your own is a 30min. hike from town; start in front of the church and head south (away from the Plaza Central toward the entrance to the village), until you approach a soccer field. From there, it is a 15min. walk along the main road to the house where the path to the waterfalls start. If you don't have a guide and want one, the kids that live on the property are willing to serve as guides.

Though the rock formations are visible year-round, swimming is really only possible at Los Tercios after significant rainfall as the waterfall itself is often fairly dry. *(Horse rides US$20-25 per person, discounts for groups.)*

LA PALMA

Nestled in the cool mountains near the Honduran border, La Palma charms tourists and locals alike with its fresh breezes, colorful Naif artwork, and numerous outdoor activities. Cerro El Pital, El Salvador's tallest mountain, is just kilometers away. Within the city are numerous shops and markets selling locally made paintings, woodwork, and other crafts in the Naif style influenced by artist Fernando Llort. No stranger to tourism, La Palma is filled with picturesque lodging options and tasty, inexpensive food, making it equally pleasant as way station or as a destination unto itself.

▐ TRANSPORTATION

La Palma is small enough that it is easily navigated on foot.

Buses: All intercity buses stop at the Parque Municipal, just before the MiTur/CorsaTour office. To: **El Poy** (#119, 30min., every 30min. 6am-7pm, US$0.45); **Los Planes** (#509A, 2 per day 11am and 3pm, US$0.25-1) via **San Ignacio, Rio Chiquito,** and **Granadillas; Las Pilas** (#509, every hr. 6am-6pm, US$0.25-1) via **San Ignacio, Rio Chiquito,** and **Miramundo; San Salvador,** (#119, 2½hr., every 30min. 6am-4:30pm, US$1.60).

Mototaxis: Small and red, these mini taxis scoot travelers too lazy to walk around town. US$0.20-0.50 per ride.

◆▌ ▐ ORIENTATION AND PRACTICAL INFORMATION

Buses enter La Palma on the **Carretera Troncal del Norte,** which turns into **Calle Gerardo Barrios** when it becomes a one-way street in the town center. The **Carretera** continues out of La Palma on its way to San Ignacio. La Palma's **Parque Municipal** is bounded by Carretera Troncal del Nte./C. Gerardo Barrios on the east and **Calle Principal** on the west; the majority of restaurants and hotels are on these two streets. The two streets are connected by **Calle La Cancha,** which runs perpendicular from the police station, down past the post office, to the **Museo de Artesanias de La Palma.**

Tourist Office: (☎2335 9076), in front of Parque Municipal. Open M-F 8am-4pm, Sa-Su 9am-1pm. Internet available; they also distribute maps and information on local guides, artisan cooperatives, hotels, restaurants, and bus schedules.

Tours: ADIZAL, (☎2309 1006 or 1007). A Río Chiquito-based organization of local youths that provides guide services for the area's many trails. **Arnoldo** (☎2286 4421 or 2352 9226), who speaks English, is another local mountain guide. For tours of La Palma, **Oscar García,** owner of Piera del Bosque, can serve as a guide (☎2335 2467).

Bank: Citibank (☎2305 9330), on the corner of C. La Cancha and C. Principal. Open M-F 8:30am-12:15pm and 1pm-4pm, Sa 8:30am-noon. **24hr. ATM.**

Police: C. Gerardo Barrios, in front of the Parque Municipal. Open 24hr.

Pharmacy: Farmacia San Rafael, C. El Principal (☎2305 8477), in front of the Parque Municipal. Open daily 7am-6pm.

Medical Services: Laboratorio-Clinica La Palma, C. Gerardo Barrios (☎2300 7433), next to Mini-Super La Palma. Open M-F 7am-5pm, Sa 7am-noon.

Internet: Palma City OnLine, C. Principal, Barrio El Centro (☎2305 8674). Photocopies US$0.04. Internet US$0.75 per hr. Open daily 8:30am-7pm.

Post Office: C. La Cancha (☎2305 8519), 50m from Citibank. Open M-F 8am-noon and 2pm-5pm, Sa 8am-Noon.

ACCOMMODATIONS

There are only a few accommodations in La Palma; most hotels are located on the **Carretera Troncal del Norte,** along which buses travel from the junction at Amayo to San Ignacio. There camping and lodging options closer to hiking trails at Miramundo, a small village near Cerro El Pital and other local trails.

Hotel y Restaurante La Palma, Carretera Troncal del Nte., Km 84 (☎2335 9012), at the entrance to town, where the road forks between C. Principal and C. Gerardo Barrios. Easily the nicest option in town, this hotel has cool, chalet-style housing with private hot-water baths. The older section, which overlooks the main complex, has vaulted ceilings with high windows, while the lower, newer rooms have bright murals on the walls and hammocks on the porch. On-site restaurant (open daily 7am-10pm; breakfast US$4-5; dinner US$4-12), pool, and TV area with free Wi-Fi. Rooms US$15 per person. Cash only. ❸

Hotel y Restaurante de Montaña Paseo Pital, C. Gerardo Barrios (☎2305 9344). The cheapest option in town, this hotel has basic rooms with fans and private hot-water bathrooms. There is free on-site parking and a pool for guest use (closed rainy season, usually May-Aug.). The restaurant with purple and seafoam green booths and jungle murals serves up cafeteria style *comida típica* at reasonable prices. Restaurant open daily 6:30am-6pm. Entrees US$2-5. Rooms US$5 per person. Cash only. ❷

Hotel y Restaurante La Posada Real, C. Gerardo Barrios (☎2335 9009 or 7482 0600). Its rooms are a bit musty, with simple whitewashed walls and older fixtures, but the clean private hot-water baths, fans, convenient location, and on-site restaurant with reasonably priced breakfast (US$3) and dinner (US$5-10) make it a good choice for those on a tight budget. Rooms US$8 per person. Cash only. ❷

FOOD

La Palma is full of *comedores*, cafeterias, and *pupuserías* serving up *comida típica*. It's hard to find anything other than rice, tortillas, and meat here. Most hotels have their own restaurants attached, which serve similarly priced Salvadoran and Central American food. Those desperate for something different can go to **Mini-Super La Palma** at C. Gerardo Barrios. (☎2305 9403. Open daily 7:30am-7:30pm. Cash only.)

Restaurante y Pupusería La Palma, C. Principal, Barrio El Centro (☎2335 9063). Popular with locals, this restaurant—which has no connection to the hotel and restaurant of the same name—serves up hearty portions of *comida típica* at its wooden picnic tables with plastic-covered tablecloths and fans to keep the breeze going. Entrees US$2-4.50. Open M-Sa 8am-8pm. Cash only. ❷

Restaurante del Pueblo, C. Gerardo Barrios (☎2305 8503), just past Hotel Montaña. The options at this family-run eatery are limited, but the portions are hearty and cheap. The atmosphere is one of the most pleasant in town, with medieval-style chairs flanked by a mix-and-match decor that includes an old xylophone, religious icons, modernist paintings, a few strands of Christmas lights, and the occasional urn. Sandwiches US$1.25. Breakfast US$2.50-3. Entrees US$3-5. Open daily 7am-8pm. Cash only. ❷

Cafe de Cafe, C. El Principal (☎2335 9190), across from Telecom. Serving coffee (US$0.75-1.50), *licuados* (US$1.25), and desserts (US$1-1.25), this small cafe has a few cushy leather chairs, bar-style seating, and picnic tables. Guests come to lounge and make use of the town's only free Wi-Fi. Open M-Sa 8am-7:30pm. Cash only. ❷

Cartagena's Pizza, Barrio El Centro, Entrada La Palma (☎2305 9475 or 2301 7986). Serving up pizza (US$2-12), tacos (US$1.10-2.50), enchiladas (US$0.40-0.50), and

ON THE MENU

PLATOS TÍPICOS: THE SALVADORAN BREAKFAST OF CHAMPIONS

It's 9 am in El Salvador, and your bleary eyes spot platos *típicos* on the breakfast menu. Although it literally translates to "typical dishes," your usual breakfast fare is nowhere to be found—no pancakes, no omelettes, and no granola! What could have possibly taken the place of your eggwiches, your crullers, and your French toast? A enormous platter of refried pinto beans, sour cream, cheese, and plátanos fritos over rice and scrambled eggs, that's what.

Platos típicos, available almost any restaurant serving breakfast, is a Salvadoran smorgasbord of national favorites, including *huevos picados* (eggs scrambled with vegetables) and casamiento (white rice fried with black beans, onions, garlic, and spices). Served with a side of toast or warm tortillas, try wrapping the breakfast fixings into a breakfast burrito, or use the bread to mop up the breakfast mess. Wash it all down with café de maíz, made by brewing toasted corn kernels in hot water, or a traditional Mayan atole, a warm, thick, and creamy elixir made with corn and cinnamon and sweetened with sugar. You'll never settle for cornflakes and coffee again.

burritos/quesadillas (US$1-1.50), Cartagena's has a little something different from the usual *comida típica*. Open M-Th and Sa-Su 6am-8:30pm. Cash only. ❷

Típicos y Cocteles María Luisa, C. al Instituto Nacional (☎2352 1127). A small corner-shop dining area with green cinderblock walls, fans, and Spanish-language TV; low on atmosphere but heavy on variety. A hodgepodge of Chinese dishes (US$1.50-4.50), seafood (US$3.75-4.50), *comida típica* (US$2.50-4.50), and a variety of *licuados* (US$0.80-1.30). Open daily 7am-8pm. Cash only. ❷

◉ SIGHTS

In addition to its famed outdoor activities, La Palma is an artistic center in El Salvador; along with nearby towns San Ignacio and Chalatenango, it is home to several artisan cooperatives producing paintings, woodwork, and other local crafts. You can see evidence of this work in the bright, Naif murals covering the walls of almost every house and building in town.

COPAPASE. The oldest established artisan cooperative, Copapase includes artists from both San Ignacio and La Palma. It has an office and **museum** on C. La Cancha, one block past the post office, with information about the cooperative, examples of its work, and a history of the organization. (☎2305 9376. Open M-F 8am-5pm, Sa-Su 8am-noon.)

ASOCIACIÓN COOPERATIVA LA SEMILLA DE DIOS. Those with a hankering to see more than the final product can contact artisan cooperative Semilla de Dios, which has a store in La Palma, but will also arrange tours of its production process for individuals and groups. (3a C. Pte. and 5a Av. Nte., Barrio San Antonio. ☎2335 9010; coopsem@turbonett.com, Open daily 8am-4pm. Call or email for information about tours.)

ARTESANOS UNIDOS. This group of 12 local artisans can give a more personalized presentation of local artistic culture, from production to distribution. (For information on tours or the art itself, call ☎2300 2485.)

▣ DAYTRIPS FROM LA PALMA

CERRO EL PITAL. El Salvador's highest mountain (2730m), Cerro El Pital offers panoramic views of El Salvador's volcanoes and of nearby Honduras, whose border is just kilometers away. The climb can be muddy and steep, but does not require any technical skills. There is a camping area at the summit. Be prepared to start your climb early, especially during the rainy season; the rain is usually worse in the afternoons and on the mountains, making for a muddy walk if the weather gets bad. *(Bus 509 leaves from the Parque Municipal in La Palma every hr. 6am-6pm, stopping in Río Chiquito; ask the driver to let you off at El Pital (1hr., US$0.80). From this point, it is only a 1½hr. hike to the peak. To be safe, either hike in a group or get a local guide to accompany you. From the main road in Río Chiquito, turn left on the dirt road (where the town's few houses are), and continue along a steep road until you reach the peak, bearing right at any forks along the way. You'll pass three barbed-wire gates. During the rainy season, this road can become quite muddy. At the top, a US$1 entrance fee is required. There is a camping area with a toilet (US$2 per person including admission). Bring your own gear and come prepared for chilly temperatures.)*

MIRAMUNDO. This small town, high up in the mountains, is right next to hiking trails, waterfalls, and rivers. Most tourist activity here originates at **Hostal Miramundo,** which has log-cabin style lodging, a restaurant, karaoke bar, and guides for hikes. **Emely Tours,** based at the hostel, offers trips to the Río Sumpul, Cerro El Pital, and Las Pilas. The hostel arranges transportation from San Ignacio; package deals (one-day trip US$26) include transportation, meals, and hiking around the area. *(Miramundo is 2km from Río Chiquito and 10km from San Ignacio. Hostal Miramundo arranges transportation from San Ignacio; contact them in advance to arrange pick up. Using public transportation, take bus #509 from La Palma (every hr. 6am-6pm, US$0.45), and get off at Miramundo; you can also hike from Río Chiquito, but the 2km trudge uphill is not that fun with luggage. Be sure to bring warm clothes; this is one of the only parts of the country where temperatures get close to freezing. Hostal Miramundo ☎ 2219 6252 or 6251; www.hotelmiramundo.com. Rooms with private hot-water bath and TV. 2-4 person rooms US$50, 2 person cabins US$50.)*

LAS PILAS. Las Pilas is the capital of agriculture in this mountainous region, and has one of the best markets around, full of fresh fruit and vegetables; in fact, you may even be able to pick the fruit yourself. There is a nice hike from Las Pilas to the **Río Sumpul,** a river that forms the border with Honduras and originates at El Pital. Turn right in the center of town, and make the 20min. walk to the river, where you can find pleasant bathing pools. *(Bus #509, which also services Río Chiquito, San Ignacio, and Miramundo, terminates in Las Pilas (1hr., every hr. 6am-6pm, US$0.50). Make sure that you finish up in time to catch a bus back to La Palma; the last one leaves at 5pm.)*

WESTERN EL SALVADOR

Hilly terrain covered by national parks, lakes, volcanoes, and coffee plantations make the west one El Salvador's most captivating regions. Santa Ana, the
country's most pleasant city, boasts a newly renovated theater and impressive
cathedral, while the small towns of Apaneca, Juayua, and Nahuizalco offer
an idyllic mountain escape. Traces of the region's history are visible at the
archaeological site of Tazumal. For a more extreme escape, head into the cloud
forest of Parque Nacional Montecristo, near Metapán in the north, or visit El
Salvador's last untouched wildlife reserve at Parque Nacional El Imposible.

APANECA

Surrounded by forests and coffee plantations, Apaneca is a peaceful village
that has remained largely untouched by tourists. Founded in 1525, the coffee industry has supported Apaneca for over 400 years, employing a majority of the population. The least touristy of the Ruta De Flores villages, Apaneca is a surprisingly calm place with not much more than beautiful scenery,
cool air, and good home cooking.

▟ TRANSPORTATION

Buses heading towards **Ahuachapan** and **Ataco** leave from 2a C. Pte.; those going
towards **Juayua** and **Sonsonate** stop on 3a Av. Nte. before heading out of town.
Both directions are served by bus #249 (every 15min., daily 5am-7pm, US$0.30-
1); Ataco and Ahuachapan are also served by **minibuses** (every 10 min, daily
5am-5pm, US$0.25-0.50).

▟▟ ORIENTATION AND PRACTICAL INFORMATION

Apaneca has two main roads, **Calle Menéndez** and **Avenida Central** which intersect
one block east from the southeast corner of the **parque central** to form the center of the town's grid system.

Tourist Information: Casa de la Cultura, C. Menéndez/Av. 15 de Abril (☎2433 0163).
Open M-F 8am-4pm.

Police: 3a C. Ote. and Av. Central (☎2433 0347).

Pharmacy: Farmacia San Agustin, Av. Central Nte. #8 (☎2433 0085). Open daily 7am-6pm.

Internet: Cyber Cafe, (☎2443 0625), in front of the Parque Municipal. Internet US$1
per hr. Open daily 8am-6pm.

Post Office: 3 C. Ote./Av. 15 de Abril Nte. (☎2433 0430). Open M-F 8am-noon and
2-5pm, Sa 8am-noon.

▟ ACCOMMODATIONS

Though Apaneca has few accommodation options, most (like the ones below)
offer unforgettable quirks.

Hostal Rural Las Orquideas, Av. Central Sur #4 (☎2433 0061). Run by friendly owner
Roberto Aguirre and his wife, Las Orquideas has clean rooms with private hot-water
baths situated around a courtyard. The long porch has hammocks for lounging, and the
walls have painted murals and mini-doors; duck before you head into the courtyard.
Singles US$15; doubles US$20. Cash only. ❸

Hotel El Paraiso, Av. 15 de Abril Sur (☎7296 2055). A collector's dream, Paraiso is beautifully decorated with wrought-iron sculptures, colorful fabrics, and huge collections of key chains, mugs, plates, and beer cans lining the walls. The comfortable rooms have vaulted ceilings, private hot-water baths, phones, and in some rooms, cable TV. There is a courtyard, parking, and several large meeting rooms and lounge areas for guest use. Singles and doubles US$30; triples and quads US$40. AmEx/D/MC/V. ❺

🖪 FOOD

Enjoy typical Salvadoran dishes like *pupusa* while absorbing the spectacles offered at each of the following restaurants.

☒ **La Cocina de Mi Abuela,** 1a Av. (☎2433 0100), 2 blocks north of the *parque central*. People from all over the country come to enjoy a gourmet meal at one of the wooden tables in Grandma's Kitchen; admire the antique photographs, plates, and railings. Live music and beautiful gardens accompany the exquisite *típico*. Meals US$12-15. Reservations required. Open Sa-Su 11am-7pm. AmEx/D/MC/V. ❺

Mercado Municipal, on the east side of the *parque central*. The Mercado Municipal is home to several *comedores* and pupuserías serving up *comida típica* to locals and tourists at checkered picnic tables next door to little *artesanías*. Pupusas US$0.20-0.60. Entrees US$2-5. Open daily 6am-5pm. Cash only. ❶

👁 🏞 SIGHTS AND OUTDOOR ACTIVITIES

Two hikes into the volcanic region leave from points just outside of town. Note that the trip isn't safe to make alone. Fortunately, the local police (☎2433 0037), located two blocks west of the *parque*, are happy to guide and protect travelers.

LAGUNA VERDE. A 7km walk from Apaneca, Laguna Verde is a beautiful and popular crater lake surrounded by pine slopes. *(From the highway at the edge of town heading towards Ataco, take the dirt road to the right of the Jardín de Flores garden center; this road winds up and around the mountain, and passes some views of Ahuachapán. The trip should take 3hr. total.)*

LAGUNA LAS NINFAS. The smaller Laguna Las Ninfas, a 45min. walk from town, has good bird-watching. The laguna area has nice views but dries up in times of low rainfall. It's easy to get lost—arrange a guide at Casa de la Cultura or the police station. *(Head straight from the garden center and then, after about 20min., bear right onto a dried-out creek bed.)*

JUAYUA

Quickly becoming a backpacker's hotspot, Juayua (why-YOU-a) is a cobblestone town set in a valley surrounded by volcanoes and coffee fields. Though the hiking, waterfalls, and caffeine are reasons enough to visit, the real star is the weekly *Feria Gastronómica*, the weekend food-festival that transforms several town blocks into a dining extravaganza at bargain prices.

🖪 TRANSPORTATION

Buses drop-off and depart from the town entrance across the street from Scotiabank. Two buses service Juayua, going to:

Ahuachapan/Sonsonate: Bus #249. Every 15min. 5am-6:30pm, stopping in **Ataco** (30min., US$0.55), **Apaneca** (20min., US$0.40), and **Nahuizalco** (25min., US$0.40). All buses leave from the same spot, so ask the driver which direction the bus is going before getting on.

Santa Ana: Bus #238. 3hr.; 5 per day 5:30, 8, 9am, 2, and 4pm; US$2.

⚞ 🔁 ORIENTATION AND PRACTICAL INFORMATION

The entrance to Juayua is the **Calle a Salcoatitlán**, which intersects with **4a Calle Oriente** at the corner where there's a Scotiabank. The **Catedral** and **parque central** are two blocks east of this intersection. The center of Juayua's grid is one block north and one block east of the *parque*'s northeast corner, where **Avenida Daniel Cordon** meets **Calle Merceditas Caceres.**

Bank: Scotiabank,C. a Salcoatitlán and 4a C. Pte. (☎2452 2007). Open M-F 8am-4pm, Sa 8am-noon. **24hr. ATM** accepts international credit cards. Currency exchange.

Police: C. Merceditas Caceres Pte.#1 (☎2452 2455).

Pharmacy: Farmacia Cristo Negro, 4a C. Pte. (☎2452 2954), across from the *parque central.* Open daily 8am-9pm.

Internet Access: Ciber y Equipment, 1a Av. Sur #1-2 (☎2452 2769). Internet US$1 per hr. Open daily 8am-7pm.

Post Office: Av. Daniel Cordón Sur #1-2 (☎2452 2709). Open M-F 8am-5pm, Sa 8am-noon.

⚞ ACCOMMODATIONS

Juayua is developing into quite the backpacker scene. As a result, dorm rooms are increasingly becoming common. Luckily, quieter and more private options are also available. Hotel owners are supportive of each other and will refer you to another place if they are full; if you have your heart set on a specific location, call ahead—especially if you plan to stay on a weekend.

Hotel Anahuac, 1a C. Pte. and 5a Av. Nte. (☎2469 2401). The most popular backpacker spot in town. Offers a bit of paradise for those on a budget. The extremely helpful staff makes the upscale dorm rooms and clean hot-water bathrooms seem even nicer. The porch with chairs, hammocks, kitchen, and a book exchange overlooking a small courtyard garden adds to the relaxing atmosphere. The staff also runs tours to local hikes, organic coffee farms, and Nahuizalco's Mercado Nocturno (US$5-20). Dorm US$7; singles US$15; doubles US$25; triples US$35. AmEx/D/MC/V. ❷

Hotel El Mirador, 4a C. Pte. (☎2452 2432), 1 block west of the Catedral. Juayua's premier hotel, El Mirador has the best location; only 2 blocks from the center, its rooftop viewing area offers spectacular views of volcanoes and churches, while rooms have clean, private hot-water baths, cable TV, Wi-Fi, and the occasional balcony. For a real splurge, romantics can stay in the honeymoon room, which has extra decor, room service for breakfast and lunch, and includes a bottle of wine (US$85). Dorms US$7; singles US$17.50; doubles US$27-31; triples US$47.50. AmEx/D/MC/V. ❷

Casa Mazeta Hostal, 1a C. Ote. and 2a Av. Nte. (☎2406 3403). The newest addition to Juayua's backpacker options, Casa Mazeta has sparkling dorms and private rooms with impressively clean hot-water bathrooms and a host of common areas including an internet station, cable TV and DVD room, kitchen, garden, hammocks, and garage. Dorms US$7; doubles with shared bath US$20, with private bath US$25. Cash only. ❷

Casa de Huéspedes Doña Mercedes, 2a Av. Sur and 6a C. Ote. (☎2452 2287). Run by the hospitable Doña Mercedes, this small hotel is a nice break from the backpacker-style lodgings popularized in other areas of town. The rooms have cable TV, fans, and private hot-water baths, located far enough away to offer some peace and privacy. Singles and doubles US$25. Cash only. ❺

⚞ FOOD

Juayua's specialties are Salvadoran staples with exotic twists. Luckily for travelers, this means reasonable prices and some surprising vegetarian options.

For groceries, visit **Selectos Market,** C. Merceditas and Av. Cordón (☎2469 2582). Open M-Sa 7am-8pm, Su 7am-6:30pm.

Restaurante R&R, C. Merceditas #1-4 (☎2452 2083). Enter through the doors of this indoor jungle, replete with plants and murals on every wall, to enjoy gourmet Salvadoran fusion cuisine; the food offers traditional Salvadoran dishes with little twists and extra-fresh ingredients, along with vegetarian options. Entrees US$5-12. Beer US$1-2. Open M-Th 10am-5pm, F-Su 8am-9pm. Cash only. ❸

Daysis Grill, 6a Av. Sur #2 (☎2452 2932). Specializes in sandwiches (US$2.50-4.50) and burgers (US$3-4.50). Daysis delivers American home cooking in a Mediterranean-style villa with with some elements of Salvadoran cuisine thrown in for good measure. The results are delicious; follow and complement the taste with a cold beer (US$1-1.50) or glass of wine (US$1.75). Open Tu-Su 11am-9pm. Cash only. ❷

Pupusería Esmeralda, Urb. La Esmeralda #6 (☎2452 2931). *Pupusas* are standard fare in El Salvador, but this family-run shop turns normal into exotic with an amazingly large variety of *pupusas* (US$0.25-1), from the standard beans, cheese, and *chicharrón* to more unusual versions with squash, shrimp, berries, and other local vegetables. It's a Juayua institution, and the prices are so low you shouldn't resist. Open M-Sa 6am-8pm. Cash only. ❶

👁 🏔 SIGHTS AND OUTDOOR ACTIVITIES

TEMPLO DEL SEÑOR DE JUAYUA. Juayua's most famous sight is the Templo del Señor de Juayua. Built in 1957, the building has an impressive nave and black marble columns that frame the main attraction: the statue of **El Cristo Negro** behind the altar. Carved by Quiro Cataño, the sculptor of the world famous Cristo Negro de Esquipulas, this statue displays the same artistic expertise. *(3 Av. between 2 and 4 C. Open daily during daylight hours. Free.)*

LA FERIA GASTRONOMICA. With music, art, and over 50 different *platos típicos* available in covered patios lining the three blocks around the *parque central,* the Feria Gastronómica is a feast for the eyes and mouth. Enjoy specialties including fried *yucca* (US$1), fresh *licuados* (US$1.50), grilled frog (US$4), and stewed rabbit (US$4), along with more standard dishes. Once a month, the festival showcases a specific country's food, music, and culture. *(Platos US$1-4. Open Sa-Su 10am-5pm.)*

LA RUTA DE LAS CINCO CASCADAS. The most popular trek in the area available is to the Ruta de las Cinco Cascadas. This day hike leads to a number of waterfalls, including Salto Papalunate (80m), and ending at Los Chorros. The first two waterfalls are man-made dams and less pretty, but are the only ones with clean water; the other, prettier waterfalls are fine for hiking, but are used by locals for sewage disposal. Swimming is discouraged. *(☎2452 2916. Guides US$2-8, call the day before; the hike can be done without guides as it is well marked; aks for directions in town. Open Sa-Su.)*

🔀 DAYTRIPS FROM JUAYUA

NAHUIZALCO

Only 25min. away from Juayua on the Ruta de Flores. Bus #249 going to Sonsonate passes through Nahuizalco (25min., every 15min. from 5am-6:30pm, US$0.40).

Known for its *artesanía,* Nahuizalco is a picture-perfect town on the Ruta de Flores. Unfortunately, the town lacks accommodations and dining options. Fortunately, its convenient distance from Juayua makes it easily accessible.

Visitors can stop at both *artesans'* workshops and the famous **Mercado Nocturno**, a candle-lit food market that runs each night from 7:30-9:30pm, offering up delicious plates of *típico* food. Guides can be arranged at the **Casa de la Cultura** (3 C. and 1a Av. ☎2453 0129. US$0.50). Visitors coming from Juayua can arrange transport and guides through **Hotel Anahuac** (☎2469 2401. US$7) in Juayua.

SANTA ANA

Santa Ana is picturesque, wealthy, and surrounded by tourist gems like Parque Nacional Cerro Verde, Volcano Izalco, Volcano Santa Ana, the Tazumal ruins, and Lago de Coatepeque. The city itself has seen grander days, and today the streets are marked by hot dust and street vendors as much as by Neo-Gothic architecture and breezy palm trees, but the charm still hasn't worn off. The fertile volcanic soil is ideal for farming and the plethora of coffee plantations have made this area one of the richest in the nation, and while the extravagance of San Salvador's elite neighborhoods isn't as prevalent here, neither is the poverty of its slums. The result is a city that is beautiful yet gritty and accessible while authentic.

▉ TRANSPORTATION

Buses: Within Santa Ana, buses connect to main points in the center and popular stops such as **Metrocentro.** The 2 main routes are **#51** and **#55. #51** is the main north-south route, although it does a lot of east-west travel as well, passing 1 block south of the cathedral and eventually heading to the Metrocentro on the southern edge of town. The #55 is the main east-west route, passing 1 block south of the cathedral and then to the hospital on the city's eastern edge. Both routes have various sub-routes, marked by letters that only increase the confusion. Most indicate their main stops on the front. Both buses pass near the bus terminal and run 6am-8pm daily (US$0.20), though it's better to take a taxi after dark. There are 2 **intercity** bus terminals in Santa Ana:

Main Terminal: 10a/14a Av. Sur and 12a/15a C. Pte.; incoming buses drop off outside the terminal on 14a Av. Sur, while outgoing ones depart from inside on 10a Av. Sur. To: **Ahuachapan** (#210. 1hr., every 15min. 4am-7pm, US$0.90); **Juayua** (#238. 3hr.; 3 per day 9, 11am, and 1pm; US$2); **Lago de Coatepeque** (#220, 1hr., every 30min. 4am-4pm, US$0.45); **Metapan** (#235. 1½hr., every 15min. 4am-6pm, US$1.15); **San Cristobal** (#236. 1hr., every 15min. 5:30am-7pm, US$0.50); **San Lorenzo** (#277. 2hr., every 15min. 6am-6pm, US$1.25); **San Salvador** (#201. 2hr.; every 10min. 4am-7pm; US$1, *especial* US$1.50); **Sonsonate** (#216. 1½hr., every 15min. 5am-6pm, US$0.80).

Terminal Transportes La Vencedora: 11 C. Pte./Av. Fray Felipe, 1 block west of Parque Colón. To: **Cerro Verde** (#248. 1½hr.; M-Th 5 per day 8:40am-3:30pm, US$0.90; F-Su extra bus at 7pm, US$0.90); **El Congo** (#51. 20min., every 15min. 5am-7pm, US$0.25); and **Guatemala City** (4hr., every hr. 5am-5pm, US$8).

Taxis: ☎2441 1661. Cabs are clustered on the north side of Parque Libertad, outside Metrocentro, and behind the Alcaldía. US$3-4 around town. If you are outside the *centro* or Metrocentro at night, you'll have to call one.

◼❷ ORIENTATION AND PRACTICAL INFORMATION

Santa Ana uses the same grid system as other Salvadoran cities. The center of the grid is in the northern end of the city, on the southwest corner of **Parque Libertad,** where **Avenida Independencia** meets **Calle Libertad.** The **Palacio Municipal** is on the west side of the *parque*. Av. Independencia runs south all the way to **Metrocentro,** where buses from San Salvador enter the city. The other main arteries are **10a Avenida Sur** and **14a Avenida Sur,** which service the bus station.

Tourist Office: Maps and info at the **Teatro Nacional** (☎2447 6268), on the north side of Parque Libertad at 2 C. Pte. and Av. Independencia Nte. Maps US$1.75. Open M-F 8am-noon and 2-6pm, Sa 8am-noon.

Bank: Scotiabank, C. Libertad Pte. and 2a Av. Nte. (☎2447 1969). Open M-F 8am-5pm, Sa 8am-noon. Does cash advances and exchanges travelers' checks;**24hr. ATM** accepts all international cards. Second location in Metrocentro mall.

Beyond Tourism: Salva Span Spanish School, 5a C. Pte. and 4a/6a Av. Sur (☎7015 4171; www.salvaspan.com). Offers Spanish classes and tutoring based out of Santa Ana office. For more **Beyond Tourism** opportunities, see p. 313.

English-Language Bookstore: La Ceiba (☎2440 8115), in Metrocentro. Open M-Sa 10am-7:00pm, Su 10am-5pm. AmEx/D/MC/V. Decent selection of well-priced English-language books in addition to a Spanish selection.

Police: 25 C. Pte. and 14a Av. Sur (☎2440 8327 or 2447 7179).

24hr. Pharmacy: Farmacia Moderna,3 C. Pte. and Av. Independencia Sur (☎2448 1212). Open M-Sa 8am-7pm, Su 8am-noon.

Hospital: Hospital Cader, 5 C. Ote./13 Av. Sur #10 (☎2452 7400). Open 24hr.

Internet Access: Ciber La Web.com,10a Av. Sur #103 (☎2440 0321). Internet US$1 per hr. Open daily 8am-7pm.

Santa Ana

🏠 ACCOMMODATIONS

Hotel Livingston, **9**
Hotel La Casita, **2**
Hotel La Posada
    del Rey, **3**
Hotel Tazumal, **1**

🍎 FOOD

Los Horcones, **5**
Pastelería Ban Ban, **6, 7**
Restaurante El
    Sin Rival, **4**

Post Office: 9 C. Pte. #30 (☎2441 0084). Open M-F 8am-5pm, Sa 8am-noon.

ACCOMMODATIONS

In Santa Ana there are many motels that offer comfortable budget accommodations, as long as you don't mind "working girls" occasionally checking in with their clients for a couple of hours. If you don't want to listen to your neighbor and his "friend," you'll have to pay a little extra for nicer hotels.

Casa Frolaz, 29 C. Pte. and 10a Av. Sur (☎2440 5302). The clear backpackers' choice, Casa Frolaz offers cheap dorm rooms (US$7 per person) in a beautiful home with a kitchen, TV room with DVD collection, and hot water bathrooms. Laundry US$2.50. Free Wi-Fi. Cash only. ❷

Hotel Tazumal, 11 C. Pte. #35 (☎2440 2830). Only a few blocks from Livingston, Tazumal offers slightly cheaper rooms with basic conveniences like cable TV, fans, and private baths in a no-frills atmosphere. Singles US$10; doubles US$15. Cash only. ❷

Hotel La Cosita, 4 C. Ote. #9, 3/5 Av. Nte. (☎2441 1039), near Parque Libertad. Cozy rooms with fans, private baths, and cable TV. Room size varies, so ask to see several rooms before checking in. English spoken. Singles US$12; doubles US$15. Cash only. ❸

FOOD

Though its colonial grandeur suggests a more cosmopolitan atmosphere, dining options in Santa Ana remain fairly generic; the usual *comedores* and *pupuserias* abound near the market and bus station, and more upscale spots are primarily located near Parque Libertad to the north and around Av. Independencia and Metrocentro to the south. For groceries, visit **SuperSelectos,** in Metrocentro. (☎2440 6553. Open M-Th 8am-10pm, F-Su 7am-8:30pm. AmEx/D/MC/V.)

La Antorcha, 4a Av. Sur between 25/27 C. Pte. (☎2448 3246), A popular spot for *típica*, La Antorcha runs on a truly Salvadoran schedule, open during lunch hours and again in the evening to serve *licuados* (US$1-1.50), *tortas*(US$1.50-2.50), and the ever popular *pupusas* (US$0.20-0.40) to a local crowd. Open Tu-F 11:30am-2pm and 5-9pm and Sa-Su noon-9pm. Cash only. ❷

El Sin Rival, Av. Independencia #33 (☎2448 1443). Considered the best ice cream around, the popular chain of *sorbeterías* is based here in Santa Ana. Choose from a large selection of delicious, chilly sorbets and ice creams to escape the heat. Ice cream US$0.60-3. Open daily 10am-7pm. Cash only. ❷

Pasteleria Ban Ban, Av. Independencia and C. Libertad/1 C. (☎2447 1865), second location in Metrocentro. Ideal for breakfast, Pasteleria has the best coffee in town (US$1.25) and a selection of sumptuous pastries (US$0.33-1.15). The soda-pastry-sandwich combo (US$2.50-3) is great for a quick lunch. Open daily 8am-7pm. ❷

Restaurante Los 44, Av. La Independencia and 23 C. (☎2440 3133 and 7390 6331). One of Santa Ana's more upscale establishments, Los 44 is popular with local businessmen and parties, but it also has great lunch deals on its executive menu (US$4-5). Usual menu of gourmet Salvadoran cuisine. Salads US$3-6. Entrees US$6-12. *Bocas plates* US$5.50. Open daily 10am-10pm. AmEx/D/MC/V. ❷

Super Marina, Av. Independencia and 31 C. Pte. (☎2338 4243). With quick delivery and a comfy air-conditioned dining area, this spot serves up reasonably priced seafood, from cocktails and *ceviches* (US$4-7) to fried shrimp (US$8). Entrees US$4-9. Open daily 11am-9pm. AmEx/D/MC/V. ❷

Deli Cafe, 10a Av. Sur and 25 C. Pte. (☎2440 0115). An eclectic decor of green picnic tables surrounded by bright, elaborate floral arrangements makes Deli Cafe a great stop for smoothies (US$1.40-1.60), coffee (US$0.50-1.65), cakes (US$0.20-1.50), or for a break from the toil and sun of the market. Open daily 9am-6pm. Cash only.

Los Horcones (☎2447 2038), on the east side of Parque Libertad, close to the Catedral. With some of the prettiest views in town and a breezy upstairs dining area perfect for an evening meal or beer (US$1.25-2), Los Horcones remains a constant favorite among local and visiting customers. Meat entrees US$2-10. Seafood entrees US$9-13. Open daily 10:30am-10pm. AmEx/D/MC/V. ❷

Restaurante Lover's Steak House, 33 C. Ote. (☎2440 8510). A little pricier than most places in Santa Ana, but a great place for a romantic splurge or just a self-indulgent treat. The wide selection includes meats (steaks US$8-12), seafood, Chinese, Italian, and traditional food. An appetizer comes with every beer you order (US$1.50-3). Open M-Th 11:30am-10pm, F-Sa 11:30am-11:30pm, Su 11:30am-9pm. AmEx/D/MC/V. ❸

👁 SIGHTS

CATEDRAL DE LA SEÑORA SANTA ANA. This is one of the most impressive neo-Gothic cathedrals in the area. Built in 1905, it is a testament to the once-great aspirations of local coffee magnates. There is a marble altar to the Virgin Mary. The cathedral exhibits a mix of Gothic elegance and Byzantine strength: the imposing interior holds statues dating back to the 16th century. *(On the northeast corner of the parque. Open daily 6am-6pm. Free.)*

TEATRO NACIONAL DE SANTA ANA. Another architectural beauty on Parque Libertad, the Teatro Nacional is an impressive Renaissance-style structure housing some of Santa Ana's best theater and art exhibitions. *(On the north side of Parque Libertad. ☎2447 6268 or 2448 1094. Open M-F 8am-noon and 2-6pm, Sa 8am-noon.)*

PALACIO MUNICIPAL. The largest of the colonial buildings on Parque Libertad, the Palacio Municipal presides over the west side of the *parque.* Its biggest draw is the lush, palm tree-lined courtyard with fountains and walkways. *(On the west side of Parque Libertad. Open M-F 8am-noon and 2-5pm, Sa 8am-noon. Free.)*

MUSEO REGIONAL DEL OCCIDENTE. Santa Ana's premier museum, the Museo Regional, houses rotating exhibits on indigenous and pre-colonial culture and on the history in El Salvador. Those curious about Salvadoran money before the infiltration of the US dollar can head downstairs to the bank vault, where the history of Salvadoran money is on permanent display—from the Spanish *real,* through the various editions of the *colón.* *(On Av. Independencia Sur, 1 block south of Parque Libertad, in the old Federal Reserve Bank. ☎2441 1215. Open Tu-Sa 9am-noon and 1-5pm. US$0.50.)*

IGLESIA EL CARMEN. Two palm trees frame the bell tower that looks like it's straight out of a Hollywood movie. The church itself is small, but with its bright colors and elevated position at the top of white stairs, it's still worth a visit, if only to snap a few photos. *(On 7 C. Oriente between Av. Independencia and 3 Av. Sur. Open during daylight hours and religious celebrations. Free.)*

🏞 OUTDOOR ACTIVITIES

PARQUE NACIONAL CERRO VERDE AND ENVIRONS

Buses leave Santa Ana for Cerro Verde daily (#248, 1¾hr., 8:40am-3:30pm, US$0.70), dropping off at a small building where you have to pay US$1 to continue walking up to Cerro Verde. In Santa Ana, the #248 bus leaves from La Vencedora terminal. Info on the park is available at the San Salvador ISTU office (☎2222 8000). The park has recently re-opened and is now very well organized for tourists. Written explanations in English describe the attractions and numerous guides lead visitors to the different sites (unaccompanied

WESTERN EL SALVADOR

walks to any site are forbidden). Daily trips to the Santa Ana and Izalco volcanoes leave at 11am; if you want to fit both in, you'll have to call at least a day in advance to arrange an earlier guide. If you decide to do both hikes, you'll have to be efficient; the last bus back leaves by 3:30pm. The park information desk is open daily 8am-5pm. ☎ 2873 3594.

From the El Congo junction, 15km southeast of Santa Ana, a road heads to Cerro Verde, a long-extinct 2030m volcano that has recently been transformed into a national park. The road that reaches all the way to the crater makes the park one of the most accessible in the country.

There are three main trails within Cerro Verde. **Una Ventana a la Naturaleza** ("A Window on Nature") is a 45min. walk looping around the Cerro Verde crater. Two lookout platforms present impressive views of Volcán Santa Ana and Lago Coatepeque respectively. Several signs in both English and Spanish explain different aspects of the forest life. **El Orquediario** ("The Orchid Path") is a 30min. trail among 37 different orchid species; the best times for this hike are in December, January, April, and May when most of the flowers are blossoming. **Caminata al Hotel** ("Walk to the Hotel") is a 15min. walk to the Hotel de Montana, which offers an outstanding view of Volcán Izalco.

Nearby, Volcán Santa Ana and Volcán Izalco are still active. The three volcanoes in such close proximity to one another provide a fascinating lesson in volcanic development. Rich vegetation covers Cerro Verde (the oldest), while Izalco (the youngest) remains almost entirely composed of rough volcanic rock. Santa Ana is the middle child, with both plant life and volcanic stone.

VOLCÁN SANTA ANA. With its last eruption in 1904, Volcán Santa Ana (2365m) is a young, though not very active, volcano. The clearly marked trail to the volcano departs from the Ventana a la Naturaleza trail, about 100m after the *mirador*, toward the volcano. It heads 200m down to a farm, behind which a narrow path leads up to the volcano. The trail is a creek bed so you will have to navigate among the rocks. As you reach the top, an enormous abyss unfolds; 500m deep and 1km in diameter, the crater is filled with grayish water and spews out clouds of sulfuric vapor. The highest point of the volcano is on the opposite side. Circling around, views of Volcán Izalco, the coast, Apaneca, Santa Ana, Lago, and finally Cerro Verde open up in front of you. This volcano, while forested at its base, is mostly bare rock and volcanic sediment at the top. The ascent is mildly strenuous (about 3hr. round trip from Cerro Verde, plus another 1½hr. if you want to walk around the rim).

VOLCÁN IZALCO. The trail to Volcán Izalco is just a few meters above the bus drop-off from Santa Ana. For an idea of what the other volcanoes looked like in their infancy, and to complete a three-stage tour of volcanic evolution, head to Volcán Izalco, one of the youngest volcanoes in the world. Legend says it formed on Feb. 23, 1770 and kept erupting without interruption for 183 years, giving it the name of "The Lighthouse of the Pacific." The hike is the most dramatic and intense in the park, with the barren cone rising up to the southwest of Cerro Verde. A marked path leads off the road just before the Cerro Verde parking lot; this path is the start of the 1km hike through the forest to the base of Izalco. The ascent begins from there, and involves strenuous rock climbing at times. For other stretches, you may struggle for footing among the loose, tumbling rocks. The view of the coast and the contrast between barren lava and lush forests make the trip more than worth it. Steam and sulfuric gas force their way up through holes in the rock. The descent is terrifying at first, but can be fun if you learn the technique and let yourself go: dig in your heels with toes up, lean back, and slide. The entire trek to and from Cerro Verde takes 4hr. and requires sturdy shoes.

DAYTRIPS FROM SANTA ANA

LAGO DE COATEPEQUE

Bus #220 leaves from the terminal in Santa Ana and heads for the lake (1hr., every 30min. 5am-4pm, US$0.45). If you miss the last bus back to Santa Ana at 4pm, take a bus to the bridge in El Congo. From the bridge, walk down to the highway on the side furthest from Coatepeque, and catch any of the buses passing by; they all stop in Santa Ana. Coming from San Salvador, catch the #201 toward Santa Ana and get off in El Congo, where you can catch the #220 for the 5km down to the shore. Buses to Coatepeque pass along the hillside rim of the lake before heading downhill along its shores on a slow dirt road. Most restaurants, hotels, and beach access points are near the end of this road. The lake has little in the way of sandy beaches, but you can swim off the docks of restaurants and hotels, provided you pay an entrance fee or order food.

Roughly 16km from Santa Ana, the Lago de Coatepeque, formed by an ancient volcanic crater and surrounded by lush slopes, seems almost eerily tranquil compared to the surrounding areas' bustling commerce and busy buses. Though easily accessible from Santa Ana and San Salvador, the lake's peaceful waters, expensive villas, and breezy porch dining areas on the water seem eons away from the hubbub of both cities. The lake attracts San Salvadoran weekend visitors, who justifiably claim that it is among the most beautiful lakes in Central America. Although much of the prime real estate here is occupied, there are still places where you can stop and soak up the scenery. There are a few less-than-clean public spaces at the end of the bus' route, but the best option is to eat at a waterfront restaurant, stay at a local hotel, or just pay the entrance fee for the day (usually around US$1). The lake is great for swimming, and most hotels and restaurants have boats and jet-skis available for rent.

Hostal 3er Mundo (3rd World) ❷, a 10min. ride from where the buses turn on to the lake road, has accommodations and a restaurant overlooking the water, replete with separate open air *cabañas* with hammocks, picnic tables, and foosball. There's a small pool in the front and an extensive library and used bookstore for guest use, along with a TV room shared with the owner's family. The premises are open to non-guests for US$1 or the purchase of a meal at the restaurant. (☎2441 0608. Dorms US$8-9; singles and doubles with private bath US$20-25 depending on view. Cash only.) Next door, **Hotel y Restaurante Rancho Alegre** ❶ offers fresh, delicious, and large portions of *comida típica*, including more unusual options like grilled rabbit (US$6.50) on its 2-story patio on the water. The upstairs is the most comfortable, with lounging chairs and couches to go with incredible views of the lake and the occasional live accordion soundtrack. Alegre also has rooms above the first floor of the lower patio; rooms are simple with shared baths in the restaurant. (☎2441 6071. Singles US$20; doubles US$25. Entrees US$5-15. Jet ski rental US$60 per hr. Restaurant open daily 9:30am-8pm. Cash only.)

METAPÁN

Situated below the mountainous juncture of El Salvador, Honduras, and Guatemala, on the cloud-ensconced Cerro de Montecristo, Metapán survived the civil war yet remains in relative isolation. Ranching is the main livelihood; here older *vaqueros* still mosey into town on horseback. The town is mostly commercial and agricultural, but with convenient access to the cloud forests of Parque Nacional de Montecristo, it's also a great stop for those seeking to get far off the beaten path and into the woods.

▣ TRANSPORTATION

The bus terminal is on the main highway, between C. El Tamarindo and 2 C. Ote. **Buses** go to:

Citalá/Frontera El Poy: #463. 3½hr.; 5am, noon, 2:30pm; US$2.30.

Anguiatú/Frontera Guatemala: #211A. 30min., every 30min. 5am-4:30pm, US$0.50.

Santa Ana: #235. 1½hr., every 15min. 4am-6:15pm, US$0.90.

San Salvador: #201A. 2hr., 7 per day 4am-3pm, US$1.65.

✈ ☷ ORIENTATION AND PRACTICAL INFORMATION

The road to Metapán comes in from the south and passes the eastern border of the town before heading north to the Guatemalan border. The bulk of the town is on **Calle 15 de Septiembre** and **2 Calle,** which run parallel to each other, perpendicular to the highway, and lead downhill five blocks to the **parque central.**

Bank: Banco Scotiabank, C. 15 de Septiembre and Av. Gómez (☎2402 7911). Open M-F 8am-5pm, Sa 8am-noon. Currency exchange. **24hr. ATM** takes international credit cards.

Police: Km 112 (☎2442 0101), on the highway to Santa Ana.

24hr. Pharmacy: Farmacia San Pedro, Av. Isidro Menéndez #4 (☎2442 0207). Open daily 7am-6pm; emergencies 24hr.

Hospital or Medical Services: Hospital Nacional de Metapán, Km112 (☎2402 0937), on the highway to Santa Ana. Open 24hr.

Internet Access: Ciber Cafe, 8a Av. Nte. and C. 15 de Septiembre (☎2415 7021). Internet US$1 per hr. Open daily 7am-6pm.

Post Office: 2 C. Ote. #2 (☎2442 0217). Open M-F 8am-noon and 2-5pm, Sa 8am-noon.

▣ ACCOMMODATIONS

Metapán is usually visited as a stopover on the way to Guatemala; there aren't many lodging options in town, but the range is enough to find something for every budget.

Hotel California (☎2442 0561), 500m from the bus terminal outside of town. To get there, walk out from the bus terminal. Facing town, turn right on the highway and walk about 500m; the hotel is on the left just before the ESSO station. The most budget oriented of Metapán's lodging options, California is still pretty nice; it has plenty of room, a green patio, and clean and simple rooms with private baths and fans. Singles US$10; doubles US$15. Cash only. ❷

Hotel Christina, 6a Av. 2/15 de Septiembre C. (☎2442 0044), 2 blocks west of the terminal. A more upscale, but still convenient, option. Offers clean rooms with fans, private cold-water baths, phones, and cable TV. For better sun, ask for a room on the top floor, which has a rooftop terrace with chaise lounges. Doubles US$20. Cash only. ❹

Hotel San Jose (☎2442 0556), 1km after the hospital on the highway to Santa Ana. If you need to be near Metapán but still want your creature comforts, San Jose offers the most luxurious rooms around, with a private hot-water bath, cable TV, phone, and A/C in every room. The only downside is the location; you'll need a taxi or a good pair of walking shoes to get into town from here. Singles US$35; doubles US$40. AmEx/D/MC/V. ❺

▣ FOOD

Metapán is not set up for tourists, and dining options are sparse. There is only one restaurant in town, and a few *comedores* and *pupuserias* that serve the standard Salvadoran fare. For groceries, visit **Supermarket Palí,** in front of the park. (☎2402 1834. Open M-Sa 7:30am-8pm, Su 8am-6pm).

Restaurante Antojitos La Nueva Esperanza, C. Marcia and Av. Valiente (☎2454 1602). The only full service restaurant in Metapán, Antojitos sticks to the basics: Salvadoran favorites (US$3-8) and Mexican tacos, fajitas, and *tortas* (US$3-6). Open daily 11am-9pm. Cash only. ❷

TropyJugos, 2 C. Pte., 4 blocks west of the highway. Huge, super-fresh fruit drinks (US$1-1.40) are a great cool-down after a long bus ride, and there are uber-affordable sandwiches and hamburgers for those craving something a bit more filling. Sandwiches US$1.50-2. Open daily 7:30am-8pm. Cash only. ❷

Comedor y Pupuseria La Esperanza, 2 C. Ote. #12 (☎2402 0625). It's basic, but consistent, serving up plates of *típica* and *pupusas* to a large local crowd. *Pupusas* US$0.20-0.50. Entrees US$2-4. Open daily 7am-8pm. Cash only. ❶

◙ SIGHTS

Metapán's church, the **Iglesia de San Pedro,** located in front of the park between 1 and 3 C. Pte., dates to 1743. Restored in 1963, the church has a vaulted ceiling, elaborate golden side altars, and **catacombs,** one of which is easily accessible via a wooden trap door in the tiled floor of the center aisle. To tour the catacombs, stop by after 9am during the week and ask for the caretaker, who can show you around and explain the history of the church (in Spanish only). During the last week of June, the church is decorated with flowers for the nine-day **Festival de San Pedro,** celebrating the town's patron saint. The days of processions, music, carnival, and an acclaimed rodeo conclude with a closing parade, complete with fireworks and marching bands.

▶ DAYTRIP FROM METAPÁN

LAGO DE GÜIJA

Take bus #235 south toward Santa Ana and ask to get off at Desagüe, an unmarked but well-known village about 20min. south of Metapán (US$0.30). Walk about 100m along a dirt road, bearing right at the fork. Follow the railroad tracks across the bridge on the left; then leave the tracks and continue on the trail as it slopes to the right. You will pass through a small village before coming to the lake. The walk is about 2km and fairly well marked; ask a local for directions if you get lost.

Scenic and tranquil, the Lago de Güija allows you to swim in both El Salvador and Guatemala; you can also take a *lancha* around the calm waters. The edges of the lake are lined by **Cerro de Las Figuras,** a series of faded pre-Columbian rock carvings on the boulders lining the lake's small peninsula. Though the most impressive and well-preserved carvings now sit in museums, there are still many interesting carvings of snails and men. You can view the carvings up close, touching the ancient art and hunting for new designs. Don't be fooled by the clever forgeries: the peace sign carved into one of the rocks is probably not pre-Columbian. If you look closely, you may notice some obsidian fragments, pieces of tools, or pottery along the shore. The walk out to the point along Cerro de las Figuras' west shore is a pleasant 30min. stroll encompassing all of the major carvings, as well as views across the lake to Guatemala. *Lanchas* are usually available for lake tours; ask local fishermen, who will take you around for about US$5-7 per hr. The last bus passes Desagüe around 6pm.

WESTERN
EL SALVADOR

PARQUE NACIONAL MONTECRISTO

The cloud forest reserve Parque Nacional Montecristo covers the northwestern corner of El Salvador and sprawls across the border into Honduras and Guatemala. The three countries converge in the cloudforests of El Trinifio on **Cerro Montecristo,** the park's highest peak, which overlooks the Salvadoran town of Metapán. The park protects an amazing variety of wildlife—quetzals, guans, agoutis, porcupines, and anteaters, to name a few. The two hour hike to the uppermost part of the park gives you the opportunity to hop from El Salvador to Guatemala to Honduras without having to pay border guards. Plus, hiking in the cloud forest is one of the only chances left in El Salvador to glimpse such sprawling forests and diverse wildlife. During breeding season, from May to October, the higher areas of the park are closed. Get a permit in San Salvador if you plan on camping.

TRANSPORTATION

From **Metapán** (p. 355), a treacherous **dirt road** climbs 20km to the main tourist area of the park at **Los Planes.** Beginning in Metapán, the road to the park branches right from the highway and continues 4km along a dirt road to the park's entrance at the **Caseta de Información.**
Getting to the park is a difficult task; public transportation from Metapán will only take you within 12km of the park (1hr., 5 per day leaving between 5am and noon, US$0.60). There are no private cars at this point, so you'll have to hike the rest of the way in. The bus drops off at hte Casco Colonial Visitors' Center. The best way to cover the rocky road is to hire a pickup from Metapán to Los Planes; a round-trip, including waiting while you hike, should cost no more than US$40-45. Next-day pick up should cost about US$75-90. Be prepared to bargain.

ORIENTATION AND PRACTICAL INFORMATION

Visitors need to pay the **US$6 fee** plus **US$1 per vehicle.** From the Caseta, the road winds 3½km to the visitor center, known as the **Casco Colonial.** At the foot of Trifinio, 12km past the Casco Colonial, the **Los Planes visitors' area** has campgrounds, picnic areas, and bathrooms. A number of well-maintained trails depart from the two visitor areas, heading to waterfalls, viewpoints, and rivers. The **Caseta de Información** is staffed 24hr., but entry hours are generally 7am to 3pm; if you want to camp for the night, you must arrive before 3pm. Camping is allowed only in the Los Planes campgrounds, and **permits** are required if you plan to spend the night. A permit must be obtained at the **Ministerio de Agricultura, Servicio de Parques Nacionales** in San Salvador. If you plan to visit just for the day and arrive without a permit, the guards will let you pay the entrance fee and continue on. You will have to pay the entrance fee for your driver as well. Officials at the Caseta will radio ahead and arrange for a **guide** to meet you at the Casco Colonial or Los Planes (free, but tips are appreciated). Guides are required for hiking in these areas, but they only speak Spanish.

CAMPING

Los Planes is the only location within the park where camping is allowed. Camping expenses are included in the entrance fee. You need permission from the Ministerio de Agricultura in San Salvador to camp in the *parque.* The three campgrounds at Los Planes are well-equipped with bathrooms, running water, and cooking pits, as well as plenty of trails through secondary pine and cypress forest. Camping areas #2 and #3 are smaller and more tranquil. Warm clothes are essential to fight off nighttime cold. There are a couple of small stores run by locals where you can restock on camping supplies. Each day in the *parque* is US$6.

SIGHTS

CASCO COLONIAL VISITORS CENTER. The well-preserved *hacienda* Casco Colonial is surrounded by beautiful flowers and lined with cobblestone streets. The interpretative center in the back explains the history of the park, gives the cultural background of its inhabitants, and provides information on animal specimens found here. From the visitors center there are also two short trails: the first, **Sendero de Curiosidades de la Naturaleza,** is a 20min. stroll that begins in front of the buildings; the other, **Sendero de los Pioneros,** is a slightly more interesting 35min. hike through a secondary forest that leads to a 15m-high lookout tower and the remains of a 1992 plane crash. To reach the second trail, go over the footbridge near the visitors center and continue a few minutes on the dirt road until you see signs for the *sendero*. Smaller paths wind behind the center around the stream trickling by. *(Open daily 8am-3pm.)*

TRAILS FROM THE MAIN ROAD. Along the road up to Los Planes, ask your guide to direct the driver to nearby sights that you can get out and explore. At Km 12, a road forks off and continues 1km to a 17m high *mirador* known as **Desvío de la Torre.** This *mirador* provides impressive views of the surrounding jungle. The tower is manned by a *vigilante* keeping his eyes peeled for forest fires. There is another *mirador* at Km 13, with views of a beautiful waterfall, and a third at Km 15 looking over Metapán and the Lago de Güija. Around Km 19, there is a dirt road which forks left and continues 7km up to Trifinio. This trail is a rewarding and intense hike; the trail leading to Trifinio from Los Planes is a more convenient starting point.

TRAILS FROM LOS PLANES. Twenty kilometers along the main road (after 1½hr. of driving), you will come to Los Planes. Once there, find **El Jardín de Cien Años** with trails winding through a well-kept garden of orchids and tall ferns. There is an educational center where each of the 74 species of orchids is labeled.

Several winding trails leave from Los Planes. **Sendero Maravillas y Procesos de la Madre Naturaleza,** a 45min. loop leaving from the soccer field at the campgrounds, passes a striking *mirador*. Another trail, **Sendero El Río Hondurano,** starting from camping area #2, continues for 1hr. before it ends outside the park at a pleasant swimming area on a river. If you head out around dusk and stay quiet you're bound to come across plenty of animals. The trail heading up to Trifinio leaves from the road next to the *jardín*. The trail climbs from 1850m above sea level to 2418m over the course of 7km and should take a little less than two hours. Guides should accompany you.

EASTERN EL SALVADOR

The region most severely devastated by the civil war, Eastern El Salvador is still recovering from its days as the FMLN stronghold. Economic recovery is well on its way, even though the government still tends to favor the less rebellious West. San Miguel, with its long and rich history, is the biggest city in the "Wild East" and an ideal transportation hub to most sites. Perquín's Museo de la Revolución Salvadoreña and La Ruta de la Paz shock and humble visitors through stark and powerful civil war testaments. The eastern beaches west of the Golfo de Fonseca are rather underdeveloped in terms of tourist facilities, but some of them, especially El Espino, are among the most beautiful in Central America. Finally, do not forget to stop by Ilobasco on your way east; their ceramics are internationally renowned.

SAN VICENTE

Situated in the Torre Vicentina valley, San Vicente is surrounded by hilly coffee plantations, the double peak of Volcán Chichontepec, and the nearby Laguna de Apastepeque. San Vicente offers a variety of outdoor excursions for those eager to get out of town and a consistently beautiful view for those who choose to stay in it. When visiting San Vicente, you may notice that it is more open to GLBT life than other areas in El Salvador. Still, this reputation has not led to an increase in GLBT services or establishments, and same-sex couples should follow the same level of discretion that applies to the rest of the country. The town also offers a comfortable city atmosphere for travelers passing through. San Vicente is also a good base for setting out on some long hikes—the trek up Volcán Chichontepec can take up to 9 hours.

▐ TRANSPORTATION

San Vicente is relatively small, so it's not too difficult to get around. Tourists in need of a **taxi** should head to the east side of the *parque central*, where most taxis line up. **Buses** come into town on Av. Cornejo; the easiest spot to get off is in front of the *parque*. The official bus station is on the corner of 15a Av. and 6 C., but you can also catch buses on 1a Av. Nte., between 3a C. Pte. and 7 C. Pte. Buses stop in front of the Cathedral, on the east side of the *parque* before leaving town, but most seats will be full at this point; expect to wait in line and stand on the bus. Buses from San Vicente go to:

Ilobasco: Bus #530. 50min.; 3 per day 7, 11am, 4pm; US$0.60.

San Salvador: Bus#116. 1½hr., every 10min. 4:30am-7pm, US$0.90.

Santa Clara and Laguna de Apastepeque: Bus#157A and 157B. 1½hr., every 20min. 6am-6pm, US$0.80.

Zacatecoluca: Bus #177. 50 min., every 15 min. 4:30am-5:30pm, US$0.60.

Tepetitán: Bus #191. 30 min., every 30 min. 5:30am-6:30pm, US$0.40.

▐ ▐ ORIENTATION AND PRACTICAL INFORMATION

Buses enter San Vicente on **Avenida Cornejo,** on the west side of the **parque central.** One block south of the park's southwest corner, Av. Cornejo intersects with **Calle Alvaro** and **1 de Julio 1823,** which forms the starting point for San Vicente's grid layout. **1a Avenida,** which runs north to south one block west of the *parque central,* is lined with most of the town's banks and is a good spot to catch buses before they get too full. The **market** can be found where **1a Avenida** and **3a Avenida** intersect with **Calle Alvaro**. The **Cathedral** is on the east side of the *parque central;* buses stop here before heading out of town, but they are often standing room only at this point.

Bank: Banco Procredit, corner of 1a C. Pte. and 1a Av. Nte. Open M-F 8am-5pm, Sa 8am-Noon. **24hr ATM** accepts international Visa. Western Union services.

Police: Corner of 1a Av. Nte. and 1a C. Ote. (☎2399 3800).

Pharmacy: Farmacia Alfalfa, 1a C. Pte. Contiguo #5a (☎2393 1103), just off the *parque central.* Open M-Sa 8am-7pm, Su 8am-4pm. AmEx/D/MC/V.

Hospital: Hospital Santa Gertrudis, 2a Av. Sur and 4a/6a C. Ote. (☎2393 0267). Open 24hr.

Internet Access: Ciber Line World, 3a Av. Sur #24a (☎2393 3283). Open M-F 8am-7pm, Sa-Su 9am-4pm. Internet US$0.75 per hr.

Post Office: 3a Av. Nte. #22 (☎2393 3226), past the Pollo Campero. Open M-F 8am-5pm, Sa 8am-noon. **Postal Code:** 1701.

ACCOMMODATIONS

Hotel y Restaurante Central Park (☎2393 0383), Av. Cornejo on the west side of the park. Hotel, restaurant, and bar all-in-one, Central Park is right in the middle of everything. Rooms are unattractive but functional, with cable TV, fans or A/C, and private cold-water baths to match the peeling or worn-away paint on the concrete walls. Rooms overlooking the plant-filled courtyard offer more privacy; those in the 2nd-floor hallway also get traffic to the terrace bar. Wi-Fi. *Comida a la vista* US$1-3. Singles US$10, with A/C US$15; doubles US$15/20. Restaurant open daily from 6:30am-9pm. ❷

FOOD

For groceries, visit supermarket **Super Selectos,** 2a Av. Sur, one block south of the Cathedral. (☎2393 0073. Open M-Sa 7:30-9, Su 7:30-8pm. MC/V.)

Comedor Rivoly, 1a Av. Sur #15 (☎2393 0492). Cafeteria-style dining area surrounded by gardens. Fresh, cheap meals US$1-3. Comedor Rivoly has the best *comida a la vista* in town. The well-lit, spacious dining area is conveniently located 3 blocks from the *parque central.* Grab a delicious *licuado* (US$1) with your meal. Open daily 6am-7pm. Beer US$1. Cash only. ❷

Restaurante y Pastelería Betania, 3a Av. Sur #20 (☎2393 0392), next to the post office. Covered al fresco seating at picnic tables next to a small courtyard. Serves large portions of Salvadoran favorites (US$1.50-3) and a huge menu of delicious *licuados* (US$1). Open M-Sa 6am-5pm. Cash only. ❷

Restaurante "Casa Blanca," 2 C. Ote., 2/4 Av. Sur (☎2393 0549). The jungle-like atmosphere and colonial-style architecture of this restaurant may be mismatched, but the food is the most upscale in town, with meat and fish platters (US$4-10) accompanied by live music. Beer US$1.25. Open daily 11am-8:30pm. Cash only. ❸

SIGHTS

VOLCÁN CHICHONTEPEC. The "easiest" approach to finding this volcano begins at its base in Tepetitán, reachable by bus #191 from C. Osorio at 9 Av. (30min., every 30min. 5:45am-6:30pm, US$0.30.) Once in Tepetitán, walk for about 2hr. along the **stone road** that begins two blocks north of the *parque.* You will pass the Finca Camón, one of the best coffee plantations in the country, owned by former President Cristiani, signer of the 1992 Peace Accords. Where the stone road begins to descend, a **dirt road** branches uphill. Because of an earthquake, the final stretch of this road is rocky and uneven. One more hour on this path will bring you to the peak. Remember to bring water and food for the trek (and for your escorts, if you have them). Nahuat for "mountain of two breasts," Chichontepec has two peaks, one cone-shaped and the other flat, rising 2200m. Though the top is marred by a military helicopter deck, it still affords a panorama that encompasses the Pacific Coast, San Salvador, and the Honduran border. It takes at least three hours to get up the volcano, and afternoons often bring rain, so start early. If the whole trek doesn't appeal to you, check out the **hot springs**—or *infernillos*—only an hour into the hike, whose sulfuric smoke makes the volcano's dormant state seem questionable. If hiking without a large group, contact the police in San Vicente for an escort.

ALEGRÍA AND THE LAGUNA

Serene, clean, and removed from the hustle and bustle of El Salvador's commercial towns, Alegría beckons tourists and Salvadorans alike with its beautiful views, neat rows of pastel-colored houses, cobblestone streets, and the icy but gorgeous Laguna de Alegría.

TRANSPORTATION. Traveling to Alegría can be complicated. The town is serviced by buses from **Santiago de María** (#348. 20min., 1 per hr. from 5am-5pm, US$0.35), **Usutlán** (#348. 1hr., every hr. 5:30am-4:30pm, US$0.75), and **San Salvador** (#301A. 3hr., 1 per day; leaves Alegría at 2:30pm, bus from San Salvador arrives at 5pm; US$3.15). Buses are often off schedule; ask locals about departures for more information. Buses enter Alegría on the main drag, C. Mansferrer, stopping in front of Restaurante Pueblito, across the street from the tidy *parque central*.

ORIENTATION AND PRACTICAL INFORMATION. Alegría is easily traversed on foot, though its hilly streets can be tiring for those not accustomed to the mountain air. The center of the town's grid is the intersection of **Calle Mansferrer** and **Calle Araujo** with **Avenida Motiño** on the northwest corner of the **parque central**. The **Cathedral** is on the southwest corner of the *parque*, on **Calle Romero**. To get to the laguna, follow C. Romero to the east, where signs point you in the direction of Laguna de Alegría, 2km away.

Though Alegría is still small, it is becoming more popular with travelers and the services available in town are improving. The nearest **bank** is in Santiago de María, but there is a **police station** on 4a Av. Sur, next to the school. (☎2628 1016. Open 24hr.) **Farmacia El Pilar** is on Av. Pedro Motiño and 3a C. Pte. (Open M-Sa 7am-6pm, Su 7am-noon.) The **tourist office**, in front of the *parque central*, has plenty of info about the village and surrounding sites. (www.alegria.gob.sv. Open daily 8am-5pm.). Another source of information is the **Centro de Desarrollo Cultural** (☎2628 1038; open daily 9am-5pm), next to the church, where **Narciso Marroquín** runs a guided service to the volcano, the laguna, and hikes to flower nurseries in the area. (US$8-15 per day depending on the hike.)

ACCOMMODATIONS AND FOOD. Alegría has a surprising number of accommodations, and most are fairly comfortable. **Hostal y Cafe Entre Piedras** ❸ (☎2313 2812) is located on the east side of the *parque central* and has rooms with Wi-Fi, cable TV, and hot baths. Two rooms share a bath, while the other is completely private. There is also has a pool for guest use, as well as an outdoor cafe serving coffee, wine, desserts, and panini. (Food US$1-2. Rooms US$16 per person. Cash only.) **Cabañas La Estancia de Daniel** ❷, C. Araujo (☎2628 1038) is perfect for more privacy and a lighter budget.

The friendly owners have log cabins with private hot-water baths, cable TV, free coffee, and orange juice. Rooms US$10 per person. There's also a small nursery inside the complex. (Cash only.)

Restaurante Mi Pueblito ❸, C. Mansferrer, is located across from the *parque central* (☎2628 1038). The most popular restaurant in town serves up heaping plates of fresh-cooked meat with salad, potatoes, rice, and vegetables (US$5-10) in its multiple *ranchos* (covered patios) overlooking the valley below. Popular with families and groups, the menu changes each day. If you're lucky, there might be live guitar and accordion music from local musicians; just remember to tip if they serenade your table! (Open daily 8am-5pm. AmEx/D/MC/V.)

Restaurante El Portal ❸ (☎2628 1144) on the west side of the *parque central*. This restaurant grants a chance to watch the park's constant parade of visitors while indulging in large portions of *comida típica* (US$4-8), a relaxing cup of coffee (US$0.50-1.25), or beer (US$1-1.25). Take it all in at its picnic tables and outdoor patio seating. (Open daily 9am-9pm. Cash only.)

◙ ⚑ SIGHTS AND OUTDOOR ACTIVITIES. Though most visitors come to Alegría for the Laguna, the mountain views at **Mirador de Cien Grados,** which is at the end of 2a Av. Nte., just off of C. Araujo, are also spectacular. **The Laguna,** is 2km south of town, at the end of a 45 min. hike through coffee *fincas.* To get there, head east on C. Romero, where you will see signs marking the cobblestone turnoff that is the start of the trail. The green crater lake has icy waters that are alternately considered medicinal or deadly, depending on which townsperson you ask. Local legend has it that a *sirena* lures young and old men to the lake, keeping them there forever. Local history affirms several drownings in the lake. Visitors are discouraged from swimming in the waters. You can camp here, though a latrine and fire pit are the only comforts available outside of town. At the entrance to the laguna is a trail going up the volcano ridge, from which you can see both the lake and the surrounding mountains, volcanoes, and valleys; it's a 1½ hr. hike to the top. Both of these trips are considered safe to do without escorts. (Entrance to the Laguna US$0.50. Camping US$5 per person. Open 8am-5pm for visitors, unless camping. Cash only).

PERQUÍN

A tiny mountain town, Perquín (pop. 6000) located in the northern region of Morazán (2hr. from San Miguel). The peaceful village has a unique concern with preserving its tragic history for present and future generations. Perquín served as Farabundo Martí National Liberation Front headquarters during the war; the mountains surrounding the town saw some of the fiercest fighting, including the massacre of El Mozote. Every year on December 9th, the town comes together to remember the 1000 people killed by 800 US-trained Salvadoran troops. When the war ended, the town resolved to never forget its past, erecting the powerful Museo de la Revolución Salvadoreña and the monument at El Mozote. Perquín is one of six towns in La Ruta de la Paz, which was created to celebrate local culture and peace.

⎗ TRANSPORTATION

Though Perquín has a lot to offer historically, the transportation options in the city are limited mainly to road travel. Luckily, it is a tiny town and easily traversed on foot. Buses pick up and drop off on the north side of the *parque municipal.* You can also catch them anywhere along the highway heading into or out of town. See below for details:

Buses: All buses heading south from Perquín go to **San Miguel** (2hr.; 5, 6:30, 6:45, 7:45, 8:15, 10:45am, 1, 3:45, 4pm; US$1.25). If you miss these bus times, a **pickup** service to **San Francisco Gotera** departs regularly from the park's north side as well; pick-ups are covered and coordinated by a collective (1hr., every 30min. 5am-6pm, US$0.75). From **Gotera**, buses depart every 30min. for **San Miguel** (1¼hr., 6am-5pm, US$0.75).

✦ ⁊ ORIENTATION AND PRACTICAL INFORMATION

Perquín is a tiny town without street names and with few services. The *carreterra* from San Miguel and San Francisco Gotera enters the town from the south, continuing three blocks until it reaches the north end of town where it curves right toward San Fernando. The **Municipal Square** is one block northwest of the town's entrance; follow the one-way road that heads to the *carreterra*, southbound from town. Most services are centered around the Municipal Sq.; there is no bank or currency exchange in Perquín, so bring cash with you, the nearest bank is in Gotera. Some hotels accept credit cards.

Tourist Offices: Prodetur (☎2680 4086; www.perkintours.ya.st), next door to Alcadia Municipal, on the west side of the Sq. Maps, info, and guide services to sights in Perquín, El Mozote, and Río Sapo, among others. Open M-F 8am-5pm.

Tourist Police: (☎2680 4040), at the intersection of the road into town and the *carreterra* to San Fernando. Open 24hr.

Pharmacy: Farmacia La Luz, (☎2680 4082), on the south side of the Municipal Sq. Open M-F and Su 6:30am-7pm. Cash only.

Internet Access: Cyber Center Christopher (☎2680 4352), 1 block north of Perquín Real on the road into town. Internet US$0.75 per hr. Open M-Th and Su 8am-9pm. Cash only.

Post Office: (☎2680 4165), in the tourist office, on the west side of the Municipal Square and *parque central*. Open M-Tu and Th-F 8am-noon and 1-4pm.

Telephones: Telecom (☎2680 4111), on the north side of the Municipal Park. Open M-F 8am-noon and 2-5pm, Sa 8am-noon and 2-4pm.

⌂ ACCOMMODATIONS

Though there are several nice hotels and lodges on the highway to Perquín, the options within walking distance of town are sparse. Expect to splurge a bit for comfort or hanker down with a shared bath and bare room; there isn't much else to choose from.

▨**Hotel Perkin Lenca,** Km 209.5 on the *carreterra* to Perquín (☎2680 4080; www.perkinlenca.com), 1km from entrance to Perquín. Easily the nicest option around. Comfortable rooms with fans, private hot-water baths, phones, and porches with hammocks. On-site restaurant with breakfast (US$3-5), a small gift shop, and the beginnings of a book exchange. Singles US$20; doubles US$30; triples US$40. Restaurant open 6am-8pm daily. Entrees US$5-9. AmEx/D/MC/V. ❸

Hostal Perquín Real y La Cocina de Mama Toya y Mama Juana (☎2680 4045), at the entrance to town where the road splits into one way streets. Privacy is difficult to find at this hotel, where rooms open directly onto the popular cafe area with hammocks, tables, Spanish soaps, and local teenagers hanging out. The prices are dirt cheap (US$6 per person) and the rooms spare but clean, though you'll have to share your bathroom with restaurant visitors as well. Restaurant open 7am-9pm. Cash only. ❶

La Muralla (☎2680 4314), 1 block north of the *parque central*. Set off from the highway and other major roads. Quiet, simple rooms overlooking a garden. More expensive rooms have private hot-water baths; cheaper rooms have shared baths. The attached *comedor* serves up Salvadoran favorites from 6am-6:30pm. Rooms with private bath US$20 per person, with shared bath US$10 per person. MC/V. ❸

▐ FOOD

Despite its appeal to tourists, Perquín is a tiny village with few commodities; there are a couple under-stocked *tiendas* in town, but if your interests go beyond potato chips and fruits you'll have to look elsewhere. The town center has the standard *comedores* and *pupuserías*. Hotels have their own restaurants, and most tourists eat there.

▧**Restaurante Perkin Lenca** (☎2680 4080), 1km south of the entrance to town, on the *carreterra* from San Miguel. Connected to the hotel, this restaurant has the biggest variety in town, especially if you're craving something other than *pupusas*. The tacos (US$6) are delicious. A variety of pasta dishes (US$5-7) and *comida tipica* (US$4-9), all served in the friendly log-cabin style dining area. Breakfast (US$3-5) is especially noteworthy. Open daily 6am-8pm. AmEx/D/MC/V. ❷

Antojitos Marisol (☎2615 8919), on the main road into town, across from the internet cafe. With the standard variations of *comida típica* (US$1.50-4), *pupusas* (US$0.50-0.60), *licuados* (US$1.25), and beer (US$1), this *comedor* keeps it simple, friendly, and cheap. Open daily 7am-5pm. Cash only. ❷

◎ ▐ SIGHTS AND OUTDOOR ACTIVITIES

CACAOPERA. Descendants of the Lenca and Ulua tribes, the inhabitants of Cacaopera proudly preserve their artistic, cultural, and folkloric traditions. The town is renowned for handmade cotton and *henequén* hammocks, pottery, and sugarcane sweets. The Museum Winakirika highlights the artistic achievements of the town. (☎2651 0251. Open Sa afternoon and all day Su.) A 1hr. walk from town leads to colorful hieroglyphics in Cueva Unamá. Find a guide and info at the tourist office (open M-Sa 8am-4:30pm) in front of the *parque*. *(To get to Cacaopera, take a pick-up from Perquin to San Francisco Gotera. 1hr., every 30 min. from 6am-5pm, US$0.75. From Gotera, buses leave for Cacaopera every 30min. from 6am-4:30pm, US$0.60.)*

RUTA DE LA PAZ. The areas around Perquín were once the epicenter of the country's 12-year civil war. They now form the Ruta de la Paz (Route of Peace). In honor of the tranquility of recent years, the *pueblos* of Perquín, Arambaia, Villa del Rosario, Joateca, Cacaopera, Corinto, and Guatajiagua invite tourists to come and see first-hand an area whose wounds are still too fresh to be called "historical." Locals share their personal war stories and the newly thriving cultural traditions of their towns; visitors can see local artisans making hammocks and pottery while enjoying the beautiful and tiny mountain towns. *(Public transportation between these towns is irregular or nonexistent. Prodetur can arrange guides (US$20 per person) to the towns; tours including transport US$30 per person with pick-up, US$50 with A/C minibus.)*

▧**MUSEO DE LA REVOLUCION SALVADOREÑA.** The Museo de la Revolución Salvadoreña vividly tells El Salvador's tragic military history. Events are told from the Farabundo Martí National Liberation Front perspective, explaining their take on the causes of the war and the main struggles. Exhibits are in Spanish and English, though the ex-guerrilla tour guides only speak Spanish. A visit will give every hill and village in the area new meaning. *(Across from the Cerro and Mirador de Perquín; head west on the carreterra at the north of town, in the opposite direction of San Fernando. The museum is 4 blocks down. ☎2610 6737. Open Tu-Su 8am-5pm. US$1.25.)*

EL MOZOTE. Commemorating the 1981 massacre of townspeople by American-funded government troops, the metal silhouettes the members of a family—father, mother, daughter, and son holding hands—is accompanied by the inscription "They did not die. They are with us, with you, and with all humanity." *(Prodetur can arrange visits to El Mozote in conjunction with or separate from trips to Río Sapo. Tour US$20 per person, with transport US$30. There is only 1 bus per day to El Mozote; it leaves at 7:30am from the desvío 1½km south of Hotel Perkin Lenca. Be prepared to stay around for a while; the only bus back is at 1pm. To walk to El Mozote takes 1½hr.; follow the signs heading to Alameda for 20min., and then walk the main road about 1hr. Remember to bring an umbrella; rain comes suddenly in the mountains.)*

RÍO SAPO. Río Sapo has opportunities for hiking, mountain biking, rappelling, and camping. The two main hikes are **Secretos de la Naturaleza** (45min.) and **Manquilha del Bosque** (30min.). Unfortunately, guides are required for entrance to the area. If arriving on your own, you can get one at the site. Alternatively, organize one in advance via the tourist office in Perquín (US$15 per day). Camping facilities have shower, toilets, and kitchens. (US$12 per person, includes guide and one hike; food can be prepared, but call the tourist office in Perquín in advance.) *(From Perquín, Río Sapo is accessed by car or minibus, which you can arrange through the tourist office. Transportation and guide US$30 per person. To get there on your own, take Bus#332E (2hr., US$1) from San Miguel heading toward Joateca; ask to be let off at the Río Sapo.)*

LA UNIÓN AND GOLFO DE FONSECA

La Unión, a port city near the border with Honduras, is conveniently near the beaches of Eastern El Salvador. A major transportation hub, La Unión's affluence has unfortunately been curbed by the forced closure of its port during the 12-year civil war. Today, the Golfo de Fonseca and its 30 islands are shared between Honduras, El Salvador, and Nicaragua, and La Unión is struggling to regain its former glory. The charm isn't entirely gone from its green park and breezy water-front eateries, but the dusty streets and worn-down buildings belie a tenuous future for the once-prominent city. While La Unión may still play second fiddle to nearby San Miguel in prosperity and economic growth, it is still the best base for reaching El Salvador's eastern beaches and the islands of the Golfo de Fonseca.

▐ TRANSPORTATION

Buses: La Unión has several bus terminals, though most serve only a couple of destinations.

Main Terminal: 3 C. and 4/6 Av. serves buses to and from major cities. To: **San Miguel** (#324. 1½hr., every 10min. from 4am-6pm, US$1), **Santa Rosa de Lima** (#342. 1hr., every 15min. 4am-6pm, US$1), and **San Salvador** (#304. 4hr., every 30min. 4am-3pm, US$3).

Terminal de Playas: 2a C. and Av. Morazan, serves buses to beaches. Buses to Las Playitas leave from the parking lot closer to the market, those to Tamarindo leave from the front lot. To: **Las Playitas** (#418. 25min., every 30min. 6am-5:30pm, US$0.25), and **Tamarindo** (#383. 1½hr., every 20min. 4:30am-5pm, US$1) via **Playa Las Tunas** (45min., US$0.60) and **Playa Jaguey** (1hr., US$0.75).

Boats: Leave from the waterfront between 1/3 Av.; get times and price information from the *comedor* at the end of the dock (open daily 6am-4pm). Boats go to **Potosí, Nicaragua** (2-3hr.; US$10-20 per person; no set schedule, check at the dock. Private boats US$200 per boat). Before leaving, get an exit stamp at the immigration office (Av. Cabañas/5 C.; open daily 6am-8pm).

▐▌ ORIENTATION AND PRACTICAL INFORMATION

The center of La Unión's grid system is at the southwest corner of the **parque central,** where **Calle San Carlos** and **Calle General Menéndez** meet **Avenida General Cabañas.** The **cathedral** is on the east side of the *parque central,* on **1a Avenida,** which stretches south to the market and north down to the bay. Incoming buses enter from the west on 1 C. Pte., dropping passengers off at the corner of 1a C. Pte. and 4a Av. Nte., before heading to the terminal one block north.

Bank: Banco Procredit, 2a Av. Nte. and 1a C. Pte. (☎2604 1719 or 0050). Open M-F 8am-5pm, Sa-Su 8am-noon. Western Union services and **24hr. ATM.** International Visa accepted.

Police: 1a Av. Nte. and 3a C. Ote. (☎2665 9222).

Hospital or Medical Services: Hospital Nacional de La Unión, 9a Av. Nte. #8 (☎2604 0326). Open 24hr.

Internet Access: Cyber Galaxy, 2a C. Ote. and 3a Av. Sur (☎2664 2134). Internet US$1 per hr. Open daily 8:30am-6pm.

Post Office: Av. Cabañas and 3/5 C. (☎2604 4002). Open M-F 7:30am-5:30pm, Sa 7:30am-noon.

Telephone: Telecom, 1 C. Ote. and 5a Av. Nte. (☎2604 2842). Open M-Sa 8am-7pm, Su 8am-noon.

ACCOMMODATIONS

Despite its proximity to several popular tourist areas, La Unión lacks comfortable lodgings. Still, there are several generally safe and reasonably priced options in town.

Hotel Portobello, 1 C. Pte. and 4a Av. Nte. (☎2604 4113). The spacious rooms with fans, hammocks, cable TV, and porch access compensate for the small, outdated bathrooms. Conveniently, Hotel Portobello is only 20ft. from where incoming buses drop off passengers, and its within 3 blocks of the *parque central* and the bay. A/C from 7pm-7am. Free parking. Singles and doubles US$10, with A/C and bath US$21. Cash only. ❷

Hotel San Francisco, C. Menendez and 9/11 Av. Sur (☎2604 4159). With its own greenery-filled compound with multiple courtyards, this is easily the most pleasant accommodation in town. Clean and pleasant rooms with private baths and cable TV, but the prices aren't much of a bargain. On-site parking. Singles with A/C US$35; doubles US$40, with fan US$20; triples US$50. Cash only. ❹

Boarding House Night & Day, 11a Av. Sur and 2/4 C. Ote. (☎2604 3006). The most basic option in town; simple rooms with beds and fans. Private baths that are each little more than a faucet and toilet. Made more appealing by low prices, friendly family-owners, and quiet location. Free parking. Singles and doubles US$10. Cash only. ❷

FOOD

Seafood is the name of the game in La Unión. Shrimp, lobster, and fish are local favorites, but you can also find pizza, chicken, and Mexican options in town as well. For groceries, visit **Selectos Market,** 3a Av. Sur/6a C. Ote. #2/3. (☎2604 1812. Open M-F 7am-8pm, Sa-Su 7am-7pm. MC/V.)

Comedor Maurita, Av. Cabañas and 3a C. Pte. (☎2604 4254). The most famous seafood place in town, Maurita's serves traditional seafood dishes (US$8-12), breakfast (US$3), soups (US$4), and *licuados* (US$1) in an old-fashioned dining area with dark-wood tables and checkered tablecloths. Check out the rows of figurines, collectibles, and old beer bottles. Open daily 6am-4pm. Cash only. ❷

Restaurante El Dragon, 3a Av. Sur and 4a C. Ote. (☎2604 2856). Surprisingly upscale, this Chinese restaurant has an extensive menu of Chinese favorites (US$4-7.50). The cool dining salons are tastefully decorated and a welcome break from the town's sweltering heat. Free parking. Open daily 9am-9pm. AmEx/D/MC/V. ❷

All American Burgers & Mexican Tacos, 4a Av. Nte. and 1/3 C. Pte. (☎2604 6497). This family restaurant is a tribute to foreign sports teams. Indulge in reasonably-priced Mexican food (US$3-5), hamburgers (US$3.50-4.50), and pizza (US$3-12) in the shadows of Patriots jerseys, Red Sox pennants, and Barcelona banners. Games shown on the big-screen TV. Open 10am-7:30pm daily. ❷

Caviotas Restaurant and Karaoke Bar, 3a Av. Sur and 4a C. Ote. (☎2604 0692), across the street from Restaurante El Dragon. Restaurant by day and karaoke bar by night. A variety of Mexican food (US$3-4.50), meat (US$5-7), and seafood dishes (US$4-10), including shrimp, lobster, and fish. Beer US$1-2.50. Drinks US$2-4. Karaoke 9pm nightly. Open daily 8am-2am. Cash only. ❷

SIGHTS AND OUTDOOR ACTIVITIES

LAS PLAYITAS. The closest beach to La Unión, Las Playitas is a small beach with a row of *comedores* behind it, serving up the standard *pupusas* (US$0.35-0.60) and *refrescos* (US$0.50-1) to a mostly local crowd. (*To Las Playitas, take bus #418 (25min., every 30min. 6am-5:30pm, US$0.25). It leaves from the parking lot behind the market at the corner of 1a Av. Sur and 2a C. Ote.*)

ISLANDS OF THE GULF. The gulf islands **Isla Zacatillo, Isla Martia Pérez, Isla Conchagüita,** and **Isla Meanguera** have deserted beaches and are accessible by ferry from La Unión. Martia Pérez and Meanguerra are the most highly recommended beaches; **El Mirador** on Meanguerita provides the option to stay the night (C. Ppal. Ote., ☎2648 0072). (*Most public lanchas (US$1-2.50) travel to and from the islands before 10am, with an afternoon trip to Zacatillo. Comedor Montecristo on the harbor has plenty of lancha information (at the end of 3a Av. Nte., just before the pier. Open daily 6am-5pm). A daytrip to any of the islands departs around 6am and returns around 3pm. US$40-100 per person, discounts for big groups; prices negotiable.*)

PLAYAS JAGUEY, LAS TUNAS, AND TAMARINDO. Popular with Salvadorans because their milder surfs are safer for swimming, the eastern beaches can be somewhat underwhelming for tourists. Though the views are amazing, the beaches aren't always clean and can be crowded, especially on weekends. Playa Jaguey is your best bet at avoiding the crowds. Las Tunas has a lot of reasonable dining options, but its beach is completely submerged at high tide. Tamarindo is the furthest away, the biggest, and the most popular, with several resort-style hotels and a wide, busy beach. As always, be careful with your belongings and pay attention to the tide. The riptide is a concern as always in El Salvador, but the calmer waters of the east can be full of jellyfish and stingrays, so look and shuffle before you step. (*Bus #483 leaves from 2a C. Ote. between Av. Morazán and 1a Av. Sur; 1-1½hr., every 15min. 5am-5:30pm, US$1. The last bus back to La Unión leaves Tamarindo at 4:30pm and Las Tunas at 5pm; be sure to make them or you'll be stuck on the beach.*)

NICARAGUA

Nicaragua, known as the "land of lakes and volcanoes," is a dream come true for many travelers: a tropical paradise largely undiscovered by tourists, complete with picturesque colonial towns, spectacular natural phenomena, and a vibrant, welcoming population. At peace for more than a decade, Nicaragua is shedding its reputation from the Contra War of the 1980s, and you'll find that outside the messy urban jungle of Managua, the country clearly deserves recognition as one of the most beautiful and fascinating places on the continent.

Though Nicaragua is the most populous country in Central America (5.5 million people), its land mass (also largest in the region) makes it one of the least densely populated. More than 90% of citizens live in the Pacific lowlands and less than 15% of its territory. Unfortunately, it also remains the poorest country in the region, in part due to political unrest over the past few decades, and also because of the devastation unleashed by Hurricane Mitch in November 1998. As the tourism industry is practically nonexistent in many parts of the country, exploration requires initiative and courage. Volcanoes on the Pacific coast, beaches on the Caribbean, and tracts of rainforest dwarf even Costa Rica's park system, and yet remain largely untouched. Those willing to leave the tourist trail and tolerate fewer amenities will find Nicaraguan destinations extremely rewarding.

ESSENTIALS

PLANNING YOUR TRIP

PASSPORTS, VISAS, AND CUSTOMS.
Passport. Required of all visitors. Must be valid for a full 6 months after arrival.
Visa (p. 370). Not required of citizens from the US, UK, EU, Canada, Australia, New Zealand, and Ireland. However, tourist card (US$5) required of all visitors; good for 30 days.
Onward Ticket. Required of all visitors.
Work Permit (p. 39). Required for all foreigners planning to work in Nicaragua.
Required Vaccinations. Travelers who have visited nations with endemic yellow fever need proof of vaccination.
Driving Permit. Valid driver's license from your home country or an International Driving Permit required.
Departure Tax. US$32.

EMBASSIES AND CONSULATES

For a list of embassies in Nicaragua, see the **Practical Information** section for Managua (p. 380).

Canada: Consulate, 4870 Doherty Avenue, Montréal, PQ H4V (☎+1 514-484-8250).

NZ: Consulate, 50 Clonbern Road Auckland, 1005 (☎+64 9373 7599).

UK: Embassy, Suite 31, Vicarage House, 58-60 Kensington Church Street London W8 4DP (☎+44 020 7938 2373).

US: Embassy, 1627 New Hampshire Avenue NW, Washington DC 20009 (☎+1 202-939-6570). **Consulates** located in Houston, Los Angeles, Miami, New York, and other American cities.

VISA INFORMATION

All visitors must purchase a **tourist card** (US$5) upon entering Nicaragua. Countries with which Nicaragua has a *visa librado* agreement (US, UK, select European countries) may then stay up to 90 days. Citizens of Canada, Australia, and New Zealand may only stay for 30 days with a tourist card. However, extensions are often permitted upon arrival. The often dysfunctional website of the **Ministry of Immigration and Foreign Affairs** (www.migracion.gob.ni) can provide more details.

For those wishing to **work** or **study** in Nicaragua, a **resident visa** is required. To apply for residency, travelers may enter with a passport and obtain a letter

NICARAGUA

from the school or employer. This, plus a medical certificate, birth certificate, and police record should be submitted to the Immigration Office in Managua.

TOURIST OFFICES

The **Instituto Nicaragüense de Turismo (INTUR; ☎+505 254-5191; www.intur.gob.ni** or www.visitnicaragua.com) offers resources for travelers to Nicaragua, including suggestions on destinations and accommodations. The websites aren't very good; it might be worth a trip to the office in Managua.

MONEY

CÓRDOBAS(C)	AUS$1 = C15.3	C1 = AUS$0.07
	CDN$1 = C17.5	C1 = CDN$0.06
	EUR€1 = C27.1	C1 = EUR€0.04
	NZ$1 = C12.2	C1 = NZ$0.08
	UK£1 = C31.0	C1 = UK£0.03
	US$1 = C19.1	C1 = US$0.05

The currency chart above is based on August 2009 exchange rates. The Nicaraguan unit of currency is the **córdoba** (C). There are 100 **centavos** to one *córdoba*. Colloquially, *córdobas* are sometimes referred to as *pesos* and 10 *centavos* are referred to as one *real*. Coins come in 1 and 5 *córdoba* pieces. Large bills are hard to break. US dollars are usually accepted and welcome at larger banks, hotels, stores, and even street vendors or markets. Changing dollars to *córdobas* is never a problem, and most banks will exchange at the official rate. Nicaragua's **coyotes,** guys on street corners with a calculator in one hand and a wad of bills in the other, will also change dollars at comparable rates. This is technically illegal. Though the black market is usually not dangerous, *Let's Go* does not recommend you interact with *coyotes*. Avoid changing currency at night, and make sure the bills are genuine.

Many Nicaraguan cities have at least one bank that changes **traveler's checks.** Watch out for long lines, forms, and service charges. Most hotels and restaurants do not accept traveler's checks, though some take credit cards. Coyotes are less willing to change traveler's checks than cash. Most cities have **Western Union** offices, but some still route their orders by phone to Managua, sometimes with a one-day delay. **ATMs** are found in Managua and most other big cities. ATMs are linked to Visa, Master Card, American Express, and Cirrus. There's no withdrawal charge, but there is a 2000C maximum withdrawal per day. Tipping policies vary—use discretion. For more info, see **Tipping and Bargaining**, p. 9.

PRICE DIVERSITY

Our researchers list establishments in order of value from best to worst, honoring our favorites with the Let's Go thumbs-up (🖼). Because the best *value* is not always the cheapest *price*, we have incorporated a system of price ranges based on a rough expectation of what you will spend. For **accommodations,** we base our range on the cheapest price for which a single traveler can stay for one night. For **restaurants,** we estimate the average amount one traveler will spend in one sitting. The table below tells you what you'll *typically* find in Panama at the corresponding price range, but keep in mind that no system can allow for the quirks of individual establishments.

ACCOMMODATIONS	RANGE	WHAT YOU'RE *LIKELY* TO FIND
❶	Under C118 (Under US$6)	Hammocks and rented mattresses in some hostels; you'll be providing the sheets.
❷	C118-237 (US$6-12)	Dorms at hostels in tourist-heavy areas and single rooms in lower-end family hotels. Bathrooms are usually shared.
❸	C257-395 (US$13-20)	Nicer family hotels and some singles at larger hotels. You should definitely expect a private bathroom, and amenities such as cable TV and complimentary breakfast.
❹	C415-890 (US$21-45)	Large rooms with all the amenities as a ❸; possibly phone access or Wi-Fi.
❺	Over C890 (Over US$45)	Large, upscale hotels and chains. This should be the best of the best. Sizeable rooms, big beds, and all the perks you could want.

FOOD	RANGE	WHAT YOU'RE *LIKELY* TO FIND
❶	Under C59 (Under US$3)	Probably street food or smaller meals from local *comedors* (street vendors). You aren't going to get high quality foodstuffs or particularly exotic flavors, but these establishments are a good idea if you're hungry and low on cash.
❷	C59-99 (US$3-5)	Meals from local restaurants, usually serving typical Nicaraguan fare or regional dishes.
❸	C118-178 (US$6-9)	Local favorites and fast food restaurants imported from the US or elsewhere. A greasy, oversized, American hamburger? Yep, it's a bit more down here.
❹	C198-257 (US$10-13)	More upscale restaurants that have a wider selection of dishes and more exotic flavoring. You should also be able to find international options.
❺	Over C257 (Over US$13)	This should be gourmet, exquisitely prepared food in a restaurant that prides itself on ambiance. A dress code may be imposed, and there's likely to be an extensive bar. Enjoy!

COSTS

Accommodations in Nicaragua are notably more expensive than those in other parts of Central America. While basic rooms and dorms can certainly be found for under 100C, more safe and comfortable lodgings are 150C-200C. Food is cheap, with *típico* (a standard meal) usually 15C-30C. While the assiduous traveler may be able to scrape by on 200C-300C per day, a safer bet would be 400C-500C, excluding transportation.

TRANSPORTATION

Buses are the primary mode of transportation in Nicaragua. Most of Nicaragua's bus fleet is composed of **"chicken buses,"** yellow school buses retired from North America. Buses usually leave from one main terminal in town (except Managua, where there are five terminals), and each terminal has a small office with info on schedules. Nearly every town and certainly every city has a local bus system.

For more information on driving in Nicaragua, see **Essentials,** p. 20. Within cities, **taxis** are the easiest mode of transport.

La Costeña (☎+505 263-2142; www.lacostena.com.ni) offers flights to several destinations in Nicaragua, including Bluefields, the Corn Islands, Puerto Cabezas, and San Carlos. The main office is in Managua, but most travel agencies sell tickets.

BORDER CROSSINGS

Travelers can cross into Nicaragua by land or sea. Remember to carry enough money to pay any entrance or exit fees.

COSTA RICA. There is one land crossing. **Peñas Blancas/Sapoá** is 36km southeast of Rivas, near Liberia, Costa Rica (p. 500). There is also a river crossing at Los Chiles, south of San Carlos.

HONDURAS. There are three land crossings. **Guasaule** is 77km north of Chinandega, near Choluteca, Honduras (p. 224). **San Marcos/El Espino** is 25km west of Somoto, near Choluteca, Honduras. **Las Manos** is 25km north of Ocotal, and 150km east of Tegus, Honduras. It's also possible to cross by boat via the Caribbean port town of Puerto Cabezas.

SAFETY

As always, you should stay alert and check the latest travel advisories before departing. Managua, like any large city, demands a certain degree of caution and common sense, especially to avoid pickpockets. Touristed areas see a lot of petty crime; poorer neighborhoods and political demonstrations are best avoided entirely. Avoid traveling alone in rural areas. Sporadic armed violence is reported throughout the country, and bandits have been known to operate on the roads, especially in the rural northeast. See **Safety and Health,** p. 10, for more info.

HEALTH

Prophylaxis for **malaria** is recommended for travelers going to the outskirts of Managua and other rural areas.

LIFE AND TIMES

HISTORY

FROM INDIGENOUS TO INDEPENDENT (PRE-COLUMBIAN–AD 1838). Before the arrival of the Spanish, three distinct cultural groups inhabited the territory known today as Nicaragua: the **Niquirano**, the **Chorotega**, and the **Chontal**. Columbus was the first European to visit, coasting by in 1502. In 1524, the rival towns of Granada and León were founded, marking the beginning of permanent Spanish settlement. The Spaniards also gave Nicaragua its name, likely after powerful Niquirano chief Nicarao. Great Britain entered the scene in 1655 when it claimed authority over the Caribbean-facing **Mosquito Coast** (named both for the local Miskito tribe and for the pesky blood-sucking insects). Nicaragua remained a Spanish colony until 1821, when a wave of revolutions swept through Central America. It was then that Nicaragua joined the United Provinces of Central America. Only with the collapse of that union in 1838 did Nicaragua gain full autonomy.

ANGLO-AMERICAN ADVENTURING (1838-1857). After the Spanish departed, British and American influence grew in Nicaragua. In 1847, American transportation magnate **Cornelius Vanderbilt** established the Accessory Transit Company, which carried thousands of prospectors through Nicaragua to California during the Gold Rush of the 1850s. In 1855, American freebooter **William Walker** took advantage of domestic Nicaraguan strife. Invited by liberals in León to help capture the conservative capital at Granada, Walker decided to stick around. Soon, he had taken control of the national army and declared himself president. But in 1857 when Walker drew Vanderbilt's ire by seizing property from the transit company, the combined forces of the British Navy and four Central American governments expelled him from Nicaragua.

AUTOCRATS AND ASSASSINATIONS (1857-1979). The city of Managua, a geographic compromise between León and Granada, was selected as the capital after Walker's forced departure. Conservatives held power in Managua until an 1893 liberal revolt installed dictator José Santos Zelaya in power. Zelaya's actions included driving the British out of the Mosquito Coast and offering Japan canal-building rights in Nicaragua, drawing the ire of the US government, which proceeded to consequently sponsor the first of many rebellions in 1909 to overthrow Zelaya. US Marines remained in the country from 1912 until 1933, when they departed after a gruesome six-year struggle against revolutionaries under General Augusto Sandino. In their wake, they left the brutal US-trained militia, the **Guardia Nacional**, in the hands of **Anastasio Somoza García** (a.k.a. "Tacho"), who had Sandino assassinated in 1934 and promptly assumed dictatorial power. The Somoza family ruled brutally for the next half-century, repressing their opposition through torture, murder, and "disappearances." In 1972, a major earthquake struck, killing some 10,000 Nicaraguans and destroying 90% of Managua. Sadly, the ruling Somoza dictator, Anastasio Somoza Debayle, embezzled most the international aid dollars: his estimated worth rose to $400 million as his country sunk further into poverty. Finally, in 1979, a popular revolution against the Somozas began in earnest. The revolt was led by the socialist **Frente Sandinista de Liberación Nacional (FSLN)**, which took its name after the assassinated Sandino. By the time the Sandinistas took the capital on July 19, 1979, the revolution had cost around 50,000 lives and left 500,000 homeless.

SANDINISTAS AND CONTRAS (1979-1990). In the depths of Cold War anxiety, US President Ronald Reagan envisaged communist trouble lurking behind the Sandinista government. US money and CIA expertise began pouring in to assist the actions of counter-revolutionary groups, known as the **Contras**, against the leftist Sandinistas. The struggle plunged Nicaragua back into chaos. Over 30,000 were killed amid rampant human-rights violations, food and supply shortages, and staggering 30,000% inflation. Despite more than $100 million of US aid and CIA agents mining Nicaraguan harbors, the Contras failed to overthrow the government. The election of opposition candidate **Violeta Chamorro** in 1990 over incumbent Daniel Ortega ended Sandinista rule democratically, and the majority of the Contras disbanded.

NICARAGUA

TODAY

Though Nicaragua still suffers today from the physical and economic destruction of the 20th century, it appears to have secured a modest level of domestic tranquility. Chamorro's presidency saw an effective restoration of peace in the early 1990s after she reintegrated former fighters into society with unconditional amnesties and an extensive campaign to buy back and destroy weapons used in the war. The end of the fighting also brought relative economic stability. Unfortunately this stability did not lead to prosperity. In 1998, Hurricane Mitch dealt the country another devastating blow by wreaking a billion dollars of damage, killing 3,000, and displacing 870,000 Nicaraguans from their homes. Though **President Arnoldo Alemán** managed to lead the country through the storm, he was convicted after leaving office of embezzling $100 million with the help of his family and was sentenced to 20 years in prison in 2003.

In 2006, Daniel Ortega was re-elected President at the head of the still-powerful Sandinista party. Though Ortega had run as the Sandinista candidate in every presidential election since 1990, this marked the first time he and his party had captured the nation's highest office since the end of the civil war. Despite gaining only 38% of the vote, Ortega held a ten-point lead over his closest opponent, a margin that enabled him to narrowly avoid a runoff, one of the electoral reforms introduced in 2000.

As his commitment to the capitalist economic status quo demonstrates, the socialist Ortega has moved towards the political center since the 1980s. Such policies have not, however, removed this president from the scrutiny of the United States: his friendly overtures to Iran and socialist Venezuela have invited deep suspicion in Washington. Ortega has endeavored to craft a more prominent international persona for Nicaragua in other ways as well. In June 2008, he led a failed diplomatic bid for Nicaragua to assume the presidency of the United Nations General Assembly.

Ortega's international ambitions have done little to quell domestic tensions. Only a few months after the failed UN maneuver, riots erupted in the streets after opposition parties claimed that the Sandinistas had rigged hundreds of mayoral elections across the country. The governing party incited further controversy in January of 2009 when the Nicaraguan Supreme Court overturned former President Alemán's corruption conviction. Opponents claimed the ruling had been rigged in a political deal which let Alemán off in exchange for congressional support from his Liberal Party.

ECONOMY AND GOVERNMENT

Despite a massive influx of international aid in the 21st century, Nicaragua's economy is still on the rocks. Unemployment afflicts more than half of the country's population. The per capita income of the country is one of the lowest in the Western Hemisphere, with Haiti's falling just above. The **Heavily Indebted Poor Countries Initiative** provided around $4.5 billion dollars in debt relief for Nicaragua in 2004, followed by more help from a **Poverty Reduction and Growth Facility** program headed by the International Monetary Fund in 2007. Agriculture remains important, employing a third of the country's working population even after the damage reaped by human and natural disasters from 1980 to 2000. Coffee exports and tourism constitute the nation's top two industries. The textile and clothing industry—together comprising almost 60% of Nicaragua's exports—round out the list of Nicaragua's most profitable economic endeavors.

The political scene in Nicaragua is currently dominated by the socialist **Sandinistas**, who hold the presidency and a plurality of seats in the legislative National Assembly. Their main rivals are the two liberal parties, the **Constitutionalist Liberal Party (PLC)** and the **Nicaraguan Liberal Alliance (ALN)**. The latter split from the PLC in 2005 over controversy concerning Alemán's continued power despite his corruption conviction and the political alliance (named "El Pacto") with Ortega. Recent proposals to transform the Nicaraguan government into a parliamentary government with a separate president and prime minister may enable both men to run Nicaragua simultaneously.

PEOPLE

DEMOGRAPHICS

Nicaragua has a population of 5½ million people whose racially and ethnically diverse composition reflects nation's rich history. *Mestizos*, who comprise almost 70% of the country's population, almost exclusively occupy the western half of the country, living in and around urban centers. Descendents of European settlers make up about 17% of the population, while descendents of African slaves comprise another 5%. Only 5% of the modern-day citizenry is accounted for by the nation's indigenous peoples, the largest groups of which are the Miskito, Rama, and Sumu.

LANGUAGE

Like most countries in Central America, Nicaragua's primary language is Spanish—or **Nicañol,** as Nicaraguan Spanish is sometimes called—and is spoken by 90% of the population. Although there is some English along the Caribbean coast due to lingering British influences and American commercialization, it is better to be safe than sorry and always have your translator—human, dictionary, or otherwise—at hand. The Nicaraguan accent and dialect are different from those of other Spanish-speaking nations. *Nicas* are likely to drop the "s" from many words, making it harder for you to understand but easier for them to speak. Though much less common, the indigenous languages of Somo, Rama, and Miskito are still used, the latter being the most prevalent of the three.

RELIGION

Religion, predominantly **Roman Catholicism**, is an important part of Nicaraguan culture. Aside from Catholics and indigenous peoples, who follow their own ancient religions, the rest of Nicaragua's inhabitants are largely **Protestant**. Though still very much a minority religion, Protestantism has expanded rapidly in Nicaragua since the 1990s.

CULTURE

MUSIC. An important trades top, Nicaragua is home to a blend of cultures and nationalities. Nicaragua's music and dance hail from a wide array of cultural origins including traditions of indigenous tribes, European settlers, and African slaves. Surprisingly, all musical genres are not only accepted but also embraced in this country. Home to such popular singers as Reggaeton artists Torombolo and J. Smooth, Nicaraguans listen primarily to modern Latin American music as well as Reggae groups like Kali Boom. One is likely to see people dancing to another nation's popularized beats, like Colombia's *cumbia* or the Dominican Republic's *bachata*, in addition to the *salsa* and *mambo*, but there is no shortage of local musical flair. The *marimba*, a percussion instrument with keys arranged like a piano, is a staple of native bands whose music style embodies the soulful ethnic core of Nicaraguan culture.

LITERATURE. Nicaragua's literary history can be traced to pre-colonial times where its oral traditions of myth and folklore originated. The most famous Nicaraguan story, first orated by an anonymous author, was passed down from the 16th century until it was finally recorded in the early 1900s. This satire, called "El Güegüense", depicts Nicaragua before Columbian settlement. The story is a masterful rendering of indigenous dance, customs, and music. The majority of Nicaraguans only recently became literate thanks to the Sandista's literacy campaign of the 1980s. Few modern Nicaraguan writers gain international literary recognition. Modernist poet Rubén Darío (1867-1916), whose poetry started the new movement of "Modernismo" in Nicaraguan literature, is an exception to this trend. As is Pedro Joaquin Chamorro (1924-1978), whose activism against the Somoza dynasty led to his assassination in 1978.

VISUAL ARTS. Nicaragua's art history has experienced remarkable change with the country's political revolutions. Its native arts are essentially unpracticed now, except for a few remaining rituals observed in isolated indigenous areas. Most of the art one sees today is of a style pioneered by Ernesto Cardenal, a Sandinista priest and leader. He created a small community on the island of Solentiname, where he encouraged Nicaraguans to create experimental and imaginative paintings and murals. While the creative styles of these pieces were not traditional, Cardenal's technical influence did include some features typical of indigenous art such as strong emotion and bold colors. Though much of this art was censored and eventually burned by the National Guard after the 1979 Revolution, this inventive, colorful painting style became Nicaragua's most popular form of visual art.

LAND

GEOGRAPHY. It may be the largest country in Central America, but Nicaragua is only about the size of New York State. The country has three distinct regions: the **Pacific Lowlands**, the **North-Central Highlands**, and the **Atlantic lowlands**. The Pacific Lowlands are hot, fertile plains punctuated by the bubbling volcanoes of the Marrabio mountain range. The North-Central Highlands are marked by rugged mountain terrain and mixed oak and pine forests. The Atlantic lowlands are fondly and all-too truthfully known as La Costa De Mosquitos (the Coast of Mosquitos). As well as the majority of its pesky, blood-sucking insects, these lowlands contain the majority of Nicaragua's famously stunning rainforests.

WILDLIFE. The wildlife of Nicaragua is unlike that of any other country. Perhaps best known for its sea turtles, thousands of whom lay eggs on the country's beaches each year, Nicaragua is also inhabited by about 700 bird species, jaguars, Tamandus anteaters, and fresh-water bull sharks. Nicaragua is also home to the three-toed sloth, a creature that moves so slowly that it is literally impossible to miss.

WEATHER. Nicaragua's climate is primarily tropical, especially during the dry season which lasts from December to May, when the temperature can reach 100°F. Though you'll still be hot and sweaty from June to November, the temperature will drop toward the 80s. The northern mountain regions boast a much cooler climate, but one still warm enough to allow frolicking in Nicaragua's beautiful outdoors.

CUSTOMS AND ETIQUETTE

GREETINGS

Nicaraguans are friendly people, but like most of us they cherish their personal space. A simple handshake will suffice between men and generally between men and women as well. A brief hug and a single cheek kiss are usually reserved for close friends and family. Depending on whom you are interacting with, don't be offended if they don't look you in the eye or try to shake your hand. Typically, people of lower classes will not make eye contact upon formal introduction. But don't be frightened if you catch some staring at you, especially in rural areas; *Nicas* like to people-watch like the best of us.

GESTURES AND MANNERS

Don't be afraid to use the finger! No, not *that* one—a finger wag is a common way to motion toward something, such as a taxi or a passing bus, and rubbing fingers together usually signifies you want to pay for something.

Nicas value politeness and avoid conflict whenever they can. Try not to say "no" if you can handle the consequences of saying "yes," and never take off your shoes unless you are told to do so.

FOOD AND DRINK

Nicaraguan cuisine is based on rice, beans, meat, and tortillas. Nicaragua is not for the heart-healthy or carb-wary, as everything is cooked in oil and fried into oblivion. Though this may seem scary at first, it is undeniably delicious. These starch-heavy loads are balanced with an abundance of tropical fruit and *ensaladas* of cabbage, tomatos, and beets. Even fruit can be fried, and plantains are no exception—they are often served greasy and sweet as *maduros* or crispy and brittle as *tostones*. As for the thirsty, national beers can be found everywhere, and it wouldn't be surprising if they came dripping out of your faucet. **Flor de Cana**, the favorite local rum, is produced from evaporated sugarcane and will provide an extra punch to any drink.

BEYOND TOURISM

VOLUNTEERING

Building New Hope, 106 Overton Lane, Pittsburgh, PA 15217, USA (☎412-421-1625; www.buildingnewhope.org). Volunteers must be able to commit to the organization for at least a month, and should have an intermediate knowledge of Spanish. You may work as a teaching assistant, animal technician, chef, or tutor to a teenage student. For details on volunteering, email donna@buildingnewhope.org.

Experiential Learning International (ELI), 2828 N. Speer Blvd. Suite 230, Denver, CO 80211, USA (☎+303-321-8278; www.eliabroad.org). Offers Spanish language immersion programs for students of all levels. ELI offers fun and low-key Spanish lessons in

Granada, as well as a 2-week "Expanded" Spanish program including both practical and theoretical lessons. 1-week Spanish lessons US$250; 2-week Expanded Spanish US$725; each additional week US$200-380.

Proyecto Mosaico, 3a Av. Nte. #3, Casa de Mito, Antigua, Guatemala (☎502 7832 0955; www.promosaico.org). A German nonprofit organization offering volunteer programs in Nicaragua and Guatemala. Project Mosaic Nicaragua (PMN) works to combat the poverty in Nicaragua, a nation politically aligned with Germany. Volunteer projects include working with the elderly and undernourished or disabled children. Visit the "Volunteering" section of the website to request information.

VISA INFORMATION. To visit Nicaragua, you must have a valid passport, and will have to pay US$5 for a tourist card upon arrival. If you plan to stay for more than 90 days, you need permission from Nicaraguan immigration authorities. Also, there is a departure fee of US$32 that may be included in the price of the airline ticket.

STUDYING

AMERICAN PROGRAMS

Helping Hands in Health Education, 948 Pearl Street, Boulder, CO 80302, USA (☎303 448 1811; www.helpinghandsusa.org). An organization that works to reduce the child mortality rate in Nicaragua, offering volunteer programs in both summer and winter. Volunteers work in a local health clinic. US$2700 (includes travel, room and board, and scheduled excursions).

NICARAGUAN PROGRAMS

The Institute for Central American Development Studies (ICADS), Dept. 826, P.O. Box 025216, Miami, FL , 33102-5216, USA (www.icads.org). In Nicaragua, ICADS has a field course in resource management and sustainable development, as well as a semester-long internship and research opportunity. Tuition, room and board (without lunch included) US$9850. Programs also available in Costa Rica.

LANGUAGE SCHOOLS

La Mariposa Spanish School and Eco-Hotel (☎505 418-4638; www.mariposaspanishschool.com). A truly unique learning environment for Nicaraguans and expats, La Mariposa offers a relaxed learning environment where you choose the duration of your stay. Offers a variety of outings on foot, public transportation, and horseback. Information on volunteer opportunities is also available on the website. US$300 per week per person; US$1000 per month per person.

Viva Spanish School, (☎505 2 270 2339; www.vivaspanishschool.com). Owned by an American living in Nicaragua, Viva Spanish School in Managua offers intensive and semi-intensive Spanish language courses. Homestays are offered for US$115 per week. Provides a fixed schedule of affordable activities and tours (US$2-10).Spanish courses US$90-175 per person per week. Also offers online Skype courses for US$11 per hour.

NICARAGUA

MANAGUA

With a series of massive, disorganized *barrios* in place of tall buildings, the city feels more like an overgrown suburb than the capital of Central America's largest country. Downtown Managua was leveled by an earthquake in 1972; what remained was then left to the mercy of the revolution. Today, empty dirt lots surround shopping centers and bustling markets border gutted buildings. Nonetheless, Managua remains the entertainment, commercial, and transportation hub of Nicaragua. Although it may be less safe than other parts of Nicaragua and its cultural life is suffering—many museums and galleries have closed due to inadequate funds—Managua does have bright spots: the famous Teatro Rubén Darío and the impressive Palacio Nacional.

◼ INTERCITY TRANSPORTATION

FLIGHTS

Managua International Airport (Augusto Sandino International Airport), 12km east of the city. Accessible by bus. All buses headed to Roberto Huembes pass by the airport, just ask the driver to drop you off on the way. **International** airlines include: **Aerocaribbean** (☎2277 5191); **Aeroméxico** (☎2266 6997); **American** (☎22559090); **Contitnental** (☎2278 7033); **Copa** (☎2267 0045); **Delta** (☎2254 8130); **Helinica** (☎2263 2142); **Iberia**(☎506 441 2591); **Nature Air** (506 358 2395); **Serper AA** (☎2270 7863); **Spirit** (☎2233 2884 86); **Taca** (☎2266 3136). **Domestic flights** are all on **La Costeña** airlines. Open M-F 7am-6pm, Sa 7am-3pm, Su 8am-3pm. Counter M-F 5am-5pm, Sa 5am-3pm, Su 5am-3pm.

INTERNATIONAL BUSES

International buses can be found at the **Ticabus Bus Station** (www.ticabus.com. two blocks east of the Antiguo Cine Dorado, Barrio Bolonia). Buses travel to: **San José, Costa Rica** (9-10hr., 6am, C480) via **Granada** (9-10hr., noon, C480); **San Pedro Sula, Honduras** (12-13hr., 5am, C780); **San Salvador, El Salvador** (11-12hr., 5am, C730); **Tegucigalpa, Honduras** (7-8hr., 5am, C480).

DOMESTIC BUSES

Buses depart from four scattered markets: **Mercado Roberto Huembes** and **Mercado Israel Lewites** in the southwest part of the city, and **Mercado Ivan Montenegro** and **Mercado Mayoreo** in the eastern part of the city. It's best to take a taxi or a local bus from one station to another. Note that fares and times for buses change often, so you should always double check with the driver when you board.

Ivan Montenegro: (☎2253 2879). To **Bluefields** (6¾hr., 9pm, C350) and **El Rama** (5hr., 9pm, C150).

Israel Lewites: To: **Carazo** (1¼hr., every 20min. 5:10am-7pm, C18); **Chinandega** (2hr., every 30min. 4:30am-6pm, C50); **Corinto** (2¾hr., 6:30am, C65); **Jinotepe** (1¼hr., every 20min. 5am-7pm, C18); **León** (2½hr., every 45min. 5am-7pm, C30); **Masatepe** (1¾hr.; 1, 3, 5:30, 6:10pm; C20); **Pochomil** (1¼hr., every 20min. 5:10am-7pm, C22).

Mayoreo: Buses bound for the northern half of Nicaragua can be caught from the **Rigoberto Cabezas** bus station, more commonly known as **Mercado Mayoreo** (which is the name of the market surrounding the station). To: **Boaco** (every 30min. 5:30am-6:30pm, C30); **Estelí** (every hr. 5:45am-5:45pm, C60); **Jinotega,** (every 1½hr. 4am-5:30pm, C75); **Matagalpa** (every hr. 3:30am-6pm, C60); **Nueva Guinea,** (every hr. 3:30am-9:30pm, C150); **Rama** (every 2hr. 5am-10pm, C120); **Somoto** (7:15, 9:45am, 12:45, 1:45, 3:45, 4:45pm; C78); **Uigalpa** (every hr. 5:30am-5:30pm, C30).

Roberto Huembes: To: **Rivas** (1½hr., every 30min. 4am-6pm, C50); **Granada** (1½hr., 6am-8pm, C20); **Masaya** (1hr., 6am-8pm, C14); **Masatepe** (1hr., 6am-8pm, C16); **Tipitapa** (30-45min., 6am-8pm, C8).

OTHER TRANSPORTATION

Rental Car Companies: All rental car company offices can be found inside the international wing of the Managua International Airport.

Avis (☎2233 3013; www.avis.com.ni). Open daily 5am-last flight. AmEx/D/MC/V.

Alamo (☎2244 3718; alamocentroamerica.com). Open daily 6am-9:30pm. AmEx/D/MC/V.

Dollar Rent a Car (☎2233 2192; www.dollar.com.ni). Open daily 5am-9pm. AmEx/D/MC/V.

Hertz (☎2233 1237; www.hertz.com). Open daily 5am-9pm. AmEx/D/MC/V.

Budget (☎2263 1222; reserve@budget.com.ni). Open daily until last flight.

✳ ORIENTATION

UPON ARRIVAL

Arriving by air, you'll land at the **Managua International Airport,** also known as the **César Augusto Sandino International Airport,** 12km east of the city on the **Carretera Norte.** Taxis from the airport to hotel-rich barrio **Martha Quezada** cost between C200 and 400, with prices rising after dark. For a less-expensive ride to your hostel, walk 100m right or left after exiting the terminal and head toward the highway where you can get a non-airport certified taxi; these guys are much cheaper (C200-300). This is not suggested if you arrive after dark, as Managua can be dangerous at night. Arriving by international bus from another Central American capital, you'll most likely be at the well-situated **Ticabus** terminal in Martha Quezada, just a few blocks from **Plaza Inter** and numerous hotels. **Sirca** buses from San José arrive in the south part of the city on **Avenida Eduardo Delgado.** Arriving by **domestic bus,** you'll find yourself at one of four markets scattered about the city. Crowded local buses go between the markets and the hotel areas; taxis are usually easier to find (C30-50).

WATCH OUT! Managua is far from the world's safest city. Theft and muggings are common, and as a tourist you look like a walking wallet. Problem spots include all of Managua, although the Barrio Martha Quezada is relatively safe. The city's parks and crowded streets can present the risk of pickpockets and grab-and-run thefts, so hold on to your belongings. Be especially careful at the bus stations and markets, as they are always packed with people. After sunset, the safest way to get around is by taxi, especially for women traveling alone.

LAYOUT AND ADDRESSES

Managua doesn't have street names; helpful, we know. "Addresses" are given in terms of proximity to landmarks—a Texaco station, a statue, where a cinema used to be—and their proximity to the **Rotunda. Al sur** means south, **al lago** is

Managua Center

ACCOMMODATIONS
Casa Vanegas, 8
Hospedaje Quintana, 4
Hotel El Conquistador, 5

FOOD
Ananda, 1
Café Mirna, 9
Comedor Sara, 3
Doña Pilar, 6

NIGHTLIFE
Amatl Café, 11
KTV Discotheque, 7
El Quetzal, 12
La Ruta Maya, 2
Shannon's Irish Pub, 10

"al lago"
(north: toward the lake)

"abajo" ←→ "arriba"
(west)   (east)

"al sur" (south)

Lago de Managua
(Xolotlán)

Malicón

PLAZA DE LA FÉ
JUAN PABLO II

SAN SEBASTIAN

Teatro
Rubén Darío

Casa Presidencial

C. el Triunfo

PLAZA DE LA
DEMOCRACIA

The Old
Cathedral

Palacio de
Comunicaciones

Palacio
Nacional

Centro Cultural
(de Managua)

Dupla Norte

JUILIO
BUITRAGO

SAN
ANTONIO

Parque
Luis Alfonso
Velásquez

C. 15 de
Septiembre

Paseo
Salvador
Allende

Dupla Sur

TO ✈ (12km)

Estadio
Nacional

19 DE JULIO

Av. Bolívar

Av. Colón

TO ❶ & MONTOYA
STATUE (400m)

C. Colón

MARTHA
QUEZADA

Av. Julio Buitrago Urroz

TO ❷

C. 27 de Mayo

Plaza
Intercontinental

Casino
Royale

Tica

Hotel
Intercontinental

Av. Williams Romero

ℹ

Laguna
de Tiscapa

0   300 meters
0   300 yards

Hospital
Militar

C.
José
Martí

BOLONIA

BOSQUES DE
BOLONIA

SERRANO

Rotonda
El Güegüense

Av. Casimiro Sotelo

Av. Rubén Darío
(Carretera a Masaya)

Pista Benjamin Zeledón

PLAZA
ESPAÑA

JONATHAN
GONZALEZ

TO ⓬, ⓯ (2km),
METROCENTRO (1km)

MANAGUA

toward the lake and north, **arriba** is east, and **abajo** means west. For example, *"Del Tica Bus una cuadra abajo y media cuadra al lago,"* means from the Tica Bus Station walk one block west and half a block toward the lake (north).

Managua lies on the south shore of **Lago de Managua;** the locals call it **Lago Xolotlán.** Managua expands in all directions away from the lake. Near the *malecón* (lakefront), you will find many of Managua's sights. El viejo Catedral, La Casa Presidencial, Teatro Nacional Rubén Darío and the Rubén Darío monument are all located lake's shores. The effective center of the city is the pyramid-like Hotel Crown Plaza. Just north of the hotel is **Plaza Inter,** a US-style shopping mall complete with specialty stores, a cinema, and a food court. Just west of the Inter, **Avenida Bolívar** runs north to south 1km north from the hotel to the lakeshore and the old city center, where it meets **Teatro Rubén Darío.** Along the way, it passes the **Asemblea Nacional,** the **Bank of America** skyscraper, the **Palacio Nacional,** and the **Santo Domingo Cathedral.** Across Av. Bolívar from the Inter is the **Intur** tourist office of Managua. **Martha Quezada** is the neighborhood that houses most of Managua's budget hotels and *hospedajes.* Situated in the center of this *barrio* is the **Ticabus Station. Avenida Williams Romero,** with the now-defunct **Casino Royale,** forms the western border of Martha Quezada. The northern border of the *barrio* is formed by **Calle 27 de Mayo.** Both of these streets are larger and busier than the bumpy byways of Martha Quezada. Eight blocks south of C. 27 de Mayo, on Av. Williams Roberto, is the **Plaza de España,** home to a number of banks, several travel agencies, and a supermarket. Most of the discos, chain restaurants, and the **Metrocentro Mall** are located on the **Carretera a Masaya.**

▐ TRANSPORTATION

Transportation in Managua is unreliable and often unsafe. Your best bet is to grab a cab, especially at night. Should you need to take a bus within the city, don't take anything valuable with you; keep what small amount of cash you do carry in a money belt or in you shoe. No matter where you go within the city limits, be sure there is a way for you to get back to your accommodation; ask your driver when and from where the last bus back departs. Getting stuck in an unfamiliar neighborhood after dark in Managua almost guarantees disaster.

▐ PRACTICAL INFORMATION

TOURIST AND FINANCIAL SERVICES

Tourist Offices: Ministerio de Turismo INTUR (☎2254 5191; www.intur.gob.ni), 2 blocks south and 1 block west of Plaza Inter. English spoken. Sells a variety of maps and guides. Open M-F 8:30am-12:30pm and 1:30-5pm.

Tours: Most sights in Nicaragua are safer when visited through tours.

Ecotours de Nicaragua, 123 Del Hotel Crowne Plaza (☎2266 8523; www.centralamericanexcursions.com), 2 block south and half a block west.

Tours Nicaragua, 110 Shell Plaza El Sol (☎2252 4035; www.toursnicaragua.com), 1 block south and 120m. Offers a variety of tour packages from ecotourism to beach vacation packages.

Ecole Travel, Planes de Altamira (☎2278 2572 or 6919; www.carelitours.com). Offers several different organized tours of Nicaragua. Packages include History and Culture, Adventure, Ecotrips, and Beaches.

Embassies: For more information see, **Essentials** p. 369. **U.S. Embassy,** Carretera Sur (☎2252 7100). Ask for the American Citizens Services Unit. Open 7:30am-4:15pm. **Canadian Embassy,** Costado Oriental de la Casa Nasareth, Una Cuadra Arriba, C. El Noval. (☎2268 0433 or 3323) Open M-F 7:30am-4:30pm, Fri 7:30am-1pm. The **Brit-**

MANAGUA

ish Embassy in Nicaragua closed in 2004, but you can contact the **British Honorary Consul** (in Managua) in case of emergency; **Dr. José Evenor Taboada,** Taboada & Asociados, Av. Bolívar 1947, del Hospital Militar (☎2254 5454 or 3839).

Currency Exchange and Banks: There are banks located throughout Managua; almost all have **ATMs.** You can usually also find an ATM in most busy, commercial centers. The Plaza Inter, next to the Barrio Martha Quezada, has several ATMs outside the shopping center on the ground floor.

BanPro, Plaza Inter (☎2255 9595). Open M-F 10am-6pm, Sa 10am-noon.

BDF, Av. Bolivaracross (☎2240 3001), across the street from Plaza Inter. Open M-F 8:30am-4:30pm, Sa 8:30am-12:30pm. **24hr. ATM.**

Citibank (☎2271 9212), inside the MetroCentro Mall. Open M-F 8:30am-4:30pm, Sa 8:30am-12:30pm. **24hr. ATM** located next to the food court.

Western Union, Plaza Inter, ground floor. Open daily 10am-7pm.

SHOPPING

Markets and Malls: Metrocentro Mall, across the street from La Nueva Catedral. This is *the* mall of Managua. You can find brand name stores and eat from one of the many food court options (McDonald's, Pizza Hut, Burger King, Subway, and Quizno's). There are also ATMs.

Centro Comercial Las Américas, in Barrio Bello Horizonte. Another big shopping center, complete with food court, a multi-level shopping area, grocery store, and movie theater.

EMERGENCY AND COMMUNICATIONS

Police: (☎2277 4130, emergency 118), across the street from the MetroCentro Mall, at the Plaza del Sol. Open M-F 8am-5pm, although there is always an officer present at the station. There are 8 different Police districts within the city of Managua; in case of an emergency, contact the dispatch nearest you.

District 1: **Ciudad Sandino** (☎2269 9290 or 9318).

District 2: **Linda Vista** (☎2266 4718 or 1427).

District 3: **Altagracia** (☎2265 0651 or 0659).

District 4: **Mercado Oriental** (☎2249 8340-41 or 8342).

District 5: **Colonia Centroamérica** (☎2278 8934).

District 6: **La Subasta** (☎2233 1118 or 1621).

District 7: **San Rafael del Sur** (☎2293 3319 or 3231).

District 8: **Tipitapa** (☎2295 3229).

Pharmacy: Farmacia del Buen Pastor (☎2222 6462), 1 block north and half a block west from Ticabus. Open M-Sa 8am-6:30pm. AmEx/D/MC/V. **Medco Pharmacy** (☎2254 1000), on the bottom floor of Plaza Inter. Open daily 10am-9pm. AmEx/D/MC/V.

Hospital: Hospital Bautista (☎2249 7070 ext. 4002; www.hospitalbautistanicaragua.com), Barrio Largaespada. **Hospital Privado Salud Integral** (☎2266 1707; www.hospitalsaludintegral.com.ni), Barrio Javier Cuadra Montoya, 1 block north and 1 block west.

Internet: Western Union Internet Cafe, inside the Plaza Inter, bottom floor. Internet C30 per hr. Open daily 10am-9pm. Cash only. **Cyber A. J.** (☎2222 7030), Barrio Martha Quezada, 1 block north from Cafe Mirna. Internet C11 per hr. Open M-Sa 9am-9pm. Also offers international calls. Cash only.

Post Office: Correos Central (☎2222 1060). Edificio Jorge Navarro, to the west of Teatro Nacional Rubén Darío. Open M-F 8am-5pm, Sa 8am-noon.

◪ ACCOMMODATIONS

Managua is a big city, so we've narrowed our search for the best accommodations to the central neighborhood of **Martha Quezada**. It's a quiet, residential neighborhood full of family-run restaurants and small- to medium-sized hotels. Here you can find everything from a night backpacker's hostel for C140 to an upscale hotel for C1000. The neighborhood is close to Ticabus station, the Plaza Inter shopping center, and the tourist office INTUR. While Martha Quezada is relatively safe by Managua's standards, you should still be careful, especially at night. Bear in mind when hunting for hotels or hostels here that the Nicaraguan address system still applies—you'll be placing everything in perspective from the Ticabus. Just remember, *al lago* (to the lake) is north, *abajo* (down) is west, *arriba* (up) is east, and *al sur* (south) is to the south.

BETWEEN LOS HEROES AND THE UNIVERSITY

◪ **Hostal Dulce Sueño** (☎2228 4125), 75m west of Ticabus. Nicer than most of the hostels near the station. The common area, with yellow and green walls, has free purified water and a TV. Kitchen use. Laundry C40. Checkout noon. Rooms C160 per person. Cash only. ❷

◪ **Casa de Huespedes Santos** (☎2222 3713 or 8962 4084; www.casadehuespedes-santos.com), 1½ blocks east of Ticabus. A giant, 2-story building with great patios. All rooms have fans, baths, and small TVs. Breakfast C30-50. Internet access. Checkout 10am. Rooms C140 per person. Call a day in advance to reserve. Cash only. ❷

Hotel Los Cisneros (☎2222 3535; www.hotelloscisneros.com), 1 block north and 1½ blocks east from Ticabus. All of the rooms here are essentially small apartments, and come with private bath, cable TV, a kitchenette, and Wi-Fi; some have patios with hammocks. Breakfast C60. Checkout 11am. Singles with fan C600; with A/C C900; matrimonial C800/1100. Also rents by the week and month. AmEx/D/MC/V. ❹

Hotel El Conquistador, 1 block west from INTUR. With all the hand-painted jungle murals and a garden in the courtyard, it almost feels like you've left Managua. Clean rooms, each with hot-water bath, cable TV, and a mini-refrigerator. Breakfast included. Free Wi-Fi. Checkout at noon. Singles C1100; doubles C1300; triples C1500. AmEx/D/MC/V. ❺

Hospedaje Casa Blanca (☎8637 1350), 10m north from Ticabus, right off the street from the bus station. All rooms with baths and cable TVs. Checkout 9am. Doubles C100 per person. ❶

Hospedaje El Molinito, is half block north from Ticabus. Singles with shared bath C120; doubles with shared bath C240; triples with private bath and TV C300. Cash only. ❶

Hospedaje El Viajero (☎2228 1280), half a block west from Ticabus. A light pink building, Traveler's Hostel offers basic accommodations. Singles C140 per person; the apartment (really just a large room with multiple beds) costs C200 per person. Cash only. ❷

◪ FOOD

Nicaraguan cuisine is made out of basic ingredients—beans, rice, and corn tortillas. The *fritangas* (food joints) often offer the same dishes as the traditional Nicaraguan restaurants. There's certainly enough *gallo pinto* (rice and fried beans mixture) to go around. Still, Managua also has its fair share of international eateries. There's also a food court at the Metrocentro for those who miss their happy meals.

There is a **supermarket** on Av. Central, C. 11/13. (Open daily 6:30am-midnight. AmEx/MC/V.) You can also try **La Colonia,** in Centro Comercial Las Américas, Barrio Bello Horizonte. (☎2277 7710. Open daily 8am-9pm.)

▓ **Doña Pilar** (☎2222 6016), 1 block west and half a block north from Ticabus. A Nicaraguan culinary experience. Come by Doña Pilar's restaurant on Sunday at noon for *Baho*, a steaming hot conglomeration of all things good (meat, eggplant, yucca, plantains, and salad all cooked together in a single bowl). Large plate C40, with rice C50. Cash only. ❶

Cocina de Doña Haydée (☎2249 5494), Carretera Nte., 1 block east of La Rotunda Bello Horizonte. One of Managua's most popular traditional food spots decorated in a rancho style. Delicious House specialty, *Enchiladas Doña Haydée* C45. Entrees C45-170. Open M-Su 7am-10pm. AmEx/D/MC/V. ❷

El Grillito 1 (&2) (☎2266 8567 or 8958 4706), across the street from INTUR. A spacious open-air porch decorated with murals of masks, faces, and half-naked women. Hot wings C70. Mixed plates C189. If it's too crowded when you arrive, don't worry—just head up the block to its twin, **El Grillito 2.** Open daily 3pm-6am. Cash only. ❶

Restaurante del Rey (☎2222 4475), 1 block west and 1 north from Ticabus. Spanish soft rock and ranchero music sets the mood here. Beer C16. Steak in garlic sauce C75. Fruit salad C40. Open M-F 10am-10pm, Sa-Su 10am-midnight. Cash only. ❷

Bar Los Chepes (☎8649 0083), 1 block north and 2 west from Ticabus. A tin roof over a few plastic tables on the sidewalk, Bar Los Chepes doesn't have a menu—you'll just have to look at the handpainted signs on the walls. Catering to the backpacker crowd, this bar offers pancakes, french toast, and omelettes for breakfast. Steak in Jalapeño sauce C46. Open M-Sa 9am-9pm. Cash only. ❶

◉ SIGHTS

The sights in Managua surround the **Plaza de la Democracia** (formerly Plaza de la Revolución), on the northern end of Av. Bolívar, near the lake. From Martha Quezada to the plaza, walk 12 blocks north or take bus #109 from the corner of Av. Bolívar and C. Julio Buitrago. Head to the plaza for the **colorful light** show choreographed to classical music in the central fountain at 6 and 9pm nightly.

EL VIEJO CATEDRAL. This cathedral is a testament to Nicaragua's volatile geology. Nearly destroyed by the 1972 earthquake that ravaged Managua, it's now closed to the public, and for good reason—it looks as if it could fall at any moment. Yet, despite being cracked, it remains a beautiful and poignant spot to visit. *(Plaza de la Democracia, next to La Casa Presidencial and El Palacio Nacional.)*

MUSEO NACIONAL. Occupying the first floor of the Palacio Nacional, Nicaragua's national museum showcases the country's geology, paleontology, and cultural heritage. There are some great fossils, pre-Colombian statues unearthed near Juigalpa, and costumes used in Nicaraguan folk festivals. *(Plaza de la Democracia. ☎2222 3845; www.inc.gob.ni. Open T-Sa 9am-4pm, Su 9am-3:30pm. C80. Camera use C20. Video use C40.)*

RUBÉN DARÍO MONUMENT This monument commemorates Nicaragua's national poet. A white-marble Rubén Darío stands atop a stone pillar with an angel, harp in hand, behind him. Swans and a boat with women blowing trumpets occupy the fountain below. Lines of Darío's poetry decorate the sides of the pillar upon which he stands. *(In a quiet plaza, right next to the Casa Presidencial.)*

CATEDRAL DE LA INMACULA CONCEPCIÓN. This new cathedral has certainly departed stylistically from its Gothic predecessors. An enormous, concrete box, it looks a bit like an open egg-carton, with a ceiling full of egg-shaped domes. These same domes, when viewed from the inside, have small skylights at their tops. The sign inside commemorates those who helped fund the construction of the cathedral. *(Across from the Metrocentro Mall. Open daily 7am-6pm. Mass Su 8, 11am, and 6pm.)*

TEATRO NACIONAL RUBÉN DARÍO. The largest theater in Central America, Teatro Rubén Darío is a multi-level edifice with the *salón de las cristales*, named for its pair of enormous crystal chandeliers. *(Down on the edge of Lake Managua, across from the Malécon. ☎ 2222 7426; www.tnrubendario.gob.ni. Box office open M-F 9am-5pm, or until 7pm if there's a show, Sa-Su 10am-3pm. Tours of the theater in the afternoon C20. No shorts, flip-flops, or tank tops.)*

ARBORETUM NACIONAL. Come sit and read on one of the many benches situated throughout this verdant park. An oasis in an otherwise cold and concrete city, the Aboretum is especially beautiful in March with the national flower, the *sacuanoche*, is in bloom. *(Av. Bolivar, 2 blocks north of Plaza Inter. ☎ 2222 2558. Guided tours available, call in advance. Open M-F 8am-5pm.)*

◤ NIGHTLIFE

ZONA 1

- ▦ **Bar & Restaurante Irlandés** (☎ 2222 6683), 1 block east and 1 south from Ticabus. A reincarnation of the once popular Shannon Bar. Fried mozzarella sticks C80. Guinness C85. Grolsch C40. An extensive liquor selection.

- ▦ **Casa de los Mejía Godoy** (☎ 2222 4866), on the west side of the Hotel Crown Plaza, next to Plaza Inter. A open-air bar and restaurant for musical and cultural events. Nicaraguan artists perform on stage here Th-Sa 9pm-midnight. Sit down at a table, grab a beer, and enjoy the music. Open M-W 8am-11pm, Th-Sa 8am-midnight. AmEx/D/MC/V.

PACIFIC LOWLANDS

The Pacific lowlands, stretching from Chinandega in the north to Rivas in the south, is Nicaragua's population center. A long string of volcanoes along the coast has made the lowlands the most fertile farmland in the country. Shielded from the Caribbean rains by the mountains, the lowlands are hot and dry. For a breeze, migrate to any body of water—Lago de Nicaragua or the Pacific. León, where student radicals keep things lively, and Granada, a tourist favorite for its architectural wonders, are both steeped in history.

LEÓN

The streets of Leon (pop. 130,000) blend colonial with modern at every step. Horse-drawn carriages and liberal students fill the streets, while bells from the 19 churches compete with taxi horns and *camionetas*. Prayer to saints is never far from town parties where spirituality is easily forgotten. Despite the constant mixing of eras, echoes of the town's Spanish founders ring loud and clear.

León Viejo was founded on the shore of Lake Xolotlán in 1524. Destroyed by an earthquake in 1610, León (full name: León Santiago de los Caballeros) was rebuilt 30km to the west. After a slow beginning, the new León soon became a cultural and intellectual stronghold, and acted as the capital of Nicaragua for more than 300 years. The heady atmosphere fueled the imagination of its favorite son, Rubén Darío, whose poetry launched the Modernist movement in Latin America. As bumper stickers on many cars proclaim, León is *orgullosamente liberal* (proudly liberal). The Universidad Nacional Autónoma de Nicaragua (UNAN), the country's first university, sharpens León's politics to a keen radical edge.

▐ TRANSPORTATION

Buses: The main terminal is 6 blocks north and 7 blocks east of the *parque central*. To get there take a taxi (C15) or a camioneta (C3). To: **Chinandega** (1hr., every 15min. 4:30am-6pm, C12-15); **Estelí** (3hr.; 5:20am, 12:45, 2:15, 3:30pm; C60); **Managua** (1½hr., every hr. 4am-4pm, C24); **Matagalpa** (2hr.; 4:20am, 7:30am and 2:45pm; C24). Buses also leave from "El Mercadito," on the western side of town, to the beaches of **Poneloya** and **Las Peñitas** (1hr., every hr. 6am-6pm, C10).

▐▐ ORIENTATION AND PRACTICAL INFORMATION

One of the few cities in Nicaragua where street names are used in directions, León is surprisingly easy to navigate. Like many other cities in Nicaragua, León's center is the **parque central**. If you're standing in the *parque* with the fountain of lions, the massive **cathedral** is to the east, and the imposing **ENITEL** antenna is to the west. León's *calles* run east and west and its *avenidas* run north and south. **Calle Central Rubén Darío** fronts the north side of the parque. **Avenida Central**, León's main thoroughfare, runs north-south straight through the city, broken only by the *parque central*. León's nineteen churches dot the landscape every few blocks and are frequently used as reference points for directions farther away from the *parque* and the cathedral. **La Iglesia de La Merced**, one block north of the *parque's* northwest corner, and **La Iglesia de La Recolección**, 1 block east and 2 blocks north of the *parque's* northeast corner, are useful landmarks. The **bus terminal** sits on the edge of town, 6 blocks north and 7 blocks east of the *parque central*. To get to town from the bus station, take a right onto the main street that you came in on, walk past the market, and continue for several blocks before taking a left on 1 Av. Noreste. The walk to the center of town can be a hot and dusty 20min. trek, but it's manageable. Take advantage of the shade provided by overhangs, or hop in a taxi to skip the whole thing for C15.

Tourist Office: Intur (☎2311 3682), 1½ blocks north of the *parque*. Provides tourist information and brochures. Open M-F 8am-noon and 2-5pm. **Office of Tourist Information** (☎8647 4521), 20m north of the Cathedral. English spoken. Open M-F 8:30am-7pm, Sa 9am-5pm.

Tours and Agencies:

Tierra Tour (☎2315 4278 or 8966 3482; www.tierratour.com), 3 blocks north of the northwest corner of the *parque central*. Offers a wide array of excursions, from a simple tour of León City (C300-400) to sandboarding the Cerro Negro (C560) and exploring the Isla Juan Venado.

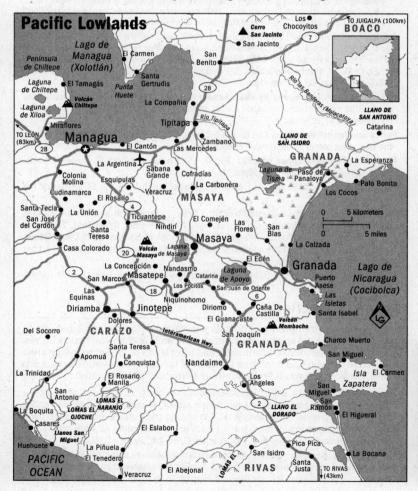

Pacific Lowlands

PACIFIC LOWLANDS

Tours generally depart twice daily: once in the morning and once in the afternoon. Open M-F 8am-7pm, Sa-Su 8am-6pm.

Quetzal Trekkers (☎2311 6695; www.quetzaltrekkers.com), 1½ blocks east of Iglesia La Recolección. A non-profit tour company specializing in hikes of the surrounding volcanoes. All proceeds go to help **Las Tías**, an organization dedicated to helping orphans and homeless children. Volunteer opportunities available. Open M-Sa 9am-5pm, Su 1-5pm.

Nicasí Tours (☎8414 1192 or 8999 4754; www.nicasitours.com). An alternative to conventional tour companies offering a variety of social and cultural tours. Cooking workshop with a local family C400 per person. History of the Revolution tour. Most tours leave from ViaVia hostel.

Vapues Tours (☎2315 4099; www.vapuestours.com), half a block east of the north side of El Laborio Church. Offers maps tours of León and the surrounding area, as well as a León-Granada shuttle service.

Pathways Tour Co. (www.greenpathways.com), across the street from Bigfoot hostel. 3-day whale watching tour in Cosigüina C3000 per person, min. 4 people. 1-day combination Cerro Negro, León Viejo, and Laguna de Asososca tour C1000 per person. 6hr. Isla de Juan Venado tour C600 per person. Bike rentals C200 per day. Open M-Sa 10am-6pm.

Banks: BanCentro (☎2311 0991), half a block south of the cathedral. **24hr. ATM.** Open M-F 8:30am-4:30pm, Sa 8am-noon. V only. **BanPro** (☎2311 3445), 30m south of the Iglesia La Recolección. **24hr. ATM.** Open M-F 8:30am-4:30pm, Sa 8:30am-noon. AmEx/D/MC/V. **Banco ProCredit,** 2½ blocks east of the *parque central.* Open M-F 8:30am-4:30pm, Sa 8:30am-1pm.

Beyond Tourism: Metropolis Spanish School (☎8932 6686; www.metropolisspanish. com), 30m north of the northeast corner of *parque central.* One-on-one instruction, homestays, and activities.

Police and Tourist Police: (☎118 or 2311 3137), 1 block east and 2 blocks north from the northeast corner of the *parque central.*

Pharmacy: Farmacia Lopez (☎2311 3363), 1½ blocks west from El Calvario Church. Open daily 8am-noon and 1-5:30pm.

Hospital: (☎2311 6990 or 2311 6934), 2 blocks south from the SE corner of the *parque central.*

Internet Access: Cyber La Cegua (☎8895 1116), 1 block north and 1½ blocks west of the *parque central.* Internet C10 per hr. Open M-F 8am-6pm. **Cyber Fast,** 2½ blocks north of Parque de las Poetas. Internet C8 per hr. Open M-Sa 9am-8pm. **Cyber Home. net,** 1½ blocks west from the southwest corner of the *parque central.* Internet C10 per hr. Open M-F 8am-9pm, Sa 8am-6pm.

Post Office: (☎2311 6655), 3½ blocks north of Iglesia San Francisco. Open M-F 8am-5pm, Sa 8am-noon.

ACCOMMODATIONS

León may have more hotels and hostels per square mile than any other city in Nicaragua, resulting in an abundance of great hostels and several luxury hotels. Larger hostels have tourist information and offer tours of the surrounding area. If you arrive in León and don't like the look of the first place you stop at, keep moving: chances are you'll find something better around the corner.

Hostal Colibri (☎2311 3858; iguana.colibri@yahoo.com), ½ block left of La Iglesia de la Recolección. Large rooms. Free kitchen access. Breakfast and unlimited coffee included. Free internet access and Wi-Fi. The shaded patio area in front and the hammocks under the thatched palm hut out back are a great place to enjoy all the free coffee. Reception 24hr. Singles C200; doubles C260-280; triples C360. ❷

Hostal Tortuga Booluda (☎2311 4653; www.tortugabooluda.com), 3½ blocks west of the southwest corner of the *parque central.* Winner of hostelworld.com's "best hostel in Nicaragua 2008" award, Tortuga Booluda lives up to its reputation by providing clean,

León

ACCOMMODATIONS
Casa Ivana, 28
Casona Colonial
Guesthouse, 4
Hostel Vía-Vía, 13
Hotel Avenida, 2
Hotel Los Balcones, 16
La Clínica, 29

FOOD
Casa Vieja, 8
Cafe la Rusta, 12

El Buen Gusto, 25
El Sesteo, 20

NIGHTLIFE
Divino Castigo, 5
Don Señor, 14
El Álamo/El Mirador, 15
El Bohemio, 18
Plaza Siglo Nuevo, 11

Centro de Arte, 22
Galería de Héroes y
Mártires, 9
Museo Insurreccional, 24
Museo Rubén Darío, 21

CHURCHES
Capilla y Colegia
la Asunción, 26
Catedral de la Asunción, 23
El Colvario, 17

Iglesia de San Felipe, 1
La Merced, 10
Recollecíon, 6
San Francisco, 19
San Juan, 3
San Juan de Dios, 27
San Nicolas de Laborio, 30
San Sebastian, 31
Zaragoza, 7

MUSEUMS

DIRECTION ABBREVIATIONS
NE (Norte Este) = North East
NO (Norte Oeste) = North West
SE (Sur Este) = South East
SO (Sur Oeste) = South West

PACIFIC LOWLANDS

cheap accommodations and plenty of perks. Free kitchen use and coffee. Breakfast included. Internet available. One-on-one Spanish instruction C100 per hr. Dorms C120; singles C200-480. ❷

Hostal El Nancite (☎8834 2256 or 2311 4117), 2½ blocks south of the Iglesia San Juan. More like a hotel than a hostel, Hostal El Nancite is brand-new, and has the sparkling bathrooms and glossy, comfortable bedspreads to prove it. Only the prices make it seem like a hostel. Check-out 11am. Singles and doubles C300; suites for up to 4 people C900. Cash only. ❸

ViaVia (☎2311 6142; www.viavia.com), 75m south of Banco ProCredit. Clean dorms. The lively bar (open until 11:30pm) is a great place to connect with fellow travelers in León. F nights live music. Dorms C100; private rooms with bath C300-500. Cash only. ❶

Hostal El Albergue (☎8894 1787; www.hosteltrail.com/elalbergueleon), 50m west of the Petronic. A locally owned and operated hostel, this is your ultimate budget stop. Free coffee and kitchen use. Talk to the owner about city tours and volunteer opportunities. Check-out 11am. Dorms C60-120. Cash only. ❶

Bigfoot Hostel (☎8977 8832; www.bigfootnicaragua.com), 75m south of Banco Pro-Credit. Another backpacker favorite. Mini-park, complete with mini pool in back. Dorms C120; singles C260. ❶

Lazybones Hostel (☎2311 3472; www.lazybonesleon.com), 1 block west and 2½ blocks north from the NW corner of the *parque central*. Comfortable dorms. Amenities include a pool, pool table, and TV. Free internet and Wi-Fi. Dorms C160; private rooms C380-560. Check-out 11am. Cash only. ❷

Casona Colonial (☎2311 3178), ½ block west of Parque San Juan. A perfect spot for couples or honeymooners, the Casona Colonial takes its name to heart. Rooms feature elaborate furnishings and beautiful bed frames. Checkout 11am. Singles with private baths C400; doubles C600. Cash only. ❸

Hotel La Posada del Doctor (☎2311 4343; www.laposadadeldoctor.com). Lovely inner courtyard with stone pathways and even a fountain. Free Wi-Fi. Singles with fan C800, with A/C C1000; 5-person suite C1400/1700. AmEx/D/MC/V. ❶

Hotel La Perla (☎2311 2279 or 2311 3125), 2½ blocks north of the *parque central* on the right. A completely converted and restored colonial mansion, Hotel La Perla is now the lodging of choice for travelers wishing to indulge. Impeccably clean rooms come with enormous beds, private bathrooms, A/C, and flatscreen TVs. Free access to the pool. Free Wi-Fi. Rooms C1400-3600. AmEx/MC/V. ❺

Casa Marbella (☎2833 0827 or 2709 8011), between the Tortuguero Information Center and Dorling's Bakery. Beautiful views and friendly owners make this small bed and breakfast a charming and comfortable option. Each of the 4 rooms has high ceilings, soft beds, and solar-powered hot water. Breakfast included. Singles in high season C700, in low season C600; doubles C800/700; triples C1000/900. ❶

🔲 FOOD

Like any college town, León has plenty of pizza joints. Thankfully, most restaurants here also provide an equally enjoyable atmosphere and quality food. Try the traditional Nicaraguan eateries on the south side of the market and by Bigfoot Hostel for a cheap and tasty meal. For groceries, visit **Salman Supermercado**, 1 block north and 3 blocks west of the *parque central*. (☎2311 5027. Open M-Sa 7am-9pm, Su 8am-8pm.)

Comedor El Buen Gusto, on the south side of El Mercado. Serves great food in enormous quantities on the cheap. Heaping plate of *típico* with a coke C45-80. Open M-Sa 10am-10pm. Cash only. ❷

▓ **Cocinarte** (☎2315 4099 or 8854 6928), a bit of a hike from the center of town, on the south side of El Calvario Church. Vegetarians rejoice: finally a restaurant catering specifically to you that offers more than rice and beans. Entrees (Bami Maní; Indonesian noodle plate with steamed veggies and peanut sauce) C90-130. Natural fruit juice C15-20. F nights live music. Open daily 11am-10pm. ❸

Mediterraneo (☎8895 9392), 2½ blocks north from the Parque de las Poetas. Great ambience matched by great food. *Espagueti* Doña Petrona with prawns in a white wine sauce C160. Extensive international wine list. Open T-Su 5:30-11pm. AmEx/D/MC/V. ❸

Comedor Lucia (☎2311 4932), ½ block south of Banco ProCredit, next to both Bigfoot hostel and ViaVia. Buffet style breakfasts and lunches (C35-60) are tasty and filling. Open M-F 7am-9pm, Sa 7am-4pm. Cash only. ❶

El Sesteo (☎2311 5327), on the NW corner of the *parque central*. Open-air restaurant makes a great vantage point for people-watching. *Nactamales* C88. Burgers and hotdogs C64-110. Cool down with a banana split C60. Open daily 8am-10pm. AmEx/D/MC/V. ❷

La Terraza M (☎8458 1374) 2½ blocks north of Parque de las Poetas. Mediterraneo's little brother, La Terraza M caters to the cafe crowd with sandwiches (hot or cold C45) and crepes. Palm trees, dim lighting, and a fountain with goldfish make for a pleasant atmosphere. Open T-Su 7:30am-11pm. AmEx/D/MC/V. ❶

Café La Rosita, ½ block west of the *parque central*. Grab a bagel (C25) or donut (C12), and wash it down with one of La Rosita's coffee concoctions. Cappucinos C22. Open M-Sa 7am-10pm, Su 11am-2pm. Cash only. ❶

◎ SIGHTS

CENTRO DE ARTE. Housed in two colonial buildings, this private collection, owned by the Ortiz Guardian Foundation, has a wide selection of art on display. From pre-Columbian ceramics to European religious paintings to modern art, the Centro is a must-see. *(Two blocks east and 15m south of the northeast corner of the parque central. ☎2311 7225; www.fundacionortizguardian.com. Open Tu-Su 10:30am-6:15pm. C20.)*

CATEDRAL DE LA ASUNCIÓN. This cathedral is the largest in Central America: a reputation the imposing facade won't let you forget. Rubén Darío rests here; his tomb is guarded by one of the cathedral's enormous lion statues. Cathedral de la Asuncíin is also famous for the *Stations of the Cross,* a series of paintings by Antonio Sarria. At the time of publication, these paintings were being restored by local art students. *(On the east side of the parque central. C40 to climb the stairs to the top of the church.)*

MUSEO ARCHIVO RUBÉN DARÍO. This museum, honoring the country's favorite and most respected poet, Rubén Darío, is befittingly housed in Darío's former abode. The museum has collected are some of his clothes, paintings of his family, his death mask, many of his manuscripts, and first editions of several of his works. Unfortunately, there is not much information given about these items; the little info available is entirely in Spanish. With permission, you can read the books in the archive. *(3 blocks west of the parque. ☎2311 2388; www.unanleon. edu.ni. Open Tu-Sa 9am-noon and 2-5pm, Su 9am-noon. Donations encouraged.)*

MUSEO ENTOMOLOGICO. Featuring rotating exhibits of both native and foreign insects, this museum allows you to get up close and personal with everything from incandescent butterflies to giant pincer beetles. *(1½ blocks from El Calvario Church. ☎2311 6586; www.bio-nica.com. Open M-Sa 8am-noon, 2-5pm. C10.)*

MUSEO DE LEYENDAS Y TRADICIONES. Through the pleasant garden in front may lead you to believe otherwise, this building was a prison for Somoza's political enemies from 1921-1979. Converted into a museum in 2000, it now contains a mixture of superstitious tales and artifacts from León's violent past. Paintings on the prison walls depict various scenes of guard brutality. Ask one of the guides to explain the history of the prison. *(Three blocks south and ½ block east of the cathedral's southwest corner, across from San Sebastián Church. Open Tu-Sa 8:30am-noon and 2-5:30pm, Su 8:30am-3pm. C10.)*

LEÓN VIEJO. "Old León" lies 30km southeast of León, on the shores of Lago de Managua. Founded in 1524 by Francisco Hernández de Córdoba, it was the colonial capital of Nicaragua until early 1610, when Volcán Momotombo, standing at the edge of town, caused an earthquake that destroyed the city. Hurricanes have since taken their toll on the partially-excavated ruins. To prevent further damage, UNESCO has covered the remaining brick foundations so only footprints of buildings remain. A Spanish-speaking guide will relate the story of their past splendor. Tours take 45min. and begin at the foundations of the cathedral, a 5min. walk past the museum, where a statue marks the spot of Hernández de Córdoba's beheading. Córdoba's remains were exhumed from the Iglesia de La Merced in May 2000 and are now entombed below the statue. *(From León, take a bus to La Pax Centro (1hr., every 35-40min. 5:50am-6:40pm, C8). Then, catch a bus for the town of Momotombo and ask to be let off at "Las Ruinas" (30min., 9 buses per day 6:30am-5pm, C6). From Managua, take a bus from Mercado Israel Lewites to La Paz Centro (1¼hr., every 20min. 4am-6pm, C10). Buses return to La Paz Centro every 1-2hr (8 buses 8am-5pm, C5). Once in Momotombo, follow the blue-and-white signs to Las Ruinas de León Viejo; the walk takes 10min. Open daily 8am-5pm. C10, with ISIC C5.)*

▨ ♫ NIGHTLIFE AND ENTERTAINMENT

León really comes alive at night. University students spend weekend nights dancing until dawn—or at least until authorities shut the clubs down (at 1 or 2am), after which the party moves to bars. Popular areas are well lit and patrolled by vigilantes (local watchmen hired by the town). The larger hostels host frequent parties: Quetzal Trekkers hosts a combination party and fundraising raffle on select weekends. The local tourist board sponsors **Tertulias Leonesas** in the *parque* every few Saturdays. The events—part concert, part culture, and part fiesta—are free to the public and draw huge crowds. Artisans and street vendors set up mid-afternoon, and a music show starts around 6:30pm.

Bar y Restaurante "Baro" (☎8820 4000), 1 block west of the *parque central*. Popular with both tourists and locals. Serves more than 50 mixed drinks, such as the *Despertador* (alarm clock). Fish fingers and fries C80. The owner, an Israeli ex-pat, swears that his hummus (C115) is the best in Central America.

ViaVia (☎2311 6142; www.viavia.com), 75m south of Banco ProCredit. The bar at ViaVia is a happening place, but people staying there shouldn't worry: it shuts down early. Specialty nights include M trivia night, W themed music night, and F live music. Open daily 7:30-11:30pm. Cash only.

Oxygene (☎2311 0748), 75m west of the *parque central*. Despite having a name that sounds like a pair of aerated Levis (it's French), Oxygene is the club du jour for dancing. Pulsing electronica fills the place with people on the weekends. Beer C20. Mixed drinks C30-40. Oxygene Margarita C55. Cover F-Sa C30. Open Tu-Su 4pm-2am. D/MC/V.

Don Señor (☎2311 1212) 1 block north of the northwest corner of the *parque central*. Bar bordering the street downstairs; disco and dance floor upstairs. Salsa dominates the playlist. Cover up to C40. Open Tu-Su 8pm-2am. AmEx/D/MC/V.

Restaurante Cactus (☎2311 3591), 15m west from La Merced Church. A great place to scope out local music and dance. W-Sa nights live music, ranging from Nicaraguan rock to folklore. The enormous open-air space and sparsely arranged tables make getting a good view easy. Hamburgers and chicken sandwiches C60. Cactus plate C150. Open M-Sa 10am-2am. AmEx/D/MC/V.

Malibu Bar & Restauarante (☎2311 6327), 2½ blocks north of the Parque de las Poetas. Decorated with model sailboats and lit by revolving beer signs. W 3-6pm beer C16. Mixed drinks C50. Open Tu-Th 4pm-midnight, F-Su 4pm-2am. AmEx/D/MC/V.

SANDBOARDING THE CERRO NEGRO

Take advantage of one of several tour companies that do sandboarding tours, including **Tierra Tours** (p. 389) and **Bigfoot Hostel** (p. 392). The drive each the volcano takes 1hr. each way. At the entrance point, you will have to pay C100 (some tours cover this fee). You'll then grab the boards and begin the trek to the rim of the crater. The hike itself isn't too step, but the loose rocks can make things difficult. It can get extremely windy at the top, so be careful. From the top you can see the entire Maribos Volcano chain. Look into the sulfurous, still-smoking crater of the Cerro Negro, whose last eruption was in 1993. Then, when you're ready, head over to the "sandy" side (on the opposite side of the volcano) and get ready to throw yourself down the mountain. You can ride standing up or sitting down. No matter how you ride, you're bound to get covered in dust. It's also possible to get some serious road rash if you fall, so jeans and a tucked in shirt are recommended.

VOLCANOES

León is situated near several breathtaking volcanoes, all of which can be scaled in guided treks. Treks range from half-day walking tours to three-night camping excursions. Your best bet is to go with the **Quetzal Trekkers** (p. 390), a group of friendly international volunteers who donate all of their proceeds to a local charity. Try a relatively untaxing overnight trip to **Cerro Negro**, whose last eruption occurred just 15 years ago. A pleasant hike up **Telica** includes swims in volcanic pools. More hard core camping and trekking tours to **Cosiguina** (3 days; minimum donation C1300) and **Momotombo** (2 days; minimum donation C1100) are only for travelers in decent shape. Local tourism offices and hostels can arrange other treks and guides.

GRANADA

Granada's prime location makes it hands-down the most touristed city in Nicaragua. Worlds away from the chaos and grime of neighboring Managua, Granada is a peaceful city with astonishing beauty. Palm tress share wide boulevards with colorful colonial houses, ribboned horse-drawn taxis rattle by, and vendors hawk eccentric wares in the *parque central*.

▐ TRANSPORTATION

Buses: Express buses leave for **Managua** from just beyond the *parque central* on C. Vega. Buses leave for **Masaya** across from El Mercado on C. Atrevesada. Buses leave for **Rivas** just past El Mercado on C. Atrevesada.

Bike Rental: Bearded Monkey, C. 14 de Septiembre (☎2552 4028), 1 block from La Libertad. C100 (US$5) per day.

▪▪ ❖ ORIENTATION AND PRACTICAL INFORMATION

Granada is built around the attractive *parque central*. The major streets **El Consulado, Real Xalteva, La Libertad,** and **La Calzada** all begin on the *parque's* edges. Many of the tourist hostels, hotels, and restaurants are clustered on and

LOCAL LEGEND

THE WICKED WITCHES OF NICARAGUA

The wicked witch **La Ceuga** is a well-known figure in Nicaragua legend. She is said to wear a dress of plantain leaves while her long, dark hair cloaks her ghoulish face. She passes through the jungle at night, unbounded by the laws of physics, floating or passing through objects on her mission to haunt the unfortunate. Sometimes La Ceuga goes naked, using her seductive silhouette to lure men into the jungle. La Cegua's whispers are so ghastly that the men to whom she speaks go crazy and never recover.

Those who manage to escape La Ceuga's grasp must still be wary of **La Mocuana.** She is the beautiful daughter of a local chief, who once fought the Spaniards. The chief hid his treasure and shared the secret with his daughter before defeating the enemy. Some time later, a Spaniard who had fought against the villagers settled peacefully in the area and fell in love with La Mocuana. The enamored chief's daughter took the treasure to help her start a new life with her lover. The Spaniard, however, preferred the gold to La Mocuana, and made off with it after sealing La Mocuana in a cave. The heartbroken girl escaped and began to roam the landscape in sorrow. She wanders around, exacting vengeance on the lustful, unfaithful, and unsuspecting men who make her acquaintance.

around La Calzada. **Bus stations** and **El Mercado** are both located to the south of town. When in doubt, simply ask someone to direct you to your destination. If they don't know, have them point you back to *parque central* and try again.

Tourist Office: Intur (☎ 2552 6858; www.visitanicaragua.com). From the *parque central,* walk to the end of the Plaza de la Independencia. From there, walk 2 blocks to the right. Open M-F 8am-12:30pm and 2-5pm.

Tours: Nica Adventures (☎2552 8461; www.nicaadventures.com), on La Calzada, 1½ blocks from the Cathedral. Runs a daily shuttle to Managua airport, San Jorge, and San Juan del Sur. Offers tours of the surrounding area, including a kayaking trip on Lake Nicaragua. Also exchanges dollars and euros. Open M-Sa 8am-6pm. AmEx/D/MC. **Tierra Tours** (☎2552 8723; www.tierratour.com), on La Calzada, 2 blocks from the Cathedral. Tour of Granada C300 (US$15). Open M-F 8am-7pm, Sa-Su 8am-5pm. AmEx/D/MC/V.

Bank: Banco America Central (BAC), on the corner of Atrevesada and La Libertad. Open M-F 8:30am-4:30pm, Sa 8:30am-noon. **24hr. ATM.** AmEx/MC/V. **Banpro,** on the corner of El Consulado and La Atrevesada. Open M-F 8:30am-4:30pm, Sa 8:30am-noon. **24hr. ATM.** MC/V.

Beyond Tourism:

Centro de Arte (☎8616 7322; www.nicasagas.com), 25m up La Calzada from the Cathedral, on the left. Owned and operated by American artist Amy. Painting classes W, F, and Su 9am-noon; C100 US$5. Mosaic classes M-Sa 1-4pm; C100 US$5 per hr. Cash only.

One on One Spanish and English tutoring (☎2552 6771; www.1on1tutoring.net), 5 blocks down La Calzada from the Cathedral. Offers a personalized schedule of Spanish classes. C400 (US$20) per day; C1900 (US$95) per week. Open daily 8am-noon, 1-8pm. Cash only.

Nicaragua Mía Spanish School (☎2552 8193 or 2755; www.nicaraguamiaspanish.com), 3½ blocks east, down El Caimito from the *parque central.* Open daily 8am-noon and 1-5pm. C100 (US$5) per hr. lesson; C2000 (US$100) per week.

Spanish School Xpress (☎2552 8577), 2½ blocks from the northwest corner of Parque Central.

La Esperanza Granada (☎2432 5420; www.la-esperanza-granada.org), ½ block east from the corner of C. La Libertad and C. Miguel de Cervantes. Help local school systems by donating your time, skills, or money. Open M-F 9am-5pm.

English-Language Bookstore: Mockingbird Books (☎2552 2146), on La Libertad just off the *parque central.* Used books in English from C80 (US$4). Open M-Sa 9am-5pm, Su 11am-5pm.

Laundromat: Mapache Laundry Service (☎2552 6711). Open M-F 7:30am-6pm, Sa 7:30am-4:30pm.

Under 5lb C70 (US$3.50); up to 20lb. C200 (US$10). Extensive assortment of free flyers, brochures, and maps.

Emergency: Cruz Roja (☎552 2711), on La Calzada, just past Iglesia de Guadalupe.

Police: (☎552 2977 or 552 2929), 1½ block east of the Parque Sandino.

Pharmacy: (☎552 5726 or 552 7679), on C. Xalteva, 2 blocks from the *parque central*. Open M-Sa 7am-7pm, Su 7:30am-7pm. AmEx/D/MC.

Hospital: (☎552 2719).

Internet Access: Cyber Games, on C. Estrada, 10m east of C. Atrevesada, across the street from Hostal Oasis. Internet C20 (US$1) per hr. International calls C1 (US$0.05) per min. Open 8am-10pm daily. **Internet Transfer and Tours** (☎2552-441; hewleto8@ hotmail.com), on the corner of La Libertad and C. Miguel de Cervantes. Internet C15 (US$0.75) per hr. International calls C1 (US$0.05) per min. Cash only.

Post Office: (☎2552 2776), from the Iglesia San Francisco, half a block down C. el Arsenal. Open M-F 8am-noon and 1-5pm, Sa 8am-noon.

ACCOMMODATIONS

Hotels and a scattering of hostels line C. La Calzada, the long road that runs east from the *parque* to the lake shore. Wander up and down it long enough and you're bound to find something.

Hostal Oasis, C. Estrada (☎2552 8006 or 8005), half a block from C. Atrevesada. Spotless high-ceilinged dorms and small, but functional, private rooms. Quiet, out-of-the-way location. Exchange for books and movies. Free daily 10min. international phone call. Free internet and Wi-Fi. Reception 24hr. Dorms C160 (US$8). Cash only. ❷

Hotel America, (☎2552 3914), 3 blocks down C. La Calzada on the left. Warm colors and polished wood furniture make for attractive decor and great ambience. Singles with bath C500 (US$25), with A/C C560 (US$28); doubles C700 (US$35)/C760 (US$38); triples C900 (US$45)/C960 (US$48). D/MC/V. ❹

Hotel Colonial, (☎552 758 182), 25m from the *parque central* on La Libertad. Luxurious as accommodations come in this touristed city. All rooms feature fans, cable TVs, and lockboxes. Pool. Free Wi-Fi. Singles C1200 (US$60); doubles C1500 (US$75); suite C2400 (US$120). ❺

The Bearded Monkey, C. 14 de Septiembre (☎2552 4028), 1 block from La Libertad. A lively social center with every amenity a backpacker could hope for. Great place to share stories with fellow travelers. Bulletin boards full of brochures and flyers for things to do in Granada, including Spanish lessons and volunteer opportunities. Free Wi-Fi. Bike rental C100 (US$5) per day. Hammocks C80 (US$4); dorms C120 (US$6); singles C220 (US$11); doubles 380 (US$19); triples 520 (US$26). ❶

Hospedaje Cocibolca (☎2552 7223), 3 blocks down La Calzada, on the right. A favorite of backpackers. Free Wi-Fi and kitchen use. Singles with bath C300 (US$15); doubles 360 (US$18); quads C560 (US$28). AmEx/D/MC/V. ❸

FOOD

Tired of eating *gallo pinto* and fried plantains? Fortunately for you, Granada is home to an international restaurant scene. For groceries, visit supermarket **Palí,** just past El Mercado on C. Atravesada. (☎2552 7110. Open M-Sa 8am-8:30pm, Su 8am-5pm. Cash only.)

Imagine Restaurant and Bar (☎2454 1602), 1 block from the *parque central*. The owner, a native New Englander, grows produce in his own private garden. Vegetarians will love the Vegetable Fantasy Spectacular, and with dishes like the Pacific Coast Mahí

Mahí in a papaya lime cilantro salsa, carnivores are in good hands. Entrees from C220 (US$11). Open daily 5-11pm. ❷

El Zaguán (☎2552 2522), 1 block down La Calzada street. Try the *brocheta el bramadero,* or beef kebab (260C, US$13). Drinks 40C (US$2). Open noon-11pm daily. AmEx/D/MC/V. ❶

Nuestra Casa (☎2552 8469), 1½ blocks down C. El Consulado. The bull horns above the door don't lie: this is the South in the... uh, other South. Jimmy, Alabama native and owner, does his ribs right. Entrees from C140 (US$7). Open 6-9:30pm daily. Cash only. ❷

O'Shea's Irish Pub and Restaurant, 2 blocks down La Calzada on right. The Irish flag outside is no gimmick: the fish and chips C90 (US$4.50) are authentic. Open 10am-late. Cash only. ❶

Chocolate Cafetería (☎2552 3400), 1½ blocks up Calzada on the left from the Cathedral. Coffee from C15 (US$0.75). Salads C80 (US$4). Sandwiches and hamburgers C60-100 (US$3-5). Open 24hr. AmEx/D/MC/V. ❶

⚓ SIGHTS

We thought we'd change it up here and give you a sort of walking tour through Granada. This should take you about two hours to complete; wear comfortable shoes because you'll be covering about 20 blocks of the city.

Begin your tour of the city at **Iglesia La Merced**. The outer facade of this building is a testament to Nicaragua's volatile history. Climb the bell tower for the best view in town; you'll see the lake, Volcán Mombacho, and Granada's school children playing soccer in church's concrete plaza (Open 5am-7pm daily. C20/US$1) Next, head down Real Xalteva until you get to La Atrevesada. Then, turn right, and walk two blocks to **El Mercado Municipal;** you'll find bootleg wares and fresh fruit and vegetables here. When you're done shopping around, pack up your purchases head back toward Atrevesada. Walk about four blocks to C. El Artesenal. Turn right and follow Arsenal for two blocks until you reach **La Iglesia San Francisco**, commissioned by the filibuster William Walker in 1856. The stunning **Antiguo Convento San Francisco** (☎2552 5535), right next door, is a must-see. The building is a piece of art in and of itself, with a grand staircase and set of bells. Inside, surrounding palm tree

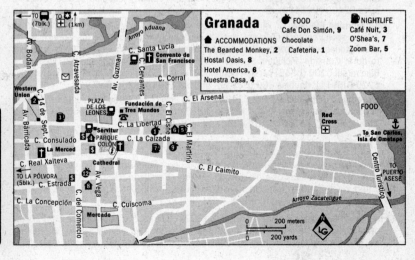

courtyards, is an impressive collection of art. Some of the pieces, including statues taken from the surrounding islands, dates all the way back to AD 800. (Open M-F 8am-5pm, Sa-Su 9am-4pm. C40/US$2. Cash only.) After a long afternoon at the museum, head across the street to **Kathy's Waffle House** where you can take down some tasty Belgian Waffles. Enjoy a complimentary coffee with your meal. (☎2552 8401. Open 7am-2pm daily. C81-102/US$4-5.) Heading back down El Arsenal, take a left at **Plaza de la Independencia.** Be sure to stop off at **Casa de los Tres Mundos** (☎2552 4176; www.c3mundos.org), a multicultural center that provides music and art lessons and info on upcoming events in the city. The *parque central* is right at the end of the Plaza. You'll notice the beautiful yellow and white **Cathedral.** Walk down C. La Calzada (right next to the Cathedral), stop in at one of the many cafés, and grab a scrumptious espresso. End your tour at **Iglesia de Guadalupe** (about five blocks down C. La Calzada), which was originally built as a fort.

NIGHTLIFE AND ENTERTAINMENT

Café Nuit (☎2552 7376; www.granadaparty.com), on C. La Libertad, 2½ blocks from the *parque central.* A cafe turned discoteque. The DJ and live music (merengue anyone?) will have you dancing all night long. Mixed drinks from 40C (US$2). Beer from 25C (US$1.25). Open M and W-Su 8pm-3am. Cover F C10 (US$0.50), Sa C20 (US$1). Cash only.

Be Karaoke (☎2552 4209; www.begranada.com), on the corner of C. Atrevesada and C. La Libertad, across the street from the Banco America Central. Chances are you'll hear this place before you get to it. More than 40 mixed drinks (from C30, US$1.50) provide ample liquid courage. Open T-Su 7pm-6am. AmEx/D/MC/V.

Roadhouse Drinks and Food (☎2552 8459), C. La Calzada, 2 blocks from the Cathedral. Baseball themed sports bar. Drinks C20-80 (US$1-4). Food C120-220 (US$6-11). Open daily 11am-2am. AmEx/D/MC/V.

Zoom Bar, (☎89 858 0913), on La Calzada 3 blocks from Parque Central. A Sports Bar with a great location. Claims to serve the best hamburger in Granada C80 (US$4). Open M-Th 11:30am-midnight, F-Su 8am-midnight. Cash only.

FESTIVALS

With its beautiful colonial buildings and tourist-friendly atmosphere, Granada is a wonderful place to celebrate Nicaragua's culture.

International Poetry Festival (www.festivalpoesianicaragua.com). Since 2005 celebrated poets from many different countries have been getting together in Granada for a week of readings, presentations, and poetry.

Hípica. A once-a-year occurrence, the Hípica is a celebration of the patron saint of each city. In Granada, that means an all-day party for La Virgen Concepción de María.

Día de la Independencia, Sept. 14-15. Nicaragua and Central America celebrate their liberation from Spain.

La Gritería, Dec. 7-8. A celebration of the Virgin Mary's conception, Nicaraguans light off enough fireworks to worry a pyrotechnic teenager.

DAYTRIPS FROM GRANADA

VOLCÁN MOMBACHO

To get to Volcán Mombacho, head down past the market in Granada and hop on a bus to Rivas. Let your driver know that you wish to be let out at "el volcán." From there you'll have to catch one of the park's transport services, or else suffer the long (3hr.) hike to the visitors center. Transport runs M-W at 10:30am, and Th-Su at 8, 10am, and noon.

Three main hikes await visitors to Volcán Mombacho. The crater hike (2hr.; C100, US$5) takes you for a loop around the crater. The "Tigrillo" hike (2½ hr.; C200, US$10) takes you to a higher elevation than the crater hike. The Puma hike (4hr.) is the most physically demanding. It takes you around both craters and to higher elevations still for some of the best views of the surrounding area. Tack on an extra C100 (US$5) for a bilingual guide.

LAS ISLETAS
There are many "unofficial" tour guide companies down at the Malecón that are willing to take you on a trip through Las Isletas. Zapatera tours (☎ 2479 9944; www.zapateratours. com), run by Kevin from Imagine Restaurant and Bar, is a more "off the beaten path" tour.

Kevin will take you out on his boat for a tour of any part of the surrounding area. Take a half-day trip to Las Isletas and stop on a beach for lunch. If you want something a little more adventurous, have him show you around **Isla Zapatera**, an important archaeological site, to see the ancient petroglyphs. For the truly intrepid, he's even willing to take you on an overnight trip to camp on the lake itself. Prices range from C200 (US$10), depending on the size of group and the length of trip.

SAN JUAN DEL SUR

In the days of the gold rush, before the Panama Canal, San Juan del Sur served as a transportation hub for prospectors shuttling between the Atlantic and the Pacific. No longer a layover for money-hungry sailors, modern San Juan del Sur is a relatively undiscovered beach town. A popular surfer hangout for decades, this humble beachfront town has a lot to offer, even if your itinerary does not include riding the waves. The city's beach forms a large half circle, with beautiful cliff faces framing either side. Come here to grab a cheap drink and watch a spectacular beach sunset. Prices drop progressively with added distance from the sand; the small, local eateries and accommodations located inland from the beach are budget traveler's best bets.

▐ TRANSPORTATION

Despite its history, San Juan del Sur is no longer a major transportation hub.

Buses: The **bus station** is on Av. Central, across the street from El Mercado. To: **Managua** (5, 6, 7am) and **Rivas** (every ½hr., 7am-5pm).

Shuttles: Hostel Casa Oro offers a daily shuttle to **Playa Maderas** (departs 10am, 12:30, 3:45pm; returns 10:45am, 1, and 5pm).

Taxis: To **Granada** C1000 (US$50). To **Rivas** or **San Jorge** C300-400 (US$15-20).

◼ ◼ ORIENTATION AND PRACTICAL INFORMATION

Located on the Pacific ocean and boasting some of the best waves around, San Juan del Sur is a surfer's dream. Unsurprisingly,, the town revolves around the coast. **El Paso del Rey** runs along the shore; *avenidas* **El Albinal, Central and Real** branch inland.

Bank: Banco America Central (BAC) ATM, on the beachfront, in front of the Casablanca Hotel. Open 24hr. AmEx/MC/V. **Banco de Finanzas (BDF),** on the coastal end of Calle Real. Open M-F 8:30am-noon, 1-4:30pm. Su 8:30am-12:30pm. **24hr ATM.**

Beyond Tourism: Playas del Sur Spanish School (☎8668 9334; www.playasdelsur-spanishschool.com), about 50m south on beachfront from Banco de Finanzas. 1week with 20hr. of class C2000 (US$100), with homestay C3500 (US$175). Also offers activities such as dancing, cooking, and trips to the beach. Open M-Sa 8am-5pm, Su 8am-noon. **Spanish School House Rosa Silva** (☎8682 2938; www.spanishsilva.com), 30m seaward from Market. 1hr. lesson C140 (US$7); 1 week with 20hr. of class C2500 (US$125), with homestay C4500 (US$225). **Nica Spanish** (☎505 832 4668; www.nicaspanish.com), on the corner of Av. Real and C. Vanderbilt. 1week with 20hr. of class and homestay C2000 (US$100). Collaborates with volunteer organizations throughout Nicaragua.

English-Language Bookstore: El Gato Negro (☎8678 9210; elgatonegronica.com), 1 block inland from El Albinal. New and used English-language books. Open daily 7am-3pm.

Laundromat: Nica Spanish Laundry Service (☎832 4668), on the corner of Av. Real and C. Vanderbilt. 12 pieces C70 (US$3.50).

Red Cross: (☎2563 3415).

Police: (☎2563 3732).

Pharmacy: Farmacianic (☎8411 3330), half a block south of Texaco. Open M-Sa 8am-5pm.

Hospital: (☎2563 3301, 3615, or 3415).

Internet Access: Cyber Cool Welcome, Av. Central (☎2568 3037), half a block inland from the shore. All computers have webcams and Skype. Internet C40 (US$2) per hr. International calls to most places C1 (US$0.05) per min. most places. Also sells camera memory cards and data disks. **Cyber Leo's,** C. Vanderbilt, south of C. El Albinal. Internet C20 (US$1) per hr. International calls to the US C2 (US$0.10) per min. Open daily 7am-9pm..

Post Office: (☎2568 2560), on the southern end of the beachfront. Open M-F 8am-4pm.

ACCOMMODATIONS

Accommodations in San Jan del Sur are geared toward the beach-loving backpacker crowd. As expected, the closer you are to the beach, the more expensive your hotel is going to be.

▨ **Casa Oro Hostel** (☎2568 2415; www.casaeloro.com), on the corner of C. Vanderbilt and C. Real. A hostel and tourist office all in one, Casa Oro is your hookup to goings-on in San Juan del Sur. With surfing lessons, beach transport (including a cheap shuttle that runs 3 times daily), sea turtle expeditions, and canopy tours, they've got you covered. Dorms C150-170; singles C340-380; doubles C500. Discounts to local establishments available. ❷

▨ **Hostal South Seas,** C. Tropezón (☎2568 2084; www.thesouthseashostal.com), just beyond the fork of C. Tropezón with C. Albinal. This completely refurbished building boasts clean, comfortable rooms, spotless shared bathrooms, and a small but refreshing pool. Rooms C300. Discounts for a stays exceeding 1 week. AmEx/D/MC/V. ❸

Hostel Esperanza (☎8423 6869; www.hostelesperanza.com), half a block down the beachfront from the Banco de Finanzas. This clean and friendly newcomer offers the cheapest beachside accommodations around, and locals and travelers alike know it: the hostel is almost always full. Free water, coffee, kitchen use, and internet. Hammocks and tents C100; dorms C200-300; private rooms C400. Cash only. ❶

Hotel La Estación (☎2568 2304; www.laestacion.com.ni), on the corner of C. Paseo del Rey and C. Central. A sparkling hotel right on the beachfront with numerous amenities. Large, air-conditioned rooms with cable TV, private baths with hot water, and balconies overlooking the beach. Breakfast included. Free Wi-Fi. Singles C1100-1200; doubles C1400. AmEx/D/MC/V. ❺

Hospedaje Delfin (☎2568 2373), 1½ blocks north of the market. Another reasonable option close to the beach. Free kitchen use. International calls available, with discounts for guests. Checkout 1pm. Rooms with private bathroom C140; with TV C200. Cash only. ❷

FOOD

As with accommodations, the closer your restaurant is to the beach, the more likely it is to be expensive. Whether or not they boast beachfront views, international options are plentiful. For groceries, visit the **town market,** on the corner of C. Gaspar García Laviana and C. Central.

■ **El Gato Negro** (☎8678 9210; www.elgatonegronica.com), 1 block inland, on El Albinal. An eclectic cafe with more personality than you'll know what to do with. The food is organic and local whenever possible. Extensive selection of tasty vegetarian options. In-house bookstore sells brand-new English-language books (C100-500). Vegetable sandwich (avocado, tomato, onion, cucumber, lettuce and melted cheese) C95. Local, organic coffee C30. Decadent specialty drinks (Dark Chocolate Raspberry Truffle Latté; C50-60). Open 7am-3pm daily. ❷

Big Wave Dave's (☎2568 2151), just before El Gato Negro, on El Albinal. With its international American fare, Big Wave Dan's is apparently where the Americans who live in San Juan del Sur come to hang out. Hamburgers with mashed potatoes or fries (C90). Chicken and beef nachos (C45). Vegetarian options include fresh Caesar salad. Open 7:30am-11pm daily. AmEx/D/MC/V. ❷

Soda Mariel (☎2568 2466), half a block towards the shore from El Mercado. Definitely one of the cheapest options in town. The pink and purple interior will grow on you when you realize how much cash you are saving. Vegetarian tacos C30. Entrees C65-90. Soda C10. Open M-Sa 8am-8pm, Su 10am-3pm. Cash only. ❶

Restaurante El Globo (☎505 568 2478), across the street from the Banco de Finanzas. One of many beachfront options, El Globo provides a great view, but at a price. Chicken *cordon bleu* C170. Lunch special C85. Open M-F 10am-10pm, Sa-Su 10am-midnight. AmEx/D/MC/V. ❸

OUTDOOR ACTIVITIES

■ **Arena Caliente Surf Shop,** C. Gaspar García Laviana (☎8815 3247; www.arenacaliente.com), half a block north of the Market. The oldest surf company in San Juan del Sur. 1hr. lesson, 24hr. board rental, roundtrip transportation, and rashguard shirt C600. Boogie board C100 per day; skimboard C120 per day. Cash only.

■ **San Juan Surf and Sport,** Av. Central (☎2984 2464 or 8402 2973; www.sanjuandelsurf.com), 20m west of the market. Although all the hype would have you to believe that you're in for a rowdy excursion, San Juan Surf and Sport's "Booze Cruise" (daily 3:30-5:30pm, C300) is actually more of a lesson in ecotourism than a party. A combination of sightseeing and sportfishing, passengers scout for sea turtles and watch the sunset over the ocean. After you've made your catch, guides are happy to direct you to restaurants where can have it seasoned and cooked. Open 8am-6:30pm daily. AmEx/D/MC/V.

Nica Surf, C. Vanderbilt (☎2568 2626), just south of Av. Central. Offers 3hr. surf lessons with board rental included C800. Transportation to surf spots C100. Open M-Sa 8am-6pm. AmEx/MC/V.

Good Times Surf Shop, C. Vanderbilt (☎8976 1568), just south of Av. El Albinal. 1hr. lesson, 24hr. board rental, and transportation C600. They'll take you to the beach; you decide when to come back. Surfboard rental C200. Transportation C100.

CHINANDEGA

Chinandega (pop. 120,000), 36km northwest of León, is located in one of Nicaragua's hottest, driest, and flattest regions. A bustling commercial center, it has little to offer tourists save its chaotic *mercado* and ample stock of the famous rum, *flor de caña*. The only compelling reason to linger is to climb San Cristóbal, the country's tallest volcano.

TRANSPORTATION. From the terminal in León, take the **bus** (1¼hr., every 15min. 4:30am-6pm, C12-15). For a faster and more comfortable trip, take the **minibus**, which departs from the terminal in León throughout the day as soon as it fills (40min., C20). Once you arrive in Chinandega, take a taxi or bus to the center of town.

All **buses** from Chinandega leave from the "El Bisne" bus terminal. Buses go to: Ciudad Darío (5:20am and 2:14pm); Corinto (every 15min. 4:30am-6pm); Guasaule, Honduras (every hr. 4am-5pm); León (every 15min., 4:30am-6:00pm); Managua (every hr. 4am-5:20pm); Matagalpa (4:20am, 5:20am, 2:45pm). **Minibuses** depart when full for Managua, León, Guasaule, and Corinto (daily 4am-5pm).

PRACTICAL INFORMATION. The tourist office, **Intur**, is located 1 block east and ½ block south of the *parque central*. (☎2341 1931. Open M-F 8am-12:30pm, 2-5pm.) **Farmacia Lisseth** is 2½ blocks east of the *parque* (open M-Sa 8am-6:30pm.) **Internet access** is available at **Satcom**, 2 blocks east of the *parque*. (☎2241 8481. C10 per hr. Open daily 8am-8pm.)

ACCOMMODATIONS. Hotel Cosigüina ❸, 2 blocks east and ½ block south from the SE corner of the *parque*, is the nicest (and most expensive) hotel in Chinandega. All rooms come with cable TV, hot water, and private bathrooms. (☎2341 3636; www.hotelcosiguina.com. Free Wi-Fi. Singles C800; doubles C1000; triples C1250. AmEx/D/MC/V.) In front of El Gallo más Gallo, **Hotel Casa Grande ❷** offers basic rooms. The owner speaks English and offers tours of San Cristobal, where he owns a farm. (☎2341 4283. Free laundry service. Checkout 11:30am. Singles and doubles C200-400; triples C300-500. Cash only.) **Hotel Glomar ❷**, 1 block south of the *mercado central*, has well-lit rooms with fans. Some come with cable TV and private baths. (☎2341 2562. Checkout 2pm. Singles C200-300; doubles C300-500; triples C450-600. Cash only.)

FOOD. Chinandega is not exactly a thrill-ride for your taste buds. The best food here is the *fritanga* (fried food), served from a line of small huts on the east side of the *parque central*. **Fritanga La Parrillada ❶**, 1 block south of the SE corner of the *parque*, serves *comida corriente* that is delicious C30-75. (☎2341 2132. Open daily 10am-10pm. Cash only.) For groceries, visit **Palí**, on the east side of the *parque*. (☎2341 1007. Open M-Sa 7:30am-8pm, Su 8am-6pm.) **Deliburguer ❶**, a small white and green hut on the east side of the *parque*, serves cheap eats; and, yes, that's actually how the name is spelled. (☎2341 2779. Jumbo hot dog C22. Open daily 11am-midnight.) At **Buffet Doña Jiima ❶**, Chinese rice and a drink will set you back C65. (3 blocks east and ½ block south from the *parque*, in Chinandega's small food court. ☎2341 0378. Open M-Sa 11:30am-3pm. Cash only.)

OUTDOOR ACTIVITIES

SAN CRISTÓBAL VOLCANO

From Mercado Bisne in Chinandega, take the bus headed toward Guasaule on the Honduran border. Ask to be let off at the Campusano stop in El Ranchería (40min.; every 30min.

4am-7:30pm, return every 30min.; C8). Buses leave for El Bolsa from El Mercadito in Chinandega (30min., every hr. 5am-6pm, C6).

The highest volcano in Nicaragua (1786m), San Cristóbal affords amazing views. From Chinandega, the climb is difficult. It's likely that you will have little time to look around if you want to get up and back before nightfall. **Hiring a guide is a must**, since following a random trail will likely take you nowhere. The 8-10hr. round-trip hike is steep and mostly above the tree line. There are two routes to the top, the first via **El Ranchería**. From the bus stop in Chinandega, walk along the highway toward Guasaule. Turn right where you see the few houses in the area and ask locals to show you where the *guardabosque* responsible for the area lives. He should be able to find you guide and horses. Come early, or the guide will probably refuse to take you to the top because hiking past nightfall is not advisable. (Guide and horses C110-140, plus tip).

The other route to the volcano is via **Las Bolsas**. From Las Bolsas, it's 11km up the road to **Hacienda Rosas,** at the foot of the volcano. No buses pass this way, so if you don't have a car you'll either have to walk or borrow a horse from **Socorro Pérez Alvarado** (☎8883 9354) who lives at the Las Bolsas stop. It's best to go with a guide to the summit. **Vincente Pérez Alvarado** (Socorro's brother) is knowledgeable and can arrange to meet you. The walk from Las Bolsas to the summit takes 9hr.; from the base of the volcano, the climb takes 5hr. round trip. There is no water on either route, so bring plenty.

LAGO DE NICARAGUA

Fed by more than 40 rivers, streams, and brooks from Nicaragua and Costa Rica, Lago de Nicaragua is the largest lake in Central America and the tenth-largest freshwater body in the world. Hundreds of islands—430 to be exact—dot the lake's surface, notable as much for the water's wildlife as for the myths of the pre-Columbian petroglyphs. The lake is home to the bullshark, the only freshwater shark in the world. Many years ago these animals migrated up Río San Juan from the Caribbean Sea and slowly adapted to the freshwater environment.

Farther south, the Archipiélago de Solentiname is renowned for both its natural beauty and the minimalist paintings it has inspired. On the southeastern side of the lake sits San Carlos, where the Río San Juan begins its lazy trek toward the Caribbean. Four hours from Granada, some of Nicaragua's most treasured spots—two enormous volcanoes and the paradise of the Isla de Ometepe—sit in waiting.

ISLA DE OMETEPE

In Náhuatl, the ancient language of the Aztecs, *ome* means "two" and *tepetl* means "hills" or "volcanoes." Ometepe is a freshwater island with the highest altitude in the world. The island has twin volcanoes, the active **Volcán Concepción** (1610m) and the extinct **Volcán Maderas** (1394m), which houses an exquisite crater lake.

Ometepe is certainly one of Nicaragua's jewels, with pre-Columbian petroglyphs, fresh fish dinners, and above all, natural beauty. An adventure junkie's dream, Ometepe teems with energy. Homegrown tour agencies, which bombard tourists arriving from the port at Moyogalpa, offer activities ranging from hikes up the volcano, to tours on horseback, to kayaking on the lake. After you've come back to your hotel, grimy, sweaty and smiling, know that this island is no stranger to nightlife. Although you won't find the techno discoteque that prevails in Granada, there are plenty of bars.

The only thing more inspiring than the scenery is the fact that local nature reserves are making conscious efforts to preserve it; you'll find more signs here urging you to clean up after yourself than you will in Managua. Even if you've always had an aversion to the outdoors, come to Ometepe and you'll be sure to find something that will amaze you.

▛ TRANSPORTATION

The easiest way to get around the island is to grab a **taxi** or **bus** from the station, just past the port as you walk in. Buses coordinate with the local **ferries** and head around the island, leaving from Moyogalpa hourly throughout the day. Taxis are bound to be more expensive, but offer the perks of faster travel and comfort. For the truly adventureous, there are many **dirtbike** rental places clustered around the port at Moyogalpa.

Car and Bike Rentals: UGO (☎8901 5587). Manual C700 per 12hr. Automatic C900 per 12hr. **OmetepExpeditions** (☎8933 4796). Dirtbikes C700 per 12hr. Scooters C900 per 12hr. **Parradero Tours** (☎8363 5796). Bikes C500 per 12hr.

⚓ ORIENTATION

La Isla de Ometepe's imposing skyline can be intimidating from the ferry. Fortunately, it's not too complicated to get around. All of the island's towns and roads are situated on the edges of the island, and roads traverse the gap between the two volcanoes. All parts of Ometepe can be reached in close to two hours by taxi. **Moyogalpa,** on the western side of the island, has a spectacular view of **Volcán Concepción. Altagracia** and **Santo Domingo** also populate the western half of the island, while the incredible ◼**San Ramón waterfall** and **Volcán Maderas** occupy the eastern portion. On the whole, moving around is fairly easy, despite the often poor road conditions. Just know that if you do decide to ride the bus, or even the faster and more comfortable taxis, you are in for a bumpy ride.

🛈 PRACTICAL INFORMATION

MOYOGALPA

Tour Companies: Several different tour companies are located just inside the port of Moyogalpa, but "unofficial" guides can be found all around the island. Ask around for the best price.

UGO: Unión Guías de Ometepe (☎8901 5587; www.ometepeguides.com). UGO hands out a large map of the island and a helpful brochure. It also runs 10 different guided tours of the entire island. Tours of Volcán Concepción (up 1000m to a lookout point) C300 each for a group of 6. Hikes to the summit of Volcán Maderas (9hr.) C400 each for a group of 6. Horse tours around the island C120 per hr. 4hr. kayak tour C400 per person. Manual motorcycle C700, automatic C900. Open daily 9am-6pm.

OmetepExpeditions (☎8933 4796), just off the port on the left. 3-4 person tour of Volcán Maderas C600. Fishing tour C400 per hr. per person. Kayak and horse tours. Dirtbike rental C700. Scooter rental C900. Open daily 9am-6pm.

Parrandero Tours (☎836 35796), across the street from UGO and OmetepExpeditions. Fun, laid-back tours in English or Spanish. Just tell them what you want to do. Trip up to the lookout on Concepción C200. Motorcycle C500 per day.

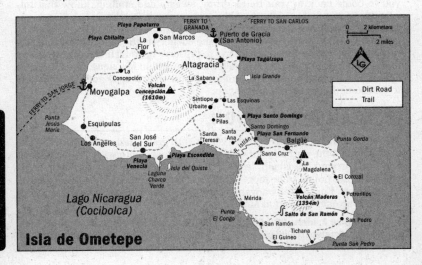

Bank: Banco ProCredit (☎883 6393 or 883 8786), 3 blocks up from the Port, just past Cyber Arcia. **24hr ATM.** Open M-F 8:30am-4:30pm, Sa 8:30am-1pm.

Pharmacy: Farmacia Jany, 3½ blocks up from the port, on the left. Open M-F 8:30am-noon, 2-6pm.

Internet: Arcia Cyber Cafe (☎2569 4110), 2½ blocks from the port, on the right. Internet C10 per 30min. Open M-Sa 8am-8pm.

Post Office: Half a block left of the *parque central.* Open M-F 8am-noon, 1-4pm.

ALTAGRACIA

Internet: Hotel Castillo, 1 block south of the *parque central,* has the only reliable internet access in town. Internet C25 per 30min.

Pharmacy:Farmacia Jany, on south side of the *parque central.* Open M-F and Su 7:30am-10pm.

◪ FOOD

Food on Ometepe does not stray far from the Nicaraguan norm. Here, your culinary experience is enhanced with fresh ingredients. Chances are that your fish came directly from the lake. Most vegetables sold are grown locally and organically in Ometepe's nutrient-rich volcanic soil. For groceries, head to **Comercial Hugo Navas.** It's no Palí, but it covers the basics (☎2569 4244; open M-Sa 7:30am-5:30pm).

MOYOGALPA

▧ **Los Ranchitos** (☎2569 4112), 3 blocks up from and half a block to the right of the port. Dirt floor and a lovely thatched roof with wicker lampshades. Recommended by every local around. Breakfast C45-75. Lunch and dinner C110-150. Open 7am-9:30pm daily. Cash only. ❸

Chidos (☎8359 7546), 3 blocks up, and a half block to the left of the port. Watch sports on the big screen TV inside or enjoy the fresh air on the patio. Personal pizza C80; extra large pizza C260. Calzones C100. Beer C20. Cash only. ❷

Comedor Mar Dulce (☎8667 5261), 2½ blocks up from the port, right before Banco ProCredit, on the left. Red and white tablecloths and multicolored plastic lawn chairs. A classic family restaurant serving hearty home-cooked meals. Open daily 7am-7:30pm. Cash only. ❷

ALTAGRACIA

▧ **Comedor Nicarao,** across from the *parque central.* Big plates heaped with fresh, flavorful Nicaraguan fare. Beef, chicken, or fish with *gallo pinto* C45. Open 7am-10pm. ❶

ON THE MENU

GALLO PINTO

Nationalist rivalries come to fore in the celebration of *gallo pinto* ("painted rooster"), the official dish of both Nicaragua and Costa Rica. Though both countries claim to have created the dish, it is not known which country's version came first.

Nicaraguan *gallo pinto* consists of fried red beans and fried brown rice, mushed together and fried again with vegetables and spices such as onions, peppers and cilantro. The shade the beans dye the rice is similar to the red crest and coloring of a rooster, explaining the origin of the dish's name. Costa Rican *gallo pinto* is nearly identical, though with slight local variations. A fairly simple recipe, it is made using ample amounts of oil and is cooked over a wood fire, making its taste difficult to replicate in a modern kitchen.

The dish is eaten for breakfast, lunch, dinner, or all three meals, sometimes with sides of meat, bread, or cheese. If a meal fried three separate times doesn't satisfy your saturated fat craving, it can be served refried for extra crispiness.

In fall of 2008, Nicaragua competed with Costa Rica for the honor of the world's largest gallo pinto at Pharaoh's Casino. The event, which took place on Nicaragua's annual **Gallo Pinto Day,** provided enough *gallo pinto* to feed 22,200 attendees.

SANTO DOMINGO

The best way to grab cheap beach grub on Santo Domingo is, unsurprisingly, to make your way to the beach. Walk along it in either direction and chances are you'll quickly find a good *comedor*.

> **Comedor Gloriana,** just down the beach from Finca Santo Domingo. This little lakeside eatery serves standard fare, but it's cheap and the view can't be beat. Entrees C40-120. Drinks C10-25. Open 7am-9pm. Cash only. ❶

📷 SIGHTS

▓SAN RAMÓN WATERFALL. Located on a private ecological preserve, the *cascada* (waterfall) is well known around the island: local guides will know how to reach it. Pay C60 to enter and make the 1½ hour trek up as early as possible, both to beat the heat and avoid the crowds. Getting there takes you through some pristine jungle, where you can hear howler monkeys calling and see exotic birds flying overhead. It's bound to be hot and humid in any season, so bring lots of water. The hike itself is fairly easy going; it's only the last quarter of the 3km jaunt that the trek gets rocky and steep. It's worth all the effort, however, when you get there. Turning a corner, you suddenly come upon the San Ramón waterfall. A sheer, gray cliff face rises seemingly out of nowhere. Water, falling down and crashing off the rocks, collects in a small pool at the bottom. The best part is that you can simply walk right up to the edge of the waterfall and cool off under its spray. The pool never gets deeper than around 3 ft. The hike back down only takes about two-thirds of the time needed to ascend.

VOLCÁN MADERAS. Reaching Maderas's summit requires an early start: it's 5-8hr. (closer to the 8hr. end) of fairly steep hiking to the top and back, not including stops. The hike passes through tropical dry forest, then dense tropical rainforest, and finally cloud forest, so be prepared for muddy and physically taxing conditions. Hiking down into the lagoon in the crater, you may see howler and white-faced monkeys alongside colorful wildflowers. Be prepared: the higher you get, the colder it gets, so bring a jacket, even if you think you're not going to need it. It is possible to continue down into the crater with a rope to assist you, though this is better attempted with a guide. Unless you're planning on staying overnight, get started early. Ask the bus driver to drop you off at the entrance to Magdalena, from which a 15min. walk up the path leads to **La Finca Magdalena ❸** (☎8855 1403; www.fincamagdalena.com), an organic coffee farm with spectacular views, selling quality cups of joe and 100% pure bee honey. Workers live off the ecologically friendly solar energy system. It has a *hospedaje*, where tourists can stay in their hammocks or campgrounds (C60), or upgrade to a three-person dorm (C320) or a four-person wooden cabin (C1110). The restaurant serves delicious, traditional food (C60-100), and you can get 1lb. of roasted, ground coffee for C120.

VOLCÁN CONCEPCIÓN. The taller of the two volcanoes (1610m), Concepción is said to have the most perfect conical shape of all the volcanoes in Central America. Concepción is still active and the terrain near the top consists primarily of loose rocks and sand, making it less popular than Maderas for climbing. Low visibility, especially during the rainy season, often makes reaching the crater challenging (and pointless). If you do plan on hiking Concepción, bear in mind that it is very steep, and you need to be just as careful coming down as going up. The lower half of the volcano is covered with tropical dry forest. **Floreana** (about 2hr. to the top) is a good destination and offers the first clear, breathtaking vista from the volcano. Most hikes begin at **La Flor**, 6km northeast of Moyogalpa and reachable by bus (6:30, 10am, 1:30pm; returns every hr. 12:10-5:10pm.) Trails also start at **Cuatro Cuadras**, 2km from Altagracia; **La Concha**, 4km from Moyogalpa on the road to La Flor; **La Sabana**, a 1km walk from Altagracia; and **San Ramón**. A guide is essential; paths on Concepción are unmarked and hard to find.

MUSEO DE OMETEPE Sadly, Altagracia's one real claim to fame is in a sad state of disrepair. What should be an interesting, engaging collection of ancient ceramic and *petroglyphs* (rock carvings) is in need of a good cleaning and some serious reorganization. It's still worth a peek if you're in town. *(1 block west of Parque Central, Altagracia. Open M-F 8am-noon, 1-4:30pm, Sa 9am-3pm, Su 9am-1pm. C30, permission to take photos of the exhibits C35.)*

SALA ARQUEOLOGICA, MOYOGALPA. This salon exhibits a private collection of pre-Colombian pieces found all over Ometepe, including ancient ceramics and grindstones. Some objects date back as far as 300 BC. *(2½ blocks from the port on the right. ☎ 2569 4225. Open daily 9am-9pm. C40)*

PLAYA SANTO DOMINGO. Come to Ometepe to explore; come to Playa Santo Domingo to rest afterwards. With its long stretches of white sand, a lake with amazing views, and cheap eats, Santo Domingo is a wonderful place to relax. This long beachfront is home to several different hotels. The lake water is warm, comfortable, and safe to swim in.

CHARCO VERDE. Charco Verde, or the "green lagoon," is another tourist hotspot on Ometepe located in a private nature reserve. A hotel with lakefront beach access awaits all those who come to see the lagoon and discover they just can't leave. As an added bonus, the C10 entrance fee to the park is waived for guests of the hotel. Walking around, checkout massive termites hard at work and iguanas lurking in tree tops. A quiet, shady trail circles the lagoon. There is also a hike to a nearby hill to witness it from above, where its green color is supposedly at its most vibrant. After you've explored the lagoon, grab a beer and enjoy the hotel's spacious table seating, or cool off by jumping in the lake.

Hotel y Restaurante Charco Verde (☎8927 2892; www.charcoverde.com), on the route to Altagracia from Moyogalpa. Rooms with private baths and A/C. Checkout at noon. Doubles C910; triples C1110. AmEx/D/MC/V.

GIVING BACK

ISLAND SCHOOL

For those looking to contribute to the communities they visit during their stay in Nicaragua, the bilingual school on Ometepe may provide the perfect opportunity for their efforts.

The school is located in the small town of Mérida, on the slopes of Volcán Maderas. Founded in 2007 by Alvaro Molino, proprietor of the Hacienda Merida, the school requires a minimum committment of two weeks. The school offers free langue courses to the 50 students enrolled. Volunteers can expect to teach as many as three 2hr. English classes to 10 or more students each day; there is no school on Sunday. Sometimes class involves kayaking, hiking, or other field trips; these trips engage kids in discussions regarding local biodiversity. In this way, the school promotes the preservation of habitats and wildlife on Ometepe.

The fee for volunteers is US$150 for two weeks, which covers lodging in the hacienda as well as three meals per day. You do not have to be able to speak Spanish to participate as a volunteer.

Interested in helping out? Send your basic information and work experience details via email to **Alvaro** (alvaronica@gmail.com); be sure to include the dates you can work and the reasons why you are interested in volunteering.

PETROGLYPHS. Affording a unique glimpse into the pre-Columbian world, most of the petroglyphs lie between Balgüe and Magdalena on the Maderas side of the island. Another group is located near El Porvenir, a 30min. walk from Santo Domingo and 10min. from Santa Cruz and La Palma. Carved between the 11th and 13th centuries, these simple etchings contain spirals and circles of unknown significance. Find them yourself by renting a bike or car and asking around (most children will be willing to show you the way for a few córdobas), or hire a guide.

RÍO SAN JUAN

The gorgeous Río San Juan runs over 200km, connecting Lake Nicaragua and its river tributaries to the Caribbean Sea. It also marks the border between Nicaragua and Costa Rica. Swirling, expanding, and churning from San Carlos to San Juan del Norte, its waters have washed away history and legends since the 16th century. Since its days as a conduit between the Atlantic and the Pacific for slave-trading ships, the region's growing ecotourism market has blossomed. While some might cry foul at the commercialization of this natural wonder, nearly of the tours are geared toward a better appreciation of the area's beauty, with an eye for helping preserve its pristine condition.

The Río San Juan has counted many admirers, including the American author Mark Twain. The lucky visitor who makes it out to see this wonder will find a mini-Amazon full of untouched flora and fauna, including the *Sábalo Real* (a giant fish, known in English as the Tarpon) and endless tropical flora like *lechuga*, a type of lettuce that grows on floating vegetation. Apart from the main attractions, there are many hidden places along the river—farms, mountains, pueblos, and *comarcas* like Boca de Sábalos and Raudal del Toro. Travel down the Río San Juan and experience some of Nicaragua's most remote settlements, namely Boca, El Castillo Viejo, and San Juan del Nicaragua.

⌶ TRANSPORTATION

BOCA DE SÁBALOS

Boats: Take any of the boats heading from San Carlos to El Castillo; they all make a stop at Boca de Sábalos. C65. Daily departures at 6:30, 8, 10am, noon, 12:30, 3:30, 4:30pm.

Water Taxis: C5-10 depending. Ask one of the people waiting at the docks for someone to take you across the river in a wooden canoe.

EL CASTILLO

Boats: Boats leave from San Carlos to El Castillo daily (6:30, 8, 10am, noon, 12:30, 3:30, 4:30pm; C75). Boats returning to San Carlos (2hr. 20min; 5, 6, 7am, 2pm; C80; express 1hr. 20min.; 5:20am, 11am, 3:30pm; C120).

SAN JUAN DE NICARAGUA

Boats: Public *lanchas* come and leave town only twice a week from San Carlos (9-12hr.; Tu and F 6am, return Th and Su 5am; 160C) and El Castillo (Tu and F 10am, return Th and Su 2pm).

❖ ORIENTATION

The Río San Juan runs from its southwestern joining point with Lago de Nicaragua at the dull city of **San Carlos,** and flows east all the way through to the Atlantic Ocean and **San Juan de Nicaragua.** The towns of **Boca de Sábalos** and **El Castillo,** as well as **Refugio Bartola** and the **Indio Maíz nature preserve,** lie along the river between these two points. Boca de Sábalos comes first, sitting on the mouth of a tributary ("boca" meaning mouth). El Castillo, an additional 15-30min. upriver by boat, is all located on one bank and sits on top of a large hill. Six kilometers farther upstream takes you to Refugio Bartola, located on the edge of the Indio Maíz nature preserve. From there, it's a straight 8hr. boat ride to San Juan de Nicaragua.

❷ PRACTICAL INFORMATION

BOCA DE SÁBALOS

Tourist Office: (☎8123 3190), in a small shack on the docks. Ask for Julío Murillo. Offers 12 different tours, including a hot springs tour (C700 for a group of 5); a steamboat tour, where you can observe the remains of an over 200-year-old steamboat abandoned on the Río San Juan (2½-3hr.; C850 for a group of 5); and an epic, 6-day kayak trip to San Juan de Nicaragua (C5050 per person). Open M-Sa 7am-noon, 1-5pm.

Tour Companies: Hotel Sábalos, across the river from the Tourist Office. Canoe tour up the Río Sábalos in a traditional wooden canoe C200. 2hr. horseback tour C400. Steamboat tour C700. San Juan Plantation tour C900. 2hr. Caymen tour C300 per person. Tour of Cocoa Plantation (price varies). Full-day tour of El Castillo and Reserva Indio Maíz, which takes you first to El Castillo to see La Fortaleza Immaculada de la Concepción, and then continues on an into the nature reserve, C3000 for a group of 4-5.

Pharmacy: "Farmacia Flor de Liz," 1½ blocks up the hill on the left. Open M-Sa 7:30am-10pm, Su 7:30-11:30am.

EL CASTILLO

Tourist Office, 20m from the docks. Provides information about the town and the surrounding area, and offers several different tours. Caymen night tour (C800 for a group of 4). Tours of Reserva Indio Maíz (4hr.; C1300 for a group of 6). This tour showcases the natural beauty of the area, with virgin forests, birdwatching, monkeys, and medicinal plants. Trails are very well marked. Fishing tours also available, consult office for prices. Guides speak some English.

Pharmacy: Venta Social de Medicamentos Inmaculada Concepción, 3 blocks south of the docks. Take a right at the playground; its on the left. Open M-F 8am-noon, 2-5pm.

Internet: Hotel Albergue. Internet C15 per hr. **Border's Coffee.** Internet C20 per hr. International calls to the US C10 per min.

❖ ACCOMMODATIONS

When exploring the Río San Juan, you'll most likely end up staying at one of the area's two river towns, Boca de Sábalos and El Castillo. There are plenty of small hostels and family hotels in both cities, although El Castillo is more tourist-oriented than Boca de Sábalos. For groceries, head to **Mini Super San Antonio** in El Castillo, 2 blocks south of the docks. This small shop sells basic produce, snacks, and toiletries. (☎8690 0681. Open daily 6:30am-9pm.)

BOCA DE SÁBALOS

☑ **Hotel Sábalos** (☎8659 0252 or 2894 9377; www.hotelsabalos.com), at the entrance to Boca de Sábalos, on the opposite bank of the Río San Juan. The impressive deck, strewn with chairs and hammocks, will make you want to stay here just so you can hang out outside. Clean and comfortable rooms with fresh linens and hot water. The owner, Rosa Elena, is a great source of information about the surrounding area, and the hotel offers various tours. Breakfast included. Singles from C300; doubles from C600. AmEx/D/MC/V. ❸

Hotel Kateana (☎8633 8185 or 2583 0178), about 1½ blocks up from the dock on the left. A smaller and less expensive option than Hotel Sábalos. A small market downstairs means you can get all your snacks for the day before you head out. Checkout 10am. Singles with shared baths C150, with private baths C200; doubles C200/250. Cash only. ❷

EL CASTILLO

☑ **Hotel El Albergue** (☎8924 5608; mrcrsls116@yahoo.com), from the dock, 1 block east up the stairs. Spacious, open interior filled with comfortable wood-paneled rooms. Breakfast included. Internet C15 per hr. Wi-Fi C20 per hr. Singles C300. Cash only. ❸

Hotel Richarson (☎8644 0782), 350m east of the docks. Basic, clean rooms, each with a private bath and fan. Breakfast included. Singles C200; doubles C400. ❷

Hospedaje Marantial (☎8843 7033), 75m from the docks. Breakfast C35. Singles C80. Discounts available for groups. ❶

Hotel Refugio Bartola (☎8880 8754; refugiobartola@yahoo.com), 6km downriver from El Castillo. On the edge of the Bartola nature reserve, next to La Reserva Indio Maíz. For those who really, really want to "get away from it all." Large "rancho" space available for group events. Breakfast included. Individual cabins C1000 per person. ❺

SAN JUAN DE NICARAGUA

Tío Poon's Place, on C. Primera across from Disco Fantasía. Rooms with shared baths 60C. ❶

◘ FOOD

Small *comedors* (diners) and *sodas* (cafés) constitute the majority of the food options on the Río San Juan. Your best bet is to opt for some fresh fish, such the local favorite, the tarpon, and have it cooked to your liking.

BOCA DE SÁBALOS

Comedor Gomez (☎8446 7447), ½ block up from the docks, on the right. A Mom and Pop establishment. Serves a quick plate of whatever's hot with a soda (C50). Open daily 6am-8pm. ❶

Soda "El Buen Gusto" (☎8991 1158), 1 block up from the docks, on the left. Cheap, classic Nica food. Entrees C40-100. Sodas C10. Beer C20. Open daily 7am-8:30pm. Cash only. ❶

EL CASTILLO AND SAN JUAN DEL NICARAGUA

☑ **Border's Coffee** (☎2583 0110 or 8408 7688; borderscoffee21@yahoo.com), off of the docks, on the right. Try the vegetarian pasta (C120) or a milkshake made with real, locally grown cocoa (C40). Owner Yamil Obregón is a wonderful resource for information on the town and boat schedules. Open daily 7am-10pm. Cash only. ❷

Comedor Vanessa (☎8408 0279 or 8447 8213), about 4 blocks south of the docks. Entrees C120-C220. *Comidas rápidas* C20-80. Beer C20. Open daily 7am-8:30pm. ❷

Bar y Restaurante los Delicias del Indio, on C. Primera in San Juan de Nicaragua. Serves cheap corriente (20C) under a gazebo along the Río Indio. ❶

◎ SIGHTS

EL CASTILLO

LA FORTALEZA INMACULADA DE LA CONCEPCIÓN. Constructed in the 17th century by the Spanish at a strategic point on the *El Diablo* rapids, this fortress is now a national landmark. No tourist excursion down the Río San Juan would be complete without a stroll around its ancient walls. Climb up the stairs and cross over the drawbridge (yes, it has a drawbridge) of this over 300-year-old structure. The top of the fortress, where the Nicaraguan flag proudly flies, is a perfect spot for taking photos of the surrounding area. The public library for El Castillo is located in the Fortress. *(Open M-F 8am-noon, 2-5pm. C40.)*

LA FORTALEZA INMACULADA DE LA CONCEPCIÓN MUSEUM. At the top of a hill, just before the final push to the fortress, is the fortress's museum. This new building features several attractive displays, holding artifacts ranging from ancient grinding stones to glass bottles and pistol handles pulled out of the river. Each display is accompanied by an elaborate explanation in Spanish and a smaller explanation in dubious English. Stroll through before heading up to the monument and to get a crash course in the history of the region. *(On the top of the hill, just before the monument. C40, pictures C25 extra.)*

REFUGIO BARTOLA AND THE INDIO MAÍZ NATURE PRESERVE. Up river from El Castillo, toward San Juan de Nicargua, lies El Refugio Bartola and La Reserva Indio Maíz, a nature preserve that houses some of the most untouched wilderness in the world. The hot, steamy jungles of the Río San Juan are filled with exotic flora and fauna. A stay at the **Hotel Refugio Bartola** (p. 412), 6km downriver from El Castillo, affords travelers an opportunity to immerse themselves completely in these jungles.

▧**FESTIVALS.** On March 19th, El Castillo celebrates its patron saint, San Jose de la Montaña, with *hípica* (horse parades), dancing, and parties. From September 13-15, the town hosts an international fishing tournament for *Sábalos Real* (Tarpon).

CENTRAL HIGHLANDS

The central highlands are a region of rugged mountains accessible by steep, curving, scenic roads. They were the political stronghold of the Contras during the late 1980s, and fighting continued here long after it had died out in the lowlands. Nearly every individual over age 25 has a story to tell about the war's impact. The fiercely free-thinking highlanders have always been difficult for the government to control, with passionate viewpoints spanning the political spectrum.

Estelí, the largest city in the north, has some compelling reminders of the war and is easily visited en route from Managua to the Honduran border along the Interamerican Hwy. South of Estelí is a turnoff for the beautifully situated town of Matagalpa—gateway to Selva Negra, one of Nicaragua's most accessible forest preserves. A separate highway running east from Managua toward the Caribbean coast passes near Boaco, a mountainous cowboy town, before reaching Juigalpa, a good place to stop if you're making the trip all the way to the coast.

ESTELÍ

The agricultural town of Estelí (pop. 201,000), about halfway between Managua and the Honduran border, is a welcome escape from the heat of lowland cities. While it is the largest town in northern Nicaragua, its cobbled streets turn to dirt roads just a few blocks from the Avenida Central, and the nearby countryside remains fairly unsettled. The colonial Cathedral, Nuestra Señora del Rosario, towers over the surrounding streets, providing an excellent example of the past that this town zealously tries to preserve. Estelí is the tobacco center of Nicaragua, producing volumes of hand-rolled cigars that rival the quality of those made in Cuba. The town also has a lively coffee industry. Fiercely patriotic, Estelí celebrates its own revolution on the 16th of July, three days before the rest of the country's, with an enormous party in the *parque central*, full of music, flags, and screaming people.

▐ TRANSPORTATION

Buses: Cotran Norte, on the PanAm highway, on the south side of town. To: **Managua** (3hr.; 5:20, 6:20, 11:20am; C60); **León** (2hr. 20min., 3:10pm, C60); **Masaya** (3hr., 2 and 3:10pm, C60); **Jinotega** (3½hr.; 4:45, 7:30, 8:30am; C45); **Ocotoal** (2¼hr., every hr. 6-11am, C25); **Somoto** (2hr., every hr. 5:30-10:30am, C25); **Jalapa** (5½hr., 4:10am, C76); **Wiwili** (8hr.; 3, 4, 5, 7:35, 8:30am; C85). **Cotran Sur,** on the PanAm highway, about 200m south of Cotran Norte. To **Managua** (regular: 3hr. 10min., C45; express: 2hr. 10min., every 30min. 3:30am-6pm, C60), **León** (2½hr., 6:50am, C60), and **Matagalpa** (1¾hr., every 30min. 5:20am-5:30pm, C25).

✈ ▐ ORIENTATION AND PRACTICAL INFORMATION

Avenidas run north-south and *calles* run east-west. **Avenida Central,** which spans the length of the city, and **Calle Transversal** run near the center of town one block south of the *parque*. The **Interamerican Highway** runs along the eastern edge of town, six blocks east of Av. Central. The **Esquina de los Bancos** (financial district) sits at the intersection of Av. 1 SO and C. Transversal. The town is divided into **quadrants (NO, NE, SO, SE)** that originate from the four corners of the **parque central.** The **Terminal Norte** is at the south end of town; three blocks up is **Terminal Sur.**

Central Highlands

HONDURAS

Jalapa
FILA EL VENADO
VALLE SAN DIEGO
El Paraiso
Las Manos
Santa María
Volcán Viejo
Dipilto
Cerro el Tizal
Santa Clara
San Fernando
Murra
El Jícaro
Susucayan
Cerro California
Cerro Chachgua
FILA DE BUENA
Cerro el Perro
Wiwilí
Cerro el Marimacho
Macuelizo
Mosonte
Ocotal
Ciudad Antigua
RÍO COCO
Totogalpa
Cerro Montañita de Santa María
Telpaneca
Quilalí
Cerro el Careto
Río Coco
Yalagüina
Palacagüina
San Juan de Río Coco
El Espino
Somoto
Ducualí
FILA LAGUNA
Río Coco
Las Praderas
San Marcos
San Lucas
Pueblo Nuevo
Condéga
Cerro la Ilusión
La Rica
Pueblo las Sabanas
Río Estelí
San Sebastián de Yalí
SIERRA LOS CEDROS
San José de Cusmapa
El Bosque
El Miraflor
Asturias
La Dalia
San Francisco del Norte
LLANO VALLUCÚN
El Regodío
LLANO SANTA ANA
San Rafael del Norte
Laguna de Apanás
Río Tuma
San Juan de Limay
La Concordia
Río Negro
LOMA LA PEÑA DE AGUA SARCA
Estelí
Jinotega
El Tuma
San José de Achuapa
El Salto de Estanzuela
Santa Cruz
Selva Negra
La Trinidad
Matagalpa
San Ramón
El Sauce
San Nicolás
San Isidro
Interamerican Hwy.
Sebaco

0 10 kilometers
0 10 miles

Tourist Office: Cafe Luz (☎8405 8919; www.cafeluzyluna.com) has the best tourist information in Estelí. **Intur** (☎2713 6799; www.visitanicaragua.com), ½ block south of the western corner of the *parque central*. Has some tourist information and brochures. Open M-F 8am-noon and 2-5pm.

Tours: UCA Miraflor (☎2713 2971 or 8855 0585), 2 blocks east and ½ block north of the eastern corner of the *parque*. Has information and makes reservation services for the Miraflor reserve.

Banks: BanPro, BDF, ProCredit, and **BAC** are located on the *esquina de los bancos* (bank corner), 1 block south and 1 block west of the *parque central*. All have **24hr. ATMs.** All are open M-F 8:30am-4:30pm, Sa 8:30am-noon.

Beyond Tourism: Cenac Spanish School (☎2713 5437; www.spanishschoolcenac.com), by the stoplights on the PanAm highway. Offers 4hr. Spanish classes. **Texoxel Spanish School** (☎8487 4106), 5 blocks east on right from the Shell Estelí. C100 per hr. or C3430 per week. Funds go to help support a cancer research group based in Managua.

Emergency: Cruz Roja (☎2713 2330 or 119).

Police: (☎2713 2616 or 118).

24hr. Pharmacy: Farmacia Las Segovias (☎2713 6654), 1 block south and ½ block west from the southwestern corner of *parque central*. Open M-Sa 8am-8:30pm. Cash only. **Farmacia Estelí** (☎2713 2531), 1 block south on C. Central from *parque central*. Open daily 8am-8pm. Cash only.

Hospital: (☎2713 6305).

Internet Access: Conectate, ½ block west from the southwestern corner of the *parque central*. Internet C12 per hr. Open daily 8am-10pm. **Estelí@Net,** across the street from Farmacia Las Segovias. Internet C12 per hr. Open daily 8am-10pm.

Post Office: Ave. 2nd NE, between 5a SE and 6a SE. Open M-Sa 8am-noon and 1-4pm.

ACCOMMODATIONS

Hospedaje Luna (☎8405 8919; www.cafeluzyluna.com), 1 block east of Hotel Mesón. Guests of the hotel get free tea and coffee at Cafe Luz (below). Attentive staff provides you with tourist info and gives tours of the city's murals and cigar factory. Wi-Fi available. Dorms C140; singles C200, with bath C240; doubles C340/400; triples C420/480. Cash only. ❷

Hotel El Mesón (☎2713 2655), 1 block north from the Cathedral on the *parque central*. Eye-catching bright blue and maroon exterior. Rooms come with private baths, hot water, fans, and cable TVs. Pleasant garden courtyard with tables and palm-thatch huts. Wi-Fi in lobby. Checkout 2pm. Singles C300, with A/C C500; quads C640. AmEx/MC/V. ❸

Hotel Los Arcos (☎2713 3830). This is Estelí's luxury option. Convenient location only ½ block away from the *parque central*. Large rooms, each with TV, bath, hot water, and complimentary candy. Lovely garden. Singles C800, with A/C C1000; doubles C900/1100; Presidential Suite C1700. AmEx/D/MC/V. ❹

Hotel Nicarao (☎2713 2490), 1½ blocks south of the *parque central*. Well-decorated rooms; some with TVs. Sells tasty-looking donuts all day in the lobby. Dorms C140; rooms C200-600. Cash only. ❷

FOOD

Estelí has some of the best *comida extranjera* (foreign food) in Nicaragua. For groceries, visit **Palí**, 3½ blocks south on C. Central. (☎2713 2963. Open M-Sa 7:30am-8pm, Su 8am-7pm. Cash only.)

Cafe Luz (☎8405 8919; www.cafeluzyluna.com). Café Luz is not to be missed. The varied menu contains several flavorful vegetarian options. Smoothies, made with milk and fresh house yogurt, come in a variety of fruit flavors (C30-35). The inside of this eclectic cafe is filled with shelves selling local chocolate, coffee and handicrafts. All profits from the cafe go to the Miraflor foundation. ❶

Casa Italia (☎2713 5274), 3 blocks north and ½ blocks east of Hotel El Mesón. Sit down for authentic Italian cuisine in the chef's house and play complimentary pool, darts, cards, or dominos while you wait for your food. Delicious pizzas (C100-150) and appetizers (garlic bread; C20), handmade from scratch. Open Tu-Su noon-2pm, 4-10pm. Cash only. ❸

La Casita (☎2713 4917), 500m south down the highway past the curve. Healthy and tasty food. Try a *merienda* (a small loaf of homemade whole wheat bread) with hummus and cucumber for C26. Fresh fruit juices and coffee. Open M 2-7pm, Tu-Su 9am-7pm. Closed 1st M of every month. Cash only. ❶

Rincón Pinareño (☎2713 0248), 1½ blocks south from the southeastern corner of the *parque central*. Specializes in Cuban food. Get your pork fix here. Smoked roasted pork leg

CITY OF ESTELÍ

C100. Roasted pork sandwich on a crispy baguette half C55, whole C75. Refresh yourself after the meal with a *mojito cubano* (C55). Open Tu-Su 10am-11pm. AmEx/D/MC/V. ❷

La's Carreta Buffet (☎8608 3783), next to Farmacia Las Segovias. A traditional Nica buffet and lunchtime hangout. 3-course plate C30. Open M-Sa 7am-4pm. Cash only. ❶

Yúsvar (☎8412 3713), ½ block west from the *parque central*. This small juice bar serves fresh smoothies. Cooling cucumber, watermelon, and mint leaves C25-35. Fruit salads C15. Open M-Sa 8am-7pm. Cash only. ❶

Café Repostería Mamilou (☎2713 2878), 20m south of Bancentro. Secluded cafe with fountains, prompt service, and multiple comfortable seating areas. Coffee and soda C5-28. Pies C5-25. Small meals C45. Open M 10am-7pm, Tu 10am-5pm, W-Sa 10am-7pm, Su 1-7pm. ❶

🎵 🎭 NIGHTLIFE AND ENTERTAINMENT

Rincón Legal (☎8438 6336 or 8423 3721), on the PanAm highway, on the south end of Estelí. This bar is a standing tribute to the revolution, with murals of Sandino, Fonseca, and other heroes, as well as Che Guevara. The entryway is decorated with war relics, including helmets and machine guns. Beer C20. Rum C50. Open Th-Sa 5pm-3am. Cash only.

Cinema Estelí (☎2713 2293), on the south side of the *parque central*. Shows recently released movies. Showings M-Th 6 and 8pm; Sa-Su 3, 6, and 8pm. C30.

Los Semáforos (☎2713 3659), on the south side of town, 400m south of the hospital. 2 dance floors and 2 bars make this discotheque popular with locals. F-Sa live music. DJs spin when the bands aren't playing. Beer C24. Rum shot C20. Open Th-Su 7pm-2 or 3am. Cash only.

👁 SIGHTS

CIGAR TOUR. The tour guides are knowledgeable of the cigar-making process and explain it in great detail. Walking through the factory, you'll see tobacco in its multiple manifestations, from being "cured" in great stacks (to make it flexible for rolling) to watching workers roll the cigars. You'll also see the workers who roll the cigars. For real cigar aficionados, the company sells its product in any size or brand (C20 per cigar). Grab a box to take home. *(The easiest way to go on a tour of the cigar factory is to inquire at Café Luz. The tours leave at 9am and take about 2hr. Includes guide, tour, taxi ride, and a free stogie. C100.)*

CATEDRAL NUESTRA SEÑORA DEL CARMEN. Built in a modern style, this cathedral's floor tiles, colorful windows, and wooden ceiling panels are worth a look. *(On the east side of the parque central.)*

OTHER SIGHTS. Casa de Cultura showcases local art. Wander the gallery downstairs to see if any of the artists are at work. La Casa de Cultura also runs dance and theater classes; call María (☎8362 5294) for more info. The **Museo de Heroes y Martínes** covers history of the revolution of 1979 through photographs and soldier memorabilia. *(1 block south of the parque central. ☎2713 3021. Both are open M-F 8am-noon and 1-4pm. Free. Donations encouraged.)*

🏔 OUTDOOR ACTIVITIES

EL SALTO DE ESTANZUELA. This sight may be reason enough to come to Estelí. The waterfall is spectacular, spilling over the edge of the cliff and filling a small pool perfect for swimming. The area on the cliff around the water is covered in green moss, which makes for a great photo opportunity. Visitors can swim right up to the waterfall and feel the water crash down around them. There is also a small overhang to the left of the waterfall in case you want to stay up close but avoid the spray. The pool under the waterfall drains into a small stream that heads off into the jungle. *(Take the bus from Terminal Norte (1hr, 6:30am and 1:30pm, C20) all the way to the waterfall, or take a taxi to the hospital south of town and then walk 5km up the dirt road (1½hr.). C15.)*

MIRAFLOR. Just outside of Estelí is the nature reserve Miraflor, a collection of 44 different communities, all of them populated by subsistence farmers and coffee producers. Five of the communities are open for tourist homestays, and some offer *cabaña* accommodations. The outdoor opportunities around Miraflor are endless: with jungles, waterfalls, and caves, you won't be a bored hiker here. The real joy in visiting Miraflor, however, lies in getting to know the people that live there. Staying with a family in a simple cement and wood home and experiencing their day-to-day activities is a once-in-a-lifetime experience. *(Arrange a reservation at the UCA Miraflor office (see Practical Information, p. 414). Homestays C30; meals included. Cabañas C100.)*

MATAGALPA

Matagalpa (pop. 77,000) has an extraordinary location in the heart of coffee country. Those arriving from hotter climates will be refreshed by the pleasantly cool days and downright chilly nights. Originally settled in the 19th century by European immigrants, Matagalpa was an FSLN (Sandinista National Liberation Front) stronghold during the revolution and the birthplace of Carlos Fonseca—a founding member of the FSLN. As a result, locals take their politics seriously. The majority of visitors come to Matagalpa for the spectacular Selva Negra National Park, a short bus ride from the city, but visitors should also check out El Castillo de Cacao, the chocolate factory just outside of town.

TRANSPORTATION

Buses: 2 blocks south and 5 blocks west of Parque Rubén Darío. To: **Chinandega** (2½hr., 2pm, C60); **Estelí** (2hr., 2 per hr., C25); **Jintogea** (1½hr., 2 per hr., C25); **León** (2½hr., 3 and 4pm, C60); **Managua,** (2hr., every hr., C60); **Selva Negra** (45min.-1hr., C15)

ORIENTATION AND PRACTICAL INFORMATION

Matagalpa has two *parque centrals:* **Parque Rubén Darío** in the south and **Parque Morazán** in the north, across the Cathedral. The downtown area lies between them. The main street, **Calle de los Comercios,** begins at the northwestern corner of Rubén Darío and continues north for seven blocks before ending in the middle of Parque Morazán. One block east, **Avenida de los Bancos** (Avenida Central) also connects the two parks and contains most banks. The **bus terminal** is five blocks west and two blocks south of Parque Darío, along the river.

Tourist Office: Intur (☎2772 7060; www.visitanicaragua.com), 1½ blocks from Citibank. Attentive staff answers questions about the surrounding area. No English spoken. Great map of Matagalpa C50. Open M-F 8am-5:30pm.

Tours: Matagalpa Tours (☎2772 0108 or 8647 4680; www.matagalpatours.com), 1 block south and ½ block east from Parque Morazán. A great tour company that specializes in ecotours and hikes of the surrounding area. Offers visits to cacao and coffee farms, as well as trips to the indigenous village of "Chile" 30km away. City tour (C740) focuses on Nicaraguan social life. Hike in the cloud forests of Cerro El Arenal nature preserve (3-5hr., C700 per person). Ask about more intense, week-long hikes up into the untouched rainforests near Siuna. Open M-F 8am-6pm, Sa 9am-2pm.

Bank: Banco ProCredit (☎2772 6501), 2 blocks east from Parque Morazán. Open M-F 8:30am-5:30pm, Sa 8:30am-1pm. **24hr. ATM.**

Beyond Tourism: Escuela Español Matagalpa, inside Matagalpa Tours. One-on-one language classes. C140 per hr. Homestay packages available.

Police: (☎2772 3870), on the south side of Parque Morazán. **Red Cross:** (☎2772 2059), across the river from the bridge, near Parque Morazán.

Hospital: Cesar Amador Molina (☎2772 2081), on the north end of town.

Pharmacy: Farmacia Arevalo (☎2772 0988), ½ block from the southwestern corner of Parque Darío. Open M-Sa 7am-9pm, Su 7am-1pm.

CENTRAL HIGHLANDS

Internet Access: Excell Cyber (☎2772 3173), on the west side of Parque Morazán. Internet C14 per hr. Open daily 8am-8:30pm. **Cyber G-Net** (☎2772 2214), 1 block north from the northwest corner of Parque Darío. Internet C12 per hr. Open M-Sa 8am-9pm.

Post Office: (☎2772 2004), 1 block south and ½ block east from Parque Morazán. Open M-F 8am-5pm, Sa 8am-noon.

🔐 ACCOMMODATIONS

There is no shortage of accommodations in Matagalpa. Expect clean, family-run hotels and a mostly Nicaraguan clientele.

- **Hostal El Rey** (☎2772 3435 or 2772 3762). A new hostel and a great budget option. All rooms with TVs. Kitchen available. 2-person dorms C100 per person; private rooms with baths and hot water C200 per person. Cash only. ❶

- **Hotel Apante** (☎2772 6890), next to Gallo más Gallo, on the west side of Parque Darío. Family-run hotel with free coffee and purified water (score!). Incredible views from the 2nd floor. Singles with bath and hot water C150; doubles C220; triples 350. Cash only. ❷

- **Hotel Alvarado** (☎2772 2830). Owned by a nice elderly couple. Each room comes with a fan, but more importantly, a bedspread that you might actually need. Curfew 10:30pm. Checkout 10am. Singles have shared baths; all other rooms come with private baths. Singles C150; matrimonials C300; doubles C350; triples C400. Cash only. ❷

- **Hotel Soza** (☎2772 3030 or 8928 1941), 2½ blocks from the northwest corner of Parque Darío. Tight hallways and low head clearances. Clean and comfortable rooms. Checkout 10am. Rooms C140 per person, with TV C200 per person. Cash only. ❷

- **Hotel 24 Horas** (☎8607 6164), 1 block south of Juan Morales. One of the newest hotels in Matagalpa. Clean and modern rooms. Be warned: guests have been known to get locked out at the not-so-late-hours of the night. TV in common room. Balcony on the 2nd floor. Checkout 9am. Matrimonials C200; doubles C300. Cash only. ❷

🍴 FOOD

For groceries, visit **Supermercado La Matagalpa**, 2½ blocks from the northwest corner of Parque Darío (☎2772 2664 or 2772 5312; open daily 8am-9pm). You're in the heart of coffee country, so enjoy it! There are several small cafes scattered about Matagalpa where you can get a cup of freshly brewed joe.

- **Comedor Oasis** (☎2772 3833), 1½ blocks east of Parque Darío. Tasty and filling 3 course meals, complete with corn tortilla and *refresco* (juice drink; C40). Try the Maracuya and carrot drink; it's cool and refreshing. Open M-F 7am-8:30pm, Sa 7am-3pm. Cash only. ❶

- **La Vita é Bella** (☎2772 5476), 2 blocks east and 1½ blocks north from northeast corner of Parque Morazán. Great homemade pasta and pizza await at this tucked-away restaurant. Pizzas small C40-60, large C130-160. Try the Pasta Vita Bella (with your choice of spaghetti, penne, or bowtie noodles), with bacon, tomato sauce, olives, and mushrooms. All pastas come with homemade garlic bread. Open Tu-Su noon-10:30pm. AmEx/D/MC/V. ❷

- **Casa Grande** (☎2772 0988), 1½ blocks from Iglesia San Jose. A local favorite. Balcony seating available. Try *Caballo Ball* (a platter with chicken, beef, pork, green and ripe plantains, tortillas, cheese, *gallo pinto*, and salad; C350). Beer C15-40. Appetizers C80. Main plates C150-205. Open daily 11am-11pm. AmEx/D/MC/V. ❸

- **Maná del Cielo** (☎2772 5686), 1½ blocks south of Av. de los Bancos. Convenient buffet and breakfast joint. Plates of ham and cheese C50. Open daily 7am-10pm. AmEx/D/MC/V. ❶

CAFES IN MATAGALPA

◪ **Simo's Cafe** (☎2772 0020), 75m west of the southwest corner of Parque Darío. A modern cafe, with padded chairs, comfy couches, A/C, and great coffee. Wi-Fi available. A cup of joe C12. Arabic coffee and cappuccino C20-25. Sandwiches and breakfast plates C30-50. Open daily 8am-9pm. AmEx/D/MC/V.

Cafe Barista (☎2772 6790), on the north side of the cathedral. Espresso C15. Mocha frappe C30. Nutella crepe C40. Daily paper and Wi-Fi available. Open M-Sa 8:30am-9pm, Su 9am-9pm. AmEx/D/MC/V.

👁 SIGHTS

◪**EL CASTILLO DEL CACAO.** Nicaragua's chocolate company offers a tour of its headquarters that covers the history of cacao and describes the process of turning the tiny beans into a sweet, finished product. Five women produce 400-500 candy bars by hand each day. The best part about the tour, however, is that when you're done, you'll receive the best brownies of your life, accompanied by coffee and juice. (*4 blocks north of Esso Las Marías on the carretera to Tuma. Taxi ride C20. ☎2772 2002. C100. For tours in English, call ahead.*)

◪**MUSEO CASA CUNA CARLOS FONSECA AMADOR.** Located in the house of Fonseca Amador's birth, this museum pays tribute to the local hero, martyr, and revolutionary. Fonseca Amador was one of the founding fathers of the Sandinista National Liberation Front and a key member of Nicaragua's revolution, which he didn't live to see—he was killed in a gunfight in 1976. The museum displays several of his personal items, including his typewriter and machine gun. Check out the newspaper articles, published by the Somozan government that chronicle his death, albeit with a serious bias. (*☎8655 6304. Open M-Sa 8:30am-8pm.*)

MUSEO DEL CAFÉ. El Museo del Café showcases old coffee roasting equipment and exhibits photos of past mayors of Matagalpa. (*Av. del Comercio, 1½ blocks south of Parque Morazán. ☎2772 0587. Open M-F 8am-noon, 2-5pm.*)

CATEDRAL SAN PEDRO. What must be one of the most freshly-painted cathedrals in Central America; the cathedral in Matagalpa features intricate ceilings and a beautiful wooden altar. (*On the north side of the Parque Morazán. Open daily 5:30am-9pm. Mass M-Sa 6am and 7pm, Su 6, 10am, 4, 7pm.*)

🎭 🎵 NIGHTLIFE AND ENTERTAINMENT

Matagalpa has a social scene that far exceeds its small-town status. Even though the movie theater closed down, you can still catch a documentary at the **Centro Cultural Guanuca** on Friday nights. In terms of bars and discotheques, Matagalpa has its fair share. **Artesanos Bar,** next to Matagalpa Tours, is the most popular bar in town. **Rancho Escondido,** a disco to the west of Parque Darío, also gets packed on the weekends. On the last weekend of every month, the local restaurants set up shops at one of the *parques* for **Noches Matagalpinas,** a weekend full of traditional dance and music (Sa-Su 5-11pm). Local festivals include the **Fiesta Patronales de la Merced** on September 24, and the **Festival de Polkas, Mazurcas y Jamaquellos** during the last weekend of September.

◪ **Artesanos Café Bar,** C. La Calzada (☎2552 8459), 2 blocks from the cathedral. Baseball themed bar with blasting A/C. Entrees C115-215. Drinks C20-80. Open daily 11am-2am. AmEx/D/MC/V.

DJ's Sports Bar (☎8601 0219), 25m west from the northwest corner of Parque Darío. Watch the game on this sports bar's flatscreen TV while you enjoy a refreshingly cold beer (C20-35). Try the Alitas Buffalo Wins C80. Open daily 11am-11pm. Cash only.

Centro Cultural Guanuca (☎2772 3562). A women's center that encourages equality between the sexes. F documentary screenings. Sa live music. Open F from 7:30pm until the end of movie, Sa 8pm-midnight.

El Rancho Escondido (☎2772 6432), 2 blocks west of the southwest corner of Parque Darío. A bar and dance floor decorated with palm fronds. Beer C20. Rum shots C20. Half-bottle of rum C130. Open Th-Su 6pm-2am.

⬛ DAYTRIPS FROM MATAGALPA

⬛SELVA NEGRA

While it's possible to get private transportation with a tour company (such as Matagalpa Tours) getting to Selva Negra on your own isn't that difficult. Take a Jinotega-bound bus from Matagalpa (45min.-1hr., 2 per hr., C15) and tell the driver that you want to be let off at the entrance to the park. You'll know you're there when you see the old tank, now covered in rainbow graffitti, that was abandoned by the Somozan army during the revolution. From there, it's about a 1km walk to the entrance of the hiking area. C25, with dessert and coffee C50.

The "Black Jungle," 12km north of Matagalpa, is a coffee plantation and forest reserve. Nearly 80% of the 2000-acre estate is protected and has a network of labeled hiking paths. Vibrant toucans, howler monkeys, and even the elusive quetzal inhabit the 150m of dense foliage. If you're spending the night, try the **Selva Negra Ecolodge ❹**, a family-run ecolodge with excellent rooms and cabins, the largest of which feature spiral staircases and fireplaces. Each room comes with a private bath, hot water, fresh towels, and complimentary bottled water. The larger cabins boast upstairs lofts with lots of natural sunlight. The dorms are comfortable too and are decorated with murals painted by local artists. (☎2772 3883 or 2772 5713; www.selvanegra.com.ni. Dorms C600; double cabins C1240; 12-person suites C3615. AmEx/D/MC/V.) To experience the jungle mists at the park's second highest point, try the **Peter and Helen** trail (1¾hr.). Bear in mind, however, that the higher you go in this humid jungle, the muddier it gets. In other words, be careful where you step and be prepared to get dirty. All of the hikes can be completed alone; however, *Let's Go* warns against hiking alone, especially for women. Signs are in English, and a free map of the trails is available at the hotel desk. If there is one disappointing thing about the Selva Negra Ecolodge, it's that the food from the **restaurant ❹** doesn't come cheap. Entrees exceed C200, and the seafood is even more expensive. However, you can get a delicious dessert, such as an orange-chocolate cake, for C50-60. (Open 9am-9pm. AmEx/D/MC/V.)

CARIBBEAN COAST

Nicaragua's Caribbean coast is unlike the rest of the country, and the fact that it is only reachable by boat or plane only broadens this gap. The region is part of a geographical area known as the Mosquitia (Mosquito Coast), a sparsely populated expanse of rainforest, plains, and coastland extending the length of Nicaragua's east coast and north into Honduras. The Mosquitia is home to the country's largest group of indígenas, the Miskitos, who maintain their own language and have a semi-autonomous government system. Other indigenous groups, including the Sumos, Garífunas, and Ramas, also reside here. Most Caribbean-coast residents identify more strongly with their West Indian heritage or indigenous community than with a Nicaraguan identity.

Travel here is tricky, as there are almost no roads. Unless you're flying, getting from one place to another involves a great deal of puttering around in small boats. The extra effort is rewarded by relaxing beaches and colorful villages. Be aware that the remote nature of the Atlantic coast means little policing in some areas, so exercise extra caution.

BLUEFIELDS

Bluefields (pop. 48,000) is Nicaragua's most important Caribbean port, though the port itself is actually across the bay in Bluff. The city is a fascinating urban jungle: the streets are full of a delightful mix of Caribbean-tinged English, Spanish, and Miskito. Since Bluefields lacks beaches for swimming and big tourist attractions, it is most often used as a launch pad to the Corn Islands or other remote points on the Caribbean coast. You can fly in from Managua or Puerto Cabezas, or take the road to Rama, and follow that with a boat ride to Bluefields. Unfortunately, the area is plagued with a large drug problem: bags of drugs abandoned by smugglers in the Gulf of Mexico have been known to wash up on shore. Be safe, keep a watchful eye on your belongings, and always take a taxi at night.

▶ TRANSPORTATION

Flights: The airport at Bluefields is located about 3km south of the city center. **La Costeña** airline flies from Managua to **Bluefields** (1hr.; M-Sa 6am and 2pm; one-way C1165, round trip C2560). To **Managua** (50min.; daily 7:10, 8:40, 11:10am, 1:10, 4:10pm), **Puerto Cabezas** (50min., M, W, F 11:10am) and **Corn Island** (20min.; daily 7:40am and 3:10pm; one-way C1300, round trip C1990). From **Puerto Cabezas** to **Bluefields** (50min.; M, W, F 12:10pm; one-way C1950, round trip C2990). From **Corn Island** to **Bluefields** (20min., daily 8:10am and 3:40pm).

Buses: Managua Bus Station Rigoberto Cabezas (otherwise known as **Mercado Mayoreo**). Buses go to **Rama** at 5, 6, 7:30, 8:45, 11:30am, 2, 6, and 10pm (C150).

Boats: At the small docks a few blocks north of the Moravian Church. To **El Rama** (6hr., daily at 4am, C150) and **Big Corn Island** (Tu 9am, C4300).

423

◪ 🔢 ORIENTATION AND PRACTICAL INFORMATION

Tourist Office: (☎2572 0221), 1 block west, ½ block north of Hotel South Atlantic II. Brochures describing the area and hotel information. Open M-F 8am-noon and 1:30-5pm.

Bank: BanPro, across the street from the Moravian Church. **24hr ATM.** Open M-F 8:30am-4:30pm, Sa 8:30am-noon. MC/V.

Police: (☎2572 2448), 1 block south of Hotel Caribbean Dream .

Pharmacy: Farmacia Nueva Lucha (☎8628 1377), across the street from Hotel Costa Sur. Open daily 7am-9pm.

Internet Access: (☎2572 1900), ½ block west of Cima Club and Karaoke Bar. C10 per hr. International calls available. Open M-Sa 8am-8:30pm.

Post Office: 1 block west of Los Pipitos. Open M-F 8am-5pm, Sa 8am-noon.

┏ ACCOMMODATIONS

During high season (January-May), it's a good idea to make reservations: the nicer hotels in Bluefields become considerably crowded and prices rise.

▧ **Mini Hotel Cafetín Central** (☎2572 2362), ½ block south from the Moravian Church. The best deal for your buck. Large, comfortable rooms, all with A/C, fans, private baths, and Wi-Fi. The 2nd fl. patio above the street is charming as well. Rooms C200-250. Cash only. ❷

Hospedaje Los Pipitos (☎2572 1590; terezaperezmai@yahoo.com), from the Moravian Church, 1½ blocks south. A cozy family-run hostel. Clean rooms with spring mattresses. Private bath and A/C available in the pricier rooms. Offers 2 smaller rooms with a shared living space. Rooms C200-500; rooms with shared living space C160 per person. Cash only. ❷

Hotel Caribbean Dream (☎2572 0107; reyzapata1@yahoo.com), the big green building 2 blocks south of the Moravian church on the right. Spacious rooms come with A/C, cable TVs, and private baths. You get what you pay for. Check-out noon. Singles C550; doubles C650; triples C750. MC/V. ❸

Oasis Hotel and Casino (☎2572 0665 or 2572 2812; www.oasiscasinohotel.net). Cornered from the docks is Bluefields' (and possibly eastern Nicaragua's) most luxurious hotel. Each spotless, well-decorated room boasts an enormous, apartment-like space with a huge balcony, full kitchen, A/C, flatscreen TV, Wi-Fi, and private bath with hot water. Casino downstairs. Free transport to the airport is provided for all guests. Check-out noon. Singles C1275; doubles C1860; Presidential Suite C3700. AmEx/D/MC/V. ❺

Hotel South Atlantic II (☎2572 1022), next door to the Moravian Church. All rooms have A/C, cable TVs, and private baths. If you can ignore the unattractive furniture in the lobby, it's a comfortable place to stay the night. Singles C500-560; doubles C1000; triples C1200. AmEx/D/MC/V. ❸

Hotel Costa Sur (☎2572 2452), ½ block west from Mini Hotel Cafetín Central. Your die-hard budget option. 13 small rooms with tiny TVs, shared baths, and lumpy mattresses. Singles C160; matrimonial suite C200. Cash only. ❷

◖ FOOD

For groceries, visit the **market**, a group of small booths two blocks east of Los Pipitos, each with a different selection of fruits and vegetables.

▧ **Comedor Arlen** (☎2572 2741), ½ block west and ½ block north from the post office. This hole-in-the-wall is a local favorite for delicious, cheap meals. C50 gets you a heaping plate of steaming Nica food. Open M-F 11:30am-2pm and 5-9pm. Cash only. ❷

Salón Siu (☎2552 2511), across the street from Intur. A relaxing place to hang out and grab some cheap eats—nothing on the menu here is more than C70. Breakfast (eggs, sausage, and pancakes) C50. Open daily 7am-8pm. Cash only. ❷

Restaurante La Ola (☎2572 2779), 2 blocks south and 1 block west from the Moravian church. Fresh fish plates, complete with rice, salad, and french fries C90. Yes, you're eating your meal at a plastic chair and table, but the food is tasty and the restaurant is out of the sun. Open daily 8am-midnight. V. ❷

👁 SIGHTS

MUSEO HISTÓRICO CULTURAL (BLUEFIELDS INDIAN & CARIBBEAN UNIVERSITY). This government-sponsored museum showcases exhibits from private donations. Highlights include the interesting display of the Caribbean and missionary influenced culture as well as the collection of old currency. *(Located in Barrio Punta Fría, by the police station and ½ block south of Pesca Frita. ☎2572 2735 or 8658 5607; museobicu@yahoo.com. Open M-F 8am-noon and 2-5pm. Free. Donations appreciated.)*

🎵 NIGHTLIFE

Cima Club and Karaoke Bar, 1 block inland from Hotel South Atlantic II. 2-story discoteque and karaoke bar. Open Th-Su 7pm- 3am.

🚩 DAYTRIP FROM BLUEFIELDS

LAGUNA DE PERLAS
Pangas leave the main pier each morning for Laguna de Perlas (1hr, 3 boats per day 6-10am, 70C). Pangas return to Bluefields at 6am, noon, and occasionally 10pm, C70.

Pearl Lagoon is a small community on the southern edge of a large lagoon of the same name, 80km north of Bluefields. The 1-2hr. trip is an excellent way to get a look at Caribbean coastal culture and local **wildlife.** The pearl cayes—18 uninhabited, white-sand tropical islands with coral off the coast—are ideal for **snorkeling.** There is also a waterfall in the area, and tour companies offer hikes to go swim in its pool. Contact Canadian Ray Beloin (☎780 956 3334) to organize your own tour. **Green Lodge Guesthouse ❷,** has basic, clean rooms with fans and outside baths (C85) and excellent food (shrimp C30). Electricity is limited. Bring your own snorkeling equipment, food, and drinks. In the village, local boats can take you to even smaller villages around the lagoon (C1600-1920 for the *panga*). About 1hr.

FROM THE ROAD

NICARAGUA BY NUMBERS

As I move across Nicaragua, five weeks into my trip, I thought it would be appropriate to compile a little numbers list, a collection of the hard facts that have made this trip what it is.

0: The number of hotels or hostels I've been at where the internet hasn't crashed or cut out at least once.

1½: The number of times I've "washed" my clothing.

3: Volcanoes climbed.

4: The sum total of all of my articles of clothing.

6: The number of once-a-week anti-malarial tablets I've taken, starting from one week before I left.

8: The highest number of people I've had to ask when trying to find a building.

15: The number of hours since I last took a shower.

30: The SPF of my sunscreen.

68: The number of geckos crawling along the walls of my hostel.

1000: The average temperature in Nicaragua.

Countless: Miles I've walked.

south from Bluefields by boat, **Ramaqui** is a small island community home to descendants of the Rama. Corrugated metal buildings stand next to traditional bamboo huts, and canoes pull up next to more modern fishing vessels. Though the island sees few visitors, local families are usually willing to host guests for a negotiable price. (You'll have to hire your own boat; it's a good idea to recruit a group to split the cost, C600-700.)

THE CORN ISLANDS

The Corn Islands, 70km off the coast from Bluefields, offer white sand beaches, warm turquoise water, and a uniquely untouristed Caribbean atmosphere. Most visitors stay on Big Corn Island (pop. 10,000), with a small but reasonable selection of hotels and restaurants. With no resorts and no cars or roads, splendid Little Corn Island (pop. 700), 18km away, feels even more untouched and noticeably safer. The islands, populated by English speakers of British West Indian descent, have excellent fishing and colorful coral reefs, but most of all they simply offer the chance to curl your toes in pure Caribbean sands and do absolutely nothing. Unfortunately, safety is as much of a concern on the Corn Islands as in Bluefields; violence and robbery are both common. Paying more for increased security is a good idea, and absolutely worth it.

BIG CORN ISLAND

The Corn Islands are an undiscovered oasis of Caribbean beauty lazing off Nicaragua's east coast. It's also an oasis of beautiful deals—it's still possible to find a hotel for C200 (US$10) per night and to get your meals for even less. The larger of the two islands, Big Corn Island, is home to a small airstrip, roads, and cars. Although it may seem more accessible, it's also more polluted and dangerous than Little Corn Island. Whichever Corn you're drawn to, beautiful beaches and pleasant accommodations await you.

◪ TRANSPORTATION

Flights: La Costeña airlines. Open M-F 5am-5pm, Sa-Su 5am-3pm. From **Managua** to **Corn Island** (1½hr.; daily 6:30 am and 2pm; one-way C2140, round trip C3300). From **Corn Island** to **Managua** (1½hr., daily 8:10am and 3:40pm). From **Bluefields** to **Corn Island** (20min.; daily 7:40am and 3:10pm; one-way C1300, round trip C1980). From **Corn Island** to **Bluefields** (20min., daily 8:10am and 3:40pm).

Boats: Boats leave from **Bluefields** to **Big Corn** Tu 9am (C250). Pangas from **Big Corn** to **Little Corn** daily 10am and 4:30pm. From **Little Corn** to **Big Corn** daily 7am and 2pm (C110).

WET AND WILD. The boat ride over to Little Corn can jar even the steadiest of sea legs. Locals know that the best places to avoid being thrown up and down by the waves and getting soaked by the spray are the middle seats, preferably on the left side.

◪ ⁊ ORIENTATION AND PRACTICAL INFORMATION

Big Corn Island is approximately 6 sq. km. The island's main road runs all the way around its coast, and a few dead-end drives branch off either inland or out to the ocean. The **airstrip** runs southwest to northeast, marking off **Brig Bay** and the western quarter of the island, where most of the businesses and hotels are located. In the eastern part of the island are the beach communities of **North End** and **South End,** with **Sally Peachie Beach** in between. Pick up maps of the island at **Nautilus Ecotours,** about 5 blocks north of Fisher's Cave Restaurant.

Tours: Nautilus Water Sports (☎2575 5077; divebigcorn.com), just north of the Enitel. Come here for tourist info about the island. Scuba courses: basic PADI instruction+dive (C1600), 2 dives (C1300-1900), 1 night dive (C1200), 10 dives package (C6000).

Offers 3-day open-water PADI dive course (C5600) and 2-day advanced course (C4650). Snorkeling on Big Corn (2hr., C400) and Little Corn (1hr., C900). Glass-bottomed boat tour: 3 shipwrecks and coral reef (2hr., C400). All equipment included. V.

Bank: BanPro, Barrio Brig Bay (☎2575 5107). Open M-F 8:30am-4:30pm, Sa 8:30am-noon. **24hr ATM. Western Union,** Brig Bay (☎2575 5074), in front of Reggae Palace. Offers **currency exchange.** Open M-Sa 8am-5pm.

Police: Brig Bay (☎2575 5201), a few blocks north of Fisher's Cave restaurant.

Pharmacy: Taylor Drugs Store (☎8417 7247), just south of the airport. Open M-Sa 7am-7pm, Su 7am-noon.

Internet: Cyber Cafe Island Spring (☎2575 5053), a few blocks north of the Police station. C30 per hr. International phone calls to USA C3 per min., Europe C10 per min.

◪ ACCOMMODATIONS

Expect to spend more on Big Corn than on the mainland. Hotels here run from C200-1000 per night, and chances are you'll want a hotel somewhere in the middle of the island.

▣ **Hotel & Restaurante Morgan** (☎2575 5052 or 8835 5890), at the North End. A beautiful hotel with handmade pillars and courtyard. Large and comfortable rooms all with TVs and fans; some with A/C and private baths. Singles C300, with A/C and bath C500; doubles C600/800. Internet access. Check-out 2pm. Additional 5% tax. AmEx/D/MC/V. ❸

Sunrise Hotel (☎8828 7835 or 8420 5468; southendsunrise@yahoo.com), at the South End, across the street from Casa Canada. It may not be *right* on the beach (it's actually across the street), but if it's comfort you're looking for, the Sunrise Hotel will meet all of your expectations. Spacious and immaculate rooms with white tile floors and modern baths. Each room comes with cable TV, A/C, and a private bath. Rooms C700-1100. Check-out 2pm. ❹

Hotel G&G (☎2575 5017 or 8824 8237; hotelg.gcornisland@hotmail.com), at Brig Bay, next to the Pasanic. Big rooms with fresh, clean linens, high water pressure, and (best of all) a bottle opener attached to the wall of every room. Bar and restaurant right next door. Rooms C600. MC/V. ❹

Casa Canada (☎8644 0925), on the south side of the island. Casa ▣Canada is a resort-like hotel. Each room has a private bath, hot water, cable TV with DVD, A/C, and a minibar. Unfortunately, it also comes with a resort price. Restaurant and bar on the premises. Check-out 2pm. Singles C1800; doubles C2000. Additional 5% tax. AmEx/D/MC/V. ❺

Hotel Creole (☎8356 4719), at Brig Bay, just north of Cyber Cafe Island Spring. For those on a tight budget, Hotel Creole rents basic rooms with baths for C150-200. Call in advance—the rooms are often full with long-term boarders. ❸

◪ FOOD

Food on the islands is generally good, and the seafood is always excellent. Try the Caribbean-influenced dishes, such as the "Run down," a combination of fruits (plantian, breadfruit, and coconut) and seafood (lobster or shrimp) stewed together in a big pot so that the flavors "run down" into the dish. Fresh and usually cheap lobster and shrimp can also be found at most restaurants, and it's up to you how you want them prepared. Impatient personalities beware: Big Corn's "relax, take it easy" attitude often applies to its leisurely restaurant service. For **groceries,** visit supermarket Miscelanea Aquileo Martinez, just after the big runway loop, Brig Bay. (☎2575 5126. Open M-Sa 6am-6pm, Su 6am-midnight).

▣ **Fisher's Cave,** right off the docks, Brig Bay. Decked out in crabs and coconuts, Fisher's Cave is a favorite of tourists and locals waiting for the panga to Little Corn. Try the

"Fisher's Cave" breakfast (ham or bacon, bread, butter, a pancake, *gallo pinto, huevo entero,* and coffee or juice; C125). Open daily 7am-11am. Cash only. ❷

Hotel and Restaurante Morgan (☎2575 5052 or 8835 5890), at the North End. Classy restaurant with fresh, tasty food. The owner is ready to answer any questions you might have about the area. Filet Mignon C270. Pasta with Lobster C180. Checkout the 6 ft. tall baseball trophy inside. Open daily 7am-9pm. AmEx/D/MC/V. ❸

🎵 NIGHTLIFE

Nico Bar (☎8827 1894), at the South End. A nondescript yellow wooden building overlooking the beach. Handpainted pictures of Bob Marley and a small balcony overlooking the ocean make for a fun atmosphere. Don't miss this local favorite. Beer C20. Rum shots C30.

🏔 OUTDOOR ACTIVITIES

A walk around the island is worthwhile and takes about 4½hr. Be careful around **Bluff Point,** on the south side of the island, the area is known for drug-related crimes and is unsafe for walking. The **Picnic Center** should also be avoided. **Long Bay,** just south of South End, is a sweeping crescent of white sand, turquoise water, and coconut palms, perfect for sunbathing and relaxing. Water currents, however, make the swimming less than ideal. The best snorkeling site is **Sally Peachie Beach,** on the east side of the island: swim among schools of iridescent fish and drift over reefs teeming with marine life. Be sure to explore the sunken ships on the west side of the island. A number of places rent snorkel equipment. Remember to check equipment for quality. Half-day guided hikes around the island run about C64; boat excursions cost C1040-2000.

Marcus Gómez at Hospedaje Sunrise, in Sally Peachie. Rents new gear C60 per day, C160 deposit.

Yellow Tail House, in Sally Peachie. Rents gear C80 per day, C160 with a 2hr. tour.

Nautilus Ecotours (☎ 285 5077), 5 blocks north of Fisher's Cave Restaurant. Activities for experienced divers. 2 tank dive C720. Rents snorkel gear (½-day 64C, full day C110), new bikes (C60-C95), and horses (½-day C190).

LITTLE CORN ISLAND

A thirty minute *panga* ride from Big Corn Island takes you to Little Corn island, where there are no cars, no bikes after dark, and pristine beaches all around. Add to this local islanders who are community-oriented and kind to visitors, and you've got the new hotspot in Nicaraguan tourism. Dirt footpaths wind through lush palm forests and reach uninhabited beaches where coral reefs sit just offshore. The swimming and snorkeling are great, and there are several dive companies on the island where you can get cheap PADI certification. On the far side of the island, a shipwrecked fishing boat—just visible above the surface of the reef—awaits exploration. The 50ft. lighthouse on the island's highest point yields a gorgeous vista. Sportfishing is excellent: snag some giant barracuda (or even just a few yellowtails) and get a free dinner. Little Corn Island as a general rule is very safe, but be wary of your surroundings after dark, especially on the more remote eastern side of the island.

🚍 TRANSPORTATION

Boats: 4 daily *panga* rides run daily between the islands. From **Little Corn** to **Big Corn** 7am and 2pm. From **Big Corn** to Little Corn 10am and 4:30pm (30min, C110).

◻ ▱ ORIENTATION AND PRACTICAL INFORMATION

Little Corn island is essentially divided into three different areas. The majority of the island's hotels and restaurants are on its **western side.** There is a collection of assorted beach cabins on the quieter, more deserted **eastern side.** Additional accommodations are scattered across the northern tip of the island, including **Farm Peace Love** and **Derek's Place.** It's hard *not* to find a beautiful beach, but there are some particularly impressive ones on the north side of the island— **Otto's Beach** is a favorite. Just make sure to ask Otto if you can have some of his coconuts before you take them.

Tours and Agencies: ◼**Dolphin Dive** (☎8690 0225 or 8917 0717; info@dolphindivelittlecorn.com), 2 blocks south of the dock. Wide variety of scuba-diving activities, including recreation as well as PADI courses. Offers 1 tank dive (C700), 2 tank dive (C1300), 5 dives package (C3000), 10 dives package (C5650), and refresher dive (C1300). PADI courses (C1300-12,800). 4 night hotel stay plus PADI certification C800 per person. Underwater digital camera rental C400; includes a day's use and a CD with your pictures. **Dive Little Corn** (www.divelittlecorn.com), just south of the dock. PADI scuba certification C6870. Snorkel trips C300, C200 with your own gear. Bike rental C300 per 24hr. All instructors speak English and Spanish.

Hospital: Just south of Los Delfines. Open M-F 8am-4pm. Always open for emergencies.

Internet: Upstairs of the Los Delfines Hotel, next to the restaurant. C60 per hr. Open 11am-7pm.

▰ ACCOMMODATIONS

Little Corn Island has some surprisingly great budget options. Most hotels with modern amenities can be found on the western side of the island. Looking for a little cabaña on the beach? Head to the more remote eastern side.

◼ **Sunshine Hotel** (☎8495 6223; www.sunshinehotellittlecornisland.com), just north of the docks. Each dorm and room with private bath has cable TV and A/C. Guests get full access to the game room with pool, ping pong and card tables, as well as video games. DVD player with movie rental (C100 per day), snorkel gear rental (C60 per day), and snorkel trips (C200 per person, min. 4 people). Dorms C100; rooms C200. ❷

Elsa's Place Hotel and Restaurant (☎8333 0971), on the eastern half of the island. Collection of brightly-colored beach *cabañas* on a beautiful, quiet stretch of beach. Restaurant on site. *Gallo pinto*, eggs, coconut bread or pancakes, and coffee C60. Singles C200, with bath C500; doubles C600. Cash only. ❷

Hotel Los Delfines (☎8836 2013), south of the docks, on the western side of the island. A series of *cabañas*, each comprised of 2 rooms stacked on top of one another. Rocking chairs on the porch or patio. All rooms have private baths, cable TVs, and A/C. The green and white paint job goes well with the park-like atmosphere. Singles C600-700; doubles C1000. AmEx/D/MC/V. ❹

Lobster Inn (☎8847 1736 or 8927 0710), about 2 blocks south of the docks on the western side of the island. Lives up to its name with a color scheme that could only be described as Pepto-Bismol pink. Clean rooms with private baths and balconies with ocean views. Restaurant downstairs. Rooms for C400-500, with cable TVs C500-600. Discounts for groups. ❸

Grace's Place Cool Spot (☎8948 7725), on the eastern half of the island, right next to Elsa's place. Basic beach *cabaña* option. The rooms are small, and if you got one in the back without the ocean breeze, they feel like tin incubators. Kitchen use C100. The shared bathrooms are 2 tiny shacks that share a small outside sink. The "mosquito nets" are really just old tarps tied above the beds. Singles and doubles with shared bath C300; matrimonial with private bath C500. ❸

◪ FOOD

Food on the island is generally fresh, if a bit unimaginative. You'll get lots of great fish, but you'll be hard-pressed to find it prepared any way other than the island's preferred method—deep fried. That being said, there are a few fantastic restaurants, and asking the locals is always an effective way to figure out where to head for dinner. For groceries, visit **Comercial Los Delfines,** just past Dive Little Corn, south of the docks. As well as having fresh and canned goods, this small supermarket also carries a large selection of hardware and a building supplies section (open daily 6:30am-7:30pm).

▧ **Mango's Pizza** (☎8495 9268), just past Los Delfines, south of the dock. Serves tasty pizzas at a great price underneath palm huts. Try a calzone, with toppings (such as fresh pineapple) and a flaky crust (small C100, large C150). Grab a pizza and add the toppings (C7-18) at your leisure. ❷

Sweet Oasis, 50m south of Dive Little Corn, right next to Comercial Los Delfines. If you're into big breakfasts, you'll be in heaven at this bright restaurant. Get a typical island breakfast: a generous portion of *gallo pinto*, a pile of plantain chips, and an entire fried fish (C120). Coffee C12. There are also delicious, cheap hot dogs at the little stand across the sidewalk. Open daily 7am-9pm. AmEx/D/MC/V. ❸

Restaurante Glorieta ("La Sabrosicima") (☎8354 5716 or 8354 5715), 1 block north of the Sunshine Hotel. A kitchen surrounded by plastic tables under a tin roof. Great food for a decent price. Meat plates C150-180. Try the *espaguety* (with fish or lobster; C130-180). Open daily 6am-9pm. Cash only. ❸

◪ ♫ NIGHTLIFE AND ENTERTAINMENT

Las Aguilas, a few blocks north of the Sunshine Hotel on the western side of the island. This small dance club-billiard hall is popular with locals on the weekends. Show up on Mother's or Father's day to witness (or take part) in the impromptu boxing matches. Seriously. Beer C25.

COSTA RICA

The Spanish explorers who first arrived at this "rich coast" in 1502 named the region for the decorative gold bands worn by its native inhabitants and for the fortunes they hoped to attain there. Despite this optimistic view, later explorers found themselves unable to discover gold—or material riches of any sort—anywhere along the coast. Indeed, the country's only riches seemed to be its endless armies of mosquitoes and its unforgiving jungles, neither of which colonial settlers found in short supply. These days, however, most visitors to Costa Rica would probably attest that its initial name was not such a misnomer after all. Its well-oiled tourist industry is only too happy to recount the country's impressive statistics: though it covers only 0.03% of the world's territory, Costa Rica is home to 6% of its plant and animal species. From camouflaged vine snakes to Jesucristo lizards that "walk on water" in fantastic 50 yd. dashes, the wildlife here is truly entertaining. Many Costa Rican creatures come off as performers, and there is something decidedly exhibitionist about their homeland as well. The terrain seems to include all possible landforms: volcanoes, jungles, beaches, coral reefs, hidden caves, and deserted islands all lie within a day's (or even an hour's) travel of one another.

Sometimes it feels like the only thing this country can't offer is a corner that travelers haven't already found and conquered—leaving fusion bistros and high-tech canopy tours in their wake. Fortunately, rustic spots never lie too far away, and Costa Rica's national character has remained surprisingly visible beneath the trappings of its tourist infrastructure. Though you'll find plenty of *gringos* lounging on the beaches of the Pacific, you'll find vacationing *tico* families enjoying them as well. Their *tico* friendliness only adds to the charm of the country.

ESSENTIALS

PLANNING YOUR TRIP

PASSPORTS, VISAS, AND CUSTOMS.

Passport. Required of all visitors. Must be valid for a full 6 months after arrival.

Visa (p. 433). Not required of citizens from the US, UK, EU, Canada, Australia, NZ and many other countries. Valid for 90 days.

Onward Ticket. Required of all visitors.

Work Permit (p. 39). Required for all foreigners planning to work in Costa Rica for more than a year.

Required Vaccinations. Travelers who have visited nations with endemic yellow fever need proof of vaccination.

Driving Permit. International Driving Permit (p. 20) or valid American or Canadian driver's license and passport required.

Departure Tax. US$26.

EMBASSIES AND CONSULATES

For a list of embassies in Costa Rica, see the **Practical Information** section for San José (p. 453). The following are Costa Rican embassies and consulates abroad.

Australia: Consulate, De la Sala House, Piso 11, 30 Clarence Street, New South Wales, 2000 (☎+61 29261 1177).

Canada: Embassy, 325 Dalhousie Street, Suite 407, Ottawa, Ontario, K1N 7G2 (☎+1 613-562-2855). Open M-F 9am-5pm.

UK: Embassy, Flat 1, 14 Lancaster Gate London W2 3LH (☎+44 020 7706 8844). Open M-F 10am-3pm.

US: Embassy, 2114 "S" Street NW, Washington, DC 20008 (☎+1 202-234-2945 or 2946). Open M-F 10am-6pm.

VISA INFORMATION

Citizens of the US, UK, Australia, New Zealand, Canada, the EU, and Ireland are permitted to stay in Costa Rica for 90 days without a visa. Citizens of other select nations can stay without a visa for up to a month. Everyone else must apply for a visa. For a **visa extension,** travelers need to contact the **Office of Temporary Permits** in the **Department of Immigration** in San José (☎+506 2299 8026; www.migracion.go.cr).

A **work permit** is required for all foreigners planning to work in Costa Rica for more than one year. Most short-term study, work, and volunteer programs do not require special visas. Standard tourist visas will be valid. Foreign students registered in recognized educational institutions planning to **study** in Costa Rica for more than six months should apply for **temporary residence** (US$100 deposit required, waived under special circumstances) at the embassy upon entering the country. Long-term study-abroad programs requiring special entry documentation often process forms for their participants. Double-check on entrance requirements at the nearest embassy or consulate.

TOURIST OFFICES

The **Costa Rica Tourism Board** (from the US and Canada ☎1-866-26782 7422) provides a wealth of information on the country. The spiffy new website (www.visitcostarica.com) is probably the most helpful resource for travelers. The **tourist office,** in San José at Plaza de Cultura, Calle 5 between Avenida Central & Avenida 2, (☎+506 223 1733) is also helpful.

MONEY

COLONES (¢)		
AUS$1 = ¢462	100¢ = AUS$0.22	
CDN$1 = ¢529	100¢ = CDN$0.19	
EUR€1 = ¢815	100¢ = EUR€0.12	
NZ$1 = ¢369	100¢ = NZ$0.27	
UK£1 = ¢933	100¢ = UK£0.11	
US$1 = ¢576	100¢ = US$0.17	

The currency chart above is based on August 2009 exchange rates. The unit of currency in Costa Rica is the **colón,** which is divided into 100 *céntimos*, though these coins are becoming increasingly less useful as Costa Rican currency

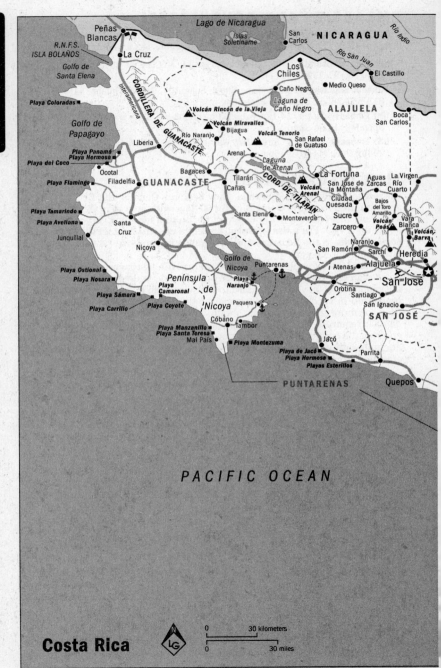

Costa Rica

PACIFIC OCEAN

0   30 kilometers

0   30 miles

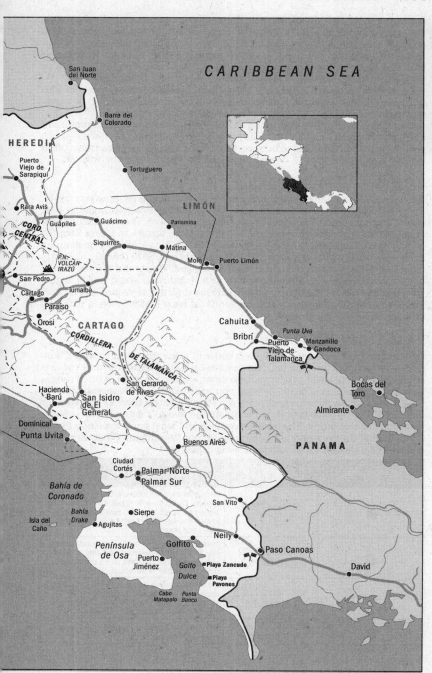

CARIBBEAN SEA

San Juan
del Norte

Barra del
Colorado

HEREDIA

Puerto
Viejo de
Sarapiquí

Tortuguero

Rara Avis

LIMÓN

CORD.
CENTRAL

Guápiles

Guácimo

Parismina

Siquirres

Mátina

P.N.
VOLCÁN
IRAZÚ

Molń

Puerto Limón

San Pedro

Cartago

Turrialba

Paraíso

Orosi

CARTAGO

CORDILLERA

Cahuita

Bribrí

Punta Uva

Puerto
Viejo de
Talamanca

Manzanillo
Gandoca

DE TALAMANCA

Bocas del
Toro

Hacienda
Barú

San Gerardo
de Rivas

San Isidro
de El
General

Almirante

Dominical

Punta Uvita

Buenos Aires

PANAMA

Ciudad
Cortés

Palmar Norte

Palmar Sur

Bahía de
Coronado

San Vito

Bahía
Drake

Sierpe

Isla del
Caño

Agujitas

Neily

Paso Canoas

Península
de Osa

Golfito

Puerto
Jiménez

Golfo
Dulce

Playa Zancudo

Playa
Pavones

David

Cabo
Matapalo

Punta
Banco

depreciates on the global market. Paper notes circulate in the following amounts: 50, 100, 500, 1000, 2000, 5000, and 10,000. Youou might hear them referred to as *rojo* (1000) or *tucán* (5000). Travelers should take care to retain credit card receipts and check accounts regularly. Many of Costa Rica's more touristed destinations (large nature reserves, the Nicoya Peninsula, much of the Central Valley) are full of establishments that prefer US dollars

Costa Rica's streets (particularly in San José) are full of money vendors who will pass off counterfeit US dollars and *colones*. Visitors should also be sensitive to the possibility of credit card fraud, which is widespread.

Costa Rica levies a 13% **sales tax** on all purchases. In addition, restaurants add a 10% **service charge** on all bills. Usually these charges are included in the prices posted, but ask beforehand to be sure. Checks in Costa Rican restaurants often include two price columns: one with tax-inclusive prices and one without.

COSTS

Trip cost will vary considerably, depending on where you go, how you travel, and where you stay. The rainy season (May-Nov.) typically brings the best deals. Transportation in remote areas can be expensive. The most significant expenses will probably be your round-trip (return) airfare to Costa Rica. To give you a general idea, a bare-bones day in Costa Rica (camping or sleeping in hostels, buying food at supermarkets) costs about US$15 (¢6500); a slightly more comfortable day (sleeping in hostels or guest houses and the occasional budget hotel, eating one meal per day at a restaurant, going out at night) would cost US$30 (¢13,000). For a luxurious day, the sky's the limit. Don't forget to factor in emergency reserve funds (at least US$200) when planning how much money you'll need.

PRICE DIVERSITY

Our Researchers list establishments in order of value from best to worst, honoring our favorites with the Let's Go thumbs-up (🖑). Because the best *value* is not always the cheapest *price*, we have incorporated a system of price ranges based on a rough expectation of what you will spend. For **accommodations,** we base our range on the cheapest price for which a single traveler can stay for one night. For **restaurants** and, we estimate the average amount one traveler will spend in one sitting. The table below tells you what you'll *typically* find in Costa Rica at the corresponding price range, but keep in mind that no system can allow for the quirks of individual establishments.

ACCOMMODATIONS	RANGE	WHAT YOU'RE LIKELY TO FIND
❶	Under ¢7500 (US$1-13)	Campgrounds, dorm rooms, and very rustic *cabinas*. Expect bunk beds and a communal bath, but you might get lucky with private baths and singles. You may have to bring your own or rent towels and sheets.
❷	¢7600-14,500 (US$14-25)	Upscale hostels, small hotels, and *cabinas*. You may have a private bathroom with cold or warm water, or a sink in your room and a communal shower in the hall. Most include fans and TVs.
❸	¢14,600-29,000 (US$26-50)	A small room with a private hot-water bath or a *cabina* with a full kitchen. Should have decent amenities, such as phone, A/C, and TV. Breakfast may be included in the price of the room.
❹	¢29,100-46,400 (US$51-80)	Similar to a ❸, with more amenities or a more convenient location.

ACCOMMODATIONS	RANGE	WHAT YOU'RE LIKELY TO FIND
⑤	Over ₡46,500 (Over US$80)	Large hotels, lodges, or upscale chains, usually found in heavily touristed areas. If it's a ⑤ and it doesn't have the perks you want, you've paid too much.

FOOD	RANGE	WHAT YOU'RE LIKELY TO FIND
①	₡Under 2900 (US$1-5)	Mostly *sodas* serving inexpensive *comida típica*, street food, or fast-food, but also university cafeterias and bakeries. May be only takeout, though limited seating is often available.
②	₡2900-5800 (US$5-10)	Some high end *sodas*, sandwiches, pizza, appetizers at a bar, or low-priced entrees. Most ethnic eateries are a ②. Either takeout or a sit-down meal, but only slightly more fashionable decor.
③	₡5900-10,400 (US$11-18)	Mid-priced entrees, seafood, and exotic pasta dishes. A bit more expensive, but chances are you're paying for a change from *comida típica*. More upscale ethnic eateries. Since you'll have the luxury of a waiter, tip will set you back a little extra.
④	₡11,000-14,500 (US$19-25)	A somewhat fancy restaurant. Entrees may be heartier or more elaborate, but you're really paying for decor and ambience. Few restaurants in this range have a dress code, but some may look down on T-shirts and sandals. These places tend to be in more-touristed areas.
⑤	Over₡14,500 (Over US$25)	Your meal might cost more than your room, but there's a reason—it's something fabulous, famous, or both. Expect delicious food with great service and a spectacular view. Otherwise, you're paying for nothing more than hype. Don't order a PB&J!

TRANSPORTATION

Domestic air travel is more expensive, but also more convenient than traveling by bus. Smaller, less regulated airlines do offer domestic flights, but it is recommended that you use the two larger airlines: **Sansa** (from the US ☎877-767-2672, in Costa Rica 506-2290-4100; www.flysansa.com) and the pricier but more reliable **NatureAir** (toll-free ☎1-800-235-9272; www.natureair.com), have flights connecting San José with destinations throughout Costa Rica.

The **bus** system in Costa Rica is thorough, cheap, and reliable. From San José, you can travel almost anywhere in the country for under US$6. However, it's not always immediately clear where the buses arrive, when they leave, or how much they cost. Costa Rica's bus system is labyrinthine; every destination is served by a different company, and each company is located in a different part of town. You can find the most accurate bus information, including detailed schedules and maps, at the **Instituto Costarricense de Turismo (ICT;** ☎+506 223 1733 or 800-343-6332 from the US). You can find ICT representatives at the base of the stairs just before you exit the airport in San José (p. 453).

Boats are a fairly common mode of transportation along the Caribbean Lowlands—ranging from *lanchas* (water taxis) to larger ferries. These modes of transportation are just as reliable and much more quaint than a bus ride. On the other hand, boats are almost always open to the elements, with little shelter from bad weather. Public boat transport is available daily out of Limón, but it might be easier to stick to pre-arranged packages set up by a hotel or by tour operators.

For information on **driving,** see **Essentials,** p. 20.

BORDER CROSSINGS

Travelers can cross into Costa Rica by land or sea. Remember to carry enough money to pay any entrance or exit fees.

NICARAGUA. There is one land crossing at **Peñas Blancas/Sapoá,** 75km north of Liberia and near Rivas, Nicaragua. There is a more pleasant **boat crossing** at **Los Chiles** that goes to San Carlos, Nicaragua.

PANAMA. There are three land crossings: (p. 619) is 18km southeast of Ciudad Neily, near David, Panama; it is sometimes blocked by protesting banana workers. **Sixaola/Guabito** (p. 629) is on the Caribbean coast 1½hr. from Puerto Viejo de Talamanca, near Changuinola, Panama. A third crossing at **Río Sereno,** east of San Vito, is rarely used.

SAFETY

LOCAL LAWS AND POLICE. Costa Rica is a democratic republic and maintains a strong emphasis on human rights and democracy. Costa Rican law requires that all foreigners carry their passports with them at all times and be able to demonstrate proof of legal entry. The country's police force is domestic; there is no military. The **Practical Information** section for each town lists the location and number of the local police station. In case of an emergency, dial ☎**911.**

NATURAL DISASTERS. The rainy season in Costa Rica occurs between May and November, contributing to an average rainfall of 250cm per year. There are often **floods** during this time, especially near the Caribbean coast and areas surrounding major rivers. For more information on volcanoes and earthquakes, see **Essentials,** p. 11.

HEALTH

Malaria is especially common in the Alajuela, Limón, Guanacaste, and Heredia provinces. Travelers going to these places should seek preventive treatment.

THE OUTDOORS

Costa Rica's extensive national park system provides good hiking and camping opportunities. If camping, be sure to do your research ahead of time as some parks do not offer camping facilities. There are restrictions on how many people can be in a given park at the same time. Camping outside of official camping areas is usually not permitted. The **Ministerio del Ambiente y Energía** (Ministry of Atmosphere and Energy), commonly known as **MINAE,** is a government organization devoted to encouraging sustainable development in Costa Rica. MINAE has a strong presence in many of the natural sights of Costa Rica. In some cases it is required that you have a guide; inquire at the local MINAE office.

The *parques nacionales* are the foundation of the ecotourism industry in Costa Rica. There are twenty national parks spread across the country, drawing visitors from all over the world. While attracting large crowds every year, the national park system still manages to preserve most parks from significant human impact. Entrance fees vary by park, but are generally US$5-10. Not all parks are easily accessible by foot.

LIFE AND TIMES

HISTORY

BEFORE COLUMBUS

Costa Rica's development actually follows a dynamic timeline that both mirrors and defies the typical story of Central America. Spanish explorers arrived in Costa Rica at the dawn of the 16th century and found upwards of 25,000 people from five distinct native groups. The history of the country predates their arrival by several hundred years, with the oldest archeological site in Costa Rica dating back to 1000 BC. The area that is now Costa Rica played an important historical role as a meeting place for various pre-Columbian civilizations, such as the Mesoamericans to the north and the Andeans to the South. The Spanish conquest, while often characterized as a peaceful settlement, was in fact especially destructive to the native cultures and peoples. Following Columbus' arrival in Costa Rica in 1502, new settlements and diseases drastically reduced the native population to 120,000 by 1521, to 10,000 by 1611, and to only 500 by 1675. Today, only 1% of Costa Rica's population descends from its original indigenous inhabitants.

THE COLONIAL PERIOD

Costa Rica was not settled until explorer Gil Gonzalez Davila set off from Panama to settle the region in 1522. The golden bands the natives wore in their ears and noses inspired him to name the region Costa Rica, or the "Rich Coast." The early settlement years were tumultuous, marked by ongoing conflict between European settlers and native residents as well as recurring attacks from British pirates along both coasts. In 1564, Juan Vásquez de Coronado finally managed to establish himself in the Central Valley and proclaimed the city of Cartago as his capital. Due to its status as a remote outpost within the Spanish colonial kingdom, Costa Rica had the opportunity to develop under weaker colonial influence than that of many of its neighbors.

LIBERATION AND "EL GRANO DE ORO"

Although Central America officially gained independence from Spain on September 15, 1821, Costa Ricans didn't hear about it until a month later, when the news arrived by mule from Mexico. Predictably, liberation led to a power struggle. While Costa Rica's four largest cities (San José, Cartago, Heredia, and Alajuela) vied to govern the country from within its borders, nearby nations (Guatemala, Mexico, and Nicaragua) vied to govern it from beyond them. Costa Rica eventually became a member of the United Provinces of Central America and was one of the first to become its own country when the collective dissolved in 1838.

Much of Costa Rica's socio-economic development during the 19th century was defined by the export of coffee and bananas, two fruits that, surprisingly, were not native to the country. For 70 years, coffee was the country's only major export, obstructing the growth of even basic foodstuffs. It remained dominant until the 1870s, when Minor Keith, an American engineer building a railroad connecting San José and Puerto Limón, began to plant banana trees along the sides of the train tracks.

INVASION AND DICTATORSHIP

The only serious external threat to Costa Rican national security during the late 19th century came from William Walker, a rogue gold miner from Tennessee who wanted to annex the country as a slave-holding American state. The Costa Rican people had been asked by an enemy of Walker's, Cornelius Vanderbilt, to stop Walker's mission. The Costa Rican army invaded Guanacaste in 1856. Fueled by a newly forged sense of territorial pride, the Costa Rican army drove Walker's forces back to Rivas, Nicaragua, where a drummer boy and precocious military strategist named Juan Santamaría set fire to Walker's troops' impromptu barracks, ending their deluded campaign and launching himself into the sparsely populated ranks of Costa Rican national heroes. Costa Ricans now celebrate the day Juan Santamaría sacrificed his life to burn the Mesón de Guerra and secure national freedom annually on April 11.

General Tomás Guardia, one of Costa Rica's only dictators, seized power soon after in 1870 in order to end the rule of the coffee barons. During Guardia's 12 years in power, his ambitious, iron-fisted policies modernized the country in important ways, though they cost Costa Ricans their civil liberties and accrued a sizable deficit. After his dictatorship, the country saw a peaceful transition back to democracy. In 1889, Costa Rica conducted the first legitimate large-scale elections in Central American history, though women and African descendants were not allowed to vote.

DOMESTIC REFORM AND CIVIL WAR

Costa Rica underwent a rather ungraceful transition into the 20th century. These years were marked by border disputes with Panama and another dangerous flirtation with autocracy. In the 1914 elections, the people of Costa Rica were unable to give a majority vote to any candidate. As a result, congress chose Alfredo González as a compromise, but he was soon overthrown by the reactionary General Federico Tinoco. The dictatorship was unpopular and brief, however, and the decades to follow were smooth and prosperous. A powerful, and probably highly caffeinated, coffee elite continued to ensure that income taxes were low (as they still are today), though social discontent grew among laborers and radicals. Moderate president Rafael Ángel Calderón Guardia implemented important labor reforms, including health care and minimum wage for laborers, but he lost popular support soon after World War II. In 1944, he annulled the results of the election and installed a puppet president instead.

A disaffected middle class rose up against this puppet regime during the War of National Liberation in 1948 under the leadership of José Figueres Ferrer, a wealthy coffee farmer and intellectual. Widely known as "Don Pepe," Figueres appealed to a popular distrust of communism's foreign ideology and called for the renewal of Costa Rican democracy. Backed by US CIA forces looking to stop communism, Figueres defeated the government's machete-clad forces in six weeks before inaugurating the Founding Junta of the Second Republic and instituting a wide range of political reforms. In 1949, he banned the Communist party and wrote a new constitution that gave women and African descendents the right to vote. It abolished the Costa Rican military, making Costa Rica the first country ever to operate under a democratic system without an army. All that remains of the army today is the Civil Guard, a government police force composed of only 8400 members. After 18 months in power, Figueres stepped down and handed over the presidency to Otilio Ulate, the initial winner of the incendiary 1944 election. Widely admired for his actions, Figueres was elected president in 1953. Once in office, he instituted a number of leftist reforms—like nationalizing banks and unions—similar to those that had motivated civil war in the first place.

GLOBAL ROLES AND NOBEL LAURELS

Since dissolving its army in 1949, Costa Rica has enjoyed peace, political stability, and a relatively high degree of economic comfort, earning it the nickname "Switzerland of the Americas," a title it bears with pride. It has not, however, been unaffected by civil strife in nearby nations. Thousands of refugees (some Salvadorean, most Nicaraguan) have crossed the border each year since the late 1970s, causing unemployment, and tensions to rise.

The 1980s were a tough period for Costa Rica. In addition to the internal crisis of currency devaluation and soaring welfare and oil costs, the country faced plummeting prices in the coffee, sugar, and banana markets, as well as a nearby civil war in Nicaragua. In 1987, however, then-former president Oscar Arias earned the Nobel Peace Prize when he achieved a consensus among Central America leaders with the Plan de Paz Arias, negotiated a cease-fire agreement, and laid the groundwork for a unified Central American Parliament. In 1988, he increased his commitment to democracy by creating the Arias Foundation for Peace and Human Progress.

TODAY

Today, Costa Rica is one of the most prosperous countries in Latin America. Its well-educated population maintains a strong democratic spirit and displays an admirable level of collective sensitivity to issues surrounding ecological conservation, democratic development, and commercial vitality. In 2006, following the passage of a constitutional amendment that allowed for the re-election of presidents, former president and Nobel Laureate Oscar Arias was re-elected as president in one of the closest elections in Costa Rican history. Economically, the country has experienced relatively stable growth and a slow reduction in inflation. Though unemployment, poverty, and the management of an emerging welfare state are still pressing issues, Costa Rica has consistently managed to sustain generally positive economic trends.

ECONOMY

Costa Rica has a strong agricultural history, and its economy has traditionally been based on the exportation of bananas and coffee. Today, though agriculture continues to be important to the economy, with the addition of pineapples to the export market, the economy has been greatly diversified. After economic trouble in the 1980s, the economy has begun to turn around, and Costa Rican wealth is fairly well distributed among the different social classes.

In order to protect Costa Rica's environment and its ecotourism industry, the government has banned all open-pit mining. In 2004, Costa Rica became an observer in the Asia-Pacific Economic Cooperation Forum and began to widely increase its trading with South East Asia.

Today, Costa Rica's export-oriented economy relies primarily on tourism, and the industry is growing. Statistics have recorded a significant increase in tourism from year to year, making it even more important. Governmental development strategies for Costa Rica have been geared increasingly toward environmental and social sustainability, as tourists mainly come to Costa Rica for two reasons: its wilderness and its reputation for convenience and safety.

ECOTOURISM

The official slogan of Costa Rica's tourist industry—"Costa Rica: No Artificial Ingredients"—reveals just how intentional the country has been about continuing its reputation as a natural and eco-friendly tourist environment. Ecotourism has made the Costa Rica famous worldwide. It remains a huge draw for foreign tourists, promoting sustainable, responsible travel to natural sites, as well as encouraging low-impact cultural and environmental exploration that will generate income for farther conservation. In fact, Costa Rica has even been awarded and honored by the Sustainable Tourism Certification program for its sustainable approach to tourism.

One of the most unique elements of Costa Rica's ecotourism industry is its opportunity for turtle-watching. Visitors come from all over the world to watch turtles come ashore to lay their eggs at night on various Pacific and Caribbean beaches. Some of the most important nesting sites for turtles in the western hemisphere are located in Tortuguero (p. 542) and Parismina, a smaller, less-touristed town 50km south, home to a turtle conservation organization which draws hundreds of volunteers each year to protect the eggs from poachers. In addition to the turtles, Costa Rica boasts 6% of the world's biodiversity even though it covers only 0.03% of the world's surface.

Though proponents of the industry maintain that it benefits the environment and travelers alike, Costa Rican ecotourism remains a delicate endeavor. While there has been a push to move tourism toward luxury ecotourism in order to attract wealthier travelers seeking comfortable wilderness adventures, conservation groups are concerned that larger facilities will put an unreasonably heavy burden on the nation's ecosystems.

COSTA RICA AND NICARAGUA

Two issues continue to strain Costa Rican-Nicaraguan relations: conflicts over use of the San Juan River and illegal immigration from Nicaragua. Dating back to 1858, the **Cañas-Juarez Treaty** holds that the San Juan River constitutes the border between Costa Rica and Nicaragua but belongs to Nicaragua, though Costa Rica was granted perpetual free commercial access to its waters. Negotiations continue as both countries try to reach a consensus about what constitutes "commercial use." The borders of both countries are paying the price for this tension, as the political conflict impedes investment and development.

The issue of migration between these two countries also remains an urgent one. Because Costa Rica is prosperous and economically stable, it has drawn massive numbers of illegal immigrants from Nicaragua. Many come to work because of better job opportunities, and a significant portion of the Costa Rican population is made up of Nicaraguans. Both the Costa Rican and the Nicaraguan government have made attempts to resolve the disputes, but their isolation and political pride have made resolution an elusive concept. In the midst of this tension, *ticos* tend to look down upon their Nicaraguan neighbors, commonly known as *nicas*. Immigrant *nicas* are accused of stealing jobs, bringing violent crime, and using up many of the country's social resources.

PEOPLE

DEMOGRAPHICS

Out of nearly 4.3 million inhabitants, indigenous people comprise less than 1% of the population, while individuals of African descent make up only 3% and are concentrated on the Caribbean coast. A staggering 94% of the population is of European and *mestizo* descent, making Costa Rica one of the most racially homogeneous countries in Latin America.

Most of the eight groups of *indígenas* in Costa Rica who wish to protect their traditional lifestyles and languages do so on one of the 22 reserves scattered throughout the country. Reserve boundaries are often disrespected, however, and indigenous lands are constantly threatened. Other ethnic groups, including Germans, Americans, Italians, Britons, Chinese, and other Latin Americans have immigrated to Costa Rica over the past 150 years and have established communities. The town of Monteverde, for example, was founded by Quakers and is now home to a community that supports itself with cheese production.

LANGUAGE

Spanish is the official language, though Costa Ricans speak with a characteristic *tico* twist in accent and usage. Rare in other regions of the country, English is common along the Caribbean coast, where a Caribbean Creole dialect is used. Indigenous groups maintain their traditional languages.

Costa Rica has more country-specific vocabulary than many larger nations, generally known as *tiquismo*, which comes from adding the diminutive "-ito" or "-ico" to words in order to make them more friendly. They have ventured into the realms of the phonetically implausible by turning the word *chiquito* (small) into *chiquitico*, and they use this ending so often that *"ticos"* has come to refer to Costa Ricans in general. The country's most popular phrase, *pura vida* (literally "pure life"), is extremely versatile and may be used to mean "hello," "goodbye," "awesome," or "good luck." While the phrase is not used too often in major cities, it is kept alive by rural communities, enthusiastic tourists, and a thriving souvenir industry. Some other common words include: *tuanis*, the spanglish pronunciation of the English phrase "too nice"; *mae* (dude); and *rico/a*, an adjective often used to describe excellent food.

RELIGION

Costa Rica is a politically secular country with weak links between church and state. Though the constitution provides for religious freedom, **Roman Catholicism** is the official religion, practiced by almost 77% of the population. As such, only Catholic marriages receive state recognition—all others must have a civil ceremony. Semana Santa (Holy Week), a national holiday culminating on Easter Sunday, is a balance of piety and partying. Protestantism has a presence, though it has yet to gain the ubiquity it has in other Central American countries. There are small numbers of Jehovah's Witnesses, Jews, Mennonites, Quakers, and people of other denominations throughout the country.

FOOD AND DRINK

If it doesn't have **rice and beans,** it isn't **tico!** Rice and black beans infiltrate almost every meal. In one day, it's possible to have them for breakfast as **gallo pinto,** (literally, "spotted rooster"; rice and beans fried with spices and served with meat or eggs), then take a **casado** for lunch and have a hearty bowl of black bean soup for dinner. "Casado" literally means "married," and it refers to the hearty combination plates (usually rice and beans with meat, plantains, cabbage, and tomato). *Tamales, empanadas,* and *tortas* are also typical dishes. **Comida típica** (native dishes) in Costa Rica are usually mild and can even be bland. As if to answer this need for flavor, *lizano salsa,* a slightly sweet and spicy sauce of vegetables, has become Costa Rica's most popular condiment.

Informal restaurants called *sodas,* which serve flavorful, home-style cooking at inexpensive prices, dominate the landscape. Larger and generally more expensive *restaurantes* are slightly less common. If you're far from the city, you may find yourself at a small *soda* where they only offer you a spoon. This is because *campesinos* (rural field workers) often eat only with this utensil. Don't be embarrassed to ask for a fork and knife. Many meals come with bread or corn tortillas, both of which you can hold and eat with your hand.

In terms of popularity, nothing can compete with the widespread appeal of Costa Rica's world-class **coffee.** *Ticos* young and old enjoy a big mug of *café* (usually mixed with milk) multiple times a day. Despite the high quality of Costa Rican blends, most *ticos* seem to prefer a sweetened brew. For a stronger cup of joe, look for restaurants and cafes that cater to tourists, or buy your own beans. Ask for *café sin leche* or *café negro* to skip the cream and sugar.

Though coffee has captured the hearts of Costa Ricans, alcohol is still putting up a fight for their livers. **Guaro,** made from sugar cane and similar-tasting to rum, is the national liquor. It mixes well with anything, though *coco loco* (*guaro* with coconut juice) is a popular choice. When it comes to lower proof options, Imperial, Pilsen, and Bavaria beers are popular among *ticos.*

CUSTOMS AND ETIQUETTE

BEING COSTA RICAN. *Ticos* are very family oriented. Kids live with their parents through their college years and generally don't leave home before marriage. Close extended families are common and contribute to fairly cohesive communities, particularly in rural areas. Costa Ricans are known for their relaxed temperament, as well as their willingness to lend a hand — or even a home — in times of need. The phrase *quedar bien,* which means "stay on good terms," is one of the essential tenets of Costa Rican lifestyle values. Costa Ricans will often want to *quedar bien* by saying "yes" when they mean "no" in order to avoid conflict. This may also mean that promises made during face-to-face interactions are more symbolic than authentic; a friendly gesture is emphasized over a desire for particularly deep or intimate friendship.

HOUSEGUEST MANNERS. Gratefulness is an admirable quality in houseguests, and hospitality should be received with articulated gratitude (say *"gracias,"* and say it often). Middle- and upper-class families will often have an *empleada,* a young girl or woman who lives in the house and gets paid to help with house chores. Nonetheless, hosts appreciate if guests offer to help serve others or clean after a meal is over, especially if they're doing the work.

BEING POLITE. When speaking Spanish in Costa Rica, you'll find an important distinction between the *usted, vos,* and *tú* forms of verbs. Use *usted,* the third person singular, or *ustedes,* the third person plural, when speaking to a stranger or someone older; it is more formal and respectful. Costa Ricans are distinct for using *usted* very broadly: with family, friends, children, and even pets. It is important to use *Don* or *Doña* before an older person's name; call a friend's father Don Alberto and not just Alberto.

Machismo has left a mark on Costa Rican gender relations. Out of tradition, men are very chivalrous, often assuming a protective role, though women might also find themselves subjected to unwanted male attention on the streets. It is considered good manners for men to open doors and help carry bags.

DRESS CODE. Costa Ricans are always very conscious about looking presentable and tidy when they go out. People often dress much more conservatively than the warm weather would call for. Men usually wear slacks, jeans, t-shirts, polo shirts, or button-down shirts. Women usually wear pants, jeans, or skirts in the city. Travelers should try not to wear shorts in the city; shorts are acceptable in more rural areas and at the beach. When in doubt, it's a good idea for visitors to present themselves in a fairly conservative manner.

TICO TIME. People in Costa Rica tend to be very laid-back—being on time is not a major point of concern. *Ticos* can be late for almost everything, which often comes as a surprise to foreigners accustomed to punctuality. While it is usual for people to be 15-30min. late for business appointments, a meeting with friends can be delayed by up to several hours.

THE ARTS

Unlike some of its other Central American neighbors, Costa Rica is not known for its artistic heritage. Typical artifacts include **statues** in gold, jade, and stone, as well as breastplates featuring stylized jaguars, crocodiles, and hook-beaked birds from the Pre-Columbian era. Some of the most famous and mysterious artifacts are the more than 300 almost perfectly spherical **Diquis stones,** called *Las Bolas* by locals, which are found in the southern territories. The stones are arranged in geometric formations that point to earth's magnetic north and are estimated to be around 1600 years old. Archaeologists still are confounded by their origin. With the arrival of Spanish colonial rulers, Costa Rica's arts and culture were dominated by European norms for centuries. In the modern era, Costa Ricans have begun to take an active interest in their pre-Columbian history and culture, and excavations have fueled this process of rediscovery.

While periodicals rule the reading market, Costa Rica does have a colorful literary history. Before the 20th century, Costa Rican literature drew largely from European models, though it also gained inspiration from folk tales and colloquial expression in a movement known as *costumbrismo*. Despite the strength of this early movement, Costa Rican literature didn't find its expressive voice until the 20th century, when it began dedicating itself to political and social criticism. **José Marín Cañas's** *Inferno verde*, a depiction of the Chaco War between Paraguay and Bolivia, bolstered anti-imperialist sentiment. **Oreamuni's** *La ruta de su evasión* explored inter-generational tensions and the subtleties of Latin American *machismo*. Writer **Fabián Dobles,** winner of the Premio Nacional, Costa Rica's highest distinction for artistic and intellectual achievement, has also gained recognition beyond the borders of the country; and **Carlos Salazar Herrera** is one of the nation's premier artists, working as a painter, poet, and professor. Costa Rica also serves as a haven for expat writers and artists from around the world, offering inspiration or simply a secluded backdrop.

COSTA RICA

BEYOND TOURISM

VOLUNTEERING

SAVE THE ANIMALS

With an increasing number of tourists visiting Costa Rica every year, there is a greater need to protect the wildlife. Programs mainly focus on protecting turtles from poachers or helping out in a wildlife refuge.

Earthwatch, 3 Clock Tower Pl., Ste. 100, Box 75, Maynard, MA 021754, USA (☎+1 800-776-0188 or +1 978-461-0081; www.earthwatch.org). Arranges eco-friendly programs in Costa Rica and provides the opportunity to participate in cutting-edge scientific research. Volunteers have the opportunity to gather data about the effects of climate change on leatherback turtles or caterpillars; alternatively, volunteers can help Costa Rican coffee farmers develop environment-friendly methods of production. Fees vary; average US $2800.

Volunteer Visions, Casa Roja de Dos Pisos, Playa Samara, Guancaste, Costa Rica (US ☎+1 330-871-4511; www.volunteervisions.org). Provides affordable volunteer opportunities for adventurous individuals. Based in Costa Rica, Volunteer Visions's wildlife conservation project in the Guancaste region of Costa Rica strives to reintroduce birds, monkeys, and other animals to the wild. Volunteers help to care for the animals. Trips range from 2 weeks (US$650) to 26 weeks (US$3340). Fee includes food, accommodations (homestay or dorm), orientation, and excursions.

World Endeavors, 3015 E Franklin Ave., Minneapolis, MN 5540, USA (☎+1 612-729-3400 or +1 866-802-9678; www.worldendeavors.com). Opportunities for volunteers to rescue and rehabilitate parrots, macaws, and other native tropical birds in Atenas. Programs range from 2 weeks (US$1455) to 3 months (US$2877); includes housing, 3 meals per day with a family, and cultural activities. Placements longer than 1 month receive 2 weeks of Spanish language classes.

SAVE THE TREES

Costa Rica is one of the most environmentally diverse places on earth. Numerous organizations work to protect the national parks, tropical forests, and beaches from unsustainable farming practices and tourist practices. The following programs offer volunteer opportunities ranging from trail maintenance and reforestation to teaching sustainable farming techniques.

Punta Mona Center (www. puntamona.org), located 5km south of Manzanillo. A huge organic farm and educational center dedicated to sustainable agriculture. Interns live in houses built completely of fallen trees, and using solar-powered, eco-friendly energy. 100+ varieties of tropical fruits, vegetables, and medicinal herbs are grown at the farm., Meals (mostly vegetarian) included. Internships (US$600 per month) begin the first day of each month.

Asociación Preservacionista de Flora y Fauna Silvestre (APREFLOLFAS), P.O. Box 917 2150, San José, Costa Rica (☎2240 6087; www.apreflofas.or.cr). A non-profit volunteer organization, also called "The Raccoon," provides a wealth of information on ecotourism in Costa Rica's parks. The organization promotes reforestation and works to guard Costa Rica's natural resources from illegal exploitation.

Asociación de Voluntario de Areas Protegias Silvestres (ASVO), Apdo. 11384-1000, San José (☎2258 4430; www.asvocr.org). Your link to virtually every national park in Costa Rica. Although some parks prefer that volunteers contact their conservation areas directly, you can always reach a specific park through this office. Live and work in the same conditions as the park rangers. US$17 per day to cover lodging and meals.

FARMING

The export of crops if an important part of Costa Rica's economy, and there is a plethora of opportunities for involvement in this industry.

Finca Lomas, (☎506 2224 6090 or 506 2224-0911; ww.anaicr.org). An environmentally friendly farm in the Talamancan Lowland Rainforest. Works to establish sustainable economic and environmental groups and encourage community self-sufficiency. Email info at anaicr.org for more details.

uVolunteer (Volunteer Costa Rica), Apartado 280-4250, San Ramon, Alajuela, Costa Rica (☎+1 971 252 1334; www.uvolunteer.org). Strives to create a sustainable, conservative method of farming that is realistic for Costa Rican farming communities. Volunteers' responsibilities may include organic gardening, constucting nature trails, and caring for animals.

World-Wide Opportunities on Organic Farms (WWOOF), P.O. Box 2154, Winslow, Buckingham MK18 3WS, England, UK (www.wwoof.org). A network that connects volunteers with organic farms in Costa Rica, and around the world. Promotes sustainable, organic farming by providing travelers with information on farms that will host them for free. Membership fee (US$16) to receive a book of host farms from which you'll choose.

STUDYING

AMERICAN PROGRAMS

American Field Service (AFS), 198 Madison Ave., 8th fl., New York, NY 10016, USA (☎+1 800-237-4636; www.usa.afs.org). Offers homestay exchange programs in Costa Rica primarily for high school students and graduating seniors planning on taking a gap year. Summer US$5900-6900; semester US$7900; full year US$8900.

American Institute for Foreign Study (AIFS), River Plaza, 9 W. Broad St., Stamford, CT 06902, USA (☎+1-866-906-2437; www.aifs.com). Organizes programs for college students through Veritas Unviersity in San José. 12-week programs without airfare US$7495; 16-week program without airfare US$8995.

Council on International Educational Exchange (CIEE), 300 Fore St., Portland, ME 04101, USA (☎+1-207-553-4000 or 800-40-STUDY/407-8839; www.ciee.org). One of the most comprehensive resources for work, academic, and internship programs around the world, including Costa Rica, where you can study ecology in Monteverde. Summer fee US$6500; semester fee US$12900.

COSTA RICAN PROGRAMS

Instituto Monteverde, Apdo. 69-5655, Monteverde, Puntarenas, Costa Rica (☎2645 5053 or 2645 5365; www.mvinstitute.org). This non-profit association provides educational and cultural resources for the local community. Learn about sustainability and community health, as well as Spanish language and culture. Email info@mvinstitute.org for further details.

University of Costa Rica Rainforest Adventure, World Class Adventures in Education 17812 SH 16 S, Pipe Creek, TX, 78063, USA (☎+1 800-321-7625; www.educationabroad.com). A tropical field ecology program for English-speaking undergraduates at Costa Rica's main national university. Students take Spanish lessons and stay with Costa Rican families. Credit accepted by many US universities. US$8500.

SAN JOSÉ

At first, Costa Rica's capital is sure to frustrate the tourists eager to experience the country's natural beauty. Modern concrete structures encroach on the city's surviving examples of colonial architecture. Smog and grime dominate the capital, while piercing car horns never stop blaring. During the summer rainy season, travelers should expect daily downpours.

Still, San José is filled with the energy of a young and bustling city. As irritating as the fast-food joints on every corner may be for someone attempting to escape civilization, the neon facades demonstrate how rapidly the city is modernizing. Internet cafes have sprung up on nearly every corner. Luxury hotels and restaurants offering international cuisine provide the discerning traveler with a plethora of culinary options. But have no fear, loyal lovers of *comida típica*—the authentic *casado* can still be found just about anywhere.

For those seeking nightlife, bars and clubs in San Pedro and El Pueblo are alive with energy and music until the wee hours of morning. San José is home to approximately 300,000 people (over 1 million including the suburbs), and most of them will show you up on the dance floor—the speed and elegance of *salsa* takes most gringos by surprise.

The transportation and economic hub of Costa Rica, San José offers a glimpse into the country's future. Surrounded by mountains and perched 1132m above sea level, San José was first settled in 1736, though it spent much of the colonial era as a tobacco-farming town. In 1823, San José replaced Cartago as the capital of Costa Rica and came into its own as the nexus of the coffee trade. As an ever-changing city, it is a worthy stop between the two coasts. Be sure to give yourself enough time; there's plenty to see here in bustling San José.

◼ INTERCITY TRANSPORTATION

FLIGHTS

International Flights: Juan Santa María International Airport (SJO), about 15km northwest of San José in Alajuela. Most cheaply accessible by bus from San José to Alajuela. Official **airport taxis** to and from San José charge ¢13,366 (US$23). The taxi driver will meet you at the airport exit to confirm a price and will then take you to the window on your left to pay the fare. **Grayline Tours** (☎2291 2222; www.graylinecostarica.com) runs an **airport shuttle** that picks up travelers across the street and upstairs from the airport exit and drops off at many mid-range and top-end hotels around town for ¢5,811 (US$10). Online booking available. Airlines include: **American** (☎2223 5426); **Continental** (☎2296 4911 or 0800 044 0005); **Copa** (☎295 7400); **Delta** (☎2257 4141 or 1-800-221-1212); **Iberia** (☎2441 2591); **Mexicana** (☎2257 6334); **Taca,** through **Sansa** (☎2221 9414); **United** (☎2220 4844 or 2441 8025). Arriving at the airport 2½hr. early is recommended for all international flights. **Sansa** (☎2666 0307; www.flysansa.com) offers the cheapest domestic flights from a terminal just to the left of the international terminal (¢39,514-56,947/US$68-98). Departures and one-way fares for Sansa: **Barra de Colorado** (1 per day M, F, Sa; ¢45,907/US$79); **Drake Bay** (2 per day, ¢56,367/US$97); **Golfito** (4 per day, ¢55,205/US$95); **Liberia** (6 per day, ¢55,205/US$95); **Nosara** (1 per day, ¢55,205/US$95); **Palmar Sur** (3 per day, ¢50,555/US$87); **Puerto Jimenez** (6 per day, ¢55,205/US$95); **Quepos** (9 per day, ¢32,541/US$56); **Samara** (1 per day, ¢56,948/US$98); **Tamarindo** (6 per day, ¢55,205/US$95); **Tambor** (5 per day, ¢43,583/US$75); **Tortuguero** (1 per day, ¢45,907/US$79).

Tobías Bolaños Airport, in Pavas, 20min. from San José by taxi. Serves **NatureAir** (☎2229 6000, US reservations +1-800-235-9272; www.natureair.net).

Domestic Flights: Online reservations available. Departures and one-way fares for NatureAir: **Arenal** (1 per day, ¢43,001/US$74); **Bocas del Toro** (1-2 per day M, W, F, Su; ¢76,705/US$132); **Drake Bay** (2 per day, ¢63,340/US$109); **Golfito** (1 per day, ¢61,597/US$106); **Liberia** (4 per day, ¢61,597/US$106); **Limón** (1 per day M, W, F, Su; ¢47,650/US$82); **Nosara** (1-2 per day, ¢61,597/US$106); **Palmar Sur, Dominical** (1 per day, ¢55,785/$96); **Puerto Jiménez** (5 per day, ¢63,340/US$109); **Punta Islita** (1 per day, ¢63,340/US$109); **Quepos** (3 per day, ¢35,447/US$61), **Tamarindo** (3 per day, ¢61,597/US$106); **Tambor** (2 per day, ¢45,907/US$79); **Tortuguero** (1 per day, ¢50,556/US$87). When booking online, you may find cheaper deals with more restrictions.

BUSES

Buses to almost everywhere in the country arrive and depart from the city's stops and terminals. Many depart from around **Terminal Coca-Cola,** between Av. 1/3, C. 16/18. The schedule is available at the **Instituto Costarricense de Turismo (ICT)** at the **Museo de Oro** (p. 460). Times often change, so double-check with your hostel. Fares for domestic trips are not listed and change frequently, but expect rides under 4hr. to cost ¢2000 or less, with longer trips under ¢4000. **All fares must be paid in colones, so carry small bills or change.**

Domestic Buses:

Alajuela-Airport: TUASA, Av. 2, C.12/14 (☎2442 6900). 35min.; every 10min. 4:30am-10pm, every 30min. 10-11pm.

Cahuita: Terminal Caribe, Av. 13, C. Central (☎2257 8129). 4hr.; 6, 10am, 2, 4pm.

Cariari: Terminal Caribe, Av. 13, C. Central (☎2222 0610). 2hr., 9 per day 6:30am-8:30pm.

Cartago: Empresa Lumaca, Av. 10, C. 5 (☎2537 2320). 45min., every 10min. 5:05am-midnight.

Fortuna: Auto Transportes, Av. 7/9, C. 12 (☎2255 0567). 4hr.; 6:15, 8:40, 11:30am.

Golfito: Tracopa, Av. 18/20, C. 5 (☎2221 4214). 8hr.; Su 7am, 3:30pm.

Guápiles: Empresarios Guapileños, Av. 13, C. Central. 1½hr., every hr. 5:30am-7pm.

Heredia: Transportes Unidos 400, Av. 7/9, C. 1. Other locations at Av. Central, C. 8 and Av. 5/7, C. 4. 30min., every 10min. 5am-11pm (5am-3am from Av. 7/9, C. 1).

Jacó: Transportes Morales, Terminal Coca-Cola, Av. 3, C. 16 (☎2223 1109). 2hr.; 6am, every 2hr. 7am-7pm.

Liberia: Pulmitan, Av. 5/7, C. 24 (☎2256 9552). 4½hr., 8 per day 6am-10pm.

Limón: Caribeños, Terminal Caribe, Av. 13, C. Central (☎2221 0610). 2½hr., every hr. 5am-7pm.

Monteverde: Autotransportes Tilarán, Atlántico Nte. Terminal, Av. 7/9, C.12 (☎2222 3854). 5hr., 6:30am and 2:30pm.

Playa Nosara and Garza: Tracopa-Alfaro, Av. 3/5, C. 14 (☎2222 2666). 6hr., 5:30am.

Playa Panamá: Tralapa, Av. 1/3, C. 20 (☎2221 7202). 6hr.; 3:30pm. Return 3pm.

Playa Tamarindo: Tracopa-Alfaro, Av 5, C. 14/16 (☎2222 2666). 5hr., 11:30am and 3:30pm. Tralapa, Av. 3/5, C. 20 (☎2221 7202), 4pm.

Playas del Coco: Av. 5/7, C. 24 (☎2222 1650). 5hr.; 8am, 2, 4pm. Return 4, 8am, 2pm.

Puntarenas: Empresarios Unidos de Puntarenas, Av.12, C. 16 (☎2222 8231). 2hr.; every hr. 6am-7pm; return every hr. 4-7pm.

Quepos and Manuel Antonio: Transportes Morales, Terminal Coca Cola, Av. 3, C. 16 (☎2223 5567). Direct 3hr.; 6, 9am, noon, 2:30, 6, 7:30pm. Return 4, 6, 9:30am, noon, 2:30, 5pm. Indirect 5hr.; 7, 10am, 2, 3, 4pm. Return 5, 8am, 2, 4pm. Only direct buses continue to Manuel Antonio.

Siquirres: Terminal Caribe, Av. 13, C. Central (☎2222 0610). 1hr.; 11 per day 6:30am-6pm.

Turrialba: Transtusa Av. 6, C. 13 (☎2222 4464). 1hr.; every hr. 5:15am-10pm; return 7am, 9pm.

Volcán Irazú: Av. 2, C. 1/3. 2hr.; Sa-Su 8am. Return Sa-Su 12:30pm.

San José Overview

Volcán Poás: TUASA, Av. 2, C. 12/14 (☎2222 5325). 2hr.; 8:30am. Return 2:30pm.

International Buses:

El Salvador: TicaBus, Av. 2/4, C. 9 (☎2221 8954; www.ticabus.com/ingles). 48hr. with 1 night in Managua; 6, 7:30am, 12:30; ₡23,244 (US$40).

Guatemala: TicaBus, Av. 26, C. 3. 60hr. with 1 night in Nicaragua and 1 night in El Salvador; 6, 7:30am, 12:30pm; ₡32,541 (US$56).

Tegucigalpa, Honduras: TicaBus, Av. 2/4, C. 9. 48hr. with 1 night in Managua; 6, 7:30am, 12:30pm; ₡20,338 (US$35).

San Pedro Sula, Honduras: TicaBus, Av. 2/4, C. 9. 48hr. with 1 night in Managua; 6, 7:30am, 12:30pm; ₡27,311 (US$47).

Nicaragua: TicaBus, Av. 26, C. 3. 8hr.; 6, 7:30am, 12:30pm; ₡8,135 (US$14).

Panamá City: TicaBus, Av. 26, C. 3 (☎2221 8954). 20hr.; midnight and 11pm, US$26. Panaline, Av. 3/5, C. 16 (☎2256 8721, www.panalinecr.com). 18hr., 1pm, ₡13,365 (US$23).

✈ ORIENTATION

San José's design follows a typical Costa Rican grid: *avenidas* run east-west and *calles* run north-south. Directions in San José, as well as in other large cities, are usually given by listing the street and cross street where a destination

SAN JOSÉ

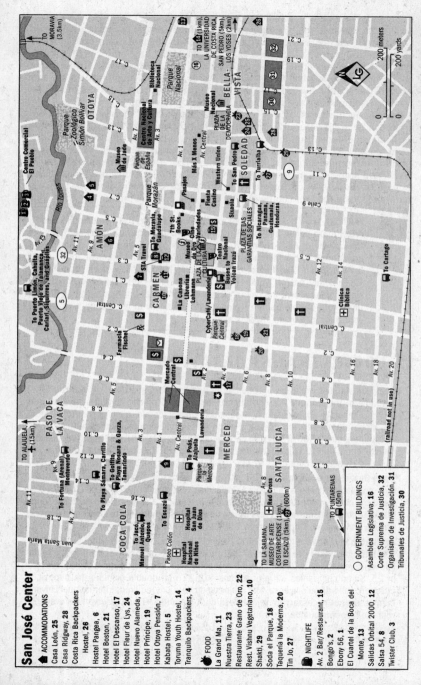

San José Center

⚑ ACCOMMODATIONS
Casa León, 25
Casa Ridgway, 28
Costa Rica Backpackers
  Hostel, 26
Hostel Pangea, 6
Hotel Boston, 21
Hotel El Descanso, 17
Hotel Fleur de Lys, 24
Hotel Nuevo Alameda, 9
Hotel Príncipe, 19
Hotel Otoya Pensión, 7
Kabata Hostel, 5
Toruma Youth Hostel, 14
Tranquilo Backpackers, 4

❧ FOOD
La Grand Ma, 11
Nuestra Tierra, 23
Restaurante Grano de Oro, 22
Rest. Vishnu Vegetariano, 10
Shakti, 29
Soda el Parque, 18
Taquería la Moderna, 20
Tin Jo, 27

■ NIGHTLIFE
Av. 2 Bar/Restaurant, 15
Bongo's, 2
Ebony 56, 1
El Cuartel de la Boca del
  Monte, 13
Salidas Orbital 2000, 12
Salsa 54, 8
Twister Club, 3

○ **GOVERNMENT BUILDINGS**
Asamblea Legislativa, 16
Corte Suprema de Justicia, 32
Organismo de Investigación, 31
Tribunales de Justicia, 30

is located. For example, a building located at Av. 2, C. 5/7 would be located on Av. 2, somewhere in the block between C. 5 and 7. **Avenida Central** (called Paseo Colón north of C. 22) is the main drag, with a shopping and eating area blocked off to traffic between C. 2 and C. 5. Just west of the city center is the frantic **Mercado Central,** bordered by Av. Central/1 and C. 6/8. Four blocks further west of the market is **Terminal Coca-Cola,** on Av. 1, C. 16/18. Many streets are not labeled; the staff at stores rarely knows their own address, so counting blocks between destinations and relying on landmarks is helpful.

Barrio Amón, northeast of Av. 5 and C. 1, and **Barrio Otoya,** slightly east of Amón, are the most architecturally interesting neighborhoods in the city center, housing Spanish colonial buildings dating back to the 19th century. West of downtown, past C. 42, **La Sabana** contains the large **Parque Metropolitano La Sabana.** Five kilometers farther west, the quiet suburb of **Escazú** is home to gorgeous B&Bs and some of San José's most posh restaurants. Other upscale regions include **Los Yoses,** east of downtown past C. 3, and **San Pedro,** home to the University of Costa Rica and some of the city's best entertainment.

WATCH OUT! Although San José is relatively safe, theft, prostitution, and drugs make some areas a bit risky. Problem spots include: **Terminal Coca-Cola,** south of Av. 8 between C. 2 and 14, Av. 4 to 6 between C. 4 and 12, areas north of the **Mercado Central,** and areas around the mall and C. de la Amargura in **San Pedro.** Generally, areas beyond a few blocks from San José's center pose a greater threat after dark. The city's parks and crowded streets can present the risk of pickpockets and grab-and-run thefts, so hold on to your belongings. After sunset, the safest way to get around is by taxi, especially for women traveling alone.

⊟ LOCAL TRANSPORTATION

Buses: Local buses run every 5-10min. from 5am to 10pm and travel all over San José, including to the suburbs and the airport. There are no official printed schedules and timing is generally approximate. Ask locals and drivers for info or check bus fronts. Most bus stops are marked with the destination they serve. As local destinations generally run no more than ₡300, it's best to carry small change. Major bus stops include **Escazú** (Av. 1/Central and C. 16), **Guadalupe** and **Moravia** (Av. 3, C. 3/5), and **San Pedro** (Av. 2, C. 11/13 and Av. Central, C. 9/11).

Private Buses: Grayline Tours (☎2220 2126; www.graylinecostarica.com). Offers **buses** to and from popular destinations throughout Costa Rica (one-way ₡14,527-24,987/US$25-43). Buses run once or twice daily between **San José** and **Arenal, Conchal, Golfo Papagayo, Jacó, Manuel Antonio, Monteverde, Playa Hermosa, Playa Tamarindo, Puerto Viejo de Talamanca, Rincón,** and **Sámara.** Most leave daily 7:30-10:30am. AmEx/D/MC/V.

Car Rental: Prices range from ₡11,622/US$20 (for a small manual sedan) to ₡61,015/US$105 (for a 4x4) per day. Avis and Economy tend to offer some of the lowest rates. Minimum rental age is 21, although a few companies require drivers to be at least 23 or 25. Some companies will rent to those 18-21 with double or triple the deposit. A passport, valid driver's license, and major credit card are required; International Driver's Permits are not necessary for rentals less than 3 months. Online reservations available with the following companies:

Avis (☎2232 9922; www.avis.co.cr), at the Hotel Corobicí, north of the Parque La Sabana on C. 42, and at the airport (☎2442 1321). Minimum rental of 48hr. Minimum age 23.

Budget, Paseo Colón, C. 28/30 (☎2255 4240; www.budget.co.cr), and at the airport (☎2440 4412). Open M-Sa 7am-6pm, Su 7am-4pm; airport office open daily 6am-10pm. 21+. Offers combination packages with specific hotels. Rents to ages 18-21 for surcharge.

Economy (☎2299 2000; www.economyrentacar.com), in Sabana Nte. and at the airport (☎2442 8100). Open daily 7am-10pm, airport office open 5am-2am. Rents to ages 18-21 for surcharge.

Europcar, Paseo Colón, C. 36/38 (☎2257 1158; www.europcar.co.cr), and at the airport (☎2440 9990). Open daily 8am-6pm; airport office open daily 5am-midnight. Surcharge 5-6am and 10pm-midnight.

Hertz, Paseo Colón, C. 38 (☎2221 1818; www.hertz.com). Open M-F 7am-6pm, Sa-Su 7am-5pm. 25+.

National Car Rental, Av. 7, C. 36 and (☎ 2242 7878, toll-free from US +1 800-227-7368; www. natcar.com), at the airport (☎2440 0085). Also at the Hotel Irazu and Hotel Real Intercontinental in San José. Main office open daily 7:30am-6pm; airport 6am-10pm. 21+.

🔢 PRACTICAL INFORMATION

TOURIST AND FINANCIAL SERVICES

Tourist Offices: Instituto Costarricense de Turismo (☎2299 5800, from US or Costa Rica 1-866-COSTARICA/267-8274). Offices located at Av. Central/2, C. 5 (☎2222 1090; open M-F 9am-1pm and 2-5pm), next to El Museo del Oro, and Av. Central/1, C. 5, 2nd fl. (☎2257 8064; open M-F 8:30am-5:30pm). Free country and city maps, intracity bus schedules, and brochures. Another office in the post office (Oficina de Correos). **OTEC Viajes,** an office of **STA Travel,** Av. 1/3, C. 3 (☎2256 0633, www.otecviajes.com), can help you makes changes to your STA ticket, but cannot book new ones. ISIC card available for purchase. Open M-F 8am-6pm, Sa 9am-1pm.

Tours:

Costa Rica Expeditions, Av. 3, C. Central/2 (☎2257 0766 or 2222 0333; www.costaricaexpeditions.com), 1 block east of the post office. Tours throughout the country in collaboration with other companies. Class III and IV whitewater rafting on the Río Pacuare ¢86,584 (US$149) per person. 2-day rafting trip ¢165,614 (US$285). 10% student discount. English spoken. Open daily 8am-5pm. AmEx/D/MC/V.

Costa Rica Nature Escape, Av. Central/1, C. 5, 2nd fl. (☎2257 8064, 24hr. line 8381 7178; www. crnature.com). Student rates for all sorts of adventure, relaxation, and ecotourism packages. One-day Tortuguero tour ¢79,030 (US$136), students ¢74,380 (US$128). Class III white-water rafting on the Río Reventazón or Río Sarapiquí ¢43,582 (US$75), students ¢40,677 (US$70). Class IV white-water rafting on the Río Pacuare from ¢57,529 (US$99), students from ¢48,812 (US$84). Open M-F 8:30am-5:30pm. Cash only for student discounts. MC/V.

Ecole Travel, Av. Central, C. 5/7 (☎2223 2240; www.ecoletravel.com), inside Edificio Plaza de la Cultura, 2nd fl. A reputable and relatively inexpensive tour company. Tours to Tortuguero (2 days from ¢121,450 (US$209), 3 days from ¢167,937 (US$289), Volcán Arenal and Monteverde (4 days from ¢188,857/US$325). Online booking available. Open M-F 8am-5pm, Sa 9am-1pm.

Ecoscape Nature Tours (☎2297 0664, US and Canada +1 866-887-2764; www.ecoscapetours. com). The Highlights Tour for travelers short on time (¢49,393/US$85). The 1-day tour involves visits to Volcán Poás and its surrounding cloud forest, La Paz, San Fernando Waterfalls, Selva Verde Rainforest Lodge, a boat ride on the Río Sarapiquí, and a drive through Braulio Carillo National Park. A 2-day tour is available as well (¢122,030/US$210, with rafting ¢139,464/US$240).

Embassies: See **Essentials,** p. 433.

Currency Exchange and Banks: There are dozens of banks all over San José; nearly all of them have Cirrus/Plus/V **24hr. ATMs,** sometimes labeled "ATH." All require photo ID to exchange currency, and most require passport and charge 1% commission to cash travelers' checks. Listed below are the main offices.

Banco Central, Av. Central/1, C. 2/4 (☎2243 3333). Open M-F 9:20am-4pm.

Banco de Costa Rica, Av. Central/2, C. 4/6 (☎2287 9000). Open M-F 8:30am-6pm.

Banco Nacional, Av. 1/3, C. 4 (☎2212 2000). Open M-F 10:45am-3:45pm. **ATM** daily 5am-10pm.

Banco de San José, Av. 3/5, C. Central (☎2295 9797). Open M-F 8am-7pm.

BANCO B.C.T., Av. Central/1, C. Central (☎2212 8000). Open M-F 8:15am-5pm.

Banco Popular, Av. 2 and C. 1 (☎2202 2020). **ATM** daily 6am-11pm. Open M-F 8:15am-7pm, Sa 8:15-11:30am.

HSBC, Av. 1, C. Central (☎2287 1111). M-F 9am-6:30pm, Sa 9am-6pm. **24hr. ATM,** Av. 2, C. Central/2, next to KFC, across from the *parque central.*

American Express: Sabana Sur, Edeficio #1 (☎2242 8585). Passport required to cash traveler's checks. M-F 8am-6pm.

Western Union: Av. 2/4, C. 9 (☎+1 800-777-7777). International ID needed. **Currency exchange.** Open M-F 8:30am-5pm, Sa 9am-12:30pm.

Beyond Tourism: For complete listings, see p. 446.

WORK IT OUT. Crowded streets, small parks, and cars that don't stop for pedestrians make the San José center a terrible place for jogging. If you want to get some exercise, take the bus from Av. 2, C. 3 (¢140) to the huge Parque Metropolitano in La Sabana. While there, check out the new national soccer stadium, scheduled to be completed in late 2009.

LOCAL SERVICES

English-Language Bookstore: 7th Street Books, Av. Central/1, C. 7 (☎2256 8251). Sells a selection of new and used fiction and nonfiction English-language books. Foreign newspapers and maps available. New books ¢5000-10,000, used ¢900-2500. Open M-Sa 9am-6pm, Su 10am-5pm. AmEx/MC/V. **Librería Lehmann,** Av. Central, C. 1/3 (☎2522 4848). Large selection of reading and stationery supplies. Second-floor **Café Latino** is a delightful spot to read while sipping a cappuccino. Open M-F 8am-6:30pm, Sa 9am-5pm, Su 11am-4pm.

Pasajes Plazavenidos: Av. Central, C. 7/9, diagonally across from Fiesta Casino. Two levels of souvenir shops, ATMs, and fast food restaurants. Bathrooms located upstairs in the back (¢150).

Laundromat: Leavened Lavandería, Av. Central/1, C. 8 (☎2258 0621), to the left of the Gran Hotel Imperial. ¢4000-¢6000 per load. Open M-F 8am-6pm. **Sixaola,** Av. 2, C. 7/9 (☎2221 2111). ¢1000 per kg. Same-day service if in by 10am. Open M-F 8am-6pm, Sa 8am-noon. AmEx/MC/V.

Public Toilets: There are sparkling restrooms on Av. Central, C. 5, underground at the Plaza de la Cultura, next to the Museo de Oro. Some fast food restaurants along Av. Central will allow non-customers to use the *sanitarios,* but they have long lines. Librería Lehmann (above), 1 block north from the Museo de Oro on Av. Central, has a free bathroom in its cafe.

EMERGENCY AND COMMUNICATIONS

Emergency: ☎911.

Police: ☎911. To report a theft, contact the **Organismo de Investigación Judicial (OIJ),** Av. 6/8, C. 15/17 (☎2295 3643). To report a theft in person, proceed east on Av. 6, then turn right onto the walkway paved with square tiles. The entrance is on the right, at the ATM. Follow the signs to the Oficina Denuncias. Ask for an English speaker, if necessary. Open 24hr. During business hours, contact the **Crime Victims Assistance Office** (☎2295 3565), on the 1st floor of OIJ. Open M-F 7:30am-noon and 1-4:30pm. To report a sexual or life-threatening assault, call ☎2295 3493.

Pharmacy: Farmacia Fischel, Av. 3, C. 2 (☎2275 7659), near the center of town. Large selection of pharmaceutical and beauty products. ATM inside. Open daily 7am-8pm.

AmEx/D/MC/V. Smaller location at Av. 2, C. 5. (☎2233 0231). Open M-F 7:30am-7:30pm, Sa-Su 8am-7pm.

Medical Services: Hospital San Juan de Dios,Paseo Colón, C. 14/16 (☎2257 6282), in the building where Av. Central becomes Paseo Colón, after C. 14. **Clínica Bíblica,** Av. 14/16, C. 1 (☎2522 1000). English spoken. **24hr. emergency service** and pharmacy.

Telephones: Card and coin phones are all over town, especially along Av. Central. Most phones accept ¢5 and ¢10 coins. Most *ticos* buy phone cards from street vendors. Cards charge around ¢5 per min. for local calls and ¢100 per min. for calls to the US. **Radiográphica,** Av. 5, C. Central/1 (☎2287 0087; www.racsa.co.cr). Collect calls ¢1,743 (US$3). Also has AT&T Direct, MCI, and Sprint service. Sells prepaid Internet cards. Open M-F 7:30am-4:30pm, Sa 9am-1pm. Directory assistance ☎113.

PHONE HOME. The easiest way to make both domestic and international calls from a pay phone in Costa Rica is by using a **phone card.** Pick one up at the airport, pharmacy, or from a street vendor; scratch off the silver backing to find your phone card number; and follow the instructions on the back of the card. The cheapest way to reach home is to use a VoIP phone service, such as **Skype,** to place calls from either your computer or one of the many internet cafes around San José.

Internet Access: Internet cafes abound in San José. Here are 2 near the city center:

Café Digital, C. 7, Av. Central/1, 2nd fl. (☎2248 0701). New computers. Internet ¢400 per hr. Scanner, printing, and copies ¢100-200 per page. Skype and webcams available. Calls to the US ¢60 per min. Open M-Sa 8am-9pm, Su 9am-8pm.

Cybernético, on the corner of Av. Central and C. 4, 4th floor. Internet, video, faxing, scanning, and international internet calls. Internet ¢350 per hr. Copies ¢90. Open daily 7am-10pm.

Post Office: Av. 1/3, C. 2 (☎2223 9766), in the large green building. San José has no street mailboxes, so all mail must be sent from here. Open M-F 8am-6pm, Sa 7:30am-noon. Letter to the US ¢160. **Postal Code:** 1000.

▛ ACCOMMODATIONS

San José has hundreds of accommodations for every budget, from bare-bones hostels to Holiday Inns. That said, it's best to steer clear of the cheapest lodgings; paying the relatively "pricey" ¢5000-6800 (US$10-13) for a dormitory bed is worth it for clean, comfortable lodgings, relatively hot water, and a friendly atmosphere. Avoiding the city center is worth the inconvenience, as it offers an escape from noisy crowds. The accommodations listed below are divided into four categories by location. Staying east of the *parque central* is highly recommended as accommodations here tend to be safe and comfortable. Hotels south of the *parque central* are generally reasonably priced but are often louder because of their proximity to bars. Though they are often the cheapest options, try to avoid places north and west of the *parque*, as these tend to be the areas with the highest concentration of prostitutes, drunken bar patrons, and criminal activities. Pleasant alternatives to staying downtown are found in **San Pedro,** a 10min. bus ride from San José, and the suburb of **Escazú,** a 20min. bus ride, which offers splurge-worthy B&Bs.

BY LOCATION

EAST OF PARQUE CENTRAL

▨ **Hostel Pangea,** Av. 7, C. 3/5 (☎2221 1992; www.hostelpangea.com). Walls with dark jungle colors, metal accents, and a location near the city center create an urban feel. Plenty of social space makes this a great place to meet travelers. Free lockers with deposit, unlimited coffee, and international calling available. The staff is extremely helpful, especially in arranging tours. Potential downsides are the wristbands guests must wear at all times and the lack of outlets in the dorm rooms. Breakfast ¢2900 (US$5). Laundry ¢5220 (US$9). Free internet and Wi-Fi. 24hr. airport transport on the hostel's shuttle (¢10,440/US$18). Reception 24hr. Dorms ¢6960; private rooms ¢17,400. Additional location at Av. 11, C. 3/5 with fewer amenities, and a resort in Arenal. ❶

▨ **Costa Rica Backpackers Hostel,** Av. 6, C. 21/23 (☎2221 6191; www.costaricabackpackers.com). Packed with young, swimsuit-clad vacationers, this inexpensive backpacker magnet adds tropical flair to what feels like a spacious college dorm. Though it's a walk from the city center, the spotless rooms, shared hot-water bathrooms, night guard, communal kitchen, flat-screen TVs with cable, tourist info, free Wi-Fi, and swimming pool will make you want to stay forever. Guests often spend their mornings laying out under the sun or swinging in hammocks near the pool while munching on breakfast. Laundry ¢3,486 (US$6). Reception 24hr. Check-out 11am. Dorms ¢7004; doubles ¢16,342. ¢2,334 key deposit. MC/V, ¢11,673 minimum. ❶

▨ **Casa Ridgway,** Av. 6/8, C. 15 (☎2233 2693; www.amigosparalapaz.org), on a quiet cul-de-sac off C.15 between Av. 6 and 8. Owned by Quakers, Casa Ridgway offers the best value for peaceful, beautifully decorated accommodations. Each room is unique and often painted with a quote representative of the establishment's ideals. Guests have access to the communal kitchen, dining area, meeting room, and library. An active Quaker peace center is attached. Breakfast included. Public phone (☎2255 6399). Storage available. Laundry ¢2,905 (US$5). Internet. Reception 7am-10pm. Dorms ¢8171; singles ¢11,090; doubles ¢17,510. MC/V/US$/¢. ❷

Kabata Hostel, Av. 9/11, C. 7 (☎2255 0355; www.kabatahostel.com). Clean, quiet accommodations just blocks from some of San José's nicest parks. Shared hot-water baths, cable TV in the lobby, and free use of kitchen and dining room. Downstairs rooms have large windows and get the most sunlight. The owners are attentive to each guest's needs. Breakfast included. Free Wi-Fi. Free parking. Check-out 10am. Dorms ¢7004, group of 5 or more ¢6420; singles with shared bathroom ¢9338; doubles ¢18,676. Cash only. ❶

Tranquilo Backpackers, Av. 9/11, C. 7 (☎2223 3189 or 2222 2493; www.tranquilobackpackers.com). Bright rooms with hot showers, cable TVs, and access to a communal kitchen. Dorm rooms contain tall plain-wood bunk beds and ceiling windows. Open and sunny common room. Pancake breakfast included. Laundry ¢3000. Free internet. Reception 24hr. Dorms ¢7004; doubles ¢15,175. 2nd location in Santa Teresa/Mal País. Cash only. ❶

Casa León, Av. 6, C. 13/15 (☎2221 1651). Traveling east along Av. 2, turn right onto C. 13, and take a left to follow the train tracks; it's on the left. Casa León is a quiet and comfortable house, although the alley outside is littered with trash. Internet and communal kitchen. Laundry available. Up to 6 people per dorm. Dorms ¢8171; singles ¢14,007, with private bath ¢17,510; doubles ¢17,510-23,346. Cash only. ❷

SOUTH OF PARQUE CENTRAL

Hotel Boston, Av. 8, C. Central/2 (☎2221 0563). Spacious, mint-green rooms have sturdy beds, cable TV, and clean private baths with hot water. A good choice south of the city center and San José's thriving bar scene. Reception 24hr. Singles ¢5000; doubles ¢8000; triples ¢10,000. AmEx/DC/MC/V. ❶

NORTH OF PARQUE CENTRAL

Hotel Otoya Pensión, Av. 5, C 1 (☎2221 3925 or 2221 6017). Shares entrance with an internet cafe; on the 2nd floor. The Pensión is located only 1 or 2 blocks south of one of San José's less desirable neighborhoods. Minimal amenities such as a TVs in the room and fans. Backpackers congregate in a smoky sitting area inconveniently located behind the reception desk. Microwave, fridge, and coffeemaker available for use. Laundry service available. Reception 24hr. Check-out 1pm. All rooms with shared baths. Singles ¢5000; doubles ¢8000; triples ¢10,000. Cash only. ❶

WEST OF PARQUE CENTRAL

Hotel Nuevo Alameda, Av. Central/1, C. 12 (☎2233 3551; www.hotelnuevoalameda.com). Housed in a yellow building on C. 12, near the corner of Av. Central, near the *mercado central.* Clean rooms for 1-4 people with large windows, TVs, and private hot-water baths. Ask to be on the west side for a better view. Inner rooms are quieter. A volcano mural decorates the lobby. Wheelchair-accessible. Reception 24hr. Check-out noon. Singles ¢8,716 (US$15) per person. Cash only. ❷

Hotel El Descanso, Av. 4, C. 6 (☎2221 9941), entrance on C. 6. Safe, clean lodgings close to the *parque central.* Upstairs, the carved wooden doors, multicolored walls, and spacious hallways create a comfortable and private atmosphere. Some rooms are not well-maintained. Reception 24hr. Check-out noon. Singles ¢8755; doubles ¢17,510; triples ¢26,264. Cash only. ❷

SAN PEDRO

▧ **Toruma Youth Hostel (HI),** Av. Central, C. 29/31 (☎2234 8186), between San José and San Pedro. Take the San Pedro bus (¢190) from Av. Central, C. 9/11, and get off at Kentucky Fried Chicken; it's the yellow building across the street. Run by the same brothers who own Hostel Pangea, Toruma's offers an escape from the city. Be prepared to walk 1½km or to take a taxi to get to San Pedro or San José. Has a restaurant, pool, cable TV, and computers with free high-speed internet. Shared hot-water baths. Airport shuttle ¢10,505. Dorms ¢7004; singles and doubles ¢20,427. ❶

◖ FOOD

Black beans, white rice, and chicken remain staples, though American fast food joints have found their way into the mix. Vegetarian and international cuisines are popular, offering respite from the monotony of chain-dining and *comida típica*. Authentic *tico* fare like *casados* and *gallo pinto* are sold in *sodas* throughout the city. Most have cheap lunch and dinner specials (¢1400-2200). Take advantage of the various options and consider doing a little diner-hopping.

BY AREA

SAN JOSÉ

The *mercado central* sells cheaper meals that you can cook in your own hostel kitchen. For a more extensive selection, head to the local supermarkets like **Más X Menos,** Av. Central, C. 11/13 (open daily 6:30am-midnight; AmEx/MC/V) and **Automercado,** at Av. 3, C. 3, on the other side of town (☎2233 5511; open M-Sa 7am-8pm, Su 8am-3pm). Most of the higher-quality, more pleasant *sodas* and restaurants are in the vicinity of Av. Central.

▧ **Restaurante Grano de Oro,** Av. 2/4, C. 30 (☎2255 3322). An international dining experience at one of San José's best hotels. The pleasant meal begins with attentive service and ends just as sweetly with a chocolate truffle. Start with an arugula, spinach, and parmesan salad (₡3300), then continue with filet mignon (₡12,100), or for vegetarians, ravioli with spinach and goat cheese (₡6500). For an undeniably romantic setting, dine at dusk in the garden courtyard. Open daily 6am-10pm. AmEx/D/MC/V. ❸

◪ **Nuestra Tierra,** Av. 2, C. 15 (☎2258 6500). Candle-lit wooden tables decorated with newspapers from the early 1900s, *vaquero*-uniformed waiters, and meals served on palm leaves. Try the *gallo pinto* breakfast with delicious fried eggs (₡2500). For lunch or dinner, order the house cocktail (₡4900) and a steak (₡6800). There are no vegetarian options. Service is temperamental. Parking available across C. 15. Menu in Spanish and English. Open 24hr. AmEx/D/MC/V. ❸

Restaurant Tin Jo, Av. 6/8, C. 11. (☎2221 7605; www.tinjo.com). Broad selection of exotic Asian fusion cuisine, and an elegant ambience comprised of an indoor fountain and warm-colored tapestries on the walls. Vegetarian-friendly menu. Unique desserts include fried banana tempura with vanilla or coconut ice cream (₡2200) and lemon cheesecake with blackberry sauce. The waitstaff is friendly, attentive, and good-looking. Start out with satay (₡2800) or sushi (₡3300-5600). Curries and pad thai ₡4200-7800. Open M-Th 11:30am-3pm and 5:30-10pm, F-Sa 11:30am-3pm and 5:30-11pm, Su 11:30am-10pm. AmEx/D/MC/V. ❷

Shakti, Av. 8, C. 13 (☎2222 4475). This haven of healthy goodness serves only vegetarian dishes and white meat, a change from the typical fare of *gallo pinto* and fried meat. Frutas Shakti offers a light mix of fruit, yogurt, and granola (₡2200). *El Vampiro* (the vampire) combines oranges, sugar beets, and carrots (₡750). The avocado sandwich is delicious and comes with salad (₡1800). In keeping with its healthful mission, no alcohol is served. While waiting for your food, read up on the healthy and sanitary processes used to produce your meal. Various herbal supplements, breads, and cookies sold at the counter. *Especiál* (main dish, soup, salad, and drink) ₡2400. Open M-F 7:30am-7pm, Sa 7:30am-6pm. D/MC/V. ❶

Cafe Mundo (☎2233 6272). A romantic restaurant that won't break your bank. The Italian-fare is served by candlelight; the outside setting overlooks a small pond (look closely for the large fish). Pastas ₡2800-5500. Chicken dishes ₡4200-5000. Desserts include crepes with strawberries, flan, and tiramisu (₡1200-2200). Open M-Th 11am-10:30pm, F 11am-11:30pm, Sa 5-11:30pm. AmEx/D/MC/V. ❶

La Grand Ma, Av. 1, C. 1/3 (☎2221 3996). Packed with locals on their lunch breaks, La Grand Ma serves a wide variety of Costa Rican comfort foods. *Casados* with chicken, beef, and fried fish (₡2250) are popular, as is the selection of *almuerzos caribeñoes*, all of which come with rice and beans (₡3150-3650). Plate of the day with drink ₡2000. Open M-F 8am-5:30pm, Sa 9am-4pm. MC/V. ❶

Restaurant Vishnu Vegetariano, Av. 1, C. Central/1 (☎2256 6063). A variety of appetizing salads available (₡2100-3000). The *ensalada de frutas,* a tropical fruit salad with granola and ice cream or yogurt, is a favorite. Veggie burger combos (₡1700) and vegetarian pizza (₡2500). Don't leave without trying the yogurt smoothie *morir soñando* ("die dreaming"; ₡1400). Open M-Sa 7am-9pm, Su 9am-7pm. Other locations include Av. 4, C. 1 (next to the Banco Popular); Av. 8, C. 11/13; and Av. Central, C. 14. AmEx/MC/V. ❶

Soda El Parque, Av. 4/6, C. 2 (☎2258 3681). El Parque's round-the-clock hours draw suit-clad businessmen for lunch and late-night revelers just before dawn. Everyone comes for the same reason: cheap and tasty *comida típica*. The spacious seating area with large ceiling fans provides an escape from the heat or rain. Breakfast ₡700-3000. *Casados* ₡2500-7000. Sandwiches ₡1650-4200. Open 24hr. AmEx/MC/V. ❶

Jicaras del Campo (☎2520 1757). Take a taxi or the Escazú bus to the south side of La Sabana, 150m west from La Contrabría. Enjoy a gigantic selection of *casados* (₡2495) or go for one of the many chicken dishes (₡950). Spacious seating, arched windows, and music from a *marimba* add to the pleasant *tico* ambience. Beer ₡880. Open daily 1-10pm, buffet 1-3pm. AmEx/MC/V. ❶

Taquería La Moderna, C. 2, Av. 6/8 (☎2223 0513), near the corner of Av. 6. This tiny restaurant is easily missed—look for the line of benches with bright fruit tablecloths and colorful mural inside. Offers incredibly cheap eats, but the portions are just as small as the prices. Tacos ₡400. Hot dogs ₡450. *Casados* ₡1500. *Empanadas* ₡350. Open M-Sa 7am-9pm, Su 8am-7:30pm. ❶

SAN PEDRO

The heart of San José's student scene, San Pedro is full of inexpensive cafes and restaurants. From San José, catch a bus to San Pedro from Av. Central, C. 9/11 (10min., every 5-10min., ₡190), pass **Mall San Pedro**; get off when you see the outlet mall to your right. The main drag into San Pedro is **Avenida Central**. The street running perpendicular next to the outlet mall is **Calle Central**. Walk north down C. Central with the **Parque John F. Kennedy** to your left and the outlet mall behind you. The first street on your right leads to C. de la Amargura; a left on C. 3 leads to the University, and a right leads back down to Av. Central. This loop is packed with students all year.

▨ **Jazz Cafe** (☎2253 8933; www.jazzcafecostarica.com), 200m east of C. 3 on Av. Central. An upscale place with live performances every night and meals named after jazz singers and their songs. "Round Midnight" is the filet mignon (₡6300). The food is tasty, but it's the mixed drinks (₡1750-2750), like the Jazz Cocktail (a mix of rum and fruit juice), that really attract large late-night crowds. A different Costa Rican jazz or blues band performs every night. Cover ₡2500-3000. Open daily 6pm-2am. AmEx/MC/V. ❸

▨ **La Oliva Verde** (☎2280 2908), Av. Central, near OmniLife, 300m west of JFK Park. Fresh salads and wraps are made before your eyes in this Mediterranean sandwich shop. Try the Pita Oliva Verde (₡2500), with grilled vegetables, feta cheese, olives, and pesto sauce on soft pita bread. Salad ₡3375. Reduced calorie sauces and nutritional information on every meal. Fruit smoothies from ₡975. Shots of vitamins and minerals from ₡450. Open M-Sa 11am-7:30pm. AmEx/MC/V. ❷

Pizzería Il Pomodoro (☎2224 0966), 25m north of JFK Park on C. Central. The aroma of garlic drifts into the street, drawing those tired of rice and beans into this welcoming Italian eatery. Generous portions of crispy thin-crust pizzas (₡2200-4200) and pastas (₡2000-3500). Beer ₡950. Wine ₡1250. Open M and

ON THE MENU

COMPONENTS OF A CASADO

Although Costa Rica offers various cheap meals, the best for your stomach is the *casado*. Traditionally, wives would prepare this traditional *campesino* dish for their husbands to take to the fields. Today, the dish is enjoyed all over Costa Rica, in basic *sodas* and gourmet restaurants. Most often a lunch option, *casados* are also filling enough for dinner. They include a combination of the following:

Meat: The most common type used is steak, although chicken and fish are almost always available as substitutes. A *casado mexicano* features spicy steak or pulled pork. Vegetarians can ask for any casado "sin carne."

Rice and Beans: These Costa Rican staples—black or red beans and fried or steamed white rice—are sometimes mixed together as *gallo pinto*, or served separately. If you're lucky, your rice and beans may be spiced up with some sautéed onions or scallions.

Fried Plantains: Known as *plátano maduro* or *plátano dorado*, this delicious side is perhaps the best part of the casado. Sometimes served whole, sometimes served sliced, *plátano maduro* is always delicious.

Salad: Loosely interpreted, the salad can be anything—a sliced cole slaw-like concoction, or an elaborate array of local produce dressed in zesty lemon sauce.

W-Su 11:30am-11pm. Only pastas and salads are available between 2:30pm and 6pm. AmEx/D/MC/V. ❶

Restaurante Vegetariano (☎2224 1163), 150m north of JFK Park on C. Central. Identifiable only by a worn sign over the entrance, this small restaurant offers a surprisingly comprehensive selection of healthy vegetarian meals. Try one of the 8 different vegetable soups on the menu (from ₡1550) or go for the house special *"Plato Fuerte,"* with brown rice, salad, and avocados (₡2200). MC/V. ❶

◙ SIGHTS

▓TEATRO NACIONAL. Small but exquisite, the National Theater is a must-see. In 1897, the construction of the theater was inspired (and funded) by Costa Rican citizens clamoring for more cultural venues. Because it was originally a product of their interest and money, *ticos* take a great deal of pride in this site. The theater is graced with sculpted banisters overlaid in 22½-carat gold, marble floors, and frescoes. Designed by sculptor Pitro Bulgarelli, statues representing Dance, Music, and Fame adorn its facade. The lobby features Costa Rica's most famous mural, a collage of the crops that brought the country its prosperity—bananas and coffee. A grand staircase inspired by the Paris Opera ascends toward bright overhead reliefs. Performances include ballet, drama, classical music, and opera. *(Av. 2, C. 3, southwest corner of the Plaza de la Cultura. ☎ 2258 5135; www.teatronacional.go.cr. Open M-Sa 9am-4pm. 30min. tours available in English or Spanish on the hr., except at noon; ₡2909 (US$5). Ask about performances (often 3 per week) and ticket prices at the ticket window.)*

MUSEO NACIONAL. This museum offers an overview of Costa Rican history and early Costa Rican life. The building has been transformed from a military headquarters (the Cuarto Bellarista) into the home of a collection of artifacts. Though the front is still riddled with bullet-marks from the 1948 Revolution, the interior is full of pre-Columbian art, along with exhibits on Costa Rican history, archaeology, and geology. Don't miss the view of San José from the fort's highest point, and the butterfly garden on the lowest level. *(Av. Central/2, C. 17. ☎2257 1433 or 2256 4139. Open M-Sa 8:30am-5pm, Su 9am-4:30pm. ₡2325/US$4, students ₡1,162/US$2.)*

MUSEO DE ORO. Founded in 1950 by the Central Bank of Costa Rica, the Museo de Oro houses a three-part exploration of Costa Rican culture underneath the Plaza de Cultura. The museum's most impressive exhibit is its enormous collection of pre-Columbian gold from AD 500. Another exhibit houses 16th-century bills, coins, and *boletos de café* (coffee tokens), while the final hall displays temporary arts and archaeological exhibits. *(Av. Central, C. 5. ☎2243 4216. Open daily 9am-5pm. ₡5130, students ₡2850.)*

MUSEO DE JADE. Costa Rica's Social Security building is an unlikely location for, reportedly, the world's largest collection of American jade. The emerald-colored mineral was of particular importance to Costa Rica's indigenous groups, who used it for jewelry and talismans. The museum also has a small collection of tools and weapons dating back to pre-Columbian times. The exhibits have English- and Spanish-language explanations; ask the security guards for more in depth information. *(Av. 7, C. 9/1. ☎2287 6034. Open M-F 8:30am-3pm, Sa 9am-1pm. ₡1,162/US$2. MC/V.)*

PARQUE DE ESPAÑA AND PARQUE MORAZÁN. Complete with well-manicured lawns, benches, and a majestic dome that appears to have been taken straight from a Shakespearean play, these neighboring parks are a tranquil place to rest aching feet. Sudden downpours draw crowds of students, couples, and businessmen looking to stay dry under Morazán's dome. You might even get to see some locals practicing their juggling skills. (Av. 3/7, C. 5/13. Free.)

MUSEO DE ARTE COSTARRICENSE. Housed in a terminal of San José's old airport, this small museum is filled with temporary modern art exhibitions and a permanent collection of Costa Rican nationalist art from the 19th and 20th centuries. Those with time on their hands can explore the walls of the Salón Dorado, carved and painted to look like gold, with the history of Costa Rica depicted across all four sides. Check out the sculpture garden behind the museum. For a better view of the stone courtyard and Parque La Sabana, go out on the terrace. (Paseo Colón, C. 42, on the eastern edge of Parque La Sabana. ☎ 2222 7155; www.musarco.go.cr. Open M-F 9am-5pm, Sa-Su 10am-4pm. M-Sa ¢2909/US$5, students ¢1,743/US$3; Su free.)

SNEAK PEAK. The **Centro Nacional** houses the national Companies of Dance and Theater. Even if there are no performances scheduled during your visit, you will likely see the dancers, actors, or gymnasts practicing if you quietly and unobtrusively enter the building from the **Parque de España.**

CENTRO NACIONAL DE ARTE Y CULTURA. This impressive fortress of the arts, between Parque de España and the National Library, offers cultural events in some of Costa Rica's oldest edifices. These buildings that have survived everything from earthquakes to civil unrest. Two active theaters share space with the Museo de Arte y Diseño Contemporaneo, which hosts rotating exhibits by contemporary artists in a warehouse-like space. Stop by to see if a performance is running; schedules are on the lowest level near the press office and at the airport. (Av. 3, C. 15/17. Enter from the southeast corner for the museum and the west side for performances. ☎ 2257 7202; www.mad.ac.cr. Open M-F 10:30am-5:30pm. Tu-Su ¢1,162/US$2, students ¢300, M free. Performance prices vary.)

PARQUE ZOOLÓGICO Y JARDÍN BOTÁNICO NACIONAL SIMÓN BOLIVAR. Little more than a run-down, packaged version of the natural splendor that has made Costa Rica famous, this *parque* features spectacular creatures in cramped cages. See jaguars, squirrel monkeys, agoutis, reptiles, and tapirs. Few of the displays are in English. Consider going before you set out into the country's rainforests to know what you should be aware of in the natural setting. (Av. 11, C. 7, 300m north and 175m northwest of Parque Morazán in Barrio Amón. ☎ 2256 0012. Open daily 9am-4:30pm. ¢1500, ages 3-6 ¢1000, under 3 free.)

GOOD TIMES, GOOD CONSCIENCE. Located 2km west of Hospital Mexico in La Uruca, San José, Parque Nacional de Diversiones is the only amusement park in the world that gives all of its profits to charity. The park started as a fair to raise funds for a Children's Hospital in 1964. Built after a polio epidemic that hit Costa Rica when the country had few youth medical facilities, the current hospital still runs on funding from the park. These days, its *diversiones* are more diverse than ever, including roller coasters, water rides, a flight simulator, and a theater. (Free bus to the park at Av. Central/2, C. 8. ☎ 2242 9200; www.parquediversiones.com. Open F-Su 9am-7pm. ¢5400.)

⌐ SHOPPING

San José's size and high concentration of tourists make buying everything from basic necessities to souvenirs easier—and sometimes cheaper—than in other Costa Rican towns. You'll find the best selection of Costa Rican art, woodwork, jewelry, clothing, hammocks, and other souvenirs in a strip of vendors on Av. Central/2, C. 13/15 near the **Plaza de la Democracia.** (Most vendors open M-Sa 8am-6pm, some open Su.) Another option is **La Casona,** C. Central, Av. Central/1, where several souvenir stores are clustered under one roof. (Most stores open daily M-Sa 9:30am-6:30pm, some open Su.) Serious art collectors should check out San José's wonderful art galleries, many along Av. 1 between C. 5 and 13. **Las Arcadas,** with an entrance on C. 3 between Av. Central/2, and on Av. 2 between C. 3/5, houses clothing stores, beauty salons, an ICT office, and internet/laundry facilities in a two-story plaza. For a standard Western selection of clothing and sportswear (not to mention food courts), take a San Pedro-bound bus to **Mall San Pedro** or the **Outlet Mall.** (Both open daily 10am-8pm.)

🏛 **Galería Namu,** Av. 7, C. 5/7 (☎2256 3412; www.galerianamu.com). For authentic crafts, visit the only fair-trade gallery in Costa Rica. Namu purchases works from the country's 8 indigenous groups and from folk artists. Check out the carved wood masks (from ¢70,038), colorful tiles (¢11,673), and paintings (¢81,711). Each piece comes with a page on its origins. Ships internationally. Open M-Sa 9am-6:30pm, Su 1:15-4:30pm. MC/V.

♫ ENTERTAINMENT

A number of 24hr. casinos have opened in San José, many in hotels on Av. 1 near C. 5. Movie theaters throughout San José show US releases with Spanish subtitles.

Fiesta Casino, Av. Central, C. 7/9. Tables and slots if you want to try your luck. You must be 18 or older to gamble.

Cine Variedades, Av. Central/1, C. 5 (☎2222 6108), downtown. M-Tu and Th-Su ¢1000, W ¢500. MC/V.

Sala Garbo (☎2223 1960) and **Teatro Laurence Olivier** (☎2222 1034), both on Av. 2, C. 28, 100m south of the Paseo Colón Pizza Hut. Show a varied selection of older films from Latin and North America (¢2000).

Multicines San Pedro (☎2280 0490), on the 3rd floor of San Pedro Mall. Modern theaters with digital sound (¢1800, children ¢1500). MC/V.

Salón de Patines Music, 200m west of JFK Park in San Pedro. Rollerskate (¢2000 with rental skates) and listen to pop music. Skating for kids and parents Sa-Su 10am-12:30pm. Open daily 7-10pm.

♠ NIGHTLIFE

San Pedro pulses with life at night: the dances are *salsa* and *merengue,* and the drinks are *cervezas* and *guaro* cocktails. The scenes range from karaoke bars full of *ticos* belting Latin tunes, to American sports bars packed with tourists playing pool and swapping gringo wit. **Calle de la Amargura** is always hopping and is the best place to meet young *ticos.* Most establishments have ¢1000-1500 covers (sometimes more for men), though they are somewhat negotiable and typically include drinks. Dress is casual; a T-shirt is fine in San Pedro bars, but you might want to throw on some dressier threads to go to the El Pueblo and

San José clubs. It's a good idea to bring your ISIC card or passport out with you because most clubs and bars will require a valid ID for entrance.

CENTRO COMERCIAL EL PUEBLO

A 15min. ride north of San José center, El Pueblo is the place to find wild nights of dancing and drinking. The gift shops, bars, and dance clubs usually pick up after 11pm. El Pueblo is easily accessible by taxi (¢800-1200). Since the complex is saturated with tourists, petty crime is not uncommon. Beware of thieves who target drunken revelers as they exit the complex. Likewise, be wary of cab drivers who charge too much for pickup inside the complex. Walk out to the road for a taxi, but be cautious.

Ebony 56 (☎2223 2195), on your right in the main parking lot. This sleek, ultra-modern club attracts a mix of travelers and locals, mostly in their 20s. Brave revelers dance on a silver stage while the rest watch from space-age couches made of leather and metal piping. Music ranges from reggae and rave to *salsa* and pop, depending on the night and mood. Th Ladies' night. Beer ¢800. Mixed drinks ¢1500. Cover ¢1000-2000. Open daily 6pm-6am.

Twister Club (☎2222 5746), toward the back and on the left of El Pueblo. Attracts a late-20s crowd that gets hot and heavy on the dance floor. Crowds form early, but house beats pumping loud enough to hear from the end of the line keep bodies moving. Gringos are well-accepted and may be pleased with the American music selection. Beer ¢800. Mixed drinks ¢1000-1500. Open daily 6:30pm-3am.

Bongo's (☎2222 5746), around the corner from its sister club, Twister. A mixed-age crowd gathers to socialize and dance to house music. Bongo's offers TVs and foosball tables; more seating but less dancing than Twister. Beer ¢800. Mixed drinks ¢2000. Cover ¢1000-2000. Open daily 5pm-4am.

NEAR THE CITY CENTER

San José's center is crawling with bars and clubs, many of them hidden between *sodas* and shops. Bars and clubs often remain shuttered during the day, only to emerge at night with lit signs, loud music, and raucous laughter. Many host a wide range of ages chatting over drinks, while others blast popular Latin hits for expert dancers; most places have a little bit of both.

Salsa 54, Av. 1/3, C. 3 (☎2223 3814). A meeting place for seasoned dance veterans. The soundtrack is a hodgepodge of love songs, 60s hits, *salsa*, and reggae. Many of the dancers are experts, but don't let that stop you from joining them on the dance floor. Beer ¢800. Mixed drinks ¢1200-1800. Cover around ¢1500. Open M-Sa 7pm-late, Su 2-9pm.

Salidas Orbital 2000, Av. 1/3, C. 3 (☎2233 3814), above Salsa 54. A younger crowd of 20-somethings grooves to pop, tango, *salsa*, and *merengue* on 3 small stages amid a sea of plush red cocktail tables. Male and female models wearing almost nothing dance in the Model Revue. Karaoke depending on the mood. Cover ¢1500. Beer ¢800. Mixed drinks ¢1200-1800. Open F-Sa 7pm-late.

El Cuartel de la Boca del Monte, Av. 1, C. 21/23 (☎2221 0327). Restaurant by day and party spot by night. A good place for large groups—VIP area and lots of seating. Features local bands on Monday and on several other weekends. Rock on Sa. M women no cover; cover ¢2000 for live music. Beer ¢800. Mixed drinks ¢1500. Open daily 11:30am-3pm and 6pm-3am.

Acapulco, Av. Central, C. 17/19 (☎2221 2586), 1 block east of the northeast corner of the Museo Nacional. A strong local following gathers early for drinks. Later in the night on weekends, flashing lights and thumping music attract those hoping to show off their *salsa* and *merengue* skills. Sandwiches ¢900-1300. Entrees ¢800-1800. Beer ¢650. No cover. Open M-Sa 11am-1am.

SAN PEDRO

Though the enormous bar scene near the University in San Pedro is student-oriented, it's casual and diverse enough to accommodate just about anyone. People and music overflow into the streets, making the area relatively safe, though partiers should still take precautions. C. 3, north of Av. Central, known as **Calle de la Amargura,** is the heart of the college scene. There are fewer tourists, making it easier to meet outgoing *tico* students. All bars on C. de la Amargura may close early on weeknights, depending on turnout.

Caccio's. Contains a breezy outdoor patio. Beer ¢800. No cover. Open M-Sa 11am-1am.

Bar Tavarúa. A surf and skate bar that opens up a back room for dancing on crowded nights. Beer ¢650. Open M-Sa 11am-2am.

Terra U. A large student hangout often blasting reggaeton. Beer ¢650. Pitchers ¢1550 before 6:15pm, ¢2000 after. Open daily 10:30am-2am. AmEx/MC/V.

⚡ OUTDOOR ACTIVITES

Museums and city parks aren't your style? Costa Rica is the place for you. Even from the largest city, there are plenty of opportunities for outdoor adventure.

Tropical Bungee (☎2248 2212 or 2221 4944; www.bungee.co.cr). Jumps offered at the 80m Colorado River Bridge. 1st jump ¢37,872, 2nd jump ¢17,479. Join the "addict club" by making 2 jumps in 1 day, and your third is only ¢17,479. T-shirt and video included. Leads 1-day rappelling trips (US$65). Transportation included. Discounts for groups. AmEx/D/MC/V.

Ríos Tropicales (☎2233 6455; www.riostropicales.com). Introductory and advanced kayaking and rafting trips on rivers across Costa Rica. One-day rafting on the Reventazón River ¢43,700. Two days kayaking in Tortuguero ¢262,192. Mountain biking ¢43,700. All meals included. AmEx/D/MC/V.

Aventuras Naturales, Av. 5, C. 33/35 (☎2225 3939; www.pacuarelodge.com). Offers rafting, hiking, biking, and canopy tours. One-day Pacuare River trip ¢55,351; 2-day ¢168,385. Canopy tour can be added to multiple-day Pacuare trips for ¢23,306. English spoken. Open daily 8am-8pm. AmEx/D/MC/V.

CENTRAL VALLEY

The Central Valley, or *Meseta Central*, makes up the heart of Costa Rica, composing its demographic as well as geographic center. Cordoned off by the two great volcanic ranges that divide the country, this valley is home to four of the nation's five largest cities and almost two-thirds of the entire *tico* population. But the cities and coffee fields cover up the explosive truth: two of the region's towering volcanoes (Irazú and Poás) are still active and have caused the valley's residents heartache on multiple occasions. And yet, residual volcanic ash has secured much of the region's livelihood, blessing these temperate plains and rolling hills with enough fertile soil to cultivate crops and rich coffee.

Many travelers skip over the landlocked Central Valley and rush to more-touristed vacation spots on either coast, but those with a few extra days will not regret exploring Costa Rica's interior. Even the largest cities, like San José and Alajuela, are only a short drive from more-picturesque, agricultural communities like Sarchí and Grecia, as well as national parks and pre-Columbian ruins. Visitors can experience urban conveniences while keeping massive volcanoes, butterfly gardens, and the country's wildest rafting a daytrip away.

ALAJUELA

Alajuela, 3km from the international airport and 17km northwest of San José, is perhaps the cleanest and calmest of Costa Rica's cities. Small restaurants and B&Bs anchor the city's family-oriented environment. The town is a good base for pleasant wildlife excursions. For those who simply want to stay put and soak up the scenery, Alajuela's *parque central*, which spreads out in front of a colonial red-domed cathedral, is a good place to sit and relax. As is generally the case, the area closest to the *parque central* is the safest. Tourists should avoid wandering too far afield at night. Still, Alajuela maintains a sunny character with inviting people, and is a perfect final destination before a flight out of the country.

TRANSPORTATION

Buses: From the **TUASA station,** Av. Central/1, C. 8 (☎2442 6900), 350m west of the southwest corner of the *parque central,* buses go to **San José** (45min., every 5min. 4am-10pm, ¢370) and **Volcán Poás** (1hr.; M-Sa 9:15am, return 2:30pm; ¢1750 round-trip). Buses to **Sarchí** depart 200m west of the *mercado central* (1hr.; M-Sa every 25-30min. 4:55am-10:15pm, Su every 25min. 5:15am-10:15pm; ¢605).

Taxis: A ride to or from the airport should cost no more than ¢1500.

ORIENTATION AND PRACTICAL INFORMATION

Arriving at the TUASA bus station, turn right onto the *avenida* at the top of the station, then walk 350m until you reach the **parque central,** boxed in by **Avenida Central/Avenida 1** and **Calle Central/Calle 2.** Look for the white **cathedral** on the far end and a white dome-like shelter over a stage. The streets of Alajuela form the standard Costa Rican grid, but street signs are rare, so it's best to count the blocks or use landmarks, as locals do.

Banks: Banco Nacional, Av. Central/1, C. 2 (☎2440 9200). Open M-F 8:30am-3:45pm. **Scotiabank,** Av. 1/3, C. 2 (☎2441 1131). Open M-F 8:30am-6pm. Both have MC/V

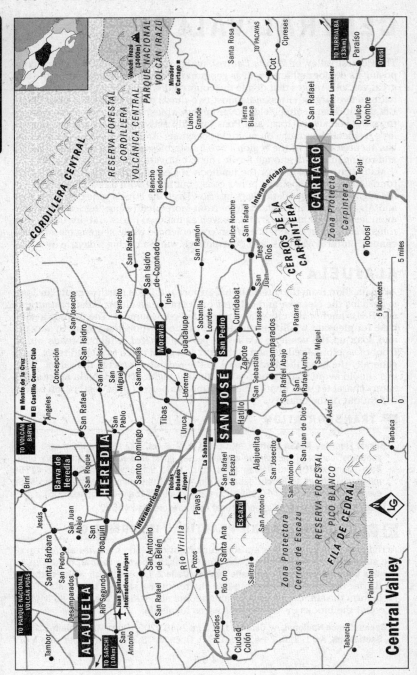

Central Valley

ATMs open 5am-10pm. Scotiabank changes Citibank and V traveler's checks; 1% commission. **Bac San José,** Av. 3, C. Central/1 (☎2443 4380), changes AmEx Travelers Cheques for a 1% commission. Open M-F 9am-7pm, Sa 9am-1pm. There is a **BCAC/Bancrédito 24hr. ATM** on Av. Central/2, C. 2, and **24hr. ATMs** inside both Palí and MegaSuper. Open M-F 10am-6:30pm, Sa 9am-5pm. **Western Union** (☎2442 6392) is inside Palí. Open M-Sa 8:30am-1pm and 2-7pm, Su 10am-1:30pm and 2-5pm.

Bookstore: Goodlight Books, Av. 3, C. 3/5 (☎2430 4083; www.goodlightbooks.com). Enjoy *espresso* (¢400) or a dessert (¢350-500) while browsing the selection of new and used English-language books and maps. Internet ¢500 per hr. Free map of the city. Open daily 9am-6pm. **Libros Chiloé,** Av. 5, C. 2/4 (☎2242 7419), across from Hotel Cortez Azul. Buys and sells used books (¢500-3000). Open M-Sa 8:30am-6pm.

Laundry: La Batea, Av. 5/7, C.4 (☎2440 2691). Open M-F 7am-5pm, Sa 7am-4pm. AmEx/D/MC/V.

Public toilets: At the *mercado central*. ¢100.

Police: (☎2440 8889, or 911), 1 block north and 4 blocks east of the *parque's* northeast corner, around the corner from the fire station. Some English spoken. Open M-F 9am-5pm. Emergencies 24hr.

Pharmacy: Farmacia Santa Lucia, Av. Central/2, C. 1 (☎2440 0404). Open M-F 8am-8pm, Sa 9am-6pm. MC/V.

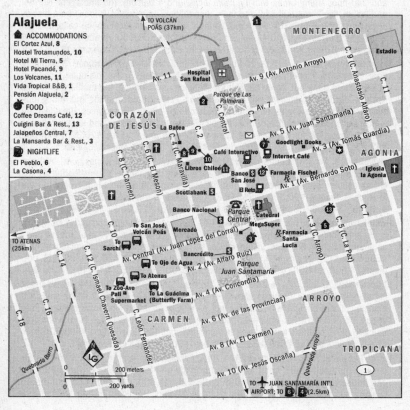

Alajuela

🏠 **ACCOMMODATIONS**
El Cortez Azul, **8**
Hostel Trotamundos, **10**
Hotel Mi Tierra, **5**
Hotel Pacandé, **9**
Los Volcanes, **11**
Vida Tropical B&B, **1**
Pensión Alajuela, **2**

🍴 **FOOD**
Coffee Dreams Café, **12**
Cuigini Bar & Rest., **13**
Jalapeños Central, **7**
La Mansarda Bar & Rest., **3**

🎵 **NIGHTLIFE**
El Pueblo, **6**
La Casona, **4**

Hospital: Av. 9, C. Central/1 (☎2436 1001), 5 blocks north of the northeast corner of the *parque*, facing Parque de las Palmeras. Open 24hr.

Telephones: Both coin- and card-operated phones are available around the *parque.*

Internet Access: El Reto, Av. 1, C. Central/1 (www.elretocr.com). New computers with Skype and headsets. Internet ¢250 per 30min., ¢350 per hr. Calls to the US ¢50 per min. M-Sa 8am-10pm, Su 10am-7pm. **Conexion,** Av. 3/5, C. 1. Computers with headsets as well as private international calling booths with fans. Internet ¢350 per hr. Calls to the US ¢60 per min. Open daily 7am-7pm. AmEx/D/MC/V. **Café Interactivo,** Av. 3, C. Central/1 (☎2431 1984), is small with older computers. Internet ¢250 per 30min., ¢350 per hr. Open M-Sa 9am-9pm.

Post Office: Av. 5, C. 1 (☎2443 2653), 2 blocks north and 1 block east of the northeast corner of the *parque.* Open M-F 8am-5:30pm, Sa 7:30am-noon. **Postal Code:** 2101. MC/V.

ACCOMMODATIONS

Vida Tropical B&B (☎2443 9576; www.vidatropical.com), 100m east and 300m north of the hospital, across from the Academia de Natación. Decorated in bright tropical colors, this comfortable B&B feels just like home. Five cozy rooms share 2 beautiful baths; 1 room at the back of the garden has a private bath. Guests enjoy pleasant 1st- and 2nd-floor sitting areas with TV, hammocks, and a balcony. The managers, Norman and Isabel, live in the building, and their hospitality is unmatched. Choose from breads, eggs, and tropical fruits for breakfast. Laundry ¢1740. Free local phone calls, internet, and Wi-Fi. Singles ¢17,400; doubles ¢26,100; triples ¢31,900; quads ¢37,700. Children under 12 free. Ask about reduced rates for extended stays. Cash only. ❸

Hotel Mi Tierra, Av. 2, C. 3/5 (☎2441 1974 or 4022; www.hotelmitierra.net). A swimming pool, communal kitchen, and cozy sitting room with cable TV make this hotel a comfortable place to hang out. When he isn't landscaping and painting, the multilingual owner, Roberto, provides a wealth of info about the town. Personalized kayaking and rafting tours available, often at a cheaper price than those offered by large companies. Breakfast and airport transportation included. Wi-Fi in common area. Free parking and luggage storage. Package discounts for families and students. Singles and doubles ¢20,300, with bath ¢23,200; triples ¢23,200/29,000; quads ¢29,000/31,900. AmEx/MC/V. ❸

Los Volcanes, Av. 3, C. Central/2 (☎2441 0525; www.hotellosvolcanes.com). Welcoming fountains and cream-colored walls accentuate the subtle sophistication of this classy accommodation. Breakfast and airport transportation included. Free Wi-Fi and local calls. Singles ¢20,300 (US$35), with hot-water bath ¢26,680 (US$46); doubles ¢26,680/34,800 (US$46/60); triples ¢34,800/42,920 (US$60/74). MC/V. ❸

Hostel Trotamundos, Av. 5, C. 2/4 (☎2430 5832; www.hosteltrotamundos.com). This backpacker hangout is family-owned and offers free internet, cable TV in all rooms, and a communal kitchen. Breakfast included. Free baggage storage and tour information. Dorms ¢6960 (US$12); singles ¢14,500 (US$25), with hot-water bath ¢20,300 (US$35); doubles ¢14,500/20,300 (US$25/35); triples ¢23,200/26,100 (US$40/45). MC/V. ❷

El Cortez Azul, Av. 5, C. 2/4 (☎2443 6145). The common area is filled with the English-speaking manager's artwork. Common kitchen, small backyard, clean rooms, 2 sitting areas with modern couches and cable TV. Services include whitewater rafting trips, tours to Volcán Poás, Volcán Arenal, the La Paz Waterfalls, and the area around Alajuela. Wi-Fi in common area. Tour info at his brother's website, www.hotelmitierra.com. Single-sex dorms ¢5800 (US$10); singles and doubles ¢14,500 (US$25), with bath ¢20,300 (US$35). AmEx/MC/V. ❶

Hotel Pacandé, Av. 5, C. 2/4 (☎2443 8481; www.hotelpacande.com). A spiral staircase at the back of this hotel leads to a brightly painted loft (with private bath) that can house up to 4 people (US$40-60/¢23,200-34,800, depending on group size). Outside common area is surrounded by flower bushes. Breakfast of fruit and coffee is

CENTRAL VALLEY

served on the patio. All rooms have mirrors and towels. Free internet, local calls, and transportation from the airport. Singles and doubles ¢16,240 (US$28), with bath ¢23,200 (US$40). Their second location, Pacandé Villa, is located 2.5km north of town toward Volcan Poás. AmEx/MC/V. ❷

Hotel 1915, Av. 5/7, C. 2 (☎2441 0495 or 2440 7163; www.1915hotel.com). Formerly the home of the owner (and of her parents and grandparents before her), 1915 was recently converted into a hotel and renovated. Fancy sitting area and pleasant rooms. Breakfast (think French toast) included. All rooms have A/C; some have fridge, TV, and balcony. Café connected to reception. Free internet. Singles ¢26,100-37,770 (US$45-65); doubles ¢31,900-49,300 (US$55-85); triples ¢37,700-58,000 (US$65-100). Apartment with kitchen available just down the block ¢58,000-69,600 (US$100-120). 16% service charge with credit card. AmEx/MC/V. ❸

Hotel Charly's Place, Av. 5, C. Central/2 (☎2440 6853; www.charlysplacehotel.com). A rainbow of colors on the sheets and walls brighten up the simple dorm that has a row of bunk beds and a shared bath. Rooms have private hot-water baths and TVs. Friendly service. Breakfast with toast and fruit included. ¢300 per piece of laundry. Wi-Fi. Dorms ¢5800 (US$10); singles ¢14,500 (US$25); doubles ¢20,300 (US$35); triples ¢26,100 (US$45). AmEx/MC/V. ❶

Pensión Alajuela (☎2441 6251; www.pensionalajuela.com), 4 blocks north of the *parque,* across from the judicial court and hospital. Fans and tropical murals. Attached bamboo bar. TV and towels available. Breakfast included. Laundry ¢2000 per load. Free Wi-Fi. Internet ¢500 per 30min. Reception 24hr. Check-out noon. Singles ¢14,500 (US$25), with bath ¢17,400 (US$30), with A/C ¢23,200 (US$40); doubles ¢20,300/23,200/34,800 (US$35/40/60); triples ¢26,100/31,900/37,700 (US$45/55/65); quads ¢34,800 (US$60), with bath ¢43,500 (US$75). Reservations recommended. Weekly and monthly rates available. 6% charge for credit cards. Traveler's checks accepted. AmEx/MC/V. ❷

⬛ FOOD

The largest supermarket in town is **Palí,** four blocks west and one block south of the southwest corner of the *parque.* (☎2442 6392. Open M-Th 8:30am-7pm, F-Sa 8am-8pm, Su 8:30am-6pm.) **MegaSuper,** on the south side of the *parque* at Av. Central, C. Central/2, is smaller but closer to the town center. (☎2441 1384. Open M-Th 8am-9pm, F-Sa 7am-9pm, Su 7am-8pm.) The *mercado central,* two blocks west of the *parque,* is a crowded collection of meat, cheese, fruit, and vegetable stands. (Open M-F 7am-6pm, Sa 6am-6pm.)

🔲 Cuigini Bar and Restaurant, Av. Central, C. 5 (☎2440 6893). Photos of Italian celebrities line the walls of this 2nd floor restaurant. Menu mixes Southern Italian with American classics. Appetizers range from french fries (¢1150) to Sicilian shrimp (¢3560). Entrees include pasta (¢2200-6500) and the Frank Sinatra burger (¢2670). Live *troba* 3 nights per week. Extensive liquor selection from the bar. Open M-W 11:30am-10pm, F-Sa 11:30am-11pm, Su 4-10pm. Bar open until midnight or later. AmEx/MC/V. ❶

🔲 Coffee Dreams Café, Av. 1/3, C. 1 (☎2430 3970). It's not just the coffee that's a dream in this homey cafe. Dark wood tables and chairs and black-and-white photos of coffee farmers blend European style with Costa Rican authenticity. Choose from several satisfying entrees, such as the chicken lasagna, served with salad, garlic bread, *refresco natural,* and a delicious dessert (¢2500). Large selection of vegetarian dishes including salads, pies, and crepes (¢1800). Broccoli quiche ¢2500. A wide variety of coffee drinks (¢1400, without liquor ¢900) go great with the *tres leches* (¢1100) or strawberry cheesecake (¢1300). Open M-F 8am-8pm. MC/V. ❶

◪ **Jalapeños Central,** Av. 3/5, C. 1 (☎2430 4027), 50m south of the post office. Mexican *ponchos* and *sombreros* decorate the walls of this popular tourist restaurant. The Columbian owner, Norman, grew up in New York City and serves delicious Tex-Mex food, including burritos (¢1750) and quesadillas (¢1800). Try the excellent *sopa Azteca* (¢2000), with cheese, guacamole, and tortillas. Taco salad ¢3250. Takeout and vegetarian options available. Open M-Sa 11:30am-9pm. AmEx/MC/V. ❶

La Mansarda Bar and Restaurant (☎2441 4390), 25m south of the southeast corner of the *parque*. A large 2nd floor restaurant whose dining area has plenty of tables with balcony seating. No Costa Rican meal is complete without *ceviche* (¢4010-5290) or steamy *sopa de mariscos* (seafood soup ¢5450). Chicken dishes ¢3200-5950. Wine ¢2000 per glass, ¢6000 per bottle. Open daily 11:30am-1am. AmEx/D/MC/V minimum ¢3000. ❷

Café Ambrosia, Av. 5, C. 2 (☎2440 3440). This simple, open-air cafe serves *típico* meals, as well as 4 types of lasagna (chicken, beef, *palmito,* and sweet corn with ham; ¢2200) and sandwiches (¢1350). Entrees come with lightly dressed salads. Coffee ¢600-850. Milkshakes ¢750. Beer ¢800-1200. Open daily 9am-6:30pm. MC. ❶

La Tacareña Bar and Restaurant, Av. 7, C. 2 (☎2441 2662). Quick service and tasty food. Burgers (¢2000) are served in the glow of a big-screen TV and posters of volcanoes and rock groups. Entrees ¢2800-4000. Personal pizzas ¢4500-7000. Beer ¢850. Open daily 11am-2am. V. ❶

🎭 🎵 NIGHTLIFE AND ENTERTAINMENT

The center of town is relatively deserted at night, and there are few nightlife options. Relax at the bar of one of the neighborhood restaurants or take a taxi (¢1300) to one of the lively, expensive bars across the street from the airport, which are packed with tourists. Though Alajuela is considered one of Costa Rica's safer cities, it is best to travel in a group or take a taxi after 9pm.

Cuigini Bar and Restaurant (☎2440 6893). Many of the waiters and patrons here speak English. Enormous selection of local and imported liquors. The restaurant upstairs serves delicious Italian-American and Southern cuisine. Don't miss the owner's special piña colada. Beer ¢700-900. Mixed drinks ¢1200-4200. Open Tu-Sa 11:30am-midnight or later, Su 4pm-midnight. AmEx/MC/V.

La Mansarda Bar and Restaurant (☎2441 4390), 25m south of the southeast corner of the *parque,* on the right. Primarily a restaurant, but the bar here sees some local action at night. Sa-Su live alternative rock music. Beer ¢700. Mixed drinks ¢1500. Open daily 11:30am-1am. AmEx/MC/V.

El Pueblo (☎2442 4270), past Fiesta Casino, on the road from the airport to Alajuela. Karaoke M-Sa 10pm, Su 4pm. Ask about the Bacardi 2-for-1 offer. Beer ¢1000. Mixed drinks ¢1500. Open M-Th and Su 9am-1am, F-Sa 9am-2:30am.

La Casona (☎2442 0066), on the road between Alajuela and the airport, across the street from El Pueblo. Popular with both tourists and locals, this spacious bar has a fountain and a big-screen TV. A large back room is sometimes used for live music and private functions. The menu includes seafood entrees (¢2600-7300) and a few Peruvian soups and *ceviches* (¢2500). Beer ¢1162. Mixed drinks ¢1740-2320. Open M-Th and Su 11am-midnight, F-Sa 11am-1am.

Fiesta Casino, by the airport, between Denny's and Rosti Pollo. Live music 8pm. Poker and VIP room. Beer ¢1740 (US$3). Mixed drinks ¢2900 (US$5). M Ladies' night. 18+. Open 24hr.

DAYTRIPS FROM ALAJUELA

VOLCÁN POÁS

Take a taxi and arrive when the park first opens (1hr., ¢20,000 round-trip). Buses depart daily from San José's TUASA station, Av. 2, C. 12/14 (2hr., 8:30am, round-trip ¢22,250). They stop at the TUASA station in Alajuela at 9:15am (1hr., round-trip ¢1750) and arrive at Volcán Poás around 10:30am. The return bus leaves the park at 2:30pm. You may be done seeing the park before the return bus arrives; bring something to amuse yourself. Park open daily Dec.-Apr. 8am-4:30pm, May-Nov. 8am-3:30pm. ¢5800 (US$10), kids ¢11,600 (US$20).

Fifty-five kilometers northwest of San José, Parque Nacional Volcán Poás is a cloud forest accessible by trails lined with moss, orchids, and dangling bromeliads. Poás is the most-visited national park between Mexico and Panama because of its proximity to San José and Alajuela. A steam-belching crater at the top of active Volcán Poás (2574m) forms the park's main attraction. Inside the massive crater (1320m across and 300m deep) is a turquoise acid pool and *fumaroles* (vents in the earth's crust) that release bursts of volcanic steam. The cone looks like a rainbow carved into the terrain, with vibrantly colored layers of gray, white, and red earth that trace the history of the volcano's eruptions.

The **visitor center** features a small **museum** that educates guests about sustainability and eco-friendly practices. There is also a souvenir shop and a cafe with more than 20 flavors of cappuccino (¢900) and a smattering of lunch items and pastries (¢700-1000).

The most direct route to the crater is a 10min. walk up a gentle, paved path from the visitor center. **Laguna Botos,** the water-filled collapsed cone of a former volcano, is a 15min. walk beyond the crater. Look for the paved trail marked "Laguna Botos" just before the crater viewing area. It is an easy uphill walk. From there, return to the main trail or follow the more indirect Sendero Escalonia back to the parking area. Poás is most enjoyable in the morning, especially from May to November, as clouds and rain obscure the view by noon. Try to avoid visiting on Sundays, when the park is usually packed. The path to the crater is wheelchair-accessible and an ambulance is available.

OROSI

Regrettably overlooked by travelers scurrying away to the more touristed coasts, this small and welcoming village allows you to quietly appreciate Costa Rica's natural beauty. While the peaceful streets, amiable residents, and comfortable lodgings in town certainly deserve a visit, the true gems here are the nearby nature reserves, waterfalls, hot springs, and rivers. Orosi's seclusion, tucked away among the coffee plantations of the Central Valley, make it well worth the trip from San José. Don't miss the town's church, the community's most prized building.

TRANSPORTATION

Buses: Buses to Orosi leave Cartago from Av. 1/3, C. 6 (40min.; every 30min. M-Sa 5:30am-10pm, Su 7am-10pm; ¢360), and return to Cartago from the northeast corner of the soccer field on the main road (40min.; every 15min. M-Sa 4:45am-9:10pm, Su 5:45am-9:10pm; ¢360).

Taxis: (☎2379 3993). Taxis leave from the northeast corner of the soccer field.

CENTRAL VALLEY

Bike Rental: Moto Tours and Rental (☎2533 1564; www.costaricamoto.com), 100m east and 600m south, for ¢2900 (US$5) for a half day, ¢5220 (US$9) for a full day. Motorcycles ¢5800 (US$10) per hr. Open daily 8am-6pm.

ORIENTATION AND PRACTICAL INFORMATION

Despite the lack of street names, Orosi is easily navigable if you use the soccer field and the **church** as landmarks. Buses and taxis arrive on the main drag, which runs from north to south through town, turning east as they leave town to the south. **La Iglesia de San José Orosi** is on the west side of the field and the police station is on the north side. **Parque Nacional Tapantí** is about 12km east of town on the main road.

Tourist Office: The **Orosi Tourist Info and Adventure Center** (☎2533 3614), 300m south of the southwest corner of the soccer field, offers tourist info, as well as the only mailbox in Orosi. Recently opened to serve as a cultural exchange for locals and visitors, the center offers Spanish school classrooms, a kitchen, and dance classes as well as poetry nights and concerts. An attached restaurant serves breakfast and lunch. Open M-Sa 6:30am-6pm, Su 8am-5pm.

Tours: Many accommodations in town arrange horseback riding and tours to Parque Nacional Tapantí, Volcán Irazú, and Casa del Soñandor.

Currency Exchange and Banks: Groceries, phone cards, fax, and photocopy service are available at **Super Anita #2** (☎2533 2128), 250m south of the southeast corner of the soccer field. The Super may exchange US dollars if you purchase something. Open M-Sa 7:30am-8pm, Su 7:30am-5pm. MC/V. Orosi's **Banco Nacional,** where you can change money and traveler's checks, is located next to Super Anita #2. Open M-F 8:30am-3:45pm. Some MC/V debit cards work in the **24hr. ATM** outside.

> **TIP**
>
> **CASH MONEY.** In smaller towns such as Orosi, hold on to your smaller bills and change. Many local *sodas* and convenience stores will have trouble changing large-denomination *colones* notes.

Police: (☎2533 3082), directly north of the soccer field. Open daily 6:30am-noon.

Emergency: In case of emergency, call the **Red Cross** (☎2551 0421) in Paraiso.

Pharmacy: Farmacia Tabor (☎2533 3395), 150m east of the southeast corner of the soccer field. Also sells phone cards. Open M-Sa 8am-noon and 1-8pm, Su 8:30am-noon. AmEx/MC/V.

Medical Services: The **medical clinic** (☎2533 3052) is next door to the police station. Open M-F 7am-4pm.

Internet: Available at **PC Orosi**, 200m south of the southwest corner of the soccer field. Internet ¢200 per 30min., ¢300 per hr. Printing black and white ¢50; color ¢150. Open M-Sa 8:30am-8:30pm, Su 8am-5pm.

Laundry: Montaña Linda offers laundry service for non-guests. Drop off laundry before 9:30am for ¢4640 (US$8), or after 9:30am for ¢5800 (US$10). Pick up between 5-6pm at the hostel.

ACCOMMODATIONS

▨ **Montaña Linda** (☎2533 3640; www.montanalinda.com), 200m south and 200m west of the southwest corner of the soccer field. A patchwork of tin and bamboo roofs and open-air sitting areas with hammocks. Guests love the shared hot-water baths and kitchen with unlimited coffee (¢580, US$1). Spanish classes include meals and a room. Laundry ₡2320 (US$4). Camping ₡1740 (US$3) per person, with tent ₡2320 (US$4); dorms ₡4350 (US$7.50); singles ₡7250 (US$12.50); doubles ₡11,600 (US$20). Cash only. ❶

Montaña Linda Guest House (☎2533 3640; www.montanalinda.com), up the street from Montaña Linda. Private baths and killer mountainside views. Laundry ₡2320 (US$4). Guesthouse rooms ₡17,400 (US$30). Cash only. ❷

Orosi Lodge (☎2533 3578; www.orosilodge.com), 400m south and 100m west of the southwest corner of the soccer field. Modern rooms have fridges, coffeemakers, fans, and private hot-water baths. Balconies look out over nearby volcanoes and the hotel's garden. The attached cafe has a small selection of pastries and snacks. Internet and Wi-Fi available. Book exchange. Reception and cafe open 7am-7pm. Breakfast ₡3480 (US$6). High-season doubles ₡30,740 (US$53), low season ₡27,840 (US$48); triples ₡36,540/33,640 (US$63/58); private chalet ₡49,300/45,240 (US$85/78). AmEx/D/MC/V. ❸

Hotel Reventazon (☎2533 3838; www.hotelreventazon.com), 300m south and 25m west of the southeast corner of the soccer field. This small hotel is owned and operated by Tiffany and Frank, a friendly couple from Florida. Rooms include sparkling tile floors and private hot-water baths. Nicer rooms include extra seating, paintings, larger beds, and fridges. Free Wi-Fi, though the signal is weak. Reception 24hr. Laundry ₡5000. Breakfast included at adjoining restaurant. Singles, doubles, and triples ₡17,000-25,000. AmEx/MC/V. ❸

Cabinas Sueños de Oro (☎2533 3476 or 8822 6830), 200m south of the southeast corner of the soccer field. Despite its less-than-appealing location above a butcher shop (which doubles as the reception), Cabinas Sueños de Oro offers pleasantly sized accommodations at affordable prices. Each of the spacious rooms, with lace curtains and smooth tiled floors, is equipped with a kitchenette, small private hot-water bath, and cable TV. Relax on the 2nd-floor patio. Singles and doubles ₡17,400 (US$30); triples ₡18,560 (US$32). AmEx/D/MC/V. ❷

◼ FOOD

Bar Restaurante Coto (☎2533 3032), at the northeast corner of the soccer field. Satisfying hunger since 1952, this restaurant serves heaping portions of *comida típica* on its palm-filled terrace. Go for the mixed meat plate of pork cracklings, chicken strips, loin with pepper, and fish (₡4500). More affordable options like sandwiches (₡1100-1400), soups, and salads (₡2200-2500) are also tasty. Beer ₡950-1600. Mixed drinks ₡1500. Open daily 8am-midnight. AmEx/MC/V. ❷

Bar Anita (☎2533 3846), a 20min. walk down the main road, across from the F.J. Orlich coffee factory. Taxi ₡1000. A popular weekend trip for cheap, tasty seafood. *Ceviche* and fish dinners ₡1000-2000. *Bocas* ₡700. Prices vary. Open M-Th 10am-9pm, F-Sa 10am-10:30pm, Su 10am-8pm. MC/V. ❶

Hotel Reventazón Bar and Restaurant (☎2533 3838), 300m south and 25m west of the southeast corner of the soccer field. Though the menu and prices cater to tourists, the bamboo roof and hand-painted wooden menus add rustic charm. For dessert, try the huge, fluffy crepes with ice cream and chocolate sauce (₡1585). Salads ₡1500-2800. Hamburgers and sandwiches ₡900-1800. Beef, chicken, and fish entrees ₡2500-4900. Free Wi-Fi. Open daily noon-11pm. AmEx/MC/V. ❷

Soda Luz (☎2533 3701) 100m north of the northwest corner of the soccer field. Serves generous portions of *comida típica* in a cheerful atmosphere. *Gallo pinto* ₡1500. Hamburger ₡1100. Open M-F 7am-4pm, Sa-Su 7am-9pm. Cash only. ❶

Rancho San José Cabecar (☎2533 2411), 200m south of the southeast corner of the soccer field. Try out your western Spanish accent at this *rancho* of food. Cowboy-themed and surrounded by benches and bamboo walls. Finish it up with a fruit or carrot drink

(¢400). Can prepare vegetarian food if requested. *Casados* ¢2100 including drink. Sandwiches ¢900-1500. Breakfast ¢1400-1600. Open daily 8:30am-7pm. Cash only. ●

🕶 SIGHTS

LA IGLESIA DE SAN JOSÉ OROSI. Built in 1743, this church, the most important structure in the city, is remarkable both for its status as one of the country's oldest operational churches and for its architectural fortitude—it has survived earthquakes that decimated nearby villages. The church is reputed to be Costa Rica's only east-facing church. The worn, whitewashed walls, red terra-cotta tiled roof, and ornately carved wooden altar display its colonial roots and make Sunday mass (7, 9:30am, 6pm) a memorable experience. The Museo Franciscano adjoins the church and houses a collection of Christian relics dating back to 1560, including religious paintings, several friar's robes, and wooden replicas of Christ. *(West of the soccer field. Open Tu-F 1-5pm, Sa-Su 9am-5pm. ¢350, children ¢200.)*

BALNEARIO TERMAL OROSI. The more accessible of Orosi's two hot mineral baths, this facility has a lap pool, two small pools, and a kiddie pool all heated at 35°C (95°F). Basic showers and a **restaurant** are available. Have a piña colada (¢2400) at the bar. *(☎ 2533 2156. 300m south and 100m west of the southwest corner of the soccer field, next to Orosi Lodge. Open daily 7:30am-4pm, additional evening hours Th-F 6-10pm for groups with reservations. Pool use ¢1200. Breakfast ¢1300-2200. Sandwiches ¢1700-2500. Casados ¢2200-2300. Restaurant accepts MC/V.)*

BALNEARIO DE AGUAS TERMALES LOS PATIOS. Slightly farther away and more scenic than Balneario Termal Orosi, Los Patios has six warm pools and two cold pools above the Orosi Valley. *(☎ 2553 3009. 1km south out of town along the main road; 15min. walk. Comida ¢800-3015. Open Tu-Su 8am-4pm. ¢1300.)*

LA CASA DEL SOÑADOR. This old-fashioned, intricately designed "Dreamer's House" is the masterpiece of late Costa Rican sculptor Macedonio Quesada, who built the bamboo and wooden *casita* in 1989. Now maintained by Quesada's sons Hermes and Miguel. A handful of assistants also look after the house and seem to be constantly working away downstairs carving figurines out of coffeewood (from US$9). The house is filled with nativity scenes and *campesino* figures. These figures hang out of the windows, displaying a mix of Latin-American, indigenous, and East-Asian influences. Everything in the house, from the doors to the window shutters, is carefully chiseled from sticks of bamboo. *(11km from Orosi on the road to the town of Cachí. From Orosi, cross the foot bridge over the river just east of town. Turn left and follow the main road. La Casa del Soñador is about 8km down on the right, just past the town of Cachi. A taxi from Orosi (☎ 2379 3993), with a visit to the nearby Ruinas de Ujarrás, ¢8500 round trip.)*

LAS RUINAS DE UJARRÁS. The village of Ujarrás was abandoned after it was destroyed by floods and earthquakes in 1833. The ruins of the 17th-century church continue to draw a constant flow of tourists, mostly on tours with Orosi hotels. In a park surrounded by coffee plantations, the church is said to have been built after a man found a wooden box, containing statue of the Virgin, in the river nearby. The statue, known as La Virgen de Candelaria, has since been moved to the town of Paraíso, along with the rest of Ujarrás's residents. Locals continue to celebrate their sacred Virgin with an annual parade marching from Paraíso to Ujarrás in late March or early April. *(From Orosi, catch a bus to Paraíso from the northeast corner of the soccer field. (20min., every 30min. 4:45am-9:15pm, ¢155.) From Paraíso, buses leave every 20-30min. for Cachí. Ask the driver to let you off at the north end of the road to Ujarrás. From there, it's about a 2km walk. Return to the main road to hail a bus. Or take a taxi and visit nearby La Casa del Soñador as well, ¢8500 round trip. Open daily from 8am-5pm. Free.)*

CENTRAL VALLEY

 DAM IT. To gain an understanding of how Costa Rica hopes to achieve carbon neutrality by developing renewable sources of energy, stop at **La Represa de Cachí,** a massive hydroelectric dam at the northeast end of the lake that separates Cachí from Orosi. Take a bus from Orosi to Paraíso (¢155), then get on a bus to Cachí (¢140). Alternatively, visit the dam between visits to Las Ruinas de Ujarrás and La Casa del Soñador.

NIGHTLIFE AND ENTERTAINMENT

Orosi isn't exactly a hopping hub of nightlife, though it does offer a few solid options for a fun night on the town.

Bar Restaurante El Nido (☎2533 3793), 200m north of the northeast corner of the soccer field. A favorite among locals. Simple decor with plastic tables and chairs, but ample space for socializing and a varied playlist. Beer ¢700. Mixed drinks ¢400-900. *Arroz con* a varied meat selection ¢1500-2100. Open daily 11am-2am. Cash only.

Bar Zepelin, 200m east of the southeast corner of the soccer field. Also popular among locals, TVs broadcast music videos from the 60s to the present; ask to see the list and make a request. Beer ¢850. *Bocas* ¢700-1200. Meat and rice dishes ¢1200-2500. Open M-Sa noon-10pm, Su 11am-11pm. Cash only.

Pooles Orosi, 150m east of the southeast corner of the soccer field. Come here for chill game of pool (¢100 per table per game), foosball (¢50 for 6 balls). No alcohol served. Open M-Sa noon-2am, Su 11am-2am. Cash only.

GUIDED TOURS

Orosi hotels work with local tour and outdoor adventure companies to arrange trips to local attractions. **Montaña Linda** (p. 472) offers whitewater rafting and guided tours of Orosi Valley, Volcán Irazú, and Monumento Nacional Guayabo. (Rafting ¢37,700/ US$65. Orosi ¢2900/US$5. Irazú ¢11,600/US$20, not including park fee; 3-person minimum. Monumento Nacional Guayabo ¢23,200, US$40 including park fee; 2-person min.) Montaña Linda also offers directions to a swimming hole, natural hot springs, waterfall, scenic walks, and awesome panoramic views of the Orosi and Cachí Valley; check out the 3-4hr. "Yellow Church Walk." The Orosi Lodge arranges combined tours of Volcán Irazú, Mirador Orosi, and La Basílica de Nuestra Señora de los Ángeles (¢34,800/US$60); Parque Nacional Tapantí (¢8700/US$15); Orosi Valley, a sugar cane mill, La Casa del Soñador, and the Lankester Botanical Gardens (¢20,300/US$35). **Orosi Funhouse** (☎2533 4000), next to Bar Restaurante Coco, offers rafting down the class III Grande Orosi river (¢23,200/US$40 includes lunch, transportation, and guide) and a hiking tour of a coffee farm and the Tapanti (¢23,200/US$40).

DAYTRIP FROM OROSI

PARQUE NACIONAL TAPANTÍ

The lengthy 12km hike from Orosi to Parque Nacional Tapantí passes by rolling coffee plantations. Head south along the main road from Orosi; the first half of the hike is fairly flat, but the road gets steeper and rockier near the park. If you're short on time or energy, you can take a cab (one-way ¢6000), and walk back down or arrange for the cab to pick you up. ☎2551 2970. Open daily 7am-5pm. ¢5800 (US$10).

Parque Nacional Tapantí is a 61 sq. km former wildlife refuge famous for having the highest average rainfall (7m per year) in Costa Rica. The resulting 150 rivers and streams criss-cross a pristine rainforest inhabited by an enormous diversity of wildlife: 45 species of mammals, including tapirs, pacas, jaguars, and kinkajous; 211 species of birds; 32 species of reptiles and amphibians, including three types of vipers; and an average of 80-160 species of trees per hectare. The enormous amounts of rainfall that Tapantí receives are used to generate hydroelectric power for most of San José's population downstream at **La Represa de Cachí.**

From the park entrance, it is 4km upward on the wide **Camino Principal** to a scenic lookout point. You are unlikely to see much wildlife on the main trail, so veer left onto the **Arboles Caídos** (2km) trail for the best chance to see animals. The **La Pava** trail branches a short way off the Camino Principal and leads to the Río Grande. Swimming in the river is not possible, and the waterfall can be seen from the Catarata branch at the summit of the Camino Principal, so skip La Pava unless you have plenty of time. Before leaving the park, cool off by following the **Oropéndola** trail to the river and taking a dip. Although camping is not permitted, the park offers very basic rooms in a 15-person cabin. The communal showers have lukewarm water. Bring a sleeping bag and food to cook in the kitchen. (¢1500 per person. Call ☎2551 2970 in advance to secure a bed.) Spanish- and English-language maps are available at the ranger station. Insect repellent is necessary: the mosquitoes at the park are ravenous, particularly by the river.

TURRIALBA

Those who visit Turrialba love its down-to-earth feel and its location amid world-class rivers and stunning mountains. Nearby Ríos Reventazón and Pacuare have brought the town international fame; both are packed with Class III-V rapids and some of the world's best river runs. Whitewater rafters and kayakers of all abilities ride the waters during the rainy season; other travelers stay here on their way to Costa Rica's most significant archaeological site, Monumento Nacional Guayabo. But those uninterested in adventure tours should also consider paying Turrialba a visit; it retains a small-town feel while offering the comforts of a city. During the day, locals hang out in the attractive *parque central,* and at night they fill the restaurants and bars singing. Due to Costa Rica's economic development projects, an increasing number of rivers may soon be dammed for hydroelectric power. Adventurers should take advantage of these natural resources while they still can.

▐⁼ TRANSPORTATION

Buses: Turrialba's bus terminal (☎2557 5050), 350m southwest of the *parque central,* on Av. 4. Tickets may be purchased at the terminal window prior to departure. Leave for **San José** (direct 1hr., indirect 2hr.; every hr. 5:15am-9pm; ¢1105) and pass through **Cartago** (1hr., ¢660). Available to **Siquirres** (2hr.; M-Th every hr. 6am-6:15pm, F-Su every hr. 6am-7pm; ¢920); **La Suiza** (30min.; M-F 5:30, 9, 11:20am, 1, 2, 2:30, 3:30, 3:50, 5, 6pm; Sa 9, 11:30am, 1, 2:30, 3:30pm, every hr. 5-10pm, Su 3:50, 4:50pm; ¢220); **Santa Cruz/Parque Nacional Volcán Turrialba** (1hr., ¢320). On weekends and in the high season you might have to buy tickets to San José a day or so in advance to grab a seat. Buses also leave from the terminal for **Monumento Nacional Guayabo** (1hr.; M-Sa 11:15am, 3:10, 5:30pm; return 5:15, 6:30am, 12:30, 4pm; Su 9am, 3, 6pm, return 6:30am, 12:30, 4pm).

Taxis: (☎2556 7070). Line up at the corner of Av. Central and C. Central. One-way ¢7000; round-trip (includes 1hr. wait) ¢15,000.

✈🛈 ORIENTATION AND PRACTICAL INFORMATION

In Turrialba, 62km east of San José, *calles* run perpendicular to *avenidas*, but none of the streets run exactly north-south or east-west. With the **parque central** as a reference point, most businesses and sights aren't too tough to find.

Tourist Office: There is a tourist office located next to La Feria, but it has variable hours. Patricia or Luis at **Hotel Interamericano** (below) are also able to provide information about the town and nearby sights in English.

Banks: All banks listed have **24hr. ATMs. Banco de Costa Rica** (☎2556 0472), 2 blocks south and 2 blocks east of the park. Open M-F 9am-4pm. **Banco Nacional** (☎2556 1211), a few meters west of Banco de Costa Rica. Open M-F 8:30am-3:45pm. Long lines tend to build up at the tellers. **Banco Popular** (☎2556 6098), on Av. 4, just east of Popo's. Open M-F 8:45am-4:30pm, Sa 8:15-11:30am. **BanCredito** (☎2556 4141), next to Cafe Azul and across the street from Turribasicos. Open M-F 8am-4pm, Sa 8am-11:30pm. **Western Union** (☎2556 0439), 100m south and 50m east of the south corner of the *parque*, is inside of Tienda La Moda. Open M-Sa 8am-6:30pm.

Bookstore: (☎2556 1697), diagonally across from the post office, north of the *parque* on C. Central. A wide selection of secondhand books (¢2000-5000) in English, French, German, Portuguese, and Spanish are sold in this tiny bookstore. Owner speaks English. Hours are flexible; usually M-F 8:30-11:30am and 2:30-5:30pm.

Emergency: ☎911.

Police: (☎2556 0030 or 8265), 500m south of the town center on C. 4.

Pharmacy: Farmacia Santa Catalina (☎2556 8983), Av. 6 and C. 2. Open M-Sa 8am-8pm, Su 4pm-7pm. MC/V. **Farmacia San Buenaventura** (☎2556 0379), Av. 2 and C. 1, one block west of the *parque* on Av. 6. Open M-Sa 8am-7:30pm, Su 8:30am-1pm. AmEx/MC/V.

Hospital: (☎2558 1311). Walk up the stairs at the west end of Av. 2, or drive west on Av. 4 past the bus station and turn left into the hospital. Open 24hr.

Internet:

Eca Internet, across C. 1 from the *parque*, upstairs past Mama Mía's. Internet ¢300 per hr. Skype and webcams are available. Open M-F 8:30am-10pm, Sa-Su 9am-9pm.

@Internet (☎2556 2857), just east of Hotel Wagelia on Av. 4. Internet ¢300 per hr. Black-and-white copying ¢20. Printing ¢100-600. Open M-F 8am-10pm, Sa-Su 9am-9pm.

Cafe Internet (☎2256 4575), Av. 2 and C. 4. Modern computers, A/C. Internet ¢300 per hr.

Phone Cards: Available at **Pague aquí su Luz y Teléfono,** across the street from BanCredito. Open M-F 7:30am-5:30pm, Sa 8am-5pm.

Post Office: (☎2556 1679), 200m northwest of the north corner of the *parque*, across from the bookstore. Open M-F 8am-5:30pm. MC/V. **Postal Code:** 7150.

🏠 ACCOMMODATIONS

Although most of Turrialba's hotels are pricier, they may offer a nice place to rest and will arrange trips to nearby sights.

🏨 **Hotel Interamericano** (☎2556 0142; www.hotelinteramericano.com), bright coral-and-orange building 3 blocks south and 1 block east of the *parque*, just behind the row of palm trees. The owners speak English and have a wealth of info about sights, guides, and restaurants. Amenities include hot-water showers, Wi-Fi (best near the balcony), and a large sitting area with cable TV. Breakfast and laundry service (wash ¢1500 per kg, dry ¢1000 per load) available. Towels are included, but bring your own for rafting. Reception 24hr. Singles ¢6380, with bath ¢14,500; doubles ¢12,800/20,300; triples ¢19,100/31,900; quads ¢25,500/37,700. V. Traveler's checks accepted. ❶

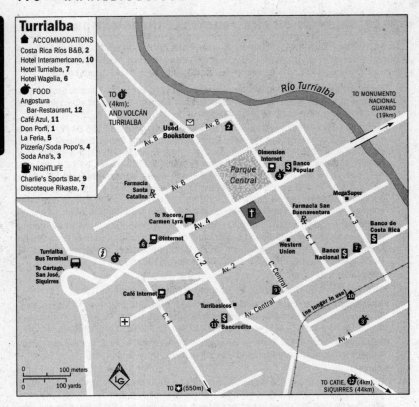

Turrialba

🏠 ACCOMMODATIONS
Costa Rica Ríos B&B, **2**
Hotel Interamericano, **10**
Hotel Turrialba, **7**
Hotel Wagelia, **6**

🍴 FOOD
Angostura
  Bar-Restaurant, **12**
Café Azul, **11**
Don Porfi, **1**
La Feria, **5**
Pizzería/Soda Popo's, **4**
Soda Ana's, **3**

🍷 NIGHTLIFE
Charlie's Sports Bar, **9**
Discoteque Rikaste, **7**

Río Turrialba

TO ①
(4km);
AND VOLCÁN
TURRIALBA

TO MONUMENTO
NACIONAL
GUAYABO
(19km)

Av. 8
Av. 8
Used
Bookstore
Av. 8

Parque
Central

Dimension
Internet
Banco
Popular

MegaSuper

Farmacia
Santa
Catalina
Av. 6

Farmacia San
Buenaventura

Banco de
Costa Rica

To Recore,
Carmen Lyra
Av. 4

@Internet

C. 3

Turrialba
Bus Terminal
To Cartago,
San José,
Siquirres

ⓘ
⑤

C. 2
Av. 2

Western
Union

Banco
Nacional

⑦

C. 1

C. Central

Café Internet
⑧

Turribasicos

Av. Central

(no longer in use)

⑩

C. 4

⑨

⑪
Bancredito

Av. 1
③

0   100 meters
0   100 yards

TO ☕ (550m)

TO CATIE, ⑫ (4km),
SIQUIRRES (44km)

🏨 **Costa Rica Ríos Bed and Breakfast** (☎2256 6651; www.hotelturrialba.com). Renovated in a Spanish colonial style, Costa Rica Ríos primarily houses those on the week-long adventure tour, but all are welcome. Named after surrounding rivers, the 10 airy rooms come with private hot-water baths, parking, free international calls, free self-service laundry, full breakfast, and Wi-Fi. Dinner can be requested for ₡8700. A few hang-out areas include a living room with board games, hot-tub, pool table, computer with internet, and mini-library. The rooftop deck has an amazing view of Volcán Turrialba. Reception 8am-6pm. Singles₡20,300; doubles ₡31,900; triples ₡43,500. AmEx/MC/V. ❸

Volcán Turrialba Lodge (☎2273 4335 or 0194; www.volcanturrialbalodge.com), about 1hr. from Turrialba and only a few km from the volcano's summit. Incredible views of the volcano and the valley from any of their lovely, cabin-style rooms. Perfect for those more interested in the outdoors than the town. Take advantage of the horseback, birdwatching, and hiking tours (p. 481). Common room with TV and comfortable couches. Electric heaters provided. One meal included. Homey singles, doubles, and triples, as well as a 4-bedroom cabin. ₡26,100 per person per night for any room combination. Busiest June-Oct.; reserve in advance. AmEx/MC/V. ❸

Hotel Wagelia (☎2556 1596; www.hotelwageliaturrialbacom), 1 block south of park, 1½ blocks west on Av. 2. 18 comfortable rooms surrounding a mini-garden and a bright outdoor common area. All rooms come with private hot-water baths with soap dispensers, A/C, and cable TV. A phone and safe deposit box are available. The attached restaurant-bar serves moderately priced entrees. Breakfast included. Laundry and tour service available. Wi-Fi. Check-in 2pm. Check-out noon. Singles ¢31,900; doubles ¢45,200; triples ¢48,700. AmEx/MC/V. Traveler's checks accepted. ❹

Hotel Turrialba (☎2556 6654), 100m south and 150m west of the *parque*. Murals decorate the hallways. All the rooms are simple, with wood-paneled walls, clean private hot-water baths, TVs, and ceiling and floor fans. Some rooms lack windows. Reception 24hr. Can place international calls. A/C ¢3000. Singles ¢7500; doubles ¢12,000; triples ¢15,000. AmEx/MC/V. ❷

◪ FOOD

Dining options are limited to pizza, *comida típica*, and a few less-than-authentic Chinese restaurants. For fresh produce, check out the **farmer's market** along Av. Central. (Open every F and Sa.) The local **MegaSuper** (☎2556 1242) is 100m south and 100m east of the west corner of the *parque*. (Open M-Sa 7am-9pm, Su 7am-7pm. AmEx/D/MC/V.) **Turribasicos**, on C. 2, near the corner of Av. Central/C. 2, has a pharmacy and bakery inside. (☎2556 0933. Open M-Sa 7am-9pm, Su 8am-4pm.)

▨ **Restaurante Don Porfi** (☎2556 9797), 4km outside of town on the road to Volcán Turrialba. Well worth the ¢2000 cab ride. Up the hill from Turrialba, Don Porfi is popular with locals but generally unknown to tourists. Excellent dishes include mixed seafood platters (¢3850-7000), beef tenderloin (7 varieties; ¢6200-6900), and chicken in garlic sauce (¢3600). The *batidos* are large and the service is highly professional. Try the house dessert, a fried banana crepe with ice cream (¢2000). Open M-Sa 11am-11pm, Su 11am-8pm. Reservations recommended during the high-season, especially on weekends. D/MC/V. ❸

▨ **La Feria** (☎2557 5550), 200m west of the south corner of the *parque* past Hotel Wagelia, at intersection of Av. 2 and C. 4. Run by a superb chef in a charming setting—local artists' work decorates the walls along with maps of Costa Rica and Turrialba, and soothing jazz plays in the background. Ancient Costa Rican artifacts are on display as well. Affordable gourmet fare includes filet mignon (¢5150), *casados* (¢1700), club sandwiches (¢2250), Fish La Feria (¢4850) and a wide variety of fruit drinks (¢575) and milkshakes (¢750). Plenty of veggie options, like the fantastic cream of tomato soup with toast (¢1900). Open M and W-Su 11:30am-9:30pm, Tu 11:30am-2:30pm. AmEx/MC/V. ❶

▨ **Soda Ana** (☎2557 2397), behind Hotel Interamericano on Av. 1. Though this soda has only a few tables and a very short menu, you most likely will not find a better *casado* (¢2000) in town. Rice and beans (¢2000) served F-Su. Ask one of Ana's sons to pull out their guitar from behind the counter and serenade you with classic Latin tunes. Open daily 6am-10pm. Cash only. ❶

Angostura Bar-Restaurant (☎2556 5757), 4km outside of town in the opposite direction of Don Porfi. Though not as elegant or well-established as Don Porfi, this restaurant with similar prices does dish out some nice plates. With a bottle of wine ready at each table, you can have the filet mignon (¢3800) or chicken in a cream mushroom sauce (¢4000). It can get cool in the open-air seating during the rainy season so consider bringing a light jacket. Taxi to the restaurant ¢2500-3000. Open M and W-Sa 11am-10pm. Su 11am-9pm. MC/V. ❸

Pizzería/Soda Popo's (☎2556 0064), on the east side of the *parque*. Known for its simple fare. If rafting has left you too tired to walk, you can order delivery until 11pm. Pizzas ¢2800-4000, ¢700 per slice. You may have to wait approximately 20min. for a small pizza. Burritos topped with ketchup, mustard, and mayo ¢600-850. Open daily 7am-11pm. V. ❶

⊙ SIGHTS

VOLCÁN TURRIALBA. The scenic road to the summit is steep and winding, and it becomes especially rocky after the town of Santa Cruz. Previously impassable by automobile, the last few kilometers have recently been repaved, so that it is now possible, though not exactly easy, to drive all the way up the volcano. The road, still bumpy and narrow, is most safely tackled in a four-wheel-drive taxi. (From Turrialba 1-2hr.; roundtrip ¢25,000, includes wait time). The Santa Cruz bus stops at the entrance to the park, 18km from the summit (1hr., ¢320). It is best to make the trip early in the morning to avoid mid-day rains and to catch the sun rising over the valley. Bring a sweatshirt and pants, since it is often surprisingly cold at the summit.

Turrialba stands out among Costa Rica's volcanoes. Unfortunately, the path down into the crater is now closed, as the volcano is still active, but you can look down into the crater as the smoke blows away in the opposite direction. It is relatively untouched, and there is no information station or entrance fee. For a guided tour by horseback or on foot, check out **Volcán Turrialba Lodge** (p. 481).

🎭 🎵 NIGHTLIFE AND ENTERTAINMENT

Discoteque Rikaste (☎2556 8081), Av. Central, C. 1/3, beside Banco Nacional, 2nd floor. Dance the night away with locals and tourists on Sa. Cover depends on time and size of crowd, but may be up to ¢1500. *Ticos* come to sit in the outside area and drink beer with friends during the day. *Cervezas* ¢600. Sandwiches ¢1000-1500. *Platos fuertes* ¢1700-3000. Restaurant/bar open M-F and Su 11am-12:30am, Sa 11am-2:30am. AmEx/D/MC/V.

Charlie's Sports Bar (☎2557 6565), Av. Central, C. Central, at the back of the complex. Modern neon lighting, loud Latin music, and TVs make this new sports bar the perfect place to catch a *fútbol* game. Buffalo wings ¢3700-5900. Hamburgers and sandwiches ¢2150-4490. Mixed drinks ¢2000. Shots ¢1500. Th Ladies' night. Open M-W and Su 4pm-midnight, Th-Sa 4pm-late.

Pocho's, on the main road in La Suiza. A bus goes to La Suiza every hr. until 10pm (30min., ¢205), but you'll have to take a taxi back if you're staying out later. This popular local bar draws *ticos* and tourists alike. The energetic owner entertains customers by juggling beer bottles and a machete. Look for signs in Turrialba that advertise periodic Sa night disco parties with Costa Rica's most popular DJs. Beer ¢700. Open daily 11am-late.

 TAKE COVER! During the rainy season, the lack of tourists means that those who brave the daily afternoon showers can often get into bars and clubs without paying a cover.

🧗 📷 OUTDOOR ACTIVITIES AND GUIDED TOURS

Capitalizing on Turrialba's legendary rafting and kayaking opportunities, tour operators offer adventure trips for all abilities. A day on the rapids is expensive, but the experience is unforgettable, especially on the Pacuare, the most popular and beautiful of the area's rivers. If you have your own equipment or rent from one of the tour companies, your hotel should be able to arrange transportation to a nearby river. Ask about the nearby serpent farm (**Serpentario Viborana**; 10km away; ☎2538 1510), Volcán Turrialba, and the Aquiares waterfall.

Ríos Locos (☎2556 6035; www.whiteh2o.com). Not one of Turrialba's largest companies, but it is one of the friendliest. 12 years of experience. These self-proclaimed Río Pacuare specialists offer rafting trips, horseback rides, and boat tours. They prefer small groups but will accommodate groups of up to 36 with advance notice. Class III-IV rafting on the Pacuare, Pejibaye, and Reventazón (half-day ¢29000, full-day ¢49,300). Photographer accompanies raft down river; photos available for negotiated price. Full day horseback tours along a jungle train line near the Peralta River (¢31,900). Can arrange a trip to Monumento Nacional Guayabo (¢23,200). Cash only.

Tico's River Adventures (☎2556 1231; www.ticoriver.com). A small local company that offers friendly service and years of experience. Specializing in rafting trips, Tico arranges day trips to the Pacuare (Class IV), Reventazón (Class II, III, or IV depending on trip), and Pascua (Class IV). Single-day trips ¢43,500 (US$75); include lunch. Special student rate of ¢34,800 (US$60) per person for groups of 10 or more. An all-inclusive 2-day Pacuare trip is also available (¢162,400/US$280 per person, includes hiking). Cash only.

Costa Rica Ríos (☎2556 9617; www.costaricarios.com), 10m north of the *parque*. Considered the most reputable rafting and kayaking operator and owns the largest fleet of water sports equipment in Central America. Offers exclusively pre-booked, all-inclusive, week-long adventure tours. Eight-day adventure (includes rafting, kayaking, canopy tour, and snorkeling) trip from ¢1,043,420 (US$1799); 8-day river-only (rafting and kayaking) trip from ¢927,420 (US$1599). The B&B provides a good place to relax after a week's worth of adventures. AmEx/MC/V.

Volcán Turrialba Lodge (☎2273 4335; www.volcanturrialbalodge.com). Offers a horseback tour to the top of Volcán Turrialba for ¢20,300 (US$35; 4-5hr. includes horse, guide, and snack). 2hr. hiking and birdwatching tours available (¢11,600/US$20). Mountain biking ¢17,400 (US$30). Rates do not include park entrance fees. AmEx/MC/V.

🔆 DAYTRIP FROM TURRIALBA

MONUMENTO NACIONAL GUAYABO

Buses to the entrance leave from the Turrialba bus terminal on Av. 4. (1hr.; M-Sa 11:15am, 3:10, 5:30pm; return 5:15, 6:30am, 12:30, 4pm; Su 9am, 3, 6:30pm; return 6:30am, 12:30, 4pm). Taxis are available (☎2556 7070); one-way ¢7000; round-trip ¢15,000, includes 1hr. wait. ☎2559 0117. Open daily 8am-3:30pm. US$6, children under 12 ¢580/US$1. Guided tour in English 1-3 people ¢5800 (US$10), 4-10 people ¢14,500 (US$25), 11-20 people ¢17,400 (US$30); in Spanish, ¢4000/7000/11,000.

Located 19km northeast of Turrialba, Monumento Nacional Guayabo is Costa Rica's most important archaeological site and the country's only National Monument. The park covers 218 hectares, although the archaeological site is just 20 hectares, and only four of those 20 have been excavated. Much remains unknown about the civilization that built and abandoned the site, though current estimates suggest that approximately 10,000 people lived here from 1500 BC to AD 1400, with most of the construction occurring after AD 800. Some say that the Guayabo people migrated to Colombia; in fact, many indigenous Columbians claim to have ancestors with similar traditions. The mysterious first inhabitants left records of their sophistication: their houses were built on large *montículos* (circular foundations), and they constructed *calzadas* (long causeways), a bridge, and an aqueduct system that still works today. The remnants of these structures can be found at the end of an easy 1½km trail called **Los Monticulous Path.** The path leads through rainforest to the focal point of the site, though you will pass a monolith, coffin graves, and several intricate petroglyphs along the way. **El Cando de Agua** (1km) leads from the park entrance to a rushing stream. Both trails, especially the shorter one, are very muddy in the rainy season; be sure to bring boots and rain gear. Take a copy of the pamphlet and ask if a guide can give a tour. The ruins are interesting, but there's not much else to see. There's a campsite (¢2320/US$4 per person) that has a toilet and a cold-water shower.

If you find yourself waiting for the bus, head down the road 500m to the **Guayabo Butterfly Garden.** Check out the meshed enclosure filled with 15 different specides of colorful butterflies, caterpillars, and cocoons. Osvaldo Salazar, the owner, can point out camouflaged butterflies and explain the entire growth process (30min.). There is also a guesthouse at the garden with access to a living room and fully equipped kitchen (☎8832 3586; open daily 8am-4pm; ¢2320. Guesthouse ¢17,400 per person). Also visit the neighboring restaurant **La Calzada Guayobo ❶** (☎2559 0437, open M-Tu, and Th-Su 8am-6pm). It is a bright and cheery place, decorated with farm implements leaning against the walls and painted wagon wheels hanging from the ceiling. Go for the grilled chicken breast (¢1950) or the rice and beans (¢1995).

NORTHERN LOWLANDS

Though it lacks the beachside glamour of other tourist hot spots, Costa Rica's mountainous northern region is home to a plethora of climates and travel destinations, from mountains and rolling green pasture to tropical rainforests and lagoons. Visitors to the lowlands will encounter a staggeringly diverse collection of wildlife, and those interested in more extreme adventure will find opportunities for windsurfing, rappelling, spelunking, and white-water rafting. Plus, while areas like Fortuna and Arenal see a huge influx of tourists every year, other parts of the lowlands are surprisingly untouristed, with a rich *campesino* culture mixed with city life in towns like Ciudad Quesada and Los Chiles. A gateway to Nicaragua and both the Atlantic and Caribbean coasts, the lowlands contain some of Costa Rica's most well-conserved examples of tropical rainforests, cloud forests, and marshlands. You can hike through the pristine jungles of Tirimbina Reserve or La Selva, drift along the swampy mangroves of Refugio Nacional Caño Negro, watch the lava flow on Volcán Arenal, and climb through the winding, bat-filled tunnels of the Venado Caves. Whether in search of extreme sports or a morning of relaxing sportfishing or birdwatching, visitors to the Northern Lowlands can strike a balance between tourism opportunities and authentic rural culture in an area distinguished for the richness and diversity of its natural wonders.

PUERTO VIEJO DE SARAPIQUÍ

Puerto Viejo de Sarapiquí is rapidly becoming a top destination for nature-lovers and thrill-seekers alike. The Río Sarapiquí, which runs just 200m from the main road, has opportunities for both wildlife sightings and river rafting. Numerous adventure ranches offer mountain biking and canopy trips for those who prefer land-based action. Despite the myriad outdoor opportunities available, the influx of tourists to the former banana town have had a minimal impact on the town itself; Puerto Viejo remains very small, with one main street and only a handful of hotels and restaurants. With world-class wildlife reserves such as Tirimbina and La Estación Biológica La Selva less than 30min. from town, Puerto Viejo is an ideal base for budget travelers looking to experience the natural wonders of the region.

▌ TRANSPORTATION

Buses: All leave from the station opposite the northwest corner of the soccer field. A schedule is posted inside next to the ticket counter. To: **Ciudad Quesada** (2hr., 12 per day 4:40am-8pm, ¢1230); **Guápiles** (1hr., 11 per day 5:30am-6:30pm, ¢785); **La Virgen** (30min., every hr. 6am-6pm, ¢350); **Río Frío** (1hr., 10 per day 7am-6pm, ¢500); **San José** (10 per day 5am-5:30pm, ¢1610) via **El Tunel Zurquí** or via **Vara Blanca** (5, 7:30, 11:30am, 4:30pm). Tell the cashier at the ticket counter if you want to get off before the final stop; some express buses do not stop at intermediate destinations.

Taxis: Line up along the main street just north of the soccer field. To La Virgen ¢5000.

◤ ▐ ORIENTATION AND PRACTICAL INFORMATION

Puerto Viejo extends along one main street for about 300m. A **soccer field** bordering this street marks the town center. The **bus station** marks the northwest side of this field, while the large stucco **church** sits on the southwest corner.

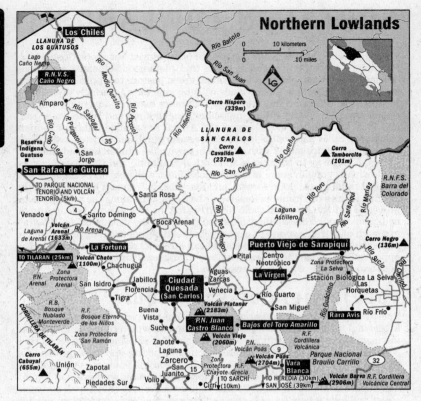

Northern Lowlands

Los Chiles
LLANURA DE LOS GUATUSOS
Lago Caño Negro
R.N.V.S. Caño Negro
Amparo
Reserva Indígena Guatuso
San Jorge
San Rafael de Gutuso
TO PARQUE NACIONAL TENORIO AND VOLCÁN TENORIO (5km)
Venado
Santo Domingo
Laguna de Arenal
Volcán Arenal (1633m)
La Fortuna
TO TILARAN (25km)
Volcán Chato (1100m)
Chachagua
P.N. Arenal
Zona Protectora Arenal
San Isidro
R.B. Bosque Nublado Monteverde
R.F. Bosque Eterno de los Niños
Zona Protectora San Ramón
Cerro Cabuyal (655m)
Unión
Zapotal
Piedades Sur
CORDILLERA DE TILARÁN
Jabillos
Florencia
Tigra
Buena Vista
Sucre
Zapote
Laguna
Zarcero
San Juanito
Volio
Ciudad Quesada (San Carlos)
Venecia
Aguas Zarcas
P.N. Juan Castro Blanco
Volcán Platanar (2183m)
Volcán Viejo (2060m)
Volcán Poás
Zona Protectora R.F. Chayote Grecia
TO SARCHÍ
Cirrí
TO HEREDIA (30km)
SAN JOSÉ (39km)
Río San Juan
Río Bartolo
Cerro Níspero (339m)
LLANURA DE SAN CARLOS
Cerro Cavallón (237m)
Río San Carlos
Río Tres Amigos
Pital
Centro Neotrópico
La Virgen
Río Cuarto
San Miguel
Bajos del Toro Amarillo
P.N. Cordillera Volcánica
Volcán Poás (2704m)
Vara Blanca
Volcán Barva (2906m)
Puerto Viejo de Sarapiquí
Río Toro
Río Sarapiquí
Río Marías
Laguna Astillero
Zona Protectora La Selva
Estación Biológica La Selva
Las Horquetas
Rara Avis
Río Frío
R.F. Cordillera Volcánica
Parque Nacional Braulio Carrillo
R.F. Cordillera Volcánica Central
Cerro Tamborcito (101m)
R.N.F.S. Barra del Colorado
Cerro Negro (136m)
Río Sicio
Río Guácimo
Río Tres Amigos
Cerro Negro
9
15
32
4
35
4
0   10 kilometers
0   10 miles

About 1km west of town, the main road forks south toward Guápiles and the entrance of **Estación Biológica La Selva,** and southwest toward La Virgen and the entrances of the **Centro Neotrópico Sarapiquís** and the **Serpentario.** About 150m east of the bus station, a small road to the right leads to the **Super Sarapiquí** supermarket. Two hundred and fifty meters east along the main road from the bus station, the road splits yet again, heading northwest on the left and toward the Río Sarapiquí port on the right.

Tourist Information: For the most comprehensive tourist info, talk to William Rojas of ■ **Oasis Nature Tours** (☎2766 6108 or 6260; www.oasisnaturetours.com), 50m west of the soccer field through a green doorway just a couple doors past the bus station. Don William arranges scenic river trips of the Río Sarapiquí all the way to Tortuguero and Nicaragua. Alex Martínez, the owner of **Posada Andrea Cristina** (see **Accommodations**), is a former hunter who is now considered by many to be the region's most knowledgeable and passionate naturalist. He is a good source for info on birdwatching and other nature tours.

Banks: Exchange travelers' checks and US dollars at the **Banco Nacional** (☎2766 6012), at the intersection of the main road and the road to the port. Open M-F 8:30am-3:45pm. **Banco Popular** is 20m east of the soccer field. Open M-F 8:45am-3pm, Sa 8:15am-11:30am. Both have **24hr. ATMs.**

Police: (☎2766 6575 or 2766 6485, emergencies 911), just off the main street along the port turnoff, next to the post office.

Pharmacy: Farmacia Alfa (☎2766 6348), 1 block east of the soccer field on the left. Open M-Sa 8am-8pm. MC/V.

Red Cross: (☎2766 6212 or 2766 6254), 250m west of the soccer field. Open 24hr.

Internet: Sarapiquí Internet (☎2766 6223), 300m west of the soccer field, past the Red Cross. Internet ¢400 per hr. Open daily 8am-8pm. Internet is available in **Mi Lindo Sarapiquí** (below) for ¢400 per hr. Open daily 7am-10pm. Wi-Fi is available at **Restaurante El Surco.**

Post Office: (☎2766 6509), across from Banco Nacional at the port turn off. Open M-F 8am-noon and 1-5:30pm. **Postal Code:** 31001.

⛺ ACCOMMODATIONS

Although the area around Puerto Viejo has become a popular destination, the town itself does not have many options for travelers. Luckily, the few hotels that do exist are within walking distance of the bus station, making them convenient choices for those looking to take daytrips to the many attractions just outside of town.

Posada Andrea Cristina (☎2766 6265; www.andreacristina.com), 1km west of the town center. From the bus station, follow the road west toward La Virgen for about 1km; the B&B is on the right. With spacious wood bungalows scattered throughout a beautifully landscaped garden, Andrea Cristina offers a unique and peaceful lodging option for those who don't mind being a bit of a walk from town. The cabins share communal cold-water baths, but the comfy beds and tasty vegetarian-friendly breakfast make up for it. Breakfast included. Singles ¢14,500 (US$25); doubles ¢26,100 (US$45); each additional person ¢8700 (US$15). 10% discount on stays longer than 4 nights. Camp on the grounds for ¢5800 (US$10). MC/V. ❶

Mi Lindo Sarapiquí (☎2766 6281), west of the soccer field and directly opposite the bus station. This conveniently located restaurant-hotel-internet-cafe offers sunny, spacious rooms that each have a twin and double bed, ceiling and wall fans, a TV, and private hot-water baths. Laundry ¢150 per item. Singles ¢9500; doubles ¢15,000; triples ¢22,100. AmEx/D/MC/V. ❷

Cabinas Laura (☎2766 6316), 100m down the road to the port. Though its location down a dark alley next to a casket store is less than ideal, this hotel has good prices for those traveling in pairs; A/C and cable TV make it even better. Singles and doubles ¢8000; doubles and triples with A/C ¢10,000-14,000. MC/V. ❷

🍴 FOOD

While many of the resorts a few kilometers outside of town serve mouth-watering cuisine, the options in town are limited. Aside from the restaurants at hotels Mi Lindo Sarapiquí and Restaurante El Surco, the only other eating spots available are *sodas* and ice cream shops.

Restaurante Mi Lindo Sarapiquí, attached to the hotel of the same name. Provides tasty *comida típica* to a busy crowd of locals. Though all of the dishes are reasonably priced, the *bocas* menu offers some particularly good deals (¢700-1500). Rice dishes ¢1600-3900. Breakfast ¢950-2500. Open daily 8am-10pm. AmEx/D/MC/V. ❶

Restaurante El Surco (☎2766 6005), in Hotel Bambú. With vaulted fan-filled ceilings under a tin roof, El Surco is the closest Sarapiquí gets to fine dining. The dishes are standard Costa Rican fare, but the atmosphere is casually elegant. *Bocas* ¢1100-1800.

Casados ₡1850-4250. Seafood dishes ₡4800-9000. Pastas ₡1700-4000. Free Wi-Fi. Open daily 6am-10pm. AmEx/MC/V. ❷

Mister Pizza (☎2766 6138), on the east end of the soccer field. This small, fast food and pizza joint offers escape from *comida típica* in town. The pizza crust has an oddly sweet flavor, but the topping options are extensive, ranging from Hawaiian to veggie. Don't miss the combo menu (₡1400). Pizzas ₡1400-5000. Open daily 8am-10pm. ❷

OUTDOOR ACTIVITIES

Hacienda Pozo Azul (☎2438 2616; www.haciendapozoazul.com), at the bridge in La Virgen. One of the most comprehensive adventure destinations in Puerto Viejo. The sprawling ranch offers canopy tours (US$45), horseback rides (2hr., US$35), rappelling (US$28), rafting (Class II and III rapids US$50, Class IV rapids US$70), mountain biking (half-day US$45), and guided hiking treks (US$15). The ranch was originally a dairy farm, and you can still take a tour of the ranch (US$10) or camp at the on-site facilities (US$25 plus US$20 for 3 meals per person). Alternatively, stay at the pricier jungle lodge (US$60 per person).

Aventuras del Sarapiquí (☎2766 6768 or 8399 3509; www.sarapiqui.com), 15min. west of town on the bus toward La Virgen. These guys opened the first rafting company in the region nearly 20 years ago. The fun-loving group of experienced, bilingual guides leads daily Class II and III rafting trips down the Río Sarapiquí (US$50, includes fruit snack). One of the owners, Pongo, organizes the annual Sarapiquí Adventure Race (www.sarapiquiadventurerace.com), a 2-day competition in Oct. that brings participants to raft, hike, and mountain bike 60km for a charitable cause. (Entrance fee US$50 per person, equipment included.)

Aguas Bravas (☎2292 2072; www.aguas-bravas.co.cr), on the road between Puerto Viejo and La Virgen. Offers a Class II and III rafting trip (US$65) and a Class IV trip for more experienced rafters (US$85).

DAYTRIPS FROM PUERTO VIEJO

TIRIMBINA RAINFOREST PRESERVE

From Puerto Viejo, take a bus to La Virgen and ask the driver to let you off at the entrance to Tirimbina (30min., ₡320). Buses returning to Puerto Viejo stop at the Preserve approx. on the hour. A taxi from Puerto Viejo costs ₡5000. On foot from La Virgen, walk 1.6km north along the road to Puerto Viejo de Sarapiquí; the entrance to the park is on the right, 300m past the Serpentario. ☎2761 1579 or 1576; www.tirimbina.org. Self-guided tour ₡8700 (US$15), students ₡5800 (US$10); guided tour ₡12,760/9860 (US$22/17); approx. 2hr. Several tours leave each day (8, 10am, 1:30, 3pm), though it is recommended to call in advance. Chocolate tour ₡11,600 (US$20), students ₡8700 (US$15); offered in the morning and afternoon. Reservations required.

Although about 90% of its land remains pristinely undeveloped, without even the most basic trails, the 350-hectare Tirimbina Rainforest Preserve offers one of the most varied selections of tourism opportunities in the Sarapiquí area. Its 9km of paved trail and more extensive collection of rougher trails can be explored with or without a guide, and the views of primary forest and the Sarapiquí River afforded by the 266m **Puente Colgante** (Hanging Bridge) are some of the best around. The 4km that can be explored without a guide takes approximately 2hr. to properly hike; the other 5km requires a guide given that dangerous animals including snakes, tapirs, and even lions have been known to chow down along the path. A spiral staircase descending from El Puente Colgante leads to an island formed by **Río Sarapiquí,** where adventurers can take a swim when the river isn't too high. A few trails cross the island, and otters and kingfishers are often spotted on the riverbanks.

For those tired of the usual wildlife-spotting, the Preserve offers several specialized tours, which must be booked in advance. The **bat tour** is a hit with those seeking a glimpse of these nocturnal rainforest residents (7:30pm), and chocoholics' mouths will water on the chocolate tour, which takes guests through a natural chocolate plantation, demonstrates traditional methods of producing chocolate, and concludes with a tasting. Insect repellent, long pants, and hiking boots are recommended for all hikes or walks. An open-air **restaurant** serves meals to guests at the lodge and will also make lunch or dinner for large groups; call the Preserve in advance to arrange a meal before or after a hour.

Though most visitors to the center stop by for only a day or two, Tirimbina also accepts volunteers and researchers for long-term stays of at least two weeks. The Preserve has lodging space for ten volunteers, most of whom help out in the general day-to-day operations of the Preserve, though Spanish speakers may also have the opportunity to help in conservation and ecology classes taught for local primary school kids. Researchers interested in studying the wildlife at Tirimbina are also welcome to stay at the Preserve. Room and board for volunteers and researchers is US$10 per night, though some financial assistance is available. Contact the Preserve for more information on current volunteer and research openings.

Tirimbina also has 12 **rooms** on the grounds available for visitors. The rooms have either a double and twin bed or three twin beds as well as private hot-water baths, Wi-Fi, and A/C. Lodging includes free access to the trails as well as breakfast in the park's restaurant. (Singles and doubles ₡34,800/US$60, students ₡29,000/US$50.)

ESTACIÓN BIOLÓGICA LA SELVA

From Puerto Viejo, take the 6:45am or 12:15pm bus headed to Río Frío (15min., ₡260) to make the 8am or 1:30pm tours. Buses to Guápiles also pass this way. Ask the driver to let you off at the Estación Biológica La Selva. From this stop, follow the dirt road on your right 1km to the station's gates; signs mark the way. To get back to Puerto Viejo, have the station call you a cab (₡3000) or wait at the bus stop on the main road for one of the buses that passes by about every 30min. (less often on Su) on their way back to Puerto Viejo. ☎ 2524 0628; www.ots.ac.cr. Private tours 2hr. Birdwatching tours begin at 5:45am, night tours 6pm; ₡18,560-22,040 (US$32-38). Make reservations online or by phone several days in advance for any of the tours.

Only 6km south of Puerto Viejo, La Selva is one of the three centers of the **Organization for Tropical Studies (OTS)**, a non-profit consortium of universities and research institutions founded on the principles of investigation, education, and conservation. La Selva borders **Parque Nacional Braulio Carrillo** to the south. The park boasts 1614 hectares of primary and secondary rainforest. Hundreds of scientists and students come to La Selva each year to study the staggering number of plants and animals here, several of which the Estación has helped bring back from the edge of extinction. Though the station has an extensive collection of concrete and dirt trails, the paths can only be accessed without a guide by those staying at the lodge. The station has many guided walks and workshops to offer. Two 3½hr. walking tours leave each day (8am, 1:30pm; ₡16,240-18,560/US$28-32). Some trails are accessible to those with physical disabilities. The station also offers private tours, including a birdwatching tour, a night tour, and a workshop on rainforest photography, all of which must be arranged several days in advance.

CENTRO NEOTRÓPICO SARAPIQUÍS

Next to Tirimbina (p. 486). ☎2761 1004; fax 2761 1415; www.sarapiquis.org. Open daily 9am-5pm. The tour schedule varies; call ahead for reservations. Entry to museum, archaeological site, and botanical gardens ¢4640 (US$8). Reception open daily 6am-8:30pm. Archaeological site and gardens open 6am-4pm. Museum open 6am-6pm. Tour of museum with guide ¢8700 (US$15), archaeological site ¢5220 (US$9).

The non-profit, private Centro Neotrópico Sarapiquís is a preserve dedicated to interactive cultural, biological, and ecological awareness and conservation. The center offers **three exhibits** to tourists: a **museum** on pre-Columbian culture, an **archaeological dig** with reconstructed 15th-century pre-Columbian buildings, and a **botanical garden** featuring medicinal and edible plants. The museum is well-kept, with neat displays of masks, shamanic implements, and a film on the relationship between man and nature in pre-Columbian societies. Unfortunately, the rest of the center is not as well-organized. Much of the writing on the signs identifying the plants in the botanical gardens has been washed away by the frequent rains, and the archaeological site is quite small, with a sample home, funerary site, and replica statues constituting the majority of the exhibit. Visitors should also beware of the rock pathways in the botanical gardens and archaeological site: the stones get quite slippery when wet, making walking in the rain feel a bit like ice skating in tennis shoes.

The Center was built in a pre-Columbian village style using sustainable technologies like solar power, local natural materials, and a waste-water treatment system. The on-site ecolodge, restaurant, and bar overlook the preserve and follow the *Palenque* architectural style. Large, round huts each house eight **cabins,** all with private hot-water baths, fans, and phones. Safe deposit boxes and laundry services are also available. Eight of the 40 rooms have A/C. (High-season singles and doubles ¢60,320/US$104, triples ¢74,820/US$129; low-season ¢56,260/60, 320, US$97/104.) The center runs an extensive **education program** with over 2000 local children and hundreds of foreign volunteers, teachers, and ecologists; for information on getting involved, contact the center (see the information above). Spanish skills are helpful for most jobs, though not necessary.

REFUGIO NACIONAL CAÑO NEGRO

Where there's water, there's life, and Refugio Caño Negro has plenty of both. The refuge gets 3.5m of rain every year, and 85% of its land (100 sq. km) is flooded during the rainy season from May to December. In the heart of this aquatic wonderland is the enormous **Laguna Caño Negro,** a 9 sq. km lake that refills every summer when the banks of the Río Frío and Río Caño Negro overflow. The labyrinth of mangroves, rivers, and harbors here has been declared the world's fourth most important biological zone, with 160 species of mammals and over 315 species of birds. Reptiles like crocodiles, iguanas, turtles, and snakes abound, and rare fish, including the prehistoric gaspar, swim the waters. On the banks of the *laguna*, 23km southwest of Los Chiles, lies the village of Caño Negro. Despite its small size and remote location down a gravel road, this town is the gateway to the Refugio Caño Negro. Caño Negro is part of the protected area of the **Conservación Arenal Huetar Norte,** an organization that focuses on the improvement of the socioeconomic conditions of the community by creating sustainable development programs. Tourism in the area is largely dictated by the water; during the dry season (February to April), you can explore the *laguna* on foot. When the lake is filled, there are two options for exploring. When rains are sufficient, the park can be explored by boat. Otherwise, the easiest way to explore the park is on the consistently accessible

Río Frio. To find out what is available, ask at the entrance or check with tour operators. (Park open daily 8am-4pm. US$10.)

▆ TRANSPORTATION

By **car,** the best way to get to Caño Negro from San José is to head north on the road toward Los Chiles. The entrance is 1km after the Tanques Gas Zeta (19km before Los Chiles); then take the 19km unpaved road. The entire trip should take around 4hr. Despite the road conditions, **buses** leave from Los Chiles to **Upala** through **Caño Negro** (1½hr.; M-F 5am, noon, 4pm; Sa 5am, 2pm; Su 5am; ¢1100). Buses leave for **Los Chiles** (1½hr.; 3 per day M-F 6am, 12:30pm, and 5pm; Sa 6am, 5pm; Su 12:30pm; ¢1100). Buses leave for **Upala** daily at 11:30am, or approximately 1½hr. after they leave from Los Chiles. The best place to wait for the bus is in front of the mini-super, where you can see traffic coming in and out of town. Buses also stop in front of the hotels along the road to the town's entrance.

▆ ▆ ORIENTATION AND PRACTICAL INFORMATION

The bus enters the village on the **main road,** making a loop around the **parque central** before heading back out at the northwest corner of the *parque,* next to the **school.** Just north of the school is the church and, 25m to the north, a **mini-super** (☎2461 1500; open M-Sa 7am-7pm, Su 7am-5pm.) The refuge entrance is on the southeast corner of the *parque.*

The **MINAE** office (☎2471 1309, open daily 8am-4pm), 200m west of the mini-super, provides tourist information. There is **no bank,** and the nearest medical facility is **Hospital Ebais** (☎2471 1531), a small clinic 50m east from the mini-super. The **police station** (☎2471 1802) is on the southeast side of the *parque.* The town has two **public telephones,** at the mini-super and in front of the police station.

▆ ▆ ACCOMMODATIONS AND CAMPING

It is possible to **camp** on the grounds of the Caño Negro MINAE office, which have access to cold-water showers and bathrooms. (¢1000 per person.)

Albergue Caño Negro (☎2471 2029), 200m north of the northwest corner of the *parque,* on a grassy *finca* on the banks of the Laguna Caño Negra. Simple cabins on stilts come with two twin beds, wall fans, linens, and padlocked doors. Communal cold-water baths located downstairs. Each cabin has a porch overlooking the *finca* and the *laguna.* ¢7000 per person. ❸

Cabinas Martín Pescador (☎2471 1369 or 1116), 100m past the MINAE office, in the field at the end of the road. The reception is across the street from the north side of the *parque* in the small goods store next to the *Cabinas Martín* sign. Cabins with covered porches and hot-water baths; some also have A/C and cable TV. Singles ¢11,600 (US$20); doubles ¢17,400 (US$30); each additional person ¢5800 (US$10). ❸

Natural Lodge Caño Negro (☎2471 1426; www.canonegrolodge.com), 300m north and 50m west of the mini-super. Elegant rooms decorated with abstract paintings have queen beds, A/C, safe deposit boxes, and spacious bathrooms. Amenities include a pool and hot tub. Breakfast included. Helpful and informed staff can schedule various tours. High-season doubles ¢58,000 (US$100), low-season ¢46,400 (US$80); triples ¢63,8000/¢52,220 (US$110/90); quads ¢69,600/¢58,000 (US$120/100); each additional person ¢5,800 (US$10). AmEx/D/MC/V. ❺

Hotel de Campo (☎2471 1012; www.hoteldecampo.com), on the *laguna* side of the road to the village, 400m before Albergue Caño Negro. Tidy, well-equipped rooms in stucco cottages. A manicured garden leads to the lagoon. Hot water and A/C. Break-

MUCHAS MARIPOSAS

Over a decade ago, the **Women's Association of Caño Negro** started the mariposario project. The project aimed to grow colonies of butterflies and sell them. Today, you can visit four different mariposarios in Caño Negro.

1. **La Asociación de Mujeres de Cano Negro** offers one of the biggest, most accessible gardens in town, and sells fresh bread and pastries in its bakery next door.

2. **Dona Claris** has a smaller atrium that features the beautiful blue morpho butterfly. (☎2471 1450. ¢1000.)

3. **Belsis Gracia** has the newest, best constructed mariposario in town. (☎2471 1315. ¢1000.)

4. **La Reinata's** convenient garden has brightly colored mariposas that flutter around lush vegetation. (☎2471 1301. ¢1000.)

fast included. Pool for guest use. Rooms ¢49,300 (US$85). Ask about the ecological and fishing tours. AmEx/D/MC/V. ❺

FOOD

Soda la Palmera (☎2471 1045), on the southeast corner of the *parque*. Though the menu offers few options, La Palmera cooks up tasty *comida típica* for a local clientele in its cottage-style dining area. *Gallo pinto* with eggs, an avocado slice, and coffee ¢1200. Entrees ¢2000 with drink. Bathroom use ¢100. Open daily 7am-8pm. ❶

Restaurante Danublo Azul (☎2471 1295), on the southeast side of the *parque*. A quiet spot during low season. In high season, its eating area overlooking the *laguna* becomes a popular disco. *Guapote* fish ¢3600. *Casados* of gaspar (the special lake fish) come with rice, beans, and salad ¢3500. Entrees from ¢2000. Open daily 10am-2am. ❷

Restaurante Jabirú (☎2471 1426), located in the Natural Lodge Caño Negro. The fanciest and priciest food in town. Pasta entrees (fettucine with broccoli sauce, ¢2800). Meat and seafood dishes ¢3500-5800. Imported beer ¢1300-2600. Mango juice ¢600. Continental breakfast with bread, marmalade, coffee/tea, and orange juice ¢2800. Open daily 6am-10pm. ❷

Restaurante El Pueblo (☎2471 1419), located right before the rooms of Cabinas Martín Pescador. This restaurant serves large breakfasts for ¢3500. *Casados* (chicken, fish, or steak, includes salad and bread) ¢4000. Open daily 7am-6pm. ❷

VISITING THE REFUGE

The park is easily reached from Caño Negro village and is best seen by boat. A 1½km trail starts near the office; others emerge as the lake dries up. **Pantanal Tours**, a small unlabeled office across from Soda La Palmera (above), offers several tours in Spanish and English. (Kayaks ¢17,4000/US$30 per 4 hr.; Fish and ecological tours for 2-3 people ¢29,000/US$50 per 2hr.; horseback riding ¢11,600/US$20 per 2hr.) Open daily 6am-5pm. Antonio at **Cabinas Martín Pescador** (p. 489) takes people fishing on his canopied *lancha*. (1-4 people, ¢29,000/US$50 per 2hr.; each additional person ¢5800/US$10.) **Natural Lodge Caño Negro** runs tours of turtle and butterfly farms (¢14,5000/US$25) and 3 hr. tours of the lake (¢25,520/US$44, includes park entrance fee). There is also the **Tour and Fishing Info Office** (☎8823 4026) shortly past the Natural Lodge Caño Negro which offers fishing, butterfly and turtle tours, camping, trails, and horseback riding. Larger tour operations run out of La Fortuna and Los Chiles. Prices typically do not include park entrance (¢5800, US$10 per day) or fishing licenses (2 months ¢17,400, US$30). You can pay the ranger for park entry in the kiosk at the entrance on the southeast corner of the *parque*. **Fishing** is prohibited April through July. A license requires a photocopy of your passport and two passport-size photos. To get one, pay ¢17,400 (US$30) in any Banco Nacional and pick up your package at any MINAE office; there is one 100m north and 200m west of the northwest corner of the *parque* in Caño Negro. You can also pay at the office. Licenses purchased within the last two months are accepted at Caño Negro. Call the **Area de Conservación Huetar Norte** with questions (☎2471 1309).

Bring waterproof boots—biting ants and 10 of Costa Rica's 17 types of venomous snakes await. For more on **Wilderness Safety**, see p. 28.

SIGHTS BEYOND THE REFUGE

There are five *mariposarios* (butterfly farms) in Caño Negro. **La Asociación de Mujeres de Caño Negro (The Women's Association of Caño Negro; ASOMUCAN)** founded the original, located 50m south and 200m west of the mini-super. They also have a *Panadería* and Deli, **Pan y Café Caño Negro,** where you can get fresh bread. (☎2471 1450. Open daily 6am-6pm. Farm entrance ¢1000.)

NORTHWESTERN COSTA RICA

The two mountain chains that stretch across northwestern Costa Rica guard some of the country's most famous attractions. The world-renowned Monte-verde Reserve protects what remains of the cloud forests that once covered all of the Cordillera de Tilarán, while the Cordillera de Guanacaste holds three spectacular national parks farther north. Volcán Arenal, Central America's most active volcano, oozes magma at a cratered peak nestled between these two majestic ranges. Though the arid lowlands of Guanacaste cannot offer such natural beauty, they have a *sabanero* (cowboy) charm all their own. They serve as good base camps for nearby attractions like Volcán Tenorio, Volcán Miravalles, and the national parks that make up the Area de Conservación de Guanacaste, which holds 65% of Costa Rica's species. The region has witnessed

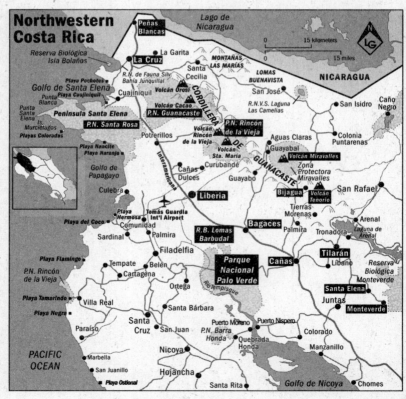

Northwestern Costa Rica

everything from annexation to invasions, and its dynamic history fosters a rich folkloric tradition that is constantly unfolding and expanding. While larger numbers of Nicaraguan immigrants have made diversity a source of regional pride and tension in more southern cities like San José, Guanacastan towns have managed to thrive on the harmony and vitality of their mixed populations.

MONTEVERDE AND SANTA ELENA

The Monteverde region, located 184km northwest of San José and due north of Puntarenas, is the reason that many travelers come to Costa Rica in the first place. Dry season guarantees more animal sightings and fewer lightning cancellations, but it also attracts many more tourists, making reservations a must for almost everything. Conversely, the rainy season offers a leisurely schedule and more exhilarating adventures as the zip lines are significantly faster in the rain. Private reserves in the area, including the famous **Monteverde Cloud Forest Reserve,** protect some of the country's last remaining primary cloud forest, which provides refuge for iridescent *quetzals*, foraging *coatis*, and a host of other creatures. Tourists flock to Monteverde to observe its array of flora and fauna. Others travel to these forests longing to fly through canopies on ziplines and watch sunsets on horses. Still others seek retreat, finding peace in the hikes, waterfalls, and art galleries that the region has to offer.

The town of **Monteverde** was founded in 1951 when a group of American Quakers, many of whom had served jail time for refusing to enlist in the armed forces, exiled themselves to the region. They used existing oxcart trails to bring in cows and to start up a successful cheese business. Though the largely English-speaking town has retained a sense of its roots, its population these days is as diverse as the nearby wildlife. There is a mix of *ticos*, tourists, eco-friendly expats, artists, biologists, and students gathered together in a sundry array of jungle lodges, local dives, and ordinary residential communities. The small town of **Santa Elena** hosts many of the area's tourist facilities and practical amenities while retaining an intimate ambience. Its central location provides a launching point to nearby reserves, including **Monteverde Reserve, Santa Elena Reserve,** and **El Bosque Eterno de los Niños.** Most are connected by dirt roads, preserving a dependent community throughout the region without infringing on the area's natural splendor. Beware its spell: many visitors have been known to extend their stays indefinitely.

⬛ TRANSPORTATION

Direct **buses** to **Santa Elena** and **Monteverde** run from **San José** (4hr.; 6:30am, 2:30pm; ₡2350), **Puntarenas** (3.5hr.; 7:50am, 1:50, 2:15pm; ₡1235), and **Tilarán** (3hr., 12:30pm, ₡1400). From **Liberia,** you can take a San José-bound bus as far as **Lagarto,** and then take a bus to **Monteverde** (8:30am, 3:00pm; ₡1200). Alternatively, go to **Puntarenas** and catch a bus from there to Monteverde. To get to Monteverde Reserve, you must change buses in **Santa Elena** (approximately 20min., times listed under Monteverde Reserve; purchase tickets for ₡600 on the bus to the Reserve).

Leaving Monteverde, buses head to: **San José** (4hr.; 6:30am, 2:30pm; ₡2350), **Puntarenas** (3hr.; 4:30am, 6, 3pm; ₡1235), and **Tilarán** (3hr., 7am, ₡1400). Buy return tickets from Monteverde to Puntarenas the morning of your bus; if going to San José, purchase the day before at the **Transmonteverde B.S.A. ticket office,** located across the street from Camino Verde in Santa Elena (☎2645 5159. Open M-F 5:45-11am and 1:30-5pm, Sa-Su 5:45-11am and 1:30-3pm.)

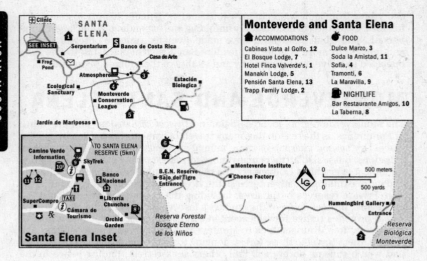

Monteverde and Santa Elena

🏠 ACCOMMODATIONS

Cabinas Vista al Golfo, **12**
El Bosque Lodge, **7**
Hotel Finca Valverde's, **1**
Manakín Lodge, **5**
Pensión Santa Elena, **13**
Trapp Family Lodge, **2**

🍴 FOOD

Dulce Marzo, **3**
Soda la Amistad, **11**
Sofia, **4**
Tramonti, **6**
La Maravilla, **9**

🍺 NIGHTLIFE

Bar Restaurante Amigos, **10**
La Taberna, **8**

Many companies offer more adventurous ways to reach popular destinations. **Jeep-Boat-Jeep** (US$25) and **Horse-Boat-Car** are offered through Aventuras El Lago. **Taxis** wait outside the church in Santa Elena. Be wary of taxi-drivers looking to charge tourists unreasonable fares. Ask the tourist office what it should cost to take a taxi to your destination; it shouldn't be more than ₡5000.

⚔️🔟 ORIENTATION AND PRACTICAL INFORMATION

Buses arrive in the town of Santa Elena, which has affordable local services, hotels, and restaurants. From here, an unpaved road heads 6km southeast to the Monteverde Reserve. The actual settlement of Monteverde is strung along this road, and has more expensive restaurants and hotels. Unless otherwise noted, the following services are in Santa Elena.

Tourist Information and Tours: Camino Verde Information & Reservation Center (☎2645 6304; www.exploringmonteverde.com), across from the bus stop, offers friendly assistance when arranging a tour. Open daily 6am-9pm. Those searching for tour companies will find no shortage along the main street; it's worth shopping around as commissions vary widely. **Camara de Turismo** (☎2645 6565; fax 2645 6464), at the end of the street across from Supermercado La Esperanza, is the official tourist center. Both book reservations to the Santa Elena and Monteverde Reserve, nearby canopy tours, ATV rides, and more. Open daily 8am-8pm. Most accommodations have their own information and tour deals; often they do not receive commission and some offer refunds for tour cancellations.

Bank: Banco Nacional (☎2645 5027; www.bncr.fi.cr), around the corner from the bus station. Changes traveler's checks and US$ and gives cash advances on MC and V with passport. Open M-Sa 8:30am-3:45pm. ATM available. **Banco de Costa Rica**, up the main road toward Monteverde Reserve, next to Sapo Dorado. Open M-F 9am-4pm.

Supermarket: SuperCompro (☎2645 5068), south of the bus station, across the street from Camara de Turismo. Open M-Sa 7am-8pm, Su 7am-8pm. AmEx/D/MC/V.

Bookstore: Librería Chunches (☎2645 5147), across from Banco Nacional and Pensión Santa Elena. Overpriced and photocopied US newspapers (NY Times ₡5000) and plain overpriced magazines (US Weekly ₡5500), new and used books and music, local information, and coffee (₡600). Also sells souvenirs, batteries, blank CDs, and envelopes. Free Wi-Fi. Open M-F 8am-6:30pm, Sa 8am-6pm. MC/V.

Laundry: Most hotels and some hostels offer laundry services; more options line the main road. Available at **Librería Chunches** for ₡3000 per load.

Emergency: Red Cross (☎128 or 2645 6128).

Police: (☎2645 6248; emergency 911), across from SuperCompro, next to the Vitosi pharmacy.

Pharmacy: Vitosi (☎2645 5004), next to the police station. Open M-Sa 8am-8pm, Su 9am-8pm. AmEx/D/MC/V.

Medical Services: Clínica Monteverde (☎2645 5076), 50m west and 150m south of the sports field. Open M-F 7am-4pm, Sa-Su 7am-7pm.

Telephones: Public telephones are everywhere, including outside SuperCompro and in the Visitors Center at the Reserve.

Internet Access: Pura Vida Internet, 50m northwest of Banco Nacional. Internet ₡1600 per hr. Open daily 11am-9pm. **Atmosphera Internet Cafe** (☎2645 6555), halfway down the road to Monteverde Reserve from Santa Elena. ₡1740 per hr. Also has free coffee, gourmet meso-American food, an art gallery, and a licensed spa. Free internet access for customers of the restaurant or art gallery. 12% discount for customers carrying *Let's Go* with them.

Post Office: Up the first hill on the way to Monteverde, beyond the Serpentarium. Open M-F 8am-4:30pm, Sa 8am-12pm. V. **Postal Code:** 5655.

ACCOMMODATIONS

With dozens of lodgings to choose from, travelers of all kinds can find a temporary home that fits their personality and budget in the cloud forests. Pricier hotels line the road to Monteverde, while most budget accommodations are in or near Santa Elena. Making reservations ahead of time is a good idea during the high season, but low-season visitors will find enterprising crowds waiting to solicit them at the bus stop. No need to be wary—most representatives are just trying to keep their businesses afloat. Prices are usually fixed. Most establishments list prices in US$ because the value of the *colón* is depreciating so rapidly, but most are happy to accept *colones* as well.

SANTA ELENA

Cabinas Vista al Golfo (☎2645 6321; www.cabinasvistaalgolfo.com), 5min. walk down the dirt road heading away from time, past the police station. The extremely amicable owners Jorge and Anali and their extended family treat their fun-loving guests as close friends from the start. Sink into the snug beds and see the beautiful view of the Monteverde mountains from the enormous bedroom windows. If that's not enough, the communal kitchen, dining tables, and hammocks upstairs all boast some of the best panoramic views of the Nicoya Gulf. Many guests have hailed their stay at Vista al Golfo as their best experience in Costa Rica. Laundry and hot water available. Free Wi-Fi and internet access, coffee, tea, and towels. Quiet after 10pm. Singles with shared bath ₡8700 (US$15); with private baths ₡11,600 (US$20); doubles ₡11,600/14,500 (US$20/25); quads ₡5800/6960 (US$10/12) per person. Apartments (with private bath, kitchen, fridge, and dining table): 2 people ₡29,000 (US$50), 3 or more ₡11,600 (US$20) each. AmEx/D/MC/V. ●

■ **Pensión Santa Elena** (☎2645 5051; www.pensionsantaelena.com; shannon@pension-santaelena.com). Young, adventure-bound backpackers flock to this ultra-social hostel just down the street from Banco Nacional. Though some locals believe it to be somewhat unsavory, it has one of the best communal kitchens around, dining tables in the reception area, and a hammock on the porch. Travelers live and mingle like family—even with the staff. Owners and siblings Shannon and Ran spend quality time with guests to answer questions, give frank suggestions, and offer words of wisdom. Early nights may not be an option as the guests tend to loosen up in the evening. Night guard makes sure only guests enter. Laundry and hot water available. Internet free for guests. Dorms ¢3480 (US$6); singles ¢6960 (US$12); doubles ¢12,760 (US$22), with private baths ¢15,080 (US$26); *cabinas* ¢20,300 (US$35). ❷

Hotel Finca Valverde's (☎2645 5157; www.verde.co.cr), down the road from Santa Elena's center en route to Monteverde. Take a small bridge over the creek to this upscale oasis, where spacious cabins are connected by stone walkways and metal bridges shaded by plantain and banana leaves. A small, private trail alongside a babbling brook provides an immediate escape. The reception area hosts a bar and restaurant serving tasty mixed drinks and affordable *tico* delights (¢4060-¢18,560/US$7-32). Cable TV, coffee maker, and fridge in every room. Complimentary breakfast. Parking available. Singles ¢40,600 (US$70); doubles ¢23,200 (US$40); triples ¢19,720 (US$34); quads ¢16,820 (US$29); *cabinas* with bathtub ¢40,600 (US$70). AmEx/D/MC/V. ❸

MONTEVERDE

■ **Manakín Lodge** (☎2645 5080; www.manakinlodge.com), about 1km from Santa Elena toward the Monteverde Reserve. 3rd-generation owner Mario and his children make guests feel like part of the family, offering town gossip, healthy veggies, and organic meals (homemade granola, omelettes, and special requests). The porches of these beautiful rooms face the edge of the forest, where white-faced monkeys wait for bananas from guests. Horse tours (¢17,400, US$30) and trips to local *fincas* available. Breakfast included. Private bath, hot water, cable TV, and fridge. Free internet access. Singles ¢11,600 (US$20); doubles ¢17,400-23,200 (US$30-40); triples ¢26,100-34,800 (US$45-60); quads ¢34,800-46,400 (US$60-80). D/MC/V. ❸

Trapp Family Lodge (☎2645 5858; www.trappfam.com). The closest hotel to the Monteverde Cloud Forest Reserve, though its distance from town necessitates transport by car, taxi (¢5000), or bus (¢600). With tall, A-frame ceilings, huge floor-to-ceiling windows, a warm orange lodge, spacious rooms, and a gorgeous location, it's easy to feel like you're already in the cloud forest. Watch the clouds roll in from the plush chairs in your room. Great restaurant on premises (entrees ¢4640-11,600, US$8-20). Parking available. Rooms with 2 double beds ¢49,300 (US$85); mountain suites (slightly higher elevation, TV, fridge, larger windows, and bathtub) ¢58,000 (US$100). AmEx/D/MC/V. ❺

El Bosque Lodge (☎2645 5221; fax 2645 5129; www.bosquelodge.com), behind Tramonti's, halfway between Santa Elena and the Monteverde Reserve. Private rooms are connected by a series of paths and bridges that weave through lovely landscaped gardens speckled with butterflies, hummingbirds, white-face monkeys, and *aguatis*. This lodge's apparent seclusion is an illusion—it is actually located right off the main road. All rooms have coffee maker, refrigerator, and hair dryer. Singles ¢26,100 (US$45); doubles ¢31,900 (US$55); triples ¢37,770 (US$65); quads ¢43,500 (US$75). D/MC/V. ❹

▣ FOOD

SANTA ELENA

■ **La Maravilla** (☎2645 6623), right across from the bus station. Serves *comida típica* to locals and tourists alike. Its convenient location and lightning-fast service make it easy to grab a ham and cheese omelet (₡1600) or a *casado* (₡2300-2850). Salads, sandwiches, soups, and seafood (fish fillet in garlic sauce ₡3450). Mango milkshake (₡800). Open daily 6:10am-9pm. AmEx/D/MC/V. ❶

■ **Soda La Amistad** (☎2645 6108), down the dirt road past the police station and next to Cabinas Vista al Golfo. Miss your *mama?* Your dynamic surrogate is waiting to serve you the most mouthwatering *tico* delights right from her personal kitchen. Cándida will plop herself down at one of the 3 tables in her home to offer warm advice and ask when she should expect you tomorrow. She can provide all of your meals: *gallo pinto* (₡1600) for breakfast, a *casado* for lunch (₡2500-3500), and vegetable spaghetti for dinner (₡1800). Open daily 6am-9pm. Cash only. ❶

■ **Coffee Bar** (☎2645 5757), in the alleyway across from the church on the main road, next to Bar Restaurante Amigos. It's all in the name: several hot coffee drinks are available (₡550-950); on warm days, the iced coffee is delightful (₡1350). Great deals include pizzas with various toppings (₡2150), burritos (₡1650), and fried garlic potatoes with bacon dressing (₡1450). Open daily 11am-10pm. ❶

MONTEVERDE

■ **Sofia** (☎2645 7017). Take a right at Atmosphera Internet C@fé and walk up 50m on the left. Indulge in creative *nueva latina* food while guitar instrumentals strum in the background. Mango-ginger mojitos ₡2900 (US$5) are a heavenly prelude to innovative fusion dishes like the Seafood Chimichanga with shrimp and tender sea bass, guacamole, sweet potato puree, and *chayote picadillo* ₡8120 (US$14). Appetizers are a cheap, delicious treat (skewered shrimp with fresh fruits and ginger, US$5). Entrees US$12-16. Open daily 11:30am-9:30pm. AmEx/D/MC/V. ❸

Pizza Tramonti (☎2645 6120), in front of El Bosque Lodge on the main road to Monteverde Reserve. Unlike many other pizzerias in town, this one maintains authenticity through its native Italian owner, Gianni. Savor Italian specialties made with imported ingredients like Pizza Tramonti with asparagus, mushrooms, ricotta, and gorgonzola cheese ₡8700 (US$15). *Spaguetti con Pesto* ₡5800 (US$10). Open daily for breakfast 6:30-8:30am, lunch 11:30am-10pm. MC/V. ❸

Dulce Marzo (☎2645 6568), next to Moon Shiva on the road to Monteverde Reserve. The kindly American owner visited the quirky cafe and was so enamored that she bought it and moved to Monteverde. Indulge in the tantalizing chocolate creations, including cheesecakes, staggeringly large cookies, or the specialty hot chocolate (a secret homemade blend of cocoa and spices; ₡1225) and you might want to buy the place too. To temper an anticipated sugar high, the small, inventive lunch menu offers daily specials of soups, pastas, and the popular curry (₡1500). Th salsa lessons with free chips, guacamole, and of course, salsa (2hr., ₡2000). Open daily 11am-7pm. ❶

 LOCAL FLAVOR. US$4 *casados* beyond your budget? Shop like a *tico* at the weekly farmer's market, *La Feria*, Sa 7am-noon at the Santa Elena School, 1 block past Restaurante El Marquez, on the road to Santa Elena Reserve. Grab 3 avocados for ₡580, 3kg of mangos for ₡1160, and homemade bread, all while supporting local farmers.

■ NIGHTLIFE

If you're too exhausted from your daytime excursions to hit the dance floors, don't feel guilty: you're not missing much. The nightlife in Monteverde is minimal. A few small-scale clubs host modest crowds where *ticos* and American tourists engage in awkward courtship rituals and heat up on hesitant dance floors. Even so, the few modest options can be entertaining.

La Taberna (☎2645 5883), 300m from Banco Nacional on the road to the Reserve. This hip *discoteca* strewn with Bob Marley and Beatles murals attracts a large crowd of *ticos* and travelers who hit the small dance floor in the main room, dancing to everything from rap to *merengue*. On quiet nights, a young crowd lounges in a room with large couches. Beer ₡800. Open daily 4pm-2am. MC/V.

Bar Restaurante Amigos (☎2645 5071), across from the church on the main road, about 20m down a small dirt road. Drawing the largest crowds in town on the weekends, Bar Amigos resembles a sports bar with some TVs, a full menu until 10pm (chicken nachos ₡1500), and a plethora of drink options. F night live salsa, merengue, and *marcao* (a tango-esque melody unique to Costa Rica). Open daily 12pm-2am. D/MC/V.

Chancho's Bar (☎2645 5926), connected from behind with La Taberna. This small, psychedelic hangout plays *trova* (Cuban protest music), alternative rock, reggae, and house, but not too loudly. A small space in the middle of the bar allows for some *tico-turista* grinding or salsa dancing (music requests accepted). During the dry season, BBQs are held in the firepit in back. If you're lucky, Chancho may invite your group to do a welcome shot. Daiquiris ₡2500; beers ₡800-1000. Open daily 7pm-3am. Wheelchair-accessible. AmEx/D/MC/V.

▩ THE RESERVES

RESERVA BIOLÓGICA MONTEVERDE

The reserve is 6km uphill from Santa Elena. Walk, take a taxi (₡3500), or take a public bus from Santa Elena outside Camino Verde (every 2hr.; 6:15, 7:40am, 1:20, 3pm; return buses 6:45, 11:30am, 2, 4pm; ₡600). The Visitor Center (☎2645 5122; www.cct.or.cr) provides general info, maps, and binoculars. ₡9860 (US$17), students or ages 6-12 ₡5220 (US$9), under 6 free. 2½hr. guided tours daily 7:30am, noon, 1:30pm; ₡9860 (US$17) per person; proceeds benefit an environmental education program geared toward rural communities, as well as a recycling program. Reservations a day in advance recommended during dry season. Many local hotels and hostels arrange private tours. The Reserve only lets in 180 people at a time; get there early if you don't want to wait for entry. Open daily 7am-4pm. Night hikes 7:30pm, ₡11,600 (US$20) with transportation; if you've already been to the reserve that day, you don't have to pay the fee again. The Visitor Center lodge has dorms with 40 beds and 6 communal showers (3 female and 3 male). Prices include entrance fee and 3 meals. Private room and bath ₡37,120 (US$64), shared room ₡30,740 (US$53); includes entrance fee and 3 meals.

Positioned directly on the continental divide, this enthralling private reserve encompasses 4025 hectares of land and provides protection for over 2500 plant species and over 400 animal species. The population of this wildlife sanctuary includes jaguars, mountain lions, peccaries, and the elusive quetzal. This last animal is a shimmering red-and-green-colored bird that falls backward off perches when startled. Though visitors frequently see animals like coatis and white-faced monkeys, spotting the other inhabitants of this dense forest can prove difficult; many visitors find that guides can prove invaluable as nature-translators or human binoculars, able to pick out creatures hidden in the trees and hear monkey calls from the ground. Other visitors find that these mystical forests cloaked in clouds and bathed in mist are best appreciated uninterpreted and are content to wander unaccompanied through the dwarf elfin woodlands and the towering canopies of the higher cove forests. Reserve highlights include **La Ventana lookout** (along the continental divide; take Sendero Bosque Nuboso directly to it) and a **long suspension bridge** (on the Sendero Wilford Guindon). At some points, it is possible to stand on either side of the continental divide, with one foot on the Caribbean slope and the other on the Pacific.

RESERVA SANTA ELENA

Reserva Santa Elena is 5km northeast of Santa Elena village. Walk on the road north from Banco Nacional, take a taxi (one-way ¢5000), or catch a minibus to the reserve in front of the bus stop (6:30, 8:30, 10:30am, 12:30pm; return buses 9, 11am, 1, 3, 4pm; ¢580). Make reservations for buses through Camino Verde after 6am (☎2645 6296). The reserve information center in town is 200m north of Banco Nacional (☎2645 5390); there is also a Visitor Center at the entrance. Open daily 7am-4pm. 3hr. guided tours 7:30, 11:30am; ¢8700 (US$15) not including entrance fee; must be arranged 1 day in advance. Entrance fee ¢8120 (US$14), students and ages 6-12 ¢4060 (US$7), under 5 free.

The often-overlooked **Santa Elena Reserve** was established in 1992 to diffuse Monteverde's tourism burden. During the dry season, Santa Elena makes for a less-crowded, equally beautiful alternative to Monteverde. Encompassing primary and secondary forests, it offers similar flora and fauna on more sparsely populated trails, where howler monkeys make a ruckus in the liana vines that dangle from the trees. There are **four main trails** in this old growth cloud forest, all short enough (1-5km) to be done as day hikes (45min.-5hr.). From some lookouts you can see **Volcán Arenal** 14km away. Morning hikes make for better weather (especially during the wet season), views, and animal watching. Informed professional guides help identify hidden animals and plants. Unlike the Monteverde Reserve, this Reserve is government-owned. Proceeds from the entrance fee go toward the local high school.

👁 🏔 SIGHTS AND OUTDOOR ACTIVITIES

🌳**CANOPY TOURS.** Canopy tours are one of Monteverde's ecotourism highlights. These tours lead potential Tarzans through forests with less intrusion than other activities. **Original Canopy Tour,** the pioneer of this arboreal activity, provides tours, but the newer tour companies offer larger coverage and cheaper prices. In addition to ziplines, suspension bridges crossing extensive distances of canopy immerse visitors in the forest while they scout for glimpses of spectacular birds, animals, insects, and plants. Five companies offer zipline tours. Three of these companies also offer walking canopy tours. The canopy tours lead visitors along a network of bouncing suspension bridges nestled in or near the canopy of the Santa Elena Reserve. **Aventura, Selvatura, Sky Trek,** and **Extremo** all offer similar packages with harrowing ziplines, though each company has its own style. Adrenaline junkies rave about the Aventura "Tarzan swings," the "Superman," mid-forest location, and rappelling apparatus, while others prefer mixing up various lengths and speeds on Selvatura or Sky Trek cables. Sky Trek boasts the highest and longest cable among its 11 (named for popular characters like "Speedy Gonzalez"). Though Sky Trek's iron platforms offer stunning vistas and combo packages with Sky Tram gondolas, some prefer tours with less-obtrusive infrastructure. In both zipline and walking tours, be prepared for sustained exposure to the elements, especially in the afternoon during the rainy season. (*Aventura* ☎2645 6959. *Zipline tour ¢23,300 (US$40), students ¢17,400 (US$30). Original Canopy Tour* ☎2645 5243; www.canopytour.com. *¢26,100 (US$45), students ¢20,300 (US$35). Sky Trek & Sky Tram* ☎2645 5238; www.skytrek.com. *¢34,800 (US$60), students ¢27,840 (US$48), children ¢23,200 (US$40). Selvatura* ☎2645 5929; www. selvatura.com. *US$40, students US$30, children US$25. Extremo* ☎2645 6058; www.monteverdeextremo.com. *¢23,300 (US$40), students ¢17,400 (US$30), children ¢14,500 (US$25). Natural Wonders Tram* ☎2645 5960; www.telefericomonteverde.com. *Aventura, Selvatura, and Sky Trek* have discounted packages for ziplines and walks on the same day. Aventura Bridges or Selvatura Walkway ¢14,500 (US$25), students ¢11,600 (US$20); Sky Walk & Sky Tram ¢29,000 (US$50), students ¢23,200 (US$40).)

ECOLOGICAL SANCTUARY. The banana and coffee plantations that once operated here have been transformed into private reserves. Four different loop trails pass stunning lookouts and several cascading waterfalls, taking anywhere from 30min. to 3hr. to hike. Because the climate is hotter here than in the reserves, there are more animals to see. The forest is home to coatimundis, three-wattled bell birds, sloths, monkeys. The sanctuary is also home to the quick-footed *agoutis*, a small barking mammal that seems to walk on tiptoe as it crosses the trails. Night visits offer a very different experience than daytime walks, frequently featuring porcupines, sloths, tarantulas, kinkajous, and lots of insects. (The well-marked turnoff from the Monteverde road is right by Atmosphera C@fe, almost 1km from Santa Elena. ☎ 2645 5869; www.ecologicalsanctuary.com. Open daily 6:30am-5pm. Guides recommended. Call a day ahead. Guides ¢14,500/US$25 for 3hr. tour, entrance fee included. Night tour 5:30-7:30pm, arrive around 5pm; ¢8700/US$15, includes entrance fee. Free printed guides available at the Visitor Center. Entrance ¢5800/US$10, students ¢4640/US$8, Costa Rican nationals and children under 10 ¢2900/US$5.)

COFFEE TOURS. Coffee lovers everywhere will gain a new appreciation for their morning cup-o-joe on a coffee tour. Start off this educational adventure at one of Monteverde's *fincas* to see how the beans are harvested, from the drying to the roasting process, in the olden days and now. At the end of the tour, visitors can taste the different types of coffee. (Monteverde Coffee Tour; ☎ 2645 7090; www.cafemonteverde.com. Tours 8am and 1:30pm. Don Juan Coffee Tour; ☎ 2645 7100; www.donjuancoffeetour.com. Irapiche Tour; ☎ 2645 5271. Tours 9:45am and 2:45pm.)

LIBERIA

As the commercial center of Guanacaste and the cultural heart of this dusty cowboy region, Liberia (pop. 40,000) is more visibly entrenched in history than many other Costa Rican towns. Paradoxically, it still strives to appease a trendier crowd; surfer stores and local *sodas* line the street in Spanish-style, white-washed colonial houses while a flag waves above the *parque central*. Guanacaste maintains a strong sense of regional autonomy and identity. In suit, Liberia celebrates Guanacaste Day, which commemorates the annexation of the "Partido de Nicoya," now known as Guanacaste, from Nicaragua in 1824. The eight-day festival, culminating on July 25th, features the traditional *tope* (horse parade). Constant fiestas, dancing, concerts, bullfights, and cattle auctions in front of the University of Costa Rica make this a highly anticipated week, drawing crowds from around the country. Apart from seasonal festivities, there's not much to see in Liberia; it's more of a transportation hub than anything else. The city also serves as an excellent base for visits to national parks like Rincón de la Vieja, Santa Rosa, and Palo Verde.

⊏ TRANSPORTATION

Flights: The **Daniel Oduber Quiros International Aiport (LIR),** 13km west of Liberia, can be reached by taxi or public transportation from the 200m north of Hotel Guanacaste. **Sansa** (☎+1-877-767-2672; www.flysansa.com). Flights to **San José** (1hr.; Nov. 20-Apr. 19 7, 10:22am, 1:13, 5:18pm; Apr. 20-Nov. 19 7, 10:22am, 1:10, 3:34, 4:54pm; round-trip ¢110,200/US$190).

Buses: Schedules often change but buses are reliable; check at either the **Pulmitán** or **Central station ticket booths.** Buy tickets in advance for **Playa Hermosa, Playa**

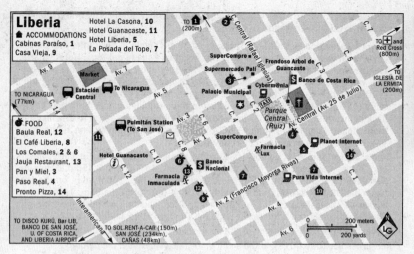

Liberia

⏶ **ACCOMMODATIONS**
Cabinas Paraíso, **1**
Casa Vieja, **9**
Hotel La Casona, **10**
Hotel Guanacaste, **11**
Hotel Liberia, **5**
La Posada del Tope, **7**

🍴 **FOOD**
Baula Real, **12**
El Café Liberia, **8**
Los Comales, **2 & 6**
Jauja Restaurant, **13**
Pan y Miel, **3**
Paso Real, **4**
Pronto Pizza, **14**

Panama, Playa Tamarindo, Playa Flamingo, Nicoya, and all international buses. Other-wise, pay on the bus. Buses fill up quickly; arrive about 30min. early. Unless otherwise noted, buses leave from **Estación Central**, across from the market, to: **Cañas** (1hr., every hr. 5am-5:30pm, ¢550); the Nicaraguan border at **Peñas Blancas** via **La Cruz** (1hr., every 2hr. 5:30am-7pm, ¢1200); **Playa Tamarindo** (1hr., 15 per day 3:50am-6pm, ¢1180); and **Playa Flamingo** (1hr., 15 per day 3:50am-6pm, ¢1165); **Playa del Coco** (1hr.; every hr. 5am-11am, 12:30, 2:30, 6:30pm; ¢350); **Puntarenas** via **Cañas** (3hr.; 5am, every hr. 8:30am-3:30pm; ¢1125); **Nicoya** via **Santa Cruz** and **Filadelfia** (2hr., every 30min. 4:30am-7:30pm, ¢785); **Playa Hermosa** and **Playa Panama** (1hr., 9 per day 4:45am-5:30pm, ¢580). Three companies depart for Nicaragua from Hotel Guanacaste (☎2666 0085), 2 blocks south of Estación Central. **Rivas, Las Virgen San Juan del Sur, Nandaime, Granada, Masaya,** and **Managua** can be reached on **Central Line** (8:30am, ¢12,000) or **Transnica** (9:30am, ¢11,400). Transnica continues to **San Salvador, El Salvador** (¢45,700). Buses to **San José** via **Bagaces** leave from the **Pul-mitán** terminal (☎2666 0458), 1 block south of the main terminal (4hr.; M-F every hr. 3am-8pm, Sa every hr. 4am-8pm, Su every hr. 5am-8pm; 9am and 3pm buses stop at Playa Coco; ¢2005).

Taxis: Line up at the north side of the *parque*, as well as by the Estación Central. **Taxi Liberia** (☎2666 7070 or 3330). **Taxi Porteadores** (☎2665 5050 or 5051).

Car Rental: Sol Rent-a-Car (☎2666 2222 or +1-800-SOL-RENT/2765 7368; www. solrentacar.com), 250m south of the Toyota dealership, on the Interamericana Hwy. in Hotel Bolero. From ¢23,200 (US$40) per day. Open daily 7:30am-5pm. Multiple rental options are also available on the road to the airport.

✈ 🔢 ORIENTATION AND PRACTICAL INFORMATION

The city is built on a typical grid with **Avenida Central** (or Av. 25 de Julio) acting as the southern border of the *parque central*, officially known as **Parque Ruiz**. Streets, however, are not well marked. **Calle Central**, or Calle Ruben Iglesias, is split by the *parque*. The oldest *barrios* of **Cerros, Los Angeles, Condega,** and **La Vic-toria** do justice to Liberia's other name, Pueblo Blanco, with their white-washed colonial buildings. In front of the church in the main plaza sits the **Frondoso Arbol** de Guanacaste, the tree after which the province was named. The **Universidad de Costa Rica** is on the west side of town.

Tourist Information and Guided Tours: Most of the hotels in town offer info on the city and on tours of nearby national parks. **Hotel La Posada del Tope, Hotel Liberia, La Casona,** and **Hotel Guanacaste** offer transportation and, during the dry season, various activities in the national parks. La Posada del Tope offers rafting trips (¢26,100/US$45), trips to Palo Verde in the dry season (¢29,000/US$50), canopy tours (¢26,100/US$45), and full adventure tours (tubing, canopy tour, and horseback riding; ¢49,300/US$85). These hotels also provide bus service to **Rincón de la Vieja** (depart 7am, return 4pm; ¢12,600) and **Santa Rosa** (depart 6am, return 3pm; ¢12,600); arrange at least a day in advance.

Banks: Banco Nacional (☎2666 1036), 3 blocks west of the *parque*. Exchanges travelers' checks. Cash advances on V. **24hr. ATM.** Open M-F 8:30am-3:45pm. **Banco de San José** (☎2666 2020), across the Interamericana Hwy., 100m down on the left, under Bar LIB. Cirrus **ATM.** Cash advances on MC/V. Open M-F 8am-6pm, Sa 9am-1pm. **Banco de Costa Rica** (☎2665 6530), north of the church. Exchanges currency and traveler's checks. Cash advances on AmEx/MC/V. Open M-F 9am-4pm.

Police: (☎2666 0213, emergency 911), 800m south of the *parque*, on the Interamericana.

Red Cross: (☎2666 0016), 200m south of the hospital, east of the *parque*.

Pharmacy: Farmacia Lux (☎2666 0061), 100m west of the *parque*'s southwest corner. Open M-Sa 8am-10pm, Su 8am-4pm. AmEx/D/MC/V. **Farmacia La Inmaculada,** Av. 25 de Julio (☎2666 7657), 50m west of Banco Nacional. Open M-Sa 8am-9:30pm, Su 10am-12pm and 4-8:30pm. AmEx/D/MC/V.

Hospital: (☎2666 0011, emergency ext. 325, or 911), 1km northeast of the *parque*.

Internet: Ciberm@nia (☎2666 7237), on the north side of the *parque*. Printing (black and white ¢100; color ¢300), international calls (¢100 per min. to US), and internet (¢300 per 30min., ¢550 per hr.). Open daily 8am-10pm.

Post Office: (☎2666 1649), 3 blocks west and 1 block north of the *parque*. Open M-F 8am-5:30pm, Sa 8am-noon. **Postal Code:** 5000.

⚑ ACCOMMODATIONS

There are many options in the city center. Some more luxurious hotels line the Interamericana Hwy. Rates may increase during the high season (Dec.-Apr.).

▪ **Casa Vieja** (☎2665 5826), 2 blocks south and 50m east of the southwest corner of the *parque*. Offers the best lodging in town without hurting your wallet. Plush couches, a full kitchen, and a covered patio with snug chairs. Dark wooden doors open up into fresh rooms with elegant curtains, private bathrooms, and cable TV. Wi-Fi and internet. Reception 24hr. Singles ¢10,000; doubles ¢17,000; triples ¢21,000. Cash only. ❷

La Posada del Tope (☎2666 3876), 1 block south of the *parque*. Entering the rustic courtyard of this 150-year-old building is like stepping into a time warp. Beds come with mosquito nets (for decorative purposes only). All rooms have cable TV. No hot water. Wi-Fi. Offers tours during the dry season and transportation to Rincon and Santa Rosa (¢12,760/US$22). Singles ¢8000, ¢12000 with private bath. Cash only. ❷

Hotel Liberia (☎2666 0161), 1 block south of the *parque*'s southeast corner. Simple rooms separated from the street by the hotel's tiled patio. Backpackers gather around the TV in the common area, chatting, drinking beer, and lounging on hammocks. Tours during dry season and transportation to parks. Laundry ¢1200 per kg. Wi-Fi. Parking available. Reception 24hr. Check-out noon. Singles ¢6300, with private bath ¢7400-8600. MC/V. 16% charge for credit cards. ❶

Hotel Guanacaste (☎2666 0085; www.higuanacaste.com), 500m west and 100 m north of the *parque*. Private rooms, as well as small shared rooms where you can fight with fellow backpackers over rights to the top bunk. No hot water. Tours to nearby volcanoes (¢11,600/US$20 per person) and national parks (¢11,600/US$20 per person to Santa Rosa, min. 4 people). Sells tickets for buses heading to Nicaragua. On-site restaurant; entrees ¢1800-4500. Wi-Fi. Shared room ¢4500; singles ¢6600; doubles ¢14,000; triples ¢19500. AmEx/D/MC/V. ❶

⚡ FOOD

For an adventurous food experience, try the sweet traditional drink called *chan*, made from coyol or flower seeds, which can look like frog eggs in water. Also ask restaurants about the popular snack *chorreadas*—a corn pancake eaten with cream or cheese. Those shopping for supplies can browse the outdoor **street market,** five blocks west and three blocks north of the *parque*. (Open M-Sa 7am-5pm.) **SuperCompro** is one block west of the *parque*'s southwest corner. (☎2666 5242. Open daily 8am-9pm.) **Supermercado Palí** is in front of the Palacio Municipal. (☎2666 4730. Open M-F 8am-7:30pm, Sa 8am-8pm, Su 8am-6pm. AmEx/D/MC/V.)

■ **Los Comales** (☎2665 0105), 3 blocks north of the northeast corner of the *parque*. Coopeingua RL, a cooperative of 25 women striving to bring back regional traditions and improve the lives of females, runs this authentic place. Serves hearty Guanacaste *típico* to locals. It's easy to miss this hole-in-the-wall, as there's no sign outside. The *arroz de maíz* (¢1600) is not actually rice, but broken corn chips cooked with chicken. *Pollo de salchichon* (long sausage) ¢1300. Open daily 6am-10pm. Open M-Sa 7am-5pm. MC/V. ❶

■ **El Café Liberia** (☎2665 1660), a few blocks southwest of the *parque*. The only European-style cafe you'll find in Liberia. Serves freshly roasted Guanacastan coffee (roasted in an antique machine in the dining area) alongside homemade delicacies. Share hummus and olives (¢3000) with a friend or go solo with a toasted pesto, goat cheese, and tomato sandwich (¢3000). Finish up with some homemade cheesecake (¢1500). Free Wi-Fi, multilingual book exchange, world music, and sporadic live performances. Themed movie showings (Th 7pm). Open M-F 8:30am-7pm, Sa 10am-6pm. Cash only. ❷

Pan y Miel (☎2666 0718), on the corner next to Palí and a Musamanni. The loaves of fresh bread stacked behind the counter are replenished often, as swarms of locals deplete the shelves of favorites like *pan danes* (¢1200). Pastries and cakes are also on sale. The 4 small tables don't allow much room for sit-down dining, so you may want to get your goodies to go. A less sweet but still popular option is the pan pizza topped with ham and cheese (¢1050). Open M-Sa 6am-8:30pm, Su 7am-5pm. AmEx/MC/V. ❶

◎ SIGHTS

Iglesia de la Ermita, six blocks east of the *parque* along Av. Central, is the oldest church in town (open daily 3-6pm, but hours vary). Enthusiastic locals converge each weekend on **Rancho Santa Alicia,** 20min. from Liberia, on the Interamericana Hwy. toward San José, where horse races, rodeos, and unrelenting heat come together to form a unique and sweaty attraction. The large horse statue at the entrance and the roaring of the crowd within make it difficult to miss (☎2671 2513; open Tu-Su).

◐ NIGHTLIFE

Ticos hailing from surrounding villages make up the bulk of the minimal party scene here. Even with the University of Costa Rica nearby, the young crowd flocks to the beach towns for more exhilarating nights.

Disco Kurú (☎2666 0769), 300m past Burger King, across the Interamericana Hwy. One of the busiest late-night spots in Liberia. Draws include 2 bars and a dance floor with mirrors. Blasting tunes feature a mix of *merengue,* salsa, *cumbia,* and hip hop. Beers ¢1100. 18+. Open daily 9:30pm-6am. AmEx/MC/V.

Bar LIB (☎2665 0741), across the Interamericana Hwy., 100m on the left above the bank. Quieter music makes for a more talkative crowd. Tropical beats on the dance floor provide lively ambience for diners. Entrees (rice, meat, ceviche) ¢5000. Occasional live music events. Cover ¢1000-2000. Open W-Sa 5pm-2:13am. AmEx/MC/V.

PARQUE NACIONAL SANTA ROSA

Established in 1971, Santa Rosa preserves one of the largest remaining tropical dry forest in Central America. Encompassing most of the Península Santa Rosa, this park has managed to keep its beaches, famous for great surfing and turtle-watching, relatively tourist-free. In addition to its status as a **UNESCO World Heritage Site,** the park is part of the **Area de Conservación Guanacaste (ACG),** one of 11 conservation areas in Costa Rica. The unique flora here includes the Guanacaste, Pochote, Naked Indian, and Caoba trees, as well as 115 species of mammals, 9600 species of butterflies and moths, 460 species of birds, and more than 30,000 species of insects. There are a number of enchanting *miradores* (lookout points) on the natural and man-made trails.

The park also houses a famous historical site, **Hacienda Santa Rosa** (La Casona). On March 20, 1856, a ragtag Costa Rican army defeated invading troops sent from Nicaragua by American imperialist William Walker. Though the event consisted of only 14 minutes of fighting, this battle is one of the most famous in Costa Rican history. Invasions were again prevented in 1919 and 1955. Sadly, La Casona did not withstand its most recent invasion, on May 20, 2001, when two vindictive deer hunters snuck into the park and set fire to the site, reducing over half of the fort to ashes. The arsonists, apparently angered by recent hunting restrictions, were caught and convicted. Costa Ricans raised ¢200,350,000 to rebuild the fort. La Casona now stands restored, with roof tiles dating from 1886 and a state-of-the-art fire alarm system. Out front, you can watch cattle going through immersion baths in preparation for their truck journey from the *embarcadero* to the *corrales de piedra* (stone corrals).

TRANSPORTATION. About 12 **buses** per day pass along the Interamericana Hwy. and stop at the entrance station at La Casetilla. No buses run the 7km stretch to the administration center or along the dirt road to the beach, so those without wheels will need to find alternative means of transportation (walking takes about an hour). **Hotel Guanacaste** (p. 503), **Hotel La Posada de Tope** (p. 502), and **Hotel Liberia** (p. 502) arrange transportation but often require a minimum number of people (¢12,760/US$22 per person). Hotel Liberia is the only hotel that arranges transportation for solo travelers (¢20,300/US$35). It may be cheaper for groups to find their own **taxi** (¢34,800/US$60 round-trip).

ORIENTATION AND PRACTICAL INFORMATION. The national park's **entrance station** is 35km north of Liberia and 24km south of La Cruz, on the west side of the Interamericana Hwy. From here, a dirt road leads 7km to the park's **administration center** which houses **MINAE offices** and an **information center.** A bit farther to the left is the campground; to the right, past the cabins, is the *comedor* (cafeteria). Beyond the administration center is a four-wheel-drive road (often closed to traffic during the rainy season) leading to the coast, 12km away. The road forks after 7km; the left branch leads 4km to **Playa Naranjo**, a popular campsite and famed surfing beach; the right heads 8km to **Playa Nancite**. Access to Playa Nancite requires special permission given to formal researchers. Contact the park for volunteer opportunities, mostly available before and during the turtle-hatching (June-Dec.; reservaciones@acguanacaste.ac.cr).

The park's **Sector Murciélago,** spread over the isolated northern coast of Península Santa Rosa, isn't accessible from the rest of the park (open 8am-5pm). To visit, start at **Cuajuniquil,** 8km off the Interamericana Hwy., which can be reached by taking a bus from La Cruz or Liberia. You will either need to walk 7km down the dirt road to the sector's ranger station or traverse the bumpy stretch with a four-wheel-drive vehicle. Information is available at the **administration center** (☎2666 5051, ext. 219; www.acguanacaste.ac.cr). Open daily 8am-4pm. For reservations, contact reservaciones@acguanacaste.ac.cr. The park is open daily 8am-4pm. Entrance fee $10; beaches $15; camping $2 extra. Discounts offered to those working on conservation efforts.

▐ ▐ ACCOMMODATIONS AND FOOD. The park offers lodging in small houses near the main offices and decent meals in the *comedor.* An on-site snack bar selling sandwiches, drinks, and bagged cookies is open to all. Reserve lodging at least one month in advance. (☎2666 5051. Lodging $12 per person. Meals $6 per day. Breakfast 6:30-7:30am; lunch 11:30am-1pm; dinner 5:30-6pm. Ask in the morning to have your lunch or dinner prepared.) A campground near the administration center has drinking water, toilets, and cold-water showers. The campground at Playa Naranjo has toilets and non-potable water. Ask about camping at the administration center.

◪ ▧ SIGHTS AND HIKING. La Casona, near the administration center (follow signs past the administration center to the left), is a museum featuring historic rooms with accompanying information and an exhibition about the Area de Conservación Guanacaste. (Open daily 8am-11:30am and 1-4pm. Free.) The **Monument to the Heroes of 1856 and 1955** lies beside La Casona and offers a windy view of nearby volcanoes in Orosi, Cacao, and Rincón de la Vieja. The lookouts **Mirador Tierras Emergidas,** halfway to the administration center from the entrance on the way to the coast, and **Mirador Valle Naranjo,** starting 6km after the administration center on the way to the coast, feature stellar views of the mountains and the beach. All trails and points of interest are marked on a useful **map** available at the entrance (¢100). The short 1km **Sendero Indio Desnudo** (a.k.a. Gringo Pelado, or "Peeled Gringo") begins on the north side of La Casona next to the museum; it winds around an impressive array of regional flora. Many of the trees in this region lose their leaves during the dry season, so it's not unusual to see them bare. Look out for indigenous carvings and monkeys high in the trees. **Sendero Los Patos** (3km), 5km beyond the administration center on the road to the coast, is one of the best trails for spotting birds and the blue morpho butterfly, and features **Mirador al Cañon del Tigre.** The 2km **Sendero Palo Seco** lies 300m before Playa Naranjo. The 6km **Sendero Carbonal** also lies 300m before Playa Naranjo and leads to **Laguna El Limbo,** a crocodile hangout. On the coast, you can swim at **Bahía El Hachal, Bahía Danta** (temporarily closed), **Coquito** (temporarily closed), **Santa Elena,** and **Playa Blanca** (17km long), or hike the 600m **Poza del General** to view birds and monkeys. **Camping** is permitted in the area, but check with the park office to see if there is space, especially during *Semana Santa* (☎2666 5051). No potable water is available.

◪ BEACHES. The famous fast waves of **Piedra Bruja** (Witch Rock) break onto a stone off **Playa Naranjo.** Though there are great waves on the shoreline, serious surfers may want to seek out sandbars where the estuary meets the ocean at Piedra Bruja; these are best from December to April. Bring a mosquito net if you plan to use the **campground** at Playa Naranjo; beware of biting *chitras* on the beach at dawn and dusk. **Playa Nancite** hosts the country's second-largest population of Olive Ridley turtles. The nesting season, lasting from July to December, is at its height from October to November and reaches its zenith during the eight days of the crescent moon. During this time, thousands of turtles arrive at 800m of beach each night around 9pm. Access to Playa Nancite is granted by permission only, and swimming is not allowed. Bring water to these beaches. Lodging is open only to researchers and students ($10 per person, up to 20 people). Call the **administration center** (☎2666 5051, ext. 233) 20 days ahead to reserve **camping** near the beach (US$2 per day; max. 25 people per day).Driving to Nancite is not allowed. Drop the vehicle off at Playa Naranjo, where a guard will watch it for you.

🚌 PEÑAS BLANCAS: BORDER WITH NICARAGUA

Liberia is only 1hr. away from the border at Peñas Blancas, a small frontier featuring a few houses and whole lot of police along the tree-lined road to Nicaragua. **Buses** run frequently from Liberia's **Estación Central** to the border (every hr. 5:30am-7pm, ¢1200). Buses from Liberia that continue into Nicaragua stop in front of **Hotel Guanacaste** (5hr., 3 per day 7:30-9:30am, ¢12,180). To reach Peñas Blancas from **San José**, take a bus from C. 14, Av. 3/5 (every hr. 3am-7pm, ¢4600). If you are traveling into Costa Rica, buses run from Peñas Blancas to **La Cruz** (every hr. 5am-6:30pm, ¢550), **San José** (every 1½hr. 5:30am-5:30pm, ¢4600), or **San Carlos** (5hr.; 6:30am, 2pm; ¢2800).

Crossing the border into Nicaragua usually takes about 30min.; if arriving on a bus, the process is slightly more prolonged. After getting your passport stamped at the **Costa Rica Immigration Office** (☎2677 0230 or 0064; open 6am-10pm), drive or walk to the actual crossing about 100m down the road. **Banco de Costa Rica** (open M-F 9am-4pm, Sa 9am-1pm), next to the immigration office, can exchange money and traveler's checks. Agents that catch you right as you get off the bus can also exchange money; they often offer a better deal than the bank, but **watch out for counterfeit bills.** Rates for changing US dollars to *cordobas* are better on the Nicaraguan side of the border, while rates for changing *colones* to *cordobas* are worse. **Hotel Guanacaste** in Liberia will also change money. Snack vendors line the road to the border. **Restaurante de Frontera,** connected to the immigration office, serves more substantial food (hamburgers ¢1000; *casados* ¢2000-2500; AmEx/D/MC/V).

Buses from the Nicaraguan border run to **Rivas** (1hr., every 30min. 4am-5:30pm; ¢20) and continue to **Managua**. To get to **San Juan del Sur,** catch the **Rivas bus** and change in Rivas for San Juan (30min., every 30min. 5am-5pm, ¢20).

NICOYA PENINSULA

The trip can be long, and the roads difficult, but the gorgeous beaches, nature reserves, and world-class waves of the Nicoya Peninsula will convince most travelers that it's worth the trek. Surfers come from across the world to surf at Tamarindo and Playa Negra, while the reef at El Coco draws novices and experienced divers alike. Though the inland region is often overlooked by travelers, its villages offer a rugged charm, with streets full of ambling cowpokes and *pueblos* where the residents guard a proud history. Larger cities like Santa Cruz and Nicoya are frequently used as transportation jump-offs but can offer rich cultural performances and a chance to experience authentic *tico* lifestyle. Since activities in these towns are scarce, it's likely you'll find yourself itching for the crashing waves and vast expanses of sand farther west.

PLAYA HERMOSA

Known as a prime swimming and diving beach for its calm waters and diverse marine life, Playa Hermosa offers beach-goers the chance to see eels, octopi, and seahorses, as well as breathtaking sunsets. With its location just outside of the Papagayo Gulf and its designation as the next "it" spot for tourism, Hermosa is experiencing tremendous growth. More villas, beachside condos, and gated communities sprout up every day. Fights to prevent environmental damage have dominated the Supreme Court for years. Despite the chaos of continual construction, Hermosa offers a peaceful and relaxing experience described by travelers and locals alike as *muy tranquilo* (very calm)—particularly in comparison to its rowdy neighbor, Playa del Coco.

⌐ TRANSPORTATION

Buses: Buses to Hermosa depart from **San José** on Av. 5/7, C. 12, one block north of the **Atlántica Norte Terminal** (6hr., 3:30pm, ¢2000) and from **Liberia** (1hr., 8 per day 4:30am-5:30pm, ¢1200). To get to San José from Hermosa, catch any bus to Liberia and transfer at the central bus station, or catch the **directo** (5am, ¢4000). Buses from **Playa Panamá** to Liberia stop in **Sardinal** (6, 7:30, 8:30, 10am, 2, 4, 5, 7:10pm; ¢1200).

Taxis: Taxis shuttle visitors from **Playa del Coco** to Playa Hermosa (15min., ¢5000).

⚹ 🛈 ORIENTATION AND PRACTICAL INFORMATION

Playa Hermosa has two entrances, both within walking distance of each other. From Playa Hermosa, **Playa Panamá** is a 3km walk along the main road to the north. **MiniSuper Dayi**, 150m south of the second Hermosa entrance, sells food products, basic amenities, beer, wine, and other liquor. (☎2672 0032; open M-Sa 7am-8pm, Su 7am-5pm.) **Lupero**, the closest *supermercado*, sits on the main road between the two entrances (☎2672 0303; open M-F 7:30am-8pm, Sa 7:30am-8:30pm, Su 8am-7:30pm). Most other services beyond those listed are available in nearby Playa del Coco and in Sardinal.

24hr. ATM: in the small complex of shops on the main road near the 1st entrance.

Telephones: 150m east of the beach, at the second entrance, next to **Pescado Loco**.

Internet Access: at **Villa Huétares**. Two computers. Internet ¢1000 per hr. Open daily 7am-10pm. Many of the hotels and restaurants have free Wi-Fi.

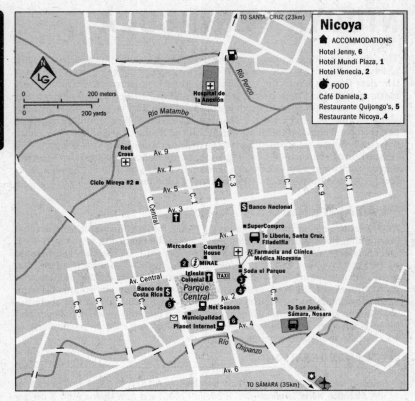

Nicoya

🏠 **ACCOMMODATIONS**
Hotel Jenny, **6**
Hotel Mundi Plaza, **1**
Hotel Venecia, **2**

🍎 **FOOD**
Café Daniela, **3**
Restaurante Quijongo's, **5**
Restaurante Nicoya, **4**

🏠 ACCOMMODATIONS

⬛ **Cabinas la Casona** (☎2672 0025), 500m west of the 2nd entrance and 20m north on the road before the beach. Friendly owners and spacious rooms with private baths, cable TV, and fully-equipped kitchens offer the best deal on the beach. Apartments for 2 with large beds, futons, and A/C provide temporary havens from the heat. Low-season singles ₡14,500 (US$25), high-season ₡17,400 (US$30); doubles ₡17,400/23,200 (US$30/40); 6-person rooms ₡43,500/49,300 (US$75/85); apartments for 2 ₡43,500/52,200 (US$75/90). Cash only. ❺

⬛ **Villa Huétares** (☎2672 0052), 300m west of the 2nd entrance to the beach. Comfortable rooms. You will be pleased with the familial owners. A/C, cable TV, pool and jacuzzi, Wi-Fi, and internet. On-site restaurant. Low-season doubles ₡26,100 (US$45), high-season ₡37,700 (US$65); triples ₡52,200/72,500 (US$90/125); quads ₡81,200 (US$140). ❹

Ecotel (☎2672 0175), walk 500m down the road from the 2nd beach entrance and turn left at the last road before the beach. The cheapest place to stay in town, suitable for nature-lovers or those willing to rough it. Options include bunk rooms, indoor lofts, and beds in the communal space. Snorkel and canoe use included. Bunk rooms and singles from ₡8700 (US$15); doubles from ₡14,500 (US$25). Camping ₡5800 (US$10) per tent, when available. ❷

Hotel El Velero (☎2672 0036; www.costaricahotel.net), on the beach. This beautifully decorated hotel has wide, whitewashed hallways, decorative fountains, bold draperies of Costa Rican fauna, and a small aquatic-themed pool. Common area on the 2nd floor has wicker rocking chairs and a book exchange. A/C and several rooms with beach views. Sailboat tours (5hr. sunset tour ¢34,800/US$60; day tour ¢46,400/US$80 per person; both include snorkeling and open bar). Massages ¢23,200/US$40 per hr. Yoga classes ¢4060/US$7. Doubles ¢43,500/US$75, each additional person ¢5800/US$10. Ask about student discounts. Prices jump in high season. Children 9 and under stay free. AmEx/D/MC/V. ●

🍴 FOOD

For once, *comida típica* is not the norm: restaurants are geared almost exclusively toward tourists and, accordingly, are pricier. Penny-pinchers will appreciate **Soda Dayi** right next to **MiniSuper Dayi**, where breakfast combos (¢2000-2500), burgers (¢1500), and other *comida rápida* leave both stomachs and wallets pleasantly full (open M-Sa 6am-7pm, Su 7am-3pm; cash only).

Finisterra (☎2672 0227; www.finisterra.net). At the 1st beach entrance, follow the signs to the restaurant by walking 700m toward the beach, taking a left, and walking 250m up the steep hill. Perched on a cliff, this popular Caribbean restaurant has some of the best views and food in town. Trained in Peru, the local-born chef cooks up creative dishes, including long-time favorites like purée of yucca with seared tuna, leeks, onion, and soy (¢5800) and Thai curry (¢81,200). Soak up your surroundings over the unforgettable passionfruit pie (¢2900). Free Wi-Fi. Open M and W-Su 5-10pm. AmEx/D/MC/V. ❸

Ginger (☎2672 0041), on stilts, off the main road. A delightful, unique tapas experience which purports to combine "all the flavors of the world on a small plate." In reality, the food is a hodgepodge of Asian and Mediterranean influences. The chef uses ample amounts of ginger, lemon-grass, cilantro, mint, and soy. Ahi Tuna (a pepper-crusted fillet served over ginger slaw and drizzled with citrus mayonnaise) ¢4000. Mojitico (guaro, passion fruit, basil, and soda) ¢2800. Large selection of wines. Open Tu-Su 5-10pm. MC/V. ❸

Pescado Loco Bar y Restaurant (☎2627 0017), 500m toward the beach (from the 2nd entrance), 50m to the right. Local food at reasonable prices served under a large wooden fish. Interesting options include squid in its own ink (¢4000), octopus *ceviche* (¢3800), and orange shrimp (¢6500). Frequented by beer-drinking locals. *Casados* ¢2800. Open daily 9am-10pm. ❷

🌀 WATERSPORTS

If it rains heavily the day before, don't plan on seeing many fish when snorkeling; Pacific tides wash phytoplankton toward the shores of the Nicoya Peninsula, which reduces visibility. By and large, however, Hermosa's calm, clear water is ideal for diving, kayaking, and waterskiing.

Diving Safaris (☎2672 1259; www.costaricadiving.net), 500m west of the second entrance to the beach. Specializes in diving and snorkeling tours. Morning dives and snorkeling 8:30am-1:30pm. 2-tank dives ¢55,100/US$95, includes equipment. Beginner day-long classes and dives ¢72,500/US$125. Snorkeling ¢23,200/US$40, includes boat. For equipment only, rentals are ¢2900/US$5 per 2hr. Arranges day sails and sunset sails with open bar and the option of snorkeling, jet-skiing, or sportfishing (from ¢58,000/US$100). Also books surfing trips to Witch's Rock and Ollie's Point (7:30am-3pm; ¢174,000/US$300, 5 person max.; experienced participants only). PADI certification course available. Open daily 7am-5pm.

Aqua Sport (☎2672 0500), follow the signs from the beach's 2nd entrance. Rents kayaks (¢5800/US$10 per 3-4hr.), pedal and paddleboats (¢5800/US$10 per person), boogie boards (¢2900/US$5 per 3hr.), and sailboats (¢17,400/US$30 for 2 people per 2hr.). Snorkeling gear and tours (¢17,400/US$30 per 3hr.; includes water, fruit, kayak, and guide). Trips to Witch's Rock (¢116,000/US$200 for 4 people per 8hr.). Fishing tour (¢116,000/US$200 per 5hr.; includes water, fruit and beer). Open M-Sa 6am-9pm.

NICOYA

Nicoya, 78km south of Liberia, is the main settlement on the peninsula. The town was named after Chorotegan Indian Chief Nicoya, who ruled the region and welcomed the Spanish in 1523. In many museums throughout Europe, Nicoya is one of the main places marked on early colonial navigation maps. Though it sees less traffic these days, Nicoya still has its charms. The *parque central* is home to ancient stone benches, cobblestone barriers, and one of Costa Rica's oldest churches. The city serves as a good base for spelunking in Parque Nacional Barra Honda. Nicoya also features more tourist services and transportation options than nearby towns, though many find that the city lacks the personality to be a destination in and of itself.

TRANSPORTATION

Buses: The **main station** is 200m east and 200m south of the *parque*. Buses leave for: **Nosara** (3hr.; 5, 10am, noon, 3, 5:30pm; ¢1000); **Playa Sámara** (1hr., every hr. 8am-9:30pm, ¢800); **San José** (4hr. via ferry, 8 per day 3am-5pm, ¢2430; 5-5½hr. via Liberia, 7:30am and 3pm, ¢4190). Buy tickets for San José at the window at least a day in advance to guarantee a seat. (☎2685 5032. Open daily 7am-5pm.) From another stop 100m north and 150m east of the *parque*, buses run to **Filadelfia** (1hr.; 10pm, additional bus Su and holidays; ¢680) and **Liberia** (2hr.; M-Sa 55 per day 3:30am-9pm, Su and holidays 9 per day 5am-7pm; ¢1000) via **Santa Cruz** (45min., ¢310).

Taxis: (¢17130/US$30 to Sámara) line up just about anywhere, including in front of the bus station, *parque*, and hospital.

ORIENTATION AND PRACTICAL INFORMATION

The two landmarks in the city center are the **parque central** and the main road, **Calle 3,** which runs north-south a block east of the *parque*. The bus might drop you off at various locations, so your best bet is to ask for the *parque central*. Once in the *parque*, Hotel Venecia is north, the *municipalidad* is south, Banco de Costa Rica is west, and Soda el Parque is east.

Tourist Information: MINAE (☎2686 6760), on the north side of the *parque*. Info on the national parks in Guanacaste. Open M-F 8am-4pm.

Banks: Banco de Costa Rica (☎2685 5010), on the west side of the *parque* with Visa/Plus **ATM,** cashes traveler's checks and gives Visa cash advances. Open M-F 9am-4pm. **Banco Nacional** (☎2685 3366), next to the Super Compro. Open M-F 8:30am-3:45pm. **24hr. ATM.**

Police: (☎2685 5559, emergency 911), 150m south of the bus station, near the airport.

Red Cross: (☎2685 5458, emergency 911), 500m north and 50m west of the *parque*.

Medical Services: Hospital de la Anexión (☎2685 8400), 100m east and 600m north of the *parque*. **Farmacia and Clínica Médica Nicoyana** (☎2685 5138), 100m east and 10m south of the northeast corner of the *parque*. Pharmacy open daily 8am-7pm, Sa 8am-6pm. Clinic open M-Sa 8am-5pm.

Internet Access: Planet Internet (☎2685 4281), 100m south of the southeast corner of the *parque*. Internet ¢500 per hr. Open M-Sa 8am-10pm, Su 10am-9pm. **Good**

Times Internet (☎8893 8891), on the south side of the *parque*, has new flatscreen computers. Internet ¢400 per hr. Black and white copies ¢100, color ¢250-1000. Open daily 9am-10pm. **Cyber Center** (☎8886 0730), below Hotel Jenny. ¢500 per hr. Black and white copies ¢100, color ¢250 and up. **Cyber Plus Internet** (☎2686 7607), 100m south of the southeast corner of the *parque*, has webcams and headphones. Internet ¢400 per hr. Open daily 8am-10:30pm.

Post Office: (☎2686 6402), across from the southwest corner of the *parque*. Open M-F 8am-5:30pm, Sa 7:30am-noon. **Postal Code:** 5200.

ACCOMMODATIONS

Unless you're willing to completely empty your wallet for a room in the truly impressive **Hotel Tempisque,** lodging options here are not the height of luxury.

Hotel Mundi Plaza (☎2685 3535 or 6702), 50m north of Banco Nacional. Pastel pink hallway and mirrors lead to bright, comfortable rooms with blue tiled floors and matching toilet-sink sets; some have balconies with mountain views. A/C and cable TV. Breakfast included. Towels provided. Secure parking. Singles ¢14,276 (US$25); doubles ¢23,984 (US$42); triples ¢34,263 (US$60). AmEx/MC/V. ❷

Hotel Jenny (☎2685 5050 or 867 5309), 100m south of the southeast corner of the *parque*. Rattier than Hotel Mundi, but becomes a real bargain if you're traveling in a group. Simple rooms with small beds, decent baths, A/C, and cable TVs. Parking available. Singles ¢10,000; doubles ¢14,000; triples ¢18,000; quads ¢20,000. AmEx/MC/V. ❷

Hotel Las Tinajas (☎2685 5081), across from the bus station to Liberia. Simple but clean rooms with small desks, shelves, and cable TVs. Public telephone available. Singles ¢6950, with A/C ¢9965; doubles ¢9800/13,600; triples ¢13,400/17,300; quads with A/C ¢22,000; quints ¢25,000; 6-person rooms without A/C ¢22,400. MC/V. ❶

Hotel Venecia (☎2686 5325), on the north side of the *parque*. High ceilings. Basic rooms with shared baths and a fan. TV and A/C also available. If you don't need a TV or A/C, this is the most economical option, though not the most comfy or sanitary. If you're going to spring for these amenities, look elsewhere. Free Wi-Fi. Lockout midnight. Singles ¢7000, with TV ¢9000, with TV and A/C ¢12,200; doubles ¢9000/10,200/13,500; triples ¢11,000/12,700/15,500. Cash only. ❷

FOOD

Casados and Chinese food joints dominate Nicoya. Pick up groceries at **Super Compro,** next to Banco Nacional. (☎2686 6314. Open M-Sa 8am-8pm, Su 8am-noon.) **Country House,** north of the northeast corner of the *parque*, sells produce. (☎2686 4800. Open M-F 8am-7pm, Sa 7am-7pm.)

Café Daniela (☎2686 6149), 100m east and 50m south of the northeast corner of the *parque*. The most popular spot for *comida típica*, with vegetarian *casados* (¢1800) that come with large green salads—a rarity in *sodas*. Large meat *casados* (¢1800-2700) come with beans, salad, rice, tortilla, and pasta. The fresh lemonade (¢800) is incredible. Open M-Sa 7am-9pm. MC/V. ❶

Cafeteria D'Melon (☎2658 4674), 100m east of the *parque*, on Av. 2. Cute coffee shop with lime green and orange walls has 67 options for hot or cold coffee, tea, and hot chocolate. Creative drinks include the Shiver *café* (coffee, chocolate cookie, vanilla ice cream, and milk; ¢1600) and the mint choco-orange (¢1000). Breakfast combo (¢2900) served with pancakes, juice, and fruit. Free Wi-Fi. Open M-Sa 9am-7pm. ❶

Restaurante Nicoya (☎2658 5113), next to Café Daniela. With the best Chinese food in town, Restaurante Nicoya is a local favorite. Large portions of fresh seafood with various

Asian and Indian flavors, like sweet-and-sour shrimp (₡3480) and chicken and shrimp with cashews (₡4000). Open daily 10:30am-3pm and 5-10:30pm. MC/V. ❷

Restaurante Madonna's Bar (☎2685 4142), on the west side of the *parque*. Don't cry for her, Costa Rica—Madonna has made it to small towns here, if only in poster form. Try the *casado* (₡1900) or the fried chicken with fruit and veggies (₡1600). Entrees ₡1500-2000. Open daily 11am-2am. ❶

La Castellana Panaderia and Reposteria (☎8861 4205), across from the Banco Nacional. Locals come for the pan pizza (₡800) and bread with pineapple and coconut (₡700). Americans feeling homesick will feel better after a slice of chocolate cake (₡600). There isn't much seating, so take it to go. Open M-Sa 5am-7pm, Su 6am-1pm. ❶

◉ SIGHTS

Iglesia Colonial, on the northeast corner of the *parque*, is one of the oldest churches in Costa Rica. It was constructed in 1644 from stone, brick, and *cal*, a unique local sand. The church was damaged by earthquakes in 1822 and rebuilt in 1831. Several religious artifacts, including a baptismal font and a 16th-century confessional booth, are worth a look. (Open to visitors M-F 8am-4pm, Sa 8am-11pm, Su 8am-5pm.) The folks at **Ciclo Mireya #2,** 400m north of the northwest corner of the *parque*, rent bikes, the perfect way to explore the surrounding countryside. (☎2685 5391. Bikes ₡8000 per day; mountain bikes ₡15,000.) Nicoya is full of shops, selling imported Panamanian clothes at unbeatable prices.

OSTIONAL

This gritty strip of black-sand beach is Costa Rica's most important breeding ground for olive ridley turtles. During the moon's fourth quarter, female turtles flock here by the thousands to lay their eggs. During this time, the tiny town comes to life: the few modest hotels in the area fill up and the fires at the two restaurants remain lit. Luckily, daytrips to Ostional from Nosara, Sámara, and even Tamarindo are available.

🚍 **TRANSPORTATION.** The trip between Nosara and Ostional (8km) makes for a pleasant 1hr. **bike** ride over dirt roads lined with cow pastures; bring a buddy. Alternatively, hop on one of the many **buses** from the bigger hotels in the surrounding towns. One bus makes the bouncy 3hr. ride between **Santa Cruz** and Ostional, leaving from Cabinas Guacamaya in Ostional and stopping at all the small towns along the way. (5, 7am, 4pm; from the *mercado* in Santa Cruz 12:30 and 4pm. It passes through Restaurante Las Tucas in **Paraíso** at 1pm (₡2100). The bus can't make the trip during heavy rains. Some travelers report finding rides, though *Let's Go* never recommends hitchhiking. Inquire for a **taxi** at local businesses, like Soda Conchito.

🏠 🍴 **ACCOMMODATIONS AND FOOD. Cabinas Guacamaya ❶,** 150m south of Soda La Plaza, is the best deal in Ostional, with spacious orange rooms that have private baths, fans, and large patios. (☎2682 0430. ₡4000 per person.) **Arribadas ❷,** across and slightly to the left of Soda La Plaza (p. 513), offers more amenities for a higher price. Each of the five rooms has a private bath with hot water and large windows. (☎8816 9815; www.hostcasaatmos.com. Breakfast included. Kitchen available. Two computers with internet available. Free Wi-Fi. Rooms ₡14,313/US$25 per person.) **Cabinas Ostional ❷,** across from Soda La Plaza, has simple triples and quads with private baths, a few hammocks, and small, private porches. The reception area is hidden, so just walk straight across from Soda La Plaza. (☎2682 0428. ₡5000 per person.) **Camping ❶** is allowed during the summer for ¢2,290/US$4 per day. You'll need to speak with the guard and pay at the ADIO booth, 150m to the left of Soda La Plaza when facing the beach. (Portable outdoor toilet.) When accommodations in Ostional get busy during the *arribada*, try San Juanillo, which has several B&Bs and a few restaurants.

The central **Soda La Plaza ❶** is one of the few restaurants in town and has a menu of all the *típico* staples at bargain prices. (*Casados* ¢2500. *Batidos*—fresh fruit juice shakes—¢500. Open daily 7am-8:30pm.) An attached **pulpería** stocks snacks and very basic cooking supplies. (Open daily 6:30am-noon and 2-7pm.) **Tony ❷**, next door to Cabinas Guacamaya, is your only other option and a break from the ubiquitous *casado*. Favorites include the Thai chicken (¢3900) or one of the many pizzas (¢4200). Free Wi-Fi for customers. (Open daily noon-10pm.)

🏄 OUTDOOR ACTIVITIES. Turtles come almost every night in small numbers, beginning around 9pm. During the moon's fourth quarter is the **arribada** or **flota**, the synchronized arrival of thousands of turtles to a specific section of the beach. In those special periods (generally 3-8 days) when the *arribada* occurs, most turtles arrive at the beach between 3pm and 7am. They travel from as far away as Peru and Baja California to give their offspring a chance to begin life in the same place they themselves were born. This makes Ostional the second largest olive ridley sea turtle breeding ground in the world. During the *arribada*, the sand is barely visible beneath the massive number of turtles digging cozy holes for their eggs. With guides holding red lights, you can watch a mother turtle dig a hole, drop all her eggs, scramble to cover the hole, and then camouflage it. This fascinating process takes about 30min. Including the ascent to the laying spot and return to the water, expect a viewing to last about an hour and fifteen minutes. Sometimes the beach gets so full with turtles that they overflow onto the town's roads. To make sure you don't miss this event, contact biologist Rodrigo Morera (☎ 682 0470; www.ostionalcr.tripod.com/index.html) at **La Asociación de Desarollo Integral de Ostional**, 100m north of Soda La Plaza. The **National Wildlife Directorate** (☎8233 8112 or 8222 9533) can also provide information about the *arribada*. You can also check in with the tourist agencies in Nosara or Sámara. If you do miss the *arribada*, wait a few weeks to see the baby turtles make their way to the water. During the *arribada* and at night, **guides are required.** Contact Rodrigo Morera, who can refer you to a guide, or any tourist agency in the area. (¢5,725/US$10. 10-person maximum per group. Flash cameras, flashlights, and surfing are prohibited during the *arribada*.) You will not be able to see the many crabs that roam the beach in the dark, so wear closed-toed shoes. To learn more about the volunteer opportunities available here, contact Rodrigo Morera. Fore more information on volunteering in Costa Rica, see **Beyond Tourism**, p. 446.

MAL PAÍS AND SANTA TERESA

Don't be fooled by the name of this remote surfing village near the southern tip of the Nicoya Peninsula; with long, empty beaches, stunning rock formations, and scenic coves, Mal País is hardly a "bad country." Settled by a small community of locals and currently home to a growing contingent of foreigners, this area is slowly developing into a haven for excellent ethnic restaurants and unique accommodations. You'll find more hotels, restaurants, and shops clumped together in Santa Teresa. Bad roads can make travel to Mal

País difficult and time-consuming, but the constant surf and peaceful vibe make the trip worth the effort.

TRANSPORTATION

Buses: Most travelers take the **ferry** from Puntarenas to **Paquera** and drive directly to Mal País, or take buses directly to **Cóbano** (2hr., 7 per day 6am-7pm, ¢1200). If you're lucky, there may be extra space on the **San José** bus coming off the ferry that will go directly to Mal País. You can also head first to **Montezuma** and then take buses to Mal País. From Montezuma, take the bus to **Cóbano** (15min., 6 per day 5:30am-4pm, ¢300) and catch a connecting bus from the same stop to **Santa Teresa** via **Mal País** (1hr.; 10:30am; 2:30pm; ¢700). Return buses leave from Santa Teresa and pick passengers up at hotels and the main crossroads by Frank's Place before heading back to **Cóbano** (7:30, 11:30am, 3:30pm). Buses leave from Frank's Place to **San José** (M-F 5:45am, Sa-Su 5:45, 8:15am, 3:45pm; ¢6500). Ask your accommodation for more information about bus stops in town.

Taxis: Taxis drive around town but are not common. If you can't find one, call a local taxi (☎8819 9021). Taxis to **Cóbano** ¢8588 (US$15) leave from the intersection.

Private Transportation: Bad roads and infrequent public transportation make moving on from Mal País time-consuming and complicated, so transfer services, though expensive, may prove well worth it for the convenience. **Montezuma Expeditions** (☎2642 0919), which can be booked at Tropical Tours (☎2640 0384) by the crossroads, has shuttles to major destinations (Arenal, Jacó, Manuel Antonio, Monteverde, San José, Tamarindo; ¢22,900-25,763/US$40-45) and can arrange other shuttles. Most leave around 8am.

Car Rental: Alamo (☎2640 0526), on the right, on the road into town from Cobano. Rentals from ¢22,900 (US$40). 21+. Open daily 8am-5pm. **Budget** (☎2640 0500), 100m from Frank's Place on the road to Santa Teresa. Rentals from ¢25,763 (US$45). 21+. Open M-Sa 8am-6pm, Su 8am-4pm.

Bike and ATV Rentals: Getting around Mal País is easiest with a **bike** or **4WD vehicle**. **Alex's Surf Shop** (☎2640 0364), 600m toward Santa Teresa from the main intersection, rents bikes for ¢5725/US$10 per day and quads for ¢34,350/US$60 per day. Open daily 8am-6:30pm. MC/V. In Mal País, **Isla Red Snapper** (☎2640 0490), 400m south of Mal País Surf School and Resort. Look for a sign that says "bikes, sportfishing, snorkeling." Low-season bikes ¢4580 (US$8); high-season ¢5725 (US$10). **Tropical Tours** (☎2640 0384). ATVs for ¢25,763 (US$45) per 6hr., ¢31,488 (US$55) per 10hr., ¢42,938 (US$75) per 24hr.

ORIENTATION AND PRACTICAL INFORMATION

The area that most surfers and locals refer to as Mal País is actually three separate beaches stretching along 6km of shoreline on the southwest corner of the Nicoya Peninsula, 11km southwest of Cóbano. Buses from Cóbano stop first at the **crossroads**, which marks the center of the bumpy **dirt road** that runs parallel to the beaches. All accommodations and services are off this main drag. The closest thing you'll find to a town center is at this main crossroads and just to the right into **Santa Teresa**, which stretches 3km north. On the opposite end from the crossroads, **Mal País** stretches 3km south, ending at the tiny marina where fishermen unload their daily catch. Establishments are pretty spread out in Mal País. **Playa Carmen** is 100m west, down a gravel road in front of the bus stop.

Tourist Office: Tropical Tours (☎2640 0384 or 1900). 2 locations, 1 by Frank's Place and the other by Super Ronny. The most comprehensive tourist information center, offering private transportation, internet, and organized tours. Open daily 8am-8pm. Hotels and various surf shops are also glad to help with information and book tours.

Currency Exchange: Banco Nacional (☎2640 0640), in the Playa Carmen Mall, 50m north of the main intersection. **24hr. ATM.** Open M-Sa 1pm-7pm. **Banco Costa Rica** (☎2640 1019), to the left of Frank's Place. **Currency exchange** and **ATM.** Open M-F 9am-4pm.

Laundry: Many hotels and hostels do laundry for their guests, but locals often offer cheaper rates. Heading north toward Santa Teresa from the main intersection, look for the many signs on the right advertising laundry. Most places charge around ¢1000 per kg.

Gas Station: Tano (☎2641 0009), 3km toward Santa Teresa. Open M-Sa 7am-5pm.

Police: ☎911 or 117.

Pharmacies: Amiga Farmacia (☎2640 0539), next to the Banco Nacional. Open M-Sa 8am-8pm. AmEx/MC/V.

Medical Services: Costa Rica Medical Response (☎2640 0976 or 2417), in the Playa Carmen Mall. The only clinic in the area. English spoken. Open 24hr.

Telephones: Several along the main drag, at the crossroads, and at Super Santa Teresa. Super Ronny's (p. 517) sells phone cards.

Internet Access: Tropical Tours, next to Super Ronny's. ¢1500 per hr. Open daily 8am-9pm. **Frank's Place** has similar rates. Open daily 8am-6pm. Other options throughout Santa Teresa. Many restaurants offer free Wi-Fi with purchase of a meal.

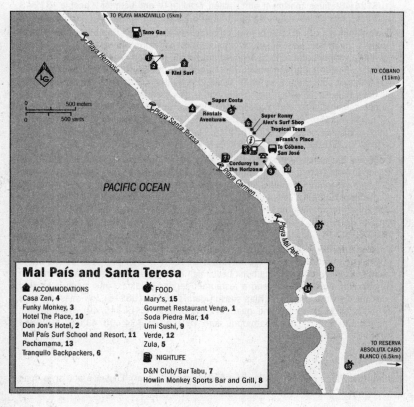

Mal País and Santa Teresa

🏠 **ACCOMMODATIONS**
Casa Zen, **4**
Funky Monkey, **3**
Hotel The Place, **10**
Don Jon's Hotel, **2**
Mal País Surf School and Resort, **11**
Pachamama, **13**
Tranquilo Backpackers, **6**

🍽 **FOOD**
Mary's, **15**
Gourmet Restaurant Venga, **1**
Soda Piedra Mar, **14**
Umi Sushi, **9**
Verde, **12**
Zula, **5**

🎵 **NIGHTLIFE**
D&N Club/Bar Tabu, **7**
Howlin Monkey Sports Bar and Grill, **8**

Post Office: Closest full-service office is in Cóbano, but there's a **mailbox** at **Pizza Tomate,** 1.5km toward Santa Teresa.

ACCOMMODATIONS AND CAMPING

Santa Teresa is where you'll find most of the budget places, while Mal País has several newer and more upscale options. Many rooms come equipped with full kitchens to accommodate surfers, many of whom stay for weeks at a time. A few camping areas provide sandy grounds for the bare-bones traveler. **Zenelda's Cabinas y Camping ❶** is a good option on the beach. Sites have bathrooms, showers, and water. (☎2640 0118. ₡2000 per person.)

SANTA TERESA

Casa Zen (☎2640 0523; www.zencostarica.com), 1km down the road to Santa Teresa. The highlight of this peaceful palace is its centerpiece: a 2-story, octagonal common area and Thai restaurant with elephants painted on the walls. In high season, Zen offers massages and nightly shows, including live music, trapeze artists, and fire entertainment. Small climbing wall on-site. Th and Su free movie nights. Yoga classes ₡4015 (US$7) per class or ₡14,338 (US$25) for 5 classes. Laundry ₡800 per kg. Internet ₡1200 per hr. Dorms ₡6882 (US$12); private rooms for 2-5 people ₡13,764-27,528 (US$24-48); huge apartment with kitchen, satellite TV, and bath for 2 people ₡31,543 (US$55), can accommodate up to 14 for ₡83,158 (US$145). ❶

Funky Monkey (☎2640 0272; www.funky-monkey-lodge.com). One of the town's most popular surfer hangouts. Two-story, unpainted wooden dorms are spacious and include gardens, showers, and sinks. Bungalows are similar, with floor-length shutters that open up onto porches with hammocks. The lounge area has a pool table and mattresses for lying out on while you watch TV. Close to a good surf break. The on-site restaurant is open daily for breakfast and dinner and serves sushi Tu and Sa. Wi-Fi, a pool, and a communal kitchen also available. High-season dorms ₡9750 (US$17); bungalows ₡45,880 (US$80). Low-season dorms ₡6882 (US$12); bungalows ₡34,410 (US$60). Each additional person ₡5735 (US$10). Apartments for 4 with ocean view ₡57,350 (US$100), with A/C ₡68,820 (US$120). V. ❶

Tranquilo Backpackers (☎2640 0614; www.tranquilobackpackers.com), 400m down the road from Frank's Place in Santa Teresa. The rooms aren't fancy, but live music during high season, a communal kitchen, cable TV, free internet, a pool table, and plenty of hammocks draw a social bunch of backpackers. The young and helpful staff offers complimentary coffee and tea and flips free pancakes every morning. ₡2000 room key and linens deposit. Security guard 6:30am-6:30pm. Dorms ₡6309 (US$11), with bath ₡7456 (US$13); doubles ₡17,205/20,073 (US$30/35). ❶

Don Jon's Hotel (☎2640 0700), past Pizzeria Tomate on the road to Santa Teresa. Tight-fisted but simply can't live without A/C? You're in luck. This hotel boasts brand new, spacious dorms with log bunk beds, high ceilings, and, yes, A/C. Common room shows surf movies all day, and a restaurant serving breakfast and lunch is located on-site. Communal kitchen. High-season dorms ₡8603 (US$15), low-season dorms ₡6882 (US$12); triples and quads ₡25,808/22,940 (US$45/40). Two-bedroom apartment with kitchen, bathroom, and DVD payer ₡34,410/43,013 (US$60/US$75). Cash only. ❶

MAL PAÍS

Hotel the Place (☎2640 0001; www.theplacemalpais.com). Elegance and style don't have to come at prohibitive prices. The modern, outdoor lounge next to the swimming pool has low tables, chairs, and pillowed seats, all accented with African and Costa Rican masks and patterns. The private bungalows all have their own themes: from "Mediterranean Breeze" and "Out of Africa" to "El Nido de Amor" (The Love Nest). The chic bar serves just about any drink you could want. Rooms come with A/C, private baths, and Wi-Fi. Satellite TV in common area. Doubles ₡40,145 (US$70); quads ₡45,880 (US$80); bungalows for 4 ₡57,350 (US$100); 2-bedroom house ₡114,700 (US$200). Discounts in low season and for stays of 6 nights or more. MC/V. ❹

▨ **Mal País Surf School and Resort** (☎2640 0061; www.malpaissurfcamp.com), 500m down the road to Mal País. Prides itself on a relaxed surfer atmosphere. Has rooms for all budgets. Its 10 acres of land feature a bar, restaurant, 17m pool, gym, and pool and ping-pong tables. With a flat-screen TV showing surfing videos and a projection screen for movies at night, there's always something to watch. Surf lessons (₡22,940/US$40), board rental, tours, and laundry also available. Check-out noon. Surfer package with 3 meals, board rental, and basic accommodations ₡34,410 (US$60). High-season open-air dorms ₡8603 (US$15); cabins for 2 ₡20,073 (US$35); villas for 4 ₡48,748 (US$85); suite with kitchen and living room ₡86,025 (US$150). Low-season dorms ₡5735 (US$10); cabins for 2 ₡14,338 ($25); villas for 4 ₡37,278 ($65); suite with kitchen and living room ₡57,350 ($100). AmEx/D/MC/V. ❶

Pachamama (☎2640 0195; www.pacha-malpais.com), 1km from Frank's Place, toward Mal País. Lemon, mango, and papaya trees surround the buildings, while monkeys move in the treetops. A 30m trek up to the hotel's lookout point offers the most breathtaking sunset view in the area. The friendly Austrian owner, Franz, offers fishing trips, kitesurfing, and board rentals. Three bungalows sleep 2-5 and have private hot water baths, kitchens, and porches with hammocks. Bigger groups will love the 2-story house, which sleeps 5 and includes a kitchen, bath, BBQ pit, outdoor dining area, loft, and porch. Free Wi-Fi. Adjoining bungalows ₡34,410 (US$60); standalone bungalows ₡45,880 (US$80); house ₡80,290 (US$140). 3-floor tipi ₡5735 (US$10) per person. Cash only. ❸

▨ FOOD

The long road running through Mal País and Santa Teresa is sprinkled with cafes, restaurants, and *sodas*. Many keep unpredictable hours despite their "official" schedules. Additionally, some restaurants close entirely in the low season. Those looking to cook at home can go to **Super Ronny's**, about 750m down the road to Santa Teresa. (☎2640 0297. Open daily 7am-9pm.) Farther into Santa Teresa is **Treble Maya Super.** (☎2640 0645. Open daily 7am-9pm.) **Super Costa** is across the street from Casa Zen. (☎2640 0530. Open daily 7am-9pm.) An **organic produce market** is held every Saturday afternoon near the main beach entrance of Playa Carmen.

SANTA TERESA

Zula, 700m down from Frank's Place toward Santa Teresa. This Israeli restaurant comes highly recommended. Hummus served with falafel (₡3500) or chicken on homemade pita bread (₡3500) are fantastic. Vegetarians will drool over the delicious avocado pita (₡3000). Larger dishes come with salad and fries. If you're feeling adventurous, try the *shakshuka*, a traditional meal with eggs poached in tomato sauce (₡3600). Free Wi-Fi. Glass of house wine ₡2000. Shisha ₡2500 per tablet. Open M-F and Su 10am-4pm and 6:30-10pm. ❷

Umi Sushi (☎2640 0968), in the Playa Carmen Mall, at the intersection of the road to Cóbano. The cool Japanese decor and extensive sushi menu will make you forget you're in Costa Rica. Eat indoors or under an umbrella in the pebble-filled courtyard. Sushi

(¢1750-2780) and sashimi (¢2650-5150) are made with both local and imported fish. Start with edamame (¢1900) or miso soup (¢1155), and sip on an imported Sapporo (¢2250). Open daily 11:30am-10:30pm. MC/V. ❷

Soda La Amistad (☎2640 0452), slightly past Casa Zen. This small soda comes highly recommended by surfers. Owner Stanley serves yummy *comida típica*. Casados ¢2000-2200. Rice with seafood ¢3000. Open daily 8am-10pm. ❶

Burger Rancho (☎2640 0583), 200m south from Funky Monkey, in front of the *futból* pitch. "Free Love" is listed on the menu, but chicken sandwich (¢2900) and hummus and pita (¢2600) are better bets. Daily specials listed on the black board. Belgian meatballs ¢4500. Free Wi-Fi for customers. Open daily 9am-11pm. ❷

MAL PAÍS

🗷 **Mary's** (☎2640 0153), 3km down the road to Mal País. Hand-made lanterns made of pressed flowers hang over private booths. The wood oven bakes delicious red snapper; the seared yellowfin tuna is scrumptious as well. All of the fish are caught by fishermen in Mal País. Pizzas (¢5000-6500) are all made with their special tomato sauce. Entrees ¢4500-6500. Open M-Tu and Th-Su 5:30-10pm. ❷

🗷 **Soda Piedra Mar** (☎2640 0069), 2km down the road to Mal País and then 200m down a dirt path toward the beach. Set back from the main road and nestled between the rocks and waves that crowd the beach, this quiet *soda* remains hidden from most travelers. The standard *típico* entrees are as scrumptious as they are affordable. Sit out on the patio and enjoy spectacular ocean views and picture-perfect sunsets. Ask about fishing trips and kite-fishing lessons. *Casados* ¢1800-2000. Chicken fajitas ¢3000. Breakfast pancakes with honey ¢1800. Fruit drinks ¢900-1000. Open M-Sa 8am-8pm. ❶

Ritmo Tropical (☎2640 0174), 700m down to the road to Mal País. Come here for good Italian food. Sit under the palm-leaf umbrellas and listen to the ocean in the distance. Pizza ¢3600-5200. Four-cheese pasta ¢4000. Open daily 8am-11:45am and 5-10:30pm. ❷

📷 NIGHTLIFE

In general, the surfer lifestyle makes for subdued nights in Mal País. That said, three main bars still get crowded on some nights.

La Lora (☎2640 0132), 3km up the road to Santa Teresa. The place to be on Th nights for reggae. Latin dance music separates the foreigners from the *ticos* on Sa. Cover ¢2000-3000 for live music events. Open daily in high season noon-2:30am, in low season 6pm-2:30am.

D&N Club (☎2640 0353), right off the beach, just south of the town center. Formerly Bar Tabu, D&N hosts full-moon parties with fire dancers, trapeze artists, and trippy techno music during the high season. M night reggae. W Latin night. Sa electronica. The club also holds BBQs on the beach and is planning to set up night lighting for surfers. Open daily 4:30pm-2am.

Good Vibrations (☎2640 0007), just south of the Playa Carmen Mall at the main intersection. Formerly Howling Monkey Sports Bar and Grill. Not much of a party scene unless the reggae (or Beach Boys) is blasting, but has a flatscreen TV permanently tuned to surfing or big sports games. Tasty bar food ¢3000-4800. F 10pm jam sessions. Beer ¢1000. Happy hour 5-7pm, beer ¢800. Open daily 11am-2am.

BEACHES AND SURFING

The Mal País area is known as a **world-class surf spot** with consistent waves and a faithful crowd. Its location between the Central Pacific coast and Guanacaste creates big southern swells in the rainy season and gnarly offshore breaks in the dry season. The currents are strong here, so swimming can be dangerous. There are several surf spots along the coast with slightly different conditions. South of the crossroads, **Playa Mal País** is inconsistent and better for tide pool exploration. Three kilometers south of the crossroads, **Punta Barrigona** at Bar Mar Azul develops great waves around the point when the swell is big. One kilometer farther south is **Playa de Los Suecos** (or Sunset Reef). The break here is shallow, inconsistent, and for high caliber surfers only. **Playa El Carmen,** directly ahead of the crossroad, has a long right wall. The best spot on **Playa Santa Teresa** is 3km north of the crossroad behind Cabinas Santa Teresa. The A-frame break here is more powerful and consistent than El Carmen; it also holds a better wave at low tide. **Playa Hermosa,** the next beach north of Santa Teresa, has almost no crowds and fast peaks rise along the beach. This beach is becoming increasingly popular for kite-surfing. The beach farthest north in the area is Playa Manzanillo, an idyllic spot 8km from the crossroads. It has an offshore reef and less hairy waves than its neighboring beaches. It's only accessible by 4WD or a 1hr. bike ride on rough roads and through shallow rivers. Still, it's worth the daytrip just to see the unspoiled scenery.

Several surf shops in Mal País and Santa Teresa rent boards and provide instruction. **Kina Surf,** 2.2km down the road to Santa Teresa, next to Pizzeria Tomate, is one the best-run surf shops, with plenty of boards and gear to pick from and a knowledgeable, friendly staff. It also sells pop art made from items found on the beach. (☎2640 0627; wwww.kinasurfcostarica.com. Surfboard rental ¢5735/US$10 per day; 2-3hr. surf lessons plus day board rental ¢20,073/US$35. Open M-Sa 9am-5pm, Su 10am-4pm.) **Alex's Surf Shop,** 200m toward Santa Teresa from Frank's Place, rents boards (¢5735/US$10 per day) and offers lessons (private ¢28,675/US$50, group ¢20,073/US$35), which include board rental. (☎2640 0364. Open daily 8am-6:30pm. MC/V.)

⚠ ⛱ OUTDOOR ACTIVITIES AND GUIDED TOURS

Although the hollow beach break is what most people come to town for, the Mal País area offers an array of outdoor activities for non-surfers; even die-hard wave-riders might find themselves diverted by the plethora of beach activities. **Fishing** is the second-most popular activity around here. The small marina at the end of the road to Mal País is always bustling with fishermen and tourists counting their catches. The adventurous and bus-weary can walk 2.5km along the road to Mal País until they reach the fork in the road, then turn left and continue 9km more to the **Reserva Natural Absoluta Cabo Blanco.** Otherwise, rent a snorkel and explore the **tide pools** just behind Sunset Reef Hotel. To get there, walk 2.5km down the road to Mal País, turn right at the fork, and continue another 500m until you see the hotel at the end of the road. Those with a bit more cash can take one of the package tours or organized trips offered around town. Check out a wide range of options at **Tropical Tours.** They offer **canopy tours** (¢20,073/US$35), **snorkeling** at Isla Tortuga from Montezuma with BBQ and drinks (¢25,808/US$45), and daytrips to Monteverde and Arenal (☎2640 1900; www.tropicaltoursmalpais.com). Located on the beach next to D&N Club, **Adrenaline Surf and Kite School** offers kite-surfing lessons to beginners and advances surfers alike. (☎8324 8671. 2hr. beginner lesson ¢57,350 (US$100); 4hr. ¢103,230 (US$180). You can also talk to Franz, the owner of **Pachamama,** about kite-surfing tours up to Nicaragua; he also knows about some inexpensive **sportfishing** (☎2640 0195; www.pacha-malpais.com).

CENTRAL PACIFIC COAST

The Central Pacific shore is Costa Rica's poster child: snapshots of its sunsets grace the covers of travel brochures and postcards, man-sized marlin lure sportfishermen from all over the world, and rugged rainforests sprawl just steps from the region's soft, sandy beaches. From vacationing *ticos* and foreign backpackers to resort-hopping honeymooners, a diverse group of travelers flocks to costal towns where they can take advantage of a well-developed tourist infrastructure. Popularity brings inevitable drawbacks, and major beach towns like Jacó, Quepos, and Manuel Antonio are invariably more crowded and more expensive than Costa Rica's more remote Caribbean side. Diehard peace-seekers, however, need only move on to Playa Esterillos Oeste or Uvita for magnificent, unspoiled scenery and long stretches of deserted beach.

JACÓ

Swimmers might be intimidated by the waves that beat against Jacó's cinnamon-colored sands, but surfers from around the world flock here to enjoy the consistent conditions and energetic atmosphere. Beginners will find that this is a great spot to pick up surfing skills, as the waves are not as enormous as other Pacific beaches, and surfing lessons are almost as common as the *casado*. Even during the low season, the town bustles with activity as surfers hit the water and tourists enjoy the numerous shops on Jacó's main drag. On the weekends, *ticos* flock to Jacó for the parties and waves. Of course, all this popularity comes with a price: restaurants charge a little more, budget accommodations aren't quite as cheap, the streets are littered with tour agencies, the beaches are not as pristine as they once were, and drugs and prostitution grow more common with each passing year. The party scene is fast-paced and runs from dusk until dawn every night. To avoid trouble, always walk with friends or take a taxi at night. Travelers looking to relax can find more peace on the black sands of Playa Hermosa, a getaway just a few kilometers south.

▗ TRANSPORTATION

Buses: Buses to **San José** (Transportes Jacó S.A., ☎2290 2922; 3hr.; 5, 7, 9, 11am, 1, 3, 5pm; ₡1510) arrive and depart from Plaza Jacó, opposite the Best Western, 1km north of the town center on Ave. Pastor Diaz. Buy tickets early from the office at the southeast corner of the plaza. Other buses stop at various locations along the main road so ask around for the nearest stop; a good place to catch them is from the benches near the Más X Menos. Buses to **Orotina** (1½hr.; 4:30, 5:30, 7, 9am, noon, 2, 4pm; ₡1000) and **Puntarenas** (3hr.; 6, 9am, noon, 2, 4:30, 5, 7pm; ₡1350) stop on the east side of the street, and buses to **Quepos** (1hr.; 6:30, 9:30am, 12:30, 2, 4, 6pm; ₡800) stop on the west side.

Taxis: (☎2643 1919, 2643 2121, or 2643 2020) line up in front of Más X Menos (Playa Herradura ₡3500; Playa Hermosa ₡3000). Except for those coming from San José and Puntarenas, buses drop off passengers along the main road. Otherwise, buses passing

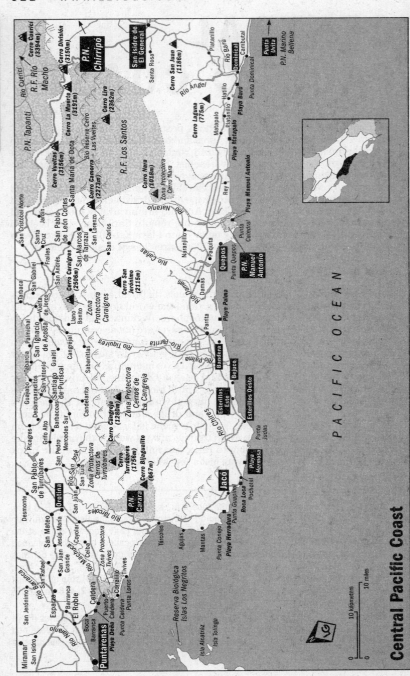

Central Pacific Coast

near Jacó along the Costanera Sur Hwy. stop at the south end of town. It is a 1km walk or a ¢600 taxi ride to Jacó center.

⊠ 🛈 ORIENTATION AND PRACTICAL INFORMATION

Jacó center stretches about 1km along the main road, which runs northwest to southwest, parallel to the beach. For simplicity's sake, we describe the road here as north-south, with the northernmost end of town marked by the Best Western and bus station and the far south end by the post office. Several side roads and paths branch west off the main road and lead to the beach. Playa Herradura is 7km north of Jacó; Playa Hermosa is about 5km south.

Tourist Information: Jacó has no official tourist office, but many tour operators and shop owners are attentive and speak English. Maaike, the attendant at **Pacific Travel and Tours** (☎2643 2520; open M-F 9am-6pm, Sa 10am-1pm), arranges tours and transportation, and provides maps and other general information.

Banks: Banco Nacional, in the center of town. Open M-F 8:30am-3:45pm. **BAC,** ion the top floor of the Il Galeone shopping center. Open M-F 11am-6pm. **Banco Popular,** 100m north of Banco Nacional next to Il Galeone. Open M-F 8am-4pm, Sa 8:30-11:30am. All have **24hr. ATMs.** A **Western Union** office is located next door to Mexican Joe's. Open M-Sa 9am-1pm and 2-6pm.

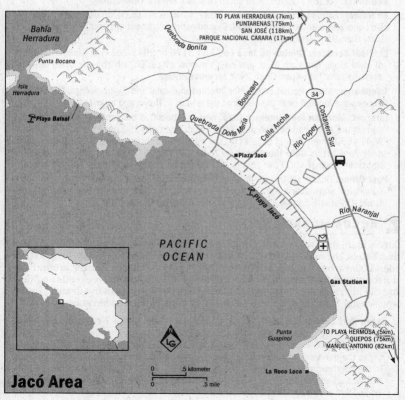

Jacó Area

Car Rental:

Budget Car Rental (☎2643 2665; www.budget.co.cr), in the Pacific Shopping Center, 50m north of the Jungle Bar. 21+. Drivers 18-20 pay ₡11,600 (US$20) extra per day. ₡435,000 (US$750) deposit. Cars in high season from ₡578,600 (US$57) per day, ₡208,800 (US$360) per week; in low season from ₡19,100/134,560 (US$33/232). Open daily 8am-5:30pm. AmEx/D/MC/V.

Economy Rent a Car (☎2643 1719), on the north side of town across from W.O.W. Surf. 18+ for Costa Rican residents, 21+ for non-residents. ₡1,160,000 (US$2000) deposit. Open daily 8am-6pm.

Laundry: Lava Max (☎2643 1617), just north of Mexican Joe's. Self-service wash and dry ₡4000 per 5kg; full-service ₡5000 per 5kg. Pick-up and delivery service also available. Open daily 8am-5pm. AmEx/MC/V. **Aqua Matic Lavandería** (☎2643 2083), 50m south of Banco Nacional. Self-service wash and dry ₡3000 per 5kg; full-service ₡3400 per 5kg. Open M-Sa 7:30am-5pm. AmEx/MC/V.

Parking: in El Paso Parqueo on C. Bohio across from Hotel Poseidon. ₡600 per hr., ₡400 per hr. for 24hr.

Emergency: ☎911.

Police: (☎2643 3011 or 2643 1881), in front of the Plaza de Futbol. Take C. Bohio down to the beach and walk 50m north. Open 24hr. An office for the transit police is located next to Clínica de Jacó.

Red Cross: (☎2643 3090), 50m south of Más X Menos. Open 24hr.

Pharmacy: Farmacia Fischel (☎2643 2089; www.fischel.co.cr), on the ground floor of Il Galeone. Has a knowledgeable staff. Remedies for jellyfish stings and board burn. Open daily 9am-9pm. AmEx/MC/V.

Medical Services: Clínica de Jacó (☎2264 3176 or 2643 3667), a 5min. walk south of town along the main road, just past the post office. English spoken. Open daily for consultations 7am-4pm. Open 24hr. for emergencies.

Telephones: Most internet cafes offer international calls and Skype access. **Public telephones** are located near the beach at the end of C. Bohio and all over town.

Internet: Mexican Joe's Internet Café, next to Tabacon in the center of town. 2nd location on the north end of town near W.O.W. Surf. Internet ₡250 per 15min., ₡700 per hr. Wi-Fi ₡550. International calls ₡100 per min. Private rooms available for Skype. Open daily 7am-11pm. **Cafe Internet @** (☎2643 2089 or 2643 1518), just north of Banco Nacional. Internet ₡500 per 15min., ₡1000 per hr. International calls ₡80 per min.

Post Office: On the south side of town, near the clinic. Follow the main road south as it curves left and make a right in front of the *municipalídad;* turn right on the 2nd side-street. Open M-F 8am-4:30pm, Sa 8am-noon. **Postal Code:** 4023.

ACCOMMODATIONS

Jacó's main drag and its surrounding side streets are lined with small *cabinas* and hotels, the majority of which have budget or mid-range rooms located less than 200m from the beach. A few more luxurious places cluster around the northern and southern ends of town. Rooms fill quickly on weekends and during the high season; it's not a bad idea to reserve a few days in advance. In the low season, bargain down the prices for groups and extended stays.

Rutan Surf Cabinas (☎2643 3328), 400m north of the bridge. Turn toward the beach at Mexican Joe's; the cabinas are on the left just past Isaga. Formerly known as Chuck's Cabinas (and still known by that name to locals). Myriad surf-slang bumper stickers testify to the hundreds of surfers who have crashed here. There's always a handful relaxing in the courtyard and giving free advice to beginners. Rents beginner epoxy boards from W.O.W. Surf across the street for ₡1740 (US$3) per hr., ₡8700 (US$15) per day. Free Wi-Fi. Dorms ₡5800 (US$10) per person; doubles ₡130,500 (US$15). ❶

CENTRAL PACIFIC COAST

Hostel Las Camas (☎8377 3459), 50m north of the bridge across from Plaza Coral. This 4-story complex with brightly painted walls and funky accents is a haven for backpackers. Well-equipped common area and rooftop patio with spectacular views of the mountains to the east and the ocean to the west. Each room has A/C, cable TV, and lockers. Wi-Fi. Check-out 11am. Dorms ¢8120 (US$14); doubles ¢17,400 (US$30). ❶

Cabinas Los Ranchos (☎2643 3070; fax 2643 1810), 100m down the first sidestreet south of the bridge. A beautiful complex just 50m from the beach with private patios, lazy-day hammocks, and a pool surrounded by towering palms. Simple, spacious rooms with comfy beds, overhead fans, and private hot-water baths. All rooms are quads. Wi-Fi available. Check-in 8am-10pm. Check-out noon. Rooms ¢26,100 (US$45), with kitchen ¢31,900 (US$55). Discounts for long stays and in the low season. AmEx/D/MC/V. ❷

Cabinas Sol Marena (☎2643 1124), next door to Rutan. High-ceilinged rooms with cable TVs, fridges, and private baths are kept cool by overhead fans or A/C. Internet access available. Singles ¢10,000 with fan, with A/C and hot-water ¢20,000; doubles ¢15,000/18,000; triples ¢18,000/30,000. ❷

▸ FOOD

A wide range of food options, from traditional *tico* fare to sushi and Argentinean steaks, are available in Jacó. This variety comes with a price: even the *sodas* in Jacó are more expensive than normal. Watch out for nightly tourist-trap promotions. For those looking to cook for themselves, the **Más X Menos** (☎2643 2528) supermarket, just south of Banco Nacional, is well stocked. (Open daily 8am-10pm. AmEx/MC/V.). A **Megasuper** (☎2643 2764) is also located in Plaza Coral just north of Budget Car Rental. Open daily 8am-10pm.

Soda Jacó Rústico (☎2643 1721), 50m down the south side of Pancho Villa's. Inexpensive, but tasty, *típico*. Filling buffet-style lunch and dinner with rice, beans, your choice of meat, salad, and drink ¢2000. Open daily 7am-7pm. ❶

Bar and Restaurant Isaga (☎2643 1467 or 2643 1412), on the north end of town, across from Rutan's Hostel. *Gallo pinto* ¢1500. *Ceviche* ¢2700. *Casados* ¢1600-2300. Beer ¢700. Free Wi-Fi. Open daily 10am-2am. ❶

Tsunami Sushi (☎2643 3678), upstairs in the Il Galeone complex, 100m north of Banco Nacional. Classic Japanese dishes like California rolls (¢3045), dragon rolls (¢6400), and shrimp and vegetable tempura (¢4900). Tu 2-for-1 tuna roll special. Watch your rolls being made in the open sushi-making area. Open daily 5-11pm. MC/V. ❷

Rioasis (☎2643 3354 or 2643 0119), 25m down C. Cocal, on the side street just north of Banco Nacional. Creatively topped wood-oven pizzas. Munchies pizza with ham, onions, sweet pepper, salami, and oregano ¢5209. Mexican burrito ¢3000. Tortellini alfredo ¢5890. Free delivery in Jacó for any order over ¢5000. Open daily 11:30am-10pm. ❷

Caliche's Wishbone Restaurant and Bar (☎2643 3406). Signed surf boards and a palm tree motif constitute the decor at this popular eatery. Stuffed potatoes with cheese and choice of chicken or broccoli ¢3300. Wishbone pizza (BBQ chicken, onion, cilantro, mozzarella; ¢6100). Guacamole and chips ¢3800. Open M-Tu and Th-Su noon-10pm. ❷

Jugos Naturales Pura Vida (☎2643 6221), in the Pacific Shopping Mall. This small juice shop concocts thirst-quenching drinks with fresh produce. Drinks ¢1000. Fruit salad topped with condensed milk, cornflakes, and granola ¢1600. Open daily 7am-8pm. ❶

▸ GUIDED TOURS

King Tours (☎2643 2441, toll-free from the US 800 213 7091; www.kingtours.com), 150m north of Banco Nacional. Friendly, knowledgeable staff arranges tours to satisfy all manner of adventure cravings. Tours to Isla Tortuga (¢69,600, US$120), Manuel

CENTRAL PACIFIC COAST

Antonio (¢51,600, US$89), Poas (¢72,500, US$125), and Volcán Arenal (¢72,500, US$125) include lunch and transportation. Canopy tours ¢49,300 (US$85). Rafting ¢69,600 (US$120). Dolphin-watching ¢40,020 (US$69). Horseback riding ¢43,500 (US$75). Open daily 8am-8pm. AmEx/D/MC/V.

Green Tours (☎2643 1984 or 2643 1021), directly across from Il Galeone. Extensive selection of tours and services. Canopy tours at Vista Los Sueños and crocodile tours ¢31,900 (US$55). Rafting near Quepos ¢58,000 (US$100). Rainforest ATV tours ¢40,600 (US$70). Meals, water, and A/C transportation included. Transportation services to Manuel Antonio ¢16,800 (US$29) per person. Full-day sportfishing tours with meals, drinks, bait, and transportation provided ¢377,000 (US$650). Open daily 8:30am-8pm.

Ricaventura ATV Tours and Motorcycle Rentals (☎2643 5720; www.ricaventura.com), just north of the bridge next to Subway. Arranges comprehensive ATV tours. Tours include waterfall views and swimming time in naturally formed pools. (2hr. tour ¢37,700/US$65; 3hr. ¢49,300/US$85; 4hr. ¢63,800/US$110. Scooters ¢17,400 (US$30) per day. Motorcycles ¢34,800 (US$60) per day. Open daily 8am-6:30pm.

An Xtreme Rider (☎2643 3130 or 8867 5089; www.axroad.com), just north of the Red Cross across from Pancho Villa's. Runs ATV tours and rents motorbikes, scooters, bicycles, and surfboards. Bicycles ¢5800 (US$10) per day, ¢17,400 (US$30) per week. Scooters ¢23,200 (US$40) per day. Motorbikes ¢40,600 (US$70) per day. Credit card required to rent. Open daily 8am-7pm.

🖻 NIGHTLIFE

Jacó has no shortage of clubs and bars: nightlife here is serious business. Be aware that Jacó's drug problems are on the rise and prostitutes linger in many bars at night.

Le Loft (☎2643 5846), across from Lappa Verde St. Up-and-coming bar with Asian-inspired decor. Plays all types of music, but if you want to salsa, head elsewhere. Open bar W midnight-2:30am. Cover for men only ¢3000. Open 9:30pm-2:30am.

Jungle Bar and Grill (☎8643 3911), 50m north of Payless Car Rental, above Subway. Live DJ plays mostly Latin and Reggaeton to accompany revelers on the enormous dance floor. Pool and beer pong tables. Tu and Sa Ladies nights 10pm-midnight (free tequila, vodka, and rum). W Latin night. Open 6pm-2:30am.

Tabacon (☎2643 3097), in the center of town opposite C. Bohio. Classy, relaxed atmosphere is a welcome break from the high-party feel of its peers. But that doesn't mean that you won't find a party here: live rock and reggae bands on weekends draw a dance crowd. Tasty drinks include the Jamaica banana (¢2500) and the mango and peach margarita (¢2200). Appetizers ¢2700-5800. M Ladies night 10pm-midnight. Open daily noon-midnight.

Pancho Villa's (☎2643 3571), toward the southern end of town across from the Red Cross. After the other bars close, a largely male crowd stumbles to this all-night joint for pricey grub and gambling on the in-house slot machines. Mariachis regularly stop by. Free Wi-Fi. Appetizers ¢2000-6500. *Casados* ¢2000. Lobster ¢16,500. Open 24hr. Loosely affiliated with **Divas Night Club** (☎2643 1978), an adult entertainment lounge located upstairs. Cover ¢4000; includes 2 beers. Open daily 8pm-3am.

Bar Oz (☎2643 2162), down a side-street across from Más X Menos. Large, airy bar. Pool tables, darts, and TVs playing American sports. Open daily 10am-2:30am.

🖻 BEACHES AND SURFING

Long renowned as some of Costa Rica's best surfing, the waters around Jacó have some of the country's most consistently diverse waves. Jacó's main beach has gentler swells that mellow southward—ideal conditions for beginners and intermediates. Experts craving more challenging surf head to the mouth of the river, north past Plaza Jacó, or to La Roca Loca, a sizable right break about 1.5km south of Jacó that crashes over a large submerged rock on Punta Guapinol (read: no beginners). **La Roca Loca** is a 30-45min. walk from the center of Jacó Beach—just head south and climb out over the rocks. Or make the 5-10min. drive and tiptoe down a gnarly cliff. Just 5km away, Playa Hermosa (p. 507) has a challenging beach break also popular with advanced surfers. Farther south of Jacó are **Esterillos Oeste, Esterillos Centro, Esterillos Este, Playas Bandera,** and **Bejuco.** North of Jacó is **Boca Barranca.** Most of these beaches have isolated surf spots.

Jacó is a popular daytrip for surfers from all over the country, and most surf tourists pay it a visit. The main road is loaded with surf shops that buy, rent, sell, trade, and repair boards. Most offer similar services and prices, but some unusual deals exist.

W.O.W. Surf (☎2643 3844 or 2643 1108; www.wowsurf.net), on the northernmost part of the main road, 50m past Beatle Bar. The largest selection of surfboards, boogie boards, and surf gear in town. Beginner epoxy boards ¢8700 (US$15) per 24hr., fiberglass boards ¢11,600 (US$20) per 24hr. ¢464,000 (US$800) credit card deposit. Surf lessons (¢37,700/US$65 for a 3hr. group lesson, ¢69,600/US$120 for a private lesson). Open M-Sa 8am-8pm, Su 8am-6pm. AmEx/MC/V.

El Pana (☎2643 2125), directly across from Tabacon. Great deals on board rentals (¢5800, US$10 per day). One of the most affordable places to buy a used board in good condition (from ¢58,000/US$100). Pana himself is almost always around to help you make the best selection. Open daily 7am-9pm.

El Roka Loka (☎2643 1806), 50m south from Pana. Good selection of used boards (from ¢87,000/US$150). Board rentals ¢8700/US$15 per 24hr.

Jacó Surf School (☎8829 4697 or 2643 1905 after 7:30pm; www.jacosurflessons. com). Operates out of a small tent on the beach at the end of Bohio Rd. Run by Gustavo Castillo, a pro who spent a decade with the Costa Rican national team, this school offers the best, most comprehensive surf lessons in town. If you don't stand up, you don't pay. All instructors are certified lifeguards and speak English and Spanish. 3hr. group lessons (¢29,000, US$50 per person) include water, fruit, and full-day board use. Private lessons ¢43,500 (US$75).

PARQUE NACIONAL CARARA

Encompassing over 5200 hectares, Parque Nacional Carara features the only remaining transitional rainforest in Costa Rica, where the drier rainforest of the North Pacific meets the humid rainforest of the South Pacific. The highly varied flora of these two distinct ecosystems provides homes for numerous rare and endangered species, including the giant anteater, the white-faced monkey, the scarlet macaw, and over 50 American crocodiles that lounge on the banks of the Río Tarcoles and the Meándrica Lagoon. Archaeological sites in the surrounding area have dug up artifacts of ceramic, rock, and jade. The park's well-maintained trail system also features **Acceso Universal,** the first and only wheelchair-accessible trail in any national park in Central America.

AT A GLANCE

AREA: 5242 hectares. Approx. 10% trail-accessible.

CLIMATE: Mean annual temperature 27˚C. Annual rainfall 2.8m.

HIGHLIGHTS: Fully paved, wheelchair-accessible trail; several rare and endangered species; the only remaining transition forest in Costa Rica; crocodiles.

FEATURES: Río Tárcoles, Meándrica Lagoon.

GATEWAYS: **Jacó** (p. 521), Orotina.

CAMPING: Not allowed in the park.

FEES: Admission ₡5735 (US$10), children 6-12 ₡574 (US$1), children under 3 free; Costa Rican nationals ₡1147 (US$2).

TRANSPORTATION

Buses traveling along the **Costanera Highway** pass by the reserve regularly. From **Jacó** or **Playa Hermosa,** take any Puntarenas-, Orotina-, or San José-bound bus (see **Transportation** sections), and ask the driver to let you off at the park entrance. In case your driver is forgetful, watch for the sign and large white ranger station. From **Puntarenas** or **Orotina,** take any Jacó- or Quepos-bound bus. **To return,** you'll have to rely on the buses that pass along the highway from San José or Puntarenas to Jacó or Quepos. A schedule of buses is posted on the information desk at the entrance to the park. Buses to Jacó and San José typically pass by every hour starting at 7am. Buses to San Jose pass by every 2hr., and to Jacó or Quepos, every hour. Because buses pass by on different schedules, you may find yourself waiting anywhere from 10min. to 2hr. for the correct bus. (The park is open daily from Dec. to Apr. 7am-4pm; from May to Nov. 8am-4pm. Last tickets sold at 3pm.)

ORIENTATION

Located 17km northeast of Jacó and 90km west of San José, Parque Nacional Carara was originally created to facilitate scientific studies and investigations. Three of its trails leave from the main entrance and are good for casual hikers, as they are easily traversed, evenly sloped, and well-shaded. The fourth, **Sendero Laguna Meándrica,** is a bit more challenging, especially during the wet season.

WHEN TO GO. Because most of the trails take about 1-2hr. to walk, Carara is best visited as a short daytrip. Get an early start and bring insect repellent, food, and water. Birdwatching is best in the morning (as soon as the park opens). Crocodiles are most likely seen at midday; scarlet macaws and monkeys are usually visible between noon to 2pm on the Laguna Meándrica trail. The **ranger station** has bathrooms, a picnic area, and potable water but no food.

HIKING

Only 10% of Carara is accessible by trail, but these trails are all well-marked and maintained. One trail leaves from the main ranger station and connects with two others, while the fourth, Sendero Laguna Meándrica, leaves from a trailhead off the highway 2km north of the main entrance. Wheelchair-accessible **Acceso Universal,** or **Sendero Cemento,** is a flat, paved 1.2km loop that takes about an hour to hike. It begins at the ranger station, moves through primary rainforest, and connects to **Sendero Quebrada Bonita.** Bonita is 1.5km long and takes about 1hr. to complete. It begins after a small metal bridge and is linked to a third trail, the 1.2km loop of **Sendero Las Aráceas,** by another small bridge. While all trails pass through similar primary forest, you're more likely to see wildlife on the Bonita trail. The less-trodden fourth trail, **Sendero Laguna Meándrica,** begins at the yellow gates 2km along the Costanera from the ranger station, where even more animals are to be found. Meandering alongside the **Río Grande de Tárcoles** for 4km, Laguna Meándrica leads to a lagoon **viewpoint,** which is the best place in the park to spot monkeys, scarlet macaws and crocodiles. This trail, however, offers little shade and is muddy year-round due to the high waters of the lagoon, so the rangers recommend rubber boots (¢1000 for rental at the ranger station). When the lagoon floods in September the trail becomes impassable. All visitors to the park must **register** and buy their **tickets** at the **MINAE office** (☎8383 9953) before hiking. Freelance guides can be hired to spot creatures and help keep your feet dry; they are recommended for visitors taking the Laguna Meándrica path. (¢11,470/US$20 per person. Guides available in English, French, German and Spanish. Antonio Vindas, ☎2645 1064, is recommended by the park, and during the dry season he can guide overnight backpacking trips into the park for ¢57,350/US$100, up to 15 people.) Scouts will guard cars for tips (recommended contribution ¢2868/US$5). There is also a secure parking lot (guarded M-Sa 8am-2pm) lot near the station if you don't mind walking to the farther trails. Don't leave valuables in the car. Carrying them is no safer, as **muggings** have been known to occur.

👁 SIGHTS

The **Río Tárcoles Bridge** is about 3km north of Parque Nacional Carara's ranger station on the highway to Puntarenas and San José. It is known more commonly as the **Puente de los Cocodrilos** (Crocodile Bridge) because of the scores of crocodiles that reside in the muddy waters of the river and doze along its banks. The rangers say that the crocodiles prey on farm animals that roam the surrounding pastures. While there have been a few (probably apocryphal) reports of people being eaten alive or having their limbs chewed off, the animals can be safely viewed from the edge of the bridge. If you're lucky, you might see a crocodile lumbering around or floating log-like down the river, but it's more likely you'll see 20-40 crocodiles lounging immobile by the water. Locals sometimes stir up activity by throwing plants or even live chickens into the water (not recommended). The bridge is hardly worth its own visit, but if you're passing by on the highway you might stop for a quick peek. Just look for several people peering off the edge. If you want a closer look, call **Jungle Crocodile Safari** (☎2236 6473 or 2385 6591; www.junglecrocodilesafari. com) in Tarcoles for a 2hr. tour down the Río Tárcoles, complete with a bilingual guide who will perform some daring crocodile tricks. (¢14,338/US$25. Tours at 8:30, 10:30am, 1:30, and 3:30pm.)

SOUTHERN COSTA RICA

With the notable exception of Parque Nacional Chirripó, this relatively isolated area doesn't really cater to tourists. In its small towns, which are either business hubs of fruit producers or gateways into the secluded wilderness of the region, foreigners often receive inquisitive stares, or an emphatic "hellooooo" and laughter from children practicing their English.

SAN ISIDRO

One hundred and thirty-eight kilometers southeast of San José, the city of San Isidro de El General, also known as Pérez Zeledón, is an urban centered circumscribed by rural villages. Though the urban streets are unusually clean and friendly, the attractions of the asphalt terrain pale in comparison to the living greenness of nearby parks. The city makes an ideal springboard for trips into the surrounding national parks and other areas of southern Costa Rica, where you can get away from the bustle of city life and relax amidst natural splendors. Shoe fanatics may find it difficult to leave San Isidro, however; *zapaterías* line every corner, making it likely that you will finally find those blue sneakers with neon green laces you've always known, deep down, that you needed.

▐▛ TRANSPORTATION

While finding the right **bus** out of San Isidro is complicated by the fact that the five different companies that share the town don't share destinations, all five have well-staffed and well-marked stations, which makes travel a bit easier. From the local bus terminal on the south side of the *mercado*, buses leave to nearby villages including **Quedabras** (15min., 11 per day 6:45am-7:25pm, ¢250) and **San Gerardo** (1hr., 2pm, ¢900). Another bus to San Gerardo leaves from the west side of the *parque* at 5am.

Musoc (☎2771 0414). Buses go to **San José** from the terminal on the Interamericana Hwy. between C. 2 and 4 (3hr., M-F 4:30am and daily every hr. 5am-6:30pm, ¢2190). Bathroom ¢150. Ticket office open daily 4:30am-6pm.

Transportes Blancos (☎2771 2550), on the curve between Av. 2 and Av. 4 on the east side of town. Marked by a Soda Quepos sign. Buses to: **Dominical** (1½hr.; 7, 9am, 4pm; ¢800); **Puerto Jiménez** (6hr.; 6:30am, 3pm; ¢2300); **Quepos** (3½hr.; 7, 11:30am, 3:30pm; ¢1300); **Uvita** (2hr.; 9am, 4pm; ¢950). Ticket office open daily 6:15-11am and 1:30-4pm.

Tracopa (☎2771 0468), on the corner of the Interamericana Hwy. and C. 3. Service to **Golfito** (3½hr.; 10am, ¢3760; 6pm, ¢5800); **San Vito** (3½hr.; 5:30am, 2pm; ¢3995); the Panamanian border at **Paso Canoas** (4hr.; direct at 10am, ¢7000; indirect at 2, 4, 7:30, 9pm, ¢3760). Ticket office open M-Sa 4:30am-7pm, Su 4:30am-3pm.

Gafeso (☎2771 0097), next to Transportes Blancos. Buses to **Buenos Aires** (1½hr.; direct at 5:15, 7:20, 10am, 12:15, 3, 5pm; indirect at 6, 8:30, 11:30am, 1:30, 4, 7:45, 10pm; ¢685).

Taxis: On the north and west sides of the *parque central,* south of Av. 6 between C. Central and C. 1. Next to the MUSOC bus terminal. To San Gerardo ¢10,000.

▟✦ ▐ ORIENTATION AND PRACTICAL INFORMATION

Unlike most other towns in Costa Rica, San Isidro has well-marked streets with signs on almost every corner. Avenida Central and Calle 0 meet at the northwest

Southern Costa Rica

corner of the *parque central.* Overlooking the eastern side of the *parque central,* the spires of the large modern cathedral, visible from most places downtown, serve as useful landmarks. The Interamericana Highway forms the northern boundary of the *parque* and is a good reference for finding other streets.

Tourist Information:

CIPROTUR, Av. 1/3, C. 4 (☎2771 6096 or 2771 2003; www.camaradecomerciopz.com), in the back of the blue Coopealianza building. Provides free maps. Answers questions about San Isidro and offers information about tours and activities in the surrounding area. Internet access ¢300 per hr. Open M-F 7:30am-noon and 1-5pm.

Selva Mar, Av. 2/4, C. 1 (☎2771 4582; www.exploringcostarica.com; www.selvamar.com). Information on kayaking, canopy, and snorkeling tours to Bahía Drake, Delfines, Golfo Dulce, Isla del Caño, Parque Nacional Chirripó, Parque Nacional Corcovado, and Tortuguero. Open M-F 7:30am-5:30pm, Sa 8am-noon. AmEx/MC/V.

Oficina Regional de Cultura-Zona Sur (☎2771 5273; dirculturazonasur@gmail.com), inside the *mercado* near the entrance to the bathrooms and buses. Works to support cultural activities within southern Costa Rica. Provides information on artisan groups and other cultural events in the area. Open M-F 8am-4pm.

Banks: All offer currency exchange and have **24hr. ATMs.**

Banco Nacional de Costa Rica (☎2785 1000), on the northeast corner of the *parque* at Av. Central, C. 1. Changes traveler's checks and gives V cash advances. Open M-F 8:30am-3:45pm.

Banco de Costa Rica, Av. 4, C. 0/2 (☎2770 9996). Open M-F 9am-6pm.

BAC San José, Av. 4, C. 0/1(☎2771 3080 or 2295 9797). Open M-F 9am-6pm, Sa 9am-1pm.

Western Union, Av. 2, C. 0/2 (☎2771 8535 or 2771 3534), on the 2nd fl. of the large yellow building. Open M-F 7:30am-4:30pm, Sa 7:30am-noon.

Bookstore: Librería San Isidro (☎2771 7802; www.libreriasanisidro.com), next to the BAC San José on Av. 4. Office supplies and copying services available on the 1st fl. (black and white ¢12, color ¢290). 2nd fl. has books, magazines, and posters, mostly in Spanish. Open M-F 8am-7pm, Sa 8am-6pm. AmEx/MC/V.

Library: Biblioteca Municipal (☎2771 3816), on the corner of Av. Central and C. 2. Travelers can read in the pleasant, well lit library but cannot check out books. Open M-F 8am-7pm, Sa 8am-noon.

Laundry: Av. Central, C. 4 (☎2771 4042). ¢800 per kg. Open M-Sa 8am-6pm.

Public Toilets: On the north and south sides of the *mercado*. ¢150. Open M-Sa 6am-6pm, Su 6am-4pm. Additional location on the north side of the cathedral. Open M-F 7am-5:30pm.

Police: (☎2771 3608 or 2771 3447), less than 1km from the *parque;* walk 200m to a small bridge over Río San Isidro, then 300m farther on the left, or speak with one of the many officers on duty around town.

Red Cross: Emergency ☎911. Toll-free ☎128. Ambulance ☎2771 0481.

Pharmacy: Farmacia San Isidro (☎2771 1567), on Av. Central, north of the *parque*. Open M-Sa 7am-8:30pm. AmEx/MC/V.

Hospital: Hospital Clínica Labrador (☎2771 7115 or 2772 6464), 5 blocks south of the cathedral on C. 1. Open daily 7am-8pm for appointments and 24hr. for emergencies. Some English-speaking doctors.

Internet Access:

Connect@ Internet Café, Av. 10, C. 0/2 (☎2771 6023), across from the soccer stadium, 400m from the *mercado*. Computers are Skype-capable. Internet access ¢350 per hr. Open daily 8:30am-10pm.

Fofo's Internet, Av. 1 & C. 4 (☎2770 1186), 1 block south of Hotel Diamante Real. Internet ¢350 per hr. Wi-Fi ¢200. International calls to the U.S. ¢50 per min. Printing services black and white ¢50, color ¢300. Open M-F 7am-10pm, Sa 7am-7pm, Su noon-8pm.

Post Office: Av. 6/8, C. 1 (☎2771 0346). Offers fax service. Open M-F 8am-5:30pm, Sa 9am-1pm. MC/V. **Postal Code:** 11901.

ACCOMMODATIONS

Most of San Isidro's budget and mid-range accommodations are clustered around the *parque central.* Other, more expensive accommodations line to the perimeter of town.

Hotel Chirripó, Av. 2, C. 0/1 (☎2771 0529), on the south side of the *parque*. Behind a small restaurant of the same name. Large windows light up pleasant, peach-walled and tiled hallways. Bright rooms have fans, cable TVs, and hot-water baths. Wi-Fi available. Singles with shared baths ¢6500, with private baths ¢9500; doubles ¢10,000/16,000; triples ¢20,000; quads ¢27,000. ❶

Hotel El Valle, Av. Central/2, C. 2 (☎2771 0246), 1 block west and 1 block south of the *parque's* northwest corner. Well kept establishment lined with signs commanding *"silencio,"* especially after midnight. A "no visitors, no exceptions" policy. Parking available. Singles with shared baths ¢6000, with private baths and cable TV ¢8000; doubles ¢9000/12,000; triples ¢18,500. ❷

Hotel Astoria (☎2771 0914), on Av. Central facing the north side of the *parque*. 2nd entrance on the Interamericana Hwy. across from the courthouse. Somewhat institutional feel. Small rooms with just as small armoires may lack windows, limiting ven-

tilation to a small space near the ceiling. Singles ¢4000, with private baths ¢6000; doubles ¢13000; triples ¢12,000, with private bath and cable TV ¢18,000. ❶

🍴 FOOD

In addition to *sodas* and restaurants, you can stock up on essentials at **Supermercado La Corona** on Av. 2 between C. 3 and the Interamericana Hwy. (☎2771 5252; open M-Sa 7:30am-9pm, Su 8am-7pm; AmEx/MC/V) or at the even larger **Supermercado Central Coopeagri**, just south of the local bus terminal. (☎2785 0227. Open M-Sa 7pm-9pm, Su 8am-4pm.) Dominated by *sodas*, raw meat shops, and produce vendors, the **Mercado Municipal** smells of fish and fried food all day. (Located between Av. 4/6, C. 0/2. Open M-Sa 5am-6pm, Su 5-11am.)

Kafe de la Casa, Av. 3 between C. 3 & 4 (☎2771 7000). Homey coffee shop. Extensive menu features everything from cinnamon pancakes (¢1800) and banana chocolate coffee (¢2000) to eggplant stuffed with meat (¢3500) and baked potatoes filled with spinach (¢3500). Leave your mark by writing your thanks on one of the walls. Open M-F 6am-9pm, Sa 6am-7pm, Su 8am-5pm. MC/V. ❷

La Cascada Bar & Restaurant, Av. 2 and C. 2 (☎2771 6479). This open-air restaurant always hosts hungry customers munching on chicken kebabs (¢4000), Caesar salad (¢4200), or stroganoff tenderloin (¢5500). Mixed drinks and virgin daiquiris ¢2500-3000. Open daily 11am-2am. ❷

Soda Chirripó, Av. 2, C. 1 (☎2771 8287), on the southeast corner of the park. Catering mostly to locals watching sports on its small TV, this restaurant feels more like a diner than a traditional *soda*. Cheese and ham omelettes ¢1800. *Casados* ¢1950-3200. Also has a less expensive fast-food menu (¢1200-1850). Open daily 6:30am-6pm. MC/V. ❶

🅶 SIGHTS

COMPLEJO CULTURAL. This cultural center hosts local shows and performances. Dates and times posted on an announcement board just outside the building. *(On Av. 1, C. 2, next to the municipal library. ☎2771 2336 . ¢1500).*

FUNDACIÓN PARA EL DESARROLLO DEL CENTRO BIOLÓGICO LAS QUEBRADASN (FUDEBIOL). This reserve is managed by a group of devoted volunteers. Learn about conservation at Las Quebradas, hike through bird-filled trails to impressive waterfalls, visit the reserve's butterfly garden, or simply enjoy its streams and lagoon. Its isolated location makes this reserve as relaxing as it is educational. Up to 30 people can stay at the center's **mountain lodge** (¢7000 per night). Join the staff every Sunday for a traditional *tico* breakfast (Su 8-11am; ¢3000). Ask about volunteer opportunities. *(In the mountains above the Quebradas River Basin, 7km from downtown San Isidro. Take the bus to Quebradas from the main bus station (every hr., 15min. past the hr., starting at 8:15am) and get off at the last stop. Walk 2.5km up to the dirt road, turning right at the FUDEBIOL sign, and continue until the end of the road. ☎2771 4131 for information and reservations. Open M and W-Th 7am-3pm. US$2 entrance fee.)*

CHIRRIPÓ AND SAN GERARDO DE RIVAS

A popular destination for nature enthusiasts, Parque Nacional Chirripó is home to the tallest peak in Costa Rica and the second tallest peak in Central America, Cerro Chirripó (3820m). A well-marked route to the summit ascends through steep pastures before winding through cloud forest and into alpine-tundra-like *páramo*. The name Chirripó means "land of eternal waters" and is well-suited to the many rivers that originate from sparkling lagoons on its summit and rush down glacial valleys to both the Pacific and Caribbean. If the weather cooperates (during high season Jan.-Apr., or very early in the morning), you can see both the Atlantic and Pacific Oceans from Cerro Chirripó. The 20km trip up the mountain is an manageable climb for the average traveler in three days, though the especially experienced and motivated can make it in two. Sports extremists and foolhardy masochists from around the world come to challenge the mountain every year for the Chirripó Marathon in February; the record to beat for the 29km to and from Base Crestones stands at just over 3hr. San Gerardo, the gateway to Parque Nacional Chirripó, although unavoidably situated on steep hills, is otherwise geared toward accommodating the sore legs and hungry bellies of visiting hikers. Since the park's opening in 1975, the families of San Gerardo have learned to embrace tourism while still maintaining their rural authenticity. To the weary hiker, the town offers natural hot springs, local trout and coffee, home-grown vegetarian food, and an abundance of hospitality.

🄵 TRANSPORTATION

The **bus** from San Isidro (5:30am or 2pm) will drop you off at the edge of town in front of the ranger station (2km from the trailhead), or at the town center in front of the soccer field. Catch the return bus at the ranger station (1½hr.; 7am, 4pm; ¢900) or from the church (5min. before the ranger station bus).

⚡ 🛈 ORIENTATION AND PRACTICAL INFORMATION

San Gerardo stretches for 2km along an uphill section of road from the ranger station at the bottom to the park entrance at the top. The town center consists of a large yellow church and a school with a soccer field across from the *pulpería* (small grocery store) **Las Nubes** (☎2742 5045; open daily 6:30am-8pm). Another smaller *pulpería* is at Hotel El Urán. The owner, Hans Arias, and his family can provide a wealth of information about San Gerardo and the national park.

Tourist Information: Extensive tourist and volunteer information can also be found online at www.sangerardocostarica.com.

Public phones: outside the ranger station and in front of Las Nubes. Both establishments also have free restrooms.

Internet Access: Reserva Talamanca (☎2742 5080), 1km uphill from the soccer field. ¢3000 per hr. Open M and W-Su 11am-10pm.

Taxis: ☎2770 1066.

🛏 🍴 ACCOMMODATIONS AND FOOD

After arriving in town, some travelers get dropped off at the ranger station, check in, and then find a nearby hotel. Most others prefer to find a hotel near the trail, stash their gear, and then walk down to check in at the ranger station. Reservations are recommended for those planning to stay at hotels near the trail during the high season (Jan.-Apr.).

🏠 **Casa Mariposa** (☎2742 5037; www.hotelcasamariposa.com), 50m from the trailhead. This unique stone and bamboo structure offers the closest beds to the trailhead. Cozy dorms have great window views of the rainforest and the surrounding mountains. All rooms have access to shared hot-water showers, a communal kitchen, and a relaxing gazebo with hammocks. The owners, John and Jill, are a wonderful source of information on the area. Free tea and coffee complement the priceless hospitality. Provides transportation to and from the ranger station upon request. Laundry ¢2500 per load. Internet ¢350 per hr. Dorms ¢6000 (US$12); singles ¢8000 (US$16); doubles ¢12,500 (US$28). ❶

Hotel El Urán (☎2742 5003 or 2742 5004; www.hoteluran.com), 25m below Casa Mariposa. Picks up visitors from the ranger station for free. The on-site **restaurant** ❶ offers hearty *comida típica* (*casados* ¢2000-2400, sandwiches ¢850-1200, pancake breakfast with fruit ¢1200, coffee ¢350; open 4:30am-8pm), while the attached grocery store sells bread, eggs, milk, spaghetti, beans, and snacks for the trek up. Free pick-up from the ranger station. Free internet access for guests; for others, ¢600 per hr. Free parking. Sleeping bag rentals ¢1500 per night. Stoves ¢1500. Dorms ¢6000; singles ¢11,300; doubles ¢16,950; triples ¢23,000. ❶

Cabinas El Descanso (☎2742 5061). Small, pastel rooms with cramped, shared hot-water baths. The owner, Francisco, has run the race up the mountain 21 times (check out his impressive trophy cabinet). On-site **restaurant** ❶ (open daily 5am-9pm) serves coffee (¢500), vegetarian dishes made with homegrown produce (spaghetti with vegetables ¢2000), and fresh *batidos* (milkshakes ¢800). Free parking and complimentary rides to the trail entrance after 5am. Trail maps provided upon request. Laundry ¢400 per item. Internet ¢1000 per hr. Sleeping bags ¢2000 per night. Stoves ¢3000 for 2 nights. Camping on the lawn or on Francisco's nearby coffee farm ¢2320. Rooms ¢5800 per person, with private baths ¢8700 per person. ❶

Cabinas El Bosque (☎2742 5021), across from the ranger station. Basic cement-floored rooms with access to hammocks on the 2nd fl. balcony. The attached **restaurant** ❶ serves *comida típica* (open daily 10am-9:30pm; earlier upon request). Breakfasts ¢1600-1800. *Arroz con pollo* ¢2300. Salads ¢2400-2700. Chicken fingers ¢2600. Rents sleeping bags for ¢2000 per night. Doubles ¢5000; each additional person ¢5000. ❶

Hotel El Marin (☎2742 5091), next to the ranger station. Transportation to the park at 5am. Restaurant open 5am-10pm. *Casados* ¢2500-2700. Omelettes ¢1200. Doubles ¢14,000. ❶

OUTDOOR ACTIVITIES

PARQUE NACIONAL CHIRRIPÓ. Hikers almost always stay at **Base Crestones,** a rugged, well-equipped lodge at the base of the peak, as a layover point on their way to the summit. Reservations are required as only 40 spaces are available, but cancellations are frequent. You may be able to nab a spot from the San Gerardo rangers. It's usually easier to reserve in the rainy season (May-Nov.). Reservations can be made one month in advance by calling the San Gerardo ranger station (☎2742 5083; M-F 6:30am-4:30pm) and then making a direct deposit into a P.N. Chirripó Banco de Costa Rica account. Reservations can also be made in person one day in advance. (Ranger station open daily 6:30am-4:30pm. Park admission ¢8700 per night plus ¢5800 for lodging at Base Crestones and ¢3000 for camping.)

> **! CLOSED GATES.** During two weeks in May and the entire month of Oct., the park closes to allow for trail and facility maintenance. Visitors can still check with the rangers in San Gerardo to find out if any trails are open.

Most hikers take two or three days to summit the mountain and return using Base Crestones as a stopping point. The 14.5km to Base Crestones is almost entirely uphill and takes a good hiker anywhere from 6-10hr. To ensure that hikers get an early enough start to reach the shelter before night falls, the park entrance is open only between 5am and 10am, and rangers suggest starting as early as possible. Make sure you keep an extra keen lookout for the park entrance on the right; you will have gone too far if you hit the Cloudbridge research station. Rangers also discourage hiking in the dark because of jaguars and other dangerous wildlife that emerge at night. When hiking in the wet season, it is especially important to start early, as rain can begin as early as noon and often continue throughout the afternoon.

Base Crestones, officially named Centro Ambientalista el Páramo, is a top-of-the-line facility, located 500m vertically below the summit. It offers dorm beds with mattresses, bathrooms with running water and extremely cold showers, a communal kitchen with cooking utensils (but no stoves), a phone, and high-speed internet. The facility is powered by solar energy and has electrical light beginning at 6pm. One thing it doesn't have is heat—the temperature at the base can drop to 3°C (45°F) at night from May to December and as low as 0°C (32°F) from January to April—so plan accordingly. The lodge can provide blankets and stoves in an emergency, but in general, sleeping bags and stoves should be rented from hotels in San Gerardo. Most offer rentals for around ¢2000 per night.

DAYHIKES FROM BASE CRESTONES. The trail up Chirripó is not the only hike from Base Crestones. **Cerro Crestones** is another popular summit located 1.7km from Base Crestones. Topped by towering exposed rock, it is the most recognizable rock formation in the park. A popular day-long route is to climb Cerro

Chirripó early to watch the sunrise, and then take the other turn at Valle de Los Conejos that leads over **Cerro Terbi** (3760m) and to Los Crestones for the sunset. Hikers may then stay in a shelter nearby and hike down to Base Crestones in the morning. Other hikers may opt to take the extremely steep hike up from Base Crestones (2hr., 2.5km) and try to scale La Aguja ("The Needle"), a 60m vertical face for advanced rock climbers. Sendero Ventisqueros (6km) leads to the *cerro* of the same name. Other trails include the flatter hike to the Valle de Las Morenas (Valley of the Moraines; 7km), where lagoons reflect the mountains, Sabana del Los Leones (The Lion's Savannah; 3.9km) flanked by paramo flowers in the wet season (May-Nov.), and Laguna Ditkebi (3.3km).

AN ALTERNATIVE ROUTE. Serious hikers—only about 80 per year compared with the 8000 others who hike Chirripó—have recently begun exploring a three-day, 40km hike along the **Cordillera Talamanca**, the highest mountain range in the country (Chirripó is one of its peaks). This range divides the Atlantic and Pacific sides of the country, and 80% of the trail (about two days) consists of a ridge path that offers stunning views of both coasts. Some say that Cerro Urán, a distinctive two-peaked mountain, provides an even more beautiful view of the country than Chirripó does. The trail, **Urán Chirripó**, originates in the village of Herradura, 3km uphill from the San Gerardo Ranger Station. The rangers require that hikers take a guide from Herradura with them. Contact Rudalfo Elizondo of Herradura (☎2742 5006), a knowledgeable, kind man who can set you up with guides and lodging in Herradura. (Up to 10 people US$50; 11-16 people US$65.)

BEYOND CHIRRIPÓ. Although the more athletic or motivated can make a round trip in two full days, most overnight trekkers spend three days in the park: the first to hike to **Sirena,** the second to explore using Sirena as a base (the route to Los Patos is most popular), and the third to hike out. Rangers arrange lodging options and meals. (Breakfast US$10. Lunch and dinner US$15. Dorm beds US$8; bring sheets and mosquito net. Camping US$4 per person; only allowed in designated areas at the stations.) Where the *colectivo* truck stops in Carate, there are last-minute meals (coffee ₡300; *gallo pinto* ₡1500; steak and eggs ₡2000). A public restroom is available for ₡300.

If your legs have enough energy left for a bridge crossing on Río Blanco and another steep hike, you'll be rewarded by soothing *aguas termales* atop a nearby hill, where hot water (32.5°C/97°F) from a natural spring bubbles up into two stone pools. These **thermal waters** are popular in the dry season (Jan.-Apr.) but often under-touristed during the wet season. Take the road that forks left at the large cement bridge for 100m. Proceed uphill about 500m to a bridge well-marked as the entrance to Aguas Termales. Don't forget your towel! The ₡1500/US$3 entrance fee is collected at the small *soda* at the top of the hill run by Gerardo Alvarado and his family (☎2742 5210. Open daily 7am-5pm.). Gerardo also has three small *cabinas* for rent (₡15,000 per night).

Francisco Elizondo of Cabinas El Descanso (p. 535) and his family offer guided treks in English through their Finca El Mirador **coffee farm,** complete with views of the entire valley and a lesson on coffee harvesting and production (3hr., ₡11,600 per person). Francisco will also guide Chirripó hikes for small groups (₡23,200), although you may have to ask him to take it slowly; he's run the Chirripó Marathon over a dozen times. He can also arrange **horseback rides** and other tours throughout the area (price varies depending on duration and group). **Truchero los Cocolisos,** a short walk up the left fork 200m past the church, offers **trout fishing** at its farm. Visitors can take fish to cook later, or, on weekends, the owner will fry them up for you.

Arrive before 4pm to be guaranteed trout action. (☎2742 5054 or 2742 5023; ¢3,000 per person; open Sa-Su 9am-6pm.)

For less-adventurous nature enthusiasts and those exhausted from Chirripó's relentless inclines, the **Cloudbridge Reserve** (www.cloudbridge.org) offers mellower hikes. The Reserve's goal is to preserve and reforest former pasture lands. Researchers study the ecology of the surrounding cloud forest at the reserve year-round. Ask for volunteer opportunities through the website. For hiking, follow the main road 1km past the Chirripó trailhead until it ends at the Cloudbridge Station. Hikes make 1hr., 3hr., and day-long loops. Eric, a Seattle native at the first house past the Chirripó trailhead, is available to guide tours. It is best to contact him in advance through the Cloudbridge website. For those who only have one day but want to experience both Chirripó and Cloudbridge, a solid 5-6hr. day hike starts at the park entrance and ends 7km at the Refugio Llanto Bonito, a resting point with a bench table and some toilets. On the return from this point, about 150m past the 4km mark, you can take the more scenic trail on your right into Cloudbridge Reserve, which leads back to the main road and affords several waterfall sightings.

CARIBBEAN LOWLANDS

PARISMINA

Drier, dustier, and even more secluded than its northern neighbor, Tortuguero, the tiny island hamlet of Parismina (pop. 400) attracts hundreds of leatherback, green, and hawksbill turtles every year, along with surprisingly small numbers of tourists. Where Tortuguero has developed an ecotourism industry based on short-term stays and guided tours, Parismina has created several volunteer programs that allow visitors to become "park rangers," doing 4hr. night watchman shifts while living with local families in homestays. Visitors looking to enjoy the island's calm ambience for only a few days will also find Parismina a welcoming stop; locals drink with tourists at the Mono Carablanca Lodge, and everyone who can stand the heat joins in the impromptu soccer games that pop up continually on every flat surface available.

◧ TRANSPORTATION

Boats: Parismina has no roads and is only accessible by boat. From Caño Blanco, a public boat meets the bus and shuttles passengers to Parismina (8min., ₡1000).

If you arrive at Caño Blanco from Siquirres by taxi (¢17,400, US$30) or private car, you can hire a private boat from the Caño Blanco dock to Parismina (¢14,500, US$25) or take one of the public boats leaving that day (8min., ¢1000). Be sure to arrive at Caño Blanco at least 30min. before 6pm as boats leave the dock early and there are no overnight facilities. Coming from farther south, hop on a boat from Moín to Tortuguero and tell the captain you only need to go to Parismina. Jumping on an already hired boat should run about ¢14,500 (US$25) to Moín and ¢11,600 (US$20) to Tortuguero. The tourist info center can arrange a pick-up for 5pm; notify them by 3pm that day. Public boats usually pass by each day in each direction between 10:30am and noon. Private boats organized on Parismina will cost upwards of US$100 for the trip; as usual, the best way to go is to buddy up or join another traveling group. To return to Siquirres, take the boat from Parismina to Caño Blanco (open M-F 5:30am and 2:30pm, Sa-Su 8:30am and 4:30pm; ¢1000) and catch the bus back to Siquirres (open M-F 6am and 3pm, Sa-Su 10am and 5pm).

Buses: From the Gran Terminal Siquirres, where the bus drops off, walk to the old bus station on the north side of the soccer field and catch a bus to Caño Blanco, from where a boat heads to Parismina (2hr.; M-F 4am and 1pm, Sa-Su 6am and 2pm; ¢300).

Tour agencies: From Parismina, the easiest way to continue onto Tortuguero or south to Moín is to contact one of the Tortuguero tour agencies, most of which arrange round-trip transportation from Moín to Tortuguero. The agencies will notify the boat captains heading in each direction that they should stop for passengers at Parismina.

✈ ❼ ORIENTATION AND PRACTICAL INFORMATION

Though the island of Parismina is quite long, the town itself is small and easy to navigate. There are two main docks in town; both are 100m west of the main path. Just south of town, the first docks service boats to Caño Blanco, while the second dock, about 250m north, services private boats including those going to Moín and Tortuguero. The main path stretches from the Caño Blanco docks in the south and ends at Sayleen del Caribe, where a right turn leads east toward the waterfront and the soccer field. There is a *pulpería*, 100m east and 50m south of Sayleen del Caribe (open daily 7am-5pm). There are **no banks or ATMs in town,** and the only place that accepts credit cards is **Mono Carablanca Lodge and Restaurant** (MC/V), so plan accordingly.

Tourist Office: The **Parismina Information Center,** located 200m north of the Caño Blanco docks, has a poster board with up-to-date info about traveling to and from the island as well as volunteer opportunities. The center also has a English and Spanish **book exchange** (open M-Sa 2-5pm).

Internet: The information center houses the only computer with internet in town (¢1500 per hr.; be prepared for lines).

Medical Services: There is no clinic in town, but a **doctor** visits every few days; details of the visits are posted in the Information Center.

Telephones: in front of both docks.

⌂ ACCOMMODATIONS

Though most visitors to Parismina are students on school trips or long-term volunteers participating in homestay programs, the town has several good value budget options for short-term, independent travelers.

- ▨ **Carefree Ranch Lodge** (☎2710 3149), east of the Information Center. This small B&B-style lodge feels like home, with peach-colored sideboards and forest-green doors. Offers some of the most comfortable accommodations in town, with high ceilings, private hot-water baths, and wide balconies. A charming on-site restaurant serves family-style meals. Rooms ¢5800 (US$10), with 3 meals ¢15,660 (US$27). ❶

Cabinas La Iguana Verde (☎2798 0828), 100m east of Salon Naomi. The yard of this small hotel looks like a jungle: the resident parrot erratically spouts greetings to passersby, and massive beetles hang continually from tree branches near the fence. The rooms, however, are animal-free, with private hot-water baths and large beds. Rooms ¢5500, with A/C ¢10,000. ❷

Mono Carablanco Lodge (☎2798 1031), 200m east of Sayleen El Caribe, just past the soccer field. The stark blue block of rooms is easily outshined by the *cabana*-style bar and restaurant, small blue pool, and palm-tree-filled lawn. All rooms have fans and private cold-water baths. ¢5000 per person, with A/C ¢7000. ❶

🔆 📷 FOOD AND NIGHTLIFE

Because most visitors to Parismina have meals with their home-stay families, the options for food and nightlife are pretty basic. Expect a lot of *comida típica* and not much else.

Restaurante Mono Carablanca (☎2798 1031), in the Mono Carablanca Lodge. Serves upscale versions of staples. Popular for locals and tourists looking for a beer between soccer games (¢500-1800). Breakfasts ¢3000. *Casados* and rice dishes ¢3000. Open daily 8am-8:30pm. MC/V. ❷

Rancho La Palma (☎2798 0259), in front of the docks where boats depart for Tortuguero. An older crowd enjoys Parismina's cheapest, most basic eats in this open-air dining area. *Casados* ¢2500. Sandwiches ¢1200. Open daily 5am-7pm. ❶

Carefree Ranch Restaurant (☎2710 3149), in the Carefree Ranch. Home-cooked, family-style meals. Drop by during breakfast hours for scrambled eggs, fruit, fresh bread, cheese, coffee, and orange juice (¢2500). Lunch and dinner ¢3000. ❷

Salon Naomi, in the center of town. The Salon is the only disco in Parismina, though the size of the local population means that the cavernous building only starts to fill on weekends or when a particularly large tourist group is in town. Beer ¢700. Mixed drinks ¢1000-2000. Dancing on Sa night. Open daily 11am-10pm. ❶

Soda Xine, in the center of town near Salon Naomi. *Casados* ¢2400-3600. Hamburgers ¢1500. *Gallos* ¢1000. Rice and beans ¢2800. Open daily 8am-7pm. ❶

🏔 OUTDOOR ACTIVITIES

There are no official tourist agencies with offices in Parismina, but you can get information and phone numbers for tour guides at the Information Center. Parismina's biggest tourist attraction is the *deshove* (turtle nesting), whose high season runs between March and September, though turtles nest sporadically throughout the year. Green turtles primarily nest between June and October, leatherbacks from February to June, and hawksbills at various times. Visitors can explore the wildlife-filled canals around Parismina village and go whitewater rafting, hiking, fishing, and horseback riding.

Rainforest World (☎2556 0014 or 2556 2678; www.rforestw.com). Runs 2- and 3-day all-inclusive rafting and turtle-watching trips down the Reventazon to Parismina, where guests stay in Rainforest World guide Rick Knowles's hotel Iguana Verde. 2-day, 2-night packages start at ¢150,800 (US$260). Whitewater rafting on the Pacuare or Reventazon ¢52,500-72,500 (US$90-125) per day.

La Asociación de Boteros de Parismina. A small, private group of boat captains that offers tours of the river canals from Caño Blanco. Several captains are bilingual and excellent at spotting the wide variety of wildlife lurking on the river banks. Prices range from ₡2900 (US$5) for the short ride to Parismina to ₡87,000 (US$150) for a round-trip ride to Tortuguero. Look for the boat captains at the Caño Blanco docks; be sure to get there by 5:30pm at the latest.

Mola Fish (☎2798 1034 or 8308 5518; www.molafish.com). Daniel, the owner, has offered sportfishing trips for the past four years in Parismina. 1-day trip $580 (₡336,400) for 1 person, $780 (₡457,000) for 2-people. All equipment is provided. English spoken.

Paradise Island (☎2298 0989; www.junglejessietours.com), near Mono Carablanca. Jorge Alberto has 30 years of experience offering sportfishing (₡145,000/US$250) and wildlife tours at sea (₡11,600/US$20; min. 6 people). English spoken.

TORTUGUERO VILLAGE

Famed for the vast number of turtles that nest on its beaches every year, the small village of Tortuguero has managed to parlay its ecological wealth into a thriving tourism industry that has both improved the local economy and reduced the impact of poaching. Completely separated from the mainland by a maze of canals and situated on the shores of the Caribbean, Tortuguero cannot be conveniently accessed from San José or any of Costa Rica's major transport hubs, but the effort required to get here is entirely worth it. Though the village is charming and the sunbathing quite pleasant, the real reason for visiting Tortuguero is a night-long event: the *deshove* (turtle nesting). From June to September, visitors to Tortuguero can witness the impressive efforts of nesting leatherback, green, and hawksbill turtles on the shores of Tortuguero village and the adjacent Tortuguero National Park. For those who don't get their fill of animal watching at the *deshove*, Tortuguero has many opportunities for boat, canoe, and kayak trips in its surrounding canals, where visitors can get practically face-to-face with caimans, monkeys, turtles, and a fantastically diverse array of birds.

Though thousands of tourists follow the turtles to Tortuguero's beaches each year, the onslaught of *cabinas* and tourist information centers has not completely destroyed its small-town appeal. Here, ecotourism has truly taken hold, and many of Tortuguero's residents are employed in the tourism industry. The influx of tourist money that comes from the nightly *deshove* has stabilized the local community and helped to decrease the prevalence of turtle poaching in the area.

⬛ TRANSPORTATION

Flying from San José (p. 448) to the airstrip, a few kilometers north of Tortuguero, is the most convenient way to get to the village, but it is also the most expensive. **Sansa** offers flights from San José and from Juan Santa María International Airport in Alajuela. (☎2221 9414; www.flysansa.com. Approx. US$100.) **NatureAir** departs from Tobías Bolaños Airport in Pavas. (☎2220 3054, reservations from US +1-888-535-8832. Approx. US$100/₡58,000.) Except for flying, all routes into Tortuguero require a boat trip, as the island is separated from the mainland by a network of canals. There are two main starting points for transport into Tortuguero: **Cariari**, in northeastern Costa Rica, and **Moín**, next to Limón on the Caribbean coast.

From Cariari: Buses leave each morning for Cariari from the **Terminal de los Caribeños** in San José (☎2221 2596; 2hr.; 9 per day). Once in Cariari, there are 2 options for transport to Tortuguero. The cheapest route from Cariari is by bus to Pavona (1hr.; 6, 11:30am, 3pm; ₡1100). Take this bus to the end of the line at the river's edge, where **lanchas** (small boats) will speed you through a swampy river to Tortuguero's main docks (1hr.; departs upon bus arrival; ₡1600, buy tickets on board). If you are traveling by **car**, park your car in Pavona and then take the boat to Tortuguero.

From Moín: The trip to Tortuguero from Moín is completed entirely in a boat and is known for providing opportunities for crocodile, bird, and monkey sightings. *Lanchas* depart early in the morning for Tortuguero from Moín's small dock behind **Restaurante Papá Manuel** (10am and 3pm, but try to arrive at least 1hr. early to bargain prices and get a captain). The *lancha* trip is 3-5hr. through canals teeming with wildlife (¢20,300/US$35). It's best to arrange in advance, either at the docks or through a hotel or tour company in Tortuguero. If you're traveling alone, a tour guide may request up to ¢87,000 (US$150) for the trip; arrive early to buddy up with other travelers (see **Tour Smart,** p. 546).

From Tortuguero: Private boats depart from Tortuguero at almost any hour desired, though boats are only allowed to travel in the area's waterways from 6am to 6pm. Most tour companies in Tortuguero organize return trips to Moín, Parismina, and Cariari via Pavona. To schedule a trip, talk to any of the tour companies listed; prices should run about ¢14,500 (US$25) per person to **Moín,** ¢11,600 (US$20) per person to **Parismina,** and ¢5800 (US$10) to **Pavona** and on to **Cariari.** Boats depart regularly for Pavona from the main docks at 6am, 11:30am, and 3pm, where a bus waits to travel the rest of the way to Cariari. Make sure to book in advance to ensure an available boat, and be aware that prices may become much steeper if traveling alone. By booking in advance, you can join a group and pay a significantly lower price.

Tour Companies: Most tour companies in Tortuguero can arrange transportation from San José or cities along the Caribbean coast to Tortuguero. However, there are several companies throughout Costa Rica that offer pre-arranged trips to the park. **Fran and Modesto Watson's tours** (☎2226 0986; www.tortuguerocanals.com) on their riverboat, *Francesca*, are highly recommended. Their most popular trip to Tortuguero includes round-trip transportation from San José to Moín in a van and from Moín to Tortuguero in a boat, in addition to 2-day, 1-night lodging at the Laguna Lodge, 5 meals, a canal boat tour, a turtle tour, a visit to Caribbean Conservation Center, and park entrance fees (¢95,700-113,100/US$165-195) per person. **Turtle Beach Lodge** (☎2248 0707; info@turtlebeachlodge.com) also offers transportation from San Jose (7½hr.; 6am; ¢20,300/US$35).

✦ 🛈 ORIENTATION AND PRACTICAL INFORMATION

The main village of Tortuguero is only about 500m long, with sandy gravel paths winding their way through the scattered buildings. The airstrip is a few kilometers north of town and is only accessible by boat. Most travelers arrive at the dock in the center of town. From the docks, with your back to the water, north is to your left and south is to your right. The docks lead on to the canals and rivers, and across the island, only about 200m from the docks, is the Caribbean Sea. The main path, **Calle Principal,** runs from the **Caribbean Conservation Center** at the far north end of the village all the way to the **ranger station** at the park entrance on the southern end of town. If you are walking around at night, you should consider bringing a flashlight; there are very few streetlights, and the paths through town beyond the main road near the docks are mostly dark and covered by trees.

Tourist Office: Tortuguero boasts an impressive number of buildings along the river's edge purporting to be "free information centers," each of which adjoins a for-profit tour company. Information guru Victor Parientes runs the 📲**Tortuguero Information Center** (☎2709 8015), opposite the church, 100m north of the docks. At the **Sansa Ticket Office** (☎2709 8015 or 8838 6330), in the same building, you can arrange plane, bus, and boat reservations, as well as rafting, hiking, and turtle-watching excursions. Open daily 8am-1pm and 2-7pm.

Banks: There are no banks or ATMs in Tortuguero, so try to stock up on *colones* before you arrive. If you are in a bind, the **Super Morpho,** located in the town center across from the docks, gives cash back on credit card or debit card purchases. (Open daily 7am-9pm. AmEx/MC/V).

Police: The **police station** (☎2767 1593), in the blue building, 75m north of the dock to the left of the C. Principal.

Medical Services: For medical emergencies, call ☎8841 8404 or 8304 2121. For serious emergencies, the Sansa ticket office can arrange charter flights to the hospital in San José.

Telephones: Available at **Miss Junie's,** the Super Morpho in front of the docks, and in front of the **ICE office,** 25m south of the police station. Local calls ¢20 per min. International calls require a calling card; some phones require a calling card regardless of destination.

Internet Access: Internet Cafe, 150m north of the main dock on the right. Offers 6 computers with sometimes-slow internet (¢2000 per hr.). Open daily until 9pm.

ACCOMMODATIONS

Despite its remote location, Tortuguero Village has an extensive selection of accommodations, most of them well within a student traveler's means. Hot-water baths and fans are standard fare on the island, and many *cabinas* have on-site breakfasts and hammocks available. Because of the large number of tourists visiting the island, it is important to make reservations in advance if you wish to stay at a particular place, especially during the Tortuguero's high season (July-Oct.). Those who aren't too fond of bugs should remember that the buildings near the canals, where the water is slow-moving, are much more mosquito-friendly than those closer to the drier air and quicker currents of the beach. **Camping** is not allowed on the beach. Backpackers can pitch tents for US$12 (¢6960) per person at the Jalova ranger station (includes park entry, accessible only by boat) or at Hotel Meriscar in Tortuguero Village (includes access to kitchen and hot-water showers).

Cabinas Aracari (☎2709 8006). From the docks, head south on the path and take the 1st left after the mini shopping center; Aracari is at the end of the path. Though its prices are relatively low, the *cabinas* scattered throughout the tropical garden are spotless, with tile floors, private hot-water showers, fans, and porches. Singles ¢5800 (US$10); doubles ¢9260 (US$16); triples ¢13,920 (US$24). ❶

Casa Marbella (☎8833 0827 or 2709 8011), between the Tortuguero Information Center and Dorling's Bakery. Beautiful views and a friendly owner make it a charming option, but swarming mosquitoes detract from the experience. Each of the 10 rooms has high ceilings, soft beds, and hot water. Breakfast included, as well as access to the fridge and microwave. Free Wi-Fi. Singles ¢17,400-29,000 (US$30-50); doubles ¢20,300-31,900 (US$35-55); triples ¢26,100-37,700 (US$45-65). ❸

Miss Miriam's (☎2709 8002), on the soccer field, next door to Miss Miriam's Caribbean restaurant. A 2-story house with sunny, yellow-walled rooms with private, but temperamental, hot-water baths and fans. Across the soccer field, at **Miss Miriam's II,** 9 slightly larger cabins with similar amenities are just as close to the ocean but farther from the traffic. Singles ¢11,600 (US$20); doubles ¢14,500 (US$25); triples ¢17,400 (US$30). ❷

Cabinas y Restaurante La Casona (☎2709 8092 or 8860 0453), on the northeast corner of the soccer field. The best deal at this popular complex is the *casita,* a 3-bedroom apartment with its own kitchen, hot-water bath, and open-air porch with stellar views of the Caribbean beach. Breakfast included. Free Wi-Fi and internet. Reserve in advance. *Casita* ¢4060 (US$7) per person for up to 8 people; singles ¢13,340 (US$23); doubles ¢17,400 (US$30); triples ¢23,200 (US$40). AmEx/D/MC/V. ❷

◘ FOOD

Though a small town, Tortuguero has a fair number of restaurants, most of which are on the expensive side as they cater to an almost entirely tourist clientele. To pick up your own trimmings, head to **Super Morpho**, directly opposite the docks (open daily 7am-9pm; AmEx/D/MC/V), **Super Las Tortugas** (☎27098022), 200m north of the docks (open daily 7am-9pm; AmEx/D/MC/V), or **Super Bambu** (☎2709 8108), 200m south of the docks (open daily 7am-9pm; AmEx/D/MC/V).

▧ **Miss Junie's,** 250m north of the docks. When it is not overrun by tourist groups, this Caribbean restaurant conjures up fresh and flavorful regional specialties. Breakfast ¢1160-4060 (US$2-7). Entrees ¢5220-8120 (US$9-14). Open daily 7am-10pm. ❸

▧ **Miss Miriam's** (☎2709 8002), next door to Miss Miriam's *cabinas* on the north side of the soccer field. Serves family-style "make your own *casado*" meals with coconut-simmered rice, salad, *gallo pinto,* french fries, and a variety of Caribbean-flavored proteins including whole fish, chicken, steak, and pork chops (¢4400 per person). Stop by in the morning for a traditional *tico gallo pinto* breakfast with a kick of coconut flavoring (¢3300). Call out if no one is in sight. Open daily 7:30am-9pm. ❷

Cabinas y Restaurante La Casona, on the northwest corner of the soccer field. Nestled in a thatched-roof porch in the gardens of Cabinas La Casona, this relaxing restaurant prepares a variety of tasty dishes for customers at picnic-style wooden tables. Hanging plants and the sweet smell of burning incense add to the intoxicating vibe. Delicious *casados* ¢3200, heart of palm lasagna ¢4200, and garlic and butter grilled shrimp with rice ¢5600. Open daily 7:30-11am and 1:30-8:30pm. AmEx/D/MC/V. ❸

Buddha Bar (☎2709 8084), 50m north of docks. Though its prices are a bit higher than those of other restaurants in town, the lounge-like atmosphere, spacious riverside terrace, and pleasant ambient music bring a fair-sized crowd to the relaxed Buddha Bar. Guests can relax on couches in the night-club-style interior or enjoy their meal *al fresco* at the dock-side tables along the river. *Batidos* ¢2000-2800. Pizza ¢4000-8000. Lasagna ¢3800. Crepes ¢3700-4300. Sangria ¢2800. Desserts (¢2000-2700) are tasty, though tiny. Reservations recommended for after 6pm. Open daily 11:30am-8:30pm. AmEx/D/MC/V. ❷

♫ NIGHTLIFE

Punto Encuentro, 100m north of the docks. Look for writing on the left side of the wall. The hippest place in town, right on the water's edge. Just try not to fall in after too many cold *Imperiales* (¢1000). Large screen displays music videos showcase old-school Caribbean music and Latin pop. Rice and shrimp ¢2500. Open daily 11am-2am. AmEx/D/MC/V.

Mala Culebra, across from the SuperMorpho at the docks. Not as busy as Punto Encuentro. Groups of tourists gather to show off their moves to the reggae-heavy soundtrack. *Imperial* ¢1000. Open daily 11am-2am.

◈ SIGHTS

CARIBBEAN CONSERVATION CORPORATION NATURAL HISTORY VISITOR CENTER. Before going to see the turtles, check out the non-profit Caribbean Conservation Corporation Natural History Visitor Center (CCC). Founded by Archie Carr, who later prompted the creation of Tortuguero National Park, the CCC specializes in research and education on sea turtles. The center has videos, exhibits, and information on the decimation of the sea turtle population and the efforts taken by conservationists to save the endangered animals. In the 50 years since its inception, the CCC has tagged over 50,000 turtles, making it the world's largest green-turtle-tagging program. Visitors can "adopt" a turtle with a ¢14,500 (US$25) donation and, in turn, receive an adoption certificate, photograph, turtle fact sheet, and information about the tagged turtle when it is found. Those who want to get up close and personal with the turtles can sign up for the center's internship positions, where interns hole up in research facilities and aid the center's scientists in their work. Interns can pick which type of turtle they want to research. Prices for internships run ¢816,000-1,573,800 (US$1400-2700) for 1-3 week programs. The center's admission fee is used to further the efforts of the CCC. *(At the north end of town. Head north on the main path for about 200m, where you will see the center's signs; turn right and follow the path a few hundred meters further until you reach the center. ☎ 2709 8091; www.cccturtle.org. Open M-Sa 10am-noon and 2-5:30pm, Su 2-5:30pm. US$1/¢580. MC/V.)*

TOUR SMART. While tourism has certainly reinvigorated the local economy in Tortuguero, it has also resulted in a wave of new tour agencies, some of which hire unqualified guides and require travelers to patronize certain establishments. To ensure that you are getting your money's worth, ask about a guide's qualifications before signing up for a tour and try to compare the offers of several individuals or companies before making a decision. Keep in mind that tours that uncover the sand where eggs are located disrupt the hatching process, kill the newly hatched baby turtles, and are illegal.

PARQUE NACIONAL TORTUGUERO

Sheltering the most important nesting site for marine turtles in the Western Hemisphere, Parque Nacional Tortuguero encompasses 261 sq. km of coastal territory and 501 sq. km of marine territory 84km north of Limón. It is almost exclusively accessible and navigable by boat. The park's 35km beach, where thousands of turtles return each year to lay their eggs, has brought the park international fame and thousands of visitors. Not content to surrender the show, howler monkeys echo in the treetops, toucans coast overhead, and caimans glide through the canals that flow into the park's swampy regions.

Despite decades of research, scientists still do not know why the turtles flock in such numbers to Tortuguero or how they are able to find their way back here to nest over 30 years after they first hatched. They do know that as the turtle leaves the beach, it records the details of the beach and its location relative to its next destination. Despite an extinction scare in the 1960s brought on by poaching and egg-stealing, conservation efforts have tremendously helped the turtle population, and the famous green turtles continue to nest in the park (from the end of June to Sept.), along with leatherbacks (Mar.-July), hawksbills (May-Sept.), and loggerheads (June-Oct.). All of these species are endangered, though the recent focus on ecotourism in the area has helped the turtles considerably; they are now worth more as a tourist attraction than as an ingredient in turtle soup. However, the turtles still face an immense number of natural predators. If they make it to the sea, baby turtles are prime meat for sharks, big fish, and other sea creatures. In the end, only one out of 1000 sea turtles will make it. To help save the baby turtles from human predators, proceeds from designated turtle stickers ¢2320 (US$4) sold at souvenir shops and tourist booths fund the guards who watch over the eggs.

Today, researchers tag turtles and use satellite tracking to determine patterns of birth dates, routes, and travel patterns in an attempt to uncover the mystery behind these forever-returning females. Tagging turtles has revealed amazing information about their migratory and mating habits: one turtle tagged near Tortuguero was found just one month later on the coast of Senegal, Africa, and many reports show that female turtles, after visiting hundreds of beaches around the world, return to their birth site to nest 30 years later.

⌐ TRANSPORTATION. Tortuguero Village is the gateway for Parque Nacional Tortuguero. See p. p. 542 for transportation to and from Tortuguero. The entrance to the park, at the Cuatro Esquinas Ranger Station, is a 400m walk south of the main docks in Tortuguero Village. The less-frequented Jalova Ranger Station is accessible by a 1½hr. boat ride—arrange transportation at the main docks.

WHEN TO GO. Tortuguero has an average yearly rainfall of 5-6m. The rainy season is officially June-Oct., but expect it to rain a lot year-round. The driest months are Feb.-May. Unlike most of Costa Rica, high season in Tortuguero is during the rainy season, when the four different species of turtles come for the *deshove* (turtle nesting). The famous *tortugas verdes* nest on Tortuguero's 35km beach June-Sept.; leatherbacks nest Mar.-July; hawksbills nest May-Sept.; and loggerheads nest June-Oct. Be sure to bring good, waterproof footwear (rubber boots work well), rain gear, sunblock, insect repellent, a hat, and cash. Frequent blackouts in rainy season make a flashlight highly advisable.

▨ PRACTICAL INFORMATION. Most journeys into the park begin at the **Cuatro Esquinas Ranger Station,** where rangers sell entrance tickets, provide maps, and answer visitors' questions. The entrance is open daily 5:30am-6pm. Although the park closes at 6pm, tickets must be purchased before 4pm, and the last entry is at 4pm. If planning a boat trip, remember that many of the canals around Tortuguero are part of the national park and thus are only open daily 6am-6pm. Most of the canals also have speed and motor restrictions; check with the park rangers (☎2709 8086) for more details. Entrance ₡5800 (US$10); children ₡580 (US$1).

▨▣ HIKING AND GUIDED TOURS. There are two official land hikes in Tortuguero National Park. Starting from the Cuatro Esquinas Ranger Station, **Sendero El Gavilán** (1hr., 2km) used to be the only hike available, but it is currently under construction. Though it is not a difficult hike, it can be muddy and buggy. The trail winds through the forest and ends on the beach, where you can take a left and walk back to town. Rubber boots are required for the hike and can be rented for ₡580 (US$1) per person at a hotel or tourist center. If it is still under construction, you can take the **Sendero Jaguar,** a 4 km (1½hr.) circular hike that both begins and ends at the Ranger Station. Venomous snakes can be found on both trails, but will not attack unless aggravated. **Caño Harold** is one of the best waterways in the Park for caiman, turtle, monkey, and kingfisher sightings.

The best way to explore the park is by canoe or kayak on its numerous canals and rivers. Although it's possible to go alone, hiring a guide makes for a much more informative and fun experience. Keep in mind, however, that guides abound in Tortuguero, and the competition between guides can be fierce. If you want a particular guide, stick with them, even if competitors try to mislead you. Most guided boat tours cost about ₡8700 (US$15) per person, plus park entry fees. The hike to the top of Cerro Tortuguero offers one of the most spectacular views of Parque Nacional Tortuguero, but is under-frequented due to its location across the canals from the village. Guided tours of the hike last about 3hr. and include transportation (¢11,600, US$20 per person).

Tinamon Tours (☎2709 8004 or 8842 6561; www.tinamontours.de), in the purple house 100m past Cabinas Tortuguero. Owner Bárbara Hartung leads canoe, hiking, and village tours in English, French, German, and Spanish. She prefers groups of four to five people. Tours ¢2900 (US$5) per hr. per person. Book several days in advance as tours fill up quickly.

Mundo Natural Tours (☎8341 1359 or 8811 7919), next to the cafe. Owners Jorge and David offer canoe trips (¢8700, US$15), turtle night walks (¢11,600/US$20), a frog night tour on private trails (¢8700/US$15), and an 8hr. "extreme adventure" tour (¢34,800/US$60).

Bony Scott (☎2709 8139 or 8320 5232), 50m south of the docks. Offers canoe tours each morning (3hr.; ¢145,000/US$25, includes park entrance fee). Kayak rentals ¢9800/US$18 per day; includes park entrance fee.

ECO-FRIENDLY TOURS. Visitors should always exercise responsibility and sensitivity when exploring the wildlife. Official park rules require boats to switch from gas to electric motors, which do not disturb the animals as much as the roar from loud gas engines. Tour boats should also glide along the canals extremely slowly to avoid causing wakes, which disrupt animal and insect life on the shores. Most tour guides observe these rules, but some ignore them for financial reasons. As an informed and eco-sensitive tourist, do your best to ask non-rule-abiding guides to slow down and be quiet.

TURTLE WATCHING. The park's feature presentation is the nightly *deshove*, when turtles come to lay their eggs. The female turtle emerges from the sea and makes her way up the sand, pausing frequently to check for danger. When she finds the perfect spot, she uses her flippers to dig a body pit about 1ft. deep, and then a smaller pit for her eggs. After laying her eggs and using her flippers to bury them in the sand, she leaves them, never seeing the final product. The intriguing process lasts about 2hr.

Visitors must be with a guide certified by the park (ask to see a license). The beaches are guarded by 18 rangers whose sole job is to find and protect the turtles; if you try to watch the *deshove* without a guide, they will throw you out. (Tours leave nightly around 8 and 10pm. ¢11,600/US$20 per person. Park entrance ticket required for beaches south of Cuatro Esquinas Ranger Station.)

Talk to any of the guides mentioned above to arrange a tour or ask around town to find an experienced local guide. It is best to find a guide in town before 4pm because the guides must purchase permits before the park closes. Wear good walking shoes and dark clothing (light clothes may scare the turtles). Flashlights are useful for the hike to the beach, but cameras and flashlights cannot be turned on once at the beach, as the light disturbs the turtles and causes them to stop the nesting process. Make sure to bring a bottle of water along with you, as some of the hikes are upwards of 2km long, and you may end up waiting up to an hour for the first turtle to arrive. Official park rules state that once a tour group has seen the egg-laying process, they must leave, regardless of whether or not the two hours have elapsed. The park rangers take any offenses very seriously and may deny future entry to any visitor who violates the rules.

⚠ **CERRO TORTUGUERO AND CAÑO PALMA BIOLOGICAL STATION.** Located just off the canals en route to Tortuguero Village from Pavona, **Caño Palma Biological Station** offers similar naturalist attractions and fauna to Tortuguero without the large numbers of tourists. Staffed by a small group of employees and volunteers from the non-profit **Canadian Organization for Tropical Education and Rainforest Conservation (COTERC)**, the station has numerous hiking trails for day visitors and opportunities for long-term volunteer work. Though technically part of Barra del Colorado Wildlife Refuge, the entrance to Caño Palma is more easily accessed from Pavona or Tortuguero. (☎2709 8052; www.coterc.org. 1st week ¢145,000/US$250, each additional week ¢104,400/US$180; includes dorm-style lodging, meals, hiking, and pickup from Cariari or Tortuguero. Station admission ¢1160/US$2.)

From Pavona, take the boat heading for Tortuguero and ask to be dropped off at the station (30min.; 9am, 1:30pm; ¢1600). From Tortuguero, catch any of the boats heading back to Pavona and ask to be dropped off at the station (30min.; 6, 11:30am, 3pm; ¢1600).

PANAMA

True, the Panama Canal might be one of the greatest human-made wonders of the world. Put that aside for the moment and consider Panama's other wonders: lush mountain forests, Caribbean beaches surrounded by coral reefs, a thriving and skyscraping metropolis, vast ranches of highland villages. Panama's 2.5 million people create a diverse culture, including vibrant indigenous groups and recent international immigrants. Far east in San Blas and Darién, dugout canoes provide access to hidden remote villages and images of Western pop culture's fashions are replaced by Kuna molas, traditional patched cloth panels. Pristine Caribbean shores and untouched forests are within a few hours' drive of Panama City, Central America's most modern city. The political situation in Panama is stable and the tourist and national park infrastructure is unmatched.

ESSENTIALS

PLANNING YOUR TRIP

PASSPORTS, VISAS, AND CUSTOMS.

Passport. Required of all visitors. Must be valid 3 months after arrival.

Visa (below). Not required of citizens from the UK or EU. For others, visa is valid for 30 days, with possible 60-day extension. In place of a visa, tourist cards (US$5) are available upon arrival.

Onward Ticket. Required of all visitors.

Work Permit (p. 39). Required for all foreigners planning to work for a Panamanian business in Panama. Employees of international corporations do not need a permit.

Required Vaccinations. Travelers coming from nations with endemic yellow fever need proof of vaccination.

Driving Permit. Valid driver's license from your home country or an International Driving Permit required.

Departure Tax. US$20.

EMBASSIES AND CONSULATES

For embassies in Panama, see the **Practical Information** section for Panama City (p. 565). The following are Panamanian embassies and consulates abroad.

Australia: Consulate, 1/234 Slade Road, Bexley North NSW 2207 (☎+61 02 9150 8409; fax 02 9150 8410). Open M-F 9am-3pm.

Canada: Embassy, 130 Albert Street, Ottawa, Ontario K1P 5G4 (☎+1 613-236-7177).

NZ: Consulate, 61 High Street, Auckland Central, Auckland (☎+64 9379 8550).

UK: Embassy, 40 Hertford Street, London W1J 7SH (☎+44 20 74934646).

US: Embassy, 2862 McGill Terrace NW, Washington, DC 20008 (☎+1 202-483-1407). Open M-F 9am-5pm.

VISA INFORMATION

Citizens from the EU and UK can travel in Panama for 30 days without a visa. Residents of other nations must obtain a multiple-entry visa from the nearest consulate before arriving, or purchase a US$5 **tourist card** upon arrival. It is possible to extend your stay another 60 days through an application at any immigration office. To stay past 90 days, you must apply for a **change of migratory status.** You will be charged US$250 and will probably need the help of a Panamanian lawyer.

If you are working for a foreign company in Panama, you do not need a **work permit.** If you are hired by a Panamanian company, you will need a permit from the Ministry of Labor. These are good for one year and are renewable. You must also have a passport, a police record notarized by the nearest Panamanian Consulate, an original birth certificate, six passport-sized photos, and a negative HIV test. If married, you must show a certificate. Alternately, if you live in Panama legally for five years, you can become a resident alien with working rights.

TOURIST OFFICES

La Autoridad de Turismo Panamá (☎507 526 7000; www.visitpanama.com) runs the tourism show in Panama. They offer maps and a wealth of information about what to do and where to go. They also have a ton of helpful info on Panama's national parks.

MONEY

US DOLLARS ($)		
AUS$1 = US$0.80		US$1 = AUS$1.24
CDN$1 = US$0.92		US$1 = CDN$01.09
EUR€1 = US$1.41		US$1 = EUR€0.71
NZ$1 = US$0.64		US$1 = NZ$1.56
UK£1 = US$1.62		US$1 = UK£0.62

The currency chart above is based on August 2009 exchange rates. All prices in this section are quoted in US dollars, as the Panamanian currency, the **balboa,** is directly linked to the US dollar. Panama uses actual US bills but mints its own coins. A huge 50¢ piece, known as a *peso,* is used regularly, and a nickel is often called a *real.*

ATMs (marked by red Sistema Clave signs) are everywhere in Panama City and throughout David. Though uncommon in rural areas, they are also found in a number of towns west of Panama City. Note that these machines don't always accept foreign cards.

There are several **Western Union** offices around the country. Some more pricey hotels and department stores accept **traveler's checks,** but few budget establishments or businesses will honor them. Many banks are willing to exchange American Express checks and sometimes other types. Bring proper ID and be prepared to pay a fee unless you are exchanging at the AmEx office.

PANAMA

Panama

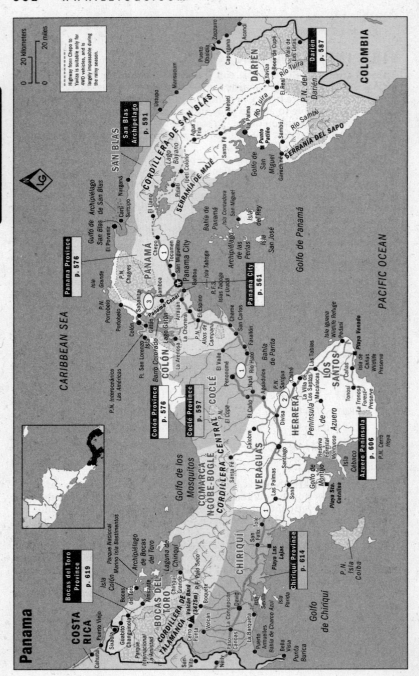

0 20 kilometers

0 20 miles

Highway from Chepo to Yaviza is suitable only for 4WD vehicles, and is largely impassable during the rainy season.

CARIBBEAN SEA

PACIFIC OCEAN

COLOMBIA

COSTA RICA

Bocas del Toro Province p. 619

Colón Province p. 576

Coclé Province p. 597

Chiriquí Province p. 614

Azuero Peninsula p. 606

Los Santos

Herrera

Veraguas

Panama Province p. 576

Panama City p. 561

San Blas Archipelago p. 591

Darién p. 587

CORDILLERA DE SAN BLAS

SAN BLAS

DARIÉN

SERRANÍA DE MAJÉ

SERRANÍA DEL SAPO

COMARCA NGÖBE-BUGLÉ

CORDILLERA CENTRAL

CORDILLERA DE TALAMANCA

BOCAS DEL TORO

CHIRIQUÍ

Golfo de los Mosquitos

Golfo de Chiriquí

Golfo de Panamá

Bahía de Panamá

Bahía de Parita

Archipiélago de las Perlas

Península de Azuero

Outside Panama City, national banks satisfy money needs, but at border crossings, money is exchanged at bad rates; bring US dollars. **Visa** and **Mastercard** are easier to use than other cards, but many hotels and restaurants only accept cash. Visitors can often obtain AmEx/MC/V **cash advances,** and there are a number of US banks (Citibank, Fleet, HCSB) where commissions and fees may be less substantial. All international debit cards work, but PINs should be in combinations to accommodate letter-less keypads. Tipping, 10% at least in the big cities, is generally expected. "Free" travel guides usually expect a tip. For more info, see **Tipping and Bargaining,** p. 9.

COSTS

The most significant costs for travelers in Panama will be accommodations. While basic rooms or dorm beds can usually be found for under US$7, more elaborate lodgings are US$10-15. Private singles with some amenities cost at least US$20. Food is cheap, with easily-found *típico* (a standard meal) US$1-$3. While the assiduous traveler may be able to scrape by on US$15-$20 per day, a safer bet would be US$25-$30, without transportation.

PRICE DIVERSITY

Our Researchers list establishments in order of value from best to worst, honoring our favorites with the Let's Go thumbs-up (👍). Because the best *value* is not always the cheapest *price*, we have incorporated a system of price ranges based on a rough expectation of what you will spend. For **accommodations,** we base our range on the cheapest price for which a single traveler can stay for one night. For **restaurants,** we estimate the average amount one traveler will spend in one sitting. The table below tells you what you'll *typically* find in Panama at the corresponding price range, but keep in mind that no system can allow for the quirks of individual establishments.

ACCOMMODATIONS	RANGE	WHAT YOU'RE *LIKELY* TO FIND
❶	Under US$5	Campgrounds and dorm rooms, both in hostels and actual universities. Expect bunk beds and a communal bath. You may have to provide or rent towels.
❷	US$5-15	Hostels in heavily-touristed areas or shabby hotels. Sometimes private bathrooms, but most likely communal facilities. May have a TV.
❸	US$16-25	A comfortable room with a private bath. Should have decent amenities such as A/C and TV. Breakfast may be included.
❹	US$26-50	Bigger rooms than a ❸, with more amenities, and often in a more convenient location. Breakfast may be included.
❺	Over US$50	Large hotels or upscale chains. If it's a ❺ and it doesn't have the perks you want, you've paid too much.

FOOD	RANGE	WHAT YOU'RE *LIKELY* TO FIND
❶	Under US$2	Probably food stalls, university cafeterias, and rural Panamanian eateries. It's yummy and cheap, but you'll be reaching for the Panamanian version of Tums post pig out.

FOOD	RANGE	WHAT YOU'RE *LIKELY* TO FIND
❷	US$2-4	National restaurant chains and some international fast food. Expect typical Panamanian platters and sandwiches, food at a bar, and low-priced entrees. The average Panamanian eatery is a ❷.
❸	US$8-11	Mid-priced entrees, seafood, and exotic pasta dishes. More upscale Panamanian eateries. Check the menu to see if tax is included in prices.
❹	US$8-15	The cheapest entrees at an upscale restaurant. Entrees tend to be heartier or more elaborate, but you'll mostly be throwing down for ambiance. Few restaurants in this range have a dress code, but you'll feel out of place in a T-shirts and sandals.
❺	Over US$15	Your meal might cost more than your room, but there's a reason—it's something fabulous, famous, or both. Extensive drink options. Only found in big cities or the most heavily-touristed areas.

TRANSPORTATION

The major domestic airline is **Aeroperlas** (☎+507 315 7500; www.aeroperlas. com). There are a few smaller airlines connecting Panama City to San Blas and Darién. **Buses** are the major means of budget transport and the only means of reaching remote locations. Bus quality is generally good, and long trips tend to be served by luxury coaches. Other intercity routes are run by **mini-buses,** while in remote areas, **vans** provide service. A bus' destination is almost always written on the front. If there's no terminal, many buses linger around the *parque central.* Pay when getting off, but confirm the fare before embarking. Consider taking warm clothes on board to protect yourself from the chilling air conditioning or the constant breeze from open windows. Travelers say **hitchhiking** becomes easier the farther one gets from the Pan-American Highway, but *Let's Go* does not recommend it. Truck drivers have been known to offer *"un lif"* from gas stations.

BORDER CROSSINGS

Travelers can cross into Panama by land or (occasionally) sea. Remember to carry enough money to pay any entrance or exit fees. Border crossings in Panama are bolded, and adjacent border towns are always listed alongside their respective country names.

COSTA RICA. There are three land crossings. **Paso Canoas** (p. 618) is 50km west of David, near Ciudad Neily, Costa Rica. To get there, catch a bus from David (p. 614). **Sixaola/Guabito** (p. 618) is on the Caribbean coast 15 minutes from Changuinola, near Puerto Viejo de Talamanca, Costa Rica. **Río Sereno,** at the end of the Concepción-Volcán road, is rarely used.

COLOMBIA. The Darién gap, the only break in the Pan-American Highway, prevents land travel to Colombia. The **ferry** service between Colón and Cartagena has been discontinued, but occasional passage can be found on cargo ships from Panama. One land-sea route involves island-hopping through the San Blas Archipelago via **Puerto Obaldía,** but this is also considered unsafe due to paramilitary and criminal activity.

SAFETY

The regions west of Panama City are politically stable and safe. In Panama City, standard big-city rules apply; some neighborhoods are best avoided at night, and a few are best avoided altogether (see **Panama City: Orientation,** p. 563). Outside the free trade zone, Colón is generally unsafe—take taxis from the bus station and don't walk in the city (see **Colón,** p. 579). Guerrillas and paramilitaries are active in the **Darién** area along the Colombian border, especially since the US military left in 1999. Both US and Panamanian governments warn travelers not to enter the region. **Women travelers** will find the same *machismo*, catcalls, and stares as in the rest of Central America, though Panama is no worse than other countries (see **Women Travelers,** p. 30). While public displays of homosexuality are not accepted anywhere in Panama, **gay and lesbian travelers** shouldn't have major problems as long as they keep a low profile.

HEALTH

Malaria is a particular concern in Panama, as there are strains of mosquitoes that resist basic malaria medication. If traveling east of Panama City, be sure to take an alternative anti-malarial. Malaria risk is greatest in rural areas like Bocas del Toro, San Blas, and the Darién. **Yellow fever vaccination** is recommended.

LIFE AND TIMES

HISTORY

FROM PRE-DEPENDENCE TO INDEPENDENCE (PRE-COLUMBIAN—AD 1821). Some eleven thousand years ago, hunter-gatherers made their first appearance on the Panamanian isthmus and eventually settled in villages such as those of the Monagrillo culture, whose pottery dates back to 2500-1700BC. When Columbus landed at present-day Portobelo in 1502, he came across indigenous cultures thousands of years old. Vasco Nuñez de Balboa followed him a few years later to conquer those cultures, establish the first Spanish colony in the New World, and appoint himself governor. Most importantly, in 1513, Balboa "discovered" the Pacific Ocean just on the other side of Panama: a finding which would soon transform the isthmus into a major route for

FROM THE ROAD

GETTING AROUND

You can tell a lot about a place by its different forms of transportation. Whether you are riding up a river in a dugout canoe or cruising the roads in a retrofitted school bus, transportation in Panama depends on the environment you're in and the needs of the people trying to get around. Here's my take on the transportation offered in different parts of the country:

Darien: The dugout canoe and well—your two feet. There aren't too many roads in the Darien, so hollowed-out logs are used to navigate wide, muddy rivers.

San Blas Islands: The only way to get around here is by boat or the infrequent propeller plane.

Panama Province: The school bus dominates transportation here. These aren't just any old yellow mobiles; they have quirky paint jobs, whistles and all sorts of other noise makers.

Azuero: Residents of the Azuero Peninsula still use horses. Most of the peninsula is hilly and has few roads. It's not uncommon to see people riding their horses with a drink in each hand; it's probably best that there are little to no cars around here.

Chiriqui: The wealthiest province in the country has the nicest buses—unfortunately, A/C is unnecessary at an altitude of 2000m. The best way to get around here is by scooter. You'll look really cool and save a few bucks while you're at it.

shipping stolen Inca gold to Spain. Dutch and English pirates began to attack these trade routes in an attempt to get their hands on the precious cargo. In spite of such riches, the Spanish Empire in the New World collapsed in 1821, and Panama became part of the independent Gran Colombia, a republic that also included present-day Colombia, Venezuela, and Ecuador.

A MAN, A PLAN, A CANAL: PANAMA (1821-1914). Transportation in Panama took off with the construction of the US-sponsored Panama Railroad in 1855, the world's first transcontinental railroad. From 1880 to 1889, the French engineer Ferdinand de Lesseps made the first attempt to dig a canal through Panama, but was ultimately defeated by the fatal triad of yellow fever, malaria, and landslides. US President Theodore Roosevelt decided to take on the challenge again in 1902. Faced with a recalcitrant Colombian government, Roosevelt sent US warships to encourage Panama to declare independence from Colombia. The result of this gunboat diplomacy was the establishment of an independent Republic of Panama in 1903. Two weeks later, the Hay-Bunau Varilla Treaty gave the US ownership of the Canal Zone, and the great Panama Canal was completed, after much effort, in 1914.

INTERVENTION CENTURY (1914-1999). The new Republic of Panama not only gave the US permission to dig the Canal, but it also gave the US the right to protect it. Although Franklin D. Roosevelt officially renounced the US's authority to intervene in 1936, the US did its fair share of "protecting" in the 20th century. The quasi-fascist President Arnulfo Arias, who had formerly been Panama's ambassador to Italy, was deposed by a US-backed coup in 1941; he returned to power in 1948, only to be ousted again later that year. In 1964, riots broke out when Panamanian students were prevented by US forces from raising a Panamanian flag over a Canal Zone high school, leaving some 25 people dead and causing Panama to break diplomatic relations with the US for three months. Arias was elected for a third time in 1968, but his political ambitions were frustrated yet again, after only eleven days in office, when he was overthrown by a third military coup. His replacement, General Omar Torrijos, negotiated a treaty with Jimmy Carter to give Panama complete control over the Canal by the year 2000. Torrijos, however, died in a mysterious plane crash in 1981 and was succeeded by former CIA operative General Manuel Noriega. Noriega granted himself dictatorial powers and backed US interests in Nicaragua against the Sandinistas. He soon lost US support by becoming involved in drug-trafficking, and in 1989, the US launched "Operation Just Cause," sending 27,000 troops into Panama to take Noriega down. When the dictator fled into the Vatican embassy, US soldiers assailed him with a bizarre form of psychological torture: they blared "Voodoo Child" and other rock tunes into the compound 24 hours a day to flush him out. (We couldn't make this up even if we wanted to.) Noriega surrendered and was sentenced in Miami to 40 years in prison.

TODAY

In 1999, Panama elected its first female president, **Mireya Moscoso,** the widow of Arnulfo Arias. Despite entering office with high hopes, Moscoso's selection of officials to government positions were dogged with charges of nepotism and she ended her term with extraordinarily low approval ratings. She was succeeded by Martin Torrijos in 2004, the illegitimate son of **Omar Torrijos** who headed the helm of Panama's government thirty years earlier. Elected on a platform of reducing corruption and fostering economic growth, the younger Torrijos' presidency focused on fiscal and social reforms; however, such reforms were frustrated by significant opposition from both labor unions and the Catholic Church. Torrijos also issued several controversial decrees intended to strengthen Panama's internal security forces, which some feared would lead to a renewed influence of the military in government affairs. Opposition candidate **Ricardo Martinelli** is the favorite to win election in 2009 for a Presidential term slated to last until 2014.

Panama has made significant progress in reversing its reputation as a safe haven for drug-smugglers and money-launderers. The construction of the new **Centennial Bridge,** which opened in 2004, has markedly improved the country's infrastructure. Spanning the Panama Canal at the Gaillard Cut, the bridge now carries the six-lane **Pan-American Highway:** an impressive architectural achievement, which, along with the decrease in drug-related violence, has led to a significant increase in tourism.

Since gaining absolute sovereignty over **the Canal** in 2000, the Panamanian government has been planning to massively expand the World's Greatest Ditch. In 2006, a national referendum approved a proposal to build a third set of locks, which would enable even larger ships to cross the isthmus. At a projected cost of around US $5.25 billion, the project is expected to nearly double the capacity of the Canal. The new locks are scheduled to open in 2015, just after the Canal's centennial.

ECONOMY AND GOVERNMENT

Panama's economy is one of the fastest-growing in the region, pulling in an impressive 8.3% of GDP growth in 2008. Nearly 80% of the country's income comes from its highly developed services' sector, which includes the **Panama Canal** and the **Colón Free Trade Zone.** The Canal **expansion project** in particular is expected to fuel economic growth over the next decade. Despite these positive achievements, however, income remains unevenly distributed throughout the country, and nearly one-third of the population lingered below the poverty line in 2008. The nation's currency is technically the **balboa, fixed to equal the US dollar;** however, no *balboa* bills exist and US dollars are used for all daily money transactions.

Political parties in Panama today are more polarized by personalities than platforms. The major players include the **Panameñista Party,** long known as the Arnulfista Party in honor of its leader **Arnulfo Arias,** and the **Democratic Revolutionary Party of Torrijos,** which won the presidency and more than half of the National Assembly seats in the 2004 election. The up-and-coming **Democratic Change Party,** founded in 1998, owes its rising popularity to the charisma of its leader Ric1ardo Martinelli and his credible message of change as a candidate free from connections with Panama's political past.

PEOPLE

Ever since the Spanish conquest, the population of native populations in Panama has been declining. Though some early settlers tried to defend indigenous rights, many of the native populations fell victim to persecution and enslavement. Today the indigenous populations reside mostly in remote areas of the countryside, and constitute just 6% of the overall population. The overwhelming majority of Panama's inhabitants are **mestizo,** of mixed Spanish and native origin; they make up 70% of the population. The next largest ethnic group, at 14%, is comprised of predominantly black **West Indians.** This segment of the population grew during the first half of the 20th century, when thousands of laborers migrated to Panama from the Antilles. Many worked on the construction of the

Panama Canal, while others worked on banana plantations. A tenth of Panamanians are made up of foreigners or Americans who, for the most part, have stayed in the country since the Canal was completed.

Like most former Spanish colonies, Panama has a strong **Roman Catholic** heritage. In the early stages of colonization, many efforts were made to convert the native population to Catholicism. As a result, **Christianity** is by far the most dominant faith: Catholics account for 85% of the Panamanian population, while **Protestants,** mainly hailing from the British West Indies, make up the rest.

The official language of Panama is **Spanish.** However, many Panamanians also speak English, so you needn't worry if your high school Spanish classes have failed you—someone to interpret is probably close by.

CUSTOMS AND ETIQUETTE

Because the United States was politically involved in Panama during the construction of the Canal, Panamanians are familiar with North American customs and gestures. If you are a guest in someone's house, make sure to bring a gift for your host, and when eating a meal, do not begin until all are seated and your host has started. Also, it is important to note that because Panama has a strong Roman Catholic tradition, dressing conservatively is always the way to go. Beachwear must be strictly limited to the beach, as even shorts are considered inappropriate in restaurants and on the city streets.

When greeting people, remember to address men as Señor, married women as Señora, and unmarried women as Señorita. If you do strike up a conversation, baseball is a favorite Panamanian topic. It's best to avoid talking about politics, especially regarding foreign involvement in the construction of the Canal.

FOOD AND DRINK

Panamanian cuisine reflects the flavors of Latin America, with **rice, beans,** and **tortillas** serving as the basic ingredients for many popular dishes. Panama's significant West Indian population has brought Western Caribbean influences to the cuisine, especially to the coastal regions. One of the most popular dishes is **ropa vieja,** literally "old rope," which consists of shredded beef and peppers with plantains and rice. We recommend include **gallo pinto,** a dish of pork, rice, and beans.

Fresh **chichas,** or juices, include the ever-popular orange as well as more exotic varieties such as watermelon and pineapple. If you still want local flavor but juice isn't exactly what you had in mind, try **seco,** an alcohol distilled from sugarcane and served over milk and ice. **Beer** fans will not be disappointed in the selection of Panamanian brands: Balboa, Atlas, Panamá, Soberana, and Cristal are all popular options.

CULTURE

ART

Though indigenous people only make up a small piece of the Panamanian population, they are responsible for much of the country's art. The indigenous **Kuna,** an Amerindian people who reside mainly in the eastern regions of Panama and on islands off the Caribbean coast, create beautiful and colorful, handmade **molas.** *Molas* are intricate, embroidered garments worn by women as part of the traditional wardrobe on the front or back of a blouse.

Some *molas* take up to 100 hours to complete, and feature geometric designs that originated in the traditional art of body painting. Today, *molas* may also feature designs reflecting the local wildlife. Other indigenous crafts include hand-woven baskets, carvings, and elaborate masks.

LITERATURE

Any account of the history of Panamanian literature must begin with the **oral tradition,** passed down to new generations through the ancient art of storytelling. The Kuna people in particular are well known for their myths, songs, and fables, many of which have now been compiled into books.

Panamanian literature came into its own when the nation gained independence from Colombia in 1903. Since then, Panamanians have produced an abundance of poetry, short stories, and novels. The **Modernist** movement took off in post-independence Panama and found a champion in the poet **Darío Herrera.** During the 1930s, under the leadership of the poet **Rogelio Sinán,** *Modernismo* gave way to new styles like **Surrealism** and **magical realism.** Much of the country's 20th-century literature reflected the contemporary political and social situations in Panama, including the controversy surrounding the canal.

MUSIC

Rubén Blades ranks far above the rest as Panama's biggest musical superstar. The popular **salsa** and **Latin jazz** musician has won multiple Grammy Awards for his Afro-Cuban rhythms and politically charged lyrics. On top of his wildly successful musical career, Blades has appeared in several films and actually ran for president in 1994, garnering 18% of the vote.

The Panamanian folkloric style of music is known as **típico** and features vocals and the accordion. Other styles of music, including Colombian **vallenato** and Puerto Rican **bachata** and **calypso,** are also quite common. Today, reggaeton and rock and roll can be heard alongside these more traditional styles.

LAND

Panama is an isthmus connecting North and South America. It lies between Costa Rica on the west and Colombia on the east and between the Caribbean Sea to the north and the Pacific Ocean to the south. As the narrowest stretch of land standing between these two great bodies of water, Panama is of great strategic importance to many nations. As such, it attracted considerable controversy in the early 20th century during the construction of the Panama Canal, which spans 48 miles and bisects the country. Today, over 300 million tons of cargo pass through annually. International commerce aside, Panama's 1540 miles of **coastline** are also strategic for those seeking beautiful beaches. The interior of this narrow country is dominated by mountains formed along the continental divide.

Panama is a tropical paradise, hot and humid year round. The Pacific coast tends to be cooler than the Caribbean and temperatures are notably cooler at higher elevations inland. The length of the rainy season varies, but it usually extends from April to December. This climate supports an abundance of flora and fauna, in habitats ranging from **cloud forests** at high elevation to **rainforests** and **mangrove swamps** closer to sea level. Panama is home to a host of tropical flowers including **bromeliads** and over 1000 species of **orchid.** Highlights of native wildlife include the **giant anteater, the capybara,** and several different monkey species. Among Panama's more colorful residents are **macaw parrots** and **toucans.**

BEYOND TOURISM

VOLUNTEERING

SEAS, TREES, AND CLOUDS

School for International Training (SIT) Study Abroad, 1 Kipling Rd., P.O. Box 676, Brattleboro, VT 05302, USA (☎+1-888-272-7881 or 802-258-3212; www.sit.edu/studyabroad). Semester-long program in Panama entitled, "Tropical Ecology, Marine Ecosystems, and Biodiversity Conservation," costing approximately US$13,000 for the semester.

The Lost and Found Lodge Eco Resort (☎507 6581 9223 or 507 6636 8863; www.lostandfoundlodge.com). In the Panama Cloud Forest, this resort is perfect for the nature-loving backpacker. The lodge offers several volunteer opportunities, including maintaining organic farms, teaching English, and leading tours. Email info@lostandfoundlodge.com for further details on volunteer opportunities.

COMMUNITY OUTREACH

Global Volunteer Network Ltd., PO Box 30-968, Lower Hutt, New Zealand (☎+1 800-963-1198 from the US or Canada, 0800 032 5035 from the UK; www.volunteer.org). Founded in 2000, the Global Volunteer Network helps communities in need by supporting local organizations. Several volunteer opportunities are available in Panama, including working with children, teaching adults and children to read, and helping at a center for disabled people of all ages. Alternatively, you may help out at a local animal refuge or join a community recycling project.

Volunteers for Peace, 1034 Tiffany Road, Belmont VT, 05730, USA (☎+1-802-259-2759; www.vfp.org). Check website for volunteer programs in countries throughout the world, including Panama. Volunteers needed in Kuna, Panama to teach English to children and adults.

STUDYING

AMERICAN PROGRAMS

Institute for Tropical Ecology and Conservation (ITEC, inc.), 1023 SW 2nd Ave., Gainesville, FL, 3260, USA (☎352 367-9128; www.itec-edu.org). A research and conservation organization that operates the Bocas del Toro Biological Station in Panama. During summer and winter break, ITEC offers field courses to graduate and postgraduate students (18+). Coral reef ecology, primate ecology, and adventure photography are just a few of the courses offered. ITEC is a private institution; students will have to contact their respective universities to ensure that they can receive credit for this program. Tuition US$1650 (3 weeks) to US$1950 (4 weeks).

PANAMA CITY

Few cities in the world have a history, fortune, and character so intimately and singularly related to their geography. Permanently marked by the canal and the commerce it brings, not mention a century of partial US occupation, Panama City (pop. 800,000) is unlike anything else you'll find in the country or in the rest of Central America. It's a surprising and welcoming combination of the historic and ultra-modern, where Spanish and indigenous traditions coexist with immigrant cultures from the world over. The result is a metropolis that defines "cosmopolitan."

Panama City's location, a calm harbor on a narrow bridge between two continents, has made it a transit point for people and currency for over 300 years. Originally the gateway for all the gold from Spain's Pacific colonies, the first Panama City, known as Panamá Viejo (Old Panama), was founded by the Spanish in 1519 on the site of an Indian village. In the late 17th century,

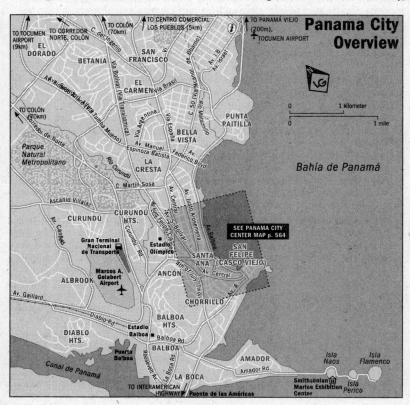

Panama City Overview

pirate invasions, infertile swamps, and numerous fires forced residents to move 8km west, to modern-day San Felipe. There, the city flourished under Spanish, French, and American occupations. During the California Gold Rush, hordes of prospectors flowed in from North America, fattening the pockets of steam-ship barons and resulting in the construction of the first railway joining the Pacific and Atlantic Oceans. The French dreamed of more ambitious inter-oceanic connection; their attempt to build a canal at the end of the 19th century ended in failure. By the early 20th century, US plans for a water passage were complete. During the canal's construction the city began to expand and spread eastward, moving to its current site. The first ship passed through the canal's Miraflores Locks in 1914. Since then, Panama has gained control over the canal, and its favorable tax regulations have made Panama City an international banking and commercial center. Today, Panama's relative stability compared to other Latin American countries continues to attract people and money. The low cost of living here has drawn retired Americans by the thousands. This influx of wealthy residents is reflected across the city, from the international cuisine to the rapidly expanding skyline.

With its first-world infrastructure, diverse population, continuing international influence, and lively nightlife, Panama City boasts all the advantages of a large, modern city. Be sure to take time and explore Panama's rainforests, Indian villages, and beautiful beaches, which are all just an hour from the city.

▮ INTERCITY TRANSPORTATION

Flights: Tocumen International Airport (☎238 2600) lies 30min. east of the city and can be reached by cab (US$15-20) or any bus marked Tocumen Corredor (US$0.35), which leave from the bus terminals at Albrook, C.50, Vía España, and Plaza 5 de Mayo. Airport serves: **American** (☎269 6022); **Continental** (☎263 9177); **Copa** (☎227 0116); **Delta** (☎214 8118); **KLM** (☎264 6395); and **Taca** (☎360 2093). **Marcos Gelabert Airport** (☎526 7990) handles all domestic flights and is a US$2 taxi ride from the Santa Ana neighborhood. **Aeroperlas** (☎315 7500; www.aeroperlas.com) has flights to **Bocas del Toro, Darien, David,** and **the San Blas islands. Air Panama** (☎316 9000; www.flyairpanama.com) serves roughly the same destinations. Flight prices and schedules change often, depending on demand. Flights are often canceled, combined, or re-directed. Trips to smaller destinations will often involve 2 or more stopovers.

Buses: Gran Terminal de Transporte (☎232 5803), is next door to the Albrook mall and near Marcos Gelabert Airport. Tickets can be bought at the booths lining the terminal. Station employees can point you in the right direction, though few of them speak English. Information booth (☎303 3040) open 24hr. The terminal has food courts, ATMs, internet, and luggage storage. Schedules are flexible; buses may wait to fill up. To: **Bocas del Toro** (10hr., 8pm, US$24) via **Almirante** (9½hr.); **Chitré** (4hr., every hr. 6am-11pm, US$7.50); **Colón** (1½hr., every 30min. 4am-midnight, US1.80; express service 1hr., 14-17 per day, US$2.50) via **Sabanitas** (1hr.); **David** (7hr., every hr. 5:30am-8:30am, US$12.60; express night service 6hr., 10:45pm and midnight, US$15), with some continuing on to **the border** with Costa Rica at Paso Canoas (9 per day 6:30am-midnight); **El Valle** (2hr., every 25min. 6am-7pm, US$3.50); **Metetí** (6hr., 14 per day, US$9); **Penonomé** (2hr., every 20min. 4am-11pm, US$4.35); **Santiago** (3½hr., every hr. 3am-1am, US$7.50,); and **Yaviza** (7hr.; 4:15, 5:15, 5:45, 6:30, 7:30am; US$14). **Tica Buses** (☎314 6385) sends buses to **San José, Costa Rica** (16hr.; 11am, 10, 11pm; US$25-35).

♦ ORIENTATION

From the international airport, take a taxi (30min.; US$28, shared taxi US$11). To find a bus, walk out of the parking lot where the cars exit, and walk through the roundabout. On the other side of the road is a bus stop. Take the Tocumen Corredor bus (45min., US$0.35), which will drop you off on C.50. The domestic airport is a US$2 cab ride from the center; alternatively, take a bus (US$0.25) from the airport to the central bus station nearby. From the bus station, there are buses to almost everywhere in the city. For Bella Vista, take the "Vía España" bus and ask the driver to let you off in Bella Vista.

Parts of Panama City are laid out in grids. Many streets have two or three names: one is often a person's name, the second some a combination of numbers and letters (i.e. C. 49A Este). As such, directions in the city are generally given in terms of landmarks and blocks. The city sprawls west to east along the **Bahía de Panamá** (Panama Bay). The **Peninsula of San Felipe** (also known as **Casco Viejo**), on the west side of the bay, is home to magnificent crumbling old buildings, some of the swankiest new restaurants, and many of the city's historical sites. At the heart of Casco Viejo is **Plaza Independencia,** from which the city's largest street, **Avenida Central,** extends northeast into **Santa Ana** (often pronounced "Santana"). Between the Plaza de Santa Ana, just north of San Felipe and **Plaza 5 de Mayo,** in the heart of Santa Ana, Av. Central becomes a pedestrian mall lined with budget shopping. Beyond the Plaza, the road runs east through Calidonia before becoming **Vía España.** Further on, the road enters **Bella Vista,** which is quickly becoming the cosmopolitan center of the city. **Avenida Balboa** intersects with Av. Central in Santa Ana, and stretches along the bay with a new park on the right and the city's fanciest skyscrapers on the left. Passing through **Marbella,** which borders Bella Vista, Av. Balboa continues through a bulge in the bay known as **Punta Paitilla** and **Punta Pacífica,** which are home to some of the most expensive apartment buildings and the best hospital in town.

SAFETY. Though Panama City is welcoming to visitors, all cities have their dangers, and Panama definitely has its share. Problems have been reported in San Felipe, Santa Ana, Panamá Viejo, and Calidonia, especially at night. **After dark, avoid walking long distances, try to stick to busier roads, and don't flaunt your wallet, watch, camera or any other item that marks you as a tourist.** Women traveling alone will probably feel most comfortable in Bella Vista. The city's poorest and most dangerous section, El Chorillo, borders San Felipe and Santa Ana to the west. Panamá Viejo basically shuts down at night. Americans in particular are advised to avoid Panamá Viejo, since US troops burned many area residences to the ground during the 1989 invasion, stirring up anti-American sentiment. Curundu, San Miguel, and Santa Cruz, north of Santa Ana and Calidonia are all best avoided. If traveling long distances, take a taxi.

▤ LOCAL TRANSPORTATION

Buses: Stops are often unmarked, and there aren't any route maps. Still, buses are the cheapest way to get around. **City buses** (old American school buses with loud mufflers) have their final destination painted on the front windshield; to wave one down just stick out your hand. Most buses run through **Plaza 5 de Mayo,** or along **Avenida Perú, Calle 50,** or **Vía España.** Buses marked *"directo"* make fewer stops. It's a good idea to let

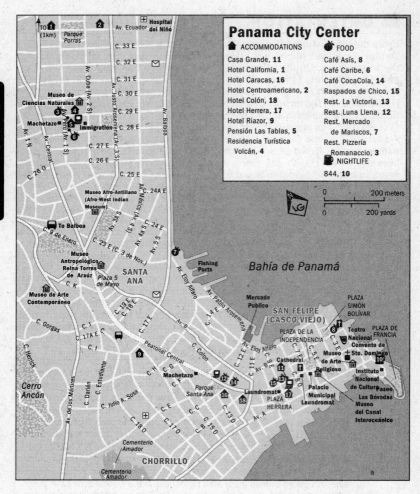

Panama City Center

ACCOMMODATIONS

Casa Grande, **11**
Hotel California, **1**
Hotel Caracas, **16**
Hotel Centroamericano, **2**
Hotel Colón, **18**
Hotel Herrera, **17**
Hotel Riazor, **9**
Pensión Las Tablas, **5**
Residencia Turística
   Volcán, **4**

FOOD

Café Asís, **8**
Café Caribe, **6**
Café CocaCola, **14**
Raspados de Chico, **15**
Rest. La Victoria, **13**
Rest. Luna Llena, **12**
Rest. Mercado
   de Mariscos, **7**
Rest. Pizzería
   Romanaccio, **3**

NIGHTLIFE

844, **10**

your driver know your destination. The cost within the city is always US$0.25 (Tocumen Airport US$0.35); pay the driver or the bus jockey as you get off. **Express buses** (US$0.75-1) have *"corredor"* marked on the front next to their destination; these buses are more expensive because they take toll roads and sometime have A/C. If the bus doesn't stop where you want, yell *"¡Parada!"* Buses run from 4am-11pm.

Taxis: Taxis can be found everywhere. Fares are based on a 6-zone system spanning from **Balboa** to just beyond the **Río Abajo**. Rides within a zone for 1 person should cost no more than US$1.35; every zone boundary crossed adds US$0.15. Each additional passenger costs US$0.25. A US$0.40 surcharge applies for called cabs (**Radio Taxi Express** ☎221 3142; **Radio Taxi Rey** ☎254 1880). These rules are loosely followed. A trip from San Felipe to Vía España costs around US$1.50. To Albrook Airport, the mall, or the bus station US$2-3. To Amador Causeway US$3-5. Taxi drivers can be picky;

depending on traffic or destination, you may have to try another cab. Always settle on a price before getting in; tourists are prime targets for scams.

Car Rental: Prices range from US$40-100 per day, depending on car size and insurance. At major chains, drivers must be 25 or older, although some go as low as 23 if you pay with a credit card. Website reservations are usually easier; sometimes you can get better deals online. All chains have locations near or along Vía España in Bella Vista. Companies include **Alamo** (☎229 5257; www.alamopanama.com); **Avis** (☎278 9444); **Budget** (☎263 8777; www.budgetpanama.com); **Dollar** (☎270 0335); **Hertz** (☎260 2111; www.rentacarpanama.com); **Thrifty** (☎264 2613).

🔢 PRACTICAL INFORMATION

TOURIST AND FINANCIAL SERVICES

Tourist Information: Autoridad de Turismo Panama (ATP; ☎526 7000; www.visit-panama.com). National office in a large black building on Av. Samuel Lewis, in front of the Comosa building, though this office is of little practical resource. Their website serves as a good database of phone numbers and services. Other branches, at Albrook (☎526 7990; open 6am-6pm everyday) and Tocumen (☎238 8356; open daily 8am-midnight) airports and in Plaza Concordia (open M-F 8am-4pm, Sa 8am-1pm) are more useful. The **Autoridad Nacional del Ambiente (National Environmental Authority),** known commonly as **ANAM,** (☎500 0839) has an office housing its Areas Protegidas (protected areas) division near the Albrook Airport. They have limited info about the parks. More thorough info is available at regional offices and at the park headquarters. Open M-F 7:30am-3:30pm.

Travel Agencies and Tour Companies: Ancon Expeditions, C. Elvira Méndez at C.49A Este (☎269 9415; www.anconexpeditions.com), in Edificio El Dorado. A wide range of options for ecological trips throughout the country. Prices run about $100 per day per person. Open M-F 8am-5pm, Sa 9am-1pm. **Viajes y Destinos** (☎264 8461; www.viajesydestinos.com.pa), across the street from the Hotel Continental and the Banco Transatlantico on C. Manuel Maricasa. Popular travel agency with English-speaking staff. Books everything from international flights to domestic tours. Open M-Sa 8am-5pm. **Mirador Adventures** (☎6401 6278; www.miradoradventures.com), operates out of La Jungla Hostel, and is an outfitter for everything outdoors.

Embassies and Consulates: Canada, Edificio World Trade Center, 1st fl. (☎264 9731; www.panama.gc.ca), in Marbella, C.53 Este near C.50. Open to public M-F 8:30am-1pm. **Costa Rica** (☎264 2980), on Av. Samuel Lewis, behind El Rey on Av. España. Open 8am-1pm. **UK** (☎269 0866; www.britishembassy.gov.uk/panama), in Marbella in the MMG buiding on C.53. Open M-Th 7:30am-3:30pm and F 7:30am-12:30pm. **US,** 783 Av. Demetrio B. Lakas (☎207 7030; www.panama.usembassy.gov), in Clayton. Open M-F 8am-noon and 1:30pm-3:30pm. Closed last Th of each month and on US holidays.

Banks: The city is littered with banks, especially in Bella Vista along Vía Espana. **Sistema Clave** 24hr. **ATMs** accept the most debit and ATM cards, and can be found throughout the city, and in many pharmacies and grocery stores. **Banco General,** in Santa Ana, in the pedestrian mall on Av. Central. Open M-F 8am-3pm. **HSBC,** on Vía España across from Hotel Panama. English-speaking staff. Cash advances on major credit cards. Open M-F 8am-8:30pm, Sa 9am-noon.

American Express: (☎264 2444), in Centro Commercial, Vía Pacífica, in Punta Paitilla next to Lumi Centro. Open M-F 8am-5pm, Sa 8am-10:30am.

Western Union: Plaza Concordia, across from the Supermercado El Rey in Bella Vista. Open M-Sa 8am-7pm. Another in the Albrook Mall. Open M-Sa 10am-7:30pm, Su 10:30am-7pm.

LOCAL SERVICES

Luggage Storage: In the bus terminal. Walk out the end of the terminal on the side that buses enter, take a left, and then another left into a narrow hallway; it's on the left. US$1.50-US$4 per day depending on size. Open M-Sa 7am-9pm, Su 8:30am-7pm.

Bookstores: Exedra Books (☎264 4252), on Vía España and Vía Brazil. The best bookstore in Panama, with a large selection of English-language books. Nice cafe with Wi-Fi. Open M-F 9:30am-8:30pm, Sa 9:30am-7pm. **Gran Morrison** (☎202 0029), next to El Rey in Bella Vista, across from Plaza Concordia. Limited English-language selection relative to the rather large Kama Sutra section.

Laundromats: Most hostels offer laundry service for a small fee (US$3.50-5), but there are also *lavamáticos* (machine laundromats) and *lavanderías* everywhere. **Lavamático,** on C.13 between Av. A and Av. B, just off the plaza in Santa Ana. Full service US$4. Wash US$1; dry US$0.75. Soap US$0.30. Open M-Sa 7:30am-3pm, Su 8:30am-2pm. **Milena Lavandería & Lavamático,** just next to the Blockbuster on Vía España in Bella Vista. Wash and dry US$2. Open M-Sa 7:30am-8pm, Su 9am-4pm.

EMERGENCY AND COMMUNICATIONS

Emergency: ☎104.

Police: Tourist Police (☎211 3365); **National Police** (☎511 7000); **Bella Vista** (☎511 9439); **Calidonia, San Felipe, Santa Ana** (☎511 9427).

Red Cross: ☎228 2187.

Pharmacy: Pharmacies are everywhere in Panama City. **Farmacia Arrocha** (☎223 4505), in Bella Vista, just off Vía España, near HSBC. Open daily 7:30am-11pm. Another branch (☎262 1068) on Av. Central on the Pedestrian Mall in Santa Ana. Open M-Sa 7am-8:15pm, Su 8:30am-4:45pm.

Hospital: Hospital Punta Pacifica (☎204 8000), near the Multiplaza. English spoken.

Telephones: Public phones are everywhere, though they may not always work. **Phone cards,** for sale at supermarkets and pharmacies, are a good option since public phones rarely give change.

Internet Access: Internet cafes are common in most parts of the city, especially Calidonia and Bella Vista. Around US$1 per hr. **Internet Panama Cafe,** in Santa Ana on the plaza, at the end of the pedestrian mall. Internet US$0.75 per hr. Open daily 9am-9pm. Another cafe in Bella Vista in Plaza Concordia. Internet US$0.50 per 30min. Open M-F 8am-8pm, Sa 9am-5pm.

Post Office: (☎511 6232), inside Plaza Concordia. Open M-F 7:15am-4:45pm, Sa 8:15am-12:45pm.

▐ ACCOMMODATIONS

Accommodations in Panama City run the gamut, from dark and dreary *pensiones* that do business by the hour to glitzy glass high-rises catering to the jetset crowd. Quality hostels and establishments on the backpacker circuit lie in Casco Viejo and the neighborhoods east of Bella Vista; these are on opposite sides from the center of the city, but within walking distance. Hotels closer to the city center, in Santa Ana and Calidonia, cost more and have fewer amenities. It's advisable to book in advance, especially during the high season (December-March).

SAN FELIPE (CASCO VIEJO)

San Felipe, popularly know as Casco Viejo, is in a constant state of transition. Crumbling colonial buildings lay vacant next to beautifully restored buildings. Lodgings in Casco Viejo reflect this duality, offering the most bohemian hostels and some of the shadiest hotels. During the day, it's safe to walk around, but at night the neighborhood is sort of a ghost town, so it is a good idea to either stick to main roads (Av. Central) or take cabs.

🔲 **Luna's Castle,** C. 9NA, Este 3-28 (☎262 1540; www.lunascastlehostel.com). From Av. B and C.9, walk east toward the water. From the public market, walk up the ramp; it's the 2nd house on the right. Housed in a beautifully renovated old mansion and chock-full of modern art, sofas, and hammocks, this place is a backpacker's paradise. A popular bar, a movie theater, and views of the ocean and the glamorous high-rises across the bay round out the deal. Breakfast and lockers included. Laundry US$5. Free internet. Reservations recommended. Dorms US$12; doubles with shared bath US$28; triples US$36. ❷

Hospedaje Casco Viejo, C.8a and Av. A (☎211 2027; www.hospedajecascoviejo. com). Walk west away from the plaza; it's on the left. A renovated colonial mansion, this new hostel lacks the homey atmosphere and the amenities of its competitors, but its hard to beat the price. Very little communal space and clean, standard rooms. Bathrooms very small and a bit dirty. Kitchen and lockers available. Free Wi-Fi. Dorms US$9; singles US$16, with bath US$18. ❷

Casa Grande, C.8 and Av. Central (☎211 3316), in an old yellow and white building. Cheapest rooms in Casco Viejo. Common baths, tiny showers, and high ceilings with fans. Many of the guests are long-term, so it can be hard to get a room. Private rooms US$6, with balcony US$7. ❶

SANTA ANA

Noisy, bustling Santa Ana is closer to the city center, and has a number of good hotels, but nothing nearly as charming or bohemian as Casco Viejo. Streets are a lot more crowded, and considered by most to be a little more dangerous, so stick to Av. Central if you stay here. Most of the hotels are within a block or two of Plaza de Santa Ana and the Pedestrian mall on Av. Central.

Hotel Colón, C.B and C.12 (☎228 8506). From the pedestrian mall at Plaza Santa Ana, follow the trolley tracks 1 block toward San Felipe and turn right. Peeling paint and a general air of neglect add to the mystique of this enormous 5-story hotel that's been around since 1915. Large, beautiful common rooms and a rooftop terrace with views over Casco Viejo and the bay. Rooms come with fans. Singles US$11, with bath US$15.40, with A/C and bath US$10.90; doubles US$13.20/18.70/24.20. ❷

Hotel Caracas (☎228 7229). When facing the church in Plaza Santa Ana, it's on the left. Three floors of big rooms. Singles US$10, with A/C US$15; doubles US$12/16; triples US$18/24. ❷

Hotel Riazor, C.16 and Av. 1 (☎228 0777), around the corner from the Banco Nacional building in the pedestrian mall. A good deal in a central, though noisy location. Forty-six comfortable and spotless rooms, each with a fan, hot water, towels, and free coffee. Singles US$25; doubles US$28; triples US$40. ❸

CALIDONIA

Calidonia, running east of Playa 5 de Mayo along Av. Central, has many options, but don't expect the best values in town. US$12 will get you a queen size bed with a fan a shared bath. Expect to pay twice as much for a private bath and air conditioning.

Mamallena, C. 38 and Av. Central (☎6676 6136; www.mamallena.com). Head toward Plaza 5 de Mayo on Av. Central and turn right at the Govimar building. Closer to downtown but far from some of the sights. Friendly, English-speaking staff. Rooms are a little rough around the edges, but all have A/C. Breakfast included. Laundry US$3.25. Free internet and Wi-Fi. Singles US$11; doubles with shared bath US$27.50. ❷

Hotel Backpacker Inn (☎225 7283, reservations 227 1522), north of Av. Justo Arosemana on C. 33, near Hotel Roma. The closest thing to a hostel in Caladonia and the best value in the area. Rooms are simple but clean; all come with private bath, hot water, A/C, and cable TV. Free transportation to the international airport. Free Wi-Fi. Singles US$25; doubles US$35. MC/V. ❸

Pensión Las Tablas, Av. Perú between C. 28 and C. 29, across from Machetazo. Small, clean rooms with fans, TVs, and an uncommonly festive paint job. Rooms on Av. Perú are noisy. Rooms US$12, with bath US$15; doubles US$18. ❷

Residencia Turística Volcán (☎225 5263), on C. 29 between Av. Perú and Av. Cuba. Recently renovated, Volcán's woodwork, tiles, and bright paint job brighten up the otherwise basic and clean rooms. The mattresses are a little stiff. All rooms have A/C. Singles US$25; doubles US$30. ❸

BELLA VISTA

The Bella Vista district is a large swath of land east of the city center. This area encompasses a number of smaller neighborhoods that stretch along Vía España, including (from west to east) Bella Vista, El Congrejo, and El Carmen. Not quite as old and charming as Casco Viejo, nor as glamorous as the buildings along the waterfront, Bella Vista is home to some of the best restaurants and nightlife in town.

⊠ Hostal La Casa de Carmen (☎263 4366; www.lacasadecarmen.net), on C.1 in El Carmen. It's on the street parallel to Vía España, off Vía Brazil. A beautiful backyard garden, a spacious lounge, and homey rooms make this a pleasant respite from the bustle and heat of the city. All rooms have A/C. Showers, kitchen, and library on-site. Breakfast included. Wash US$1; dry US$1. Free Wi-Fi. 6-bed dorm US$12; singles US$30, with bath US$38; studio US$55. ❷

La Jungla (☎6668 5076; www.miradoradventures.com), on C. 49A west of Vía Arentina, 3 buildings up the hill from Hotel Las Huacas, on the 5th fl. A new, welcoming hostel with a laid-back environment in a quiet residential neighborhood. People congregate on the balcony to sip on beer and discuss their escapades. The owner is an outdoorsman and a valuable resource for anyone looking to head into the jungle. Dorms US$16; singles US$26; quads with A/C and bath US$80. ❸

Voyager International Hostel (☎260 5913). From Vía Argentina, turn right at the Subway restaurant; the hostel is on the 2nd fl. Great location on the Vía Argentina is the main selling point, but a full array of amenities adds to the appeal. Rooms comes with cable TV and hot water. Bathrooms are a little dirty. Kitchen available. Breakfast included. Free Wi-Fi. Reception 24hr. 12- and 5-person dorms US$10; 4-person dorm with A/C US$13; private doubles US$27. ❷

☐ FOOD

Given the variety of cultures that have left their mark here, it isn't surprising that Panama City is the capital of international cuisine in Central America. Prices are diverse, from the cheap (US$1-2) *comida típica* found in cafeterias, to the international flavors of Bella Vista, Marbella, and El Congrejo. Throughout the city, street vendors sell hot dogs, *empanadas, frituras,* fresh fruit, and *chichas* (a sweet fruit juice concoction). You can find most vendors around C. 13, the pedestrian mall, Playa 5 de Mayo, in the *mercadito* at Av. Perú and C.34, or at the grand **market** on Av. Alfaro.

Panama City is filled with supermarkets. **El Rey** is a popular chain; there's one on Vía España across from the Plaza Concordia in Bella Vista (open 24hr.). **Machetazo,** a gargantuan five-story department store, has a supermarket inside. There is one on the Pedestrian Mall near Plaza Santa Ana (open M-Sa 8:30am-7pm) and another on Av. Perú between C.29 and C.30 (open M-Sa 8:30am-8pm).

The **seafood market** on the coast at Av. Balboa and C. 24E is worth a visit; there's nothing like the sound of hundreds of butcher knives gutting the day's catch. (Open daily from dawn until the early afternoon.) Just up the hill on Av. Balboa is **El Mercado Público,** a large warehouse with stalls selling meat and vegetables. The market is surprisingly clean and sanitary considering the bloody cow parts. Food starts coming in from the countryside as early as 3:30am; the place empties out by 4pm.

SAN FELIPE (CASCO VIEJO)

Food options in San Felipe range from chic gourmet cafes to cafeteria-style *típicos,* with little else in between. Restaurants are spread fairly evenly throughout the area. If you're really on a budget, it may be worth a trek up to Santa Ana for more affordable options.

René, on Plaza Catedral. High-class, 5-course meals at affordable prices. The kitchen is open, allowing you to watch the chef prepare each course. The fixed 5-course meal (from US$8.25) comes with salad, appetizer, rice, your choice of entree, and dessert. Open M-Sa 11:30am-3pm and 6:30-10pm. ❸

Casablanca, at Av. B and C.4, on Plaza Bólivar. Grab a table on the historic plaza at this classy establishment. Their specialties, ribs and seafood, are probably a little pricey for most. Cheaper options like veggie burgers (US$6) and sandwiches (US$5) are also available. Casablanca is also a great place to grab a beer (US$2.75). Be sure to try 1 of their 10 different mojitos (US$5). Open daily 10am-1am. MC/V. ❷

Cafe Perdue, on Av. A and C.4. Probably the most affordable non-*típico* restaurant in Casco Viejo. Throwback tunes (Ace of Base, anyone?) and the best pizza (US$4-6) in the neighborhood. Breakfast US$2-4. Subs US$3.50. Open Tu-Sa 8:30am-10pm. ❷

Habana Club, at the corner of Av. B and C.5. Looks like a Havana saloon from the playboy 50s. Does more business as a bar than a restaurant, but the food is good, the portions decent, and the prices agreeable. Hamburgers US$6.50-9. *Ceviche* US$7-8. Sandwiches US$7-8. Restaurant open daily 8am-4pm. Bar open 4pm-midnight. MC/V. ❸

Conajagua, on Av. B between C.11 and C.12. Though its just one of the many *fondas* in the neighborhood serving cafeteria-style *típico,* Conajagua is a bit friendlier and cleaner than the rest. Grab a tray and point to what you want. Large portions US$1.50-2.00. Open daily 4am-4pm. ❶

SANTA ANA

More crowded and less historic Santa Ana has many more budget options than San Felipe. A variety of street stall offerings, ice cream, pizza, and fast food (God bless America), as well as plenty of cheap *típico.* Most of the eateries line the Pedestrian mall from Plaza Santa Ana to Plaza 5 de Mayo.

Restaurante Mercado de Mariscos, part of the Seafood Market where Av. Balboa hits the San Felipe entrance. Head indoors and up the stairs. Seafood that practically crawls off the boats and onto your plate. Seafood cocktails US$4. Fish US$5-8. Shrimp and calamari US$7-10. Lobster US$20-30. Open M-Sa 11am-7pm, Su 11am-4pm. ❸

Café CocaCola, Av. Central and C.12, across from Plaza Santa Ana. Supposedly the oldest cafe in Panama, this is a gathering spot for old men wearing Panamanian caps and *guayaberas* (the traditional 4-pocket shirts). Seafood cocktails US$3.50. Spaghetti US$2.50. Fish US$4-7. Open daily 7:30am-11:30pm. ❷

Restaurante Cheyl, on the pedestrian mall on Plaza Santa Ana, directly across from the church. Cafeteria-style *típico* with a little bit of Chinese flair. Cheap and hearty portions. Large order of *patacones* US$0.50. Fried chicken with rice US$1-2. Open daily 6:30am-8pm. ❶

CALIDONIA

Calidonia's establishments serve similar fare as those in Santa Ana, though many close a bit earlier. Eateries cluster on C.28-32, between Central and Arosemana.

Café Caribe, on C. 28 and Av. Perú, inside Hotel Caribe. A popular place with locals, Caribe is one of the only non-cafeteria establishments in the area. Cheap *típico* made all the better by A/C. Sandwiches US$3-5. Fish US$8. Open M-Sa 7am-9pm, Su 7am-3pm. AmEx/MC/V. ❷

Restaurante Pizzería Romanaccio, on C. 29 and Perú. Delicious pizza popular with locals. Mini pizza US$4, for 2 US$6. Whole pizza US$11. Open daily 11am-11pm. MC/V. ❷

BELLA VISTA

Bella Vista is dubbed the "restaurant district" for a reason. The thriving culinary scene here caters to the thousands of resident expats. From sushi and crepes to tacos and gelato, you can find almost anything here. The greatest concentration of restaurants is on Av. Argentina, up the hill from Vía España. Be prepared to shell out for anything but fast food.

New York Bagel Cafe. Heading up Vía Argentina, turn right at the Subway restaurant; pass Voyager, it's 10m up on the right. The closest thing to a New York deli this side of the Tropic of Cancer, this delicious diner serves hearty omelettes (US$6) and a large selection of bagels (with cream cheese US$2; dozen US$9). Free Wi-Fi with purchase. Open M-F 7am-8pm, Sa 8am-8pm, Su 8am-3pm. MC/V. ❷

La Novena, up Vía Argentina near C. 49B. Sophisticated, friendly, and vegetarian. Watch your food be prepared in the open kitchen. Enjoy your meal while listening to classical music and admiring the fabulous local art. Soups US$4-5. Entrees US$6-8. Open M-Sa 10am-10pm. MC/V. ❷

Dolce, on Vía Argentina, a few blocks up from Vía España. The Canadian owner, Angel, boasts that there is no internet, TV, or even a cash register. Come here to devour delicious meals, brownies, beer, and participate in the booming book exchange. Breakfast US$2-4. Sandwiches US$4-5. Open M and W-Sa 8am-10pm, Su 8am-6pm. ❷

Beirut, Ricardo Arias at C. 52, near the Marriott Hotel. Great Middle Eastern fare with hookah (US$10.50) and live performances F and Sa night 9pm-midnight. Appetizers US$4-6. Entrees US$8-15. Beer US$3. Open daily 11am-4am. AmEx/MC/V. ❸

◐ SIGHTS

Most travelers pass through Panama City to see other parts of the country, but for history buffs and art-lovers Panama City is the place to be. Casco Viejo has the greatest concentration of museums, ruins, and art galleries. With beautiful

Bellavista

🏠 ACCOMMODATIONS
Hostal La Casa de Carmen, 1
Hotel California, 13
Voyager Int'l Hostel, 7

🍴 FOOD
El Pavo Real, 10
El Trapiche, 2
La Casa de las Costillitas, 3
Niko's Cafe, 5
Pita Pan Kosher, 17
Restaurant Fu Yuan, 6
Restaurant Vegetariano
  Mireya, 8
Rock Burgers, 14

🍷 NIGHTLIFE
Bacchus, 9
BLG, 16
El Pavo Real, 12
Liquid, 11
S6is, 15
Space, 4

colonial churches, the fabulous Canal Museum, and splendid views of the new city across the bay, Casco Viejo alone deserves a day of wandering around. A trip to the new Museo Antropológico Reina Torres De Araúz, just a few minutes outside of the city, is also well worth the trip.

SAN FELIPE (CASCO VIEJO)

The second "Panama City" was founded on January 21, 1673, after pirate greed and a fire destroyed the original city. Known today as Casco Viejo, this area is a striking blend of beautifully restored colonial buildings and crumbling, decrepit buildings. Old Spanish colonial churches blend in among the houses with iron balconies, inspired by the French when they undertook the initial Canal construction effort. In 1997, UNESCO declared the area a **World Heritage Site** for its rich architectural diversity. Though the whole neighborhood seems to be under endless renovation, it's loaded with worthwhile memorials, ruins, and museums. Begin at **Plaza de la Independencia** (Plaza Catedral), on Av. Central and C. 7, which honors Panama's founders, among them the first President of the Republic, Manuel Amador Guerrero.

CATHEDRAL. Facing the Plaza de la Independencia is the huge Cathedral, which features a chiseled stone facade enclosed by whitewashed towers. The inside is simple, but be sure to check out the intricate sacrament. The cathedral has been around since 1798 and was one of the few buildings in the city to survive the 1882 earthquake. *(If the front is closed, try one of the side entrances. Open daily 8am-2pm. Su services 10:30am.)*

MUSEO DEL CANAL INTEROCEÁNICO. Though rivaled by the exhibit at Miraflores, this is probably the best museum in Panama. Housed in what used to be the headquarters of the French company that first worked on the Canal, the building itself is fascinating. The museum explains in detail the canal's construction, history, and operations; in tracing the early history of the Canal, it also manages to cover the history of the colonization of Panama. The museum has a vast collection of primary artifacts, from a Panama Railway depot's original benches to the colonial weapons from the *Camino de Cruces* (see **Portobelo Sights,** p. 583). Displays are well organized and informative, accompanied by videos and diagrams. All descriptions are in Spanish—even if you can't read them, though, there's plenty to see. *(With your back to the cathedral, the museum is on your right. ☎ 211 1650; www.sinfo.net/pcmuseum. Open Tu-Su 9am-5pm. US$2, students with ISIC card and children US$0.75. English-language tours available, but book in advance; US$5 per person.)*

PASEO LAS BÓVEDAS. This walkway, with fabulous views of the Pacific, was once used as a buffer against pirates and prisoners. Today the arbor-covered footpath offers shade and a great place to stroll. At the end of the Paseo lie the *bóvedas*, vaults which once held prisoners but now house a fancy restaurant and the small **Instituto Nacional de Artes Visuales** (National Institute of Visual Arts), which showcases rotating exhibits by local artists. The gallery faces **Plaza Francia,** built in honor of the Frenchmen who died during the 19th-century canal attempt. Walk around the semicircle to learn more about the history leading up to the Canal's construction and the men who came to build it (keep in mind it's all in Spanish). Chamber orchestras occasionally play in the park's small plaza. *(From Plaza de la Independencia, walk south away from the Cathedral along Av. Central until the street winds past the Pacific. Free. Gallery open M-F 9am-5pm. Free.)*

CHURCH AND CONVENT OF SANTO DOMINGO. Dating back to 1678, the church's **Arco Chato** was famous for its mortar construction and lack of internal supports—right until it collapsed in 2003. Panamanian leaders used the arch's age to prove the country was earthquake-proof, important in the campaign to get the Canal built there. Connected to the old church ruins, the **Museo de Arte Religioso Colonial** contains a gigantic altar, sculptures, and religious paintings. *(Av. A and C. 3, 1 block south and 2 blocks east of the Plaza de la Independencia. At the time of publication, both were undergoing renovation, but they are slated to reopen at the end of Dec. 2009. ☎ 228 2897. Open Tu-Sa 9am-4:30pm. US$0.75, students US$0.25.)*

OTHER SIGHTS. Parque Simón Bolívar features a monument honoring the namesake liberator with friezes depicting his feats. *(1 block east and 1 block north of Plaza de la Independencia.)* There are a number of cafes here with seating arranged on the square (see **Food,** p. 568). The Moorish-style **Palacio Presidencial,** also known as the "Palace of Herons," is home to Panama's president; you won't be able to get anywhere near it. *(On Av. Alfaro, 2 blocks north of Plaza de la Independencia.)* The **Iglesia de San José** houses the **Altar de Oro.** According to legend, a priest covered the magnificent golden altar in mud to disguise its worth from pirate Henry Morgan, who sacked Panama Viejo in 1671. The Church was built just a few years later. *(Av. A and C. 8, 1 block south and 1 block west of the Plaza.)* **Casa Góngora,** built in 1756, is one of the oldest buildings in Panama and the only one with a preserved interior. The building has been beautifully restored with its original architecture and floor. The wall space is used for rotating art exhibits. *(C. 4 and*

Av. Central. ☎ *506 5836. Open M 8am-4pm, Tu-Su 10am-6pm. Free.)* For everything from fresh fruit to Spanish textbooks head to **Sal Si Puede** (literally "get out if you can"), which runs from Av. Alfaro to the pedestrian mall at the Plaza de Santa Ana. Note the name and take precautions against pickpockets and thieves.

OUTSIDE CASCO VIEJO

Most of the museums outside of San Felipe are concentrated around **Plaza 5 de Mayo,** connected to San Felipe via the busy pedestrian mall. The mall itself is a piece of history, erected in honor of firemen who battled the flames from a gunpowder warehouse that exploded in 1914. Although none of the museums are particularly eye-opening, wandering through them is a nice way to while away a day.

MUSEO DE ARTE CONTEMPORÁNEO. This museum houses a small rotating exhibition space for modern artists from around the world, with a focus on Latin America. The first floor is child-oriented. *(West of Plaza 5 de Mayo on Av. de los Mártires.* ☎ *262 8012. Open Tu-Su 9am-5pm. US$3, students US$2, children US$1.)*

MUSEO AFRO-ANTILLIANO. Housed in a tiny gray church, this stand-out one-room museum was once the chapel of the Christian mission, around which Panama's Afro-Indian population first organized. The small museum expertly recounts their history with photos, antiques, and parts of the old Panamanian railroad, the construction of which attracted immigrants looking for work. The museum also pays tribute to the important cultural, religious, and economic contributions these cultures have made to Panama. *(From Plaza 5 de Mayo, continue east 1-2 blocks along Av. Justo Arosemana.* ☎ *501 4130. Open Tu-Sa 8:30am-3:30pm. US$1, students US$0.75.)*

MUSEO DE CIENCIAS NATURALES. Though it's no Smithsonian, the museum offers small exhibits on paleontology, geology, and vertebrate taxonomy. One exhibit on indigenous wildlife has a wide variety of stuffed birds and mammals. This might be the only way to experience the Panamanian outdoors without mosquitoes, but unless you're a biology or taxidermy buff, the Museo de Ciencias Naturales might be worth a pass. *(Av. Cuba, C. 30 Este.* ☎ *225 0642. Open M-F 9am-3:30pm. US$1.)*

PANAMA VIEJO

Founded in 1519, Panamá Viejo—the original Panama City—was the first European New World city on the Pacific coast. As the starting point for Spanish expeditions to the rest of the continent, the city quickly became linked to international transport and trade. It flourished as the Pacific terminus of Spain's **Camino Real.** The Camino functioned as the transisthmian pipeline for Spain's Pacific colonies. This importance was short-lived, however, and after near-destruction at the hands of pirate Henry Morgan in 1671 and the fire that followed, Panamá Viejo was abandoned. Today, it offers an intriguing peek into a 16th-century city. The modern **museum** has two floors with materials on the city's history and archaeology; a fair amount of the information is in English. The first floor even has a surprisingly lighthearted exhibit on pirates.

Panamá Viejo includes ruins, a fort, several convents, a hospital, and other structures sprawled along a lovely 1km boardwalk that follows the bay. The stretch is conveniently delineated by two impressive landmarks, the 15m **cathedral tower** at the far end, and the Bridge of Kings, one of the oldest bridges in the Americas, just before the modern museum. At the end of the road is the **Mercado Nacional de Artesanías,** which houses loads of touristy mini-shops that all seem to sell the same stuff, though they claim it comes from different regions around the country. *(Take any city bus with the "Panamá Viejo" sign from Casco Viejo on Av. B and C. 12, just in front of the police station, and along Av. Balboa. 30min., 7am-11pm, US$0.25. Info center ☎ 226 8915. Open daily 9am-5pm. Entrance to the museum and ruins U$6, ruins US$3, under 17 US$0.50. Market open daily 9am-6pm.)*

🎵 NIGHTLIFE

Whether you're looking to strut your stuff on the dance floor or to just sit back and watch the locals, Panama City has it all. Panamanians dress well most of the time, especially so for nightlife: men wear long pants and collared shirts. Around here, women aren't afraid to show some skin. Jeans and short-sleeve shirts are acceptable for bars and discos, but shorts and sandals are not. You must be 18 or over to enter; be ready to show ID, though most places don't card.

Trendy San Felipe can be a blast, but take extra care at night—if you're alone, stick to taxis and avoid walking. Bella Vista's happening scene, concentrated around C. Uruguay and Vía Argentina, is considerably more safe. **Calle Uruguay** is the undisputed nightclub zone. If you aren't looking to dance, Vía Argentina has a more bar-oriented scene. On the Amador Causeway, there are a number of bars where you can sit at a table, grab a few drinks, and admire massive yachts. The action in clubs usually picks up around 11pm, but they tend to stay open as long as there are people, and there usually are. Panamanians don't consider it a night without some serious dancing. On average, beer costs US$2, mixed drinks US$4-5, and a bottle of Panamanian alcohol US$30.

For live music, head to **Restaurante Las Bóvedas** on Plaza de Francia. This spot is housed in a 17th-century fort turned torture chamber turned classy jazz club. (☎228 8058. Open W and Sa 9pm-midnight.) For traditional *típico* music, **Las Tinajas**, Av. Frederico Boyd and Av. 3 Sur, has traditional performances Tu-Sa at 9pm. (☎263 7890. Cover US$5. Open M-Sa 11am-11pm. AmEx/MC/V.)

El Pavo Real, 3 blocks up Vía Argentina. A hugely popular bar that attracts locals and expats alike. Recently relocated, the loyal clients were so attached that they brought pieces of the old bar to the new location. Free pool tables. F-Sa live music. Open M-Sa 5pm-late. MC/V.

People (☎263 0104; www.peoplepanama.com), on C. Uruguay. One of the many trendy, pumping nightclubs on the block. Outdoor patio to cool off and a 2nd floor deck that overlooks the dance floor. They play "crossover" music, which is essentially electronic, salsa, hip hop, or anything else that keeps people dancing. Th women free before 11pm. If you're in a group, call ahead and see if you can get the cover waived. Cover US$10. Beer US$3. Mixed drinks US$4-7. Open 9pm-5am or late. MC/V.

The Londoner, on C. Uruguay. A haven for expats and travelers. With authentic English ambience (one of the owners is from the UK) and anywhere from 12-15 types of imported beer (US$5), this place attracts a slightly older crowd looking to have a good time. 70s and 80s rock, with an occasional live performance. Beer US$3. Open M-Sa 5pm-2am. AmEx/MC/V.

Relic, inside of Luna's Castle (p. 567). Appropriately named, this new bar is housed in the basement and courtyard of a 1905 mansion. Unlike other places in the area, drinks are cheap (beer US$1; drinks US$2). Not the place to go if you're looking to meet locals, but a great place to share stories and drinks with some eccentric travelers. Open F-Sa 7pm-late.

Baños Publicos, on Plaza Herrera. Epitomizes Casco Viejo, reclaiming the old public bathrooms (hence the namesake) as a laid-back bar with a small stage for performances. Live music F-Sa. Music ranges from hip hop to Latin and rock. Beer US$1. Open W-F 6pm-late, Sa-Su noon-late.

⚠ OUTDOOR ACTIVITIES

PARQUE NATURAL METROPOLITANO

Metropolitano is within walking distance of the Albrook Mall and the bus station, and is easily accessible by bus. Take any Albrook Station bus headed for the Gran Terminal (US$0.25) and ask the driver to let you off at the Universidad de Panamá at Curundo, just before the station. Facing the forest across the street, turn left. Walk along the road for 100m and go right at the 1st fork. The ranger station will be on your left. Taxis cost about US$2-3. Park and ranger station open daily 7am-5pm. Early morning and late afternoon are the best times to watch wildlife. During the rainy season, come in the early morning. ☎ 232 5516 or 5552; www.parquemetropolitano.org. Trails US$2. Map US$1.50. Guides US$5 per person with a minimum of 5 people.

Panamanians claim this is "the most accessible rainforest in the world," which just might be true. Metropolitano occupies 232 hectares (almost a square mile) of forest within the city limits, 75% of which is fragile Pacific dry forest, an ecosystem almost extinct in the region. The park is just minutes from downtown and is somehow still home to hundreds of plant and animal species like the **two- and three-toed sloth**, trogon, toucan, and Geoffrey's tamarin. Without the drone of cars whizzing by on the nearby highways, this urban escape might as well be in the Darién.

There are five **trails** in the park. In order of increasing difficulty, trails include: **Los Momótides** (900m, 30min.), named after the motmot bird; **El Roble** (700m, 30min.), named for the oak tree; **Los Caobos** (900m, 1hr.), named for the *Caoba* (mahogany) tree; **Mono Tití** (1.1km, 1½hr.), named for the *tití* monkey; and **La Cienaguita** (1.1km, 1hr.), named for its swamp. This last trail leads you to the top of a hill, 150m above sea level, that offers spectacular views of the city, canal, and bay. From the ranger station, you can make a loop including almost all of these routes (1½-2hr.).

PANAMA AND COLÓN PROVINCES

PANAMA PROVINCE

PANAMA CANAL

The Panama Canal is the world's greatest shortcut, chopping 8000 miles off the voyage from the Pacific to the Caribbean. Although the locks are designed to raise and lower two boats at the same time, for logistical reasons they tend to move boats in the same direction and alternate every hour. On the Pacific side, boats go through a series of two locks, the Miraflores and Pedro Miguel, that elevate the ships a total of 26m above sea level, to the altitude of the Gatún Lake. From the locks, the boats pass through a narrow section of highland rainforest known as the Gaillard Cut, and finally enter the expansive Gatún Lake before they are lowered on the Atlantic side by the Gatún Dam. Boats use their own propulsion, but when passing through the locks, electric locomotives align them and keep them in position. Ships are charged based on their weight; the average cost to pass is around US$90,000. Around 36 boats pass through every day. More than a technological marvel, the Canal has also determined much of Panama's history, from its colonial exploitation to its recent economic growth. Today it continues to be a central part of the Panamanian economy.

TRANSPORTATION. To get to the canal, you can take a taxi (US$5-6) or take a bus from the Gran Terminal just outside Panama City toward **Gamboa** (M-F 14 per day 5am-10:30pm, Sa-Su 9 per day 5:45am-10:30pm; US$0.65) or **Paraíso** (M-F 12 per day, Sa-Su fewer; US$0.35) and ask the driver to stop at Miraflores. Buses to **Chilibre** also pass by Miraflores.

ORIENTATION AND PRACTICAL INFORMATION. From the bus stop, turn left toward the canal and cross the bridge. It is about a 10min. walk to the air-conditioned **visitor center.** (☎276 8617. Entrance US$5, with access to the museum and theatre US$8; students US$3/5. Open daily 9am-5pm. AmEx/MC/V.) Partial boat tours of the canal run by **Canal and Bay Tours** leave Saturdays at 7:30am from Isla Flamenco on the Amador Causeway behind Mi Ranchito. (☎209 9000. US$115 per person, full tours first Sa of every month US$165.)

SIGHTS. Few people pass through Panama without paying tribute to the canal at the Miraflores Locks, the largest on the canal and the closest to the Panama city. The visitor center includes a four-story museum, a film about the canal, an expensive restaurant (entrees US$18-30), a souvenir shop, and a fourth-story deck with a commanding view over the impressive operation. When boats pass, presentations in English and Spanish on the viewing deck explain how it works. When boats are not passing, a 10min. film alternates between English and Spanish to recount the history of the canal. The best (though priciest) way to see the canal is to experience it yourself by taking a partial or full tour. Panama City travel agents book the tour, but the main operator is **Canal and Bay Tours** (above).

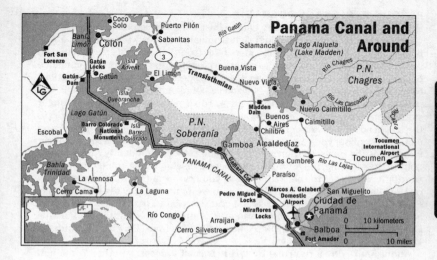

THE ROAD TO GAMBOA

Traveling along the canal out of Panama City, you'll eventually come to Gamboa, where Río Chagres feeds into Gatún Lake. A short hike in Soberanía or a stop in Summit Gardens makes a great daytrip from Panama City. Unless you want to camp or shell out some serious cash, spending the night in the area is difficult.

To access the area, take a Gamboa-bound bus from the Gran Terminal in Panama City (40min.; M-F 14 per day 5am-10:30pm, Sa-Su 9 per day 5:45am-10:30pm; US$0.65) or you can take a Chilibre bus and ask to get off at the ANAM station at the entrance to Gamboa. If your first stop is Miraflores, you can also take a Paraíso bus. These also leave from the terminal frequently.

Nine kilometers from the city is the turnoff to the Miraflores Locks. Another 2.5km along the road are the Pedro Miguel Locks, which are harder to see and less tourist-friendly. Beyond these lies the small town of Paraíso, the last town before the birdwatching paradise of **Parque Nacional Soberanía** (p. 578). Following the cut-off for Gamboa, the road skirts along between the canal and the park, passing the Summit Botanical Gardens and Zoo on the continental divide. The road crosses the Río Chagres and then finally enters the sleepy town of Gamboa, the entrance to one of the park's best hikes and a point of departure for boat trips on the Río Chagres or Lago Gatún.

The ritzy **Gamboa Tropical Rainforest Resort** (take a right after the bridge in to town or stay on the bus while it passes through the town and loops around to the resort) is a good (if pricey) place to arrange tours of the park trips up the Chagres or activities on Lago Gatún. (☎314 5028; www.gamboaresort.com. 2hr. rainforest tram US$52, 40min. river tour US$15). Another destination is **Barro Colorado**, a densely forested island in Lago Gatún operated by the Smithsonian Tropical Research Institute. (Follow the road straight through town. When it bends right, continue straight; it's a 5min. down on the left. ☎212 8903. Trips to the island including the boat launch, a guide, and lunch. Call in advance to make a reservation. US$70 for a full day up to 5 people.)

PARQUE NACIONAL SOBERANÍA

Spanning 19,540 hectares on the canal's east bank and encompassing the Río Chagres, part of Lago Gatún, and rich tropical rainforest, Soberanía is a fantastic day trip from Panama City, just 25km from Panama City. In addition to several good trails, it protects the canal's watershed and harbors an abundance of wildlife and birds. The park also hosts 105 species of mammals, 79 reptiles, 55 amphibians, and more than 1,300 species of plants.

Buses going to Chilibre pass the park. You'll need to get off at the ranger station, pay the entrance fee, and wait for another bus or alternate transport to the trailheads. Or, head off on foot; the zoo is about a 25min. walk. If you're on a bus to Gamboa, you can get off the bus to pay the entrance fee and a collect a map, but the buses to the trailheads come rather infrequently (about every hour in the morning, longer in the afternoon); disembarking could mean a long wait before you get to the trailheads. If you don't want to wait, you can stay on the bus and get off at the trailhead; you won't have to pay the entrance fee. From the road, Chilibre is to the right and Gamboa to the left. Guides can be arranged in advance through the ranger station or with outfitters in Panama City. (Ranger station ☎232 4192. Open daily 7am-5pm. Park US$5, students US$3. Camping US$3 per day.)

About 5min. down the road by bus is **Summit Gardens**. Another 7min. and you'll come to the first trailhead for the **Plantation Loop**. The trail takes you past the funky **Canopy Tower** (www.canopytower.com), a former US radar station, now a pricey hotel and birdwatching mecca. The moderately difficult trail leads 4 mi. into the forest and terminates in the middle of the Camino de las Cruces. Another few minutes by car down the road lies the short and easy **El Charco** trail, a short but well-maintained loop through the forest. It follows a creek and ultimately leads to a waterfall and pond where you can swim. The walk takes an hour at a leisurely pace, but is quite crowded on weekends. The **Camino de Oleoducto** (Pipeline Road), which traces the path of a pipeline built by the US in WWII to transport oil from the Caribbean, is said to be one of the best places to birdwatch in all of Panama. To get there, get off the bus in Gamboa, another 10min. down the road (passing over the Río Chagres), and continue straight through the town. When the road bends right, stay straight to get to the trailhead. Although the trail is technically the longest in the park, you can only head up 6km through secondary and primary rainforest. Strikingly colorful butterflies, howler monkeys, and phenomenal bird life inhabit the hilly forests around the path.

In Soberanía, you can also hike one of the only remaining and maintained sections of the historic **Camino de Las Cruces,** which was constructed by the Spanish in the 16th century to transfer goods, primarily gold, across the isthmus. The difficult 6.2-mile (10km) trail has stone steps and terminates at the ruins of **Venta de Cruces,** a former resting spot along the Río Chagres. The trailhead is along the road to Chilibre, so after checking in at the ranger station, catch one of the frequent buses towards Chilibre and get off about 7km up the road. Unless you do a difficult round-trip hike (12.4 miles), you will need to arrange a boat on the Chagres to pick you up from the ruins. If you hire a guide, this will be taken care of for you. Felipe Cabezoni, a local Embera man, offers tours, though he only speaks Spanish (US$40). Elvira Cabrera, a local Embera woman who also only speaks Spanish, can also arrange a boat. (☎6704 0380. US$3.50 one way, US$7 round trip.)

COLÓN   ☎981

Mention Colón to most Panamanians and they'll tell you not to go there. If you choose to come anyway, most people will advise you to leave. Colón has been in a downward spiral since its splendor in the early 20th century. Today the city is plagued by poverty and the highest crime rates in the country. Muggings occur in broad daylight despite the numerous armed policemen who patrol the streets. Aside from shopping in **Colón 2000**, the cruise port, or the **Zona Libre** (the second largest free trade zone in the world), there is not much to do in Colón. If you don't mind the real possibility of getting mugged, however, wandering the streets (with all your belongings locked in your room) can be an interesting experience. Despite the squalor, Colón has its own color and gritty vibrancy. Whether it's kids playing baseball in the streets, men playing checkers in the alleys, women fixing their hair, or drunk homeless men picking through trash, everyone seems to be outside, yelling, joking, and bringing the streets alive.

▐ TRANSPORTATION

Buses: Leave from the bustling terminal on C. 13 and Av. Bolívar. Buses to: **Coco Solo** (35min., every 30min. 6am-7pm, $0.30); **La Guaira** (2hr.; M-Sa every hr. 9:30am-3:30pm, fewer Su; $2.50); **Panama City** (1½hr., every 30min. 4am-midnight, $1.80; express service 1hr., every hr. M-F 4:45am-10pm, Sa-Su 7am-9pm, US$2.50); **Portobelo** (1½hr.; every 20min. M-F 4:30am-6pm, Sa-Su 7am-6pm; $1.30); **Sabanitas** (45min., every 30min. 5am-12am, $0.35).

Trains: By far the classiest way to travel. Vintage train complete with wood paneling and an open-air viewing deck. Runs through the jungle and skirts the canal. Trains (☎317 6070; www.panarail.com) leave from the **Albrook station** in Panama City and arrive near the **Cristóbal Colón port** in Colón. (1hr. Leave from Panama City weekdays at 7:15am; return from Colón at 5:15pm. One-way $22.)

Boats: From the port at **Coco Solo** you can try to get a boat to the San Blas Archipelago and on to Colombia. These trips are negotiated with the vessel captains. They can be dangerous as this route is frequented by drug traffickers. For the best info about safer boat travel, inquire at hostels in Panama City.

Car Rental: Located in Colón 2000. **Hertz** (☎441 3272, open M-F 8am-5pm and Sa 8am-4pm). **Budget** (☎263 8777, open M-Sa 8am-12:30pm and 1:30-5pm).

◼ ▐ ORIENTATION AND PRACTICAL INFORMATION

Colón is laid out in a north-south grid pattern. The city is situated on a roughly square piece of land that was once an island. In general, *avenidas* run north-south, connected by numbered east-west *calles;* C. 1 is to the north, while C. 16 is to the south. Very few of the roads are labeled, but **Avenida Central** runs through the center of the island with a wide median—stick to this *avenida* for the safest walking routes. West of Av. Central is **Avenida Guerrero** and then **Avenida Bolívar**. The **Zona Libre** (closed Sunday) occupies the southeast corner; the **Port of Cristóbal** is in the southwest. The **Colón 2000** shopping complex is on the far east side of town at the ends of C. 9-11. The **airport** is reached by a bridge from the Zona Libre. Outside of the Zona Libre, most of the neighborhoods are unsafe. There is a cluster of budget eating and lodging options between C. 9 and C. 11 on Av. Guerrero.

Tourist office: ATP (☎475 2301), in a small building on the waterfront facing C. 1 just west of Av. Central. Provides basic information on the city. Little English spoken. Open M-F 7:30am-3:30pm.

Banks: Although there are banks and **ATMs** all over Colón, the safest options are in Colón 2000 and Zona Libre, where a bank is on almost every block. If you need a bank closer to the center of town, you can try the **HSBC** on C. 11 and Av. Barboa, which has an **ATM;** open M-F 8am-3:30pm, Sa 9am-noon. For safety reasons, have a taxi waiting for you. **Western Union,** C. 13 and Av. Central (☎441 1309), on the 2nd floor. Open M-F 8am-5pm, Sa 8am-1pm.

Laundry: Most hotels will do laundry (usually around US$5). Numerous *lavamáticos* and *lavanderías*. **Luis N-2,** near a cluster of cheap hotels and restaurants on Av. Guerrero south of C. 11. Open daily 7am-5pm.

Police: (☎473 0365; emergencies 104), temporarily at Fuerte Davis; main branch is under renovation.

Pharmacy: Farmacia Itzel (☎441 7940) is one of 2 pharmacies at the intersection of C. 11 and Av. Guerrero. Open M-Sa 7am-11pm, Su 8am-10pm.

Hospital: Amador Guerrero (☎475 2211), next to Colón 2000 on C. 11, is clean.

Internet: Dollar Rent-A-Computer, on the 2nd floor above **Cafetería Nacional** (p. 580).

Post Office: (☎475 3043), in a particularly seedy section of C. 9, west of Av. Bolívar. Open M-F 7:15am-4:45pm and Sa 8:15am-12:45pm.

ACCOMMODATIONS

Let's Go recommends that you make Colón a daytrip from Panama City or stop by on your way to Portobelo. If you decide to stay, there are two good options with decent amenities and security; neither is particularly budget-friendly.

Hotel Carlton (☎447 0111), on C.10 2 blocks east of Av. Central, a few blocks north of Zona Libra. Clean and basic rooms come with TV and A/C. You're mostly paying for proximity to the Zona Libra and amenities: in-house laundry, pharmacy, and restaurant. Staff speaks English. Singles $39-44; doubles $44-50; triples $55; quads US$66. Higher prices for rooms with a balcony. ❹

Hotel Internacional (☎445 2930), near the bus station on C.11 and Av. Bolívar. Similarly basic rooms with internet, TV, and A/C. Also has its own restaurant-bar (open M-F 7:30am-10:30pm, Sa 8am-11pm). They offer a free shuttle to the Zona Libre in the morning. Singles $35; doubles $45. ❹

FOOD

There is no shortage of places to eat in Colón, although it's probably a good idea to eat at or near your hotel if possible. The main dishes are *criolla*-style chicken or fish, but other cheap standbys like American fast food and Chinese food are easy to find. Supermarkets abound throughout the city, many of which are open 24 hours. Try **El Rey** on C.7 and Av. Central and **Super 99** in Colón 2000. Both have ATMs.

La Cabanita, on Av. Central and C.8. Serves local *criolla*-style fried chicken ($3.50), shrimp ($6), and fish ($6-8). Totally decked out in strange animal remains, including giant sets of jaws, snake skins, and stuffed heads. Open M-Sa 11am-5pm. ❷

Restaurante Dominicano, next to Pensión Acropolis. Offers up cheap, delicious Dominican chicken ($3) and meat ($4). Open M-Sa 7am-7:45pm. ❷

Cafetería Nacional, south along Av. Guerrero at the intersection with C.11. A strange combination of Chinese and local food. Heavily air-conditioned. Breakfast $1.50. Sandwiches $1.75-3.50. Full meals $3-6. Open daily 9am-9:30pm. ❷

🔲 DAYTRIP FROM COLÓN

GATÚN LOCKS. Just 10km south of Colón, the Gatún Locks and Dam may be the best place to see the Panama Canal in operation; together they make for a great half-day trip from Colón. The **Gatún Locks,** the longest of the three sets of locks, raise and lower ships 26m between the Caribbean and Lago Gatún. The two sets of locks are designed to allow boats to come in and out at the same time. Boats going in the same direction move together, alternating every hour. For a better idea of how massive the locks really are, you can walk across the small bridge at the bottom of the lowest lock and come within meters of the massive iron walls. It's less glamorous than its Miraflores counterpart, but the **visitor center,** a tower above the middle of the three locks, has some of the best views of the canal operation. The guides speak perfect English and are eager to share all there is to know about the canal. Observe as the electric locomotives, known as *mulas,* guide the ships steadily through the canal. Jump on one of the original, retired *mulas* at the visitor center exit. *(From the main bus terminal in Colón, catch a bus to Cuipo or Costa Abajo (both 15 min., every hr. 5am-10pm, $0.75) and let the bus driver know you want to get off before crossing the locks or a few min. down the road at the dam. From the bus stop at the locks, go left up the hill, keeping the canal on your right until you reach the visitor center, a white building with an ATM in front of it.* ☎ *443 8878. Open daily 8am-4pm. $5).*

GATÚN DAM. Two kilometers up the road from the locks is the massive the **Gatún dam.** When it was constructed in 1906, it was the largest earth dam in the world and created the largest artificial body of water to date, Lago Gatún. The dam's construction caused the Rio Chagres to flood, covering villages, the Panama Railroad, and 262 hectares of forest. Today, the dam actively regulates the water level of the lake and generates enough power to operate the entire canal system. If you're lucky, some of the 14 spillways will be open; you can watch as millions of gallons of water flow out, changing the water level and powering one of the greatest engineering feats in the world. *(To reach the dam, you can catch the bus ($0.25) across the locks, or walk 20min. If you choose to walk, go left after crossing the locks and bear right when the road forks. Beware that the Canal Police are not always excited to have people walking near the locks or the dam, so they may ask you to take the bus. Buses return to Colón at least once an hr., though they do not stop if they are full. If you get tired of waiting for the bus, there are usually taxis ($10-15) that will pick you up.)*

PORTOBELO ☎981

Lush hills gently bend through Spanish colonial ruins to meet crisp Caribbean waters here in alluring Portobelo (pop. 8000). For 200 years after its founding in 1597, Portobelo was a commercial center of the Spanish colonies. It hosted famous fairs mingling the Old and New Worlds, where Spanish traders came to collect gold and silver in exchange for European goods to be introduced into the Americas. For several weeks a year, the streets of Portobelo would host these huge exchange markets whose spirit of commerce and vigorous enterprise is today echoed in the **Colón Free Trade Zone.** Forts were built to protect outgoing gold supplies against pirates and the English Navy. Eventually though, the fort failed, and the port met its demise. Today, this laid-back, economically depressed town comes to life twice a year for some of the best festivals in all of Panama. Ruins, diving, snorkeling, and mangrove tours draw crowds on the weekends and in the dry season, but in the low season Portobelo enters a lull; most establishments close during this time.

TRANSPORTATION

To get to Portobelo, take any **bus** from Panama City toward Colón and ask your driver to let you off at **Sabanitas** (look for shops with "Sabanitas" signboards, or for the McDonald's on the left side of the road. From the turnoff in front of El Rey supermarket, catch a **Portobelo** or **Costa Arriba** bus (1hr.; every 30 min. 5:30am-7pm, fewer on Su; $1), though these buses are often standing-room only. In Colón, buses to Portobelo leave from the **bus terminal** (1½hr.; every 30min. 4:30am-6pm, less on Su; $1.30). From Portobelo, buses leave for Colón (1½hr.; every 45min. 4:30am-6pm, less on Su; $1.30) and stop in Sabanitas, where you can catch buses headed for Panama City all day. There are buses east to **Guaira** (30min., every 2hr. 11am-5pm, $2), the jump-off point to **Isla Grande.** Be sure to check with the driver before boarding, as onlt a few Costa Arriba buses stop at Guaira. There are **taxis** waiting in town; a trip to the resorts on the outskirts of town will cost $2, but on the way back you'll have to take a bus ($0.25).

ORIENTATION AND PRACTICAL INFORMATION

Portobelo town lies on the south side of the tranquil Bay of Portobelo, 34km east of Sabanitas. All the watersport activities and high-class establishments are located a few kilometers before town on the main road. To skip town and go directly to one of these places, get off the bus when you see the "Scuba Portobelo" or "Coco Plum" signs on your left. From **Scuba Portobelo**, the small town is a 40min. walk east along the main road through the **Santiago de la Gloria ruins.** The town itself is centered around two squares. The first, the **parque central,** is in front of the **Aduana,** the distinctive historic building with arches. The main road continues on to the main square, which sits in front of a large white church, **El Nazareno.**

Tourist Office: IPAT (☎448 2200), located in a new building 20m west of the **Aduana,** across the street from the municipal offices. Open M-F and Su 7:30am-3:30pm.

Police: ☎448 2033, 2km west of the town in front of Pirate's Cove resort.

Medical Services: Ministerio de Salud (☎448 2033), runs a **clinic** in Barrio Guinea. From the main road, take a right up the hill. There is another clinic, **Caja de Seguro Social** (☎448 2729), just outside of the town, on the main road heading east. Neither are open at night, so you may have to go to Sabanitas in case of a nighttime emergency.

Internet: A cafe just after the IPAT office. Internet $1.50 per hr. Open M-F 8am-4pm. **Internet Enilda** (☎448 2439), across from Restaurante Ida. Internet $1.25 per hr. Open M-F 8:30am-9pm, Sa-Su 10am-8pm.

ACCOMMODATIONS

Although the bulk of the places to stay are on the road on the way into Portobelo, the town proper has three options. If you can't afford resort prices but want to stay outside of town, a family rents out a few **basic rooms** ❷ with fans and baths just past Coco Plum. (☎448 2400. Rooms $15-20.)

Mercado Andy (☎448 2332), in front of El Nazareno. Rents out 4 clean rooms with fan and shower. Rooms $15. ❷

Hospedaje Saigu (☎448 2204) on the main road up a hill to the east. Putting the "bare" in "barebones." Rooms with fans have beds on a concrete floor. Angel, the friendly owner, is willing to negotiate his already low prices. Rooms $7-10. ❷

Hospedaje Aduana (☎448 2925), next to the *aduana,* above a bar. A few basic, if damp, rooms with floor fans. Doubles $12, with bath $14, with A/C $20. ❷

Coco Plum Eco-Lodge and Resort (☎264 1338; www.cocoplum-panama.com). The best resort outside of town with large, overly decorated rooms. It's situated among a beautiful grove of palms, with plenty of hammocks and a small beach. All rooms have A/C, private bath and TV, and there is an adjoining restaurant. Rooms $45 plus 10% tax; $10 for each additional person. ●

Scuba Panama (☎261 3841 www.scubapanama.com), further down the road. Nice rooms with A/C and bath for typical resort rates. A full array of aquatic activities offered, including rides to nearby pristine beaches ($4-10), snorkel rental ($10), dives (starting at $18; equipment $21), and an incredible value 4-5 day PADI certification class that includes equipment and lodging ($175). Doubles $50; 4-person cabana $61. ●

🍴 FOOD

All the budget eateries are in town; nicer places with more options lie on the outskirts. In town, both **Restaurante Arith ●** on the *parque*, and **Restaurante Ida ●** near El Nazereno, serve cheap and delicious local food. Try the fried meat, chicken, or fish with rice, beans, and plantains ($3). On the edges of town, prices double. There are several **mercaditos,** one on each square, and one on the outskirts of town before the dive shop.

Restaurante Los Cañones (☎448 2980), a few feet west of Scuba Portobelo. Superb place for conch and other Caribbean delights. Named after the rusting cannons that dot the Portobelo region, the restaurant has a great bay view. Fish *ceviche* $4. Seafood with salad and rice $8-10. Beer $1.50. Open 9am until empty, usually around 6:30pm. ●

Restaurante El Torre (☎448 2039), just west of the police station. A great lunch spot with fantastic fresh juices ($1.50), *empanadas* (6 for $4), and typical seafood dishes ($8-11). ●

🎎 FESTIVALS

The **El Nazareno statue** first arrived in Portobelo in 1646 en route to Cartagena, Colombia. During a furious storm, the ship captain tossed everything overboard, including a statue of Christ. Miraculously, the cholera epidemic that had been ravaging Portobelo disappeared at the same time that fishermen recovered the lost statue. On October 21, after the outbreak had ended, the 40 men left carried the statue to town on a heavy platform. This same procession, now ritualized, occurs throughout the year, notably for **Cristo Negro** on October 21, when thousands of Panamanians sporting purple robes descend on Portobelo to celebrate what is one of Panama's most important religious traditions. Another lively festival celebrates **congo,** an upbeat Afro-Caribbean dance performed during **Carnaval** (February). The dance commemorates the liberation of the thousands of slaves brought from Africa. Women wear long dresses and men decorate themselves with odds and ends: bottles, old radios, just about anything they can find. They then take their turn dancing with the appointed *rey* and *reina* (king and queen) of Carnaval.

👁 SIGHTS

FORTRESSES AND RUINS. Gold from Spain's South American colonies was carried by mule from Panama City to Portobelo on the Camino de Cruces and down the Rio Chagres. The gold made Portobelo a prized target for pirates and the British Navy, so the Spanish built (and constantly rebuilt) a number of castles, battlements, and forts on either side of the bay. Built in the 1600s, **Santiago de la Gloria** is located on the left as you enter the town. Across the street, climb on top of what is left of the 18th-century **Castillo de Santiago** for a beautiful view of the bay. From the dock next to Santiago de la Gloria, catch a boat to **San Fernando,** an impressive three-tiered battlement built in 1753. The highest tier commands the best view of the whole bay. Be sure to arrange a pick-up time to return; allow at least 30min. for exploration. *($5 round-trip.)* The statue of **San Felipe** once guarded the entrance to the harbor, but was dismantled early in the 20th century to provide stones for the Gatún Locks (p. 581) of the Panama Canal and the breakwater at Colón. The hillside above Portobelo is dotted with other ruins including **La Trinchera** and **La Batería de Buenaventura.** The jungle seems to have reclaimed the path to these ruins, so making your way extremely difficult at best. In town, **San Gerónimo,** with cannons, vultures, and a view of the harbor, rests behind the **Aduana.** In a famous surprise attack in 1668, the Welsh pirate Henry Morgan (the namesake of your favorite spiced rum) stowed his boats on the other side of the mountain in Buenaventura, marched his men over the mountain and took Santiago de la Gloria. Morgan took priests and nuns hostage in exchange for the San Gerónimo Castle. **El Nazareno** (p. 582), the sacred statue of Christ carrying the crucifix, rests in the large, white church of San Felipe.

ADUANA. The royal customs house, built in 1630 out of the same coral reef used for the forts, was used to store gold. For a century, more than one-third of the world's gold passed through this building. The building underwent a joint Panamanian-Spanish renovation in 1998. There are two museums on the first floor: one houses historical artifacts and the other features an informative video and helpful diagrams about the history of Portobelo. *(Materials in English and Spanish. Both open daily 8am-4pm. $1, provides entry to both.)* Entry also gets you access to the **Museum of Negro Cristo** behind the church of San Felipe, which displays scores of the purple cloaks worn by El Nazareno; the statue is dressed in a new cloak each year.

ISLA GRANDE   ☎981

Just 100m off the coast, Isla Grande is a quiet Caribbean island that comes to life on the weekend, attracting a crowd of Panamanians on vacation. The island offers lovely beaches and great surfing. This is a great place to lay back and enjoy a drink with friendly locals, *extranjeros* (foreigners), and *capitalianos* (those from Panama City).

▐ TRANSPORTATION

During daylight hours, **boats** travel frequently between Isla Grande and **Guaira,** its sister town on the mainland (5min., $1.50). **Buses** go to Guaira from Colón (M-Sa every 2hr. 9:30am-3:30pm, fewer Sunday; $2.50) via **Sabanitas** (connections to and from Panama City) and **Portobelo.** They return on the same route (6:30, 7:30, 9am, 12:30pm).

◀▐ ⑦ ORIENTATION AND PRACTICAL INFORMATION

All the hotels and restaurants spread across a short 2km strip on the southern face of the island. Opposite the **main dock** sits the small but whimsically-named market **Bodega Super Jackson.** The store has a large selection of alcohol and a small selection of groceries. Facing inland, walk 100m to the right (east) for a medical clinic, the **Sub-Centro de Salud** (open M-F 8am-3pm, Sa-Su 11am-6pm; no emergency service). There is a public **phone** two houses past the clinic.

▐ ACCOMMODATIONS

A number of great hotels are sprawled along the coast, with prices ranging from $20 for rooms with a fan, to $75 for a little more. **Nido del Postre** (see

Food, below) rents out a few rooms in an old thatched building (doubles and triples $75). The cheapest, but certainly not the safest, option is to camp on the beach. (Free. Bring a mosquito net.) Try the point just beyond the neglected **Hotel Isla Grande.** Extreme caution is recommended if you camp on the beach; it is not advisable to do it alone.

Hotel Sister Moon (☎236 8489; www.hotelsistermoon.com), at the eastern end of the island. Sister Moon rents a number of private *cabañas* overlooking some of the best surf on the island. The beach is rocky, but the hostel has a small fresh water pool with a tiled deck. Each room comes with a hammock. Doubles $50; triples $75. ❹

Cabañas Cholitas (☎448 2962; cholitas@cwpanama.com), about half the distance to Sister Moon. Probably the best bang for your buck, with clean and simple rooms. One of the most lively places on the island. All rooms have A/C. Singles $20; doubles $25. MC/V. ❸

Cabañas Candy Rose (☎448 2947), right next to Bodega Super Jackson. Rents out a number of colorful rooms. The friendly, enterprising owner is willing to negotiate when business is slow. Doubles with fan $30, with A/C $40. ❹

FOOD

The scrumptious *comida típica* of Isla Grande is fresh fish fried with coconut rice. A dozen or so places dotting the coastline serve some combination of chicken, meat, or fish; most of them are affiliated with one of the hotels. A cut above the rest is ◼**Nido del Postre** ❺ (☎448 2061). Though expensive by local standards, the savory gourmet Mediterranean food (dinner $18-25) is a welcome change of pace from the local restaurants. Call ahead, so Olga can spend the afternoon preparing your meal. If dinner here is out of your budget, stop by in the morning for a cappuccino and some fresh fruit with yogurt and granola (US$5). Olga's French husband, François, speaks a little English and is full of stories from his travels around the world. The best value is **Restaurante Teletón** ❷, where they serve chicken ($3) and seafood served with *patacones* ($7). Built on stilts, **Restaurante-Bar El Congo** ❷ has good food, two parrots, and smooth Caribbean music. Their well stocked bar attracts a crowd on the weekends. (Seafood meals $7-10. Open 11am-8pm, later on weekends.) Sip on a piña colada ($5) without even getting out of the water at **Cabañas Cholitas** ❸ (see above). They also cook fabulous fish ($8). In the high season (Dec.-Feb.), **Restaurante La Punta** ❷, in the wooden shack on the sandy spit near Hotel Isla Grande, serves drinks and cheap lunches ($3-4).

SIGHTS

For the best **beaches,** turn left from the dock and head west for 10min. For a pleasant **hike,** turn left up the hill before you get to Hotel Sister Moon. The trail takes you through the thick forest, so it's a good idea to bring sturdy shoes—a must in the rainy season. It's a 20min. hike to the top of the mountain, which is marked by a cell tower and an abandoned lighthouse. If you walk past the lighthouse, a **lookout** materializes over the expansive Caribbean. If you're still feeling adventurous, find the trail heading down the other side. Its a hazardous 20min. walk along the ridgeline down to a secluded **cove.** The rocky beach and strong surf make it too dangerous to swim, but you can cool off in the tidal pool. From the cove, the safest route is to retrace your way back.

NIGHTLIFE

Nightlife on Isla Grande consists of sitting, talking above loud music, and downing mixed drinks. During the week in the low season, the bars are empty and sometimes don't even bother to open, but in the winter and during the weekends they're open late. Side-by-side **Cholitas** (p. 585) and **Ensueño** are popular places on the water, as is **El Congo**. Decorated like a shrine to Bob Marley, **Pupy's**, just before El Congo, plays reggae until the wee hours and attracts a more local crowd. It's usually only open on the weekends, or whenever Pupy feels like it.

OUTDOOR ACTIVITIES

Surfing is possible on the eastern part of the island, in front of Hotel Sister Moon (p. 585). **Snorkeling** is another popular activity, especially on the reef in front of Villa Ensueño, where schools of fish gather around the striking white crucifix in the water. The crucifix stands near a breach in the reef where the current is strong, so be careful. The best reefs are on the western part of the island. Walk west to the beach point and then swim 200m across the inlet toward the pink house on the hill. Beware: this can be a hard swim. Unless you're fit, it's probably not worth it. In front of the house are the best reefs on the island. **Villa Ensueño** (☎448 2964) rents snorkeling equipment ($1.50 per hr.). **Isla Grande Diving Center** (☎775 9127 or 570 0500; www.panamadive.com), a blue and yellow house west of the dock, just past a small bridge, has quality snorkeling gear ($10 per day), snorkeling trips ($35 for a 3hr. tour), and scuba trips ($85-125). Andres, the English-speaking owner, also offers a four-day course ($350; call in advance). **Kayaking** is another option; **Hotel Isla Grande** (☎448 2019) rents two-person kayaks ($10 per hr.). **El Congo** has the cheapest kayaks on the island ($5 per person).

DARIÉN

The Darién is quite literally the end of the road, the only gap in the entire Inter-american Highway from Northern Alaska to Tierra del Fuego in Argentina. It's a vast expanse of wild virgin jungle and one of the last few unexplored places on earth—an actual heart of darkness. Many who come are lured by the mystique and risk associated with crossing the dangerous Darién Gap into Colombia. *Let's Go* strongly discourages any attempt to cross the gap, which is home to, aside from two indigenous groups, a motley collection of drug smugglers, para-military groups, and bandits—not to mention the poisonous animals. Travelers in the gap have been abducted and murdered as recently as 1994. That said, it is also home to **Parque Nacional Darién**, one of the most biologically rich areas in the world, part of which is safe to explore.

The Interamerican Highway leads from Panama City through Metetí and ends near **Yaviza**, from where you can get a *piragua* (a wooden canoe) to **El Real** and hike into Parque Nacional Darién. Alternatively, you can turn off at Metetí, take a side road and a short boat ride to **La Palma** on the Golfo de San Miguel on the Pacific Ocean. Between the reserve and La Palma is the village of **Mogué**, which is remarkably touristy for a traditional village. On the other side of the reserve on the way to Garachiné is the **Río Sambu**, lined with indigenous villages. South along the Pacific coast from the Garachiné coast lie **Casa Vieja** and the isolated village of **Playa Muerto**. Even farther south is **Bahía Piña** and then, practically in Colombia, **Jaqué**.

Traveling in the Darién requires a lot of patience, money, or luck, and more often than not, a bit of all three. There are few roads, so almost all transport is by boat, either on rivers or on the Pacific Ocean. Buses and boats rarely run on a timetable, and even if they do, they are subject to change at any moment—ask around to make sure you won't be stranded. Issues of safety, transporta-tion, and local knowledge make planning a trip here difficult, so it might be wise (if pricey) to take a guided tour of the region. **Ancon Expeditions** has exten-sive experience in the region. If the areas of Garachiné and Sambú are what interest you most, fly in directly and avoid the hassle of waiting for a boat.

YAVIZA

The Interamerican Hwy. comes to an unceremonious end at Yaviza, the begin-ning of the infamous 150km-long Darién gap. Yaviza remains the best starting point for intrepid, fearless souls looking to cross the gap, although we can't emphasize enough how dangerous and suicidal this would be. If civil unrest and guerrilla warfare aren't enough to dissuade you, the border police will not permit you to go any farther than **Boca de Cupe**, 30km farther along; good luck finding a guide to take you the rest of the way. If you bring camping equipment, the trek to Boca de Cupe is safe.

TRANSPORTATION. Buses arrive in Yaviza from **Panama City** if there are enough passengers; otherwise, they let you off in Metetí and pile you into an overcrowded minibus for the last hour of the journey. **Minivans** leave Yaviza (1hr., every 30min.-1hr., US$5). Between Yaviza and **El Real**, *piraguas* (1hr., US$5) pass throughout the day, but your best bet is in the morning. If you're lucky, you might get a faster *panga* (fiber glass boat; 20min.). Special trips cost US$30, but are usually unnecessary unless you arrive in the late after-noon. Boats and buses meet at the dock.

⬛ PRACTICAL INFORMATION. Continue straight and turn left at the **post office** (open M-F 8am-noon and 1-2:45pm, Sa 8am-noon), which has **internet,** to get to the **police station,** where you should check in upon arrival. Past the police office is the **ANAM office,** where you will need to stop if you want to go to the **Pirre Station** of **Parque Nacional Darién** (see p. 590). (☎299 4495; open M-F 8am-4pm; call during the week if you plan to come during the weekend). If you instead turn right at the post office, cross a narrow suspension bridge and turn left to find the **hospital.** (Open 24hr.; pharmacy open 8am-4pm.) Behind the basketball court in the center of town is the **Visitor Center,** which has lots of information about surrounding communities and events. They can arrange a guide for nearby hikes (US$5) and volunteer opportunities in villages. (☎299-4469; www.cegel.com. Open daily 8am-4pm.)

⬛⬛ ACCOMMODATIONS AND FOOD. If you have to spend the night, the new **Hotel Yadarien ❷,** a yellow building just past the dock, offers spare, clean rooms with private baths. (☎299 4334. Doubles US$15, with A/C US$20; triples US$20/25.) A decent enough option is **Pensión Americas ❷,** across from the basketball court. They have four no-nonsense rooms with a shared bath. Sheets are provided, but it's probably a good idea to bring your own. (☎299 4439. Rooms US$12, with A/C US$15.

There are **restaurants** clustered around the dock, all serving basically the same *típico* for US$2 during the day. They open for breakfast around 6am and stay open for dinner, closing around 7pm.

EL REAL

El Real (pop. 1500) is the gateway to Parque Nacional Darién and the Pirre station. The main part of town the town is a built on a small grid of paved paths around a decaying plaza with a church. Most of the services are on a paved path leading out from the river.

⬛⬛ TRANSPORTATION AND PRACTICAL INFORMATION. Coming from the river, you will enter through one of two ports: **El Mercado** is for larger boats and is used all day, while **Gallital** is on a small stream and can only accommodate dugout canoes at high tide. Boats leave town throughout the day, but not on any regular schedule; ask around near the docks for departure times. In the morning you won't have to wait more than an hour, but you'll have a harder time in the afternoon.

Along the path leading outside the town (turn right when you get off the boat), you will find a **Centro de Salud** with a small **pharmacy.** (☎299 6589. Open 24 hr. Pharmacy open 7am-3pm.) Farther along you will find a **post office** and the **police station,** where you should check in before and after you go to Pirre.

⬛⬛ ACCOMMDATIONS AND FOOD. If you spend the night, **Hotel El Nazareno ❶,** an attractive blue and white building one block from the central plaza, is your only option. Rooms have fans and private baths, but the town has serious water problems, so don't expect water after noon; they have a bucket full of water for rinsing off. (☎299 5033. Singles US$7; doubles US$10; triples US$15; quads US$20.)

There is a **restaurant** around the corner serving the dish of the day—usually fried chicken, rice and beans (US$2).

LA PALMA

La Palma (pop. 6000) is the province's capital and largest town, but don't get the wrong idea—it's little more than a few houses strewn over a hillside or on stilts above the water. Though it offers scenic views, it's not a destination in itself, and most travelers stay a single night on their way through. From La Palma, you can access the villages along **Río Tuira**, the most prominent of which is the traditional Emberá village of **Mogué**. Its tourist infrastructure is more extensive than that of other villages in the region, but you'll probably still be the only guest.

TRANSPORTATION. There is an airstrip 20min. outside of town in **Miraflores**, which is served by **Air Panama** on Tuesday and Saturday if there is demand. The booking agent, Serafina Sugasti (☎6529 6446) has an office at the airstrip, but she is usually in town. She can also give you a lift to the airport for US$1. La Palma can be reached by **bus** to Metetí (6hr.), by **minibus** to La Quimba (25min., every 20-30min. 5am-5pm, US$1.50), and by **boat** (20min., every hr. 5am-5pm, US$3). Onward transportation to Sambú or Garachiné is difficult to find; ask around about hiring a boat (US$150-250). Boats head to **Garachiné** (M, W, F 10am). If you want to leave on a day without scheduled departures, the best thing to do is wake up early (5:30-6am) and head for the dock to see where boats are leaving for. The only way to get reliable information is to ask on the day of; if you want to get to Garachiné or other towns directly, look into direct flights, which are often cheaper. Private boats to **Mogué** cost $100.

IT'S ALWAYS BETTER WHEN WE'RE TOGETHER. Hiring a private boat by yourself can be terribly expensive. Chat up your hostel-mates and other travelers you encounter and see if they're heading to the same place; splitting the trip can save you a lot, and traveling in groups means that the crocodile might not eat you first.

PRACTICAL INFORMATION. You will arrive on a concrete ramp, which serves as the dock. Walking right from the dock, you'll encounter the **ANAM office** (☎299 6373; open 8am-4pm), though the tourist office, **ATP**, inside the Ministerio de Comercio e Industrias (☎299 6337; open M-F 8am-4:30pm) farther down the road is much more helpful. They also have free **internet**. Across the street, the **Banco Nacional** has an **ATM**. (Open M-F 8am-3pm, Sa 9am-noon.) Earlier on the same path is the **police station**. To get to the **hospital** (☎299 6219) and **pharmacy**, hop on the minibus (US$0.25) that passes through town in the direction right from the dock, and they will drop you off.

ACCOMMODATIONS. To the left, you'll find **Hotel Guacamayra ❷**, unmarked above the mini-market Ramaldy. It offers wood-paneled and attractive rooms on the second floor with two open-air lounges, one with a hammock overlooking the water and one with satellite TV looking down on the street. Rooms and baths are clean and have free drinking water. (☎299 6224. Singles US$10, with A/C and private bath US$20; each additional person US$5.)

SAMBÚ

The muddy waters of the Río Sambú open up to the Pacific between Garachiné and Punta Patiño. The river is lined with traditional Emberá villages that form the backbone of the **Comarca Emberá Sambú**, the first of which is the village of **Puerto Indio** and the neighboring village of Sambú. From these two joined villages (connected by a narrow suspension bridge), adventurous souls trek up the jungle's river.

TRANSPORTATION. By far the easiest way to get to Sambú is by plane. **Air Panama** flies in (T, Th, Sa; US$60). To make a reservation on a flight, show up the night before or morning of at 8am. You can also take a **boat** from **La Palma,** though finding a boat directly to Sambú is difficult. You're more likely to find a boat to **Garachiné** (1hr., US$10), from where some travelers hitch a ride (1hr. US$3) on the road that connects them; *Let's Go* never recommends hitchhiking. You can also book a private boat for around US$200 between Sambú and La Palma.

PRACTICAL INFORMATION. Sambú, connected to Puerto Indio by a narrow suspension bridge, has a **police station** and **medical clinic** (open 24hr.), both visible from the runway that cuts through the middle of town. There's also a **public phone** at the end of the runway, but you'll need to bring a phone card.

ACCOMMODATIONS. Villa Fiesta ❸, at the end of the runway, has pleasant rooms and an affable English-speaking owner. Rooms have two queen size beds and clean private bathrooms, sheets, and towels. (US$20, with A/C US$25.)

SIGHTS. For a trip up the Río Sambú, arrange for a guide and a *piragua* in Sambú. The journey is hot and tiring and modern amenities, such as mattresses, electricity, and running water, are virtually non-existent. Make sure to bring water. Guides can arrange for a place to spend the night, but you will need a hammock or a sleeping pad, and a mosquito net is recommended. The farthest village up the river is **Pavarandó.** A trip there and back will cost US$100-150, including the guide, boat, and gasoline. If you spend the night, expect to pay US$10-15 for food and a place to sleep for you and your guide.

PARQUE NACIONAL DARIÉN

The Rancho Frío ranger station is a 3hr. walk from El Real, depending on conditions on the trail. Another option is to hire a piragua (US$30-50) to take you to the village of Piji Basal, where you can find the trail for the last hour. Guides are a must—ask around El Real, or at the ANAM office in Yaviza. There is a dormitory at the station (US$15 per person) and a campsite (US$10). The park is accessible at Rancho Frío, Sambú, and Garachiné. These entry points are generally safe, though check on the current status at one of the many police stations in the region. There is a little solar electricity and a propane stove, as well as an outhouse with running water, but you need to bring your own food, flashlight and sleep sheet. The water is safe to drink, but bring a filter or purification tablets to be safe. Entrance fee US$5. Wear hiking boots at all times—there are snakes.

With 576,000 hectares of old-growth tropical forest, Parque Nacional Darién is so dense that the midday sun looks like dusk. The Park's neotropical biodiversity is bested only by the Amazon, and more migrating birds cross the isthmus through its boundaries than any other place in the world. Among the 450 species of birds are the toucan, parrot, and Harpy Eagle, the national bird of Panama. The Park is most easily accessible at **Rancho Frío,** though it's still a hike just to enter. At Rancho Frío, there are enough trails to keep a hike-happy visitor busy for days. One of the highlights is a summit of the **Cerro Ridge,** which is best done over two days, so bring a tent. Whether you have a day or a week, be sure to go to the nearby **waterfall,** just 20min. from the station. Crisp, pure water flows off the rocks into a serene pool, while the thick canopy opens above just enough to let in a few direct rays of light—it's a true jungle oasis, especially after the sweaty walk in, and you can slide down the waterfall. A few friendly rangers run the station. They each spend a month there at a time with little to do, so they will be happy to see you.

SAN BLAS

SAN BLAS ISLANDS   ☎981

With traditional, indigenous tribes, pristine beaches, and an abundance of coconuts, fish, and hammocks, the San Blas Archipelago (pop. 32,000) may be the closest anyone can come to true paradise. Formally known as the *Comarca Kuna Yala* ("Land of the Kuna"), the Caribbean archipelago stretches between Colón and Colombia, and is one of two autonomous political regions in Panama. The Islands are owned and operated entirely by the region's indigenous inhabitants, the Kuna. Although they use the mainland for corn, mangos, *Yucca,* and other agricultural products, almost all the Kuna are concentrated on the islands. The near-absense of mosquitoes and wild animals makes for a healthy and safe environment. Although you'll have to shell out a little extra cash to stay here, it's well worth it. Come get a tan and learn more about the culture of one of Central America's most independent indigenous peoples while you're at it.

HISTORY

By the 1500s, the Kuna had migrated into Daríen from Colombia. By the 19th century, war with the Spanish and the rival Emberá tribe had forced the Kuna onto the San Blas Islands. Here, the Spanish left them in comparative peace. In the early 20th century, however, a newly independent Panama launched attempts to "civilize" the Kuna. Fed up with mistreatment, on February 25th, 1925, the Kuna revolted against the Panamanian police force in the **Nele Kantule Revolution** (named in honor of their leader) and, with the help of a US battleship offshore, successfully gained autonomy. In 1938, Kuna land was further secured by the organization of the *comarca*, or district; in 1952 San Blas was officially recognized by the Panamanian government as a self-governing entity. The Kuna are not subject to Panamanian taxation, they own the entire region, and they send two representatives to the National Assembly. Even so, the older generation is fighting once again (this time without violence) to preserve traditions in the face of growing Westernization. In many Kuna town congress halls, banners proclaim, "People who lose their tradition lose their souls." Still, modernization continues to infiltrate the islands. While the Kuna once survived by trading coconuts with Colombian ships, today the *balboa* (US dollar) reigns supreme, with tourists as the new trading partners. As a result, the number of amenities and establishments on the Archipelago is constantly on the rise. Although it appears that each generation is becoming more Westernized, most of the Kuna lead simple, traditional lives.

CULTURE AND CUSTOMS

The *comarca* is governed by three *Cacinques*, who are the equivalent of provinicial governors and act as elected intermediaries between the Kuna and the Panamanian government. Every village has its own smaller **Congress,** the *"Casa de Congreso,"* which is headed by the **Sáhila.** The community celebrates religious ceremonies, resolves disputes, and makes important decisions in the *Casa de Congreso.*

The Kuna have their own language, but many speak at least some Spanish. Men typically wear Western clothes, while women wear distinctive clothing styles with golden earrings, nose piercings, bright colored bracelets, and skirts with blouses featuring the famous *mola*. The *mola* is a piece of colorful cloth stitched by hand. Although traditional *molas* have only abstract designs, modern ones are often decorated with animals and scenes from daily life. One of the most sophisticated and sought-after handicrafts in Latin America, the *mola* is sold to tourists everwhere in Kuna Yala (prices depend on quality, size, and age; US$5-10 per small panel).

With few exceptions, the Kuna live on the beach, only using the inland as a sort of grocery store for fresh produce and wood. Despite the presence of Christian missionaries, most of the Kuna maintain traditional piety. Kuna theology revolves around a divine human, **Iberogum**, sent to teach them how to live based on the principle of sharing within a community. More recent events, such as battles fought against the Emberá, the Spanish, and the Panamanian army, have become part of semi-mythic Kuna cosmology. Kuna Yala culture includes customary puberty rituals, marriage ceremonies, funeral rites, and traditional medicine. If you hang around long enough, you could run into a **chica fuerte** feast. *Chica fuerte* is an alcoholic drink made from sugarcane juice and maize and flavored with *cacao;* like the name suggests, it's not recommended for the faint of heart. The biggest parties of the year are in February: the 25th of the month is the anniversary of the 1925 Kuna revolution.

Travelers, particularly if visiting the more isolated islands, should learn about the Kuna before coming. Those arriving on an island that has no hotel need to see the **sáhila** to ask permission to stay (an entrance fee of US$1-3 is typically charged, irrespective of duration). Meeting the *sáhila* also provides an opportunity to ask about meals or accommodation options on the island. If you want to spent the night on an uninhabited island (an amazing experience), you s hould arrange a trip through one of the hotel owners, who may be able to talk with the owner of the island and work out a deal. **And don't forget to arrange a pick up.**

▪️ VISITING SAN BLAS

Due to its remoteness and the high price of gasoline and commodities, San Blas is not the easiest place in which to stay within a budget. Thanks to a newly improved road and growing budget accommodation options, it is becoming relatively more accessible to the student traveler. (Round-trip jeep US$50, boat transfer US$15; US$20 per night.) **Lodging** options are extremely limited. A stay on a densely populated island with vibrant Kuna life is just a short boat ride away from the mainland. Staying on an uninhabited, fairly remote island filled with nothing but coconuts, hammocks, and a few Kuna huts for you to rent, is more expensive to access. Most accommodations include three meals and many include tours of nearby islands. At higher prices, you are mostly paying for a little more comfort: Western-style toilets, a shower, and better, larger quantities of food. Although almost everywhere has a solar panel for electricity, only the higher-end places have lights inside the rooms.

There isn't much value in doing a highlights tour of the islands; the attractions on each are fairly similar, and picking one or two nearby will give you a good sense of what Kuna Yala is all about. **Guided tours** of the archipelago are best booked in Panama City (p. 565), but are only worth the expense if you're looking for a specific bonus, such as sailing or fishing. All visitors should keep in mind that most Kuna islands require visitors to pay a US$1-3 fee; this may be paid at governmental offices or with the local *Sáhila*. Even uninhabited islands are privately owned, and often require a fee. There's also a rule in most towns prohibiting walking around with only bathing suits on. In addition, photographers will normally be charged US$1, sometimes per shot.

◰ GETTING THERE AND AROUND

FLIGHTS

Flights to the San Blas Islands are easy, short, and fairly cheap, though prices depend on the price of fuel. Beware, destinations vary almost daily. At the time of publication, **Aeroperlas** and **Air Panama** were the only two airlines flying to San Blas. Flights go to **Cartí** or **Porvenir** (usually alternating depending on the conditions of the runway), **Corazón de Jesus** and **Playon Chico,** and **Puerto Obaldía** near the Colombian border. For more information, see **Panama City: Transportation,** p. 562. Since planes make multiple stops in the islands, they are occasionally available for island hopping, depending on demand. If you're planning to island-hop by plane, check with the airline before you arrive. Note that airports are often not on the destination itself; if you know where you are staying, arranging connection transportation with your hotel is the easiest and cheapest way to get where you are going. Alternatively, every arriving plane is met with enthusiasm by **boats** and **guides** from as far as an hour away. It is usually not that difficult to get where you are going—just be very clear on the name of the island and the specific accommodation. Agree on the price before you get on the boat. Boat rides largely depend on distance, from US$1 for an island that you could swim to versus US$10-15 for an hour-long trip. For much longer trips expect to shell out some serious cash. Since there is little chance of sharing a boat, you will be expected to pay for the gas need to travel to your destination and back, whether or not you return (up to US$75).

JEEPS

Thanks to new improvements, the once impassible Llano-Cartí Road can now be navigated by jeep. Jeeps from Panama city cost US$25 in each direction (3hr.); they'll pick you up at your hotel. The easiest way to book this is through your hotel or hostel; La Jungla, Mamallena, and Luna's are all known to book jeeps.

BOATS

There are two options for long-distance boat travel: one is expensive and usually safe and the other is cheap and less safe. Wealthy travelers take yachts from Panama, usually embarking near Colón at Puerto Lindo, passing through the San Blas islands and ending in Cartagena, Colombia. Similar trips can be arranged through travel agents or hostels. The best hostels have extensive information about boats. Prices usually run around US$350-450 for a five-day, all inclusive tour.

▨ THE ISLANDS

It seems as though there is a picturesque island for every day of the year in the San Blas Archipelago. Surrounded by reefs ideal for scuba-diving and snorkeling, and almost entirely isolated, these sandy gems make for perfect getaways. Keep in mind, that the islands farther afield are notorious stopping points for drug runners from Colombia. Arrange your visit with a hotel owner who knows which islands are safe—Arnulfo Robinson of Cabañas Robinson is one of many who would be happy to help.

The most densely populated islands tend to be the closest to larger pieces of land (the population is dependent on it for most of its food), and those farther afield are usually uninhabited—though few are more than a few kilometers from the mainland. Almost every island has two names: one Kuna and one Spanish; some even have an English name. For example, **Achutupu** is the same as **Isla Perro** which is sometimes called **Dog Island. Leading to even more confusion, some of the islands have the same name—make sure you and your boat captain are talking about the same place.** The western part of the archipelago has the greatest density of islands and the most accommodations. This area is the most easily accessible thanks to the road connection and the two airports on Cartí and Porvenir.

WESTERN ISLANDS. El Porvenir, the farthest west access point, is right next to the well-touristed **Wichub Wala** and **Nalunega,** both densely populated and rather traditional. Twenty minutes south, Cartí is a group of four similarly dense and slightly less traditional islands. Among them, **Cartí-Sugtupu** offers the most services, including a clinic. East of Cartí are **Río Sidra** and **Nusadup,** also densely inhabited and just off the coast. Directly north lie the budget-friendly islands of **Naranja Chico** (Narasgandup), **Dupasenika.** Also north is the more expensive **Kuanidup.** Farther north lies **Isla Pelicano,** with just four huts for rent. Still farther north, and a bit west, lies another group of islands. These are mostly uninhabited, though there are *cabañas* for rent on **Isla Diablo** and **Achutupu** (also known as Isla Perro). Note there is another Achutupu halfway to Colombia; don't get the two confused. Between Isla Diablo and Achutupu there is an easily accessible shipwreck perfect for snorkeling. To the west **Coco Blanco** has a few simple accommodation options. All of these islands, plus many more uninhabited ones, make up the western *comarca,* and are reasonably accessible from one another (at most 1½hr.).

OTHER ISLANDS. Farther northeast, the **Cayos Holandéses** (Holland Cayes) are a large group of completely uninhabited, picturesque islands popular with Yachties. A trip here is expensive (round-trip US$45-70). Farther east (up to 2½hr. by boat) are the fairly Westernized **Corazón de Jesús** and **Narganá.** The more traditional **Isla Tigre** and **Tikantiki** even farther east. From there, in order of increasing distance, are **Playón Chico, Yandup, Isla Tupile, Achutupo,** and the **Port of Obaldía.**

EL PORVENIR

Just barely large enough to fit an airstrip, Porvenir serves as a popular jumping-off point to the western archipelago. This island is also a required stop for any boat passing on its way to or from Colombia; as a result, it tends to always be flanked by yachts. The island itself has little to offer—this is not the place to see a Kuna village and the beaches are better elsewhere—but it is practically within a stone's throw of Wichub Wala and Nalunega, which each offer comfortable accommodations among densely populated bamboo and thatch huts.

F TRANSPORTATION. Although it is not official policy, it seems that the airports at Cartí and Porvernir alternate as the local airport. At the time of publication, the Porvenir airport was closed, but slated to open shortly (when the Cartí airport was closing). Flights coming in from Panama City arrive around 6:45am or later depending on what stops they make first. Make reservations a day in advance to fly to other islands; internal flights are subject to demand. Go to the government building a day before your flight and put your name on the list of people leaving, especially if you haven't bought a ticket. Hotels often take care of this for guests. When arriving by plane, sign in with immigration or the police official who meets each flight. (Entry fee US$6.) **Boats** to **Wichub Wala** cost US$1-2, though hotels will often pick you up for free.

▓ ▤ ORIENTATION AND PRACTICAL INFORMATION. Directly in front of the docks, a government building houses the **police station** (☎ 299 9124), **immigration office** (theoretically open 9am-4pm, though you may have to go look for the officer), **marine office,** and **public phones** (☎ 299 9000). To get any of the offices by phone, call the public phone and someone will try to find who you are looking for. The **airport** serves as a **post office**; give letters to the pilot heading out on the morning flight to Panama City (he'll buy stamps, if necessary).

▣ ▢ ACCOMMODATIONS AND FOOD. The only hotel on the island is **Hotel Porvenir ❶,** practically on the tiny airstrip. This hotel offers contiguous concrete rooms with private baths. (Local cell ☎ 6692 3542, in Panama City 221 1397. Daytrips and meals included. US$45 per person). Hotel Porvenir also operates a small snack bar with surprisingly cheap bottles of liquor. A brand new restaurant, **Nan Magrlya ❶,** is owned by Congreso General Kuna, the unified government of the different Kuna Villages. Its a great place to grab a coffee (US$0.35) or a mid-afternoon snack (fish and rice US$3) before your early morning flight. (Open from 7am until last customer.)

WICHUB WALA

This small, densely populated island is not a beach destination. If it's a Kuna village you seek, this charming assembly of traditional homes will suit you fine. Join local kids playing basketball with hoops attached to palm trees, or watch women put in long hours on their *molas.* The island has a **health center** (open M-F 7:30am-3:30am, Sa-Su 8am-noon), but in a bigger emergency you will need to go to Cartí. There are a number of small markets, including a community-run **store** just past the public docks. (Open daily 6am-9pm.) There are two good accommodations for those visiting Wichub Wala; only one is actually on the Island. **Hotel Ukuptupu ❺** is a 5min. canoe ride farther west, on a tiny island, halfway to Nalunega. The island is actually manmade. A former Smithsonian research island, this island is now occupied by the family of Juan García, an amiable man who speaks English. The hotel here has clean, breezy rooms, and common bathrooms constructed on stilts over water. García and his wife go out of their way to make you feel welcome, especially when it comes to food; you can even handpick the lobster you want for dinner. Rates include three meals, tours of other islands, and all-night electricity. (Panama City ☎ 290 6650, cell 6514 2788; www.ukuptupu.com. US$55 per person.) Among the cluster of thatch houses on the main island of Wichub Wala, **Kuna Niskua Lodge ❹** has a beautiful two-story bamboo-thatch building. All rooms have private baths, and there is electricity all night. Rooms include three meager meals and tours. (☎ 6029 6255 or 6662 2239. Snorkeling equipment US$6 per day. US$50 per person.)

NALUNEGA

A short trip west from Wichub Wala, Nalunega is slightly more spread out, but equally populated. It is home to the well-known **Hotel San Blas ❹,** the oldest hotel on the Archipelago, which offers Kuna-style cabins with sand floors as well as a newer concrete building. Luis Burgos, the aged owner, speaks English and Spanish. The place has ample hammocks and benches. If you are not staying at the hotel, you can still go on the daily tours for US$25. The hotel rents snorkeling masks (US$3) and flippers (US$6). (☎ 344 1274, cell 6661 4609. Rooms US$10. Tour and 3 meals an additional US$40.) There is a small one-room **museum** marked by a door made of washed up cans and bottles. Inside is a collection of impressive wood carvings. Teodoro Dorez is the creator of most of the work. Dorez is deeply disturbed by the amount of trash found in the water; for this reason, he dedicates himself to collecting trash in his museum. He hopes to some day construct a new building from the trash he gathers.

CARTÍ-SUGTUPU

Cartí is a group of four densely populated islands just off the mainland. **Cartí-Sugtupu, Cartí-Tupile,** and **Cartí-Yantupu** are the three largest ones. Of these, Cartí-Sugtupu (pop. 2000) is the largest and most thickly settled, and offers the most services.

TRANSPORTATION. Daily flights from Panama City arrive in Cartí airport when it is not closed, which appears to be about half the time. The airport is on the mainland, a 5min. boat ride from the island. The airplanes land on the northern terminus of the El Llano-Cartí road, the only overland road to the entire Archipelago. Although the road has recently been upgraded, don't expect actual pavement; the trip still requires good four-wheel-drive vehicle and possibly a snorkel. Jeeps making the journey daily from Panama City can be booked by most of the hostels (one-way US$25).

ORIENTATION AND PRACTICAL INFORMATION. The busy island is crossed by **two east-west footpaths.** The **public docks** are on the north side, near the middle of the island; walk straight on a nearby path to run in to the two main footpaths. The town's **health center** is one of the biggest in the whole archipelago, though the competition isn't that steep; in an off-hours emergency, you may have to find the medics in town. (☎6041 3611. Open M-F 7:30am-12pm and 1pm-3:30pm, Sa-Su 8am-noon.) There are **public phones** next to the dock (☎299 9002).

ACCOMMODATIONS AND FOOD. If you head right on the first footpath, you will find the **Cartí Homestay Backpacker Inn,** one of the cheapest places in the area. The second floor has a number of beds, separated by partition walls; it's essentially one big dorm with plenty of hammocks. Eulogio Pérez, the English-speaking owner, runs **San Blas Adventures,** where you can book reasonably-priced tours throughout the islands, though tours and food are included in the price of a room at the inn. (Panama City ☎257 7189, cell 6517 9815. US$30 per person.) Cartí-Sugtupu boasts a friendly community-run **dormitorio** and **cafeteria,** though at the time of publication it was undergoing renovations. Rooms do not include food. The bathroom is built in the Kuna style: a toilet seat over a hole in the floor. (☎6065 0098. Open 7am-10pm. Meals US$3.50. Rooms US$8.) There are no fewer than four *tiendas* in town, all of which sell basic items such as soap, toilet paper, and beer.

SIGHTS. Also in town is the one-room **Kuna Museum,** 5min. east of the public dock on the northern road. The room is filled with Kuna artifacts, in an attempt to preserve and educate about Kuna life. Owner, curator, and guide José Davies leads visitors through the Kuna artifacts and his own illustrations of Kuna myths and rituals. Tours are in Spanish, and, if necessary, broken English. If he is not there or your Spanish is limited, his son (who speaks perfect English) can direct you. (☎6732 1899 or 6668 6821. Open daily 7am-10pm.)

SAN BLAS

COCLÉ AND VERAGUAS

EL VALLE DE ANTÓN

It's no wonder that Panamanians flock here on the weekends. The main attraction of El Valle (pop. 6200), which is surrounded by mountains and fields of flowers, is the climate. A tranquil town situated 600m up on the crater floor of an ancient volcano, El Valle has temperate weather year-round, a godsend in the sweltering summer. Nearby attractions include hot springs, hikes, and waterfalls.

⌐ TRANSPORTATION

Buses: Buses in El Valle fill up quickly, so it's best to pick them up at the market. You can usually get them to stop anywhere along the main road leading east of town. They head to **Panama City** (2½hr., every 45min. 3:30am-4pm, US$3.50). For later departures, take the bus to **San Carlos** (40min., every 20-25min. 4am-6pm, US$1.50); from there you can go just about anywhere. Buses to **La Mesa** (10min., every 25-30min., US$0.75) head west of town passing by **El Macho** (US$0.25).

Public Transportation: There is 1 local bus, labeled **"La Compañia El Halto,"** which loops through the town's few streets (US$0.25)

Taxis: Around town. Fares around US$2.

✦ 🔋 ORIENTATION AND PRACTICAL INFORMATION

El Valle is about 40min. up a twisty road off the Interamerican Highway from the cut-off at Las Uvas. The **main road** enters town from the east and runs west; almost everything is either along this road or a short walk off it. The open **mercado** is in the middle of town. Generally, sights are outside of town to the west; lodgings are to the east of town.

Tourist Office: (☎983 6474), in a small pavilion in front of the market. Free maps and basic info about transportation and nearby activities. Some English spoken. Open Tu and Th-Su 7:30am-3:30pm. **ANAM** (☎983 6411). Take a left about 1½km before town at the sign. Info about nearby hikes in Monumento Cerro Gaital and the surrounding areas. Open daily 8am-4pm.

Tours: Proyecto de Eco-Turismo (☎983 6472), about 500m before town. Turn left following signs for the Orchid Center. Take any bus (US$0.25) heading east from town back toward the highway. Based out of the Orchid center, they offer guide services for nearby attractions. English guides available. Prices include transportation, and range from US$10 for a guided trip to El Macho to US$35 for longer hikes.

Library: After the market and before the church. Terminals and Wi-Fi US$1 per hr. Open M-F 8:30am-4:30pm, Sa 8:30am-3pm, Su 9:30am-12:30pm.

Laundromat: Lavamático La Libertad, about 500m before town on the main road. Wash US$0.75. Dry US$1. Tips appreciated. Open M-Sa 8am-4pm.

Public Toilets: In the market. US$0.25.

Police: (☎983 6216), on the way in to town. Turn right as if going to El Níspero.

Pharmacy: Mi Farmacia, 500m before town, next to Lavamático La Libertad. Open M-Sa 8am-4pm. MC/V.

Medical Clinic: Centro de Salud (☎983 6112), behind the church. Open M-F 7am-3pm. **24hr. emergency care.**

Internet Access: FSR technology Systems (☎908 7003), before town next to the Lavamático and pharmacy. Wi-Fi US$1 per hr. Open M-Sa 8am-6pm, Su 11am-3pm.

Post Office: Behind the market. Open M-F 8am-4pm. **Postal Code:** 1001.

▌ ACCOMMODATIONS

El Valle is a weekend retreat for wealthy Panamanians, but there are plenty of options for budget travelers, too. Since the town is temperate year-round, hot water is standard, but A/C isn't. Some hotels jack up their prices on the weekends.

▨ La Casa de Juan (☎6453 9775), about 1.5 km before town; take a left at the sign. Señor Juan rents out a few rooms in his funky house. Under the large roof is an outdoor kitchen and and eating area where backpackers sit around and sip beer. Rooms are clean and have private baths with hot water. Old mountain bike rentals US$5. 6-person dorms US$10; private rooms US$20. Cash only. ❷

Cabañas Potosi (☎983 6181). Follow the road west of town. After it curves right, turn left at the store and continue straight for 10min. Some of the most affordable cabins in the valley, situated in a beautiful park-like atmosphere. The charcoal grill is perfect for an afternoon picnic. Rooms are simple, sleep up to 3, and have hot water, mini-fridges, and fans. Rooms US$43. Cash only. ❹

Santa Librada (☎6591 9135), in Restaurante Santa Librada. The cheapest private rooms in town are small and have a bit of a bug problem, but they come with private bathrooms and towels. Singles US$12; doubles US$20; triples US$30. Cash only. ❷

Don Pepe (☎983 6425), in the 3-story yellow and green building just before town. A good deal for a big group. Rooms are clean and have hot water baths and TVs. Laundry US$6. Internet US$2 per hr. Bikes US$2 per hr. Don Pepe can also arrange nearby tours (US$10 per hr.) and horseback riding (US$8 per hr.). Singles US$35; doubles US$40; 6-person room US$70. MC/V. ❹

▐ FOOD

Food in El Valle is more expensive than in Panama City, but it's still possible to get cheap *típico* without breaking the bank. If you have access to a kitchen, your best option is to buy some produce from the market. For groceries, visit **Supercentro Yin,** across the street from the market. (Open daily 7am-1pm and 2-7pm.)

Pinocchio's (☎983 6715), just past town. Mario, the grandson of italian immigrants, carries on the tradition in delicious pizzas (US$5-8) and pasta (US$5-6). The weekend crowd raves about the food. Open W-Su noon-9pm. Cash only. ❷

Hotel Anton Valley (☎983 6097), across the street from the church. This cute, American-owned B&B opens its doors to the public for breakfast. The dining room (the "Orchid Room") has a fountain and cozy seating. Coffee US$0.50. French Toast US$3.50. Wi-Fi. Open daily 7am-9:30am. MC/V. ❷

Restaurante Santa Librada (☎6591 9135), 100m before town on the right. An appealing little restaurant with outdoor seating. Specializes in seafood and meat dishes *al carbón*. Entrees US$6-8. Open daily 7am-9pm. Cash only. ❷

Caravan.com is Going Places in Costa Rica from $995.

This map presents the best selling **10 day** all inclusive tour, starting at only $995.

Caravan makes it so easy - and so affordable - for you to explore the magnificent rainforests, beaches and volcanoes of Costa Rica. Your Caravan Costa Rica tour includes all meals, all activities, all hotels, a great itinerary, all airport transfers, and all transportation and excursions within Costa Rica.

Join the smart shoppers and experienced travelers who rely on Caravan to handle all the details while you and your friends enjoy a well-earned, worry-free vacation in Costa Rica.

Caravan.com

Or Call 1.800.CARAVAN   Fully Escorted Tours, #1 in Value

Restaurante Mar de Plata (☎983 6425), just before town, across from Supercentro Yin and inside Hotel Don Pepe. Serves a wide variety of *típico* and a selection of Peruvian dishes. Try the *sancocho* (traditional Panamanian chicken soup with rice; US$4). Entrees US$4-8. Open M-Th 7am-9pm, F-Su 7am-11pm. MC/V. ❷

Doña Nelia (☎9087 0075), across from the market. Cafeteria-style *típico* attracts the locals from the market across the street. Open daily 7am-3:30pm. Cash only. ❶

👁 SIGHTS

MUSEO DEL VALLE. The museum is a large room with ancient artifacts and local crafts, accompanied by an explanation of the geological events that created the valley. Some explanations are in English. *(Behind the church. ☎6437 8639. Open during business hours. US$0.50)*

MERCADO EL VALLE. El Valle is known for its Sunday market, one of the most popular in Panama. Indigenous artisans gather from surrounding farms to sell sculpted pots, carved soapstone figurines, wooden toys, and woven baskets. There is also a large selection of delicious fruit, wholesome vegetables, and gorgeous plants; it's a pity that customs agents don't look kindly on botanical imports. Between August and October, the national flower—**Flor de Espíritu Santo** (Flower of the Holy Spirit)—is on sale. *(In the middle of town. Open 7am-5pm.)*

EL NÍSPERO. A well-maintained zoo and botanical garden, El Níspero makes for a lovely afternoon stroll. Animals include ocelots, titi monkeys, iguanas, scarlet macaws, giant sleeping tapirs, and jaguarundi. *(Take a right about 500m before town by the ATM. From there, walk straight and take a right after the fire station. ☎983 6142. Open 7am-5pm. Adults US$3, children US$2.)*

POZOS TERMALES. El Valle is one of the few places in Panama cool enough to make hot springs attractive. The pleasant grounds include natural pools, mudbaths, and hot springs. Admission includes a packet of mineral-rich mud for your face. *(☎6621 3896. Turn left following the signs when the road curves right outside of town; it's about 7min. farther down the road. Open 8am-5pm. US$1.)*

EL MACHO. An impressive 85m rainforest waterfall over black volcanic rock, El Macho is one of El Valle's greatest attractions. It's a 5min. hike via bouncy suspended walkways, overlooking Río Guayago and Amarillo (El Valle's two water sources) and lush virgin forest. The viewing station is 20m away; it is forbidden to bathe or get too close to the waterfall. There is a 2hr. hike through the surrounding **Refugio Ecológico Chorro El Macho** that loops above the waterfall and comes down the other side. Guides are required for the hikes. The *refugio* also runs **Canopy Adventures**, which operates a system of zip lines that crisscross in front of the waterfall and through dense forest *(☎983 6547. Follow the main road west of town for 30min.; there are plenty of signs. Or, take the La Mesa bus (US$0.25). Open daily 8am-5pm. US$3.50, children US$1.75. Natural bathing pool US$3.50. Guided hike for wildlife observation US$35. Zip lines US$52.50 per person with a guide.)*

PIEDRA PINTADA. One of El Valle's most prized sights is a bit underwhelming unless you are a petroglyphs buff, but it's a nice walk regardless. Nearby is a splendid waterfall. Less famous but more accessible than El Macho, hiking Piedra Pintada is free. Some travelers jump into the crisp pool at the bottom. It's also the beginning of the trail up the India Dormida (p. 600). *(Follow the road out of town to the west. Continue as it bends to the right and turn left at the sign. Continue straight until the road comes to a T, then turn right; it's through an open gate to the left. The 10m rock is 5min. past the road. For the waterfall, continue up the path keeping the river to your left. Except during school hours, you will find little boys waiting to guide you; US$1 tip recommended.)*

INDIA DORMIDA. You can't spend a day in El Valle without someone pointing out La India Dormida. Legend has it that when the *indígena* maiden daughter of legendary Indian Chief Urracá, Flor del Aire, fell in love with a conquering Spaniard, her previous lover Yaraví killed himself. The girl, tormented and disgraced, wandered into the hills to die, lying down to stare forever at the skies. With a little imagination, her silhouette can be deciphered by visitors in the hills to the west of El Valle. *(The more difficult of two trails passes through incredible rainforest. Follow the signs to Piedra Pintada (p. 599) and continue up the trail keeping the river to your left. The hour-long hike is steep and slippery. The signs in town for La India Dormida lead to the other way up, a less exciting route. Follow the road west out of town; when it turns right, hang a left. At the 1st street take a right, and then at the next street, a left. Its a 15min. walk from town to the start.)*

SANTIAGO

Halfway between Panama City and David, along the Interamerican Highway, Santiago (pop, 74,680) is a convenient base for forays into the fabulous province of Veraguas. Filled with waterfalls, wilderness areas, beaches, and small traditional villages, this area is gorgeous. Aside from the *Fiesta Patronal de Santiago Apóstol* (July 22-25), Santiago itself doesn't offer much to visitors.

◧ TRANSPORTATION

Situated on the Interamerican Highway, Santiago is a transportation hub, so you'll probably have to pass through whether you want to or not.

Buses: Transportes David-Panamá (☎998 4006), next to Hotel Piramidal on the Vía Americana, east of the fork. To **David** and **Panama City** (3hr., every hr. 9am-11pm, US$7.50). Buses leave from the main terminal on C. 10 halfway between Av. Central and the Interamerican Hwy. to: **Atalaya** (20min., every 30min. 6am-9pm, US$0.75); **Las Palmas** (1½hr., every hr. 5:15am-6:45pm, US$2.60); **Puerto Mutis** (45min., every 20min. 5:15am-10:10pm, US$1.10); **San Francisco** (30min., every 25min. 6:05am-8:15pm, US$0.75); **Santa Fé** (1½hr., every 30min. 5am-7pm, US$2.40); **Soná** (1hr., every 20min. 5:40am-9:20pm, US$1.25).

Taxis: Rides around town US$1.25.

Car Rental: Budget Rent-a-Car (☎998 1731), next to the McDonald's on the Interamerican Hwy., near the fork. Open M-Sa 8am-5pm. AmEx/MC/V.

◧ ⁊ ORIENTATION AND PRACTICAL INFORMATION

The main road, **Avenida Central**, branches off from the Interamerican Highway and runs west about 2km to the cathedral and the town's **parque central**. *Calles* run north-south between Av. Central and the Interamericana, starting with C. 1 beyond the cathedral and C. 10 about halfway between the **cathedral** and the fork. To get to the *parque* from the main bus terminal, turn right on C.10 in front of the terminal and continue for about 4 blocks; turn right at Av. Central and continue straight to the cathedral.

Tourist Office: ATP (☎998 3929), in Plaza Palermo on Av. Central. No English spoken. Open M-F 7:30am-3:30pm. **ANAM** (☎994 7313), across from the Hotel Gran David on the Interamerican Hwy. They operate cabins on Isla Coiba; call in advance to reserve one. Open M-F 8am-4pm.

Bank: HSBC, on Av. Central and C. 7. **24hr. ATM.** Open M-F 8am-5pm, Sa 9am-noon. There is **Western Union** (☎998 5431) inside Servicios Martinez on C. Eduardo Santo, across the street from the Escuela Normal. Open M-F 8am-5:30pm, Sa 8am-5pm.

Luggage Storage: In the main terminal on C. 10. US$0.75-6.50 per day. Open 24hr.

Laundromat: Lavamático La Espuma, 4 blocks north of Av. Central on C. 9. Wash US$0.50; dry US$0.50. Full service US$1.50. Open M-Sa 8am-8pm.

Police: (☎958 2400), 500m east of the fork on the Interamerican Hwy.

24hr. Pharmacy: Farmacia Veraguas (☎958 6844), in the same bus stop as Restaurante Tucanes on the Interamerican Hwy.

Hospital: (☎999 3070 and 3146), about 4km east of town on the Interamerican Hwy.

Internet Access: F1 Computers, across from the bus station on C.10. Internet US$0.60 per hr. Open M-F 8am-6pm, Sa 8am-1pm

Post Office: (☎998 4293), on C. 8, 8 blocks north of Av. Central. Open M-F 7am-5:45pm, Sa 7am-4:45pm. **Postal Code:** 0923.

ACCOMMODATIONS

Most people pass through Santiago without spending the night. If you do have to spend the night, there are plenty of options, ranging from comfortable (along the highway) to basic and a bit dodgy (in the middle of town).

Hotel Gran David (☎998 4510), west of the fork on the Interamerican Hwy. One of Santiago's best hotels. Comfortable rooms have phones, private baths with hot water, and access to a 24hr. restaurant and pool. Internet US$1 per hr. Singles US$11, with cable and A/C US$20; doubles US$15/26, triples with A/C US$34. MC/V. ❷

Hotel Piramidal (☎998 3124), next to the David-Panama bus terminal on the Interamerican Hwy., just east of the fork. The surprisingly chic lobby has Wi-Fi, and there is a large pool in back. Plain rooms come with hot water, A/C, and cable. Singles US$25; doubles US$33; triples US$37. AmEx/MC/V. ❸

Hotel Santiago (☎998 4824), 1 block south of the southwestern corner of the Cathedral. With your back to the rear of the cathedral, turn left and walk 20m. A step up from the group of sketchy accommodations downtown. Don't be tricked by the attractive facade—the rooms in back are seriously neglected. Rooms have private baths, but the plumbing doesn't always work. Singles US$7.70; doubles US$11, with A/C US$17. Cash only. ❷

FOOD

You can find *típico* all over town. Fast food joints cluster around the Interamerican. For groceries, visit **Super99**, on C.10, just off Av. Central. They also have a **24hr. ATM** and a **pharmacy.** (☎998 3939. Open 24hr. MC/V.)

Cocina del Abuelo (☎933 4041), 1km east of the fork on the Interamerican Hwy., inside the Hotel Plaza Gran David (not to be confused with Hotel Gran David). Although it's a bit touristy, this restaurant serves delicious international cuisine, difficult to find in Santiago. People come for live performances Sa-Su night. The attached tavern is a sports bar. Entrees US$6-12. Beer US$1.50. Open daily 11am-11pm. Tavern open daily 5pm-1am. MC/V. ❷

Los Tucanes (☎958 6490), just west of the fork on the Interamericana. A popular stop for long-distance buses. Basically a large cafeteria with cheap sandwiches (US$1.25) and *típico* (US$1.25-2). Open 24hr. Cash only. ❶

SIGHTS

There isn't much to explore in Santiago, but the ◪**Escuela Normal Juan Demóstenes Arosemana** is worth a stop. Built between 1936 and 1938, this school for teachers boasts dazzling architecture, sculptures, and paintings. The facade is a gorgeous hodgepodge of stone carvings hiding miniature figures of *pollera*-clad girls. Head through the archway of the entry hall, framed by the Allegory of Time and Philosophy (Plato and Aristotle lean on the clock) and through the doors to the Aula Máxima. This huge room was painted by **Roberto Lewis,** the famous painter who decorated the Palacio Presidencial in Panama City. *(On C.7, 4 blocks north of Av. Central. Shorts and sleeveless shirts prohibited. Open 7am-3pm. Free.)*

◾ DAYTRIPS FROM SANTIAGO

◾IGLESIA SAN FRANCISCO DE LAS MONTAÑAS. Thirty minutes down the road to Santa Fé is the small town of San Francisco, built around a pretty square and this beautiful church. Unlike the abundant white-washed churches in the rest of the region, this 18th-century masterpiece has a stone exterior with a single white steeple and an ornate wooden interior. If you're headed to Santa Fé and have a little time to kill, it's certainly worth the stop. *(Take a bus to San Francisco or Santa Fé from Santiago. Turn right off the main road after the Protecion Civil building on the left. The entrance to the church is on the side. Open Tu-Sa 10am-6pm.)*

SANTA CATALINA

Santa Catalina, recognized as one of the best year-round surfing spots in the Americas, is a small fishing town 110km south of Santiago. Today it is fighting fiercely against developers and businessmen to maintain its small-town atmosphere. For the most part it has kept its laid-back feel. People from all over the world come to Panama and hop on a bus for six to seven hours to get straight to Catalina. Although the vast majority of these crazies are surfers, nearby fishing, diving, and snorkeling attract other nature-lovers. It's also a good leap-off point to Pacific islands like Cébaco, Gobernadora, and ◾Coiba.

◾ TRANSPORTATION

To get to Santa Catalina by **bus,** you have to travel through Soná. From the terminal, **buses** leave for **Santa Catalina** (1½hr., 4 per day 5am-6pm, US$3.80). Though Soná is closer to David than it is to Santiago, you'll probably have to pass through Santiago to get to Soná. Within Santa Catalina there is no public transportation. Fortunately, nothing is much more than a 30min. walk. For a **taxi,** talk to David (see **Ocean Tour,** p. 603).

◾ ◾ ORIENTATION AND PRACTICAL INFORMATION

There are only **two main roads** in town. The one from Soná leads to the heart of town and ends at the town's beach. The other, a dirt track, takes you to **Playa Estero.** Between the cut-off for Estero and the beach, there are **four side roads** on your right that also lead to the water. Services are extremely limited in town. There are still **no landlines here,** and cell phone service is only availiable a few kilometers up the road. There is **no bank,** so bring plenty of cash.

Tours:

Scuba Coiba (☎6575 0122; www.scubacoiba.com), on the beach. A professional full-service, PADI-certified scuba outfitter. Runs frequent trips to Isla Coiba. Open 8am-6pm. Full-day trip to Coiba with 2 dives US$100. Two-day trip US$420 (min. 2 people). You can hop on daytrips as a non-diver for US$60.

Fluid Adventures Panama (☎832 2368; www.fluidadventurespanama.com), on the beach next to Scuba Coiba. If nobody is there, check at the home next to Big World Villas; the owners are usually only in town Dec.-May. A young Canadian couple, one a former Outward Bound instructor and the other a yoga instructor, run this kayak, surf, and yoga outfit. They offer all sorts of different packages from kayaking in Coiba (US$85 per person with 4 people; overnight US$200 per person, minimum 4 people) to a combination surf and yoga camp.

Ocean Tour (☎6915 5256; www.2oceanpanama.com; david2670@gmail.com), next to Restaurant Tropical Beach, on the left on the way down to the beach. David takes people out on fishing, surfing, and snorkeling adventures. Fishing trip US$50 per hr. A trip to Coiba is US$280 or US$50 per person. A surfing trip to Cébaco is US$200 for up to 10 people. David also has a taxi service; a trip to Soná is US$30. As his cell phone rarely works, it's best to use email.

Laundromat: 20m from the main road toward Playa Estero. Two washing machines under a shelter. US$1. Open 24hr.

Police: Across the street from Rolo's, in the heart of town.

Internet Access: Big World Villas, in town across the street for the turn off for Playa Estero. The office for a nearby real estate development lets people use its satellite Wi-Fi connection. Bring your laptop. Free. Available 10am-6pm.

▚ ACCOMMODATIONS

There are more than a dozen places to stay in this small town. Most accommodations are located along the road to Playa Estero. For travelers on a tight budget, there are a few reasonably priced dorm rooms (US$10). Those looking for more seclusion and comfort can get excellent lodgings for US$40-50. Most places are operated by foreigners, so English is widely spoken. From December through March, reservations are recommended.

▨ **Oasis Surf Camp.** From town, take the road to Playa Estero all the way to the end; it's across a small stream that you can cross in a car, except at high tide. A series of removed *cabañas* are strewn across an extensive black sand beach. There is a volleyball court, a communal area with satellite TV and Wi-Fi, and a restaurant serving exquisite Italian food. Every *cabaña* has its own thatch *ranchito* out front. Surfboard rentals US$10-15. Surfing classes US$25 per hr. Singles US$15; doubles US$25; triples US$45; room for 6 US$70. US$10 for A/C. Prices rise in high season. Cash only. ❷

▨ **Hibiscus Garden** (☎6615 6097; www.hibiscusgarden.com), a 7min. drive outside town down a dirt road (follow the signs). A series of beautiful new buildings lining a tranquil bay. Rooms combine chic style with natural wooden touches. For their impeccable style and quality, they're a great deal. Shared kitchen available. Breakfast US$3-5. Dinner US$7-10. Slow internet available. Shuttle service into town round-trip US$3.50; 3 or more US$1.50 per person. Singles US$15; doubles US$25. Large double with its own porch, A/C, and private bath US$39. Cash only. ❷

La Buena Vida (☎6635 1895; www.labuenavida.biz), in town 50m before the road to Playa Estero. A young American couple has 3 *cabañas* and a restaurant. Though a bit pricier than the other options in town, you won't find attention to detail and craftsmanship like this for a better price anywhere. All the finishes were done by the couple; it's apparent that they've put a lot of love into their business. Detached private rooms have private baths, A/C, and hot water. Rooms US$55-75. ❺

Boarder's Paradise, next door to La Buena Vida and operated by the same people. One of the best deals in town. There are just 2 rooms, each with 2 beds; there's a good chance you'll have the place to yourself, especially in the off-season. They have a communal kitchen and clean shared baths with hot water. Their restaurant is worth the few extra dollars, so stop by for a hearty bowl of fruit topped with yogurt and homemade granola (US$5). Rooms US$10 per night. Cash only. ❷

Campin' (☎6579 1504), along the road to Playa Estero; head down the small driveway marked "Campin" just after the turn off for Los Piebes. After turning right, turn right again at the 2 CDs hanging on the post. Someone from the Camarena family will most likely be there to great you. This extraordinarily friendly family opens up their rustic home to backpackers and campers. The bathroom is a tiny building made from palm leaves;

you'll have to bathe from a bucket. The cute, old mother cooks dinner for a few dollars. Camping US$3 per person; thatched hut US$5 per person. Cash only. ❶

Cabañas Rolo (☎6598 9926), at the end of the road in town. One of the most popular places for surfers. A surfer himself, the owner Rolo is also one of the most influential people in the community, constantly fighting to fend off development and preserve the laid-back environment. Clean dorm rooms have fans and outdoor shared baths. There is a communal kitchen and plenty of hammocks. Rolo also arranges reasonably priced tours in a safe, comfortable boat. Dorms US$10; doubles US$40; triples US$45. Cash only. ❷

Surfer's Paradise (☎6709 1037). Take the 3rd right along the road to Playa Estero. This spot, situated on a bluff overlooking the best break in town, has the best views by far. They also offer the best access to the break and an easy walk to a good beach. As of summer 2009, this accommodation was in the process of being remodeled. The basic rooms come with A/C and baths. Shared rooms US$15 per person; private rooms US$22. Cash only. ❷

▶ FOOD

For a small fishing town with a few surfers, Santa Catalina offers impressive cuisine, with everything from seafood to pizza. Entrees are reasonably priced. Many of the hotels cook decent meals. By law, places have to close by 10pm; establishments more removed, like those along the road to Playa Estero, often disregard this rule when there's a crowd. There is one small grocery store with minimal offerings, **Mini-Super Elisa,** at the turn off for Playa Estero in town, below Hotel Costa America. (Open daily 7am-9:30pm.)

▨ **Los Pibes.** From the road to Playa Estero, follow the sign at the 2nd right. The Argentinian owner grills up burgers and other savory delights, served at open-air tables under a small roof. Non-stop surfing videos to entertain the crowd. Try the famous #3 burger, with bacon, cheese, and peppers (US$6). Fish special US$7-9. He'll also grill up your day's catch for free. National beers US$1. Open 6:30-10pm. Cash only. ❷

Donde Viancka, along the road to Playa Estero before the turn off for Los Pibes. Viancka, the bubbly former Panamanian surfing champ, serves delicious fresh seafood caught in the waters offshore. Vegetarian options available. Entrees US$5-7. Open daily in low season 2-10pm, in high season earlier for breakfast. Cash only. ❷

Pizzeria Jammin. From the road to Playa Estero, take the 2nd right. Pizza cooked in a wood-burning oven brings gringos and other expats here by the dozen. They have a few ranchitos out on a lawn and a lively area under the main roof where people hang out until late. The hammocks are perfect for sleeping off the booze. Pizza US$5-8. Open 4-10pm or later. Cash only. ❷

The Dive, just before the end of the main road, in front of Rolo's. The newest spot in town is a great place to grab a beer and meet other travelers. Beers are a bit steep (US$2), but they come with a shot. Drink up, since closing time is early. They also serve good tacos, burritos, and other Mexican food for US$3-5, with plenty of vegetarian options. Open until 10pm. Cash only. ❷

Restaurante Tropical Beach, on the main road from Soná, 60m up from the beach in an unmarked building advertising fresh fruit and vegetables. A popular spot with locals and backpackers alike. Delicious típico. You can get 2 small whole fried fish for just US$2. Open 7am-8pm. Cash only. ❶

◉ SURFING

There are five breaks within walking distance of Santa Catalina. The most famous break, known simply as **La Punta,** is a rocky break left of the town's main beach. You can get there by going left from town or by going right from

Surfer's Paradise. **Playa Estero** is a long sandy beach with intermediate waves, good for beginning surfers. To get there, take the dirt road left from the main road all the way to the end; it's about a 30min. walk. Left along the beach from Estero is **Punta Brava.** Between Estero and La Punta and below Surfer's Paradise is **Indicador,** another rocky break. **Punta Roca** is right of the town's main beach.

DAYTRIPS FROM SANTA CATALINA

ISLA COIBA. The gem of Panama's Pacific Coast, Isla Coiba, named a **UNESCO World Heritage site** in 2004, is home to the best snorkeling, diving, and fishing in Panama. Coiba is a tropical paradise, almost completely untouched by humans, thanks to the fact that until recently it was a notorious penal colony (think *Lord of the Flies*); the most violent and undesirable were sent to the island, and the name Coiba struck fear in the hearts of Panamanians. Today there are only four prisoners remaining on the island. Don't worry—not only are they far from the ANAM cabins, they're also probably the most laid-back prisoners you've ever met, employed to maintain the island and sell crafts and fruit to tourists. There are three trails on the island. The **observatory trail** starts at the main beach and leads to a lookout point less than an hour away. **Sendero (Monkey Trail)** is about an hour-long hike, and the new **Sendero del Parque (Park Trail)** is a 3hr. trek across the island. You need a boat to access all but the observatory trail. Tourism is just starting to pick up there; few services exist on the island, and it's expensive to get to. On the island, there are a series of recently renovated **cabins** with A/C operated by ANAM. They charge US$20 per night in addition to the US$20 entry fee. *(Leave from Puerto Mutis or Santa Catalina. From Puerto Mutis, you may be able to arrange a fishing boat, but you will most likely need to hire a private boat. Sr. Camarena (☎ 999 8103) charges US$135 per day plus gas, which runs around US$100 each way. In Santa Catalina, there are a number of tour organizers that charge around US$50 per person per day for a group of 8. To find a group, call in advance to see if they have any trips going out. Your best chances are on weekends and during the high season (Dec.-Mar.). See Santa Catalina Practical Information, p. 600, for outfitters.)*

AZUERO PENINSULA

The Azuero Peninsula is Panama's heartland. It is the home of *típico* music, the *pollera* (traditional Panamanian dress), and Panama's grandest fiestas, which involve bullfighting, drinking, traditional music, drinking, religious processions, and drinking. The peninsula is still heavily agrarian, with large green pastures filled with herds of cattle that frequently impede the flow of traffic. Many people travel by horse, the men often wear *guayaberas* (traditional 4-pocket shirts) and old-style straw hats, and the biggest crowd on a Saturday night is at the local cockfight. When a festival is not taking place—which doesn't seem to happen often—travelers are lured by the natural attractions. The peninsula has over 270km of mostly undeveloped beaches, perfect for seclusion in the sun. Off Isla Iguana, the snorkeling and diving is top-notch; Playa Venao has world-class surfing; thousands of sea turtles nest on Isla Cañas; and in a country known for its fishing, the nearby waters are believed to be among the best. The towns of interest—Chitré, Las Tablas and Pedasí—all lie on the eastern side of the peninsula and are linked by the Carretera Nacional, which branches off the Interamerican Hwy. at Divisa. Santiago is farther west along the highway, inland from the peninsula, and halfway between David and Panama City.

CHITRÉ

The largest town on the Azuero Peninsula (pop. 42,467), Chitré itself doesn't offer much, but it's an important jumping off point for nearby villages, where you can watch locals make traditional crafts, taste some scrumptious local bread, or, if you time it right, party until the sun rises. Many travelers continue farther down the peninsula to Las Tablas and from there visit the endless expanses of unexplored Pacific beach. Chitré explodes during the Fiesta Patronal de San Juan on June 24th, to celebrate the feast day of John the Baptist. They close all the main streets for a seemingly endless procession of horses, bands, and icons of the saint, all the while carousing and dancing to live music.

▉ TRANSPORTATION

The Carretera Nacional cuts right through the city center, making Chitré an excellent transportation hub.

Buses: Leave from a station 15min. south of town. To town, taxis run US$1.50, local buses US$0.15. **Tuasa** (☎996 2661) operates buses to **Panama City** (4hr., every 1½hr. 2:45am-6pm, US$7.50) via **Penonomé** (1½hr., US$4). Other buses go to: **Aguadulce** (1hr., every 20min. 6am-5:40pm, US$2.50) via **Divisa** (30min., US$1.25); **Las Tablas** (40min., every 10min. 6am-9pm, US$1.25) via **Guararé** (30min., US$1); **Monagre** (25min., every 40min. 6am-6:30pm, US$1); **Ocú** (1hr., every 30min. 6am-6:30pm, US$2.50); **Parita** (15min., every 20min. 6am-6pm, US$0.70); **Santiago** (1¼hr., every 30min. 4am-6:30pm, US$2.30); **Tonosí** (2hr., every 1½hr. 10am-4pm, US$4). Some buses run less frequently on Su and holidays, so check in advance. Local buses south to **Los Santos** (5min., US$0.25) and west to **La Arena** (5min., US$0.25) can be found at the bus terminal and in town on C. Manuel Correa, 2 blocks north of the cathedral. Any buses heading in those directions will drop you off for the same fare.

Taxis: (☎996 8700). Fares around town run US$1-2.

AZUERO PENINSULA

⊞ 🄸 ORIENTATION AND PRACTICAL INFORMATION

All cars and buses arrive in Chitré from the west along the **Carretera Nacional,** (Highway 2), which becomes **Calle Manuel Correa** as it comes into town. Near the center of town, C. Manuel Correa intersects **Avenida Herrera** (or **Avenida Central**), which runs north-south. Just about everything in town can be found along these two roads. Two blocks south of the intersection is the **cathedral,** next to the **parque.** Three blocks farther south, Av. Central bends southeast onto **Los Santos** and **Las Tablas.** To reach the *parque* from the bus terminal, turn left out the front parking lot and continue 500m. Turn left on the Carretera Nacional, passing by the hospital on the right. About 200m farther, take a right at the fork and the cathedral and *parque* are three blocks up.

Tourist Office: ATP (☎974 4532; www.visitpanama.com), near the industrial park south of the Carretera Nacional in La Arena. Take any bus for La Arena and tell the driver you are going to IPAT (the old name for ATP), or ask for Parque Industrial. Open M-F 8am-4pm. **ANAM** (☎996 7675), northeast of town near the Universidad de Panama. Local buses stop at the university; get off just before at Mini-super Zheng. It's on the left. Open M-F 8am-4pm.

Bank: Citibank, on Plaza de Las Banderas, 1 block west and 1 block north of the *parque.* **ATM.** Open M-F 8am-pm. Sa 9am-noon.

Laundry: Lavamático Azuero (☎996 7411), 1 block east and 3 blocks south of the cathedral, just off Carretera Central east of town. Wash US$0.50. Dry US$1. Full service US$2.50. Open M-Sa 7:30am-7pm, Su 7:30am-1pm.

Police: Policia Nacional: (☎996 2810), between Chitré and La Arena on the Carretera Nacional.

Pharmacy: Farmacia Universal (☎996 4608), across the street from the cathedral. Open daily 8am-8pm.

Hospital: Hospital Cecilio Castillero (☎996 4444), along the Carretera Nacional east of town. Follow Av. Central south behind the cathedral and take a left at the Carretera Nacional; it's 100m up on the left. Open 7:30am-3:30pm. Open 24hr. for emergencies.

Internet Access: Sanchi Computer Internet, (☎996 2134). Half a block north of the cathedral on Av. Central. US$0.50 per hr. Open 8am-midnight.

Post Office: Heading west on C. Manuel Correa, walk past the Museo de Herrera (on the left) and take a right on the next street. Its inside the Cable and Wireless building on the right. Open M-F 7am-6pm, Sa 7am-5pm. **Postal Code: 0601.**

🄵 ACCOMMODATIONS

Hotels in Chitré aren't anything to write home about, and you'll have a hard time finding anything cheaper than US$15. Prices rise during festivals, so it's a good idea to call ahead. Most of the hotels crowd around the center of town in front of the cathedral.

Hotel Bali Panama (☎996 4620; www.balipanama.com), half a block north of the cathedral. Not the cheapest in town, but definitely the best value. The rooms lack character and could use a bit more lighting, but come with cable TV, private baths with hot water, desks, and A/C. Wi-Fi. English and Indonesian spoken. Singles US$20; doubles US$27; triples US$34. ❸

Hotel Versalles (☎996 4422; www.hotelversalles.com), a 15min. walk west of town on the Carretera Nacional. Walk or take the La Arena bus (US$0.15). A tropical, festive, white-washed motel. Rooms open onto a garden with beautiful flowers and a pool. Wi-Fi, hot baths, and cable TV in all the rooms. Singles can sleep 2 if you don't mind sharing a bed. Singles US$33; doubles US$50. ❹

Pensión Central (☎992 0059). Might be the cheapest place in town. Rooms have A/C and private baths, but are dark, dreary, and a tad dirty. The Wi-Fi only works in the lobby. Solo travelers are better off elsewhere, but it's a good deal for groups. Doubles US$18; triples US$23. ❸

🍴 FOOD

Food in Chitré is decent and cheap. Nearby La Arena is famous for its bread, so *panaderías* are a common sight. For groceries, visit **Supercentro Willians**, half a block north of C. Manuel Correa on Av. Central. (Open daily 6:30am-9pm.)

- 🍴 **Restaurante Chiquita** (☎996 2411), half a block north of C. Manuel Correa on Av. Central. This restaurant's offerings are anything but *chiquita*. It's basically a long counter, with stations for *típico*, bread, pizza, sweets, and ice cream. It's easy to get addicted to their fruity empanadas (US$0.30), baked fresh throughout the day. Open daily 5am-10:30pm. Cash only. ❶

- **Restaurante El Prado** (☎996 4620), inside Hotel Bali Panama. Globalization at its best, this restaurant is the product of a Panamanian-Indonesian marriage, serving Indonesian specialties with local spices mixed in. Meals aren't huge. Try the *sate ayam* (chicken kebabs with peanut sauce; US$3.50). Open daily 7am-8pm. Cash only. ❷

- **La Estrella** (☎996 7811), on the corner across the street from the cathedral. Similar to Chiquita, but with a greater emphasis on *típico*. Its central location and cheap prices make it popular with the locals. Open daily 6am-9pm. Cash only. ❶

- **Restaurante El Aire Libre** (☎996 3639), on the opposite side of the *parque* from the cathedral. Friendly restaurant with a wide variety of *típico*. Fish US$4-5. Sandwiches US$1-2. Entrees US$2-4. Open 6:30am-10pm. Cash only. ❷

👁 SIGHTS

IGLESIA SAN JUAN BAUTISTA. The cathedral in town features a beautiful gilded mahogany altar. On the 24th of June, it's the center of festivities for the feast day of John the Baptist. *(On Av. Central.)*

EL MUSEO DE HERRERA. The town's museum has exhibits on the archaeology, history, and traditions of the Herrera province. *(☎966 0077. On Av. Manuel Correa, 2 blocks west of Av. Central and on Plaza de Las Banderas. Open Tu-Sa 8am-4pm.)*

🔀 DAYTRIP FROM CHITRÉ

GUARARÉ. For a full dose of traditional Azuero music, stop by this otherwise sleepy town on September 24th for the the **Festival de la Mejorana**. The festival features many traditional instruments, including the accordion, tambourines, and the *mejorana* (a small guitar-like instrument made from mango wood). Guararé's **Semana Santa** festivities are more intricate than most. Dancing and singing form the backdrop for an Easter story reenactment, culminating in a bonfire where an effigy of Judas is burned amid great celebration. If you happen to be there when Guararé returns to its usual state of tranquility, visit **Casa-Museo Manuel F. Zárate**, former home of the festival's creator. It is filled with *polleras*, masks, costumes, and a photo of the chosen *reína* (queen) from each year of the festival's 59 years. *(Take a bus to Las Tablas, which leave every 30min. (US$1); and ask to be dropped off. From the road, take a left; the main plaza is 2 blocks down.)*

PEDASÍ

A small fishing town in the southeast corner of the Azuero Peninsula, Pedasí (pop. 3620) is a great place to spend a few days. Despite its small-town charm and quiet *parque central*, most people come here to fish, hoping for the catch of a lifetime. Even for the least experienced fishermen, it's a thrill: there's a good chance you'll come back with a fish half your size. The town is the birthplace of Panama's first female president, Mireya Moscoso. Pedasí has been a well-kept secret until recently, but today the word is getting out, and the town has seen millions of investment dollars pour in. Fortunately, the development hasn't yet spoiled the town—the only indication of it is the billboards along the road.

Pedasí is walking distance from miles of empty of Pacific beaches, and is the main jumping-off point for the picturesque Isla Iguana. Good surfing is another 30min. farther at Playa Venado, which has some of the best waves in the Americas. Even farther is Isla Cañas, where thousands of turtles go to lay eggs from July to November.

⟲ TRANSPORTATION

Buses: Buses to **Las Tablas** head up Av. Central (40min., every 25min. 6:30am-5pm, US$2). Note that not every bus from Las Tablas to Cañas passes through Pedasí. One bus passes through to **Cañas** around 7am and returns at 10am; another passes around 2pm and returns are 3pm. These buses pass by the entrance to **Playa Venado,** but stop short of Isla Cañas (not to be confused with the town of Cañas).

Taxis: Go to nearby beaches (US$2.50), to Playa Venado (US$15-20), and to the port for Isla Iguana (US$20-25).

⊿ ⁊ ORIENTATION AND PRACTICAL INFORMATION

From Las Tablas, the Carretera Nacional hugs the east coast of the peninsula for 41km before entering Pedasí, where it becomes **Avenida Central,** the main north-south strip in town. The **parque central** is one block east of the main road. Most streets have signs, making it perhaps the best-labeled town in the country.

Tourist Office: IPAT/ATP (☎995 2339). Take the 2nd left after entering town; it's in a barely marked 2-story building on the right on the road to Playa El Arenal. Open M-F 8am-4pm.

Tours: Dive-N-Fish Pedasi (☎995 2894; www.dive-n-fishpanama.com), on Av. Central behind Pedasí Sports Club. A variety of services from fishing, spear fishing, and scuba diving to kayaking and horseback riding. Spearfishing trip US$85 per person (2 person minimum). Kayaks US$40 per day. Horseback riding US$55 per day.

Bank: Banco Nacional, just before town in the large white building on the right. **24hr. ATM.** Open M-F 8am-3pm, Sa 9am-noon. Plan ahead, as people withdraw cash to pay the fishermen and the machines sometimes run out.

Police: (☎995 2122), before the Banco Nacional building just outside of town, on the right.

Pharmacy: Centro Commercial Pedasí (☎995 2182), on Av. Central across from Dim's Hostel. Open M-F 7am-9:30pm. Sa-Su 7am-10pm.

Medical Services: Centro de Salud, C. Las Tablas (☎995 2127). Take a left off Av. Central. It's 3 blocks down past the *parque.* Open daily 7am-3pm; 7am-7pm for emergencies. After hours, seek medical attention in Las Tablas.

Internet Access: Los Macaraquenos #2, C. Agustin Moscoso (☎6788 4352). Take a left off Av. Central; it's 10m up on the left. Internet US$1 per hr. Open M-Sa 8am-8pm, Su 8am-2pm.

Post Office: (☎995 2221). Turn left after Centro Commercial Pedasí on to Av. Central. Open M-F 8am-3pm, Sa 8am-1pm. **Postal Code:** 0749.

ACCOMMODATIONS

In the past few years, the number of accommodations in Pedasí has doubled, and it seems that prices have followed suit. During Carnaval, most places hike up their prices, and you have to call far in advance to get room. The cheapest, but definitely not the safest, place to sleep any time of the year is on the beach; be sure to bring a tent and mosquito net.

Dim's Hostel (☎995 2303). One of the original spots and still the one of the coolest. Rooms are on the 2nd floor of a building decorated with logs and branches. The backyard has a thatch hut built around a tree, and although it may look like an unsuspecting spot, it's apparently ground zero for millions of dollars in local real estate deals. All rooms have A/C and hot water baths. Breakfast included. Free Wi-Fi. Singles US$33; each additional person US$15. Cash only. ❹

Hotel Residencial Pedasí (☎995 2490 or 6747 5363), on Av. Central, on the left as your enter town. Clean, brightly painted rooms open onto a large lawn with a few hammocks. Rooms have A/C, hot-water baths, and Wi-Fi. Singles US$25-30; doubles US$30-40; triples US$50. Cash only. ❸

Hostal Doña Maria (☎995 2916; www.hostaldonamaria.com). Charmingly decorated rooms with perfectly upholstered furniture. The best part is the large backyard, which has an open-air *cabaña*, hammocks, lounge chairs, and a BBQ for grilling your day's catch. Rooms have hot water baths and TVs. Breakfast US$5. Free Wi-Fi. Singles US$39; doubles US$44; triples US$54. Cash only. ❹

Hospedaje Moscoso (☎995 2203), on Av. Central just past C. Las Tablas. Sra. Moscoso is a relative of the former president Mireya Moscoso. More importantly, she rents out the cheapest rooms in town. They're nothing special, but they are clean and come with all the necessary amenities, including A/C, private baths, and TVs. Rooms along the road can be a little loud. Doubles US$25; triples US$30; quads US$35. Cash only. ❸

FOOD

Restaurants pop up overnight here, but unlike with hotels, it's still possible to eat well for cheap. *Típico* is the cheapest option, but you can get fresh fish for just a little more. For groceries, visit **Centro Commercial Pedasi** on Av. Central across from Dim's Hostel. (☎995 2182. Open daily M-F 7am-9:30pm, Sa-Su 7am-10pm.) **Abernathy's** is the best fishing supplies store in town, just across from the Centro de Salud, past the *parque* on C. Las Tablas. (☎995 2779. Open daily 8am-5pm. MC/V.)

Dulcería Yely (☎995 2215), off Av. Central. Take a right on C. Ofelia Reluz. A huge assortment of fresh, delicious cakes (US$0.35). They also have renowned *flan*, cheap sandwhiches (US$1.50), and spectacular empanadas (US$0.30). Ask for the *chicheme*, a delicious sweet corn drink popular all over Panama. Open daily 8am-9pm. Cash only. ❶

Restaurante Angela (☎995 2207), on Av. Central just past Dim's Hostel. One of the original restaurants in Pedasí, Restaurante Angela serves fast, delicious, and cheap food. Granola and yogurt US$1.25. Be sure to try the day's catch. Fish US$4. Open M-Sa 7am-9pm, Su 7am-7:30pm. Cash only. ❷

Restaurante Pedasieño (☎6707 9945), next to the Accel gas station on Av. Central. A friendly spot serving great, cheap *típico*. Fast food US$2. Fish US$3.50. Open daily 6am-7pm. Cash only. ❶

Pizzeria Tiesto (☎995 2812), on the east side of the *parque*. A lovely spot with *arte-sanía*-covered walls and seating that opens up to the plaza. Pizzas (US$3-4) are a good deal. Open M and W-Su 8am-10pm. Cash only. ❷

BEACHES

Although Pedasí itself is not on the beach, it is only a few kilometers from endless expanses of secluded sandy beaches. Most people head for **Isla Iguana** or **Playa Venado,** but on the weekends these can be more crowded. If all you're looking for is a wide stretch of your own, **Playa El Toro** and **La Garita** are just 3km from town. The water isn't as sparklingly clear here as on Isla Iguana, but these beaches are cheap and accessible. A taxi will charge you US$3 to get there, and if you want a pick-up you will have to arrange it,. The walk is also an easy 45min. jaunt.

FISHING

The waters around Pedasí are a goldmine of wahoo, tuna, mahi mahi, marlin, and other delicious fish. People come from all around the world to fish off the coast. **Pedasifishing.com** arranges complete tours, while **Dive-N-Fish Pedasí** has a wide array of day trips. If you want to spearfish, you'll have to book through one of them. A cheaper option is to go directly through local fisherman. They will take you out for US$50 per day, plus gas, which usually runs another US$50. You can comfortably fit 5 people in the boat, and if you get a good catch, you'll come home with enough fish to feed you for a few days. Everyone who comes to Pedasí has their favorite fisherman, but not all of them have equipment. **Avidel** (☎6509 3783) comes highly recommended. He'll supply all the equipment and has a jeep, so he can pick you up. If you think you might get seasick, bring dramamine. It's also a good idea to bring plenty of sunscreen, snacks, and drinks because you'll probably be out all day. Make sure not to bring bananas on board, as the superstitious fishermen believe it's bad luck.

DAYTRIPS FROM PEDASÍ

ISLA IGUANA. Pedasí's big draw is nearby **Refugio de Vida Silvestre Isla Iguana,** a diving, snorkeling, and fishing hotspot 7km from Pedasí's nearest beach. The island has two pristine beaches with crystal water, and lies within feet of one of the largest coral mass on the Pacific Coast, which covers an impressive 16 hectares. The rest of the coast is made up of dark rocks that look like baked sandcastles. The island is home to huge flocks of birds; a recent study has identified at least 20 different species. Boats let you off on the larger **Playa El Cirial,** where you pay to enter. Boats can also bring you 200m to the opposite side of the island to **Playita El Faro,** a smaller, more secluded beach with better snorkeling. There are two short paths, teeming with iguanas (hence the island's name). Those paths are surrounded by occassional bomb holes left over from the days when it was occupied by the US navy during WWII. The new **ANAM visitor center** has a pleasant view of the beach below; it also has information about the local plants and animals and a good map of the island. *(Hotels in Pedasí can arrange transportation to the island. The ANAM park ranger on the island, Analio, is also more than happy to bring you over. ☎6654 4716. The price of transportation to the island is US$50 (up to 8 people). The boats all leave from Playa El Arenal (also called El Bajadero), a 5min. car ride from the gas station at the northern end of Pedasí or a 45min. walk. From the beach it's a 20min. ride by boat. As soon as you disembark on the island, you will be asked for the entry fee; US$10, Panamanians US$4. There is an outhouse and a roof over a concrete floor where you can string up a hammock or post a tent; US$10, Panamians US$4.)*

PLAYA VENADO. Thirty minutes southeast of Pedasí, "Playa Venao" (as the locals call it) has one of the best surfing breaks in all of Panama. Despite its fame, Playa Venado remains uncrowded. Even on a weekend there are only a few dozen people around, and there is almost no infrastructure to speak of. Venado's waves are big (2-3m, breaking both ways), so casual swimming is sometimes impossible. The 1.5km cresent of dark sand is flanked by two land points and backed by endless green hills, making for a stunning drive in.

At of 2009, there were no formal accommodations on the beach. Many choose to camp out in their cars or along the beach. If you choose to string up a hammock, make sure to bring a mosquito net. **Restaurante Playa Venao ❷** is along the beach at the entrance, and serves cheap fish (US$3) with rice and beans or fries. You can also get *sancocho* (US$2.50), a chicken, yucca, and veg-etable stew. (Open daily 6:30am-9pm.) About 1km up the road toward Cañas is **⬛Hospedaje Eco Venao ❷**, on top of a green hill. They have a volleyball court, an outdoor kitchen, and a game room. Bunked dormitories filled with surfers are surrounded by hammocks. You'll sleep well on the thick mattresses knowing that the hostel is part of a reforestation project for the surrounding 346 acres. (☎832 0530; www.venao.com. Dorms US$11; private rooms with shared bath US$27.50; private *cabañas* US$35. Campsite US$5 per person.) *(Buses from Las Tablas to Cañas are infrequent; there are 2 per day (30min., US$2) that arrive in Pedasí between 7-8am and 2-3pm. Ask to get off at Venao. It's a 5min. walk from the road to the beach. For current info ask at the gas station. The easiest way to get there is to hire a taxi (US$15), or hitchhike, though Let's Go does not recommend hitchhiking.)*

ISLA DE CAÑAS. West of Pedasí, Playa Venado, and the town of Cañas lies Isla de Cañas, an island off the southern coast of the Azuero. The sugarcane-cov-ered island is scarcely populated. You arrive on the island's north side, a stone's

throw from the mainland; the main beach is on the opposite side, a short 5min. walk away. It is on this beautiful 14km beach where five of the world's eight species of sea turtles come to lay eggs. The reproductive antics climax in **arriba-das,** when more than 10,000 turtles hit the beach in just two or three nights to lay eggs. The main egg-laying season is July-November; most of the *arribadas* occur in October. Apart from the *arribadas*, there are many nights in the egg-laying season when 100 or more turtles spawn on the beach. The island is managed cooperatively by ANAM and the local community, which subsists mainly on turtle egg sales. The community has a nursery program: 1.5km of protected land on the beach means that about 15,000 nests are left untouched. The rest of the eggs are given to those who work with the program for profit.

Since the turtles are only around at night, you'll probably have to stay on the island. Unfortunately, the only accommodation is pretty unappealing. On the walk toward the beach, there is a **yellow house ❶** on the left. Ask for Neri Perez, who rents two bare rooms in an unattractive concrete structure behind her house. Each room has four beds and a private bath. (☎6918 3204. US$5 per person, with A/C US$10 per person.) A better option is to bring a tent, but high tide makes the beach a bad campsite. Boats let you off at an unmarked **restaurant,** where you will often find loud music and a few drunk men. Fulvilla, the cook, serves whatever they have—usually you'll have the option of beef, pork, or some sort of seafood. (☎6971 2957. US$2.50-4, including rice and a small salad. Open 6am-10pm.) She can also get in touch with a local **tour guide** (US$10-15). The **ANAM office,** in the middle of the island, can also arrange tours. Open M-F 8am-4pm. They answer the public phone in front of the office (☎995 8002). *(The easiest transportation is to take a taxi from Pedasí (US$20-25 each way). Alternatively, take a bus from Las Tablas toward Tonosí and get off at the entrance to the dirt road for the port. It is a 3km walk along the road; some travelers report that you can catch a ride from a passing car (though Let's Go does not recommend hitchhiking). There are 3 buses a day from Las Tablas directly to the port, leaving at 6, 10am and 2pm, and returning at 7:30, 11:45am, and 3pm; all these buses pass through the town of Cañas. Check with the bus drivers in Las Tablas for the latest schedule. Buses pass through Pedasí for the town of Cañas (see Pedasí Transportation, p. 609). Island admission US$10, for Panamanians US$4. The ANAM office is closed on the weekends.)*

CHIRIQUÍ PROVINCE

Located on the southwest extreme of Panama, Chiriquí is the Central American traveler's dream: enticing rainforests, endless beaches, and sky-scraping volcanoes. Choose your own kilometer of beach on Playa Las Lajas or head to the Golfo de Chiriquí and see some impressive wildlife. The northern highlands have striking views of Volcano Barú, the highest point in Panama. In these cloud-covered hills above the valley hold hot springs, lakes, and the elusive quetzal. Remote villages, only a few hours north from the provincial capital **David**, sit at the base of gorgeous mountain trails. Even if you're not a hiker, Boquete and **Cerro Punta** are pleasant spots to spend a few days. After a grueling day outside, you can sit down to world-renowned coffee, mounds of strawberries, and locally-grown beef. *Chiricanos* are proud of their land and their origins, and it's easy to see why.

DAVID

David (pop. 124,500) is the second largest city in Panama and the capital of the rich commercial and manufacturing province of Chiriquí. Hot and humid year-round, with impressively few tourist attractions for its size, David functions for most as a pit stop to Bocas del Toro, the Chiriquí highlands, and San José, Costa Rica. Fitness gyms, low-rider trucks, and a Top-40 radio station hint at the town's cosmopolitan aspirations, though its nightlife and cuisine pales in comparison to Panama City. David wakes from its slumber for 10 days in mid-March for the rowdy festival of its patron saint, La Feria de San José. Visitors from other provinces and Costa Rica join to celebrate.

TRANSPORTATION

David is the transportation hub of the region. The large, bustling bus station has bathrooms, restaurants, internet, and luggage storage.

Flights: Aeropuerto Enrique Malek, 4km south of the city. **Aeroperlas** (☎721 1195), on C. Central between Av. A and Av. B Este. Open M-F 8am-5pm, Sa 8am-3pm. Flights to **Bocas del Toro** (30min.; M, W, F 11:20am; US$52) and **Panama City** (1hr.; M-F 7:55am, 12:55, 5:35pm; US$98). **Air Panama** (☎721 0841) on Av. 2 E and C.D N. Open M-F 8am-5pm, Sa 8am-3pm. Flights to: **Panama City** (1hr.; M-F 7:45am, 1:15, 5:15pm, Sa-Su 10:30am, 5:15pm; US$98); **San Jose** (45min.; M, W, F 10:30am; US$175).

Buses: North of Av. Obaldía on Av. 2E. From the main terminal, buses leave for: **Almirante** (4hr., every 30min. 3:30am-7pm, US$7); **Boquete** (1hr., every 30min. 5am-7pm, US$1.50); **Cerro Punta** (2hr., every 15min. 5:30am-8pm, US$2.90) via **Volcán** (1½hr., US$2.50); **Changuinola** (4½hr., every 30min. 3:15am-6:30pm, US$8) via **Chiriquí Grande** (2½hr., US$5); **Divisa** (3½hr., US$7.85); **Panama City** (7hr., every hr. 5:45am-8pm, US$12.60; express 6hr., 10:45pm and midnight, US$15) via **Santiago** (3hr., US$7.50); **Penonomé** (5hr., US$9.90); **Puerto Armuelles** (1½hr., every 15min. 3:45am-10:30pm, US$3) via the **Costa Rican border at Paso Canoas** (1¼hr., US$2.25); **San José, CRA** (8hr., daily 8:30am, US$16). **PADAFRONT** (☎774 9205) has a terminal on Av. 1E (9 de Enero), just south of Av. Obaldía. Buses go to **Panama City** (7hr., every 1½hr. 7:30am-7:45pm, US$12.50; express 6hr., 10:45pm and midnight, US$15).

Car Rental: Most major rental agencies have offices at the airport 4km outside of the city. **Budget** (☎775 5597; open M-Sa 7am-7pm, Su 8am-11am) and **Hertz** (☎775 8471) next to the Super 99 in San Mateo. **National** (☎721 0000) and **Thrifty** (☎721 2477) have better rates online. Cars from US$20 per day.

⚡🛈 ORIENTATION AND PRACTICAL INFORMATION

David is laid out in a grid, cut off from the *parque central* by the busy diagonal **Av. Obaldía** and to the northwest by the **Interamerican Highway.** North-south *avenidas* are numbered with *oeste* (west) and *este* (east) designations, starting on either side of **Avenida Central.** East-west *calles* have similiar *norte* (north) and *sur* (south) designations with letters increasing to the north and south from **Calle Central.** Many of the streets are now labeled by names instead of numbers—for example, Av. 3E is now Av. Bolivar, Av. 1 E is 9 de Enero, and C. A Sur is called Ruben D. Samudio, but locals stick to the old alphanumeric combinations. Few of the roads are actually labeled. The *parque central,* **Parque Cervantes,** lies between Av. 3/4 E. and C. A/B N. Most services are south of the *parque,* while the bus terminal and most of the shopping are north.

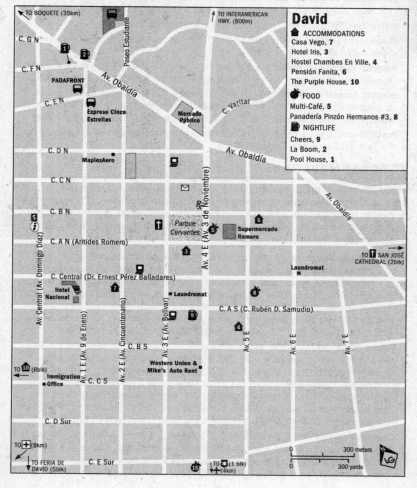

David

🏠 ACCOMMODATIONS
Casa Vego, **7**
Hotel Iris, **3**
Hostel Chambes En Ville, **4**
Pensión Fanita, **6**
The Purple House, **10**

🍎 FOOD
Multi-Café, **5**
Panadería Pinzón Hermanos #3, **8**

🎵 NIGHTLIFE
Cheers, **9**
La Boom, **2**
Pool House, **1**

Tourist Office: ATP (☎775 2839), on C. Central between C. 5E and Av. 6E. Has some maps. Little English spoken. Open M-F 7:30am-3:30pm. **ANAM** (☎775 3163), on the road to the airport. Turn left onto Av. 8E at the Delta gas station. The main office for Parque Internacional La Amistad and Volcán Barú. May be able to arrange a guide at some of the ranger stations. English spoken. Open M-F 8am-4pm.

Consulate: Costa Rica C. B N. and Av. 1 E. (☎774 1923), 2 blocks west of the *parque*, across the street from the Policlinica on the 2nd floor. Open M-F 8am-12pm and 1-3pm.

Bank: Citibank, Av. Central and C. B N. (☎775 3988). Open M-F 8am-3pm, Sa 9am-noon. **24hr. ATM. Western Union,** inside Supermercado Romero in San Mateo. Open M-Sa 9am-1pm and 2-6pm.

Luggage storage: At the bus station. US$0.50-2 per piece. Open 6am-8pm.

Laundromat: Lavamático Los Primos (☎6908 3926), C. E N. between Av. Central and Av. 1 E. Wash US$0.75; dry US$0.75; soap US$0.25. Open M-Sa 7am-8pm, Su 9am-8pm.

Police: (☎775 2210), on C. F Sur and Av. 4 Este (Av. 3 de Noviembre).

Pharmacy: Farmacia Revilla (☎777 8515), on the northeast corner of the *parque*. Open daily 7am-11pm. AmEx/MC/V.

Hospital: Hospital Chiriquí, C. Central and Av. 3 Oeste (☎774 0128). A modern, private hospital. Non-emergency service M-F 9:30am-1:30pm and 2:30-6:30pm, Sa 9am-1pm.

Internet Access: Speed Explorer, C. Central (☎730 3541), between Av. 2 E and Av. 3 E. Internet US$0.75 per hr. Open M-Sa 8am-midnight, Su 10am-11pm. **Río Internet Cafe,** on Av. Bolívar between C. D N. and C. C N. Internet US$0.75 per hr. Open 24hr.

Post Office: C. C N. (☎775 4261), 1 block north of the *parque.* Open M-F 7am-5:30pm, Sa 7am-4:30pm. **Postal Code:** 0426.

◤ ACCOMMODATIONS

There are numerous sleeping options in David, especially around the *parque central.* They range from expensive hotels to cheap *pensiones.* The two good hostels in town are both a bit of a hike from the town center in safer, more residential neighborhoods. Make reservations in advance if visiting during March, when the city's festival takes place.

Purple House Hostel (☎774 4059 or 6428 1488; www.purplehousehostel.com), on C. C Sur and Av. 6 Oeste. True to its name, this homey building is completely covered in purple—even the staff wears purple clothing. It's a popular spot for people passing through, and offers Wi-Fi, TV, free coffee, a book exchange, a public kitchen, cheap laundry service, luggage storage, and huge binders of information about destinations around Panama. The friendly American owner is a good source of info herself. Watch out for her mischievous dog, Cutsie. Dorms US$7.70; private room US$20, with A/C US$25. MC/V. ❷

Bambu Hostel (☎730 2966; www.bambuhostel.com), on C. Virgencito. With the Super 99 in San Mateo to your back, walk right and bear left at the gas station. Turn left after a junkyard and then right at the small store. Whew. A long walk from the city center and about 5min. from nearby services, but a nice place to stay if you're just passing through. The backyard pool is a great way to combat David's year-round humidity. Other amenities include free coffee, pancake mix (cook them yourself in the kitchen), Wi-Fi, and computers. Dorms US$8; private rooms with A/C US$28, with bath US$30. ❷

Chambres En Ville (☎6404 6203), Av. 5 E, between C. B and C. A Sur. A friendly family has opened up a number of rooms onto their large backyard, which is home to an outdoor public kitchen and a pool. Clean rooms sleep up to 3 and come with hot water, private baths, and Wi-Fi. Rooms US$15-25, with A/C US$20-30. Prices rise in high season. ❸

Hotel Iris (☎775 2251), on the south side of the *parque*. Iris has been around for more than 30 years, longer than most of the buildings in the area. Clean but unremarkable rooms come with hot water and TVs. Doubles US$18, with A/C US$25; triples US$25/40. MC/V. ●

Pensión Fanita (☎775 3718), on C. B N., just off Av. 5 E. A green facade masks a labyrinth of rooms, a sheltered courtyard, and an attached restaurant (*comida corriente* US$2). Conveniently located near the *parque*, this *pensión* has the cheapest rooms in David. Fan US$1. US$5 per person, with bath US$7.50, with A/C US$9. ●

🛏 FOOD

Comida típica is everywhere, but there isn't too much in the way of international cuisine aside from the occasional pizza shop or Chinese place. You can buy groceries at **Supermercado Baru**, Av. 3 Oeste and C. D N. (☎774 4344. Open M-Sa 7:30am-11pm, Su 8am-9pm. MC/V.) There is also a 24hr. **Super 99** (☎777 3694) in San Mateo with a pharmacy, bank, and several **ATMs.**

Java Juice (☎730-3794), on Av. Francisco Clark north of the bus station, and in San Mateo across from the Super 99. Great health food. On the menu are salads (US$1.60), burgers (US$1.80-3), and all-natural veggie-burgers. Amazing *batidos* (shakes) are made with 100% natural ingredients. Wi-Fi. Open M-Sa 10am-11pm, Su 10am-2pm. ●

Restaurante Multi Café (☎775 4695), on the *parque*, underneath Hotel Occidental. Very popular, very cheap *típico*. Eclectic—the food is a blend of Chinese (chicken lo mein US$1.80) and Panamanian dishes. Try *guacho*, a local soup with rice (US$1.50). Open daily 6am-10pm. AmEx/MC/V. ●

Panadería Pinzón Hermanos #3 (☎775 5194), on Av. 5E across from Pensión Costa Rica. By day a mild-mannered bakery (pastries US$0.50), by night a happening sandwich and burger joint (US$1.30-2.50), with a few *típico* options (US$1-2). Open M-Sa 7am-9pm, Su 9am-7pm. ●

Restaurante Casa Vegetariana (☎6903 4465), on C. Central and Av. 2E. Super cheap cafeteria-style vegetarian dishes. Servings US$0.30. Open M-Sa 6:45am-4pm. ●

Tambu Country (☎774 4951), on the corner of Av. 4 Este and Av. E Sur. A popular local pizza place serves all kinds of pasta, light salads, and sandwiches. Recently renovated with indoor and outdoor seating. Entrees US$4-8. Delivery available. Open daily 11am-11pm. AmEx/MC/V. ●

🎵 🎬 ENTERTAINMENT AND NIGHTLIFE

If you don't feel like hitting the dance floor, catch a movie at **Multicines Nacional,** on Av. 1 E, C. A Sur, adjacent to the Hotel Nacional. (☎774 7889. Tickets US$3.50, M-W US$2.50.)

Opium (☎775 2849), at Av. 4 Oeste and C. Miguel A. Brenes, across the street from the Crown Casino. The swankiest club in David, popular with university students. The music is loud, and covers everything from electronica and reggaeton to salsa and merengue. Wear long pants and shoes. Cover men US$5, women US$3. W ladies night; free entry 9-11pm. F university night; US$1 for students. Open W, F, Sa 9pm-4am. Cash only.

Top Place Billars (☎774 2129), on C. Miguel A. Brenes across from the Super 99. Second-floor billiards bar that consistently attracts a local crew. Drinks are cheap and pool tables plentiful. Beer US$0.60. Mixed drinks US$1. Open 11am-late. Cash only.

Crown Casino (☎775 4447), at Av. 4 Oeste and C. Miguel A. Brenes, across the street from Super 99 in San Mateo. Panamanians love to gamble, and this is the hottest spot to roll the dice. They also have a popular sports bar. Beer US$1. Open 24hr. AmEx/MC/V.

CHIRIQUÍ

✖ BORDER CROSSING AT: COSTA RICA

CHIRIQUÍ

PASO CANOAS

Unappealing Paso Canoas, on the Interamerican Highway, is the principal crossing between Panama and Costa Rica. To get to the border, take one of the frequent **buses** from David, 50km east of Paso Canoas. They may ask you to show proof of onward travel; either an onward plane or bus ticket will suffice. They also may ask for proof of sufficient funds, so you may have to show that you have at least US$300; this can be done with cash or a bank statement.

Entering Costa Rica, you first need to stop at the Panamanian **Servicio Nacional de Migración** (☎727 6508; open daily 7am-11pm), the large building in the middle of the road where the bus lets you off. They will ask to see your **passport** and the **tourist card** you received upon entering Panama. Then you must walk 100m along the road to the Costa Rican Equivalent, **Dirección General de Migración** (☎2732 2150; open 6am-10pm), where you will need to present your **passport, proof of onward travel,** and **proof of sufficient funds.** If you do not have an onward ticket from Costa Rica, you will need to buy a bus ticket, so it is best to prepare for this beforehand. For proof of funds, a bank statement with US$300 is best, though cash will also do. Entering Panama, the process is the same, but you must buy a tourist card for US$5 at the **Autoridad de Turismo** (☎727 6524; open 7am-11pm) inside the same building as immigration. Customs may ask to search your bags on either side of the border.

In Panama, the **police** are a few feet from the border. (☎727 6521.) **Bolsijeros,** identifiable by the leather purses slung across their chests, congregate around the *Migración* building on the Panamanian side and offer good rates for currency exchange. There are also numerous **ATMs.** To get to **Banco Nacional de Panamá,** turn left before the crossing and walk 50m. They have a **24hr. ATM.** (☎727 6522. Open M-F 8am-3pm, Sa 9am-noon. MC/V.) The Panamanian **post office** is on the second floor of the main building. (Open M-F 8am-5pm, Sa 8am-4pm.) On the Panamanian side, just before the border, **Tourist Travel Internet,** above Café Raúl, has Wi-Fi and computers. (☎727 7220. US$0.75 per hr. Open 8am-midnight.)

In Costa Rica, the police are just across the border. (☎2732 2402.) Next to the police building is a bank, which offers *colones* (right machine) and US dollars (left machine). On the left is the Costa Rican post office. (Open M-F 8am-noon and 1-5pm.)

There aren't many places to spend the night, but **Cabinas Familiares ❷,** tucked away across the street from the Costa Rican Migración building, has a group of rooms opening onto a surprisingly nice garden. Parking available. Rooms have private baths. (☎732 2653. Singles ¢5000; doubles ¢10,600, with A/C ¢18,000; triples ¢15,000. US dollars accepted.) There is an overabundance of *típico* and men hawking fried food and fruit. For some tasty bread and a quick escape from the bustle of the border, try **Musmanni,** a small bakery behind the Costa Rican post office. (☎2732 1782. Empanadas ¢375. Open 5am-9pm.)

BOCAS DEL TORO PROVINCE

North of Chiriquí Province, the archipelago of Bocas del Toro (pop. 89,000) gives its name to the province and capital. Drawing travelers with an entirely different siren song than its southern neighbor, Bocas del Toro doesn't promise cool temperatures or high-altitude thrills, but rather its own distinct Caribbean allure. You'll hear Spanish give way to a dense mix of English creole and indigenous languages known as *Guari-guari*. Watch rugged forests and ranchlands melt into beaches, mangroves, and mossy docks that frame island life. The banana industry made Bocas del Toro a point of entry for immigrants and money in the 19th century. Today it attracts foreigners with its natural wonders: white sand islands, coral-rich underwater views, hikes through untouched vegetation, and great surfing spots. In addition to the Ngöbe (NO-beh), Bribrí, and Naso tribes, inhabitants include a mix of Latino and Afro-Caribbean peoples. Many islands, reflecting the local multi-lingual stew and Columbus's overzealous naming practices, have more than one name.

The archipelago is made up of six large islands (Colón, Bastimentos, Cristóbal, Popa, Cayo Nancy, and Cayo Caranero) and several smaller ones. Called "Bocas Isla" by the *bocatoreños*, Isla Colón is the main base for visiting the archipelago. It is also ground zero for Panama's backpacker scene. If you're looking for all-night partying, an international crowd, great cuisine, and hostels, look no further. If you prefer a laid-back Caribbean vibe, Bastimentos, just a few minutes away by boat, is the place to go.

BOCAS DEL TORO AND ISLA COLÓN

Bocas is equal parts Caribbean village and international backpacker destination. The island gives off a lazy island vibe, but still offers some of the best nightlife, food, and hostels in Panama. The slow pace of life here is infectious—Bocas is notorious for persuading visitors to put their travel plans on hold. Ambitious travelers can work in a few side trips during their stay, to Isla Bastimentos, Boca del Drago, and other nearby islands. The town swings its hips a little on November 16, when a parade celebrates the founding of the province.

TRANSPORTATION

Flights: The airport is on Av. F and C. 6. From the park, walk 1 block north and 3 blocks west. **Nature Air** (☎6692 1983; www.natureair.com) flies to **San Jose** (1hr.; W, F, Su 12:30pm; US$158). **Air Panama** (☎757 9841; open 6:45am-5pm) has daily flights to **Panama City** (1hr., 8am and 4:45pm, US$98). **Aeroperlas** (☎757 9341, open 7am-5pm) has flights to **Changuinola** (15min., daily 7:30am and 4pm, US$22) and **Panama City** (1hr., daily 9am and 5pm, US$98). Call ahead to check schedules, as they change frequently.

Ferries: (☎6615 6674). Leave from the southern tip of town (1½hr., M-Sa 4pm, US$1.50).

Local Boats: Locals with boats hang out at the public docks south of the police station or at the Bocas Marine Tours pier on C. 3. Most fares are set. To: **Isla Carinero** (US$1) and **Old Bank** (US$3). Prices higher at night. Armando (☎6439 7439) is reliable, friendly, and fair.

Water Taxis: Bocas Marine Tours (☎757 9033), on C.3 between Av. B and C. **Taxi 25,** next to the police station on C.1. Water taxis go to Almirante (30min., every 30min. 6am-7:30pm, US$4).

Ground transportation: Getting around the island can be done by taxi or *colectivo*. Taxis charge US$0.50 per person within town, but special trips across the island cost upwards of US$15. *Colectivos* leave from the *parque* to **Bocas del Drago** (35min., 7 per day 5am-5:30pm, US$2.50). **Caribe Shuttle** (☎757 7048; www.caribeshuttle) runs daily trips from Bocas to **Puerto Viejo, CRA** (daily 8:30am, US$32). Caribe Shuttle also offers door-to-door service for any of the nearby islands. Book a day in advance with your destination hotel and passport.

Rentals: Ixa's Bicycle World (☎6717 5379), on Av. H Norte. Bikes US$2 per hr., US$10 per day. Open M-Sa 8am-6pm. **Lau's Bicycles and Scooters,** on C. 3 across from the park. Bikes and rusting scooters US$15 per hr., US$45 per day. **Bocas Water Sports** (☎757 9541; www.bocaswatersports.com), on C. 3 near Bocas Marine Tours. Single kayak US$3 per hr., US$10 per ½-day, US$18 per day. Double kayak US$5 per hr., US$20 per half-day, US$35 per day. MC/V.

✹🔃 ORIENTATION AND PRACTICAL INFORMATION

Bocas is laid out in an L-shaped grid. Numbered *calles* run north-south and lettered *avenidas* run east-west, though you won't find too many street signs. Directions are usually given by landmarks. With the docks behind you, north is to the right and south is to the left. Just about everything is on **Calle 3,** the wide main street, or on **Calle 1,** farther east. The water cuts across the grid from C. 3 at the south end of town to C. 1 at the east end. A small park lies between C. 2 and 3 and Av. D and E. **Avenida G,** at the northern end of town, is the main strip leading to the rest of the island.

Tourist Office: (☎757 9642), near the police station in a large yellow and white wooden house on C.1. Maps of the city and some information exhibits. English spoken. Open M-F 7:30am-3:30pm. **ANAM** (☎757 9244), next to Barco Hundido on C.1. Runs the Parque Nacional Marino Isla Bastimentos. Entry US$10, students US$5. Camping US$10.

Bank: Banco Nacional Panama, C. 4 and Av. E (☎757 9230). **24hr. ATM.** Open M-F 8am-2pm, Sa 9am-noon. There is also a 24hr. ATM next to the police station.

Laundromat: Lavamático Don Pardo (☎757 9487), next to Mondo Taitú on Av. G. Wash and dry US$3.50 per load. Open M-Sa 8am-8pm.

Police: (☎757 9217), on the southern end of C.1 before it ends at the water.

Pharmacy: Farmacia Rosa Blanca (☎757 9566), on C. 3 south of the *parque* near Bocas Marine Tours. Open M-Sa 8:30am-9pm, Su 10am-noon and 7-9pm. Cash only.

Hospital: Av. G (☎757 9201). From the park, walk north to Av. G (Hostal Mondo Taitú), then turn left and walk a few blocks west. Open M-F 7am-4pm. Emergency service 24hr.

Internet: Bocas Internet Cafe (☎757 9390), on C. 3 next to the supermarket Isla Colón. Internet US$0.50 per 15min. **Internet Micro,** next to La Buga. Skype, Wi-Fi, and new computers. US$2 per hr. Open M-Sa 9am-10pm, Su 9am-7pm. **Boca's Cyber Shop** (☎757 7035), across the street from the police. US$1 per hr.

Post Office: (☎757 9321), inside the government building on the northern side of the *parque*. Open M-F 8am-noon and 1-3pm.

🏚 ACCOMMODATIONS

Bocas is blessed with excellent hotels, not to mention the best hostels in Panama. Dorm rooms range from US$10-12, and private rooms start at US$20. Accommodations fill up in the high season (Dec.-Apr.), so make reservations. If you can't find a room, many families will rent out rooms in their house, so ask around.

■ **Casa Max** (☎757 9120), north of town at the beginning of Av. G and across from Mondo Taitú. Attractive, well-kept wooden rooms and ample outdoor space. All rooms have private baths with hot water. Splurge for the Caribbean-style deck with a hammock. Free Wi-Fi. Doubles US$25, with decks US$35; triples US$35. D/MC/V. ❸

Mondo Taitú (☎757 9425), north of town at the beginning of Av. G. B. A maze of wooden rooms and staircases built around a tree, Mondo has a cult following among backpackers. Free bike rentals, make-your-own pancake sessions every morning, and one of the most popular bars in town all ensure that the legacy lives on. If you want a good night's sleep, it might not be the best spot. Next-door, they have quieter rooms with A/C. Free Wi-Fi. Dorms US$10; rooms US$12. ❷

Hostal Gran Kahuna (☎757 9038 or 6732 2345; www.grankahunabocas.com), on C. 3 south of the *parque*. This recently remodeled hostel has a less party-oriented atmosphere. Probably the best spot for a good night's sleep. Large common area has computers (US$1.75 per hr.), games, and a kitchen. Shell out for the upstairs rooms, which are breezier and have balconies. Lockers included. Free Wi-Fi. Rooms US$10-12. Cash only. ❷

Hostal Heike (☎757 9708), on C. 3 just off the park. Mondo Taitú's cleaner, somewhat quieter sister hostel has a great rooftop deck with a lounge area and computers. Downstairs is a kitchen and a book exchange. All rooms are dorm style, with shared baths and lockers. Ask about their free Spanish lessons. Free Wi-Fi in lobby. Rooms US$10, with A/C US$12. ❷

Hotel del Parque (☎757 9008), on the eastern side of the *parque*. One of the quietest spots in town, despite its central location. A step above the rest. A pleasant front garden complements a back deck with hammocks. Rooms have A/C, fans, hot water, cable TV, and large orthopedic mattresses. Kitchen available. Free Wi-Fi. Doubles US$50; triples US$55. ❹

▐ FOOD

Bocas has everything from fast-food and *típico* to classy Italian and Asian fusion. The prices might inspire a little sticker shock—even the produce and supermarkets are a bit more expensive than on the mainland. The cheapest food is local *bocatareño* food, usually seafood or chicken with coconut-lime sauce and coconut rice. Bocas doesn't have clean tap water, though some places have filters. For groceries, visit **Isla Colon,** on C. 3 just south of the *parque.* (☎757 9591. Open daily 7am-11:30pm.) Around the corner, they also operate a produce stand. (Open daily 8am-10:30pm.)

■ **La Casbah,** next to Mondo Taitú at the northern end of C. 3. Fresh food cooked with Mediterranean flair. Though the prices may not be the friendliest, they could easily charge more for the quality. Fish of the day US$9. Entrees US$8-12. Open Tu-Sa 6pm-10pm. Cash only. ❹

Lili's Café (☎6829 4600), near the police station above the water, on the diagonal connecting C. 1 and C. 3. Breakfast all day—try Lili's Omelette (US$7.50), the house special, with "killin' me, man" sauce. Open M-F 7am-11pm, Sa 7am-4pm, Su 7am-1pm. Cash only. ❸

Om Café (☎6624 0898), behind the municipal building between C. 1 and C. 3. Locally celebrated by long-term gringo residents, Om deserves the attention. Authentic Indian cuisine and ambience—feels closer to Goa than Bocas. Entrees US$7-11. Beer US$1.50. Open Tu and F-Su 8am-noon and 6pm-10pm. Cash only. ❹

Lemongrass Restaurant and Bar, next to Lili's Café near the police station. Asian fusion (like Thai tacos) on the breezy deck of a wooden building. The chef uses fresh produce and fish, so the menu changes daily. Dinner (US$10-12) is pricey, but lunch (US$5-6) is a good value. Cash only. ❸

Starfish Coffee, on the southern part of C. 3 along the water, next to La Buga. The best coffee shop in town has a cozy interior with books and a large selection of National Geographics. They serve the best breakfast in town. Coffee US$1.25. Salads US$7. Sandwiches US$5. Entrees US$8-12. Open M-Sa 8am-10pm, Su 9am-10pm. Cash only. ❹

The Reef (☎757 9336), at the southern end of C. 3. Tasty *bocatareño* food right by the sea. Excellent seafood is accompanied by rice, potatoes, or *patacones* (US$6-8). Beer US$1.25. Open daily 10am-10pm. Cash only. ❸

Golden Grill (☎757 9650), on C. 3 next to the *parque*. If food prices around town have got you on the bread diet, Golden Grill will be your salvation. The best value in town—cheaper than a lot of *típico* options. Free Wi-Fi. Fast food US$4. Open daily 7am-10pm. Cash only. ❷

🔘 SIGHTS

From Bocas town, Av. G leads west and eventually bends right across a small isthmus to the main body of the island. From here, the road forks: the left side leads 15km through the middle of the island past La Gruta to Boca del Drago, while the right side follows the eastern coast, passing through Big Creek, Playa Paunch, and Playa Bluff along the way. Many of these beaches are infested with *chitras* (tiny sandflies with an irritating bite), especially in the late afternoon. Biking is a great way to get around the island, though you should make sure your wheels are in working order, as the roads are hilly and often muddy. There are also *colectivos* and mini-buses that go to Bocas del Drago and back a few times per day.

EASTERN BEACHES. Just north of town is a string of relatively easily accessible beaches. **Playa Paunch** is a surf spot, popular with locals, who can be territorial about the waves. The best of these beaches, farther north, is relatively *chitra*-free **Playa Bluff**. The sandy beach stretches almost 2km, with good surfing and casual swimming when the surf isn't too strong. Between May and July, the beach attracts sea turtles laying their eggs; ask ANAM (p. 620) for information. *(Playa Bluff is about 8km north of Bocas town; biking takes around 45min. Taxis US$10-15.)*

BOCA DEL DRAGO. On the western side of the island, 8km past La Gruta on a hilly road, you'll find laid-back Boca del Drago. Beautiful beaches and a coral reef are just a few meters from shore. There are only a few buildings along the water, and almost no services. For parts of the year, you may be able to stay overnight at **Cabañas Estefany**. From May 15 to August 15 and from December to January, the *cabañas* are generally rented out to the Institute of Tropical Ecology, but you may be able to scrounge an extra room of camp on the property. *(Minibuses leave for Boca del Drago. 35min., 7 per day 5am-5:30pm, US$2.50. Biking takes more than an hour, and it's a hilly ride. Cabañas Estefany ☎6624 9246; ask for Chino or Fátima. Camping US$5; dorms with seperate bath US$15; private cabins with bath and kitchen US$35.)*

ISLA DE PÁJAROS OF SWAN CAYE, WRECK ROCK, AND SAIL ROCK. About 15min. by boat from Boca del Drago, Isla de Pájaros, part of the greater Swan Caye, attracts hundreds of seabirds which circle a huge rock and a few hardy trees. There's a coral reef with excellent deep-water snorkeling right off the island, but the water isn't always clear, especially after it rains. Just past Pájaros are two smaller rocky islands: Wreck Rock, which looks like the wreck of a ship, and Sail Rock, a phallic rock sticking straight out of the water. *(Tour operators in Bocas all offer trips here; contact them for transportation.)*

LA GRUTA CAVE. A series of two long, dark caves with plenty of bats and even more bat guano, La Gruta is a religious shrine and the site of an annual pilgrimage celebrating Nuestra Señora de la Gruta, la Virgen del Carmen. The celebration of the Virgin occurs on July 16th, with the procession to the cave on the following Sunday. *(La Colonia Santeña, where a short trail leads to the cave, is about 6km* *from town. Bring a flashlight and good boots. If you haven't had enough after the first cave, a dark, wet 50m walk, there is another one about 30min. farther along the trail. US$1 per person.)*

ISLA CARENERO. Just a few hundred meters east of Bocas town, *chitra*-infested Isla Carenero is practically on Isla Colón. On the eastern point of the island, black rock is a popular surfing break good for beginners. Most of the restaurants on the island are rather expensive and cater to the yachting crew, but if you need to grab something to eat, the prices at **Restaurante Doña Maria ❸** are fairly reasonable. (☎757 9551. Sandwiches US$5. Salads US$7. Entrees US$7-10. Open 7am-10pm. MC/V). Most backpackers come to the island for **Aqua Lounge** (see **Nightlife**, below), which throws the biggest parties around. Believe it or not, people also stay here, though you probably won't get much sleep if you do. (www.bocasaqualounge.com. Dorms US$10.) They have a diving board and a waterside trampoline. *(Local boatmen take you to the isle; US$1.)*

🎵 NIGHTLIFE

Bocas town is one of the biggest party destinations in Central America for backpackers, especially between December and February. That said, there are only a few spots in town where it really goes down. It's a small island, so those spots won't be hard to find. If you're looking for something more relaxed, most restaurants have full-service bars. On Sunday night, there's usually a drum circle in the park. You might catch the locally-famous Beach Boys de Bastimentos, a calypso band rumored to have once played for 15hr. straight. Ask around to see if they are playing.

Aqua Lounge (www.bocasaqualounge.com), on Isla Carinero. Boats to the island US$1. Parties every night. Crowds of people, mostly gringos, take the short boat ride and dance until the wee hours of the morning. The dance floor is along the water. There's even a diving board (maybe try it before the 3rd drink). Beer US$2.

Barco Hundido, on C.1 just east of the park near Taxi 25. Keeps the party going until late. Most of the serious dancing is done on land, but you can also head off onto the series of interconnected floating docks surrounding a sunken boat just off the shore. When the party really gets crazy, it sometimes moves onto *Barco Loco*, a party boat (well, a platform on top of 2 canoes). Beer US$2. Mixed drinks US$3. Open M-Tu and Th-Su 9am-3am.

Mondo Taitú (p. 621). This hostel has one of the most popular bars in town. It's a great spot to meet fellow travelers, and beer is cheap (US$1). Happy hour 7-8pm; beer US$0.50. Cocktail hour 8pm-9pm; US$1 off. Open until midnight.

Bar El Encanto, across the street from Hostal Gran Kahuna. A wooden building over the water attracts a local crowd. A good place to meet townies, though women may feel a little too welcome. Beer US$0.70. Open M-F 12:30pm-midnight, Sa-Su 12:30pm-3am. Cash only.

📷 WATERSPORTS AND GUIDED TOURS

DIVING AND SNORKELING. As the local economy is almost entirely dependent on tourism, nearly every hotel, restaurant, dock, shack, and patch of grass offers some form of rental. The archipelago is covered in dive spots. For beginners, the closer spots are best. **Hospital Point** is a great spot for divers and snorkelers alike, with a 100 ft. deep wall to explore. **Barco Hundido** is an artificial reef the Smithsonian Institute created by sinking a boat near Isla Colón. Just south of Bocas town is **Punta Manglar**. The **Playground** is the nearest dive, though its proximity means that it's often crowded, and the fish are better elsewhere. Around Bastimentos, **La Covita,** on the north side, has underwater caverns.

South of Cayo Nancy (Isla Solarte) is a huge coral reef with great visibility. One of the best dives around, **Tiger Rock,** is on the far eastern side of Bastimentos.

There are many dive schools in town, with prices generally around US$60 for a half-day, two-tank dive, as well as certification and trips for non-certified divers. The newest, PADI-certified **La Buga,** on C.3 between Av. A and B, has good instructors and new equipment. For certified divers, a half-day two-tank dive costs US$60, and a night dive (1 tank) is US$50. They also offer a certification course for US$265 and a full-day discovery crash course for non-certified divers for US$90. Dives change daily depending on time of year and conditions, though they try to accomodate diver requests. (☎757 9534; www.labugapanama.com. AmEx/MC/V.) For snorkeling, most dive shops run tours (US$20-25) with gear included.

SURFING. Crowds of surfers come to Bocas for the large waves, which are best in the winter months. On Isla Colón, **Playa Bluff** is the most popular spot for tourists, while **Playa Paunch,** a bit closer, has a territorial local crowd. On the eastern side of Isla Carenero, **Black Rock** can be a good place for beginners. **Wizard's Beach** and **Playa Larga,** on the northern side of Bastimentos, have some of the biggest waves, though they are not recommended for beginners, as the riptides are strong. **Hostal Gran Kahuna** (p. 621) offers lessons and rents boards (US$10-15). La Buga Dive Center also runs classes. Ask for Panama's national champ Juan Pi Caraballo. (Full day US$89, half US$49.)

CATAMARAN SAILING AND SNORKELING. One family runs daily catamaran tours that stop at some of the best destinations for snorkeling and fishing. Boats leave from Av. Sur at the southern tip of the island at 9:30am and return at 5pm. Prices include lunch, fruit, and a drink. (☎757 9710 or 6464 4242; www.bocassailing.com. US$40 per person or US$33 for students.)

ISLA BASTIMENTOS

If the flood of party-oriented backpackers on Bocas doesn't appeal to you, Bastimentos offers a sample of authentic Caribbean life with a lot fewer tourists. Most boats arrive in the small town of Old Bank, from which it is a short walk to kilometers of beautiful beach. The island is also home to a Ngöbe village and Parque Nacional Marino Bastimentos, the region's best protected natural area, though getting there is either an expensive boat ride or a very long walk.

▗ TRANSPORTATION

Getting to Isla Bastimentos from Bocas del Toro is easy. Local **boats** leave from the pier of Bocas Marine Tours on C. 3 and head to Old Bank (6am-6pm, more frequent in the morning; US$2 per person, after dark US$5). To reach **Cayos Zapatillos** or the other side of the island, your best bet is the tour operators, who generally leave in the morning between 9-10am.

▦ ▛ ORIENTATION AND PRACTICAL INFORMATION

The village of Old Bank has no roads, only a semi-paved footpath running along the water. With your back to the water, east is to your right and west to the left. The little park is toward the western end, as are most of the docks, where you can catch a boat to the end. The island is crisscrossed by trails, most of which are hard to follow and poorly marked.

Tours: The Dutch Pirate (☎6567 1812; www.thedutchpirate.com), at the far eastern end of the trail over the water. Leads scuba tours and certification courses in Dutch, English, German, and Spanish. 2-tank dive US$55. Certification course US$225, includes 2-tank dive at the end. Surfboard rental US$10.

Police: (☎ 757 9757), in front of the main dock.

🍴 FOOD

🍲 **Island Time Thai Restaurant** (☎ 6844 7704; islandtimethairestaurant.com), up a hill 7min. from town. Follow the signs from the town center. Authentic Thai cuisine up in the hills overlooking nearby jungle and the ocean. All meals are US$6, a steal for the high quality. Wash it down with some soothing Thai tea (US$1). If you would like to stay (and you probably will), they rent 2 handsome wooden cabins (US$35 per night) with private baths, hot water, decks, and TVs. Open M-Sa noon-8pm. ❷

🍲 **Up in the Hill Shop** (☎ 6570 8277; www.upinthehill.com), just past Island Time Thai. An amazing find in a garden paradise. An Argentinian-Scottish couple do everything home-style, from the organic farm and the hand-built house to the beautiful craftsmanship. They sell all-natural body products like insect repellents and soap. Many people just stop by for some organic coffee (US$1) and the unbelievably good cacao-brownies (US$2.50). ❷

Bar and Restaurant Roots (☎ 6754 1624), over the water across from Hotel Midland. Locals and gringos kick back to reggae, sip on cold beers, and enjoy some delicious local coconut rice and fish. Chicken US$4. Beer US$1. *Cuba libre* US$2. Open daily noon-9pm. ❷

Tacos by Face. Follow the signs from the western end of the path, situated on the windward side of the island. This breezy spot is a great place to cool off. The owner, Face, cooks fish tacos (US$6.50), chicken burritos (US$6), and quesadillas (US$3.50), though beer (US$1.50) is probably the most popular order. Occasional live music. Open daily noon-last customer. ❷

👁 SIGHTS

BEACHES. The island's beaches lie in a string on the northern and eastern coast, and are connected by a series of poorly-marked trails. To get to **Playa Primera,** or "Wizard Beach," follow the sign from the eastern part of Old Bank's main concrete path and proceed 20min. over the island and down the other side. You can also get there along the path that passes Island Time Thai Restaurant and Up in the Hill Shop. The next beach is **Playa Segunda,** also known as "Red Frog Beach" for its amphibian inhabitants. This is a favorite tour destination from Bocas and a good surfing spot in the dry season (30-40min. past Wizard Beach). The next beach is **Playa Polo,** followed by the extensive **Playa Larga,** part of the **Parque Nacional Marino** (p. 627). Beware: extremely strong currents make swimming dangerous at all of these beaches. Furthermore, these beaches are known for harboring thieves, especially Wizard Beach. Leave your watch and other valuables at home and always keep your belongings within sight.

At the opposite end of the island from the town of Old Bank lies **Punta Vieja,** a secluded beach with astonishingly clear water and awesome snorkeling. Many turtles nest here during the night. *(Tour operators in Bocas generally run tours to both the reef and Salt Creek for US$20-25. Entry to Salt Creek US$6 per person.)*

CAYO NANCY. Isla Solarte (or Cayo Nancy) is south of Old Bank. It is most famous for Hospital Point, named after the United Fruit Company hospital that was once located there, and one of the best, most accessible places for snorkeling in the area. You'll find a variety of corals, some barely submerged, others 100 ft. deep. Many tours go to Hospital Point, but any boat can take you there. There are a few good places to snorkel in the protected waters between Bocas, Isla Carenero, Isla Bastimentos, and Cayo Nancy. If you go by boat, make sure you have a ride back, as all of these sites are in open water. ❧

🎵 NIGHTLIFE

Cantina La Feria. Bastimentos' main party spot and the best place in the archipelago to hang out with locals. F is reggae night, but "Blue Monday" is when the party really goes down. Beers US$0.75. Party starts at 9pm.

ALMIRANTE

People visit small, run-down Almirante either to hop on a boat out to the Bocas del Toro archipelago or to take a bus to Changuinola or David. Bananas are a big business in this small town. In recent years, the famous banana train has been cast to the wayside in favor of a flood of banana trucks, bringing the harvest from Changuinola to be loaded onto banana ships. There's not much to do in town, but if you have some time to kill waiting for a ferry, enjoy the view of the Almirante while throwing back a few bananas.

▐ TRANSPORTATION

Buses: There are 2 terminals in Almirante. Buses to and from **Changuinola** (45min. every 20min. 5:50am-9pm, US$1.20) leave from the station near to town. With your back to the docks, turn left, and when the road dead ends walk to the right 100m. Buses to **David** (4hr., every 30min. 4am-7pm, US$7) and **Panama City** (11hr., 8am and 7pm, US$23) leave from a bus station about 10min. outside of town on the road between Chiriquí Grande and Changuinola. To get there, instead of turning right after walking from the docks, turn left and continue straight; the station is on the left. Buses to Changuinola also pass by this station.

Ferries: (☎6615 6674). Leave from the opposite side of town (M-Sa 8am, US$1.50).

Water Taxis: Taxi 25 (☎757 9028) and **Bocas Marine Tours** (☎758 4085) go to **Bocas del Toro** (30min., every 30min. 6am-7pm, US$4).

Taxis: Charge US$0.50 within town, and US$1 between the David station and the docks.

▐ 📍 ORIENTATION AND PRACTICAL INFORMATION

The main strip in town runs east-west. It begins west of town at the intersection with the road between Chiriquí Grande and Changuinola and ends in the east at the Puerto de Almirante. The bus station to David, at the western intersection, is a 10min walk from town. With your back to the station, turn right and continue straight into town. To get to the dock, take another right about 10min. down the road before a roadside inspection station. If you continue straight and then take the second right after the Changuinola bus station at the large blue Movistar sign, you will arrive in the center of town. Most of the services are within a block of the center.

Bank: Banco Nacional de Panama (☎758 3718). Turn right into town, then take your 1st left and walk 2 blocks. **24hr. ATM.** Open M-F 8am-2pm, Sa 9am-noon.

Police: (☎758 3714), next to the port at the far eastern part of town.

Pharmacy: Farmacia San Vicente (☎758 3535), 2 blocks south of the main road in town just past the supermarket. Open M-Sa 8am-8pm, Su 9am-5pm. MC/V.

Hospital: (☎758 3754), at the southernmost point of town. Turn as if going in to town and continue straight for 3 blocks. Open 7am-3pm. Emergency service 24hr.

Post Office: (☎758 3650), 1 block past the bank. Open M-F 7am-6pm, Sa 7am-2:30pm. **Postal Code:** 0104.

~~CCOMMODATIONS~~

~~Puerto Almirante~~ (☎758 3786), across from the bank. If for some reason you
get to Bocas, Almirante offers adequate, if barren, rooms with wooden floors, pri-
~~b~~aths, and TVs. Some water and electricity problems, so don't count on either.
~~e~~s US$15; triples with A/C US$25. ❸

~~D~~

~~e~~ plenty of *típico* options and fruit markets in town. Since groceries
~~ive on Isla Colón, it may be worth stocking up at **Supermercado 888,** in
~~of town, one block south of the main road. (Open daily 6am-9pm.)

~~rante Bocas Marina~~ (☎6697 6175). Walk to the far eastern part of town along
~~main road. With the port in front of you, turn right. A great place to pass the time
~~h~~ile waiting for the ferry, with arguably the best view of Almirante Bay. Sandwiches
US$1-3. Entrees US$4-6. Open daily 8am-midnight. ❷

SIGHTS

PARQUE NACIONAL MARINO ISLA BASTIMENTOS

Covering 13,156 hectares, of which only 1,630 are land, Parque Nacional Marino
Isla Bastimentos comprises much of the interior of Basimentos, all the mangroves to its south, the two precious Cayos Zapatillos farther southeast, and
all of the surrounding open water. The park is on the opposite end of the island
from Old Bank, and although it is possible to hike to it in 3-4 hours (each way),
the trail can be complicated without someone who knows the way. The best
way to see the park is on one of the many tours that leave from the docks in
the morning. **Playa Larga,** a spectacular 14km beach on the northern part of the
park, is an important turtle nesting site from April to September. The interior
of the island is home to some fantastic wildlife, including monkeys, sloths,
and crocodiles. Farther south is a forest trail that leads to golden beaches
and underwater cave formations. There are two ranger stations, one on the
more southern of the two Cayos Zaptillos and one on Playa Larga. Camping is
allowed (US$10 per night), though you will need to bring everything, including
mosquito nets, water, and food. For more professional tours, talk to **ANCON
Expeditions** (☎757 9600; www.anconexpeditions.com) on Av. G in Bocas. They
run expensive tours to the park as well as to a nearby Ngöbe village.

CHANGUINOLA

Changuinola is hot and dirty, but is home to the border crossing into Costa Rica.
It's a good place to run errands and complete any necessary paperwork. The city
survives off merchants and banana plantations, many of which offer tours.

▟ TRANSPORTATION

Flights: The airport is at the north end of town; turn right past the gas station. **Air Panama** (☎758 9841) flies to **Panama City** (1hr.; M-Sa 7:15am and 3:50pm; Su 3:50pm;
US$98) via **Bocas del Toro** (15min., US$22.40). **Aeroperlas** (☎758 7521) also flies
to Panama City (1hr., 8:35am and 4:40pm, US$98).

Buses: Changuinola has 2 bus terminals within 300m of each other on opposite sides
of the street. Terminal La Piquera, next to the Shell station in the center of town, han-

dles short-distance travel. There's no timetable, but buses come frequently to: **Almirante** (45min., every 20min. 5:40am-9:45pm, US$1.20); **Chiriquí** (1½hr., every hr. 7am-2pm, US$5.50); **El Silencio** (20min., every 20min 6am-8 US$0.65); **Las Tablas** (30min., every 25min. 5:30am-8pm, US$0.80) via the **Rican border at Guabito**. Terminal Urraca (☎758 8455), north of Terminal La Pi To **David** (4hr., every 30min. 3:15am-7pm, US$8) and **Panama City** (12hr., 7am 6pm, US$24).

Taxis: *Taxis colectivos* next to Terminal La Piquera. A faster, more comfortable option **Guabito** (20min., US$1.20).

✚ 🔁 ORIENTATION AND PRACTICAL INFORMATION

Changuinola is strung along the road from the Guabito border in the northwes to Almirante in the southeast. The road to Almirante curves along a traffc circle and turns left to intersect with the main strip. The center of town is marked by the Shell gas station, right next to the Terminal La Piquera. Facing the gas station from **Avenida 17 de Abril**, the town's main street, north is to the left and south is to the right.

Tourist Offices: ANAM (☎758 6603). Head 2 blocks north of La Piquera and turn left at the Western Union sign. Turn left again at the 1st intersection and then right at the mosque. They run the San-San wetlands and the Wetzo entrance to Parque Internacional La Amistad. Open M-F 8am-4pm.

Bank and Currency Exchange: HSBC (☎758 6163), between the 2 terminals. **24hr. ATM.** Open M-F 8am-3:30pm, Sa 9am-noon. Most of the large stores lining the main road will change *colones* for you. **Almacen Zona Libre** (☎758 5468), just south of the terminal. **Western Union** (☎758 9155), inside Super Deportes Sammy, just past the HSBC. Open M-F 8:30am-7:30pm, Sa 8:30am-8:30pm, Su 9:30am-2:30pm. MC/V.

Police: (☎758 2800), at the traffic circle east of the main strip.

Hospital: (☎758 8232). Facing the police station, go right 1 block.

Internet Access: Foto Centro Arco Iris (☎758 8457), across from the terminal on the north side. US$1 per hr. Open M-Sa 8am-7pm. MC/V.

🏠 ACCOMMODATIONS

Changuinola has no shortage of digs, but none of them is spectacular. Electricity and water in Changuinola can be erratic.

Hotel Carol (☎758 8731), 2 blocks south of Terminal La Piquera. Some of the cheapest rooms in town. They seem a bit unfinished, with partially concrete floors and other touches missing, but they all have private baths and much needed A/C. Singles US$14, with TV and hot water US$23; doubles US$16/25. Cash only. ❸

🍴 FOOD

Cheap *típico* dominates the menus, but there are a few surprises mixed in. For groceries, visit **Romero**, just south of the traffic circle, 1 block east from Hotel Carol. (☎758 9834. Open 24hr.) They also have a bakery and pharmacy.

🔲 **El Buen Sabor** (☎758 8422), hidden behind some foliage across the street from Paraíso de Batidos, between the 2 bus stations. This bakery is the best Changuinola has to offer. A wide variety of flaky, fresh-from-the-oven treats neatly sorted into wooden boxes—all for less than a dollar. They also sell pizzas (US$3.25), and a large variety of cool shakes. Cash only. ❶

☒ GUABITO: BORDER WITH COSTA RICA

Guabito is 16km from Changuinola (30min. by bus and 20min. by taxi); Sixaola is across the border in Costa Rica. *Taxis colectivos* (US$1.20) are the fastest way to travel between the two. The Panamanian side of the border is open daily from 8am-6pm and the Costa Rican side is open daily from 7am-5pm. The difference is due to the change in time zones at the border. When entering Panama, you must get an **exit stamp** from the Panamanian immigration, then go across a rickety bridge (the border is technically halfway along the bridge), and get an entrance stamp from the other side at the Costa Rican Immigration (☎2754 2044). When entering Panama, the process is the same, but on the Panama side, you need to buy a **tourist card** from the tourist office (☎759 7985; next to the Immigration Office). Both countries require that you show proof of onward travel; make sure to bring an onward bus or flight ticket. They also may ask you for a copy of your passport and proof of sufficient funds for travel—a bank statement with at least US$300 is best.

For those entering Panama, frequent buses run to Changuinola (30min., every 25min., US$0.80). Catch one at the junction 200m past the border next to the police station. *Taxis colectivos* (US$1.20) are faster. **El Caiman Internacional** and **Mini Super El Poderoso,** both on the left side of the border crossing, change money. The **immigration office** is just before the bridge, and the **police station** is 200m farther down the road. Before the police station on the left is **Abby's Internet.** (US$1 per hr. Open 9am-9pm, Su 10am-3:30pm.) The **post office** is across from the police station. (☎759 7997. Open M-F 8am-5pm, Sa 8am-noon.) On the Costa Rican side, the **police station** (☎2751 2160) is just over the bridge. Guabito has no accommodations and almost no restaurants; Sixaola, just across the border, has better options.

APPENDIX

CLIMATE

AVG. TEMP. (LOW/ HIGH), PRECIP.	JANUARY			APRIL			JULY			OCTOBER		
	°C	°F	mm	°C	°F	mm	°C	°F	mm	°C	°F	mm
Belize City, Belize	19-27	66-80	137	23-30	73-86	56	24-31	75-87	163	22-30	71-86	305
Guatemala City, Guatemala	12-23	53-73	8	14-28	57-82	31	16-26	60-78	203	16-24	60-75	173
San Salvador, El Salvador	16-32	60-89	8	18-34	64-92	43	18-32	64-89	292	18-31	64-87	241
Managua, Nicaragua	20-31	68-87	5	23-34	73-93	5	22-31	71-87	134	22-31	71-87	59
Tegucigalpa, Honduras	14-25	57-77	12	17-30	62-86	26	18-27	64-80	70	17-27	62-80	87
San José, Costa Rica	14-24	57-75	15	17-26	62-78	46	17-25	62-77	211	16-25	60-77	300

MEASUREMENTS

Like the rest of the rational world, Central America uses the metric system. The basic unit of length is the **meter (m)**, which is divided into 100 **centimeters (cm)** or 1000 **millimeters (mm)**. One thousand meters make up one **kilometer (km)**. Fluids are measured in **liters (L)**, each divided into 1000 **milliliters (mL)**. A liter of pure water weighs one **kilogram (kg)**, which is divided into 1000 **grams (g)**. One metric ton is **1000kg**.

MEASUREMENT CONVERSIONS	
1 inch (in.) = 25.4mm	1 millimeter (mm) = 0.039 in.
1 foot (ft.) = 0.305m	1 meter (m) = 3.28 ft.
1 yard (yd.) = 0.914m	1 meter (m) = 1.094 yd.
1 mile (mi.) = 1.609km	1 kilometer (km) = 0.621 mi.
1 ounce (oz.) = 28.35g	1 gram (g) = 0.035 oz.
1 pound (lb.) = 0.454kg	1 kilogram (kg) = 2.205 lb.
1 fluid ounce (fl. oz.) = 29.57mL	1 milliliter (mL) = 0.034 fl. oz.
1 gallon (gal.) = 3.785L	1 liter (L) = 0.264 gal.

LANGUAGE

PRONUNCIATION

The letter **X** has a baffling variety of pronunciations: depending on dialect and word position, it can sound like English "h," "s," "sh," or "x." Spanish words receive stress on the syllable marked with an accent (´). In the absence of an accent mark, words that end in vowels, "n," or "s" receive stress on the second to last syllable. For words ending in all other consonants, stress falls on the last syllable. Spanish has masculine and feminine nouns, and gives a gender to all adjectives. Masculine words generally end with an "o": *él es un tonto* (he is a fool). Feminine words generally end with an "a": *ella es bella* (she is beautiful). Pay close attention—slight changes in word ending can cause drastic changes in meaning. For instance, when receiving directions, mind the distinction between *derecho* (straight) and *derecha* (right).

PHONETIC UNIT	PRONUNCIATION	PHONETIC UNIT	PRONUNCIATION	PHONETIC UNIT	PRONUNCIATION
a	ah, as in "father"	rr	trilled	ñ	ay, as in "canyon"
e	eh, as in "pet"	h	silent	Mayan ch	sh, as in "shoe"
i	ee, as in "eat"	y and i	ee, as in "eat"	gü	goo, as in "gooey"
o	oh, as in "oh"	j	h, as in "hello"	g before e or i	h, as in "hen"
u	oo, as in "boot"	ll	y, as in "yes"	gu before e	g, as in "gate"

PHRASEBOOK

ESSENTIAL PHRASES

ENGLISH	SPANISH	PRONUNCIATION
hello	hola	O-la
goodbye	adiós	ah-dee-OHS
yes/no	sí/no	SEE/NO
please	por favor	POHR fa-VOHR
thank you	gracias	GRAH-see-ahs
you're welcome	de nada	deh NAH-dah
Do you speak English?	¿Habla inglés?	AH-blah een-GLESS
I don't speak Spanish.	No hablo español.	NO AH-bloh ehs-pahn-YOHL
Excuse me.	Perdón/Disculpe.	pehr-THOHN/dee-SKOOL-peh
I don't know.	No sé.	NO SEH
Can you repeat that?	¿Puede repetirlo?/¿Mande?	PWEH-deh reh-peh-TEER-lo/MAHN-deh
I'm sorry/forgive me.	Lo siento	lo see-EN-toe

SURVIVAL SPANISH

ENGLISH	SPANISH	ENGLISH	SPANISH
good morning	buenos días	How do you say (dodgeball) in Spanish?	¿Cómo se dice (dodgeball) en español?
good afternoon	buenas tardes	What (did you just say)?	¿Cómo?/¿Qué?/¿Mande?
goodnight	buenas noches	I don't understand.	No entiendo.
What is your name?	¿Cómo se llama?	Again, please.	Otra vez, por favor.
My name is (Jessica Laporte).	Me llamo (Jessica Laporte).	Could you speak slower?	¿Podría hablar más despacio?
What's up?	¿Qué tal?	Where is (the bathroom)?	¿Dónde está (el baño)?
See you later.	Hasta luego.	Who?/What?	¿Quién?/¿Qué?
How are you?	¿Qué tal?/¿Cómo está?	When?/Where?	¿Cuándo?/¿Dónde?
I'm sick/fine.	Estoy enfermo(a)/bien.	Why?	¿Por qué?
I am hot/cold.	Tengo calor/frío.	Because.	Porque.
I am hungry/thirsty.	Tengo hambre/sed.	Go on!/Come on!/Hurry up!	¡Ándale!
I want/would like...	Quiero/Quisiera...	Let's go!	¡Vámonos!
How much does it cost?	¿Cuánto cuesta?	Look!/Listen!	¡Mira!
That is very cheap/expensive.	Es muy barato/caro.	Stop!/That's enough!	¡Basta!

Is the store open/closed?	¿La tienda está abierta/cerrada?	maybe	tal vez/puede ser
Good morning.	Buenos días.	How do you say (I love Let's Go) in Spanish?	¿Cómo se dice (Me encanta Let's Go) en español?

INTERPERSONAL INTERACTIONS

ENGLISH	SPANISH	ENGLISH	SPANISH
Where are you from?	¿De dónde viene usted?	Pleased to meet you.	Encantado(a)/Mucho gusto.
I am from (Europe).	Soy de (Europa).	Do you have a light?	¿Tiene luz?
I'm (20) years old.	Tengo (veinte) años.	He/she seems cool.	Él/ella me cae bien.
Would you like to go out with me?	¿Quiere salir conmigo?	What's wrong?	¿Qué le pasa?
I have a boyfriend/girl-friend/spouse.	Tengo novio/novia/esposo(a).	I'm sorry.	Lo siento.
I'm gay/straight/bisexual.	Soy gay/heterosexual/bisexual.	Do you come here often?	¿Viene aquí a menudo?
I love you.	Te quiero.	This is my first time in Mexico.	Esta es mi primera vez en Mexico.
Why not?	¿Por qué no?	What a shame: you bought *Lonely Planet*!	¡Qué lástima: compraste *Lonely Planet*!

YOUR ARRIVAL

ENGLISH	SPANISH	ENGLISH	SPANISH
I am from (the US/Europe).	Soy de (los Estados Unidos/Europa).	What's the problem, sir/madam?	¿Cuál es el problema, señor/señora?
Here is my passport.	Aquí está mi pasaporte.	I lost my passport/luggage.	Se me perdió mi pasa-porte/equipaje.
I will be here for less than six months.	Estaré aquí por menos de seis meses.	I have nothing to declare.	No tengo nada para declarar.
I don't know where that came from.	No sé de dónde vino eso.	Please do not detain me.	Por favor no me detenga.

GETTING AROUND

ENGLISH	SPANISH	ENGLISH	SPANISH
How do you get to (the bus station)?	¿Cómo se puede llegar a (la estación de auto-buses)?	Does this bus go to (Guanajuato)?	¿Esta autobús va a (Guanajuato)?
Which bus line goes to..?	¿Cuál línea de buses tiene servicio a...?	Where does the bus leave from?	¿De dónde sale el bús?
When does the bus leave?	¿Cuándo sale el bús?	How long does the trip take?	¿Cuánto tiempo dura el viaje?
Can I buy a ticket?	¿Puedo comprar un boleto?	I'm getting off at (Av. Juárez).	Me bajo en (Av. Juárez).
Where is (the center of town)?	¿Dónde está (el centro)?	Please let me off at (the zoo).	Por favor, déjeme en (el zoológico).
How near/far is...?	¿Qué tan cerca/lejos está...?	Where is (Constitución) street?	¿Dónde está la calle (Constitución)?
I'm in a hurry.	Estoy de prisa.	Continue forward.	Siga derecho.
I'm lost.	Estoy perdido(a).	On foot.	A pie.
I am going to the airport.	Voy al aeropuerto.	The flight is delayed/canceled.	El vuelo está atrasado/cancelado.
Where is the bathroom?	¿Dónde está el baño?	Is it safe to hitchhike?	¿Es seguro pedir aventón?
Where can I buy a cell-phone?	¿Dónde puedo comprar un teléfono celular?	Where can I check email?	¿Dónde se puede chequear el correo electrónico?
Could you tell me what time it is?	¿Podría decirme qué hora es?	Are there student dis-counts available?	¿Hay descuentos para estudiantes?

ON THE ROAD

ENGLISH	SPANISH	ENGLISH	SPANISH
I would like to rent (a car).	Quisiera alquilar (un coche).	north	norte
How much does it cost per day/week?	¿Cuánto cuesta por día/semana?	south	sur
Does it have (heating/air-conditioning)?	¿Tiene (calefacción/aire acondicionado)?	public bus/van	bús
stop	pare	slow	despacio
lane (ends)	carril (termina)	yield	ceda
entrance	entrada	seatbelt	cinturón de seguridad
exit	salida	(maximum) speed	velocidad (máxima)
(narrow) bridge	puente (estrecho)	dangerous (curve)	(curva) peligrosa
narrow (lane)	(carril) estrecho	parking	estacionamiento, parking
toll (ahead)	peaje (adelante)	dead-end street	calle sin salida
authorized public buses only	transporte colectivo autorizado solamente	only	solo
slippery when wet	resbala cuando mojado	rest area	área de descansar
danger (ahead)	peligro (adelante)	do not park	no estacione
do not enter	no entre	do not turn right on red	no vire con luz roja

DIRECTIONS

ENGLISH	SPANISH	ENGLISH	SPANISH
(to the) right	(a la) derecha	near (to)	cerca (de)
(to the) left	(a la) izquierda	far (from)	lejos (de)
next to	al lado de/junto a	above	arriba
across from	en frente de/frente a	below	abajo
(Continue) straight.	(Siga) derecho.	block	cuadra/manzana
turn (command form)	doble	corner	esquina
traffic light	semáforo	street	calle/avenida

ACCOMMODATIONS

ENGLISH	SPANISH	ENGLISH	SPANISH
Is there a cheap hotel around here?	¿Hay un hotel económico por aquí?	Are there rooms with windows?	¿Hay habitaciones con ventanas?
Do you have rooms available?	¿Tiene habitaciones libres?	I am going to stay for (4) days.	Me voy a quedar (cuatro) días.
I would like to reserve a room.	Quisiera reservar una habitación.	Are there cheaper rooms?	¿Hay habitaciones más baratas?
Could I see a room?	¿Podría ver una habit-ación?	Do they come with private baths?	¿Vienen con baño privado?
Do you have any singles/doubles?	¿Tiene habitaciones simples/dobles?	I'll take it.	Lo acepto.
I need another key/towel/pillow.	Necesito otra llave/toalla/almohada.	There are cockroaches in my room.	Hay cucarachas en mi habitación.
The shower/sink/toilet is broken.	La ducha/la pila/el servicio no funciona.	(The cockroaches) are biting me.	(Las cucarachas) me están mordiendo.
My sheets are dirty.	Mis sábanas están sucias.	Dance, cockroaches, dance!	¡Bailen, cucarachas, bailen!

EMERGENCY

ENGLISH	SPANISH	ENGLISH	SPANISH
Help!	¡Socorro!/¡Auxilio!/¡Ayúdeme!	Call the police!	¡Llame a la policía!
I am hurt.	Estoy herido(a).	Leave me alone!	¡Déjame en paz!
It's an emergency!	¡Es una emergencia!	Don't touch me!	¡No me toque!
Fire!	¡Fuego!/¡Incendio!	I've been robbed!	¡Me han robado!
Call a clinic/ambu-lance/doctor/priest!	¡Llame a una clínica/una ambulancia/un médico/un padre!	They went that-a-way!	¡Se fueron por allá!

APPENDIX

I need to contact my embassy.	Necesito comunicarme con mi embajada.	I will only speak in the presence of a lawyer.	Sólo hablaré con la presencia de un(a) abogado(a).

MEDICAL

ENGLISH	SPANISH	ENGLISH	SPANISH
I feel bad/worse/better/okay/fine.	Me siento mal/peor/mejor/más o menos/bien.	My (stomach) hurts.	Me duele (el estómago).
I have a headache/stomachache.	Tengo un dolor de cabeza/estómago.	It hurts here.	Me duele aquí.
I'm sick/ill.	Estoy enfermo(a).	I'm allergic to (nuts)	Soy alérgico(a) a (nueces)
Here is my prescription.	Aquí está mi receta médica.	I think I'm going to vomit.	Pienso que voy a vomitar.
What is this medicine for?	¿Para qué es esta medicina?	I have a cold/a fever/diarrhea/nausea.	Tengo gripe/una calentura/diarrea/náusea.
Where is the nearest hospital/doctor?	¿Dónde está el hospital/doctor más cercano?	I haven't been able to go to the bathroom in (4) days.	No he podido ir al baño en (cuatro) días.

OUT TO LUNCH

ENGLISH	SPANISH	ENGLISH	SPANISH
breakfast	desayuno	Where is a good restaurant?	¿Dónde está un restaurante bueno?
lunch	almuerzo	Can I see the menu?	¿Podría ver la carta/el menú?
dinner	comida/cena	Table for (one), please.	Mesa para (uno), por favor.
dessert	postre	Do you take credit cards?	¿Aceptan tarjetas de crédito?
drink (alcoholic)	bebida (trago)	I would like to order (the chicken).	Quisiera (el pollo).
cup	copa/taza	Do you have anything vegetarian/without meat?	¿Hay algún plato vegetariano/sin carne?
fork	tenedor	Do you have hot sauce?	¿Tiene salsa picante?
knife	cuchillo	This is too spicy.	Es demasiado picante.
napkin	servilleta	Disgusting!	¡Guácala!/¡Qué asco!
spoon	cuchara	Delicious!	¡Qué rico!
bon appétit	buen provecho	Check, please.	La cuenta, por favor.

MENU READER

SPANISH	ENGLISH	SPANISH	ENGLISH
a la brasa	roasted	frijoles	beans
a la plancha	grilled	leche	milk
al vapor	steamed	legumbres	legumes
aceite	oil	licuado	smoothie
aceituna	olive	lima	lime
agua (purificada)	water (purified)	limón	lemon
ajo	garlic	limonada	lemonade
almeja	clam	lomo	steak or chop
arroz (con leche)	rice (rice pudding)	maíz	corn
birria	cow brain soup, a hangover cure	mariscos	seafood
bistec	beefsteak	miel	honey
café	coffee	mole	dark chocolate chili sauce
caliente	hot	pan	bread
camarones	shrimp	papas (fritas)	potatoes (french fries)

carne	meat	parrillas	various grilled meats
cebolla	onion	pastes	meat pie
cemitas	sandwiches made with special long-lasting bread	pasteles	desserts/pies
cerveza	beer	pescado	fish
ceviche	raw marinated seafood	papa	potato
charales	small fish, fried and eaten whole	pimienta	pepper
chaya	plant similar to spinach native to the Yucatán	pollo	chicken
chorizo	spicy sausage	puerco/cerdo	pork
coco	coconut	pulque	liquor made from maguey cactus
cordero	lamb	queso	cheese
(sin) crema	(without) cream	refresco	soda pop
dulces	sweets	verduras/vegetales	vegetables
dulce de leche	caramelized milk	sal	salt
empanada	dumpling filled with meat, cheese, or potatoes	sopes	thick tortillas, stuffed with different toppings
ensalada	salad	tragos	mixed drinks/liquor
entrada	appetizer	Xtabentún	anise and honey liqueur

A P P E N D I X

NUMBERS, DAYS, & MONTHS

ENGLISH	SPANISH	ENGLISH	SPANISH	ENGLISH	SPANISH
0	cero	30	treinta	weekend	fin de semana
1	uno	40	cuarenta	morning	mañana
2	dos	50	cincuenta	afternoon	tarde
3	tres	60	sesenta	night	noche
4	cuatro	70	setenta	day	día
5	cinco	80	ochenta	month	mes
6	seis	90	noventa	year	año
7	siete	100	cien	early	temprano
8	ocho	1000	mil	late	tarde
9	nueve	1,000,000	un millón	January	enero
10	diez	Monday	lunes	February	febrero
11	once	Tuesday	martes	March	marzo
12	doce	Wednesday	miércoles	April	abril
13	trece	Thursday	jueves	May	mayo
14	catorce	Friday	viernes	June	junio
15	quince	Saturday	sábado	July	julio
16	dieciseis	Sunday	domingo	August	agosto
17	diecisiete	day before yesterday	anteayer	September	septiembre
18	dieciocho	yesterday	ayer	October	octubre
19	diecinueve	last night	anoche	November	noviembre
20	veinte	today	hoy	December	diciembre
21	veintiuno	tomorrow	mañana	2010	dos mil diez
22	veintidos	day after tomorrow	pasado mañana	2011	dos mil once

SPANISH GLOSSARY

aduana: customs
agencia de viaje: travel agency
aguardiente: strong liquor
aguas frescas: cold fresh juice/tea
aguas termales: hot springs
ahora: now
ahorita: in just a moment
aire acondicionado: air-conditioning (A/C)
al gusto: as you wish
almacén: (grocery) store
almuerzo: lunch, midday meal
altiplano: highland
amigo(a): friend
andén: platform
antro: club/disco/joint
antojitos: appetizer
arena: sand
arroz: rice
artesanía: arts and crafts
avenida: avenue
azúcar: sugar
bahía: bay
balneario: spa
bandido: bandit
baño: bathroom or natural spa
barato(a): cheap
barranca: canyon
barro: mud
barrio: neighborhood
bello(a): beautiful
biblioteca: library
biosfera: biosphere
birria: meat stew, usually goat
bistec: beefsteak
blanquillo: egg
bocaditos: appetizers, at a bar
bodega: convenience store or winery
boetería: ticket counter
boleto: ticket
bonito(a): pretty
borracho(a): drunk
bosque: forest

botanas: snacks, frequently at bars
bueno(a): good
buena suerte: good luck
burro: donkey
caballero: gentleman
caballo: horse
cabañas: cabins
cajero automático: ATM
cajeros: cashiers
caldo: soup, broth, or stew
calle: street
cama: bed
cambio: change
caminata: hike
camino: path, track, road
camión: truck
camioneta: small pickup-sized
campamento: campground
campesino(a): person from a rural area, peasant
campo: countryside
canotaje: rafting
cantina: bar/drinking establishment
capilla: chapel
carne asada: roasted meat
carnitas: diced, cooked pork
caro(a): expensive
carretera: highway
carro: car, or sometimes a train car
casa: house
casa de cambio: currency exchange establishment
casado(a): married
cascadas: waterfalls
catedral: cathedral
cenote: fresh-water well
centro: city center
cerca: near/nearby
cerro: hill
cerveza: beer
ceviche: raw seafood marinated in lemon juice, herbs, vegetables
cevichería: ceviche restaurant

chico(a): little boy (girl)
chicharrón: bite-sized pieces of fried pork, pork rinds
chuleta de puerco: pork chop
cigarillo: cigarette
cine: cinema
ciudad: city
ciudadela: neighborhood in a large city
coche: car
cocodrilo: crocodile
colectivo: shared taxi
colina: hill
coliseo: coliseum, stadium
comedor: dining room
comida corrida: fixed-price meal
comida del día: daily special
comida típica: typical/traditional dishes
computador: computer
con: with
concha: shell
consulado: consulate
convento: convent
correo: mail, post office
correo electrónico: email
cordillera: mountain range
corvina: sea bass
crucero: crossroads
Cruz Roja: Red Cross
cuadra: street block
cuarto: room
cuenta: bill, check
cuento: story, account
cueva: cave
cuota: toll
curandero: healer
damas: ladies
de paso: in passing, usually refers to buses
desayuno: breakfast
descompuesto: broken, out of order; spoiled (food)
desierto: desert
despacio: slow

de turno: a 24hr. rotating schedule for pharmacies
dinero: money
discoteca: dance club
dueño(a): owner
dulces: sweets
duna: dune
edificio: building
ejido: communal land
embajada: embassy
embarcadero: dock
emergencia: emergency
encomiendas: estates granted to Spanish settlers in Latin America
entrada: entrance
equipaje: luggage
estadio: stadium
este: east
estrella: star
extranjero: foreign, foreigner
farmacia: pharmacy
farmacia en turno: 24hr. pharmacy
feliz: happy
ferrocarril: railroad
fiesta: party, holiday
finca: farm
friaje: sudden cold wind
frijoles: beans
frontera: border
fumar: to smoke
fumaroles: holes in a volcanic region that emit hot vapors
fundo: large estate or tract of land
fútbol: soccer
ganga: bargain
gobierno: government
gordo(a): fat
gorra: cap
gratis: free
gringo(a): Caucasian
habitación: a room
hacer una caminata: take a hike
hacienda: ranch
helado: ice cream
hermano(a): brother (sister)
hervido(a): boiled
hielo: ice
hijo(a): son (daughter)

hombre: man
huevo: egg
iglesia: church
impuestos: taxes
impuesto valor añadido (IVA): value added tax (VAT)
indígena: indigenous person, refers to the native culture
ir de camping: to go camping
isla: island
jaiba: crab meat
jamón: ham
jarra: pitcher
jirón: street
jugo: juice
ladrón: thief
lago/laguna: lake, lagoon
lancha: launch, small boat
langosta: lobster
langostino: jumbo shrimp
larga distancia: long distance
lavandería: laundromat
lejos: far
lento: slow
librería: bookstore
licuado: smoothie, shake
lista de correos: mail holding system in Latin America
llamada: call
loma: hill
lomo: chop, steak
lonchería: snack bar
loro: parrot
madre: mother
malo(a): bad
malecón: pier or seaside boardwalk
maletas: luggage, suitcases
manejar despacio: to drive slowly
manzana: apple
mar: sea
mariscos: seafood
matrimonial: double bed
menestras: lentils/beans

menú del día/menú: fixed daily meal often offered for a bargain price
mercado: market
merendero: outdoor bar/kiosk
merienda: snack
mestizaje: crossing of races
mestizo(a): a person of mixed European and indigenous descent
microbús: small, local bus
mirador: an observatory or lookout point
muelle: wharf
muerte: death
museo: museum
música folklórica: folk music
nada: nothing
naranja: orange
niño(a): child
norte (Nte.): north
nuez/nueces: nut/nuts
obra: work of art, play
obraje: primitive textile workshop
oeste: west
oficina de turismo: tourist office
oriente (Ote.): east
padre: father
palapa: palm-thatched umbrella
pampa: a treeless grassland area
pan: bread
panadería: bakery
papagayo: parrot
parada: a stop (on a bus or train)
parilla: various cuts of grilled meat
paro: labor strike
parque: park
parroquia: parish
paseo turístico: tour covering a series of sites
pelea de gallos: cockfight
peligroso(a): dangerous
peninsulares: Spanish-born colonists

pescado: fish
picante: spicy
plátano: plantain
playa: beach
población: population, settlement
poniente (Pte.): west
policía: police
portales: archways
pueblito: small town
pueblo: town
puente: bridge
puerta: door
puerto: port
queso: cheese
rana: frog
recreo: place of amusement, bar-restaurant on the outskirts of a city
refrescos: refreshments, soft drinks
refugio: refuge
reloj: watch, clock
requesón: cottage cheese
río: river
ropa: clothes
sábanas: bedsheets
sabor: flavor
sala: living room

salida: exit
salto: waterfall
salsa: sauce
scabé: paved, elevated roads found in many ruins.
seguro(a): lock, insurance; adj.: safe
selva: jungle
semáforo: traffic light
semana: week
Semana Santa: Holy Week
sexo: sex
SIDA: AIDS
siesta: mid-afternoon nap; businesses often close at this time
sillar: flexible volcanic rock used in construction
sol: sun
solito(a): alone
solo carril: one-lane road or bridge
soltero(a): single (unmarried)
supermercado: supermarket

sur (S.): south
tarifa: fee
tapas: bite-size appetizers served in bars
telenovela: soap opera
termas: hot mineral springs
terminal terrestre: bus station
tienda: store
timbre: bell
tipo de cambio: exchange rate
tortuga: turtle
trago: mixed drink/shot of alcohol
triste: sad
turismo: tourism
turista: tourist, tourist diarrhea
valle: valley
vecindad: neighborhood
vegetariano(a): vegetarian
volcán: volcano
zócalo: central town plaza
zona: zone

INDEX

MAP INDEX

MAP INDEX

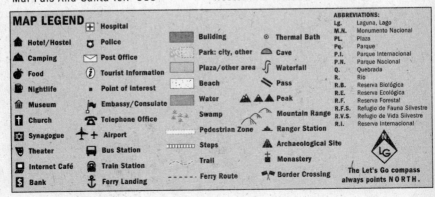

MAP LEGEND

✚ Hospital	
🏠 Hotel/Hostel	🚔 Police
⛺ Camping	✉ Post Office
🍴 Food	ⓘ Tourist Information
🎵 Nightlife	▪ Point of Interest
🏛 Museum	🚩 Embassy/Consulate
⛪ Church	☎ Telephone Office
✡ Synagogue	✈ Airport
🎭 Theater	🚌 Bus Station
💻 Internet Café	🚂 Train Station
$ Bank	⚓ Ferry Landing

Building		⊙ Thermal Bath	
Park: city, other		⌂ Cave	
Plaza/other area		∫ Waterfall	
Beach		Pass	
Water		▲▲▲ Peak	
Swamp		Mountain Range	
Pedestrian Zone		⛰ Ranger Station	
Steps		▲ Archaeological Site	
Trail		✚ Monastery	
Ferry Route		Border Crossing	

ABBREVIATIONS:
Lg. Laguna, Lago
M.N. Monumento Nacional
PL. Plaza
Pq. Parque
P.I. Parque Internacional
P.N. Parque Nacional
Q. Quebrada
R. Rio
R.B. Reserva Biológica
R.E. Reserva Ecológica
R.F. Reserva Forestal
R.F.S. Refugio de Fauna Silvestre
R.V.S. Refugio de Vida Silvestre
R.I. Reserva Internacional

The Let's Go compass
always points NORTH.

ABOUT LET'S GO

THE STUDENT TRAVEL GUIDE

Let's Go publishes the world's favorite student travel guides, written entirely by Harvard students. Armed with pens, notebooks, and a few changes of clothes stuffed into their backpacks, our student researchers go across continents, through time zones, and above expectations to seek out invaluable travel experiences for our readers. Because we are a completely student-run company, we have a unique perspective on how students travel, where they want to go, and what they're looking to do when they get there. If your dream is to grab a machete and forge through the jungles of Costa Rica, we can take you there. If you'd rather bask in the Riviera sun at a beachside cafe, we'll set you a table. In short, we write for readers who know that there's more to travel than tour buses. To keep up, visit our website, www.letsgo.com, where you can sign up to blog, post photos from your trips, and connect with the Let's Go community.

TRAVELING BEYOND TOURISM

We're on a mission to provide our readers with sharp, fresh coverage packed with socially responsible opportunities to go beyond tourism. Each guide's Beyond Tourism chapter shares ideas about responsible travel, study abroad, and how to give back to the places you visit while on the road. To help you gain a deeper connection with the places you travel, our fearless researchers scour the globe to give you the heads-up on both world-renowned and off-the-beaten-track opportunities. We've also opened our pages to respected writers and scholars to hear their takes on the countries and regions we cover, and asked travelers who have worked, studied, or volunteered abroad to contribute first-person accounts of their experiences.

FIFTY YEARS OF WISDOM

Let's Go has been on the road for 50 years and counting. We've grown a lot since publishing our first 20-page pamphlet to Europe in 1960, but five decades and 54 titles later our witty, candid guides are still researched and written entirely by students on shoestring budgets who know that train strikes, stolen luggage, food poisoning, and marriage proposals are all part of a day's work. This year, for our 50th anniversary, we're publishing 26 titles—including 6 brand new guides—brimming with editorial honesty, a commitment to students, and our irreverent style. Here's to the next 50!

THE LET'S GO COMMUNITY

More than just a travel guide company, Let's Go is a community that reaches from our headquarters in Cambridge, MA all across the globe. Our small staff of dedicated student editors, writers, and tech nerds comes together because of our shared passion for travel and our desire to help other travelers get the most out of their experience. We love it when our readers become part of the Let's Go community as well—when you travel, drop us a postcard (67 Mt. Auburn St., Cambridge, MA 02138, USA), send us an e-mail (feedback@letsgo.com), or sign up on our website (www.letsgo.com) to tell us about your adventures and discoveries.

For more information, updated travel coverage, and news from our researcher team, visit us online at www.letsgo.com.

HELPING LET'S GO. If you want to share your discoveries, suggestions, or corrections, please drop us a line. We appreciate every piece of correspondence, whether a postcard, a 10-page email, or a coconut. Visit Let's Go at **http://www.letsgo.com,** or send email to:

feedback@letsgo.com, subject: "Let's Go Central America"

Address mail to:

Let's Go Central America, 67 Mount Auburn St., Cambridge, MA 02138, USA

In addition to the invaluable travel advice our readers share with us, many are kind enough to offer their services as researchers or editors. Unfortunately, our charter enables us to employ only currently enrolled Harvard students.

Maps by Let's Go copyright © 2010 by Let's Go, Inc.

Distributed by Publishers Group West.
Printed in Canada by Friesens Corp.

ISBN-13: 978-1-59880-296-2
ISBN-10: 1-59880-296-8
Tenth edition
10 9 8 7 6 5 4 3 2 1

Let's Go Central America is written by Let's Go Publications, 67 Mount Auburn St., Cambridge, MA 02138, USA.